UNIVERSITY OF ST. THOMAS LIBRARIES

Contemporary Philosophy of Art

READINGS IN ANALYTIC AESTHETICS

Contemporary Philosophy of Art

READINGS IN ANALYTIC AESTHETICS

Edited by

John W. Bender
Ohio University

H. Gene Blocker
Ohio University

PRENTICE HALL, *Englewood Cliffs, New Jersey 07632*

Library of Congress Cataloging-in-Publication Data

Contemporary philosophy of art : readings in analytic
  aesthetics / edited by John W. Bender and H. Gene Blocker.
     p.   cm.
  Includes bibliographical references.
  ISBN 0-13-018086-6
  1. Aesthetics.   2. Aesthetics, Modern—20th century.   I. Bender,
John W., (date).   II. Blocker, H. Gene.
BH39.C666   1993
111'.85—dc20   92-30165
                                                                    CIP

Acquisitions editor: Ted Bolen
Editorial/production supervision and
   interior design: Colby Stong
Copy editor: Patricia Daly
Cover designer: Carol Cenedi
Prepress buyer: Herb Klein
Manufacturing buyer: Bob Anderson

"Kasaner" 1968 by Kenzo Okada. Oil on canvas, 73" × 63". National Gallery of Art, Washington. Collection of Mr. and Mrs. Paul Mellon.

 © 1993 by Prentice-Hall, Inc.
A Simon & Schuster Company
Englewood Cliffs, New Jersey 07632

All rights reserved. No part of this book may be
reproduced, in any form or by any means,
without permission in writing from the publisher.

Printed in the United States of America
10 9 8 7 6 5 4 3 2 1

ISBN 0-13-018086-6

Prentice-Hall International (UK) Limited, *London*
Prentice-Hall of Australia Pty. Limited, *Sydney*
Prentice-Hall Canada Inc., *Toronto*
Prentice-Hall Hispanoamericana, S.A., *Mexico*
Prentice-Hall of India Private Limited, *New Delhi*
Prentice-Hall of Japan, Inc., *Tokyo*
Simon & Schuster Asia Pte. Ltd., *Singapore*
Editora Prentice-Hall do Brasil, Ltda., *Rio de Janeiro*

Contents

Preface   xi

PART I   HAS ANALYTIC AESTHETICS A FUTURE?

1   Taking Stock   1

RICHARD SHUSTERMAN
Analytic Aesthetics: Retrospect and Prospect   10
ANITA SILVERS
Letting the Sunshine In: Has Analysis Made Aesthetics Clear?   19
JOSEPH MARGOLIS
The Eclipse and Recovery of Analytic Aesthetics   34
NICHOLAS WOLTERSTORFF
Philosophy of Art After Analysis and Romanticism   55

2   The Postmodern Challenge   67

HUGH J. SILVERMAN
The Philosophy of Postmodernism   74

JANE TUMAS–SERNA
Art, Culture, and Postmodern Expression: A Communicative Aesthetic   78

DONALD KUSPIT
The Contradictory Character of Postmodernism   93

PEGGY ZEGLIN BRAND
Feminism in Context: A Role for Feminist Theory in Aesthetic Evaluation   106

3 Case in Point: Expressiveness and Art   123

BENEDETTO CROCE
Intuition and Expression   128

WILLIAM E. KENNICK
Does Traditional Aesthetics Rest on a Mistake?   134

SUSANNE K. LANGER
Expressiveness   145

STEPHEN DAVIES
Is Music a Language of the Emotions?   150

NELSON GOODMAN
Exemplification and Expression   159

ALAN TORMEY
The Concept of Expression: A Proposal   164

PART II   ONGOING ISSUES AND NEW PERSPECTIVES IN CONTEMPORARY PHILOSOPHY OF ART

4 The Particularity of Art and the Generality of Theory   171

IMMANUEL KANT
Critique of the Aesthetical Judgment   176

MORRIS WEITZ
The Role of Theory in Aesthetics   191

ARTHUR DANTO
The Artistic Enfranchisement of Real Objects: The Artworld   199

GEORGE DICKIE
What Is Art? An Institutional Analysis   207

WILLIAM L. BLIZEK
An Institutional Theory of Art   219

HAROLD OSBORNE
What Is a Work of Art?   225

5 Art and Its Properties   233

MONROE BEARDSLEY
Regional Qualities   239

FRANK N. SIBLEY
Aesthetic Concepts   243

GORAN HERMEREN
The Variety of Aesthetic Qualities   260

GUY SIRCELLO
Expressive Properties of Art   268

KENDALL WALTON
Categories of Art   282

6 What Sorts of Things Are Works of Art?   303

RICHARD WOLLHEIM
From *Art and Its Objects: An Introduction to Aesthetics*   309

JOSEPH MARGOLIS
The Ontological Peculiarity of Works of Art   317

NICHOLAS WOLTERSTORFF
Toward an Ontology of Art Works   322

JERROLD LEVINSON
What a Musical Work Is   338

JOHN W. BENDER
Music and Metaphysics: Types and Patterns, Performances and Works   354

7 Aesthetic Experience and Art's Value   367

GEORGE DICKIE
The Myth of the Aesthetic Attitude   373

MONROE C. BEARDSLEY
The Aesthetic Point of View   384

NELSON GOODMAN
The Activity of Aesthetic Experience   396

MONROE BEARDSLEY
In Defense of Aesthetic Value   402

GEORGE DICKIE
Instrumental Cognitivism   406

ARTHUR DANTO
Aesthetic Responses and Works of Art   412

8 Questions of Interpretation   419

ARNOLD ISENBERG
Critical Communication   424

MONROE C. BEARDSLEY
The Testability of an Interpretation   433

ROBERT J. MATTHEWS
Describing and Interpreting a Work of Art   444

JOSEPH MARGOLIS
Reinterpreting Interpretation   454

M. M. VAN DE PITTE
Hermeneutics and the 'Crisis' of Literature   471

H. GENE BLOCKER
Interpreting Art   481

9 Evaluating Art and the Relativism Controversy   493

MONROE C. BEARDSLEY
The Refutation of Relativism   500

JOSEPH MARGOLIS
Robust Relativism   506

DAVID NOVITZ
Towards a Robust Realism   516

RUBY MEAGER
Art and Beauty   531

FRANK SIBLEY
General Criteria and Reasons in Aesthetics   535

GEORGE DICKIE
Beardsley, Sibley, and Critical Principles   546

10 Art, Science, and Knowledge: Knowing the World
    through Art   557

  LOUIS ARNAULD REID
  Art and Knowledge   563
  HAROLD OSBORNE
  Interpretation in Science and in Art   570
  NELSON GOODMAN
  Art and the Understanding   580
  HILARY PUTNAM
  Literature, Science, and Reflection   582
  DAVID NOVITZ
  Fiction and the Growth of Knowledge   585
  JOHN W. BENDER
  Art as a Source of Knowledge: Linking Analytic Aesthetics and
     Epistemology   593

Preface

As the subtitle of this anthology suggests, we have tried to select the best contemporary work of aestheticians in the analytic tradition and have sought an arrangement of chapters and an ordering of readings within each chapter that reflect the relationships among the central aesthetics concerns of recent years. In some cases, we have found it advisable, either for contrast or historical perspective, to include readings from earlier periods, but these are few.

Our selection process for this book has been, one might say, empirical. That is, although both of us had at the outset our own selection of preferred topics and texts, as well as our own sense of the effects in recent years of the challenge of Postmodernism, we nonetheless set about to explore the literature thoroughly to find out whether our initial biases and preferences were indeed borne out by the actual scholarly contributions to aesthetics over the past fifteen years or so. In some cases, our initial assumptions were confirmed, and in others they were not. On the whole, we found a lively, mature, sophisticated, pluralistic, and developing literature and a healthy dialogue with Postmodern trends that so often are conceived as in tension with analytic aesthetics. We also found more change and evolution within analytic aesthetics than we had initially supposed. As we argue in our introductions to Chapters 1 and 2, we think the record shows that analytic aesthetics is neither dead, nor dying, nor defensively circling the wagons, but is alive and well and enjoying and benefiting from a vigorous debate with contributors from other traditions. The "state of the art" is healthy and robust, in our estimate.

Although recent work has been extremely diverse in style and content, we have tried to arrange the material in a logically coherent manner, both as a pedagogical device offering students guidance through some extremely complex issues, and to give a better sense of the interactive nature of philosophical debate that is characteristic of analytic aesthetics and, indeed, philosophy in general. Contemporary aesthetics is not characterized by the dominance of one or two great figures whose views are emulated and expanded on by others, nor by isolated figures patiently developing their own positions and unconcerned with the views of others, but rather by a group of able philosophers of art who are constantly engaged with one another, challenging, criticizing, modifying, and enlarging on each other's positions. By putting together clusters of writers discussing each other's ideas and proposals, we hope to give some sense of this active and ongoing critical exchange.

Let us look briefly at the overall plan of the book as we see it. Part I, consisting of the first three chapters, concerns the assessment of analytic aesthetics' contributions and future. In Chapter 1, we offer the reflections of several prominent philosophers of art on this issue. In Chapter 2, we examine the challenge of Postmodernism and how it may or may not affect the future of analytic aesthetics. Chapter 3 is intended as a case study that measures the progress in handling the problem of expression in the arts. These selections move from the early "programmatic" rejection of the idealistic, wooly essentiality of Croce, through a variety of constructive but very different contributions, to the more specific question of exactly *how* expression works in the arts. We think that something of the evolution and expansion of analytic aesthetics from its postwar beginnings to its current state is indicated in this chapter.

The bulk of the book, Part II, takes up a broad range of interesting and ongoing abstract issues in analytic aesthetics. First, in Chapter 4, is the fundamental question of whether there can be a general theory of art at all. From the early position of Kant that there could be no cognitive science of aesthetics, and the early anti-essentiality of analytic aesthetics, which seemed to preclude the possibility of any definition and thereby any general theory of art, analytic aesthetics has evolved considerably and enlarged its range of options to include the possibility of theorizing about art in an expanded social context of the "artworld." Moving beyond the old dichotomy of properties of the object versus features of the subject, these new approaches contextualize art in a new cultural, sociological configuration.

This carries over into expanded possibilities for new ways of looking at the properties of artworks (Chapter 5) and from that to an enriched perspective on the nature of artworks themselves (Chapter 6). Again, moving beyond dead-end dichotomous alternatives that aesthetic properties are either properties of physical objects or subjective feelings in the minds of their perceivers, much interesting work has been done in recent years looking at aesthetic properties as relational properties, which are "culturally emergent," just as is the artwork itself.

This expanding cultural, sociological contextualization leads, in turn, to a reexamination of aesthetic experience, which we explore in Chapter 7. It is a concept that has been rejected by Dickie, refined by Beardsley, redefined by Goodman, and recontextualized by Danto.

Recontextualizing the concepts of the artwork, its properties, and our experience of it also realigns questions of our interpretation and evaluation of art, which we consider in Chapters 8 and 9. If the artwork is best seen as culturally emergent and enveloped in complex and various relations, then our interpretations and evaluations of art must be understood in a similarly relational fashion, in which publicly perceptible features of the artwork, the human psychology of the audience, and the social conventions and artistic institutions and traditions are seen to interact. And finally, this relational understanding of art has opened up new possibilities for recognizing a kind of knowledge of the world through art, which we examine in the last chapter. Insofar as we see art as a culturally emergent product of social institutions and conventions, it has the power to speak to us about and through those institutions and conventions.

Many of the chapters are highlighted by pairs and triplets of articles that record specific topical debates and replies to criticisms. These clusterings substantially enliven the issues and should significantly heighten students' appreciation of the subtlety of the problems. The most obvious of these clusters involve Dickie and Blizek in Chapter 4;

Wolterstorff, Levinson, and Bender in Chapter 6; Beardsley, Goodman, and Dickie in Chapter 7; Beardsley, Margolis, and Novitz in Chapter 9, as well as Sibley and Dickie, again in that chapter. Some interesting similarities and contrasts are also to be found in the Putnam, Novitz, and Bender essays contained in Chapter 10. These dialogues should give the student a clear sense of the way in which philosophers debate issues and should indicate how mini-traditions develop within a field of philosophy.

J. W. B.
H. G. B.

Contemporary Philosophy of Art

READINGS IN ANALYTIC AESTHETICS

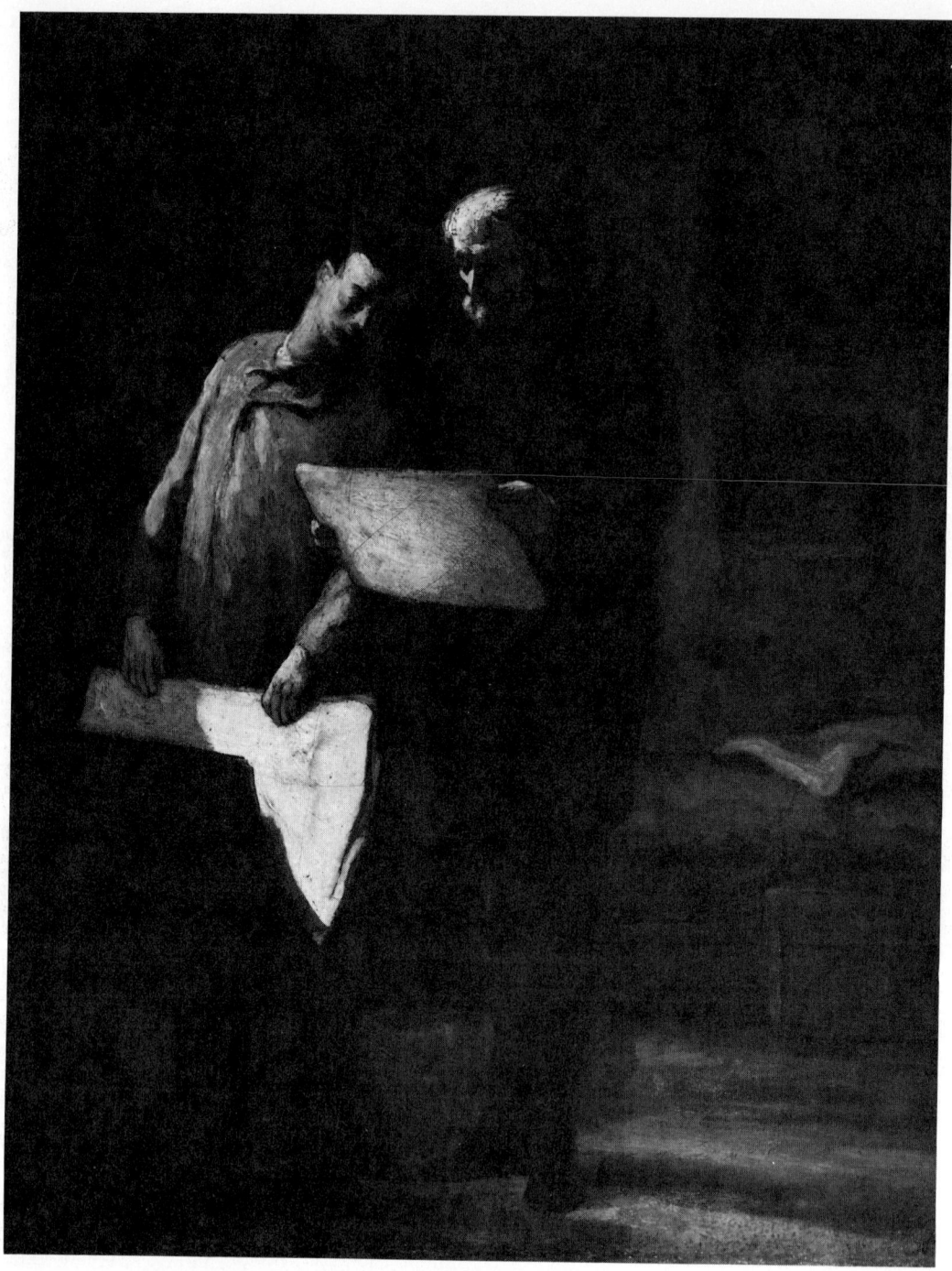

Advice to a Young Artist, Honore Daumier (French). Painted probably after 1860. National Gallery of Art, Washington, D.C.

PART I

Has Analytic Aesthetics a Future?

CHAPTER 1
Taking Stock

I

We write this at a time that many consider a significant turning point in philosophy and perhaps an even more fateful time for analytic aesthetics. The so-called Postmodern turn is radically characterized by some as the death of all philosophy, but even if this claim is judged as implausible and hyperbolic, there appears to be a higher level of concern about the continuing vigor of analytic aesthetics. The issues involved are numerous and complex, as are the practices and interests of working analytic aestheticians; consequently, overgeneralized and overheated characterizations are predictable, and the romance of a supposed intellectual revolution is difficult, as always, to resist. Without blanketly denying the force of more general Postmodern influences, some of which we characterize in due course, we suggest in this introduction that there are strong internal and predictable maturational forces at work within analytic aesthetics which, far from threatening its continued existence and value, ensure its lively future. There is good reason, we believe, to interpret much of the change in contemporary aesthetics in terms of the field's maturation and the usual waning and waxing of certain well-established emphases, rather than in terms of its yielding to the next, Postmodernist, order. Analytic aesthetics is not a *style* of philosophy in the sense that Bauhaus is an architectural style; it is, in its greater open-endedness and room for development and substantive change, a *form* of philosophy, as democracy or socialism is a form of government.

But clearly, the interpretation one offers, either maturational or revolutionary, is subordinate to one's understanding of the scope of analytic aesthetics and to one's characterization of the Postmodern challenge. The latter is notoriously difficult to clarify, while what is meant by analytic aesthetics is open to ambiguity and vagueness. We begin with these last points.

II

All agree that analytic aesthetics began in earnest around 1946 and by the early 1950s had achieved self-sustaining momentum. It was an early goal of what Silvers (see "Letting the Sunshine In" in this chapter) calls the analytic "program" to be rid of the romanticism, idealism, essentialism, and the perceived consequent soft-headedness of the aesthetic theorizing of the earlier half-century. The tools of close logical and conceptual analysis were to be implemented in the elimination of the three major sources of what John Passmore famously described as the field's "dreariness": confused and obscure ideas, overgeneralizations based on overly particular features of certain aesthetic experiences, and the unfounded presupposition that art in its variety nonetheless shares a philosophically important "essence."

Construed as "negative" goals of elimination, and directed against known offenders (presumably writers such as Croce, Collingwood, Santanya, Maritain, Bell, Parker, and perhaps even Dewey), these directives are reasonably sharp, and the analytic program is consequently defined as a short-lived polemical "mission." But clearly, when understood as positive methodological directives for an ongoing, improved philosophy of art, these concerns are both incomplete as a characterization of analytic aesthetics and open-ended and ripe for elaboration, variation, and evolution. For example, the broad demand for clarity helps to determine analytic philosophers' proclivity for working on "close" piecemeal topics rather than concerning themselves with larger system building but does not, of itself, set the agenda. Moreover, the demand for clarity easily evolves from a practice of internal, conceptual clarification to more revisionist or constructivist activity. Early analytic ideals of engaging in value-free logical analysis of literary and art criticism, for instance, are modified as it becomes obvious that clarification of concepts regularly exposes latent norms and values that are amenable once revealed.

Similarly, the caution against overgeneralization naturally brings forward questions concerning the role of generalities in aesthetic cognition, description, interpretation, and evaluation. And an antiessentialism about art can hardly fail to lead to ontological investigations of the various arts as well as to questions about art's categories and context-embeddedness. Pluralistic and pragmatic tendencies come into ascendency rather predictably.

Our point here is that the characterizations of early analytic aesthetics, such as Silvers offers, may well be accurate early portraits, but they are more correctly seen as offering time-slices of ongoing and developing research. Emphasizing the evolving and dialectical character of the discussion within the analytic community, to say nothing of its multifaceted diversity, goes a considerable way toward addressing the deficiencies or problematic features attributed to the field by Shusterman (see "Analytic Aesthetics: Retrospect and Prospect" in this chapter). Those features are (1) a view of itself as a logic-centered, metacritical activity (i.e., an activity focused on the clarification of the methods and language of literary and art criticism); (2) its non-normative, or normatively noncommittal character; (3) its ahistorical, noncontextualist, and isolationist approach; (4) its lack of pluralism in regard to critical practices; and (5) a lack of pragmatist elements in its philosophizing about art.

The nature of criticism and interpretation has always been a central issue in analytic aesthetics, as, indeed, it remains today, and there certainly was a period in the late 1950s and early 1960s when the constellation of philosophical questions surrounding the activities of criticism, interpretation, and evaluation of artwork laid claim to center stage. However, whether this literature was ever *exclusively* focused on value-free matters of internal logical consistency and clarity is doubtful, in our view, but not worth the quibble.

It may, however, be worth pointing out that the view of philosophy of art as metacriticism has much in common with the contemporaneous view of ethics as metaethics: Both descriptions seem to be products of the dominant "linguistic turn" in philosophy at the time, and both are, at best, partial truths. For just as the ethicists of the time did not cease producing theories of right and wrong even as they worried about the analysis of "right," so too philosophers of art remained engaged in many first-order issues in aesthetics, many of which were not restricted to the problems of interpretation and criticism. There was concurrent and continuing interest in the nature of aesthetic experience, questions about the representational function of art, the role of expression, the alleged autonomy of the artwork, and the importance of the artist's intentions. There was interesting new work in the semiotics of art and music and the never-flagging debate over the desire for a definition of art. A positivistic and logicistic interest in literary criticism never exhausted the aesthetic interests of analytic philosophers.

Nor were pragmatic or pluralistic strains ever wholly absent in the analytic tradition, even if they have seen growth in recent years. One only has to reflect on the early claims by numerous philosophers that the function of critical discourse is best viewed as nonargumentative, or on the debates over the question of whether interpretations can reasonably be construed as correct or uniquely correct, to appreciate that pragmatic and pluralistic elements may in fact have had something of a head start in aesthetics when compared to their development in areas such as epistemology or metaphysics, for instance.

The always-present diversity and *doctrinal* disagreements within the analytic conversation in aesthetics, coupled with the complementary (not contrary) fact that this conversation has exhibited and continues to exhibit an intellectual continuity, a continuity of growth, revision, and refinement, suggests that it is more appropriate to view Shusterman's list not as an accounting of essential flaws in the analytic strategy but rather as a map of the more important directions of the current growth of the field.

We conceive of analytic aesthetics broadly, not as a set of dogmas or manifestoes but as a combination of methods and problems, as the activity of working philosophically on certain core problems in aesthetics, or at least on certain aspects, instances, or implications of those problems, using the analytical methods of careful and focused argumentation, linguistic analysis, the examination of the structure and force of competing arguments, the testing of claims through example and counterexample, and the identification of telling logical consequences of claims. There is a symptomatic prizing of logical clarity and precision to the degree that it may be attainable, a predisposition toward objectivity when it is not illusory to strive for it, and an embracing of the notion that philosophy of art is a kind of *theorizing* about fundamental issues concerning art and the artworld, to which standards of truth, consistency, and argumentation apply, at least to a significant degree.

III

There is no reason to deny a distinct overlap between the identifiable currents now present in analytic aesthetics and the characteristics thought symptomatic of the Postmodern turn. It may be instructive to comment on these characteristics from the perspective of analytic aesthetics, by way of placing this maturing field in the broader philosophical whirl. This will do little more than orient the reader and perhaps indicate our own position on matters that are far too extensive and difficult to handle adequately within an introduction.[1]

1. Rejection of Truth. The denial of any classical version of the concept of truth as a correspondence or relation between beliefs, claims, descriptions, or theories, and Reality, the Facts, the Way the World is, or Things in Themselves is the most fundamental and far-reaching tenet of Postmodernism. It is this rejection that motivates and underlies many of the other symptomatic features of Postmodernism. According to the proponents of Postmodernism, our signs and symbols connect us to other signs and symbols and are open to interpretation, but their referential function, their ability to connect us and our ideas to the world is denied, critiqued, or downplayed.

Difficulties over truth are, of course, hardly new and have posed challenges in every philosophical tradition, analytic philosophy prominent among these. But more specifically, the place of truth in the arts, art criticism, and art evaluation has generated debate within analytic aesthetics since its inception. Whether interpretation of the arts requires or resists the application of the concept of truth has never been a settled matter within the tradition, and nay-sayers have been many, from Hospers to Margolis to Robert Matthews. In other words, this has been an instance in which internal questioning of whether the goal of truth is appropriate to the issues has itself a substantial tradition. Furthermore, because the arts have, for literally hundreds of years, been conceived of as generally expressive, perspectival, subjective, interpretational, and value-laden in nature, rather than descriptive or factual, the Postmodern rejection of truth is less of a threat to the future of analytic aesthetics than it may be thought to be for epistemology or philosophy of science. This is not to say that aestheticians are moving to any consensus about the role of truth in the arts, but only that their ongoing discussion is likely to broaden to include any novel and relevant Postmodern argument or contribution.

2. Rejection of Foundationalism. There are no Archimedean intellectual points, no rock bottom, indubitable bases or unassailable foundations, no uninterpreted given on which we can rely in securing our knowledge of reality, our world view, according to Postmodern thought. This has long been a major contention within contemporary analytic theory of knowledge and can hardly be claimed as a new contribution of continental Postmodernism. Once we progress past the Cartesian, rationalistic desire for certainty (a very old idea, by most epistemologists' lights), the arguments over sophisticated foundationalism, coherence theories, and pragmatist theories of knowledge are the stuff of technical, analytical epistemology and have not, in truth, had a major influence on philosophy of art. In fact, surprisingly little attention has been given to the rich possibilities of applying analytic epistemology to aesthetics.

Foundationalism, then, has not had its strongest showing in the arena of aesthetics. It has its most obvious appearance, perhaps, in attempts to distinguish descriptions of artworks from interpretations of them, a distinction which might be construed as a form of the Myth of the Given. Frank Sibley's efforts to distinguish a work's aesthetic from its nonaesthetic properties is an instance. It is notable, however, that Sibley's views were immediately criticized by as many analytic aestheticians as have been inspired by them.

A more radical thesis than nonfoundationalism has also been suggested by some Postmodern writers. The view of knowledge as a representation of an independent world of stable, factual nature has been deconstructed into changing, pragmatically governed views, interpretations, language games, forms of life, and expressions of power by advocates of Postmodernism who have been deeply influenced by Nietzsche, Wittgenstein, and others. Included are thinkers such as Rorty, Derrida, Foucault, Lyotard, and Gadamer.

These various forms of antirealism may well have one of their most plausible applications (relatively speaking) within aesthetics. It is commonplace to think of art as providing various and alternative ways of viewing things, new perspectives or interpretations through different eyes, presentations of different human possibilities, and so forth rather than as a window (mirror?) through which to view the real way the world is. But again, since it is not at all clear that analytic aesthetics was ever a stronghold of realism, any revolution on this count is a rather quiet matter. It is, however, an exciting prospect to look ahead to the further working-out of these ideas and a clarification of their relationship to other proposals, such as Wolterstorff's "worlds of art" thesis.

3. Emphasis on the Contingency and Conventionality of the Rules and Practices of Rational Thought and Judgment. A related emphasis on the pragmatics, politics, and poetics of natural language, rather than the purely logical and semantic leanings of the analytic as well as the structuralist traditions, marks Postmodernism. Contingency and convention replace foundationalism and human universals or claims to essentiality, according to Postmodern thinking. Dealing with the contingencies of our ways of life and thought supplants the metaphysical quest for the final vocabulary, according to Rorty and others.

These are ideas that are not alien to analytic aesthetics, especially that of most recent vintage. The role of the critic and the expert in initiating others into the language games, institutional conventions, and intellectual community of the artworld has been emphasized against the competing image of expert as teacher of uncovered truth or knowledge.

Wolterstorff (in "Philosophy of Art after Analysis and Romanticism" in this chapter) speaks provocatively, if sketchily, about reception practices, our learned modes and abilities for art appreciation. Walton, Levinson, and others have stressed that the conventions of genre and style, as well as the aesthetic and historical context, affect the properties correctly ascribable to works. And issues of contingency and pluralism surfaced even earlier in the various debates over the objectivity, incommensurability, and cognitive content of interpretations and evaluations of art.

4. Critique of the Rational, Sovereign, Disengaged, and Self-Transparent Self, and of the Related Humanistic Ideals of the Enlightenment: Autonomy, Self-Knowledge, Rationality, and Impartiality. The autonomy of the artwork, the freedom and expressivity of the artist, the impartiality, disengagement, or "distance" characterizing the truly aesthetic experience—each are familiar, if contested, issues in aesthetics, harkening back to Kantian and Romantic roots. But no one could rightfully suggest that analytic aesthetics' picture of either the artist or the audience was that of a self-knowing, isolated Cartesian ego. Perhaps the closest approach to such a picture is found in some of Beardsley's passages, in which the appreciator of art appears engaged in a private, detached, introspective assessment of a work's presented formal and regional qualities.

In general, however, there has been too much recognition of the inability of artists to speak with much clarity or in any but anecdotal ways about the creative process, too much understanding of the subliminal, suggestive, and allusive power of the arts, too much sympathy toward application of psychoanalytic principles to aesthetic matters to support the notion that analytic aesthetics harbors the Enlightenment concept of the self. If anything, a more Romantic image of the self has been substantially retained, as Wolterstorff has argued.

5. Ascendency of Rhetoric within Philosophical Discourse. Hans Blumenberg has argued that with the weakening of the grip of eternal truths and demonstrable certainties on the philosophical mind, rhetoric, broadly conceived of as intellectual methods for reaching consensus in situations in which definitive evidence is lacking, should be viewed more positively by philosophy as a form of rationality, a means of coming to terms with the provisionality of reason.

Paul Ricoeur and many others have given new centrality to the theory of metaphor. Ricoeur has argued that metaphor is involved in the mode of understanding that is presupposed by, rather than secondary to, explanation.

Analytic aesthetics, we would argue, has maintained stronger connections to the issues of rhetoric and metaphor than have other areas of analytic philosophy and harbors no principled animosity to these Postmodern interests. The logic and function of metaphor have intrigued numerous analytic writers from the start, and credence is given to a variety of treatments of, and perspectives on, the problems. The rhetorical aspects of analytical argument and theorizing are slowly becoming more appreciated by their practitioners, largely as a result of recent French and continental hermeneutical and deconstructive influences. But earlier threads can also be traced back to the huge discussion within analytic aesthetics of the so-called institutional theory and to the provocative claims of Arthur Danto about the relation between art and philosophy.

Concern for, and interest in, rhetoric and metaphor do not, of course, entail endorsement of the view that rhetoric can or should replace analytic-style argumentation in philosophy, or, as Rorty seems to suggest, that literature, or at least a more literary philosophy, should, because of a greater forcefulness and effectiveness, supplant philosophy as it has been executed in the analytic tradition of this century. Blumenberg may believe that we must proceed "rhetorically" as soon as we move beyond the embrace of definitive certainties, but the average analytic philosopher, we believe, would respond by pointing out that all scientific as well as philosophical theorizing is or involves inductive, hypothetical, fallibilistic, and revisable reasoning. However, this does not establish that a concern for consensus and agreement is the only legitimate goals of theorizing. Nor does the fallibility of our knowledge and theories undermine the need for clear, precise, analytical argumentation or establish the primacy of rhetoric over such argument.

IV

In sum, then, there is—at least from our perspective within the analytic tradition—a continuity to the discussions in aesthetics, even as the contributions of Postmodernist writers are assimilated and critically examined for their applicability to the field's central questions. We do not see Postmodern issues as signaling the demise of analytic aesthetics; nor do we find much justification for viewing these influences as external, alien, hostile, or particularly revolutionary, for the most part. Hostility arises only if Postmodern themes are presented as dogma; and what would strike analytic philosophers as most alien is not a call for considering these themes, but rather any suggestion that active debate of the alternatives is somehow inappropriate or passé. This would amount not so much to a natural death of analytic philosophy as to attempted murder by intellectual neglect.

In our view, however, there should be no fear that the issues represented in this anthology are on the verge of abandonment. Aesthetics, like other areas of philosophy, is experiencing in the closing years of this century a widening, or perhaps a dissolution, of territorial boundaries, a greater openness to pluralism, and an enlivened attempt to synthesize discourses which may have seemed disparate and exclusionary several years ago. Slow transformation of the field is, in the end, an inevitability and an almost trivial truth about any intellectually active area. And transformations are much more exciting to look forward to than a death notice.

V

As is obvious by now, ours is a positive view of the contributions and future of analytic aesthetics. Equally obviously, other philosophers' interpretations of the history and limits of this field will vary interestingly. The following selections represent some of this variation. Because we think that self-criticism is generally more informed, precise, and aimed at improvement than are critiques from farther afield, the pieces included here all come from within the tradition, and a number of them initially were published together in the summer 1987 special issue of the *Journal of Aesthetics and Art Criticism*.

Shusterman argues that although analytic aesthetics rebelled against the older romantic, idealist theories and was, indeed, anti-essentialist for the most part, it never succeeded in ridding aesthetics of some central romantic notions, and thus it marginalizes the social contextuality of the practices of art.

Silvers assesses the early history of analytic aesthetics and concludes that it did rescue us from the dreariness of obscurity and confusion, but only at the price of introducing a new kind of dreariness: analytic tedium. Analytic aesthetics failed, partly for this reason, to engage the interests of art historians and critics and still less to reform their practices. The problem, Silvers finds, lies in attempting to analyze critical discourse by a logical standard without inquiring more directly about how critical discourse functions in the context of the many institutions and practices of the artworld.

Margolis sees the "eclipse" of analytic aesthetics in terms of the rejection by different philosophers of various parts of the analytic "canon" (he deftly examines four philosophers in detail: Beardsley, Goodman, Danto, and himself), and he views the "recovery" of analytic aesthetics as involving the recognition that there are no privileged, ahistorical foundations for philosophy and in terms of a rapprochement between analytic and continental perspectives.

Margolis summarizes his reaction to (and recovery from) the antianalytic movement as follows: (1) There is no way to avoid the constative function of discourse; that is, there is no way to talk about things without making assertions which one presumably believes to be true; and (2) all such discourse must submit to some form of critique; that is, there is no way to talk about things without establishing rules concerning what is to count as legitimate or illegitimate assertion. No such critique can be privileged or guaranteed to be valid from a point of view outside the field of discourse. All critiques are internalist, and we must learn to do philosophy in a nonprivileged way.

Wolterstorff characterizes analytic philosophy as basically neo-Kantian, against continental philosophy's basic neo-Hegelianism. Among the neo-Kantian traits of analytic philosophy are the reliance on a scheme of concepts applied to a given content and emphasis on the concept of necessity; the role of the analysis of concepts in one's characterization of knowledge, science, morality, and rationality; and an assumption of foundationalism.

This neo-Kantian model, however, has virtually no direct application to art (are there, after all, conceptual schemes in painting and music, as there are in science?), and this fact may well explain the absence, according to

Wolterstorff, of "any great analytic philosophy of art." As a result, analytic aesthetics took up the task of analyzing concepts where it could find them (namely, in art criticism), but this second-order task turned out, in Wolterstorff's estimate, to be largely boring and useless.

Such analytic pursuits retained strong connections to romanticism—on this point Wolterstorff agrees with Shusterman. And, like Shusterman and Silvers, he suggests that the corrective is to be found in looking at art in its broader social, cultural, and historical context. Wolterstorff suggests that we apply MacIntyre's analysis of socially embedded "practices" to our study of the fine arts.

However, Wolterstorff is not endorsing a return to a Hegelian-inspired historicism in our philosophy of art, and neither is he in agreement with Rorty's relativist and skeptical interpretation of the Postmodern turn. Rather, he suggests that his own particular brand of realism is a way of transcending the swing of the Kantian–Hegelian pendulum.

NOTE

1. The characterizations of Postmodernism offered here roughly follow the introductory discussion in the fine recent anthology, *After Philosophy, End or Transformation*, K. Baynes, J. Bohman, and T. McCarthy, eds., MIT Press, 1987.

Analytic Aesthetics: Retrospect and Prospect

Richard Shusterman

I

What, if anything, particularly characterizes what we call analytic aesthetics, and in what way can we speak at all of an analytic movement, or at least an analytic method or style, in aesthetics? How much and in what manner does analytic aesthetics differ from its antecedents and rivals? Has it lived up to the hopes of radical transformation and philosophical progress which informed many early analytic attempts at demolishing the projects and theories of traditional aesthetics? How has its own program been pursued and modified over the years; and can it point to any achievements of which philosophy can be proud? . . .

If so-called continental theory has successfully challenged the analytic hegemony in Anglo-American aesthetics, this seems less a reason for dismay than a promise of wider and more fruitful aesthetic dialogue. . . . How then should we conceive the present and future role of the philosophy of art, and what if any function do the specific techniques, strategies, and problems of analytic aesthetics have to play here?

Such questions are easier to ask (and to multiply) than to answer. For even the non-evaluative definition of a philosophical genre or domain like analytic aesthetics is a philosophical problem itself, and shares the resolute irresolution of philosophy. . . . The definitive critical history of analytic aesthetics remains to be written; and it is perhaps impossible to write if, for all its apparent fall from grace, analytic aesthetics remains what Gallie (himself an influential analytic aesthetician) termed an essentially contested concept. . . . I shall offer with maximal brevity (hence minimal argument) some of my own general views on how analytic aesthetics and its career may be understood.

II

1. A very basic issue in understanding analytic aesthetics is determining its scope. The question is whether to construe this notion as including all the aesthetic writings of philosophers in the twentieth-century analytic tradition . . . or whether . . . analytic aesthetics should be much more narrowly taken as a specific program (originating in the late forties and reaching full force by the late fifties and through into the sixties) which involved only some of the analytic philosophers writing aesthetics and only some of their writings. The narrow scope provides a sharper historical focus and makes it easier to provide convincing (but perhaps still not exceptionless) generalizations about analytic aesthetics. . . .

However, the former approach has the undeniable advantage of giving analytic aesthetics greater breadth and richness, and of including important analytic philosophers whose writings on aesthetics were very influential but preceded or succeeded the nar-

---

From *The Journal of Aesthetics and Art Criticism*, 46 (1987), Special Issue. Reprinted by permission of The American Society for Aesthetics. Footnotes have been renumbered.

rowly defined analytic movement. Philosophers like Danto, Goodman, and Wollheim would be excluded or marginalized by the narrow conception, and so would Wittgenstein, whose remarks and lectures on aesthetics predated analytic aesthetics as narrowly defined yet enormously influenced it. Another first-rank analytic philosopher who wrote significantly on aesthetics but is consistently and most unfortunately ignored in even the most generous construals of analytic aesthetics is G. E. Moore. Though Moore's approach often sharply deviates from that of typical analytic aestheticians (e.g., his preoccupation with beauty), a case can be made for his enduring importance to analytic aesthetics and even for his indirect influence (chiefly through Wittgenstein) on analytic aesthetics narrowly construed. But I will not make this case here.

2. As its name indicates . . . analytic aesthetics is a consequence (though perhaps not a mere epiphenomenon) of the analytic approach to philosophy introduced by Moore and Russell and continued by Wittgenstein and others through the various phases of logical atomism, logical positivism, and ordinary language analysis. All analytic philosophers would probably agree with Russell's claim that analysis rather than the construction of philosophical systems is the major aim of philosophy.[1] But as Isenberg perceptively and honestly noted[2] there was not only disagreement and unclarity about what precisely should be analyzed (concepts, meanings, propositions), there was also the problem, acutely formulated in Langford's famous "paradox of analysis," of how a general standard of accurate and yet informative analysis could be defined.[3] With his enthusiastic faith in the general superiority and promise of the analytic approach and his evident pride in its already achieved results, Isenberg dismissed these difficulties as ultimately manageable and in no way precluding objectivity and agreement as to what is in particular cases a good analysis.

However, a further problem is that there are at least two quite different modes of analysis. One is reductively breaking down a concept, fact, or putative entity into more basic components or properties which are its necessary and sufficient conditions. Such analysis was usually pursued for metaphysical reductions (e.g., objects into sense-data, the average man into a quotient of real men). But there is also a form of analysis not aimed at reductive definition but simply at clarifying vague and problematic notions, distinguishing such a notion's complexities and different senses, even if failing to emerge with a precise, univocal definition of its essential conditions. Is analytic aesthetics to be limited to reductive definitional analysis or is it also to include attempts at clarification which do not provide such precise analytic definitions of necessary and sufficient conditions (which certain aesthetic concepts apparently preclude) but do nonetheless afford philosophical understanding? Different answers will yield very different pictures of the field. This tension of analysis between precisionist definitional reduction versus complex clarification of our aesthetic concepts is also reflected in the tension between ordinary language analysis and the Carnapian analytic project of rational reconstruction. If analysis reveals our aesthetic concepts as troublingly vague, why not proceed from analysis to make them better and more precise. Goodman frequently takes this constructivist line (as in his definitions of musical and literary works of art[4]), and if we exclude all rational reconstruction from the analytic program then it becomes very hard to classify Goodman's aesthetics as analytic, though it has inspired two decades of analytically oriented philosophy of art.

3. Clearly, then, analytic aesthetics cannot be properly understood without reference to the various analytic methods and achievements first established in other branches of philosophy. But no less essential for its understanding is a grasp of the background of aesthetic theory against which it sharply and successfully rebelled. Such theory was highly transcendental and idealistic in tone, and largely dominated by the romantic idealist aesthetic of Croce with its distinction-demolishing essentialism that all art is

simply expression and that there is no substantial classificatory distinction to be made between different expressions, every expression being completely unique. The vigorous mid-century burgeoning of analytic aesthetics was as much due to the perceived failures and woolly dreariness of Crocean idealism and other romantic essentialisms (e.g., the Bell-Fry "significant form" theory) as to the perceived achievements of the analytic method.[5] One of Isenberg's most basic arguments in his report is simply that since other aesthetic philosophizing has left things in such a muddle, analytic aesthetics, even if still unproven, deserves a chance. But if analytic aesthetics developed by opposing romanticism's essentialism and godlike view of the artist as determiner of meaning, it did not . . . rid itself altogether of romantic tenets, such as the uniqueness, gratuitousness, and autonomy of works of art.

4. Anti-essentialism about art[6] and the quest for clarity (distinctively through close concern with language) are probably the most common and distinctive features of analytic aesthetics, and though distinguishable they are clearly related. The murky confusion of traditional aesthetics was imputed to its assumption that the arts shared a common essence, which once discovered by the aesthetician could also serve as an absolute standard for aesthetic judgment. Pointing out how the various arts are very different and that their subsumption under our common concept of art was not effected till the eighteenth century,[7] the analysts argued that the essentialist presumption led traditional aesthetic theories to ignore, conflate, or homogenize obvious differences between the arts and to speak in terms that are so vague, muddled, and general as to be able to conceal all those differences in a woolly mist of confusion and by an empty, ambiguous formula of essence. Thus Passmore (as also Hampshire, Kennick, Gallie, and Weitz) saw the woolly dreariness of aesthetics "as arising out of the attempt to impose a spurious unity on things, the spuriousness being reflected in the emptiness of the formulae in which that unity is inscribed": expression, representation, significant form, beauty.[8] In the aim of greater clarity and substantive theories Passmore went so far as to suggest that "there is no aesthetics and yet there are principles of literary criticism, musical criticism, etc." and that general aesthetics should be abandoned for "an intensive special study of the separate arts, carried out with . . . much respect for real differences between the works of art themselves."[9] Such concern with the close study of the separate arts and their criticism was everywhere endorsed by analytic aesthetics and points to another important feature which distinguishes it markedly from traditional aesthetic philosophy.

5. Analytic aesthetics saw itself fundamentally as a second-order discipline engaged in the clarification and critical refinement of the concepts of art and art criticism. It neither presumed to offer new manifestoes about what art should be nor revolutionary criteria about how art should be evaluated. It instead sought a more logical and systematic account of the principles of art and criticism as actually reflected in the practice of good critics. And since much practice was distinctly verbal (but often confusingly verbose), this perfectly fit analytic philosophy's special concern with language. It also neatly corresponded with analytic philosophy's role regarding its main concern and its paradigm of a worthy first-order discipline—science. As science described nature, art criticism (understood widely to include art history and theory) described art: what science was for analytic philosophy in general (preponderantly concerned with epistemological and logical foundations for scientific knowledge), art criticism—the careful, systematic, and potentially even scientific study of the arts—was for analytic aesthetics. Without art criticism as a serious first-order cognitive discipline for analysts to clarify, logically sharpen, and ground, there would be much less room or reason for analytic aesthetics to depart from traditional revisionary flights into the essence of beauty or "the aesthetic." What explains both its anti-essentialism and sudden burst of vigor in the late forties and early fifties is that by this time art criticism, music criticism,

and especially literary criticism were already established as serious and *separate* academic enterprises with scientific or at least cognitive pretensions.[10]

It is thus not at all surprising that analytic aesthetics burgeoned long after general analytic philosophy had reached (and perhaps already passed) its prime. Second-order analytic method had to wait till it found the aesthetic counterpart of science in academic art criticism. Literary criticism seemed to present the most developed of such "scientific" critical disciplines, and not surprisingly analytic aestheticians most frequently and closely concerned themselves with it. (Consider Beardsley and Weitz, probably the two most influential figures in the fifties and sixties: Beardsley's most influential essay was co-authored with a literary critic [Wimsatt], while Weitz was himself something of a scholar and practitioner of literary criticism.[11]) It should, then, be no more surprising that with post-structuralism's challenge of the scientific study of texts, and more generally of the systematic and principled accumulation of knowledge of artistic meanings, the power and appeal of analytic aesthetics has now significantly waned. . . . But even if the perceived dissimilarities of science and art criticism would eventually scuttle its grand metacritical program, analytic aesthetics was primarily and most promisingly conceived in the terms of the philosophy of art criticism. Of course, an apparently larger project, "the philosophy of art and art criticism," was sometimes expressed, but since, in second-order fashion, art was to be studied through its criticism, philosophy of art effectively collapsed into the philosophy of art criticism. There are, of course, serious limitations with this conception of aesthetics as metacriticism . . . and there are also internal tensions which trouble it. But before considering these latter, we should note two important and problematic consequences which followed from seeing aesthetics as the philosophy of criticism.

6. One consequence is obviously an overwhelming preoccupation with art rather than natural beauty. (There was no first-order aesthetic discipline of nature criticism in the fifties, though ecological hindsight suggests that perhaps there should have been.) Of course, beyond Kant and certainly since Hegel, it is hard to find aestheticians who gave greater attention and regard to nature than to art. But in analytic aesthetics the bias toward art and neglect of nature is particularly pronounced. The point is too obvious to belabor, but one example is Wollheim's castigating Kant and Bullough (and by extension countless others) for trying to understand the aesthetic attitude by means of examples from nature, where, for Wollheim, the only central, nonderivative case of the aesthetic attitude is regarding a work of art under the concept of art.[12] Perhaps this prejudice was further fueled by analytic philosophy's special concern with language. Its linguistic turn in aesthetics is evident in the relentless titling of books and articles in the form "The Language(s) of Art (Criticism, Fiction, Poetry, Painting, Music, Metaphor, etc.)." Language obviously involves intention and mind. To study the language(s) of nature and natural beauty might well have seemed naively animistic or more sinisterly theological to secularly enlightened analysts. Preoccupation with art and its criticism did not mean that analytic aesthetics totally ignored more traditional and general aesthetic topics such as defining the aesthetic attitude or aesthetic experience. But it typically tended either to challenge or undermine them (as in Dickie's radical critique of these notions) or unintentionally rendered them problematic (as in Beardsley's valiant but vain attempt to define the object of aesthetic experience in a purely perceptual, phenomenal way that would still do justice to critical discourse about what were clearly intentional and materially embodied entities).[13]

Analysis and its preponderant concern for art thus proved fatal to the traditional idea of the aesthetic. It is true that a number of serious efforts were devoted to a more general foundational quest to define the aesthetic and clearly distinguish it from the nonaesthetic (e.g., in terms of a special aesthetic situation, attitude, experience, judgment, or logically distinct breed of concepts). But all these attempts proved unsatisfactory.[14] Moreover, they seem hopelessly problematic and misguided in the face of developments in twentieth-century art which vigorously opposed the assimilation of art into the aesthetic. The notion of "aesthetic," etymologically and historically wedded to sensory perception (and traditionally suggestive of form and pleasure), hardly seems reconcilable with the artworks of Duchamp and so many others whose appreciation (or even identification) requires more than the senses can descry. Though frequently felt and somehow recognized, this tension between art and the aesthetic was usually swept deftly under the carpet by ignoring natural beauty and tacitly identifying the aesthetic with what relates to art and its criticism. But Goodman and Danto, the two philosophers who most influenced the last two decades of analytic aesthetics, have more recently strongly denounced the traditional concept of the aesthetic as a misleading repressive ideology which trivializes art as mere sensuous pleasure with no essential cognitive dimension. And Goodman's revisionary account of the aesthetic is purely and explicitly in terms of the characteristic symbolic functioning of the various languages of *art*, where aesthetic value is construed simply as cognitive efficacy in the function of symbol systems so characterized.[15]

7. Another apparent consequence of analytic aesthetics' self-construal as a second-order discipline or metacriticism was a strong tendency to avoid evaluative issues, generally by relegating them to the first-order level of criticism itself. The philosopher of art was to analyze the evaluative judgments of literary scholars and both clarify and critically examine their supporting reasoning. But it was not his role to contest their expert judgments. He might try to extract and formulate from their practice some evaluative standards, but he was not expected to offer original ones of his own. What made it even worse for evaluation was academic criticism's own great reluctance to evaluate. Since it aspired (as a university-based discipline) to some sort of scientific status, and since the then reigning dogma held science to be value neutral, academic criticism essentially confined itself to finding facts and new interpretations, and could be scathing (like Northrop Frye) in rejecting evaluation as "meaningless criticism" or "leisure-class gossip."[16]

Thus, though the influential analyst Charles Stevenson insisted that interpretation and evaluation could not be clearly separated in criticism, and though Beardsley offered not only canons of evaluation but a theoretical grounding for them in an account of aesthetic experience, analytical aesthetics gave far less attention to value than did traditional aesthetics.[17] Indeed, not only did it spend proportionally more time on topics like interpretation, the definition of art, representation, expression, fiction, the ontological status and identity of artworks, analytic aesthetics often seemed to want to skirt the question of evaluation altogether as being too traditionally muddled and fruitlessly intractable and misleading. This is starkly expressed in Wollheim's explicit refusal to discuss the question in his *Art and its Objects* (1968), and even more bluntly in Goodman's continuing refrain that excessive concentration on the question of "excellence in art has been partly to blame for the lack of excellence in aesthetics."[18] Moreover, the vast majority of analytic aestheticians insisted (against Harold Osborne) that artistic evaluations could be accurately made and justified without relying on or appealing to aesthetic theory.[19]

But probably the most striking sign of analytic aesthetics' discomfort and shrinking disengagement from the issue of evaluating art is its very distinctive attempt to distinguish a non-evaluative, merely classificatory, sense of "art" from the more characteristic evaluative or "honorific" sense of art as something at least *prima facie* valuable. Most analysts initially held with Weitz that the aesthetician's task was not to define art but to describe the logic of its concept. While Gallie suggested that what helps make art an essentially contested concept and therefore apparently impossible to define is its ineliminable evaluative dimension, Weitz made much of sharply distinguishing descriptive and evaluative senses of the concept.[20] Though he held art undefinable in either its descriptive or honorific sense, the conceptual wedge Weitz helped drive between them led many to think that analysis could factor out and ignore the so-called evaluative sense and concentrate philosophical efforts on understanding art in its purely descriptive or classificatory content. Here objectivity and definition might succeed since there would apparently be no values to obstruct and obfuscate precise, logical analysis.

We find precisely this move in Dickie's influential institutional definition of art which defines an artwork only in the classificatory sense: to wit, as an artifact given the status of a candidate for appreciation by some agent acting on behalf of a social institution called the artworld.[21] But what real value or substance can such a definition possibly have? For, as its proponents admit, the strictly classificatory sense of the judgment "This is art" has virtually no use. Moreover, the substantive aesthetic issue which motivates such definitional quests, i.e., whether or how we should appreciate a particular artifact as a work of art, is merely deferred to the artworld and its evaluational decisions and definitions. The very notion of candidate for appreciation presupposes a background where art is evaluatively appreciated, and such evaluations (as Wittgenstein stressed) take many more forms than traditional ascriptions of beauty: there is rightness, precision, importance, originality, interest, etc. Art and (the contest of) value cannot in a holistic sense be separated, which is neither to deny that art is cognitive nor to imply that other domains of cultural achievement are not also intrinsically value laden.

8. This suggests another salient feature of analytic aesthetics—its neglect of the socially charged context of art. In trying to define art in purely nonevaluative terms, analytic philosophy not only ignored something crucially important, but it misleadingly suggested that art could be properly understood without having to understand (and take a stand in) the contested field of culture. In this arena, the struggle over aesthetic valorization both reflects and bears on the struggle for larger social stakes in a very complex field of individuals and class fragments competing for social legitimation and distinction. Analytic philosophy's blindness to the complex and contested social context of art criticism, and even its own aesthetic theorizing, is paradoxically most striking . . . in its attempt to define art as a social institution.

9. A somewhat similar point might perhaps be made about analytic aesthetics' relative neglect of history, which is characteristic of analytic philosophy's general ahistorical approach to problems.[22] Such a point would, however, require significant qualifications and exceptions. Certainly Wittgenstein, Wollheim, and Danto have long emphasized the historicity of art and its appreciation; and many analytic aestheticians are also excellent scholars of aesthetics' history. But there is nothing in mainstream analytic aesthetics to match the grand historiosophical or genealogical approach which dominates continental philosophy of art since Hegel. The only thing anyway like it is Danto's recent (and avowedly Hegelian) theory of art's original disenfranchisement, evolution, and end in *The Philosophical Disenfranchisement of Art*. But this book, even if written by an analytic philosopher, is clearly very remote from analytic aesthetics as ordinarily understood and typically practiced. Moreover, it must be stressed that art's history is seen by Danto (and more generally by analytic aesthetics) as autonomous and relatively isolated from history's socioeconomic factors and struggles.[23] Analytic aesthetics will seek to justify both this "isolationist" historical perspective and its own general penchant for the isolated, piecemeal treatment of particular problems narrowly defined and logically purified, as necessary means for adequate clarity and focus. Marxian critics will instead interpret and condemn them as reflecting the social fragmentation, isolation, and reification engendered by capitalism. Analysts will counter by demanding that such charges and concepts be themselves clearly and precisely defined. This is a debate which must be introduced but not entered here.

10. I shall conclude by returning to the problematic conception of analytic aesthetics as metacriticism. This of course confined philosophy's understanding of art and the aesthetic to what criticism understood or sought to understand, thereby preventing philosophy from using its aesthetic inquiries to achieve philosophical illumination in epistemology, philosophy of mind, and philosophy of language. But apart from such problems of limitation of scope, there were problems of consistency intrinsic to the very project of critically clarifying the language and logic of criticism. There were two basic tensions at work here: the first between the ideals of clarificational descriptive accuracy and critical reform, the second between the different language-games or logics in criticism.

Analytic aesthetics as a clarificatory second-order account of the first-order discipline of critical practice assumed (and had to assume) that this practice (at least as practiced by established critics) was both worthwhile and productive of acceptable results which it was not the analyst's job to question. His role was simply to elucidate the logical form of proper critical practice and perhaps formulate and sharpen it into clear principles which critics might then use if they felt they went astray or were locked in irresolvable controversy about a particular critical question. The job was to provide a clear map or picture of a very confused and vague terrain intuitively familiar to critics who were its best explorers but had no skill in precise cartography. But if critical practice was both confusingly vague and yet essentially acceptable, what should the analyst's job of clarification be? Should it just make that practice more clear to us by tracing all its complex vagaries or should it make the practice itself more clear by criticizing such ambiguities and recommending somewhat different and clearer concepts, standards, or procedures? Descriptive accuracy versus prescriptive clarity was analytic aesthetics' irresolvable dilemma. As Wittgenstein sharply posed it, "won't it become a hopeless task to draw a sharp picture corresponding to the blurred one? . . . And this is the position you are in if you look for definitions corresponding to our concepts in aesthetics or ethics."[24] It is equally hopeless to recommend a definite reform to render critical practice less ambiguous (as Beardsley did in his anti-intentionalism and three objective canons) and then to pretend that this is not so much a substantial reform as the analytic discovery of what all good critics were really doing all along when they were doing things right.[25] Yet Beardsley's reformatory "analyses" were probably those most stimulating and influential for critics and theorists both within and outside the analytic tradition. And a more explicitly constructivist and pragmatist analyst like Goodman (who is also less committed to metacriticism) can flatly insist that analysis of antecedent practice and concepts is just a springboard for critically constructive efforts to improve or replace them. It therefore seems likely that analytic aesthetics will move in this more pragmatist, activist direction, especially since recent critical practice has taken some surprising new directions which many analytic philosophers will not wish to follow or accept as critical paradigms to which analysis as accurate second-order reflection must be faithful.

This suggests the second source of tension in the metacritical program of analysis—the plurality of contested critical practices. In accord with philosophy's traditional search for general and unifying principles, much analytic effort was devoted to uncovering the underlying logic behind the vast and complex array of different critical practices; for example, to reveal *the* basic logic of interpretation at work in the seemingly different interpretive practices of different critics (and to do the same thing for evaluation). Analysts sought to do this by close examination and accurate description of what good critics actually do when interpreting, but they arrived at very different and inconsistent accounts of interpretive logic. The reason is simply that there is no basic or essential interpretive logic; there instead are very different logics (and not merely different methods) of interpretation. Different critics play different interpretive "games" with different logics implicit in and structuring the games they practice. These different games reflect and serve different aims; and their fundamental logical variance is concealed by the fact that they are never explicitly formulated by critics and further by their sharing much the same terms "the poem," "the right interpretation," "the meaning," "justification" but using them in often very different senses. The cause of the controversy and divergence of analyses of interpretive logic is that analysts are analyzing different logics which they take as their model and from which they generalize for all interpretations.[26]

But if analysis is the clarificatory program of accurately describing the actual logic employed rather than normatively prescribing the logic that should be employed, then the analytic aesthetician has a problem. He is not justified in defending his theory of interpretive logic by rejecting all the entrenched interpretive games which do not fit his model on the grounds that they are not "true" interpretation or that they do not satisfy the true or proper ends of interpretation. For the true nature and ends of interpretation are essentially contested by critics, and thus to determine such issues would be to legislate or recommend, not neutrally to analyze. The idea that there is or must be one essential or proper interpretive logic (whether objectivist, relativist, noncognitivist, etc.) which underlies all good criticism was a vestige of aesthetic essentialism that analytic aesthetics had trouble shedding. For the faith that such a logic was there to be discovered and subsequently employed to ground and grade academic criticism was what gave that project of analysis its whole point and motive.

Of course, an analyst could maintain the ideal of neutral objective analysis by accepting the plurality of critical practices (even those he finds most unsavory) and faithfully analyzing their variant logics. Their different aims, strengths, and limitations would be indicated but no transcendental philosophical privileging would be provided, and the variant practices would be left to prove themselves by the power and appeal of their achievements. This path of analytic purism seems to converge with radical deconstruction in concluding that there is no philosophically privileged right way for criticism. But such a posture of rigorous neutrality is arguably itself a scientific prejudice involving gross self-deception. For philosophy's abnegation of normative judgment as to how texts and artworks *should be* understood for the sake of representing accurately how they *are in fact* understood seems to betray the issue that really matters to us, and instead pursues an old analytic dream of discovering and mirroring the true structure of facts, here the logical structure of criticism.

Pragmatists would argue that this dream rests on the dubious assumption that the nature of criticism (or art) is simply there to be discovered rather than to be made and remade. They would insist that it is partly a philosopher's responsibility to see that it is made right and not just left to the professional critics. Analytic aestheticians like Goodman and Margolis have shown evidence of general pragmatist leanings (albeit mainly in their nonaesthetic writings). Moreover, some analysts like Scruton show great zeal in polemically confronting continental theory on the issue of how art should be understood and experienced. Here again it seems likely that analytic aesthetics will take a more activist and interventionist role in the contest over the nature of art criticism rather than simply "clarify" (with implicit acquiescence) what the prominent critics see fit to do.

But if it pursues this direction, . . . will it still remain analytic aesthetics? Or will it be something new, something analytic only in its style, terminology, and the authors it cites? The answer to this question depends not only on the future but on how analytic aesthetics should be understood.

NOTES

1. See, for example, B. Russell, "Logical Atomism," in D. Pears, ed., *Russell's Philosophy of Logical Atomism* (London, 1972), p. 162. I wish to thank Anita Silvers for apprising me

of the original document's importance and the Rockefeller Foundation for making it available.
2. See W. Callaghan et al., eds., *Aesthetics and the Theory of Criticism: Selected Papers of Arnold Isenberg* (University of Chicago Press, 1973), pp. 285–301.
3. See C. H. Langford, "The Notion of Analysis in Moore's Philosophy," in P. A. Schilpp, ed., *The Philosophy of G. E. Moore* (Northwestern University Press, 1942), pp. 321–42.
4. See Nelson Goodman, *Languages of Art* (Indianapolis, 1968), pp. 177–221. For a more general defense of constructivism, see his "The Revision of Philosophy," in *Problems and Projects* (Indianapolis, 1972), pp. 5–23.
5. See Richard Shusterman, "Analytic Aesthetics, Literary Theory, and Deconstruction," *Monist* 69 (1986): 22–38.
6. Beardsley, however, might seem an exception to this since he regards works of art as constituting a special "function-class" of objects most suitable for producing aesthetic experience, where aesthetic experience is treated in an essentialist manner. See Monroe Beardsley, *Aesthetics: Problems in the Philosophy of Criticism* (New York, 1958), pp. 524–30. Danto also seems to embrace some sort of essentialism; see his *The Transfiguration of the Commonplace* (Harvard University Press, 1981), pp. viii, 28. I should further note that analytic aesthetics in fact displayed two kinds of antiessentialism—weak and strong. The weak held that if we follow Wittgenstein's advice "to look and see" we just won't find any essence of art, while the stronger view held that art could not possibly have any essence because of its adventurous character and the open nature of its concept. This distinction is nicely elucidated in T. J. Diffey, "Essentialism and the Definition of Art," *British Journal of Aesthetics* 13 (1973): 103–20.
7. Analysts were particularly fond of making this point by reference to the historical research of P. O. Kristeller's "The Modern System of the Arts," *Journal of the History of Ideas* 11, 12 (1951, 1952).
8. J. A. Passmore, "The Dreariness of Aesthetics," in W. Elton, ed., *Aesthetics and Language* (Oxford, 1954), p. 44. See also Stuart Hampshire, "Logic and Appreciation," W. B. Gallie, "The Function of Philosophical Aesthetics" in the same Elton volume; W. E. Kennick, "Does Traditional Aesthetics Rest on a Mistake?," *Mind* (1958), reprinted in C. Barret's anthology, *Collected Papers in Aesthetics* (Oxford, 1965), another trove of influential analytic papers; and M. Weitz, "The Role of Theory in Aesthetics," *Journal of Aesthetics and Art Criticism* 16 (1955): 27–35.
9. Passmore, pp. 50–55.
10. This dependence on the separate "scientific" study of the arts is also a reason why the mid-century analytic aestheticians were especially hard on Croce, whose essentialism was coupled with a virulent antiscientism about the understanding of art. For more on this see Shusterman, "Analytic Aesthetics."
11. Consider, for example, not only Weitz's scholarly and compendious *Hamlet and the Philosophy of Literary Criticism* (London, 1964), but his excellent study of Eliot's poetry, "T. S. Eliot: Time as a Mode of Salvation," first published in *The Sewanee Review* in 1952 and reprinted in B. Bergonzi, ed., *T. S. Eliot: Four Quartets* (London, 1969), pp. 138–52.
12. See Richard Wollheim, *Art and its Objects* (Harmondsworth, U.K., 1975), section 42.
13. See G. Dickie, "The Myth of the Aesthetic Attitude," *American Philosophical Quarterly* 1 (1964): 56–66; and "Beardsley's Phantom Aesthetic Experience," *Journal of Philosophy* 62 (1965): 129–36. See Beardsley, *Aesthetics*, pp. 29–52.
14. For more detail on this, see Richard Shusterman, "Deconstruction and Analysis: Confrontation and Convergence," *British Journal of Aesthetics* 26 (1986): 310–24.
15. See Danto, *The Philosophical Disenfranchisement of Art*, (Columbia University Press, 1986) pp. xiv–xv, 1–21; and Nelson Goodman, *Languages of Art*, pp. 248–64, and *Of Mind and Other Matters* (Harvard University Press, 1984), pp. 138–53.
16. See N. Frye, *The Anatomy of Criticism* (Princeton University Press, 1957), p. 18.
17. See C. L. Stevenson, "On the Reasons That Can be Given for the Interpretation of a Poem," repr. in J. Margolis, ed., *Philosophy Looks at the Arts* (New York, 1962), p. 124; and Beardsley, *Aesthetics*, pp. 524–43.
18. See Wollheim, sec. 65; and Nelson Goodman, *Problems and Projects*, p. 121. See also *Languages of Art*, pp. 261–62: "Excessive concentration on the question of excellence has been responsible for constriction and distortion of aesthetic inquiry. . . . And a criterion of aesthetic merit is no more the major aim of aesthetics than a criterion of virtue is the major aim of psychology." The theme is continued

(albeit in a more moderate vein) in *Of Mind and Other Matters*, pp. 164–66.
19. According to Kennick, the very assumption that a definition of art is needed or used when properly evaluating art represents the second grave mistake (after essentialism) on which traditional aesthetics rested. See W. Kennick, "Does Traditional Aesthetics Rest on a Mistake?" *Mind* 67 (1958): 317–34. For a detailed account of the views of other analysts (e.g., Hampshire, Isenberg, Macdonald, Sibley) who rejected the idea that evaluation was or should be guided by any general theory, see Richard Shusterman, "Evaluative Reasoning in Criticism," *Ratio* 23 (1981): 142–59, and more recently, "Wittgenstein and Critical Reasoning," *Philosophy and Phenomenological Research* 47 (1986): 91–110.
20. See Weitz, "The Role of Theory in Aesthetics"; and W. B. Gallie, "Art as an Essentially Contested Concept," *Philosophical Quarterly* 6 (1956): 97–114.
21. See, for example, G. Dickie, *Aesthetics* (New York, 1971), pp. 98–108. In response to numerous criticisms, the theory has gone through a number of minor revisions since first advanced in 1969. The latest version is found in *The Art Circle* (New York, 1984), and perhaps the most sustained and powerful case against the whole idea of defining art in a purely classificatory sense is in B. R. Tilghman, *But Is It Art?* (Oxford, 1984).
22. Consider, for example, Goodman's contemptuously glib dismissal of traditional aesthetic theory as hopelessly misguided and obsolete, its relation to his own contemporary aesthetics being that of the horse and buggy to the motor car (*Of Mind and Other Matters*, p. 198).
23. For Danto the factors of imperatives directing art's evolution and history are those of "its own internal development" (*The Philosophical Disenfranchisement of Art*, pp. 97–111, 204); and Roger Scruton similarly insists, against Marxian views, that art history be viewed as having the "autonomy constitutive of a genuine independent subject." See R. Scruton, "Art History and Aesthetic Judgment," in *The Aesthetic Understanding* (London, 1983), p. 167.
24. L. Wittgenstein, *Philosophical Investigations* (Oxford, 1953), par. 77.
25. *Aesthetics*, pp. 17–29, 454–70.
26. See Richard Shusterman, "The Logic of Interpretation," *Philosophical Quarterly* 28 (1978): 310–24.

Letting the Sunshine In: Has Analysis Made Aesthetics Clear?

Anita Silvers

In the middle of the twentieth century, some analytic philosophers set out to rescue aesthetics from dreariness. Although it would be an exaggeration to think of them as a self-conscious movement, as were the logical positivists of the Vienna Circle, it is not difficult to reconstruct the program to which they generally adhered in their attempt to rescue and enliven aesthetics. The body of work which I take to announce and to exemplify the program was published in a period of about fifteen years, from 1946 through 1962, in England and America.[1] Much fine work in philosophical aesthetics was done subse-

From *The Journal of Aesthetics and Art Criticism*, 46 (1987), Special Issue. Reprinted by permission of The American Society for Aesthetics.

quently, some more and some less obviously addressed to the issues raised by the program and responsive to the program's standards and objectives. But in reconstructing the theses characteristic of the program, it is not necessary to examine more than a representative sample of the exemplary, influential work done during this fifteen-year post war period.

In fact, the program succeeded in some respects, and aesthetics seems less dreary today. Ironically, what dreariness remains is blamed by some on the very techniques which the analysts promoted. When the analytic aestheticians sought to cleanse their domain of obscurity, the charge goes, they failed to recognize that the activities they promoted were drearier than those they sought to extirpate.

With probably only one single exception, that being Wimsatt and Beardsley's "The Intentional Fallacy," historians and critics of the arts treated the work of the analytic aestheticians at best as irrelevant, but sometimes as malevolent. Of course, the concern that such negative reactions provokes depends on whether philosophical aesthetics is expected to make a positive impact on art studies. Nevertheless, the failure of the analytic program to influence art studies contrasts not only with the profound influence of those whom the analytic aestheticians sought to reform—for instance, Wordsworth, Tolstoi, and Bell—but also with the influence attained by their programmatic successors like Nelson Goodman (on arts education), Arthur Danto (on postmodern art criticism), and Jacques Derrida (on literary theory).[2] Nevertheless, it might be said that analytic aesthetics provided reforms from which more substantive developments could evolve. In this essay, I want to explore whether the reforms of the analytic aestheticians were beneficial, or whether their program was defective at its core.

Did the analytic program revive aesthetics? Did it succeed on its own terms? Did it at least initiate reforms from which more substantive improvements evolved? Or was it nothing more than a sterile interlude? Resolving these questions is of more than mere historical interest, for the failure of a philosophical program can be as instructive as its success. By discovering how such a program was meant to operate and what it was meant to achieve, and then by observing what promoted and what impeded it, philosophy gains a firmer grasp of its own purpose and philosophers are aided in perfecting their craft.

To reconstruct the program of analytic aesthetics, I rely on three sources[3]: the collection of essays titled *Aesthetics and Language*,[4] the collection of essays edited by Joseph Margolis and titled *Philosophy Looks At the Arts*,[5] and a report by Arnold Isenberg titled "Analytical Philosophy and the Study of Art."[6] The earliest essay is Beardsley and Wimsatt's "The Intentional Fallacy," originally published in 1946 and included in Margolis; the most recent is Charles Stevenson's "On the Reasons That Can Be Given for the Interpretation of a Poem," which appeared for the first time in the Margolis collection in 1962. The full text of the Isenberg report has never been published, although excerpts from it appear in the posthumous collection of Isenberg's writings.[7]

That one of the earliest of these sources—Isenberg's report—was influential despite never being published in full is evidenced by the introduction Elton wrote for his own volume. Elton concludes a lengthy paragraph, in which he repeats others' charges that aesthetics is abundantly confused, barren, dull, boring, largely bogus, and desolate, with a direct quotation from Isenberg's report, which he describes as having been privately circulated in 1950 and in which Isenberg refers to the "present stone age of aesthetics."[8] The report also is footnoted by Vincent Tomas, in an essay first published in 1952 and subsequently included in the Margolis collection.[9]

To reconstruct the program of "analytic aesthetics" from these sources in no way is to assess the essays collected in them as the best or most important examples of analytic aesthetics. Many well-known names and influential articles are not included.[10] But there is an advantage in using these anthologies as sources from which to derive the salient characteristics of the program. The essays they contain were selected both to exemplify and to promote the analytic approach to aesthetics. The editors of both collections proclaim this. Moreover, very many of the authors of the essays in both collections refer to what they conceived of as the work of their programmatic predecessors, and they also cite work written by their contemporaries which they take to be programmatically connected with their own. Consequently, it is fair to view these collections as the primary source books for analytic aesthetics, which is how they were viewed by students in the 1960s.[11]

In diagnosing the causes of dreariness in aesthetics, the source writings converge in advocating the reformation of aesthetic as guided by three theses. Although these are related to each other, none entails any of the others. Here is the first and most general directive.

1. Aesthetics must be reformed by replacing its typically obscure and confused ideas with clear ones.

How is this thesis applied? W. B. Gallie,[12] for instance, demonstrates the method he proposes by analyzing Wordworth's *Preface to the 1815 Edition of the Lyrical Ballads* to expose what he thinks of as contradictions and confusions. Gallie assesses the *Preface* (and the *Essay Supplementary* of the same year) as "great"; nevertheless he applies his "logical tools" to reveal how Wordsworth gets himself "into a muddle." He does not, however, blame Wordsworth as much as pity him. That is, Gallie diagnoses the contradictions into which he thinks Wordsworth falls as faults resulting from Wordsworth's lack of logical sophistication in treating the complex aesthetic phenomena he was aesthetically sensitive enough to recognize. Wordsworth's observations are valuable, Gallie admits, but their value is obscured by Wordsworth's apparently contradicting himself by suggesting both that the processes of imaginative abstraction necessarily falsify and also provide us with new truths.

This theme is encountered as well in "The Intentional Fallacy."

Certainly it need not be with a derogatory purpose that one points out personal studies, distinct from poetic studies, in the realm of literary scholarship. Yet there is danger of confusing personal and poetic studies.[13]

Isenberg sounds a similar note by saying,

The best thing that philosophy can do for the art studies is to bring some clarity to those issues with which modern criticism is rife—which have arisen "naturally," as it were, out of recent aesthetic preoccupations.[14]

Subsequently, Isenberg analyzes a passage of criticism of *Hamlet* and comments:

Broad remarks about the fundamental purpose of criticism, narrow rules of thumb which have been useful to the author in his work, a few objections to prevailing practices among contemporaries, a few intelligent suggestions as to paths of thought that deserve to be opened up, some ideas of theses that belong *in* the field rather than in an essay about it, some inconclusive examples (often minutely analyzed) which are supposed to prove general principles about the distinction between creativity and criticism or the relation of art and knowledge or the bearing of historical erudition upon critical judgment—all these are scrambled together with a fine disregard for logical order and coherence. . . .
The same topics, in the hands of persons trained in logical analysis, could be treated with unexampled clarity and rigor.[15]

Deploring confusion and advocating the increased clarity afforded by applying logical tools lead analytic aesthetics to a second characteristic thesis.

2. Aesthetics must be reformed by prohibiting the practice of generalizing insights gained from experience of particular artworks and then expecting the generalizations to function as rules in aesthetic arguments.[16]

This message runs throughout. It is an

outcome of the injunction to be clear. Of the murky phenomena of aesthetic discourse, the analytic aestheticians find the field's unrequited enchantment with formulating rules among the most obscure. Noticing that what passes for aesthetic rules or principles systematically falls short of success, they suspect that to argue aesthetically by appealing to generalizations is to masquerade.

In "Logic and Appreciation," Stuart Hampshire concludes,

when in Aesthetics one moves from the particular to the general, one is travelling in the wrong direction.[17]

And, in "Arguments Used By Criticism of the Arts," Margaret Macdonald writes:

But to attempt to legislate for art is to invite successful infringement of any law, as the "Unities" showed. Criticism is, therefore, I suggest, an indefinite set of devices for "presenting" not "proving" the merits of works of art. It has none of the stability of logical truth, scientific method, legal and moral law.[18]

In "Critical Communication," Arnold Isenberg writes:

Is it reasonable to expect better evaluations of art after a thousand years of criticism than before? . . . I think we have already numerous passages which are not to be corrected or improved upon. And if this opinion is right, then it could not be the case that the validation of critical judgments waits upon the discovery of aesthetic laws. . . . We are not more fully convinced in our own judgment because we know its explanation; and we cannot hope to convince an imaginary opponent by appeal to this explanation, which by hypothesis does not hold for him.[19]

And in "The Interpretation of a Poem," Charles Stevenson writes,

The inconclusiveness of the reasons mentioned (and they are inconclusive even when used collectively) suggests that they are not premises in an argument that is strictly deductive.[20]

The formulation of the various versions of this thesis are developed by the analytic aestheticians in the process of clarifying the way aesthetic discourse actually functions. In his or her own way, each notes how claims which typically might be taken as aesthetic principles, or as resting on aesthetic principles, never enjoy results compatible with their functioning as major or minor premises in sound arguments. Where someone proposes to generalize from the properties which seem responsible for value or meaning in the case of one work or one small group of works of art, the generalization fails to create conclusive conviction when applied beyond the initial case. Although some proportion of failure, even a high one, could pass without remark, the categorical inability of aesthetic debate to achieve the force of sound argument indicates to the aesthetic analysts that aesthetics is systematically and profoundly confused.

A special source of confusion lies in what analytic aesthetics takes as the traditional cause of misguided generalization—the desire to be definitive about art.[21] This diagnosis leads to a third characteristic thesis, the only one of the three addressed not to aesthetic discourse only but also to art itself.

3. Aesthetics must be reformed by recognizing that art admits of no essential properties.

The most influential of the essays pursuing this thesis is Morris Weitz's "The Role of Theory in Aesthetics." Here is a sketch of the position to which so many of Weitz's successors felt called upon to respond.

Theory has been central in aesthetics and is still the preoccupation of the philosophy of art. Its main avowed concern remains the determination of the nature of art which can be formulated into a definition of it. . . .

In this essay I want to plead for the rejection of this problem. I want to show that theory—in the requisite classical sense—is *never* forthcoming in aesthetics, and that we would do much better as philosophers to supplant the question, "What is the nature of art?" by other questions, the answers to which will provide us with all the understanding of the arts there can be. . . . Aesthetic theory—all of it—is wrong in principle in thinking that a correct theory is possible because it radically misconstrues the logic of the concept of art. Its main contention that "art" is amenable to real or any kind of true definition is false.[22]

And in "The Dreariness of Aesthetics," J. A. Passmore remarks:

Woolliness of this sort seems to have a natural habitat in certain fields. . . . Why should these particular fields be thus distinguished by so fine an array of empty formulae? . . .
The woolliness of education, of sociology, of metaphysics, is understandable, then, as arising out of the attempt to impose a spurious unity on things, the spuriousness being reflected in the emptiness of the formulae in which that unity is described. We can easily understand the passions which lie behind this anxiety to reconcile. But why should the same sort of thing happen in aesthetics?[23]

What justifies the program's directions for reform? In general, the analysis starts with an observation that form apparently does not fulfill function. The development of the second thesis, prohibiting generalizations which take the form of rules, provides a good illustration of how this process works.

In formulating this position, Isenberg and Macdonald contend that, although critical discourse contains expressions that have the form of major premises, these expressions do not function successfully in that capacity.[24] Then it is assumed that the mismatch of function and form results in dysfunction, which in turn explains why aesthetics seems incapable of escaping dreary futility. Thus, Macdonald, Isenberg, and others rely on their readers agreeing with them that not only has there never been a successful categorical principle of art, but also that no sophisticated person expects there to be such. They deplore aesthetics' history of pursuing such principles—a kind of activity which to them is not merely futile, but, worse, is patently so.

Having noted that expressions possessing the form of aesthetic rules or principles fail to perform according to form, it remains for contributors to the program both to explain why and to recommend an appropriate remedy. Different ways of accounting for this phenomenon are offered. These typically are claims about how critical discourse functions. For instance, in "The Use of 'Good' in Aesthetic Discourse" Helen Knight appeals to what we do and do not say.

One picture is good for one sort of thing, and another for something quite different. . . . We praise the brightness and clarity of an Impressionist painting, but do not condemn a Rembrandt for lacking those qualities. It is clear that we look for something different in each case. . . . And how do we praise a realistic picture? We say that the artist has caught the exact pose, the kind of thing one might see at any moment. And the very banality of that pose (in the case of Degas) is a merit. But we do not condemn Botticelli because we fail to meet his goddesses and nymphs as we walk through the street. On the contrary, we praise him for imagination of the ideal. And we praise him for his flowing rhythm, but do not condemn Byzantine art for being rigid, nor Cezanne for being ponderous.[25]

Within the program of analytic aesthetics, the futility of proposing categorical rules for judging or understanding art is not explained in terms of the nature of art, or of aesthetic experience. Earlier philosophers who arrived at analogous conclusions, such as Kant, Collingwood, or Dewey, were inclined to appeal to ontological or epistemological considerations to support and inform their opposition to aesthetic rules. But, of the analytic aestheticians, it is Margaret Macdonald, I think, who forges furthest beyond appealing simply to "what we say and do" when we talk about art when she insists that:

It is often said that a great artist is reinterpreted in every age and no doubt by some of these interpretations he would be much astonished. Yet even the apparently bizarre interpretations are often illuminating. It seems to follow that interpretation is partly subjective invention, but about this there could be endless argument of the sort that would hardly be necessary about the description of a chair or horse, except perhaps in extreme borderline cases. Certainly, the critic claims to be interpreting the work, not supplying his own fancies. But the work is what it is interpreted to be, though some interpretations may be rejected. There seems to be no work apart from *some* interpretation.[26]

Macdonald here begins by referring to the discourse "It is often said that . . . " and "about this there could be endless argument of the sort that would hardly be necessary about the description of a chair." However, she continues by making an epistemological claim to the effect that we interpret artworks whereas we only describe chairs, and an ontological claim to the effect that artworks exist only as interpretations. This is atypical for analytic aestheticians, who characteristically operate as if it is easier to substantiate claims about how critical discourse works (that is, about how we talk) than claims about what art objects really are (that is, about what we talk about) and how we can know them.

Compare this with Paul Ziff's approach in "Art and the 'Object of Art'" in the same volume,[27] wherein Ziff proposes to dissolve such claims by showing that the seemingly incompatible attributions which lead some philosophers to accord special status to art objects should be explained not epistemologically or ontologically, but, instead, by noticing that we employ these attributions in different discourses suited for and used in quite different contexts. Ziff proposes that so-called incompatible attributions can be treated by understanding that the discourses in which they are embedded belong to different families that are, if not incommensurable, then at least disassociated from each other. Consequently, these attributions are not inconsistent with each other, and one need not save appearances by explaining that art objects are illusory or otherwise ontologically mysterious.

To what extent does the sort of account favored by the analysts explain why aesthetic discourse is dysfunctional? Since the most typical stratagem of the analytic aestheticians is to draw attention to actual practice and to speculate cautiously on what such practice can and cannot achieve, their explanations tend to lay the blame for confusion on the doorstep of inflated expectations. We are tricked by attending to the form of expressions rather than to their use, they say. As a result, we expect aesthetic discourse to function more powerfully than it can do.

On the program of analytic aesthetics, such mistakes must be rectified once their cause has been clarified. But revealing a source of an error does not necessarily disclose its remedy. And the technique used by the analytic aestheticians to diagnose aesthetics' problems creates a particular puzzle about where the solution lies.

To dispel obscurity, we are directed to observe practice carefully, to lower our expectations, and not to seek results beyond what actual practice has shown it can attain. On this program, then, existing practice sets the standard. But if existing practice is the standard, and existing practice is also obscure, against what standard should existing practice be reformed?

Here, the analytic program's most general directive appears to take precedence. If, in practice, aesthetic discourse is beclouded because form and function typically are mismatched, clarity must be imposed rigorously. To dispel confusion, either the form of the discourse should change to suit its functions, or its functions must be revised to more appropriately make use of its form.

But to urge such change must be to advocate that practice be changed. That is what the theses which constitute the analytic aestheticians' program advise. Presumably, this advice derives either from considerations internal to practice, or else from grounds logically prior to, or more fundamental than, practice itself. We also can presume that the source of the program's directives ultimately affects how serviceable the advice they offer turns out to be.

It is typical of analytic aesthetics that the reasons given for reforming practice are considerations drawn from practice itself. Passmore addresses the issue characteristically. His whistle-blowing is motivated by the suspicion that dreariness engulfs aesthetic discourse just when those who engage in the discourse distort it by imposing inappropriate models.

. . . it seems to me possible at least that the dullness of aesthetics arises from the attempt to construct a subject where there isn't one. . . . perhaps the truth is that there is no aesthetics and yet there [is] . . . literary criticism, . . . music criticism, etc.[28]

But how to identify the appropriate model? Weitz suggests that criticism works by favorably recasting features which previously have been considered either as unimportant or as defects of the discourse.

But what makes them—these honorific definitions—so supremely valuable is not their disguised linguistic recommendations; rather it is the *debates* over the reasons for changing the criteria of the concept of art which are built into the definitions. In each of the great theories of art, whether correctly understood as honorific definitions or incorrectly accepted as real definitions, what is of the utmost importance are the reasons proffered in the arguments for the respective theory, that is, the reasons given for the chosen or preferred criterion of excellence and evaluation. It is this perennial debate over these criteria of evaluation which makes the history of aesthetic theory the important study it is. . . . Thus, the role of the theory is not to define anything but to use the definitional form, almost epigrammatically, to pin-point a crucial recommendation to turn our attention once again to the plastic elements in painting.[29]

Isenberg adopts the same approach. He tries to explain why we think we are giving critical reasons when we actually are not giving critical reasons at all. He proposes that the critic uses the locutions we call reasons to direct perception of works of art.

I have perhaps overstressed the role of the critic as teacher, *i.e.* as one who affords *new* perceptions and with them new values. . . . it often happens that there are qualities in a work of art which are, so to speak, neither perceived nor ignored but felt or endured. . . . Suppose it is only a feeling of monotony, a slight oppressiveness, which comes to us from the style of some writer. A critic then refers to his "piled-up clauses, endless sentences, repetitious diction." This remark shifts the focus of our attention and brings certain qualities which had been blurred and marginal into distinct consciousness.[30]

In his report to the Rockefeller Foundation, Isenberg addresses the question of reform systematically. He justifies the reform of aesthetics and provides detailed commentary about who should do it and how it should be done. It is interesting that this report was submitted after the article "Critical Communication" was written and published, so Isenberg was experienced with analysis which criticizes one account of a critical practice and then substitutes another, more plausible account. But such an approach is noticeably absent from the Rockefeller report.

In the 1949 essay, Isenberg analyzes the use of expressions which appear to be, but do not meet the criteria for being, reasons, proposing that these expressions function instead to direct immediate attention to properties that are rewarding to perceive. In fact, Isenberg's has proven to be one of the most successful of such alternative accounts produced by analytic aesthetics. It has shown itself to be much more durable than, for example, Stevenson's analogous attempt to account for the practices of interpretation. Curiously, in contrast to the 1949 essay, in the 1950 Rockefeller Foundation report Isenberg displays hardly any concern for explaining critical practice. But he does not hesitate to call vigorously for the reform of critical practice and to propose confidently how improvement may be brought about.

What is to be reformed, and how is the reform to be effected? Isenberg begins by recommending that philosophers and critics should acquire expertise in each other's fields.

I believe we may say that the best work in the field is to be done, if it is done at all, by young and unknown people. These people will appear if and when graduate students become convinced that aesthetics is worth studying. Analytically minded students of philosophy nowadays try to learn something about sciences such as mathematics or psychology. When they believe that criticism and art history also deserve their attention, when students of literature come to feel that they must go far into logic and philosophy, there will be some prospect of advances in aesthetics. . . . The subject, analytical aesthetics, remains largely to be created.[31]

Nevertheless, as Isenberg's proposals unfold, it turns out that little hope lies in expanding the philosophical competence of even very young and unformed historians and critics of the arts.

. . . this attitude is, in my judgment, typical of the critic or scholar turned philosopher. His reflections upon method are struck off as by-products of his daily occupation. They contain a mixture of considerations of different type or level. The shop talk of the craftsman is confused with the theory of the craft. . . .[32]

So we must turn to rigorously trained philosophers, whose education and interests need only be broadened.

For logical analysts, however, the danger lies in lack of familiarity with the concrete subject-matter and its problems, leading to an excessive abstractness. Even today there are some good ideas in theoretical aesthetics which are ignored by critics and historians because of their forbidding dryness, their apparent lack of relevance to practical pursuits. A thorough acquaintance with the rich though incoherent reflections of men working in the mines are the corrective to this philosophical remoteness.[33]

How expert in art studies need an analyst be?

An analysis is usually tested against the "denotation" of the concept that is being analyzed. . . . It follows that the analyst must be at least aware of the chief specific values that are denoted by the term or idea he is analyzing. Now among the important concepts of the art studies are some which have arisen in the process of critical evaluation and which therefore denote values as well as facts. The analyst should know these values. He should know, for example, that Tennyson is considered a skillful manipulator of verse rhythms and phonetic harmonies, and why he is so considered—if he wishes to clarify the critical use of the term "technique." . . . But if, as often happens, he tries to explain what is meant by "good color" in the criticism of painting by means of examples drawn from the *worst* colorists, then (at the very least) he confuses his treatment of a normative concept by raising distracting controversies at the primary level.[34]

What is it that the analyst, able to approximate if not equal the art scholar or critic in knowledgeable perception and delicate discrimination, is expected to do about art studies?

We can at once draw a conclusion for the theory and practice of criticism. A good theory of criticism should not and could not reform critical practice from the ground up. But by separating out, from the welter of reactions that pass for criticism, those lines of thought which have proved fruitful, and by explaining their tendency, it can encourage harder and sharper attacks in the same directions.[35]

A curiosity surfaces in this remark. For the analytic aesthetician to follow this advice, that is, to illuminate criticism without reforming it from the ground up, it is necessary to distinguish fruitful critical tendencies or practices from those which are unproductive. A few pages later, Isenberg acknowledges a programmatic prescription to remove the impediments to progress in art studies.

There is, indeed, an appearance of continuity and progress. . . . But when the smoke blows away, nothing solid remains; there is no real advance towards truth. Factual study, in art history, at least makes progress towards quantitative accumulation; but literary theory makes no progress towards greater objectivity, precision, generality and comprehensiveness. . . .
Let us make it clear that the specifically *critical* effort is probably not to be judged by any canons of scientific progress. To set up the positivist ideal of "getting somewhere" for the criticism of art is to impose an aim foreign to its nature—though, we must add, an aim which many critics seem to accept when they talk about each other's works.
Yet none of these points impeaches the desirability of intellectual progress. . . . It is these au-

thors themselves, incidentally, who set up their theoretical objectives. . . . Now if we ask why interesting and important projects like these have accomplished so little, the answer is fairly simple. These writers, with no lack either of brilliance or of care, are irresponsible because there is no clear-cut subject or method to which they can be responsible.[36]

What remains unclear from this and other comments is why Isenberg is so confident in the above passages, and others, that criticism can advance toward truth, greater objectivity, precision, generality, and comprehensiveness. The latter objectives are noteworthy in view of the position he takes earlier in "Critical Communication." Complicating the puzzle is the inclusion in the Rockefeller report of comments such as the following:

Today we have a small body of remarks of piercing brilliance about the nature of poetry, bequeathed to us by writers like Goethe, Coleridge, De-Quincey, Valery. These insights were usually the fruits of a close meditation not on Poetry itself but on poems in particular; they were flung out as a sort of generalization of some direct critical *aperçu*. Commonly, they are backed up either by no theory at all or by a shadowy metaphysic. Yet by comparison with them philosophic concepts of poetry seem blunt and inapposite. It has seldom occurred to philosophers to use these great critical passages as materials for analysis, striving to bring them into connection with sound principles of semiotic and aesthetic.[37]

What is so curious about this latter passage is Isenberg's proposed remedy for clarifying criticism. In 1949, he denies that there can be effective theoretical generalizations of direct critical perceptions of particular artworks. So one would expect him to urge in 1950 that critics simply refrain from "flinging out" generalizations and thus obscuring the brilliance of their remarks about particular works. Here, however, that question remains open, and the answer is thought to lie in securing the generalizations to a foundation of sound philosophical theories. In this spirit, Isenberg calls for recognition of the methodological status of such generalizations, as if they could be legitimated just by being categorized.

There is, I suggest, one standard of limited utility by which we can try to discriminate hopeful programs in poetics from hopeless ones; and that is clarity of aim. "You say you have a theory about poetic language. To what branch of knowledge or human endeavor does this theory belong? Empirical psychology? History of literature? Criticism? Philosophical analysis? What method will you use to establish your findings and by what criteria will you want them to be judged?" Needless to say, the application of this standard presupposes that we have a good methodology of art study.[38]

And:

Now in the Introduction to Wölfflin's brilliant and influential *Principles of Art History* we find questions raised that are essentially similar to those which have been treated with such distinction by analytically trained philosophers. The difference between the philosophy of history and the philosophy of art history is not a difference in inherent promise and potentiality; it consists entirely in the fact that the problems of art history have not attracted the interest of many analysts or able ones. The thought that the ideas of a Wölfflin should be reviewed and criticized by a philosopher with the acumen of Hempel would cause eager anticipation among informed scholars.[39]

Nothing in the report exposes Isenberg's optimism as glaringly as this last comment. How realistic is it to expect that scholars in other fields will value philosophers' telling them what to do? I think that Isenberg's expectation here is mediated by his belief that analytic philosophy does not impose prescriptions on other disciplines but, instead, merely clarifies those disciplines' own preferred methods. This is the status he accords Hempel's hypothetico-deductive model.

So the purpose of the proposed review of Wölfflin's ideas seems to be to expose the logical structure of the explanatory model successful art historical research adopts, and the purpose of the proposed criticism is to demonstrate where scholarly progress is impeded by departures from the model. By discovering Wölfflin's model, philosophers would permit art historians to progress more methodically in consolidating Wölfflin's gains; by revealing Wölfflin's lapses, philosophers could enable art historians to surpass Wölfflin's achievements. It is important to notice that whatever recommendations for reform philosophers make, on Isenberg's view here the advice is to be drawn from considerations internal to the structure of critical practice itself. On its least virile interpretation, the program is not to change critical practice, but merely to aid the practitioners in sorting their practices out.

In the Rockefeller report, Isenberg speculates on the beneficial results which could be expected from well-trained philosophers of good taste reviewing and criticizing key masterworks of aesthetic discourse. To better grasp the thrust of this program, it is illuminating to follow the speculation through and explore what would occur if the directives of analytic aesthetics were implemented. Would this improve the discourse by rendering it less obscure? What, for instance, would be the result of reforming art studies as the program's second thesis directs? Would eliminating the purported mismatch between form and function eliminate some dysfunctional dimensions of aesthetic discourse and make it more successful?

Suppose we erased the generalizations "flung out" by Goethe, Coleridge, DeQuincey, and Valery from their critical writings?[40] What remains are these writers' insights about particular works of art. Suppose, as Urmson does, we correct A. E. Housman's poetics by pointing out that Housman's own examples do not support his contention that being moved by thrilling utterances makes a situation aesthetic?[41] What remains are the examples themselves, which Urmson appropriates as confirmation of his own account of what makes a situation aesthetic. Suppose, as Gallie does, we explicate Wordsworth's 1815 *Preface* so as to obtain a more rigorous theory of the imagination.[42] What remains of Wordsworth's varied but perhaps inconsistent examples of imaginative activity (subtracting properties from an object, endowing an object with properties that do not inhere in it, consolidating discrete entities into a unity and separating a thing into discrete elements, framing comparisons of expression and effect) is Gallie's summation that, unlike mathematical abstraction, poetic abstractions are inexplicit, indefinite, and vague.

In all these cases, it seems to me, clarifying criticism results only in impoverishing it. Goethe, Coleridge, DeQuincey, Valery, and Housman no longer have theories at all after their work has been clarified. Their brilliance illuminates nothing beyond the illustrations they give. And the illustrations illustrate nothing beyond themselves. On the other hand, Wordsworth's theory no longer is illuminated by the brilliance of the illustrations, since on Gallie's showing these illustrations do not all drive uniformly in the same logical direction.

To strip, or not to strip, criticism of components which fall short of being clear. What is gained, and what, if anything, is lost? It should be noted that successful analysis need not make the critical writings easier to understand, as philosophical accounts that are clear to philosophers are not necessarily clear to anyone else.

Moreover, eliminating all but the critics' discussions of individual works could restrict interest in the criticism to those acquainted with the particular works discussed. For example, Reynolds's *Discourses* command some interest from those unacquainted with the paintings Reynolds names because he generalizes, and consequently his views apply to other paintings that these readers might have seen. Remove the theories and general remarks, inadequate though they may be, and one is left with remarks one recognizes as penetrating only if one has encountered the subjects of the remarks, a condition which the audience to whom Reynolds's lectures were directed might have found difficult to satisfy.

It is hard to see how methodological clarification of the kind exemplified by these analyses of Isenberg, Gallie, and Urmson advances criticism intellectually, since none of the revisions reform anything other than their immediate object. It is also hard to see why improving criticism logically should make it less rather than more dreary. For instance, Wordsworth's 1800 *Preface* is, in his own words, supposed to be a "systematic defense of the theory" which informed the writing of the *Lyrical Ballads*. Is it systematic, and is it a defense? Margaret Macdonald comments:

In his Preface Wordsworth says that he would not wish it to be supposed that he entertained the foolish hope of *reasoning* the reader into an approbation of the *Lyrical Ballads*. . . . the Preface increased the size of the volume by more than a score of pages. Whether or not this was argument, Wordsworth evidently did not regard it as a complete waste of time.[43]

However, the lines immediately following the words Macdonald cites make clear that Wordsworth does think he is offering arguments. He makes the disclaimer to which Macdonald refers because he cannot hope for complete success.

. . . adequately to display the opinions, and fully to enforce the arguments, would require a space wholly disproportionate to a preface. For to treat the subject with the clearness and coherence of which it is susceptible, it would be necessary to give a full account of the public taste in this country. . . . I hope, therefore, the reader will not censure me for attempting to state what I have proposed myself to perform; and also (as far as the limits of a preface will permit) to explain some of the chief reasons which have determined me in the choice of my purpose.[44]

Throughout this *Preface*, Wordsworth offers reasons to justify his choice of subject matter and style, and he even goes so far as to support and reject various canons of criticism.

. . . there is a numerous class of critics, who, when they stumble upon these prosaisms . . . imagine that they have made a notable discovery, and exult over the Poet as a man ignorant of his own profession. Now these men would establish a canon of criticism which the Reader will conclude he must utterly reject. . . . it would be a most easy task to prove to him that not only the language of a large portion of every good poem . . . must necessarily . . . in no respect differ from that of good prose, but likewise that some of the most interesting parts of the best poems will be found to be strictly the language of prose. . . . The truth of this assertion might be demonstrated by innumerable passages. . . .[45]

Indeed, Wordsworth apparently has so much confidence in reasoning that the 1815 *Preface* is even more lavish in using the language of reasoning.

It is deducible from the above, that poems, apparently miscellaneous, may with propriety be arranged either with reference to the powers of mind *predominant* in the production of them; or to the mould in which they are cast; or, lastly, to the subjects to which they relate.[46]

And in the *Essay Supplementary to the Preface* he argues inductively:

Let us take a hasty retrospect of the poetical literature of this Country for the greater part of the last two centuries, and see if the facts support these inferences.[47]

If there be one conclusion more forcibly pressed upon us than another by the review which has been given of the fortunes and fate of poetical Works, it is this,—that every author, as far as he is great and at the same time *original*, has had the task of *creating* the taste by which he is to be enjoyed. . . .[48]

If we accept Macdonald's view, at worst Wordsworth contradicts himself when he uses expressions like "the Reader will conclude" and "the truth of this assertion might be demonstrated." At best, he wastes his time because, Macdonald says, no one can be argued into admiring the *Lyrical Ballads*. On either the strong or the weak ground for condemning Wordsworth's effort, the language of argument and reasoning should be removed from the *Preface*. But if this project were carried out it is hard to see what language is available to further the aim which gives the *Preface* its force and interest.

For those who did not appreciate the *Lyrical Ballads* because they had been acclimated to language embellished by rhetorical excess, directing attention to the properties of Wordsworth's poems promises to be ineffectual. Wordsworth clearly indicates his concern that the *Lyrical Ballads* will leave such persons cold unless their poetic expectations are changed. What Wordsworth tries to supply are reasons why they should alter their expectations. He points out that his style resembles the language used by Shakespeare and Milton, and he appeals to passages in predecessor works to demonstrate the value of the characteristics of his style. He also offers some generalizations about moral and cognitive value which he stipulates that the reader share and he argues that his poems promote these values.

Despite the obscure and perhaps self-contradictory methodology which, on the standards of the analytic program, mars Wordsworth's *Preface*, his poetics surely would be more rather than less dreary if purged of the language he chooses to convey and instill rational conviction. What is true of Wordsworth's *Preface* is true also of the treatises of Aristotle, Reynolds, Tolstoi, and Bell, to take some influential examples. Each provides an apologia which expands appreciation of a certain sort of artwork by arguing (whether the argument succeeds is not at issue here) that the distinguishing properties of that kind of work resemble (or have evolved out of) those found in admired predecessor works. The analytic aestheticians would have it that this form of aesthetics is illegitimate. But to eliminate or radically revise art studies that are among the most influential in the field, and perhaps to carry out such reforms on most instances of study in the field, comes perilously close to just what Isenberg warned analytic aesthetics was unauthorized to do: reform critical practice from the ground up.

What went wrong with the program should now be more transparent. Analytic aesthetics violated one of its own rules, and in doing so, exacerbated the dreariness it was meant to reduce. By limiting the grounds for reforming practice to considerations internal to aesthetic discourse, the analysts argued from form to function, but then also from function to form. Consequently, they obscured their own procedure. They appealed to practice to demonstrate that the argument forms found in traditional aesthetics do not fulfill their supposed functions. To account for the persistence of these forms, they offered explanations in terms of alternative functions, consistent with the continued use of the forms. Thus, the tactic they adopted identified the presence of the traditional forms as the source of confusion. But, because form obscures function, the program's commitment to illumination required that the misleading forms be cleared away.

Why should clearing up confusion leave aesthetics duller than before? The answer, I think, is that the analysts misjudged the relation between function and form. If form follows function, it is equally so that function depends on form. There is a vast difference between being formally equipped to fulfill a function but regularly failing to fulfill it, and not being equipped to fulfill it at all. To illustrate by analogy, a student might have formal training in geometry but nevertheless always encounter defeating conditions and always flunk the exam. In respect to having potential to pass the exam, such a student is situated differently from a student who never has learned geometry, even though the two students are indistinguishable in respect to having failed the exam. Whereas in traditional aesthetics, defeating conditions may stand between form and function, form still may serve as an enabling condition of function. If this is so, then clearing out forms that provoke confusion and logical blunders cannot help but have a reductive impact on function. The price of eliminating confusion in aesthetics seems to be the constriction of critical force and scope.

It might be objected here that this is all to the good because practices doomed to fail to function should not be retained. But this objection conflates failing to have an orientation with failing to meet a necessary condition. That is, for an activity to be functional, it need not necessarily attain its goal; it may suffice that the activity is goal-oriented.

To illustrate, suppose the function of an apprentice's activity is to acquire his master's skill, but the apprentice always fails to do so. Possibly, revising the training program will provide for success, although it is unlikely that useful reforms can be grounded in considerations internal to the inadequate practices. On the other hand, the world may be such that no one can ever equal the master's hand. If such is the case, is the program a failure? Only if drawing near to the goal has no value at all. Only if approximating the goal is completely insufficient. Imposition of such severe conditions for retaining practices seems implicit in the analytic aestheticians' procedures, but this standard may be so rigorous that complex, sophisticated human activities should not be held to it.

To decide whether to impose such a strict standard in aesthetics, we need to know whether (in practice) benefits accrue from using forms whose functions may never be fulfilled. The question is not whether the forms themselves make an irreplaceable contribution to aesthetics, but rather whether the functions these forms serve, however unsuccessfully, are integral to aesthetic discourse. To address this question requires departing from the procedures of analytic aesthetics. To decide how important it is to retain or eliminate any function of traditional aesthetics, we cannot restrict ourselves, as most of the analytic aestheticians did, to considerations internal to aesthetic discourse. We must go further than to ask, "Is the discourse coherent and clear?" Whether or not it is useful to retain any function as a goal, even if we are systematically frustrated in reaching it, depends on the benefits or drawbacks of pursuing it in the world. Consequently, to make this decision, we must advance beyond the analytic aestheticians' program and seek grounds logically prior to aesthetic discourse.

Outside of, and prior to, aesthetics is at least a world, and at most a multiplicity of worlds. This provides the subject matter of aesthetics. To explore what methods will permit aesthetics to function most productively demands not only views about how aesthetic discourse operates, but also a theory of semantics, a philosophical account of the relations between aesthetic discourse and its world(s).[49]

In addressing the prospects for reforming the theory of art studies, Isenberg is optimistic, not to say rash, about philosophy's capacity for supplying aesthetics with a rigorous methodological framework.

Now it is certainly true that no philosophical analysis can devise methods which it imposes . . . from the outside. Every idea of method must come from the study of methods already employed in the field. But those methods which have led to the best results in one part of the field may be unrecognized, or may be merely implicit, or may be mixed up with barren methods, in the rest of the field. An explicit formulation of method, then, can lead to a greater awareness of direction and aim; it can eliminate waste activity; it can increase the general efficiency of research. Such an influence of philosophy upon science is perhaps imperceptible at the present time, for the simple reason that a highly efficient "hypothetico-deductive-experimental" method has become institutionalized in the natural sciences. . . . But if we were living in the time of Bacon and Descartes, when the very idea of science was in a state of confusion, such a question as whether science concerns itself with efficient or final causes would be rather momentous for the future of science.[50]

There is an instructive reason why this comment sounds somewhat dated today. Approximately a decade after Isenberg wrote this, philosophers acknowledged that the institutionalization of a hypothetico-deductive model of scientific explanation was more the product of philosophy than of science. Perhaps the model is efficient in explaining events in the world of Newtonian physics, but the world of Darwin is as much the subject of science as the world of Descartes. In science as in aesthetics, methodologies are judged not only in respect to their internal coherence but also in respect to the adequacy for their world.

Of the theses which constituted the program of analytic aesthetics, only one addresses not only the discourse but also, inadvertently, the world. This is the thesis that art admits of no essential properties. Although this claim concerns the form of definition, it also, necessarily, makes a statement about art. After all, an essentialist definition of art is proper if and only if art has an essence. Anti-essentialism has proven to be the most durable product of analytic aesthetics. There has been no revivial of aesthetic essentialism. Because it is about art rather than about discourse about art, anti-essentialism shares with the great traditional aesthetic theories the potential to function as an apologia. If the nature of art prohibits its being defined by essential properties, then postmodern art, designed to violate whatever aesthetic principles its predecessors seem designed to confirm, can be exalted not only as accommodating but also as celebrating art's natural bent.

Analytic aesthetics benefited the field by focusing on the methodology of studying art. But the program did not acknowledge that getting clear about methodology is not the same as getting a methodology for studies which are clear. If the world with which a methodology deals is disordered and confused, then the studies it produces should reflect this state of affairs. If that world does not enjoy clearly delineated entities and conclusive outcomes, then what we learn about it is clear and conclusive only at the risk of being misleading.

With a few exceptions such as Margaret Macdonald,[51] the analytic aestheticians did not reveal what they thought the world of art was like. Possibly, some of them avoided having such thoughts, fearing to be drawn into speculation. But in detouring around the world, they also missed opportunities to talk about art itself and to illustrate their work with remarks enlightened by the piercing brilliance Isenberg praised.

Why this was so, I have argued, is attributable to a defect in the analysts' procedure. But considering this flaw from a historical perspective may also provide some light. An unacknowledged ontological boundary seems to circumscribe the thinking of most of them. As we have seen, for instance, when Macdonald turns from talking about aesthetic discourse to talking about art, she is drawn to viewing the art object as an ontological entity constituted somehow by a collection of interpretations. As in so many other matters, Isenberg's position resembles Macdonald's; he says that to give a semantics of criticism is to relate critical language to the qualities of the reader's or critic's experience, not directly to properties of art objects.[52] In "The Uniqueness of a Work of Art," Ruby Meager tries to mitigate Macdonald's position from within the framework of the analytic program. Meager explains how the configuration of features in one artwork can be aesthetically relevant in the criticism of other works. She proposes that to cite works as reasons, as we saw Wordsworth citing passages from Shakespeare and Milton, succeeds only if the objects cited resemble each other closely enough. What counts as sufficiently close resemblance to sustain critical argument? According to Meager, we can do no more than hope that what suffices to establish resemblance in one beholder's eye resembles closely enough what other eyes behold.[53]

What prevents these analytic aestheticians from stepping beyond phenomenological boundaries to think of art not only as existing in experience but also as situated in a world? In the preface to his third (substantially revised) edition of *Philosophy Looks At The Arts*, Joseph Margolis describes analytic aesthetics as "a general mode of working that departed abruptly but penetratingly from the then-dominant idealist tradition."[54] While this is so, I think it also may be the case that analytic aesthetics' departure from idealism was not abrupt and clean enough to impel the program to achieve its goals.

In the mid-1960s, work in aesthetics which directly engaged questions about worlds began to appear. In 1964, Arthur Danto published "The Artworld," initiating a major and influential project in which Danto tells us about how the artworld makes art. In 1968, Nelson Goodman published *The Languages of Art*, initiating a major and influential project in which Goodman tell us about how art makes worlds. With their expertise in art and their philosophical talent, Danto and Goodman fulfill Isenberg's programmatic recommendation[55] to integrate insightful commentary on art with rigorous philosophical argument. These contemporary asetheticians exemplify how aesthetics has brightened up because its practitioners turn their lights on the world.

NOTES

1. Of course, any stipulation of the time period during which a philosophical program is pursued is motivated by considerations of convenience as well as concern for accuracy. This does not destroy the usefulness of examining the program. For instance, it would be foolhardy to demand precise dating of the Cartesian program before its strengths, defects, and results could be examined. The dates I set here permit inclusion of most of the philosophers usually mentioned in connection with analytic aesthetics.
2. One should not overlook the fact that philosophers who are not known for their work in aesthetics also can influence art scholarship. Wittgenstein's *Philosophical Investigations* (not, apparently, his lectures on aesthetics) influenced Gombrich. John Searle's work influenced the literary theory of Stanley Fish. This listing is not intended to be comprehensive; I merely offer a few illustrative examples.
3. In her introduction to the selected essays of Arnold Isenberg (see footnote 7), Mary Mothersill comments that contributions to analytical aesthetics are few and that the same essays reappear in each new anthology (pp. xix–xx).
4. William Elton, ed., *Aesthetics and Language* (Oxford, 1954). Authors represented in this volume are W. B. Gallie, Gilbert Ryle, Beryl Lake, Arnold Isenberg, Stuart Hampshire, J. A. Passmore, O. K. Bouwsma, Margaret Macdonald, Helen Knight, and Paul Ziff.
5. Joseph Margolis, ed., *Philosophy Looks At The Arts* (New York, 1962). The authors represented in this volume are Isenberg, Ziff, Macdonald, J. O. Urmson, Vincent Tomas, Morris Weitz, Frank Sibley, Wimsatt and Beardsley, Joseph Margolis, Charles Stevenson, John Hospers, and Max Black.
6. Arnold Isenberg, "Analytical Philosophy and the Study of Art: A Report to the Rockefeller Foundation," April 1950. I am very grateful to the Rockefeller Foundation for furnishing me with a complete copy of this text.
7. William Callaghan et al., eds., *Aesthetics and the Theory of Criticism: Selected Essays of Arnold Isenberg* (University of Chicago Press, 1973), pp. 285–301. However, the parts of the report excerpted here include noticeably less than half the report. They apparently have been selected to illustrate Isenberg's views about how philosophers could and should engage in art studies.
8. Elton, p. 2.
9. Margolis, p. 43.
10. Some which probably should be mentioned are collected in Cyril Barrett, ed., *Collected Papers on Aesthetics* (Oxford, 1965). This volume includes W. E. Kennick's "Does Traditional Aesthetics Rest On a Mistake?" (first published in *Mind* [1958]) which provides one of the clearest statements of the program I describe here. It also includes Ruby Meager's "The Uniqueness of a Work of Art" (first published in *Proceedings of the Aristotelian Society* LIX [1958–59]: 49–70) and Morris Weitz's "Reasons in Criticism" (first published in *Journal of Aesthetics and Art Criticism* 20 no. 4 [1962]).
11. I base this claim on memory.
12. Elton, pp. 30–35.
13. Margolis, p. 97.
14. Isenberg, p. 2.
15. Ibid., p. 18.
16. In the essays cited in footnote 10 above, Ruby Meager and Morris Weitz seek to mitigate the force of this thesis. Meager specifically challenges Gallie, Macdonald, and Hampshire. Weitz specifically challenges Stevenson. These discussions offer good examples of debates internal to the program.
17. Elton, p. 169.
18. Ibid., p. 129.
19. Ibid., p. 135.
20. Margolis, p. 124.
21. Of course, Weitz does accept this less sweeping thesis.
22. Margolis, pp. 48–49.
23. Elton, pp. 43–44.
24. See Isenberg's "Critical Communication" and Macdonald's "Some Distinctive Features of Arguments Used in Criticism of the Arts."
25. Elton, pp. 155–56.
26. Ibid., p. 126.
27. Ibid., pp. 170–86 *passim*.
28. Ibid., p. 50.
29. Margolis, pp. 58–59.
30. Elton, p. 142.
31. Isenberg, p. 11. Isenberg was wrong in sup-

posing that the best work in the field would be done by unknown people. In this report, he cites Goodman as one of those known philosophers whose analytic work in philosophy of science offers an excellent model for aestheticians. Of course, Isenberg was not to know that, in 1968, Goodman's *Languages of Art* would help to initiate enlivened aesthetics.
32. Ibid., pp. 17–18.
33. Ibid., p. 18. This passage focuses on that aspect of Isenberg's proposal which Mary Mothersill takes to be most significant. See footnotes 3 and 7.
34. Ibid., p. 27. This passage exhibits Isenberg's view that the subject of analytic aesthetics is criticism, not art.
35. Ibid., p. 20.
36. Ibid., pp. 22–23.
37. Ibid., pp. 31–32.
38. Ibid., p. 32.
39. Ibid., p. 33.
40. Ibid., pp. 31–32.
41. Margolis, pp. 20–21.
42. Elton, pp. 30–34.
43. Ibid., p. 114.
44. William Wordsworth, *Selected Poetry* (New York, 1950), pp. 676–77.
45. Ibid., p. 694.
46. Ibid., p. 675.
47. William Wordsworth, *The Poetical Works of Wordsworth* (Oxford University Press, 1950), p. 745.
48. Ibid., p. 750.
49. In "Critical Communication," Isenberg raises the issue of semantics, but does not characterize it as addressing the relation between aesthetics and the world, art and the world, or aesthetics and art. Instead, he thinks the question is as follows: "What is the semantical relationship between the language of criticism and the qualities of the critic's or the reader's experience?" Elton, p. 143.
50. Isenberg, pp. 19–20.
51. Elton, pp. 114–30, *passim*.
52. See footnote 49 above for citation.
53. Barrett, p. 45.
54. Joseph Margolis, *Philosophy Looks At The Arts*, third edition (Temple University Press, 1987).
55. While Goodman and Danto are engaged by art-making and art studies of various sorts, it would be misleading to think of them as accepting Isenberg's advice to write criticism as part of doing philosophy. I think it more accurate to describe them as writing philosophy and, on occasion, writing philosophy as part of pursuing an art study.

The Eclipse and Recovery of Analytic Aesthetics

Joseph Margolis

Memory is mischievous and facile and demands a smug slogan. If we ask ourselves to explain the eclipse of analytic aesthetics, the short answer is ready: time has overrun all its entrenched positions. I speak with some authority as a partial victim at least, spared (if that is the term) only by running before the flood. Nevertheless, to admit this much is hardly to judge what has been gained and lost and not quite to say where the high ground will eventually reappear.

The best way to catch the change is to note

From *Analytic Aesthetics*, Richard Shusterman, ed. (Oxford: Basil Blackwell, 1989). Reprinted by permission of author and Basil Blackwell.

its effects on acknowledged exemplars; and the best economy is to link these effects jointly to the principal themes of analytic philosophies of art and analytic philosophy in general—for they should be the same. They are indeed the same, and with only negligible exception the essential themes may be drawn from the work of relatively influential members of the 'analytic' community of philosophers of art.[1] I select four specimens and four themes: Monroe Beardsley, Nelson Goodman, Arthur Danto and Joseph Margolis (myself); and, not coordinately, empiricism, extensionalism and nominalism, physicalism and (what already in an alien idiom is termed) presence. All of this will need to be explained of course. But by the economy intended, what has happened to these four theorists effectively marks what has happened to analytic aesthetics over a period of somewhat more than one (the last) generation. Each has made tell-tale adjustments, whether primarily in aesthetics or in philosophy in general, that signify accommodations favoring themes substantially subverting whatever may be fairly taken to belong to the analytic canon.

There is no explicit canon of course, but there can be little doubt that 'analysts' have always been strongly disposed to subscribe to one. Also, each of the four theorists mentioned has proceeded in a way that suggests an entirely natural enlargement and shift in their respective views: so that although analytic aesthetics has been effectively subverted, the changes favored in the views of each hardly justify a straightline application of that finding to each of them. In fact, with the exception of Beardsley, the theorists in question have clearly evolved as frank and vigorous opponents of certain themes distinctly favored in the analytic camp. It needs to be said, also, that if we do not concede within analytic aesthetics a penchant for the canonical, there would be little point in speaking of its eclipse. Since this cannot fail to be a quarrelsome matter, there is bound to be a touch of fiction about the manner of reporting here favored. Two caveats need to be mentioned. For one, both the substantive themes indicated and the disciplined manner of working that the analysts favor have come under severe fire—precisely because they are so intimately related. For another, the recovery of something not very distant from the canon is promisingly joined with options linked to the critique of the original themes. The truth is that the original analytic themes and the assured 'method' of analysis were always contested within the practice of analytic philosophy—and within analytic aesthetics. So the admission of the eclipse of analysis is already part of its anticipated recovery.

These are cryptic remarks no doubt. But they may explode the fiction that we are facing the imminent collapse of a monolithic philosophical program because of essential mistakes that ineliminably define the dogmas of the entire movement. There are no such dogmas. In fact, *none* of the themes attributed to the canon was ever permitted to run uncontested; and no one can rightly claim to formulate *the* canonical method of analysis. Certain themes and methods have of course dominated the movement. Their distinct pretensions were regularly punctured by the best and most powerful practitioners of that movement; but then, of course, those same practitioners went blithely on with their own favored projects—against their own instruction. To lose sight of the fact is to exaggerate the meaning of the 'eclipse'. To insist too casually on its 'recovery' is to miss the extent of the transformation required. To yield up the executive standing of extensionalism, nominalism and physicalism, the unity of science is, quite simply, to recover forbidden (or at least officially opposed or discouraged) conceptual fruit. And yet, the effective subversive strategies are all traceable, in an admittedly thin way, to the central work of Anglo-American analytic philosophy itself. Their recovery—and the recovery of analysis—signifies the need for a frank rapprochement between Anglo-American and Continental philosophical currents. For it is clearly among the latter that such themes as the historicist, the hermeneutic, the preformational, the structuralist and poststructuralist, the deconstructive, the genealogical, the praxical have been consistently and productively favored; and it is only by quite openly accommodating those themes (and the varieties of conceptual strategy that addressing them must subtend) that analytic philosophy and analytic aesthetics *can* be recovered at all. So the truth is that the analytic tradition has tended to impoverish itself by a kind of increasing suicidal neglect of the leading themes of cultural life—*a fortiori*, of the leading themes that inform the world of the arts. It is also to neglect the subterranean possibilities of its own best world. The irony remains that, with regard to the *pre*-analytic period, both in philosophy in general and in the philosophy of art, the themes of intentionality, historical tradition, preformative history, discontinuity and incommensurability, the impossibility of conceptual closure, the symbiosis of the individual and the societal, the denial of cognitive transparency, the critique of critique, the emergence of human culture, the priority of practices, interpretive indeterminacy and consensual tolerance, and a thousand related themes had already been in place and had already been most vigorously dissected. The hegemony of the analytic has, quite unpardonably, done as much as it could to dismiss the full complexity of these matters in its zeal to install its own executive vision. And many, notably the specimen theorists of art who by their own interest should have been alert enough to have resisted that tendency, have often been co-opted by it and, on occasion, have been quite pleased to lead compliant troops over the philosophical cliff.

So the point of the recovery is clear. The 'analytic' represents a measure of discipline that, at least saliently, at least with regard to the work of the formal and physical sciences (and whatever could fairly be associated with such work within the study of language, history, practice, art and psychology), clearly succeeded in displacing what was perceived to be the incompetence, confusion, informality and sheer error of pre-analytic philosophy. In aesthetics, the chief villain was idealism.[2] But it *was* (and it still is) unpardonable to have impoverished the field of analysis as unconscionably and as carelessly as the vanguard of analytic philosophy was prepared to do—and did do. Now, the matter haunts its progeny, and, now, many of that progeny are simply too fixed in their own prejudices to reopen the case.

So the current philosophical scene offers the spectacle of subversive talents drawn chiefly from outside the analytic tradition, that specialize in demonstrating or insinuating the inadequacy, irrelevance, unresponsiveness, sheer ignorance of a great body of *analytic* philosophy when applied to the palpable issues of any number of different sectors of bona fide interest. The disquieting truth is that many of the current critics of analytic practice are reasonably well informed regarding its best work: *they* cannot be easily counted among the *pre*-analytic innocents that the best analytic work of the early twentieth century bid fair to replace. There is a deeper innocence, now pretty well exposed, in the pioneer work of Russell and Moore in England, of the pragmatists in America, of the transplanted rigour of the positivists and logical empiricists and unity-of-science theorists of Berlin and Vienna, and of the later formal semantics of Quine and Tarski and of the followers of Quine and Tarski and Frege and Peirce and Wittgenstein, and of those attracted to ordinary-language analysis (Austin) and intuitive conceptual analysis (Ryle). None of that work is lost, nor need be lost. Some of it includes the best work philosophers have ever done. But all of it is now under fire—capable perhaps of being recast in terms more responsive to the latest attacks on both the themes and analytic strategies of the movement we are tracing (focused both within and without the tradition). These attacks are clearly too insistent to be ignored and much too compelling and too savvy to be met by old defenses.

Having said this much by way of a preface, two small warnings need to be added. First of all, the issue at stake is an eccentric and technical one, the intersecting careers of general analytic philosophy and analytic aesthetics. Since the weaknesses of analytic aesthetics are due largely to the persistence of certain entrenched commitments drawn from analysis at large, the discussion that follows may seem at times rather indifferent to the more local questions of aesthetics. Secondly, since we are primarily concerned with the threat to the future of analytic aesthetics posed by those entrenched commitments, the philosophies of art reviewed in what follows are treated essentially diagnostically. The result, frankly is that they are not particularly sympathetically described. There is something thankless about the effort, but it has its use and it invites a certain directness.

I

The most general picture of the span of analytic philosophy of the entire century—certainly of the past twenty-five years—is reasonably fixed by the conceptual linkage between W. V. Quine's well-known theory of the indeterminacy of translation and Richard Rorty's notorious recommendation that 'epistemology-centered philosophy' is (or ought to be) at an end.[3] This is not to say that either Quine or Rorty had pursued his own theme in the most perspicuous or most irresistible way. Actually, neither one has—which complicates the tale to be told. It is rather to say that what is most tenable in the accounts of each symbiotically entails that of the other, and that, at their peril, analytic philosophers of art have (until recently) tended to ignore the implied lesson. The 'eclipse' of analytic aesthetics may fairly be said to depend on ignoring that lesson; its 'recovery' depends on accommodating it. The irony is that, both in general philosophy and in aesthetics, the incompleteness of Quine's and Rorty's arguments—their frank prejudices and disinclination to explore the options they themselves have very nearly prepared—promises to enrich both analytic philosophy and analytic aesthetics in ways that could not be easily foreseen from their own exertions.

Quine is essentially a holist, a pragmatist who rejects all forms of cognitive privilege, who treats distributed claims as functioning within the space of the preformative parsings of societally entrenched 'analytical hypotheses'—hypotheses that are themselves reflexively specified only by way of more attenuated such 'hypotheses'.[4] From this and Quine's profound demonstration that there is no principled disjunction between analytic and synthetic truths, between distinctions of meaning and distinctions of fact,[5] the indeterminacy thesis ineluctably follows:

There can be no doubt that rival systems of analytical hypotheses can fit the totality of speech behaviour to perfection, and can fit the totality of dispositions to speech behavior as well, and still specify mutually incompatible translations of countless sentences insusceptible of independent control.[6]

The trouble is that Quine never satisfactorily explained how 'sentence', 'behavior', and 'fit', between sentence and behavior could be managed or reconciled with his own severe theory; or, what might be the *non*-behavioral evidence of 'incompatible translation' fitting behavior 'to perfection'; or, what 'truth' might mean under such circumstances; or, indeed, what constraints within holism itself might reasonably be proposed to facilitate the comparative assessment of rival analytical hypotheses. On all of these matters Quine is disappointingly silent—even though it is plain that he favors physicalism, favors the rejection of intentionality, favors extensionalism, behaviorism, and a general empiricist bent congenially but loosely committed to something like the unity-of-science program. The bearing of Quine's work on aesthetics rests with the double theme: (a) that analytic aestheticians (influenced by the tendencies Quine has spawned and nourished) have themselves tended to favor physicalist, extensionalist and behaviorist strategies with respect to puzzles about art and criticism; and (b) that those strategies proved to be peculiarly vulnerable in aesthetics because they were never satisfactorily secured in analytic philosophy in general and because they hobbled the chances of formulating any adequate analytic philosophy of art.

Rorty is more radical about the radical import of having taken Quine's lesson (and

Wilfrid Sellars's lesson) to heart—even against the 'failure' of those two worthies to understand that the traditional philosophy of the West is at an end as a direct result of their own labours:

> To drop the notion of the philosopher as knowing something about knowing which nobody else knows so well would be to drop the notion that his voice always has an overriding claim on the attention of the other participants in the conversation [of mankind]. It would also be to drop the notion that there is something called 'philosophical method' or 'philosophical technique' or 'the philosophical point of view' which enables the professional philosopher, *ex officio*, to have interesting views about, say, the respectability of psychoanalysis, the legitimacy of certain dubious laws, the resolution of moral dilemmas, the 'soundness' of schools of historiography or literary criticism, and the like—I do not know whether we are in fact at the end of an era—perhaps a new form of systematic philosophy will be found which has nothing whatever to do with epistemology but which nevertheless makes normal philosophical inquiry possible.[7]

Quine does not offer an explicit or satisfactory account of how we proceed with the distributed claims of any disciplined inquiry *within* his own holism; and Rorty does not satisfactorily explain what is entailed *in* his favoring the work of the sciences or other inquiries within that same constraint. Quine does not concede that *his* extreme holism disqualifies philosophy in the least; Rorty argues that it does but never shows us why. And we, caught between these two lines of argument, insist on saving whatever may be saved of the empirical sciences and other first-order inquiries we believe deserve an inning. But we too need to explain what we have salvaged in salvaging that.

Quine simply disallows programs of analysis that go against the elimination of intentionality, for instance, as in his well-known attack on Brentano:

> In the strictest scientific spirit we can report all the behavior, verbal and otherwise, that may underlie our imputations of propositional attitudes, and we may go on to speculate as we please upon the causes and effects of this behavior, but so long as we do not switch muses, the essentially dramatic idiom of propositional attitudes will find no place.[8]

But if anything is clear about the theory of art, it is clear that we cannot make sense of the structure of artworks, their cultural status, their history, the detection and interpretation of their properties without featuring intentionality. Analytic aestheticians either have actually tried to restrict themselves to a de-intentionalized idiom (Monroe Beardsley, for instance) or have been drawn in a distinctly divided way toward and against physicalism, toward and against an idiom congenial to the unity-of-science idiom (Arthur Danto, for instance). Quine's influence is unmistakable here.

Once we see matters this way, the radical incompleteness of Quine's program and the radical arbitrariness of Rorty's stare us in the face. Their joined claims, that is, the claims for which they are now regularly made the totemic bearers—holism with respect to the analytic penchant for rejecting transcendental arguments, for naturalizing epistemology, for promoting physicalism and extensionalism (Quine); and holism with respect to repudiating the viability of all epistemology and metaphysics, but for favoring in first-order discourse an inherited physicalism and extensionalism (Rorty)—signify what is popularly perceived as the 'eclipse' of analytic philosophy (*a fortiori*, the eclipse of analytic aesthetics). On the other hand, the perception of the incompleteness and arbitrariness of their respective programs signifies the beginning of the best program for the 'recovery' of analytic philosophy (and, of course, of analytic aesthetics). Rorty's claim—hardly restricted to analytic aesthetics—is that 'epistemology-centered philosophy', philosophy in the Western tradition, analytic philosophy as it has been canonically practiced, is now doomed. On the Rortyan line, Quine's program of analysis is best reinterpreted as a contribution to a supposedly radically different model of philosophy, the model of the '*conversation*' [of mankind] as the ultimate context within which knowledge is to be understood'.[9]

But what does that mean? Certainly, it means that *any* inquiry—scientific, philosophical, critical, interpretive, historical—must: (i) give up the pretense of the transparency of reality with respect to human cognition; (ii) admit the preformative and pluralized historical contingency of the conditions of understanding under which the members of any society make inquiry; (iii) concede the impossibility of drawing from the holist conditions under which we appear to dwell in the world and survive as a species any direct, distributed consequences affecting the truth of particular claims made within the space of those conditions; (iv) recognize that our critical speculations about the enabling conditions under which the sciences and other distributive inquiries prosper are themselves subject to the same tacit preconditions as are those very claims; and (v) acknowledge that our philosophical inquiries cannot be apodictic, cannot be known to be universally binding, synthetic a priori, or formulated for all conceivable conditions. To accept constraints (i) to (v) is to embrace what is convincing and common to Quine's and Rorty's views all right—to embrace what is common to pragmatism and analytic philosophy. It is also to embrace, of course, what is common to the best work of Hegel, Marx, Nietzsche, Husserl, Heidegger, Peirce, Dewey, James, Merleau-Ponty, Foucault, Derrida, Wittgenstein. *But it is not tantamount to disallowing an 'epistemology-centered philosophy' at all*—as Rorty's mentors (including Quine, Sellars and Davidson) have either implicitly grasped or at least never denied.[10]

To embrace (i) to (v) is, effectively, to disallow what has disapprovingly been called the philosophy of 'presence'.[11] But it is not—certainly it need not be—to disallow philosophy *tout court*, to disallow epistemology, metaphysics, transcendental argument in particular. It is only to insist that philosophy must henceforth confine itself within the terms of (i) to (v) or within the terms of other corollary constraints of the same sort. The point is that Quine nowhere supposes it is impossible to do so, and Rorty nowhere shows that it *is* actually impossible; *and* it may be argued both that it *is* possible and that pursuing philosophy thus offers a rational benefit, particularly conceding the destabilizing loss of privilege that (i) to (v) entails. The recovery of analytic philosophy, *a fortiori* the recovery of analytic aesthetics, is simplicity itself: merely proceed as before, or proceed as would now be congenial to how one proceeded before, under the 'new' constraints.

They are not really new constraints: they are only the old implicated constraints freshly perceived—perhaps perceived compellingly for the first time. Once one grants (i) to (v), one sees at once *why philosophy cannot be abandoned*: first, because science and philosophy are continuous, incapable of principled disjunction; second, because first- and second-order inquiries make no sense without the other and because the distinction between them is itself a second-order distinction; third, because holisms of the pragmatist sort are not intended to disqualify science, or other first-order inquiries but only to disallow any privilege regarding their cognitive standing; and fourth, because to wish to secure the continuing practice of a rigorous science (or of any other first-order discipline) is, effectively, *to* secure epistemology and metaphysics. Quine certainly concedes all this. All the pretended demonstrations favoring the abandonment of philosophy—offered by Rorty, the poststructuralists, the postmodernists, the deconstructionists, the genealogists, the anarchists, the nihilists, the sceptics—are simply manifestations of a profound *petitio*, regardless of the persistence of the disordered thinking critics of these sorts have managed to expose in the received tradition and regardless of the important differences there may be among them in exposing their own favored offenders.

The trick is to see that embracing (i) to (v) makes possible an indefinitely large, even unpredictable, variety of philosophical claims that could not have been favored under the aegis of an epistemology and metaphysics that implicitly favored privilege. Rorty makes the mistake, however, of concluding that there are no forms of epistemological, metaphysical, transcendental, second-order, legitimative inquiry *that are not inherently privileged*. But both the Anglo-American and Continental traditions (he favours) straightforwardly show *that* it is indeed possible to proceed epistemologically after having abandoned all epistemic privilege.

Analytic philosophy—*a fortiori*, analytic aesthetics—certainly has its work cut out for it. Under the radical limitations of (i) to (v), for instance, there may be no convincing reasons for preserving physicalism or extensionalism, for endorsing the rejection of intentionality, for insisting on bivalence or *tertium non datur*, for disallowing moderate or extended incommensurabilism or conceptual discontinuity, for opposing historicism, relativism, hermeneutic pluralism, the symbiosis of realist and idealist approaches to science or to any other forms of disciplined inquiry. But the whole notion of the sheer end of philosophy—hence the end of analytic philosophy, hence the end of analytic aesthetics—is nonsense, a self-inflicted wound utterly uncalled-for by the welcome philosophical epiphany of rediscovering the end of privilege. In its best form, the apparent lesson could be little more than a hoax by which to expose the easy deception of an army of grateful, self-sacrificing philosophers.

There are two distinct sorts of leverage that must be secured. They service at one and the same time the recovery of analytic philosophy in general and the recovery of analytic aesthetics. The first, of course, is the redemption of a viable and disciplined idiom that is not restricted to extensionalism, physicalism, behaviorism and the rest (in Quine's manner); and the second is the demonstration that the rejection of privilege does not entail the 'end of philosophy' (in Rorty's manner). Rorty's project, which is clearly having increasing influence on the theory of art and criticism, is peculiarly pernicious because it both fails to vindicate the 'end of philosophy' and because, in promoting that doctrine, it somehow insinuates the adequacy at (what would normally have been called) *the first-order level* of a physicalism, extensionalism and behaviorism congenial to Quine's, Sellars's and Davidson's own projects. What needs to be grasped, *contra* Rorty, is that (1) assertive or constative practices of discourse are clearly ineliminable and not in any significant respect different at first-order levels (science and literary criticism, say) and at second-order levels (philosophy and legitimation, say); (2) the offending doctrine of cognitive privilege cannot be derived merely from (1), on pain of eliminating science and criticism, in eliminating philosophy; (3) there can be no first-order work without second-order work; and (4) part of the concern of philosophy is, precisely, to clarify how the legitimation of methodological, ontological, epistemological, normative and related matters can be salvaged and fruitfully pursued under the constraints of historical existence, the loss of cognitive privilege, cultural preformation, moderate incommensurabilities and the like.

In a strange way, there is really no counter-argument needed against either Quine or Rorty. Quine is completely candid about the arbitrariness of his prejudice against intentionality, though it is true that he is entirely sanguine about the reduced idiom he prefers. Rorty simply offers no argument at all to show that (4) is not a possible or worthwhile project or in fact a project that his own mentors have regularly favored and still favor. There are indeed arguments to show that Rorty's finding is a complete *non sequitur*: that, having shown that much of traditional philosophy does secure transcendental, legitimative, epistemological, metaphysical, normative arguments by illicit privilege, Rorty overhastily concludes that there is no alternative to that sort of failure. But we cannot pause here to track down that complex issue.[12]

We may, however, offer as a metonymic but entirely characteristic clue the following remarks by Rorty regarding the theory of truth:

a pragmatist theory about truth . . . *says* that truth *is not* the sort of thing one should expect to have a philosophically interesting theory about. For pragmatists, 'truth' is just the name of a property which all true statements share. It is what is common to 'Bacon did not write Shakespeare', 'It rained yesterday', 'E equals mc²', 'Love is better than hate', *'The Allegory of Painting* was Vermeer's best work', '2 plus 2 is 4', and 'There are nondenumerable infinities'. Pragmatists *doubt* that there is *much* to be said about this common feature.[13]

These opening lines of Rorty's *Consequences of Pragmatism* convey the mixed impression that the philosophical analysis of truth has been convincingly shown to be fruitless, that all pragmatists agree about this, *and* (also) that they only have doubts about its fruitfulness and have seen little or nothing to encourage the contrary impression. There is not, in all of Rorty's work, a straightforward resolution of this wobbling or a single demonstration that the theory of truth—even pragmatist theories of truth (even Peirce's or James's or Davidson's or Putnam's theory of truth)—are not fruitfully, even essentially, connected with the fortunes of first-order inquiry (say, regarding the direction of science and literary criticism). That is to say, there is no demonstration that the dialectical rebuttal of any of these and similar theories *is not* itself philosophically productive, not merely a self-consuming argument that shows (therapeutically) the point of abandoning philosophy. The nagging proof of this is very neatly tied to the fact that Rorty's recommendation to abandon philosophy still means to leave in place something like Quine's ulterior program *at the first-order level* and to deny there is any reasoned basis for critical review (inevitably second-order) of the adequacy of such an idiom—say, for the fortunes of the criticism and appreciation of the arts. But that is preposterous.

Now, the interesting thing is that a great deal could be cleared up in philosophy in general (and in aesthetics in particular) by pursuing the import of the 'recovery' of philosophical analysis under the threat of philosophy's coming to an end. It is really a question of using the old joke of Chicken Little in order to remind ourselves of the conditions under which we live and think. The argument regarding science and philosophy is embarrassingly elementary: the courage and acumen wanted bear rather on what is to be salvaged beyond the joke, and on what new directions might bear the weight of our appetite for philosophical inquiry. The argument is simply this. We cannot consider the truth of anything without the use of statements, propositions, affirmations, constatations, claims and the like. Cognitive concerns of every kind are caught up with them. So it must be the case that science and philosophy need not presuppose or entail privilege or transparency merely in taking a constative form. There is no large practice of natural language that, in permitting us to affirm this or that as true, fails to provide for the reference or identification of that about which we speak, or fails to provide for predications or attributions regarding what is thus identified as marking what we take to be true of it; and *that* must be true, at least as far as formal considerations go, for both first- and second-order discourse. Furthermore, *if*, as both Quine and Rorty hold (however different the motive of each may be), that distributed truth-claims function and are confined within the space of some holist adjustment to the actual world—but relative to which we can never hope to exit to ensure the least measure of distributed privilege—then it is doubly clear that philosophy, concerned as it is with the conditions and legitimation of knowledge and distributed truths, *cannot possibly pretend to recover privilege or transparency* (cannot possibly affirm the philosophy of 'presence') *merely by attending to second-order questions*. Philosophy, rather like science and literary criticism, must proceed in an 'internalist' way, in a way that is entirely internal to the cognitive resources of a particular historical era reflexively identified and refined under the same circumstance. But why not? That's all there is to it. Rorty has missed the essential lesson.

One may well wonder how all of this bears on analytic aesthetics. I shall say in a moment. But to collect the import of all that has been said so far, I offer the following summation: (a) our confidence that the whole of human inquiry takes a realist form is suitably in touch with the actual world cognitively, is a *holist* theme to which all theories converge but without requiring distributed (therefore privileged) cognitive grounds and without directly yielding distributed (therefore privileged) truths; (b) the admission of (a) justifies—indeed, is meant to locate properly—practices *internal* to that holist assurance, in accord with which distributed truth-claims are and may be assessed and confirmed in realist terms; (c) the practices of (b) need make no principled distinction between *first-order* (scientific) and *second-order* (legitimative or transcendental or epistemological) claims; and (d) disputes about the truth of distributed claims within (c) may be construed in realist terms despite the *loss of* (distributed) *transparency* and therefore despite the impossibility of precluding *incommensurabilities, relativistic divergences, artefactual discontinuities* within the space of such disputes. *It is the prospects of elaborating (d) that count as the future of analytic philosophy and analytic aesthetics, and it is just those prospects that invite (and require) a rapprochement between Anglo-American and Continental philosophical currents.* Shorn of philosophy's 'accustomed' privilege, we are now *more* dependent than before on the good legitimative (second-order) guesses we are able to construct. Since there is no assured logic of discovery, there is actually an ineliminable need for transcendental speculation.

II

Turn, now, to our exemplars. All four may fairly be said to have manifested more than a touch of 'objectivism' (or 'naturalism') in that sense in which Husserl had throughout his career attempted to refine the critical function of phenomenology *vis-à-vis* the presumed fixity and reliability of the cognitive relationship between subject and object (self and world).[14] Analytic aesthetics has characteristically never shown much accommodation of the critical Husserlian theme of the preformative conditions of 'subjectivity' within which the *historically and psychologically contingent relationship of (cognizing) subject and (cognized) object emerges*—what Husserl ultimately cast in terms of the preformational, tacit, incompletely fathomable function of the encompassing *Lebenswelt* in which 'naturalistic' scientists and inquirers come to rely on their empirical resources.[15] Husserl himself, of course, pursued the delusive goal of an apodictic (phenomenological) science that his own better followers were disposed to modify along the lines of imaginative conceptual experiments that might yield, however provisionally *and* within the constraints of one's own *Lebenswelt*, some sense of an asymptotic approximation to conceptual invariance. The hopelessness of this line of (Cartesian or apodictic) speculation is, it is fair to say, the precise point of Derrida's early critique of Husserl.[16]

We are not concerned, here, to render a full and reasoned account of each of our four specimen figures; and we are not concerned (except in the way of offering a clue about the convergence of Anglo-American and Continental philosophy) to vindicate Husserl or the work of his somewhat less than completely loyal followers. Our interest lies rather in gauging the viability of analytic aesthetics in the face of certain philosophical challenges that appear to threaten its continued effectiveness—coming mainly from Continental sources and condensing in what (it may be hoped) we now see to be the pointless extravagance of Rorty's dismissal of analytic epistemology and metaphysics.

There can be little doubt that Monroe Beardsley is, of the four, the most devoted objectivist. This is the entire point of Beardsley's most widely discussed book, *The Possibility of Criticism*—which is committed to the rejection of intentionalism in criticism, the rejection of relativism in interpretation and the affirmation of the stable objective presence of literary artworks (and, of course, of artworks in general) on the admission of which depends the very 'possibility' (in the Kantian sense) of a discipline of critical reading that could be said to function as a fair analogue of the characteristic work of the empirical sciences.[17]

Beardsley never wavered in these commitments, though it is true that his own candor and inventiveness led him, first, to admit 'we can never establish . . . decisively [what is] "in" or "out" [of a given literary work]'[18]; and, secondly, to incorporate into his analysis of a poem a speech act model that installed the strong intentionalism of speech acts themselves, although Beardsley clearly hoped that the device of illocutionary acts would ultimately be dropped from his account.[19]

'If there were no principles involved in criticism,' says Beardsley, 'I do not see how it could be kept from collapsing into something purely intuitive and impressionistic'.[20] Apart from the questionable use of the phrase 'purely intuitive and impressionistic', this admirably fixes the sense in which Beardsley was a straightforward naturalist or objectivist (in Husserl's sense); it marks the point of his quarrels with E. D. Hirsch (about author's intentions) and with Joseph Margolis (about relativism in interpretation). Those two theorists, of course, may also be said to have exhibited a similar sort of objectivism, even if they disagreed with Beardsley's line of argument.[21] The essential challenge to a strong analogy between artworks and physical phenomena construed as *objects* suitably stable and determinate for the purposes of description, interpretation, criticism, and explanation (wherever and in whatever way pertinent for the disciplines in question) rests largely with the bearing of the puzzles of intertextuality on the determinate identity and intentional structure of artworks. If artworks cannot be fixed as referents for continuing critical discourse stable enough that their reidentification entails that their internal structure remains relatively fixed and finitely bounded through the very process of critical interpretation, then Beardsley's project must fail and the extension of something like the unity-of-science model to criticism is doomed. The theme of intertextuality, perhaps most floridly flaunted by Roland Barthes in the notorious manifesto, 'Every text, being itself the intertext of another text, belongs to the intertextual',[22] has by this time largely undermined any simple objectivism of Beardsley's sort in the practice of literary criticism. Whatever may be the ultimate fate of Yale deconstructive views (notably, Harold Bloom's) or reader-response theories (notably Wolfgang Iser's) or of such maverick theorists as Stanley Fish, it is precisely the intentionality and historicized existence of artworks, both opposed by Beardsley, that have forced a radical revision in the conception of the methodology of criticism.[23] In any case, although Beardsley pursued, particularly toward the end of his life, all the principal currents of Continental and Continentally inspired aesthetics, he never saw the need to modify the strong objectivism he favored, an objectivism that clearly approached (however informally) the extensionalist severities of Quine's program and of programs associated with the unity of science.[24] Nevertheless, as we have already implicitly noted, Quine's notion of 'analytical hypotheses' is itself a thin pragmatist counterpart to Husserl's major theme of preformation—the key philosophical theme that eventually yielded increasingly radical notions of intertextuality.

We must be clear that the limitation of Beardsley's form of analytic aesthetics is a dual one: it is partly the consequence of an excessively optimistic empiricism in the face of intentional, historical, interpretive, productive complexities that have taxed the ingenuity of his New Critical orientation beyond its apparent resources; and it is partly the consequence, *via* those complexities, of his never having come to terms with the preformational, intransparent, conceptually discontinuous, incommensurable features of discourse about art and culture (and, by extension, about science itself) or, indeed, the deep indeterminacies of the very ontological structure of artworks. Analytic aesthetics (like analytic philosophy) can no longer pursue such simplifications if it is to survive. That texts and artworks are *not* suitably similar to physical objects, that their intentional structure obliges us to reflect on what it means to affirm or deny that artworks *have* determinate or completely determinate structures, is certainly the single most important theoretical issue confronting all philosophies of art at the present time as well as all practices in history and criticism. The bare question makes no sense in terms of Beardsley's framework—nor, indeed, in terms of any first-order work drawn from Quine's orientation.

But, having said that, it is crucial to understand that, once the apodictic pretensions of Husserl are disallowed, there remains no effective disjunction between naturalistic and phenomenological strategies. On the contrary, *non*-phenomenologized naturalisms *are* fairly dubbed 'objectivist' in Husserl's pejorative sense; and *non*-naturalized phenomenologies *are* cognitively pointless and empty. This is, in fact, the shared discovery of Heidegger and Merleau-Ponty, who ultimately refused to support Husserl's rather mad extremes.[25] But in more general terms it is the theme common to naturalistic forms of critique (as in the Kantian, Marxist, Frankfurt School and Freudian modes) and to non-naturalistic forms of critique (as in the phenomenological, existential, deconstructive, genealogical and postmodernist modes). The pivotal issue is the one already identified, namely, that *every* form of discourse must accommodate the constative functions of reference and predication; that such discourse cannot be committed for that reason alone to some form of cognitive privilege; and that no holism (whether naturalistic or phenomenological) makes any sense if it does not provide for distributed truth-claims servicing the sciences and any other form of critical discourse (literary criticism, moral debate, for instance) that we wish to preserve. The upshot is that Beardsley's philosophical pursuit of *objectivity* is *not* a disabling weakness of his 'analytic' aesthetics: it is only his particular way of securing it (inspired by empiricism and the unity of science) that is indefensible.

In many ways, Goodman's aesthetics, particularly when qualified along the lines of his *Ways of Worldmaking* and *Of Mind and Other Matters*,[26] appears to bridge the divide between the two sorts of strategy. It does afford the possibility of an opening, but Goodman hardly has that in mind. Again, as with Beardsley, questions need to be raised about Goodman's substantive views regarding the arts as well as about the general philosophical orientation of his most recent publications. The truth is that there is no clear way of reconciling the peculiar fixities—bordering on essentialism—of *Languages of Art* with the so-called 'irrealism' of *Ways of Worldmaking*;[27] and those fixities are themselves particularly doubtful on internal grounds.

The most noticeable oddity about Goodman's general philosophy, which remains pretty constant from *The Structure of Appearance* and *Fact, Fiction, and Forecast* to the latest books (despite the incompatibility between the visions of the two pairs), is that Goodman's entire effort is centered on epistemological puzzles, although he never actually engages those puzzles in explicitly epistemological or epistemologically informed methodological terms. For instance, he raises the question of the viability of nominalism;[28] but then he both treats the matter in purely formal terms, without the least attention to biological and cultural constraints on the effective, spontaneous use of discriminated resemblances and general terms in natural-language contexts, and converts the nominalist issue into an exclusively logical matter regarding the (ontological) eliminability of nonindividual entities.[29] Or, he poses the seemingly methodological question of projectibles within the context of induction,[30] but he nowhere pursues it in cognitive terms. That theory depends inescapably on an account of 'entrenchment'—which is clearly an epistemological matter and, as such, is clearly nowhere discussed in Goodman.[31] Furthermore, although the notion of entrenchment reappears in Goodman's later writings (in fact, in the context of his aesthetics[32]), Goodman's handling of it is utterly irreconcilable with the notion developed in *Fact, Fiction, and Forecast*, remains completely undeveloped in epistemologically pertinent terms now so urgently required by his irrealism (that is, by the proliferation of plural, made, actual worlds) and is clearly at odds with the rather strong essentializing tendencies of *Languages of Art*. The matter is complicated and takes a little patience to get clear about. But is can be shown to bear in a decisive way on the structure of Goodman's aesthetics.

The clue may be grasped by reminding ourselves of the stern once-and-for-all application of the (intended) testing of would-be projectibles in a world that (once) seemed to be so steady and orderly that Goodman's well-known new riddle of induction actually appeared to capture the methodological practices of the sciences. Entrenchment seemed so palpable and straightforwardly recoverable (then) that Goodman could afford to announce:

The obvious first step in our weeding-out process in determining (true) projectibility is to eliminate all projected hypotheses that have been violated. Such hypotheses, as already remarked, can no longer be projected, and are thus henceforth unprojectible. On similar grounds, all hypotheses having no remaining unexamined instances are likewise to be ruled out. However, neither the violated nor the exhausted hypotheses are thereby denied to have been projectible at an earlier time.[33]

Of course, all of this was meant by Goodman to be read in terms of 'the passing of the possible': 'Possible processes and possible entities vanish. . . . All possible worlds lie within the actual one'.[34]

All of this is now forgotten, swept away, or reduced to an utter shambles inasmuch as (pertinently for his theory of art) Goodman now affirms:

Irrealism does not hold that everything or even anything is irreal, but sees the world melting into versions and versions making worlds, finds ontology evanescent, and inquires into what makes a version right and a world well-built. . . . How, then, are we to accommodate conflicting truths without sacrificing the difference between truth and falsity? Perhaps by treating these versions as true in different worlds. Versions not applying in the same world no longer conflict; contradiction is avoided by segregation. A true version is true in some worlds, a false version in none. Thus the multiple worlds of conflicting true versions are actual worlds, not the merely possible worlds or nonworlds of false versions. So if there is any actual world, there are many. For there are conflicting true versions, and they cannot be true in the same world.[35]

There is, however, no explanation, in Goodman, of how to individuate worlds or world-versions, or what it means to say that something is true in one (actual) world but not in another, or what it means to say that what is false is false in all actual worlds (despite the fact that what is true in one world may be in 'conflict' with what is true in another), or what it means to say that *we* can sort such different worlds. All of this amounts to a complete abandonment of the epistemological questions of entrenchment.

Goodman has found a way of *suggesting* that he is accommodating anti-analytic attacks on objectivism in the most ramified way. But it is extremely difficult to find any such accommodation and it is equally difficult to make the case that his theory remains coherent in this regard;[36] *and*, whatever its motivation, it is quite impossible to draw out of it—or reconcile with it—the salient claims of *Language of Art*. The essential point is this: Goodman's irrealism and apparent historicizing of the construction of plural worlds (in *Ways of Worldmaking*) are *never* intended to make any concessions in the direction of radically intentionalizing the world of art (or the world of science for that matter); it is simply a device for avoiding palpable contradictions in a Quinean-like unitary world governed by a nominalist and extensionalist canon. Goodman uses the device of plural actual worlds in order to make nominalism and extensionalism work *in the domain of art and culture*. This is why it is important to note that Goodman fails to address the (apparently) *historicized* puzzle of entrenching projectibles in epistemic terms. If he had, he would not have been able to avoid the problems of textuality or of intentionality or of the limits of nominalistic models.

There can be little doubt that *Languages of Art* is written in a straightforwardly objectivist spirit. There is nothing in it that manifests the slightest qualm along phenomenological or deconstructive or genealogical lines—that is, concerns about preformational forces. On the contrary, apart from the extremely important development of a semiotic idiom for the handling of philosophical issues about the arts–which certainly can and ought to be redeemed by an analytic aesthetics—Goodman is peculiarly intransigent about the *nature* and *properties* of the arts, a matter that might seem at odds both with his nominalism and his (later or at least more explicit) irrealism. Two doctrines are of particular importance. In one, he contrasts in the strongest disjunctive sense what he calls allographic and autographic arts.[37] That is, he not only introduces the formal distinction, he surveys the arts and finds that music and literature are (it seems, essentially) allographic.

The ulterior reason for the distinction may escape one's notice: it is simply meant to bring discourse about the arts into a satisfactory alignment with an extensionalist model. The autographic arts are ones in which 'even the most exact duplication of an original does not thereby count as genuine'.[38] So intentional complexities are disallowed by ensuring uniqueness of reference. The allographic arts are ones in which all apparent discrepancies, variations, differences (as of performance and printing) may be tolerated (and discounted) as far as numerical identity and individuation are concerned, provided only that the individuating marks preserved satisfy completely extensional scores or notations. Goodman struggles manfully with the notational informalities of the history of music; but he never quite comes to terms with its profoundly historical and intentional nature. He is ultimately driven to the obviously unnecessary (even intolerable) conclusion:

The innocent-seeming principle that performances differing by just one note are instances of the same work risks the consequence—in view of the transitivity of identity—that all performances whatsoever are of the same work. If we allow the least deviation, all assurance of work-preservation and score-preservation is lost; for by a series of one-note errors of omission, addition, and modification, we can go all the way from Beethoven's *Fifth Symphony* to *Three Blind Mice*.[39]

If Goodman had but found 'ontology evanescent' enough, he might have allowed intentional informalities to flower, or at any rate cognitive fixities to go more informal. For example, if one concedes that the numerical identity of a dance (as in re-identifying one and the same dance in different performances) is a function of its *stylistic* features, and if its stylistic features are profoundly intentionalized, historicized, *incapable* of being captured by any strict extensionalized notation, then it may well be that all so-called allographic arts are ineluctably autographic—and, in being autographic, irreconcilable with the severe nominalism and extensionalism Goodman means to favour.[40] The truth is that Goodman nowhere actually analyses the stylistic *properties* of artworks (with regard to their intensional complexity)—or the predicates purporting, in a logically relaxed way, to designate such properties; he never goes beyond merely insisting that any and all such properties *are* capable of being extensionally regimented. Clearly, the collapse of that claim would place Goodman's sort of analytic aesthetics in serious jeopardy.

The other large issue that Goodman addresses—tied to the present one because there is, in Goodman's work, no actual discussion of the structure of artworks—concerns the notion of exemplification. It concerns the nature of artistic expression and so borders once again on the complexities of intentionality. Goodman's key is given by the following:

Expression [in a work] is not, of course, mere possession [by the work of the putatively expressive property]. Apart from the fact that the possession involved in expression is metaphorical, neither literal nor metaphorical possession constitutes symbolization at all. . . . [But] an object that is literally or metaphorically denoted by a predicate or the corresponding property, may be said to exemplify that predicate or property. Not all exemplification is expression, but all expression is exemplification.[41]

Once again, the essential point remains that Goodman treats expression (semiotically) as metaphorical, *because* to treat the expressive property *of* an artwork as 'literally' possessed by it would entail serious complications *for any extensional treatment of art*—hence, for the autographic/allographic distinction as well. Nevertheless, Goodman nowhere justifies the *metaphorical* ascription:[42] he literally *has* no ontology of art; and he nowhere provides a suitable clue about how philosophical inquiries regarding the arts should proceed. He has no genuine analytic aesthetics.

That is, Goodman practices a variety of analytic aesthetics, but he nowhere entertains questions about the nature of philosophical strategies in the large. As a result, it is impossible to gain from Goodman's work a clear idea of how analytic aesthetics should meet the challenge of anti-analytic currents; although it remains both true and provocative that Goodman's notion of worldmaking has been seen—for instance by the phenomenologically and hermeneutically minded French philosopher Paul Ricoeur—as promising a new view of 'fiction' (Ricoeur is thinking of Goodman's symbol systems: quite another matter) as a sort of 'productive imagination' by which we 'make and remake reality' in ways that would obviously defeat any straightforwardly objectivist stance.[43] But whether Goodman would, or could, accept Ricoeur's adventurous suggestion is difficult to say. In fact, the essential irony is just that Ricoeur favors Goodman's view of worldmaking because he, Ricoeur, sees this as a powerful concession in the direction of historically preformative forces that lay a proper foundation for the admission and treatment of the intentional or hermeneutic features of artworks; whereas Goodman's motivation is to extricate a strongly anti-hermeneutic (that is, a formal semiotic) conception of artworks *for* his own favored extensionalism. There could not be a more curious marriage of ideas.

Of our four specimen analysts, Arthur Danto affords the most detailed sense of adjusting a theory of art to the actual phases of the history of contemporary art—chiefly painting. He is particularly attentive to modernist, postmodernist and especially so-called conceptual art. For that reason, he is sensibly disinclined to specify any essentialist definition of art. For instance, he is suitably brief regarding George Dickie's institutional conception of art,[44] and he ultimately dismisses Goodman's thesis of expression as metaphorical exemplification with the rather nice piece of tact: 'It would be unfortunate to conclude that expressive predicates are never literally true of works of art'.[45] He is also noticeably hospitable to Hegelian and broadly phenomenological currents. Nevertheless, it is quite clear that his general philosophical orientation is uneasily—and unsatisfactorily—divided between his appreciation of the complexities of cultural phenomena, particularly historicity and intentionality, and his residual commitment to a relatively inflexible physicalism and extensionalism. In fact, in his discussion of the issue of expression, which in the context of the rhetoric of art occupies Danto's principal attention, he actually concludes: 'The philosophical point [of the discussion of some of Cezanne's paintings and other artworks] is that the concept of expression can be reduced to the concept of metaphor, when the *way* in which something is represented is taken in connection with the subject represented'.[46] By this device, Danto recovers what Goodman does not quite accommodate—but in an ingenious way that preserves his ulterior convergence with Goodman's extensionalism and tendency toward physicalism.

This is a large and rather complicated matter, not easily grasped or conceded. Our intention here, one must remember, is to draw the thread of analytic aesthetics from a number of its principal champions in order to weigh the prospects for its continuing force. Let it therefore be said of Danto's work (in the philosophy of art) that its fatal weakness lies with Danto's failure to have resolved the analysis of what he himself had memorably identified as 'the "is" of artistic identification'.[47] The point to grasp is that Danto's difficulty with the 'is' of artistic identification (not, of course, a difficulty Danto himself feels) is both the mate of similar difficulties that surface in all of his philosophical work—in his theory of history and in his theory of action, for instance[48]—and a clue to his essential philosophical strategy. But it needs to be said, of course, that most readers of Danto do not sense the conceptual strain in his aesthetics simply because they do not take seriously enough the bearing of the 'is' of artistic identification on *all* of his otherwise most perceptive discussions of artworks. That is, *most readers accept Danto's straightforward account of the complexities of art without attempting to reconcile his critical and appreciative remarks with *his fundamental philosophical orientation*. It is not that Danto embraces the empiricism, physicalism, nominalism, extensionalism, unity-of-science orientation so characteristic of the analytic tradition: it is rather that his theory is fatally encumbered by the traces of such affiliations, that he is divided in his heart regarding the adequacy of those doctrines and their disciplined application to the world of action, history, art, language and culture, *and* that he fails (for reason of that divided allegiance) ever to resolve the puzzle of the 'is' of artistic identification.

The objective of Danto's entire strategy (going well beyond aesthetics) is to marry two somewhat disparate projects: one, the articulation of an idiom ample enough for the entire span of cultural life—notably, art, history, action, knowledge; the other, adherence to an underlying ontology, more or less faithful to the inspiration of the unity-of-science program and of a strong physicalism. *That* is what the 'is' of artistic identification is all about, and that explains why Danto takes such pains to distinguish it from the 'is' of (numerical) identity. *If*, however, *what* is *constituted* by the first 'is' *is* real as such, then the second 'is' *would* ineluctably apply to it. So the trick is that Danto manages to hold that artworks are 'constituted' as artworks by the 'is' of artistic identification all right, but that *that constitution does not yield an entity or real phenomenon about which it may be said that it is both real (in the ontological sense) and self-identical as such*. What is true of 'it' is held at arm's length from what is real, kept from capturing the actual properties of 'mere' physical phenomena (not quite the equivalent of what Danto calls 'mere real things').[49] But the motivation for that manoeuvre is still not too distant from Sartre's insistence that art is 'unreal', that is, superior to what is 'merely' real.[50]

All of this comes out reasonably clearly in Danto's recent objection to Susan Sontag's view of interpretation. Here is what he says:

Hers [that is, Sontag's objections regarding the nature of interpretation] is against a notion of interpretation which makes the artwork as an explanandum—as a symptom, for example. My theory of interpretation is instead constitutive, for an object is an artwork *at all* only in relation to an interpretation. We may bring this out in a somewhat logical way. Interpretation in my sense is transfigurative. It transforms objects into works of art, and depends upon the 'is' of artistic identification. Her interpretations, which are explanatory, use instead the 'is' of ordinary identity. Her despised interpreters see works as signs, symptoms, expressions of ulterior or subjacent realities, states of which are what the artwork 'really' refers to, and which requires the interpreter to be master of one or another kind of code: psychoanalytical, culturographic, semiotical, or whatever. In effect, her interpreters address the work in the spirit of science. . . . Mine is a theory which is not in the spirit of science but of philosophy. If interpretations are what constitute works, there are no works without them and works are misconstituted when interpretation is wrong. And knowing the artist's interpretation is in effect identifying what he or she has made. The interpretation is not something outside the work: work and interpretation arise together in aesthetic consciousness. As interpretation is inseparable from work, it is inseparable from the artist if it is the artist's work.[51]

Now, the transfigurative 'is' is meant to accommodate absolutely everything of interest that may be said about artworks, but it collects all of that only *in a relational way*. That is, it is initially the artist's intention *with respect to* a merely physical object (or, in a more relaxed, provisional sense, with respect to a 'mere real thing' that may even happen to be an artefact—a snow shovel or bottlerack, for instance); and it is subsequently, therefore, the viewer's (or aesthetic percipient's) recovery of *that* (or something like that) *constituting relationship* (the interpretation) that permits the viewer to 'see' it *as* an artwork: 'To see something as art requires something the eye cannot descry—an atmosphere of artistic theory, a knowledge of the history of art: an artworld'.⁵²

This is the reason Danto is so comfortable in declaring (as we have seen) that 'the concept of expression *can* be reduced to the concept of metaphor', after having dismissed Goodman's version of a related thesis. *Danto has a better way of holding on to all the complexity of art, while reaching for the same extensional and physicalist model Goodman is more explicitly attracted to.* But it cannot be enough *if*, as seems plain, *human persons themselves*, the paradigms of culturally complex entities, are *not* similarly reducible (by the 'is' of identity) to mere physical bodies.⁵³ After all, if persons were thus reduced, then there would be no independent entities capable of *relating* to other physical objects by suitable interpretation or theory, in such a way that those 'objects' would be imaginatively 'transfigured' (but *not* ontically transformed) into artworks—or human actions or historical events or speech or the like. Otherwise, Danto would merely be the stock figure of a reductive physicalism (would hold that artworks just are—by the 'is' of identity—physical objects), whereas (in truth) he means to be a *non*reductive physicalist.⁵⁴ But he is never sufficiently clear, ultimately, about the relationship between the intentionally complex language of human culture and the language of physicalism—which is what the true physicalist (whether reductive or nonreductive) cannot permit to remain inexplicit. That is why his account fails. More than that, his endeavour fixes the plain sense in which, for all his considerable ingenuity and perceptiveness, his version of analytic aesthetics remains essentially bound to the objectivism that we noted at the start in Beardsley's very much simpler aesthetics.

Nevertheless, it would be churlish not to admit the finesse of Danto's sustained discussion of the historical and intentional complexities of art. What Danto manages to show thereby—against his own intentions—is that, by a logically small adjustment, fatal to the older strains of analytic aesthetics, these exemplary observations could revive the analytic orientation by embracing just the kind of complication the older strains disallow. Danto is too well informed to disallow them; but he is also too loyal to those older strains to work out an explicit ontology fitted to the kind of critical remarks he himself regularly favors. Hence, he never skimps on the critic's role; but then he also never addresses the obvious theoretical pressure that it imposes on a realism essentially committed to the contraints of physicalism.

The fourth of our specimens, Joseph Margolis (myself, of course, if I dare speak in the third person), is the only one of the four to have attempted systematically to reconcile the strategies of analytic philosophy with the principal currents of anti-analytic philosophy—chiefly, with those that appear in Husserl, Heidegger, Derrida and Foucault, that is, with phenomenological and poststructuralist currents. Margolis's general argument insists that, first of all (as already remarked), there is no way to avoid the constative function of discourse; and, secondly, that all such discourse (whether first-order or second-order, whether intended to be descriptive of the world or intended to be legitimative with respect to what purports to be descriptive of the world—there being no way to disengage one from the other) must submit to some form of critique, that is, to some way of attending to the performative conditions under which constative discourse functions as such.⁵⁵ This has the effect of 'phenomenologizing' naturalistic discourse or of 'naturalizing' phenomenological or deconstructive or genealogical discourse. For the absence of the first leaves the naturalistic blind, and the absence of the second leaves the phenomenological and the deconstructive pointless and empty; *and*, for that reason, *critique* may be either naturalistic (say, Marxist or Frankfurt School) or anti-naturalistic (say, Nietzschean or Heideggerean). The important point is that critique (in this sense) is entirely 'internalist' and viable as such, that is, restricted in the same way as any first-order inquiry (say, science and literary criticism). In short, though second-order and legitimative, it utterly eschews cognitive privilege.[56]

It is a very pretty and uncomplicated consequence that the postmodernist conception of philosophy—preeminently, Rorty's view—simply fails at a stroke, that is, fails in the sense that there are no professional practices of cognitive inquiry that can escape the need for second-order, legitimative reflection, even if (or precisely because) it is the case that the 'loyalty' we may manifest with respect to such practices 'no longer needs an ahistorical backup'.[57] Rorty's point is that the metaphysical, transparent, cognitively privileged, essentialist, correspondentist, mirrored, objectivist, transcendental, presenced, logocentric idiom of Kant and Descartes is neither necessary nor defensible. Fine. He offers two options: one, a historicized and naturalistic but *not* philosophical or epistemological source of reasons and arguments for the practices in question (which he regards as a naturalized Hegelian line); the other (the 'postmodernist bourgeois liberal', also 'Hegelian'), one that simply abandons the entire need *for* a justification of practices—contenting itself with the notion that: 'On a Quinean view, rational behavior is just adaptive behavior of a sort which roughly parallels the behavior, in similar circumstances, of the other members of some relevant community'.[58]

But this is simply intellectual bankruptcy. For, for one thing, we cannot eliminate (Rorty does not wish to eliminate) constative discourse. And for a second, the *practice*—any practice, the practice of any community of inquirers—must have a rationale *regarding how to go on to new cases not included in the paradigms learned in learning the original language or practice.* Therein lies the essential disability of Goodman's nominalism and of every nominalism construed in a cognitively pertinent sense; and therein also lies the defect and defeat of the postmodernist maneuver. For the problem is not merely one of how to go on extending the scope of complex predicates in new circumstances but also one of how to go on giving rational or critical redirection to any sustained and disciplined inquiry. The first is the *pons* of nominalism; the second, of postmodernism. If analytic aesthetics is to survive—if analytic philosophy or any philosophy is to survive, if any rational inquiry is to survive—then: (1) it must be possible to bridge the difference between naturalism and phenomenology and deconstruction and genealogy and the like, and (2) it must be possible to provide for second-order legitimative discourse that does not fail in the 'Kantian' manner Rorty is at such pains to dismantle. Margolis's entire philosophical effort is committed to working out the conceptual conditions for satisfying (1) and (2), with attention particularly to the metaphysics and epistemology of culture and art. This is at least a viable proposal regarding a *new* program and orientation for analytic aesthetics—again, of course, considered here only in the spirit of tracing the prospects of analytic aesthetics. It would put into question all the older doctrines of objectivism, physicalism, nominalism, extensionalism and unity-of-science constraints; and it would embrace, at least as pertinent options, historicism, intentionality, preformation, intertextuality, relativism, cultural emergence, nonreductive materialism, critique, incommensurabilism, legitimation. The vista is large enough.

Through a marvel of innuendo but not argument, Rorty declares and insinuates at one and the same time: 'Analytic philosophy *cannot*, I suspect, be written without one or the other of these two distinctions: the "Kantian" distinctions (ambiguously) repudiated by Quine and Wilfrid Sellars respectively, namely, the "necessary-contingent" distinction and the "given-interpretation" distinction'.[59] The juxtaposition of the italicized 'cannot' and the coy 'I suspect' permits Rorty to play the enormously pleasant game of agreeing with all his critics for the sake of the ongoing 'conversation' while at the same time cutting philosophy (and science and criticism) off at the knees. So he adds, catching up the point of what we took note of before:

Behaviorism claims that if you understand the rules of a language-game, you understand *all* that there is to understand about why moves in that language-game are made. (All, that is, save for the extra understanding you get when you engage in various research programs which nobody would call epistemological—into, for example, the history of the language, the structure of the brain, the evolution of the species, and the political or cultural ambience of the players.)[60]

But that is just what one does not understand, unless one understands the rationale, the legitimative rationale, the second-order transcendental moves in accord with which we recommend—dialectically, historically, contingently, without foundations—how to go on rationally.[61] If we give up the 'Kantian' position, which we must, then we need second-order legitimative discourse more than ever—not less—because we need the best rational guess about what the conditions of inquiry and truth-claims are by which to guide ourselves in extending our practice. That is what philosophy is all about; and that is what no one has ever convincingly shown to be disposable. To be sure, 'rational' (like 'true' and 'false') also *has* a history, which complicates philosophy enormously. But it complicates it, it does not rule it out. Even Foucault rather wistfully acknowledges the point in reviewing the threatening incoherence of his own postmodernist efforts.[62] There *cannot* be a recovery of analytic aesthetics, now faced with its own stalemate, without a 'rational' second-order redirection of its energies. Rorty's is simply a counsel of despair or irresponsibility.

Margolis, then, has deliberately sought to reconcile what the objectivist and naturalistic idioms have correctly perceived—namely, that constative discourse is ineliminable and that first-order and second-order (legitimative) discourse are inseparable—with the best elements of non-naturalistic (in effect, non-'analytic') philosophy; while at the same time he abandons the objectionable logocentric or privileged discourse that the phenomenologists and poststructuralists have rightly perceived to be entrenched in most of analytic philosophy. This means that the famous 'subject/object' relationship that Husserl (and Heidegger and Derrida) so much inveigh against cannot be eliminated but, *once* placed in an appropriate preformational or critical context (*without*, then, reclaiming privilege on its own), the relationship affords a perfectly adequate and viable (and necessary) basis for recovering epistemological and metaphysical inquiry—in aesthetics as elsewhere.

It is true that Margolis has come to this rapprochement somewhat later than his characteristic accounts of the ontology of artworks, of the logic of interpretation and of relativistic judgments in general.[63] The result is that there *is* a distinct vestigial objectivism in these various discussions that needs to be exorcised. This is as it may be, a matter entirely local to Margolis's own efforts; and is of little consequence in the present context. In his more recent papers,[64] Margolis explores the ontic indeterminacies, the historicized openness, the lack of essential fixity artworks exhibit. But there is no question that all of this needs to be put into better form. That is not my present concern. The fact remains that the analysis of the nature of art and culture, of description and interpretation, of texts, of histories, of reference, of judgement, of relativistic and nonrelativistic truth-values is entirely congenial both with regard to the rapprochement sketched and the continuance of analytic aesthetics. In fact, Margolis's themes (even within a more naive epistemological framework drawn from a less developed non-foundationalist account of analytic philosophy than we are now suggesting) have characteristically been hospitable to the full recovery of intentional phenomena, the irreducibility of culture to nature, the inadequacy of both reductive and nonreductive physicalisms, the admission of emergence, the replacement of the unity-of-science program, the abandonment of a comprehensive extensionalism, the acknowledgement of the complexities of historicism, the advocacy of ontic indeterminacies, of conceptual incommensurabilities, of divergent pluralisms, of relativistic values, the rejection of closed systems, the insistence on the symbiosis of the psychological and the societal, the symbiosis of realism and idealism, and the constructive nature of selves and world. These are all themes peculiarly favorably attuned to phenomenologizing naturalism and naturalizing phenomenology—meaning by that to accommodate all forms of critique (say, the Marxist as well as the Nietzschean) that seriously address the question of the pursuit of first- and second-order inquiry under contingently preformational conditions that, at the level of both first- and second-order discourse, we cannot fathom in a privileged way.

In short, analytic philosophy—and analytic aesthetics in particular—cannot be expected to prosper without recovering (at least selectively) these and related questions within the subtler space of an inquiry that avoids the older cognitive privilege or foundationalism, or without resisting altogether the siren attraction of a know-nothing postmodernism. But there is reason already to think that the imminent future will transform these implied recommendations into a prophecy—and a fulfilment. In any case, the best prospects of analytic aesthetics depend on two adjustments: (i) the pursuit of all the themes just mentioned, that go entirely counter to the canonical tendencies of analytic philosophy but are not at all incompatible with the native discipline of such philosophy; and (ii) the ability to steer a middle course between the older tendency toward ahistorical privilege and the newest tendency to disallow, within a historicized condition, suitably adjusted versions of philosophy's legitimate legitimative concern.

NOTES

1. I have attempted several summaries of this sort before. I trust the overlap will not seem excessive. The perspective keeps changing of course. See Joseph Margolis, 'Recent Currents in Aesthetics of Relevance to Contemporary Visual Artists', *Leonardo*, 12 (1979) 111–19; 'Recent Work in Aesthetics', in Kenneth G. Lucey and Tibor R. Machan (ed.), *Recent Work in Philosophy* (Totowa, NJ, Rowman and Allanheld, 1983).
2. See, for instance, William Elton (ed.), *Aesthetics and Language* (Oxford, Basil Blackwell, 1954); and Joseph Margolis (ed.), *Philosophy Looks at the Arts* (New York, Scribner, 1962).
3. Richard Rorty, *Philosophy and the Mirror of Nature* (Princeton, NJ, Princeton University Press, 1979), p. 390.
4. W. V. Quine, *Word and Object* (Cambridge, Mass., MIT Press, 1960), pp. 15–16.
5. W. V. Quine, 'Two Dogmas of Empiricism', *From a Logical Point of View* (Cambridge, Mass., Harvard University Press, 1953).
6. Quine, *Word and Object*, p. 72.
7. Rorty, *Philosophy and the Mirror of Nature*, pp. 392–4.
8. Quine, *Word and Object*, p. 219.
9. Rorty, *Philosophy and the Mirror of Nature*, p. 389.
10. See, further, Joseph Margolis, *Pragmatism without Foundations: Reconciling Realism and Relativism* (Oxford, Basil Blackwell, 1986).
11. See Richard Rorty, 'Overcoming the Tradition: Heidegger and Dewey', in *Consequences of Pragmatism: Essays 1972–1980* (Minneapolis, University of Minnesota Press, 1982).
12. I examine the recovery of certain key philosophical projects in *Pragmatism without Foundations*; see particularly, ch. 11.
13. Rorty, *Consequences of Pragmatism*, p. xiii; italics added.
14. A brief sense of the range of Husserl's criticism may be got from Edmund Husserl, *Phenomenology and the Crisis of Philosophy*, trans. Quentin Lauer (New York, Harper and Row, 1965). Lauer brings together two independent essays of Husserl: 'Philosophy as Rigorous Science' and 'Philosophy and the Crisis of European Man'.
15. See Edmund Husserl, *The Crisis of European Sciences and Transcendental Phenomenology*, trans. David Carr (Evanston, Ill., Northwestern University Press, 1970).
16. See Jacques Derrida, *Edmund Husserl's Origin of Geometry: An Introduction*, trans. John P. Leavey, Jr (Stony Brook, NY, Nicolas Hays, 1978); and *Speech and Phenomena and Other Essays on Husserl's Theory of Signs*, trans.

David B. Allison (Evanston, Ill., Northwestern University Press, 1973).
17. See Monroe C. Beardsley, *The Possibility of Criticism* (Detroit, Mich., Wayne State University Press, 1980).
18. Ibid., p. 36.
19. Ibid., p. 14 and 'The Testability of an Interpretation' in the same volume.
20. Ibid., p. 14.
21. See E. D. Hirsch, Jr, *Validity in Interpretation* (New Haven, Conn., Yale University Press, 1967); and Joseph Margolis, *The Language of Art and Art Criticism: Analytic Questions in Aesthetics* (Detroit, Mich., Wayne State University Press, 1965). The latter volume has been considerably re-worked and enlarged as *Art and Philosophy: Conceptual Issues in Aesthetics* (Atlantic Highlands, NJ, Humanities Press, 1980), though it exhibits much the same orientation.
22. Roland Barthes, 'From Work to Text', trans. Josue V. Harari, in Josue V. Harari (ed.), *Textual Strategies* (Ithaca, NY, Cornell University Press, 1979), p. 77.
23. For an overview of these and similar currents, see Joseph Margolis, 'What is a Literary Text?' in Herbert L. Sussman (ed.), *At the Boundaries: Proceedings of the Northeastern University Center for Literary Studies*, vol. 1, 1983 (Boston, Mass., Northeastern University Press, 1984), 47–73.
24. I may say, here, that Beardsley read Roland Barthes's S/Z as a straightforward, objectivist semiotics of literature and failed completely to appreciate the subversively deconstructive intent of Barthes's essay. That is, where he was able to assimilate the poststructuralist literature, he regularly read it as something like a continuation of New Criticism—which indeed it superficially resembles. Otherwise, just as Derrida serves as a straightforward (!) deconstructionist (*On Grammatology*), Beardsley serves as a straightforward and uncompromising New Critic.
25. See, for instance, Maurice Merleau-Ponty, *The Phenomenology of Perception*, trans. Colin Smith (London, Routledge and Kegan Paul, 1962); Walter Biemel, 'Husserl's *Encyclopaedia Britannica* Article and Heidegger's Remarks Thereon', in Frederick A. Elliston and Peter McCormick (eds.), *Husserl: Expositions and Appraisals* (Notre Dame, Ind., University of Notre Dame, 1977). The rapprochement of naturalism and phenomenology and deconstruction is discussed at length in Joseph Margolis, *Texts without Referents: Reconciling Science and Narrative* (Oxford, Basil Blackwell, 1988).
26. See Nelson Goodman, *Ways of Worldmaking* (Indianapolis, Hackett Publishing, 1978); and *Of Mind and Other Matters* (Cambridge, Mass., Harvard University Press, 1984).
27. Cf. *Ways of Worldmaking*, p. x.
28. See, for instance, Nelson Goodman, 'Seven Strictures on Similarity', in Lawrence Foster and J. W. Swanson (eds.), *Experience and Theory* (Amherst, University of Massachusetts Press, 1970).
29. See Nelson Goodman, *The Structure of Appearance*, 2nd edn (Indianapolis, Bobbs-Merrill, 1966), ch. 2.
30. See Nelson Goodman, 'Prospects for a Theory of Projection', *Fact, Fiction and Forecast*, 2nd edn (Indianapolis, Bobbs-Merrill, 1965).
31. Ibid., pp. 94–9.
32. Cf. Goodman, *Of Mind and Other Matters*, pp. 32–3.
33. Goodman, *Fact, Fiction and Forecast*, p. 83.
34. Ibid., p. 57.
35. Goodman, *Of Mind and Other Matters*, pp. 29, 31.
36. See Hilary Putnam, 'Reflections on Goodman's *Ways of Worldmaking*,' *Philosophical Papers*, vol. 3 (Cambridge, Cambridge University Press, 1983).
37. See Nelson Goodman, *Languages of Art* (Indianapolis, Bobbs-Merrill, 1968), pp. 113–22.
38. Ibid., p. 113.
39. Ibid., pp. 186–8.
40. See Joseph Margolis, 'The Autographic Nature of the Dance', in Maxine Sheets-Johnstone (ed.), *Illuminating Dance: Philosophical Explorations* (London and Toronto, Associated University Presses, 1984); and Nelson Goodman, 'The Status of Style', in *Ways of Worldmaking*.
41. Ibid., p. 52.
42. Cf. Margolis, *Art and Philosophy*, pp. 12–14.
43. Paul Ricoeur, 'The Narrative Function', *Hermeneutics and the Human Sciences*, ed. and trans. John B. Thompson (Cambridge, Cambridge University Press, 1981), particularly pp. 292–3.
44. Arthur C. Danto, *The Transfiguration of the Commonplace* (Cambridge, Mass., Harvard University Press, 1981), pp. 92–5.
45. Ibid., pp. 189–97, particularly p. 192.
46. Ibid., p. 197.
47. The notion first appeared, unanalysed, in Arthur Danto, 'The Artworld', reprinted in Mar-

golis (ed.), *Philosophy Looks at the Arts*, 3rd edn (Philadelphia, Temple University Press, 1987).
48. This more ramified issue is explored in Joseph Margolis, 'Ontology Down and Out in Art and Science', *Journal of Aesthetics and Art Criticism*, 46 (1988). The relevant texts include: Arthur C. Danto, *Narration and Knowledge* (New York, Columbia University Press, 1985)—the enlarged second edition of Danto's *Analytical Philosophy of History* (1964); and *Analytical Philosophy of Action* (Cambridge, Cambridge University Press, 1973).
49. Cf. 'Works of Art and Mere Real Things', in *Transfiguration of the Commonplace*.
50. See Jean-Paul Sartre, *The Psychology of Imagination* (Secaucus, NJ, Citadel Press, n.d.); also, Arthur C. Danto, *Jean-Paul Sartre* (New York, Viking, 1975), ch. 1.
51. *The Philosophical Disenfranchisement of Art* (New York, Columbia University Press, 1986), pp. 44–5.
52. Danto, 'The Artworld', p. 162.
53. The nature of this difficulty is explored in Joseph Margolis, 'Constraints on the Metaphysics of Culture', *Review of Metaphysics*, 39 (1986), 653–73.
54. The most ingenious version of nonreductive physicalism is developed in John F. Post, *The Faces of Experience* (Ithaca, NY, Cornell University Press, 1987). Post's book is examined at some length in Margolis, *Texts without Referents*, ch. 6.
55. Cf. Margolis, *Pragmatism without Foundations*, ch. 8; and *Texts without Referents*, pt 1.
56. On 'internalist' strategies, see Margolis, *Pragmatism without Foundations*, ch. 11.
57. Richard Rorty, 'Postmodernist Bourgeois Liberalism', *Journal of Philosophy*, 80 (1983) 583–89; reprinted in Robert Hollinger (ed.), *Hermeneutics and Praxis* (Notre Dame, Ind., Notre Dame University Press, 1985); the material quoted appears on p. 216 (in Hollinger's edition).
58. Ibid., p. 217.
59. Richard Rorty, 'Epistemological Behaviourism and the De-Transcendentalization of Analytic Philosophy', *Neue Hefte fur Philosophie*, 9 (1978); reprinted in Hollinger, *Hermeneutics and Praxis*, pp. 95–6. Rorty professes to follow Lyotard, of course, in characterizing his own view as postmodern. Cf. Jean-François Lyotard, *The Postmodern Condition: A Report on Knowledge*, trans. Geoff Bennington and Brian Massumi (Minneapolis, University of Minnesota Press, 1984).
60. Rorty, 'Epistemological Behaviourism', p. 98; italics added.
61. I have tried to formulate a fresh interpretation of transcendental arguments along these lines, in *Pragmatism without Foundations*, ch. 11.
62. See, for instance, Michel Foucault, 'Questions of Method: An Interview with Michel Foucault', trans. Alan Bass, *Ideology and Consciousness*, 8 (1981); reprinted in Kenneth Baynes et al. (eds.), *After Philosophy: End or Transformation?* (Cambridge, Mass., MIT Press, 1987).
63. For instance, in *Art and Philosophy*; also, in *Culture and Cultural Entities* (Dordrecht, D. Reidel, 1984), ch. 1.
64. See, particularly, Joseph Margolis, 'What is a Literary Text?', (ed.), *At the Boundaries*, pp. 47–73; 'The Threads of Literary Theory', *Poetics Today*, 6 (1986) 75–110; 'How to Theorize about Texts at the Present Time: Deconstruction and Its Victims', in Peter J. McCormick (ed.), *The Reasons of Art* (Ottawa, University of Ottawa Press, 1985), pp. 98–111; 'Opening the Closure, and Vice Versa', in Mark Neuman and Michael Payne (eds.), *Self, Sign, and Symbol* (London and Toronto, American University Press, 1987), pp. 34–44; 'Puzzles of Pictorial Representation', in Margolis (ed.), *Philosophy Looks at the Arts*, 3rd edn., pp. 338–57; 'Reference as Relational: Pro and Contra', *Grazier Philosophische Studien*, 25/26 (1985/6), 327–57.

Philosophy of Art after Analysis and Romanticism

Nicholas Wolterstorff

It is beyond dispute that the glory of twentieth-century analytic philosophy is not revealed in the field of the philosophy of art. If one is on the lookout for analytic philosophy's greatest attainments, one must look elsewhere. Why is that?

Most of the major figures of analytic philosophy spent no time at all reflecting on the arts. As for the remaining ones, their reflections on art were rarely central to their philosophical work. The cultivation of the analytic philosophy of art was left almost entirely to figures of the second and lower ranks. Mainly, they applied to art lessons learned elsewhere. Nobody tried to apply elsewhere lessons learned in thinking about art—with the exception, perhaps, of those who applied lessons learned in thinking about poetic metaphor. The busy hive of analytic philosophy was never located in the field of philosophy of art. Why is that?

The answer cannot be that the priorities of the analytic philosopher mirrored the priorities of our culture, for in modern Western culture, art is no minor matter. So is it perhaps that what determines philosophy's attention to some component of culture is not prominence but crisis? Not that either; for in our century, art has not lacked for crises. It must be something in the character of analytic philosophy which accounts for art's minority status there, or strictly, something in

From *The Journal of Aesthetics and Art Criticism* (46) 1987, Special Issue. Reprinted by permission of The American Society for Aesthetics. Footnotes and headings have been renumbered.

the *relation* of the character of analytic philosophy to the character of art, or to the character of our modern ways of thinking about art. Perhaps the fit is poor.

I

In a good many of his writings over the past decade or so, Richard Rorty has expounded the thesis that analytic philosophy, when it was still a movement and not merely a style, was a version of neo-Kantianism. That interpretation seems to me correct. Or at least what seems to me correct is that the "ideal type" (using Max Weber's concept of *ideal type*) of analytic philosopher was a neo-Kantian with empiricist predilections.

Philosophers hold and defend theses. But deeper in their thought than the theses they hold and defend are the pictures and images which govern and guide their holding and defending. Analytic philosophy has been governed and guided by the Kantian image of structure and content: a scheme of concepts applied to a given content. Kant regarded the content as "intuitions"—*Anschauungen*. Some analytic philosophers agreed. But others thought that what is given is not just our intuitions but also items in the world; and even more held that among our concepts are to be found some that apply not to our intuitions but to items in the world—to entities independent of our subjectivity. Kant also held that concepts *structure* intuitions and that experience is *constituted* by those structured intuitions: to experience a table is (under the appropriate circumstances) to *take* one's intuitions *as* a table; it is to *conceptualize* them *as* a table. Probably most analytic philosophers did not accept this structuring/constituting thesis concerning the working of concepts. But the conviction that in thinking and speaking we apply (some part of) our conceptual scheme to some content or other has been common coinage, as was the Kantian conviction that ultimately the content is *given* to us and that we *provide* the concepts. The human mind exhibits a duality of receptivity and spontaneity. Thought—and perhaps even experience—represent the interplay of these two dimensions: receptivity and spontaneity, the given and the contributed, content and structure, awareness and concept.

Obviously there is much about our conceptual schemes and our intuitions that is contingent. But beneath the contingency there is—so argued Kant—necessity. There are connections of logical necessity among the concepts. In addition, it is necessay that human beings—or more generally, finite knowers—intuit space and time. And it is necessary that they conceptualize the intuitional given in certain ways. These modes of necessity constitute necessity's full scope. Beyond *de dicto* necessity, and *de re* necessity concerning the powers of intuiting and conceptualizing of finite knowers, there is no necessity. Further, *de dicto* necessity is not a feature of the metaphysical structure of things independent of finite knowers. It too has the status of being a limit on the powers of finite knowers; it is impossible for us to think of a proposition of the form $p \ \& \ -p$ as true. The laws of logic are the rules of thought. All necessity, then, can be thought of as pertaining to how we think and experience. Necessity is the limit on human spontaneity. This, I say, was Kant's view. Within analytic philosophy there was powerful impetus toward following Kant in this subjectivizing of necessity. Necessity represents the limits on thought, or language, or whatever.

This picture made available to Kant and the neo-Kantians an elegant way of delineating the task of philosophy among the "sciences." Philosophy deals with our conceptual scheme as such; the other sciences deal with the application of one and another part of that scheme. In philosophy, as Wittgenstein remarked, the scheme idles. More specifically, philosophy deals with the necessary structure of our conceptual scheme. Now necessity is ascertainable a priori; conducting experiments and taking polls is irrelevant to the discerning of necessity. Philosophy is thus an armchair enterprise. Philosophical knowledge is a priori knowledge. Rorty says that neo-Kantians regarded philosophical knowledge as apodictic (certain). And some did indeed not only regard genuine philosophical knowledge as a priori but as certain.

What questions do philosophers pose as they stand back to discern necessity in our conceptual scheme? Here one finds a sharp difference between Kant on the one hand and the analytic philosopher on the other. Kant's preoccupying concern was to establish that every conceptual scheme of human beings will necessarily contain certain specific concepts, such as existence, necessity, and causality, and certain types of concepts, such as those of enduring objects and of qualities. In addition, he endeavored to show that there is an ineradicable dynamic in the constitution of us human beings which leads us to think of the intuitions given to us as reality putting in its appearance to us, and which leads us to think of that reality along certain quite definite lines—this in spite of the fact that *knowledge* of that reality is in principle unattainable for us. These views on Kant's part contain and produce deep paradoxes. Of these, the analytic philosophers were well aware. Accordingly, they did their best to keep the Kantian preoccupations at arm's length. They simply avoided the question of the extent to which we human beings can do our thinking with alternative conceptual schemes, insisting only that any viable conceptual scheme will satisfy the laws of logic.

With the Kantian preoccupations thus renounced, what was it that remained for philosophers to do? Philosophers would concern themselves solely with the *internal* necessities of our conceptual schemes, i.e., with the necessary relations holding among concepts.

They would offer necessary and sufficient conditions for the application of concepts. They would *analyze* concepts. Philosophy would be the analytic of concepts. Philosophy would be conceptual analysis. As such, philosophy would finally become scientific. Its days of wandering in the sloughs of indecisiveness would be over. It would now at long last join the other sciences in the algorithmic settling of disputes.[1] At the core of the philosophical enterprise would be the activity of looking to see whether P does or does not entail Q.

What would be the point of this enterprise? What values would conceptual analysis serve? Two things especially were emphasized. The cause of clarity would be served; never has there been a philosophical movement which so prized clarity. We do not discern the logic of scientific discourse, do not discern the logic of moral discourse, do not discern the structure of one and another sort of fact. These structures are obscured from us. Language, especially language outside of science, serves other purposes than to display for us the structure of the facts. One of the consequences of its service of those other purposes is that it conceals from us that structure. The task of the philosopher is to undo that concealment, to make the hidden manifest.

It was widely held, however, that this attempt to uncover the concealed would show that some of our language, instead of stating facts obscurely, states no facts at all. It is without sense: nonsense. Eventually analytic philosophers acknowledged that some of such language might nonetheless serve valuable human purposes. It might be useful for expressing our emotions, useful for marrying people, etc. But even then the conviction remained that some of it served no useful purpose whatsoever. Especially some of the talk produced by traditional philosophers was seen as *nothing but* nonsense, parading, however, under the guise of sense, hence obfuscation. Traditional philosophy contains "metaphysics." And so, just as in Kant, the problem of demarcation became central in analytic philosophy. Usually it took the form of trying to demarcate "genuine science" from "metaphysics." For it was assumed without question that mathematics and the hard sciences are paradigms of sense. There, rationality rules. There, rationality is embodied. If, on one's analysis of rationality, the hard sciences prove not to be rational, that is to be taken as evidence against one's analysis of rationality and not as evidence against science's rationality. The central version of the problem of demarcation became that of trying to demarcate genuine science from the pseudoscience of metaphysics.

If one knew nothing directly of the movement itself, the image evoked by my description of analytic philosophy would probably be that of the philosopher wandering about aimlessly in the field of concepts, analyzing whatever struck him as unclear. In fact, analysis was not a directionless enterprise. In the first place, it was, above all, three areas of thought and discourse that drew the attention of the analytic philosopher: scientific discourse, the discourse of private morality, and discourse about knowledge and rationality. Secondly, in the first and last of these, especially, two deep assumptions determined the direction of attempts at analysis. For one thing, attempts at analysis were directed by pervasive adherence to foundationalism with respect to knowledge. Knowledge, it was assumed, has a foundational structure; some of what we know is known immediately and everything else that we know is known because we know it on the basis of that. What we know immediately, we are certain of. And we are certain of something because at that point we are directly aware of reality. This is *the given*. Secondly, attempts at analysis were directed by what may be called *concept constructivism*. All concepts, it was widely assumed, either apply to what we are directly aware of or are constructed out of such concepts by simple logical operations. The direction of analysis was foundationalist and constructivist.

II

Analytic philosophy as I have described it has now almost entirely disappeared. Images central to the project have been widely discarded; assumptions fundamental to it have come under attack and have been widely rejected. Rorty, especially, has offered a narrative of the demise—a narrative which argues that analytic philosophy deconstructed into pragmatist-Hegelianism. Shortly I shall discuss the Rortian narrative. But first, let us return to our question as to why it was that analysis never flourished in philosophy of art.

Ever since the early romantics, it has been a commonplace that high culture in the West has a science side and an art/humanities side, and that these two coexist in tension. C. P. Snow's well-known writings on the matter served to express, for our own times, a thesis already a century and a half old. Analytic philosophy emerged from the science side of our culture; almost all of its great figures were trained in science or mathematics. It was about that side of culture that they were knowledgeable, and it was in that side of culture that they were interested. Often they went so far as to express the conviction that the primary business of philosophy was to uncover the "logic" of science. And, as already mentioned, many of them embraced the goal of making philosophy itself finally scientific. Analytic philosophy was to be "scientific" philosophy. Hans Reichenbach in *The Rise of Scientific Philosophy* caught the spirit. In the preface he said that:

The present book . . . maintains that philosophic speculation is a passing stage, occurring when philosophic problems are raised at a time which does not possess the logical means to solve them. It claims that there is, always has been, a scientific approach to philosophy. And it wishes to show that from this ground has sprung a scientific philosophy which, in the science of our time, has found the tools to solve those problems that in earlier times have been the subject of guesswork only. To put it briefly: this book is written with the intention of showing that philosophy has proceeded from speculation to science.[2]

Given these attitudes, it was entirely to be expected that the standard advice given to fledgling philosophers would be to study more science and math. Nobody counseled studying more art. And likewise it was entirely to be expected that graduate departments would be especially welcoming to those who already had extensive training in science and mathematics.

Beyond this, there was something plainly ill-fitting—so it would appear, at any rate—between the project of analytic philosophy and the reality of art. The goal of the analytic philosopher was to uncover the structure of our conceptual schemes. Now in fact science consists of a great deal more than a conceptual scheme—even more than a body of theories expressed with a conceptual scheme. But at least theories and concepts are prominent in science. Art is different. Buildings, paintings, string quartets, sculptures, dances: How is the analytic philosopher to get a purchase on these? Where are the conceptual schemes? Where are the languages? In poetry and fiction and drama there is of course language, in the most straightforward sense. But the romantic tradition had long warned that here language works differently, so differently that it isn't even referential. In short, it is not evident that the philosopher committed to conceptual analysis has much of anything to do when it comes to art.

Two different strategies were adopted for coping with this difficulty. Of one, Monroe Beardsley was the most noted practitioner. Beardsley's strategy was to call attention to the difference between art and art criticism, and then to propose that aesthetics, instead of remaining the philosophy of art or the philosophy of the aesthetic dimension, should become the philosophy of art criticism. For in art criticism, one has that on which the analytic philosopher can practice his craft, i.e., a conceptual scheme. Thus Beardsley gave to his major book, *Aesthetics*, the subtitle *Problems in the Philosophy of Criticism*.[3] He said, in the opening paragraph of the introduction, that:

There would be no problems of aesthetics, in the sense in which I propose to mark out this field of study, if no one ever talked about works of art. So long as we enjoy a movie, a story, or a song, in silence—except perhaps for occasional grunts or groans, murmurs of annoyance or satisfaction—there is no call for philosophy. But as soon as we utter a statement about the work, various sorts of questions can arise (p. 1).

And in summarizing his delineation of the field he said that,

In the course of this book, then, we shall think of aesthetics as a distinctive philosophical inquiry: it is concerned with the nature and basis of criticism—in the broad sense of this term—just as criticism itself is concerned with works of art (p. 6).

Philosophical aesthetics, he said, "deals with questions about the meaning and truth of critical statements" (p. 7).

To conceive of aesthetics thus is to place it at a remove from the phenomena of art and the aesthetic. To all but the most hardened analytic philosopher that will already give pause. But perhaps it is more important to observe that the foundationalism and constructivism which gave point and direction to the work of analysis in philosophy of science had only a rather weak grip on the "Beardsleyans" in aesthetics. For example, vast amounts of time and energy were devoted to devising analyses of the concept of *work of art*. For sheer boringness, the results of these endeavors have few peers. Something interesting might have turned up if philosophers had looked into the emergence of our (modern) concepts of *the arts* and *works of art*. When and where did these concepts emerge? Why? What intellectual and social purposes did they serve? Do those purposes remain viable? Have the concepts attached to the words "an art" and "a work of art" remained steady over the years or have they altered? If they have changed, why have they changed? All such historical inquiries would, however, be regarded by the neo-Kantian analytic philosopher as mucking around in the contingent. The analytic philosopher of art, like his fellow analytic philosophers, practiced his craft with resolute ahistoricism: slicing into the conceptual scheme of art criticism at a certain moment in its history, never asking why that scheme had arisen and developed as it had, attempting just to offer analyses of the concepts critics use and uncover criteria for the warranted assertion of the statements they make, scarcely guided in his analyses even by the doctrines of foundationalism and constructivism.

There was, as I have mentioned, a second strategy for developing an analytic philosophy of art—a strategy which expanded the notion of language and then treated works of art as examples of language, on this expanded concept. Of this strategy, Langer and Goodman have been the foremost practitioners, though it must at once be said that in their writings on art, neither one has been a typical analytic philosopher. Langer argued that the language of art is an iconic language, and that works of art iconically express and communicate the dynamic dimension of the emotional life. Not surprisingly, she was attacked on the ground that an iconic language is no language. Goodman, by contrast, argued that the languages of art are entirely conventional, not at all iconic; conventionally established denotation was for him the central concept. The price he paid was to leave thoroughly obscure how and what such things as pure music and abstract painting denote. In the field of music, Goodman devoted almost all of his attention to the language of *scores* for music and said almost nothing about any supposed language of music. And in general, his contention that the arts present us with specimens of conventional (not iconic) language led Goodman to focus his attention on representational art and on notational systems for the arts, and to neglect what falls outside this net.

III–IV

Though the foundationalism and constructivism which served to give direction to analysis in the philosophy of science played little role in the philosophy of art, it must not be inferred that the philosophy of art in the analytic style was lacking in definite character. On the contrary, the analytic philosophy of art has for the most part been a species of the romantic philosophy of art. In Beardsley's case, it is easy to see why: criticism, whose language Beardsley set it as his task to "analyze," was itself for the first part of our century predominantly a species of romantic criticism. But the same has been true for those not committed to the "Beardsleyan" approach. The ideology of romanticism has reigned for most of our century over our customary modes of thinking about art. . . .

The romantic theory of the arts, I suggest, is best thought of as the ideology of our modern Western bourgeois institution of high art. The institutional realities of high art have combined with romantic theories of art to produce that picture which has shaped the analytic philosophy of art. . . .

V

Philosophy of art after romanticism must historicize romanticism. Instead of accepting the romantic claim that now, finally, art has come into its own and its essence been revealed in thought, it must insist that romantic practice and thought in the arts represent just one stage in those interlocking ever-changing social practices which are the arts. Romantic ideology is not the philosophy of the end of time in art. It is a polemic, couched in essentialist and eschatological terms, in favor of certain ways of conducting the social practices of art and against other ways.

But though the way ahead for philosophy of art after romanticism is to historicize romanticism, it does not follow that the way ahead is to become a species of historicism, or, as Rorty calls it, of pragmatism. To see what else it might become, we must glance now at the fall of analytic philosophy. Rorty has offered a narrative of that fall. But another, quite different, narrative is also possible. To set the stage, let us briefly rehearse Rorty's narrative, as offered in his *Philosophy and the Mirror of Nature*.[4]

Analytic philosophy, says Rorty, cannot be written without one or the other of such related distinctions as the necessary and the contingent, the analytic and the synthetic, the structural and the empirical, the philosophical and the scientific. "If there are no intuitions into which to resolve concepts (in the manner of the *Aufbau*) nor any internal relations among concepts to make possible 'grammatical discoveries' (in the manner of 'Oxford philosophy'), then indeed it is hard to imagine what an 'analysis' might be" (p. 172). Accordingly, says Rorty, the story he wants to tell is "how the notion of two sorts of representations—intuitions and concepts—fell into disrepute in the latter days of the analytic movement" (p. 168). In Rorty's narrative, Quine and Sellars become the central figures in the demise of analytic philosophy and the emergence of its successor—pragmatism.

The conviction that there is some sort of "given" on which the mind imposes its concepts was never very firm in the analytic tradition, says Rorty. In "Empiricism and the Philosophy of Mind,"[5] Sellars launched an all-out attack on what he called "The Myth of the Given"; but this was just the culmination of a good many queries and hesitations. By contrast, the distinction between the necessary and the contingent went unquestioned until the publication of Quine's "Two Dogmas of Empiricism."

Analytic philosophers did not follow Kant in his claim that some necessary truths are synthetic, i.e., that there are, in Kantian parlance, *synthetic a prioris*. For them, the necessary/contingent distinction coincided with the analytic/synthetic distinction. Indeed, probably most of them viewed these distinctions not only as coincident but as identical. The concept of the necessary just *is* the concept of the analytic; the concept of the contingent just *is* the concept of the synthetic. Though attempts to explain the analytic/synthetic distinction were many and diverse, there was something of a consensus around the conviction—now to use Quine's words—that synthetic truths are "grounded in fact" and *analytic* truths are "grounded in meanings independently of matters of fact."[6] One of Quine's purposes in his essay was to attack this distinction as untenable. The conclusion he drew was that "for all its *a priori* reasonableness, a boundary between analytic and synthetic statements simply has not been drawn. That there is such a distinction to be drawn at all is an unempirical dogma of empiricists, a metaphysical article of faith."[7]

Rorty's narrative thus far points to the destructive consequences, for analytic philosophy, of Quine's and Sellar's work. The scheme-content picture must be surrendered and the conviction undergirding foundationalism—that certain of our beliefs and assertions are certain and hence privileged because they report a reality to which we have direct access, viz., meanings and the intuitional given—must be given up. But Rorty continues his narration by pointing to what he sees as the positive, forward-looking element in this same work of Quine and Sellars. Here he treats them together; they both, on his interpretation, affirm "epistemological behaviorism," or pragmatism. We do indeed regard various reports about our inner life as certain. But "for Sellars, the certainty of 'I have a pain' is a reflection of the fact that nobody cares to question it, not conversely" (p. 174). So too we regard "all men are animals" and "there have been some black dogs" as certain, and Quine thinks, says Rorty, that an anthropologist would not be able "to discriminate the sentences to which natives invariably and wholeheartedly assent into contingent empirical platitudes on the one hand and necessary conceptual truths on the other" (p. 173). But this certainly too "is a reflection of the fact that nobody cares to question it, not conversely." According to epistemological behaviorism, says Rorty, "rationality and epistemic authority" are not to be explained by reference to meanings and experiential givens, to which we have direct access. "Quine thinks that 'meanings' drop out as wheels that are not part of the mechanism, and Sellars thinks the same of 'self-authenticating non-verbal episodes'" (p. 174). Rationality and epistemic authority are to be explained "by reference to what society lets us say, rather than the latter by the former." And this, says Rorty, is the essence of epistemological behaviorism, or pragmatism. The rules of the language game in which we participate allow us to say certain things under certain circumstances and not other things under those circumstances; warrant and entitlement are always and only by reference to some such rules. We can probe the historical origins of such rules, the relative usefulness of such rules, the relation of such rules to the structure of the brain, etc. But what we cannot do is "ground" such rules in a reality which we apprehend. "To be behaviorist in the large sense in which Sellars and Quine are behaviorist is not to offer reductionist analyses, but to refuse to attempt a certain sort of explanation: the sort of explanation which not only interposes such a notion as 'acquaintance with meanings' or 'acquaintance with sensory appearances' between the impact of the environment on human beings and their reports about it, but uses such notions to explain the reliability of such reports" (p. 176). "For the Quine-Sellars approach to epistemology, to say that truth and knowledge can only be judged by the standards of the inquirers of our own day is not to say that human knowledge is less noble or important, or more 'cut off from the world,' than we had thought. It is merely to say that nothing counts as justification unless by reference to what we already accept, and that there is no way to get outside our beliefs and our language so as to find some test other than coherence" (p. 178).

Rorty's reading of the character and history of analytic philosophy is that once again the fundamental Kant-Hegel dialectic has come into play. At the end of the nineteenth century, Western philosophy was Hegelian in its general character, with pragmatism being the characteristically American manifestation of this. At the turn of the century this Hegelianism was overwhelmed with a new surge of neo-Kantianism, the great figure in the Anglo-American world being Russell, that on the Continent, Husserl, and with Frege as common partrimony.[8] But once again the Hegelian dynamic asserted itself, undercutting the assumptions of twentieth-century neo-Kantianism, appearing somewhat earlier on the continent than in the ambience of analytic philosophy; but it has now appeared in the pivotal work of Quine and Sellars, so that once again there is a coalescence between European and Anglo-American philosophy. Once again, our human conceptualizing is properly seen as historicized; once again, the notion of there being limits on our conceptualizing and our thinking (these limits constituting necessity) is discarded; only this time, instead of history being seen as the attempt of Hegel's Reason to realize itself, history is seen as the attempt of human beings to find what *works*.

This, I say, is Rorty's narrative of the history of analytic philosophy; call it the pragmatist-Hegelian narrative. But a supplementary narrative, a *Realist* narrative, must be added. The Realist agrees that classic analytic philosophy was a species of neo-Kantianism—a species which absorbed some of the major themes of John Locke. The Realist also agrees that the probing of some of the assumptions of analytic philosophy which took place at the hands of such as Quine and Sellars has led to the emergence of a mode of thought which is pragmatist-Hegelian in its orientation—plus, of course, has also led simply to bewilderment in many. But the Realist contends that Rorty's narration stops too soon and is too myopic. Pragmatism is not the only successor to analytic philosophy. There is another successor. That other is Realism. The Realist refuses to participate in the dialectic of Kantianism and Hegelianism. He questions assumptions common to both. Analytic philosophy has split in two. . . .

There is a long tradition, going back at least to Plato, which holds that it is the business of the philosopher to discover and contemplate the structure of the realm of necessity, that such contemplation is of higher worth than anything else we human beings can do, and that it can serve to direct our lives in the world. After first subjectivizing necessity, Kant, in his own way, perpetuated this tradition. The sort of Realist I have in mind rejects it. Of course, it's true that that Platonic picture of the philosopher's task is *compatible* with modal realism. It is not, however, *compelled* by it, and it should, in my view, be rejected. The Realist is happy to embrace, along with the Pragmatist, Sellars's rough-and-ready formula for the task of philosophy: to discuss how things, in the most general sense of the term, hang together, in the most general sense of the term. What in part distinguishes the Realist is his conviction that to speak with any amplitude of how things hang together, we will have to speak of necessity *de re*. Necessity and essence are features of reality. The new Realist wishes to break that ancient bond between the necessary and the important. It is more important to discover the contingent social practices of art than to find the essence of art, if, indeed, art has an essence. The new Realist breaks as firmly as does the Pragmatist with the Platonic-Kantian notion that philosophers are students of necessity.

We have seen that the Realist breaks with the Kantian notion that necessity marks the bounds on human intuiting, conceptualizing, and judging. He breaks with this notion not by following the pragmatist-Hegelian line of saying that there are no such limits, but rather, by being a Realist concerning modality. But there is another rejection that the Realist executes which goes perhaps even deeper.

Kant held that we have no intellectual intuitions, no awarenesses other than sensory awarenesses—sensory of course comprising for him inner sense as well as outer sense. Kant's way of construing concepts fit this contention: Concepts are not apprehensions of predicables but modes of organization of intuitions. Intuitions are given to us; we provide the concepts. More specifically, we impose modes of organization on the disparate intuitions. The outcome of this creative blending of the given and the imposed is knowledge. Here, then, is the origin of that picture which has so powerfully dominated analytic philosophy, the picture of scheme and content, of organizing structure and intuitional given.

The pragmatist-Hegelian has various reasons for rejecting this picture. Perhaps the deepest is that he finds it incoherent. What is this stuff to which the conceptual scheme is applied? Kant thought that whatever conceptual scheme we applied would always and necessarily have the same fundamental structure. Others have spoken of alternative conceptual schemes. Either way, says the pragmatist, the picture is the same, i.e., that of applying a conceptual scheme to some stuff. But any way of thinking of that stuff already involves the use of a concept. Kant spoke of it as intuitions. That is already to conceptualize it, namely, as intuitions. Others preferred speaking of the scheme as applied to the world. But *world* too is a concept. The whole idea of a world out there, or of intuitions in here, waiting to be conceptualized, is hopelessly incoherent. Better to scrap the whole idea: it would be world and intuitions well lost. We must allow to sink into us the full force of the fact that we cannot get outside our concepts, or, if one prefers, our language. Philosophers suggest "that there is some way of breaking out of language in order to compare it with something else. But there is no way to think about either the world or our purposes except by using our language."[9] We dwell, all of us together, in the prison house of language, or of concepts. That is the image which irresistibly comes to mind when the pragmatist speaks. Of course the pragmatist would reject the image. For we cannot think of anything as being outside this prison. And what kind of prison is a prison with nothing outside? No prison. Better to use images of freedom. The inescapability of language is the inescapability of freedom. We must learn to live with pure contingency. Pragmatism

is the doctrine that there are no constraints on inquiry save conversational ones—no wholesale constraints derived from the nature of the objects, or of the mind, or of language, but only those retail constraints provided by the remarks of our fellow-inquirers. . . .

I prefer this . . . way of characterizing pragmatism because it seems to me to focus on a fundamental choice which confronts the reflective mind: that between accepting the contingent character of starting-points, and attempting to evade this contingency. To accept the contingency of starting-points is to accept our inheritance from, and our conversation with, our fellow-humans as our only source of guidance. . . . Our identification with our community—our society, our political tradition, our intellectual heritage—is heightened when we see this community as ours rather than nature's, shaped rather than *found*, one among many which men have made. . . . James, in arguing against Realists and idealists that "the trail of the human serpent is over all," was reminding us that our glory is in our participation in fallible and transitory human projects, not in our obedience to permanent nonhuman constraints.[10]

The Realist sees things differently. Though he too rejects the scheme/context picture, he does so for a reason very different from that of the pragmatist-Hegelians. For him, the basic picture is not that of taking something as so-and-so, i.e., conceptualizing something as so-and-so; but rather, that of *recognizing* something as what it is, of becoming acquainted with it. We do not just *take* some unnameable protean stuff *as* a duck. We recognize the duck before us to be a duck, sometimes, anyway. The Realist rejects the Kantian claim that we have no intellectual intuitions. He holds that there are predicables and propositions (states of affairs), and that of many of these we have a grasp. He thinks of concepts (some of them, anyway) as graspings of predicables. And he holds that some of the predicables that we grasp are instantiated and are known by us to be instantiated. Reality, though not made by us, is thus also not alien to us. Concepts are not mental representations screening reality from us. Neither are they modes of organization imposed on unorganized protean stuff. The image of conceptualizing some given stuff—doing something to it, taking it as so-and-so, imposing a mode of organization on it—is wrong, admittedly relevant for some of our contact with reality but not for all and not for what is most basic. The pragmatist-Hegelian does not remove what is wrong about this image by proposing that we scrap the notion of a stuff taken in various ways and keep just the *takings*. The smile does not come without the cat. Neither does the Realist think of believings as inclinations to assert, these governed solely by the rules of the social game (horizontally, as it were). He holds that when we believe, there is something which is the object of belief—a state of affairs. And he holds that some of the states of affairs which we believe to be the case are in fact the case. We are at home in the world, without having made it.

So at bottom, the reason the Realist does not see necessity as merely the limits on the ways we can take things, is that he does not regard the phenomenon of us taking things a certain way as at the bottom of things. We can take a design as either a duck or a rabbit. But what it really is, then, is a design—neither a duck nor a rabbit.

Much more could be said by way of delineating and advocating the position which I have been calling realism, but this must suffice.[11] Not one but two coherent philosophical visions have emergd from, and superseded, analytic philosophy in its senescence. One is the pragmatism which Rorty eloquently propounds—essentially one more manifestation of the Hegelian response to Kantianism. The other is realism, which refuses to participate in the Kant-Hegel dialectic and instead rejects assumptions shared alike by Kantians and Hegelians. Pragmatists and Realists agree in rejecting the picture of a scheme of necessities imposed on a given of contingencies. They agree in rejecting the notion that the philosopher is a specialist in necessity. They agree that philosophy is not apodictic. And though the Realist, *qua Realist,* is not opposed to classical foundationalism and concept contructivism, he is, in my judgment, well-advised to share the pragmatist's opposition to these. But from there on, they part ways. For the Realist holds that there is a reality "out there," a reality which includes necessity, to which we can be faithful or unfaithful in our beliefs—not just a social game whose shifting rules we can follow or not follow. Indeed, he regards rules, along with the persons who obey or defy them, as also part of the reality "out there" to which, in our beliefs, we can be faithful or unfaithful.

VI

The world within which the social practices of art are played out includes, as the Realist sees it, necessity and possibility and impossibility, and properties and actions and kinds and states of affairs. Down through the ages, for example, one of the things done with works of art (with some, not all) is world-projection. Never will the projected world of a work of art be our actual world, that is to say, never will it be that possible world which is the actual world. The actual world is too vast for projection. And usually what the artist projects is not even, in its totality, *part* of the actual world. Usually, in its totality, it is a merely possible state of affairs; and sometimes, in its totality, an impossible state of affairs. The writers and tellers and presenters of fiction project worlds.

In the course of fictionally projecting a state of affairs, the fictioneer will often refer to countries, persons, events, etc., which do or did exist. Customarily in those cases, the world of the work will include states of affairs which cannot occur without those entities existing. In that way, the world of the work is anchored to those entities. The world of a work of art is not a self-contained, hermetically closed, phenomenon. But in addition to this, the writer will delineate for us *types* of entities: person types, country types, city types, etc. Some of these are the fictional characters of fiction.

I think an adequate ontology of types will yield the conclusion that writers do not create characters but select and delineate them, just as I think an adequate theory of states of affairs will yield the conclusion that writers do not create states of affairs but take note of them and call them to our attention. What underlies the possibility of fiction is the human capacity for envisagement.[12]

On such a view as here alluded to, world-projection is not a way of worldmaking. But neither is it, as the old view would have it, a mode of imitation. If we reject romanticism in the arts and approach art from the side of its social practices, and if the philosophy of art we then develop rejects the Kantian-Hegelian dialectic and adopts instead a Realist orientation, then we will see the social practices of art as dealing not just with actuality but with possibility and impossibility, and not just with particulars but with properties and actions and kinds. The fictioneer neither makes a world nor imitates a world, but selects from the vast realm of possibility and impossibility a segment thereof, a "world," for us to consider. Among the many benefits of a Realist philosophy of art is that it offers us a cogent and powerful way of explaining what it is to project a world.

NOTES

1. Cf. Moritz Schlick, "The Turning Point in Philosophy," in A. J. Ayer, ed., *Logical Positivism* (New York, 1959), p. 54: "I refer to this anarchy of philosophical opinions which has so often been described, in order to leave no doubt that I am fully conscious of the scope and weighty significance of the conviction that I should now like to express. For I am convinced that we now find ourselves at an altogether decisive turning point in philosophy, and that we are objectively justified in considering that an end has come to the fruitless conflict of systems. We are already at the present time, in my opinion, in possession of methods which make every such conflict in principle unnecessary. What is now required is their resolute application."
2. Hans Reichenbach, *The Rise of Scientific Philosophy* (University of California Press, 1963).
3. Monroe Beardsley, *Aesthetics: Problems in the Philosophy of Criticism* (New York, 1958).
4. Richard Rorty, *Philosophy and the Mirror of Nature* (Princeton University Press, 1979), p. 172.
5. In *Science, Perception and Reality* (New York, 1963).
6. W. V. O. Quine, "Two Dogmas of Empiricism," in *From a Logical Point of View*, second edition, revised (New York, 1963), p. 20.
7. Ibid., p. 37.
8. Richard Shusterman's discussion in "Analytic Aesthetics: Literary Theory and Deconstruction," pp. 22–38, makes clear that the same thing happened in philosophy of art. Croce was the great Hegelian; and the analytic reaction to him was typical in its charge of dreary wooliness. See especially the articles by Gallie and Passmore in W. Elton, ed., *Aesthetics and Language* (Oxford, 1954). It may be worth repeating that on my interpretation, the reaction to Croce did not represent a rejection of a fundamentally romantic way of looking at art but the rejection of a Hegelian way of articulating the romantic vision, in favor of a neo-Kantian, analytic, way.
9. Richard Rorty, *Consequences of Pragmatism* (University of Minnesota Press, 1982), p. xix. Compare this passage, in ibid., p. xxxix: "So the question of whether such a post-philosophical culture is desirable can also be put as the question: can the ubiquity of language ever really be taken seriously? Can we see ourselves as never encountering reality *except under a chosen description* as, in Nelson Goodman's phrase, making worlds rather than finding them?"
10. Ibid., pp. 165–66.
11. For more detailed discussions of the realist/anti-realist (pragmatist) debate, see my "Realism and anti-Realism: How to Feel at Home in the World," in *Proceedings of the Catholic Philosophical Society* (1985); and "Are Concept Users World-Makers," in James Tomberlin, ed., *Philosophical Perspectives, I: Metaphysics, 1987* (Atascadero, CA, 1987).
12. These ideas about projected worlds and fictional entities are developed in detail in my *Works and Worlds of Art*.

Wexner Center for the Visual Arts, Columbus, OH. Eisenman and Trott, architects. 1989. View from the south. Photo courtesy of the Wexner Center.

Postmodern architecture often strives to synthesize classical or older themes in a contemporary context. To some extent this is also true of postmodern writing in aesthetics.

CHAPTER 2
The Postmodern Challenge

In recent years, the most fundamental assumptions of aesthetics, as it has developed in America over the past thirty years, have been called into question—not so much by philosopher-aestheticians as by literary and art theorists whose theories are derived from Continental philosophical traditions not yet well integrated into Anglo-American analytic philosophy. Despite the diversity and changes within analytic aesthetics discussed in the previous chapter, certain of its fundamental assumptions are now widely assumed to have been refuted, and have been abandoned by Postmodernist theorists as relics of an earlier period of aesthetics.

However, as pointed out in the previous chapter, it is not that these assumptions were dogmatically assumed as inviolable within analytic aesthetics. Indeed, they have been constantly debated from all sides within the analytic tradition. Nonetheless, they were never dogmatically rejected and have occupied central positions within the field's discussions.

Analytic aestheticians widely believed, for example, that the primary tasks of aesthetics were distinct from those of the artist producing art and from those of the art critic and art historian interpreting and evaluating artworks. The artist had his or her assigned task of producing artworks; the critics, in turn, attempted to interpret and criticize these artworks; and the aestheticians, finally, were self-appointed to clarify the critic's talk about the artworks. Much of analytic aesthetics thus situated itself squarely within a professional circle of university-trained academic philosophy, usually several removes from the making, buying, selling, and promotion of artworks.

Of course, it was hoped that analytic aesthetics would influence the practice of art criticism, which, in turn, would influence standards of taste and the practice of art. But this influence was anticipated to be, at best, only *indirect* and remote and with a considerable time lag from the pen of the philosopher to the brush of the painter. Analytic aesthetics also assumed a fairly narrow band of relevance for broader cultural factors thought to be pertinent to art and the talk about art.

Part of the antiessentialism of the 1950s and 1960s was to remove the discussion of art from its vague and confusing associations with psychology, religion, sociology, politics, education, economics, and so on. Not that analytic aestheticians embraced the art-for-art's-sake position of the Formalists (though as we saw in the previous chapter, the notion of aesthetic "autonomy" persisted in much of early analytic aesthetics). Most analytic aestheticians recognized the need to view the individual work of art in the larger context of other work by the same artist, the still larger context of other work done in the same style or genre, and in the light of art historical conventions governing particular art genres.

Dickie and Danto later extended the "circle of contextual relevance" to include the "institutions" of the "art world." But that was as far as most analytic aestheticians were prepared to go. Did art have some relation to economics, to general social history, to political issues, to changes in gender and racial attitudes, and so forth? Yes, of course, but analyzing this was not considered the primary job of the aesthetician.

At the same time that analytic aesthetics was taking the "high road" of meta-criticism and professional, academic philosophy, massive and very confusing changes were occurring in the artworld—in the practice of the arts and their perceived place within the larger life of the society. In most cultures and at most times, art exists in a kind of tension between, on the one hand, conventional stability, which allows communication among members who share a particular set of art and cultural conventions, and, on the other hand, the desire for creative originality, which challenges those conventions and, when successful, can produce major changes in the arts. When the search for creative originality dominates, however, racing ahead of the establishment of stable art conventions as it did in the 1960s and early 1970s, objective consensus regarding art does in fact break down and relativism and subjectivism become the norm. This, in turn, greatly affected the kinds of things art critics were saying about art.

As a result, those engaged in the analysis of culture and social change found themselves desperately searching for a "theory" to explain such radically puzzling and fundamental aesthetic changes. Looking in vain to analytic aesthetics for guidance, they turned instead to a very different Continental tradition in which art had long been discussed in terms of a much broader cultural context of social change. Phenomenology, structuralism, semiotics, hermeneutics, and later poststructuralism and deconstruction all offered cultural historians the kind of theory they were looking for—sociological and historicist, examining art in terms of a broad sociological, political context.

The result has been to isolate analytic aesthetics further from a growing consensus in art discussions outside of philosophy and based on a perspective thought to be alien in many Anglo-American philosophical circles. In discussions of literature, film, communications, and popular culture, an Americanized Postmodern "theory" was rapidly developing largely independently of the ongoing and, as we argued in the previous chapter, healthy tradition of analytic aesthetics. Thus, Postmodernism did not develop as a rebellious movement from within analytic aesthetics, nor did it develop as the work of Continental philosophers gradually came to the attention of analytic philosophers. Rather it came in "through the back door," as it were (i.e., through British and American "theorists" of film, popular culture, and communications, attempting to understand, absorb, and "Americanize" Continental philosophical traditions). In many cases, analytic aestheticians first began to hear of postmodern theories from popular magazines and from their art students.

Because these Continental philosophical theories were enormously complex and difficult, emerging, as they had, from long traditions of their own, and because those initially attracted to these theories were not trained philosophers (in either philosophical tradition), the Americanized versions of postmodern theories were often presented as far more radical than they were understood to be within European philosophical circles. As such, they were often dismissed by those analytic philosophers who had become aware of them as so much muddle-headedness, not to be taken seriously.

Thus, despite its rich historical origins in French and German philosophical traditions, Postmodernism has penetrated the domain of Anglo-American discussions of art as a series of extremely radical challenges to the very foundations of "modernist" thinking about art in the English-speaking world, both philosophical and art critical. Especially in the radical subjective relativism of Derrida and "deconstruction," Postmodernism, having disconnected language from its referential relation to the world, appears to deny the very possibility of discovering the truth about anything and thereby of making objective claims and rational arguments for such claims.

As we pointed out in the previous chapter, problems concerning truth were by no means unheard of within analytic philosophy. What is different about Postmodernism is the apparent dogmatic insistence on the absolute impossibility of any sort of cognitive reliability. It is not that analytic philosophy stands squarely on the other side of this issue, dogmatically rejecting skepticism, relativism, and subjectivism. The contrast is rather between those who allow for, and therefore debate, the possibility of some sort of cognitive reliability and those who dogmatically reject such a possibility.

Insofar as analytic aesthetics has perceived its task (in Beardsley's work, for example) as a "second order" discipline clarifying the concepts of the art critics and art historians, the philosopher of art is always in the process of tracking, always a step or two behind, the work of the art and literary critic. Part, though by no means all, of early analytic aesthetics was therefore concerned with providing a second-order analysis of the then-dominant New Criticism, with its presumptions of the autonomy of meaning and the ultimately rational objectivity of critical discourse, however difficult to achieve in actual practice. New Criticism assumed, in other words, that the meaning of an artwork is there to be discovered in the work of art; that some critical statements more truthfully describe this meaning than others, and so are more nearly correct, while others have missed the meaning and so are false and incorrect. By the same token, it was assumed that some artworks were objectively better than others and could be shown to be so.

Other important consequences follow from these New Critical assumptions: that there is a progressive evolution in art history; that there is an ascertainable "canon" of art masterpieces qualitatively judged to be superior to the mass of mediocre works, both in terms of their absolute superiority and also in terms of their contribution to the evolution of modern art; and, finally, that different interpretations and evaluations of an artwork presuppose that there is a single artwork existing over and above the various interpretations which those interpretations are about.

Were the philosopher of art, playing the role of meta-critic *à la* Beardsley, to listen in on and look over the shoulder of the art critic today, however, he or she would not hear the New Critical claims (which Beardsley heard and tried to "clarify") of objective standards of taste, a rational basis for settling interpretive disputes, an evolution in art history, and the establishment of a "canon" of masterpieces. Rather he or she would hear a plea by critics for tolerance of a plurality of relative, subjective responses, a rejection of the "canon" as a form of political dominance, the inclusion of previously "marginalized" groups systematically excluded in the past from art's mainstream by the "canon," and for a greatly expanded, neo-Marxist, "historicist" social context in which art is to be understood as an expression of political and economic and broadly sociological factors. One of the expressions of Postmodernism is a continuation of the Marxist wholesale rejection of all art as a form of manipulation by the economically powerful bourgeois to justify and maintain their position of economic power and dominance over other groups.

The most radical Postmodern claim, however, which we saw Margolis struggling with in the previous chapter, is the denial that there is an independently existing artwork available for critical assessment. If critical interpretations, or "readings," are in no way subject to critical assessment, then they cannot be judged as interpretations *of* an artwork existing over and above various interpretations of it, and so, for all practical purposes, the notion of an independently existing artwork toward which different interpretations are directed dissolves into a series of interpretations, or "readings," not one of which can be said to be any better or worse than any other. (How an interpretation can be considered, in any ordinary sense, to be an "interpretation of" that artwork, and hence an interpretation at all, is unclear.) If the referential link between art criticism and the artwork has been severed by Postmodernism, so too has the referential link between the artwork and the world it had previously been thought to describe.

Modernism assumes that art has an important role to play in the evolution of social consciousness. One of the important roles which Modernism attributes to art is to articulate evolving social norms and values. As Kandinsky expressed it in his famous image of the "triangle," before evolving social values can be stated logically, enacted legally, or even recognized by the majority, they must first be intuited and expressively explored by the artist. Despite the claims of early, "vulgar" Marxism that art was part of the superstructure determined entirely by the economic base, neo-Marxist "critical theorists" also looked to art as an important form of social criticism. Art is therefore a crucial means of understanding and critiquing social reality, according to Modernism. But by Postmodern lights, art has no epistemic accountability to social reality, and art criticism has no epistemic accountability to the artwork. Critical statements therefore virtually replace artworks.

For similar reasons, if there are or can be no objective means of assessing art critical statements, there is no longer any effective difference between the work of the art critic and that of the philosopher of art. Boundaries previously drawn between philosophy of art, art criticism, and art itself are thereby effectively erased.

Turning now to the readings, Silverman sees Postmodernism primarily as heralding the end of an era—the end of Modernism. "Postmodernism brings the modernist hegemony to closure." "Postmodernism signals the end of what has become commonplace and ordinary in the modernist outlook." This is not stated as a criticism of the shortcomings of modernism and an argument that we ought to embrace Postmodernism because it corrects these shortcomings. Silverman speaks here more as a historian than as a philosopher, announcing something which has actually taken place, though we may not have noticed it. We do not abandon Modernism because it has been shown to be inadequate, but because it is passé.

Part of Modernism which is now replaced by Postmodernism is the notion that art functions to help us understand ourselves and our world. Postmodernism announces and embraces the relativized, fragmented, pluralistic world we actually live in, including our fragmented sense of ourselves, where many different voices are heard and many different readings of each voice are given, and where none can be judged more accurate or fairer than any other. "Critics and professors of art or literature extol the [ability] of the modern artist . . . to perceive better than the rest of us; and they look to the artist for guidance as to how to articulate [this]. . . . But the *postmodern* artist has no such privileged status."

Another part of the task of Modernism now abandoned by Postmodernism is the ordering of art in an elitist hierarchy of better and worse and the articulation of a canon of masterpieces that stand as monuments to the progressive evolution of art. Whereas Modernism circumscribes high culture from the mass of cultural products through "centering" and "focusing," Postmodernism celebrates a social world which "is fragmented, discontinuous, multiple, and dispersed."

Tumas–Serna rejects the conciliatory notion that more recent analytic philosophy is moving toward Postmodernism by more widely contextualizing the questions of aesthetics. Even Dickie and Danto, and Margolis in his most recent writing on the relation of art and culture, uncritically assume too much, she argues, precisely because they do not sufficiently contextualize to see the unconscious manipulative use of art in the support of a covert political agenda which privileges the dominant elite in our society at the expense of other marginalized and disenfranchised groups. "The issue extends beyond problematic, ambiguous definitions and concepts of art to a more fundamental discontent with formerly unnoticed but operative assumptions about Culture"—in particular, the assumptions of ethnocentrism, High Culture, the classical canon of masterpieces, and the steady growth of sophisticated originality and creative inventiveness.

Postmodernism, according to Tumas–Serna, cuts through such social constructions, encouraging the marginalized and disenfranchised to speak up, leveling (deconstructing) all such dichotomies of good taste/vulgar taste, high art/low art, and High Culture/popular culture.

To understand these cultural assumptions and not be manipulated by them, Tumas–Serna tells us, we must get behind the surface appearance of things as they are offered to us and look at the whole social-cultural edifice holistically in the broad historicist, contextualist manner of Hegel and Marx. Just as Postmodernism helps us read artworks in their broadest possible historicist, contextualist setting, so Postmodernism helps us to read modernist art critics and philosophers of art *critically*, not for what they *meant* to say, but for those clues which they inadvertently, unintentionally left behind and which reveal a largely unconscious political agenda privileging a dominant elite and suppressing other groups by marginalizing them into insignificance.

When traditional aestheticians argue for a universal aesthetics of form, for example, we must learn to read this as an unconscious attempt to dehistoricize, decontextualize human beings, to pretend that we are all alike and not, as we really are, educated versus uneducated, white versus nonwhite, male versus female, rich versus poor, developed versus underdeveloped, and so on. Or when traditional aestheticians talk about aesthetic disinterestedness, we must see this *critically* as an attempt to take art out of the arena of political "interests"—or rather, to pretend it is not politically interested, when in fact it *is* interested in maintaining the dominance of the rich and powerful over other groups.

The elitism of modern art, Tumas–Serna argues, reduces the audience, or "readers," to uneducated vulgarians whose only hope is to adjust through education to the elitist standards of High Culture. Postmodernism, on the other hand, helps us to deconstruct this elaborate social construction whereby some cultural products are nominated "works of art" and others are elevated to the status of High Culture.

Deconstructed, we are left with the reality of extreme cultural relativism, epistemic skepticism, and personal subjectivism—any reading is as good as any other, and any reader is as good as any other, thereby leveling the hierarchical binaries of high and low art and placing the popular arts of marginalized groups (Hispanics, women, African-Americans) on the same plane as that of the supposed art of High Culture.

Kuspit criticizes Postmodernism for its own contradictory and impotent "criticality." By criticizing *all* art and indeed all cultural products as serving the bourgeois's purposes of maintaining control of the centers of power, Postmodernism renders art, art criticism, and aesthetics incapable of social criticism. Whereas Silverman plays down, in a conciliatory fashion, the dramatic hyperbole of Postmodern rhetoric, Kuspit insists that such rhetorical exaggeration is essential to and inseparable from Postmodernism. Indeed, Kuspit asserts that the "inflationary" nature of Postmodernist claims is a sign of significant internal weakness. Postmodernism claims to be a description of social reality, whereas, in fact, according to Kuspit, it is a propagandistic proposal for change. "Postmodernism is more of a program developed by theorists than the common reality of contemporary society and culture." Pretending to be a radical theory of the future, Kuspit argues, Postmodernism is really a sign of our loss of confidence in theory generally.

As art becomes more pluralistic, as standards become more subjective, understanding the arts and theorizing about them become more and more difficult; Postmodernism tries to make a theory out of these difficulties. As contemporary art becomes more fragmented and aesthetic communication more difficult, Postmodernism becomes, in effect, "a species of avant-garde art." Postmodernism represents, in short, "a general crisis of theory's belief in its power and influence." Unable to arbitrate theoretical disputes, Postmodernism argues for complete skepticism, subjectivism, relativism, "another sign of the theory's impotence, self-defeat." By so completely "absolutizing" its parody of modern art and culture as the unwitting tool of a dominant power elite, Postmodernism's critique of modern society is "without any teeth," and its total rejection of all culture forms as unintended parody "degenerates" into playful "decadence."

Brand's article on feminist aesthetics, like feminist aesthetics generally, follows Postmodernist analysis in some respects and abandons and rejects it in others. The part of Postmodernism which Brand and other feminists accept is the "critical" Postmodern exposure of the political agenda of mainstream, traditional aesthetics to privilege the white male elite, marginalizing and disenfranchising, suppressing and dominating other groups, especially women. Through its social constructions of High Culture, the canon of masterpieces, and the steady evolution of avant-garde art based on aggressive (i.e., male) individualistic novelty and innovation, women have traditionally been effectively excluded from art, art criticism, and philosophy of art. And when, more recently, women have been admitted into art's inner circle, their work has been trivialized as "minor," not quite making it into the canon of true masterpieces. The other main point of agreement between Brand's feminist aesthetics and Postmodern analysis is the emphasis on maximal contextualization. The main difference between the way men and women look at and do aesthetics, Brand argues, is that men tend to analyze a whole into its parts, privileging and isolating certain parts from the rest, in the case of aesthetics, analyzing and isolating aesthetic experience and activity from other sorts of experience and activity deemed unworthy of aesthetic examination. Women, on the other hand, tend to see art and aesthetic experience as part of a larger whole—holistically, contextually. Again, like Postmodernism, Brand sees women's aesthetics including, in its drive for contextualization, the politics of gender discrimination and suppression. By emphasizing disinterestedness, the autonomy of the artwork, and the centrality of its formal properties, male aestheticians, like Beardsley, try to remove art from politics or, as we said earlier, pretend that art is separable from politics when in reality it is not.

Where feminists, including Brand, generally break with Postmodernism is in refusing to accept the self-inflicted critical impotence of Postmodernism, as described by Kuspit. Unlike Postmodernism, feminists want to be able to criticize contemporary society. As such, they realize that they must hold that there are objective wrongs in society, such as gender discrimination, whose truth can be objectively established and rationally argued for. They wisely see that if no theory can be said to be any better or worse than any other, then feminism itself cannot be said to be any more truthful or any more morally just than those ideologies against which it wishes to do battle.

The Philosophy of Postmodernism

Hugh J. Silverman

Postmodernism has no special place of origin. The meaning and function of postmodernism is to operate at places of closure, at the limits of modernist productions and practices, at the margins of what proclaims itself to be new and a break with tradition, and at the multiple edges of these claims to self-consciousness and auto-reflection. Postmodernism is not as such a new style of creating artworks, of synthesizing novel self-expressions, and of justifying theoretically its aesthetic practices. Postmodernism does not open up a new field of artistic, philosophical, cultural, or even institutional activities. Its very significance is to marginalize, delimit, disseminate, and decenter the primary (and often secondary) works of modernist and premodernist cultural inscriptions.

Postmodernist thinking offers to re-read the very texts and traditions that have made premodernist and modernist writing possible—but above all it offers a reinscription of those very texts and traditions by examining the respects in which they set limits to their own enterprises, in which they incorporate other texts and traditions in a juxtapositional and intertextual relation to themselves. Postmodernist thinking involves rethinking—finding the places of difference within texts and institutions, examining the inscriptions of indecidability, noting the dispersal of signification, identity, and centered unity across a plurivalent texture of epistemological and metaphysical knowledge production.

Postmodernism brings the modernist hegemony to closure. It examines the ends, goals, hopes of modernist activity, situating it in its context of premodernist frameworks. However, just as the post-impressionism of Van Gogh and Cézanne was not an *attack upon and rejection of* the impressionism of Monet, Renoir, Manet, Degas, and Pissarro, so too postmodernism is not a simple refusal to accept modernist principles and perspectives. Rather postmodernism extends but also brings to a close the fundamental tenets and activities of a modernist outlook. This means that the lines of demarcation between modernism and postmodernism are not well-defined. A region of indeterminateness prevails such that although the Joyce of *Portrait of the Artist as a Young Man* and *Ulysses*, along with Virginia Woolf's *Mrs. Dalloway* and *To the Lighthouse*, Proust's *Remembrance of Things Past*, and Kafka's *The Trial*, are major documents of modernist literary production, Joyce's *Finnegans Wake* along with Robbe-Grillet's *Jealousy*, Beckett's *Malone Dies* and *The Unnameable*, and Borges's *Fictions* take on features of a postmodern textual practice. Indeed to be able to identify particular literary works as postmodernist as opposed to modernist is itself the kind of enterprise invoked by the modernist critic seeking to distinguish modernism from romanticism (just as romantics were set off against—and set themselves off against—those of the classical style). But postmodernism in fiction, for instance, is not the successor to modernism—rather it is modernism taken to its extremes. Postmodernism signals the end of what has become commonplace and ordinary in the modernist outlook. Postmodernist literary practice operates at the edge of the modernist manner.

From *Postmodernism: Philosophy and the Arts*, Hugh Silverman, ed. (New York: Routledge, Chapman and Hall, 1989). Reprinted by permission of the publisher.

To be modern is to break with tradition, to interrupt the endless reiteration of classical themes, topics, and myths, to become self-consciously new, to attend to the *modes* of the times, to offer a critique of the conditions of one's own culture and society, to represent reality—not as it is—objectively and devoid of evaluation, but rather as it is *experienced*—subjectively and with the transcendental or critical consciousness available especially to the artist. To be modern is to "break with the past" and to "search for new self-conscious expressive forms." Whether the "new self-expressive forms" are abstract like those of Kandinsky and Pollock, or geometrical like those of Mondrian and Josef Albers, or alienated like those of Edvard Munch and Max Beckmann, or fanciful like those of Giacometti and Paul Klee, they all give shape to the concept of modern art. The modern artist claims to take a privileged view of the social and psychological concerns of the day. Modern man and modern woman are plagued with uncertainties, despair, bureaucratization, and mechanization. Their concern is how to cope with such solidifications and preoccupations of modern times—the Charlie Chaplin film whose title gave a name to Sartre's new journal in 1945 is but a caricature of the modern condition. And the modern artist has an interior consciousness that knows how to express the realities of industrial society. Critics and professors of art or literature extol the virtues of the modern artist; they praise his or her abilities to perceive better than the rest of us; and they look to the artist for guidance as to how to articulate (if not diagnose or cure) the modern predicament. But the *postmodern* artist has no such privileged status. The postmodern artist is on the margins of things in such a way that it is not the artist who counts but rather the paintings and inscriptions themselves. And these texts and performances achieve their significance and value in their intertextual relations with other texts and performances. The postmodernist text *is* by its difference from other productions—including critical writings and alternate aesthetic or cultural genres.

The modern music of Schönberg, Bartok, Weber, and, in a different way, Stravinsky, offers a radical break with the classical styles of Bach, Beethoven, and Brahms. Where the romantic expressions of Berlioz and Mahler gave something other than the prior classical styles, they nevertheless could not be considered sufficiently radical, sufficiently modern, to be "a true break" with tradition. When Wagner introduced his music dramas, he brought together many different art forms. Although the medieval *Nibelungenlied* was the basis for his Ring cycle, just as the Romantic poets latched onto Macpherson's (imaginary and mythical sixth-century) Ossian for their inspiration, Wagner created what was hailed by Verlaine and others as *definitely* modern. Certainly he was not providing the sort of operatic work that Rossini, Mozart, Puccini, or even Verdi offered. Here was something solidly new, unquestionably modern, very much *à la mode*, praised not only by the *Revue Wagnerienne* but also by Nietzsche's 1872 *The Birth of Tragedy out of the Spirit of Music*. Nietzsche's disappointment—as elaborated later in *The Case of Wagner* (1888)—was indicative of the self-delimitation of Wagnerian modernism. But Nietzsche—identified by Michel Foucault in 1966 as a threshold figure, along with Mallarmé—was himself a spokesman for the postmodernism that had come too early, before its time, *avant la lettre*. Nietzsche's ultimate turn—away from Wagner, his view that Wagnerism was not, after all, the proper work of *his* "philosopher" Dionysus—was an early inscription of modernism's self-circumscription. But postmodernism has no place of origin—it can inscribe itself in different places, at various limit points—and Nietzsche's rereading of Wagner is only one such locus.

But what is *postmodernist thinking?* Philosophers are wont to cite Bacon and Galileo, Descartes and Malebranche, as the beginnings of modern thought. The idea that man can be an "interpreter of nature" (Bacon) or an observer of the universe through an instrument such as the telescope (Galileo), that one can reshape and control the world through science—inaugurates the "modern" world view. Descartes's further specification of the self or subject as able to distrust bodies and extended substances, as a thinking substance whose existence can be affirmed by a clear and distinct idea of its own activity, as offering a set of rules for directing the mind—these are all proclaimed to be distinctively 'modern." Although not engaged *as such* in the *querelle des anciens et des modernes* (which Boileau and other seventeenth-century critics ascribed to their new writers), Descartes nevertheless asserted his rejection of the scholastic style of philosophizing. Thus while literary debates of the seventeenth and eighteenth centuries—in France for instance—focused on the dispute between the ancients and the moderns, philosophers set the so-called modernist views of rationalism and empiricism into motion. The dichotomy between the philosophical claim that Descartes, Hume, and Kant are modern philosophers while literary scholars proclaim Joyce, Woolf, Proust, and Kafka as modern is only one indication of the effects of discipline segregation. But that Molière, La Rochefoucauld, and Fontenelle are sometimes called "modern" suggests that even among literary disciplines the extent of cooperation in naming is not very significant. Similarly, modern *art* is clearly post-romantic or more definitively post-post-impressionist, namely futurist, fauvist, abstract expressionist, cubist, surrealist, dadaist, and so forth.

While the arts do not correspond with respect to what counts as modern, where philosophy interprets itself as modern since the late Renaissance, what is to be said of nineteenth-century philosophy? Surely Hegel, Marx, Mill, and Comte are also modern—but they are modern with a twist, or several twists. Dialectic, the utilitarian principle, and positivism give a new look to the Kantian critical philosophy. So if rationalism, empiricism, critical philosophy, dialecticism, utilitarianism, Marxism, and Comtean positivism are all "modern" philosophies, then what sense does modernist thinking have? And in what respect can it be said that modernist thinking—when self-delimited—establishes the condition for a postmodernist position? If it can be said—as I shall here—that postmodernist thinking *enframes, circumscribes,* and *delimits* modernist thinking, then where are the places in which modernism in philosophy comes to an end? This closure occurs in many places and in many different ways. Postmodernism enframes modernism without identity or unity. It is fragmented, discontinuous, multiple, and dispersed. Where modernism asserts centering, focusing, continuity—once the break with tradition has already occurred—postmodernism decenters, enframes, discontinues, and fragments the prevalence of modernist ideals. But this selfdelimitation does not occur all at once. Indeed, the coordinate philosophical practices of the early twentieth century reaffirm, reconstruct, and then set the stage for their own self-circumscription. The determination of the ends of metaphysics and the paths of thinking is also the framework for the closure of modernism.

Concomitant with—and perhaps even antecedent to—the reign of twentieth-century modernist writers like Joyce, Woolf, Proust, and Kafka, certain philosophies of consciousness achieve dominance in a variety of different contexts. In concert with William James's characterization of lived time as a "stream of consciousness," and Husserl's "phenomenology of internal time-consciousness," Freud developed a view of the psychic realm which is comprised both of consciousness and of unconscious fields. Each of these philosophies of consciousness is also a theory of self-consciousness and self-reflection. The Kierkegaardian call to individual subjectivity is defined by James, Bergson, Husserl, and Freud as a field available for scrutiny, investigation, and detailed inventory. One can examine one's own field of consciousness and describe, both temporally and spatially, the flow of conscious experience as distinct from the objective, empirical data of the external world. But not that many philosophers of the twentieth century were favorably disposed to the idea of a "ghost in the machine" (as Ryle, in 1949, called it). Wittgenstein (in his earlier incarnation) wanted to remain silent about such matters. And Sarte (1936) discovered that the transcendental ego, which Husserl so steadfastly maintained (phenomenologically) at the heart of conscious life, could not be found—at least not *in* consciousness. For Sartre the ego was an object of consciousness, out there in the world, available for investigation just like any other thing. Consciousness, for Sartre (1943), was at best not anything at all, only pure freedom without any content. So along with the development of a modernist theory of self-consciousness, there are also the very seeds of its demise—in Ryle, in Sartre, and in Heidegger.

Heidegger does not provide the closure that the postmodernist will want to call for. Lacan and Derrida—to name some notable signatures—take the circumscription to its further stages of development. Heidegger's way is to call for the end of philosophy (1961, 1966). Once philosophy sets its own limits, rereads its traditions from the time of the Greeks, it can demarcate what it would be for philosophy to accomplish the tasks it sets out for itself. If philosophy could achieve, through its acts of interpretation, an understanding of philosophical writers who sought to account for the essence of truth, the disclosure of truth, the uncovering of what has remained hidden over the centuries, then the path of thinking might become evident. Hegel had proclaimed that one could bring about the end of philosophy. Philosophy could bring its own activity to absolute knowledge—the full and complete synthesis would thereby be achieved. The *telos* or goal of philosophy would be the finalization of the movement toward the place where all knowledge is encompassed by its own activity. Heidegger sought to find the place at the end of philosophy where thinking might happen. But thinking can occur only where there is a place for the disclosure of truth. For Heidegger, truth can be disclosed only where difference is located. This difference is the ontico-ontological difference where (in his 1927 version) *Dasein* is interpretation and where (in the 1950s) language speaks.

Heidegger marks the shift from a theory of consciousness and self-consciousness to a theory of language. Sartre has no place for language until the late 1940s and 1950s. Merleau-Ponty had already spoken of the embodied and gestural expression of language in his *Phenomenology of Perception* (1945), but in the late 1940s, when he began to read (and lecture on) Saussure, he incorporated the idea of a "spoken speech" and a "speaking speech" as a sign. With Merleau-Ponty, the language of the speaking subject is the elaboration of an embodied sign system. But Merleau-Ponty's phenomenology of language is not yet a theory of textuality. When Roland Barthes (1953) provides a critique of Sartre's concept of literature (1947), he sets forth a theory of writing *at degree zero*, i.e., no longer wrapped up in a complex discourse of subjectivity and authorship. Barthes proposes a theory of writing as revolutionary and yet nonhistoricist, a theory of writing which is informed by style and period but not tied down or limited to them. When Barthes later moves to a theory of the text (in the 1970s with *The Pleasure of the Text*, for instance), he sets the stage for a postmodernist theory of textuality—differential, scriptive, and semiotic—which also marks in turn the writings of Derrida, Deleuze, and Kristeva.

Art, Culture, and Postmodern Expression: A Communicative Aesthetic

Jane Tumas-Serna

> *The director [Giovanni Carandente, 1990 visual-arts director of the Venice Biennale] then vitiated any hope that he had understood the critical issues of cultural difference when he praised these Aboriginal and African artists as "the authors of a 'bridge' between primitive civilizations and the modern world, which is increasingly leading to an Esperanto of a new universal language of forms." (Vetrocq, 1990, p. 155)*

INTRODUCTION

Joseph Margolis (1987) proposes that philosophical aesthetics uses its unique position to examine the relationship of Art and Culture. A reassessment of the "ontological and methodological implications of viewing art and its appreciation as fully cultural phenomena" (p. vi), his argument challenges definitions of artworks solely as physical, perceptual, material objects of intrinsic worth and claims rather that they are "physically embodied and culturally emergent." Margolis seeks to broaden the arena of investigation from a concern with the intrinsic quality of art objects to one that includes the context of art.[1] Since philosophical aesthetics—that is, theories of taste, aesthetic judgment, aesthetic perception, aesthetic objects, and aesthetic experience—constitutes theories of art, the solution suggested is a return to the arts to revitalize philosophical discourse (Wartofsky, 1987). However, this strategy operates under unexamined assumptions about Art and Culture.

The issue extends beyond problematic, ambiguous definitions and concepts of art to a more fundamental discontent with formerly unnoticed but operative assumptions about Culture. Communication scholars and cultural theorists challenge the exclusive domain of Culture with examinations of mass culture and other folk cultures, respectively.[2] Raymond Williams (1965) makes a key contribution by working out the two competing definitions of culture that are operative. First, "culture is a state or process of human perfection, in terms of certain absolute or universal values" (p. 57). This is Culture (uppercase C) as high culture designated in this paper as "art culture" (see Clifford, 1981). Second, "culture is a description of a particular way of life which expresses certain meanings and values not only in art and learning but also in institutions and ordinary behavior" (p. 57). This is culture (lowercase C) as "other" or folk as well as mass or popular culture designated in this paper as "culture as a whole way of life" (Williams, 1965).

Critics in communication studies and cultural theory take Western Culture and its philosophical, historical, and critical framework to task for creating hierarchies of exclusion that discount forms of expression deemed to be the domain of popular or mass culture and

---

Published with permission of the author.

for perpetuating an ethnocentric bias that appropriates and decontextualizes the expression of "others" as primitive or folk cultures (Clifford, 1987; Foster, 1983; Williams, 1983).

The purpose of this paper will be to look at art culture and the limits of Margolis's proposal by examining three central assumptions of a modern formalist aesthetic. This aesthetic, systematized in Western philosophy, claims that aesthetic experience depends on universality of form, perceptual and psychological disinterestedness, and the primacy of originality and innovation. Postmodern expression challenges a modern formalist aesthetic which promotes a fixed, homogeneous, unitary art culture and is unable "to represent" the fragmented, decentered multiplicity of contemporary culture as a whole way of life.

THE CRITIC AND POSTMODERN EXPRESSION

In the modern period, the era of industrialization inaugurated the bureaucratization of social institutions, the scientific technologization of the environment, as well as the establishment of mass education and mass-mediated communication with its information explosion. There appears, in the face of unbridled optimistic belief in progress, the cultural critic who interprets the present conditions of modern civilization as symptomatic of a loss of traditional cultural values.

Two general trends in cultural criticism represent the established critical positions: conservative (those who advocate a return to the classical tradition) and radical (those who advocate fundamental changes). On one hand, the conservative position runs through the entire modern period and staunchly privileges the received "classical" canon of Arts and Letters in which intellectual, spiritual, and artistic development determine priorities (Williams, 1965). From this position the degradation of aesthetic sensibility and the corruption of good taste lead to cultural anarchy and foreshadow the destruction of Culture. The revival of Culture requires the reinstitution of the Arts and Letters grounded in the classical tradition.

On the other hand, even radical positions are critical of the conditions of contemporary Culture and likewise search for the legitimation of Cultural activity in the Arts. Modernist critical theory[3] proposes that the Arts fulfill an important function in subverting dominant bourgeois capitalism, providing some possibility of emancipation by holding back the spread of mass culture (Adorno, 1972) and later consumerism (Greenberg, 1965; Guilbaut, 1983). Art critics such as Greenberg propose that the avant garde (i.e., modern art) furnishes the last stronghold against the rising tide of consumerism. Likewise, late critical theory critics such as Habermas (1983) and Jameson (1983) warn of the danger to Culture in late capitalism. Lyotard (1984), another cultural critic, identifies these conditions of culture as post-modern.

The two sides are responding to the fragmentation and indiscriminate juxtaposition of values both social and cultural. They fear a breakdown of clearly defined values, a loss of supportable criteria of judgment, and the florescence of mass culture consumerism. Both sides fear that this fragmentation undermines the meaning structures by which Western Culture maintains cohesive cultural values. Both sides of the debate, whether conservative or critical, respond to this fragmentation and loss of legitimation by demanding retrenchment.

There is a third position of critical dialogue, which I identify as postmodern expression, that disrupts critical distinctions, locating formerly antagonistic positions within the same camp. This third position questions the authority of those who impose traditional "classical" criteria (the first position), but it attacks primarily the authority of the modern to define universal Culture (the second position). Although postmodern[4] and therefore ancillary to the modern, it shifts its critical focus and confronts the very boundaries of the art culture system.

A Postmodern Communication Aesthetic

Architecture is one of the first manifestations of postmodern expression. A mosaic of multiple stylistic traditions of postmodern architecture challenges the universalizing abstraction of the modern international style. According to Jencks (1984), modern architecture as exemplified in the international style imposes a strictly material, formal aesthetic which ignores the context and people who inhabit the structures. Rather than universal form, Jencks claims that "architecture should be looked at as communication" (p. 45). The problem is then that as communication, the international style imposes a universal signifying system. The complex coding of postmodern architecture subverts the universal language of the international style and calls into question a universalizing aesthetic. A common strain, much postmodern expression turns to the vernacular (the local ethnic cultures and popular cultures) in order to broaden the discourse in which the aesthetic participates.

As postmodern expression, the arts are a communicative activity that shapes and are shaped by culture (see Risatti, 1990). Postmodern expression is neither a temporal period, nor a categorization of style, but a critical discourse within the domain of art culture that recognizes the centrality of the aesthetic in culture but challenges the authority of the modern formalist aesthetic.[5] The aesthetic as communicative activity disrupts the absolute authority of modern formalist aesthetics as an overarching universal signifying system at the level of discourse. Many of those disenfranchised by the modernist aesthetic discourse are beginning to challenge the legitimacy of this discourse to speak for them (Hutcheon, 1988; Jardine, 1985; also Clifford, 1988). Rather than the fragmentation and devaluation of post-modern culture as in postmodernism, the target of the first two critical practices (conservative and radical), those theorists who examine specific areas of postmodern expression such as Hutcheon (1988), Huyssen (1983), and Jardine (1985) conceive of the possibility of deciphering a creative and critical postmodern practice, which I identify as the third position (postmodern expression). Those who have been excluded from mainstream aesthetic discourse—such as women, people of color, and the peoples of Third World cultures—are especially committed to excavating from within this perceived decline of Western civilization a new vision.

CHARTING MODERN AESTHETIC DISCOURSE

Philosophical aesthetics consists of a set of texts that lay out the fundamental parameters of modernist aesthetic discourse. These texts present the principal theories, definitions, and logics of theories of art and aesthetic experience through a series of statements, descriptions, analyses, and arguments by which critical hierarchies and legitimacy are established. This discourse provides a unified narrative of available knowledge about aesthetic perception and Art.

A tangible illustration of this discourse appears in the numerous anthologies produced for college courses to initiate the student of aesthetics into the discipline.[6] The familiarity of easily identifiable primary texts—standards such as Plato, Aristotle, Kant, and Hegel—and secondary texts (here the list is not so universally approved) establishes a canon. Modernist aesthetics depends primarily on its systematization in Kant with acknowledgments to the British empiricists of taste. Although Baumgarten's study of the science of secondary perception provides the designation "aesthetic" (derived from the Greek *aisthesis*, meaning "sensuous perception"), modern aesthetics traces its origins to the formalization of theories of taste and beauty in Kant's *Critique of Judgment*. Here aesthetic judgments, despite their subjective nature, claim universal validity through disinterestedness and differentiated perception of pure form. The texts that follow—Schopenhauer, *The World as Will and Idea* (1819), and Nietzsche, *The Birth of Tragedy*

(1872)—establish Art as a legitimate concern of philosophy. Other texts, such as Edward Bullough (1912) on psychical distance, Clive Bell (1914) on significant form, and Suzanne Langer (1953) on symbolic expression, shape the development of relevant topics of concern to the discipline (see Dickie & Sclafani, 1977).

Clement Greenberg represents the direction of this discourse. In *Art and Culture*, Greenberg (1965) embodies the late modernist position concerning the relationship to art and culture. The modernist avant-garde "culture," according to Greenberg, represents a "superior consciousness of history" which coincides with the scientific revolution. Detached from politics, the avant garde's "specialization of itself" is a "search for the absolute" through "abstract" or "nonobjective" art. Pure invention of space, surfaces, shapes, colors, and so on, Art can be validated solely on its own terms and superior to both folk art and kitsch (mass culture). Its purity is guaranteed through its uniqueness. Despite its self-referential status according to Greenberg, avant-garde art is the only living culture we have and it is the only hope our Culture has for survival in the face of the onslaught of mass culture (kitsch). Only the avant-garde is genuine, and mass culture is a simulacra of genuine culture. This rather brief summary of the aesthetic discourse as manifest in a number of texts provides an illustration of how modern formalist aesthetics generates knowledge through discourse.

Michel Foucault (1972), a French poststructuralist, provides a critical examination of the discursive nature of knowledge acquisition. Philosophical aesthetics can be considered such a discourse. According to Foucault, these discourses are not innocent, objective, or apolitical, and "in every society the production of discourse is at once controlled, selected, organized, and redistributed according to a certain number of procedures" (p. 216). The discourse produces formalized systems of thought through the omission and marginalization of competing positions. What appears to be a unified body of knowledge contains discontinuities and ruptures, and it is these gaps which are the condition for the possibility of calling the modernist aesthetic into question. Focusing on the discourse of modern aesthetics clarifies what is found to be problematic in Margolis's suggestion that philosophical aesthetics examines the relationship of Art and Culture.

The implications of understanding philosophical aesthetics and its constitution of a modern formalist aesthetic as discourse are numerous. We will look at three that are central to the critique of modern aesthetics and its relationship to culture.

First, this discourse naturalizes what are culturally fixed meanings (Risatti, 1990). Neither art nor the aesthetic as put forth in philosophy pertain to a natural order of things but are constructed within a discourse which makes the meaning of the aesthetic and art possible. But over and above this, the discourse itself is culturally constituted within fixed social/political positions. Knowledge is constructed. This discourse gives rise to the organization of concepts and definitions designating priority to some over others. It determines what are sound methods of inquiry and the appropriateness of their application. The discourse ascertains who has the right to speak and under what institutional auspices, including the language to be used and research style, usually a highly specified sign system of specialized terminology and a style of legitimate presentation. In addition, the correct subject position is determined by the discourse. In philosophical aesthetics, the speaking subject of the discourse maintains a disinterested, apolitical position, but the discourse itself is not disinterested. Its methodological, ontological, and epistemological claims determine what is legitimate art and what is not, what belongs in the class of perception designated aesthetic and what does not. Objects are constituted in the discourse and appear as art within the context of the discourse.

Second, this discourse constitutes a universal aesthetic of form. Although the modernist aesthetic itself is constituted in a specific historical period and within particular cultural signifying systems, it is not just art and aesthetics that the discourse constructs, but the discipline itself obeys certain rules. As a universal aesthetic, assumptions are made about the constituted objects (the art object), the perceiving subjects of those objects (the connoisseur as well as the audience), and the creating subject (the artist). A universal aesthetic decontextualizes each of the members in the communication process by reducing the field of operatives through abstraction, objectivity, and formal relations.

Third, the context is itself circumscribed by the aesthetic discourse, which is much broader than the discipline of philosophical aesthetics. Not only is art approached through other disciplines, such as art history or literary criticism, but the practice and experience of producing and distributing art define it and in turn influence the producers and distribution organizations. The modernist formal aesthetic isolates the enunciating subject of modern aesthetic expression. It favors the discursive over the nondiscursive, language over image and gesture, propositional language over rhetorical, metaphoric language and innovation over communication. There is an assumption that the arts—plastic, visual, poetic, musical—require translation or interpretation into analytical (i.e., rational) thought. In modernist formal aesthetics, this can only be done by a self-reflective subject initiated into the exclusive domain of cultivated taste—culture.

Postmodern expression generates a counterdiscourse within modern aesthetic discourse which recognizes a larger field of meaning within the social order—designated discursive practices. Postmodern expression skeptically doubts the authority of modern formalist aesthetics and challenges exclusion by problematizing its foundations and attacking the hierarchies of power (i.e., the political, historical, and subject-constituting practices of the entire artfield).

THE POLITICS OF DISINTERESTEDNESS

The strict formalism of modern aesthetics demands an apolitical stance and suppresses the political as viable aesthetic discourse. Modern aesthetics assigns primacy to the intrinsic quality of artifacts designated "art" or pertaining to art and promotes the autonomy of prescribed aesthetic discourse. It defines the art zone and dismisses the political as extrinsic to appropriate aesthetic experience. Referential content, immersed in the political instability of the present, is at best ignored or it can reduce the aesthetic force by hindering aesthetic appreciation. Picasso's *Guernica* as a work of art must stand on its formal merits; its political force as an outcry condemning the massacre of the people of Guernica is extrinsic to the aesthetic experience of the artwork.

Artists object to their disenfranchisement. Douglas Davis (1977) observes,

The artist now is not allowed to be a citizen, save at the cost to his reputation. He is expected to leave the business of the world to dealers, collectors, curators, and naturally, politicians. (p. 8)

The apolitical stance of modern aesthetics is increasingly under fire. First, in actual practice modern art has had a subversive political agenda. The Soviet Union's repression of modern art in favor of social realism is the recognition of just such an agenda. Today controversy in the United States over the subject matter of the *Pissed Christ* or Maplethorpe's oeuvre can still be defended on the basis of form, line, and figure-ground relations, but it is their content which incites controversy and political turmoil. Numerous artists have an explicit political agenda. Jenny Holzer represented the United States at the Venice Biennale, and her medium (LEDs) and content challenge the received values of American culture (Joselit, 1990). Lorna Simpson's photographs of Afro-American women (Vetrocq, 1990) or political/conceptual artists such as Dennis Adams, Group Material, Alfred Jaar, and Krzysztof Wodiczko (Cameron, 1990) work to enfranchise the artist and question the apolitical stance of modern aesthetic discourse.

However, the exclusion of political content obscures the political nature of the modernist discourse itself. An aesthetic purism negates and represses the political in the name of a higher purpose and transcendent order (Carroll, 1987). The programmatic apolitical stance is troublesome for a much more fundamental reason than the exclusion of political content and reference in specific art objects. Norris (1985) claims that the authority of modern aesthetics to establish a separate intellectual discipline maintains an ideological position and establishes the ontological and epistemological categories for art.[7]

According to Norris, philosophical aesthetics ignores concrete social and political practices and subverts criticism through the power of its discourse.[8] He claims that philosophical aesthetics subordinates criticism. First, it defines criticism and limits it to its own analytical method, which claims:

a certain regulatory role *vis-a-vis* the practice of criticism. It no longer looks to provide a full-scale ontology of art or a firm categorical grounding for the exercise of critical judgement. What it offers instead is a 'logical' account of how perceptions, reasons, and evaluative judgements hang together in a well-conducted sequence of critical argument. (Norris, 1985, p. 125)

Second, it discounts all other critical practices as deficient. From this perspective the social sciences, literary theory, and art criticism as well as the practice of artists are ill-prepared to address the discourse critically. These disciplines are limited to the description and interpretation of individual works of art. Norris claims that this modern aesthetic establishes legitimate discourse about art and its criticism and thereby maintains existing institutions and is itself political.

Likewise, Bourdieu (1987) deconstructs the assumed purity (i.e., political disinterestedness) of the modern formalist aesthetic. Bourdieu's argument challenges the claim of disinterestedness on the basis of the historicity of the experience of the actors in the artfield. Philosophical aesthetics "implicitly establishes as universal aesthetic practices the rather particular properties of an experience which is a product of privilege" (Bourdieu, 1987, p. 202). The singular experience of the philosopher (generally Eurocentric, white, male, and well endowed with what Bourdieu identifies as "cultural capital") becomes the singular experience which establishes "a transhistorical norm for every aesthetic perception" (p. 202). According to Bourdieu, the establishment of a universally pure art and transhistorical norms for aesthetic experience are not apolitical, but a product of negotiation and struggle among members of an extended artfield which includes not only philosophers, but also artists, collectors, and connoisseurs as well as curators and the entire commercial sector. Modern formal aesthetics establishes a domain of autonomy over the political milieu of the artfield not as disinterested but as a means of maintaining the power to determine who is an artist and what are the criteria for art making.

Postmodern expression in the visual arts takes up the critique of the political agenda of modernist aesthetic discourse. Joseph Beuys, a performance artist, proposes a broader definition of art that includes as a high priority the acknowledgment of the political nature of art. Beuys's political action party asserts itself not in the political world of electoral politics but in the redefinition of art (Tisdall, 1979). Beuys perceives the artist as a shaman that seeks to heal society through the teaching of the creativity of art. He says,

My objects are to be seen as stimulants for the transformation of the idea of sculpture, or of art in general. They should provoke thoughts about what sculpture can be and how the concept of sculpting can be extended to the invisible materials used by everyone:

Thinking forms	how we mould our thoughts
Spoken forms	how we shape our thoughts into words
Social sculpture	how we mould and shape the world in which we live:

Sculpture is an evolutionary process; everyone an artist. (Tisdall, 1979, p. 7)

For Beuys, art is not the medium of the political; it is itself political. The repressive ideology of modernist aesthetics necessitates a whole new definition of art. As postmodern, Beuys deconstructs "the aesthetic" in order to reconstruct art. The artist is more than a maker of objects, he or she is a teacher who maps out strategies for healing the cultural order. Beuys seeks a democratic rather than authoritarian aesthetic and the possibility of a "ideo-picto-phonographic media" (see Ulmer, 1985) which can communicate this new aesthetic. Although Beuys works within the artfield, enmeshed in the complex aesthetic of modernism, he attempts to subvert the politics of the prevailing aesthetic discourse by calling forth a populist politics which inhabits his performance pieces.

Davis (1977), another artist seeking new media of communication for a populist art, uses the electronic media. He finds that no matter what artists do to subvert object art—whether in happenings, performances, or the very body of the artist—they are each objectified within the artfield and become "commodities susceptible to trade and sale." Critical postmodern expression faults modern aesthetics as implicated in rather than a bulwark against the political (see Buchloh, 1987). Modern aesthetics supports the creation of commodities and is implicated in the very process of commodification that Greenberg suggests the avant garde can subvert—consumer mass culture. It fragments the sociopolitical force of its own practice. Depoliticizing its practice, it displaces its political force within the discourse by self-referentially establishing itself as ahistorical and part of the universal order of things.

UNIVERSAL FORM AND THE HISTORICITY OF THE AESTHETIC

Modernist aesthetic discourse produces a powerful unified narrative, a linear, cause-and-effect discourse which functions to validate its position while denying the historicality of its discourse. Caught between two contradictory positions, it covers over the living, present practices of the arts and culture. Postmodern expression calls into question the construction of a linear history which functions to cloak the past and deny tradition while using it to legitimate exclusionary culture. This unified narrative produces a privileged discourse which marginalizes through omissions and repressions opposing sites of the aesthetic. On one side, modern aesthetics sets up universals which reject tradition for the new and experimental. Knowledge is based not on traditional values but on an avant garde of future possibilities. On the other side, the discourse is validated through the ordering of events, texts, debates, and legitimate speakers in history, which make advances in aesthetic knowledge possible. The discourse establishes the origins and development of art theories while shrouding in uncertainty the legitimacy of those which it marginalizes. Established interpretations and confirmed art objects verify and justify the advance of knowledge and then constitute, through prediction, future possibilities. This was especially evident in the late 1960s and 1970s, when conceptual artists such as Kosuth and Arakawa become more and more dependent on philosophical discourse to generate art (Danto, 1986), borrowing from other discursive fields to advance in the modern aesthetic discourse. In late modernist discourse there is an end of art, or antiart. This is a recuperative strategy which provides an end in order to have a basis for a new beginning.

Modernist aesthetic discourse constructs a history of future possibilities dependent on overcoming traditional barriers and breaking conventions. This break with tradition and the conventions of the past in favor of the constant construction of new ism's with unique characteristics limits those who can decipher and understand what it is that is being accomplished. Enculturated perception is naturalized, while it divides reception between those who are part of the discourse and those who are marginalized. On one hand, there are the cultivated unique few within constituted history who may participate in the transcendental aesthetic, and on the other hand the ignorant, conventional masses immersed in the contingent present who are limited to conventional signs and symbols within communication.

Reception aesthetics addresses this aporia of the historical in modern aesthetics by asserting the role of the perceiver/reader. It extends the position of the reader to that of the reception of the work in "effective" history.[9] Reception aesthetics relocates practical and theoretical concerns toward an interactive, communicative aesthetic and provides a wedge into the exclusionary aesthetic of the modern. This interactive communication model begins with studies of the act of reading literary texts in phenomenology (see Ingarden, 1985). Under the influence of Ingarden, Iser's (1978) investigation of the reading process centers on the question of "how and under what conditions a text has meaning for a reader." Traditional interpretation privileges the text or artwork as source of meaning; whereas Iser discerns the meaning of aesthetic texts to be the result of interaction between text and reader. For Iser the aesthetic is a communicative activity accomplished by the reader, while the text (artwork) "simply offers a frame within which the reader must construct for himself the aesthetic object" (p. 107).

Reception aesthetics does not overturn modernist precepts if the reader is defined as the "model reader" who is enculturated into aesthetic discourse, but rather reveals the operative processes in aesthetic discourse by which meaning is constructed. The traditional, legitimate perceiver of the artwork is maintained by positing a model reader who maintains and is maintained by the discourse. Reception theory ratifies the administrative activity of aesthetic discourse and the privileging of enculturated perceivers, while it uncovers the operative practices and fuels a critical practice. The challenge to prevailing aesthetic discourse comes when the implications of this position are uncovered in the reader response and cultural studies (mass media) versions of reception theory, which extend the notion as to who are legitimate receivers (Holub, 1986).

In the modern view, according to Jauss (1988), history becomes a succession of styles and periods strung together by causal relationships which link work to work in a causal explanation. This account of discrete happenings is incapable of accounting for the "continuity of the aesthetic." Using Gadamer's (1975) concept of history as "effective historical consciousness," Jauss grounds the reception or constitution of the meaning of artworks in an effective historical consciousness. The effect of the work and its significance through the tradition constitutes the meaning of the artwork, which is dependent not on historical fact or causal validation but on the way that the artwork affects the discourse. As a critical practice, reception theory assails the modern concepts of a causal history of discrete objects and focuses on the discursive nature of history.

Viewed from a reception aesthetic position, art continually revitalizes the past through present activity and links works in the artfield by means of creating and receiving subjects. The historicity of artworks depends on communication between and among subjects within a culture. Understanding is possible through the intersubjectivity of human activity in a complex, multilayered tradition. The aesthetic dimension intersects all other levels in the significative field, meaning art, and it does so within a multicultural milieu within effective history. Artworks are preserved and signify as they participate in this tradition through the artwork of the present. The "new" of modernism presupposes the very tradition it denies.

Reception aesthetics interrogates an underlying presupposition in modernist aesthetics and reveals the intimate connection between art objects and their audiences. Reception theory's critique of historicism and the aesthetic it supports is crucial to postmodern expression. It breaks down the privileged worth of the art object in favor of the object's reception in an historical context. Value is not intrinsic to art objects but is constituted in the relationship of object and reception. Reception theorists make paradoxical the relation of the artwork and the audience.

The revitalization of the audience as creative is present in the works of artists first involved in happenings, earthworks, and body art and more recently in performance art. As Laurie Anderson comments, the new site of the artwork is the audience. Anderson, a performance artist, works both within the gallery circuit and the rock concert venue. Her highly successful concert tour, *USA 1-4*, and her movie, *Home of the Brave*, as well as her concert in the Brooklyn Academy of Music's Next Wave Series put her within the context of both popular and high culture. As postmodern expression, Anderson's work revitalizes art culture by acknowledging a multiplicity of perceiving positions within the effective historical consciousness of culture and challenges the bifurcation of the audience by aesthetic discourse. The art and artist take on the responsibility of extending the context of art, which recognizes that to communicate with a larger audience a self-reflective aesthetic which claims universal validity must address the multiplicity of a living culture.

ORIGINALITY AND THE PRIMACY OF INNOVATION

The unmasking of the conventions of a modernist aesthetic by postmodern expression dismantles two of the central components of modernist discourse: originality and innovation. Issues of the authenticity and the legitimacy of certain objects as art plagues modernism. According to Greenberg,

> The unique and proper area of competence of each art coincided with all that was unique to the nature of its medium. The task of self-criticism became to eliminate from the effects of each art any and every effect that might conceivably be borrowed from or by the medium of any other art. Thereby each art would be rendered "pure," and in its "purity" find the guarantee of its standards or quality as well as of its independence. (1973, p. 68)

In late modernist discourse, "the pure" requires a disinterested "pure" perceiver and abstract universal "pure" forms, which designate the unique. Originality and innovation become the primary means by which modernism sustains the legitimate status of art. Originality, authenticity, and uniqueness celebrate the styles of the individual artist. Since these artists work in nondiscursive meanings, the interpretation of works and the deciphering of their singular contribution is delivered to the culture by aesthetic discourse. The legitimate speaking subject is not the artist but the critic, philosopher, historian, or any number of actors in the field who determine, acknowledge, and are determined by the discourse. It is this discourse which initiates the artist into the artfield and legitimates the work as artwork by constituting the artist, who cannot "speak" for himself or herself, as the unique innovator. Modernist discourse displaces the speaking subject of the artist in the name of the discourse—which has the power to designate a work as an artwork. One of the main issues in poststructuralist thought is this constitution of the subject who has the power to speak and create knowledge.

According to Foucault (1973), the subject is constructed by the power structure of the discourse. Whatever is knowable and sayable is constituted in and through the discursive practice of a period. According to Foucault, from the nineteenth century forward the order of things is founded on the human subject. Human beings as we conceive of them are a product of a specific historical discourse. By challenging this discourse, Foucault suggests that we confront the definition of human as constituted in modern thought:

> Anthropology constitutes the fundamental arrangement that has governed and controlled the path of philosophical thought from Kant until our day. This arrangement is essential, since it forms part of our history; but it is disintegrating before our eyes, since we are beginning to recognize and denounce it, in a critical mode, both a forgetfulness of the opening that made it possible and a stubborn obstacle standing obstinately in the way of an imminent new form of thought. (p. 342)

Much of poststructuralist thought works to deconstruct the anthropological subject of the modern by questioning the authority to posit humans as rational subjects fully capable of constituting all knowledge about everything. What is at stake for the poststructuralist is the scientific, systematic discourse of the modern, which favors an instrumental rationality—autonomous, stable, and quantitative—and is contemptuous of qualitative interpretative reasoning. This conceptualization of the rational knowing subject marginalizes the affective, sensual, and erotic (i.e., the aesthetic) that cannot be captured by analytical aesthetic discourse. Many poststructural thinkers—Foucault, Derrida, and Lyotard—envision the arts as a means of dismantling the grip of instrumental rationality in the modern and those systems of meaning that maintain established, repressive institutions (Carroll, 1987). The individual subject as we know it, according to Foucault (1973), is not embued with essential human nature or the fundamental force of creation but is born as a subject of and subjected to the power of discourse.

Originality, authenticity, and uniqueness are celebrated in the styles of individual artists, while repetition and copying are rejected. But as Krauss (1984) suggests, repetition and copying have been a central component of modern art. She uses the example of Rodin's sculpture being recast from the original wax moulds well after the artist's death. The development of photography and sophisticated printing techniques, not to mention the skill in the reproduction of original artworks, have made the copy a standard form of modern art. This form of copying changes the scale, site, and media of communication of artworks no longer requiring the original (Krauss, 1984). Can we decide in photography what print is the original? In effect, the camera has undermined the feasibility of originality. The repeatability of the new electronic media and their technologies feeds the innovation in modern art. Eco (1985), in providing a postmodern aesthetic, addresses the problem of innovation.

According to him, an innovative aesthetic signifies art as a "scientific revolution: every work of modern art figures out a new law, imposes a *new paradigm*, a new way of looking at the world" (p. 161). Eco claims that our historical period fosters a different aesthetic—a postmodern aesthetic of seriality—in which repetition and formula are the marks of aesthetic sensibility. As seen from a modernist perspective or innovative point of view, the serial is the "indefinite variation of a theme"—a formula by which the same form is repeated with minor variations. According to Eco (1985), if we bracket the cult of originality in innovation aesthetics, then what is interesting is the variability itself. "Variability to infinity" has the characteristics of repetition and not innovation, but if done an infinite number of times then the device of variation takes on new meaning. Eco suggests that this new aesthetic of seriality demands a new audience who is comfortable with the break-up of "unicity." A new public, indifferent to the stories told, will relish the repetition and its own "microscopic variation" that needs to be received in a state of inattention, such as the typical way television is watched.

Unlike a modernist aesthetic, postmodern expression has been especially sensitive to the power of the mass media as a medium of mechanically reproducible expression. In contemporary society, most cultural expression is distributed to us in some electronic-mediated form. The classical performance arts, such as music or dance, are broadcast on public radio or television, a classical painting is made into a poster, or some visual art masterpiece appears in an advertisement. We experience the arts through some form of mechanical reproduction or electronic technology. These new media have made a marked impression on how we experience, produce, and reproduce our culture. They make available the sensuous presentation of human expression to a large, heterogeneous, mass audience. A medium that produces and reproduces audiovisual expression creates the impression of immediate experience. No longer an inert static medium, it makes available the gesture of human expression and does not require translation into print or graphic form. But the expense and voracious consumption of cultural material necessitates repeatable, serial, and formulaic forms of expression.

Today the visual and performing arts are breaking down established criteria of excellence, execution, and media. Pop, minimalism, and performance art have radically called up content in new ways, breaking the formal parameters of traditional art forms. Earthworks, performance art, and happenings rely on some form of mass distribution and photographic textualization to endure as artworks, without which they disintegrate and disappear. Video and film become new materials that influence and sometimes replace painting and sculpture. These new media reshape the working aesthetic of art. The camera's role in the mass media, film, serigraph, and photography no longer subordinates the work to the formal requirements of a modern aesthetic and challenges the criteria of formalism. And finally today, the whole phenomenon of cross-overs, between mass media and fine arts media—such as the rock music of Laurie Anderson, or the rock groups of Malcolm McLaren—not only call into question the elite premises of a modern aesthetic but also reshape popular culture forms of expression—rock and roll acts such as the Velvet Underground, The Beatles, Pink Floyd, Grace Jones, and especially punk rock (see Laing, 1985) all have been influenced by the avant garde. This intermixing leads to the breakdown of the high culture, popular culture boundaries instituted in a modern aesthetic (see Shore, 1980).

ART AND CULTURE

Much of the vitality of the innovation aesthetics of the modern is the reproduction of the cultural expression of "other" cultures. The artifacts of non-Western culture are lifted out of their cultural context and placed in the realm of fine art if their formal qualities coincide with the prevailing formal aesthetic order. Modern arts' foundations reflect the influences of the cultures of Micronesia and Africa. Early Cubists, especially Picasso and Braque, use the masks and artifacts of other cultures and by so doing reflect the fragmenting of the prevailing aesthetic.

Appropriating the artifacts of other cultures into the modern aesthetic discourse, ostensibly to rescue them from modernization and the ravages of mass culture, modern art uses the primitive to revitalize an overly abstract aesthetic.[10] So within modernism there is a contradiction between technological formalism (artifice) and primitive symbolism (authenticity). The response is to create a "synthetic," more stylized, abstracted culture over and above living culture. Clifford (1987) identifies this strategy as a salvage paradigm in Western Culture:

The salvage paradigm, reflecting a desire to rescue "authenticity" out of destructive historical change . . . names a geopolitical, historical paradigm that has organized western practices of "art-and culture-collecting." Seen in this light, it denotes a pervasive ideological complex. (p. 121)

One of the driving rationales for modern aesthetics is this salvaging of the past—to capture the sensual present and preserve it in the formal structures of rational discourse. By doing so it isolates the multiple dimensions of culture. The elite, exclusive Culture of modernist discourse preserves artifacts of human expression: encased in the museum, repeatedly performed in the symphonic orchestra hall, and sequestered in archives. Unable to withstand the onslaught of mass culture, this refined Culture falls prey to a technological determinism which rests on unexamined assumptions about the media and mass culture. Popular culture, the living culture of the people (either folk or mass), is separated from legitimate Culture and abandoned to unbridled technological forces, unable to participate in the exclusive structures of elite culture. The cultures of "other" peoples, labeled primitive, preliterate, tribal, etc., represent the majority of the peoples of the world. These cultures, disenfranchised, become just so many "natural resources" for Western multinational corporations.

Cognizant of the cultural imperialism of the past, cultural studies examine the study of culture and the arts. Levi-Strauss (1953) makes a scathing critique of traditional disciplines which posit an evolutionary theory of development to explain the relationship of our Culture (high culture) to other cultures (folk culture). In an evolutionary paradigm, Western "man" becomes the latest and most advanced stage of development. According to Levi-Strauss, the classification of societies as "primitive" or "underdeveloped" is based on a technological bias which measures the development of "man" in relationship to the sophistication of technology. However, this overriding emphasis on technical sophistication and progress limits any understanding of other cultures that might use different criteria of evaluation. Levi-Strauss (1953) suggests that our whole notion of revolutionary change might be limited by this technical bias. All other changes, which according to Levi-Strauss have most certainly come about, are only partially perceptible or seriously distorted.

Today cultural studies question the very basis on which traditional disciplines collect and organize cultural artifacts and account for cultural activity. As Clifford (1987) observes, "Anthropology no longer speaks with automatic authority for others defined as unable to speak for themselves" (p. 10), so it can also be said of philosophical aesthetics. The aesthetic discourse is produced in a particular historical period by a privileged culture which defines the parameters of that culture. In this discourse the discrepancies between art theory (a theoretical formalism) and art practice (a communicative aesthetic) are indicative of the separation of art and life which plagues modern aesthetics and those intellectual traditions which explain art—philosophy, literary theory, art criticism, and art history. By recognizing that the aesthetic and art are communicative (discursive) in the wider range of culture, aesthetic discourse can be extended to include discursive practices in the arts. Overdetermined and overcoded, the discourse of art uses gestures, movement, and extralinguistic signifying systems within the total artfield to participate in the meaning structures of the discursive practices of the whole culture. The artfield, with a central role in Western Culture as a whole way of life, is significa-

tive and as such does not transcend but participates in the wider range of culture.

In this paper we have examined briefly the tenets of modernism and its formalist aesthetic. If philosophy is going to address the relationship of art and culture, as Margolis suggests, it might examine the arts and art practice within culture as a whole way of life. The complex, multicultural milieu of contemporary culture challenges a universal, transcendent aesthetic. Postmodern expression demands a socially and politically relevant art and questions an aesthetic discourse that isolates itself from the political, historical, and subjective contingencies of a living culture.

EPILOGUE

When the historical avant garde attempted to bring art into life, they failed because their Culture insulated itself from the sensual contingencies of life in an abstract, universal formal aesthetic. Today it is perhaps those very sensual "aesthetic" activities that provide for the communicative bridge between peoples of varied cultural experiences, recognizing that life in all its multiplicity creates culture. The "aesthetic" or *aisthesis* as sensual can be used to deconstruct and then participate in the reconstruction of cultural expression capable of communicating the multiplicity of cultural meaning. Life and art are not antagonistic or mutually exclusive. Rather life is the social, political, aesthetic, economic forces that create culture (i.e., culture as a whole way of life).

NOTES

1. Dickie (1977) seeks an institutional definition of art; Danto (1986) extends the definition of art to artworlds; and Eaton (1988) frames definitions and concepts of art within art institutions.
2. Contemporary cultural studies is a multidisciplinary project which includes cultural anthropology, sociology, literary criticism, art criticism, communication, and mass culture studies. It operates within a wide theoretical

base which embraces both the social sciences and philosophy and reflects the impact of structuralism, poststructuralism, and semiotics. Its critical focus takes into account the diverse palette of critical studies which began with Kant. This consists of but is not limited to phenomenology, hermeneutics, and the critical school and includes the social science disciplines such as anthropology (Clifford, 1981, 1988), communication and mass culture studies (Carey, 1975; Hall, 1980; Haug, 1986; Pillotta & Mickunas, 1990), and sociology (Bourdieu, 1980, 1987) as well as literary theory (Huyssen, 1983; Jauss, 1982, 1988; Jameson, 1983). However, it is the new European theory, structuralism (Levi-Strauss, 1953), poststructuralism (Derrida, 1977; Foucault, 1972, 1973), semiotics (Barthes, 1977; Eco, 1979a, 1979b), and postmodern criticism (Hutcheon, 1988; Huyssen, 1983; Lyotard, 1984) which have solidified this new direction.
3. With their roots in Marxism and the Frankfurt School, critical theorists seek the material basis of social relations in the superstructure, and in so doing they turn their critical attention to the Arts. Marxism shifts focus to an examination of ideology and the production of culture in deciphering cultural hegemony, the overarching ideas of a culture central to the production of social relationships.
4. The difference between postmodern and post-modern is significant. The term divided with a hyphen, *post-modern*, maintains the priority of modernism and identifies these cultural products as a deviation from and detrimental to modernism. The term without a hyphen, *postmodern*, claims the unique contribution of postmodern expression and acknowledges the validity of its critique of modernism.
5. As Carroll (1987) points out, the major poststructuralist, post-modern critics (Foucault, Derrida, and Lyotard) address the issue of art and aesthetics in contemporary culture. Carroll identifies it as a paraesthetics, Kroker and Cook (1986) a hyperaesthetic, while Baudrillard's (1980) concept of the simulacrum attempts to deal with appearance and simulation.
6. There are many popular anthologies, for example: Rader (1979), and Dickie and Sclafani (1977).
7. Kuspit (1983) observes this authoritarian cast to modern aesthetic discourse. However, based on the working aesthetic available, he sees most alternatives as unacceptable.
8. Contemporary criticism—Bourdieu (1987) and Norris (1985)—is influenced by neo-Marxism and a shift of analysis from the base to the superstructure. This attention to the superstructure opens up the examination of the relationship of cultural expression to concrete political power.
9. Reception aesthetics is primarily developed in literary theory, so its reference is to the text. Barthes's (1977) extension of the notion of the text facilitates my equating of text and artwork, as well as the interchange of reader and viewer.
10. Gauguin writes in response to a critic, "I had then the premonition of a revolt: the conflict between your civilization and my barbarism . . . civilization from which you suffer; barbarism which is for me a rejuvenation" (in Chipp, 1968, p. 82).

REFERENCES

Adorno, T. W. (1972). Culture industry: Enlightenment as mass deception. In T. W. Adorno & M. Horkheimer, *Dialectic of Enlightenment*. New York: Seabury Press. (Original work published 1944.)

Barthes, Roland. (1977). From work to text. In *Image, Music, Text*. (S. Heath, Trans.). New York: Hill & Wang.

Baudrillard, J. (1980). The implosion of meaning in the media and the implosion of the social in the masses. In K. Woodward (ed.), *The Myth of Information* (pp. 137–48). Madison, WI: Coda Press, Inc.

Baudrillard, J. (1981). Requiem for the media. In J. Baudrillard, *For a Critique of the Political Economy of the Sign* (C. Levin, Trans. pp. 164–94). St. Louis: Telos Press. (Original work published 1972.)

Benamou, M. (1977). Introduction presence and play. In M. Benamou and C. Carmello (eds.), *Performance in Postmodern Culture* (pp. 3–7). Madison, WI: Coda Press, Inc.

Blocker, H. Gene. (1979). *Philosophy of Art*. New York: Charles Scribner's Sons.

Bourdieu, Pierre. (1987). The historical genesis of a pure aesthetic. *The Journal of Aesthetic and Art Criticism*, 46 (special issue), 201–10.

Buchloh, Benjamin. (1987). Periodizing critics. In H. Foster (ed.), *Discussions in Contemporary Culture*. Number One. Seattle: Bay Press.

Burger, Peter. (1984). *Theory of the Avant-Garde* (M. Shaw, Trans.). Minneapolis: University of Minnesota.

Cameron, Dan. (1990). Changing priorities in American art. *Art International*, 10, 86–90.

Carey, J. W. (1975). A cultural approach to communication. *Communication*, 2, 363–79.

Carroll, David. (1987). *Paraesthetics: Foucault, Lyotard, Derrida*. New York: Methuen.

Chipp, Herschel. (1968). *Theories of Modern Art: A Source Book of Artists and Critics*. Berkeley: University of California Press.

Clifford, J. (1987). Of other peoples: Beyond the "salvage" paradigm. In H. Foster (ed.), *Dia Art Foundation: Discussions in Contemporary Culture*. Number One (pp. 121–30). Seattle: Bay Press.

Clifford, James. (1981). On ethnographic surrealism. *Comparative Studies in Society and History*, 23(4), 539–64.

Clifford, James. (1988). *The Predicament of Culture: Twentieth-Century Ethnography, Literature, and Art*. Cambridge, MA: Harvard University Press.

Collins, Jim. (1989). *Uncommon Cultures: Popular Culture and Post-Modernism*. New York: Routledge.

Danto, Arthur C. (1986). *The Philosophical Disenfranchisement of Art*. New York: Columbia University Press.

Davis, Douglas. (1977). Artpolitics: Thoughts against the prevailing fantasies. In *Artculture: Essays on the Post Modern*. New York: Harper & Row.

Derrida, J. (1977). *Of Grammatology*. (Trans. Gayatri Chakravorty Spivak). Baltimore: The Johns Hopkins University Press. (Originally published 1967.)

Dickie, G. (1977). A response to Cohen: The actuality of art. In G. Dickie and R. J. Sclafani (eds.), *Aesthetics: A Critical Anthology* (pp. 196–201). New York: St. Martin's Press.

Dickie, G., & Sclafani, R. J. (1977). *Aesthetics: A Critical Anthology*. New York: St. Martin's Press.

Eaton, Marcia Muelder. (1988). *Basic Issues in Aesthetics*. Belmont, CA: Wadsworth Publishing Co.

Eco, Umberto. (1979a). *Role of the Reader*. Bloomington, IN: Indiana University Press.

Eco, Umberto. (1979b). *Theory of Semiotics*. Bloomington, IN: Indiana University Press.

Eco, Umberto. (1985). Innovation and repetition: Between modern and post-modern aesthetics. *Daedalus*, 114(4), 161–84.

Foster, Hal. (1983). Postmodernism: A preface. In H. Foster (ed.), *The Anti-Aesthetic: Essays in Postmodern Culture* (pp. ix–xvi). Port Townsend, WA: Bay Press

Foucault, M. (1972). *Archeology of Knowledge & The Discourse on Language*. New York: Pantheon Books.

Foucault, M. (1973). *The Order of Things: An Archaeology of the Human Sciences*. New York: Vintage Books.

Gadamer, H.-G. (1975). *Truth and Method*. New York: Crossroad. (Originally published 1965.)

Goldwater, Robert. (1967). *Primitivism in Modern Art*. New York: Vintage Books.

Greenberg, Clement. (1965). *Art and Culture*. Boston: Beacon Press.

Greenberg, Clement. (1973). Modernist painting. In G. Battcock (ed.), *The New Art* (pp. 66–77). New York: E. P. Dutton & Co.

Guilbaut, Serge. (1983). *How New York Stole the Idea of Modern Art: Abstract Expressionism, Freedom and the Cold War*. Chicago: University of Chicago Press.

Habermas, Jurgen. (1983). Modernity—An incomplete project. In H. Foster (ed.), *The Anti-Aesthetic: Essays on Postmodern Culture*. Port Townsend, WA: Bay Press.

Hall, S. (1980). Encoding/decoding. In S. Hall et al. (eds.), *Culture, Media and Language*. London: Hutchinson.

Haug, W. F. (1986). *Critique of Commodity Aesthetics: Appearance, Sexuality, and Advertising in Capitalist Society*. Minneapolis: University of Minnesota Press.

Holub, Robert C. (1986). *Reception Theory: A Critical Introduction*. London: Methuen.

Hutcheon, Linda. (1988). *A Poetic of Postmodernism: History, Theory, Fiction*. New York: Routledge.

Huyssen, Andreas. (1983). Mapping the Postmodern. *New German Critique*, 32(18), 5–52.

Ingarden, R. (1985). *Selected Papers in Aesthetics* (P. J. McCormick, ed.). Washington, DC: Catholic University Press of America.

Iser, Wolfgang. (1978). *The Act of Reading: A Theory of Aesthetic Response*. Baltimore: The Johns Hopkins University Press.

Jameson, F. (1983). Postmodernism and consumer society. In H. Foster (ed.), *The Anti-Aesthetic: Essays in Postmodern Culture* (pp. 111–25). Port Townsend, WA: Bay Press.

Jardine, A. (1985). *Gynesis: Configurations of Women and Modernity*. Ithaca: Cornell University Press.

Jauss, H. R. (1988). Tradition, innovation, and aesthetic experience. *The Journal of Aesthetic and Art Criticism*, 46 (special issue), 375–410.

Jauss, Hans Robert. (1982). *Toward an Aesthetic of Reception* (T. Bahti, Trans.). Minneapolis: University of Minnesota Press.

Jencks, Charles. (1984). *The Language of Post-Modern Architecture*. New York: Rizzoli International.

Joselit, D. (1990). Holzer: Speaking of power. *Art in America*, 78(10), 155–57.

Krauss, Rosalind. (1984). The originality of the avant-garde: The postmodern repetition. In B. Wallis (ed.), *Art After Modernism: Rethinking Representation* (pp. 13–30). New York: The New Museum of Contemporary Art.

Kroker, A., & Cook, D. (1986). *The Postmodern Scene: Excremental Culture and Hype-Aesthetics*. New York: St. Martin's Press.

Kuspit, Donald (1983). Authoritarian aesthetics and the elusive alternative. *The Journal of Aesthetic and Art Criticism*, 41(3), Spring, 271–88.

Laing, D. (1985). *One Chord Wonders: Power and Meaning in Punk Rock*. London: Open University Press.

Levi-Strauss, Claude. (1953). *Race and Man*. Paris: UNESCO.

Lyotard, J.-F. (1984). *The Postmodern Condition*. Minneapolis: University of Minnesota Press.

Margolis, Joseph. (1987). *Philosophy Looks at the Arts*. Philadelphia, PA: Temple University Press.

Merleau-Ponty, Maurice. (1964). Indirect language and the voices of silence. In *Signs* (Trans. R. C. McCleary). Chicago: Northwestern University Press.

Norris, Christopher. (1985). *Contest of Faculties: Philosophy Theory after Deconstruction*. London: Methuen.

Pilotta, J. J., and Mickunas, A. (1990). *Science of Communication: Its Phenomenological Foundation*. Hillsdale, NJ: Lawrence Erlbaum Associate Publishers.

Rader, Melvin. (1979). *A Modern Book of Aesthetics*. New York: H. Holt Co.

Risatti, H. (ed.). (1990). *Postmodern Perspectives: Issues in Contemporary Art*. Englewood Cliffs, NJ: Prentice Hall.

Shore, Michael. (1980, November). Punk rocks the art world: How does it look, how does it sound. *Art News*, 68–73.

Shusterman, Richard. (1988). Postmodern aestheticism: A new moral philosophy. *Theory, Culture and Society*, 5(2), Special Issue on Postmodernism, 337–56.

Tisdall, Caroline. (1979). *Joseph Beuys*. New York: The Solomon R. Guggenheim Museum.

Ulmer, Gregory L. (1985). *Applied Grammatology: Post(e)- Pedagogy from Jacques Derrida to Joseph Beuys*. Baltimore: The Johns Hopkins University Press.

Vetrocq, Marcia E. (1990). Vexed in Venice. *Art in America*, 28(10).

Wartofsky, M. W. (1987). The liveliness of aesthetics. *The Journal of Aesthetics and Art Criticism*, pp. 211–18.

Williams, Raymond. (1965). *The Long Revolution*. New York: Columbia University Press.

Williams, Raymond. (1983). *Culture and Society: 1780–1950*. New York: Columbia University Press.

The Contradictory Character of Postmodernism

Donald Kuspit

I. THE AILMENT CALLED POSTMODERNISM

"The inflationary and often contradictory use of the term 'postmodernism' does not have to concern us," writes Jochen Schulte-Sasse, "as long as it is understood that postmodernity and postmodernism refer to qualitative changes in society and their cultural manifestations."[1] Schulte-Sasse is wrong: the inflationary and often contradictory use of the term 'postmodernism' does have to concern us. The term may be more significant for what it tells us about the theorists who use it than for what it tells us about society and culture. (The contradictory character of the term expands its meaning; its inflationary character follows from this contradictoriness. That is, the inflation signals that the contradictoriness is unresolvable—an idealistic over-expansion that empties the term of material meaning. The only historical reality "postmodernism" comes to signal is that of its exaggerated significance for theorists, which is one way of understanding how it is that a term can become a signifier without reference. A so-called free signifier is a term that has been so removed from circulation—practice—by its intellectual analysis that it can only signify that analysis. It has, one might say, been over-clarified, which reduces its usefulness. It achieves ideal, rather than realistic, status.)

Is there any way Schulte-Sasse can be sure that the social and cultural changes "postmodernism" theoretically designates have not been inflated—into qualitative ones— by the term itself? The changes may not be what they seem to be in the light of the concept when the concept itself is obscure. The term "postmodernism" may pass its inflationary contradictoriness on to its object, making what may be social and cultural molehills into insurmountable mountains. It may be that our society and culture do indeed have an inflated, contradictory character[2]—and this is implicitly, if perversely, acknowledged through the inflated, contradictory use of the term "postmodernism." However, there is no way of establishing it except through an analysis of the contradictoriness of the term "postmodernism."

That Schulte-Sasse is compelled to suppress his own intellectually honest, unhappy admission of the problematic character of postmodernism should make us aware that it has ideological import and is protected by a mystique. Postmodernism is more of a program developed by theorists than the common reality of contemporary society and culture. Postmodernism is a rhapsodic, elusive, exhilarating concept, used with license, because the hopes and fears—anxious ambitions?—of theorists are riding on it. I suggest that the term "postmodernism" is deliberately kept flexible and enchanting—so rich with connotations that it dissolves on direct contact with reality—as a pretentious, pseudo-autonomous display of theory's critical power

---

From *Postmodernism: Philosophy and the Arts*, Hugh Silverman, ed. (New York: Routledge, Chapman and Hall, 1989). Reprinted by permission of the publisher.

in its bourgeois situation of social impotence.[3] The creative use of the term "postmodernism" is the product of unconscious frustration rather than unfolding conscious insight. In order to deny this frustration, the meaning of the term "postmodernism" *must* be kept open—even if it becomes so porous that it can hold no meaning. The more outwardly complex the theory of postmodernism, the less the inner truth it signifies will have to be faced: it implies the collapse of a by now true and tried (even establishment) sense of criticality, namely, that of anti-establishment modernist (avant-garde) criticality. It suggests that there is no replacement concept of criticality in sight. We may be in a transition toward a new period, or deadended in the old one. The term 'postmodernism' reflects the uncertain destiny of criticality in contemporary society and culture. This signals, I contend, a changed rationale for criticality, a change in its meaning and purpose. If criticality is to continue to be socially useful in a broad way—rather than simply serving the narcissistic needs of intellectuals—it must serve different human needs than it once did.

The *Sturm-und-Drang* debate surrounding postmodernism creates the impression that it represents some extraordinary understanding.[4] The theory of postmodernism is presented as a great critical innovation, fraught with consequences for society and culture. Its incestuous intellectual turmoil suggests that it is conceived in difficult labor: it weighs a great deal at birth. In fact, all the conflict about it, like its own contradictory character, indicates that social and cultural theorists are extremely unsure of themselves, and of the power of their theory. The theory of postmodernism represents a general crisis of theory's belief in its power and influence—theory's loss of narcissistic face, loss of elementary belief in itself, loss of self-idealizing self-esteem. The excessive conflict and contradictoriness—leading not to agreement, but to rancorous confusion—raises the suspicion that the conceptualization of postmodernism is more a matter of honor among theorists than of interpretation of phenomena. The theory of postmodernism is a kind of spectacle—another entertainment, as opaque as any in our society; it obscures more than it illuminates—and fails to provide a genuinely critical/activist understanding. The difficulties, both internal and external, of the theory of postmodernism, suggest that it reflects contemporary bourgeois society more by way of demonstrating problems involved in critical and activist engagement—activism through criticality—than by direct articulation and examination. In other words, the contradictoriness of the theory of postmodernism is not simply a matter of familiar epistemological uncertainty accompanying the attempt to fix a concept definitively. Nor does it indicate an intellectual incision along a dialectical fault. Rather, it suggests the problem that critical/activist theory has encountered in its attempt to maintain a critical cutting edge in society.

The inflationary, contradictory use of the term 'postmodernism' also suggests its esthetic use; it is an artistic phenomenon of sorts. One might even be tempted to say, however tongue-in-cheek, that the theory of postmodernism is implicated "in the aesthetic of the sublime [through which] modern art . . . finds its impetus and the logic of avant-gardes finds its axioms,"[5] making it a species of avant-garde art. Even further, it seems to be more about the problems of presenting theory, even the unpresentable in theory, than about creating a theory, if these elements can be separated at all these days.[6] It is of course harder and harder to distinguish a theory's artistic character from its cognitive character: analysis is itself a mode of narrative. And there is apparently less and less need and desire to make the distinction—perhaps another sign of theory's impotence, self-defeat. But it is worth noting that blurring the difference between the artistic character and the cognitive character of theory can be understood as a manifestation of what Freud has called "omnipotence of thought."[7] If thinking about postmodernism has become a high art, then it must involve the omnipotence of thought, like all art.[8]

If this is the case, then the theory of postmodernism is an artistic illusion serving theory's most desperate infantile needs. I have already suggested that they are generally narcissistic; now, I want to propose that they are specifically a matter of secondary narcissism, a regressive response to various social dangers, from bourgeois indifference to outright appropriation of criticality.[9] The critical/activist theorist necessarily—tautologously—believes in his or her criticality, and in the power—necessity, validity, and efficacy—of criticality as such. That is, after all, what it is to be a critical/activist theorist, and to have self-respect. The theory of postmodernism is the latest attempt to reinforce the credibility of critical thinking as an activist mode of relating to the world as well as an inherently valuable activity. It argues for the socioexistential as well as high intellectual import of critical thinking. More precisely, the theorists of postmodernism argue that there is still a significant critical culture in bourgeois society, acknowledged and advocated by, and including, them.

However, the theory of postmodernism absolutizes a bankrupt vision of the critical as parodic irony. Culture is supposed to be a parody of society.[10] This is criticality in acceptable bourgeois form. Parodic irony is criticality without its poisonous sting, the empty shell of criticality, criticality that has been castrated. The postmodernist version of criticality as parody is an attenuated, compromised conception of criticality, designed to save critical theory's face in contemporary bourgeois society. Parodic irony is not only no longer effective against it, but is itself bourgeois, a tactic of bourgeois control, a sign of the cynicism of the bourgeois status quo. In contemporary bourgeois society, parodic irony means self-compromise; it is no longer subtly rebellious self-assertion, dialectical self-consciousness, ingenious self-transformation in the face of the status quo. Parody is thus an illusion of criticality. It is criticality without any teeth.

Postmodernist theorists hang on to the old idea of avant-garde criticality or resistance to bourgeois society. They assume that to rationalize and conventionalize modernist criticality into parody—to turn confrontational avant-garde anger into witty sniping—is to propose a whole new theory of criticality. They do not recognize the *de facto* bankruptcy of avant-garde criticality. As has been much noted, it has been institutionalized and co-opted by bourgeois society. Not only is the old criticality dead and the new criticality not yet born, but its birth is hindered by the postmodernist theorists, who refuse to recognize the obsoleteness of the old criticality. This puts the fate of criticality itself in jeopardy. As we will see, it is in architecture in particular—the most public of the arts—that parodic irony is supposed to be most alive and effective. Indeed, the term "postmodernism" has been applied most unequivocally to architecture. But even there, the avant-garde idea of criticality—even in its attenuated form of parodic irony—has become beside the point, a fact which architectural historians alone seem to recognize. As we will see, they argue that what is perceived as parodic irony is nothing of the sort.

In sum, I am arguing that the fundamental postmodernist issue is what the character and meaning of criticality are in the so-called postmodernist age. The truth behind the term 'post-modernism' is that modernist criticality no longer works or makes sense in contemporary bourgeois society. The bourgeois have learned to resist it by assimilating and neutralizing—diluting—it. Their strategy of response is not unlike that of the Russians, who let invaders penetrate into their land as far as they can, until they flounder and die in the Russian winter. The bourgeois have made modernist criticality, with its confrontational melancholy and disruptive deconstruction of bourgeois modes of representation, their own.[11] They have introduced an almost overwhelmingly therapeutic—anesthetic?—response to melancholy, in effect surrounding it on all sides, creating the illusion that it is generally conquerable but in fact acknowledging its near universality.[12] And they have assimilated deconstructive modes of representation, which get their revolutionary power by playing upon the ambiguity of the difference between abstract presentation and concrete representation, as the spearhead signs of their own ideology of so-called "permanent revolution."[13] The theory of postmodernism reflects this—showing its own bourgeois character—by dogmatically advocating hypothetically deconstructive parody as therapeutic criticality, in effect combining the extremes in a single facile formulation. This innocent notion of therapeutic deconstruction plays into the hands of bourgeois society, for it amounts to criticality's self-limitation. Thus, the contradictoriness which theorists regard as a sign of the complexity of the phenomenon of postmodernism is actually the sign of the failure of critical theory to achieve a revolutionary criticality, such as avant-garde criticality claimed to be, whether in its melancholy or deconstructive modes. The real phenomenon of postmodernism is that neither theory in particular nor culture in general live up to their own great critical expectations of themselves. Theory imagines it has achieved authentic criticality—criticality serving the needs of contemporary society—by advocating a watered-down version of the old modernist idea of criticality, which today has become a quaint, historical aspect of what Harold Rosenberg called the tradition of the modern. And high culture seems to flounder in a melancholy deconstruction of all historical styles, a fact that seems especially evident in postmodernist architecture. Later, we will see that the decadence suggested by this fact means quite the opposite of what it seems to.

The inflated, contradictory use of the term 'postmodernism' also marks the degeneration of activist criticality into futile, self-righteous rage signalling nothing but its own preaching thunder. It has been argued that this is the way it exists in the Marxist writings of Frederic Jameson and Terry Eagleton.[14] Activist criticality seems to be able to exist paranoically only as rage because it unconsciously experiences itself as peculiarly illegitimate or impossible—threatened in its very existence—in contemporary bourgeois society. It is lost in a kind of no-man's-land; more precisely, it has become irrelevant because class conflict has become peculiarly irrelevant in bourgeois society, so that activist criticality has no clear side or revolutionary cause to serve. Paradoxically, this is just because social differences have become perversely irreconcilable: class conflict has become hypostatized. Philosophically, this can be regarded as the collapse of dialectic, the much-acknowledged inability to achieve totality, or rather the recognition of a perverse totalization of society through the principle of permanent contradiction. Contradiction is institutionalized as irreducible, in effect an acknowledgement of the so-called instability of and discontinuity in all social relations, and the consequent diminishing of the sense of self.[15] This simply underlines the insurmountable differences that make for a lack of social and personal cohesion.

If criticality that is worth the name—criticality that is more than rabid and finally arbitrary and pseudo-apocalyptic negation, more than a displacement of one's death wish onto the other, a blind aggression against the other—implicitly aims at reconciliation with its target, then the hardening of differences into irreconcilability signals that activist criticality is no longer a "progressive," viable approach to social conflict. If contradiction has become a principle of social "conservation" and determination, criticality can no longer work through contradiction. This perverse social and cultural stabilization—"inflation"—of contradiction in postmodernism can be regarded as an ironical apotheosis of the unconscious bourgeois belief that the "difference" between itself and all other classes can and will be overcome, but on its own terms: everyone will eventually become bourgeois, creating a homogeneous society in which the lowest common denominator conception of life will be elevated as ideal. (Supplying this conception and performing this elevation is the task of popular culture.) This is certainly one ironical way of avoiding "catastrophic" revolution, maintaining the status quo, and trivializing activist criticality as beyond the pale—marginal in the extreme. It is a major way of de-legitimatizing critical difference in general and muting activist criticality in either its conservative or anarchistic forms.[16] The inflationary, contradictory use of the term 'postmodernism' reflects this bourgeois hypostatization of irreconcilability and the simultaneous falsification of reconciliation. This theoretical as well as social and cultural triumph of the bourgeois is more than a class or ideological victory; it is a "metaphysical" triumph.

II. THE CURE CALLED POSTMODERNISM

The term 'postmodern' implies contradiction of the modern without transcendence of it. This is, I take it, what Jean-François Lyotard means when he writes that "the postmodern . . . is undoubtedly a part of the modern."[17] Clearly, part of the identity problem of postmodernism is to identify the modern. Instead, postmodernism has reified the problem of identity, absolutizing identity crisis, as it were. Postmodernism implies not simply that it is difficult but impossible and *unnecessary* to achieve what Heinz Kohut calls a core self,[18] primitive "integrity," or what Schulte-Sasse calls "a homogeneous, fortified identity."[19] This is the import of the postmodernist argument about—one is tempted to say advocacy of—schizophrenia.[20] It is the one area of consensus in postmodernist theory. At the same time, postmodernism shows itself to be violently nostalgic for the various avant-garde strategies of achieving integrity. These range from the techniques of aggressive alienation as described by Renato Poggioli[21] and as summarized by Jürgen Habermas in his statement that "modernity lives on the experience of rebelling against all that is normative"[22] to Lyotard's view that the postmodern is the neo-sublime of unpresentability, namely, a neo-estheticism in the form of neo-experimentalism.[23] Habermas, in spite of himself, is a postmodernist, or at least he faces a postmodernist issue, in addressing the problem of legitimation—and its distorted mirror image, i.e. Peter Bürger's notion is that the avant-garde is an attempt to re-integrate art and life by overcoming estheticism.[24] Postmodernism is in the contradictory position of yearning for the perhaps insane and ineffective rebellious integrity of the avant-garde—the tragic idealism of its activist criticality—and repudiating it. This is the essence of its, and unconsciously bourgeois society's, identity problem.

As I have emphasized, postmodernist theory is in a double bind: it acknowledges the social assimilation of the avant-garde as another cultural institution[25]—as noted, another bourgeois entertainment—and its dissemination in the schizophrenic field of society, yet it still clings to a belief in activist criticality that can only derive from the avant-garde. This condition of contradiction—which as I have suggested is as stable as contradiction in bourgeois society—signifies activist criticality's condition of social and cultural impasse, which is most succinctly articulated in the impasse of the self facing the problem of its own integrity. From a postmodernist perspective—which supposedly transcends pessimism and optimism—this problem is passé; yet on the individual level it is experienced as pressing, and the postmodernists indirectly acknowledge it in their theory of the individual as a schizophrenic "center" displaced by messages passing through it. The most significant aspect of postmodernist thinking—as exemplified by Habermas, who as I have suggested is more postmodernist than he realizes—is its insistence that the only way out of this impasse of activist criticality and self-criticality, the only way to establish a critical/activist relationship to society and to find a ground for personal integrity (reconciling these pressing needs or rather denying their inseparability), is through acceptance of intersubjectivity. That alone leads to critically significant individuality and social activism. The modernist rebel and experimenter refused the condition of intersubjectivity, which postmodernism embraces.

In summary, postmodernism has a double dimension: (1) desperate clinging to obsolete modes of hyper-individualistic yet conventionalized or institutionalized criticality (e.g., in the pseudo-rebel/hero of the rock world); and (2) recognition that the *locus vivendi* of activist criticality and sophisticated integrity is at once cognitive and empathic acceptance of intersubjectivity, with all its problems. In fact, the transition from the paradigm of modernist subjective consciousness to that of postmodernist intersubjectivity advocated by Habermas has been thoroughly worked out in psychoanalytic theory's transition from drive theory to interpersonalist and object-relations theory.[26] Above all, as I will maintain, with the empathic as the conduit for the cognitive—something that the historian of postmodern architecture, rather than its cultural interpreter, recognizes as a general truth of postmodernist intentionality. (Psychoanalysis has long since been postmodernist; whatever pockets of modernist thinking about the subject remain have been integrated into a postmodernist intersubjectivist perspective. I mention this because I will use postmodernist psychoanalytic concepts in order to understand what is basically at stake in postmodernist architecture.)

The difference between the two sides of postmodernism—and the correct (essentially psychosocial or intersubjectivist) interpretation of its critical/activist dimension—can be made transparently clear by contrasting a cultural theorist's with an art historian's understanding of the critical/activist character of postmodernist architecture. As Linda Hutcheon, the theorist, remarks, architecture is "the one art form in which the label [postmodern] seems to refer, uncontested, to a generally agreed upon corpus of works."[27] For Hutcheon, postmodern architecture has an unequivocally "parodic relation to the art of the past."[28] This is a supposedly critical—rather then merely parasitic—relationship: "It contests uniformity by parodically asserting ironic difference instead of either homogeneous identity or alienated otherness."[29] (The former is the normative bourgeois conception of identity, the latter the avant-garde conception, both are supposedly quaintly modernist.) The key word here is "contest," which echoes Lyotard's notion of "agonistics"[30]: without it, there is no criticality. As Hutcheon says, "contemporaneity need not signify wholesale implication without critical consciousness."[31] For her, there is a double aspect to postmodernist criticality in general: the return to the past (presumably the passive element in it), and the return to it in a parodic way (where the parodic is a way of avoiding sentimentality or directionless and speechless nostalgia, and is thus presumably the active element in it). The postmodernist return to the past is generally critical of modernism, with its presumed repudiation of the past. And the parodic relation to the past is particularly critical, for the return does not mean that one is taken in by the past, but rather that one maintains a "critical" distance from it. And to what point? Hutcheon has nothing to say about this. Parody shows that one is not taken in by the past, not really sympathetic to it, and recognizes that it is not really "appropriate" to the present. Then why bother with it? "Just as modernism (oedipally) had to reject historicism and to pretend to a parthenogenetic birth fit for the new machine age, so postmodernism, in reaction, returned to history, to what I want to call 'parody,' to give architecture back its traditional social and historical dimension, though with a new twist this time."[32] Is this just another swing of the pendulum, the inevitable return and recycling of the past that is repressed in collective modern memory?

What does this complex postmodernist criticality—the return to the past, the parodic distance from it—really amount to? As Hutcheon presents them, both the return and its parody are superficial, gratuitous, seemingly self-reflexive acts of art. Where the medium of self-reflexivity was the material medium in modernist art, in postmodernist art it is presumably conceptual—the way of conceptualizing the past, more generally history, including the history of the present. But is the reconceptualization of the past—the establishing of a new critical/activist relation to it—accomplished by this kind of mechanical reversal of the modernist orientation and the emptily ironical, purely esthetic parodying of the past, as Hutcheon presents this re-orientation to the past? Both the "reaction" and the "twist" as she understands them seem to serve no other purpose than to afford the postmodernist architect the narcissistic self-satisfaction of cleverly asserting "critical difference" from the modernist architect. They are almost foreordained moves in the game of history, the first making them gain the prestige of knowing how to play the game—understanding the timing crucial to playing it. If there is anything truly revolutionary in the postmodernist giant step toward history and the small parodic step away from it, it has been lost in Hutcheon's treatment of the steps as esthetically experimental. For her, they are implicitly the latest way of generating artistic novelty in a critically credible way. For all her insistence on the criticality of the return to history and the use of parody, she shows this trivial criticality as having no other point than to celebrate itself. It may be "reductive" to think, as Hutcheon writes, "that any recall of the past must, by definition, be sentimental nostalgia," but it is also reductive of criticality to think that the parodic "ambiguity and irony" that result from "echoing history and its multivalent meanings" is its postmodernist essence.[33] On the contrary, the parodic is criticality deadended in itself, smugly lost in the labyrinth of its own knowing subtlety—criticality with no other purpose than to score points in a game of solitaire, to play that nostalgic game of Trivia called "ironic references."[34] The parodic is modernist ambiguity and irony reduced to the purposeless cunning of a generalized reason.

It never occurs to Hutcheon that there may be other reasons than esthetically ingratiating, cannibalistic, didactic ones for returning to the past and establishing what she mistakenly interprets as a parodic relationship to it. In fact, hidden behind the self-importance of the parodic return to the past, there is an attempt to achieve some kind of intimate relationship to it. Postmodernist architecture attempts to appropriate the past not as a dead, over-estheticized form but as a living, symbolic substance, charged with contemporary significance—which is the only way the past can remain viable. The return to the past is in effect a criticism of the present's lack of integrity, and is in purpose motivated by an effort to recover that integrity in symbolic form. For authentic postmodernism, the past represents lost integrity, the "home" the subject no longer inhabits but still yearns for, namely its own sanity and general good. The past is re-enacted less in the spirit of parody than of empathy, however incomplete. Pre-emptively to interpret the postmodernist appropriation of the past as parodic—a kind of witty "off" parroting of it—is to ignore the latent empathic reasons for seeking out a relationship to it, trying to establish a kind of introspective relationship with it. That empathy may miss the full reality of that past—and may be a form of knowing mystification to some—but this reality always exists archaeologically, through its reified information-signs and ideal constructs.

Is the inflationary, contradictory use of the term "postmodernism" a reverberation from this empathic use of the past for the purposes of achieving an elusive contemporary integrity? Does it perhaps signal the difficulties of using the past as a weapon against contemporary schizophrenia or lack of subjective cohesion? Does it register the difficulty of using the past intersubjectively? Is the reluctance of cultural theorists to accept this intersubjective, empathic use of the past as a symbol of integrity—the "true self" hidden under the contemporary "false self," in D. W. Winnicott's sense of these terms[35]—responsible for the inflationary, contradictory use of the term "postmodernism"? Will such empathic searching always seem inflationary and contradictory—overreaching and unstable—from the perspective of theoretical purity? This search constitutes the critical/activist content and intentionality of postmodernism at its best.

Pure theorists are ashamed of and refuse to admit the contemporary emotional needs that motivate the postmodernist return to the past. They have in effect estheticized and emotionally sanitized critical/activist theory—removed its psychological aspect. But some art historians are ready to admit it, if indirectly. They implicitly acknowledge that postmodernism makes the past contemporary by using it to satisfy living needs symbolically. They realize the peculiar character of postmodernism's intimacy with the past—in effect a testing of its potential for symbolizing the integrity absent in the present, of making good the bad present environment[36]—and that its critical activism exists through this testing.

For them, genuinely "postmodernist" criticality is an effort to solve the problem of modernity, the problem that, it is now realized, the aggressive rebellion or antinormativeness and alienation from intersubjectivity that avant-garde activist criticality signalled. It is the problem of the apparent impossibility of achieving integrity according to existing psychosocial norms, and yet it is a felt need *for* the integrity *without* the destruction of the intersubjective matrix of society. Under the auspices of this postmodernist articulation of the felt, pressing need for integrity—for cohesion in the face of a schizophrenic, idly pluralistic world—modernist rebellion can now be understood as an attack against the character-types that bourgeois society proposes as models to be followed. From the postmodernist art-historical perspective, the so-called nostalgia of postmodernism shows that an element of profound psychological pathos—misunderstood by the parodic interpretation of postmodernist criticality—is operational in the postmodernist manipulation of fragments of past styles. What appears to be parodic is in fact a loose and limited allegorical attempt to integrate sign-fragments of the past in a way that makes contemporary emotional sense. It is an effort to give a sense of dialectical inevitability to their relationship, as though their contemporary presence could only be explained by the fact that their reconciliation was imminent. There is no actual statement of reconciliation, only its proposal or rehearsal, as it were—no actual integrity, but its intimation. The amalgamation of historical styles is in part that of a constellation in the sky, in part that of a confederation of states.

Postmodernism thus represents an expanded sense of the possibilities of the past. Cognition of the art-historical past is worked through to an empathic relationship to it. There is the gold of integrity in the empathy itself. Integrity is, as it were, prosthetically achieved through this narcissistic appropriation of the past, in effect a combination of mirror and idealizing transferences to it.[37] The appropriation of classicism in Charles Moore's Piazza d'Italia in New Orleans (1976) does not parodically empty it, as Hutcheon thinks, but in fact establishes an empathic intimacy with it—no doubt ironic from the perspective of a professional classicist or fan of popular culture—and thereby gives it a special kind of fullness and accessibility, or usefulness.

The architectural historian Heinrich Klotz is closer to an understanding of the emotional gains of postmodernist appropriation of the architectural past than Linda Hutcheon. One can regard Klotz's approach as "conservative" rather than "radical" if one wishes, but that is to miss the critical import. Klotz calls attention to the "playful and humorous" character of Moore's postmodern architecture: "here the sonorous sound of the all-powerful no longer speaks, but the wit of the human-all-too-human." What was dismissed as unserious by modernism—"human license"—is once again allowed.[38] For Klotz, postmodernist architecture has something to say about the condition of being human—the creative play inherent in being human. Integrity is realized through this play.[39]

Postmodernist architecture is not intent upon exclusivity and strict consequence, but is prepared for difficult compromises and proposes daring connections. It advocates . . . the fullness of life, not the orthodoxy of dogma. The "revolutionaries," who broke completely with history in the name of a new age, are today "revisionists" who have the dangerous purpose of reconciliation. They want to combine the memory of the long past with the pathos of innovation. . . . Revision is the third way between conservativism and revolution, which we would like to advertise as the term—already one of abuse—for "postmodern." We presuppose that an abundance of the achievements of the modern are still valid, and we presuppose that an abundance of the dogmatic, rigidified teachings of the modern are untenable. . . . Radically new, standing in sharp contrast to the program of the modern, is the demand for an architecture that no longer proclaims the abstraction of pure geometric form, but instead the diverse forms that are used to mediate contents and messages, that is, an architecture that again permits the pictorial and the imagistic [*Bildhaften und Abbildhaften*], decoration and ornament, symbol and sign.[40]

It is appropriate that architecture, the most public of arts, once again openly serve human needs—the need of being human—and that it resist the tendencies of modernist architecture to annihilate all traces of humanness. Clearly, for Klotz, postmodernist architecture at its best is an attempt to counteract the annihilative anxiety that haunts contemporary bourgeois society.[41] Where the modernist building was the metaphor for the modern ideal of robotic man,[42] the postmodernist building is an attempt to make buildings once again like essentially organic human beings, however integrated with the machine. Freud has remarked on the uncanny effect of certain automata that seem human, suggesting that certain human beings operate automatically.[43] While not denying the machine presence in contemporary life, postmodernist architecture is an attempt to restore the human to predominance. The compromises and reconciliations it proposes, from the return to decoration (inseparable from the notion of improving decor or environment) and ornament (once thought of as a "necessary accident" of human existence[44]), to the symbolizing and signing of historical human presence, are all indications of the postmodernist path to integrity of self.

The fact that an irreversible intersubjectivity is suggested by the "theatrical" turn to history, in the form of remembered architectural styles, is perhaps the most dynamic part of postmodernism. Postmodernist architecture suggests that it is never possible to be an integral subject without remembering the intersubjectivity of the past. In this sense, it is a kind of healing of the wound modernist architecture gave to the human beings who inhabited it by asking them to forget everything but the present. Modernist architecture functioned like the commissar of a brave new world ruthlessly liquidating all traces of the old worlds that once existed. Now this mechanistic inhumanity is itself eliminated as criminal by postmodernist architecture. This is correlate with the assimilation of the technological revolution that inspired modernist architecture. In however strange a way—and that it is often an apparently comic way suggests that there was a tragic aspect to the old modernist architecture—postmodernist architecture struggles to articulate a sense of human self that, while appropriate to the present, takes its cues from older statements of humanness which it struggles to remember. These become its sources. In its encyclopaedic, quasi-museumlike character, postmodernist architecture shows a hunger for old ideas of authenticity. It is like Hamlet with Yorick's skull, in search of a half-familiar, half-forgotten truth about human existence. Until it finds that truth, it remains a demonstration that there is more in the heaven of art than modernism imagined in its philosophy.

NOTES

1. Jochen Schulte-Sasse, "Modernity and Modernism, Postmodernity and Postmodernism: Framing The Issue," *Cultural Critique*, 5 (Winter, 1986–87), p. 6.
2. Charles Newman argues as much in *The Post-Modern Aura: The Act of Fiction in an Age of Inflation* (Evanston, Ill.: Northwestern University Press, 1985). For Newman, "climax inflation" characterizes postmodernism, suggesting that the inflation of contradiction, resulting in irreparable social and personal fragmentation—apparent loss of even the possibility of cohesion—is another climax of bourgeois overexpansion.
3. I am suggesting that the feeling of impotence latent in bourgeois society has finally caught up with its critics, the intellectuals who have formulated the critical theory of postmodernism and who are themselves bourgeois. I would even go so far as to say that critical activism as such is an effort to fight off and overcome this feeling of impotence—at least of extreme vulnerability generated by the rationalized anonymity of the bourgeois system, among other factors inseparable from it. Especially does the general existence of seemingly

unresolvable contradictions on every front of bourgeois activity undermine the sensitive intellectual from within, generating that peculiar kind of despair called criticality. But the feeling of impotence is as unconscious as the critical activism is conscious. As Erich Fromm writes in "Zum Gefühl der Ohnmacht," *Zeitschrift für Sozialforschung* (Paris, 1937), p. 96, "Bourgeois man, in contrast to certain types of religious individual, is usually not conscious of the feeling of impotence." Later, Fromm modified his psychosocial theory by arguing that the feeling of impotence was less the response of the authoritarian character in search of symbiotic stability and submissive unity with a surrogate parent than a narcissistic response to an annihilative danger. This accords well with my interpretation of the rationale for postmodernism's conception of criticality, which in general follows Fromm's theory. In *Escape From Freedom* (New York: Farrar & Rinehart, 1941), p. 172, Fromm argues that the need for power is the expression of impotence, a "desperate attempt to gain secondary strength where genuine strength is lacking." Criticality is secondary strength at its best. But the climactic contradictions of bourgeois society sap everyone's genuine strength, so that critical activism in bourgeois society is as close to genuine strength as it is possible to come in bourgeois society. At the same time, postmodernist criticality inflates—re-empowers—an obsolete modernist idea of criticality in response to the climactic contradictions of bourgeois society, which make critical intellectuals feel irreparably impotent.

4. For a summary of the debate see Richard Rorty, "Habermas, Lyotard et le postmodernité," *Critique* 442 (1979; March 1984), pp. 181–97. Jean-François Lyotard's critique of Habermas appears in *The Postmodern Condition: A Report on Knowledge* (Minneapolis: University of Minnesota Press, 1984), pp. 71–82.
5. Lyotard, *The Postmodern Condition*, p. 77.
6. I am here mockingly following Lyotard, p. 81.
7. In *An Autobiographical Study* (1925; New York: W. W. Norton, 1963), p. 126, Sigmund Freud describes "the principle of 'the omnipotence of thoughts'" as "the overestimation of the importance of psychical reality." Karl Abraham pointed out that omnipotence of thought meant the unconscious belief that to think something was to make it happen, or that it was the case.
8. Sigmund Freud, *Totem and Taboo* (1913; New York, W. W. Norton, 1950), p. 190:

   In only a single field of our civilization has the omnipotence of thoughts been retained, and that is in the field of art. Only in art does it still happen that man who is consumed by desires performs something resembling the accomplishment of those desires and that what he does in play produces emotional effects—thanks to artistic illusion—just as though it was something real. People speak with justice of the "magic of art" and compare artists to magicians. But the comparison is perhaps more significant than it claims to be. There can be no doubt that art did not begin as art for art's sake. It worked in the service of impulses which for the most part are extinct today. And among them we may suspect the presence of many magical purposes.

   From this point of view, postmodernist criticality is a magical attempt to produce emancipatory emotional effects in its intellectual advocates.
9. In "primary narcissism" the libido of the child is completely self-directed, not yet extending to objects in the external world, which occurs with maturity. "Secondary narcissism" is a response to pathological conditions. The libido detaches itself from external objects and reattaches itself exclusively to the self. See Sigmund Freud, "On Narcissism: An Introduction," *Standard Edition*, XIV. See also Freud, *Totem and Taboo*, pp. 88–90.
10. See Frederic Jameson, "Postmodernism and Consumer Society," *The Anti-Aesthetic*, ed. Hal Foster (Port Townsend, Wash.: Bay Press, 1983), pp. 113–4, for the distinction between pastiche and parody, and the argument for the dominance of the former in contemporary bourgeois culture. Jameson yearns for parody in what he takes to be a cultural situation of pastiche, but which others see as a special form of parody.
11. Lyotard, *The Postmodern Condition*, pp. 79–80, formulates the distinction as that between an avant-garde mode which shows "nostalgia for presence felt by the human subject, on the obscure and futile will which inhabits him in spite of everything" and the avant-garde mode which emphasizes "the power of the faculty [of presentation] to conceive, on its 'inhumanity,' so to speak . . . whether or not human sensibility or imagination can

match what it conceives" (the mode of "invention of new rules of the game"). It is the difference between the mode of melancholy and the mode of deconstruction—between "the German Expressionists, and on the side of *novatio*, [the Cubism of] Braque and Picasso." Ever since Lyotard has made his distinction, it has been unthinkingly parroted, until the melancholy mode has been understood to be naively compensatory—a typical Marxist diminishment of psychologically oriented art—and the deconstructivist mode elevated as the only critically significant, genuinely activist one. Nonetheless, Schulte-Sasse, who accepts the valorization of the polarity, has the courage to admit ("Modernity and Modernism . . . ," p. 8) that even the "mode of deconstructive *novatio*" may fall victim to the nostalgia of melancholy, namely, "mesmerizing fascination with what already exists, viewing it as the only epistemologically relevant object." This is a prelude to institutionalization, and indeed, as Schulte-Sasse acknowledges, the mode of deconstructive *novatio* has become another institutionalized avant-garde discourse. What he fails to acknowledge is that in a situation of total administrative control of the avant-garde, correlate with a situation of bourgeois hypostatization of contradiction—which can be conceived in terms of T. W. Adorno's notion of "hyper-modernism" (*Aesthetic Theory* (London: Routledge & Kegan Paul, 1984), p. 22)—that is, a situation in which dissonance approximates to consonance or irreconcilability to reconciliation, the mode of melancholy may be more to the psychosocial point than the mode of deconstructive *novatio*. The latter mode plays into the hands of a bourgeois system which uses novelty to generate contradiction—which needs deconstruction to create the novelties that overthrow all that has hitherto been presented, thus establishing the convergence of permanent contradiction and permanent revolution. The psychosocial point made by the mode of melancholy is that of endurance in the face of an unendurable world— endurance, as Freud remarked, being the first obligation of the self to itself. (Under circumstances of extreme social contradiction, the melancholy (lonely) integration of the self, assuring its endurance, can be a revolutionary act in itself. Endurance is most revolutionary when the world has become most banal, that is, banally contradictory and self-contradictory—priding itself on its bourgeois administration of its contradictions.) No doubt this also turns into an obligation to the world. But so does the revolution-generating mode of deconstruction, with its endlessly artificial novelties, which serve the world without offering any integration—however melancholy—that can resist it. In line with this, psychoanalytically speaking the deconstructivist mode looks like a manic defense for the avoidance of melancholy (sense of death, tragedy, negativity, chaos) which the Germans articulate through their Expressionistic mode. See D. W. Winnicott, "The Manic Defence," *Collected Papers, Through Paediatrics to Psycho-analysis* (London: Tavistock, 1958), p. 132.

It is worth noting that Lyotard's view of German Expressionism ultimately derives from Georg Lukács's "Grösse und Verfall' des Expressionismus" (1934), which describes it as a "qualitative increase in the sense of loss and despair" in capitalistic society, resulting from the petit-bourgeois individual's "impatient submission" [*Unterordnung*] to capitalism. Ernst Bloch's response to Lukács, in Bloch's "Diskussionen über Expressionismus" (1938), suggests an alternative conception, which I subscribe to: "But perhaps Lukács's reality . . . is not objective . . . perhaps genuine reality [totality] is also collapse [*Unterbrechung*]. Because Lukács has a closed objectivist conception of reality he turns against every artistic attempt, such as Expressionism, to articulate the world view of the broken (even if it is also the world view of capitalism)." Lukács, in other words, cannot give the subjective sense of vulnerability and impotence its full due because he has a narrow objectivist sense of the self as objectively determined and either mechanically reactionary or revolutionary in import. Thus, he cannot see the personal revolutionary potential in the feeling of impotence—cannot see that it may lead to a criticality that can transform society from within. Both quotations are from Paul Raabe, *Expressionismus: Der Kampf um eine literarische Bewegung* (Munich: DTV, 1965), pp. 264, 289.

12. Philip Rieff, *The Triumph of the Therapeutic* (New York: Harper & Row, 1966), makes this point decisively, if in psycho-philosophical terms.

13. Schulte-Sasse, "Modernity and Modernism . . . ," p. 9, points out that modernist aesthetic practice involves an "institutionally al-

14. ways already achieved . . . defusion of . . . oppositional figurations, a transformation of their critical content into nostalgic, utopian images which reconcile the opposition in an imaginary mode." This holds as much for the deconstructive mode as the melancholy mode.
14. Linda Hutcheon, "The Politics of Postmodernism: Parody and History," *Cultural Critique*, 5 (Winter 1986–87), p. 184.
15. Lyotard, *The Postmodern Condition*, pp. 14–17, especially his assertion "that each of us knows that our *self* does not amount to much" (p. 15), which confirms the psychoanalytic view of diminished self-esteem—reflecting self-fragmentation—as the major pathology of the time. It may be true, as Lyotard says, that while the self does not amount to much, it "exists in a fabric of relations that is now more complex and mobile than ever before," and that it is "always located at 'nodal points' of specific communication circuits" (p. 15), but this itself seems to confirm the absence of primary relations and self-supportive communication. What Daniel Stern, *The Interpersonal World of the Child* (Cambridge, Mass.: Harvard University Press, 1983) calls the "sense of self" and what Heinz Kohut, in *The Analysis of the Self* (New York: International Universities Press, 1971) and *The Restoration of the Self* (New York: International Universities Press, 1977), calls the archaic narcissistic self—necessities of specifically human being—are not addressed by Lyotard's view of the self, which in fact confirms the diminished sense of self in administered bourgeois society.
16. In *The Philosophical Discourse of Modernity* (Cambridge, Mass.: MIT Press, 1987), pp. 3–5, Jürgen Habermas distinguishes between the "*neoconservative* leave-taking from modernity" and the "farewell to modernity" represented by the "aesthetically inspired anarchism"—a "revolt against it once again"—under whose sign postmodernity marches. Both modes of postmodernist critical activism are branches on the same tree of critical individualism from the bourgeois perspective, and as such confirm and reinforce the triumph of the bourgeois idea of "sameness with a difference." The question, of course, is whether Habermas's own advocacy of intersubjectivity in the name of communicative competence does not do the same.
17. Lyotard, *The Postmodern Condition*.
18. Kohut, *The Restoration of the Self*, passim. See especially chapter 2, "Does Psychoanalysis Need a Psychology of the Self?"
19. Schulte-Sasse, "Modernity and Modernism . . . ," p. 13.
20. The argument for postmodernist schizophrenia is presented at its most concentrated in Jameson, "Postmodernism and Consumer Society," pp. 118–22, and even more succinctly in Jean Baudrillard, "The Ecstasy of Communication," *The Anti-Aesthetic*, pp. 132–3. It ultimately derives from Gilles Deleuze and Félix Guattari, *Anti-Oedipus: Capitalism and Schizophrenia* (1972; Minneapolis: University of Minnesota, 1983). From a psychiatric point of view, it involves a preposterous misunderstanding and misappropriation of the concept of schizophrenic pathology—a facile application of it to advanced capitalist society.
21. See Renato Poggioli, *The Theory of the Avant-Garde* (New York: Harper & Row, 1971), pp. 25–42 for an analysis of avant-gardism as a dialectic moving from activism to antagonism to nihilism to agonism.
22. Jürgen Habermas, "Modernity—An Incomplete Project," *The Anti-Aesthetic*, p. 5.
23. Lyotard, *The Postmodern Condition*, pp. 71, 81.
24. Peter Bürger, *Theory of the Avant-Garde* (Minneapolis: University of Minnesota Press, 1984).
25. Jameson, "Postmodernism and Consumer Society," pp. 111–2, discusses some of the details of this assimilation, showing how even the anti-authoritarian avant-garde acquires social authority and legitimacy, and becomes the preferred object of authoritarian desire—the basis of a new authoritarian character.
26. See Jay R. Greenberg and Stephen A. Mitchell, *Object Relations in Psychoanalytic Theory* (Cambridge, Mass.: Harvard University Press, 1983).
27. Hutcheon, "The Politics of Postmodernism," p. 180.
28. Ibid., p. 179.
29. Ibid., p. 183. See also p. 185, n. 18 for Hutcheon's criticism of Jameson's concept of parody. "Contemporaneity," says Hutcheon, "need not signify wholesale implication without critical consciousness," as Jameson seems to think. Hutcheon in general points out the misguided nature of Jameson's characterization of postmodernism, which supposedly derived "from architectural debates," followed from Jameson's own [Marxist] odd angle.

30. Lyotard, *The Postmodern Condition*, pp. 10–16. Thus aggression is brought back in the sublimated form of contesting language games and the power of messages to "displace what traverses them." Roland Barthes also uses this supposedly post-Freudian view of aggression, but one which involves death-wishing and death-dealing as much as its Freudian source.
31. Hutcheon, "The Politics of Postmodernism," p. 185.
32. Ibid.
33. Ibid., p. 192.
34. Ibid., p. 193.
35. D. W. Winnicott, "Ego Distortion in Terms of True and False Self" (1960), *The Maturational Processes and the Facilitating Environment* (New York: International Universities Press, 1965), pp. 140–52. According to Winnicott the false self is compliant yet through its compliance protective of the true self, which may be unknown or incommunicado. From this point of view, postmodernist architecture seeks out the true self hidden in the false historical styles of past self. This incommunicado self becomes the core of the contemporary true self.
36. Winnicott, "Ego Distortion . . . ," pp. 145–6 points out that the initial good-enough environment is the good-enough mother. However, the need for a good-enough, facilitating environment never diminishes throughout life, although one may become increasingly hardened to—superficially tolerant of—the variety of bad-enough environments, emotional and physical, which exist in the lifeworld. That is, one may develop a strong reality principle. From this point of view, the postmodernist pursuit of integrity through the past—a very indirect and on face value absurd, futile route—suggests the unconscious recognition that the present bourgeois environment will never be good-enough, that is, it will always subject one to new, increasingly inhuman, contradictions. The present is unconsciously perceived as totally inhuman because it is realized that it can never overcome its contradictions.
37. Kohut, *The Analysis of the Self*, chapters 2, 5, 6
38. Heinrich Klotz, *Revision der Moderne: Postmoderne Architecture 1960–1980* (Munich: Prestel Verlag, 1984), p. 9. See also Klotz, *Moderne und Postmoderne, Architectur der Gegenwart, 1960–1980* (Braunschweig: Vieweg, 1984); Paolo Portoghesi, *After Modern Architecture* (New York: Rizzoli, 1982); and Charles Jencks, *The Language of Postmodern Architecture* (New York: Rizzoli, 1985; 2nd ed.) for similar approaches to postmodern architecture.
39. Winnicott, "The Manic Defence," p. 185 sees play as an instrument of the realization of the creative impulse, that is, the impulse to integrate.
40. Klotz, *Revision der Moderne*, p. 9.
41. Heinz Kohut, *How Does Analysis Cure?* (Chicago: University of Chicago Press, 1984), p. 16 regards "disintegration anxiety" not as anxiety about "physical extinction but loss of humanness: psychological death." Psychological death is what Lyotard describes when he speaks of the self counting for nothing, and of what is behind the postmodernist account of the schizophrenia of contemporary existence. Lyotard and other postmodernist theorists almost seem to advocate such psychological death or loss of humanness. But postmodernist practice, at least as it exists in architecture, represents a refusal to accept it.
42. Ludwig von Bertalanffy, *General System Theory* (New York: George Braziller, 1968), pp. 190–1 describes the dominance of the robot model of behavior in contemporary society.
43. Sigmund Freud, "The 'Uncanny'" (1919), *Studies in Para-Psychology* (New York: Collier Books, 1963), p. 31. From this point of view, the sense of false self comes from the experience of oneself as an automaton (robot, machine). Modernist architecture presumably encourages this robotic sense of self, while postmodernist architecture repudiates it through the "poetry" of past selves it implicitly articulates. Yet it also subsumes—puts in its proper place—the robotic/technocratic self of modernism.
44. See Ananda Coomaraswamy, "On Ornament," *Selected Papers*, vol. I (Princeton: Princeton University Press, 1977), p. 242 for an account of the "inner existential necessity" of ornament as a manifestation of humanness. For Coomaraswamy, it essentializes humanness into an attribute of a particular self—an attribute conferring personhood.

Feminism in Context: A Role for Feminist Theory in Aesthetic Evaluation

Peggy Zeglin Brand

This paper will explore virgin territory: the role of recent feminist theory of art within the analytic philosophical tradition of aesthetics.[1] There is, I believe, a great deal to be gained—for both feminists and philosophers—from a meeting of the minds. Feminists may learn that the straw man they have constructed (in order to be deconstructed) of a phallogocentric father-figure of philosophy is not altogether accurate.[2] Philosophers may find that feminists are voicing interesting and legitimate challenges to traditional philosophical traditions: challenges that are failing to be heard only because they are expressed in unfamiliar jargon. Mutually beneficial dialogue is possible only if each side listens to the other.

Section I will present a sampling of two "traditional" analytic philosophers who claim that a work of art can be aesthetically appreciated in isolation from its context; contextual theories of criticism may be useful, but only within limits. Such theories, like Marxism, Freudianism, and (presumably) feminism, are considered useful only for interpretation and not evaluation because they utilize factual data which is *external* to the aesthetic object. Feminist theory, however, wants to push for that point forbidden by tradition; Section II presents their side. Feminist theory advocates evaluation of a work of art by means of reference to information *outside*

the work of art—including the artist's intentions, the gender of artist and critic, and the level of awareness of gender issues of the sociohistorical framework surrounding the work of art and its reception. Section III is the voice of newly formulated philosophical contextual theories of art, such as those of Arthur Danto, George Dickie, and Marcia Eaton. This voice, though young and developing, is strong and dominating. It consistently fails, however, to take gender issues into account. My suggestion is that the feminist's and the philosopher's voices are in concert more so than either would like to admit. In Section IV, I will argue that feminist theory plays a role that is vital to contemporary discussions in aesthetics: As a second-order contextual theory of *criticism*, it is one type of contextual critical theory that naturally and necessarily follows upon current philosophical contextual theories of *art*.

I. TRADITIONAL AESTHETICS: STOLNITZ AND BEARDSLEY

Years ago Jerome Stolnitz provided an interesting analysis of art criticism in a text entitled *Aesthetics and Philosophy of Art Criticism: An Introduction*.[3] Stolnitz claimed that criticism—the talk about art—can have different, often interrelated functions; sometimes criticism is used to ascertain reasons for supporting value-judgments (evaluative criticism) and sometimes it is used simply to describe, explain, or clarify a work of art (inter-

---

Published with permission of the author.

pretive criticism). Writing in the 1950s, during the heyday of Abstract Expressionism and Abstract Formalism, Stolnitz was perhaps little aware that he was focusing on an aspect of the artistic enterprise that would become so encompassing and animated. He naively commented on the need for interpretive criticism, explaining that some works of art are difficult to understand immediately or appreciate fully without recourse to the enlightening words of the critic. This was said at a time when John Cage, Robert Rauschenberg, and the Minimalists were just beginning to gain and hold attention. He could hardly have predicted the role such criticism would play in the various arenas of literary criticism, art criticism, and aesthetics. Interpretive criticism, in the wake of New Criticism and formalist criticism, came to have a life of its own.

Stolnitz would hardly have approved of contemporary critics' emphasis on theory. He believed that one perceived a work aesthetically (grasping only what is immediately given *in* the work) while maintaining an aesthetic attitude: gratefully and submissively accepting and enjoying the work of art "for its own sake," "no questions asked," without challenge or criticism. Such is the substance of an aesthetic experience. Such experiences give rise to appreciation and aesthetic evaluation, embodied in statements like, "This is a good work of art," or "This work is uglier than that work of art." Only when a viewer has given up the aesthetic attitude to adopt a critical attitude does the work become something to be "probed, analyzed, and wrangled over":[4] activities which give rise to the talk about art (i.e., art criticism). As stated earlier, one of the functions of criticism is to provide reasons that support aesthetic value-judgments. The interesting aspect to be investigated (for our purposes) is the *interaction* of these two types of activities: aesthetic valuing and the criticism used as reasons for those values. Stolnitz seems to be speaking inconsistently, at times, when he simultaneously holds that criticism can enhance the appreciation of a work of art and criticism is irrelevant to the appreciation of a work of art. Let us review his ideas in order to become clear on this apparent inconsistency.

Stolnitz insists on two requirements for criticism, namely, that it illuminate (via interpretation) our understanding of the work of art and that it provide workable criteria of evaluation. Within the two basic types of criticism differentiated by *function* (interpretive and evaluative), several kinds of criticism are differentiated by means of their emphases on various aspects of the work. For example, some criticism might emphasize the origins of the work (what he calls contextual criticism and a subspecies, intentionalist criticism), some might emphasize the effects of the work (impressionist criticism), and some might emphasize the intrinsic structure of the work (New Criticism).

Among the several kinds of criticism analyzed by Stolnitz, one kind expanded on at length is collectively called contextual criticism. Included among the general category of contextual criticism are Marxian and Freudian criticism, which stress the origins and effects of the work: its social, historical, and psychological contexts. Contextual criticism, it should be noted at the outset, though praised as *sometimes* extremely helpful in providing interpretive criticism, is also highly suspect: "It should not be permitted to swamp or distort aesthetic evaluation."[5] Stolnitz believes that contextual criticism can provide relevant and informative contextual-factual data with regard to subject matter and content but fails in attending to the purely artistic elements (aesthetic data) of form and medium.

Contextual criticism also fails to provide workable criteria of evaluation. Stolnitz takes issue with contextualist critics for failing to stop at the appropriate boundary (i.e., with the task of interpretation) and for presuming to be qualified to move from the activity of interpreting to the activity of evaluating. Here they commit the fallacy of transforming the concepts used to *describe* the work into concepts used to *judge* the work. In Stolnitz's words, "factual-contextual concepts are converted into criteria of evaluation."[6] As a result, Stolnitz holds these judgments to be *moral* and not aesthetic; thus they are useless in assessing the work aesthetically. Contextual criticism only sometimes fulfills Stolnitz's first requirement (that of illuminating our understanding of the work of art) and completely fails to fulfill the second (that of providing workable criteria of evaluation).

Here we come upon the resolution to the apparent inconsistency of Stolnitz's views on the role of critical evaluation: Stolnitz is really claiming that only *some* forms of criticism enhance aesthetic appreciation. Some interpretive criticism can provide knowledge that enables us to see more in a work of art, thereby enhancing one's aesthetic experience, and some can provide knowledge that causes us to devaluate a work. Similarly, some evaluative criticism can sometimes enhance appreciation and, alternatively, some evaluative criticism distorts or obliterates aesthetic evaluation. One type of evaluative criticism that distorts or obliterates aesthetic evaluation is contextual criticism. Thus Stolnitz is arguing that only certain kinds of criticism are acceptable as evaluative criticism—namely, only noncontextual criticism. Stolnitz's argument can be reconstructed as follows:

1. Aesthetic judgments utilize knowledge of internal data.
2. Moral judgments utilize knowledge of external data.
3. Either aesthetic judgments or moral judgments determine aesthetic value.
4. Moral judgments determine only moral value (i.e., they are irrelevant for determining aesthetic value).
5. Therefore, only aesthetic judgments determine aesthetic value.

Premises (1) and (2) list two types of value judgments, each of which requires support from evaluative criticism. They are distinguished by the type of data utilized by the person making the judgment and the function they serve. Stolnitz stipulates in (1) that only knowledge about the intrinsic, noncontextual aspects of the work is used in making an aesthetic judgment. The use of any other type of data (i.e., contextual-factual data that are external to the work of art "on its own" and "for its own sake") is external or extrinsic to the work. He writes,

The "context" of the work of art includes the circumstances in which the work originated, its effects upon society, and, in general, all of the relations and interactions of the work with other things, apart from its aesthetic life . . . the work, considered nonaesthetically, exists in a context.[7]

Contextual criticism (e.g., Freudian criticism) focuses on extrinsic, external factors—"all the elements which point beyond the work to 'life' "[8]—and *excludes* the intrinsic, internal, purely aesthetic considerations. These aesthetic considerations are seen to be the major constuent of the aesthetic object (i.e., they are what give rise to the aesthetic experience and are not to be glossed over, belittled, or ignored by the limited concerns of contextual criticism). Though often providing relevant and necessary factual information, contextual theories help us to understand and appreciate more fully only part of the aesthetic object. The "aesthetic life" of the work of art, on the other hand, is necessarily approached through aesthetic perception: "Aesthetic perception focuses upon the work itself, taken in isolation."[9] Similarly, the aesthetic attitude gives no thought to causes and consequences outside the object; in an aesthetic experience, the intrinsic aspects of the aesthetic object are experienced and appreciated "in isolation"—without recourse to any external considerations—in a vacuum devoid of any contextual air. Another traditionalist, Monroe C. Beardsley, contrasts the isolationist's approach to the contextualist's as follows:

Isolationism is the view that in order to appreciate a work of art, we need do nothing but look at it, hear it, or read it—sometimes again and again, with the most concentrated attention—and that we need not go outside it to consult the facts of history, biography, or anything else.
. . . contextualism holds that a work of art should be apprehended in its total context or setting, and that much historical and other knowledge "feeds into" the work of art, making the total experience of it richer than if it were approached without such knowledge.[10]

Beardsley, like Stolnitz, believes that moral judgments are judgments about the "side effects" of a work of art; they are not about a work's "immediate effect" (i.e., the aesthetic experience).[11]

Premise (3) reflects Stolnitz's and Beardsley's traditional view that only one type of judgment is relevant to a work of art's aesthetic value. In other words, one *can* appreciate a work of art fully enough without recourse to any contextual data. Certain contextual data yield moral judgments which are totally irrelevant to the determination or justification of aesthetic value.

Premise (4) embodies the traditional isolationist's reason for excluding moral judgments from the realm of aesthetic valuing: They are judgments that determine so-called moral value only. A basic underlying assumption is that moral value and aesthetic value are totally separate types of value that a work might possess and that traditional aesthetics is concerned primarily with aesthetic value; moral value is a distraction that a conscientious art viewer and theorist can best do without.

The conclusion (5), which states that only aesthetic judgments determine aesthetic value, follows from (3) and (4); it implies by means of (2) that knowledge of external data is not utilized in determining aesthetic value. It is this claim, namely, the conclusion (5), that I wish to argue against. Feminist theory will be the primary contextual theory I will use to argue against (5), but first I would like to point out a weakness in the isolationist's argument, one that I think was anticipated by Stolnitz and Beardsley both. It resides in premise (4)—in the isolationists' claim that moral judgments are irrelevant for determining aesthetic value.

At one point in arguing for (4), Beardsley presents Aestheticism and Moralism as views that point up the dichotomy of the moral and aesthetic aspects of art. Interestingly, he rejects Aestheticism as a fanatical reaction of "those, who, in their eagerness to exalt the arts, forget that they are after all human products of human activities, and must find their value in the whole context of human life."[12] He does not go on to explain the phrase "the whole context of human life." One is left guessing as to precisely what context of human life might be relevant to establishing value, as Beardsley proceeds to reject Moralism as well as Aestheticism.

Moralism is a point of view in which aesthetic objects are judged "solely, or chiefly, with respect to moral standards."[13] Moralists utilize two forms of argument by which they judge works. The first is the Argument from Reduction in which all critical evaluation is reduced to moral evaluation:

And so the whole, apparently aesthetic, question whether a particular aesthetic object is a good one or not is reduced to the (moral) question whether the feelings it arouses are good or bad.[14]

This argument is rejected because it fails to assess the separate and independent aesthetic value of a work. The second, less severe, form of argument is the Argument from Correlation by which Moralists grant the existence of a separate form of aesthetic value but make it dependent upon or correlated to moral value. In this view, a work of low moral value is necessarily a work of low aesthetic value. Beardsley is quick to reject this approach with regard to music and nonrepresentational visual art but seems less sure for cases of representational visual art, literature, and film. He cites pornography as an example of visual art that is low in both moral value and aesthetic value. He sees neither a *causal* nor a *necessary* connection between moral value and aesthetic value but admits to some "commonsense evidence to support here, in a rough way, the Argument from Correlation."[15]

Beardsley's failure to dismiss the Argument from Correlation implies a weakness in premise (4). If there is a possibility that the Argument from Correlation is at all plausible and that there is a possibility that contextual factors that determine so-called moral value are relevant in assessing the aesthetic value of a work of art, then the repercussion for traditional theories of aesthetic value is obvious: It is false to claim that aesthetic value is determined solely by internal/intrinsic factors by means of contemplation of the work in isolation.

Stolnitz wavers in his support of premise (4) as well. In discussing an example of a moral judgment of Marxist criticism, he claims that the moral evaluation (that the work is poor due to its failure to inspire social revolt) "also has an aesthetic side to it":

> Like some non-Marxist-critics, the Marxists contend that many of Ibsen's symbols are vague and unintelligible. This is a weakness in the aesthetic effectiveness of his plays. If this criticism can be shown to be sound, and if it is supported by the evidence of aesthetic experience, then it is, of course, aesthetically relevant. Again, however, the Marxist does not speak of "purely" aesthetic matters. He holds that Ibsen's symbolism illustrates the artist's "blurred and indefinite" social thinking.[16]

Stolnitz seems to be saying that the value judgment, "Ibsen's symbols are vague and unintelligible," is a value judgment which is based on legitimate internal data for the non-Marxist that becomes a *moral* value judgment when the Marxist extends the data utilized to noninternal, contextual data. Citing the mental state of the author as a reason for the evaluation automatically turns an aesthetic judgment into a moral judgment. But what can Stolnitz mean when he says that this moral judgment "also has an aesthetic side to it"? Could it possibly mean that moral judgments are not so strictly distinguishable from aesthetic judgments? If they are not, this weakens premise (4) in that the possibility is left open for a so-called moral judgment to determine aesthetic value as well as moral value.

In this section, the isolationist approach to a work of art was outlined as the approach of two recent traditional analytic aestheticians. This approach claims that all contextual data is irrelevant to aesthetic judgments of a work of art. In the next section, feminist theory will be presented as one example of a nontraditional approach; feminist theorists are contextualists who hold (contrary to the isolationists' conclusion [5]) that knowledge of external data can be relevant to determining aesthetic value.

II. CONTEXTUAL FEMINIST THEORY

Feminists writing about the arts claim that although barely two decades have elapsed, we are well beyond the first phase of feminist theorizing about the arts.[17] This first phase, labelled "the feminist critique" by Elaine Showalter,[18] sought to recapture the past by exposing numerous denigrating sterotypes of women in works by males, whether works of the visual arts or the literary arts. Another aspect of recapturing the past, what Showalter called "gynocritics," involved (re)discovering female authors and artists previously excluded from the canon and seeking the commonalities of female culture in various artistic modes of expression. In this process of discovery, feminist theorists began to seriously question the dominating ideology of the past which both erected and sustained what feminists regarded as an exclusively male canon (the "Great Masters"). In the process of deconstructing the foundations and myths of this canon, many disciplines, including art history, literature, and philosophy, came under fire. Feminists demanded to know how purportedly universal and objective criteria of aesthetic value could yield such a biased, subjective set of paradigms. Hence the present phase, marked by an obsessive interest in metacriticism and metatheory in which feminists attempt to construct an unprecedented alternative to the dominating male criteria of interpreting and evaluating art. It is nothing less than fitting that aestheticians pay some attention to these challenges to traditional modes of evaluating art, for when feminists dismantle the canon by rejecting what we've come to know as the greatest *master*pieces of all time, the entire notion of aesthetic value is at stake.

What is feminist theory? The answer is not always forthcoming from a feminist theorist since many hold that feminist theory, in virtue of being feminist and consciously attempting to avoid the mistakes of its phallocentric predecessors who thought defining a worthwhile and beneficial activity, is untheorizable. In spite of this push for open-endedness, feminists do fall into the old habit of characterizing—sometimes in intimate and laborious detail—the parameters and goals of a framework for interpreting and judging works of art in a new and unique way.

It might be helpful to piece together a characterization of feminist theory by first looking at the guiding principles of a feminist, in general. There is perhaps less hesitation to generalize what constitutes a feminist today in spite of the many factions that exist than there is in characterizing feminist theory; in 1980, one author proposed the following principles:

> Feminists are, at the very least, supposed to have committed themselves to such things as participation in consciousness-raising groups and nonhierarchical organization, . . . the inherent equality of the sexes (or the superiority of the female) and the enslavement of women as the root of all oppression.[19]

In other words, a feminist consciously strives to undo the wrongs of previous oppression as well as to prevent similar occurrences from happening in the future. Most feminists believe in *active* promotion of these principles and also believe that works of art can be an expressive and effective means of actively communicating such principles. Along the lines suggested by one philosopher, this would make feminist theory (which is based on these principles) *more* than just a theory—a theory is a system of belief or world view shared by its adherents—but once theory goes beyond advancing a world view to *prescribing* a way of life or certain actions, theory becomes ideology.[20] Feminist theory, like Marxist theory or Christianity, is not merely descriptive but also directive. As Lucy Lippard, feminist art critic and theorist, writes, "Feminism is an ideology, a value system, a revolutionary strategy, a way of life."[21]

Without reservation, some art created by women for other women or for men who need to learn the feminists' message about women, has been labelled "propaganda."[22] The term *propaganda* may ordinarily carry a negative connotation but it is defined rather neutrally as the propagation of ideas, doctrines, or practices. Women's art (art created by women) differs from feminist art (art self-consciously created or interpreted along the lines of a feminist ideology), but both can be means of disseminating feminist propaganda by means of typical artistic media.[23]

Feminist theory in its descriptive form, is similar to any other kind of theory; it is a world view or system of beliefs consisting of a formulation of apparent relationships or underlying principles of certain observed phenomena which has been confirmed to some degree. In its prescriptive form, it is not confirmable; ideologies are either practiced or not.

Basically, all works of art are subject to the dictum, "The personal is the political" (i.e., there is no nonpolitical, unbiased perspective). Beardsley might say (as he has said of Marxist principles of interpretation and evaluation) that feminists adhere to the Principle of Nonneutrality:

> The Marxist . . . judges all behavior with repect to a single goal, the advancement of the revolutionary proletariat toward a classless society . . . considerations of aesthetic value are to be subordinated to political ones, for—and this is the basic Marxist principle—aesthetic objects cannot be politically neutral.[24]

For feminists, the single goal might be the advancement of the revolutionary feminist toward a nonsexist, egalitarian, nonhierarchical society. Compare Beardsley's summary of the Marxists' adherence to the Principle of Nonneutrality to a recent suggestion by feminist theorist Gisela Ecker:

> . . . feminist aesthetic theory must insist that all investigations into art have to be *thoroughly genderised*. . . . A truly genderised perspective would mean that the sex—male *or* female—of both the artist and the critic is taken into account. This also implies their relation to gender-values in the institutions and within the theories they apply.[25]

This, in light of the picture sketched of contextual theories in Section I of this paper, is surely a contextual approach grounded in the belief that no work of art is appropriately assessed without paying attention to issues of gender. I will assume that the question of whether feminist *interpretive* criticism is an aesthetically relevant source of information is moot for both Stolnitz and Beardsley, since both have already acknowledged an acceptance of other types of contextual criticism, provided it meets their requirements. It is to the unresolved question of utilizing knowledge of contextual-factual data with regard to resultant *evaluative* criticism that we must now address ourselves.

Let us return to the argument presented in Section I in order to pursue the task of arguing against the conclusion (5) by means of feminist theory. It is the belief of feminist art theorists that the concept of an isolationist approach to a work of art is not only ludicrous but more importantly, pernicious. Given the feminist approach to a work of art, grounded in what Beardsley calls the Principle of Non-neutrality, women see it as conceptually impossible for a work of art *ever* to be "objectively" created, interpreted, or evaluated. All aesthetic objects are "'marked' by gender."[26] Consider one summary of this view, as expressed by Janet Wolff in a text entitled, *The Social Production of Art*:

> . . . the ideas, beliefs, attitudes and values expressed in cultural products are ideological, in the sense that they are always related in a systematic way to the social and economic structures in which the artist is situated. . . . Ideas and beliefs which are proposed as value-free or non-partisan are merely those ideas which have assumed the guise of universality, perceiving as natural social facts and relations which are in fact historically specific. To this extent, then, art as a product of consciousness is also permeated with ideology, although it is not reducible to ideology.[27]

If all art is permeated with ideology and marked by gender, then there is no possible way to make aesthetic judgments that do not take contextual data, like ideology and gender, into account.[28] Let us look at an example of these claims.

This example could count as the feminists' paradigm demonstrating that male critics, theorists, and aestheticians do not, in actuality, practice what the traditional isolationists preach. Consider the controversial body of work by artist Judy Chicago, the most well-known examples being her massive mid-1970s work entitled *The Dinner Party* and, more recently, her equally ambitious *The Birth Project*.[29] They are a paradigm of neglect (a fate equivalent to low aesthetic evaluation) by the established male-dominated artworld precisely because they are impossible to interpret or evaluate *fully* without recourse to knowledge of external, contextual-factual data. Most male critics have failed to write about them at all, thereby refusing to legitimize them as art. Feminist works are rarely critiqued in the major art magazines (e.g., *Art in America*, *ARTnews*, or *Artforum*) and are rarely discussed in theoretical works written by men.[30] There are two possible reasons for this. A critic, maintaining an isolationist approach, might see Chicago's images simply as poor design, unaesthetically interesting, and not worth writing about. Another possibility is that a critic actually uses external, contextual-factual data to determine *low* aesthetic value, based on Beardsley's Argument from Correlation.

What is the contextual data that could possibly cause a critic to so harshly judge these works? Possibly Chicago's avowed claim that her works constitute a new form of imagery, a new genre of representation: what she and others call cunt imagery.[31] According to Chicago, cunt imagery depicts, either literally or abstractly, the source of woman's power: female genitalia. According to Chicago and other feminist artists, only a woman can truly identify with a work of cunt imagery, thereby interpreting the color and form and cultural associations of the imagery as a symbol of female power and consolidation.

An isolationist, on the other hand, who experiences Chicago's work *can*, as Beardsley suggests, "do nothing but look at it . . . again and again, with the most concentrated attention," without consulting any facts outside the work itself. However, it is nearly impossible to fathom how an isolationist would be able to understand, interpret, or evaluate the work fairly or fully without knowing that the symmetrical, multicolored designs being viewed mean more than just symmetrical, multicolored designs. It is not that a contextualist would simply have a richer aesthetic experience of this work of art; it is that an isolationist's aesthetic judgments are seriously inadequate because they are a function of *only* those judgments which depend on internal, intrinsic, noncontextual data. Chicago's works end up undervalued much as a medieval allegorical altarpiece would be undervalued if no account was taken of its rich symbolic iconography. The conclusion (5), then, of the isolationist's argument is not only shown to be faulty in principle but is also conveniently ignored in practice when the critic's effect is to exclude certain works from aesthetic consideration.

It is appropriate at this point to ask the following two questions: (1) Is what the isolationist claims true, namely, that someone can experience a work of art fully if he or she experiences it solely for its own sake? and (2) If the answer to (1) is yes, how does one separate internal data from external data in order to ignore external data and experience an artwork solely for its own sake? The resolution of the isolationist-contextualist debate lies in the answer to these two questions, particularly the latter. But determining precisely which qualities or properties of an aesthetic object are internal and external and, hence, are relevant or irrelevant to aesthetic evaluation is hardly unproblematic in light of recent challenges to the very notions of aesthetic attitude, aesthetic experience, aesthetic quality, and aesthetic value.[32]

Even Beardsley has changed his mind, at least in one case, on what counts as a property *of* the work (i.e., internal to the work), for example, in his eventual agreement with Stolnitz regarding the skill of an artist.[33] At first, Beardsley considered skill to be external to the artwork—a property of the artist—but later decided with Stolnitz that skill is an internal property of the work that is experienced (as part of the isolationist's aesthetic experience). Skill becomes "part of the expressiveness of the work" and thus relevant to aesthetic evaluation, without leading "away from the work to biographical inquiry."[34] Beardsley, of course, would not admit to allowing external evidence to be relevant to evaluative judgments; rather he turns what was previously considered external evidence into internal evidence.

Beardsley's conversion shows most tellingly the lack of clear lines of demarcation between those properties within the work that are allowed to yield judgments about aesthetic value and those properties external to the work that are irrelevant. Once we start asking if ideology or gender is internal or external to a work of art, serious problems arise. A clearly stipulated set of criteria is needed to separate the two types of properties (if there is a separation) and to explain when properties external to a work are allowed to "become" properties internal to a work. (Two spin-off questions might be, "Can internal properties become external?" and "How would internal properties become external?")

Beardsley's change of heart reflects an attempt to move away from the traditional isolationist's approach as argued in (1) through (5). He comes to admit (in 1980), in contrast to the traditional view (which he espoused in 1958), that aesthetic value is *under*determined by aesthetic experience. One implication of this is that aesthetic value is also underdetermined by aesthetic judgments. Beardsley's revised notion of aesthetic value is as follows: "the aesthetic value of anything is its capacity to impart—*through cognition of it*—a marked aesthetic character to experience."[35] This revision moves us closer to the type of contextual theories we will look at in Section III, namely, those that rely heavily on a complex cognitive process to determine whether something is art instead of relying on perceptual experience alone. Even though Beardsley anticipates problems as to what counts as "the receiver's cognitive grasp"[36] (i.e., the proper experience), he still claims that an experience with a marked aesthetic character still remains free "from concerns about matters outside that object."[37] Contemporary contextual theorists, we shall see, depend heavily on matters outside the object.

The main point of this section was to introduce feminist theory as a type of contextual theory, excluded from traditional philosophical discussion due to the longstanding belief that contextual theories are only helpful (sometimes) in determining critical, nonevaluative judgments. In contrast, feminist theory was used to demonstrate against the isolationists' premise (4) and conclusion (5) that aesthetic value need not be a function of only aesthetic judgments and that knowledge of external, contextual data can be relevant to determining the aesthetic value of an aesthetic object. Perhaps this is what Beardsley meant when he said that the value of a work of art must be found in the whole context of human life.

III. CONTEMPORARY CONTEXTUAL THEORIES: DANTO, DICKIE, AND EATON

The newest introductory text in aesthetics, Marcia Eaton's *Basic Issues in Aesthetics*, is a good place to start for an updated perspective on contextual theories within analytic aesthetics.[38] Eaton introduces contextual theories as one type of aesthetic theory which purports to separate the aesthetic from the nonaesthetic; contextual theories are usually at odds with traditional (i.e., formalist and isolationist) theories. Some contextual theories point to institutions as necessary for providing an account of the aesthetic; others point to historic, economic, or social conditions. Eaton briefly reviews Marxist aesthetics, George Dickie's institutional theory, Danto's historical theory, and her own theory, which is heavily dependent on the role of the traditions of art criticism and history.[39] Nowhere is feminist theory mentioned.[40]

Eaton insists that formalist theories are insufficient; some kind of contextualist theory is needed to account for both the form and content of a work of art. However, she clearly voices the prejudice of traditional aestheticians when she says,

One of the problems with Marxism (and other sociologies of art) is that it assumes a connection between art and social features that has yet to be shown to exist. That is, it presupposes the existence of lawlike connections between social factors and artistic creation.[41]

Until these connections are "empirically verified" and exceptions to the connections accounted for, Eaton dismisses any such approach as "aesthetic sociology":

Marxism identifies artworks with their contexts and hence does not allow us to see what is special about them. There is a sense in which Marxist aesthetics ceases to be aesthetics at all.[42]

In his introduction to a special issue of *The Journal of Aesthetics and Art Criticism* entitled "Analytic Aesthetics: Retrospect and Prospect," Richard Shusterman berates the analytic tradition as myopic and naive.[43] It is myopic in its attempt to define art in nonevaluative terms and naive in its assumption that art can be fully understood theoretically without taking its full social context into account. His condemnation even extends to contemporary contextual theories (presumably of Danto, Dickie, and Eaton):

Analytic philosophy's blindness to the complex and contested social context of art, criticism, and even its own aesthetic theorizing is paradoxically most striking . . . in its attempt to define art as a social institution.[44]

Why does Shusterman fault contemporary contextual theories? Are they guilty of the same problems that befall other contextual theories like Marxism and Freudianism? And where does feminist theory fit into the picture? Is it more akin to Marxist theory, to be discounted as mere aesthetic sociology, or is it more like Danto's historical theory and Dickie's institutional theory, though more focused in its attentiveness to social context on issues of *gender*?

Theory is a terribly overused and abused term. In looking at the acceptance and rejection rates of contextual theories in aesthetics, it soon becomes apparent that not all contextual theories are theories in the same sense of the term. What we encounter in analyzing these theories is that although they all (in their descriptive, i.e., nonprescriptive form) are formulations of underlying principles of certain observed and verified phenomena, there are really two different levels or orders of theories operative. Let us first investigate the *differences* between these two levels or orders and then the *similarities*.

(i) There are first-order theories of *art* (e.g., those of Stolnitz, Beardsley, and Dickie, to name only a few) and there are second-order theories of *criticism* of art which depend on a first-order theory of art (again, e.g., Stolnitz, Beardsley, and now Dickie's new work, *Evaluating Art*).[45] Second-order theories of criticism depend on, follow on, or presuppose first-order theories of art since it makes no sense to utter the locution, "X is a good work of art" without first assuming some sort of criterion designating X to be a work of art. Thus, first-order theories separate art from nonart and second-order theories interpret and evaluate art.

Looking more closely at the range of first- and second-order theories available, it is appropriate to say that there are first-order *contextual* theories of art (e.g., those of Danto, Dickie, and Eaton) and second-order *contextual* theories of criticism of art (Marxism, Freudianism, and feminism). Let us designate the first-order contextual theories of art as contextual$_a$ and the second-order contextual theories of criticism as contextual$_c$. The first-order theories of Danto, Dickie, and Eaton purport to separate art from nonart, while second-order theories like Marxism and feminism do not. They are used to interpret and evaluate art (among other things). Both utilize extrinsic, factual, contextual data by which to identify and evaluate art (more on this later). The functions of the different orders differ and do not overlap. Thus an important difference is established between contextual$_c$ theories and contextual$_a$ theories, which yields an interesting and important result: The evaluation of a work of art (i.e., the utilization of a contextual$_c$ theory) presupposes a contextual$_a$ theory.

(ii) Another difference between contextual$_a$ theories and contextual$_c$ theories is that contextual$_c$ theories are more wide-ranging. That is, one can produce a Marxist or feminist critique of nonartworks as well as of works of art (i.e., of advertisements, the social structure of humankind, or the unusual antiquarian tradition of Chinese footbinding). Perhaps this is why Eaton and other philosophers are hesitant to call Marxist or feminist criteria "aesthetics." Eaton claimed that Marxism "does not allow us to see what is special" about works of art; they are simply one type of thing to be assessed according to contextualist$_c$ criteria. To point out this contrast further, it makes no sense to say that one could do a Danto-like or Dickie-like critique or analysis of anything *but* a work of art. The criteria of contextualist theories of art are primarily used to designate "art"; they are used to pick out *only* works of art.

(iii) A third difference seems at first glance apparent, though it has been challenged by feminists and others. The third difference is that contextual$_c$ theories, like Marxism and feminism, *can be* ideological (or prescriptive, in the sense outlined in Section II) whereas contextual$_a$ theories *cannot* (it is this latter claim to which some feminists object). In other words, the difference would consist in contextual$_c$ theories possibly containing a prescriptive element which contextual$_a$ theories most definitely lack. Feminists see feminism as "a way of life" (to quote Lippard) that others ought to follow; Marxists see Marxism as a theory that ought to govern human action. Theory moves beyond description to prescription—to ideology—by issuing directives as to how one ought to follow the theory.

But does it make sense to say that Dickie's theory of art is a way of life that ought to be followed? Or that Danto's view of what constitutes an artwork should govern future action? Our most immediate response, of course, is in the negative. It sounds counterintuitive to think of theories that define art in terms of anything other than in the role of analyzing the concept "art" in the most correct way, where correctness is a function of the way the concept is used in the world. Counterevidence, in the form of counterexamples, may motivate a change in the theory; that is, the description may change but it is never transformed into a guiding ideology or way of life.

As already noted, feminists and others have raised objections to past theorists who *claim* to be objective, neutral, and free of ideology. As already indicated (Section II) by Janet Wolff, some feminists believe that principles and theories which are promoted as "value-free" or "non-partisan" are merely those principles and theories which have assumed the "guise of universality." It is really the case, they believe, that phallocentric ideology, existing for centuries, masquerades as neutrality and universality, only recently exposed for what it really is. Whether or not these objections are to be taken seriously is controversial; the problem cannot be resolved in brief discussion here. I mention it only to point out a difference that seems to have at least implicitly caused the analytic tradition to consign certain contextual$_c$ theories, like Marxism and feminism, to the fringes of "objectively neutral" philosophical aesthetics. Recall Stolnitz's claim that Marxist theory is a social-political theory and Eaton's claim that Marxism is aesthetic sociology. One might surmise that it is feminist theory's prescriptive, ideological character that is at least one reason for its absence from recent analytic philosophical literature.

At this point I would like to break with feminist tradition and propose an explanation for the third difference (iii) listed, namely, why I claimed (only) that feminist contextual$_c$ theory *can be* ideological. This is a weakening of the basic strong feminist prescriptive line, such as Gisela Ecker's, that all aesthetic inquiry *must* be or *ought* to be genderized. I am proposing that the strong feminist claim can be stripped of its prescriptive import, leaving behind the following weaker claim: Works of art *can be* assessed in terms of the sex of the artist, viewer, and critic and attending sociological framework *but need not be*. For the purpose at hand, that of assessing contextual$_c$ theories, it is a more workable and marketable approach. Thus, contextual$_c$ theories can be prescriptive but need not be; this avoids the problem of feminist theory as ideology and reduces it to just theory.

Let us now focus on some *similarities* between contextual$_a$ theories and contextual$_c$ theories utilizing the theories of Danto, Dickie, and Eaton as examples of the former and feminist theory as an example of the latter.

(i′) One similarity is that both types of contextual theories stress a work of art's *nonexhibited* properties. Marcel Duchamp's *Fountain* and Andy Warhol's *Brillo Box* motivated contextualists to look beyond the (aesthetic) perception of the visible, discernible, exhibited properties of the object to its nonexhibited, relational properties in delineating a work of art from its perceptually indiscernible counterpart. Contextual$_a$ theorists believed it impossible for isolationists to distinguish a work of art from its perceptually indiscernible counterpart by simply looking at each of the two objects "as a work of art" in isolation from its invisible, imperceptible framework. Hence, Stolnitz's suggestion to aesthetically experience only what is immediately given *in* the work and Beardsley's proposal to "do nothing but look at it . . . again and again" prove to be totally inadequate. Contextual$_c$ theorists believe it is impossible to correctly or fully understand or appreciate the object designated a work of art without recourse to some invisible, imperceptible framework that it is integrally tied to the nonexhibited properties of the object. This brings us to the second similarity.

(ii′) In addition to contextual$_a$ theorists emphasizing nonexhibited properties of an object, those same properties are ones that tie the object to things or persons outside the object *by virtue of which* it counts as a work of art. For Danto, it is the appropriate causal history; for Dickie, it is the institution of the artworld; for Eaton, it is the information concerning its history of production. External, extrinsic data become essential (both necessary and sufficient) to an object's identity as a work of art; the object in question is constituted art via these relational properties. This is in stark contrast to noncontexual theories of art, like Stolnitz's, that relies only on internal, intrinsic data. What "external, extrinsic data" translates into is (to use Eaton's phrase) "social factors" or (to use Dickie's or Danto's terms) "context" or "framework." All contextual theories reject a purely formalist, isolationist approach: the traditional approach of Stolnitz and Beardsley. In Danto's words, being a work of art has "little to do with any intrinsic features of the object."[46] A work of art is inextricable from its historical and causal connections—the Artworld; "an ahistorical theory of art can have no philosophical defense."[47] For Danto, the connection is between the work of art and the social factors of its causal history, a knowing audience, and an interpretation of that work within the history of art, by which one grasps the content and form of the metaphorical nature of art. For Dickie, the connection is between the work of art and the social factors of artists' intentions, a "prepared" public, and artworld systems which make up the institutional framework known as the artworld.[48] For Eaton, criticism of the object and history of its production—both external factors—are essential in bringing us to value the traditionally appreciated intrinsic properties.[49]

An obvious conclusion to be drawn from just this brief sketch of contextual$_a$ theories is that they do in fact assume some type of essential "lawlike" connection between aesthetic and "social features." Recall that this was precisely Eaton's criticism of Marxist theories. Eaton concludes her section on contextual theories by stating that all of the theories discussed hold that "outside the context of social and cultural practices and conventions, 'art' does not make sense."[50] Not only do all three contextual$_a$ theories presuppose the existence of lawlike connections between social factors and the work of art, they flaunt those connections.[51] For it is in virtue of those connections that these theories seek to separate themselves from purely formalist, isolationist theories of art.

Returning to point (ii'), feminist theory alos looks to external, extrinsic social factors as essential to the tasks of interpretation and evaluation. Recall Gisela Ecker's suggestion that no work of art *ought* to be assessed without utilizing a "genderized" perspective: taking into account the *external* data of the sex of the artist, the sex of the viewer and critic, and the relationship between those persons and the "gender-values" of the institutional framework (of the artworld) in which they find themselves. ("Gender-value" is meant to convey the feminists' skepticism about the supposed neutrality of this framework and the theories it employs.) Stripping her claim of its prescriptive import, we might restate it as follows: Works of art *can be* assessed by means of a genderized perspective. Feminist critical theory, therefore, is consistent with Danto's notion of theory and history of the artworld but warns the appraiser of the work of art to beware of the hidden sexist and oppressive nature of this essential theoretical context.[52] Nevertheless, external factors are essential and it is probably no coincidence that the contextual$_a$ theorists and the contextual$_c$ theorists have focused on the same sorts of external data.

This section reviewed several popular contextual theories of art, outlined the distinction between theories of art and theories of criticism, and focused on the differences and similarities of contextual$_a$ and contextual$_c$ theories. Let us now move beyond differences and similarities and take our earlier discussion of first-order and second-order contextual theories one step further.

IV. A ROLE FOR FEMINIST THEORY IN PHILOSOPHICAL AESTHETICS

Since second-order theories of art criticism depend on or presuppose a first-order theory of art, could it also be the case that second-order contextual theories of art criticism presuppose a first-order contextual theory of art?

We might want to suggest that they match up better, or work together better, for the purposes of assessing a work of art than a contextual theory of criticism and a noncontextual theory of art, but are we authorized to conclude something stronger: that a contextual theory of criticism necessarily presupposes a contextual theory of art? If so, we may have found the answer to determining the role—or at least one role—of feminist theory; feminist theory is one form of contextual criticism that necessarily follows on a contextual theory of art. Feminist theory offers a set of criteria to interpret and evaluate a work of art that has achieved its ontological status by means of social factors deemed by traditional, isolationist aestheticians as external and irrelevant. Feminist theory is one type of contextual criticism that assesses a work's social factors as (1) essential to the work's being art in the first place, and (2) determinants in judging the work to be good, valuable, etc. Let us pursue this proposal by means of some examples.

At one point, Danto proposes one criterion of evaluating a work of art by means of its metaphorical nature:

> . . . the greatest metaphors . . . [are] those in which the spectator sees his or her life in terms of the life depicted: it is oneself as Anna Karenina, or Isabelle Archer, or Elizabeth Bennett, or O: . . . where the artwork becomes a metaphor for life and life is transfigured.[53]

This is precisely the type of criterion of evaluation that feminists have been proposing, namely, that of identifying with the characters or images or personae in a work of art. It was the rationale behind Judy Chicago's notion of cunt imagery: that such imagery expressed the previously oppressed power of all females and that all women would positively identify with their new-found symbol, thus enhancing the transfigurative power of that symbol or metaphor. It is the same rationale used by feminists to critique the male, "old masters" tradition of "The Reclining Venus" by arguing that women will negatively identify with the reclining nude Venus who is on display solely for the male artist and fellow male voyeuristic viewers. It is the same rationale used by some feminists to condemn pornographic images. The notion of "body identification" explains the female's negative reaction of shared oppression and exploitation with the victim in the image which the male does not feel; he does not identify with the passive female body but rather enjoys his position as the active looker, in control of the passive female.

The point is that it is reliance on factual-contextual data and external social factors that determines the interpretation and evaluation of a work previously judged to be art by means of those same external factors. Warhol's *Brillo Box* is deemed art (versus its perceptually indistinguishable counterpart) in virtue of its theoretical and historical framework that includes the intentions of the artist and the audience's knowledge of those intentions. Chicago's *Dinner Party* is deemed art (versus an imaginable perceptually indistinguishable counterpart in a typical hardcore porn magazine) in the same way. Only one of each pair exists in the artworld framework; only one of each pair becomes art in virtue of external, social factors. It is only fitting that a natural extension of the process of the object-become-art-in-virtue-of-external-factors is object-judged-art-in-virtue-of-external-factors. The most effective way to proceed to interpret and evaluate such a work is also by means of external, contextual data (e.g., the sex of the artist, viewer, critic). Thus, the most natural fit between first- and second-order levels of theories is the one proposed: Contextual$_c$ theories necessarily presuppose contextual$_a$ theories, and feminist theory is one type of contextual$_c$ theory.

To sum up this section, let us return one last time to the argument presented in Section I. Contrary to the isolationists' stance that only so-called aesthetic judgments determine aesthetic value, embodied in (5), I argued that aesthetic value need not be a function of only aesthetic judgments. It seems plain enough that aesthetic judgments that look only to internal, intrinsic factors are insufficient to fairly assess works such as Warhol's and Chicago's. What were previously called "moral" judgments are really crucial in assessing works of art, especially those whose status as art depends on external data previously held irrelevant. Not only has the isolationists' conclusion (5) been refuted, but I have also claimed something stronger: Knowledge of external, contextual data is necessarily required to assess a work of art that has been deemed a work of art by means of external, contextual data. In other words, a contextual$_a$ theory of art requires a contextual$_c$ theory of art to follow through with a thorough and fair assessment of a work of art. Feminist theory is one type of contextual$_c$ theory available.

V. CONCLUDING REMARKS

In order to argue for the role of feminist critical theory, the traditional isolationist approach to evaluating was outlined and criticized in Section I. Feminist theory itself was introduced in Section II and assessed in light of the backdrop of traditional isolationist views. Contemporary contextual theories of art were differentiated from contextual theories of criticism in Section III and their relationship explored. In Section IV, the role of feminist theory as a natural extension of recent contextual theories of art was advocated, securing the role of feminist theory in future discussions. In arguing that knowledge of external, contextual data (like that stressed by feminist theory) is relevant to the aesthetic value of a work of art, I have hoped to accomplish two things: to make feminists and philosophers aware of the commonalities of their views and to point out that more work needs to be done in both camps. Shusterman's blanket disapproval for even recent contextual$_a$ theories calls for more openness toward other, previously neglected social aspects of art. I am suggesting that gender is one aspect of contextual theories that needs to be investigated. With such changes afoot, it may not be long until feminist theory is rightfully considered an essential part of aesthetic inquiry.

NOTES

1. The territory is still virgin in spite of forthcoming ground-breaking publications such as special issues of *Hypatia, The Feminist Newsletter*, and *The Journal of Aesthetics and Art Criticism*, all of which are devoted to topics in feminist aesthetics.
2. Derrida's term "phallogocentric" has been borrowed by feminist theorists; it is a compilation of "phallocentric" (phallus-centered, i.e., a mode of representation in which the phallus is taken to be the principal signifier of the male) and "logocentric" (logic-centered, as is analytic philosophy). See Derrida's "The Purveyor of Truth," *Yale French Studies*, LII (1975), 95–97. Christie V. McDonald defines the term as "the complicity of Western metaphysics with a notion of male firstness" in "Choreographies," *Diacritics*, XII (Summer, 1982), 69.
3. Jerome Stolnitz, *Aesthetics and Philosophy of Art Criticism: An Introduction* (Boston: Houghton Mifflin Company, 1960). My main focus will be on pp. 441–92.
4. Stolnitz, *Aesthetics and Philosophy of Art Criticism*, 369. Stolnitz, foretellingly, added the following: "Indeed, there are some people who, if the truth be told, get more fun out of this sort of thing than from aesthetic perception itself."
5. *Ibid.*, 461.
6. *Ibid*,
7. *Ibid.*, 449–50.
8. *Ibid.*, 495.
9. *Ibid.*, 450.
10. Monroe C. Beardsley, "Problems in Aesthetics," *The Encyclopedia of Philosophy*, ed. Paul Edwards, I–II (1972), p. 44.
11. Monroe C. Beardsley, *Aesthetics: Problems in the Philosophy of Criticism* (2nd ed.; Indianapolis: Hacket Publishing Company, Inc., 1981), pp. 558–71.
12. Beardsley, *Aesthetics: Problems in the Philosophy of Criticism*, 563.
13. *Ibid.*, 564.
14. *Ibid.*
15. *Ibid.*, 566.
16. Stolnitz, *Aesthetics and Philosophy of Art Criticism*, 457.
17. We are either in the second or third phase, depending on how one counts. Thalia Gouma-Peterson and Patricia Mathews believe we are in the second generation—see "The Feminist Critique of Art History," *The*

Art Bulletin, LXIX (September, 1987), pp. 326–57—as does Toril Moi, *Sexual/Textual Politics: Feminist Literary Theory* (London and New York: Routledge, 1985). Another analyst of literature, K. K. Ruthven, believes feminists are in the third phase; see *Feminist Literary Studies: An Introduction* (Cambridge: Cambridge University Press, 1984).

18. Elaine Showalter, "Toward a Feminist Poetics," in Showalter, ed., *The New Feminist Criticism: Essays on Women, Literature and Theory* (New York: Pantheon Books, 1985).

19. In spite of the date of this reference from Janet Radcliffe Richards, *The Sceptical Feminist: A Philosophical Enquiry* (London: Routledge & Kegan Paul Ltd., 1980), p. 2, these basic tenets still seem to hold now, even in light of recent polls in which women prefer not to be identified as feminists. See "Onward, Women!" *Time*, Dec. 4, 1989, pp. 80–89.

20. Leslie Stevenson, *Seven Theories of Human Nature* (New York: Oxford University Press, 1987), pp. 8–9.

21. Lucy R. Lippard, "Sweeping Exchanges: The Contribution of Feminism to the Art of the 1970s," *Get the Message? A Decade of Art for Social Change* (New York: E. P. Dutton, Inc., 1984), p. 150.

22. Lucy R. Lippard, "Some Propaganda for Propaganda," *Get the Message? A Decade of Art for Social Change* (New York: E. P. Dutton, Inc., 1984), p. 116.

23. The exceptions to this claim are feminist music and feminist architecture (in contrast to producing blatantly feminist visual art, literature, performances, films, etc.) although The Women's Building designed by architect Sophia G. Hayden for the 1893 World's Columbian Exposition in Chicago is one possible example of feminist architecture.

24. Beardsley, *Aesthetics*, 567.

25. Gisela Ecker, *Feminist Aesthetics*, trans. Harriet Anderson (Boston: Beacon Press, 1985), p. 22.

26. This is Ruthven's phrase, p. 14 of K. K. Ruthven, *Feminist Literary Studies: An Introduction*. For other versions of this claim, straight from original feminist sources, see Rozsika Parker and Griselda Pollock's *Old Mistresses: Women, Art and Ideology* (New York: Pantheon Books, 1981), as well as Deborah Cherry's review of this text, "Feminist Interventions: Feminist Imperatives," *Art History*, V (1982), 503.

27. Janet Wolff, *The Social Production of Art* (London: The Macmillan Press Ltd., 1981), p. 119.

28. Actually, some feminists are not claiming simply that knowledge of external, contextual-factual data is relevant to determining the aesthetic value of an aesthetic object, but rather they are claiming something stronger (i.e., that knowledge of external data must be considered in determining aesthetic value or is the only thing to be considered in determining aesthetic value). Feminist theory is on shaky ground, I fear, with these stronger versions. In opposition to their views, I only wish to argue what *some* feminists and other contextualist theorists argue, that knowledge of external, contextual data can be relevant to determining aesthetic value.

29. For texts by Chicago chronicling and explaining these works, see *The Dinner Party: A Symbol of Our Heritage* (New York: Anchor Books, 1979), *Embroidering Our Heritage: The Dinner Party Needlework* (New York: Anchor Books, 1980), and *The Birth Project* (New York: Doubleday and Co., Inc., 1985). For commentary on *The Dinner Party*, see Lippard's article in *Art in America* (April, 1980), pp. 114–25, entitled, "Judy Chicago's 'Dinner Party.'" For a discussion of Chicago's early work, see Lippard's "Judy Chicago, Talking to Lucy R. Lippard," *Artforum* 13, No. 1 (September, 1974).

30. One qualification is in order here: Both Lawrence Alloway and Donald Kuspit have ventured to discuss feminist works of art in contextualist terms. Alloway has discussed Chicago's works as well as Lippard's criticisms of them; he has been both applauded and castigated for his venture. See the following: Lawrence Alloway, "Women's Art in the Seventies," and "Women's Art and the Failure of Art Criticism," both of which can be found in *Network: Art and the Complex Present* (Ann Arbor: UMI Research Press, 1984), pp. 273–95. The former was originally published in *Art in America* (May–June, 1976). For the feminists' responses, plus a final comment from Alloway, see "More on Women's Art: An Exchange," *Art in America* (November–December, 1976), p. 11–23.

31. As Lippard reports, Chicago and fellow artist, Miriam Schapiro, invented the phrase "cunt imagery" to describe their work of the early 1970s. It is well documented in feminist art

criticism and discussed by Alloway (see footnote 30).
32. For a brief overview, consult Sections 3, 9, and 10 in Beardsley's "Postscript 1980—Some Old Problems in New Perspectives," in *Aesthetics: Problems in the Philosophy of Criticism*.
33. The Stolnitz article that gave rise to the discussion was the 1973 article, "The Artistic Values in Aesthetic Experience," *Journal of Aesthetics and Art Criticism*, XXXII (1973), pp. 5–15.
34. Beardsley, *Aesthetics*, lxiii.
35. Beardsley, *Aesthetics*, lix. This is a revised Beardsley view in light of the date of Beardsley's 1980 "Postscript" to his 1958 text.
36. Beardsley, *Aesthetics*, lx.
37. Beardsley, *Aesthetics*, lxii.
38. Marcia Muelder Eaton, *Basic Issues in Aesthetics* (California: Wadsworth Publishing Company, 1988), pp. 5–6, 84–96.
39. The main philosophical theories I will be discussing are found in Arthur C. Danto's *The Transfiguration of the Commonplace: A Philosophy of Art* (Cambridge: Harvard University Press, 1981), George Dickie's *The Art Circle* (New York: Haven Publications, 1984), and Marcia Muelder Eaton's *Basic Issues in Aesthetics* (California: Wadsworth Publishing Co., 1988). An expanded version of the latter is found in Eaton's *Art and Nonart* (New Jersey: Associated University Presses, Inc., 1983).
40. In spite of its unpardonable lack of mention of feminist theory as a contextualist theory (even though Eaton mentions feminist works of art intermittently in the text), this is a worthwhile and useful introductory text, as it even includes a brief discussion of structuralism and deconstruction, topics usually not included in texts by analytic philosophers. For a brief review, see Patricia H. Werhane's review in *The Journal of Aesthetics and Art Criticism*, XLVI (Spring, 1988), pp. 424–25. Unfortunately, Werhane also fails to note the glaring absence of any mention of feminist theory.
41. Eaton, *Basic Issues*, 87–88.
42. Ibid., 88.
43. Richard Shusterman, "Analytic Aesthetics: Retrospect and Prospect," *The Journal of Aesthetics and Art Criticism*, XLVI (Special Issue, 1987), pp. 115–245. An expanded version can be found in Richard Shusterman, ed., *Analytic Aesthetics* (New York: Basil Blackwell Inc., 1989), pp. 1–19.
44. Shusterman, "Analytic Aesthetics," 120.
45. George Dickie, *Evaluating Art* (Philadelphia: Temple University Press, 1988).
46. Danto, *The Transfiguration*, 28.
47. Ibid., 175.
48. See Dickie's *The Art Circle* (New York: Haven Publications, 1984).
49. See Eaton's *Art and Nonart* (East Brunswick, N.J.: Associated University Presses, 1983).
50. Eaton, *Basic Issues*, 96.
51. Dickie, in fact, argues against Beardsley's theory of art evaluation based on art's detachedness from the world, by claiming that works of art are tied to the world (they have cognitive properties) of which we are immediately aware upon experiencing the work. "The most basic is the awareness that the objects we are involved with are works of art . . . [and] that the object is art of a particular kind." Dickie, *Evaluating Art*, p. 79.
52. Again, the Parker and Pollock text, *Old Mistresses*, lays out the rationale for this skepticism (known as the feminist critique) in detail (see Footnote 26) as well as the Gouma-Peterson and Mathews article (see Footnote 17). These theorists, it must be noted, do not discuss philosophical contextual theories of art like Danto's, Dickie's, or Eaton's but rather have concentrated their criticisms on the underlying principles of the "canon" of art history and of the critics of art. I have taken the liberty of extending the feminist critique to these three contextual$_a$ theories; I feel this was Shusterman's point as well.
53. Danto, *The Transfiguration*, 172.

I would like to thank the Women's Studies Program at the Ohio State University for a grant during the Summer of 1988 which helped support the writing of this paper.

Reconciliation Elegy. Robert Motherwell (American). 1978. National Gallery of Art, Washington, D.C.

As an abstract expressionist, Motherwell sought to create expressive effects but through nonrepresentational means. The expressive properties of art often are independent of their representational function.

CHAPTER 3
Case in Point: Expressiveness and Art

To get a more accurate picture of the development of analytic aesthetics, from its preanalytic beginnings through its earlier to its later stages, it is helpful to focus on a concrete example, and the example we consider here is the idea of artistic expression. As we pointed out earlier, analytic aesthetics, like much of analytic philosophy, emerges in part from the rejection of early twentieth-century neo-Hegelian idealism, the most noteworthy representative of which, as far as aesthetics is concerned, is Croce and his theory that all art is the expression of feeling.

In an artwork, Croce tells us, we find both images and feelings, but not as two distinct things. "The feeling is altogether converted into images," becoming thereby "a feeling that is contemplated and therefore resolved and transcended." Croce calls this a "lyrical intuition," which has "converted chaotic feeling into clear intuition." Somehow, an emotional sensation is given form in an image within an artwork in such a way that the emotion is elevated from a mere sensation to a contemplated image—not yet an intellectual idea but well on its way. Thus for Croce there is an "identity of intuition and expression." The difference between an emotional sensation and a lyrical intuition is that only the latter has been given form (that is, has been expressed). Hence, while one may feel the frustration of having unexpressed emotional sensations, an unexpressed intuition would be a logical contradiction. To have an intuition is already to have expressed it—though, consistent with Croce's idealist orientation, expressing an intuition for him is not yet to have communicated it physically in paint on canvas, musical notes on paper, and so on.

As Croce and others, like Collingwood, have formulated it, the theory is too vague to evaluate in any precise or detailed way. It is hard to tell what would count for or against the theory, what it includes, and what it excludes. But for Kennick and many other early "analytic aestheticians," such theories are fundamentally flawed by their reliance on an underlying assumption that it is possible and useful to attempt to answer a question as broad as the one Croce attempts—namely, "What is art?" in general. This is the first "mistake" of traditional aesthetics, according to Kennick: to hold, as Parker does (and Bell, as well), that for the term *art* to apply to every work of art, there must be "a common nature" which "applies to *all* works of art, *and to nothing else.*"

The problem, according to Kennick and other early analytic aestheticians, has nothing to do with anything peculiar to the arts. It springs rather from a misunderstanding of the meaning of general terms, such as *art* in a natural language; it is the essentialist fallacy of supposing that the meaning of every common noun must designate a feature shared by every object denoted by that word. As Wittgenstein pointed out regarding the word *game*, not only is there no such common feature in all games, but no such common feature is required for the word *game* to be meaningful. Speakers of English know how to use words like *game* and *art* (or at least they did in 1958 when Kennick wrote his article), and that is all there is to the "meaning of the word." Philosophers analyzing the meaning of the word should therefore pay attention to the "variety of uses" of the word *art*, and not, like Croce, look for some nonexistent essence shared by all artworks.

In his famous warehouse example, Kennick imagines a workman who is to be sent into a gigantic warehouse full of all sorts of objects and instructed to bring out all the artworks. As difficult an instruction as that may be for the workman (and it surely has gotten more difficult since the late 1950s), think how much more confused our workman would be if, following Croce's definition, we instructed the workman to bring us everything that had "expression," or, according to Bell's equally famous but obscure definition, we asked for everything that possessed "significant form." Clearly, "significant form" and "expression" fail as definitions of art for the simple reason that they are far less clear than the term *art* itself.

But even if we agree that the theory that all art is "expression" is to be rejected because it tries to answer the inappropriate question, "What does all art have in common?," it does not follow that other questions regarding artistic expression are inappropriate or uninteresting. Analytic aestheticians assumed that once we set aside the big definitional question, "Is art essentially expression?," more careful and illuminating work could be done on the smaller and more manageable questions, such as, "What exactly is meant by saying that a given artwork expresses a particular emotion, that this piece of music, for example, is somber or melancholy?" As a direct result of the shift of analytic aesthetics away from the essentialist, definitional quest of earlier aestheticians, such as Croce, a great deal of extremely interesting work has been done on a variety of problems relating to the artistic expression of emotion.

Susanne Langer can be regarded as a transitional figure, associated both with the older, preanalytic aesthetics and also with the early analytic movement. Though often singled out for attack by analytic aestheticians, she responded to those attacks in her later works, often seeking an intermediate position. For example, although she held that we should not merely *assume* that all the arts have something in common, she thought it possible to *find* such a unity by a very patient examination of each of the arts. And one of these common, definitional features of art she claimed to have "found" was its expressiveness. "A work of art is an expressive form created for our perception through sense or imagination, and what is expressed is human feeling."

Unlike Croce, however, Langer proceeded carefully and in a broadly analytic manner to work out precisely how works of art can express human feeling. In her famous theory of expression as "iconic isomorphosism," she developed a noncognitive, nondiscursive symbolic account of expressive form as a perceptible relation of parts which is symbolically taken to represent another whole with analogously related parts (namely, human feeling and emotion). By presenting visible and audible forms which are congruent with the forms of feeling (that is, which have the same pattern or structure, though obviously of a very different content), artworks become symbols of feeling, presenting "feeling . . . for our contemplation, making it visible or audible . . . through a symbol." Unlike discursive symbol systems in a natural language, a work of art is a "non-discursive symbol that articulates what is verbally ineffable—the logic of consciousness itself."

Stephen Davies carries forward this more sophisticated but still rather vague project of Langer that music is a kind of language of the emotions, though different from ordinary language ("non-discursive" as Langer had said). As Davies points out, we ordinarily understand music to have meaning of some sort, that is, meaning which the listener correctly understands about the music. Though part of this meaning has to do with formal and technical aspects of the music, much of it is expressive. The informed listener understands what the music expresses; therefore musical expression is part of the meaning of musical works. The philosophically interesting question for Davies, however, is "how expressive music gets its meaning." Music does not have expressive meaning as a natural language does, a thesis Langer also rejected; but neither is this musically expressive meaning explainable as a nonlinguistic symbol system, as Langer held.

Rather, Davies holds, music is "'naturally' meaningful . . . of emotions." He rejects Langer's theory as too vague and too cognitive. His account is nonetheless similar to hers in holding that the structure of music resembles that of human emotion in the sense in which a St. Bernard dog can look sad without actually being sad. But whereas for Langer the structure of the music resembles the structure of the human *experience* of emotion, for Davies the structure of music resembles the way sad people *look* and *behave*. Like other accounts of artistic expression which seek to avoid the absurd "animistic" conclusion that music, for example, *experiences* the emotion of sadness, Davies argues that emotion terms, like *sad*, refer to people in a primary sense and to music only in a secondary sense.

At the opposite extreme from those who claim a natural expressiveness in artworks and other nonhuman objects, Goodman urges a more radically conventionalist account, developing more fully the analogy of art to a natural language. Goodman analyzes expression as a complex form of *reference*, the relation a symbol bears to what it symbolizes. In so doing, Goodman systematically relates expression to other of artworks' functions, such as their representational function and their capacity to highlight or exemplify certain properties of interest.

When works of art represent things to us, they are (among other things) acting as a symbol which *denotes* the object represented. Cézanne's famous series of paintings represents Mont Sainte Victoire in part by the semantic fact that the paintings denote that mountain in France. In addition, many of those paintings not only are predominantly blue in color, but they "highlight" or "exemplify" this dense, liquid blueness. This property is exemplified in these paintings rather as the texture and color (but not the size or shape) of a material is exemplified by a tailor's swatch. Artworks exemplify properties when they both possess them and highlight them. (Goodman restates this point by saying that the predicate "is blue" denotes the Cézanne painting and the painting "refers back" to the predicate.)

Goodman takes expression to be a form of exemplification. The difference between expression and other forms of exemplification is that the expressive properties are *metaphorically* rather than literally possessed by the artwork. Predicates in our language are often literally true of a certain class of things while they are metaphorically true of a different class of things. For instance, the predicate "is airy" can be literally true of a certain room but is also metaphorically true of certain paintings or pieces of music.

When an artwork is expressive of sadness, Goodman asserts, the predicate "is sad" is true of that work, but not in the literal sense in which a grieving person is sad; rather the predicate is metaphorically true of the work, since the work is one of the objects this predicate applies to when it is functioning metaphorically. It is central to Goodman's theory that the semantical relations involved in aesthetic expression can be true independently of whether the artist had any particular emotional experience in creating an expressive work or whether the work causes such an experience in its viewers. In understanding the "languages of art," we can comprehend and appreciate art's expressive function without literally undergoing the emotions expressed.

Tormey holds that there are "expressive properties" true of artworks but that these are not to be confused with or identified with the (literal) emotional properties that are true only of live, feeling beings. A person may have the property of being anguished, for example, but an artwork can only have the *expressive* property, anguish. Confusion is easy here because we tend to use the same simple predicates to cover both cases: we say that paintings as well as persons are anguished; the music as well as the person is merry.

Tormey defines expressive properties as those properties of artworks (or natural objects) whose names also are used to designate intentional states of persons. It is Tormey's view that, with the help of the distinction between expressive properties and simple emotional properties, and with an understanding that art's expressive properties depend on the more descriptive, structural, or compositional features of the work itself, it can be concluded that artworks are *autonomously self-expressive objects*.

According to Tormey, artworks "reveal" expressive properties by "presenting" nonexpressive properties. In distinction from many writers (such as Sibley, whose views are presented in Chapter 4) who puzzle over the question of how a work's expressive properties can depend on its nonexpressive features, given that there appears to be no logical or rule-governed connection between properties at these different levels, Tormey asserts that the nonexpressive properties of an artwork are *wholly constitutive* of its expressive properties. To quote one of Tormey's examples, "the tempo, dynamics, harmonic texture, melodic contour of Ravel's *Pavane* are not merely the grounds, warrants or criteria for asserting that the work is tender, they are the *constitutents* of its tenderness."

So, as a person's behavioral and linguistic expressions may be thought partially to constitute that person's current intentional mental state, so Tormey believes that the nonexpressive features that an artwork "presents" to us are constitutive of and reveal the work's expressive properties. Revealed properties, however, do not *logically follow* from the presence of their constituting nonexpressive properties, Tormey suggests, because any set of nonexpressive properties is compatible with a *range* of expressive properties, in the way that a long face may reveal sadness, tiredness, or depression in a friend. This fact is the source of the aesthetic ambiguity so prominent and so important in the arts.

Tormey argues that this uneliminable ambiguity makes certain critical and interpretative disagreements irresolvable. Interpreting a work requires making critical *choices* within the applicable range of expressive predicates, with the understanding that alternative choices are possible and equally acceptable.

Although there is surely a need for a fuller elaboration of the idea that nonexpressive features of art are *ambiguously constitutive* of a work's expressive features (or constitutive of a range of such properties), Tormey seems to be suggesting that our understanding of, or experience of, a work's expressive properties is neither a matter of *direct* perception or intuition, nor is it a matter of *inferences* which are grounded in or based on perception of the work's nonexpressive qualities. His view, therefore, stands between traditional Expression theories and those of a more cognitive stripe, such as Langer, Goodman, and Sibley.

What we find, then, in tracing the history of analytic thinking on the problem of artistic expression is not merely the rejection of overly simplified and overly generalized theories of the nature of art, but also the steady development of a complex, sophisticated, and interesting debate on a narrower and more manageable range of philosophical questions about the way in which artistic expression actually works. It is our contention that similar progress, variety, and promise can be discovered in the other subareas of aesthetics represented in subsequent chapters.

Intuition and Expression

Benedetto Croce

POETRY AS INTUITION

If we examine a poem in order to determine what it is that makes us feel it to be a poem, we at once find two constant and necessary elements: a complex of *images*, and a *feeling* that animates them. Let us, for instance, recall a passage learnt at school: Virgil's lines (*Aeneid*, iii, 294, *sqq.*), in which Aeneas described how on hearing that in the country to whose shores he had come the Trojan Helenus was reigning, with Andromache, now his wife, he was overcome with amazement and a great desire to see this surviving son of Priam and to hear of his strange adventures. Andromache, whom he meets outside the walls of the city, by the waters of a river renamed Simois, celebrating funeral rites before a cenotaph of green turf and two altars to Hector and Astyanax; her astonishment on seeing him, her hesitation, the halting words in which she questions him, uncertain whether he is a man or a ghost; Aeneas's no less agitated replies and interrogations, and the pain and confusion with which she recalls the past—how she lived through scenes of blood and shame, how she was assigned by lot as slave and concubine to Pyrrhus, abandoned by him and united to Helenus, another of his slaves, how Pyrrhus fell by the hand of Orestes and Helenus became a free man and a king; the entry of Aeneas and his men into the city, and their reception by the son of Priam in his little Troy, this mimic Pergamon with its new Xanthus, and its Scaean Gate whose threshold Aeneas greets with a kiss—all these details, and others here omitted, are images of persons, things, attitudes, gestures, sayings, joy and sorrow; mere images, not history or historical criticism, for which they are neither given nor taken. But through them all there runs a feeling, a feeling which is our own no less than the poet's, a human feeling of bitter memories, of shuddering horror, of melancholy, of homesickness, of tenderness, of a kind of childish *pietas* that could prompt this vain revival of things perished, these playthings, fashioned by a religious devotion. . . . something inexpressible in logical terms, which only poetry can express in full. Moreover, these two elements may appear as two in a first abstract analysis, but they cannot be regarded as two distinct threads, however intertwined; for in effect, the feeling is altogether converted into images, into this complex of images, and is thus a feeling that is contemplated and therefore resolved and transcended. Hence poetry must be called neither feeling, nor image, nor yet the sum of the two, but "contemplation of feeling" or "lyrical intuition" or (which is the same thing) "pure intuition"—pure, that is, of all historical and critical reference to the reality or unreality of the images of which it is woven, and apprehending the pure throb of life in its ideality. Doubtless, other things may be found in poetry besides these two elements or moments and the synthesis of the two; but these other things are either present as extraneous elements in a compound (reflections, exhortations, polemics, allegories, etc.), or else they are just these image-feelings themselves taken in abstraction from their context as so much material, restored

---

From "Aesthetics" in *Encyclopaedia Britannica*, 14th edition, 1929. Reprinted by permission of Encyclopaedia Britannica, Inc.

to the condition in which it was before the act of poetic creation. In the former case, they are nonpoetic elements merely interpolated into or attached to the poem; in the latter, they are divested of poetry, rendered unpoetical by a reader either unpoetical or not at the moment poetical, who has dispelled the poetry, either because he cannot live in its ideal realm, or for the legitimate ends of historical enquiry or other practical purposes which involve the degradation—or rather, the conversion—of the poem into a document or an instrument.

Artistic Qualities

What has been said of "poetry" applies to all the other "arts" commonly enumerated; painting, sculpture, architecture, music. Whenever the artistic quality of any product of the mind is discussed, the dilemma must be faced, that either it is a lyrical intuition, or it is something else, something just as respectable, but not art. If painting (as some theorists have maintained) were the imitation or reproduction of a given object, it would be, not art, but something mechanical and practical; if the task of the painter (as other theorists have held) were to combine lines and lights and colors with ingenious novelty of invention and effect, he would be, not an artist, but an inventor. . . . Thus the critics of these arts advise the artist to exclude, or at least not to rely upon, what they call the "literary" elements in painting, sculpture and music, just as the critic of poetry advises the writer to look for "poetry" and not be led astray by mere literature. The reader who understands poetry goes straight to this poetic heart and feels its beat upon his own;- where this beat is silent, he denies that poetry is present, whatever and however many other things may take its place, united in the work, and however valuable they may be for skill and wisdom, nobility of intellect, quickness of wit and pleasantness of effect. The reader who does not understand poetry loses his way in pursuit of these other things. He is wrong not because he admires them, but because he thinks he is admiring poetry.

OTHER FORMS OF ACTIVITY AS DISTINCT FROM ART

By defining art as lyrical or pure intuition we have implicitly distinguished it from all other forms of mental production. If such distinctions are made explicit, we obtain the following negations:

1. *Art is not philosophy*, because philosophy is the logical thinking of the universal categories of being, and art is the unreflective intuition of being. Hence, while philosophy transcends the image and uses it for its own purposes, art lives in it as in a kingdom. It is said that art cannot behave in an irrational manner and cannot ignore logic; and certainly it is neither irrational nor illogical; but its own rationality, its own logic, is a quite different thing from the dialectical logic of the concept, and it was in order to indicate this peculiar and unique character that the name "logic of sense" or "esthetic" was invented. The not uncommon assertion that art has a logical character, involves either an equivocation between conceptual logic and esthetic logic, or a symbolic expression of the latter in terms of the former.

2. *Art is not history*, because history implies the critical distinction between reality and unreality; the reality of the fact and the reality of a fancied world; the reality of action and the reality of desire. For art, these distinctions are as yet unmade; it lives, as we have said, upon pure images. The historical existence of Helenus, Andromache, and Aeneas makes no difference to the poetical quality of Virgil's poem. Here, too, an objection has been raised: namely, that art is not wholly indifferent to historical criteria, because it obeys the laws of "verisimilitude"; but, here again, "verisimilitude" is only a rather clumsy metaphor for the mutual coherence of images, which without this internal coherence would fail to produce their effect as images. . . .

3. *Art is not natural science*, because natural science is historical fact classified and so made abstract; nor is it *mathematical science*, because mathematics performs operations with abstractions and does not contemplate.

The analogy sometimes drawn between mathematical and poetical creation is based on merely external and generic resemblances; and the alleged necessity of a mathematical or geometrical basis for the arts is only another metaphor, a symbolic expression of the constructive, cohesive and unifying force of the poetic mind building itself a body of images.

4. *Art is not the play of fancy*, because the play of fancy passes from image to image, in search of variety, rest or diversion, seeking to amuse itself with the likenesses of things that give pleasure or have an emotional and pathetic interest; whereas in art the fancy is so dominated by the single problem of converting chaotic feeling into clear intuition, that we recognize the propriety of ceasing to call it fancy and calling it imagination, poetic imagination or creative imagination. Fancy as such is as far removed from poetry as are the works of Mrs. Radcliffe or Dumas *père*.

5. *Art is not feeling in its immediacy*. . . . [T]he poet does not lose his wits or grow stiff as he gazes; he does not totter or weep or cry; he expresses himself in harmonious verses, having made these various perturbations the object of which he sings. Feelings in their immediacy are "expressed" for if they are not, if they were not also sensible and bodily facts ("psycho-physical phenomena," as the positivists used to call them) they would not be concrete things, and so they would be nothing at all. Andromache expressed herself in the way described above. But "expression" in this sense, even when accompanied by consciousness, is a mere metaphor from "mental" or "esthetic expression" which alone really expresses, that is, gives to feeling a theoretical form and converts it into words, song and outward shape. This distinction between contemplated feeling, or poetry, and feeling enacted or endured, is the source of the power, ascribed to art, of "liberating us from the passions" and "calming" us (the power of *catharsis*), and of the consequent condemnation, from an esthetic point of view, of works of art, or parts of them, in which immediate feeling has a place or finds a vent. Hence, too, arises another characteristic of poetic expression—really synonymous with the last—namely its "infinity" as opposed to the "finitude" of immediate feeling or passion; or, as it is also called, the "universal" or "cosmic" character of poetry. Feeling, not crushed but contemplated by the work of poetry, is seen to diffuse itself in widening circles over all the realm of the soul, which is the realm of the universe, echoing and reechoing endlessly; joy and sorrow, pleasure and pain, energy and lassitude, earnestness and frivolity, and so forth, are linked to each other and lead to each other through infinite shades and gradations; so that the feeling, while preserving its individual physiognomy and its original dominating motive, is not exhausted by or restricted to this original character. A comic image, if it is poetically comic, carries with it something that is not comic, as in the case of Don Quixote or Falstaff; and the image of something terrible is never, in poetry, without an atoning element of loftiness, goodness and love.

6. *Art is not instruction or oratory*: it is not circumscribed and limited by service to any practical purpose whatever, whether this be the inculcation of a particular philosophical, historical or scientific truth, or the advocacy of a particular way of feeling and the action corresponding to it. Oratory at once robs expression of its "infinity" and independence, and, by making it the means to an end, dissolves it in this end. Hence arises what Schiller called the "nondetermining" character of art, as opposed to the "determining" character of oratory; and hence the justifiable suspicion of "political poetry"—political poetry being, proverbially, bad poetry.

7. As art is not to be confused with the form of practical action most akin to it, namely instruction and oratory, so *a fortiori*, it must not be confused with other forms directed to the production of certain effects, whether these consist in pleasure, enjoyment, and utility, or in goodness and righteousness. We must exclude from art not only meretricious works, but also those inspired by a desire for goodness, as equally, though differently, inartistic and repugnant to lovers of poetry. . . .

ART IN ITS RELATIONS

The "negations" here made explicit are obviously, from another point of view, "relations"; for the various distinct forms of mental activity cannot be conceived as separate each from the rest and acting in self-supporting isolation. This is not the place to set forth a complete system of the forms or categories of the mind in their order and their dialectic; confining ourselves to art, we must be content to say that the category of art, like every other category, mutually presupposes and is presupposed by all the rest: It is conditioned by them all and conditions them all. How could the esthetic synthesis, which is poetry, arise, were it not preceded by a state of mental commotion? . . . And what is this state of mind which we have called feeling, but the whole mind, with its past thoughts, volitions, and actions, now thinking and desiring and suffering and rejoicing, travailing within itself? Poetry is like a ray of sunlight shining upon this darkness, lending its own light and making visible the hidden forms of things. Hence it cannot be produced by an empty and dull mind; hence those artists who embrace the creed of pure art or art for art's sake, and close their hearts to the troubles of life and the cares of thought, are found to be wholly unproductive, or at most rise to the imitation of others or to an impressionism devoid of concentration. Hence the basis of all poetry is human personality, and, since human personality finds its completion in morality, the basis of all poetry is the moral consciousness. Of course this does not mean that the artist must be a profound thinker or an acute critic; nor that he must be a pattern of virtue or a hero; but he must have a share in the world of thought and action which will enable him, either in his own person or by sympathy with others, to live the whole drama of human life. He may sin, lose the purity of his heart, and expose himself, as a practical agent, to blame; but he must have a keen sense of purity and impurity, righteousness and sin, good and evil. He may not be endowed with great practical courage; he may even betray signs of timidity and cowardice; but he must feel the dignity of courage. Many artistic inspirations are due, not to what the artist, as a man, is in practice, but to what he is not, and feels that he ought to be, admiring and enjoying the qualities he lacks when he sees them in others. Many, perhaps the finest, pages of heroic and warlike poetry are by men who never had the nerve or the skill to handle a weapon. On the other hand, we are not maintaining that the possession of a moral personality is enough to make a poet or an artist. . . . The *sine qua non* of poetry is poetry, that form of theoretical synthesis which we have defined above; the spark of poetical genius without which all the rest is mere fuel, not burning because no fire is at hand to light it. But the figure of the pure poet, the pure artist, the votary of pure Beauty, aloof from contact with humanity, is no real figure but a caricature.

That poetry not only presupposes the other forms of human mental activity but is presupposed by them, is proved by the fact that without the poetic imagination which gives contemplative form to the workings of feeling, intuitive expression to obscure impressions, and thus becomes representations and words, whether spoken or sung or painted or otherwise uttered, logical thought could not arise. Logical thought is not language, but it never exists without language, and it uses the language which poetry has created; by means of concepts, it discerns and dominates the representations of poetry, and it could not dominate them unless they, its future subjects, had first an existence of their own. Further, without the discerning and criticizing activity of thought, action would be impossible; and if action, then good action, the moral consciousness, duty. Every man, however much he may seem to be all logical thinker, critic, scientist, or all absorbed in practical interests or devoted to duty, cherishes at the bottom of his heart his own private store of imagination and poetry; even Faust's pedantic *famulus,* Wagner, confessed that he often had his "grillenhafte Stunden." Had this element been altogether denied him, he would not have been a man, and therefore not even a thinking or acting being.

This extreme case is an absurdity; in proportion as this private store is scanty, we find a certain superficiality and aridity in thought, and a certain coldness of action.

INTUITION AND EXPRESSION

One of the first problems to arise, when the work of art is defined as "lyrical image," concerns the relation of "intuition" to "expression" and the manner of the transition from one to the other. At bottom this is the same problem which arises in other parts of philosophy: the problem of inner and outer, of mind and matter, of soul and body, and, in ethics, of intention and will, will and action, and so forth. Thus stated, the problem is insoluble; for once we have divided the inner from the outer, body from mind, will from action, or intuition from expression, there is no way of passing from one to the other or of reuniting them, unless we appeal for their reunion to a third term, variously represented as God or the Unknowable. Dualism leads necessarily either to transcendence or to agnosticism. But when a problem is found to be insoluble in the terms in which it is stated the only course open is to criticize these terms themselves, to inquire how they have been arrived at, and whether their genesis was logically sound. In this case, such inquiry leads to the conclusion that the terms depend not upon a philosophical principle, but upon an empirical and naturalistic classification, which has created two groups of facts called internal and external respectively (as if internal facts were not also external, and as if an external fact could exist without being also internal), or souls and bodies, or images and expressions; and everyone knows that it is hopeless to try to find a dialectical unity between terms that have been distinguished not philosophically or formally but only empirically and materially. The soul is only a soul in so far as it is a body; the will is only a will in so far as it moves arms and legs, or is action; intuition is only intuition in so far as it is, in that very act, expression. An image that does not express, that is not speech, song, drawing, painting, sculpture or architecture—speech at least murmured to oneself, song at least echoing within one's own breast, line and color seen in imagination and coloring with its own tint the whole soul and organism—is an image that does not exist. We may assert its existence, but we cannot support our assertion; for the only thing we could adduce in support of it would be the fact that the image was embodied or expressed. This profound philosophical doctrine, the *identity of intuition and expression* is, moreover, a principle of ordinary common sense, which laughs at people who claim to have thoughts they cannot express or to have imagined a great picture which they cannot paint. . . . This identity, which applies to every sphere of the mind, has in the sphere of art a clearness and self-evidence lacking, perhaps, elsewhere. In the creation of a work of poetry, we are present, as it were, at the mystery of the creation of the world; hence the value of the contribution made by esthetics to philosophy as a whole, or the conception of the One that is All. Esthetics, by denying in the life of art an abstract spiritualism and the resulting dualism, prepares the way and leads the mind towards idealism or absolute spiritualism.

EXPRESSION AND COMMUNICATION

Objections to the identity of intuition and expression generally arise from psychological illusions which lead us to believe that we possess at any given moment a profusion of concrete and lively images, when in fact we only possess signs and names for them; or else from faulty analysis of cases like that of the artist who is believed to express mere fragments of a world of images that exists in his mind in its entirety, whereas he really has in his mind only these fragments, together with—not the supposed complete world, but at most an aspiration or obscure working towards it, towards a greater and richer image which may take shape or may not. But these objections also arise from a confusion between *expression* and *communication*, the latter being really distinct from the image and its expression. Communication is the fixation of the intuition-expression upon an object metaphorically called material or physical; in reality, even here we are concerned not with material or physical things but with a mental process. The proof that the so-called physical object is unreal, and its resolution into terms of mind, is primarily of interest for our general philosophical conceptions, and only indirectly for the elucidation of esthetic questions; hence for brevity's sake we may let the metaphor or symbol stand and speak of matter or nature. It is clear that the poem is complete as soon as the poet has expressed it in words which he repeats to himself. When he comes to repeat them aloud, for others to hear, or looks for someone to learn them by heart and repeat them to others . . . or sets them down in writing or in printing, he has entered upon a new stage, not esthetic but practical, whose social and cultural importance need not, of course, be insisted upon. So with the painter; he paints on his panel or canvas, but he could not paint unless at every stage in his work, from the original blur or sketch to the finishing touches, the intuited image, the line and color painted in his imagination, preceded the brush-stroke. Indeed, when the brush-stroke outruns the image, it is cancelled and replaced by the artist's correction of his own work. The exact line that divides expression from communication is difficult to draw in the concrete case, for in the concrete case the two processes generally alternate rapidly and appear to mingle, but it is clear in idea, and it must be firmly grasped. Through overlooking it, or blurring it through insufficient attention, arise the confusions between *art* and *technique*. Technique is not an intrinsic element of art but has to do precisely with the concept of communication. In general it is a cognition or complex of cognitions disposed and directed to the furtherance of practical action; and, in the case of art, of the practical action which makes objects and instruments for the recording and communicating of works of art; e.g., cognitions concerning the preparation of panels, canvases or walls to be painted, pigments, varnishes, ways of obtaining good pronunciation and declamation and so forth. Technical treaties are not esthetic treaties, nor yet parts or chapters of them. Provided, that is, that the ideas are rigorously conceived and the words used accurately in relation to them it would not be worthwhile to pick a quarrel over the use of the word "technique" as a synonym for the artistic work itself, regarded as "inner technique" or the formation of intuition-expressions. The confusion between art and technique is especially beloved by impotent artists, who hope to obtain from practical things and practical devices and inventions the help which their strength does not enable them to give themselves.

Does Traditional Aesthetics Rest on a Mistake?

William E. Kennick

It rests, I think, on at least two of them, and the purpose of this paper is to explore the claim that it does.

By 'traditional aesthetics' I mean that familiar philosophical discipline which concerns itself with trying to answer such questions as the following: What is Art? What is Beauty? What is the Aesthetic Experience? What is the Creative Act? What are the criteria of Aesthetic Judgment and Taste? What is the function of Criticism? To be sure, there are others, like: Are the aesthetic object and the work of art the same? Or, Does art have any cognitive content?—but these questions are commonly taken to be subordinate to those of the first group, which might be called the 'basic questions' of traditional aesthetics.

1. The Basic Questions as Requests for Definitions. If someone asks me 'What is helium?' I can reply: 'It's a gas' or 'It's a chemical element' or 'It's a gaseous element, inert and colourless, whose atomic number is 2 and whose atomic weight is 4·003.' A number of replies will do, depending upon whom I am talking to, the aim of his question, and so on. It is a pretty straightforward business; we get answers to such questions every day from dictionaries, encyclopedias, and technical manuals.

Now someone asks me 'What is Space?' or 'What is Man?' or 'What is Religion?' or 'What is Art?' His question is of the same form as the question 'What is helium?' but how vastly different! There is something very puzzling about these questions; they cannot be answered readily by appealing to dictionaries, encyclopedias, or technical manuals. They are philosophical questions, we say, giving our puzzlement a name although we should not think of calling 'What is helium?' a philosophical question. Yet we expect something of the same sort of answer to both of them. There's the rub.

We say that questions like 'What is Space?' or 'What is Art?' are requests for information about the nature or essence of Space or of Art. We could say that 'What is helium?' is a request for information about the nature or essence of helium, but we rarely, if ever, do; although we do use questions like 'What is helium?' as analogues of questions like 'What is Space?' to show the sort of reply we are looking for. What we want, we say, is a definition of Space or of Art, for as Plato and Aristotle taught us long ago, "definition is the formula of the essence." So, just as the traditional metaphysicians have long sought for the nature or essence of Space and of Time, of Reality and of Change, the traditional aesthetician has sought for the essence of Art and of Beauty, of the Aesthetic Experience and the Creative Act. Most of the basic questions of traditional aesthetics are requests for definitions; hence the familiar formulae that constitute the results of traditional aesthetic inquiry: 'Art is Expression' (Croce), 'Art is Significant Form' (Clive Bell), 'Beauty is Pleasure Objectified' (Santayana), and so on.

From *Mind*, 67 (1958). Reprinted by permission of the publisher.

Given these definitions we are supposed to know what Art is or what Beauty is, just as we are supposed to know what helium is if someone tells us that it is a chemical element, gaseous, inert, and colourless, with an atomic number of 2 and an atomic weight of 4·003. F. J. E. Woodbridge once remarked that metaphysics searches for the nature of reality and finds it by definition. We might say that traditional aesthetics searches for the nature of Art or Beauty and finds it by definition.

But why should it be so difficult to discern the essence of Art or Beauty? Why should it take so much argument to establish or defend such formulae as 'Art is Expression'? And once we have arrived at such formulae or have been given them in answer to our question, why should they be so dissatisfying?

To come closer to an answer to these questions, we must look at what it is the aesthetician expects of a definition of Art or Beauty. De Witt Parker has stated with unusual clarity the "assumption" of the aesthetician in asking and answering such questions as 'What is Art?'; at the beginning of his essay on "The Nature of Art" (note the title) he says:

The assumption underlying every philosophy of art is the existence of some *common nature* present in all the arts, despite their differences in form and content; something the *same* in painting and sculpture; in poetry and drama; in music and architecture. Every single work of art, it is admitted, has a unique flavour, a *je ne sais quoi* which makes it incomparable with every other work; nevertheless, there is some mark or set of marks which, if it applies to any work of art, applies to *all* works of art, *and to nothing else*—a common denominator, so to say, which constitutes the definition of art, and serves to separate . . . the field of art from other fields of human culture.[1]

2. The Assumption Questioned; the First Mistake.

The assumption that, despite their differences, all works of art must possess some common nature, some distinctive set of characteristics which serves to separate Art from everything else, a set of necessary and sufficient conditions for their being works of art at all, is both natural and disquieting, and constitutes what I consider to be the first mistake on which traditional aesthetics rests. It is natural, because, after all, we do use the work 'art' to refer to a large number of very different things—pictures and poems and musical compositions and sculptures and vases and a host of other things; and yet the word is one word. Surely, we are inclined to say, there must be something common to them all or we should not call them all by the same name. *Unum nomen; unum nominatum.*

Yet the assumption is disquieting when we come to search for the common nature which we suppose all works of art to possess. It is so elusive. We ought to be able to read a poem by Donne or by Keats, a novel by George Eliot or Joseph Conrad, or a play by Sophocles or Shakespeare, to listen to Mozart and Stravinsky, and to look at the pictures of Giotto and Cezanne and the Chinese masters and *see* what Art is. But when we look we do not see what Art is. So we are inclined to suppose that its essence must be something hidden, something that only an aesthetician can see, like the sounds that only a dog can hear, or else, as Parker, for example, supposes, that it must be something very complex, involving many characteristics (*op. cit.* p. 93). This explains why an adequate definition of Art is so hard to arrive at, why it is so much harder to answer questions like 'What is Art?' than it is to answer questions like 'What is helium?' Perhaps this also explains why there is a Philosophy of Art when there is no Philosophy of Helium?

But this explanation will not do. It will not do, that is, to suppose simply that the essence or nature of Art is elusive, very hard to detect, or very complex. It suggests that what we are faced with is a problem of scrutinizing, that what we have to do is to look long and hard at works of art, examine them carefully and diligently and, *voila!* we shall *see*. But no amount of looking and scrutinizing gives us what we want. All we see is this poem and that play, this picture and that statue, or some feature of them that catches our attention; and if we find some resemblances between poems or plays or pictures, or even between poems *and* pictures, pictures *and* musical compositions, these resemblances quickly disappear when we turn to other poems and plays and pictures. That is why in aesthetics it is best not to look at too many works of art and why, incidentally, aesthetics is best taught without concrete examples: a few will do. We can readily believe that we have seen the essence of Art when we have selected our examples properly; but when we range farther afield we lose it.

Despite the temptation to think that if we look long enough and hard enough at works of art we shall find the common denominator in question, after all the fruitless scrutinizing that has already been done, it is still more tempting to think that we are looking for something that is not there, like looking for the equator or the line on the spectrum that separates orange from red. No wonder that in aesthetics we soon begin to feel the frustration of St. Augustine when he asked himself 'What is Time?': "If I am not asked, I know; if I am asked, I know not." Something must be wrong.

What is wrong, as I see it, has nothing to do with the nature or essence of Art at all; that is, there is neither anything mysterious nor anything complicated about works of art which makes the task of answering the question 'What is Art?' so difficult. Like St. Augustine with Time, we do know quite well what Art is; it is only when someone asks us that we do not know. The trouble lies not in the works of art themselves but in the concept of Art. The word 'art,' unlike the word 'helium,' has a complicated variety of uses, what is nowadays called a complex 'logic.' It is not a word coined in the laboratory or the studio to name something that has hitherto escaped our attention; nor is it a relatively simple term of common parlance like 'star' or 'tree' which names something with which we are all quite familiar. As Professor Kristeller has shown us,[2] it is a work with a long, involved, and interesting history; a complicated concept indeed, but not for the reasons which the aestheticians suppose. Any good dictionary will indicate some of its many meanings, some of the variety of uses which the word 'art' has: but no dictionary will give us the kind of formula which the aestheticians seek. That is why we suppose that the nature of Art is a philosophical problem and why there is a Philosophy of Art but no Philosophy of Helium.

It is the complicated concepts like those of Space, Time, Reality, Change, Art, Knowledge, and so on that baffle us. Dictionaries and their definitions are of use in making short shrift of questions of the form 'What is X?' only in relatively simple and comparatively trivial cases; in the hard and more interesting cases they are frustrating and disappointing.

Doubtless there is an answer to this, and it might run somewhat as follows: "We know that the word 'Art' has a variety of uses in English. Most commonly it is used to refer to pictures alone; when we visit an art museum or consult an art critic, we expect to see pictures or to hear pictures talked about. We say that painting, painting pictures, *not* painting houses or fences, is *an* art, that cooking and sewing and basketweaving, bookbinding and selling are *arts*, but only some pictures do we call *works* of art, and rarely do we refer to dishes or garments or baskets as works of art, except honorifically. We speak of the liberal arts and the industrial arts and of the art of war. But all of this is beside the point. As aestheticians we are interested only in what are sometimes called the 'fine arts', or what Collingwood calls 'art proper'—works of art. Surely all of these have something in common, else how should we be able to separate those paintings and drawings and poems and plays, musical compositions and buildings which are works of art from those which are not?"

To answer the last question first and make a long story short: we are able to separate those objects which are works of art from those which are not, because we know English; that is, we know how correctly to use the word 'art' and to apply the phrase 'work of art.' To borrow a statement from Dr. Waismann and change it to meet my own needs, "If anyone is able to use the word 'art' or the phrase 'work of art' correctly, in all sorts of contexts and on the right sort of occasions, he knows 'what art is,' and no formula in the world can make him wiser."[3] "Art proper" is simply what is properly called "art." The 'correctly' and 'properly' here have nothing to do with any 'common nature' or 'common denominator' of all works of art; they have merely to do with the rules that govern the actual and commonly accepted usage of the word 'art.'

Imagine a very large warehouse filled with all sorts of things—pictures of every description, musical scores for symphonies and dances and hymns, machines, tools, boats, houses, churches and temples, statues, vases, books of poetry and of prose, furniture and clothing, newspapers, postage stamps, flowers, trees, stones, musical instruments. Now we instruct someone to enter the warehouse and bring out all of the works of art it contains. He will be able to do this with reasonable success, despite the fact that, as even the aestheticians must admit, he possesses no satisfactory definition of 'art' in terms of some common denominator because no such definition has yet been found. Now imagine the same person sent into the warehouse to bring out all objects with Significant Form, or all objects of Expression. He would rightly be baffled; he knows a work of art when he sees one, but he has little or no idea what to look for when he is told to bring an object that possesses Significant Form.

To be sure, there are many occasions on which we are not sure whether something is a work of art or not; that is, we are not sure whether to call a given drawing or musical composition a work of art or not. Are "Nearer My God to Thee" and the political cartoons of Mr. Low works of art? But this merely reflects the systematic vagueness of the concepts in question, or what Dr. Waismann on another occasion has called their 'open texture'; a vagueness, note, which the definitions of the aestheticians do nothing at all to remove. On such occasions we can, of course, tighten the texture, remove some of the vagueness, by making a decision, drawing a line; and perhaps curators and purchasing committees of art museums are sometimes forced for obvious practical reasons to do this. But in doing so, they and we are not discovering anything about Art.

We do know what art is when no one asks us what it is; that is, we know quite well how to use the word 'art' and the phrase 'work of art' correctly. And when someone asks us what art is, we do *not* know; that is, we are at a loss to produce any simple formula, or any complex one, which will neatly exhibit the logic of this word and this phrase. It is the compulsion to reduce the complexity of aesthetic concepts to simplicity, neatness, and order that moves the aesthetician to make his first mistake, to ask 'What is Art?' and to expect to find an answer like the answer that can be given to 'What is helium?'

What I have said about Art in this section applies, *mutatis mutandis*, to Beauty, the Aesthetic Experience, the Creative Act, and all of the other entities with which traditional aesthetics concerns itself.

Where there is no mystery, there is no need for removing a mystery and certainly none for inventing one.

3. Common Denominators and Similarities. Is the search for common characteristics among works of art, then, a fool's errand? That depends upon what we expect to find. If we expect to find some common denominator in Parker's sense, we are bound to be disappointed. We shall get ourselves enmeshed in unnecessary difficulties, and the definitions which we hope will free us from the net will be specious at best. If we say 'Art is Significant Form' we may feel momentarily enlightened; but when we come to reflect upon what we mean by 'significant form' we shall find ourselves entangled again. For the notion of Significant Form is clearly more obscure than is that of Art or Beauty, as the example of the warehouse above amply illustrates; the same holds for Expression, Intuition, Representation, and the other favored candidates of the aestheticians. Nor will it do to say, as Professor Munro does,[4] that "art is skill in providing stimuli to satisfactory aesthetic experience." This has merely a scientific *sound*, and this sound is about as close as the effort to make aesthetics scientific comes to science. The notion of aesthetic experience is fraught with the same difficulties as the notion of art. To put it dogmatically, there is no such thing as *the* Aesthetic Experience; different sorts of experiences are properly referred to as aesthetic. Do not say they must all be contemplative. Does that really help at all?

There is, however, a fruitful and enlightening search for similarities and resemblances in art which the search for the common denominator sometimes furthers, the search for what, to torture a phrase of Wittgenstein's, we can call 'family resemblances.' When we squint we can sometimes see features of an object which otherwise we should miss. So in aesthetics, when we narrow our view, when in the search for the common denominator we carefully select our examples and restrict our sight, we may not see what we are looking for, but we may see something of more interest and importance. The simplifying formulae of the aestheticians are not to be scrapped merely because they fail to do what they are designed to do. What fails to do one thing may do another. The mistake of the aestheticians can be turned to advantage. The suspicion that aesthetics is not nonsense is often justified. For the idea that there is a unity among the arts, properly employed, can lead to the uncovering of similarities which, when noticed, enrich our commerce with art. Croce's supposed discovery that Art is Expression calls our attention to, among other things, an interesting feature of some, if not all, works of art, namely, their indifference to the distinction between the real and the unreal.

Or, to take examples from critics, when F. R. Leavis says of Crabbe, "His art is that of the short-story writer,"[5] and when Professor Stechow compares the fourth movement of Schumann's "Rhenish" Symphony with certain features of the Cologne Cathedral,[6] we have something of interest and importance. Our attention is refocused on certain works, and we see them in a new light. One of the offices of creative criticism, as of creative aesthetics, is the finding and pointing out of precisely such similarities.

4. *Aesthetic Theories Reconsidered.* Philosophical mistakes are rarely downright howlers; they have a point. What I have said is, I think, correct, but it neglects an important facet of the quest for essences, a by-product of that search, so to speak, which we should not ignore. An aesthetic theory, by which I mean a systematic answer to such questions as 'What is Art?', 'What is Beauty?' and the like, frequently does something quite other than what it sets out to do. The assumption underlying traditional aesthetics, as Parker states it in the passage quoted above, is wrong, and I hope I have shown why it is wrong. It does not follow from this, however, that aesthetic theories are wholly without point, that they are merely mistaken, that formulae like 'Art is Significant Form' are worthless, useless, or meaningless. They do serve a purpose, but their purpose is not that which Parker assigns them. Considered in context, in the historical or personal context, for example, they are frequently seen to have a point which has nothing to do with the philosophical excuses that are made for them.

Take Bell's famous dictum that 'Art is Significant Form.' It does not help us to understand what art is at all, and to that extent it is a failure; its shortcomings in this direction have been exposed on numerous occasions. It is easy to beat Bell down; he is so vulnerable. But when we stop to consider that he was an Englishman and when he wrote his book on art (1913) and what the taste of the English was like then and of his association with Roger Fry, the statement that 'Art is Significant Form' loses some of its mystifying sound. It has a *point*. Not the point that Bell thinks it has, for Bell was also looking for the common denominator; another point. We might put it this way. The taste of Edwardian Englishmen in art was restricted to what we pejoratively call the 'academic.' Subject-matter was of prime importance to them—portraits of eminent persons, landscapes with or without cows, genre scenes, pictures of fox hunts, and the rest. Bell had seen the paintings of Cezanne, Matisse, and Picasso, and he was quick to see that subject-matter was not of prime importance in them, that the value of the paintings did not rest on realism or sentimental associations. It rested on what? Well, 'significant form'; lines and colours and patterns and harmonies that stir apart from associations evoked by subject-matter. He found also that he could look at other paintings, older paintings, paintings by the Venetian and Dutch masters, for example, and at vases and carpets and sculptures in the same way he looked at Cezanne. He found such looking rewarding, exciting. But when he turned to the pictures of the academicians, the thrill disappeared; they could not be looked at profitably in this way. What was more natural, then, than that he should announce his discovery by saying 'Art *is* Significant Form'? He *had* discovered something for himself. Not the essence of Art, as the philosophers would have it, although he thought that this is what he found, but *a new way of looking at pictures*. He wanted to share his discovery with others and to reform English taste. *Here* is the point of his dictum; 'Art is Significant Form' is a slogan, the epitome of a platform of aesthetic reform. It has work to do. Not the work which the philosophers assign it, but work of teaching people a new way of looking at pictures.

When we blow the dust of philosophic cant away from aesthetic theories and look at them in this way, they take on an importance which otherwise they seem to lack. Read Aristotle's *Poetics*, not as a philosophical exercise in definition, but as instruction in one way to read tragic poetry, and it takes on a new life. Many of the other dicta of the aestheticians can also be examined in this light. We know that as definitions they will not do; but as instruments of instruction or reform they will do. Perhaps that is why they have had more real weight with practising critics than they have had with philosophers. The critics have caught the point, where the philosophers, misguided from the start by a foolish preoccupation with definition, have missed it.

5. Aesthetics and Criticism; the Second Mistake. One of the prime reasons for the aesthetician's search for definitions of Art, Beauty, and the rest, is his supposition that unless we know what Art or Beauty is, we cannot say what good art or beautiful art is. Put it in the form of an assumption: Criticism presupposes Aesthetic Theory. This assumption contains the second mistake on which traditional aesthetics rests, namely, the view that responsible criticism is impossible without standards or criteria universally applicable to all works of art. The second mistake is in this way closely related to the first.

To see more clearly how this assumption operates, we can turn to a recent book by Mr. Harold Osborne,[7] *Aesthetics and Criticism*. Osborne believes that "a theory of the nature of artistic excellence is implicit in every critical assertion which is other than autobiographical record," and he thinks that "until the theory has been made explicit the criticism is without meaning" (p. 3). By a 'theory of the nature of artistic excellence' Osborne means a theory of the nature of Beauty (p. 3).

Osborne examines several theories of the nature of Beauty and finds them all wanting. His moves against them are instructive. Take, for example, his move against a version of the Realistic Theory, the theory holding that artistic excellence consists in 'truth to life'—or so Osborne states it. He correctly notes that practising critics have rarely insisted that verisimilitude is a necessary condition of artistic excellence, and we should all agree that it is not. "But," says Osborne, "if correspondence with real or possible actuality is not a necessary condition of artistic excellence, then most certainly it is not and cannot be of itself an *artistic* virtue, or an aesthetic merit, in those works of literature where it happens to occur" (p. 93). This is a curious argument. It seems to contain a glaring *non sequitur*. But what leads Osborne from his protasis to his conclusion is the assumption that the only acceptable reason offerable for a critical judgment of a work of art is one framed in terms of a characteristic which all works of art, *qua* works of art, must possess. Since we admit that not all works of art must possess truth to life or verisimilitude, we cannot use their adventitious possession of this property as a reason for praising, judging, or commending them as works of art.

Now surely this is mistaken. We can agree that correspondence with real or possible actuality, whatever that may mean, is not a *necessary* condition of artistic excellence; that is, it is *not* necessary that it appear among the reasons offerable for the judgment that a given work of art is good or beautiful. But it does not follow that therefore it does not and cannot appear as *a* reason for such a judgment. We can and do praise works of art, *as* works of art, whatever the force of that is, for a variety of reasons, and not always the same variety. Osborne's reply here is that in doing so we are being 'illogical and inconsistent.' Attacking the users of the Hedonistic Criterion, he says, "In so far as he [the critic] also uses other criteria [than the hedonistic one] for grading and assessing works of art, he is being illogical and inconsistent with himself whenever he does introduce the hedonistic—or emotional—assumption" (p. 139). But why? There is nothing whatever illogical or inconsistent about praising, grading, or judging a work of art for more than one reason, unless we assume with Osborne that one and only one reason is offerable on pain of inconsistency, which is clearly not the case in art or anywhere else.

Osborne, true to the assumptions of traditional aesthetics, is looking for that condition which is both necessary and sufficient for artistic excellence or merit. His own candidate for that condition is what he calls "configurational coherence." But if anything pointed were needed to convince us of the emptiness of the search, it is the unintelligibility of Osborne's account of "beauty as configuration." If what I have said above about the concepts of Art and Beauty is true, we should not be surprised by this. For 'art' and 'beauty' do not name one and only one substance and attribute respectively; no wonder we cannot find the one thing they name or render intelligible the felt discovery that they do name one thing. We can *make* each of them name one thing if we wish. But why should we bother? We get along very well with them as they are.

6. Ethics and Criticism; the Second Mistake Again. "But surely," someone will say, "this cannot be the whole story. We can and do say that this work of art, this picture, for example, is better than that, or that this is a good one and that one is not. Do we not presuppose certain standards or criteria when we make such judgments? And isn't this really all that Osborne and other aestheticians have in mind when they insist that criticism presupposes aesthetic theory? They are looking for the standards of critical judgment and taste in the nature of art, just as many moralists have looked for the standards of right conduct in the nature of man. They may be looking in the wrong place, but clearly they are right in assuming that there must be something to find."

My reply is this: they are not looking in the wrong place so much as they are looking for the wrong thing. The bases of responsible criticism are indeed to be found *in* the work of art and nowhere else, but this in no way implies that critical judgments presuppose any canons, rules, standards, or criteria applicable to all works of art.

When we say that a certain knife is a good knife, we have in mind certain features of the knife, or of knives in general, which we believe will substantiate or support this claim: the sharpness of the blade, the sturdiness of the handle, the durability of the metal, the way it fits the hand, and so on. There are a number of such considerations, all of which refer to characteristics of the knife and not to our feelings about or attitudes towards it, which may be said to constitute the criteria of a good knife. Special criteria may be adduced for fishing knives as opposed to butcher knives, and so on, but this does not affect the issue in question. Note first that there is no definite or exhaustively specifiable list of criteria in common and universal employment; it does not make sense to ask how many there are or whether we have considered them all. But there are generally accepted criteria with which we are all familiar which we use to support our judgments, though in cases of special instruments or implements, like ophthalmoscopes, only specialists are acquainted with the criteria. Secondly, note how the criteria are related to the purposes or functions of knives, to the uses to which we put them, the demands we make upon them. 'Knife,' we might say, is a function-word, a word that names something which is usually defined by its function or functions. The criteria, we can say loosely, are derivable from the definition. This second consideration has led some aestheticians to look for the standards of taste and criticism in the function of art.

Now take apples. They have, of course, no function. We use them, we do things with them—eat them, use them for decoration, feed them to pigs, press cider from them, and so on—but none of these things can be said to constitute the function of an apple. Depending, however, on how we use them or what we use them for, we can frame lists of criteria similar to the lists for knives. The best apples for decoration are not always the best for eating, nor are the best for making pies always the best for making cider. Now take mathematicians. A mathematician, unless he is assigned a particular work to do, again has no function. There are certain things a mathematician does, however, and in terms of these we can again frame criteria for judging, praising, grading, and commending mathematicians. Finally, take men in general. We often praise a man, *as* a man, as opposed to as a plumber or a mathematician, and we call this sort of praise moral praise. Here again, we have criteria for assessing the moral worth of men, although, theological considerations aside, we do not frame them in terms of man's function, purpose, or task, even if some moralists, like Aristotle, have tried to frame them in terms of man's end. But we make demands on men, moral demands on all men, and our criteria reflect these demands.

Let us turn now to art. The question we have to raise is this: Are critical judgments of pictures and poems logically symmetrical to the sorts of judgments we have been considering? I think they are not, or not entirely. Not because they are somehow more subjective or unreliable than other value judgments (this issue is as false as an issue can be!), but because the pattern of justification and support which is appropriate to them is of a different sort. Any critical judgment, to be justified, must be supported by reasons; this goes without saying, for this is what 'justification' means. But must the reasons offerable and acceptable in cases of critical appraisal be of the same order or type as those offerable and acceptable in cases of instruments, implements, useful objects, professional services, jobs, offices, or moral conduct? In particular, must there be any general rules, standards, criteria, canons, or laws applicable to all works of art by which alone such critical appraisals can be supported? I think not.

In the first place, we should note that only a man corrupted by aesthetics would think of judging a work of art *as* a work of art in general, as opposed to as this poem, that picture, or this symphony. There is some truth in the contention that the notions of Art and Work of Art are special aestheticians' concepts. This follows quite naturally from the absence of any distinguishing feature or features common to all works of art as such, and from the absence of any single demand or set of demands which we make on all works of art as such. Despite the occasional claim that it has, Art has no function or purpose, in the sense in which knives and ophthalmoscopes have functions, and this is an insight to be gained from the 'art for art's sake' position. This does not mean that we cannot use individual works of art for special purposes; we can and do. We can use novels and poems and symphonies to put us to sleep or wake us up; we can use pictures to cover spots on the wall, vases to hold flowers, and sculptures for paper weights or door stops. This is what lends point to the distinction between judging something *as* a work of art and judging it *as* a sedative, stimulant, or paper weight; but we cannot conclude from this that Art has some special function or purpose in addition to the purposes to which it can be put.

Similarly there is no one thing which we *do* with all works of art: some we hang, some we play, some we perform, some we read; some we look at, some we listen to, some we analyse, some we contemplate, and so on. There is no special aesthetic use of works of art, even though it may make sense, and even be true, to say that a person who uses a statue as a door stop is not using it as a work of art; he is not doing one of the things we normally do with works of art; he is not treating it properly, we might say. But the proper treatment of works of art varies from time to time and from place to place. It was quite proper for a cave man to hurl his spear at the drawing of a bison, just as it was quite proper for the Egyptians to seal up paintings and sculptures in a tomb. Such treatment does not render the object thus treated not a work of art. The attempt to define Art in terms of what we do with certain objects is as doomed as any other. From this and the first consideration it follows that there is no way by which we can derive the criteria of taste and criticism from the function of art or from its use.

The remaining parallel is with moral appraisal, and this is the most interesting of them all. It has been, and perhaps still is, a common view among philosophers that Beauty and Goodness are two species of the same genus, namely, Value, and that therefore there are at least two classes of value judgments, namely, moral judgments and aesthetic judgments. For this reason there is a tendency further to suppose that there is a logical symmetry between the two. But the supposition of symmetry is a mistake, and I am led to suspect that it does little but harm to suppose that Beauty and Goodness are two species of the same genus at all. There are clearly certain similarities between the two, that is, between the logic of statements of the form 'This is good' and the logic of statements of the form 'This is beautiful'—they are used in many of the same ways—but this must not blind us to the differences. Criticism suffers from a very natural comparison with ethics.

Moral appraisal is like the other forms of appraisal, in this respect; it expresses a desire for uniformity. It is when we are interested in uniformity of size, milk producing capacity, conduct, and so on, that standards or criteria become so important. We maintain standards in products and in workmanship; we enforce them, hold ourselves up to them, teach them to our children, insist on them, and so on, all for the sake of a certain uniformity. In morals we *are* interested in uniformity, at least in what we expect men not to do; that is one reason why rules and laws are necessary and why they play such an important role in moral appraisal. But in art, unless, like Plato, we wish to be legislators and to require something of art, demand that it perform a specified educational and social service, we are not as a rule interested in uniformity. Some critics and aestheticians are, of course, interested in uniformity—uniformity in the works of art themselves or uniformity in our approach to them. For them it is quite natural to demand criteria. For them it is also quite natural to formulate theories of Art and Beauty. Remember what we said about aesthetic theories above: the definitions in which they issue are often slogans of reform. As such they are also often devices for the encouragement of uniformity. But this merely betrays the persuasive character of many aesthetic theories, and the peculiar legislative posture of some critics and aestheticians is no warrant for the assumption that the criteria in question are necessary for responsible criticism. Nor should it blind us to the fact that we do quite well without them. Criticism has in no way been hampered by the absence of generally applicable canons and norms, and where such norms have been proposed they have either, like the notorious Unities in the case of tragedy, been shown to be absurd, or else, like the requirements of balance, harmony, and unity in variety, they have been so general, equivocal, and empty as to be useless in critical practice. Ordinarily we feel no constraint in praising one novel for its verisimilitude, another for its humour, and still another for its plot or characterization. We remark on the richness of Van Gogh's impasto, but we do not find it a fault in a Chinese scroll painting that it is flat and smooth. Botticelli's lyric grace is his glory, but Giotto and Chardin are not to be condemned because their poetry is of another order. The merits of Keats and Shelley are not those of Donne and Herbert. And why should Shakespeare and Aeschylus be measured by the same rod? Different works of art are, or may be, praiseworthy or blameworthy for different reasons, and not always the same reasons. A quality that is praiseworthy in one painting may be blameworthy in another; realism is not always a virtue, but this does not mean that it is not sometimes a virtue.[8]

Mr. Hampshire has put the reason why the criteria sought by the aestheticians are so 'elusive' and why the parallel with ethics is a mistake in this way: "A work of art," he says, "is gratuitous. It is not *essentially* the answer to a question or the solution of a presented problem" (*op. cit.* p. 162). There is no one problem being solved or question answered by all poems, all pictures, all symphonies, let alone all works of art. If we set a number of people to doing the same thing, we can rate them on how well they do it. We have, or can frame, a criterion. But not all artists are doing the same thing—solving the same problem, answering the same question, playing the same game, running the same race. Some of them may be, we do group artists together by 'schools,' and in other ways, to indicate precisely this kind of similarity; but only in so far as they are does it make sense to compare and appraise them on the same points. It is no criticism of Dickens that he did not write like Henry James. Writing a novel or a lyric poem may, in some interesting respects, be like playing a game or solving a problem, we in fact speak of artists as solving problems. But it is also different; so that if we wish to retain the analogy we must call attention to the differences by saying that not all poets or novelists are playing the *same* game, solving the *same* problems. There is indeed a certain gratuitousness in art which destroys the parallelism or symmetry between moral and aesthetic appraisal.

But there is also a gratuitousness in aesthetic criticism. Moral appraisal, like legal judgment, is a practical necessity; aesthetic appraisal is not. That is why the claim that in art it is all a matter of taste is tolerable, even if it is false, when this sounds so shocking in morals. We can live side by side in peace and amity with those whose tastes differ quite radically from our own; similar differences in moral standards are more serious. And yet, of course, aesthetic criticism is not merely a matter of taste, if by taste we mean unreasoned preferences. Taste does play an important part in the differences among critical appraisals, but we are clearly not satisfied when, in answer to our question 'Why is it good?' or 'What's good about it?,' we are told 'It's good because I like it.' Mrs. Knight correctly notes that "my *liking* a picture is never a criterion of its goodness" (*op. cit.* p. 154). That is, my liking a picture is no reason for its *being* good, though it may be a reason for my *saying* that it is good.

But if it is not all a matter of liking and disliking, why is it that a certain feature is a virtue in a given work of art? If someone tells me that a certain work of art is good for such and such reasons, how can I tell whether the reasons he offers are good reasons or not, or even if they are relevant? These questions are not easily answered, for in practice we adduce many considerations for saying that a work of art is good or that a certain feature of it is a virtue. I will make no attempt to canvass these considerations but will close with some observations on a logical feature of the problem.

We are confronted, I think, with a problem that is really two problems: there is the problem of saying why a given work of art is good or bad, and there is the problem of saying why our reasons are good or bad, or even relevant. We may praise a picture, say, for its subtle balance, colour contrast, and draughtsmanship; this is saying why the picture is good. We may now go on to raise the more 'philosophical' question of what makes balance, or this sort of colour contrast, or this kind of draughtsmanship an artistic virtue. The first sort of question, the question of why the work of art is good or bad, is decided by appeal to the 'good-making characteristics' or 'criterion-characters' of the work of art in question, that is, by an appeal to certain objectively discriminable characteristics of the work under discussion. These characteristics are many and various; there is a large variety of reasons offerable for a work of art's being a good or bad work of art. The second sort of question, the question of the worth or relevance of the reasons offered in answer to the first question, is settled by appeal either to custom or to decision. In this respect aesthetic criticism is very like moral appraisal. We either simply praise what is customarily praised and condemn what is customarily condemned or we *decide* what the criteria shall be. This does not mean that the criteria, that is, the reasons offerable for a work of art's being good or bad, are arbitrary. There may be plenty of reasons why one feature is a 'criterion-character' and another is not. Part of the reason may be psychological, part sociological, part metaphysical, or even religious and ethical. Only an aesthete ignores, or tries to ignore, the many relations of a poem or picture to life and concentrates on what are called the purely 'formal' values of the work at hand; but in doing so he *determines* what he will accept as a reason for a work of art's being good or bad. That a work of art assists the cause of the proletariat in the class struggle *is* a reason for its being a good work of art to a convinced Marxist, but it is not a reason, let alone a good reason, to the bourgeois aesthete. That a picture contains nude figures is a reason, to the puritan and the prude, for condemning it, though no enlightened man can be brought to accept it. Thus morals and politics and religion do enter into our critical judgments, even when we claim that they should not.

I noted above that there is no one use which we make of all works of art, nor is there any one demand or set of demands which we make on them. This is, I think, important, and serves to explain, at least in part, the actual relativity of aesthetic criteria. What one age looks for in painting or in literature, another age may neglect. What one group demands, another forbids. We are not always consistent in even our own demands on art, and I can see no reason why we should be. We can be interested in works of art for many reasons, and some of these reasons may be more decisive at one time or in one set of circumstances than they are at another time or in another set of circumstances. This affects the very logic of critical appraisal by determining the relevance and merit of the reasons we offer for our judgments. We are well aware of the fact that the estimate of a given poet or painter changes from period to period. El Greco's or Shakespeare's reputation has not always been what it is, and no one should be surprised if it should change in the future. But if we examine the reasons that have been offered for the different estimates, we find that they too are different. Different reasons are persuasive at different times and in different contexts. The same explanation is operative: the needs and interests that art gratifies are different from time to time and, to a lesser extent perhaps, from person to person. But as the needs and interests vary, so also will the criteria and the weight we place on them. This is a vicious relativism only to those who are morally disposed to insist on the uniformity of taste.

Summary: I have tried to show (1) that the search for essences in aesthetics is a mistake, arising from the failure to appreciate the complex but not mysterious logic of such words and phrases as 'art,' 'beauty,' 'the aesthetic experience,' and so on. But (2) although the characteristics common to all works of art are the object of a fool's errand, the search for similarities in sometimes very different works of art can be profitably pursued, and this search is occasionally stimulated by the formulae of the aestheticians. (3) Although the definitions of the aestheticians are useless for the role usually assigned to them, we must not ignore the live purpose they frequently serve as slogans in the effort to change taste and as instruments for opening up new avenues of appreciation. (4) If the search for the common denominator of all works of art is abandoned, abandoned with it must be the attempt to derive the criteria of critical appreciation and appraisal from the nature of art. (5) Traditional aesthetics mistakenly supposes that responsible criticism is impossible without a set of rules, canons, or standards applicable to all works of art. This supposition arises from an uncritical assimilation of the pattern of critical appraisal to that of appraisal in other areas, particularly morals, and from a failure to appreciate the gratuitousness of art and the manner in which reasons are operative in the justification of critical judgments.

NOTES

1. De Witt H. Parker, "The Nature of Art," *Revue Internationale de Philosophie*, July 1939, p. 684; reprinted in E. Vivas and M. Krieger, eds., *The Problems of Aesthetics* (New York, 1953), p. 90. Italics mine.
2. P. O. Kristeller, "The Modern System of the Arts: A Study in the History of Aesthetics," *Journal of the History of Ideas*, xii (1951), 496–527; xiii (1952), 17–46.
3. See F. Waismann, "Analytic-Synthetic II," *Analysis*, 11 (1950), p. 27.
4. Thomas Munro, *The Arts and Their Interrelations* (New York, 1949), p. 108.
5. F. R. Leavis, *Revaluation: Tradition and Development in English Poetry* (London, 1936), p. 125.
6. Wolfgang Stechow, "Problems of Structure in Some Relations Between the Visual Arts and Music," *The Journal of Aesthetics and Art Criticism*, 11 (1953), 325.
7. Routledge and Kegan Paul Ltd., London, 1955.
8. I owe much in this section to Helen Knight's "The Use of 'Good' in Aesthetic Judgments," *Aesthetics and Language*, William Elton, ed. (Oxford, 1954), pp. 147 ff., and to Stuart Hampshire's "Logic and Appreciation," ibid., pp. 161 ff.

Expressiveness

Susanne K. Langer

When we talk about Art with a capital 'A'—that is, about any or all of the arts: painting, sculpture, architecture, the potter's and goldsmith's and other designers' arts, music, dance, poetry, and prose fiction, drama and film—it is a constant temptation to say things about "Art" in this general sense that are true only in one special domain, or to assume that what holds for one art must hold for another. For instance, the fact that music is made for performance, for presentation to the ear, and is simply not the same thing when it is given only to the tonal imagination of a reader silently perusing the score, has made some aestheticians pass straight to the conclusion that literature, too, must by physically heard to be fully experienced, because words are originally spoken, not written; an obvious parallel, but a careless and, I think, invalid one. It is dangerous to set up principles by analogy, and generalize from a single consideration.

But it is natural, and safe enough, to ask analogous questions: "What is the function of sound in music? What is the function of sound in poetry? What is the function of sound in prose composition? What is the function of sound in drama?" The answers may be quite heterogeneous; and that is itself an important fact, a guide to something more than a simple and sweeping theory. Such findings guide us to exact relations and abstract, variously exemplified basic principles.

At present, however, we are dealing with principles that have proven to be the same in all the arts, when each kind of art—plastic, musical, balletic, poetic, and each major mode, such as literary and dramatic writing, or painting, sculpturing, building plastic shapes—has been studied in its own terms. Such candid study is more rewarding than the usual passionate declaration that all the arts are alike, only their materials differ, their principles are all the same, their techniques all analogous, etc. This is not only unsafe, but untrue. It is in pursuing the differences among them that one arrives, finally, at a point where no more differences appear; then one has found, not postulated, their unity. At that deep level there is only one concept exemplified in all the different arts, and that is the concept of Art.

The principles that obtain wholly and fundamentally in every kind of art are few, but decisive; they determine what is art, and what is not. Expressiveness, in one definite and appropriate sense, is the same in all art works of any kind. What is created is not the same in any two distinct arts—this is, in fact, what makes them distinct—but the principle of creation is the same. And "living form" means the same in all of them.

A work of art is an expressive form created for our perception through sense or imagination, and what is expressed is human feeling. The word "feeling" must be taken here in its broadest sense, meaning *everything that can be felt*, from physical sensation, pain and comfort, excitement and repose, to the most complex emotions, intellectual tensions, or the steady feeling-tones of a conscious human life. In stating what a work of art is, I have just used the words "form," "expressive," and "created"; these are key words. One at a time, they will keep us engaged.

From *Problems of Art* (New York: Charles Scribner's Sons, 1957). Reprinted by permission of Charles Scribner's Sons and Routledge & Kegan Paul Ltd.

Let us first consider what is meant, in this context, by a *form*. The word has many meanings, all equally legitimate for various purposes; even in connection with art it has several. It may, for instance—and often does—denote the familiar, characteristic structures known as the sonnet form, the sestina, or the ballad form in poetry, the sonata form, the madrigal, or the symphony in music, the contredance or the classical ballet in choreography, and so on. This is not what I mean; or rather, it is only a very small part of what I mean. There is another sense in which artists speak of "form" when they say, for instance, "form follows function," or declare that the one quality shared by all good works of art is "significant form," or entitle a book *The Problem of Form in Painting and Sculpture*, or *The Life of Forms in Art*, or *Search for Form*. They are using "form" in a wider sense, which on the one hand is close to the commonest, popular meaning, namely just the *shape* of a thing, and on the other hand to the quite unpopular meaning it has in science and philosophy, where it designates something more abstract: "form" in its most abstract sense means structure, articulation, a whole resulting from the relation of mutually dependent factors, or more precisely, the way that whole is put together.

The abstract sense, which is sometimes called "logical form," is involved in the notion of expression, at least the kind of expression that characterizes art. That is why artists, when they speak of achieving "form," use the word with something of an abstract connotation, even when they are talking about a visible and tangible art object in which that form is embodied.

The more recondite concept of form is derived, of course, from the naive one, that is, material shape. Perhaps the easiest way to grasp the idea of "logical form" is to trace its derivation.

Let us consider the most obvious sort of form, the shape of an object, say a lampshade. In any department store you will find a wide choice of lampshades, mostly monstrosities, and what is monstrous is usually their shape. You select the least offensive one, maybe even a good one, but realize that the color, say violet, will not fit into your room; so you look about for another shade of the same shape but a different color, perhaps green. In recognizing this same shape in another object, possibly of another material as well as another color, you have quite naturally and easily abstracted the concept of this shape from your actual impression of the first lampshade. Presently it may occur to you that this shade is too big for your lamp; you ask whether they have *this same shade* (meaning another one of this shape) in a smaller size. The clerk understands you.

But what is *the same* in the big violet shade and the little green one? Nothing but the interrelations among their respective various dimensions. They are not "the same" even in their spatial properties, for none of their actual measures are alike; but their shapes are congruent. Their respective spatial factors are put together in the same way, so they exemplify the same form.

It is really astounding what complicated abstractions we make in our ordinary dealing with forms—that is to say, through what twists and transformations we recognize the same logical form. Consider the similarity of your two hands. Put one on the table, palm down, superimpose the other, palm down, as you may have superimposed cut-out geometrical shapes in school—they are not alike at all. But their shapes are *exact opposites*. Their respective shapes fit the same description, provided that the description is modified by a principle of application whereby the measures are read one way for one hand and the other way for the other—like a timetable in which the list of stations is marked: "Eastbound, read down; Westbound, read up."

As the two hands exemplify the same form with a principle of reversal understood, so the list of stations describes two ways of moving, indicated by the advice to "read down" for one and "read up" for the other. We can all abstract the common element in these two respective trips, which is called the *route*. With a return ticket we may return only by the same route. The same principle relates a mold to the form of the thing that is cast in it, and establishes their formal correspondence, or common logical form.

So far we have considered only objects —lampshades, hands, or regions of the earth—as having forms. These have fixed shapes; their parts remain in fairly stable relations to each other. But there are also substances that have no definite shapes, such as gases, mist, and water, which take the shape of any bounded space that contains them. The interesting thing about such amorphous fluids is that when they are put into violent motion they do exhibit visible forms, not bounded by any container. Think of the momentary efflorescence of a bursting rocket, the mushroom cloud of an atomic bomb, the funnel of water or dust screwing upward in a whirlwind. The instant the motion stops, or even slows beyond a certain degree, those shapes collapse and the apparent "thing" disappears. They are not shapes of things at all, but forms of motions, or dynamic forms.

Some dynamic forms, however, have more permanent manifestations, because the stuff that moves and makes them visible is constantly replenished. A waterfall seems to hang from the cliff, waving streamers of foam. Actually, of course, nothing stays there in midair; the water is always passing; but there is more and more water taking the same paths, so we have a lasting shape made and maintained by its passage—a permanent dynamic form. A quiet river, too, has dynamic form; if it stopped flowing it would either go dry or become a lake. Some twenty-five hundred years ago, Heraclitus was struck by the fact that you cannot step twice into the same river at the same place—at least, if the river means the water, not its dynamic form, the flow.

When a river ceases to flow because the water is deflected or dried up, there remains the river bed, sometimes cut deeply in solid stone. That bed is shaped by the flow, and records as graven lines the currents that have ceased to exist. Its shape is static, but it *expresses* the dynamic form of the river. Again, we have two congruent forms, like a cast and its mold, but this time the congruence is more remarkable because it holds between a dynamic form and a static one. That relation is important; we shall be dealing with it again when we come to consider the meaning of "living form" in art.

The congruence of two given perceptible forms is not always evident upon simple inspection. The common *logical* form they both exhibit may become apparent only when you know the principle whereby to relate them, as you compare the shapes of your hands not by direct correspondence, but by correspondence of opposite parts. Where the two exemplifications of the single logical form are unlike in most other respects one needs a rule for matching up the relevant factors of one with the relevant factors of the other; that is to say, a *rule of translation*, whereby one instance of the logical form is shown to correspond formally to the other.

The logical form itself is not another thing, but an abstract concept, or better an *abstractable* concept. We usually don't abstract it deliberately, but only use it, as we use our vocal chords in speech without first learning all about their operation and then applying our knowledge. Most people perceive intuitively the similarity of their two hands without thinking of them as conversely related; they can guess at the shape of a hollow inside a wooden shoe from the shape of a human foot, without any abstract study of topology. But the first time they see a map in the Mercator projection—with parallel lines of longitude, not meeting at the poles—they find it hard to believe that this corresponds logically to the circular map they used in school, where the meridians bulged apart toward the equator and met at both poles. The visible shapes of the continents are different on the two maps, and it takes abstract thinking to match up the two representations of the same earth. If, however, they have grown up with both maps, they will probably see the geographical relationships either way with equal ease, because these relationships are not *copied* by either map, but *expressed*, and expressed equally well by both; for the two maps are different *projections* of the same logical form, which the spherical earth exhibits in still another—that is, a spherical—projection.

An expressive form is any perceptible or imaginable whole that exhibits relationships of parts, or points, or even qualities or aspects within the whole, so that it may be taken to represent some other whole whose elements have analogous relations. The reason for using such a form as a symbol is usually that the thing it represents is not perceivable or readily imaginable. We cannot see the earth as an object. We let a map or a little globe express the relationships of places on the earth, and think about the earth by means of it. The understanding of one thing through another seems to be a deeply intuitive process in the human brain; it is so natural that we often have difficulty in distinguishing the symbolic expressive form from what it conveys. The symbol seems to be the thing itself, or contain it, or be contained in it. A child interested in a globe will not say: "This means the earth," but, "Look, this is the earth." A similar identification of symbol and meaning underlies the widespread conception of holy names, of the physical efficacy of rites, and many other primitive but culturally persistent phenomena. It has a bearing on our perception of artistic import; that is why I mention it here.

The most astounding and developed symbolic device humanity has evolved is language. By means of language we can conceive the intangible, incorporeal things we call our *ideas*, and the equally inostensible elements of our perceptual world that we call *facts*. It is by virtue of language that we can think, remember, imagine, and finally conceive a universe of facts. We can describe things and represent their relations, express rules of their interactions, speculate and predict and carry on a long symbolizing process known as reasoning. And above all, we can communicate, by producing a serried array of audible or visible words, in a pattern commonly known, and readily understood to reflect our multifarious concepts and precepts and their interconnections. The use of language is *discourse*; and the pattern of discourse is known as *discursive form*. It is a highly versatile, amazingly powerful pattern. It has impressed itself on our tacit thinking, so that we call all systematic reflection "discursive thought." It has made, far more than most people know, the very frame of our sensory experience—the frame of objective facts in which we carry on the practical business of life.

Yet even the discursive pattern has its limits of usefulness. An expressive form can express any complex of conceptions that, via some rule of projection, appears congruent with it, that is, appears to be of that form. Whatever there is in experience that will not take the impress—directly or indirectly—of discursive form, is not discursively communicable or, in the strictest sense, logically thinkable. It is unspeakable, ineffable; according to practically all serious philosophical theories today, it is unknowable.

Yet there is a great deal of experience that is knowable, not only as immediate, formless, meaningless impact, but as one aspect of the intricate web of life, yet defies discursive formulation, and therefore verbal expression: that is what we sometimes call the *subjective aspect* of experience, the direct feeling of it—what it is like to be walking and moving, to be drowsy, slowing down, or to be sociable, or to feel self-sufficient but alone; what it feels like to pursue an elusive thought or to have a big idea. All such directly felt experiences usually have no names—they are named, if at all, for the outward conditions that normally accompany their occurrence. Only the most striking ones have names like "anger," "hate," "love," "fear," and are collectively called "emotion." But we feel many things that never develop into any designable emotion. The ways we are moved are as various as the lights in a forest; and they may intersect, sometimes without cancelling each other, take shape and dissolve, conflict, explode into passion, or be transfigured. All these inseparable elements of subjective reality compose what we call the "inward life" of human beings. The usual factoring of that life-stream into mental, emotional, and sensory units is an arbitrary scheme of simplification that makes scientific treatment possible to a considerable extent; but we may already be close to the limit of its usefulness, that is, close to the point where its simplicity becomes an obstacle to further questioning and discovery instead of the revealing, ever-suitable logical projection it was expected to be.

Whatever resists projection into the discursive form of language is, indeed, hard to hold in conception, and perhaps impossible to communicate, in the proper and strict sense of the word "communicate." But fortunately our logical intuition, or form-perception, is really much more powerful than we commonly believe, and our knowledge—genuine knowledge, understanding—is considerably wider than our discourse. Even in the use of language, if we want to name something that is too new to have a name (e.g. a newly invented gadget or a newly discovered creature), or want to express a relationship for which there is no verb or other connective word, we resort to metaphor; we mention it or describe it as something else, something analogous. The principle of metaphor is simply the principle of saying one thing and meaning another, and expecting to be understood to mean the other. A metaphor is not language, it is an idea expressed by language, an idea that in its turn functions as a symbol to express something. It is not discursive and therefore does not really make a statement of the idea it conveys; but it formulates a new conception for our direct imaginative grasp.

Sometimes our comprehension of a total experience is mediated by a metaphorical symbol because the experience is new, and language has words and phrases only for familiar notions. Then an extension of language will gradually follow the wordless insight, and discursive expression will supersede the nondiscursive pristine symbol. This is, I think, the normal advance of human thought and language in the whole realm of knowledge where discourse is possible at all.

But the symbolic presentation of subjective reality for contemplation is not only tentatively beyond the reach of language—that is, not merely beyond the words we have, it is impossible in the essential frame of language. That is why those semanticists who recognize only discourse as a symbolic form must regard the whole life of feeling as formless, chaotic, capable only of symptomatic expression, typified in exclamations like "Ah!" "Ouch!" "My sainted aunt!" They usually do believe that art is an expression of feeling, but that "expression" in art is of this sort, indicating that the speaker has an emotion, a pain, or other personal experience, perhaps also giving us a clue to the general kind of experience it is—pleasant or unpleasant, violent or mild—but not setting that piece of inward life objectively before us so we may understand its intricacy, its rhythms and shifts of total appearance. The differences in feeling-tones or other elements of subjective experience are regarded as differences in quality, which must be felt to be appreciated. Furthermore, since we have no intellectual access to pure subjectivity, the only way to study it is to study the symptoms of the person who is having subjective experiences. This leads to physiological psychology—a very important and interesting field. But it tells us nothing about the phenomena of subjective life, and sometimes simplifies the problem by saying they don't exist.

Now, I believe the expression of feeling in a work of art—the function that makes the work an expressive form—is not symptomatic at all. An artist working on a tragedy need not be in personal despair or violent upheaval; nobody, indeed, could work in such a state of mind. His mind would be occupied with the causes of his emotional upset. Self-expression does not require composition and lucidity; a screaming baby gives his feeling far more release than any musician, but we don't go into a concert hall to hear a baby scream; in fact, if that baby is brought in we are likely to go out. We don't want self-expression.

A work of art presents feeling (in the broad sense I mentioned before, as everything that can be felt) for our contemplation, making it visible or audible or in some way perceivable through a symbol, not inferable from a symptom. Artistic form is congruent with the dynamic forms of our direct sensuous, mental, and emotional life; works of art are projections of "felt life," as Henry James called it, into spatial, temporal, and poetic structures. They are images of feeling, that formulate it for our cognition. What is artistically good is whatever articulates and presents feeling to our understanding.

Artistic forms are more complex than any other symbolic forms we know. They are, indeed, not abstractable from the works that exhibit them. We may abstract a shape from an object that has this shape, by disregarding color, weight and texture, even size; but to the total effect that is an artistic form, the color matters, the thickness of line matters, and the appearance of texture and weight matters. A given triangle is the same in any position, but to an artistic form its location, balance, and surroundings are not indifferent. Form, in the sense in which artists speak of "significant form" or "expressive form," is not an abstracted structure, but an apparition; and the vital processes of sense and emotion that a good work of art expresses seem to the beholder to be directly contained in it, not symbolized but really presented. The congruence is so striking that symbol and meaning appear as one reality. Actually, as one psychologist who is also a musician has written, "Music sounds as feelings feel." And likewise, in good painting, sculpture, or building, balanced shapes and colors, lines and masses look as emotions, vital tensions and their resolutions feel.

An artist, then, expresses feeling, but not in the way a politician blows off steam or a baby laughs and cries. He formulates that elusive aspect of reality that is commonly taken to be amorphous and chaotic; that is, he objectifies the subjective realm. What he expresses, is, therefore, not his own actual feelings, but what he knows about human feeling. Once he is in possession of a rich symbolism, that knowledge may actually exceed his entire personal experience. A work of art expresses a conception of life, emotion, inward reality. But it is neither a confessional nor a frozen tantrum; it is a developed metaphor, a non-discursive symbol that articulates what is verbally ineffable—the logic of consciousness itself.

Is Music a Language of the Emotions?

Stephen Davies

In discussing musical works and their appreciation we accept that they may be understood (and misunderstood) and that a person who understands a musical work can be asked to justify his understanding. The nature of aesthetic discussions and disagreements about music indicates that we accept that music is the bearer of meaning or sense and that it is this meaning or sense which the listener comprehends when he is said to understand a musical work. Nevertheless, neither *what*

From *The British Journal of Aesthetics*, 23 (1983). Reprinted by permission of Oxford University Press.

it is that music means, nor the way in which music bears its meaning is readily apparent. It is these subjects which are considered below.

What is the meaning of a piece of music? It is whatever it is that we understand when we (can be said by others to) understand a musical work aesthetically; it is that which interests us and which we value in musical works. On the phenomenological level, a typical understanding response to music is the experience of hearing the way in which one series of notes gives rise to another. It is to recognize that a musical continuation makes 'sense' (or does not make 'sense') as a continuation of that which preceded it, even where the continuation might not have been predicted on hearing the antecedent passage. We experience music not merely as a succession of notes, and chords, but as developing, recasting and otherwise exploring its materials in a connected way. Our attempts to understand music are premised on the belief that we can attempt reasonably to justify and not merely explain the course of the music.

If music never referred us beyond itself, so that all that was involved in understanding music was an appreciation of its structure, its texture, the thematic relationships and so on, then the nature of musical understanding (and, thus, of musical 'meaning') would raise few philosophical difficulties. But music does refer beyond itself in that it is expressive of emotions, and there are considerable philosophical difficulties to be faced in attempting to account for the way in which music is expressive of emotions. Since it is arguable that the listener usually reveals his understanding of the music through his appreciation of, and response to, that which is expressed in music (in those cases where the music is expressive), such difficulties cannot be dismissed in discussing the nature of musical meaning. I do not wish to claim that all music is expressive of emotions. But the importance attached to the appreciation of such expressiveness, where it occurs, as indicating that the listener understands the music, clearly suggests that the conceptually interesting difficulties in describing music as expressive of emotion are of central importance in a consideration of the philosophically interesting cases of musical meaning.

Obviously we should not say of a person that he understood a musical work if he was unaware, for example, that its themes were related, that texturally and harmonically, some sections were denser than others, that some sections were relatively more tense than others, and so on. We would expect him to be able to give some account of such matters, though not necessarily in technical terms. But, if the music were expressive of some emotion, we would be dubious of the claim that the person understood the piece, even if he could provide a description of his experience of the relatedness of its themes, etc., if he failed to notice the expressiveness of the music. A musician with a complete grasp of the music's technical features may not be able to play it convincingly until told to play it as if in 'cheerful resignation' rather than 'tense foreboding.' Whilst not all music is expressive of emotion, our present notions of musical understanding and musical meaning would be quite other than they are if music were never experienced, and responded to, as expressive of emotion.

Sometimes we say 'This music is expressive' without feeling that we can adequately answer the question 'What, then, does it express?' A person may feel that he cannot convey in words that which is expressed in a musical work when he is describing it to another who is not familiar with the piece, but if he says that the work is sad he has conveyed something about it, although he may not have captured the quality of the sadness that he finds so interesting.[1] Now, of course, to understand a musical work is not simply to be able to name the emotional states expressed in it. To justify an understanding of some particular work it must be described in such a way as to reveal it as the sole source of our experience of the emotion expressed in it. In describing the emotion expressed in music one is led to describe the course of the music and the experience of its connectedness.

So far I have suggested that to understand the meaning of a musical work expressive of emotion will involve appreciating the emotions expressed in it, and that we are not precluded from identifying and describing these emotions. I have also suggested that there are a few philosophically interesting difficulties in accounting for the 'sense' or 'meaning' of music in which emotions are not expressed. In discussing musical meaning, I will be considering the philosophically interesting case, that of how expressive music gets its meaning. The question is: How is musical reference to the expressed 'content' secured? In the following it will be argued that music is understood neither as a (natural) language, nor as a non-linguistic symbol system, before it is suggested that music is 'naturally' meaningful (in the Gricean sense) of emotions. I will be attacking the view that our *present* notions of musical understanding and musical meaning are best to be elucidated by showing that these notions are strictly analogous to the notions of linguistic meaning or of meaning determined by the conventions of a symbol system.

Several writers have argued that, in understanding a musical work, we appreciate it as having a propositional function.[2] According to this theory, music has assertoric meaning in the way that declarative sentences have assertoric meaning; musical compositions are a means for the communication of information in the way that assertoric sentences of natural languages are. Music differs from natural languages only in that its field of reference is restricted to the world of emotions. Music, in this theory, is a semantic system with a vocabulary and a syntax.

One objection to this view is the following. To say that music is understood as having an assertoric function is to claim that music refers to emotions *and* goes on to describe the emotions to which it refers. In developing a parallel between music and language it is not sufficient to show that music may refer us to emotional states, it is also necessary to show how emotions are described in music. Whilst there may be a point to developing a description of the emotion expressed in a musical work in terms of the musical features through which the emotion is presented, it is not clear that music provides for the *completion* of one's thoughts about the expressed emotion in *the way* in which the predicate of an assertoric sentence provides for the completion of one's thoughts about the subject of that sentence. The emotion is announced through the music rather than described by the music.

The theory under consideration might attempt to meet this objection by claiming that musical 'sentences' are of the type called by Strawson 'feature-placing sentences'.[3] That is, it might be claimed that musical sentences perform the same function as a sub-class of the class of assertions found in natural languages. The assertions in this sub-class introduce neither particulars nor sortal universals (such as, fall of snow); they introduce 'feature-universals' or 'feature-concepts' as does, for example, the sentence 'It is snowing.' According to this view, 'The music is sad' can be analysed as asserting that 'There is sound and sadness here'. Feature-placing sentences are not subject-predicate sentences; they introduce a universal or a 'stuff' and place it in space and time. It might be said that in feature-placing sentences, the assertion is effected through the location of the subject.

This answer to the objection fails on two counts. First, it might be suspected that it is 'particular-placing' rather than 'feature-placing' which is required. By feature-placing the subject is transformed into a universal (or, sometimes, a 'stuff'), so that 'Sadness is here' is not equivalent to 'The (bit of) sadness in which you are interested is here.' The counter to the objection loses the fact that our interest in the expressiveness heard in music is an interest in the particular expressiveness of a particular piece of music. Second, the possibility of feature-placing sentences within a language presupposes the possibility within the language of assertions in which particulars and sortal universals are introduced.[4] That is, there could be no language, as the counter to the objection claims, in which all assertions were of the feature-placing type. The attempt to analyse 'The music is sad' as 'There is sound and sadness here' will fail. We will be forced to conclude that what is involved in musical reference is not feature-placing but, rather, something like brute 'naming'. And, as Rhees has argued, that is an idle, sense-less game except within the context of a fuller language within which it is possible for people to tell each other things.[5]

The second objection to the theory that music is understood aesthetically as a language like any other argues that musical meaning is unlike linguistic meaning in that, whereas the latter depends upon the possibility of truthful assertion, the notion of truth plays no part in the determination of the former. Two (contrasting) accounts of linguistic meaning (of an assertion) for natural languages are given in the contemporary literature. The first defines the meaning of an assertion in terms of the assertion's truth-conditions; the second defines the meaning of an assertion in terms of the assertion's verifiability conditions or justified assertability.[6] Fortunately it is not necessary that we adjudicate between these accounts before we are able to argue that music does not constitute a language of the emotions such as could answer to either of these views. Both definitions of linguistic meaning entail that language is essentially a *semantic* system, and it can be argued that music is not understood as such. Both accounts of linguistic meaning entail that the meaningfulness of linguistic utterances in all their uses depends upon the possibility of truthful assertion. The non-assertoric uses of language depend upon and follow from the possibility that those same words can have a use in the making of truthful assertions. Within the context of a semantic system by which communication can be effected, reference and meaning entail the possibility of truthful assertion. As Rhees has argued, there can be no language which admits of the possibility of non-assertoric uses of sentences which does not also admit of the possibility of an assertoric use of sentences.[7]

To understand a musical utterance is not to know whether that utterance is true or false. We do not regard musical utterances as subject to truth-conditions or as meeting standards of assertoric correctness or incorrectness of use. In respect of its meaning, music cannot usefully be compared to a language.

It might be argued that the above conclusion was reached too hastily. For, whilst music obviously is not a natural language, the appreciation of musical meaning and the appreciation of a declarative sentence may be, in important respects, analogous. It might be argued, for example, that musical reference is like reference in the sentences of a natural language to the extent that both types of reference are secured by the conventions of a symbol system. The conventions, by means of which the symbols are systematized, serve to make manifest the symbolizer's intentions and thus his meaning to his audience. According to this view, music is understood as a non-linguistic symbol system.

An account of meaning which applies both to linguistic and non-linguistic symbol systems is offered by Grice.[8] He analyses utterer's occasion-meaning—'The utterer meant by uttering x (an instance or token of an utterance type, such as a word, sentence, gesture, name or whatever) that x'—as follows: For some audience, A, U uttered x intending (a) A to produce a particular response, r; (b) A to think (recognize) that U intends (a); and (c) A to fulfil (a) on the basis of his fulfilment of (b). This definition is inadequate as it stands to cope with some of the less usual instances of utterer's occasion-meaning, but it is adequate for our purposes.

Now, if the utterance is a work of art and if the audience's interest in the work of art is an aesthetic one, then the third condition, (c), is not necessarily met. An aesthetic interest in the work of art concerns itself with the best (most aesthetically rewarding) reading of the work of art, without treating the work of art merely as a vehicle for the communication of the artist's thoughts. An aesthetic interest is an interest in what the artist has "to say," but an interest in what the artist has "to say" need not necessarily be an interest in the artist's intentions (made manifest in the work of art or by their avowal) that the work of art be read and understood in one way rather than another. The audience may respond, say, to a poem as it was intended to respond, and it may also recognize that the poet intended it to respond this way, but the response, if aesthetic, is not *determined* by the recognition of the artist's intention. That is, the acceptance of the first condition, (a), does not rest on the recognition that the second condition, (b), is fulfilled. This is a general point about the way in which aesthetic interest differs from an interest in utterer's occasion-meaning, and about the way in which the aim of aesthetic understanding differs from the aim of understanding an utterance spoken on a particular occasion as communicating a meaning intended by the utterer. This point holds true of art (such as literature and representational paintings) which *could* be understood *non-aesthetically* according to Grice's model, because they constitute or fall within symbol systems. The same argument shows that music is not understood as a non-linguistic symbol system, but leaves open the question of whether music could be so understood.

In the same paper Grice distinguishes cases of 'naturally' determined meaning from 'non-naturally' determined meaning. Non-natural meaning (meaning$_{NN}$) is secured by the conventions of a symbol system which serve within the system to make understandable the meaning that the utterer intended to convey. Non-natural meaning may be either linguistic or non-linguistic. Grice uses 'Those three rings on the bell (of the bus) mean that "the bus is full"' as his example of non-natural meaning. Natural meaning (meaning$_N$) is not determined by the conventions of a symbol system. Grice uses 'Those spots mean measles' as his example of natural meaning. Five points of difference between these two kinds of meaning are noted.

(1) '*x means that p*', with meaning$_N$ entails *p* (the person must *have* measles); but with meaning$_{NN}$ *p* is not entailed (the bus-conductor can be mistaken). (2) With meaning$_N$ we cannot argue from '*x means that p*' to 'by those spots *it* is meant that he has measles'; but with meaning$_{NN}$ we can argue from the sentence to what is meant *by* it. (3) With meaning$_N$, we cannot argue from the sentence to the conclusion that someone meant by the spots so-and-so; but, with meaning$_{NN}$, we can argue to the conclusion that someone meant that the bus was full. (4) With meaning$_N$, the sentence cannot be restated in such a way that 'mean' is followed by a sentence or phrase in reported speech (we cannot say "Those spots mean 'he has measles'"); but with meaning$_{NN}$, we can do this. (5) With meaning$_N$, the sentence can be restated beginning with 'the fact that' (as in 'The fact that he has those spots means that he has measles') without changing its meaning; but with meaning$_{NN}$, a restatement of the sentence in this form does not preserve the meaning of the original version, although both statements may be true.

Representational paintings and the statements found in literature are clearly understood as non-naturally meaningful. 'This picture of Wellington means that "Wellington looked [or ". . . ought to have looked . . .", or ". . . might have looked . . .", etc.] like this"' is substitutable for 'Those three rings on the bell mean that "the bus is full"'. Though this is not to say that an *aesthetic* interest in a portrait of Wellington is an interest in the Wellington-likeness of the painting, nor that an *aesthetic* interest in the statements found in literary works is concerned with their truth. The appreciation of that which a painting represents or that which is stated in a literary work rests on a recognition of the conventions of their respective symbol systems. However, 'This music means sadness' would seem to be more readily substituted for 'Those spots mean measles' than for 'Those three rings on the bell mean that "the bus is full",' at least in (1), (4) and (5).

Grice's second and third criteria leave vague the way in which we should treat cases where something that is naturally meaningful is given an intentional use; for example, where a person frowns intentionally. As Grice points out, our recognition that the frown was intentional would normally require understanding it as non-naturally meaningful to the extent that one's concern is with that which the frown is intended to convey rather than with the significance merely of the person's appearance. Since, usually, music presents in sound the appearance of the emotion that it was intended by the composer to present, it would seem that musical expressiveness should be analysed as non-naturally meaningful after all. But the case of musical expressiveness differs importantly from that in which a person frowns intentionally. It is because one's interest in facial expressions normally follows from a concern with their indicating how the person feels that an intentional frown becomes non-naturally meaningful, whereas an unintended frown is naturally meaningful. By contrast, the expressiveness of music does not interest us as indicating how any person feels; our concern is with the *appearance* of emotion rather than with a particular feeling as indicated in such an appearance.

Grice's second and third criteria do not suggest that all intentional 'utterances' must be understood as non-naturally meaningful. Where the meaningfulness of the utterance depends upon an appreciation of the intention, as is the case with onomatopoeic words or where intentional frowns interest us as signifying a person's feelings, non-natural meaning is involved. But where the intention may be disregarded without this thereby potentially altering the meaning of the 'utterance', the meaning of the utterance is natural rather than non-natural. In the case of musical expressiveness, the composer's intentions are essentially irrelevant. Whilst it may be the case that most music that is expressive presents the appearance of emotions that the composer intended it to present, the absence of such an intention does not affect the expressiveness heard in a musical work. Either the music presents the appearance of some emotion or it does not, independently of its being intended or not to present the appearance of this emotion. Once more there is an obvious contrast with representational painting. A painting of a man may resemble Wellington whether or not it was intended to do so. But representation (as opposed to mere resemblance) crucially involves intention. However much a painting may resemble Wellington, it does not represent him unless it was intended to represent him. The appreciation of representation involves the recognition of intention in a way that the appreciation of musical expressiveness (as the presentation of appearances of emotions) does not.

With the above argument in mind, it appears to be the case that music is naturally, rather than non-naturally, meaningful of emotions. Thus, music is not even like a language to the extent that musical reference to emotions is secured by the conventions of a non-linguistic symbol system. Musical reference to emotions is natural rather than conventional. Music does not constitute a symbol system; the means by which music is expressive are importantly unique to each piece. There are conventions in music, but they are formal and stylistic rather than semantic; that is, they do not serve to reveal the composer's intention in order that we may appreciate that which is expressed in the music. If composers have regularly expressed sadness by similar musical means, this is because those means are naturally expressive of sadness rather than because audiences have associated those means with intentions to express particular emotional states. Of course, recognizing that which is expressed in a musical work may require some familiarity with the stylistic conventions (and so it may be difficult to appreciate the expressiveness of non-Western music for example), but not because the conventions make the expressiveness understandable *as* the expressiveness that the music was intended to convey.

With words and representational pictures we can ignore what was meant or what was represented and consider the meanings that may be put upon the words or that which the picture is experienced as resembling. It is because we can distinguish between what is meant and what is "said" that an *aesthetic* interest in literature and representational pictures may ignore the artist's intentions as determining *the* meaning of his creation. Symbol systems which primarily serve the end of communication provide for the possibility of an interest in the meanings of "utterances" which does not concern itself with *intended* meanings. But we cannot make a similar distinction between that which a musical work expresses and that which it is intended to express (except by means of independently conveyed information about the composer's intentions). Music does not lend itself to the Gricean analysis of utterer's occasion-meaning in respect of its expressiveness. There is no way of recognizing the composer's intention to express some emotion within the context of the music except by taking that which is actually expressed as realizing the composer's intention. Because it does not constitute a symbol system, the audience cannot fulfil (b), the second part of Grice's analysis of utterer's occasion-meaning, when appreciating the expressiveness of a musical work. The composer's intentions as regards the expressiveness of his work drop out at the second level of Grice's account of utterer's occasion-meaning, and thus music could not be understood non-aesthetically as conveying such a meaning. Whereas, in the case of literature and representational painting, the second level in Grice's analysis becomes irrelevant only where an aesthetic interest leads the audience to ignore the third level of intention.

Having claimed that music is naturally meaningful of the emotions expressed in it, it remains to demonstrate an appropriate connection between the music and the emotional states to which it refers us. Obviously the connection is not a causal one, as is often the case with meaning$_N$ (where, for example, smoke means fire, or where a groan wrung from a person means that he feels sad). Already I have suggested that music expresses emotions by presenting or exemplifying the appearances of emotions. How could a connection be established between appearances of emotion and the human world in which emotions are felt? That is, how can music refer to emotions by exemplifying their appearances?

The fact that a musical work exemplified some property, for example harmoniousness, would not normally lead us to say that it thereby *refers* to harmoniousness. Music presents many properties without thereby referring beyond itself. Why, where the features presented are expressive, are we inclined to understand the music as referring to the world in which emotions are felt? Normally we are interested in appearances of emotion as indicating how the "owner" of the appearance *feels*; our interest in the appearances of emotions is parasitic on a more fundamental concern with the feelings indicated in such appearances. Even where we interest ourselves in the appearances of emotions for themselves, a reference to the world of feelings remains implicit. We may divorce our interest in the particular appearance of some emotion, sadness say, from a concern with the particular sadness felt by the "owner" of this appearance, but the appearance alone could sustain such an interest only where it was taken as referring to sadness *in general*. So it is, I think, that the emotions expressed in music refer generally to emotions although they are not taken as signifying any particular person's feeling of an emotion, and so it is that we regard musical expressiveness as worthy of interest.

It remains to show how appearances of emotion may be presented in the sounds which comprise a musical work. Before sketching my own answer to this difficulty I will consider briefly the theory proposed by Susanne Langer. Although I wish to reject Langer's theory, it is of the type required by the preceding argument. That is, she argues that music is naturally meaningful of emotions and that it refers to them by means of presenting their 'appearances' or forms.

In the writings of Susanne Langer we find an attempt to analyse music as naturally meaningful (in her terms, as a presentational symbol).[9] She specifically rejects the view that music is non-naturally meaningful (a 'discursive' or 'propositional' symbol). According to Langer, a presentational symbol brings to mind a conception of the subject symbolized. The appropriate response to a presentational symbol is a thought; not a thought about the subject referred to, but, rather, an idea or conception of the *nature* of that subject. One thing, S, can be a presentational symbol of another thing, O, by virtue of the fact that the *form* of S is 'iconic' with the *form* of O. No feature of a thing can be dismissed *a priori* as irrelevant to its form. The form of an object can be abstracted from it in thought (it can be known), but not in practice (it cannot be described except ostensively). Where two forms are iconic, the essential relation between the elements of the two objects is identical, even though the 'materials' of which the elements are comprised may be unlike. Thus the relation between the aural elements of a musical work can be the same as the relation between the thoughts and sensations which comprise a feeling. When a composer symbolizes some feeling in his music he 'transforms' the relation between the elements of that feeling to a relation between auditory elements by applying the appropriate 'laws of projection'. He could not state these laws; they are applied unconsciously and intuitively. And when his audience appreciates his music as a presentational symbol of that feeling, they recognize the iconicity between the form of the feeling and the form of the music unconsciously and intuitively. Where one form is recognized as a transformation of another with which it is iconic, the audience becomes aware of the first form-bearer as a presentational symbol of the second form-bearer.

Langer's theory is founded on a questionable characterization of the nature of emotions and it might be attacked on this and many other grounds. However, in the following discussion it is the notion of a presentational mode of symbolism which is confronted. The central concepts of Langer's theory—indescribable forms, undemonstrable iconicity and unstatable laws of projection—are unintelligible. If 'unintelligible' means here 'cannot be explained in language,' Langer would agree. But, we might continue, the problem that her theory "answers" is such that it demands an explanation which can be given in language and, therefore, that the unintelligibility of her theory is a crucial weakness. It is not nonsensical to ask how art can be a natural bearer of emotions in the way that it is nonsensical to ask how (genuine) groaning can be expressive of, say, sadness. Because it is not obvious how (non-sentient) works of art can be bearers of (disembodied) emotions, the first question requires an answer where the second does not. By denying the possibility of an answer to the first question Langer deprives her theory of significant content. Rather than solving the problem, as it purports to do, Langer's theory restates the apparent fact to which the nature of aesthetic discourse testifies—that we hear emotions in music, that music is naturally meaningful of emotions—in new and misleading terms.

Presumably Langer would claim that the ultimate and only real test of her theory is that, once we have understood what presentational symbols are like, we recognize that, in appreciating works of art as expressive, we are appreciating them as presentational symbols; that is, as conveying conceptions of emotions. However, when her claims are tested against our experience of the expressiveness of the music, they prove to be false. The expressiveness of music sometimes seems to demand an emotional response from the listener. Whilst it is obvious that the presentation of an emotion in a musical work might sometimes compel an emotional response from the listener, it is not at all obvious that the presentation of the *conception* of an emotion would ever compel an emotional response. Langer's theory removes emotion from art, replacing it with conceptions of emotions. In so doing, her theory removes the basis for emotional responses to musical works and makes mysterious the power of music to evoke emotional responses. That is to say, her theory severs the connection between emotions in music and emotions in life upon which an acceptable characterization of the nature of aesthetic responses and interest depends. In responding emotionally to musical works as we do, we are not responding to them as natural signs conveying *conceptions* of emotions.

Rather than arguing (as Langer did) that it is the forms of music and emotions which resemble each other, one might argue that music is naturally expressive because the dynamic character of music is experienced as significantly similar to human behavior in which emotions are expressed. Movement is heard in music. The relative highness and lowness of notes provides a dimension in aural space within which music moves through time. Thus, if the characteristic behavioral expression of an emotion, X, has the dynamic form, Y, and if a musical work is heard as having the same dynamic form, then X is heard in the music.

Such a theory faces a major objection. However close may be the analogy between one's experience of musical movement and the dynamics of human behavior, it could never be the case that musical movement expresses emotions such as those expressed by human behavior, since there is no felt-emotion which finds expression in music. Because music is non-sentient, musical movement could not be heard as expressive *just as* human behavior may be seen as expressive, since, in the paradigmatic cases, our recognition of the expressiveness of human behavior is founded on our understanding of the expressiveness of that behavior as the expression of something that is *felt*. The objection rightly points out that emotion-words do not retain their primary use (that of denoting the experience of an occurrent emotion) when used in describing musical expressiveness. The primary use of emotion-words cannot be learned solely from musical examples, and key distinctions, such as that between pretended and genuine expressive behavior, do not arise in the musical case. Furthermore, it will not be possible to meet the objection by arguing that emotion-words are given a special, secondary use applicable only to musical expressiveness. Unless the sadness heard in music can be connected somehow to the sadness that people feel and express, our interest in the expressiveness of music will be inexplicable. If it is only by chance that emotion-words are given this special, aesthetic use, there is no *reason* why we should not be uninterested in musical expressiveness.

However, the objection can be met if we can show that there is a secondary use of emotion-words which applies to people and that it is this same use which is applied to musical expressiveness. While admitting that the use of emotion-words in connection with music is secondary, it will be possible to demonstrate that this use preserves the meanings that the words have in their primary use by explaining how the same secondary use in connection with sentient beings is parasitic on the primary use. Now, there is a secondary use of emotion-words which does not involve (even implicit) reference to felt-emotions. In this use we talk of the expressive character of an appearance; usually a person's or animal's appearance. Thus, one might say that a Saint Bernard is a sad-looking dog without meaning that Saint Bernards feel sad any more often than other breeds of dog. So, it might be possible to argue that music is naturally meaningful of the emotions expressed in it by showing that musical 'reference' to emotions is secured by virtue of the fact that musical movement mirrors the bearing, carriage or gait of people in that *both* music and people are experienced as wearing appearances which present emotion-characteristics. That is, one might argue that the recognition in music of emotional expressiveness depends upon an analogy between the experience of hearing expressiveness in music and seeing bearings, carriages and gaits as presenting appearances of expressiveness (which pay no regard to what is felt).[10]

Of course, the view advocated above must be argued in detail. In particular it will be crucial to explain *how* it is that music can be experienced as presenting the appearance of emotions; that is, how the dynamic character of music is appreciated as analogous to actions rather than to mere movements. Elsewhere I have tried to demonstrate that such explanations are possible.[11] Here the concern has been to indicate that a consideration of the nature of musical meaning leads us towards a theory of the kind proposed above.

NOTES

1. This argument derives from R. Wollheim, *Art and Its Objects*, Sec. 48–49, and from R. Scruton, *Art and Imagination* (1974), pp. 78–83.
2. See especially D. Cooke, *The Language of Music* (1962); L. Meyer, *Emotion and Meaning in Music* (1970).
3. *Individuals* (1964), pp. 202–217.
4. Ibid., pp. 214–225.
5. 'Wittgenstein's Builders', *Proceedings of the Aristotelian Society* (1959–1960).
6. I have in mind the views of Donald Davidson and of Michael Dummett.
7. Rhees, op. cit.
8. 'Meaning', *The Philosophical Review* (1957).

9. See especially *Philosophy in a New Key*.
10. In *Languages of Art* (1968), Goodman analyzed expressiveness in art as involving reference through *metaphorical* exemplification. Whilst my own view retains the key notions of reference and exemplification, I have rejected in the above the claim that the predication of emotion-words to works of art is metaphorical. It is an extremely narrow view of meaning which concludes that all non-primary uses of words are metaphorical; a view which fails to recognize that live metaphors die at the time when they are taken into general use. Emotion-words have a general, perfectly licit (although secondary) literal use when predicated of works of art.
11. 'The Expression of Emotion in Music', *Mind* (1980).

Exemplification and Expression

Nelson Goodman

A DIFFERENCE IN DIRECTION

Before me is a picture of trees and cliffs by the sea, painted in dull grays, and expressing great sadness. This description gives information of three kinds, saying something about (1) what things the picture represents, (2) what properties it possesses, and (3) what feelings it expresses. The logical nature of the underlying relationships in the first two cases is plain: the picture denotes a certain scene and is a concrete instance of certain shades of gray. But what is the logical character of the relationship the picture bears to what it is said to express?

A second look at the description may raise some question about the line between possession and expression of a property. For instead of saying the picture expresses sadness I might have said that it is a sad picture. Is it sad, then, in the same way that it is gray? A notable difference is that since, strictly speaking, only sentient beings or events can be sad, a picture is only figuratively sad. A picture literally possesses a gray color, really belongs to the class of gray things; but only metaphorically does it possess sadness or belong to the class of things that feel sad.

Expression, then, can be tentatively and partially characterized as involving figurative possession. This may explain our feeling that expression is somehow both more direct and less literal than representation. For possession seems more intimate than denotation, while the figurative is surely less literal than the literal. Yet to say that expression involves figurative possession seems at once to assimilate it to possession and to contrast it with possession. "Figurative" seems to imply "not actual". In what sense can expression involve possession but not actual possession? Some analysis of the nature of the figurative, or at least of the metaphorical, will have to be undertaken presently; for although what is metaphorically true is not literally true, neither is it merely false. Yet what distinguishes metaphorical truth from literal truth on the one hand and from falsity on the other?

Before going into that question, we had better examine actual possession more closely. An object is gray, or is an instance of or possesses grayness, if and only if "gray"

From *Languages of Art* (Indianapolis: The Bobbs-Merrill Co., 1968). Reprinted by permission of Hackett Publishing Co. and the author. Footnotes have been renumbered.

applies to the object.¹ Thus while a picture denotes what it represents, and a predicate denotes what it describes, what properties the picture or the predicate possesses depends rather upon what predicates denote it. A picture cannot be said to denote those properties or predicates except in the upside-down way that a local newspaper was said to have 'acquired new owners'. The picture *does not denote* the color gray *but is denoted by* the predicate "gray".

Thus if representation is a matter of denotation while expression is somehow a matter of possession, the two differ in direction as well as (or perhaps rather than) in domain. Whether or not what is represented is concrete while what is expressed is abstract, what is expressed subsumes the picture as an instance much as the picture subsumes what it represents.

Expression is not, of course, mere possession. Apart from the fact that the possession involved in expression is metaphorical, neither literal nor metaphorical possession constitutes symbolization at all. To denote is to refer, but to be denoted is not necessarily to refer to anything. Yet expression, like representation, is a mode of symbolization; and a picture must stand for, symbolize, refer to, what it expresses. The symbolization or reference here runs, as we have seen, in the opposite direction from denotation—runs up from rather than down to what is denoted. An object that is literally or metaphorically denoted by a predicate, and refers to that predicate or the corresponding property, may be said to exemplify that predicate or property. Not all exemplification is expression, but all expression is exemplification.

EXEMPLIFICATION

Although encountered here rather incidentally in the course of our inquiry into expression, and seldom given much attention, exemplification is an important and widely used mode of symbolization in and out of the arts.

Consider a tailor's booklet of small swatches of cloth. These function as samples, as symbols exemplifying certain properties. But a swatch does not exemplify all its properties; it is a sample of color, weave, texture, and pattern, but not of size, shape, or absolute weight or value. Nor does it even exemplify all the properties—such as having been finished on a Tuesday—that it shares with the given bolt or run of material. Exemplification is possession plus reference.² To have without symbolizing is merely to possess, while to symbolize without having is to refer in some other way than by exemplifying. The swatch exemplifies only those properties that it both has and refers to. We may speak of it as exemplifying the bolt or the run in the elliptical sense of exemplifying the property of being from the bolt.³ But not every piece of the material functions as a sample; and something else such as a painted chip of wood may have, and be used to exemplify, the color or other properties of the material.

If possession is intrinsic, reference is not; and just which properties of a symbol are exemplified depends upon what particular system of symbolization is in effect. The tailor's sample does not normally function as a sample of a tailor's sample; it normally exemplifies certain properties of a material, but not the property of exemplifying such properties. Yet if offered in response to a question about what a tailor's sample is, the swatch may indeed exemplify the property of being a tailor's sample. What startles and amuses us in Ring Lardner's remark that one of his stories "is an example of what can be done with a stub pen"⁴ is that the story, although it may have the property that its manuscript was written with a stub pen, does not in the context, or in any usual context, exemplify that property.

So far I have spoken indifferently of properties or predicates as being exemplified. This equivocation must now be resolved. Although we usually speak of what is exemplified as redness, or the property of being red, rather than as the predicate "(is) red", this leads to familiar troubles attendant upon any talk of properties. Socrates discussing philosophy in Athens is a rational animal, a featherless biped, and a laughing mammal; but his exemplifying the first property does not imply his exemplifying the other two. Perhaps that is because the three properties, while coextensive, are not identical. But a figure that exemplifies triangularity, though always trilateral, does not always exemplify trilaterality. If trilaterality is not identical with triangularity, what is? And if the two properties are identical, then identical properties may differ in what exemplifies them. We seem to need a different property for every predicate.

Let us, then, take exemplification of *predicates* and other labels as elementary. In so speaking, say of a chip as a sample of "red" rather than of redness, we must remember that what exemplifies here is something denoted by, rather than an inscription of, the predicate. What a symbol exemplifies must apply to it. A man, but not an inscription, may exemplify (every inscription of) "man"; an inscription, but not a man, may exemplify (every inscription of) "'man'".

Yet to insist that "exemplifies redness" must always be regarded as a sloppy equivalent of "exemplifies 'red'" is too strict. To Plato, Socrates hardly exemplified "rational" but rather the corresponding Greek predicate; and a paint chip exemplifies "rouge", not "red", to a Frenchman. Even within English, we may hesitate to say that a sample refers to one rather than another among alternative predicates. What we need is an interpretation of "exemplifies redness", in terms of exemplification of predicates, that gives more latitude.

Suppose we construe "exemplifies redness" as elliptical for "exemplifies some label coextensive with 'red'". To say that Socrates exemplifies rationality is, then, to say only that Socrates exemplifies some label coextensive with "rational." This provides enough latitude, but seems to provide too much. For if Socrates exemplifies rationality, and "rational" is coextensive with "risible", then Socrates will also exemplify risibility. He *does not*, indeed, therefore exemplify "risible". But must we choose between an interpretation so wide as to let in risibility and one so narrow as to shut out the Greek equivalent of "rational"?

The answer is that the lines may be drawn with any degree of looseness or tightness. While "exemplifies rationality", taken by itself, says only "exemplifies *some* label coextensive with 'rational'", the context usually tells us a good deal more about what label is in question. When a paint chip exemplifies redness to a Frenchman, or Socrates exemplifies rationality to Plato, the predicates are pretty clearly not English ones. In talk among English-speaking people about painting a house, a sample of redness exemplifies "red" or perhaps some or all of a few predicates used interchangeably with "red" in such discussions. In saying that Socrates exemplifies rationality to me, I am surely not saying that he exemplifies a Greek word that I do not know. But am I saying he exemplifies "risible"? I may comply with such a request to be more specific about the label or labels exemplified, or I may rest with what amounts to the indefinite statement that Socrates exemplifies some label coextensive with "rational". If I choose the latter course, I am not entitled to complain about the indefiniteness of my answer. In short, we can be as specific or as general as we like about what is exemplified, but we cannot achieve maximum specificity and maximum generality at the same time.

Earlier I said that what is exemplified is abstract. Now I have interpreted exemplification as obtaining between the sample and a label—for instance, between the sample and each concrete inscription of a predicate. Such a label (i.e., its inscriptions) may indeed be 'abstract' in having multiple denotation; but a singular label may equally well be exemplified by what it denotes. And a label, whether with plural or singular or null denotation, may of course be itself denoted. The 'difference in domain' discussed earlier thus reduces to this: while anything may be denoted, only labels may be exemplified.[5]

SAMPLES AND LABELS

Although exemplification is reference running from denotatum back to label, by no means every case of reference is a case of denotation or exemplification. An element may come to serve as a symbol for an element related to it in almost any way. Sometimes the underlying relationship is not referential, as when the symbol is the cause or effect of (and so sometimes called the sign of), or is just to the left of, or is similar to, what it denotes. In other cases reference runs along a chain of relationships, some or all of them referential. Thus one of two things may refer to the other *via* predicates exemplified; or one of two predicates refer to the other *via* things denoted. Some familiar types of symbolization can be distinguished in terms of such underlying relationships or chains; but no nonreferential relationship, and no chain, even (since reference is nontransitive) where each element refers to the next, is sufficient by itself to establish reference by its first element to its last. Each or either or neither of the two may refer to the other. And of course an element may symbolize another in more than one way. . . .

MODES OF METAPHOR

Metaphorical possession and exemplification are likewise parallel to their literal counterparts; and what was said earlier about predicates and properties applies here as well. A picture is metaphorically sad if some label—verbal or not—that is coextensive with (i.e., has the same literal denotation as) "sad" metaphorically denotes the picture. The picture metaphorically exemplifies "sad" if "sad" is referred to by and metaphorically denotes the picture. And the picture metaphorically exemplifies sadness if some label coextensive with "sad" is referred to by and metaphorically denotes the picture. Since, as we have seen, the features that distinguish the metaphorical from the literal are transient, I shall often use "possession" and "exemplification" to cover both literal and metaphorical cases.

EXPRESSION

What is expressed is metaphorically exemplified. What expresses sadness is metaphorically sad. And what is metaphorically sad is actually but not literally sad, i.e., comes under a transferred application of some label coextensive with "sad".

Thus what is expressed is possessed, and what a face or picture expresses need not (but may) be emotions or ideas the actor or artist has, or those he wants to convey, or thoughts or feelings of the viewer or of a person depicted, or properties of anything else related in some other way to the symbol. Of course, a symbol is often said to express a property related to it in one of these ways, but I reserve the term "expression" to distinguish the central case where the property belongs to the symbol itself—regardless of cause or effect or intent or subject-matter. That the actor was despondent, the artist high, the spectator gloomy or nostalgic or euphoric, the subject inanimate, does not determine whether the face or picture is sad or not. The cheering face of the hypocrite expresses solicitude; and the stolid painter's picture of boulders may express agitation. The properties a symbol expresses are its own property.

But they are acquired property. They are not the homely features by which the objects and events that serve as symbols are classified literally, but are metaphorical imports. Pictures express sounds or feelings rather than colors. And the metaphorical transfer involved in expression is usually from or *via* an exterior realm rather than the interior transfer effected in hyperbole or litotes or irony. A pretentious picture does not express the modesty that may be sarcastically ascribed to it.

Properties expressed are, furthermore, not only metaphorically possessed but also referred to, exhibited, typified, shown forth. A square swatch does not usually exemplify squareness, and a picture that rapidly increases in market value does not express the property of being a gold mine. Normally, a swatch exemplifies only sartorial properties while a picture literally exemplifies only pictorial properties and metaphorically exemplifies only properties that are constant relative to pictorial properties.[6] And a picture expresses only properties—unlike that of being a gold mine—that it thus metaphorically exemplifies as a pictorial symbol. Daumier's

Laundress so exemplifies and expresses weight but not any metaphorical property dependent upon the physical weight of the picture. In general, a symbol of a given kind—pictorial, musical, verbal, etc.—expresses only properties that it metaphorically exemplifies as a symbol of that kind. . . .

In summary, if *a* expresses *b* then: (1) *a* possesses or is denoted by *b*; (2) this possession or denotation is metaphorical; and (3) *a* refers to *b*.

No test for detecting what a work expresses has been sought here; after all, a definition of hydrogen gives us no ready way of telling how much of the gas is in this room. Nor has any precise definition been offered for the elementary relation of expression we have been examining. Rather, it has been subsumed under metaphorical exemplification, and circumscribed somewhat more narrowly by some additional requirements, without any claim that these are sufficient.[7] The concern has been to compare and contrast this relation with such other major kinds of reference as exemplification, representation, and description. So far we have succeeded better with expression than with representation and description, which we have not yet been able to distinguish from one another.

NOTES

1. Extensionality is preserved in this formula; truth-value is unaffected when "gray" is replaced by any coextensive predicate.
2. Ostension, like exemplification, has to do with samples, but whereas ostension is the act of pointing to a sample, exemplification is the relation between a sample and what it refers to.
3. Likewise, to say that a car on the showroom floor exemplifies a Rolls-Royce is to say elliptically that the car exemplifies the property of being a Rolls-Royce. But such ellipsis can be dangerous in technical discourse where to say that *x* exemplifies a *B* means that *x* refers to and is denoted by a *B*. See further below.
4. In *How to Write Short Stories (with Samples)* (New York, Charles Scribner's Sons, 1924), p. 247.
5. If such abstract entities as qualia are recognized, these—although not labels—may indeed be exemplified by their instances, which are concrete wholes containing these qualia. But exemplification of other properties would still have to be explained as above in terms of exemplification of predicates; and simplicity of exposition for our present purposes seems best served by treating all exemplification in this one way.
6. A property is thus constant only if, although it may or may not remain constant where the pictorial properties vary, it never varies where the pictorial properties remain constant. In other words, if it occurs anywhere, it also occurs whenever the pictorial properties are the same. The constancy here in question obtains between the metaphorical extension of the expressed property and the literal extension of the basic pictorial properties; but a property thus constant also itself qualifies as a pictorial property.
7. But some superficially odd cases meeting the stated requirements seem entitled to admission; many a work, I think, may quite appropriately be said to express eloquently its unintentional clumsiness or stupidity.

The Concept of Expression: A Proposal

Alan Tormey

1. Philosophical concern with the expressive dimension of art has taken many directions, and it would serve no clear purpose to attempt to survey or assess them all, even if that were an attainable goal. Rather, the aim of the present chapter is limited to an extension of some of my earlier arguments and conclusions to the structuring of a proposal for comprehending and describing the expressive character of art works.

2. It is transparently evident that it would make no sense to assert that a work of art literally *had* e.g. the property anguish or longing or sadness—that it *was* anguished or sad (or else, as E. F. Carritt once remarked, we should have to cheer the poor thing up); and yet it is common enough to claim that an art work is *expressive of* anguish or longing or sadness. And we have seen in the preceding chapter that there are good reasons for taking 'is expressive of _____,' not as a relational predicate linking an art work to something external to it, but as an incomplete one-place predicate which, properly completed, is descriptive of some feature of the art work. It will be convenient to refer to the properties denoted by predicates of this sort as *expressive properties*. Thus, a work expressive of anguish will be said to have the *expressive* property anguish rather than simply the property anguish, the modification serving both to indicate affinities with instances where 'anguish' has unqualified application and to obviate absurdities engendered by taking art to exhibit full-blooded sentient states. The question then becomes one of establishing the connection between a property γ and the expressive property γ and explaining the apparent fact that expressive properties are not merely garden variety properties belonging to special classes of objects.

The analysis developed in earlier parts of this study suggests the following proposal: expressive properties are those properties of art works (or natural objects) whose names also designate intentional states of persons. Thus 'tenderness,' 'sadness,' 'anguish,' and 'nostalgia' may denote expressive properties of art works because they also denote states of persons that are intentional, and thus expressible in the fullest and clearest sense. This proposal imposes limitations on what shall be counted as an expressive property, and to that extent is to be regarded as a stipulation. But it is a stipulation that I believe can be defended and shown to have important advantages over alternative ways of understanding the expressive dimension of art.

Restricting our attention to art works then, an expressive property γ will be understood to be any property of an art work denoted by a predicate which also denotes intentional states of persons. Nonexpressive properties will constitute a complementary class defined merely by exclusion. (That duration, pitch, color, weight, being-the-portrait-of-X, being-a-six-voice-motet, and the like, are nonexpressive properties of art works is evident from the fact that none of these properties is designated by predicates which also denote intentional states of persons.) The dichotomy is

---

From *The Concept of Expression* (Princeton: Princeton University Press, 1971). Reprinted by permission of the publisher.

rough-hewn and cuts across distinctions that are common in aesthetic analysis, but it will enable us to raise some important questions about the internal relations among properties commonly ascribed to art works.

3. The relation between the expressive and the nonexpressive properties of an art work is obviously an intimate one. Ravel's *Pavane pour une infante défunte* is often characterized as tender or nostalgic, and these expressive properties are dependent, in some way, upon such nonexpressive properties of the piece as the contour of the melodic line, the quasi-modal harmonic structure, the moderate tempo, and the limited dynamic range. Similarly, the animated opening bars of "Parade" from Benjamin Britten's *Les Illuminations*, though not expressive *of* animation, can be heard as expressive of apprehension, and apprehension would be an expressive property of the piece.

It is this relation between expressive and nonexpressive properties that I intend to explore, and in virtue of which I shall suggest that art works can be thought of as autonomously self-expressive objects, *viz.* that the complex of relations among the properties of an art work is such that it can be seen as presenting some of its properties and revealing others; those properties which are its expressive properties themselves being revealed through the presentation of varying sets of nonexpressive properties.[1]

All this of course demands both clarification and defense; and we have first to justify the retention of an expression vocabulary to characterize the relation. The choice results in part from the elimination of alternatives. The relation between expressive and nonexpressive properties is more intimate than would be implied by reference to necessary conditions, critical warrants, or rule-governed regularities, all of which leave open the possibility that the relata are logically independent. But more positive reasons can be derived from arguments presented earlier for taking the behavioral and linguistic expressions of a person to be *partially constitutive* of his intentional states. It was argued there that certain observable aspects of behavior are logically proper parts of the complex referents of such predicates as 'anger,' 'jealousy,' 'joy,' and 'fear,' and thus partially constitutive of the intentional states denoted by predicates of this sort. And since we have already stipulated that expressive properties of art works are the aesthetic correlates of intentional states of persons, it follows that the relation between nonexpressive and expressive properties of art works is analogous to the relation between human (or animal) behavior and the intentional states of which the behavior is partially constitutive.

The aesthetic situation is analogous, however, with the important difference that the nonexpressive properties of an art work are *wholly* constitutive of its expressive properties, there being no "inner" aspects of art comparable to the ostensibly private states of persons. And since there is nothing "hidden" from us in an art work, there is no room for the construction of inferences from some of its properties to others. (There is nothing *essentially* private in an art work, but what is not essentially private need not be essentially obvious. Significant works of art have a perceptual thickness, and the critical task is to see *into* them, not through them or beyond them.) To recall an example, the tempo, dynamics, harmonic texture, melodic contour of Ravel's *Pavane* are not merely the grounds, warrants or criteria for asserting that the work is tender, they are the *constituents* of its tenderness. This relation of constituency is the aesthetic analogue of the expression of full-blooded intentional states of persons, and furnishes, I believe, at least provisional justification for describing art works as self-expressive objects ('*self*-expressive' to prevent relapse into the language of the Expression theory with the attendant implications that what is expressed belongs to something, or someone, other than the work itself). The tenderness of the *Pavane* and the apprehensiveness of "Parade" are properties of the works themselves expressed in, or through, the differing complexes of tempo, texture, and structure.

A serious difficulty may appear to arise here, for if a given set [c] of nonexpressive properties is wholly constitutive of an expressive property γ it might appear that [c] is equivalent to a set of necessary and sufficient conditions for γ. And it would follow from this that we should need only to establish the presence of [c] in a particular work to conclude that it was necessarily expressive of γ, since [c] would entail γ. But it has been persuasively and plausibly denied that such sets of conditions can be assumed to exist, on the grounds that it would render the detection of expressive properties a quasi-mechanical process available to anyone with normal perception, and obviate the need to develop particular aesthetic sensibilities, or to exhibit good "taste" as opposed to good sight or good hearing.[2]

However, it would be a mistake to assume that the present argument implies an equivalence of [c] with a set of necessary and sufficient conditions for γ. For such an equivalence to hold, [c] must be unambiguously correlated with γ. But the relation between sets of nonexpressive properties and the expressive properties of art works is such that a given set of nonexpressive properties may be compatible with, and constitutive of, any one of a *range* of expressive properties, just as a given set of gestures or movements may be compatible with (and partially constitutive of) more than one intentional state of a person. That is, [c] will not be uniquely constitutive of γ; and thus, while the nonexpressive properties of an art work are wholly constitutive of its expressive properties they are *ambiguously* constitutive. And this ambiguity is the source of our inability to determine decisively whether, for example, the Ravel *Pavane* is more truly expressive of tenderness or of yearning or of nostalgia, since all of these may fall within the compatibility range of the work's nonexpressive properties. Moreover, the ambiguity is symmetrical. Not only will [c] be compatible with more than one expressive property, but more than one work may be justifiably described as tender without it following that they possess identical sets of nonexpressive properties. In consequence, the relation is not one of necessary and sufficient conditions nor of sufficient conditions alone, and no encouragement is lent to the fear (or the hope) that rule books and check lists will replace the exercise of "taste" and herald the triumph of the philistine.

Consequently, moreover, it will not do to attempt to explain the relation between expressive and nonexpressive properties as a rule-governed relation of the form: Whenever [c], predication of 'γ' is warranted. And this is not only, as is frequently argued, because no such rules can be formulated in practice, but rather because *any* rule of this sort would fail to provide for the two most relevant features of the relation. The concept of a rule-governed relation is at once too weak and too strong—too weak because it fails to account for constituency and too strong because it fails to allow for ambiguity. More generally, the language of rules, conditions, and criteria is simply inadequate to capture the relation we are considering.

4. I have argued that the relation between the nonexpressive and the expressive properties of an art work is one of ambiguous constituency. There are good reasons, moreover, for believing that the resultant expressive ambiguity is essentially uneliminable and that, consequently, critical disagreements of at least one sort are, of necessity, irresoluble.

There are no uniquely decisive procedures for adjudicating between critical judgments that a work W displaying the set [c] of nonexpressive properties is expressive of γ rather than δ, or δ rather than ϑ, so long as the relevant grounds for such claims are recognized to lie in the work itself, and as long as [c] remains compatible with a range of expressive properties which includes γ, δ, and ϑ.[3]

Moreover we cannot confirm, or disconfirm, claims about the expressive properties of art works in the same way we frequently confirm claims that a *person* is expressing a particular intentional state. There is no access to independent evidence comparable to a person's avowals of his feelings or his subsequent behavior. Paintings, unlike people, remain silent in the face of our persistent misjudgments of them; and the possibility of disagreement over the expressive properties of art works remains essentially and necessarily open.

It may be suggested that there are, after all, means available to us for eliminating or accommodating critical disputes resting on the expressive ambiguity of art works. We may be tempted, for example, to resolve the issue by conceding that a work has *all* the expressive properties falling within the relevant compatibility range. But this is an excessively generous concession, and it is open to the objection that *some* of the expressive properties falling within a particular compatibility range may be psychologically or aesthetically incongruent. It might be extremely difficult to say, for instance, of a particular drawing by Käthe Kollwitz whether it was expressive of despair, anxiety, resignation, or fear. But to attempt to resolve the difficulty by attributing to the work a conjunction of such properties, or predicating of it some complex property ⟨despair-anxiety-resignation-fear⟩ would not only be to abandon all efforts at critical discrimination, it would do violence to our common understanding of these qualities. The converse alternative would be to assign members of the compatibility range of expressive properties disjunctively to the work. This, however, while logically inoffensive, is also aesthetically pointless. One must make critical choices *within* the range of available predicates, and it could hardly be thought aesthetically enlightening to be told that the Kollwitz drawing was actually expressive of ⟨despair or anxiety or resignation or fear⟩. Expressive ambiguity can neither be eliminated nor accommodated by such critical strategy, and resort to either conjunctive or disjunctive descriptions of the expressive properties of art works is an evasion and not a resolution of the critical problem.

There is a further and perhaps more decisive reason for believing the expressive ambiguity of many art works to be essentially uneliminable. The expressive "gestures" of art often occur in an aesthetic space devoid of explicit context and intentional objects. And it is the absence or the elusiveness of intentional objects that impedes our critical attempts to dissolve the ambiguity and disclose an unequivocal expressive quality in the art work. It may be true that we cannot tell from a smile, isolated from its context, whether it is a smile of parental benevolence directed toward a sleeping child or a smile of sadistic satisfaction directed toward a suffering victim.[4] But these are uncertainties that could theoretically be resolved by uncovering the intentional context. In contrast, many art works are intentionally incomplete. There are no further contexts to be uncovered and no intentional objects to be disclosed. We are free of course to invent contexts, to wrap the art work in fictions that would yield intentional objects. But is one invention more accurate, one fiction closer to the truth than another? Is there any question of *justifying* our inventions? The resolution of expressive ambiguity would require that there were.

It is not a contingent failing of art or ourselves that we frequently cannot discover what the expressive gestures of a work are *about* (toward, for, against, etc.); it is a common and aesthetically relevant condition of much of our art. Consider, for example, the expressive ambiguity of the vocabulary of modern dance movements isolated from specific dramatic contexts. Abstract dance forms consisting of context-neutral series and clusters of such movements are no less expressive than the explicitly narrative patterns of classical ballet; they are only more ambiguously expressive.[5] And there are innumerable works of art of which it would be pointless even to raise the question of intentional contexts or intentional objects—of Miro's *Painting, 1933* or the trio sonata from *The Musical Offering*, for example, and this should strengthen the suspicion that whatever expressive ambiguity such works display is not an aesthetic flaw but an inherent condition.

Now, in contrast with Baroque trio sonatas, abstract dance forms, and much contemporary visual art, many art works commonly classed as representational present us with intentional contexts (contexts in which intentional objects can be identified) as integral parts of their content. Most theatrical works exemplify this. In Euripides we are shown not only the tears of Medea; we are shown what the tears are about. In this respect Greek tragedy and Baroque instrumental music are worlds apart. The world of the drama encompasses intentional objects while the world of the trio sonata precludes them.

To the extent that intentional contexts are available then it might appear that expressive ambiguity can be circumscribed or decisively removed. But the appearance is chimerical. In works of representational art we can, and should, distinguish between the expressive properties *of* the work and contained or represented expressions *in* the work. Among the things a representational art work may represent are acts of expression, and failure to distinguish between represented acts of expression and expressive properties of the work itself will generate crucial confusions. It has been said, for example, of Bernini's *David* that it expresses a concentrated and intense determination. But this is misleading. The *work* does not express this. David does. The Bernini work *represents* David-expressing-intense-determination. And it does not follow from this that intense determination is an expressive property of the work itself. It does not follow that it is *not* an expressive property of the work either. Identical predicates *may* apply to work and represented content alike, but each predication is independent of the other, and false hopes for regenerating a corollary of classical expression theories may arise here if there is failure to notice the ellipsis when one goes on (incorrectly) to describe the work itself as expressing David's determination.

There is a limited though instructive parallel between this situation and that of the actor. It was argued earlier that it would be a distortion to describe an actor portraying Lear as expressing Lear's grief and despair—that we should say that he was portraying or representing Lear-expressing-Lear's-despair. And where an action is both an expression and a representation of an expression we have grounds for distinguishing between actor and character as discrete logical subjects of the expressions. Now art works, like actors, may portray *inter alia* acts of expression; and in both cases distortions will be avoided only if reference to represented expressions is distinguished from reference to properties correctly attributable only to the representing *agency*—the actor or the art work.

In general, it is only the contained or represented expression whose ambiguity is dissolved by the availability of intentional contexts in the art work. We may, given the circumstances of the action of a drama, be justifiably certain that the cries of the protagonist are an expression of remorse, but this leaves unanswered the question of the expressive properties of the *play*. The drama itself may project pity, horror, or contempt toward the remorse of the protagonist. That is, it may have as one of *its* expressive properties pity, horror, or contempt, and thereby comment expressively on the represented acts of expression. Acts of expression cannot themselves be expressed in art, but they can be depicted, described, reflected upon, or judged, and all these possibilities lie within the province of one or several of the representational arts. The distinction we have been considering should in fact explain the capacity of representational arts, generally, to make expressive comments on their represented content. While the availability of intentional contexts may help to obviate ambiguity in the represented expressions then, it may do little or nothing to alleviate critical discord resting on the expressive ambiguity of an art work itself, even where the work is incontestably representational and contains intentional contexts as an integral part of its content.

5. Expressive ambiguity is an inherent feature of most if not all of our art. And it is a continuing dilemma of critical practice that we are faced with the necessity of making and defending choices from a range of available alternatives for describing the expressive character of particular art works—choices that must be made in the absence of any clearly decisive means for eliminating alternative and competing descriptions. This dilemma

is, I believe, inescapable since it rests on the aesthetic need for making *some* critical choices conjoined with the impossibility of establishing the necessity for making just those choices that we do make. And it is this that makes the exercise of critical judgment so intriguing to those whose tolerance for indeterminacy is high and so frustrating to those for whom the quest for certainty is always paramount.

Finally, then, to the extent that our aesthetic concerns are with the expressive dimension of art, I would suggest that art works be thought of as ambiguously self-expressive objects. The virtue I would like to claim for this way of thinking of art is that it commits us to neither of the disjuncts of the prevalent assumption that a reference to expression in art is either (*a*) a reference to something lying behind or beyond the work—a thought, feeling, mood, or attitude to which the work stands in some external relation—or (*b*) a reference to something immediately presented to perception as an aesthetic "surface." There are, I think, decisive objections to this antithesis. If the argument of Chapter IV is correct, critical appreciation of the expressiveness of an art work is clearly not an inductive or an inferential procedure. It does not follow, however, that if we are not engaged in searching out something behind the art work then its expressiveness must lie openly and obviously on the surface; for if that were the case, we would be at a loss to explain the continuing divergence of informed judgment concerning the expressive qualities of art works.

The alternatives have been misstated. Discerning the expressive properties of art is neither a matter of scanning surfaces with the naïve eye nor sounding hidden depths with delicate inference tools, and the conception of art works as ambiguously self-expressive objects offers at least an escape from the correlative mistakes of the antithesis and, hopefully, a more promising way of both elucidating the expressive dimension of art and of accounting for the legitimacy of critical disagreement. The discerning of expressive properties requires the fusion of perception and choice. And that is perhaps, after all, what is entailed in the exercise of taste.

NOTES

1. Guy Sircello, in an interesting article, "Perceptual Acts and Pictorial Art: A Defense of Expression Theory," *Journal of Philosophy*, LXII (1965), 669–77, reaches what seems to me a view similar to this, though it is stated and developed quite differently. There are limitations to Sircello's position, however, that I should not like to accept. Aside from the difficulty of conceiving of expressiveness as arising from "virtual acts of perception" which occur in the art work but which are admittedly performed by no one, acts of perception—virtual or otherwise—are not among the things that can sensibly be said to be *expressed*. Also, Sircello's claims are supported entirely by reference to representational art works, and it is doubtful whether the arguments, even if sound, could be extrapolated to account for the expressiveness of nonrepresentational art works. Apparently, also, on Sircello's view an art work may express such things as truthfulness and frankness, though no justification is given for regarding these as specifically *expressive* (or expressible) properties. On my view, of course, they are not expressive properties since 'truthfulness' and 'frankness' do not denote intentional states of persons.
2. Most effectively by Sibley in "Aesthetic Concepts," Philosophical Review, LXVII (1959), 421–50.
3. The membership of particular compatibility ranges is flexible and subject to continuous revision, as we can note from the commonplaces of art history and art criticism. We now "see" Bambara antelope figures in ways in which no one would have seen them before Cézanne and Modigliani, and we "hear" the Mahler symphonies quite differently after exposure to Schoenberg and Stockhausen. The actual membership of particular compatibility ranges must of course be determined by aesthetic or critical judgment and not by philosophical theory.
4. L. Wittgenstein, *Philosophical Investigations*, paragraph 539, p. 145^e.
5. They may also of course be merely expressive in the intransitive sense discussed in Ch. IV.

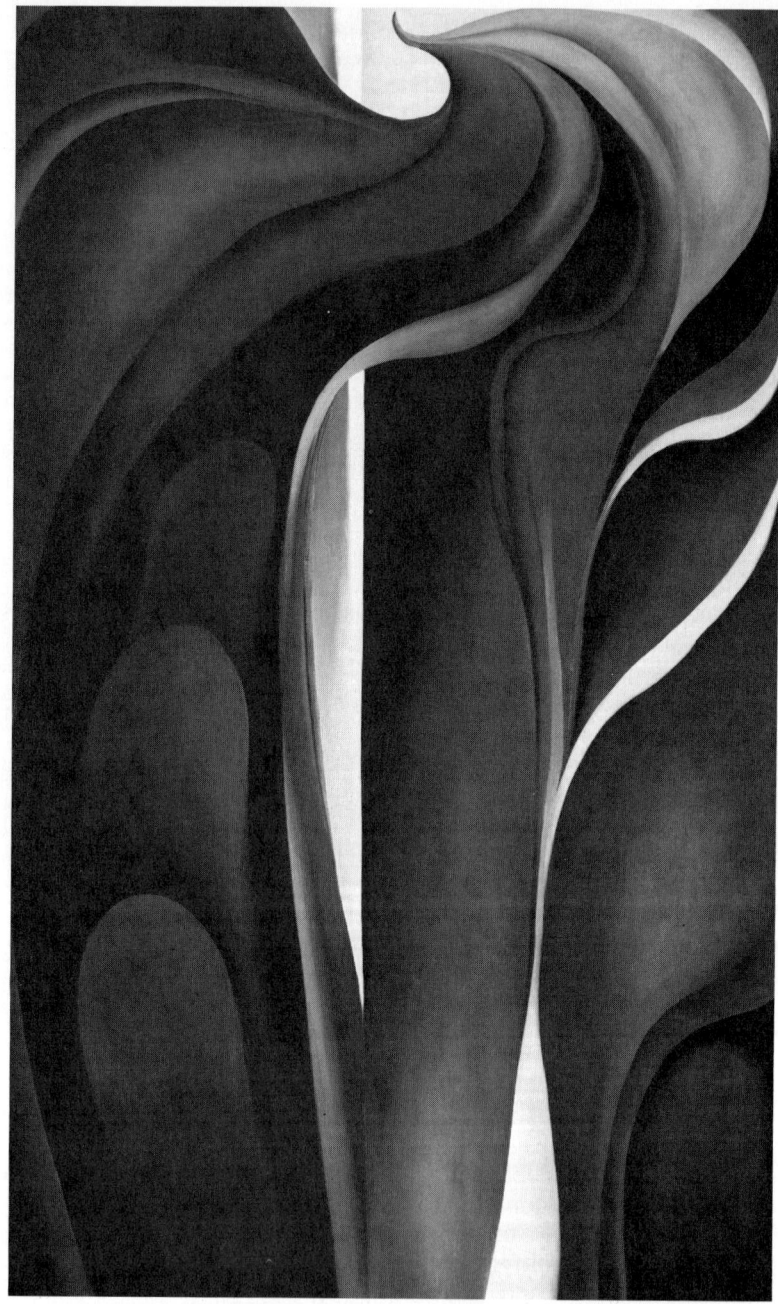

Jack-in-the-Pulpit No. V, Georgia O'Keefe (American). 1930. National Gallery of Art, Washington, D.C.

By her representationally accurate close-up of a particular woodland flower, O'Keefe produces an image of generalized, but indefinite, significance.

PART II

Ongoing Issues and
New Perspectives in Contemporary
Philosophy of Art

CHAPTER 4
The Particularity of Art and the Generality of Theory

Philosophers of art have, at least since the time of Kant, realized the problem of theorizing about art. To theorize about anything is to generalize, placing many different individual entities into the same category where they are all treated essentially alike, according to lawlike rules or principles.

The problem in theorizing about art is that each work of art is so unique and our approach to works of art seems so subjective, private, and individualistic that it seems inherently false to the nature of art and our response to it to reduce it to a generalized schema.

For Kant (whom we include here because of the power of his influence on contemporary aestheticians), judgments of beauty cannot be ordinary conceptual judgments, as Hutcheson and other British "Taste theorists" had supposed, simply recognizing that a particular object falls under the general class or kind defined by the concept "beauty." To judge beauty in this way, Kant argued, would be to confuse aesthetic judgments with cognitive judgments. To judge something as beautiful is not just to recognize intellectually that it falls within that category of things we call beautiful, but to appreciate its beauty, to respond subjectively to its beauty, to be affected positively by its beauty. A person incapable of aesthetic sensibility could learn to call beautiful what the rest of us call beautiful, but such a person could never really see or feel the beauty of anything in the sense of being able to enjoy its beauty.

Of course, as Kant acknowledged, we can make cognitive, classificatory judgments that a certain object is judged by members of our language group as beautiful of its kind. I can judge that an individual hairless cat is beautiful (in the sense that I recognize that it is the best specimen of its kind) without myself being in the least affected by (that is, enjoying, appreciating) its beauty, especially as I personally find such cats extremely repulsive. Kant called these judgments of *dependent* beauty.

Judgments of *pure* beauty, on the other hand, Kant held to be completely noncognitive, judging the mere form of the object to be as though (purposively) designed to accommodate the pleasurable interplay of my subjective cognitive faculties. Suppose I am listening to a piece of music which I judge to be beautiful—that is, universally pleasing to any human subject. I am making the judgment that these sounds seem to have been perfectly organized to stimulate, engage, excite, organize, expand, and harmonize my intellectual, imaginative, and sensual mental equipment in a perfectly delightful way. Since these mental faculties of mine are, essentially, the same in all people, so far as I know, I judge that the music *should* have, and I therefore *expect* it to have, a similar effect on any and every other human being who should happen to hear it.

Aesthetic judgments, then, do possess a kind of universality, but it is not the universality of a scientific law. Rather, it is the fact that we think our judgments of the beautiful should have force or efficacy for others; they are not, Kant claims, simply statements of our subjective preferences or private pleasures. And yet, they are not judgments which, like scientific predictions, can be deduced from conceptualizing the work of art as falling under some universal laws or principles of beauty. The uniqueness and particularity of works of art thwart any attempt at such subsumption under aesthetic laws. The deep lesson that we learn from Kant, then, is that there cannot be anything like a deductive science of aesthetic judgments.

If we cannot have a "science of the beautiful," can we not at least engage in general philosophical theorizing about the nature of art? Even if there are no lawlike rules for making aesthetic evaluations, we may still believe that the various kinds of art share a common nature, a nature which we must be aware of when we react aesthetically to those works.

But as we mentioned earlier, the idea that philosophy can uncover the essential nature of art—the very idea that art has some shared nature—came under vigorous attack in the early days of analytic aesthetics. However, with what is a characteristically "analytic" strategy, the discussion was couched in linguistic rather than ontological terms, and thereby the question of the nature of art was converted into the question of the *definability* of the concept of art in terms of concise and informative, logically necessary, and sufficient conditions. The answer given by many analytic aestheticians was that the concept of art was *not* amenable to any such definition. This, then, was a way of claiming that art had no fixed and essential nature.

Weitz, perhaps the best-known advocate of this view, follows Wittgenstein's anti-essentialist injunction to seek the meanings of words in the role they play in various "language games" and *not* to look for what all objects denoted by the same word have in common. Wittgenstein imagines that we start off wrongly assuming that if a word (for example, *game*) has meaning and refers to numerous particular things, its meaning can only consist of a feature which is common to all games. Once we have found this feature or features, we can articulate the essence or nature of games in our definition of the word.

But in fact, Wittgenstein shows us, there *is* no such common feature. Yet far from implying that the word has no meaning, this negative result leads us to look for the meaning elsewhere by examining the ways in which we use the word *game* in different contexts in everyday conversation.

For a similar reason, Weitz argued that aesthetics' traditional enterprise of proposing theories about art based on the assumption that there is something essential which all art must share was necessarily doomed to failure. But when Weitz looked to see how we use the concept "art," he went beyond Wittgenstein's general suggestion and argued that the concept "art" is especially open-ended, or, as Gallie said, an "essentially contested" concept. Our concept of art is one which recognizes and celebrates its constant evolution through innovative and creative artistic revolutions. Hence the concept "art" must be kept *open* for further changes in the future. Any attempt to limit art to some common set of properties which all works have in common would wrongly close off the concept to the addition of new features or the elimination of old features in the art of the future.

Danto found in the "conceptual art" of the 1960s even greater problems in defining art essentially by reference to commonly shared features. When Kennick imagined a workman going into the warehouse to bring out all the artworks, he imagined that the workman would have some initial, prereflective idea of what works of art were. Kennick was arguing that the definitions of the aestheticians would not help the workman, giving him less information about what to look for than he already had. He therefore has some idea of what works of art are going to look like—some are pictures in frames, others are sculptured figures, and so on. But the workman would have no way of knowing that an ordinary necktie, a hat rack, a urinal taken from a Parisian men's room were works of art, as the history of art has shown them to be. Here the difficulty is increased by a quantum leap.

The art Danto is talking about in his discussions of "indiscernibles" is art which becomes art, if it does at all, only by being christened as such by the theory which says that it is art. Otherwise, in the absence of any such theory, the necktie is just that and not a work of art. As we will have occasion to point out later, this is a reversal of the usual relation held to exist between the concepts of artwork and aesthetic experience. Most aestheticians have held that a work of art must be recognized by its capacity to stimulate aesthetic experience; Danto argues just the reverse, that, at least in the case of "concept art," we must first know that it is a work of art before we know whether it is appropriate to experience it aesthetically. Before I reflect on the aesthetic possibilities of the hat rack, I must first be sure it was put there as an art object and not simply as a convenient place in the gallery to hang one's hat. We need the contexts provided by the artworld not only to *see* that some things (sometimes quite strange things) can be treated as art, but also to *make* them art. It is a mistake to try to discern some inherent nature within every work of art that is independent of these artworld contexts.

This idea, however, sparked a new and different kind of life into the search for a definition of art. Perhaps the past failures in definitions were caused by mistakenly focusing on the work's perceptual or experiential features, when the true nature of art is to be found in certain *conventional* or *institutional* properties.

In his widely discussed institutional definition of art, Dickie elaborates on this idea and defines art in terms of the theories and practices that those who participate in the institutions surrounding the arts engage in. In his formulation in the 1974 paper reproduced here, "A work of art in the classificatory sense is (1) an artifact (2) a set of the aspects of which has had conferred upon it the status of candidate for appreciation by some person or persons acting on behalf of a certain social institution (the artworld)." Any general theory of art based on this definition would begin from the realization that a work's status as art is an institutional or cultural status; aesthetics begins to embrace the sociology of art.

Many writers have criticized Dickie's definition, and Blizek touches on many of these criticisms. First, Blizek asks, what is meant by "artworld"? In particular, how widely or narrowly should its boundaries be drawn? Who confers or can confer the status of "candidate for appreciation" on a work? The artist or the critics and curators? What if there is violent disagreement? Moreover, the status of candidate for appreciation certainly is not as clearly institutional as, say, one's marital status, nor is it as rule- or practice-bound as is, say, "Democratic candidate for governor."

Blizek also wonders what Dickie means by "appreciation." Again, to avoid the charge of excessive narrowness, Dickie has left the term deliberately broad and open-ended, but at the cost of excessive vagueness. Surely, Blizek asks, Dickie does not mean to include just any sort of appreciation, and however problematic it may turn out, Blizek suggests that it would be better to limit appreciation to *"aesthetic* appreciation," but Dickie has already, in earlier work, rejected the notion of aesthetic appreciation as naming a nonexistent mythical entity (see Chapter 6).

Finally, to avoid foreclosing on artistic creativity, so important to Weitz and others, Dickie has been at pains to include in his concept of "artifact" found art and readymades (e.g., a piece of driftwood or a necktie). But Blizek wonders if the artifactuality of found art and readymades really involves the same sort of creativity as that displayed in traditional sculpture, where the artist actually manipulates and transforms the art medium.

According to Osborne, the question "What is a work of art?" is a single form of words used to raise two distinct questions, often confused with one another—first, "What things in the world around us are correctly designated as works of art?" and second, "What is meant by calling anything at all a work of art?" The first is a factual question concerning the criteria used to choose the correct denotation of the term; the second is a philosophical question asking for the meaning of the words used. According to Osborne, institutional theories point to the "rather trivial fact that the answer to the former of these questions is a matter of social convention." But this does not answer the philosophical second question, which involves clarifying and articulating what we intuitively (and perhaps confusedly) have in mind when we call something a work of art.

Acknowledging a range of problems attending any and all attempts to define art, Osborne returns in this article to his old standby—defining art, as Beardsley also continued to do, in terms of aesthetic experience. "Whatever among natural objects is capable of arousing and sustaining aesthetic experience in suitably endowed persons we call beautiful; and whatever among artifacts is capable of arousing and sustaining aesthetic experience in suitably prepared subjects we call a work of art." Of course, Dickie has, as we mentioned earlier, denied the very existence of an aesthetic experience, but Osborne takes this as a challenge to sharpen, strengthen, and clarify the concept—not to abandon it altogether. Osborne offers by way of clarification the further gloss, reminiscent of Beardsley, that art arouses aesthetic experience in the sense that it "is capable of stimulating such self-rewarding awareness and sustaining perception at higher than the ordinary levels of intensity and fullness." (Detailed and various treatments of the aesthetic experience appear in Chapter 7.)

Critique of the Aesthetical Judgment

Immanuel Kant

FIRST DIVISION
Analytic of the Aesthetical Judgment

FIRST BOOK
Analytic of the Beautiful

FIRST MOMENT
Of the Judgment of Taste, According to Quality

1. THE JUDGMENT OF TASTE IS AESTHETICAL

In order to distinguish whether anything is beautiful or not, we refer the representation, not by the understanding to the object for cognition, but by the imagination (perhaps in conjunction with the understanding) to the subject and its feeling of pleasure or pain. The judgment of taste is therefore not a judgment of cognition, and is consequently not logical but aesthetical, by which we understand that whose determining ground can be *no other than subjective*. Every reference of representations, even that of sensations, may be objective (and then it signifies the real element of an empirical representation), save only the reference to the feeling of pleasure and pain, by which nothing in the object is signified, but through which there is a feeling in the subject as it is affected by the representation.

2. THE SATISFACTION WHICH DETERMINES THE JUDGMENT OF TASTE IS DISINTERESTED

The satisfaction which we combine with the representation of the existence of an object is called "interest." Such satisfaction always has reference to the faculty of desire, either as its determining ground or as necessarily connected with its determining ground. Now when the question is if a thing is beautiful, we do not want to know whether anything depends or can depend on the existence of the thing, either for myself or for anyone else, but how we judge it by mere observation (intuition or reflection). . . . We wish only to know if this mere representation of the object is accompanied in me with satisfaction, however indifferent I may be as regards

---

From *Critique of Judgment* by Immanuel Kant, translated by J. H. Bernard. Copyright © 1951 by Hafner Press, a Division of Macmillan Publishing Co. Inc., and reprinted with their permission. Headings have been renumbered.

the existence of the object of this representation. . . .

3. THE SATISFACTION IN THE PLEASANT IS BOUND UP WITH INTEREST

. . . If a determination of the feeling of pleasure or pain is called sensation, this expression signifies something quite different from what I mean when I call the representation of a thing (by sense, as a receptivity belonging to the cognitive faculty) sensation. For in the latter case the representation is referred to the object, in the former simply to the subject, and is available for no cognition whatever, not even for that by which the subject *cognizes* itself.

In the above elucidation we understand by the word "sensation" an objective representation of sense; and, in order to avoid misinterpretation, we shall call that which must always remain merely subjective and can constitute absolutely no representation of an object by the ordinary term "feeling." The green color of the meadows belongs to *objective* sensation, as a perception of an object of sense; the pleasantness of this belongs to *subjective* sensation by which no object is represented, i.e., to feeling, by which the object is considered as an object of satisfaction (which does not furnish a cognition of it).

Now that a judgment about an object by which I describe it as pleasant expresses an interest in it, is plain from the fact that by sensation it excites a desire for objects of that kind; consequently the satisfaction presupposes, not the mere judgment about it, but the relation of its existence to my state, so far as this is affected by such an object. Hence we do not merely say of the pleasant, *it pleases*, but, *it gratifies*. I give to it no mere assent, but inclination is aroused by it; and in the case of what is pleasant in the most lively fashion there is no judgment at all upon the character of the object, for those persons who always lay themselves out for enjoyment (for that is the word describing intense gratification) would fain dispense with all judgment.

4. THE SATISFACTION IN THE GOOD IS BOUND UP WITH INTEREST

Whatever by means of reason pleases through the mere concept is *good*. That which pleases only as a means we call *good for something* (the useful), but that which pleases for itself is *good in itself*. In both there is always involved the concept of a purpose, and consequently the relation of reason to the (at least possible) volition, and thus a satisfaction in the *presence* of an object or an action, i.e., some kind of interest.

In order to find anything good, I must always know what sort of a thing the object ought to be, i.e., I must have a concept of it. But there is no need of this to find a thing beautiful. Flowers, free delineations, outlines intertwined with one another without design and called conventional foliage, have no meaning, depend on no definite concept, and yet they please. The satisfaction in the beautiful must depend on the reflection upon an object, leading to any concept (however indefinite), and it is thus distinguished from the pleasant, which rests entirely upon sensation. . . .

However, notwithstanding all this difference between the pleasant and the good, they both agree in this that they are always bound up with an interest in their object. . . . For the good is the object of will (i.e., of a faculty of desire determined by reason). But to wish for something and to have a satisfaction in its existence, i.e., to take an interest in it, are identical.

5. COMPARISON OF THE THREE SPECIFICALLY DIFFERENT KINDS OF SATISFACTION

The pleasant and the good have both a reference to the faculty of desire, and they bring with them, the former a satisfaction pathologically conditioned (by impulses, *stimuli*), the latter a pure practical satisfaction which is determined not merely by the representation of the object but also by the represented connection of the subject with the existence of the object. It is not merely the object that pleases, but also its existence. On the other hand, the judgment of taste is merely *contemplative*; i.e., it is a judgment which, indifferent as regards the existence of an object, compares its character with the feeling of pleasure and pain. But this contemplation itself is not directed to concepts; for the judgment of taste is not a cognitive judgment (either theoretical or practical), and thus is not *based* on concepts, nor has it concepts as its *purpose*.

The pleasant, the beautiful, and the good designate then three different relations of representations to the feeling of pleasure and pain, in reference to which we distinguish from one another objects or methods of representing them. And the expressions corresponding to each, by which we mark our complacency in them, are not the same. That which *gratifies* a man is called *pleasant*; that which merely *pleases* him is *beautiful*; that which is *esteemed* or *approved* by him, i.e., that to which he accords an objective worth, is *good*. . . . We may say that, of all these three kinds of satisfaction, that of taste in the beautiful is alone a disinterested and *free* satisfaction; for no interest, either of sense or of reason, here forces our assent. Hence we may say of satisfaction that it is related in the three aforesaid cases to *inclination*, to *favor*, or to *respect*. Now *favor* is the only free satisfaction. An object of inclination and one that is proposed to our desire by a law of reason leave us no freedom in forming for ourselves anywhere an object of pleasure. All interest presupposes or generates a want, and, as the determining ground of assent, it leaves the judgment about the object no longer free. . . .

Explanation of the Beautiful Resulting from the First Moment

Taste is the faculty of judging of an object or a method of representing it by an *entirely disinterested* satisfaction or dissatisfaction. The object of such satisfaction is called *beautiful*.

SECOND MOMENT
Of the Judgment of Taste, According to Quantity

6. THE BEAUTIFUL IS THAT WHICH APART FROM CONCEPTS IS REPRESENTED AS THE OBJECT OF A UNIVERSAL SATISFACTION

This explanation of the beautiful can be derived from the preceding explanation of it as the object of an entirely disinterested satisfaction. For the fact of which everyone is conscious, that the satisfaction is for him quite disinterested, implies in his judgment a ground of satisfaction for all men. For since it does not rest on any inclination of the subject (nor upon any other premeditated interest), but since the person who judges feels himself quite *free* as regards the satisfaction which he attaches to the object, he cannot find the ground of this satisfaction in any private conditions connected with his own subject, and hence it must be regarded as grounded on what he can presuppose in every other person. Consequently he must believe that he has reason for attributing a similar satisfaction to everyone. He will therefore speak of the beautiful as if beauty were a characteristic of the object and the judgment logical (constituting a cognition of the object by means of concepts of it), although it is only aesthetical and involves merely a reference of the representation of the object to the subject. For it has this similarity to a logical judgment that we can presuppose its validity for all men. But this universality cannot arise from concepts: for from concepts there is no transition to the feeling of pleasure or pain (except in pure practical laws, which bring an interest with them such as is not bound up with the pure judgment of taste). Consequently the judgment of taste, accompanied with the consciousness of separation from all interest, must claim validity for every man, without this universality depending on objects. That is, there must be bound up with it a title to subjective universality.

7. COMPARISON OF THE BEAUTIFUL WITH THE PLEASANT AND THE GOOD BY MEANS OF THE ABOVE CHARACTERISTIC

As regards the pleasant, everyone is content that his judgment, which he bases upon private feeling and by which he says of an object that it pleases him, should be limited merely to his own person. Thus he is quite contented that if he says, "Canary wine is pleasant," another man may correct his expression and remind him that he ought to say, "It is pleasant *to me*." And this is the case not only as regards the taste of the tongue, the palate, and the throat, but for whatever is pleasant to anyone's eyes and ears. To one, violet color is soft and lovely; to another, it is washed out and dead. One man likes the tone of wind instruments, another that of strings. To strive here with the design of reproving as incorrect another man's judgment which is different from our own, as if the judgments were logically opposed, would be folly. As regards the pleasant, therefore, the fundamental proposition is valid: *everyone has his own taste* (the taste of sense).

The case is quite different with the beautiful. It would (on the contrary) be laughable if a man who imagined anything to his own taste thought to justify himself by saying: "This object (the house we see, the coat that person wears, the concert we hear, the poem submitted to our judgment) is beautiful *for me*." For he must not call it *beautiful* if it merely pleases him. Many things may have for him charm and pleasantness—no one troubles himself at that—but if he gives out anything as beautiful, he supposes in others the same satisfaction; he judges not merely for himself, but for everyone, and speaks of beauty as if it were a property of things. Hence he says "the *thing* is beautiful"; and he does not count on the agreement of others with this his judgment of satisfaction, because he has found this agreement several times before, but he *demands* it of them. He blames them if they judge otherwise and he denies them taste, which he nevertheless requires from them. Here, then, we cannot say that each man has his own particular taste. For this would be as much as to say that there is no taste whatever, i.e., no aesthetical judgment which can make a rightful claim upon everyone's assent. . . .

8. THE UNIVERSALITY OF THE SATISFACTION IS REPRESENTED IN A JUDGMENT OF TASTE ONLY AS SUBJECTIVE

This particular determination of the universality of an aesthetical judgment, which is to be met with a judgment of taste, is noteworthy, not indeed for the logician, but for the transcendental philosopher. It requires no small trouble to discover its origin, but we thus detect a property of our cognitive faculty which without this analysis would remain unknown.

First, we must be fully convinced of the fact that in a judgment of taste (about the beautiful) the satisfaction in the object is imputed to *everyone*, without being based on a concept (for then it would be the good). Further, this claim to universal validity so essentially belongs to a judgment by which we describe anything as *beautiful* that, if this were not thought in it, it would never come into our thoughts to use the expression at all, but everything which pleases without a concept would be counted as pleasant. In respect of the latter, everyone has his own opinion, and no one assumes in another agreement with his judgment of taste, which is always the case in a judgment of taste about beauty. I may call the first the taste of sense, the second the taste of reflection, so far as the first lays down mere private judgments and the second judgments supposed to be generally valid (public), but in both cases aesthetical (not practical) judgments about an object merely in respect of the relation of its representation to the feeling of pleasure and pain. Now here is something strange. As regards the taste of sense, not only does experience show that its judgment (of pleasure or pain connected with anything) is not valid universally, but everyone is content not to impute agreement with it to others (although actually there is often found a very extended concurrence in these judgments). On the other hand, the taste of reflection has its claim to the universal validity of its judgments (about the beautiful) rejected often enough, as experience teaches, although it may find it possible (as it actually does) to represent judgments which can demand this universal agreement. In fact it imputes this to everyone for each of its judgments of taste, without the persons that judge disputing as to the possibility of such a claim, although in particular cases they cannot agree as to the correct application of this faculty.

Here we must, in the first place, remark that a universality which does not rest on concepts of objects (not even on empirical ones) is not logical but aesthetical; i.e., it involves no objective quantity of the judgment, but only that which is subjective. For this I use the expression *general validity*, which signifies the validity of the reference of a representation, not to the cognitive faculty, but to the feeling of pleasure and pain for every subject. (We can avail ourselves also of the same expression for the logical quantity of the judgment, if only we prefix "objective" to "universal validity," to distinguish it from that which is merely subjective and aesthetical.)

A judgment with *objective universal validity* is also always valid subjectively; i.e., if the judgment holds for everything contained under a given concept, it holds also for everyone who represents an object by means of this concept. But from a *subjective universal validity*, i.e., aesthetical and resting on no concept, we cannot infer that which is logical because that kind of judgment does not extend to the object. But, therefore, the aesthetical universality which is ascribed to a judgment must be of a particular kind, because it does not unite the predicate of beauty with the concept of the object, considered in its whole logical sphere, and yet extends it to the whole sphere of judging persons.

In respect of logical quantity, all judgments of taste are *singular* judgments. For because I must refer the object immediately to my feeling of pleasure and pain, and that not by means of concepts, they cannot have the quantity of objective generally valid judgments. Nevertheless, if the singular representation of the object of the judgment of taste, in accordance with the conditions determining the latter, were transformed by comparison into a concept, a logically universal judgment could result therefrom. E.g., I describe by a judgment of taste the rose that I see as beautiful. But the judgment which results from the comparison of several singular judgments, "Roses in general are beautiful," is no longer described simply as aesthetical, but as a logical judgment based on an aesthetical one. Again the judgment, "The rose is pleasant" (to use) is, although aesthetical and singular, not a judgment of taste but of sense. It is distinguished from the former by the fact that the judgment of taste carries with it an *aesthetic quantity* of universality, i.e. of validity for everyone, which cannot be found in a judgment about the pleasant. It is only judgments about the good which, although they also determine satisfaction in an object, have logical and not merely aesthetical universality, for they are valid of the object as cognitive of it, and thus are valid for everyone.

If we judge objects merely according to concepts, then all representation of beauty is lost. Thus there can be no rule according to which anyone is to be forced to recognize anything as beautiful. We cannot press upon others by the aid of any reasons or fundamental propositions our judgment that a coat, a house, or a flower is beautiful. People wish to submit the object to their own eyes, as if the satisfaction in it depended on sensation; and yet, if we then call the object beautiful, we believe that we speak with a universal voice, and we claim the assent of everyone, although on the contrary all private sensation can only decide for the observer himself and his satisfaction.

We may see now that in the judgment of taste nothing is postulated but such a *universal voice*, in respect of the satisfaction without the intervention of concepts, and thus the *possibility* of an aesthetical judgment that can, at the same time, be regarded as valid for everyone. The judgment of taste itself does not *postulate* the agreement of everyone (for that can only be done by a logically universal judgment because it can adduce reasons); it only *imputes* this agreement to everyone, as a case of the rule in respect of which it expects, not confirmation by concepts, but assent from others. The universal voice is, therefore, only an idea (we do not yet inquire upon what it rests). It may be uncertain whether or not the man who believes that he is laying down a judgment of taste is, as a matter of fact, judging in conformity with that idea; but that he refers his judgment thereto, and consequently that it is intended to be a judgment of taste, he announces by the expression "beauty." He can be quite certain of this for himself by the mere consciousness of the separating off everything belonging to the pleasant and the good from the satisfaction which is left; and this is all for which he promises himself the agreement of everyone—a claim which would be justifiable under these conditions, provided only he did not often make mistakes, and thus lay down an erroneous judgment of taste.

9. INVESTIGATION OF THE QUESTION WHETHER IN THE JUDGMENT OF TASTE THE FEELING OF PLEASURE PRECEDES OR FOLLOWS THE JUDGING OF THE OBJECT

The solution of this question is the key to the critique of taste, and so is worthy of all attention.

If the pleasure in the given object precedes, and it is only its universal communicability that is to be acknowledged in the judgment of taste about the representation of the object, there would be a contradiction. For such pleasure would be nothing different from the mere pleasantness in the sensation, and so in accordance with its nature could have only private validity, because it is immediately dependent on the representation through which the object *is given*.

Hence it is the universal capability of communication of the mental state in the given representation which, as the subjective condition of the judgment of taste, must be fundamental and must have the pleasure in the object as its consequent. But nothing can be universally communicated except cognition and representation, so far as it belongs to cognition. For it is only thus that this latter can be objective, and only through this has it a universal point of reference, with which the representative power of everyone is compelled to harmonize. If the determining ground of our judgment as to this universal communicability of the representation is to be merely subjective, i.e., is conceived independently of any concept of the object, it can be nothing else than the state of mind, which is to be met with in the relation of our representative powers to each other, so far as they refer a given representation to *cognition in general*.

The cognitive powers, which are involved by this representation, are here in free play, because no definite concept limits them to a definite rule of cognition. Hence the state of mind in this representation must be a feeling of the free play of the representative powers in a given representation with reference to a cognition in general. Now a representation by which an object is given that is to become a cognition in general requires *imagination* for the gathering together the manifold of intuition, and *understanding* for the unity of the concept uniting the representations. This state of *free play* of the cognitive faculties in a representation by which an object is given must be universally communicable, because cognition, as the determination of the object with which given representations (in whatever subject) are to agree, is the only kind of representation which is valid for everyone.

The subjective universal communicability of the mode of representation in a judgment of taste, since it is to be possible without presupposing a definite concept, can refer to nothing else than the state of mind in the free play of the imagination and the understanding (so far as they agree with each other, as is requisite for *cognition in general*). We are conscious that this subjective relation, suitable for cognition in general, must be valid for everyone, and thus must be universally communicable, just as if it were a definite cognition, resting always on that relation as its subjective condition.

This merely subjective (aesthetical) judging of the object, or of the representation by which it is given, precedes the pleasure in the same and is the ground of this pleasure in the harmony of the cognitive faculties; but on that universality of the subjective conditions for judging of objects is alone based the universal subjective validity of the satisfaction bound up by us with the representation of the object that we call beautiful.

That the power of communicating one's state of mind, even though only in respect of the cognitive faculties, carries a pleasure with it, this we can easily show from the natural propension of man toward sociability (empirical and psychological). But this is not enough for our design. The pleasure that we feel is, in a judgment of taste, necessarily imputed by us to everyone else, as if, when we call a thing beautiful, it is to be regarded as a characteristic of the object which is determined in it according to concepts, though beauty, without a reference to the feeling of the subject, is nothing by itself. . . .

We now occupy ourselves with the easier question, in what way we are conscious of a mutual subjective harmony of the cognitive powers with one another in the judgment of taste—is it aesthetically by mere internal sense and sensation, or is it intellectually by the consciousness of our designed activity, by which we bring them into play?

If the given representation which occasions the judgment of taste were a concept uniting understanding and imagination in the judging of the object, into a cognition of the object, the consciousness of this relation would be intellectual. . . . But then the judgment would not be laid down in reference to pleasure and pain, and consequently would not be a judgment of taste. But the judgment of taste, independently of concepts, determines the object in respect of satisfaction and of the predicate of beauty. Therefore that subjective unity of relation can only make itself known by means of sensation. The excitement of both faculties (imagination and understanding) to indeterminate but yet, through the stimulus of the given sensation, harmonious activity, viz., that which belongs to cognition in general, is the sensation whose universal communicability is postulated by the judgment of taste. An objective relation can only be thought, but yet, so far as it is subjective according to its conditions, can be felt in its effect on the mind; and, of a relation based on no concept (like the relation of the representative powers to a cognitive faculty in general), no other consciousness is possible than that through the sensation of the effect, which consists in the more lively play of both mental powers (the imagination and the understanding) when animated by mutual agreement. A representation which, as individual and apart from comparison with others, yet has an agreement with the conditions of universality which it is the business of the understanding to supply, brings the cognitive faculties into that proportionate accord which we require for all cognition, and so regard as holding for everyone who is determined to judge by means of understanding and sense in combination (i.e., for every man).

Explanation of the Beautiful Resulting from the Second Moment

The *beautiful* is that which pleases universally without requiring a concept.

THIRD MOMENT
Of Judgments of Taste, According to the Relation of the Purposes which are Brought into Consideration in Them

10. OF PURPOSIVENESS IN GENERAL

If we wish to explain what a purpose is according to its transcendental determinations (without presupposing anything empirical like the feeling of pleasure), we say that the purpose is the object of a concept, in so far as the concept is regarded as the cause of the object (the real ground of its possibility); and the causality of a *concept* in respect of its *object* is its purposiveness (*forma finalis*). Where then not merely the cognition of an object but the object itself (its form and existence) is thought as an effect only possible by means of the concept of this latter, there we think a purpose. The representation of the effect is here the determining ground of its cause and precedes it. The consciousness of the causality of a representation, for *maintaining* the subject in the same state, may here generally denote what we call pleasure; while on the other hand pain is that representation which contains the ground of determination of the state of representations into their opposite of restraining or removing them.

The faculty of desire, so far as it is determinable to act only through concepts, i.e., in conformity with the representation of a purpose, would be the will. But an object, or a state of mind, or even an action is called purposive, although its possibility does not necessarily presuppose the representation of a purpose, merely because its possibility can be explained and conceived by us only so far as we assume for its ground a causality according to purposes, i.e., in accordance with a will which has regulated it according to the representation of a certain rule. There can be, then, purposiveness without purpose, so far as we do not place the causes of this form in a will, but yet can only make the explanation of its possibility intelligible to ourselves by deriving it from a will. Again, we are not always forced to regard what we observe (in respect of its possibility) from the point of view of reason. Thus we can at least observe a purposiveness according to form, without basing it on a purpose (as the material of the *nexus finalis*), and remark it in objects, although only by reflection.

11. THE JUDGMENT OF TASTE HAS NOTHING AT ITS BASIS BUT THE FORM OF THE PURPOSIVENESS OF AN OBJECT (OR OF ITS MODE OF REPRESENTATION)

Every purpose, if it be regarded as a ground of satisfaction, always carries with it an interest—as the determining ground of the judgment—about the object of pleasure. Therefore no subjective purpose can lie at the basis of the judgment of taste. But also the judgment of taste can be determined by no representation of an objective purpose, i.e., of the possibility of the object itself in accordance with principles of purposive combination, and consequently by no concept of the good, because it is an aesthetical and not a cognitive judgment. It therefore has to do with no *concept* of the character and internal or external possibility of the object by means of this or that cause, but merely with the relation of the representative powers to one another, so far as they are determined by a representation.

Now this relation in the determination of an object as beautiful is bound up with the feeling of pleasure, which is declared by the judgment of taste to be valid for everyone; hence a pleasantness merely accompanying the representation can as little contain the determining ground of the judgment as the representation of the perfection of the object and the concept of the good can. Therefore it can be nothing else than the subjective purposiveness in the representation of an object without any purpose (either objective or subjective), and thus it is the mere form of purposiveness in the representation by which an object is *given* to us, so far as we are conscious of it, which constitutes the satisfaction that we without a concept judge to be universally communicable; and, consequently, this is the determining ground of the judgment of taste. . . .

12. ELUCIDATION BY MEANS OF EXAMPLES

Aesthetical judgments can be divided just like theoretical (logical) judgments into empirical and pure. The first assert pleasantness or unpleasantness; the second assert the beauty of an object or of the manner of representing it. The former are judgments of sense (material aesthetical judgments); the latter as formal are alone strictly judgments of taste.

A judgment of taste is therefore pure only so far as no merely empirical satisfaction is mingled with its determining ground. But this always happens if charm or emotion have any share in the judgment by which anything is to be described as beautiful.

Now here many objections present themselves which fallaciously put forward charm not merely as a necessary ingredient of beauty, but as alone sufficient to justify a thing's being called beautiful. A mere color, e.g., the green of a grass plot, a mere tone (as distinguished from sound and noise), like that of a violin, are by most people described as beautiful in themselves, although both seem to have at their basis merely the matter of representations, viz., simply sensation, and therefore only deserve to be called pleasant. But we must at the same time remark that the sensations of colors and of tone have a right to be regarded as beautiful only in so far as they are *pure*. This is a determination which concerns their form and is the only element of these representations which admits with certainty of universal communicability; for we cannot assume that the quality of sensations is the same in all subjects, and we can hardly say that the pleasantness of one color or the tone of one musical instrument is judged preferable to that of another in the same way by everyone. . . .

"Pure" in a simple mode of sensation means that its uniformity is troubled and interrupted by no foreign sensation, and it belongs merely to the form; because here we can abstract from the quality of that mode of sensation (abstract from the colors and tone, if any, which it represents). . . .

In painting, sculpture, and in all the formative arts—in architecture and horticulture, so far as they are beautiful arts—the *delineation* is the essential thing; and here it is not what gratifies in sensation but what pleases by means of its form that is fundamental for taste. The colors which light up the sketch belong to the charm; they may indeed enliven the object for sensation, but they cannot make it worthy of contemplation and beautiful. In most cases they are rather limited by the requirements of the beautiful form, and even where charm is permissible it is ennobled solely by this. . . .

Emotion, that is a sensation in which pleasantness is produced by means of a momentary checking and a consequent more powerful outflow of the vital force, does not belong at all to beauty. And thus a pure judgment of taste has for its determining ground neither charm nor emotion—in a word, no sensation as the material of the aesthetical judgment.

13. THE JUDGMENT OF TASTE IS QUITE INDEPENDENT OF THE CONCEPT OF PERFECTION

Objective purposiveness can only be cognized by means of the reference of the manifold to a definite purpose, and therefore only through a concept. From this alone it is plain that the beautiful, the judging of which has at its basis a merely formal purposiveness, i.e., a purposiveness without purpose, is quite independent of the concept of the good, because the latter presupposes an objective purposiveness, i.e., the reference of the object to a definite purpose.

Objective purposiveness is either external, i.e., the *utility*, or internal, i.e., the *perfection* of the object. That the satisfaction in an object, on account of which we call it beautiful, cannot rest on the representation of its utility is sufficiently obvious from the two preceding sections; because in that case it would not be an immediate satisfaction in the object, which is the essential condition of a judgment about beauty. But objective internal purposiveness, i.e., perfection, comes nearer to the predicate of beauty; and it has been regarded by celebrated philosophers as the same as beauty, with the proviso, *if it is thought in a confused way*. It is of the greatest importance in a critique of taste to decide whether beauty can thus actually be resolved into the concept of perfection.

To judge of objective purposiveness we always need, not only the concept of a purpose, but (if that purposiveness is not to be external utility but internal) the concept of an internal purpose which shall contain the ground of the internal possibility of the object. Now as a purpose in general is that whose *concept* can be regarded as the ground of the possibility of the object itself; so, in order to represent objective purposiveness in a thing, the concept of *what sort of thing it is to be* must come first. . . . The formal element in the representation of a thing, i.e., the agreement of the manifold with a unity (it being undetermined what this ought to be), gives to cognition no objective purposiveness whatever. For since abstraction is made of this unity as *purpose* (what the thing ought to be), nothing remains but the subjective purposiveness of the representations in the mind of the intuiting subject. And this, although it furnishes a certain purposiveness of the representative state of the subject, and so a facility of apprehending a given form by the imagination, yet furnishes no perfection of an object, since the object is not here conceived by means of the concept of a purpose. For example, if in a forest I come across a plot of sward around which trees stand in a circle and do not then represent to myself a purpose, viz., that it is intended to serve for country dances, not the least concept of perfection is furnished by the mere form. But to represent to oneself a formal *objective* purposiveness without purpose, i.e., the mere form of a *perfection* (without any matter and without the *concept* of that with which it is accordant, even if it were merely the idea of conformity to law in general), is a veritable contradiction.

Now the judgment of taste is an aesthetical judgment, i.e., such as rests on subjective grounds, the determining ground of which cannot be a concept, and consequently cannot be the concept of a definite purpose. Therefore by means of beauty, regarded as a formal subjective purposiveness, there is in no way thought a perfection of the object, as a purposiveness alleged to be formal but which is yet objective. And thus to distinguish between the concepts of the beautiful and the good as if they were only different in logical form, the first being a confused, the second a clear concept of perfection, but identical in content and origin, is quite fallacious. For then there would be no *specific* difference between them, but a judgment of taste would be as much a cognitive judgment as the judgment by which a thing is described as good; just as when the ordinary man says that fraud is unjust he bases his judgment on confused grounds, while the philosopher bases it on clear grounds, but both on identical principles of reason. I have already, however, said that an aesthetical judgment is unique of its kind and gives absolutely no cognition (not even a confused cognition) of the object; this is only supplied by a logical judgment. On the contrary, it simply refers the representation, by which an object is given, to the subject, and brings to our notice no characteristic of the object, but only the purposive form in the determination of the representative powers which are occupying themselves therewith. The judgment is called aesthetical just because its determining ground is not a concept, but the feeling (of internal sense) of that harmony in the play of the mental powers, so far as it can be felt in sensation. On the other hand, if we wish to call confused concepts and the objective judgment based on them aesthetical, we will have an understanding judging sensibly or a sense representing its objects by means of concepts both of which are contradictory. The faculty of concepts, be they confused or clear, is the understanding; and although understanding has to do with the judgment of taste as an aesthetical judgment (as it has with all judgments), yet it has to do with it, not as a faculty by which an object is cognized, but as the faculty which determines the judgment and its representation (without any concept) in accordance with its relation to the subject and the subject's internal feeling, in so far as this judgment may be possible in accordance with a universal rule.

14. THE JUDGMENT OF TASTE, BY WHICH AN OBJECT IS DECLARED TO BE BEAUTIFUL UNDER THE CONDITION OF A DEFINITE CONCEPT, IS NOT PURE

There are two kinds of beauty: free beauty (*pulchritudo vaga*), or merely dependent beauty (*pulchritudo adhaerens*). The first presupposes no concept of what the object ought to be; the second does presuppose such a concept and the perfection of the object in accordance therewith. The first is called the (self-subsistent) beauty of this or that thing; the second, as dependent upon a concept (conditioned beauty), is ascribed to objects which come under the concept of a particular purpose.

Flowers are free natural beauties. Hardly anyone but a botanist knows what sort of a thing a flower ought to be; and even he, though recognizing in the flower the reproductive organ of the plant, pays no regard to this natural purpose if he is passing judgment on the flower by taste. There is, then, at the basis of this judgment no perfection of any kind, no internal purposiveness, to which the collection of the manifold is referred. Many birds (such as the parrot, the humming bird, the bird of paradise) and many sea shells are beauties in themselves, which do not belong to any object determined in respect of its purpose by concepts, but please freely and in themselves. So also delineations *à la grecque*, foliage for borders or wall papers, mean nothing in themselves; they represent nothing—no object under a definite concept—and are free beauties. We can refer to the same class what are called in music phantasies (i.e., pieces without any theme), and in fact all music without words.

In the judging of a free beauty (according to the mere form), the judgment of taste is pure. There is presupposed no concept of any purpose which the manifold of the given object is to serve, and which therefore is to be represented in it. By such a concept the freedom of the imagination which disports itself in the contemplation of the figure would be only limited.

But human beauty (i.e., of a man, a woman, or a child), the beauty of a horse, or a building (be it church, palace, arsenal, or summer house), presupposes a concept of the purpose which determines what the thing is to be, and consequently a concept of its perfection; it is therefore adherent beauty. Now as the combination of the pleasant (in sensation) with beauty, which properly is only concerned with form, is a hindrance to the purity of the judgment of taste, so also is its purity injured by the combination with beauty of the good (viz., that manifold which is good for the thing itself in accordance with its purpose). . . .

FOURTH MOMENT
Of the Judgment of Taste, According to the Modality of the Satisfaction in the Object

15. WHAT THE MODALITY IN A JUDGMENT OF TASTE IS

I can say of every representation that it is at least *possible* that (as a cognition) it should be bound up with a pleasure. Of a representation that I call *pleasant* I say that it *actually* excites pleasure in me. But the *beautiful* we think as having a *necessary* reference to satisfaction. Now this necessity is of a peculiar kind. It is not a theoretical objective necessity, in which case it would be cognized *a priori* that everyone *will feel* this satisfaction in the object called beautiful by me. It is not a practical necessity, in which case, by concepts of a pure rational will serving as a rule for freely acting beings, the satisfaction is the necessary result of an objective law and only indicates that we absolutely (without any further design) ought to act in a certain way. But the necessity which is thought in an aesthetical judgment can only be called exemplary, i.e., a necessity of the assent of *all* to a judgment which is regarded as the example of a universal rule that we cannot state. Since an aesthetical judgment is not an objective cognitive judgment, this necessity cannot be derived from definite concepts and is therefore not apodictic. Still less can it be inferred from the universality of experience (of a complete agreement of judgments as to the beauty of a certain object). For not only would experience hardly furnish sufficiently numerous vouchers for this, but also, on empirical judgments, we can base no concept of the necessity of these judgments.

16. THE SUBJECTIVE NECESSITY, WHICH WE ASCRIBE TO THE JUDGMENT OF TASTE, IS CONDITIONED

The judgment of taste requires the agreement of everyone, and he who describes anything as beautiful claims that everyone *ought* to give his approval to the object in question and also describe it as beautiful. The *ought* in the aesthetical judgment is therefore pronounced in accordance with all the data which are required for judging, and yet is only conditioned. We ask for the agreement of everyone else, because we have for it a ground that is common to all; and we could count on this agreement, provided we were always sure that the case was correctly subsumed under that ground as rule of assent.

17. THE CONDITION OF NECESSITY WHICH A JUDGMENT OF TASTE ASSERTS IS THE IDEA OF A COMMON SENSE

If judgments of taste (like cognitive judgments) had a definite objective principle, then the person who lays them down in accordance with this latter would claim an unconditioned necessity for his judgment. If they were devoid of all principle, like those of the mere taste of sense, we would not allow them in thought any necessity whatever. Hence they must have a subjective principle which determines what pleases or displeases only by feeling and not by concepts, but yet with universal validity. But such a principle could only be regarded as a *common sense*, which is essentially different from common understanding which people sometimes call common sense (*sensus communis*); for the latter does not judge by feeling but always by concepts, although ordinarily only as by obscurely represented principles.

Hence it is only under the presupposition that there is a common sense (by which we do not understand an external sense, but the effect resulting from the free play of our cognitive powers)—it is only under this presupposition, I say, that the judgment of taste can be laid down.

18. HAVE WE GROUND FOR PRESUPPOSING A COMMON SENSE?

Cognitions and judgments must, along with the conviction that accompanies them, admit of universal communicability; for otherwise there would be no harmony between them and the object, and they would be collectively a mere subjective play of the representative powers, exactly as scepticism desires. But if cognitions are to admit of communicability, so must also the state of mind—i.e., the accordance of the cognitive powers with a cognition generally and that proportion of them which is suitable for a representation (by which an object is given to us) in order that a cognition may be made out of it—admit of universal communicability. For without this as the subjective condition of cognition, cognition as an effect could not arise. This actually always takes place when a given object by means of sense excites the imagination to collect the manifold, and the imagination in its turn excites the understanding to bring about a unity of this collective process in concepts. But this accordance of the cognitive powers has a different proportion according to the variety of the objects which are given. However, it must be such that this internal relation, by which one mental faculty is excited by another, shall be generally the most beneficial for both faculties in respect of cognition (of given objects); and this accordance can only be determined by feeling (not according to concepts). Since now this accordance itself must admit of universal communicability, and consequently also our feeling of it (in a given representation), and since the universal communicability of a feeling presupposes a common sense, we have grounds for assuming this latter. And this common sense is assumed without relying on psychological observations, but simply as the necessary condition of the universal communicability of our knowledge, which is presupposed in every logic and in every principle of knowledge that is not sceptical.

19. THE NECESSITY OF THE UNIVERSAL AGREEMENT THAT IS THOUGHT IN A JUDGMENT OF TASTE IS A SUBJECTIVE NECESSITY, WHICH IS REPRESENTED AS OBJECTIVE UNDER THE PRESUPPOSITION OF A COMMON SENSE

In all judgments by which we describe anything as beautiful, we allow no one to be of another opinion, without, however, grounding our judgment on concepts, but only on our feeling, which we therefore place as its basis, not as a private, but as a common feeling. Now this common sense cannot be grounded on experience, for it aims at justifying judgments which contain an *ought*. It does not say that everyone *will* agree with my judgment, but that he *ought*. And so common sense, as an example of whose judgment I here put forward my judgment of taste and on account of which I attribute to the latter an *exemplary* validity, is a mere ideal norm, under the supposition of which I have a right to make into a rule for everyone a judgment that accords therewith, as well as the satisfaction in an object expressed in such judgment. For the principle which concerns the agreement of different judging persons, although only subjective, is yet assumed as subjectively universal (an idea necessary for everyone), and thus can claim universal assent (as if it were objective) provided we are sure that we have correctly subsumed the particulars under it.

This indeterminate norm of a common sense is actually presupposed by us, as is shown by our claim to lay down judgments of taste. . . .

Explanation of the Beautiful Resulting from the Fourth Moment

The *beautiful* is that which without any concept is cognized as the object of a *necessary* satisfaction. . . .

SECOND BOOK
Analytic of the Sublime

20. OF THE METHOD OF DEDUCTION OF JUDGMENTS OF TASTE

A deduction, i.e., the guarantee of the legitimacy of a class of judgments, is only obligatory if the judgment lays claim to necessity. This it does if it demands even subjective universality or the agreement of everyone, although it is not a judgment of cognition, but only one of pleasure or pain in a given object, i.e. it assumes a subjective purposiveness thoroughly valid for everyone, which must not be based on any concept of the thing, because the judgment is one of taste.

We have before us in the latter case no cognitive judgment—neither a theoretical one based on the concept of a *nature* in general formed by the understanding, nor a (pure) practical one based on the idea of *freedom*, as given *a priori* by reason. Therefore we have to justify *a priori* the validity, neither of a judgment which represents what a thing is, nor of one which prescribes that I ought to do something in order to produce it. We have merely to prove for the judgment generally the *universal validity* of a singular judgment that expresses the subjective purposiveness of an empirical representation of the form of an object, in order to explain how it is possible that a thing can please in the mere act of judging it (without sensation or concept) and how the satisfaction of one man can be proclaimed as a rule for every other, just as the act of judging of an object for the sake of a *cognition* in general has universal rules. . . .

21. THERE IS NO OBJECTIVE PRINCIPLE OF TASTE POSSIBLE

By a principle of taste I mean a principle under the condition of which we could subsume the concept of an object and thus infer, by means of a syllogism, that the object is beautiful. But that is absolutely impossible. For I must immediately feel pleasure in the representation of the object, and of that I can be persuaded by no grounds of proof whatever. Although, as Hume says, all critics can reason more plausibly than cooks, yet the same fate awaits them. They cannot expect the determining ground of their judgment [to be derived] from the force of the proofs, but only from the reflection of the subject upon its own proper state (of pleasure or pain), all precepts and rules being rejected.

But although critics can and ought to pursue their reasonings so that our judgments of taste may be corrected and extended, it is not with a view to set forth the determining ground of this kind of aesthetical judgments in a universally applicable formula, which is impossible; but rather to investigate the cognitive faculties and their exercise in these judgments, and to explain by examples the reciprocal subjective purposiveness, the form of which, as has been shown above, in a given representation, constitutes the beauty of the object. . . .

22. OF THE PROBLEM OF A DEDUCTION OF JUDGMENTS OF TASTE

The concept of an object in general can immediately be combined with the perception of an object, containing its empirical predicates, so as to form a cognitive judgment; and it is thus that a judgment of experience is produced. At the basis of this lie *a priori* concepts of the synthetical unity of the manifold of intuition, by which the manifold is thought as the determination of an object. These concepts (the categories) require a deduction, which is given in the *Critique of Pure Reason*; and by it we can get the solution of the problem: how are synthetical *a priori* cognitive judgments possible? This problem concerns then the *a priori* principles of the pure understanding and its theoretical judgments.

But with a perception there can also be combined a feeling of pleasure (or pain) and a satisfaction, that accompanies the representation of the object and serves instead of its predicate; thus there can result an aesthetical noncognitive judgment. At the basis of such a judgment—if it is not a mere judgment of sensation but a formal judgment of reflection, which imputes the same satisfaction necessarily to everyone—must lie some *a priori* principle, which may be merely subjective (if an objective one should prove impossible for judgments of this kind), but also as such may need a deduction, that we may thereby comprehend how an aesthetical judgment can lay claim to necessity. On this is founded the problem with which we are now occupied: how are judgments of taste possible? This problem, then, has to do with the *a priori* principles of the pure faculty of judgment in *aesthetical* judgments, i.e. judgments in which it has not (as in theoretical ones) merely to subsume under objective concepts of understanding and in which it is subject to a law, but in which it is itself, subjectively, both object and law.

This problem then may be thus represented: how is a judgment possible in which merely from *our own* feeling of pleasure in an object, independently of its concept, we judge that this pleasure attaches to the representation of the same object *in every other subject*, and that *a priori* without waiting for the accordance of others?

It is easy to see that judgments of taste are synthetical, because they go beyond the concept and even beyond the intuition of the object, and add to that intuition as predicate something that is not a cognition, viz. a feeling of pleasure (or pain). Although the predicate (of the *personal* pleasure bound up with the representation) is empirical, nevertheless, as concerns the required assent of *everyone* the judgments are *a priori*, or desire to be regarded as such; and this is already involved in the expressions of this claim. Thus this problem of the *Critique of Judgment* belongs to the general problem of transcendental philosophy: how are synthetical *a priori* judgments possible?

23. WHAT IS PROPERLY ASSERTED A PRIORI OF AN OBJECT IN A JUDGMENT OF TASTE

That the representation of an object is immediately bound up with pleasure can only be internally perceived; and if we did not wish to indicate anything more than this, it would give a merely empirical judgment. For I cannot combine a definite feeling (of pleasure or pain) with any representation, except where there is at bottom an *a priori* principle in the reason determining the will. In that case the pleasure (in the moral feeling) is the consequence of the principle, but cannot be compared with the pleasure in taste, because it requires a definite concept of a law; and the latter pleasure, on the contrary, must be bound up with the mere act of judging, prior to all concepts. Hence also all judgments of taste are singular judgments, because they do not combine their predicate of satisfaction with a concept, but with a given individual empirical representation.

And so it is not the pleasure, but the *universal validity of this pleasure*, perceived as mentally bound up with the mere judgment upon an object, which is represented *a priori* in a judgment of taste as a universal rule for the judgment and valid for everyone. It is an empirical judgment [to say] that I perceive and judge an object with pleasure. But it is an *a priori* judgment [to say] that I find it beautiful, i.e. I attribute this satisfaction necessarily to everyone.

24. DEDUCTION OF JUDGMENTS OF TASTE

If it be admitted that, in a pure judgment of taste, the satisfaction in the object is combined with the mere act of judging its form, it is nothing else than its subjective purposiveness for the judgment which we feel to be mentally combined with the representation of the object. The judgment, as regards the formal rules of its action, apart from all matter (whether sensation or concept), can only be directed to the subjective conditions of its employment in general (it is applied neither to a particular mode of sense nor to a particular concept of the understanding), and consequently to that subjective [element] which we can presuppose in all men (as requisite for possible cognition in general). Thus the agreement of a representation with these conditions of the judgment must be capable of being assumed as valid *a priori* for everyone. That is, we may rightly impute to everyone the pleasure or the subjective purposiveness of the representation for the relation between the cognitive faculties in the act of judging a sensible object in general.

Remark

This deduction is thus easy, because it has no need to justify the objective reality of any concept, for beauty is not a concept of the object and the judgment of taste is not cognitive. It only maintains that we are justified in presupposing universally in every man those subjective conditions of the judgment which we find in ourselves; and further, that we have rightly subsumed the given object under these conditions. The latter has indeed unavoidable difficulties which do not beset the logical judgment. There we subsume under concepts, but in the aesthetical judgment under a merely sensible relation between the imagination and understanding mutually harmonizing in the representation of the form of the object—in which case the subsumption may easily be deceptive. Yet the legitimacy of the claim of the judgment in counting upon universal assent is not thus annulled; it reduces itself merely to judging as valid for everyone the correctness of the principle from subjective grounds. For as to the difficulty or doubt concerning the correctness of the subsumption under that principle, it makes the legitimacy of the claim of an aesthetical judgment in general to such validity and the principle of the same as little doubtful as the alike (though neither so commonly nor readily) faulty subsumption of the logical judgment under its principle can make the latter, an objective principle, doubtful. . . .

The Role of Theory in Aesthetics

Morris Weitz

Theory has been central in aesthetics and is still the preoccupation of the philosophy of art. Its main avowed concern remains the determination of the nature of art which can be formulated into a definition of it. It construes definition as the statement of the necessary and sufficient properties of what is being defined, where the statement purports to be a true or false claim about the essence of art, what characterizes and distinguishes it from everything else. Each of the great theories of art—Formalism, Voluntarism, Emotional-

From *The Journal of Aesthetics and Art Criticism*, 15 (1956). Reprinted by permission of The American Society for Aesthetics.

ism, Intellectualism, Intuitionism, Organicism—converges on the attempt to state the defining properties of art. Each claims that it is the true theory because it has formulated correctly into a real definition the nature of art; and that the others are false because they have left out some necessary or sufficient property. Many theorists contend that their enterprise is no mere intellectual exercise but an absolute necessity for any understanding of art and our proper evaluation of it. Unless we know what art is, they say, what are its necessary and sufficient properties, we cannot begin to respond to it adequately or to say why one work is good or better than another. Aesthetic theory, thus, is important not only in itself but for the foundations of both appreciation and criticism. Philosophers, critics, and even artists who have written on art, agree that what is primary in aesthetics is a theory about the nature of art.

Is aesthetic theory, in the sense of a true definition or set of necessary and sufficient properties of art, possible? If nothing else does, the history of aesthetics itself should give one enormous pause here. For, in spite of the many theories, we seem no nearer our goal today than we were in Plato's time. Each age, each art-movement, each philosophy of art, tries over and over again to establish the stated ideal only to be succeeded by a new or revised theory, rooted, at least in part, in the repudiation of preceding ones. Even today, almost everyone interested in aesthetic matters is still deeply wedded to the hope that the correct theory of art is forthcoming. We need only examine the numerous new books on art in which new definitions are proffered; or, in our own country especially, the basic textbooks and anthologies to recognize how strong the priority of a theory of art is.

In this essay I want to plead for the rejection of this problem. I want to show that theory—in the requisite classical sense—is *never* forthcoming in aesthetics, and that we would do much better as philosophers to supplant the question, "What is the nature of art?," by other questions, the answers to which will provide us with all the understanding of the arts there can be. I want to show that the inadequacies of the theories are not primarily occasioned by any legitimate difficulty such e.g., as the vast complexity of art, which might be corrected by further probing and research. Their basic inadequacies reside instead in a fundamental misconception of art. Aesthetic theory—all of it—is wrong in principle in thinking that a correct theory is possible because it radically misconstrues the logic of the concept of art. Its main contention that "art" is amenable to real or any kind of true definition is false. Its attempt to discover the necessary and sufficient properties of art is logically misbegotten for the very simple reason that such a set and, consequently, such a formula about it, is never forthcoming. Art, as the logic of the concept shows, has no set of necessary and sufficient properties, hence a theory of it is logically impossible and not merely factually difficult. Aesthetic theory tries to define what cannot be defined in its requisite sense. But in recommending the repudiation of aesthetic theory I shall not argue from this, as too many others have done, that its logical confusions render it meaningless or worthless. On the contrary, I wish to reassess its role and its contribution primarily in order to show that it is of the greatest importance to our understanding of the arts.

Let us now survey briefly some of the more famous extant aesthetic theories in order to see if they do incorporate correct and adequate statements about the nature of art. In each of these there is the assumption that it is the true enumeration of the defining properties of art, with the implication that previous theories have stressed wrong definitions. Thus, to begin with, consider a famous version of Formalist theory, that propounded by Bell and Fry. It is true that they speak mostly of painting in their writings but both assert that what they find in that art can be generalized for what is "art" in the others as well. The essence of painting, they maintain, are the plastic elements in relation. Its defining property is significant form, i.e., certain combinations of lines, colors, shapes, volumes—everything on the canvas except the representational elements—which evoke a unique response to such combinations. Painting is definable as plastic organization. The nature of art, what it *really* is, so their theory goes, is a unique combination of certain elements (the specifiable plastic ones) in their relations. Anything which is art is an instance of significant form; and anything which is not art has no such form.

To this the Emotionalist replies that the truly essential property of art has been left out. Tolstoy, Ducasse, or any of the advocates of this theory, find that the requisite defining property is not significant form but rather the expression of emotion in some sensuous public medium. Without projection of emotion into some piece of stone or words or sounds, etc., there can be no art. Art is really such embodiment. It is this that uniquely characterizes art, and any true, real definition of it, contained in some adequate theory of art, must so state it.

The Intuitionist disclaims both emotion and form as defining properties. In Croce's version, for example, art is identified not with some physical, public object but with a specific creative, cognitive and spiritual act. Art is really a first stage of knowledge in which certain human beings (artists) bring their images and intuitions into lyrical clarification or expression. As such, it is an awareness, non-conceptual in character, of the unique individuality of things; and since it exists below the level of conceptualization or action, it is without scientific or moral content. Croce singles out as the defining essence of art this first stage of spiritual life and advances its identification with art as a philosophically true theory or definition.

The Organicist says to all of this that art is really a class of organic wholes consisting of distinguishable, albeit inseparable, elements in their causally efficacious relations which are presented in some sensuous medium. In A. C. Bradley, in piece-meal versions of it in literary criticism, or in my own generalized adaptation of it in my *Philosophy of the Arts*, what is claimed is that anything which is a work of art is in its nature a unique complex of interrelated parts—in painting, for example, lines, colors, volumes, subjects, etc., all interacting upon one another on a paint surface of some sort. Certainly, at one time at least it seemed to me that this organic theory constituted the one true and real definition of art.

My final example is the most interesting of all, logically speaking. This is the Voluntarist theory of Parker. In his writings on art, Parker persistently calls into question the traditional simple-minded definitions of aesthetics. "The assumption underlying every philosophy of art is the existence of some common nature present in all the arts."[1] "All the so popular brief definitions of art—'significant form,' 'expression,' 'intuition,' 'objectified pleasure'—are fallacious, either because, while true of art, they are also true of much that is not art, and hence fail to differentiate art from other things; or else because they neglect some essential aspect of art."[2] But instead of inveighing against the attempt at definition of art itself, Parker insists that what is needed is a complex definition rather than a simple one. "The definition of art must therefore be in terms of a complex of characteristics. Failure to recognize this has been the fault of all the well-known definitions."[3] His own version of Voluntarism is the theory that art is essentially three things: embodiment of wishes and desires imaginatively satisfied, language, which characterizes the public medium of art, and harmony, which unifies the language with the layers of imaginative projections. Thus, for Parker, it is a true definition to say of art that it is ". . . the provision of satisfaction through the imagination, social significance, and harmony. I am claiming that nothing except works of art possesses all three of these marks."[4]

Now, all of these sample theories are inadequate in many different ways. Each purports to be a complete statement about the defining features of all works of art and yet each of them leaves out something which the others take to be central. Some are circular, e.g., the Bell-Fry theory of art as significant form which is defined in part in terms of our response to significant form. Some of them, in their search for necessary and sufficient properties, emphasize too few properties, like (again) the Bell-Fry definition which leaves out subject-representation in painting, or the Croce theory which omits inclusion of the very important feature of the public, physical character, say, of architecture. Others are too general and cover objects that are not art as well as works of art. Organicism is surely such a view since it can be applied to *any* causal unity in the natural world as well as to art.[5] Still others rest on dubious principles, e.g., Parker's claim that art embodies imaginative satisfactions, rather than real ones; or Croce's assertion that there is nonconceptual knowledge. Consequently, even if art has one set of necessary and sufficient properties, none of the theories we have noted or, for that matter, no aesthetic theory yet proposed, has enumerated that set to the satisfaction of all concerned.

Then there is a different sort of difficulty. As real definitions, these theories are supposed to be factual reports on art. If they are, may we not ask, Are they empirical and open to verification or falsification? For example, what would confirm or disconfirm the theory that art is significant form or embodiment of emotion or creative synthesis of images? There does not even seem to be a hint of the kind of evidence which might be forthcoming to test these theories; and indeed one wonders if they are perhaps honorific definitions of "art," that is, proposed redefinitions in terms of some *chosen* conditions for applying the concept of art, and not true or false reports on the essential properties of art at all.

But all these criticisms of traditional aesthetic theories—that they are circular, incomplete, untestable, pseudo-factual, disguised proposals to change the meaning of concepts—have been made before. My intention is to go beyond these to make a much more fundamental criticism, namely, that aesthetic theory is a logically vain attempt to define what cannot be defined, to state the necessary and sufficient properties of that which has no necessary and sufficient properties, to conceive the concept of art as closed when its very use reveals and demands its openness.

The problem with which we must begin is not "What is art?," but "What sort of concept is 'art'?" Indeed, the root problem of philosophy itself is to explain the relation between the employment of certain kinds of concepts and the conditions under which they can be correctly applied. If I may paraphrase Wittgenstein, we must not ask, What is the nature of any philosophical *x*?, or even, according to the semanticist, What does "*x*" mean?, a transformation that leads to the disastrous interpretation of "art" as a name for some specifiable class of objects; but rather, What is the use or employment of "*x*"? What does "*x*" do in the language? This, I take it, is the initial question, the begin-all if not the end-all of any philosophical problem and solution. Thus, in aesthetics, our first problem is the elucidation of the actual employment of the concept of art, to give a logical description of the actual functioning of the concept, including a description of the conditions under which we correctly use it or its correlates.

My model in this type of logical description or philosophy derives from Wittgenstein. It is also he who, in his refutation of philosophical theorizing in the sense of constructing definitions of philosophical entities, has furnished contemporary aesthetics with a starting point for any future progress. In his new work, *Philosophical Investigations*,[6] Wittgenstein raises as an illustrative question, What is a game? The traditional philosophical, theoretical answer would be in terms of some exhaustive set of properties common to all games. To this Wittgenstein says, let us consider what we call "games":

I mean board-games, card games, ball-games, Olympic games, and so on. What is common to them all?—Don't say: 'there *must* be something common, or they would not be called "games"' but *look and* see whether there is anything common to all.—For if you look at them you will not see something that is common to *all*, but similarities, relationships, and a whole series of them at that . . .

Card games are like board games in some respects but not in others. Not all games are amusing, nor is there always winning or losing or competition. Some games resemble others in some respects—that is all. What we find are no necessary and sufficient properties, only "a complicated network of similarities overlapping and crisscrossing," such that we can say of games that they form a family with family resemblances and no common trait. If one asks what a game is, we pick out sample games, describe these, and add, "This and *similar things* are called 'games'." This is all we need to say and indeed all any of us knows about games. Knowing what a game is is not knowing some real definition or theory but being able to recognize and explain games and to decide which among imaginary and new examples would or would not be called "games."

The problem of the nature of art is like that of the nature of games, at least in these respects: If we actually look and see what it is that we call "art," we will also find no common properties—only strands of similarities. Knowing what art is is not apprehending some manifest or latent essence but being able to recognize, describe, and explain those things we call "art" in virtue of these similarities.

But the basic resemblance between these concepts is their open texture. In elucidating them, certain (paradigm) cases can be given, about which there can be no question as to their being correctly described as "art" or "game," but no exhaustive set of cases can be given. I can list some cases and some conditions under which I can apply correctly the concept of art but I cannot list all of them, for the all-important reason that unforeseeable or novel conditions are always forthcoming or envisageable.

A concept is open if its conditions of application are emendable and corrigible; i.e., if a situation or case can be imagined or secured which would call for some sort of *decision* on our part to extend the use of the concept to cover this, or to close the concept and invent a new one to deal with the new case and its new property. If necessary and sufficient conditions for the application of a concept can be stated, the concept is a closed one. But this can happen only in logic or mathematics where concepts are constructed and completely defined. It cannot occur with empirically-descriptive and normative concepts unless we arbitrarily close them by stimulating the ranges of their uses.

I can illustrate this open character of "art" best by examples drawn from its sub-concepts. Consider questions like "Is Dos Passos' *U.S.A.* a novel?," "Is V. Woolf's *To the Lighthouse* a novel?," "Is Joyce's *Finnegan's Wake* a novel?" On the traditional view, these are construed as factual problems to be answered yes or no in accordance with the presence or absence of defining properties. But certainly this is not how any of these questions is answered. Once it arises, as it has many times in the development of the novel from Richardson to Joyce (e.g., "Is Gide's *The School for Wives* a novel or a diary?"), what is at stake is no factual analysis concerning necessary and sufficient properties but a decision as to whether the work under examination is similar in certain respects to other works, already called "novels," and consequently warrants the extension of the concept to cover the new case. The new work is narrative, fictional, contains character delineation and dialogue but (say) it has no regular time-sequence in the plot or is interspersed with actual newspaper reports. It is like recognized novels, $A, B, C \ldots$, in some respects but not like them in others. But then neither were B and C like A in some respects when it was decided to extend the concept applied to A to B and C. Because work $N + 1$ (the brand new work) is like $A, B, C \ldots N$ in certain respects—has strands of similarity to them—the concept is extended and a new phase of the novel engendered. "Is $N + 1$ a novel?," then, is no factual, but rather a decision problem, where the verdict turns on whether or not we enlarge our set of conditions for applying the concept.

What is true of the novel is, I think, true of every sub-concept of art: "tragedy," "comedy," "painting," "opera," etc., of "art" itself. No "Is X a novel, painting, opera, work of art, etc.?" question allows of a definitive answer in the sense of a factual yes or no report. "Is this *collage* a painting or not?" does not rest on any set of necessary and sufficient properties of painting but on whether we decide—as we did!—to extend "painting" to cover this case.

"Art," itself, is an open concept. New conditions (cases) have constantly arisen and will undoubtedly constantly arise; new art forms, new movements will emerge, which will demand decisions on the part of those interested, usually professional critics, as to whether the concept should be extended or not. Aestheticians may lay down similarity conditions but never necessary and sufficient ones for the correct application of the concept. With "art" its conditions of application can never be exhaustively enumerated since new cases can always be envisaged or created by artists, or even nature, which would call for a decision on someone's part to extend or to close the old or to invent a new concept. (E.g., "It's not a sculpture, it's a mobile.")

What I am arguing, then, is that the very expansive, adventurous character of art, its ever-present changes and novel creations, makes it logically impossible to ensure any set of defining properties. We can, of course, choose to close the concept. But to do this with "art" or "tragedy" or "portraiture," etc., is ludicrous since it forecloses on the very conditions of creativity in the arts.

Of course there are legitimate and serviceable closed concepts in art. But these are always those whose boundaries of conditions have been drawn for a *special* purpose. Consider the difference, for example, between "tragedy" and "(extant) Greek tragedy." The first is open and must remain so to allow for the possibility of new conditions, e.g., a play in which the hero is not noble or fallen or in which there is no hero but other elements that are like those of plays we already call "tragedy." The second is closed. The plays it can be applied to, the conditions under which it can be correctly used are all in, once the boundary, "Greek," is drawn. Here the critic can work out a theory or real definition in which he lists the common properties at least of the extant Greek tragedies. Aristotle's definition, false as it is as a theory of all the plays of Aeschylus, Sophocles, and Euripides, since it does not cover some of them,[7] properly called "tragedies," can be interpreted as a real (albeit incorrect) definition of this closed concept; although it can also be, as it unfortunately has been, conceived as a purported real definition of "tragedy," in which case it suffers from the logical mistake of trying to define what cannot be defined—of trying to squeeze what is an open concept into an honorific formula for a closed concept.

What is supremely important, if the critic is not to become muddled, is to get absolutely clear about the way in which he conceives his concepts; otherwise he goes from the problem of trying to define "tragedy," etc., to an arbitrary closing of the concept in terms of certain preferred conditions or characteristics which he sums up in some linguistic recommendation that he mistakenly thinks is a real definition of the open concept. Thus, many critics and aestheticians ask, "What is tragedy?," choose a class of samples for which they may give a true account of its common properties, and then go on to construe this account of the chosen closed class as a true definition or theory of the whole open class of tragedy. This, I think, is the logical mechanism of most of the so-called theories of the sub-concepts of art: "tragedy," "comedy," "novel," etc. In effect, this whole procedure, subtly deceptive as it is, amounts to a transformation of correct criteria for *recognizing* members of certain legitimately closed classes of works of art into recommended criteria for *evaluating* any putative member of the class.

The primary task of aesthetics is not to seek a theory but to elucidate the concept of art. Specifically, it is to describe the conditions under which we employ the concept correctly. Definition, reconstruction, patterns of analysis are out of place here since they distort and add nothing to our understanding of art. What, then, is the logic of "X is a work of art"?

As we actually use the concept, "Art" is both descriptive (like "chair") and evaluative (like "good"); i.e., we sometimes say, "This is a work of art," to describe something and we sometimes say it to evaluate something. Neither use surprises anyone.

What, first, is the logic of "X is a work of art," when it is a descriptive utterance? What are the conditions under which we would be making such an utterance correctly? There are no necessary and sufficient conditions but there are the strands of similarity conditions, i.e., bundles of properties, none of which need be present but most of which are, when we describe things as works of art. I shall call these the "criteria of recognition" of works of art. All of these have served as the defining criteria of the individual traditional theories of art; so we are already familiar with them. Thus, mostly, when we describe something as a work of art, we do so under the conditions of there being present some sort of artifact, made by human skill, ingenuity, and imagination, which embodies in its sensuous, public medium—stone, wood, sounds, words, etc.—certain distinguishable elements and relations. Special theorists would add conditions like satisfaction of wishes, objectification or expression of emotion, some act of empathy, and so on; but these latter conditions seem to be quite adventitious, present to some but not to other spectators when things are described as works of art. "X is a work of art and contains *no* emotion, expression, act of empathy, satisfaction, etc.," is perfectly good sense and may frequently be true. "X is a work of art and . . . was made by no one," or . . . "exists only in the mind and not in any publicly observable thing," or . . . "was made by accident when he spilled the paint on the canvas," in each case of which a normal condition is denied, are also sensible and capable of being true in certain circumstances. None of the criteria of recognition is a defining one, either necessary or sufficient, because we can sometimes assert of something that it is a work of art and go on to deny any one of these conditions, even the one which has traditionally been taken to be basic, namely, that of being an artifact: Consider, "This piece of driftwood is a lovely piece of sculpture." Thus, to say of anything that it is a work of art is to commit oneself to the presence of some of these conditions. One would scarcely describe X as a work of art if X were not an artifact, or a collection of elements sensuously presented in a medium, or a product of human skill, and so on. If none of the conditions were present, if there were no criteria present for recognizing something as a work of art, we would not describe it as one. But, even so, no one of these or any collection of them is either necessary or sufficient.

The elucidation of the descriptive use of "Art" creates little difficulty. But the elucidation of the evaluative use does. For many, especially theorists, "This is a work of art" does more than describe; it also praises. Its conditions of utterance, therefore, include certain preferred properties or characteristics of art. I shall call these "criteria of evaluation." Consider a typical example of this evaluative use, the view according to which to say of something that it is a work of art is to imply that it is a *successful* harmonization of elements. Many of the honorific definitions of art and its subconcepts are of this form. What is at stake here is that "Art" is construed as an evaluative term which is either identified with its criterion or justified in terms of it. "Art" is defined in terms of its evaluative property, e.g., successful harmonization. On such a view, to say "X is a work of art" is (1) to say something which is taken to mean "X is a successful harmonization" (e.g., "Art *is* significant form") or (2) to say something praiseworthy *on the basis* of its successful harmonization. Theorists are never clear whether it is (1) or (2) which is being put forward. Most of them, concerned as they are with this evaluative use, formulate (2), i.e., that feature of art that *makes* it art in the praise-sense, and then go on to state (1), i.e., the definition of "Art" in terms of its art-making feature. And this is clearly to confuse the conditions under which we say something evaluatively with the meaning of what we say. "This is a work of art," said evaluatively, cannot mean "This is a successful harmonization of elements"—except by stipulation—but at most is said in virtue of the art-making property, which is taken as a (the) criterion of "Art," when "Art" is employed to assess. "This is a work of art," used evaluatively, serves to praise and not to affirm the reason why it is said.

The evaluative use of "Art," although distinct from the conditions of its use, relates in a very intimate way to these conditions. For, in every instance of "This is a work of art" (used to praise), what happens is that the criterion of evaluation (e.g., successful harmonization) for the employment of the concept of art is converted into a criterion of recognition. This is why, on its evaluative use, "This is a work of art" implies "This has P," where "P" is some chosen art-making property. Thus, if one chooses to employ "Art" evaluatively, as many do, so that "That is a work of art and not (aesthetically) good" makes no sense, he uses "Art" in such a way that he refuses to *call* anything a work of art unless it embodies his criterion of excellence.

There is nothing wrong with the evaluative use; in fact, there is good reason for using "Art" to praise. But what cannot be maintained is that theories of the evaluative use of "Art" are true and real definitions of the necessary and sufficient properties of art. Instead they are honorific definitions, pure and simple, in which "Art" has been redefined in terms of chosen criteria.

But what makes them—these honorific definitions—so supremely valuable is not their disguised linguistic recommendations; rather it is the *debates* over the reasons for changing the criteria of the concept of art which are built into the definitions. In each of the great theories of art, whether correctly understood as honorific definitions or incorrectly accepted as real definitions, what is of the utmost importance are the reasons proffered in the argument for the respective theory, that is, the reasons given for the chosen or preferred criterion of excellence and evaluation. It is this perennial debate over these criteria of evaluation which makes the history of aesthetic theory the important study it is. The value of each of the theories resides in its attempt to state and to justify certain criteria which are either neglected or distorted by previous theories. Look at the Bell-Fry theory again. Of course, "Art is significant form" cannot be accepted as a true, real definition of art; and most certainly it actually functions in their aesthetics as a redefinition of art in terms of the chosen condition of significant form. But what gives it its aesthetic importance is what lies behind the formula: In an age in which literary and representational elements have become paramount in painting, *return* to the plastic ones since these are indigenous to painting. Thus, the role of the theory is not to define anything but to use the definitional form, almost epigrammatically, to pin-point a crucial recommendation to turn our attention once again to the plastic elements in painting.

Once we, as philosophers, understand this distinction between the formula and what lies behind it, it behooves us to deal generously with the traditional theories of art; because incorporated in every one of them is a debate over and argument for emphasizing or centering upon some particular feature of art which has been neglected or perverted. If we take the aesthetic theories literally, as we have seen, they all fail; but if we reconstruct them, in terms of their function and point, as serious and argued-for recommendations to concentrate on certain criteria of excellence in art, we shall see that aesthetic theory is far from worthless. Indeed, it becomes as central as anything in aesthetics, in our understanding of art, for it teaches us what to look for and how to look at it in art. What is central and must be articulated in all the theories are their debates over the reasons for excellence in art—debates over emotional depth, profound truths, natural beauty, exactitude, freshness of treatment, and so on, as criteria of evaluation—the whole of which converges on the perennial problem of what makes a work of art good. To understand the role of aesthetic theory is not to conceive it as definition, logically doomed to failure, but to read it as summaries of seriously made recommendations to attend in certain ways to certain features of art.

NOTES

1. D. Parker, "The Nature of Art," reprinted in E. Vivas and M. Krieger, *The Problems of Aesthetics* (N.Y., 1953), p. 90.
2. Ibid., pp. 93–94.
3. Ibid., p. 94.
4. Ibid., p. 104.
5. See M. Macdonald's review of my *Philosophy of the Arts*, *Mind*, Oct., 1951, pp. 561–564, for a brilliant discussion of this objection to the Organic theory.
6. L. Wittgenstein, *Philosophical Investigations* (Oxford, 1953), tr. by E. Anscombe; see esp. Part I, Sections 65–75. All quotations are from these sections.
7. See H. D. F. Kitto, *Greek Tragedy* (London, 1939), on this point.

The Artistic Enfranchisement of Real Objects: The Artworld

Arthur Danto

Hamlet: Do you see nothing there?
The Queen: Nothing at all; yet all that is I see.

—Shakespeare: Hamlet, Act III, Scene IV

Hamlet and Socrates, though in praise and deprecation respectively, spoke of art as a mirror held up to nature. As with many disagreements in attitude, this one has a factual basis. Socrates saw mirrors as but reflecting what we can already see; so art, insofar as mirrorlike, yields idle accurate duplications of the appearances of things, and is of no cognitive benefit whatever. Hamlet, more acutely, recognized a remarkable feature of reflecting surfaces, namely that they show us what we could not otherwise perceive—our own face and form—and so art, insofar as it is mirrorlike, reveals us to ourselves, and is, even by Socratic criteria, of some cognitive utility after all. As a philosopher, however, I find Socrates' discussion defective on other, perhaps less profound grounds than these. If a mirror image of o is indeed an imitation of o, then, if art is imitation, mirror images are art. But in fact mirroring objects no more is art than returning weapons to a madman is justice; and reference to mirrorings would be just the sly sort of counterinstance we would expect Socrates to bring forward in rebuttal of the theory he instead uses them to illustrate. If that theory requires us to class these as art, it thereby shows its inadequacy: "is an imitation" will not do as a sufficient condition for "is art." Yet, perhaps because artists *were* engaged in imitation, in Socrates' time and after, the insufficiency of the theory was not noticed until the invention of photography. Once rejected as a sufficient condition, mimesis was quickly discarded as even a necessary one; and since the achievement of Kandinsky, mimetic features have been relegated to the periphery of critical concern, so much so that some works survive in spite of possessing those virtues, excellence in which was once celebrated as the essence of art, narrowly escaping demotion to mere illustrations.

It is, of course, indispensable in Socratic discussion that all participants be masters of the concept up for analysis, since the aim is to match a real defining expression to a term in active use, and the test for adequacy presumably consists in showing that the former analyzes and applies to all and only those things of which the latter is true. The popular disclaimer notwithstanding, then, Socrates' auditors purportedly knew what art was as well as what they liked; and a theory of art, regarded here as a real definition of 'Art,' is accordingly not to be of great use in helping men to recognize instances of its application. Their antecedent ability to do this is precisely what the adequacy of the theory is to be tested against, the problem being only to make explicit what they already know. It is *our* use of the term that the theory allegedly means to capture, but we are supposed able, in the words of a recent writer, "to separate those objects which are works of art from those

From *The Journal of Philosophy*, 61 (1964). Reprinted by permission of *The Journal of Philosophy* and the author.

which are not, because . . . we know how correctly to use the word 'art' and to apply the phrase 'work of art.'" Theories, on this account, are somewhat like mirror images on Socrates' account, showing forth what we already know, wordy reflections of the actual linguistic practice we are masters in.

But telling artworks from other things is not so simple a matter, even for native speakers, and these days one might not be aware he was on artistic terrain without an artistic theory to tell him so. And part of the reason for this lies in the fact that terrain is constituted artistic in virtue of artistic theories, so that one use of theories, in addition to helping us discriminate art from the rest, consists in making art possible. Glaucon and the others could hardly have known what was art and what not: otherwise they would never have been taken in by mirror images.

I. Suppose one thinks of the discovery of a whole new class of artworks as something analogous to the discovery of a whole new class of facts anywhere, viz., as something for theoreticians to explain. In science, as elsewhere, we often accommodate new facts to old theories *via* auxiliary hypotheses, a pardonable enough conservatism when the theory in question is deemed too valuable to be jettisoned all at once. Now the Imitation Theory of Art (IT) is, if one but thinks it through, an exceedingly powerful theory, explaining a great many phenomena connected with the causation and evaluation of artworks, bringing a surprising unity into a complex domain. Moreover, it is a simple matter to shore it up against many purported counterinstances by such auxiliary hypotheses as that the artist who deviates from mimeticity is perverse, inept, or mad. Ineptitude, chicanery, or folly are, in fact, testable predications. Suppose, then, tests reveal that these hypotheses fail to hold, that the theory, now beyond repair, must be replaced. And a new theory is worked out, capturing what it can of the old theory's competence, together with the heretofore recalcitrant facts. One might, thinking along these lines, represent certain episodes in the history of art as not dissimilar to certain episodes in the history of science, where a conceptual revolution is being effected and where refusal to countenance certain facts, while in part due to prejudice, inertia, and self-interest, is due also to the fact that a well-established, or at least widely credited theory is being threatened in such a way that all coherence goes.

Some such episode transpired with the advent of post-impressionist paintings. In terms of the prevailing artistic theory (IT), it was impossible to accept these as art unless inept art: otherwise they could be discounted as hoaxes, self-advertisements, or the visual counterparts of madmen's ravings. So to get them accepted *as* art, on a footing with the *Transfiguration* (not to speak of a Landseer stag), required not so much a revolution in taste as a theoretical revision of rather considerable proportions, involving not only the artistic enfranchisement of these objects, but an emphasis upon newly significant features of accepted artworks, so that quite different accounts of their status as artworks would now have to be given. As a result of the new theory's acceptance, not only were post-impressionist paintings taken up as art, but numbers of objects (masks, weapons, etc.) were transferred from anthropological museums (and heterogeneous other places) to *musées des beaux arts*, though, as we would expect from the fact that a criterion for the acceptance of a new theory is that it account for whatever the older one did, nothing had to be transferred out of the *musée des beaux arts*—even if there were interna rearrangements as between storage rooms and exhibition space. Countless native speakers hung upon suburban mantelpieces innumerable replicas of paradigm cases for teaching the expression "work of art" that would have sent their Edwardian forebears into linguistic apoplexy.

To be sure, I distort by speaking of a theory: historically, there were several, all, interestingly enough, more or less defined in terms of the IT. Art-historical complexities must yield before the exigencies of logical exposition, and I shall speak as though there were one replacing theory, partially compensating for historical falsity by choosing one which was actually enunciated. According to it, the artists in question were to be understood not as unsuccessfully imitating real forms but as successfully creating new ones, quite as real as the forms which the older art had been thought, in its best examples, to be creditably imitating. Art, after all, had long since been thought of as creative (Vasari says that God was the first artist), and the post-impressionists were to be explained as genuinely creative, aiming, in Roger Fry's words, "not at illusion but reality." This theory (RT) furnished a whole new mode of looking at painting, old and new. Indeed, one might almost interpret the crude drawing in Van Gogh and Cézanne, the dislocation of form from contour in Rouault and Dufy, the arbitrary use of color planes in Gauguin and the Fauves, as so many ways of drawing attention to the fact that these were *non-imitations*, specifically intended not to deceive. Logically, this would be roughly like printing "Not Legal Tender" across a brilliantly counterfeited dollar bill, the resulting object (counterfeit *cum* inscription) rendered incapable of deceiving anyone. It is not an illusory dollar bill, but then, just because it is non-illusory it does not automatically become a real dollar bill either. It rather occupies a freshly opened area between real objects and real facsimiles of real objects: it is non-facsimile, if one requires a word, and a new contribution to the world. Thus, Van Gogh's *Potato Eaters*, as a consequence of certain unmistakable distortions, turns out to be a non-facsimile of real life potato eaters; and inasmuch as these are not facsimiles of potato eaters Van Gogh's picture, as a non-imitation, had as much right to be called a real object as did its putative subjects. By means of this theory (RT), artworks re-entered the thick of things from which Socratic theory (IT) had sought to evict them; if no *more* real than what carpenters wrought, they were at least no *less* real. The Post-Impressionist won a victory in ontology.

It is in terms of RT that we must understand the artworks around us today. Thus Roy Lichtenstein paints comic-strip panels, though ten or twelve feet high. These are reasonably faithful projections onto a gigantesque scale of the homely frames from the daily tabloid, but it is precisely the scale that counts. A skilled engraver might incise *The Virgin and the Chancellor Rollin* on a pinhead, and it would be recognizable as such to the keen of sight, but an engraving of a Barnett Newman on a similar scale would be a blob, disappearing in the reduction. A *photograph* of a Lichtenstein is indiscernible from a photograph of a counterpart panel from *Steve Canyon*; but the photograph fails to capture the scale, and hence is as inaccurate a reproduction as a black-and-white engraving of Botticelli, scale being essential here as color there. Lichtensteins, then, are not imitations but *new entities*, as giant whelks would be. Jasper Johns, by contrast, paints objects with respect to which questions of scale are irrelevant. Yet his objects cannot be imitations, for they have the remarkable property that any intended copy of a member of this class of objects is automatically a member of the class itself, so that these objects are logically inimitable. Thus, a copy of a numeral just *is* that numeral: a painting of 3 is a 3 made of paint. Johns, in addition, paints targets, flags, and maps. Finally, in what I hope are not unwitting footnotes to Plato, two of our pioneers—Robert Rauschenberg and Claes Oldenburg—have made genuine beds.

Rauschenberg's bed hangs on a wall, and is streaked with some desultory house-paint. Oldenburg's bed is a rhomboid, narrower at one end than the other, with what one might speak of as a built-in perspective: ideal for small bedrooms. As beds, these sell at singularly inflated prices, but one *could* sleep in either of them: Rauschenberg has expressed the fear that someone might just climb into his bed and fall asleep. Imagine, now, a certain Testadura—a plain speaker and noted philistine—who is not aware that these are art, and who takes them to be reality simple and pure. He attributes the paintstreaks on Rauschenberg's bed to the slovenliness of the owner, and the bias in the Oldenburg bed to the ineptitude of the builder or the whimsy, perhaps, of whoever had it "custom-made." These would be mistakes, but mistakes of rather an odd kind, and not terribly different from that made by the stunned birds who pecked the sham grapes of Zeuxis. They mistook art for reality, and so has Testadura. But it was meant to *be* reality, according to RT. Can one have mistaken reality for reality? How shall we describe Testadura's error? What, after all, prevents Oldenburg's creation from being a misshapen bed? This is equivalent to asking what makes it art, and with this query we enter a domain of conceptual inquiry where native speakers are poor guides: *they* are lost themselves.

II. To mistake an artwork for a real object is no great feat when an artwork is the real object one mistakes it for. The problem is how to avoid such errors, or to remove them once they are made. The artwork is a bed, and not a bed-illusion; so there is nothing like the traumatic encounter against a flat surface that brought it home to the birds of Zeuxis that they had been duped. Except for the guard cautioning Testadura not to sleep on the artworks, he might never have discovered that this was an artwork and not a bed; and since, after all, one cannot discover that a bed is not a bed, how is Testadura to realize that he has made an error? A certain sort of explanation is required, for the error here is a curiously philosophical one, rather like, if we may assume as correct some well-known views of P. F. Strawson, mistaking a person for a material body when the truth is that a person *is* a material body in the sense that a whole class of predicates, sensibly applicable to material bodies, are sensibly, and by appeal to no different criteria, applicable to persons. So you cannot *discover* that a person is not a material body.

We begin by explaining, perhaps, that the paintstreaks are not to be explained away, that they are *part* of the object, so the object is not a mere bed with—as it happens—streaks of paint spilled over it, but a complex object fabricated out of a bed and some paintstreaks: a paint-bed. Similarly, a person is not a material body with—as it happens—some thoughts superadded, but is a complex entity made up of a body and some conscious states: a conscious-body. Persons, like artworks, must then be taken as irreducible to *parts* of themselves, and are in that sense primitive. Or, more accurately, the paintstreaks are not part of the real object—the bed—which happens to be part of the artwork, but are *like* the bed, part of the artwork as such. And this might be generalized into a rough characterization of artworks that happen to contain real objects as parts of themselves: not every part of an artwork A is part of a real object R when R is part of A and can, moreover, be detached from A and seen *merely* as R. The mistake thus far will have been to mistake A for *part* of itself, namely R, even though it would not be incorrect to say that A is R, that the artwork is a bed. It is the "is" which requires clarification here.

There is an *is* that figures prominently in statements concerning artworks which is not the *is* of either identity or predication; nor is it the *is* of existence, of identification, or some special *is* made up to serve a philosophic end. Nevertheless, it is in common usage, and is readily mastered by children. It is the sense of *is* in accordance with which a child, shown a circle and a triangle and asked which is him and which his sister, will point to the triangle saying "That is me"; or, in response to my question, the person next to me points to the man in purple and says "That one is Lear"; or in the gallery I point, for my companion's benefit, to a spot in the painting before us and say "That white dab is Icarus." We do not mean, in these instances, that whatever is pointed to stands for, or represents, what it is said to be, for the *word* "Icarus" stands for or represents Icarus: yet I would not in the same sense of *is* point to the word and say "That is Icarus." The sentence "That *a* is *b*" is perfectly compatible with "That *a* is not *b*" when the first employs this sense of *is* and the second employs some other, though *a* and *b* are used nonambiguously throughout. Often, indeed, the truth of the first *requires* the truth of the second. The first, in fact, is incompatible with "That *a* is not *b*" only when the *is* is used nonambiguously throughout. For want of a word I shall designate this the *is of artistic identification*; in each case in which it is used, the *a* stands for some specific physical property of, or physical part of, an object; and, finally, it is a necessary condition for something to be an artwork that some part or property of it be designable by the subject of a sentence that employs this special *is*. It is an *is*, incidentally, which has near-relatives in marginal and mythical pronouncements. (Thus, one *is* Quetzalcoatl; those *are* the Pillars of Hercules.)

Let me illustrate. Two painters are asked to decorate the east and west walls of a science library with frescoes to be respectively called *Newton's First Law* and *Newton's Third Law*. These paintings, when finally unveiled, look, scale apart, as follows:

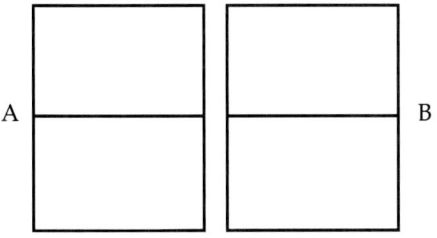

As objects I shall suppose the works to be indiscernible: a black horizontal line on a white ground, equally large in each dimension and element. B explains his work as follows: a mass, pressing downward, is met by a mass pressing upward: the lower mass reacts equally and oppositely to the upper one. A explains his work as follows: the line through the space is the path of an isolated particle. The path goes from edge to edge, to give the sense of its *going beyond*. If it ended or began within the space, the line would be curved; and it is parallel to the top and bottom edges, for if it were closer to one than to another, there would have to be a force accounting for it, and this is inconsistent with its being the path of an *isolated* particle.

Much follows from these artistic identifications. To regard the middle line as an edge (mass meeting mass) imposes the need to identify the top and bottom half of the picture as rectangles, and as two distinct parts (not necessarily as two masses, for the line could be the edge of *one* mass jutting up—or down—into empty space). If it is an edge, we cannot thus take the entire area of the painting as a single space: it is rather composed of two forms, or one form and a nonform. We could take the entire area as a single space only by taking the middle horizontal as a *line* which is not an edge. But this almost requires a three-dimensional identification of the whole picture: the area can be a flat surface which the line is *above* (*Jet-flight*), or *below* (*Submarine-path*), or *on* (*Line*), or *in* (*Fissure*), or *through* (*Newton's First Law*)—though in this last case the area is not a flat surface but a transparent cross section of absolute space. We could make all these prepositional qualifications clear by imagining perpendicular cross sections to the picture plane. Then, depending upon the applicable prepositional clause, the area is (artistically) interrrupted or not by the horizontal element. If we take the line as *through* space, the edges of the picture are not really the edges of the space: the space goes beyond the picture if the line itself does; and we are in the same space as the line is. As B, the edges of the picture can be *part* of the picture in case the masses go right to the edges, so that the edges of the picture are *their* edges. In that case, the vertices of the picture would be the vertices of the masses, except that the masses have four vertices more than the picture itself does: here four vertices would be part of the artwork which were not part of the real object. Again, the faces of the masses could be the face of the picture, and in looking at the picture, we are looking at these faces; but *space* has no face, and on the reading of A the work has to be read as faceless, and the face of the physical object would not be part of the artwork. Notice here how one artistic identification engenders another artistic identification and how, consistently with a given identification, we are *required* to give others and *precluded* from still others; indeed, a given identification determines how many elements the work is to contain. These different identifications are incompatible with one another, or generally so, and each might be said to make a different artwork, even though each artwork contains the identical real object as part of itself—or at least parts of the identical real object as parts of itself. There are, of course, senseless identifications: no one could, I think, sensibly read the middle horizontal as *Love's Labour's Lost* or *The Ascendency of St. Erasmus*. Finally, notice how acceptance of one identification rather than another is in effect to exchange one *world* for another. We could, indeed, enter a quiet poetic world by identifying the upper area with a clear and cloudless sky, reflected in the still surface of the water below, whiteness kept from whiteness only by the unreal boundary of the horizon.

And now Testadura, having hovered in the wings throughout this discussion, protests that *all he sees is paint*: a white painted oblong with a black line painted across it. And how right he really is: that is all he sees or that anybody can, we aesthetes included. So, if he asks us to show him what there is further to see, to demonstrate through pointing that this is an artwork *(Sea and Sky)*, we cannot comply, for he has overlooked nothing (and it would be absurd to suppose he had, that there was something tiny we could point to and he, peering closely, say "So it is! A work of art after all!"). We cannot help him until he has mastered the *is of artistic identification* and so *constitutes* it a work of art. If he cannot achieve this, he will never look upon artworks: he will be like a child who sees sticks as sticks.

But what about pure abstractions, say something that looks just like A but is entitled No. 7? The 10th Street abstractionist blankly insists that there is nothing here but white paint and black, and none of our literary identifications need apply. What then distinguishes him from Testadura, whose philistine utterances are indiscernible from his? And how can it be an artwork for him and not for Testadura, when they agree that there is nothing that does not meet the eye? The answer, unpopular as it is likely to be to purists of every variety, lies in the fact that this artist has returned to the physicality of paint through an atmosphere compounded of artistic theories and the history of recent and remote painting, elements of which he is trying to refine out of his own work; and as a consequence of this his work belongs in this atmosphere and is part of this history. He has achieved abstraction through rejection of artistic identifications, returning to the real world from which such identifications remove us (he thinks), somewhat in the mode of Ch'ing Yuan, who wrote:

Before I had studied Zen for thirty years, I saw mountains as mountains and waters as waters. When I arrived at a more intimate knowledge, I came to the point where I saw that mountains are not mountains, and waters are not waters. But now that I have got the very substance I am at rest. For it is just that I see mountains once again as mountains, and waters once again as waters.

His identification of what he has made is logically dependent upon the theories and history he rejects. The difference between his utterance and Testadura's "This is black paint and white paint and nothing more" lies in the fact that he is still using the *is* of artistic identification, so that his use of "That black paint is black paint" is not a tautology. Testadura is not at that stage. To see something as art requires something the eye cannot descry—an atmosphere of artistic theory, a knowledge of the history of art: an artworld.

III. Mr. Andy Warhol, the Pop artist, displays facsimiles of Brillo cartons, piled high, in neat stacks, as in the stockroom of the supermarket. They happen to be of wood, painted to look like cardboard, and why not? To paraphrase the critic of the *Times*, if one may make the facsimile of a human being out of bronze, why not the facsimile of a Brillo carton out of plywood? The cost of these boxes happens to be 2×10^3 that of their homely counterparts in real life—a differential hardly ascribable to their advantage in durability. In fact the Brillo people might, at some slight increase in cost, make their boxes out of plywood without these becoming artworks, and Warhol might make *his* out of cardboard without their ceasing to be art. So we may forget questions of intrinsic value, and ask why the Brillo people cannot manufacture art and why Warhol cannot *but* make artworks. Well, his are made by hand, to be sure. Which is like an insane reversal of Picasso's strategy in pasting the label from a bottle of Suze onto a drawing, saying as it were that the academic artist, concerned with exact imitation, must always fall short of the real thing: so why not just *use* the real thing? The Pop artist laboriously reproduces machine-made objects by hand, e.g., painting the labels on coffee cans (one can hear the familiar commendation "Entirely made by hand" falling painfully out of the guide's vocabulary when confronted by these objects). But the difference cannot consist in craft: a man who carved pebbles out of stones and carefully constructed a work called *Gravel Pile* might evoke the labor theory of value to account for the price he demands; but the question is, What makes it art? And why need Warhol *make* these things anyway? Why not just scrawl his signature across one? Or crush one up and display it as *Crushed Brillo Box* ("A protest against mechanization . . .") or simply display a Brillo carton as *Uncrushed Brillo Box* ("A bold affirmation of the plastic authenticity of industrial . . .")? Is this man a kind of Midas, turning whatever he touches into the gold of pure art? And the whole world consisting of latent artworks waiting, like the bread and wine of reality, to be transfigured, through some dark mystery, into the indiscernible flesh and blood of the sacrament? Never mind that the Brillo box may not be good, much less great art. The impressive thing is that it is art at all. But if it is, why are not the indiscernible Brillo boxes that are in the stockroom? Or *has* the whole distinction between art and reality broken down?

Suppose a man collects objects (readymades), including a Brillo carton; we praise the exhibit for variety, ingenuity, what you will. Next he exhibits nothing but Brillo cartons, and we criticize it as dull, repetitive, self-plagiarizing—or (more profoundly) claim that he is obsessed by regularity and repetition, as in *Marienbad*. Or he piles them high, leaving a narrow path; we tread our way through the smooth opaque stacks and find it an unsettling experience, and write it up as the closing in of consumer products, confining us as prisoners: or we say he is a modern pyramid builder. True, we don't say these things about the stockboy. But then a stockroom is not an art gallery, and we cannot readily separate the Brillo cartons from the gallery they are in, any more than we can separate the Rauschenberg bed from the paint upon it. Outside the gallery, they are pasteboard cartons. But then, scoured clean of paint, Rauschenberg's bed is a bed, just what it was before it was transformed into art. But then if we think this matter through, we discover that the artist has failed, really and of necessity, to produce a mere real object. He has produced an artwork, his use of real Brillo cartons being but an expansion of the resources available to artists, a contribution to *artists' materials*, as oil paint was, or *tuche*.

What in the end makes the difference between a Brillo box and a work of art consisting of a Brillo Box is a certain theory of art. It is the theory that takes it up into the world of art, and keeps it from collapsing into the real object which it is (in a sense of *is* other than that of artistic identification). Of course, without the theory, one is unlikely to see it as art, and in order to see it as part of the artworld, one must have mastered a good deal of artistic theory as well as a considerable amount of the history of recent New York painting. It could not have been art fifty years ago. But then there could not have been, everything being equal, flight insurance in the Middle Ages, or Etruscan typewriter erasers. The world has to be ready for certain things, the artworld no less than the real one. It is the role of artistic theories, these days as always, to make the artworld, and art, possible. It would, I should think, never have occurred to the painters of Lascaux that they were producing *art* on those walls. Not unless there were neolithic aestheticians.

IV. The artworld stands to the real world in something like the relationship in which the City of God stands to the Earthly City. Certain objects, like certain individuals, enjoy a double citizenship, but there remains, the RT notwithstanding, a fundamental contrast between artworks and real objects. Perhaps this was already dimly sensed by the early framers of the IT who, inchoately realizing the nonreality of art, were perhaps limited only in supposing that the sole way objects had of being other than real is to be sham, so that artworks necessarily had to be imitations of real objects. This was too narrow. So Yeats saw in writing "Once out of nature I shall never take/My bodily form from any natural thing." It is but a matter of choice: and the Brillo box of the artworld may be just the Brillo box of the real one, separated and united by the *is* of artistic identification. But I should like to say some final words about the theories that make artworks possible, and their relationship to one another. In so doing, I shall beg some of the hardest philosophical questions I know.

I shall now think of pairs of predicates related to each other as "opposites," conceding straight off the vagueness of this *demodé* term. Contradictory predicates are not opposites, since one of each of them must apply to every object in the universe, and neither of a pair of opposites need apply to some objects in the universe. An object must first be of a certain kind before either of a pair of opposites applies to it, and then at most and at least one of the opposites must apply to it. So opposites are not contraries, for contraries may both be false of some objects in the universe, but opposites cannot both be false; for of some objects, neither of a pair of opposites *sensibly* applies, unless the object is of the right sort. Then, if the object is of the required kind, the opposites behave as contradictories. If F and non-F are opposites, an object o must be of a certain kind K before either of these sensibly applies; but if o is a member of K, then o either is F or non-F to the exclusion of the other. The class of pairs of opposites that sensibly apply to the $(ô)$ Ko I shall designate as the class of *K-relevant predicates*. And a necessary condition for an object to be of a kind K is that at least one pair of K-relevant opposites be sensibly applicable to it. But, in fact, if an object is of kind K, at least and at most one of each K-relevant pair of opposites applies to it.

I am now interested in the K-relevant predicates for the class K of artworks. And let F and non-F be an opposite pair of such predicates. Now it might happen that, throughout an entire period of time, every artwork is non-F. But since nothing thus far is both an artwork and F, it might never occur to anyone that non-F is an artistically relevant predicate. The non-F-ness of artworks goes unmarked. By contrast, all works up to a given time might be G, it never occurring to anyone until that time that something might both be an artwork and non-G; indeed, it might have been thought that G was a *defining trait* of artworks when in fact something might first have to be an artwork before G is sensibly predicable of it—in which case non-G might also be predicable of artworks, and G itself then could not have been a defining trait of this class.

Let G be "is representational" and let F be "is expressionist." At a given time, these and their opposites are perhaps the only artrelevant predicates in critical use. Now letting "+" stand for a given predicate P and "−" for its opposite non-P, we may construct a style matrix more or less as follows:

F	G
+	+
+	−
−	+
−	−

The rows determine available styles, given the active critical vocabulary: representational expressionistic (e.g., Fauvism); representational nonexpressionistic (Ingres); nonrepresentational expressionistic (Abstract Expressionism); nonrepresentational nonexpressionist (hard-edge abstraction). Plainly, as we add artrelevant predicates, we increase the number of available styles at the rate of 2^n. It is, of course, not easy to see in advance which predicates are going to be added or replaced by their opposites, but suppose an artist determines that H shall henceforth be artistically relevant for his paintings. Then, in fact, both H and non-H become artistically relevant for *all* painting, and if his is the first and only painting that is H, every other painting in existence becomes non-H, and the entire community of paintings is enriched, together with a doubling of the available style opportunities. It is this retroactive enrichment of the entities in the artworld that makes it possible to discuss Raphael and De Kooning together, or Lichtenstein and Michelangelo. The greater the variety of artistically relevant predicates, the more complex the individual members of the artworld become; and the more one knows of the entire population of the artworld, the richer one's experience with any of its members.

In this regard, notice that, if there are m artistically relevant predicates, there is always a bottom row with m minuses. This row is apt to be occupied by purists. Having scoured their canvasses clear of what they regard as inessential, they credit themselves with having distilled out the essence of art. But this is just their fallacy: exactly as many artistically relevant predicates stand true of their square monochromes as stand true of any member of the Artworld, and they can *exist* as artworks only insofar as "impure" paintings exist. Strictly speaking, a black square by Reinhardt is artistically as rich as Titian's *Sacred and Profane Love*. This explains how less is more.

Fashion, as it happens, favors certain rows of the style matrix: museums, connoisseurs, and others are makeweights in the Artworld. To insist, or seek to, that all artists become representational, perhaps to gain entry into a specially prestigious exhibition, cuts the available style matrix in half: there are then $2^n/2$ ways of satisfying the requirement, and museums then can exhibit all these "approaches" to the topic they have set. But this is a matter of almost purely sociological interest: one row in the matrix is as legitimate as another. An artistic breakthrough consists, I suppose, in adding the possibility of a column to the matrix. Artists then, with greater or less alacrity, occupy the positions thus opened up: this is a remarkable feature of contemporary art, and for those unfamiliar with the matrix, it is hard, and perhaps impossible, to recognize certain positions as occupied by artworks. Nor would these things be artworks without the theories and the histories of the Artworld.

Brillo boxes enter the artworld with that same tonic incongruity the *commedia dell'arte* characters bring into *Ariadne auf Naxos*. Whatever is the artistically relevant predicate in virtue of which they gain their entry, the rest of the Artworld becomes that much the richer in having the opposite predicate available and applicable to its members. And, to return to the views of Hamlet with which we began this discussion, Brillo boxes may reveal us to ourselves as well as anything might: as a mirror held up to nature, they might serve to catch the conscience of our kings.

What Is Art? An Institutional Analysis

George Dickie

I

The best-known denial that "art" can be defined occurs in Morris Weitz's article "The Role of Theory in Aesthetics."[1] Weitz's conclusion depends upon two arguments which may be called his "generalization argument" and his "classification argument." In stating the "generalization argument," Weitz distinguishes, quite correctly, between the generic conception of "art" and the various subconcepts of art such as tragedy, the novel, painting, and the like. He then goes on to give an argument purporting to show that the

From *Art and the Aesthetic: An Institutional Analysis* (1974). Cornell University Press. Reprinted by permission of the publisher.

subconcept "novel" is open, that is, that the members of the class of novels do not share any essential or defining characteristics. He then asserts without further argument that what is true of novels is true of all other subconcepts of art. The generalization from one subconcept to all subconcepts may or may not be justified, but I am not questioning it here. I do question, however, Weitz's additional contention, also asserted without argument, that the generic conception of "art" is open. The best that can be said of his conclusion about the generic sense is that it is unsupported. All or some of the subconcepts of art may be open and the generic conception of art still be closed. That is, it is possible that all or some of the subconcepts of art, such as novel, tragedy, sculpture, and painting, may lack necessary and sufficient conditions and at the same time that "work of art," which is the genus of all the subconcepts, can be defined in terms of necessary and sufficient conditions. Tragedies may not have any characteristics in common which would distinguish them from, say, comedies *within the domain of art*, but it may be that there are common characteristics that works of art have which distinguish them from nonart. Nothing prevents a "closed genus/open species" relationship. Weitz himself has recently cited what he takes to be a similar (although reversed) example of genus–species relationship. He argues that "game" (the genus) is open but that "major-league baseball" (a species) is closed.[2]

His second argument, "the classification argument," claims to show that not even the characteristic of artifactuality is a necessary feature of art. Weitz's conclusion here is something of a surprise, because it has been widely assumed by philosophers and nonphilosophers alike that a work of art is necessarily an artifact. His argument is simply that we sometimes utter such statements as "This piece of driftwood is a lovely piece of sculpture," and since such utterances are perfectly intelligible, it follows that some nonartifacts such as certain pieces of driftwood are works of art (sculptures). In other words, something need not be an artifact in order to be correctly classified as a work of art. I will try to rebut this argument shortly.

Recently, Maurice Mandelbaum has raised a question about Wittgenstein's famous contention that "game" cannot be defined and Weitz's thesis about "art."[3] His challenge to both is based on the charge that they have been concerned only with what Mandelbaum calls "exhibited" characteristics and that consequently each has failed to take account of the nonexhibited, relational aspects of games and art. By "exhibited" characteristics Mandelbaum means easily perceived properties such as the fact that a ball is used in a certain kind of game, that a painting has a triangular composition, that an area in a painting is red, or that the plot of a tragedy contains a reversal of fortune. Mandelbaum concludes that when we consider the nonexhibited properties of games, we see that they have in common "the potentiality of . . . [an] . . . absorbing nonpractical interest to either participants or spectators."[4] Mandelbaum may or may not be right about "game," but what interests me is the application of his suggestion about nonexhibited properties to the discussion of the definition of art. Although he does not attempt a definition of "art," Mandelbaum does suggest that feature(s) common to all works of art may perhaps be discovered that will be a basis for the definition of "art," if the nonexhibited features of art are attended to.

Having noted Mandelbaum's invaluable suggestion about definition, I now return to Weitz's argument concerning artifactuality. In an earlier attempt to show Weitz wrong, I thought it sufficient to point out that there are two senses of "work of art," an evaluative sense and a classificatory one; Weitz himself distinguishes these in his article as the evaluative and the descriptive senses of art. My earlier argument was that if there is more than one sense of "work of art," then the fact that "This piece of driftwood is a lovely piece of sculpture" is intelligible does not prove what Weitz wants it to prove. Weitz would have to show that "sculpture" is being used in the sentence in question in the classificatory sense, and this he makes no attempt to do. My argument assumed that once the distinction is made, it is obvious that "sculpture" is here being used in the evaluative sense. Richard Sclafani has subsequently noted that my argument shows only that Weitz's argument is inconclusive and that Weitz might still be right, even though his argument does not prove his conclusion. Sclafani, however, has constructed a stronger argument against Weitz on this point.[5]

Sclafani shows that there is a third sense of "works of art" and that "driftwood cases" (the nonartifact cases) fall under it. He begins by comparing a paradigm work of art, Brancusi's *Bird in Space*, with a piece of driftwood which looks very much like it. Sclafani says that it seems natural to say of the piece of driftwood that it is a work of art and that we do so because it has so many properties in common with the Brancusi piece. He then asks us to reflect on our characterization of the driftwood and the *direction* it has taken. We say the driftwood is art because of its resemblance to some paradigm work of art or because the driftwood shares properties with several paradigm works of art. The paradigm work or works are of course always artifacts; the direction of our move is from paradigmatic (artifactual) works of art to nonartifactual "art." Sclafani quite correctly takes this to indicate that there is a primary, paradigmatic sense of "work of art" (my classificatory sense) and a derivative or secondary sense into which the "driftwood cases" fall. Weitz is right in a way in saying that the driftwood is art, but wrong in concluding that artifactuality is unnecessary for (the primary sense of) art.

There are then at least three distinct senses of "work of art"; the primary or classificatory sense, the secondary or derivative, and the evaluative. Perhaps in most uses of Weitz's driftwood sentence example, both the derivative and the evaluative senses would be involved: the derivative sense if the driftwood shared a number of properties with some paradigm work of art and the evaluative sense if the shared properties were found to be valuable by the speaker. Sclafani gives a case in which only the evaluative sense functions, when someone says, "Sally's cake is a work of art." In most uses of such a sentence "work of art" would simply mean that its referent has valuable qualities. Admittedly, one can imagine contexts in which the derivative sense would apply in cakes. (Given the situation in art today, one can easily imagine cakes to which the primary sense of art could be applied.) If, however, someone were to say, "This Rembrandt is a work of art," both the classificatory and the evaluative senses would be functioning. The expression "this Rembrandt" would convey the information that its referent is a work of art in the classificatory sense, and "is a work of art" could then only reasonably be understood in the evaluative sense. Finally, someone might say of a seashell or other natural object which resembles a man's face but is otherwise uninteresting, "This shell (or other natural object) is a work of art." In this case, only the derivative sense would be used.

We utter sentences in which the expression "work of art" has the evaluative sense with considerable frequency, applying it to both natural objects and artifacts. We speak of works of art in the derived sense with somewhat less frequency. The classificatory sense of "work of art," which indicates simply that a thing belongs to a certain category of artifacts, occurs, however, very infrequently in our discourse. We rarely utter sentences in which we use the classificatory sense, because it is such a basic notion: we generally know immediately whether an object is a work of art, so that generally no one needs to say, by way of classification, "That is a work of art," although recent developments in art such as junk sculpture and found art may occasionally force such remarks. Even if we do not often talk about art in this classificatory sense, however, it is a basic concept that structures and guides our thinking about our world and its contents.

II

It is now clear that artifactuality is a necessary condition (call it the genus) of the primary sense of art. This fact, however, does not seem very surprising and would not even be very interesting except that Weitz and others have denied it. Artifactuality alone, however, is not the whole story and another necessary condition (the differentia) has to be specified in order to have a satisfactory definition of "art." Like artifactuality, the second condition is a nonexhibited property, which turns out to be as complicated as artifactuality is simple. The attempt to discover and specify the second condition of art will involve an examination of the intricate complexities of the "artworld." W. E. Kennick, defending a view similar to Weitz's, contends that the kind of approach to be employed here, following Mandelbaum's lead, is futile. He concludes that "the attempt to define Art in terms of what we do with certain objects is as doomed as any other."[6] He tries to support this conclusion by referring to such things as the fact that the ancient Egyptians sealed up paintings and sculptures in tombs. There are two difficulties with Kennick's argument. First, that the Egyptians sealed up paintings and sculptures in tombs does not show that they regarded them differently from the way in which we regard them. They might have put them there for the dead to appreciate or simply because they belonged to the dead person. The Egyptian practice does not establish so radical a difference between their conception of art and ours that a definition subsuming both is impossible. Second, one need not assume that we and the ancient Egyptians share a common conception of art. It would be enough to be able to specify the necessary and sufficient conditions for the concept of art which we have (we present-day Americans, we present-day Westerners, we Westerners since the organization of the system of the arts in or about the eighteenth century—I am not sure of the exact limits of the "we"). Kennick notwithstanding, we are most likely to discover the differentia of art by considering "what we do with certain objects." Of course, nothing guarantees that any given thing we might do or an ancient Egyptian might have done with a work of art will throw light on the concept of art. Not every "doing" will reveal what is required.

Although he does not attempt to formulate a definition, Arthur Danto in his provocative article, "The Artworld," has suggested the direction that must be taken by an attempt to define "art."[7] In reflecting on art and its history together with such present-day developments as Warhol's *Brillo Carton* and Rauschenberg's *Bed*, Danto writes, "To see something as art requires something the eye cannot decry—an atmosphere of artistic theory, a knowledge of the history of art: an artworld."[8] Admittedly, this stimulating comment is in need of elucidation, but it is clear that in speaking of "something the eye cannot decry" Danto is agreeing with Mandelbaum that nonexhibited properties are of great importance in constituting something as art. In speaking of atmosphere and history, however, Danto's remark carries us a step further than Mandelbaum's analysis. Danto points to the rich structure in which particular works of art are embedded: he indicates *the institutional nature of art*.[9]

I shall use Danto's term "artworld" to refer to the broad social institution in which works of art have their place.[10] But is there such an institution? George Bernard Shaw speaks somewhere of the apostolic line of succession stretching from Aeschylus to himself. Shaw as no doubt speaking for effect and to draw attention to himself, as he often did, but there is an important truth implied by his remark. There is a long tradition or continuing institution of the theater having its origins in ancient Greek religion and other Greek institutions. That tradition has run very thin at times and perhaps even ceased to exist altogether during some periods, only to be reborn out of its memory and the need for art. The institutions associated with the theater have varied from time to time: in the beginning it was Greek religion and the Greek state; in medieval times, the church; more recently, private business and the state (national theater). What has remained constant with its own identity throughout its history is the theater itself as an established way of doing and behaving, what I shall call . . . the primary convention of the theater. This institutionalized behavior occurs on both sides of the "footlights": both the players and the audience are involved and go to make up the institution of the theater. The roles of the actors and the audience are defined by the traditions of the theater. What the author, management, and players present is art, and it is art because it is presented within the theaterworld framework. Plays are written to have a place in the theater system and they exist as plays—that is, as art—within that system. Of course, I do not wish to deny that plays also exist as literary works—that is, as art within the literary system: The theater system and the literary system overlap. Let me make clear what I mean by speaking of the artworld as an institution. Among the meanings of "institution" in *Webster's New Collegiate Dictionary* are the following: "3. That which is instituted as: (a.) An established practice, law, custom, etc. (b.) An established society or corporation." When I call the art-world an institution I am saying that it is an established practice. Some persons have thought that an institution must be an established society or corporation, and, consequently, have misunderstood my claim about the artworld.

Theater is only one of the systems within the artworld. Each of the systems has had its own origins and historical development. We have some information about the later stages of these developments, but we have to guess about the origins of the basic art systems. I suppose that we have complete knowledge of certain recently developed subsystems or genres such as Dada and happenings. Even if our knowledge is not as complete as we wish it were, however, we do have substantial information about the systems of the artworld as they currently exist and as they have existed for some time. One central feature all of the systems have in common is that each is a framework for the *presenting* of particular works of art. Given the great variety of the systems of the artworld it is not surprising that works of art have no exhibited properties in common. If, however, we step back and view the works in their institutional setting, we will be able to see the essential properties they share.

Theater is a rich and instructive illustration of the institutional nature of art. But it is a development within the domain of painting and sculpture—Dadaism—that most easily reveals the institutional essence of art.

Duchamp and friends conferred the status of art on "readymades" (urinals, hatracks, snow shovels, and the like), and when we reflect on their deeds we can take note of a kind of human action which has until now gone unnoticed and unappreciated—the action of conferring the status of art. Painters and sculptors, of course, have been engaging all along in the action of conferring this status on the objects they create. As long, however, as the created objects were conventional, given the paradigms of the times, the objects themselves and their fascinating exhibited properties were the focus of the attention of not only spectators and critics but of philosophers of art as well. When an artist of an earlier era painted a picture, he did some or all of a number of things: depicted a human being, portrayed a certain man, fulfilled a commission, worked at his livelihood, and so on. In addition, he also acted as an agent of the artworld, and conferred the status of art on his creation. Philosophers of art attended to only some of the properties of the created object acquired from these various actions, for example, to the representational or to the expressive features of the objects. They entirely ignored the nonexhibited property of status. When, however, the objects are bizarre, as those of the Dadaists are, our attention is forced away from the objects' obvious properties to a consideration of the objects in their social context. As works of art Duchamp's "ready-mades" may not be worth much, but as examples of art they are very valuable for art theory. I am not claiming that Duchamp and friends invented the conferring of the status of art; they simply used an existing institutional device in an unusual way. Duchamp did not invent the artworld, because it was there all along.

The artworld consists of a bundle of systems: theater, painting, sculpture, literature, music, and so on, each of which furnishes an institutional background for the conferring of the status on objects within its domain. No limit can be placed on the number of systems that can be brought under the generic conception of art, and each of the major systems contains further subsystems. These features of the artworld provide the elasticity whereby creativity of even the most radical sort can be accommodated. A whole new system comparable to the theater, for example, could be added in one fell swoop. What is more likely is that a new subsystem would be added within a system. For example, junk sculpture added within sculpture, happenings added within theater. Such additions might in time develop into full-blown systems. Thus, the radical creativity, adventuresomeness, and exuberance of art of which Weitz speaks is possible within the concept of art, even though it is closed by the necessary and sufficient conditions of artifactuality and the conferred status.

Having now briefly described the artworld, I am in a position to specify a definition of "work of art." The definition will be given in terms of artifactuality and the conferred status of art, or more strictly speaking, the conferred status of candidate for appreciation. Once the definition has been stated, a great deal will still remain to be said by way of clarification: A work of art in the classificatory sense is (1) an artifact (2) a set of the aspects of which has had conferred upon it the status of candidate for appreciation by some person or persons acting on behalf of a certain social institution (the artworld).

The second condition of the definition makes use of four variously interconnected notions: (1) acting on behalf of an institution, (2) conferring of status, (3) being a candidate, and (4) appreciation. The first two of these are so closely related that they must be discussed together. I shall first describe paradigm cases of conferring status outside the artworld and then show how similar actions take place within the artworld. The most clearcut examples of the conferring of status are certain legal actions of the state. A king's conferring of knighthood, a grand jury's indicting someone, the chairman of the election board certifying that someone is qualified to run for office, or a minister's pronouncing a couple man and wife are examples in which a person or persons acting on behalf of a social institution (the state) confer(s) *legal* status on persons. The congress or a legally constituted commission may confer the status of national park or monument on an area or thing. The examples given suggest that pomp and ceremony are required to establish legal status, but this is not so, although of course a legal system is presupposed. For example, in some jurisdictions common-law marriage is possible—a legal status acquired without ceremony. The conferring of a Ph.D. degree on someone by a university, the election of someone as president of the Rotary, and the declaring of an object as a relic of the church are examples in which a person or persons confer(s) nonlegal status on persons or things. In such cases some social system or other must exist as the framework within which the conferring takes place, but, as before, ceremony is not required to establish status: For example, a person can acquire the status of wise man or village idiot within a community without ceremony.

Some may feel that the notion of conferring status within the artworld is excessively vague. Certainly this notion is not as clearcut as the conferring of status within the legal system, where procedures and lines of authority are explicitly defined and incorporated into law. The counterparts in the artworld to specified procedures and lines of authority are nowhere codified, and the artworld carries on its business at the level of customary practice. Still there *is* a practice and this defines a social institution. A social institution need not have a formally established constitution, officers, and bylaws in order to exist and have the capacity to confer status—some social institutions are formal and some are informal. The artworld could become formalized, and perhaps has been to some extent in certain political contexts, but most people who are interested in art would probably consider this a bad thing. Such formality would threaten the freshness and exuberance of art. The core personnel of the artworld is a loosely organized, but nevertheless related, set of persons including artists (understood to refer to painters, writers, composers), producers, museum directors, museum-goers, theater-goers, reporters for newspapers, critics for publications of all sorts, art historians, art theorists, philosophers of art, and others. These are the people who keep the machinery of the artworld working and thereby provide for its continuing existence. In addition, every person who sees himself as a member of the artworld is thereby a member. Although I have called the persons just listed the core personnel of the artworld, there is a minimum core within that core without which the artworld would not exist. This essential core consists of artists who create the works, "presenters" to present the works, and "goers" who appreciate the works. This minimum core might be called "the presentation group," for it consists of artists whose activity is necessary if anything is to be presented, the presenters (actors, stage managers, and so on), and the goers whose presence and cooperation is necessary in order for anything to be presented. A given person might play more than one of these essential roles in the case of the presentation of a particular work. Critics, historians, and philosophers of art become members of the artworld at some time after the minimum core personnel of a particular art system get that system into operation. All of these roles are institutionalized and must be learned in one way or another by the participants. For example, a theatergoer is not just someone who happens to enter a theater; he is a person who enters with certain expectations and knowledge about what he will experience and an understanding of how he should behave in the face of what he will experience.

Assuming that the existence of the artworld has been established or at least made plausible, the problem is now to see how status is conferred by this institution. My thesis is that, in a way analogous to the way in which a person is certified as qualified for office, or two persons acquire the status of common-law marriage within a legal system, or a person is elected president of the Rotary, or a person acquires the status of wise man within a community, so an artifact can acquire the status of candidate for appreciation within the social system called "the artworld." How can one tell when the status has been conferred? An artifact's hanging in an art museum as part of a show and a performance at a theater are sure signs. There is, of course, no guarantee that one can always know whether something is a candidate for appreciation, just as one cannot always tell whether a given person is a knight or is married. When an object's status depends upon nonexhibited characteristics, a simple look at the object will not necessarily reveal that status. The nonexhibited relation *may* be symbolized by some badge, for example, by a wedding ring, in which case a simple look will reveal the status.

The more important question is that of how the status of candidate for appreciation is conferred. The examples just mentioned, display in a museum and a performance in a theater, seem to suggest that a number of persons are required for the actual conferring of the status. In one sense a number of persons are required but in another sense only one person is required: a number of persons are required to make up the social institution of the artworld, but only one person is required to act on behalf of the artworld and to confer the status of candidate for appreciation. In fact, many works of art are seen only by one person—the one who creates them—but they are still art. The status in question may be acquired by a single person's acting on behalf of the artworld and *treating an artifact as a candidate for appreciation*. Of course, nothing prevents a group of persons from conferring the status, but it is usually conferred by a single person, the artist who creates the artifact. It may be helpful to compare and contrast the notion of conferring the status of candidate for appreciation with a case in which something is simply presented for appreciation: hopefully this will throw light on the notion of status of candidate. Consider the case of a salesman of plumbing supplies who spreads his wares before us. "Placing before" and "conferring the status of candidate for appreciation" are very different notions, and this difference can be brought out by comparing the salesman's action with the superficially similar act of Duchamp in entering a urinal which he christened *Fountain* in that now-famous art show. The difference is that Duchamp's action took place within the institutional setting of the artworld and the plumbing salesman's action took place outside of it. The salesman could do what Duchamp did, that is, convert a urinal into a work of art, but such a thing probably would not occur to him. Please remember that *Fountain*'s being a work of art does not mean that it is a good one, nor does this qualification insinuate that it is a bad one either. The antics of a particular present-day artist serve to reinforce the point of the Duchamp case and also to emphasize a significance of the practice of naming works of art. Walter de Maria has in the case of one of his works even gone through the motions, no doubt as a burlesque, of using a procedure used by many legal and some nonlegal institutions—the procedure of licensing. His *High Energy Bar* (a stainless-steel bar) is accompanied by a certificate bearing the name of the work and stating that the bar is a work of art only when the certificate is present. In addition to highlighting the status of art by "certifying" it on a document, this example serves to suggest a significance of the act of naming works of art. An object may acquire the status of art without ever being named but giving it a title makes clear to whomever is interested that an object is a work of art. Specific titles function in a variety of ways—as aids to understanding a work or as a convenient way of identifying it, for example—but any title at all (even *Untitled*) is a badge of status.[11]

The third notion involved in the second condition of the definition is candidacy: a member of the artworld confers the status of candidate for appreciation. The definition does not require that a work of art actually be appreciated, even by one person. The fact is that many, perhaps most, works of art go unappreciated. It is important not to build into the definition of the classificatory sense of "work of art" value properties such as actual appreciation: to do so would make it impossible to speak of unappreciated works of art. Building in value properties might even make it awkward to speak of bad works of art. A theory of art must preserve certain central features of the way in which we talk about art, and we do find it necessary sometimes to speak of unappreciated art and of bad art. Also, not every aspect of a work is included in the candidacy for appreciation; for example, the color of the back of a painting is not ordinarily considered to be something which someone might think it appropriate to appreciate. The problem of which aspects of a work of art are to be included within the candidacy for appreciation is a question I shall pursue later . . . in trying to give an analysis of the notion of esthetic object. The definition of "work of art" should not, therefore, be understood as asserting that every aspect of a work is included within the candidacy for appreciation.

The fourth notion involved in the second condition of the definition is appreciation itself. Some may assume that the definition is referring to a special kind of *esthetic* appreciation. I shall argue later . . . that there is no reason to think that there is a special kind of esthetic consciousness, attention, or perception. Similarly, I do not think there is any reason to think that there is a special kind of esthetic appreciation. All that is meant by "appreciation" in the definition is something like "in experiencing the qualities of a thing one finds them worthy or valuable," and this meaning applies quite generally both inside and outside the domain of art. Several persons have felt that my account of the institutional theory of art is incomplete because of what they see as my insufficient analysis of appreciation. They have, I believe, thought that there are different kinds of appreciation and that the appreciation in the appreciation of art is somehow typically different from the appreciation in the appreciation of nonart. But the only sense in which there is a difference between the appreciation of art and the appreciation of nonart is that the appreciations have different *objects*. The institutional structure in which the art object is embedded, not different kinds of appreciation, make the difference between the appreciation of art and the appreciation of nonart.

In a recent article[12] Ted Cohen has raised a question concerning (1) candidacy for appreciation and (2) appreciation as these two were treated in my original attempt to define "art."[13] He claims that in order for it to be possible for candidacy for appreciation to be conferred on something that it must be possible for that thing to be appreciated. Perhaps he is right about this; in any event, I cannot think of any reason to disagree with him on this point. The possibility of appreciation is one constraint on the definition: if something cannot be appreciated, it cannot become art. The question that now arises is: is there anything which it is impossible to appreciate? Cohen claims many things cannot be appreciated; for example, "ordinary thumbtacks, cheap white envelopes, the plastic forks given at some drive-in restaurants."[14] But more importantly, he claims that *Fountain* cannot be appreciated. He says that *Fountain* has a point which can be appreciated, but that it is Duchamp's gesture that has significance (can be appreciated) and not *Fountain* itself. I agree that *Fountain* has the significance Cohen attributes to it, namely, that it was a protest against the art of its day. But why cannot the ordinary qualities of *Fountain* —its gleaming white surface, the depth revealed when it reflects images of surrounding objects, its pleasing oval shape—be appreciated? It has qualities similar to those of works by Brancusi and Moore which many do not balk at saying they appreciate. Similarly, thumbtacks, envelopes, and plastic forks have qualities that can be appreciated if one makes the effort to focus attention on them. One of the values of photography is its ability to focus on and bring out the qualities of quite ordinary objects. And the same sort of thing can be done without the benefit of photography by just looking. In short, it seems unlikely to me that any object would not have some quality which is appreciatable and thus likely that the constraint Cohen suggests may well be vacuous. But even if there are some objects that cannot be appreciated, *Fountain* and the other Dadaist creations are not among them.

I should note that in accepting Cohen's claim I am saying that every work of art must have some minimal *potential* value or worthiness. This fact, however, does not collapse the distinction between the evaluative sense and the classificatory sense of "work of art." The evaluative sense is used when the object it is predicated of is deemed *to be* of substantial, actual value, and that object may be a natural object. I will further note that the appreciatability of a work of art in the classificatory sense is *potential* value which in a given case may never be realized.[15]

The definition I have given contains a reference to the artworld. Consequently, some may have the uncomfortable feeling that my definition is viciously circular. Admittedly, in a sense the definition is circular, but it is not viciously so. If I had said something like "A work of art is an artifact on which a status has been conferred by the artworld" and then said of the artworld only that it confers the status of candidacy for appreciation, then the definition would be viciously circular because the circle would be so small and *uninformative*. I have, however, devoted a considerable amount of space . . . to describing and analyzing the historical, organizational, and functional intricacies of the artworld, and if this account is accurate the reader has received a considerable amount of *information* about the artworld. The circle I have run is not small and it is not uninformative. If, in the end, the artworld cannot be described independently of art—that is, if the description contains references to art historians, art reporters, plays, theaters, and so on—then the definition strictly speaking is circular. It is not, however, viciously so, because the whole account in which the definition is embedded contains a great deal of information about the artworld. One must not focus narrowly on the definition alone: for what is important to see is that art is an institutional concept and this requires seeing the definition in the context of the whole account. I suspect that the "problem" of circularity will arise frequently, perhaps always, when institutional concepts are dealt with.

III

The instances of Dadaist art and similar present-day developments which have served to bring the institutional nature of art to our attention suggest several questions. First, if Duchamp can convert such artifacts as a urinal, a snow shovel, and a hatrack into works of art, why can't natural objects such as driftwood also become works of art in the classificatory sense? Perhaps they can if any one of a number of things is done to them. One way in which this might happen would be for someone to pick up a natural object, take it home, and hang it on the wall. Another way would be to pick up a natural object and enter it in an exhibition. I was assuming earlier, by the way, that the piece of driftwood referred to in Weitz's sentence was in place on a beach and untouched by human hand or at least untouched by any human intention and therefore was art in the evaluative or derivative sense. Natural objects which become works of art in the classificatory sense are artifactualized without the use of tools—artifactuality is conferred on the object rather than worked on it.[16] This means that natural objects which become works of art acquire their artifactuality at the same time that the status of candidate for appreciation is conferred on them, although the act that confers artifactuality is not the same act that confers the status of candidate for appreciation. But perhaps a similar thing ordinarily happens with paintings and poems; they come to exist as artifacts at the same time that they have the status of candidate for appreciation conferred on them. Of course, being an artifact and being a candidate for appreciation are not the same thing—they are two properties which may be acquired at the same time. Many may find the notion of artifactuality being conferred rather than "worked" on an object too strange to accept, and admittedly it is an unusual conception. It may be that a special account will have to be worked out for exhibited driftwood and similar cases.

Another question arising with some frequency in connection with discussions of the concept of art and seeming especially relevant in the context of the institutional theory is "How are we to conceive of paintings done by individuals such as Betsy the chimpanzee from the Baltimore Zoo?" Calling Betsy's products paintings is not meant to prejudge that they are works of art, it is just that some word is needed to refer to them. The question of whether Betsy's paintings are art depends upon what is done with them. For example, a year or two ago the Field Museum of Natural History in Chicago exhibited some chimpanzee and gorilla paintings. We must say that these paintings are not works of art. If, however, they had been exhibited a few miles away at the Chicago Art Institute they would have been works of art—the paintings would have been art if the director of the Art Institute had been willing to go out on a limb for his fellow primates. A great deal depends upon the institutional setting: One institutional setting is congenial to conferring the status of art and the other is not. Please note that although paintings such as Betsy's would remain her paintings even if exhibited at an art museum, they would be the *art* of the person responsible for their being exhibited. Betsy would not (I assume) be able to conceive of herself in such a way as to be a member of the artworld and, hence, would not be able to confer the relevant status. Art is a concept which necessarily involves human intentionality. These last remarks are not intended to denigrate the value (including beauty) of the paintings of chimpanzees shown at natural history museums or the creations of bower birds, but as remarks about what falls under a particular concept.

Danto, in "Art Works and Real Things," discusses defeating conditions of the ascriptivity of art.[17] He considers fake paintings—that is, copies of original paintings which are attributed to the creators of the original paintings. He argues that a painting's being a fake prevents it from being a work of art, maintaining that originality is an analytical requirement of being a work of art. That a work is derivative or imitative does not, however, he thinks, prevent it from being a work of art. I think Danto is right about fake paintings, and I can express this in terms of my own account by saying that originality in paintings is an antecedent requirement for the conferring of the candidacy for appreciation. Similar sorts of things would have to be said for similar cases in the arts other than painting. One consequence of this requirement is that there are many works of nonart which people take to be works of art—namely, those fake paintings which are not known to be fakes. When fakes are discovered to be fakes, they do not lose that status of art because they never had the status in the first place, despite what almost everyone had thought. There is some analogy here with patent law. Once an invention has been patented, one exactly like it cannot be patented—the patent for just that invention has been "used up." In the case of patenting, of course, whether the second device is a copy or independently derived is unimportant, but the copying aspect is crucial in the artistic case. The Van Meegeren painting that was not a copy of an actual Vanmeer but a painting done in the manner of Vermeer with a forged signature is a somewhat more complicated case. The painting with the forged signature is not a work of art, but if Van Meegeren had signed his own name the painting would have been.

Strictly speaking, since originality is an analytic requirement for a painting to be a work of art, an originality clause should be incorporated into my definition of "work of art." But since I have not given any analysis of the originality requirement with respect to works other than paintings, I am not in a position to supplement the definition in this way. All I can say at this time is what I said just above—namely, that originality in paintings is an antecedent requirement for the conferring of the candidacy for appreciation and that considerations of a similar sort probably apply in the other arts.

Weitz charges that the defining of "art" or its subconcepts forecloses on creativity. Some of the traditional definitions of "art" *may* have and some of the traditional definitions of its subconcepts probably *did* foreclose on creativity, but this danger is now past. At one time a playwright, for example, may have conceived of and wished to write a play with tragic features but lacking a defining characteristic as specified by, say, Aristotle's definition of "tragedy." Faced with this dilemma, the playwright might have been intimidated into abandoning his project. With the present-day disregard for established genres, however, and the clamor for novelty in art, this obstacle to creativity no longer exists. Today, if a new and unusual work is created and it is similar to some members of an established type of art, it will usually be accommodated within that type, or if the new work is very unlike any existing works then a new subconcept will probably be created. Artists today are not easily intimidated, and they regard art genres as loose guidelines rather than rigid specifications. Even if a philosopher's remarks were to have an effect on what artists do today, the institutional conception of art would certainly not foreclose on creativity. The requirement of artifactuality cannot prevent creativity, since artifactuality is a necessary condition of creativity. There cannot be an instance of creativity without an artifact of some kind being produced. The second requirement involving the conferring of status could not inhibit creativity; in fact, it encourages it. Since under the definition anything whatever may become art, the definition imposes no restraints on creativity.

The institutional theory of art may sound like saying, "A work of art is an object of which someone has said, 'I christen this object a work of art.'" And it is rather like that, although this does not mean that the conferring of the status of art is a simple matter. Just as the christening of a child has as its background the history and structure of the church, conferring the status of art has as its background the Byzantine complexity of the artworld. Some may find it strange that in the nonart cases discussed, there are ways in which the conferring can go wrong, while that does not appear to be true in art. For example, an indictment might be improperly drawn up and the person charged would not actually be indicted, but nothing parallel seems possible in the case of art. This fact just reflects the differences between the artworld and legal institutions: the legal system deals with matters of grave personal consequences and its procedures must reflect this; the artworld deals with important matters also but they are of a different sort entirely. The artworld does not require rigid procedures; it admits and even encourages frivolity and caprice without losing its serious purpose. Please note that not all legal procedures are as rigid as court procedures and that mistakes made in conferring certain kinds of legal status are not fatal to that status. A minister may make mistakes in reading the marriage ceremony, but the couple that stands before him will still acquire the status of being married. If, however, a mistake cannot be made *in* conferring the status of art, a mistake can be made *by* conferring it. In conferring the status of art on an object one assumes a certain kind of responsibility for the object in its new status—presenting a candidate for appreciation always allows the possibility that no one will appreciate it and that the person who did the conferring will thereby lose face. One *can* make a work of art out of a sow's ear, but that does not necessarily make it a silk purse.

NOTES

1. *Journal of Aesthetics and Art Criticism*, September 1956, pp. 27–35. See also Paul Ziff's "The Task of Defining a Work of Art," *Philosophical Review*, January 1953, pp. 58–78; and W. E. Kennick's "Does Traditional Aesthetics Rest on a Mistake?" *Mind*, July 1958, pp. 317–334.
2. "Wittgenstein's Aesthetics," in *Language and Aesthetics*, Benjamin R. Tilghman, ed. (Lawrence, Kans., 1973), p. 14. This paper was read at a symposium at Kansas State University in April 1970. Monroe Beardsley has pointed out to me that the relationship between "game" and "major league baseball" is one of class and member rather than of genus and species.
3. "Family Resemblances and Generalizations Concerning the Arts," *American Philosophical Quarterly*, July 1965, pp. 219–228; reprinted in *Problems in Aesthetics*, Morris Weitz, ed., 2d ed. (London, 1970), pp. 181–197.
4. Ibid., p. 185 in the Weitz anthology.
5. "'Art' and Artifactuality," *Southwestern Journal of Philosophy*, Fall 1970, pp. 105–108.
6. "Does Traditional Aesthetics Rest on a Mistake?" p. 330.
7. *Journal of Philosophy*, October 15, 1964, pp. 571–584.
8. Ibid., p. 580.
9. Danto does not develop an institutional account of art in his article nor in a subsequent related article entitled "Art Works and Real Things," *Theoria*, Parts 1–3, 1973, pp. 1–17. In both articles Danto's primary concern is to discuss what he calls the Imitation Theory and the Real Theory of Art. Many of the things he says in these two articles are consistent with and can be incorporated into an institutional account, and his brief remarks in the later article about the ascriptivity of art are similar to the institutional theory. The institutional theory is one possible version of the ascriptivity theory.
10. This remark is not intended as a definition of the term "artworld"; I am merely indicating what the expression is used to *refer* to. "Artworld" is nowhere defined in this [article], although the referent of the expression is described in some detail.
11. Recently in an article entitled "The Republic of Art" in *British Journal of Aesthetics*, April 1969, pp. 145–56, T. J. Diffey has talked about the status of art being conferred. He, however, is attempting to give an account of something like an evaluative sense of "work of art" rather than the classificatory sense, and consequently the scope of his theory is much narrower than mine.
12. "The Possibility of Art: Remarks on a Proposal by Dickie," *Philosophical Review*, January 1973, pp. 69–82.
13. "Defining Art," *American Philosophical Quarterly*, July 1969, pp. 253–256.
14. "The Possibility of Art," p. 78.
15. I realized that I must make the two points noted in this paragraph as the result of a conversation with Mark Venezia. I wish to thank him for the stimulation of his remarks.
16. I now believe that it was a mistake to claim that artifactuality can be conferred. Artifactuality is not the kind of thing which can be conferred; it must result from work of some sort. A piece of driftwood which has become art might, for example, have been picked up, transported, and hung on a wall. It is in virtue of these things being done to it that the driftwood has become an artifact, not as my original statements suggest, that the driftwood became an artifact because these actions conferred artifactuality. Similarly, a piece of driftwood might be picked up and used as a weapon and, thereby, become an artifact.
17. Pages 12–14.

An Institutional Theory of Art

William L. Blizek

Professor George Dickie has presented recently the bare skeleton of an institutional theory of art.[2] His aim is to show that works of art can be defined in terms of necessary and sufficient conditions without having those conditions foreclose on creativity in the arts.[3] To accomplish this aim Dickie offers the following definition: 'A work of art in the classificatory sense is (1) an artifact (2) upon which some person or persons acting on behalf of a certain social institution (the artworld) has conferred the status of candidate for appreciation'.[4] The goal of Dickie's theory is certainly an admirable one—expanding the scope of art without making it subjective—yet, there are several aspects of the theory that raise important questions. Since Dickie has offered only the skeleton of a theory it would be unfair to attack his account, but an examination of those aspects of the theory which appear to be problematic will facilitate a preliminary evaluation and may contribute to the further development of the theory. If Dickie is successful in achieving his goal, or if his theory can be modified so as to accomplish that objective, he will have made a significant contribution to art and the theory of art.

I

One problematic aspect of Dickie's theory is the nature of the artworld. Who is to count as a representative of the artworld; who is eligible to confer the status of candidate for appreciation? Can anyone claim membership in the artworld or is membership limited by the rules of the institution? Dickie contends that 'every person who sees himself as a member of the artworld is an 'officer' of it and is thereby capable of conferring status in its name'.[5] But this position seems to involve several difficulties. (a) It will be very difficult to determine which objects in the world are works of art if *anyone* who 'sees himself as a member of the artworld' can transform *any* object into a work of art simply by treating it as a candidate for appreciation. We simply would not know whether most of the objects we encounter had been so treated. It certainly would be more difficult to determine what is art in this case than if the membership of the artworld were limited to an easily identifiable group of persons. Works of art would become a matter of private rather than public concern and the role of art in the culture would certainly be diminished. (b) Many objects which are not generally considered to be works of art might be included in the realm of art simply because someone had at one time or another conferred upon them the requisite status. When my wife asks me whether I like her new dress, or when my neighbour paints his house, or when I present myself to the public either bearded or clean shaven, something is being offered as a candidate for appreciation. Yet we do not usually see new dresses or painted houses or people as works of art.[6] Dickie might argue that when someone presents something as a candidate for appreciation they must see themselves as acting on behalf of the artworld before what is presented becomes a work of art. But my wife, my neighbour and I may see ourselves

---

From *The British Journal of Aesthetics*, 14 (1974). Reprinted by permission of Oxford University Press.

as 'designers' and 'design as art'. In this case we see ourselves as acting on behalf of the artworld and the dress, the house and my face would become works of art. (c) If membership in the artworld is extended to everyone who 'sees himself as a member', the membership of the artworld may approximate the membership of society. In this case there is no need to introduce a special institution (the artworld); rather art can be determined by the members of society at large.[7] While Dickie contends that the artworld 'carries on its business at the level of customary practice' he also contends that such practice 'defines a social institution'.[8] When membership in the artworld is open to anyone who sees himself as a member the customary practice is likely to be diffuse and the institution it defines ambiguous.

Moving in the other direction, towards limited membership in the artworld, also raises difficulties. Imagine, for example, that membership in the artworld is limited to five hundred of the world's leading artists, fifty of the world's wealthiest collectors or patrons, and the directors of one hundred of the most famous museums, galleries and concert halls.[9] In this case the realm of art may be severely limited by the tastes and interests of this select group, the 'official' artworld. Such limitations are contrary to the goal of Dickie's theory, which is to provide greater freedom and creativity in art. Yet the above model would appear to be closer to what Arthur Danto suggests when he claims that 'to see something as art requires something the eye cannot decry—an atmosphere of artistic theory, a knowledge of the history of art: an artworld'.[10] Danto's artworld would be limited by 'an atmosphere of artistic theory' and 'a knowledge of history of art', and such limitations would strengthen the institutional character of the artworld. Dickie wants a clearly defined institution (in which case art is recognizable and public) and an open door for creativity. It appears, however, that moving towards one aspect of his theory means moving away from the other. If a compromise is effected his theory will not have the full advantages of either pole, and those are the advantages which gives the theory its initial attractiveness.[11]

Another question regarding the concept of an artworld arises in virtue of the various art forms: that is, is there a music artworld, a visual artworld, a theatrical artworld, and so on? It does appear that there are such artworlds, each characterized by its own professional association, official publications and pattern of activities.[12] If we conceive of the artworld as an informal social institution that is sociologically determinable and publicly recognizable, then Dickie may have developed several theories of art—an institutional theory of music, an institutional theory of drama, an institutional theory of literature, and so on. But what is the relation of one artworld to another? Can there be a conflict between the various artworlds? Which artworld is to have priority? What power, for example, does the literary artworld have over the theatrical artworld? If a clearly defined institution is required, then it would be possible to have several artworlds which might conflict. If a general artworld is acceptable, however, the nature of that artworld and subsequently what is art may be so amorphous as to lose its significance.

II

The concept of conferring the status of candidate for appreciation is a second problematic aspect of Dickie's theory.[13] The problem centres around the possibility of retracting conferred status. In the customary practices of the artworld it appears that the retraction of status is possible. The innovative young artist submits an unusual piece of sculpture and it is rejected by the selection committee of the museum on the grounds that it is not really art. This seems to be a commonplace occurrence in the artworld—young artists are always being rejected. It is sometimes the case that works are rejected because they are of what is judged to be inferior quality; but they are also rejected, especially in the case of something new, because they are not works of art. If the artworld can retract the status conferred by a single individual, then it can limit severely the range of art and foreclose on the conditions for creativity in the arts.

Dickie, I suspect, would be anxious to deny the power to retract the status conferred by a single individual. It is this very problem—the power of an artworld 'elite' or 'establishment'—that encourages Dickie to argue that 'the status in question may be acquired by *a single person's treating an artifact as a candidate for appreciation*'.[14] As well, Dickie contends that no *mistake* can be made in conferring status and this suggests that status conferred is status secured.[15] But these arguments seem contrary to the practices of the artworld and they suggest an artworld that is so vague that its impact on any culture would be unimportant.

Another question about retracting conferred status concerns the possibility of a revolution in the artworld. Is it possible that all of the things we now take to be works of art could be expelled from the realm of art and only broken bottles and used tires included? Or, for example, could we expel all of Shakespeare's writings? What seems clear from these examples is that the kind of interest shown in what are generally considered works of art would not subside simply because we no longer applied the term 'art' to that class of objects. We would still read Shakespeare, even if it could be demonstrated that his writings did not belong to the realm of art. Our continued interest in what is no longer art suggests that there are guidelines for deciding what is art and what is not art that are not themselves subject to arbitrary decisions in the artworld. Such guidelines need to be described in a complete theory of art.

A final question about conferring status concerns the nature of artistic activity. Dickie contends that the paintings of monkeys are works of art when they are displayed in an art museum (because someone representing the artworld—the curator of the museum—has conferred upon them the status of candidate for appreciation), but are not art when displayed by the zoo keeper.[16] Similarly when Duchamp enters a wine rack in a show it is a work of art. In the latter case it is Duchamp who is the artist—because he was creative enough to imagine this ready-made as a candidate for appreciation. In the former case, then, the curator of the museum would be the artist. But there is certainly something odd about saying that the curator of the museum is an artist. The problem is more serious if membership in the artworld is limited. Suppose a struggling young painter (not yet a member of the artworld) submitted one of his paintings to the curator of the museum. If accepted, this painting would be the work of the curator and not the painter. For Dickie, artistic activity is equivalent to conferring status and this seems to eliminate much from the realm of artistic activity that would ordinarily be included in that realm. We have, then, a form of activity which is no longer considered artistic, but one again in which we are no less interested for that.

III

The concept of appreciation is another important but problematic element of Dickie's theory. By 'appreciation' Dickie means 'something like "in experiencing the qualities of a thing one finds them worthy or valuable".'[17] But there is nothing here to limit value or worth to aesthetic value or aesthetic worth. In fact Dickie admits that 'this meaning applies quite generally both inside and outside the domain of art'.[18] Thus every can of beans on the supermarket shelf is a candidate for appreciation—and so is my wife's new dress, my neighbour's house and every individual who considers his own appearance. Suppose, for example, that an accepted art critic claims that the diary of artist X is worthy or valuable because it helps us understand the symbolism of X's painting. Here is a case in which a member of the artworld, acting on behalf of the artworld, confers the status of candidate for appreciation upon the diary of X.[19] Does the diary become a work of art? Is there not a difference between saying that the diary is valuable and is therefore art, and saying that the diary is valuable because it provides certain information? I do not see that there is anything in Dickie's theory by which to distinguish between appreciation in the case of art and appreciation in general.[20] If there is not, then the realm of art will include my wife's dress, the can of beans on the supermarket shelf, the artist's diary, and so on. Dickie might contend that appreciation in art is not different from appreciation in general, as the quotation above suggests, but then what distinguishes the painting which is art from the diary which is not is that the status (candidate for appreciation) is conferred by someone 'acting on behalf of the artworld'. This solution, however, raises several difficulties. (a) 'Acting on behalf of the artworld' is dependent to some extent upon the problems mentioned above; namely, who is a member of the artworld? (b) The case of the critic and the diary suggests that someone can act on behalf of the artworld and yet generate unusual works of art. It is not just that unusual objects become works of art, given Dickie's theory—the diary might well be an important piece of literature or the urinal might be a kind of sculpture, and that is the advantage of Dickie's theory—but it is the reason for their becoming art that is perplexing—e.g. because the diary gives insight into X's paintings. (c) If one rejects the contention that the critic above is acting on behalf of the artworld, an artworld which defines 'acting on behalf of' is one that is itself more narrowly defined than one in which anyone can be a member who sees himself as a member. The more narrowly the artworld is defined, the more likely it is that the range of art will be limited. I do not know how Dickie would respond to this criticism—that the concept of appreciation does not seem to place any limits on art—but Dickie must account for this problem in the fully developed theory.

IV

Finally, one purpose of the theory is to show that artifactuality is a necessary condition of art. Dickie argues that artifactuality is a necessary condition for art because it is a necessary condition for creativity and creativity is the key to expanding the scope and variety of art. Weitz argues that to define art by specifying necessary conditions 'is ludicrous since it forecloses on the very conditions of creativity in the arts'.[21] Dickie responds by asking: 'How could there be an instance of creativity without an artifact of some kind being produced?'[22] He concludes, of course, that there can be no creativity without artifactuality and he accepts artifactuality because creativity is so important to the enrichment of art.[23] But Dickie is willing to allow natural objects to become works of art. To make this possible he contends that artifactuality can be *conferred upon* natural objects rather than *worked on* them.[24] Natural objects can become artifactualized without the use of tools; e.g. when someone retrieves a piece of driftwood and uses it as a centrepiece. The conferrability of artifactuality serves to enlarge the scope of art by admitting found objects.

Two questions arise concerning Dickie's account of artifactuality as a necessary condition for art. First, is the creativity of someone who writes a novel or performs a concerto equivalent to the creativity of someone who notices certain qualities of a piece of driftwood? If there are two concepts of creativity (one related to productivity, the other to recognition) then artifactualizing natural objects is either unnecessary or impossible. That is, if the recognition of certain qualities of natural objects is itself a creative act, then artifactuality is not a necessary condition for creativity; and if creativity implies production, then it cannot be applied to natural objects. I take it that Dickie means by 'creativity' the creativity of production because he asks: 'How could there be an instance of creativity without an artifact of some kind being produced?'[25]

The second question is whether the concept of artifactuality which is applicable in the case of a man-made object is equivalent to the concept which is applicable to a 'man-handled' or 'man-noticed' object? If there are two concepts of artifactuality, Dickie may be unable to respond to Weitz as he seeks to do.[26] It is no rebuttal to introduce a new concept of artifactuality and then claim that a work of art is an artifact in this new sense when Weitz is utilizing some other sense of artifactuality. It appears, however, that there are two senses of artifactuality. When someone takes a piece of driftwood home he artifactualizes it and it becomes art; but when he simply notices the driftwood he does not artifactualize it and it does not become art. But there is a difference between simply noticing the piece of driftwood and calling the attention of others to it even if it remains untouched by human hand.

One sense of artifactuality, then, applies to production, but another applies to the process of publicizing an object. The second sense of artifactuality is something like 'making something an object of public attention'.[27] Although Dickie does not distinguish two senses of artifactuality and his own statements suggest that artifactuality applies to production, the problem with which he deals suggests the sense of artifactuality that applies to public objects and I believe this second sense of artifactuality may contribute to his theory. Dickie may not be able to respond adequately to Weitz (if Weitz means by 'artifact' man-made object), but he may suggest a solution to some of the problems of his theory.

V

Professor Dickie's institutional theory of art is a tantalizing one. It holds out the prospect of defining art in terms of necessary and sufficient conditions and, at the same time, expanding the scope of art. Now Dickie does offer two conditions which are necessary and sufficient for something's being a work of art—artifactuality and the status of candidate for appreciation—and if these conditions are accepted, anything may become a work of art. There are, however, two significant difficulties which need to be dealt with, given Dickie's rudimentary account of the theory. First, Dickie offers no justification for the necessity of artifactuality as a condition for art. He claims that upon reflection we 'realize' that a work of art is an artifact and he contends that artifactuality is a prerequisite for creativity. Both of these claims require supporting argument. Second, the social property of art (the status of candidate for appreciation) does not seem to place any limits on art. While the scope of art is expanded, it may be expanded beyond recognition and beyond significance.

To overcome these difficulties Dickie might show that artifactuality serves as the limiting condition.[28] If an artifact is an object of public attention, this would serve as a social condition governing the conferment of status. Dickie suggests that something's hanging in a museum is good evidence for its having had the requisite status conferred upon it.[29] So hanging might also be good evidence for its being an artifact, *i.e.* a public object. We can artifactualize natural objects by displaying them, as when we make the driftwood a centrepiece. But we can also display natural objects by making paths to them and informing people of their whereabouts, *e.g.* the Old Faithful geyser of Yellowstone National Park. What I am suggesting is that artifactuality be seen as a social property as well as status of candidate for appreciation. The result will be that art will remain in the public domain. By accepting artifactuality as a limiting condition of art we are given a reason for including artifactuality and the scope of art, while remaining open, will also be recognizable. My suggestion is contrary to Dickie's contention that 'many works of art are never seen by anyone but the persons who create them, but they are still works of art', but I believe that the price to be paid for that degree of flexibility is excessive.[30] There does remain, however, the case of the zoo keeper who sees himself as a member of the artworld. The elephant is a work of art, then, because it has been artifactualized and because it is offered as a candidate for appreciation by someone representing the artworld. To avoid this case, Dickie must define more precisely 'acting on behalf of' or 'appreciation', and attend to the hazards which accompany such definitions.

NOTES

1. This paper was originally presented to the 8th National Conference of the British Society of Aesthetics, London, September 22, 1973. I am indebted to the members of the British Society for their comments and criticism, and to Professors Jerry Cederblom, Michael Gillespie, and David Paulsen for their helpful suggestions. The writing of this paper was supported by a grant from the University Senate of the University of Nebraska at Omaha.
2. Professor Dickie first presented his theory in an article, 'Defining art', *American Philosophical Quarterly*, vol. 6, no. 3 (July 1969), pp. 253–6. He presents a slightly modified version of the theory in his recently published book, *Aesthetics: An Introduction* (1971), Chapter XI.
3. So 'defining Art' is in response to those who claim that art cannot be defined in terms of necessary and sufficient conditions. For examples see: William Kennick, 'Does Traditional Aesthetics Rest on a Mistake?', *Mind*, vol. 67 (1958), pp. 317–34; Morris Weitz, 'The Role of Theory in Aesthetics', *The Journal of Aesthetics and Art Criticism*, vol. 15, no. 1 (September 1956), pp. 27–35; and Paul Ziff, 'The Task of Defining a Work of Art', *The Philosophical Review*, vol. LXII, no. 1 (January 1953), pp. 58–78.
4. Dickie, *Aesthetics: An Introduction*, p. 101.
5. *Ibid.*, p. 104.
6. The strength of arguments (a) and (b) depends in part upon the concept of appreciation. See my discussion of appreciation later in this paper.
7. There is some hint that this may have been Dickie's original intention. In 'Defining Art' Dickie defines art as '(1) an artifact (2) upon which some *society or some sub-group of a society* has conferred the status of candidate for appreciation' (p. 254). For the italicized words in the above definition Dickie has substituted 'person or persons acting on behalf of a certain social institution (the artworld)' in *Aesthetics: An Introduction*.
8. *Aesthetics: An Introduction*, pp. 103–4.
9. This hypothetical case is an extrapolation of the sociological account of Chicago's Artworld presented by Edward M. Levine, 'Chicago's Art World', *Urban Life and Culture*, vol. 1, no. 3 (October 1972), pp. 292–322.
10. Arthur Danto, 'The Artworld', *The Journal of Philosophy*, vol. LXI, no. 19 (October 15, 1964), pp. 571–84.
11. For a discussion of other problems of membership in the artworld see Ted Cohen, 'The Possibility of Art: Remarks on a Proposal by Dickie', *The Philosophical Review*, vol. LXXXII, no. 1 (January 1973), pp. 69–82.
12. For example, The American Educational Theater Association, The American Ceramic Society, The American Musicological Society, and *Dance Perspectives, Art Journal, The Musical Quarterly, Theater Quarterly*.
13. For an account of conferring status in terms of illocutions and perlocutions see Ted Cohen's 'The Possibility of Art: Remarks on a Proposal by Dickie'.
14. *Aesthetics: An Introduction*, p. 103.
15. *Ibid.*, p. 108. Dickie does suggest that a mistake can be made *by* conferring status, that is by conferring the status of candidate for appreciation on an object that no one actually does appreciate.
16. *Ibid.*, p. 106.
17. *Ibid.*, p. 105.
18. *Ibid.*, p. 105.
19. If something is actually appreciated I take it that it is also a candidate for appreciation. I do not believe that something can be appreciated but not be a candidate for appreciation.
20. Cohen asks what qualifies a thing to receive the requisite status. This question puts its finger on the problem, but suggests that the answer will be in terms of natural properties. See Cohen, p. 72.
21. Weitz, p. 32.
22. *Aesthetics: An Introduction*, p. 107.
23. Weitz also argues against artifactuality as a necessary condition for art on the basis of the 'actual employment of the concept of art' (p. 30). We sometimes refer to natural objects as works of art; therefore some non-artifacts (natural objects) are works of art and artifactuality cannot be a necessary condition of art. Dickie argues in reply that when we refer to natural objects as works of art we do not mean to classify those objects, but rather to express our approval of them. Weitz has confused, he contends, the evaluative and classificatory senses of art.
24. *Aesthetics: An Introduction*, p. 106.
25. *Aesthetics: An Introduction*, p. 107. He also

suggests that the driftwood noticed but 'untouched by human hand', is not a work of art and not an artifact (pp. 105–6).
26. Dickie's argument for artifactuality is: 'And surely when we do so reflect, we realize that *part* of what is meant when we think of or assert of something (not in praise) that it is a work of art is that it is an artifact' (*ibid.*, p. 100). This, it seems, is a very weak argument for artifactuality.
27. The number of people needed to comprise a public is questionable.
28. This was suggested by Professor David Paulsen.
29. *Aesthetics: An Introduction*, p. 102.
30. *Ibid.*, p. 103.

What Is a Work of Art?

Harold Osborne

The question What is a work of art? is not one which we are often brought up against in daily life or in our ordinary commerce with art. On rare occasions—when, for example, we come upon a strange and novel denizen such as a lump of lard in an art exhibition or when we are concerned with the artifacts of primitive peoples who lack our concept of fine art—we may be called upon to face it and to examine our criteria for deciding whether something is or is not a work of art. But except on such occasions we are ordinarily content to accept as works of art the objects to which we are exposed in museums and galleries and artists' studios and we ask ourselves rather how good they are of their kind.

But among aestheticians the question has become a basic one around which controversy now flares and flickers. And in this context it has acquired two different meanings—or perhaps it would be better to say that the same form of words poses two alternative questions envisaging answers belonging to two different realms discourse. The question may be: What things in the world around us are correctly designated works of art? Or the words may be intended to ask: What is meant by calling anything at all a work of art? The former is a factual question relating to the correct use of language. The latter is a philosophical question. It is also the sort of question which an ordinary man would naturally suppose to be intended if he were asked out of the blue: 'What is a work of art?' He would be inclined to understand that he was being asked for a definition or a general account of what is meant by 'work of art' and the criteria applied for determining whether any particular thing is or is not a work of art. This he would naturally understand to be asked, though he would be unlikely to get very far towards finding an answer.

A great deal of futile discussion in aesthetics has arisen simply out of confusion between these two questions and the sort of answers they require. It is my hope that this paper may do something towards clearing the air of the haze of dust that has been so generated.

Though they exist on different logical planes, the two questions are linked. It seems only common sense to recognize that we cannot sensibly decide whether or not anything

From *The British Journal of Aesthetics*, 21 (1981). Reprinted by permission of Oxford University Press.

is a work of art unless we know what the term 'work of art' means. We must know the answer to the philosophical question before we can cope with the practical question, for such knowledge is presupposed in every practical decision we make. But it is equally true that philosophers cannot discover what the term 'work of art' means by the pure light of reason, by looking within themselves and exercising intuition. They can only discover what it means by examining the way in which the term is used, the criteria that are in fact applied in determining whether anything is a work of art, the sort of things which are expertly said about works of art, and so on. As often in life, we know adequately for practical purposes what we mean by calling anything a work of art until we are compelled to ask ourselves what we mean. Then we don't know. We possess practical skills and accumulated conventions which involve inarticulate knowledge not readily accessible to us. It is one of the jobs of philosophy to make such inarticulate knowledge articulate.

Let us now discuss the two questions involved.

The Institutional theories of art which have recently become popular give prominence to the rather trivial fact that the answer to the former of these questions is a matter of social convention. This is necessarily so because, however the term is ultimately unravelled, 'work of art' expresses a concept which operates within a social milieu and with social implications. Whatever else it may be a work of art is an artifact, i.e., a man-made device, which is differentiated from other things that men make by the function it serves or is intended or thought to serve among men in a social environment. Therefore the decision which artifacts are properly to be called works of art and which are not must depend on men's reactions to them. To give an analogy: the biological differences between spiders and fishes do not depend on social conventions. They are the same whatever language we use. If men generally began to eat spiders with relish and to shudder at the proximity of fishes, the biological differences between them would be unaffected. But if we are talking about *food*, a social concept, such change of eating habits would be decisive. The Institutional theories rather tritely explain that what things are and what things are not correctly denominated works of art depends on men's aesthetic eating habits —on which artifacts men generally consume and enjoy in an aesthetic way. The rank and file in any society, we are told, are guided in their aesthetic eating habits by a nucleus of experts whose main professional interest is connected with the arts and their consumption—critics, reviewers, museum men, gallery owners and dealers, collectors, connoisseurs, patrons, and so on. These constitute the core of what Dr. Diffey, reviving an old metaphor of a Republic or Commonwealth of Letters, designated the Republic of Art[1] and Arthur Danto in America more pedestrianly called the artworld.[2] Since habits and capacities for aesthetic appreciation are less dominant among men in sophisticated societies than are eating habits, the nucleus of experts exercises a correspondingly more important influence in the aesthetic field—though we still have gourmets and dietitians who wield some authority in eating matters.

Professor George Dickie's much quoted saying that an art work is anything called a work of art by the artworld[3] is a correct generalization indicating the sort of answer required by the factual question. But it is not an answer to a philosophical question. It makes no suggestion about what is *meant* by members of the artworld when they call anything a work of art. To investigate what things are and have been classified as works of art and how the nucleus of experts functions in any society is an undertaking situated within the field of social anthropology. It is not a philosophical undertaking. Whether this investigation comes within the scope of Aesthetics depends on the extension one chooses to give to the term 'Aesthetics': the decision is arbitrary and remains unimportant so long as the nature and limitations of the investigation itself are understood. If Aesthetics is regarded as a branch of Philosophy, then this sort of investigation cannot lie within its scope; for it is not philosophical. But it is certainly an important and even a necessary propaedeutic providing the factual material essential for reaching any fruitful conclusions in Philosophical Aesthetics. For it is a primary task of philosophy to make articulate the tacit concepts latent in our linguistic habits and the other conventions by which we live, to bring to the surface the submerged rationality of our social lives. So Philosophical Aesthetics must seek, not to invent a new concept of art *ab ovo*, but to articulate and to display in all its complexity the inarticulate concept of art implicit in the behaviour and conventions of the art world which the Institutional theories investigate on a factual level. In order to tackle the job it must have before it the complex social organization whose conceptual structure it hopes to elucidate.

The motive for doing this is primarily an intellectual curiosity: we like to understand ourselves and our behaviour. And philosophy is, after all, powered by a self-rewarding intellectual interest. But, as has been seen, the undertaking has practical implications also and offers incidental rewards in the practical sphere.

There are, however, philosophers who have denied that the philosophical question about the meaning of art is a legitimate one or that an answer to it is feasible. About the middle of this century it became popular for a time in some circles of English-language philosophy to decry generalizations about the nature of art, stigmatizing attempts to find a philosophical definition as false 'essentialism'. On several grounds the search for a general characteristic or set of characteristics serving to define the nature of art was held to be mistaken.

Sometimes this was argued on the ground that the several art forms are so different and there is so little conformity among the critical standards applied within the various genres of art, that a central conceptual core is unthinkable. Paul Ziff, for example, concluded that 'neither a poem, nor a novel, nor a musical composition can be said to be a work of art in the same sense of the phrase in which a painting or a statue or a vase can be said to be a work of art'.[4] The grounds for his conclusion are not new. Indeed Kant's doctrine of the 'singularity' of aesthetic judgement asserted that even within any one art form we cannot generalize from particular judgements to reach a set of characteristics which could serve as a rule guaranteeing that any artifact manifesting these characteristics is a work of art or aesthetically admirable. There are no general rules for making or judging works of art. But this goes no way at all towards proving that there is no definable concept of a work of art. Indeed the assertion itself might be held to constitute one defining characteristic inherent to all works of art.

In an influential article W. E. Kennick said: 'We are able to separate those objects which are works of art from those which are not because we know English; that is, we know how correctly to use the word "art" and to apply the phrase "work of art". . . . If anyone is able to use the word "art" or the phrase "work of art" correctly, in all sorts of contexts and on the right sort of occasions, he knows "what art is", and no formula in the world can make him wiser'.[5] But what does it mean to know how to use a language correctly? We learn a language within a social milieu by acquiring skills in its use and manipulation. When we learn a language we do not try to master the complete denotation of words ostensively: we do not have to have every fish in the world pointed out to us by language-experts before we can use the word 'fish' correctly. We acquire certain implicit principles of application. The principles may be more or less clear, more or less coherent, more or less complete. But it is in virtue of these principles of application and because language is on the whole used rationally and consistently that we are able up to a point to apply words correctly to things we have not seen before. It is because we have acquired such general principles of application that we are able, up to a point, to apply the words 'work of art' correctly to objects in Kennick's hypothetical warehouse which we have not come across before. In acquiring this skill we are acquiring rudimentary knowledge of an inarticulate concept.[6] On the other hand we do not have to have a definition of 'art' before our minds whenever we are called on to decide whether this or that artifact is a work of art, and if so, how good it is. We exercise discriminatory and appreciative skills which we have cultivated and refined on the basis of innate capacities for sensitivity in the context of socially approved conventions and habits. Underlying these skills and social conventions, including linguistic conventions, there is an inarticulate concept of what a work of art is, and it is this concept which guides and controls our aesthetic behaviour. The presence of such a concept is guaranteed by the fact that we are to some extent rational creatures, that we display a measure of consistency in our attitudes and behaviour. Without it the guidance of the art world would be arbitrary and chaotic. It is this latent concept which is the object of philosophical search.

Sometimes the argument against the possibility of there being necessary and sufficient conditions defining the nature of a work of art has been based on 'the very expansive, adventurous character of art, its ever-present changes and novel creations', which, it is said, 'makes it logically impossible to ensure any set of defining properties'.[7] This argument confuses together a number of different things, most of them important. First every successful work of art, as we now think, is creative and therefore introduces an element of novelty. But far from being a barrier to definition, this itself may be regarded as part of the modern concept of a work of art, one of its defining characteristics. Secondly, new art forms have come into being in the course of history: photography and cinema are examples in fairly recent times. New materials such as plexiglass and neon lighting offer new possibilities for aesthetic creation. Therefore the concept of art must be 'open', allowing for change and development. But an open concept is not necessarily undefinable.

The notion of change involves the existence of something which continues through change. Unless we know what this changing thing is so that we can recognize it amid change and discriminate it from other things, we cannot know that it changes. Indeed the assertion that it changes would have no sense. A concept that is 'open' in the sense that it is susceptible of change and development can, indeed must, be capable of definition. Modern science is very different from the science of ancient Greece or Egypt or India; there is every reason to suppose that the science of today and today's conception of science will develop further in the future. But we do not argue for that reason that science is undefinable. We know, and up to a point we can say, what we are talking about when we speak of science.[8] And so it is with art.

Yet it is important to recognize that both our socially conditioned habits of appreciation and our concepts of art have indeed changed radically in the course of history. This gives some insight into the complexity of our contemporary attitudes and guards against the too easy assumption that they are in any way final or sacrosanct.

It is too easy to assume wrongly that other peoples share our aesthetic habits. We cherish and admire the art and literature of ancient Greece and it comes as a surprise to many people to hear that on the basis of their own records the Greeks themselves, as Frank P. Chambers justly says, 'at the height of their greatest creative period were all unconscious of the kind of aesthetic values which we ourselves accept and understand'. He adds: 'Conscious aesthetic values would seem to be as wanting in the so-called Dark Ages or Middle Ages of Western Europe as at the height of the Greek era'.[9] Until the advent of the vogue for the picturesque wild and mountain scenery was not aesthetically admired. Today Indian music makes use of complicated rhythmical structures to which unversed European musicians are imperceptive. Examples could be multiplied.

Investigation of changes in men's concepts of art and appreciation belongs to the History of Ideas. An excellent example of this may be seen in Wladyslaw Tatarkiewicz's article

'What is Art? The Problem of Definition Today'[10] and of course in his monumental three-volume *Historia Estetyki*, which ranges much more widely than histories of philosophical aesthetics such as *A History of Aesthetics* (1956) by Katherine Everett Gilbert and Helmut Kuhn or Monroe C. Beardsley's *Aesthetics from Classical Greece to the Present* (1966).

Although the ancient Greeks produced works of art which we regard as aesthetically fine, their concepts of the nature of art were, so far as we can discover, as different from ours as were their conventions of appreciation. The distinction which we make between the fine arts on the one hand, factory production and the crafts on the other, was foreign to classical antiquity. Both the fine arts and the crafts were regarded as 'production according to rule' and both were classified as *technē*, a word which can be translated 'organized knowledge and procedure applied for the purpose of producing a specific preconceived result'.[11] This runs directly counter to the deeply ingrained insight of modern aesthetic thought that the production of fine art is not the sort of performance which can be reduced to rule or appraised in accordance with a set of rules that could be formulated. The consequential Greek idea that 'perfection' is the appropriate criterion of excellence in the fine arts as in other forms of production was expressly repudiated by Kant on the ground that the notion of perfection presupposes production in accordance with a pre-established concept or rule. Yet this conception of art held the field until the middle of the eighteenth century, when the French aesthetician Charles Batteaux heralded the modern idea that the common feature of the fine arts, distinguishing them from the crafts and the sciences, is their production of *beauty*.[12] This idea lasted until the beginning of the present century, when it began to be seen that 'beauty' itself is a highly ambiguous term, far too wide and indefinite for the purpose, while many modern artists on the other hand expressly repudiated 'beauty' because of its too narrow associations with out-moded appreciative conventions. Since 1900 a large number of putative definitions of art has emerged, each of them covering a sector of accepted critical practice but none of them, apparently, applicable to the whole of what is accepted as art by the art world. Tatarkiewicz lists and briefly discusses six such definitions and suggests several more. He concludes by recommending a *disjunctive* definition embracing a number of alternatives: 'Art is a conscious human activity of either reproducing things, or constructing forms, or expressing experiences, if the product of this reproduction, construction, or expression is capable of evoking delight, or emotion, or shock'.

Though we may properly expect a measure of consistency in the organized social institutions which we call the Republic of Art, it does not follow that they are rational through and through. It would hardly be a matter for surprise if we found that the concepts of a work of art implicit in the rules and conventions of the art world were incompletely uniform or coherent. When we remember the history of their development, the bare bones of which only have been indicated, the haphazard way in which they have evolved, the massive changes which have taken place in our attitudes of aesthetic appreciation and the many powerful influences bearing upon our artistic behaviour, it is indeed likely that several not entirely consistent or compatible conceptions of art may survive in the traditions we have inherited but not fully clarified. A 'disjunctive definition' such as Tatarkiewicz proposed is an indication that this is in fact so. It is an indication of a pretty thoroughgoing irrationality in the structure of the Republic of Art. For it means that social approval is being accorded to the adoption of the same attitudes and behaviour towards a heterogeneous selection of things discriminated by several unrelated criteria.[13] And we submit to this blindly until the philosopher opens our eyes. This must be the first step, the step which Tatarkiewicz has proposed.

But we must go further. If we look more closely, we shall see that not only do the various implicit definitions of art not hang together in a coherent group, but that many of them are internally irrational since even within the range of things which they cover they do not in fact serve to differentiate those which are conventionally accepted as works of art from those which are not. Take, for example, the theory of Expression, which came to prominence in the nineteenth century and is still influential. As we have said, and as Tatarkiewicz's 'disjunctive definition' allows, this only impinges upon some works of art. There are many recognized works of art which are no more notably 'expressive' than many other things which men make or do. But to this we must add that men make or do many many things which are expressive of experience, and are capable of evoking delight, emotion or shock, but which we do not classify as works of art. A vulgar and costly icon of the Virgin and an act of reverence before the tomb of Lenin are both in their several ways expressive of reverence. But we do not rank them as works of art. The theory of Expression does not, as it is purported to do, provide a criterion by which we can discriminate among expressive things and actions those which are works of art from those which are not. The same thing might be said about the other proposed definitions. The 'mimetic' theory holds that art is an activity of reproducing reality: but many people are delighted with their own amateur photographs. Despite 'informal' and Tachist art, much of the art we recognize conforms to the definition that art is the creation of forms: but an engineer and the illustrator of a geometrical textbook also construct forms. The old definition of fine art as the creation of beauty does not apply to much that is now recognized as fine art, but it is still too wide; it would be odd to describe the act of giving birth to a beautiful baby as a work of art. All this indicates a deeper element of irrationality in our Republic of Art, for it suggests that the way in which we talk and think about works of art does not correspond with the way in which we actually select those things which we recognize as works of art from the things which we do not so recognize. Nevertheless it would be a mark of irresponsibility to accept prematurely that the structure of our Republic of Art is so grossly irrational as this suggests. To stop at this should be only an act of ultimate despair when all else has failed, for it would undermine the belief in the ultimate rationality of humanity. First we must look more deeply to see whether there is perhaps some discriminating principle operating through all these categories, a principle by which we in fact differentiate works of art from artifacts which are not works of art.

On various occasions I have suggested aesthetic experience as such a differentiating criterion. Whatever among natural objects is capable of arousing and sustaining aesthetic experience in suitably endowed persons we call beautiful; and whatever among artifacts is capable of arousing and sustaining aesthetic experience in suitably prepared subjects we call a work of art. The idea that a work of art is distinguished as the vehicle of aesthetic experience came gradually into force from the latter part of the eighteenth century and now, in modern theory and practice, is the most generally presupposed of all. It does in fact supply the necessary discriminative principle of each of the categories. On the Expression theory, for instance, a work of art would be an artifact expressing experience and capable of arousing and sustaining aesthetic experience. Things that men make and do with expressive force but which are not capable of sustaining aesthetic experience are not works of art. The idea operates similarly through the other categories. If it is accepted, it would cut the ground from under Kennick's argument that a work of art cannot be defined because 'art has no definite function' and would refute his claim that: 'There is no single property that is common to all works of art.' Its acceptance as a criterion recognizes the basic rationality in the structure of our art world.

But it has been objected that aesthetic experience itself is a vague and ambiguous term current in many different senses. This is true. Its very existence has been denied by Dickie, though under a misapprehension as to its nature.[14] In any case it needs sharper and more precise definition. It must not be dissipated or disintegrated into pleasure, emotion or shock. It is none of these. In my own writings I have endeavoured to present aesthetic experience simply as direct awareness, perception in the wider sense of the word, undertaken for its own sake. Perception is direct cognitive contact with the world outside and within ourselves; it underlies all apprehension and provides the material for analytical and constructive thinking. When we exercise this most basic of all faculties for its own sake and not for practical or theoretical purposes we are enjoying aesthetic experience. Few things are suitable vehicles for this exercise to more than a rudimentary extent. A work of art is an artifact which, whatever else it does, is capable of stimulating such self-rewarding awareness and sustaining perception at higher than the ordinary levels of intensity and fullness.

When aesthetic experience is understood in this way it will be seen that this is how we do in fact learn to discriminate in the Republic of Art.

NOTES

1. T. J. Diffey, 'The Republic of Art', *The British Journal of Aesthetics* Vol. 9, No. 2 (1969).
2. Arthur Danto, 'The Artworld', *Journal of Philosophy* 6 (1964).
3. George Dickie, *Art and the Aesthetic* (New York, 1974).
4. Paul Ziff, 'The Task of Defining a Work of Art', *Philosophical Review* Vol. 62 (1953).
5. W. E. Kennick, 'Does Traditional Aesthetics Rest on a Mistake?' *Mind* Vol. 67 (1958).
6. There is an element of rationality in perception itself. As Aristotle already pointed out in the *Posterior Analytics*, when we perceive particular things what we perceive in them are characteristics they share with other things and characteristics discriminating them from other things. When we learn the correct applications of words in a language we do not memorize by rote an inchoate jumble of unrelated particulars but master principles telling us the sort of things to which a word correctly applies.
7. Morris Weitz, 'The Role of Theory in Aesthetics', *Journal of Aesthetics and Art Criticism* Vol. 15 (1956).
8. Weitz admits that all concepts other than those of logic and mathematics are 'open' in his sense of the word.
9. Frank P. Chambers, *Perception, Understanding and Society* (1961), pp. 183–4.
10. *The British Journal of Aesthetics* Vol. 11, No. 2 (1971).
11. J. J. Pollitt, *The Ancient View of Greek Art* (1974), p. 32. Aristotle defined *technē* as 'manufacturing skill in accordance with rational principles' (*meta logon poiētikē hexis*). Eth. Nic. 1140a9.
12. C. Batteaux, *Les Beaux-Arts reduits à un même principe* (1747).
13. For a while it was popular to appeal here to Wittgenstein's idea of 'family resemblance'. But to be meaningful this vague idea must be interpreted more concretely than 'different things having the same name'. For example: the formula A has something in common with B, B with C, C with D, etc.; but F, G, and H retain little or nothing in common with A. So interpreted, it does not apply in a significant way to the different theories of art.
14. See, for example, Robert McGregor, 'Dickie's Institutionalized Aesthetic', *The British Journal of Aesthetics* Vol. 17, No. 1.

Zirchow VII, Lyonel Feininger (American). 1918. National Gallery of Art, Washington, D.C.

Philosophers of art are interested in the varied sorts of aesthetic properties that works of art exhibit. Feininger understood his art as "expression of the deepest kind of inner longing," of an almost religious nature. But this work also exemplifies more formal properties of structural unity achieved through an interpenetration of light and substance.

CHAPTER 5
Art and Its Properties

One profitable way of distinguishing art objects from ordinary physical objects is to identify various sorts of complex properties which we believe are true of artworks but not generally true of more mundane things. It is clear, upon reflection, that artworks are more culturally and psychologically dependent entities than ordinary tables and chairs, trees and stars. Culturally mediated forms of aesthetic perception seem required to enable marks on paper to be perceived as a drawing, or sounds as music. Complex cognitive and emotional processes of both active and passive sorts are involved in our interactions with art, and as a result of them we conceive of art as capable of representing, symbolizing, expressing, and exemplifying other things, ideas, emotions, values, abstract properties, and so forth. Artworks' capacity to function in these broadly symbolic ways is clearly essential to their status as *aesthetic* objects.

But whether certain of the properties true of art can be clearly characterized as *aesthetic* properties while others are considered more neutral or nonaesthetic is a question that has led to much debate and has generated interesting theorizing about the properties of artworks and the logical and other relations among these properties.

Features of artworks that have the most obvious claim to the term *aesthetic*, such as the property of being balanced, being dignified, being elegant, being controlled, and being tense, clearly must be true of a work as the result of other, more ordinary, purely descriptive features, such as the colors used, the placement of figures, the length of sentences used, the words chosen, and the juxtaposition of contrasting elements. But the nature of this dependency is extraordinarily difficult to clarify. Yet this is a perfect example of a confusing phenomenon that calls out for analytical clarification.

For Beardsley, aesthetic properties are generally those features of artworks usually referred to as "formal" properties—that is, properties which have to do with the relationship among the (aesthetically relevant) parts which make up an artwork.

The elementary parts, which cannot be further reduced to component parts, Beardsley calls "local qualities," while properties which belong to a complex of such elementary parts he calls "regional properties." Regional qualities of greatest interest in aesthetic analysis are those which are "emergent," those, that is, which are more than the sum of their parts, as saltiness is the emergent product of sodium and cholorine but is not a property of either or the sum of the two. What this amounts to is that regional qualities introduce a measure of novelty and unexpectedness relative to the local qualities, although regional qualities nonetheless *depend* on the local properties and their relations to one another. Because they depend on ordinary qualities, aesthetic properties seem to stand in some sort of condition-governed relation to ordinary properties; but because they introduce unexpected novelty, they generally fail to be condition-governed, at least in any straightforward and obvious way. Saltiness inevitably emerges from a certain chemical combination of sodium and chlorine, whereas elegance is not the inevitable or lawlike product of a certain combination of physical properties such as the use of delicate colors and curving lines; nor, obviously, is this combination the only way of creating elegance.

The regional quality of a complex depends on the elements and their relations, and Beardsley says that this dependency determines the "perceptual conditions" for the regional quality. But these perceptual conditions are neither necessary nor sufficient for the emergence of the regional qualities. An artist cannot guarantee a certain regional quality by mechanically following a formula for placing elements in a prescribed order, though he or she can make that outcome more probable, and he or she does not necessarily give up that regional quality by abandoning those elements and their particular arrangement in favor of other elementary qualities and arrangements, though altering the elements or arrangement will *usually* result in a change in the regional quality.

Thus, for Beardsley, there is only a kind of probabilistic relation between the existence of local properties and the emergence of regional qualities. But, as we will see, even this loose logical relation is too rigid for other aestheticians, Frank Sibley being prominent among them.

In the frequently and justifiedly anthologized article, "Aesthetic Concepts," Sibley distinguishes aesthetic from nonaesthetic concepts used in discussions about works of art, in the hopes of ascertaining their relation to one another. The main distinguishing feature is that aesthetic concepts require "the exercise of taste, perceptiveness, or sensitivity," whereas nonaesthetic properties require nothing beyond normal perception.

As with Beardsley's distinction of local and regional qualities, Sibley holds that there is a dependence of the aesthetic on the nonaesthetic which provides the basis of support or justification for art critical claims. Precisely because the perception of aesthetic properties is not obvious or automatic, claims about their presence in an artwork are controversial, and because nonaesthetic properties are more obvious and less controversial, and moreover because the aesthetic properties depend on them in some sense, reasoning in art criticism is generally from the nonaesthetic to the aesthetic (that is, the presence of nonaesthetic properties is offered as a reason justifying claims about aesthetic properties).

But like Beardsley, though going farther than Beardsley, Sibley argues that nonaesthetic properties are never logically sufficient conditions for the presence of aesthetic terms. Indeed they are not condition-governed at all. As Beardsley also said, different arrangements of nonaesthetic properties can result in the same aesthetic features. Nonetheless, Beardsley argued for some sort of looser probabilistic, inductive, condition-governed relation which Sibley strongly denies: "aesthetic concepts differ radically" from all such condition-governed concepts, however loosely defined. "A painting might be garish even though much of its colour is pale."

At best, some nonaesthetic features usually count for or against the application of aesthetic terms, and so we can say, loosely, that X is graceful "because of" such and such, and "in spite of" this or that. But this is still much looser than the conditionality of nonaesthetic concepts like "intelligence," wherein some features only and always count toward intelligence and others against it, though no list of such features can ever be sufficient. In talking about art, on the other hand, nonaesthetic features only count *typically* or *characteristically* toward aesthetic features.

Even the strongest linkage of nonaesthetic to aesthetic (where the one counts typically toward the other) is weaker than Hart's notion of "defeasible" concepts, according to Sibley. Defeasible concepts are such that no list of features ever logically guarantees the applicability of the concept because there exists an indefinite number of "defeating conditions," conditions whose satisfaction makes the concept in question inapplicable, no matter what other positive conditions have been met. (For example, consider the notion that a person has great integrity. No matter how many positive relevant conditions this person meets, the disclosure that he or she was involved in money laundering or in political extortion would be enough to defeat the claim to integrity.) The most we can say about defeasible concepts is that conditions A, B, C, etc. are sufficient for the concept's application *unless* something comes along to defeat them.

Sibley insists, however, that even this weak relation is still condition-governed, while aesthetic concepts are not. The major difference is that in the case of defeasible concepts, relevant conditions are clearly positive or negative (i.e., they count only for or only against the concept's application), whereas the conditions relevant to the truth of aesthetic claims can only be said to count *characteristically* or *typically* for or against the claim. This is an interesting and complex instance of the important fact that there are very few general or universal truths or laws in art, and that creating certain aesthetic effects cannot be viewed as a rule-governed process or procedure.

Sibley notes (as did Isenberg in his equally famous article, "Critical Communication") that at least part of the reason for the failure of art critical reasons to be condition-governed is that a certain work is not, for example, delicate because of pale colors in general, but only because of *those* pale colors (i.e., the exact combination of colors exhibited in the work). Nonaesthetic terms, like *pale colors,* include but do not specify the particular instance as it exists in that particular artwork. The actual properties are far more specific than the predicates referring to them suggest. For this reason we cannot generalize from specific cases and are thus unable to come up with general rules which would enable us to argue in a condition-governed way from the presence of the nonaesthetic property (pale colors) to the presence of a certain aesthetic property (delicacy).

But if the relation of nonaesthetic to aesthetic predicates in judgments of taste are not rule- or condition-governed, how, then, do they operate? What *is* the relation between the two? The connection, Sibley argues, is that calling attention to certain nonaesthetic features of an artwork is often useful "in bringing others to see what we see" (i.e., the less obvious aesthetic properties). Sibley mentions a number of practices critics can use to get us to see things their way, aesthetically.

Hermeren provides a careful topology of different sorts of aesthetic qualities—emotion (e.g., somber), behavior (e.g., bold), gestalt (e.g., unified), taste (e.g., elegant), and reaction (e.g., shocking). Unlike reactive qualities, emotion (or expressive) qualities need not cause the viewer to experience the emotion in question. Hermeren argues (somewhat as Osborne suggested in Chapter 3) that sad music is structured in ways that are similar to the ways sad people behave and to certain features of sad experiences.

Sircello wonders why analytic philosophers, like Beardsley, have not appreciated the contributions of Croce and Collingwood and others to the expression theory, and he "conservatively" tries to recapture them, in a more analytically circumspect fashion. Analytic philosophers have a fear of *animism*, he says, a fear of attributing to artworks properties that can literally be true only of people. But Sircello argues that anthropomorphic predicates apply to artworks in virtue of what the artist *does* in the work, something Sircello calls "artistic acts." In that sense, anthropomorphic predicates applied to artworks are not like properties of ordinary physical objects, but are more like predicates for describing "verbal, gestural, and facial *expressions*" of people, such as "angry scowls, . . . sullen pouts." They are also similar in that both are "significant," that both *mean* something about the person involved (that is, in the case of works of art, the artist). Thus, Sircello avoids locating an animistic expressive quality in the inanimate artwork by locating it in the human experience of the *artist*. (Contrast this view with the more abstract and semiotic view of expression offered by Goodman, as well as Tormey's view of art as autonomously self-expressive, both in Chapter 3.)

The artistic acts performed in a work cannot always be inferred from the work's surface features, and therefore the aesthetic properties true of a work are often *contextual* and only fully understandable by knowing which artistic acts have been performed through the work. If Sircello is correct in this, we have here a powerful argument against the thesis of the *autonomy* of the artwork, a thesis discussed extensively in the earlier stages of analytic aesthetics, and one we discussed in Chapter 2.

Like Sircello, Walton is also concerned about the peculiar status of artworks, the way in which they are not just like other sorts of ordinary physical objects. And like Sircello, Walton rejects the idea that aesthetic properties are the ones directly available to perception. Because we often think they *are* simply physical objects which we enjoy looking at or listening to, we (mistakenly) tend to think that artworks' only aesthetically relevant properties are therefore properties which are directly perceptible and not other properties, more historical or contextual in nature. Walton argues forcefully that the aesthetic properties true of artworks are a function of more than those works' sensible surfaces.

Walton's analysis hinges on the distinction he draws between "standard" and "contra-standard" properties of the artwork. A standard property is one in virtue of which an artwork belongs to a given art historical or stylistic "category" (e.g., "impressionistic," "Brahmsian"). Contra-standard properties are those which tend to disqualify the work as a member of that category. The standard/contra-standard distinction is, then, obviously relative to the different possible categories in which we may be operating as we perceive the work. We perceive an artwork "as," "in," or "under" various stylistic categories; so, for example, we might perceive X as "a piece of music," "a sonata," "a romantic," or "a Brahmsian." Perceiving artworks in these categories is relative to the perceiver and the social context in the sense that it depends on the perceiver's familiarity with many other works of the same kind and familiarity with standard discussions and descriptions of such categories and the context in which various works are routinely grouped together (e.g., romantic pieces of music). "A feature of a work is standard for a particular person on a particular occasion when, and only when, it is standard relative to some category in which he perceives it."

Walton's "psychological thesis" is that the aesthetic properties which an artwork seems to have often depend on which of its features are construed as standard or contra-standard. The categories applicable to the work determine what aesthetic properties it has. A feature, for example, may be "dynamic" when it occurs in the category of painting, but not when it occurs in a holiday snapshot of roughly the same scene.

But what determines when the categories one applies to works are the correct categories? If there were no distinction between categories that are correct and those that are incorrect for a work, then the properties a work could be said to have would be a purely relative matter, and Walton does not endorse such relativism. Consequently, he offers several relevant criteria for determining if one is perceiving a work within its correct categories.

A category is correct for a work when the work has a preponderance of features standard with respect to that category, when the work is better or more interestingly perceived within that category, when the artist intended the work to be perceived in that way, or when perceiving the work in that way is socially acceptable. Clearly it is possible that only some of these criteria are met in certain cases; there admittedly is a degree of tension among these criteria, and borderline cases of correctness are possible. Walton suggests that these are simply relevant considerations for determining correctness. The last two criteria (when the artist intends it that way or when that categorization is socially acceptable) indicate that the correct way to perceive a work is partly dependent on "historical facts." Historical facts then partially determine the correct categories, and the correct categories determine what is and what is not an aesthetic property of the work in question. It follows that aesthetic properties are not in the physical object in the same way in which colors, for example, are. One reason we often imagine we "just see" aesthetic properties without any consideration for the appropriate "category" is that though the categories are presupposed and implicit in our perceptions, we often are not consciously aware of them. They are simply taken for granted; they have been tacitly learned and enculturated in us.

We can see in this chapter's readings a progressive awareness that the aesthetic properties we apply to works of art, the most sensitive and rich statements we make of them and believe true of them, cannot be simply "read off" from the perceptual surface features of the works. Aesthetic descriptions involve us in complex, nondeductive inferences based on, but in neither a logical nor psychological way exhausted by, the sensory evidence supplied to us by the work's "surface." Aesthetic properties "emerge" from this surface, but our sensitivity to this emergence is in many cases a function of our sensitivity to the broader contexts—artistic, stylistic, historical, and cultural—in which the artworks are situated.

Regional Qualities

Monroe Beardsley

ELEMENTS AND COMPLEXES

We must now turn, therefore, to the question what *would* be a good set of categories for aesthetic analysis. It is clear that in so far as the disputable [aesthetic] terms we have just discussed do refer to something verifiable about aesthetic objects, they refer to parts of those objects and their relations to one another. And it is the part-whole relation that we shall take as our basic category of analysis. In the remainder of this section, I shall lay out, rather abstractly, a small set of categories connected with the part-whole relation, leaving it to the next two sections to show that they are usable and useful.

There can be no quarrel, I think, about the meaning of the relational term "part of" when it is applied to the visual field. In a reasonably clear and obvious sense, the figure of a nude, or a patch of pink, is a part of the whole painting. It is perhaps a little less familiar to speak of a note or a melody as part of a symphonic composition, though we usually say that an entire movement, or a section of a movement, is part of it. In these cases, so long as there are heterogeneities in the object, distinctions can be made within it, between a pink part and a blue part, or between a part in the key of D minor and a part in the key of F, and whatever we find between such points of distinction is a proper part of the whole.

Any part of a sensory field is then itself a *complex* if further parts can be discriminated within it. An absolutely homogeneous part of the field is partless, and such a partless part may be called an *element* of the field. Analysis stops with the elements. You can distinguish the light and dark parts on the surface of the moon, but if within a dark patch you can find no differences, then that patch is elementary.

Such an elementary part must have some qualities, otherwise we could not perceive it: its darkness, its shape. Let us call such qualities *local qualities*. The white area inside the "O" in the word "local" is an element of this printed page, and its whiteness is therefore a local quality. But some complexes have qualities that are not qualities of their elements: the word "local" has five letters, but none of its letters does. And some complexes have qualities that are not qualities of any of their complex parts: the preceding sentence has twenty-four words, but none of its phrases or clauses does. Let us call a property, or characteristic, that belongs to a complex but not to any of its parts a *regional property* of that complex. Notice then that your having weight is *not* a regional property, in this sense, because your parts—arms and legs, for example—also have weight; but your property of weighing 150 pounds, if you do, *is* a regional property, for none of your parts weighs that much.

Some regional properties can be perceived by the senses; some cannot. Your weighing 150 pounds is not directly perceivable—it has to be measured on a scale, or inferred in some other way—but your being heavy-set or thin *is* perceivable. In our descriptions of aesthetic objects we are interested in the perceivable properties, for which we shall reserve the

---

From *Aesthetics: Problems in the Philosophy of Criticism* (Indianapolis: Hackett Publishing Co., 1981). Reprinted by permission of the publisher.

word "qualities." Thus when I speak of the regional qualities of a complex, I mean its perceptual regional properties.

It may seem that we should make a further distinction between two sorts of regional property, which are sometimes called *summative* (or additive) and *emergent*. For example, if two one-pound weights are combined on a scale, the combination will have a weight of two pounds, which, by our definition, is a regional property, since it does not characterize either part by itself. But the weight of the whole is a simple arithmetical sum of the weights of the parts. On the other hand, the saltiness of sodium chloride that is not present in its separate elements, or the wetness of H_2O when neither hydrogen nor oxygen is wet by itself, is not describable as a sum; something new and different seems to emerge from the combination. Again, we might say that the brightness of a white light made up of two white lights is summative; the color of a light made up of two different colored lights is emergent.

Intuitively, this distinction seems defensible. But unfortunately no attempt to analyze it and define it in a general way has been quite successful. You can't say, for example, that the weight in the first case could be predicted from knowing the separate weights, whereas saltiness could not be predicted from the sepa-

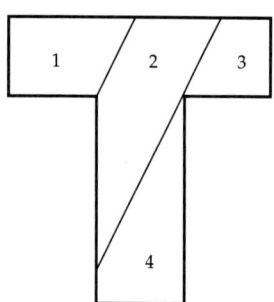

rate properties of sodium and chlorine. Actually, neither can be predicted merely from a knowledge of the parts, but both can be predicted once you have added the weights together and weighed the sums, and once you have combined sodium with chlorine.

Perhaps the difference lies merely in the degree of surprisingness, and is not a fundamental difference at all. For example, if you have nine equal cubes you can fit them into a larger cube; there is nothing very remarkable in this. But though in the well-known puzzle the four pieces combine into a T, when you are presented with them separately this is not obvious.

In certain fields of science, emergence can be defined with reference to prevailing explanatory theories. Suppose there is an accepted theory, T, and a property, P, whose presence cannot be explained by T; then P is emergent with respect to T. But this distinction does not seem to be the one we are after in analyzing aesthetic objects. In any case, it is quite certain that if the distinction between summative and emergent properties is ever satisfactorily formulated, this will be done by rather complicated methods, and with the help of some technical symbolic apparatus. Therefore, it will be convenient for us if we can say, as I think we can, that the distinction probably does not matter greatly for our purposes. What is important for discourse about art is that the regional qualities of a complex have two aspects: they have novelty, in that they are not to be found in the parts when separated, but they also depend upon the parts and their relations.

The categories that we now have on hand can be illustrated by a simple figure. Here are four small circles, lettered for convenience of reference.

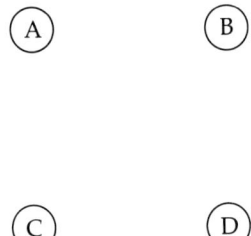

The question is, what basically different types of thing can we *say* about this figure?

First, we can describe the elements: A, B, C, and D are circles; the background is white.

Second, assuming, for convenience, a geographical coordinate system, we can describe the relations between the elements: A is 1" west of B, C is 1" west of D, A is 1" north of C, B is 1" north of D. There are other relations we could describe, of course—for example, A is northwest of D. The first four, however, are sufficient, for once they are given, they determine the figure uniquely, and consequently all the other relations among its parts.

Third, we can describe the regional qualities of the figure as a whole: this figure has a squarish character. The squarishness is a regional quality because it belongs to the complex but not to any of its parts, and a complete description of the figure would have to include the statement that this quality is present.

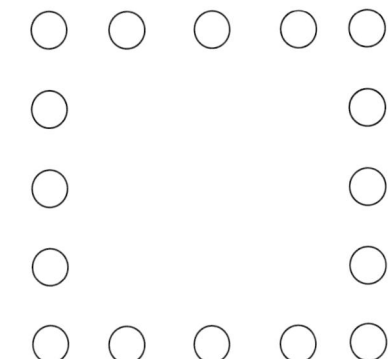

Is there anything we have left out? We could describe the elements more precisely: they are outlined in thin black lines. We could enumerate more relations: circle B is $\sqrt{4^{1}/_{2}}''$ northeast of circle C. We could say more about the qualities of the whole: the figure has a certain amount of stability, but not very much tendency to hold together. But there seems to be no new *kind* of thing that ought to be part of the description: no matter how complicated we made the figure, the true statements describing it would fall into the same basic categories. There are statements about the number and local qualities of elements, about complexes and their regional qualities, about relations between elements or between complexes.

REGIONAL QUALITIES AND PERCEPTUAL CONDITIONS

There are some points that should be noticed at once. A regional quality may be more or less *extensive*, that is, it may prevail over a larger or smaller portion of a sensory field. For example, we might make the figure and its circles larger or smaller, keeping the proportions the same. A regional quality may be more or less *intensive*. For example, we might insert more circles between the others to make the squarishness more pronounced, or on the other hand, we might increase the distances between the circles so that the squarishness becomes more and more indistinct until it disappears. A regional quality may be more or less *persistent* in time. That is, it may characterize an object, as above, or an event, or a series of events regarded as a whole in time. For example, it is not a single event on a stage, but a series of events that has a dramatic quality.

We are now in a position to introduce two other terms that will be useful in the remainder of this chapter, and later. When two elements or complexes, A and B, are both parts of a larger complex that has a relatively intense regional quality, then A and B seem to belong together in an important way. Without losing their individuality, they take on, if one may speak very metaphorically, a kind of awareness of each other; in that case, let us say they are perceptually joined. They do not merely accompany each other, but *fuse*. The four circles in our diagram, for example, take on this fusion, for each appears not just as a circle but as the corner-of-a-square-having-three-other-corners, though the fusion is less than, say, in the second figure, where each circle is even more apparently and decisively an element-in-a-row-that-forms-the-side-of-a-square-having-three-other-sides.

When the complex A-B has its own regional quality, it may be said to be a *whole*. It segregates itself for perception from its environment; it takes on individuality. Wholeness is another regional quality, which a complex may possess in various degrees, depending upon the intensity of the other regional qualities that bind its parts together; the second figure above, for example, has squarishness and stability to a higher degree than the first, and consequently it is, so to speak, more whole-ish. "Wholeness," like the names of all regional qualities, can only be ostensively defined, that is, the quality must be pointed out in examples.

It will be important for our future purposes—and it will be made clearer later on—that the existence of the regional quality of a complex depends upon the elements and their relations; they are the *perceptual conditions* of the quality. This is obvious enough in the diagram: it is because the four circles are placed in the relations they are in that the whole figure has its squarishness. If A had been southwest of B, B northwest of C, C northeast of D, and D southeast of A, then the figure would not have been squarish, but diamondish. But when we *say* that it is squarish, we are not talking about the relations between the parts; we are reporting on the consequent character of the whole. In other words, it is not a tautology, but a synthetic empirical statement, to say that the figure is squarish because of the spatial relations among A, B, C, and D.

Generally speaking, we may say two things about regional qualities and their perceptual conditions. First, if the perceptual conditions are altered, there will probably be some change in the total set of regional qualities, or in some one quality. But second, a given regional quality may persist through radical alterations of the conditions. It is possible for the same regional quality to turn up in very different perceptual conditions—as a kind of scowling look may appear on a human face or on the radiator grillwork of a car.

There are, then, two important confusions to be avoided. First, it is important to keep perceptual conditions distinct from what was called the physical basis. The statement, "Normal eyes exposed to light having a frequency of 600 mμ or over will perceive red," is a statement about the relation between a sense quality and its physical basis. But the statement, "Alternating bands of highly saturated red and green will have a flickering, restless, uneasy quality," is a statement about the relation between a regional quality and its perceptual conditions. Second, statements about perceptual conditions of regional qualities do not imply anything about ends and means. A critic may say of the Rembrandt drawing, "Rembrandt put a dark area in the upper left-hand part of the drawing, but left a light edge next to the girl's dark hair, in order to bring the head forward in space." The objective content of this statement can be rendered in the form: "The spatial orientation of the figure, with the upper part advancing (a regional quality), depends in part upon the shading in the upper left-hand part of the drawing (a perceptual condition)."

For convenience in laying out the basic terms, I have used the simplest possible diagram. How far the terms so introduced are serviceable in talking about more complex visual figures, I shall try to show in the next section. Also for convenience I have begun with an example from the visual field; it is yet another question how far the same distinctions can be applied, in the same senses, to the auditory field.

It is customary to make a distinction between two classes of art: the "space arts" of painting, sculpture, architecture; and the "time arts" of music, poetry, drama, dance. Now we must surely be prepared to find that some things that are very important in painting do not occur at all in music, and vice versa, and all the way along we must be on guard against overfacile transfers from one art to another. But we must not overstress the difference, either, for there are two general reflections that make this difference less absolute than it may seem at first: On the one hand, just as it takes time to listen to a musical composition, so it takes time to see a painting; and though that seeing-a-painting process is not so fully controlled as musical audition, it has some of the same characteristics: contrast, and a cumulative intensity based upon the recall and synthesizing of earlier stages. On the other hand, though the early bars of the music, once past, cannot be gone back to, like a part of the painting, yet to one who knows the music well all its parts are available for contemplation and comparison, and the having of them helps to give significance to every part that is heard, the parts-to-come to the parts-gone-by, just as the parts-gone-by to the parts-to-come.

There is prima-facie evidence, then, that our basic categories of description can be fruitful for music as for visual art. But we shall have to consider more carefully whether there are musical elements, relations, complexes, regional qualities, fused complexes, wholes.

Aesthetic Concepts

Frank N. Sibley

The remarks we make about works of art are of many kinds. In this paper I wish to distinguish between two broad groups. We say that a novel has a great number of characters and deals with life in a manufacturing town; that a painting uses pale colours, predominantly blues and greens, and has kneeling figures in the foreground; that the theme in a fugue is inverted at such a point and that there is a stretto at the close; that the action of a play takes place in the span of one day and that there is a reconciliation scene in the fifth act. Such remarks may be made by, and such features pointed out to, anyone with normal eyes, ears, and intelligence. On the other hand, we also say that a poem is tightly-knit or deeply moving; that a picture lacks balance, or has a certain serenity and repose, or that the grouping of the figures sets up an exciting tension; that the characters in a novel never really come to life, or that a certain episode strikes a false note. It would be natural enough to say that the making of judgments such as these requires the exercise of taste, perceptiveness, or sensitivity, of aesthetic discrimination or appreciation; one would not say this of my first group. Accordingly, when a word of expression is such that taste or perceptiveness is required in order to apply it, I shall call it an *aesthetic* term or expression, and I shall, correspondingly, speak of *aesthetic* concepts or *taste* concepts.[1]

Aesthetic terms span a great range of types and could be grouped into various kinds and sub-species. But it is not my present purpose to attempt any such grouping; I am interested in what they all have in common. Their almost endless variety is adequately displayed in the following list: *unified, balanced, integrated, lifeless, serene, sombre, dynamic, powerful, vivid, delicate, moving, trite, sentimental, tragic.* The list of course is not limited to adjectives; expressions in artistic contexts like "telling contrast," "sets up a tension," "conveys a sense of," or "holds it together" are equally good illustrations. It includes terms used by both layman and critic alike, as well as some which are mainly the property of professional critics and specialists.

I have gone for my examples of aesthetic

From *The Philosophical Review*, 67 (1959). Reprinted by permission of the publisher and the author.

expressions in the first place to critical and evaluative discourse about works of art because it is there particularly that they abound. But now I wish to widen the topic; we employ terms the use of which requires an exercise of taste not only when discussing the arts but quite liberally throughout discourse in everyday life. The examples given above are expressions which, appearing in critical contexts, most usually, if not invariably, have an aesthetic use; outside critical discourse the majority of them more frequently have some other use unconnected with taste. But many expressions do double duty even in everyday discourse, sometimes being used as aesthetic expressions and sometimes not. Other words again, whether in artistic or daily discourse, function only or predominantly as aesthetic terms; of this kind are *graceful, delicate, dainty, handsome, comely, elegant, garish*. Finally, to make the contrast with all the preceding examples, there are many words which are seldom used as aesthetic terms at all: *red, noisy, brackish, clammy, square, docile, curved, evanescent, intelligent, faithful, derelict, tardy, freakish*.

Clearly, when we employ words as aesthetic terms we are often making and using metaphors, pressing into service words which do not primarily function in this manner. Certainly also, many words *have come* to be aesthetic terms by some kind of metaphorical transference. This is so with those like "dynamic," "melancholy," "balanced," "tightly-knit" which, except in artistic and critical writings, are not normally aesthetic terms. But the aesthetic vocabulary must not be thought wholly metaphorical. Many words, including the most common (*lovely, pretty, beautiful, dainty, graceful, elegant*), are certainly not being used metaphorically when employed as aesthetic terms, the very good reason being that this is their primary or only use, some of them having no current non-aesthetic uses. And though expressions like "dynamic," "balanced," and so forth *have come* by a metaphorical shift to be aesthetic terms, their employment in criticism can scarcely be said to be more than quasi-metaphorical. Having entered the language of art description and criticism as metaphors they are now standard vocabulary in that language.[2]

The expressions I am calling aesthetic terms form no small segment of our discourse. Often, it is true, people with normal intelligence and good eyesight and hearing lack, at least in some measure, the sensitivity required to apply them; a man need not be stupid or have poor eyesight to fail to see that something is graceful. Thus taste or sensitivity is somewhat more rare than certain other human capacities; people who exhibit a sensitivity both wide-ranging and refined are a minority. It is over the application of aesthetic terms too that, notoriously, disputes and differences sometimes go helplessly unsettled. But almost everybody is able to exercise taste to some degree and in some matters. It is surprising therefore that aesthetic terms have been so largely neglected. They have received glancing treatment in the course of other aesthetic discussions; but as a broad category they have not received the direct attention they merit.

The foregoing has marked out the area I wish to discuss. One warning should perhaps be given. When I speak of taste in this paper, I shall not be dealing with questions which centre upon expressions like "a matter of taste" (meaning, roughly, a matter of personal preference or liking). It is with an ability to *notice* or *see* or *tell* that things have certain qualities that I am concerned.

I

In order to support our application of an aesthetic term, we often refer to features the mention of which involves other aesthetic terms: "it has an extraordinary vitality because of its free and vigorous style of drawing," "graceful in the smooth flow of its lines," "dainty because of the delicacy and harmony of its colouring." It is as normal to do this as it is to justify one mental epithet by other epithets of the same general type, *intelligent* by *ingenious, inventive, acute*, and so on. But often when we apply aesthetic terms, we explain why by referring to features which do *not* depend for their recognition upon an exercise of taste: "delicate because of its pastel shades and curving lines," or "it lacks balance because one group of figures is so far off to the left and is so brightly illuminated." When no explanation of this latter kind is offered, it is legitimate to ask or search for one. Finding a satisfactory answer is sometimes difficult, but one cannot ordinarily reject the question. When we cannot ourselves quite say what non-aesthetic features make something delicate or unbalanced or moving, the good critic often puts his finger on something which strikes us as the right explanation. In short, aesthetic terms always ultimately apply because of, and aesthetic qualities always ultimately depend upon, the presence of features which, like curving or angular lines, colour contrasts, placing of masses, or speed of movement, are visible, audible, or otherwise discernible without any exercise of taste or sensibility. Whatever kind of dependence this is, and there are various relationships between aesthetic qualities and non-aesthetic features, what I want to make clear in this paper is that there are no non-aesthetic features which serve in *any* circumstances as logically *sufficient conditions* for applying aesthetic terms. Aesthetic concepts are not in *this* respect condition-governed at all.

There is little temptation to suppose that aesthetic terms resemble words which, like "square," are applied in accordance with a set of necessary and sufficient conditions. For whereas each square is square in virtue of the *same* set of conditions, four equal sides and four right angles, aesthetic terms apply to widely varied objects; one thing is graceful because of these features, another because of those, and so on. Recently, philosophers have broken the spell of the strict necessary-and-sufficient model by showing that many everyday concepts are not of that type, but are governed only in a much looser way by conditions. However, since these newer models provide satisfactory accounts of many concepts, it might plausibly be thought that aesthetic concepts are of some such kind and that they similarly are governed in some looser way by conditions. I want to argue that aesthetic concepts differ radically from any of these other concepts.

Amongst these concepts to which attention has recently been paid are those for which no *necessary-and-sufficient* conditions can be provided, but for which there are a number of relevant features, A, B, C, D, E, such that the presence of some groups or combinations of these features is *sufficient* for the application of the concept. The list of relevant features may be an open one; that is, given A, B, C, D, E, we may not wish to close off the possible relevance of other unlisted features beyond E. Examples of such concepts might be "dilatory," "discourteous," "possessive," "capricious," "prosperous," "intelligent." . . . If we begin a list of features relevant to "intelligent" with, for example, ability to grasp and follow various kinds of instructions, ability to master facts and marshal evidence, ability to solve mathematical or chess problems, we might go on adding to this list almost indefinitely.

However, with concepts of this sort, although decisions may have to be made and judgment exercised, it is always possible to extract and state, from cases which have *already* clearly been decided, the sets of features or conditions which were regarded as sufficient in those cases. These relevant features which I am calling conditions are, it should be noted, features which, though not sufficient *alone* and needing to be combined with other similar features, nevertheless carry some weight and count only in one direction. Being a good chess player can count only *towards* and not *against* intelligence. Whereas mention of it may enter sensibly along with other remarks in expressions like "I say he is intelligent because . . ." or "the reason I call him intelligent is that . . . ," it cannot be used to complete such negative expressions as "I say he is *un*intelligent because. . . ." But what I want particularly to emphasize about features which function as conditions for a term is that *some* group or set of them is sufficient fully to ensure or warrant the application of that term. An individual characterized by some of these features may not yet qualify to be called lazy or intelligent, and so on, beyond all question, but all that is needed is to add some further (indefinite) number of such characterizations and a point is reached where we have enough. There are individuals possessing a number of such features of whom one cannot deny, cannot but admit, that they are intelligent. We have left necessary-and-sufficient conditions behind, but we are still in the realm of sufficient conditions.

But aesthetic concepts are not condition-governed even in this way. There are no sufficient conditions, no non-aesthetic features such that the presence of some set or number of them will beyond question logically justify or warrant the application of an aesthetic term. It is impossible . . . to make any statements corresponding to those we make for condition-governed words. We are able to say "If it is true he can do this, and that, and the other, then one just cannot deny that he is intelligent," or "if he does A, B, and C, I don't see how it can be denied that he is lazy," but we cannot make *any* general statement of the form "If the vase is pale pink, somewhat curving, lightly mottled, and so forth, it will be delicate, cannot but be delicate." Nor again can one say *any* such thing here as "Being tall and thin is not enough *alone* to ensure that a vase is delicate, but if it is, for example, slightly curving and pale coloured (and so forth) as well, it cannot be denied that it is." Things may be described to us in non-aesthetic terms as fully as we please but we are not thereby put in the position of having to admit (or being unable to deny) that they are delicate or graceful or garish or exquisitely balanced.[3]

No doubt there are some respects in which aesthetic terms *are* governed by conditions or rules. For instance, it may be impossible that a thing should be garish if all its colours are pale pastels, or flamboyant if all its lines are straight. There may be, that is, descriptions using only non-aesthetic terms which are incompatible with descriptions employing certain aesthetic terms. If I am told that a painting in the next room consists solely of one or two bars of very pale blue and very pale grey set at right angles on a pale fawn ground, I can be sure that it cannot be fiery or garish or gaudy or flamboyant. A description of this sort may make certain aesthetic terms *in*applicable or *in*appropriate; and if from this description I inferred that the picture was, or even might be, fiery or gaudy or flamboyant, this might be taken as showing a failure to understand these words. I do not wish to deny therefore that taste concepts may be governed *negatively* by conditions.[4] What I am emphasizing is that they quite lack governing conditions of a sort many other concepts possess. Though on *seeing* the picture we might say, and rightly, that it is delicate or serene or restful or sickly or insipid, no *description* in non-aesthetic terms permits us to claim that these or any other aesthetic terms must undeniably apply to it.

I have said that if an object is characterized *solely* by certain sorts of features this may count decisively against the possibility of applying to it certain aesthetic terms. But of course the presence of *some* such features need not count decisively; other features may be enough to outweigh those which, on their own, would render the aesthetic term inapplicable. A painting might be garish even though much of its colour is pale. These facts call attention to a further feature of taste concepts. One *can* find general features or descriptions which in some sense count in one direction only, only *for* or only *against* the application of certain aesthetic terms. Angularity, fatness, brightness, or intensity of colour are typically *not* associated with delicacy or grace. Slimness, lightness, gentle curves, lack of intensity of colour are associated with delicacy, but not with flamboyance, majesty, grandeur, splendour or garishness. This is shown by the naturalness of saying, for example, that someone is graceful *because* she's so light, but in *spite of* being quite angular or heavily built; and by the corresponding oddity of saying that something is graceful *because* it is so heavy angular, or delicate *because* of its bright and intense colouring. This may therefore sound quite similar to what I have said already about conditions in discussing terms like "intelligent." There are nevertheless significant differences. Although there is this sense in which slimness, lightness, lack of intensity of colour, and so on, count only towards, not against, delicacy, these features, I shall say, at best count only *typically* or *characteristically* towards delicacy. They do not count towards in the same sense as condition-features count towards laziness or intelligence; that is, no group of them is ever logically sufficient.

One way of reinforcing this is to notice how features which are characteristically associated with one aesthetic term may also be similarly associated with other, rather different aesthetic terms. "Graceful" and "delicate" may be on the one hand sharply contrasted with terms like "violent," "grand," "fiery," "garish," or "massive" which have characteristic non-aesthetic features, quite unlike those for "delicate" and "graceful." But on the other hand they may also be contrasted with aesthetic terms which stand much closer to them, like "flaccid," "weakly," "washed out," "lanky," "anaemic," "wan," "insipid"; and the features characteristic of *these* qualities, pale colour, slimness, lightness, lack of angularity and contrast, are virtually identical with the range for "delicate" and "graceful." Similarly many features typically associated with "joyous," "fiery," "robust," or "dynamic" are identical with those associated with "garish," "strident," "turbulent," "gaudy," or "chaotic." Thus an object described very fully, but exclusively in terms of qualities characteristic of delicacy, may turn out on inspection to be not delicate at all, but anaemic or insipid. The failures of novices and the artistically inept prove that quite close similarity in line, colour, or technique gives no assurance of gracefulness or delicacy. A failure and a success in the manner of Degas may be generally more alike, so far as their non-aesthetic features go, than either is like a successful Fragonard. But I need not go even this far to make my main point. A painting which has only the kind of features one would associate with vigour and energy but which even so fails to be vigorous and energetic *need* not be instead, say, strident or chaotic. It may fail to have any particular character whatever. It may employ bright colours and the like without being particularly lively and vigorous at all; but one may feel unable to describe it as chaotic or strident or garish either. It is, rather, simply lacking in character (though of course this too is an aesthetic judgment; taste is exercised also in seeing that the painting has no character).

There are of course many features which do not in these ways characteristically count for (or against) particular aesthetic qualities. One poem has strength and power because of the regularity of its metre and rhyme; another is monotonous and lacks drive and strength because of its regular metre and rhyme. We do not feel the need to switch from "because of" to "in spite of." However, I have concentrated upon features characteristically associated with aesthetic qualities because, if one could maintain that taste concepts are in any way governed by sufficient conditions, these would seem to be the most promising candidates for governing conditions. But to say that features are associated only *characteristically* with an aesthetic term *is* to say that they can never amount to sufficient conditions; no description however full, even in terms characteristic of gracefulness, puts it beyond question that something is graceful in the way a description may put it beyond question that someone is lazy or intelligent.

It is important to observe, however, that I am not merely claiming that no sufficient conditions can be stated for taste concepts. For if this were all, they might not be after all really different from one kind of concept recently discussed. They could be accommodated perhaps with those concepts which Professor H. L. A. Hart has called "defeasible"; it is a characteristic of defeasible concepts that we cannot state sufficient conditions for them because, for any sets we offer, there is always an (open) list of defeating conditions any of which might rule out the application of the concept. The most we can say schematically for a defeasible concept is that, for example, A, B, and C together are sufficient for the concept to apply *unless* some feature is present which overrides or voids them. But,

I want to emphasize, the very fact that we *can* say this sort of thing shows that we are still to the extent in the realm of conditions.[5] The features governing defeasible concepts can ordinarily count only one way, *either* for *or* against. To take Hart's example, "offer" and "acceptance" can count only towards the existence of a valid contract, and fraudulent misrepresentation, duress, and lunacy only against. And even with defeasible concepts, if we are told that there are *no* voiding features present, we can know that some set of conditions or features, A, B, C, . . . , is enough to ensure, for example, that there is a contract. The very notion of a defeasible concept seems to require that some group of features *would* be sufficient *in certain circumstances*, i.e. in the absence of voiding features. In a certain way, defeasible concepts lack sufficient conditions then, but they are still, in the sense described, condition-governed. My claim about taste concepts is stronger; that they are not, except negatively, governed by conditions at all. We could not conclude even in certain circumstances, e.g. if we were told of the absence of all "voiding" or uncharacteristic features (no angularities and the like), that an object *must* certainly be graceful, however fully it was described to us as possessing features characteristic of gracefulness.

My arguments and illustrations so far have been rather simply schematic. Many concepts, including most of the examples I have used . . . are much more thoroughly open and complex than my illustrations suggest. Not only may there be an open list of relevant conditions; it may be impossible to give precise rules telling how many features from the list are needed for a sufficient set or in which combinations; impossible similarly to give precise rules covering the extent or degree to which such features need to be present in those combinations. Indeed, we may have to abandon as futile any attempt to describe or formulate anything like a complete set of precise conditions or rules, and content ourselves with giving only a very general account of the concept, making reference to samples or cases or precedents. We cannot employ these concepts *simply* by being equipped with lists of conditions, readily applicable procedures or sets of rules, however complex. For to exhibit a mastery of one of those concepts we must be able to apply the word correctly to new individual cases, at least to central ones; and each new case may be a uniquely different object, just as each intelligent child or student may differ from others in relevant features and exhibit a unique combination of kinds and degrees of achievement and ability. In dealing with these new cases mechanical rules and procedures would be useless; we have to exercise our judgment, guided by a complex set of examples and precedents. Here then there is a marked *superficial* similarity to aesthetic concepts. For in using aesthetic terms too we learn from samples and examples, not rules, and we have to apply them, likewise, without guidance by rules or readily applicable procedures, to new and unique instances. Neither kind of concept admits of a simply "mechanical" employment.

But this is *only* a superficial similarity. It is at least noteworthy that in applying words like "lazy" or "intelligent" to new and unique instances we say that we are required to exercise *judgment*; it would be indeed odd to say that we are exercising *taste*. In exercising judgment we are called upon to examine the pros and cons, and to decide whether a quite new feature is to be counted as weighing on one side or on the other. But this goes to show that, though we may learn from and rely upon samples and precedents rather than a set of stated conditions, we are not out of the realm of general conditions and guiding principles. These precedents necessarily embody, and are used by us to illustrate, a complex web of governing and relevant conditions which it is impossible to formulate completely. To profit by precedents we have to understand them; and we must argue consistently from case to case. This is the very function of precedents. Thus it is possible, even with these very loosely condition-governed concepts, to take clear or paradigm cases of X and to say "this is X because . . . ," and follow it up with an account of features which logically clinch the matter.

Nothing like this is possible with aesthetic terms. Examples undoubtedly play a crucial role in giving us a grasp of these concepts; but we do not and cannot derive from these examples conditions and principles, however complex, which will enable us, if we are consistent, to apply the terms even to some new cases. When, with a clear case of something which is in fact graceful or balanced but which I have not seen, someone tells me what features make it so, it is always possible for me to wonder whether, in spite of these features, it really is graceful or balanced.

My point may be reinforced thus. A man who failed to realize the nature of aesthetic concepts, or who, knowing he lacked sensitivity in aesthetic matters, did not want to reveal this lack might by assiduous application and shrewd observation provide himself with some rules and generalizations; and by inductive procedures and intelligent guessing, he might frequently say the right things. But he could have no great confidence or certainty; a slight change in an object might at any time unpredictably ruin his calculations, and he might as easily have been wrong as right. No matter how careful he has been about working out a set of consistent principles and conditions, he is only in a position to think that the object is very possibly delicate. With concepts like *lazy, intelligent*, or *contract*, someone who intelligently formulated rules that led him aright appreciably often *would* thereby show the beginning of a grasp of those concepts; but the person we are considering is not even beginning to show an awareness of what delicacy is. Though he sometimes says the right thing, he has not seen, but guessed, that the object is delicate. However intelligent he might be, we could easily tell him wrongly that something was delicate and "explain" why without his being able to detect the deception. (I am ignoring complications now about negative conditions.) But if we did the same with, say, "intelligent" he could at least often uncover some incompatibility which would need explaining. In a world of beings like himself he would have no use for concepts like delicacy. As it is, these concepts would play a quite different role in his life. He would for himself, have no more reason to choose tasteful objects, pictures, and so on, than a deaf man would to avoid noisy places. He could not be praised for exercising taste; at best his ingenuity and intelligence might come in for mention. In "appraising" pictures, statuettes, poems, he would be doing something quite different from what other people do when they exercise taste.

At this point I want to notice in passing that there are times when it may look as if an aesthetic word could be applied according to a rule. These cases vary in type; I shall mention only one. One might say, in using "delicate" of glassware perhaps, that the thinner the glass, other things being equal, the more delicate it is. Similarly, with fabrics, furniture, and so on, there are perhaps times when the thinner or more smoothly finished or more highly polished something is, the more certainly some aesthetic term or other applies. On such occasions someone might formulate a rule and follow it in applying the word to a given range of articles. Now it may be that sometimes when this is so, the word being used is not really an aesthetic term at all; "delicate" applied to glass in this way may at times really mean no more than "thin" or "fragile." But this is certainly not always the case: people often *are* exercising taste even when they say that glass is very delicate because it is so thin, and know that it would be less so if thicker and more so if thinner. These instances where there appear to be rules are peripheral cases of the use of aesthetic terms. If someone did merely follow a rule we should not say he was exercising taste, and we should hesitate to admit that he had any real notion of delicacy until he satisfied us that he could discern it in other instances where no rule was available. In any event, these occasions when aesthetic words can be applied by rule are exceptional, not central or typical, and there is still no reason to think we are dealing with a logical entailment.[6]

It must not be thought that the impossibility of stating any conditions (other than negative) for the application of aesthetic terms results from an accidental poverty or lack of precision in language, or that it is simply a question of extreme complexity. It is true that words like "pink," "bluish," "curving," "mottled" do not permit of anything like a specific naming of each and every varied shade, curve, mottling, and blending. But if we were to give special names much more liberally than either we or even the specialists do (and no doubt there are limits beyond which we could not go), or even if, instead of names, we were to use vast numbers of specimens and samples of particular shades, shapes, mottlings, lines, and configurations, it would still be impossible, and for the same reasons, to supply any conditions.

We do indeed, in talking about a work of art, concern ourselves with its individual and specific features. We say that it is delicate not simply because it is in pale colours but because of *those* pale colours, that it is graceful not because its outline curves slightly but because of *that* particular curve. We use expressions like "because of *its* pale colouring," "because of *the* flecks of bright blue," "because of *the* way the lines converge" where it is clear we are referring not to the presence of general features but to very specific and particular ones. But it is obvious that even with the help of precise names, or even samples and illustrations, of particular shades of colour, contours and lines, any attempt to state conditions would be futile. After all, the very same feature, say a colour or shape or line of a particular sort, which helps make one work may quite spoil another. "It would be quite delicate if it were not for that pale colour there" may be said about the very colour which is singled out in another picture as being largely responsible for its delicate quality. No doubt one way of putting this is to say that the features which make something delicate or graceful, and so on, are combined in a peculiar and unique way; that the aesthetic quality depends upon exactly this individual or unique combination of just these specific colours and shapes so that even a slight change might make all the difference. Nothing is to be achieved by trying to single out or separate features and generalizing about them.

I have now argued that in certain ways aesthetic concepts are not and cannot be condition- or rule-governed.[7] Not to be so governed is one of their essential characteristics. In arguing this I first claimed in a general way that no non-aesthetic features are possible candidates for conditions, and then considered more particularly both the "characteristic" *general* features associated with aesthetic terms and the individual or *specific* features found in particular objects. I have not attempted to examine what relationship these specific features of a work do bear to its aesthetic qualities. An examination of the locutions we use when we refer to them in the course of explaining or supporting our application of an aesthetic term reinforces with linguistic evidence the fact that we are certainly not offering them as explanatory or justifying *conditions*. When we are asked why we say a certain person is lazy or intelligent or courageous, we are being asked in virtue of what we *call* him this; we reply with "because of the way he regularly leaves his work unfinished," or "because of the ease with which he handles such and such problems," and so on. But when we are asked to say why, in our opinion, a picture lacks balance or is sombre in tone, or why a poem is moving or tightly organized, we are doing a different kind of thing. We may use similar locutions: "his verse has strength and variety *because of the way* he handles the metre and employs the caesura," or "it is nobly austere *because* of the lack of detail and the restricted palette." But we can also express what we want to by using quite other expressions: "it is the handling of metre and caesura which is *responsible for* its strength and variety," "its nobly austere quality is *due to* the lack of detail and the use of a restricted palette," "its lack of balance *results from* the highlighting of the figures on the left," "those minor chords *make it* extremely moving," "those converging lines *give it* an extraordinary unity." These are locutions we cannot switch to with "lazy" or "intelligent"; to say what *makes* him lazy, is *responsible* for his laziness, what it is *due to*, is to broach another question entirely.

One after another, in recent discussions, writers have insisted that aesthetic judgments are not "mechanical": "critics do not formulate general standards and apply these mechanically to all, or to classes of, works of art." "Technical points can be settled rapidly, by the application of rules," but aesthetic questions "cannot be settled by any mechanical method." Instead, these writers on aesthetics have emphasized that there is no "substitute for individual judgment" with its "spontaneity and speculation" and that "The final standard . . . [is] the judgment of personal taste."[8] What is surprising is that, though such things have been repeated again and again, no one seems to have said what is meant by "taste" or by the word "mechanical." There are many judgments besides those requiring taste which demand "spontaneity" and "individual judgment" and are not "mechanical." Without a detailed comparison we cannot see in what particular way *aesthetic* judgments are not "mechanical," or how they differ from those other judgments, nor can we begin to specify what taste is. This I have attempted. It is a characteristic and essential feature of judgments which employ an aesthetic term that they cannot be made by appealing, in the sense explained, to non-aesthetic conditions.[9] This, I believe is a logical feature of aesthetic or taste judgments in general though I have argued it here only as regards the more restricted range of judgments which employ aesthetic terms. It is part of what "taste" means.

II

A great deal of work remains to be done on aesthetic concepts. In the remainder of this paper I shall offer further suggestions which may help towards an understanding of them.

The realization that aesthetic concepts are governed only negatively by conditions is likely to give rise to puzzlement over how we manage to apply the words in our aesthetic vocabulary. If we are not following rules and there are no conditions to appeal to, how are we to know when they are applicable? One very natural way to counter this question is to point out that some other sorts of concepts also are not condition-governed. We do not apply simple colour words by following rules or in accordance with principles. We see that the book is red by looking, just as we tell that the tea is sweet by tasting it. So too, it might be said, we just see (or fail to see) that things are delicate, balanced, and the like. This kind of comparison between the exercise of taste and the use of the five senses is indeed familiar; our use of the word "taste" itself shows that the comparison is age-old and very natural. Yet whatever the similarities, there are great dissimilarities too. A careful comparison cannot be attempted here though it would be valuable; but certain differences stand out, and writers who have emphasized that aesthetic judgments are not "mechanical" have sometimes dwelt on and been puzzled by them.

In the first place, while our ability to discern aesthetic features is dependent upon our possession of good eyesight, hearing, and so on, people normally endowed with senses and understanding may nevertheless fail to discern them. "Those who listen to a concert, walk round a gallery, read a poem may have roughly similar sense perceptions, but some get a great deal more than others," Miss Macdonald says; but she adds that she is "puzzled by this feature 'in the object' which can be seen only by a specially qualified observer" and asks, "What is this 'something more'?"[10]

It is this difference between aesthetic and perceptual qualities which in part leads to the view that "works of art are esoteric objects . . . not simple objects of sense perception."[11] But there is no good reason for calling an object esoteric simply because we discern aesthetic qualities in it. The *objects* to which we apply aesthetic words are of the most diverse kinds and by no means esoteric: people and buildings, flowers and gardens, vases and furniture, as well as poems and music. Nor does there seem any good reason for calling the *qualities* themselves esoteric. It is true that someone with perfect eyes or ears might miss them, but we do after all say we *observe* or *notice* them ("Did you notice how very graceful she was?," "Did you observe the exquisite balance in all his pictures?"). In fact, they are very familiar indeed. We learn while quite young to use many aesthetic words, though they are, as one might expect from their dependence upon our ability to see, hear, distinguish colours, and the like, not the earliest words we learn; and our mastery and sophistication in using them develop along with the rest of our vocabulary. They are not rarities; some ranges of them are in regular use in everyday discourse.

The second notable difference between the exercise of taste and the use of the five senses lies in the way we support those judgments in which aesthetics concepts are employed. Although we use these concepts without rules or conditions, we do defend or support our judgments, and convince others of their rightness, by talking; "disputation about art is not futile," as Miss Macdonald says, for critics do "attempt a certain kind of explanation of works of art with the object of establishing correct judgments."[12] Thus even though this disputation does not consist in "deductive or inductive inference" or "reasoning," its occurrence is enough to show how very different these judgments are from those of a simple perceptual sort.

Now the critic's talk, it is clear, frequently consists in mentioning or pointing out the features, including easily discernible non-aesthetic ones, upon which the aesthetic qualities depend. But the puzzling question remains how, by mentioning these features, the critic is thereby justifying or supporting his judgments. To this question a number of recent writers have given an answer. Stuart Hampshire, for example, says that "One engages in aesthetic discussion for the sake of what one might see on the way . . . if one has been brought to see what there is to be seen in the object, the purpose of discussion is achieved. . . . The point is to bring people to see these features."[13] The critic's talk, that is, often serves to support his judgments in a special way; it helps us to *see* what he has seen, namely, the aesthetic qualities of the object. But even when it is agreed that this is one of the main things that critics do, puzzlement tends to break out again over *how* they do it. How is it that by talking about features of the work (largely non-aesthetic ones) we can manage to bring others to see what they had not seen? "What sort of endowment is this which *talking* can modify? . . . Discussion does not improve eyesight and hearing" (my italics).[14]

Yet of course we do succeed in applying aesthetic terms, and we frequently do succeed by talking (and pointing and gesturing in certain ways) in bringing others to see what we see. One begins to suspect that puzzlement over how we can possibly do this, and puzzlement over the "esoteric" character of aesthetic qualities too, arises from bearing in mind inappropriate philosophical models. When someone is unable to see that the book on the table is brown, we cannot get him to see that it is by talking; consequently it seems puzzling that we might get someone to see that the vase is graceful by talking. If we are to dispel this puzzlement and recognize aesthetic concepts and qualities for what they are, we must abandon unsuitable models and investigate how we actually employ these concepts. With so much interest in and agreement about *what* the critic does, one might expect descriptions of *how* he does it to have been given. But little has been said about this, and what has been said is unsatisfactory.

Miss Macdonald,[15] for example, subscribes to this view of the critic's task as presenting "what is not obvious to casual or uninstructed inspection," and she does ask the question "What sort of considerations are involved, *and how*, to justify a critical verdict?" (my italics). But she does not in fact go on to answer it. She addresses herself instead to the different, though related, question of the interpretation of art works. In complex works different critics claim, often justifiably, to discern different features; hence Miss Macdonald suggests that in critical discourse the critic is bringing us to see what he sees by offering new interpretations. But if the question is "what [the critic] does and how he does it," he cannot be represented either wholly or even mainly as providing new interpretations. His task quite as often is simply to help us appreciate qualities which other critics have regularly found in the works he discusses. To put the stress upon *new* interpretations is to leave untouched the question how, by talking, he can help us to see *either* the newly appreciated aesthetic qualities *or* the old. In any case, besides complex poems or plays which may bear many interpretations, there are also relatively simple ones. There are also vases, buildings, and furniture, not to mention faces, sunsets, and scenery, about which no questions of "interpretation" arise but about which we talk in similar ways and make similar judgments. So the "puzzling" questions remain: how do we support these judgments and how do we bring others to see what we see?

Hampshire,[16] who likewise believes that the critic brings us "to see what there is to be seen in the object," does give some account of how the critic does this. "The greatest service of the critic" is to point out, isolate, and place in a frame of attention the "particular features of the particular object which *make* it ugly or beautiful"; for it is "difficult to see and hear all that there is to see and hear," and simply a prejudice to suppose that while "things really do have colours and shapes . . . there do not exist literally and objectively, concordances of colours and perceived rhythms and balances of shapes." However, these "extraordinary qualities" which the critic "may have seen (in the wider sense of 'see')" are "qualities which are of no direct practical interest." Consequently, to bring us to see them the critic employs "an unnatural use of words in description"; "the common vocabulary, being created for practical purposes, obstructs any disinterested perception of things"; and so these qualities "are normally described metaphorically by some transference of terms from the common vocabulary."

Much of what Hampshire says is right. But there is also something quite wrong in the view that the "common" vocabulary "obstructs" our aesthetic purposes, that it is "unnatural" to take it over and use it metaphorically, and that the critic "is under the necessity of building . . . a vocabulary *in opposition to the main tendency of his language*" (my italics). First, while we do often coin new metaphors in order to describe aesthetic qualities, we are by no means always under the necessity of wresting the "common vocabulary" from its "natural" uses to serve our purposes. There does exist, as I observed earlier, a large and accepted vocabulary of aesthetic terms some of which, whatever their metaphorical origins, are now not metaphors at all, others of which are at most quasi-metaphorical. Second, this view that our use of metaphor and quasi-metaphor for aesthetic purposes is unnatural or a makeshift into which we are forced by a language designed for other purposes misrepresents fundamentally the character of aesthetic qualities and aesthetic language. There is nothing unnatural about using words like "forceful," "dynamic," or "tightly-knit" in criticism; they do their work perfectly and are exactly the words needed for the purposes they serve. We do not want or need to replace them by words which lack the metaphorical element. In using them to describe works of art, the very point is that we are noticing aesthetic qualities related to their literal or common meanings. If we possessed a quite different word from "dynamic," one we could use to point out an aesthetic quality unrelated to the common meaning of "dynamic," it could not be used to describe that quality which "dynamic" does serve to point out. Hampshire pictures "a colony of aesthetes, disengaged from practical needs and manipulations" and says that "descriptions of aesthetic qualities, which for us are metaphorical, might seem to them to have an altogether literal and familiar sense"; they might use "a more directly descriptive vocabulary." But if they had a new and "directly descriptive" vocabulary lacking the links with non-aesthetic properties and interests which our vocabulary possesses, they would have to remain silent about many of the aesthetic qualities we can describe; further, if they were more completely "disengaged from practical needs" and other non-aesthetic awareness and interests, they would perforce be blind to many aesthetic qualities we can appreciate. The links between aesthetic qualities and non-aesthetic ones are both obvious and vital. Aesthetic concepts, all of them, carry with them attachments and in one way or another are tethered to or parasitic upon non-aesthetic features. The fact that many aesthetic terms are metaphorical or quasi-metaphorical in no way means that common language is an ill-adapted tool with which we have to struggle. When someone writes as Hampshire does, one suspects again that critical language is being judged against other models. To use language which is frequently metaphorical might be strange for some *other* purpose or from the standpoint of doing something else, but for the purpose and from the standpoint of making aesthetic observations it is not. To say it is an unnatural use of language for doing *this* is to imply there is or could be for this purpose some other and "natural" use. But these are natural ways of talking about aesthetic matters.

To help understand what the critic does, then, how he supports his judgments and gets his audience to see what he sees, I shall attempt a brief description of the methods we use as critics.[17]

(1) We may simply mention or point out non-aesthetic features: "Notice these flecks of colour, that dark mass there, those lines." By merely drawing attention to those easily discernible features which make the painting luminous or warm or dynamic, we often succeed in bringing someone to see these aesthetic qualities. We get him to see B by mentioning something different, A. Sometimes in doing this we are drawing attention to features which may have gone unnoticed by an untrained or insufficiently attentive eye or ear: "Just listen for the repeated figure in the left hand," "Did you notice the figure of Icarus in the Breughel? It is very small." Sometimes they are features which have been seen or heard but of which the significance or purpose has been missed in any of a variety of ways: "Notice how much darker he has made the central figure, how much brighter these colours are than the adjacent ones," "Of course, you've observed the ploughman in the foreground; but had you considered how he, like everyone else in the picture, is going about his business without noticing the fall of Icarus?" In mentioning features which may be discerned by anyone with normal eyes, ears, and intelligence, we are singling out what may serve as a kind of key to grasping or seeing something else (and the key may not be the same for each person).

(2) On the other hand we often simply mention the very qualities we want people to see. We point to a painting and say, "Notice how nervous and delicate the drawing is," or "See what energy and vitality it has." The use of the aesthetic term itself may do the trick; we say what the quality or character is, and people who had not seen it before see it.

(3) Most often, there is a linking of remarks about aesthetic and non-aesthetic features: "Have you noticed this line and that, and the points of bright colour here and there . . . don't they give it vitality, energy?"

(4) We do, in addition, often make extensive and helpful use of similes and genuine metaphors: "It's as if there are small points of light burning," "as though he had thrown on the paint violently and in anger," "the light shimmers, the lines dance, everything is air, lightness and gaiety," "his canvasses are fires, they crackle, burn, and blaze, even at their most subdued always restlessly flickering, but often bursting into flame, great pyrotechnic displays," and so on.

(5) We make use of contrasts, comparisons, and reminiscences: "Suppose he had made that a lighter yellow, moved it to the right, how flat it would have been," "Don't you think it has something of the quality of a Rembrandt?," "Hasn't it the same serenity, peace, and quality of light of those summer evenings in Norfolk?" We use what keys we have to the known sensitivity, susceptibilities, and experience of our audience.

Critics and commentators may range, in their methods, from one extreme to the other, from painstaking concentration on points of detail, line and colour, vowels and rhymes, to more or less flowery and luxuriant metaphor. Even the enthusiastic biographical sketch decorated with suitable epithet and metaphor may serve. What is best depends on both the audience and the work under discussion. But this would not be a complete sketch unless certain other notes were added.

(6) Repetition and reiteration often play an important role. When we are in front of a canvas we may come back time and again to the same points, drawing attention to the same lines and shapes, repeating the same words, "swirling," "balance," "luminosity," or the same similes and metaphors, as if time and familiarity, looking harder, listening more carefully, paying closer attention may help. So again with variation; it often helps to talk round what we have said, to build up, supplement with more talk *of the same kind*. When someone misses the swirling quality, when one epithet or one metaphor does not work, we throw in related ones; we speak of its wild movement, how it twists and turns, writhes and whirls, as though, failing to score a direct hit, we may succeed with a barrage of near-synonyms.

(7) Finally, besides our verbal performances, the rest of our behaviour is important. We accompany our talk with appropriate tones of voice, expression, nods, looks, and gesture. A critic may sometimes do more with a sweep of the arm than by talking. An appropriate gesture may make us see the violence in a painting or the character of a melodic line.

These ways of acting and talking are not significantly different whether we are dealing with a particular work, paragraph, or line, or speaking of an artist's work as a whole, or even drawing attention to a sunset or scenery. But even with the speaker doing all this, we may fail to see what he sees. There may be a point, though there need be no limit except that imposed by time and patience, at which he gives up and sets us (or himself) down as lacking in some way, defective in sensitivity. He may tell us to look or read again, or to read or look at other things and then come back again to this; he may suspect there are experiences in life we have missed. But these are the things he does. This is what succeeds if anything does; indeed it is all that can be done.

But realizing clearly that, whether we are dealing with art or scenery or people or natural objects, this is how we operate with aesthetic concepts, we may recognize this sphere of human activity for what it is. We operate with different kinds of concepts in different ways. If we want someone to agree that a colour is red we may take it into a good light and ask him to look; if it is viridian we may fetch a colour chart and make him compare; if we want him to agree that a figure is fourteen-sided we get him to count; and to bring him to agree that something is dilapidated or that someone is lazy we may do other things, citing features and reasoning and arguing about them. These are the methods appropriate to these various concepts. But the ways we get someone to see aesthetic qualities are different; they are of the kind I have described. With each kind of concept we can describe what we do and how we do it. But the methods suited to these other concepts will not do for aesthetic ones, or vice versa. We cannot prove by argument or by assembling a sufficiency of conditions that something is graceful; but this is no more puzzling than our inability to prove, by using the methods, metaphors, and gestures of the art critic, that it will be mate in ten moves. The questions raised admit of no answer beyond the sort of description I have given. To go on to ask, with puzzlement, how it is that *when* we do these things people come to see, is like asking how is it that, when we take the book into a good light, our companion agrees with us that it is red. There is no place for this kind of question or puzzlement. Aesthetic concepts are as natural, as little esoteric, as any others. It is against the background of different and philosophically more familiar models that they seem puzzling.

I have described how people justify aesthetic judgments and bring others to see aesthetic qualities in things. I shall end by showing that the methods I have outlined are the ones natural for and characteristic of taste concepts from the start. When someone tries to make me see that a painting is delicate or balanced, I have some understanding of these terms already and know in a sense what I am looking for. But if there is puzzlement over how, by talking, he can bring me to see these qualities in this picture, there should be equal puzzlement over how I learned to use aesthetic terms and discern aesthetic qualities in the first place. We may ask, therefore, how we learn to do these things; and this is to inquire (1) what natural potentialities and tendencies people have and (2) how we develop and take advantage of these capacities in training and teaching. Now for the second of these there is no doubt that our ability to notice and respond to aesthetic qualities is cultivated and developed by our contacts with parents and teachers from quite an early age. What is interesting for my present purpose is that, while we are being taught in the presence of examples what grace, delicacy and so on are, the methods used, the language and behavior, are of a piece with those of the critic as I have already described them.

To pursue these two questions, consider first those words like "dynamic," "melancholy," "balanced," "taut," or "gay" the aesthetic use of which is quasi-metaphorical. It has already been emphasized that we could not use them thus without some experience of situations where they are used literally. The present inquiry is how we shift from literal to aesthetic uses of them. For this it is required that there be certain abilities and tendencies to link experiences, to regard certain things as similar, and to see, explore, and be interested in these similarities. It is a feature of human intelligence and sensitivity that we do spontaneously do these things and that the tendency can be encouraged and developed. It is no more baffling that we should employ aesthetic terms of this sort than that we should make metaphors at all. Easy and smooth transitions by which we shift to the use of these aesthetic terms are not hard to find. We suggest to children that simple pieces of music are hurrying or running or skipping or dawdling, from there we move to lively, gay, jolly, happy, smiling, or sad, and, as their experiences and vocabulary broaden, to solemn, dynamic, or melancholy. But the child also discovers for himself many of these parallels and takes interest or delight in them. He is likely on his own to skip, march, clap, or laugh with the music, and without this natural tendency our training would get nowhere. In so far, however, as we do take advantage of this tendency and help him by training, *we do just what the critic does*. We may merely need to persuade the child to pay attention, to look or listen; or we may simply *call* the music jolly. But we are also likely to use, as the critic does, reiteration, synonyms, parallels, contrasts, similes, metaphors, gestures, and other expressive behavior.

Of course the recognition of similarities and simple metaphorical extensions are not the only transitions to the aesthetic use of language. Others are made in different ways; for instance, by the kind of peripheral cases I mentioned earlier. When our admiration is for something as simple as the thinness of a glass or the smoothness of a fabric, it is not difficult to call attention to such things, evoke a similar delight, and introduce suitable aesthetic terms. These transitions are only the beginnings; it may often be questionable whether a term is yet being used aesthetically or not. Many of the terms I have mentioned may be used in ways which are not straightforwardly literal but of which we should hesitate to say that they demanded much yet by way of aesthetic sensitivity. We speak of warm and cool colours, and we may say of a brightly coloured picture that at least it is gay and lively. When we have brought someone to make this sort of metaphorical extension of terms, he has made one of the transitional steps from which he may move on to uses which more obviously deserve to be called aesthetic and demand a more obviously aesthetic appreciation. When I said at the outset that aesthetic sensitivity was rarer than some other natural endowments, I was not denying that it varies in degree from the rudimentary to the refined. Most people learn easily to make the kinds of remarks I am now considering. But when someone can call bright canvasses gay and lively without being able to spot the one which is really vibrant, or can recognize the obvious outward vigor and energy of a student composition played *con fuoco* while failing to see that it lacks inner fire and drive, we do not regard his aesthetic sensitivity in these areas as particularly developed. However, once these transitions from common to aesthetic uses are begun in the more obvious cases, the domain of aesthetic concepts may broaden out, and they become more subtle and even partly autonomous. The initial steps, however varied the metaphorical shifts and however varied the experiences upon which they are parasitic, are natural and easy.

Much the same is true when we turn to those words which have no standard non-aesthetic use, "lovely," "pretty," "dainty," "graceful," "elegant." We cannot say that these are learned by a metaphorical shift. But they still are linked to non-aesthetic features in many ways and the learning of them also is made possible by certain kinds of natural response, reaction, and ability. We learn them not so much by noticing similarities, but by our attention being caught and focused in other ways. Certain phenomena which are outstanding or remarkable or unusual catch the eye or ear, seize our attention and interest, and move us to surprise, admiration, delight, fear, or distaste. Children begin by reacting in these ways to spectacular sunsets, woods in autumn, roses, dandelions, and other striking and colourful objects, and it is in these circumstances that we find ourselves introducing general aesthetic words to them, like "lovely," "pretty," and "ugly." It is not an accident that the first lessons in aesthetic appreciation consist in drawing the child's attention to roses rather than to grass; nor is it surprising that we remark to him on the autumn colour rather than on the subdued tints of winter. We all of us, not only children, pay aesthetic attention more readily to such outstanding and easily noticeable things. We notice with pleasure early spring grass or the first snow, hills of notably marked and varied contours, scenery flecked with a great variety of colour or dappled variously with sun and shadow. We are struck and impressed by great size or mass, as with mountains or cathedrals. We are similarly responsive to unusual precision or minuteness or remarkable feats of skill, as with complex and elaborate filigree, or intricate wood carving and fan-vaulting. It is at these times, taking advantage of these natural interests and admirations, that we first teach the simpler aesthetic words. People of moderate aesthetic sensitivity and sophistication continue to exhibit aesthetic interest mainly on such occasions and to use only the more general words ("pretty," "lovely," and the like). But these situations may serve as a beginning from which we extend our aesthetic interests to wider and less obvious fields, mastering as we go the more subtle and specific vocabulary of taste. The principles do not change; the basis for learning more specific terms like "graceful," "delicate," and "elegant" is also our interest in and admiration for various non-aesthetic natural properties ("She seems to move *effortlessly*, as if floating," "So very *thin* and *fragile*, as if a breeze might destroy it," "So *small* and yet so *intricate*," "So *economical* and perfectly *adapted*").[18] And even with these aesthetic terms which are not metaphorical themselves ("graceful," "delicate," "elegant"), we rely in the same way upon the critic's methods, including comparison, illustration, and metaphor, to teach or make clear what they mean.

I have wished to emphasize in the latter part of this paper the natural basis of responses of various kinds without which aesthetic terms could not be learned. I have also outlined what some of the features are to which we naturally respond: similarities of various sorts, notable colours, shapes, scents, size, intricacy, and much else besides. Even the non-metaphorical aesthetic terms have significant links with all kinds of natural features by which our interest, wonder, admiration, delight, or distaste is aroused. But in particular I have wanted to urge that it should not strike us as puzzling that the critic supports his judgment and brings us to see aesthetic qualities by pointing out key features and talking about them in the way he does. It is by the very same methods that people helped us develop our aesthetic sense and master its vocabulary from the beginning. If we responded to those methods then, it is not surprising that we respond to the critic's discourse now. It would be surprising if, by using this language and behavior, people could *not* sometimes bring us to see the aesthetic qualities of things; for this would prove us lacking in one characteristically human kind of awareness and activity.

NOTES

1. I shall speak loosely of an "aesthetic term," even when, because the word sometimes has other uses, it would be more correct to speak of its *use* as an aesthetic term. I shall also speak of "non-aesthetic" words, concepts, features, and so on. None of the terms other writers use, "natural," "observable," "perceptual," "physical," "objective" (qualities), "neutral," "descriptive" (language), when they approach the distinction I am making, is really apt for my purpose.
2. A contrast will reinforce this. If a critic were to describe a passage of music as chattering, carbonated, or gritty, a painter's colouring as vitreous, farinaceous, or effervescent, or a writer's style as glutinous, or abrasive, he *would* be using live metaphors rather than drawing on the more normal language of criticism. Words like "athletic," "vertiginous," "silken" may fall somewhere between.
3. In a paper reprinted in *Aesthetics and Language*, ed. by W. Elton (Oxford, 1954), pp. 131–46, Arnold Isenberg discusses certain problems about aesthetic concepts and qualities. Like others who approach these problems, he does not isolate them, as I do, from questions about verdicts on the *merits* of works of art, or from questions about *likings* and *preferences*. He says something parallel to my remarks above: "There is not in all the world's criticism a single purely descriptive statement concerning which one is prepared to say beforehand, 'if it is true, I shall *like* that work so much the better'" (p. 139, my italics). I should think *this* is highly questionable.
4. Isenberg (op. cit., p. 132) makes a somewhat similar but mistaken point: "If we had been told that the colours of a certain painting are garish, it would be *astonishing* to find that they are *all* very pale and unsaturated" (my italics). But if we say "all" rather than "predominantly," then "astonishing" is the wrong word. The word that goes with "all" is "impossible"; "astonishing" might go with "predominantly."
5. H. L. A. Hart, "The Ascription of Responsibility and Rights in *Logic and Language*," First Series, ed. by A. G. N. Flew (Oxford, 1951). Hart indeed speaks of "conditions" throughout, see p. 148.
6. I cannot in the compass of this paper discuss the other types of apparent exceptions to my thesis. Cases where a man *lacking* in sensitivity might learn and follow a rule, as above, ought to be distinguished from cases where someone who *possesses* sensitivity might know, from a non-aesthetic description, that an aesthetic term applies. I have stated my thesis as though this latter kind of case never occurs because I have had my eye on the logical features of *typical* aesthetic judgments and have preferred to over- rather than understate my view. But with certain aesthetic terms, especially negative ones, there may perhaps be some rare genuine exceptions when a description enables us to visualize very fully, and when what is described belongs to certain restricted classes of things, say human faces or animal forms. Perhaps a description like "One eye red and rheumy, the other missing, a wart-covered nose, a twisted mouth, a greenish pallor" may justify in a strong sense ("must be," "cannot but be") the judgments "ugly" or "hideous." If so, such cases are marginal, form a very small minority, and are uncharacteristic or atypical of aesthetic judgments in general. Usually, when, on hearing a description, we say "it *must* be very beautiful (graceful, or the like)," we mean no more than "it surely must be, it's only remotely possible that it isn't." Different again are situations, and these are very numerous, where we can move quite simply from "bright colours" to "gay," or from "reds and yellows" to "warm," but where we are as yet only on the borderline of anything that could be called an expression of taste or aesthetic sensibility. I have stressed the importance of this transitional and border area between non-aesthetic and obviously aesthetic judgments below.
7. Helen Knight says (Elton, op. cit., p. 152) that

"piquant" (one of my "aesthetic" terms) "depends on" various features (a *retroussé* nose, a pointed chin, and the like), and that these features are *criteria* for it; this second claim is what I am denying. She also maintains that "good," when applied to works of art, depends on *criteria* like balance, solidity, depth, profundity (my aesthetic terms again; I should place piquancy in this list). I would deny this too, though I regard it as a different question and do not consider it in this paper. The two questions need separating; the relation of nonaesthetic features (*retrousse*, pointed) to aesthetic qualities, and the relation of aesthetic qualities to "aesthetically good" (verdicts). Most writings which touch on the nature of aesthetic concepts have this other (verdict) question mainly in mind. Mrs. Knight blurs this difference when she says, for example, "'piquant' is the same kind of word as 'good.'"

8. See articles by Margaret Macdonald and J. A. Passmore in Elton, op. cit., pp. 41, 40, 118, 119.
9. As I indicated . . . above, I have dealt only with the relation of *non-aesthetic* to aesthetic features. Perhaps a description in *aesthetic* terms may occasionally suffice for applying another aesthetic term. Johnson's Dictionary gives "handsome" as "beautiful with dignity"; Shorter O.E.D. gives "pretty" as "beautiful in a slight, dainty, or diminutive way."
10. Macdonald in Elton, op. cit., pp. 114, 119. See also pp. 120, 122.
11. Macdonald, ibid., pp. 114, 120-3. She speaks of non-aesthetic properties here as "physical" or "observable" qualities, and distinguishes between "physical object" and "work of art."
12. Ibid., pp. 115-16; cf. also John Holloway, *Proceedings of the Aristotelian Society*, Supplementary Vol. xxiii (1949), pp. 175-6.
13. Stuart Hampshire in Elton, op. cit., p. 165. Cf. also remarks in Elton by Isenberg (pp. 142, 145), Passmore (p. 38), in *Philosophy and Psycho-analysis* by John Wisdom (Oxford, 1953), pp. 223-4, and in Holloway, op. cit., p. 175.
14. Macdonald, op. cit., pp. 119-20.
15. Ibid., see pp. 127, 122, 125, 115. Other writers also place the stress on interpretation, cf. Holloway, op. cit., p. 173 ff.
16. Op. cit., pp. 165-8.
17. Holloway, op. cit., pp. 173-4, lists some of these very briefly.
18. It is worth noticing that most of the words which in current usage are primarily or exclusively aesthetic terms had earlier non-aesthetic uses and gained their present use by some kind of metaphorical shift. Without reposing too great weight on these etymological facts, it can be seen that their history reflects connections with the responses, interests, and natural features I have mentioned as underlying the learning and use of aesthetic terms. These transitions suggest both the dependence of aesthetic upon other interests, and what some of these interests are. Connected with liking, delight, affection, regard, estimation, or choice—*beautiful, graceful, delicate, lovely, exquisite, elegant, dainty*; with fear or repulsion—*ugly*; with what notably catches the eye or attention—*garish, splendid, gaudy*; with what attracts by notable rarity, precision, skill, ingenuity, elaboration—*dainty, nice, pretty, exquisite*; with adaptation to function, suitability to ease of handling—*handsome*.

The Variety of Aesthetic Qualities

Goran Hermeren

INTRODUCTION

Aesthetic qualities can be compared in many respects, for example with respect to whether they are culture-dependent or not, whether the qualities are experienced as internal or external (qualities of the experienced object), whether the terms denoting them are descriptive or evaluative, and are used literally or metaphorically. Such comparisons, which I have attempted elsewhere,[1] will however, not be made here.

The purpose of the present paper is to highlight the relations between several types of aesthetic qualities, and to explain why these distinctions may be important. For example, I propose to distinguish below between

emotion qualities like 'somber', 'solemn', 'serene', 'sentimental', 'joyous', 'sad', 'melancholy', 'gay', 'brooding', 'cheerful', where neither artist nor beholder is necessarily joyous, if the work is said to be joyous, etc.,

behavior qualities like 'bold', 'nervous', 'tense', 'vital', 'vehement', 'intense', 'impatient', 'vigorous', 'exuberant', 'restrained', 'lively', 'daring', 'graceful', 'relaxed', 'vivacious', 'gentle', 'stiff', where descriptions of how people behave are applied to art by metaphorical extension,

gestalt qualities like 'unified', 'disorganized', 'coherent', 'tightly knit', 'complete', 'simple', 'balanced', 'harmonious', where the words describing these qualities refer to a quality that a complex has as a result of the relation between its parts,

taste qualities like 'elegant', 'delightful', 'harsh', 'picturesque', 'garish', 'sublime', 'beautiful', 'handsome', 'clumsy' and so forth, which are related to canons of taste internalized by critics and beholders during a particular period, and

reaction qualities (affective qualities) like 'funny', 'moving', 'tragic', 'comic', 'trite', 'surprising', 'shocking', 'mysterious', 'stirring', 'glaring', 'impressive', 'engaging', 'boring', 'trivial', which involve affective responses on the part of the beholder, or disposition to such responses, plus perhaps recognition that it is appropriate to have such dispositions.

REACTION QUALITIES

Some aesthetic qualities are in a characteristic way tied to the reactions of those who contemplate works of art. For want of a better name, I propose to call these qualities reaction qualities or simply R-qualities. "Affective qualities" might be an alternative label.

I shall now mention some qualities of this kind and I shall indicate the corresponding reaction within parentheses: funny (to be amused), moving (to be moved), frightening (to be frightened), awe-inspiring (to be inspired with awe), boring (to be bored), interesting (to be interested), fascinating (to be fascinated), provocative (to be provoked), touching (to be touched), amusing (to be amused), convincing (to be convinced), and so forth.

What kind of connection is there between these reactions and the various R-qualities? To answer this question it might be useful to compare the following pairs of sentences:

From *Aesthetic Quality and Aesthetic Experience*, Michael H. Mitias, ed. (Amsterdam: Rodopi B. V., 1988). Reprinted by permission of the publisher and the author. Footnotes have been renumbered.

X is funny	Someone is (would be) amused by X
X is moving	Someone is (would be) moved by X
X is frightening	Someone is (would be) frightened by X
X is awe-inspiring	Someone is (would be) inspired with awe by X
X is boring	Someone is (would be) bored by X
X is interesting	Someone is (would be) interested by X
X is fascinating	Someone is (would be) fascinated by X

I would like to argue that those who assert the statement expressed by the left sentence and at the same time deny the statement expressed by the corresponding right sentence do not know what "funny," "moving," "frightening," etc. mean. "Someone is (was) moved by X" is a necessary but not sufficient condition for "X is moving" (in the sense relevant here).

However, some qualifications must be made in order to avoid misunderstandings. Sometimes a critic is only making autobiographical statements when he or she writes that a particular work of art is moving, frightening, awe-inspiring, and so forth. What the critic means is then only that *he* (*or she*) was moved, frightened, inspired, or bored, by the work. In these cases "someone" in the sentences to the right above can be replaced by "I, the critic."

I would like to stress, however, that this does not mean that statements like "X is interesting, but I was bored by X" are contradictory. But they are odd and require some kind of explanation, for example, "because I was too tired when I was watching X (reading, looking at, listening to, . . .) X." But statements like "X is moving" are not always or mainly autobiographical. R-qualities involve affective responses on the part of the beholder, or dispositions to such responses, plus the recognition that it is appropriate to have such dispositions.[2] To say that, say, a painting X is moving is typically to say or suggest that anyone having a certain background and training and who is contemplating X under certain standard conditions (normal light, etc.) would be moved by X.

Thus, according to this analysis X has a disposition to produce an effect, and "would" in the previous sentence is subjunctive rather than moral (= ought to). If R is a reaction quality and r the corresponding reaction, then the connection between R and r is thus indicated by the following general statement:

(R) X has R, only if X has such properties that anyone with a certain training and looking at X under standard conditions would (1) be disposed to experience r, and (2) recognize that in his own particular culture it is appropriate to have r under these conditions.

This kind of analysis has, in my view, several advantages, and I shall now point to some of them.

In the first place, what is funny, comic, interesting, moving, etc. to one person need not be interesting or moving to another person. This is a well-known fact of ordinary life, and the analysis proposed above is compatible with this observation. For this reason it is necessary to understand the reaction as relative to personality traits as well as to a fixed cultural frame of reference (background, training, experience, and so forth). Moreover, an interesting and moving art work can go to pieces, before anyone other than a critic who is too tired to be interested or moved by it has seen it.

EMOTION (OR EXPRESSIVE) QUALITIES

Reaction qualities differ in many interesting ways from emotion or expressive qualities perceived directly in lines, shapes, colors and compositions like sad, melancholy, gay, somber, solemn, serene, joyous, sentimental, and so forth. (To avoid misunderstandings, it should be made clear at once that I do not presuppose that there is a sharp distinction between perception and interpretation, nor that interpretation is independent of cultural background and practices.[3] For short, I shall refer to these latter qualities as simply E-qualities.

The main reason for distinguishing between E-qualities and R-qualities is that the analysis proposed above of R-qualities cannot be applied to E-qualities. A tune can be sad without making the listener sad; a landscape can be melancholy without making the observer melancholy, and so forth. In the previous section I have stressed the importance of distinguishing between

(1) The tune X is melancholy
(2) The tune X makes me melancholy

The well-known psychologist James Gibson once said that it is possible that the melancholy in Mozart's string quartets has not been discovered until quite recently, but it has been there all the time. If this is correct, or close to being correct, (1) cannot be identified with (2). Nor can it be identified with a statement about the mood of the composer at the time he created the tune.

People experience emotions, but works of art do not. Most, if not all, terms used to call attention to emotion qualities are metaphors. Suppose "E" is such a term. To apply "E" to a person is then to ascribe to that person a mood or an intentional state. But to apply "E" to a work of art is not to ascribe to that work of art a mood or an intentional state. If this is so, one might wonder how statements about works of art like "X is E" are to be understood.

This is a question on which there has been a great deal of discussion, though I think it is fair to say that no solution so far proposed has been universally accepted. In my view, this is at least partly due to the failure to distinguish clearly between semantical and ontological questions.

Several scholars have called attention to the similarities or analogies between sad music and sad people. For example, O. K. Bouwsma writes as follows: "Sad music has some of the characteristics of people who are sad. It will be slow, not tripping, it will be low, not tinkling. People who are sad move slowly, and when they speak, they speak softly and low."[4] Similarly, John Hospers has written: "A work of music may be sad: that is, it may contain some of the features which characterize people when they are sad; it is soft, seldom loud; it is slow, seldom fast; it is hushed, never strident."[5] These observations are no doubt true, but it is not quite clear to me what they prove.

Suppose we look at a work of art (listen to a tune, ...) and find that it has a certain emotion quality, say, sadness. If what I have said here is roughly correct, we perceive directly that the work or the tune is sad (though I would like to stress again that I have not said, and do not want to say, that this perception is independent of the cultural background of the beholder).

Now it is important to distinguish clearly between two problems: (1) Why do we choose the term "sad" rather than any other term to characterize this E-quality? and (2) How is this E-quality to be analyzed? In particular, how is it related to our own feelings of sadness and our experiences of sad people? The first question is semantical and not ontological, whereas the second question is ontological (or phenomenological) but not semantical.

As to the first question, I think that the observations by Bouwsma and Hospers (as well as by several others) give the key to a plausible answer. The point of departure is, then, that we experience many emotions and notice features of art works for which there are no names or terms in our language. This, of course, creates a problem, if we want to talk about works of art and their qualities. How is this problem solved by critics?

We use "sad" to characterize certain states of mind of which we have first-hand knowledge by acquaintance ("I am sad") as well as the behavior of other people ("she is sad"). People who are sad typically behave in certain ways, and there is an analogy between the features of sad music and the features characterizing sad people. This is why we use the term "sad" to call attention to certain E-qualities in music. In saying this, however, I have not answered the ontological and phenomenological questions raised above.

As to the second question, it has sometimes been suggested that when we listen to sad tunes, we experience sadness and this emotion is somehow projected onto the work of art. The idea is, it seems, that our experiences of sad music and sad people have a common content. It may even be argued that this gives an answer to the semantic questions: the reason why we choose "sad" to characterize both sad music and sad people is simply that our experiences of sad music and sad people have a common content.

This account may be right but no doubt it raises several difficult problems, among others the following ones: how are the concepts of content and projection to be understood, and how are the claims of this theory to be tested? In what non-metaphysical sense can music and people possibly have a common content?

Before concluding this discussion, I would like to suggest a somewhat different analysis. It is an adverbial Chisholm-inspired approach in the sense that to experience sad music is not construed as having experiences with a certain content but rather as experiencing it *in a certain way*. To experience sad music is to experience music sadly. The difference may seem slight but I think it is important; some of the objections that can be made against the talk of projections and contents cannot be made to the approach suggested here. The important thing is that I do not assume that our experiences of sad music and sad people have a common content. What I am assuming is that I experience sad music in a way that in certain respects is similar or analogous to the way I experience sad people.

In order to be able to decide whether this theory gives an adequate answer to the ontological and phenomenological problems raised above, it has to be worked out in greater detail than I can possibly do here. But the theory advocated here[6]—that there are aesthetic qualities, and that they are perceived directly—is compatible with both the content theory and the adverbial theory; it does not imply either of them.

Simply, both of these theories are compatible with the semantic theory suggested above which is designed to explain why we choose the term "sad" rather than any other to call attention to certain E-qualities in works of art.

BEHAVIOR QUALITIES

There are a great number of other qualities in works of art which can be analyzed in roughly the same way as emotion or expressive qualities. To this group belong, for instance, 'nervous', 'vital', 'powerful', 'restrained', 'violent', 'passionate', 'vehement', 'lively', 'elegant', 'daring', 'graceful', 'vivacious'. I shall call these qualities behavior qualities or simply B-qualities.

They differ from E-qualities in the following way: when ascribed to persons, they refer to behavior rather than to moods or intentional states. Thus, if "B" is a term used to call attention to what I intend to call a behavior quality in a work of art, then to apply "B" to a person is to ascribe to that person a certain manner of acting or of appearing. A person's behavior can be nervous, vital, powerful, restrained, violent, passionate, vehement, lively, elegant, etc.

There is extensive literature on how such statements are to be understood. However, whether the dispositional analysis proposed by Ryle and his followers[7] can be applied to statements of this sort need not worry us at this point. The important thing is that these terms—when used about works of art—are metaphorical in the same way as "sad" and "melancholy" when these latter terms are used to call attention to E-qualities in art works.

Moreover, there are similarities between powerful sculptures and powerful people; some of the features which characterize the behavior of powerful people will also characterize powerful sculptures. Similarly, there are analogies between a nervous drawing (or line) and the behavior of nervous persons. Here, too, we may ask why we use certain metaphors rather than others to characterize these behavior properties of works of art, and how these properties are to be analyzed. In my view, these questions should be answered in roughly the same way for E-qualities and B-qualities.

It is possible to have different views on the exact relations between E-qualities and B-qualities. These differences can, I think, in the last analysis, be traced back to conflicting solutions of the mind-body problem. Those who are Cartesian dualists will no doubt be inclined to treat those two kinds of qualities as quite distinct sets of entities, while those who are monists will not. And those who hold that emotions and behavior are correlated, or that one depends on the other, will tend to regard one of these classes of qualities as dependent on the other.

Like the emotion qualities, the behavior qualities are culturally determined in the sense that two persons looking at the same work of art but with different backgrounds, training, expectations, etc., may experience that particular work differently: one as stiff and lifeless, the other as restrained or even passionate; one as monumental and awe-inspiring, the other as graceful and intimate.

An average European contemplating Japanese woodcuts, for example, would no doubt experience these woodcuts in a different way than most Japanese beholders would, since his cultural frame of reference is different from theirs. Similarly, an Englishman familiar with a great number of works of art and trained to notice and discern qualities in paintings may get much more out of a Monet or a Seurat than an average Englishman.

GESTALT QUALITIES

Whatever the exact relations are between E-qualities and B-qualities, both of them should be distinguished from what I propose to call structural gestalt qualities or simply G-qualities. To this group belong qualities like 'unified', 'integrated', 'chaotic', 'balanced', and so forth. Also statements to the effect that there are tensions or dynamic contrasts between certain parts of a painting refer to structural gestalt qualities.

These qualities differ from the two preceding kinds of qualities in that a work of art or a tune can have a G-quality only if this work or tune has parts which are related to each other in certain ways. A red spot or a monochrome blue painting cannot be chaotic, unified, integrated, balanced, and so forth; it does not have the required complexity; it has no structure. But a red spot or a monochrome blue painting can be gay, powerful, daring, vital, lively, and so forth.[8]

How are statements to the effect that a work of art is unified, integrated, tightly-knit, chaotic, or balanced to be understood? It may be instructive to compare the following pairs of sentences, where "P" refers to a particular person:

X is unified   P experiences (or would see) the parts of X as a unity
X is integrated   P experiences (or would see) the parts of X as integrated
X is balanced   P experiences (or would see) the parts of X as balancing each other
                    . . . etc.

How are the statements to the left related to the statements to the right?

What I am going to suggest now is in several ways analogous to what was said above about R-qualities, though G-qualities and R-qualities are quite distinct. Thus, sometimes a critic may only make an autobiographical remark when he (or she) says or writes that a work of art is unified, integrated, tightly-knit or balanced. What the critic means is, then, only that *he or she* experiences or sees that particular work as unified, integrated, and so forth. In these cases "P" can be replaced by "I, the critic."

But statements like "X is unified" are not always or mainly autobiographical. To say that X is unified or balanced is typically to say or suggest that anyone with normal eyesight, background and training who is regarding X under certain standard conditions (including normal light, absence of disturbing noise, etc.), would experience X as unified, or the parts of X as balancing each other.

This analysis can be compressed in the following general statement, where G is a gestalt quality and g the corresponding gestalt experience:

(G) X has G, only if the parts of X are related to each other in such a way that anyone—with normal eyesight, background and training—contemplating X under standard conditions and noticing the relations between these parts would have g.

The standard conditions can here (as in the analysis proposed of R qualities) be specified in different ways: by various descriptive statements indicating which these conditions are, or—as Charles Stevenson has argued[9]—by at least one normative statement. The standard conditions are, then, simply the conditions under which works of art are properly contemplated, and "properly" here contains a normative force, in addition to descriptions of culturally determined habits and conditions of viewing art works—for instance, "one ought to contemplate works of art under the conditions they are typically contemplated in (our) culture C."

In addition to many other differences between R- and G-qualities, which are obvious enough, it is tempting to suggest that people with varying (I do not say "any") cultural frames of reference might note the same G-qualities. At least, I think it is safe to say that Escher's or Reutersvard's etchings and drawings of impossible objects are frustrating across cultural barriers. In this sense G-qualities are more stable than R-qualities.

TASTE QUALITIES

It should be stressed, once again, (i) that there are no sharp boundaries between the (alleged) qualities discussed here, (ii) that many words used in criticism are ambiguous in the sense that they can be interpreted as referring to qualities of different kinds, and (iii) that many also may have multiple meanings in the sense that they can be taken to refer to several qualities at the same time.

But it seems to me that it is nevertheless possible to single out a group of qualities which more than the ones so far discussed are dependent on canons of taste. These canons vary not only between cultures but also within cultures. Words like 'elegant', 'delightful', 'harsh', 'picturesque', 'garish', 'sublime', 'beautiful', 'handsome', 'clumsy', 'depraved', 'dainty', and so forth, are often used to refer to such qualities.

These words are all value-loaded, but they are not merely value terms. Clearly, one does not contradict oneself by saying "The drawing is elegant but the work is bad," nor by saying "This work is elegant but bad," though the latter statement perhaps is a bit odd and requires some explanation. Perhaps the work is elegant but empty, elegant but superficial, elegant but unoriginal, etc.

If 'elegant', 'delightful', 'harsh', 'picturesque' and other words mentioned above are contrasted with 'unified', 'harmonious', 'balanced', 'integrated', and other words referring to gestalt qualities, it is, in my view, plain that the rules of application of the former ("elegant," etc.) are much more closely related to particular aesthetic doctrines than the rules of application of the latter ("unified," etc.).

If the former ('elegant', etc.) are contrasted with words referring to what I have called reaction qualities, it will readily be seen that they are less individual than the latter. Reaction qualities may vary from individual to individual, and their ontological and epistemological status is somewhat doubtful, to say the least. But taste concepts vary with doctrines of taste rather than with individuals.

Let us therefore, at least tentatively, try to single out a group (without sharp borderlines) of aesthetic qualities with the help of the following criterion:

X has the taste quality T, if and only if X is perceived as having T by those who have internalized the set of taste canons C.

Suppose 'aesthetic culture' is defined as follows. X and Y belong to the same aesthetic culture if they have internalized the same set of taste canons. Let us say that X and Y then share the same a-culture. Such a notion of culture is different from cultures of the kind studied by ethnologists (let us call this e-culture). In that case a-cultures may be part of e-cultures, but we must also count with the possibility that the same a-culture may be found in two (partly different) e-cultures.

Without going into the difficult problems of criteria of identity for different concepts of culture, we may conclude that taste qualities are clearly culture dependent. The extent to which this also holds for other aesthetic qualities will be discussed in a separate section below.

NATURE QUALITIES

The enumeration of qualities makes no claim of completeness whatsoever. I shall here call attention to a group of qualities which in many ways resembles the previous ones. Perhaps it is possible to see what I would like to call "nature qualities" as a separate group, parallel with (not subordinated to) emotion qualities and behavior qualities.

This group of qualities includes a number of qualities which can be found in nature, for example 'cold', 'warm', 'cool', 'bright', 'luminous', 'deep', 'rugged', 'smooth', 'soft', and 'tender'. The terms referring to these qualities can then—by metaphorical extension—be applied also to works of art. We may add terms that literally apply to physical movements and are used metaphorically of music like 'soaring', 'floating', 'sinking'.[10] The basis of division is here from what area the metaphors are drawn: behavior, emotions or nature.

Objects may be cold or warm literally, but not colors; people can be cold (or warm) literally as well as figuratively. However, colors are experienced as warm and cold. These experiences are not related to particular aesthetic doctrines or canons of taste; warm colors are neither better nor worse from an aesthetic point of view than cold ones. In this respect these qualities differ from taste qualities.

Analogously, a hole can be deep, a hand soft, a surface smooth, a steak tender. But this cannot be said literally about colors, lines or shapes. The latter can be experienced as deep, soft, rugged, and so forth, and the intersubjective agreement between reports of trained observers when asked to classify objects with respect to nature qualities of this kind is astonishing, at least as long as these observers come from the same type of geographical area.

What I want to suggest is obviously that experiences of different types of landscapes may be important in this context. It is not hard to imagine that one who has spent his entire life on the Great Plains in Kansas would classify objects (with regard to nature qualities) differently than someone from Nepal. Thus, qualities of this type are not culture dependent in the same sense as taste concepts are; they are dependent on other frames of reference, primarily on experiences of nature.

Perhaps, then, we may try to single out a group (again without sharp borderlines) of aesthetic qualities, with the help of the following tentative and crude starting point.

X has the nature quality N, if X is experienced as having N by those having a somewhat similar experience of nature.

CONCLUDING REMARKS

The qualities I have discussed here should be distinguished from both genre and style concepts like cubist, gothic, mannerist, etc. These concepts have a complex logical structure, which I am not going to discuss here; I just want to stress once again that the enumeration and discussion of various qualities in works of art here makes no claim of completeness.

In concluding this section I want to call attention to a number of differences between some of these aesthetic qualities; and these differences are important for a number of reasons. For example, an analysis of one type of aesthetic quality need not be applicable to other types of aesthetic qualities. Moreover, the relations between aesthetic and non-aesthetic qualities may be different depending on exactly what type of aesthetic quality one is thinking about. Finally, different kinds of evidence may be relevant in deciding whether a work of art has an aesthetic quality, depending on what type of aesthetic quality it is.

In concluding, I would like to elaborate briefly on some of these points. First, there do not seem to be any general logical relations between statements like "X has R" on the one hand, and "X has E," "X has B," "X has G" or "X has T" on the other. If I say something about the reaction qualities of X (that it is funny, comic, trite, interesting, fascinating, boring, exciting, frightening, etc.), I have not so far said anything at all about its gestalt qualities, nor anything about its E-, B- or T-qualities. (A surrealistic picture of a cup covered with fur can be as horrifying as a torture scene, though the B- and G-qualities of the two pictures are quite different.)

Moreover, statements of the type "X has E," "X has B" and "X has G" can be transformed to "X expresses E," "X expresses B" and "X expresses G" respectively. Instead of saying that a melody is melancholy, it is possible to say that it expresses melancholy. Similarly, instead of saying that a sculpture is harmonious, it is possible to say that it expresses harmony. (This way of speaking may be misleading but it is certainly not absurd.) But it is absurd to try to transform "X has R" to "X expresses R." To say that X is interesting is certainly not to say or imply that X expresses interest.

Finally, many aesthetic terms are ambiguous or unclear in the sense that they can be used about various kinds of qualities in works of art, and sometimes about several kinds of qualities at the same time. "Dynamic," for example, can be used to refer to both B-qualities and G-qualities. "Sentimental" can be used to refer to an R-quality as well as an E-quality. Words like "romantic" and "tragic" can be used to call attention to R-qualities, E-qualities, B-qualities and T-qualities; and "harmonious" can refer to R-qualities, E-qualities, B-qualities and G-qualities.

Thus there is no one-to-one correspondence between a certain term and a certain quality, and that is one of the reasons why it is essential to distinguish clearly between semantic and ontological questions. The fact that many aesthetic terms are unclear in the way just indicated is incidentally no objection against the distinctions proposed here. On the contrary, it is only if we make these or similar distinctions that we can describe in what ways, if any, a particular aesthetic term is unclear or ambiguous.

NOTES

1. See my *Aesthetic Qualities*, Lund: Lund University Press, 1988.
2. Cf. Joseph Margolis, *Art and Philosophy* (Atlantic Highlands, New Jersey: Humanities Press, 1980), p. 198.
3. Cf. Goran Hermeren, *Aspects of Aesthetics* (Lund: Gleerup, 1983, Acta. Royal Society of Letters at Lund, LXXVII), p. 32 and Ch. 3.
4. O. K. Bouwsma, "The Expression Theory of Art," in William Elton, ed., *Aesthetics and Language* (Oxford: Basil Blackwell, 1959), p. 99.
5. John Hospers, "Art and Emotion," in Jerome Stolnitz, ed., *Aesthetics* (New York: Macmillan, 1965), p. 54.
6. It is more fully developed in my book *Aesthetic Qualities*, Lund University Press in 1988.
7. Gilbert Ryle, *The Concept of Mind* (New York: Barnes & Noble, 1949).
8. The context is obviously important here. To forestall certain objections, it is here necessary to distinguish between a red spot X and a red spot X against a certain background Y.
9. See in particular Charles Stevenson, "Interpretation and Evaluation in Aesthetics," in Max Black, ed., *Philosophical Analysis* (Ithaca, New York, 1959), pp. 121–39.
10. Cf. Monroe Beardsley, "What is an Aesthetic Quality?" *Theoria*, 39 (1973), p. 67.

Expressive Properties of Art

Guy Sircello

Romantic ideas about mind and its relation to art did not receive their clearest expression until the twentieth century. Then philosophers like Croce, Collingwood, Cassirer, Dewey, and Langer tried to spell out exactly how it is that art can be expressive. But to many other twentieth-century philosophers, especially to those working in the various "analytical" styles whose intellectual ancestry was anything but Romantic, those philosophical discussions of expression in art were puzzling. This puzzlement can best be seen in the work of Monroe Beardsley and O. K. Bouwsma, philosophers who represent two distinct strains in recent analytical philosophy.

I think it is fair to understand the puzzlement of both Beardsley and Bouwsma in the following way. We understand relatively well what it is for a *person* to express such things as feelings, emotions, attitudes, moods, etc. But if we say that sonatas, poems, or paintings also express those sorts of things either we are saying something patently false or we are saying something true in an uninformative, misleading, and therefore pointless way. For to say of works of art that they express those sorts of things seems to imply that they are very much like persons. Therefore, unless we believe that philosophers who think of art as expression believe the unbelievable, that is, that art has feelings, attitudes, and moods

and can express them, we must believe that such philosophers are trying, however inadequately, to come to grips with genuine truths about art.

Furthermore, there is such an obvious disparity between the nature of art and the thesis that art can express the same sorts of things that people do that we cannot understand that thesis as simply a clumsy and inept way of stating some truths about art. We must understand it, rather, as a kind of *theoretical* statement, that is, as a deliberately contrived and elaborated way of construing some simple facts about art. Both Beardsley and Bouwsma thus speak of the "Expression Theory" of art.

What are the facts which the Expression Theory is meant to interpret? Although Beardsley and Bouwsma differ slightly in the way they put the point, they agree that works of art have "anthropomorphic" properties. That is, we may often properly characterize works of art as, for example, gay, sad, witty, pompous, austere, aloof, impersonal, sentimental, etc. A "theory" of art as expression, therefore, can say no more than that artworks have properties designated by the same words which designate feelings, emotions, attitudes, moods, and personal characteristics of human beings.

The nature of these properties has not been probed very deeply by analytical critics of the Expression Theory. Beardsley calls them "qualities." Bouwsma prefers to call them "characters," pointing out their affinity with the "characters" of a number of things like sounds, words, numerals, and faces. In case this suggestion is unhelpful, Bouwsma

---

From *Mind and Art: An Essay on the Varieties of Expression* (Princeton: Princeton University Press, 1972). Reprinted by permission of the publisher.

further invites us to conceive the relation of the "character" to the art work in terms of the relation of redness to the apple in a red apple. At this point he is exactly in line with Beardsley, who mentions a red rose instead of a red apple.[1]

The Bouwsma-Beardsley position on the question of expression in art is currently rather widely accepted. Indeed, John Hospers, writing in the *Encyclopedia of Philosophy* has, in effect, canonized the view.[2] Accordingly, I shall refer to it henceforth as the Canonical Position. Now despite the fact that it has illuminated the concept of expression in art, the Canonical Position is false in some respects and inadequate in others. In this chapter . . . I shall argue (1) that attributions of "characters," or "anthropomorphic qualities," to works of art come in a number of different varieties, (2) that the simple thing-property relation is not an adequate model for understanding any of those varieties, (3) that there are far better reasons for calling art "expressive" than are allowed by the Canonical interpretation of Expression Theory, (4) that the presence of "anthropomorphic qualities" in works of art is not the only fact about art which makes it expressive, and (5) that the features of art which make it expressive have precise parallels in nonartistic areas of culture such as philosophy, historiography, and science.

The Canonical Position has two incorrect presuppositions. The first is that works of art are very much like such natural objects as roses and apples as well as, I suppose, such natural quasi- and non-objects as hills, brooks, winds, and skies. The second is that the anthropomorphic predicates of art are not essentially different from simple color terms like "red" and "yellow." No one has seriously argued, as far as I know, that any art work is *just* like some natural "object." Everyone admits that there are basic differences between art and nature, most of them related to the fact that art is made by human beings and natural things are not. What the first presupposition of the Canonical Position amounts to, therefore, is that as far as the anthropomorphic predicates are concerned works of art are not different from natural objects.[3]

It is fairly easy to show that this presupposition is false by the following strategy. Anthropomorphic predicates are applied to natural things in virtue of certain nonanthropomorphic properties of those things. Of course these properties vary, depending on the particular predicate as well as on the thing to which it applies. Hills, for example, may be austere in virtue of their color, their vegetation (or lack of it), or their contours; an ocean may be angry in virtue of its sound and the force and size of its waves; a tree may be sad in virtue of the droop and shape of its branches. With respect to a number of art works to which anthropomorphic predicates are applied, I shall inquire what it is about those works in virtue of which the predicates are applicable. This strategy will yield categorial features of art which do not belong to natural things.

(1) Like most of Raphael's Madonna paintings, the one called *La Belle Jardinière* can be described as calm and serene. It is fairly clear what there is about this painting which makes it calm and serene: the regular composition based on an equilateral triangle, the gentle and loving expressions on the faces of the Mother, the Child, and the infant John the Baptist, the placid landscape, the delicate trees, the soft blue of the sky, the gentle ripples in the Mother's garments blown by a slight breeze, and, finally, the equanimity and quiet with which the artist views his subject and records the details of the scene.

(2) We might reasonably describe Hans Hofmann's *The Golden Wall* as an aggressive abstract painting. But in this painting there is no representational content in the usual sense and therefore nothing aggressive is depicted. What is aggressive is the color scheme, which is predominantly red and yellow. Blue and green are also used as contrasting colors, but even these colors, especially the blue, are made to look aggressive because of their intensity. Furthermore, by the way they are juxtaposed, the patches of color are made to appear as though they were rushing out toward the observer and even as

though they were competing with one another in this rush toward the observer.

(3) We might say of Poussin's *The Rape of the Sabine Women* (either version, but especially the one in the Metropolitan Museum of Art in New York City) that it is calm and aloof. Yet it is quite clear that the depicted scene is *not* calm and that no one in it, with the possible exception of Romulus, who is directing the attack, is aloof. It is rather, as we say, that Poussin calmly observes the scene and paints it in an aloof, detached way.

(4) Breughel's painting called *Wedding Dance in the Open Air* can be aptly if superficially described as gay and happy. In this case however it is surely the occasion and the activities of the depicted peasants which are happy. Perhaps the prominent red used throughout the painting can be called "gay." The faces of the peasants however are neither happy nor gay. They are bland, stupid, and even brutal. It is this fact which makes the painting ironic rather than gay or happy. Yet there is certainly nothing about a peasant wedding, the dull peasants, or their heavy dance which is ironic. The irony lies in the fact that the painter "views," "observes," or depicts the happy scene ironically.

(5) John Milton's "L'Allegro" is not only "about" high spirits, but it is surely a high-spirited, i.e., gay and joyful, poem. The gaiety and joy are evident in several ways. First, the scenes and images are gay and joyful: Zephir playing with Aurora, maids and youths dancing and dallying, the poet himself living a life of "unreproved" pleasure with Mirth. Second, the diction and rhythms are lighthearted: "Haste thee nymphs and bring with thee / Jest and youthful Jollity, / Quips and Cranks, and wanton Wiles, / Nods, and Becks and Wreathed Smiles."

(6) Another sort of example entirely is William Wordsworth's sentimental poem "We Are Seven." This poem is quite obviously not *about* sentimentality. It purports simply to record the conversation between the poet and a child. Neither the child nor the poet (that is, the "character" in the poem), moreover, is sentimental. The child matter-of-factly reports her firm conviction there are still seven members of her family despite the fact that two of them are dead. The poet is trying, in a rather obtuse and hard-headed sort of way, to get her to admit that there are only five. But the little girl is made to win the point by having the last word in the poem. She is thus made to seem "right" even though no explicit authorization is given to her point of view. By presenting the little girl's case so sympathetically, Wordsworth (the poet who wrote the poem, not the "character" in the poem) treats the attitude of the little girl, as well as the death of her siblings, sentimentally.

(7) The case of "The Dungeon" by Coleridge is different again. At least the first half of this poem is angry. But it is not about anger or angry persons. It is a diatribe in verse (and certainly not a poor poem on that account) against the cruelty, injustice, and wasteful ineffectiveness of prisons.

(8) T. S. Eliot's "The Lovesong of J. Alfred Prufrock" can, with considerable justice, be called a compassionate poem. In this case it is quite clear that the compassion exists in the way in which the character Prufrock is portrayed as a gentle and sensitive, if weak, victim of ugly and sordid surroundings.

(9) Suppose that we say that the second movement of Beethoven's "Eroica" symphony is sad with a dignified and noble sadness characteristic of Beethoven. In this case the sadness is in the slowness of the tempo, and the special quality of the sadness comes from the stateliness of the march rhythm, from the use of "heavy" instruments like horns and tympani and from the sheer length of the movement.

(10) A somewhat different case is presented by Mozart's music for Papageno, which is gay, carefree, light-headed and lighthearted like Papageno himself. What differentiates this case from (9), of course, is that the Mozart music is intended to suit a certain kind of character, whereas the Beethoven has no clear and explicit "representational" content. Despite this difference, however, the "anthropomorphic qualities" of the Mozart music are, like those of the Beethoven, audible in properties of the sound: in the simple

harmonies, tripping rhythms, and lilting melodies of Papageno songs.

(11) A slightly different case from either (9) or (10) is that presented by the first movement of Vivaldi's "Spring" Concerto. The first lilting, happy theme represents the joyful advent of spring. This is followed by the gentle music of the winds and waters of spring. Next, this pleasantness is interrupted by the angry music representing a thunder shower, after which the happy, gentle music returns. In this music the "programmatic" content is clear and explicit because we know the poetry from which Vivaldi composed the music.

(12) Quite different from the three cases immediately preceding is the witty Grandfather theme from Prokoviev's *Peter and the Wolf*. Grandfather's music, played by a bassoon, is large, lumbering, and pompous like Grandfather himself. But what makes it witty is that it portrays a dignified old man as just a bit ridiculous; through the music Prokoviev pokes gentle fun at the old man, fun which is well-motivated by the story itself. For in the end Peter turns out to be more than equal to the danger which Grandfather has ordered him to avoid.

(13) Finally, there is music like the utterly impersonal and detached music of John Cage, exemplified in *Variations II* played by David Tudor on (with) the piano. But where can we locate the "qualities'" of impersonality and detachment in Cage's music? They do not seem to be "properties" of the sounds and sound-sequences in the way that gaiety is a property of Papageno's music or sadness is a property of Beethoven's. Indeed, we feel that these "anthropomorphic qualities" of Cage's music depend on the very fact that the sounds themselves are completely lacking in "human" properties. They are as characterless as any of a thousand random noises we hear every day. In fact, *Variations II* does have the apparent randomness and disorganization of mere noise. But we would not be inclined to call *any* random sequences of noises "impersonal" and "detached," even if they sounded very much like the sounds of *Variations II*. The predicates "impersonal" and "detached" are not applied to Cage's music simply in virtue of some features of its sounds. These "qualities" of *Variations II* arise rather from the fact that the composer presents what sounds like mere noise as music. Cage offers this "noise" for us to attend to and concentrate upon. Moreover, he offers it to us without "comment," and with no intention that it evoke, represent, or suggest anything beyond itself. That is to say, Cage offers these noise-like sounds in a totally uninvolved, detached, impersonal way, seeking in no way to touch our emotional life.

From the preceding examples we can see that there are some respects in which anthropomorphic predicates are applied to works of art in virtue of features of those works which they share or could share with some natural things. In the Raphael it is the composition of the painting which accounts in part for the "calm" of the painting, but "composition" here refers simply to the configuration of lines and shapes, which sorts of features can of course be shared by natural objects. Similarly, the aggressiveness of Hofmann's painting is due to its colors and their arrangement. In the Beethoven and Mozart examples the anthropomorphic qualities are traceable to features of sound which can be present in natural phenomena. The ocean crashing on the shore, a twig tapping against a windowpane, the gurgle of a stream—all of these can have "tempi," "rhythms," and even "tone color." Natural "melodies" are present in the rustle of trees and the howl of winds as well as in the songs of birds. Even the anthropomorphic qualities of verbal art can be like properties of natural things. For, as the example of "L'Allegro" shows, such qualities can be attributed to poetry at least partly in virtue of the tempo and rhythm of its verses.

Some of the above examples of anthropomorphic qualities applied to art, however, show that such qualities sometimes belong to works of art in virtue of what those works represent, describe, depict, or portray. Thus the calm and serenity of the Raphael is due in part to the countryside, the sky, the garments, and the faces depicted; the gaiety of the Breughel comes from the gaiety of the depicted scene, and the high spirits of Milton's poem are due to the gay, happy scenes and images described and presented. In cases of this sort, neither paintings nor poems are comparable to natural things with respect to the way they bear their anthropomorphic qualities. And the situation is similar with respect to all other forms of representational art, whether prose fiction, drama, ballet, opera, or sculpture. Only architecture and music are generally incapable of bearing anthropomorphic qualities in this way. This is true, moreover, even for music with a sort of representation content such as the Mozart music mentioned in (10) above. For it is not due to the fact that Mozart's songs are written for a gay, lighthearted character that they are properly described as gay and lighthearted. It is rather that the songs suit Papageno precisely in virtue of the gaiety and light heartedness of their "sound" and are thereby capable of portraying him musically.

There is a second way in which anthropomorphic predicates may be applied to art works which is unlike the ways in which such predicates apply to natural things. In the discussion of (1) through (13) above we discovered the following:

(a) *La Belle Jardinière* is calm and serene partly because Raphael *views* his subject calmly and quietly.
(b) *The Rape of the Sabine Women* is aloof and detached because Poussin calmly *observes* the violent scene and *paints* it in an aloof, detached way.
(c) *Wedding Dance in the Open Air* is an ironic painting because Breughel *treats* the gaiety of the wedding scene ironically.
(d) "We Are Seven" is a sentimental poem because Wordsworth *treats* his subject matter sentimentally.
(e) "The Dungeon" is an angry poem because in it the poet angrily *inveighs* against the institution of imprisonment.
(f) "The Lovesong of J. Alfred Prufrock" is a compassionate poem because the poet compassionately *portrays* the plight of his "hero."
(g) Prokoviev's Grandfather theme is witty because the composer wittily *comments* on the character in his ballet.
(h) Cage's *Variations II* is impersonal because the composer *presents* his noiselike sounds in an impersonal, uninvolved way.

I have italicized the verbs in the above in order to point up the fact that the respective anthropomorphic predicate is applied to the work of art in virtue of what the artist *does* in that work. In order to have a convenient way of referring to this class of anthropomorphic predicates, I shall henceforth refer to what verbs of the sort italicized above designate as "artistic acts." I do not intend this bit of nomenclature to have any metaphysical import. That is, I do not mean that the viewings, observings, paintings, presentings, portrayings, and treatings covered by the term "artistic acts" all belong to a category properly called "acts." Nor do I mean that all activities properly called "artistic" are covered by my term "artistic act." As shall come out later, many artistic activities are neither identical with, constituents of, nor constituted by "artistic acts." Furthermore, I do not want to suggest that "artistic acts" have anything more in common than what I have already pointed out and what I shall go on to specify. To do a complete metaphysics of artistic acts might be an interesting philosophical job but one which would distract me from my main purpose [here].

What the preceding discussion has shown is that the view of art presupposed by the Canonical Position ignores complexities in works of art which are essential in understanding how they can bear anthropomorphic predicates. Even more significant is the discovery that anthropomorphic predicates apply to art works in virtue of "artistic acts" in these works. For, as I shall argue presently at length, it is precisely this feature of art works which enables them to be *expressions* and which thereby shows that the Canonical Position has missed a great deal of truth in classical Expression Theory.

As far as I know, no adherent of the Canonical Position, with one exception to be noted below, has recognized the existence of what I call "artistic acts," much less seen their relevance to expression in art. But it is not difficult to anticipate the first defensive move a proponent of the Canonical Position would likely make against the threat posed by "artistic acts." It would go somewhat as follows. What the "discovery" of "artistic acts" shows is merely that not all applications of anthropomorphic predicates to art works attribute qualities to those works. They merely *seem* to do so because of their grammatical form. But in fact statements of this sort say nothing at all about the art work; they describe the artist. After all, "artistic acts" are acts of the artists, and they cannot possibly be acts of (i.e., performed by) the art works themselves.

However superficially plausible this objection is, it can be shown to have little force. First, the objection presupposes a false dichotomy: a statement must be descriptive either of a work of art *or* of its artist. On the contrary, there seems to be no reason why when we talk in the above examples of the painting's aloofness, the poem's sentimentality, etc., we cannot be talking *both* about the painting or poem and about how Poussin painted or how Wordsworth treated his subject. And it is in fact the case that we are talking about both. The best proof of this is that the *grounds* for the truth of the descriptions of artistic acts in (*a*) through (*g*) above can come from the art work in question. One knows by looking at Poussin's painting that he has painted the scene in an aloof, detached way. The cold light, the statuesque poses, the painstaking linearity, are all visible in the work. Similarly, we recognize by reading Wordsworth's poem that he treats his subject sentimentally. That is just what it is to give the child, who believes that the dead are present among the living, the advantage over the matter-of-fact adult. We can also recognize the impersonality of *Variations II* by listening to its neutral, noiselike sounds. A test for statements describing art in anthropomorphic terms is always and quite naturally a scrutiny of the art, even when the terms are applied in virtue of "artistic acts."

Moreover, it is not as if this sort of attention to the work of art were merely a second-best way of testing such statements. One does not look, listen, or read in order to *infer* something about the aloof way Poussin painted, the compassionate way Eliot portrayed his hero, etc. We must not imagine that had we actually been with the artist at work, we could *really*, i.e., immediately and indubitably, have seen his aloofness, compassion, sentimentality, etc. How absurd to think that when Poussin's way of painting is described as aloof, what is meant is that Poussin arched his eyebrows slightly, maintained an impassive expression on his face, and moved his arms slowly and deliberately while he painted the picture. Or that because Eliot portrays Prufrock compassionately, he penned the manuscript of his poem with tears in his eyes. Not only would such facts not be needed to support statements about Poussin's aloofness or Eliot's compassion, but they are totally irrelevant to such statements. For even if we knew the way Poussin looked and moved when he was painting the Sabine picture or the way Eliot's face looked when he penned "Prufrock," we could not infer that the painting and poem were, respectively, aloof and compassionate in the ways we are discussing.

The foregoing considerations do not mean that the "artistic acts" in question are not truly acts of the artists, that is, are not truly something which the artists have done. Nor do they imply that these artistic acts are phantom acts, airy nothings existing mysteriously in works of art and disembodied from any agents.[4] They simply mean that these acts are not identifiable or describable independently of the works "in" which they are done. Probably nothing makes this point clearer than the fact that descriptions of artistic acts of this sort can be known to be true even when little or nothing is known about the author, much less what he looked like and what his behavior was like at the precise time that he was making his art. It can be truly said, for example, that Homer describes with some sentimentality the meeting of the returned Odysseus and aged dog Argos. And yet it would be absurd to say that the truth of that statement waits upon some detailed knowledge about Homer, even the existence of whom is a matter of considerable dispute.

Artistic acts are peculiar in that descriptions of them are at once and necessarily descriptions of art works. They are in this way distinguishable from other sorts of acts of artists which contribute to the production of works of art, e.g., looking at the canvas, chiseling marble, penning words, applying paint, revising a manuscript, thinking to oneself, etc. But artistic acts, for all their peculiarity, are not entirely alone in the universe; there are other sorts of things which people do which are analogous to artistic acts in significant ways. Note the following: A person may scowl angrily, and thereby have an angry scowl on his face; he may smile sadly and thereby have a sad smile on his face; he may gesture impatiently and thus make an impatient gesture; he may shout defiantly and produce thereby a defiant shout; he may pout sullenly and a sullen pout will appear on his face; his eyes may gleam happily and there will be a happy gleam in his eyes; he may tug at his forelock shyly or give a shy tug at his forelock. What is interesting about these clauses is that they show how an anthropomorphic term can be applied either adverbially to "acts" or adjectively to "things" without a difference in the sense of the term or of the sentences in which it is used. This sort of shift in the grammatical category of a term is clearly analogous to what is possible with respect to those anthropomorphic predicates applied to works of art in virtue of their artistic acts. Thus one may, without change of meaning, say either that Eliot's "Prufrock" is a compassionate poem or that Eliot portrays Prufrock compassionately in his poem; that Poussin paints his violent scene in an aloof detached way or that the Sabine picture is an aloof, detached painting.[5]

This grammatical shift is possible in both sorts of cases because of the inseparability of the "act" and the "thing." One does not *infer* from a smile on a person's face that he is smiling any more than one *infers* that Eliot portrayed Prufrock compassionately from his compassionate poem, and for analogous reasons. The "acts" of smiling, pouting, shouting, tugging are not even describable without also and at once describing the smile, pout, shout, or tug. Smiling, after all, is not an act which produces or results in a smile so that something could interfere to prevent the smiling from bringing off the smile. "Smiling" and "smile," we are inclined to say, are simply two grammatically different ways of referring to the same "thing."[6]

Now the parallel I want to point out is not between smile-smiling, pout-pouting, tug-tugging on the one hand, and poem-portraying, picture-(act of) painting, music-presenting, on the other. For clearly Poussin's Sabine painting is more than (is not simply identical with) Poussin's aloof way of painting the violent scene; Eliot's poem is more than his compassionate way of portraying its title character; Cage's music is more than his impersonal presentation of noiselike sounds. When we have described these artistic acts we have not by any means completely described the respective art works. The analogy rather is between smile-smiling and portrayal-portraying, presentation-presenting, treatment-treating, view-viewing, etc. Therefore, when we designate artistic acts by a noun term, those acts seem to be "parts" or "moments" of the works of art to which they pertain. We may then more properly understand the way in which an anthropomorphic adjective applies to an art work in virtue of such a "part" in something like the way in which a person's whole face is called sad in virtue merely of his sad smile or his sad gaze, or in which a person's behavior is generally angry in virtue (merely) of his quick movements and angry tone of voice. In these cases, too, it is not as if the terms "sad" and "angry" *completely* described the face or the behavior or even all parts and aspects of the face and behavior even though they can *generally* characterize the face and the behavior.

The foregoing comparison points out that not only is it the case that anthropomorphic predicates do not always apply to art works the way predicates, anthropomorphic or not, apply to natural objects, but that sometimes anthropomorphic predicates apply to works of art rather like the way that they apply to verbal, gestural, and facial *expressions*. For sad smiles are characteristic expressions of sadness in a person; angry scowls, of anger; shy tugs at forelocks, of diffidence; sullen pouts, of petulance. And this is an all-important point which the Canonical Position has missed in its interpretation of the Expression Theory of Art. Had proponents of the Canonical Position pursued their inquiry into anthropomorphic predicates further, they would have been forced to question whether such predicates apply to art in the way they apply to objects or in the way they apply to common human expressions.

Instead of pursuing this line of questioning, however, they were misled by the noun-adjective form of their favorite example—sad music—into their object-quality interpretation of Expression Theory, an interpretation which of course makes that "theory" seem very far removed indeed from the "facts" which were alleged to have motivated it. Small wonder that Beardsley's final judgment on Expression Theory is that it "renders itself obsolete" after it has reminded us that anthropomorphic predicates may reasonably be applied to art works. Even O. K. Bouwsma, who of all the proponents of the Canonical Position comes closest to the point I am maintaining, was not able to see quite where his comparison between sad music and sad faces leads. For instead of making a transition from sad faces to sad *expressions* on faces, he takes the (rather longer) way from sad faces to red apples.

There is more to the comparison between artistic acts and facial, vocal, and gestural expression than the formal or grammatical similarities just noted. Even more important are the parallels between the "significance" of things like sad smiles and angry scowls and the "significance" of aloofness or irony in paintings, sentimentality or compassion in poems, and impersonality or wittiness in music. For there are parallels between what facial, gestural, and vocal expressions, on the one hand, and artistic acts, on the other, can tell us about the persons responsible for them. In order to draw out these parallels explicitly I shall use the cases of an angry scowl and a compassionate portrayal in the mode of Eliot's "Prufrock."

First, it is obvious that an angry scowl on a person's face might well mean that the person is angry. It might be more than simply an expression of anger; it might be an expression of *his* anger. Now it should need very little argument to show that a compassionate poem like "Prufrock" might be an expression of the poet's own compassion. He might be a person with a generally sympathetic and pitying attitude toward modern man and his situation. In that case, a poem like "Prufrock," at least a poem with "Prufrock's" kind of compassion, is precisely what one could expect from the poet, just as one could expect an angry man to scowl angrily. But just as we cannot reasonably expect that *every* time a person is angry he scowls angrily, we cannot expect that every man who is a poet and who has compassion toward his fellows will produce poetry with the compassion of "Prufrock." If a man can keep his anger from showing in his face, a poet can, with whatever greater difficulties and whatever more interesting implications for himself and his poetry, keep his compassion from showing in his poetry.

Moreover, just as there is no necessity that a man's anger show in his face, there is no necessity that an angry scowl betoken anger in the scowler. There is a looseness of connection between anger and angry expressions which is matched by a looseness between compassion and compassionate poems. One reason that a man might have an angry scowl on his face is that he is *affecting* anger, for any of a number of reasons. Now although the range of reasons for affecting compassion in his poetry might be different from the range of reasons for affecting anger in his face, it is nevertheless possible that a corpus of poetry with "Prufrock's" sort of compassion might betoken nothing more than an affectation of compassion. This might be the case if, for example, the poet is extremely "hard" and sarcastic but thinks of these traits as defects. He might then quite deliberately write "compassionate" poetry in order to mask his true self and present himself to the world as the man he believes he should be.

On the other hand, both angry scowls and compassionate poetry might be the result simply of a desire to imitate. Children especially will often imitate expressions on people's faces, but even adults sometimes have occasion to imitate such expressions, e.g., in relating an anecdote. A poet might write poems with Eliot's sort of compassion in them in imitation of Eliot's early attitude. This imitation might be executed by a clever teacher in order to show more vividly than by merely pointing them out the means Eliot used to convey his special sympathy in "Prufrock." Or Eliot might be imitated because his techniques and style, together with the attitudes they imply, have become fashionable among serious poets or because these attitudes strike a responsive chord among serious poets. The latter sorts of imitation are rather like the imitations which a child might make of a person whom he regards as a model. It is not unusual for a girl who admires a female teacher, say, to practice smiling in that teacher's kind, gentle way or for a very young boy at play to "get angry" in the same way he has seen his father get angry.

A poet might write poems with the compassion of "Prufrock," not because he is either affecting or imitating the attitude of that poem, but because he is *practicing* writing poetry in different styles and different "moods." This may be just something like a technical exercise for him, or it may be part of a search for a characteristic attitude or stance which seems to be truly "his own." He thus "tries on" a number of different poetic "masks," so to speak, to see how they fit him. In a similar way, an adolescent girl grimacing before her mirror might "try on" various facial expressions to see how they "look on her" and to discover which is her "best," or perhaps her most characteristic, face: innocent sullen, sultry, haughty, or even angry.

Finally, an angry scowl on a face might be there when the person is portraying an angry person on the stage. There is a similar sort of situation in which compassionate poetry might be written not as betokening a characteristic of the poem's real author but as betokening the traits of a *character* in a play or novel who is *represented* as having written the poem. No actual examples of such a character come immediately to mind; but we surely have no trouble imagining a master of stylistic imitation writing a novelized account of modern literature in which he exhibits examples of the "Prufrock"-like poetry of an Eliot-like figure.

What I have argued so far is not that all art is expression, nor even that all art works with artistic acts anthropomorphically qualified are expression. My argument shows only that artistic acts in works of art are remarkably like common facial, vocal, and gestural expressions. It also demonstrates that precisely in virtue of their artistic acts and of the similarity they bear to common kinds of expressions, works of art may serve as expressions of those feelings, emotions, attitudes, moods, and/or personal characteristics of their creators which are designated by the anthropomorphic predicates applicable to the art works themselves. And it thereby demonstrates that one presupposition of the Canonical Position is clearly wrong: namely, that art works, insofar as they allow of anthropomorphic predicates, are essentially like natural things untouched by man. But the second presupposition of the Canonical Position, to wit, that anthropomorphic predicates of art are like simple color words, is also false. It is false with respect to all the three ways, distinguished earlier, that anthropomorphic predicates can be applied to works of art. And it is *a fortiori* false with respect to those predicates which are applied to art in two or three ways at once, as most of them are. The falsity of the presupposition can be brought out in an interesting way by showing how the three ways of applying anthropomorphic predicates to art bear a certain resemblance to color attributions which are rather unlike simply calling a (clearly) red rose red or an (indubitably) green hill green.

Suppose that a sign painter is painting a sign in three colors: yellow, red, and blue. Since the sign is large, he is required to move his equipment several times during the job. Suppose that he employs an assistant to attend to this business. Now we can imagine that the painter will have occasion to give directions to his assistant. He might say, "Bring me the red bucket, but leave the blue and yellow ones there, since I'll need them on that side later." Now if we suppose that the color of all the paint containers is black, when the painter calls for the "red bucket," he must mean "the bucket of red paint," and would surely be so understood by his assistant. In the context the phrase "red bucket" only *appears* to have the same grammatical form as "red rose." I suggest that to the extent that a painting or other representational work of art is called "gay" or "sad" solely in virtue of its subject matter or parts thereof, the latter terms function *more* like "red" in "red bucket" than in "red rose."

It is a common opinion that "sad" in "sad smile" and "gay" in "gay laughter" function metaphorically.[7] There may well be a use of "metaphor" such that the opinion is true. Whether there is such a use will not be determined until there exists a thorough philosophical study of metaphor; and I do not intend to offer one here. But even if it turns out to be true that such uses of anthropomorphic words are metaphorical, it cannot be very useful simply to say it. For such uses *appear* not to be metaphorical at all. After all, it is not as if calling a smile sad were representing the smile as, as it were, feeling sad, acting sad, weeping, and dragging its feet. To see a smile's sadness is not to discern the tenuous and subtle "likeness" between the smile and a sad person. It is much more straightforward to think that a smile is sad because it is a smile *characteristic* of a sad person who smiles; that laughter is gay because such laughter is *characteristic* laughter of persons who are gay. In this respect "sad smile" is rather like "six-year-old behavior" or "Slavic cheekbones." These phrases do not indirectly point to unexpected similarities between a sort of behavior and six-year-old children or between cheekbones and persons. They designate, respectively, behavior which is *characteristic* of six-year-old children and cheekbones *characteristic* of Slavs. And there is no inclination at all to call these phrases "metaphorical."

Yet to say that a sad smile is a smile characteristic of sad people is not to deny what the Canonical Position affirms, namely, that "sad" designates a "property" or "character" of the smile. Surely there is something about the smile which marks it as sad: its droopiness, its weakness, its wanness. But the term "sad" still has a different import from "droopy," "weak," or "wan" when applied to smiles, even though all the latter terms are also characteristic smiles of sad persons. The difference is that the term "sad" *explicitly* relates the character of the smile to sadness of persons. A comparable sort of color term might be "cherry red." "Cherry red" is like the term "bright red with bluish undertones" in that they both designate roughly the same shade of red, which is characteristic of cherries. But the former term is unlike the latter in that it *explicitly* relates the color to cherries.

It might seem that the Canonical Position would be correct in its interpretation of anthropomorphic terms as they apply to those features of works of art which they can share with natural things. For the term "sad" applied to the second movement of the "Eroica" and to a weeping willow must surely denote some properties of the music and of the tree. And they do: drooping branches in the tree; slow rhythm and "heavy" sound in the Beethoven. But "sad" differs from "drooping," "slow," and "heavy" as in the preceding case; it immediately relates the properties of the sounds and the branches to properties of other things which are sad. In these cases "sad" does function metaphorically, harboring, as it were, a comparison within itself. To find an analogy among color words, this use of "sad" is like "reddish." Like "reddish," which quite self-consciously does not denote true redness, "sad" in "sad tree" does not denote true sadness but only a kind of likeness of it. This use of "sad" is also arguably analogous to the use of "red" in "His face turned red with shame." But whether "sad tree" and "sad rhythm" are closer to "reddish clay" or to "red face" is, if determinable at all, unimportant for my point. For "reddish clay" and "red face" are equally unlike "red rose" and "red apple" when the latter refer to a full-blown American Beauty and a ripe Washington Delicious.

In this section I have argued that anthropomorphic terms, when applied to art, are *more* like "red" in "red bucket (of paint)," "cherry red" in "cherry red silk," or "reddish" in "reddish clay" than like "red" in "red rose." But, in truth, anthropomorphic predicates of art are not *very* much like any of these. The reason is that what all anthropomorphic predicates ultimately relate to are human emotions, feelings, attitudes, moods, and personal traits, none of which are very much at all like colors. But there is a point in drawing out the comparison between anthropomorphic predicates and color-terms more complicated than "red" in "red rose." The point is that "red" as applied to bucket, "cherry red," and "reddish" are all in some way relational terms in ways that "red" said of a rose is not. "Red bucket" means "bucket *of* red paint"; "cherry red" means "the red *characteristic of* cherries"; and "reddish" means "of a color *rather like* red." Had proponents of the Canonical Position troubled to refine their comparison between anthropomorphic predicates and color predicates, they might have been forced to recognize the relational aspects of the former. Eventually they might have been led to see that anthropomorphic terms finally relate to various forms of the "inner lives" of human beings. And *that* is where Expression Theory begins. The Canonical model of the red rose (or apple) ultimately fails to help us understand how anthropomorphic predicates apply to art because such predicates are not very much like simple quality-words and what they apply to are not very much like natural objects.

In spite of all the above arguments, the Canonical Position is not left utterly defenseless. Although it is the notion of "artistic acts" which is most threatening to the Canonical Position, proponents of that position have been almost totally unaware of this threat. Not totally unaware, however. There is a brief passage in Monroe Beardsley's book *Aesthetics: Problems in the Philosophy of Criticism* in which he mentions an artist's "treatment" and "handling," two examples of what I have called "artistic acts." Beardsley does not relate them, however, to the analysis of anthropomorphic terms. He discusses them under the rubric "misleading idioms," and he suggests that all talk about art concerning "handling" and "treatment" not only can be but should be translated into talk which makes no mention of these sorts of acts.[8]

These are meager clues, but from them it is possible to excogitate an objection to my notion of "artistic arts" which a defender of the Canonical Position might raise. We should first note a remark which Beardsley makes elsewhere in his book when he is concluding his interpretation of Expression Theory. He states that all remarks about the expressiveness of an art work can be "translated" into statements about the anthropomorphic qualities either of the subject matter or of the "design," i.e., roughly the properties which the work could share with natural things.[9] A defense against the notion of "artistic acts" might thus run as follows: Any statement which describes an artistic act anthropomorphically can be "translated" into a statement which describes features of the work of art other than its artistic acts. So stated, however, the defense is ambiguous; it has two plausible and interesting interpretations. First, it might mean that any anthropomorphic description of an artistic act in a work can be replaced, without loss of meaning, by a description of the subject matter and/or design of the work in terms of the same anthropomorphic predicate. Or it might mean that there are descriptions, of whatever sort, of the subject matter and/or design of a work which, given any true anthropomorphic description of an artistic act in that work, entail that description.

The first interpretation of the objection is easily shown to be false. All that is required is that some examples of art be adduced in which anthropomorphic predicates are applicable with some plausibility to an "artistic act" but which are in no other way plausibly attributable to the work. Let us look again at the works of Poussin, Eliot, and Prokoviev discussed earlier in this chapter.

In the Poussin painting of the rape of the Sabines there is nothing about the violent subject matter which could be called "aloof." Certainly the attackers and the attacked are not aloof. Romulus, the general in charge, is a relatively *calm* surveyor of the melee, but he cannot be called aloof, partly because we cannot see him well enough to tell what his attitude is. "Aloof" does not apply with regard to the formal elements of the Poussin painting either. It is difficult even to imagine what "aloof" lines, masses, colors, or an "aloof" arrangement thereof might be. The light in the painting is rather cold, and that feature does indeed contribute to the aloofness of the work. "Cold light" is not, however, the same as "aloof light," which does not even appear to be a sensible combination of words.

A similar analysis is possible with respect to Eliot's "Prufrock." If we consider the "material" elements of the poem—its rhythm, meter, sound qualities, etc.—we realize that "compassionate" simply cannot apply to those features meaningfully. Moreover, there is nothing about the subject matter of "Prufrock" which is compassionate. Certainly Prufrock himself is not compassionate; he is simply confused, a victim of his own fears and anxieties, and of the meanness and triviality of his routinized life and souless companions.

Finally, the wittiness of Prokoviev's Grandfather theme cannot be supposed to be a "property" of the music the way its comic qualities are. The music is amusing, or comic, because the wheeziness of the bassoon is funny and because the melody imitates the "structure" of a funny movement (one *must* move in an amusing way to that melody). Moreover, although Grandfather himself is funny, he is definitely not witty. What is comical, amusing, or funny is not always witty. To be witty is generally to make, say, or do something comical, amusing, or funny "on purpose." That is why Prokoviev's musical *portrayal* of a comical grandfather is witty. Similar analyses of the Breughel painting, the Wordsworth poem, and the Cage music mentioned previously could obviously be carried out. But the point, I take it, is already sufficiently well made.

The second interpretation of the hypothetical attack on the importance of artistic acts borrows any initial plausibility it possesses from the fact that anthropomorphic descriptions of artistic acts can be "explained" or "justified" in terms which neither mention artistic acts nor use any of the terms which describe them. For example, one might point out the irony in the Breughel painting discussed above by noting the combination of the gay scene and the dull faces of its participants. Or one might justify the "aloofness" he sees in the Poussin by remarking on the cold light, clear lines, and statuesque poses in a scene of violence and turmoil. And in discussing the impersonality of *Variations II* it is necessary to mention that the Cage work sounds like accidentally produced noise, which is senseless and emotionally neutral, but that this noiselike sound is to all *other* appearances music, i.e., it is scored, it is performed on a musical instrument, it is even reproduced on recordings. From these facts about the way in which anthropomorphic descriptions are justified, it might seem plausible that the statements which figure in the justification *entail* the original description. But such is not the case, as the following will show.

It has been suggested that the reason that Breughel's peasant faces are dull and stupid-looking is that the painter was simply unable to paint faces which were happy. Whether the suggestion is true or well supported by the evidence is not an issue here. What is important is that were there any reason for believing Breughel to have been incompetent in that way, then there might be (not necessarily "would be") that much less reason for believing that there is irony in Breughel's *Wedding Dance*. That is because Breughel's incompetence and Breughel's irony *can* in this case function as mutually exclusive ways of accounting for a "discrepancy" in the picture. Of course, there are ways of admitting both the incompetence and the irony. It is possible to suppose, for example, that Breughel used his particular incompetence in making an ironic "statement" about peasant existence. Such a supposition would imply that Breughel was aware of his limitation and made use of it in his work. However, were it *known* that the *only* reason for the discrepancy in the painting was Breughel's incompetence, the "irony" would disappear. It makes no difference, incidentally, that such a thing could probably *never* be known. I am making a logical point regarding the way an attribution of a certain sort to an "artistic act" relates to other aspects of a painting like the Breughel. In short, certain facts about the painting's subject matter do indeed "ground" the attribution but by no means logically entail that attribution. And that is so for the good reason that the same facts about the subject matter are consistent with a supposition about Breughel which might be incompatible with the description of the painting as ironic.

A similar point can be illustrated in Poussin's Sabine painting. In that work there is discrepancy between the violent scene, on the one hand, and the "still," clear figures, on the other. Two persons might agree about the character of the figures and the character of the depicted scene, however, and yet disagree whether these facts entail that Poussin painted the rape of the Sabines in an aloof, reserved way. One viewer might think simply that the work is incoherent, that Poussin's coldly classical means are not suited to the end he had in mind, namely, to depict the violence of the event. In this quite reasonable view, the discrepancy makes the painting "fall apart" rather than "add up" to an aloof and reserved point of view. Here then are two incompatible descriptions of a work which are equally well grounded on facts which allegedly "entail" one of the descriptions. I am mindful that it might be objected that there are other features of the Sabine painting than the ones mentioned which preclude the judgment of "incoherence" and necessitate the judgment of "aloofness." The best I can say is that there seem to me to be no such additional features contributing to the "aloofness" of the painting and that the burden of proof is upon those who disagree.[10]

Finally, let us suppose that a devoted listener of traditional Western music scoffs at the description of Cage's *Variations II* as "impersonal music." He insists that it is nothing but what it sounds like—meaningless noise. He charges that Cage is a fraud whose "music" is a gigantic hoax, a put-on, and that Cage is laughing up his sleeve at those who take him seriously, perform his "scores," record the performances, and listen gravely to his nonsense. He has, the traditional listener says, read some of Cage's "ideological" material relating to his "music" but he has noted how laden with irony it is. To him that shows that Cage is not to be taken seriously because he does not take himself seriously. Now such a doubter does not disagree with the description of *Variations II* which is used to justify calling it "impersonal." The disagreement concerns rather the way we are to assess John Cage. Are we to judge him to be a responsible and serious, albeit radically innovative, composer of music or not? It is only when Cage's seriousness is assumed that the term "impersonality" applies to his music. Otherwise, the aforementioned justification for calling it impersonal is equally justification for calling it nonsense.

What the above three cases demonstrate is that a true anthropomorphic description of an artistic act might presuppose conditions having nothing necessarily to do with the way the formal elements and/or subject matter are describable. The conditions mentioned are (1) the competence of the artist, (2) the coherence of the work, (3) the seriousness of the artist. But there are surely other examples which would bring light to other conditions of this sort. With sufficient ingenuity one could likely discover and/or construct examples of art in which anthropomorphic descriptions of artistic acts would or would not be applicable depending upon how one assessed the artist with respect to, say, his maturity, his sanity, his self-consciousness, his sensitivity, or his intelligence.

Now it is probably too rigid to regard "competence," "coherence," "seriousness," "maturity," "sanity," and the rest as denoting necessary *conditions* for the legitimate description of all artistic arts. It is probably not true that the artist *must* be serious, competent, sane, etc., and that the work *must* be coherent in order for any anthropomorphic description (of an artistic act) to apply to any work. What these terms should be taken as denoting are "parameters" according to which an artist or a work can be measured in whatever respect is relevant in a particular case. To do so would be to admit that there is probably not a single set of particular conditions of these sorts presupposed in *all* descriptions of artistic acts. Naming these parameters simply points out the *sorts* of considerations which *might* be relevant in particular descriptions of artistic acts, leaving it an open question which of these parameters are relevant, and to what degree, in particular cases.

In any event, what the recognition of such parameters means is that any attempt to save the Canonical Position by "eliminating" descriptions of artistic acts in favor of "logically equivalent" descriptions of formal elements and/or represented subject matter is doomed to fail. For the description of artistic acts in anthropomorphic terms does presuppose something about the artist which cannot be known *simply* by attending to his art. A similar point holds with respect to common expressions. The look of a sullen pout on a person's face does not mean that the person is pouting sullenly if we discover that the look results from the natural lay of his face. And thus it is that no description simply of the configuration of the person's face can *entail* the statement that the person is pouting sullenly.

But it is equally true that the assertion that a person is pouting sullenly is incompatible with the claim that the person's face has the same configuration as it does when he is not pouting sullenly. The sullen pout *must* make a difference visible on the face. Analogously, for an anthropomorphic predicate of an artistic act to be applicable to a work of art there *must* be *some* features of the material elements and/or the subject of the work which *justify* the attribution of the term, even though they do not *entail* that attribution. One thing, however, is never presupposed or implied when an anthropomorphic predicate is truly applied to a work, namely, that the predicate is truly applicable to the *artist*. In this, too, works of art are like expression.

NOTES

1. Cf. Monroe Beardsley, *Aesthetics: Problems in the Philosophy of Criticism* (New York: Harcourt, Brace, 1958), pp. 321–332; and O. K. Bouwsma, "The Expression Theory of Art," in *Philosophical Analysis*, ed. Max Black (Ithaca: Cornell University Press, 1950), pp. 75–101.
2. *The Encyclopedia of Philosophy*, ed. Paul Edwards (New York: Macmillan and The Free Press, 1967), I, 47.
3. I hope it is clear that throughout this discussion the emphasis is on "natural," not on "object." But I will, for convenience, use the terms "object" and "thing" to cover non-objects and non-things as well.
4. Nor are they "virtual," i.e., unreal, acts, as I have maintained in another place. Cf. my "Perceptual Acts and Pictorial Art: A Defense of Expression Theory," *Journal of Philosophy* LXII (1965), 669–677. Giving these acts a separate and unusual metaphysical status not only complicates the universe needlessly, it is unfaithful to the commonsense facts of the situation. There are no good reasons to deny what our ways of talking implicitly affirm, namely, that "artistic acts," perceptual and otherwise, are "acts" of the artist.
5. Of course it is true that sometimes when anthropomorphic terms are predicated of art works, they apply to subject matters and to "material" aspects of the work such as lines, colors, sounds, masses, etc., as well as to "artistic acts." My point above is only that anthropomorphic adjectives may be applied to a work only in virtue of an artistic act, in which case it is, without change of meaning, immediately applicable in adverbial form to that act.
6. It is no objection to this assertion that in virtue of the natural lay of their faces some people have perpetual "smiles," "smirks," "pouts," etc., on their faces even when they do not smile, smirk, or pout. Of course, a "smile" of this sort is different from a smile; that is what the scare quotes signify. But even though a person with such a "smile" on his face is not thereby smiling, he is, significantly, "smiling."
7. Nelson Goodman's recent theory of expression seems to depend rather heavily on the opinion that such uses of anthropomorphic predicates are metaphorical. As far as I can tell, however, Goodman merely asserts and does not argue for this opinion. Nor does he

offer anything more than the briefest sketch of a theory of metaphor, which could be used to support his assertion. See his *Languages of Art: An Approach to a Theory of Symbols* (Indianapolis: Bobbs-Merrill, 1968), pp. 50–51, 80–95.
8. Beardsley, *Aesthetics*, pp. 80 ff.
9. *Ibid.*, p. 332.
10. These statements commit me to the position that a positive judgment about the Poussin cannot be deduced from any descriptions of the painting of the sort which "ground" its aloofness. For arguments in favor of this general position see my "Subjectivity and Justification in Aesthetic Judgments," *Journal of Aesthetics and Art Criticism* XXVII (1968), 3–12.

Categories of Art

Kendall L. Walton

I. INTRODUCTION

False judgments enter art history if we judge from the impression which pictures of different epochs, placed side by side, make on us. . . . They speak a different language.[1]

Paintings and sculptures are to be looked at; sonatas and songs are to be heard. What is important about these works of art, as works of art, is what can be seen or heard in them.[2] Inspired partly by apparent commonplaces such as these, many recent aesthetic theorists have attempted to purge from criticism of works of art supposedly extraneous excursions into matters not (or not "directly") available to inspection of the works, and to focus attention on the works themselves. Circumstances connected with a work's origin, in particular, are frequently held to have no essential bearing on an assessment of its aesthetic nature—for example, who created the work, how, and when; the artist's intentions and expectations concerning it, his philosophical views, psychological state, and love life;

the artistic traditions and intellectual atmosphere of his society. Once produced (it is argued) the work must stand or fall on its own; it must be judged for what it is, regardless of how it came to be as it is.

Arguments for the irrelevance of such historical circumstances to aesthetic judgments about works of art may, but need not, involve the claim that these circumstances are not of "aesthetic" interest or importance, though obviously they are often important in biographical, historical, psychological, or sociological researches. One might consider an artist's action in producing a work to be aesthetically interesting, an "aesthetic object" in its own right, while vehemently maintaining its irrelevance to an aesthetic investigation of the work. Robert Rauschenberg once carefully obliterated a drawing by de Kooning, titled the bare canvas "Erased De Kooning Drawing," framed it, and exhibited it.[3] His doing this might be taken as symbolic or expressive (of an attitude toward art, or toward life in general, or whatever) in an "aesthetically" significant manner, perhaps somewhat as an action of a character in a play might be, and yet thought to have no bearing whatever on the aesthetic nature of the finished prod-

---

From *The Philosophical Review*, 79 (1970). Reprinted by permission of the publisher and the author.

uct. The issue I am here concerned with is how far critical questions about works of art can be *separated* from questions about their histories.[4]

One who wants to make this separation quite sharp may regard the basic facts of art along the following lines. Works of art are simply objects with various properties, of which we are primarily interested in perceptual ones—visual properties of paintings, audible properties of music, and so forth.[5] A work's perceptual properties include "aesthetic" as well as "nonaesthetic" ones—the sense of mystery and tension of a painting as well as its dark coloring and diagonal composition; the energy, exuberance, and coherence of a sonata, as well as its meters, rhythms, pitches, timbres, and so forth; the balance and serenity of a Gothic cathedral as well as its dimensions, lines, and symmetries.[6] Aesthetic properties are features or characteristics of works of art just as much as nonaesthetic ones are.[7] They are *in* the works, to be seen, heard, or otherwise perceived there. Seeing a painting's sense of mystery or hearing a sonata's coherence might require looking or listening longer or harder than does perceiving colors and shapes, rhythms and pitches; it may even require special training or a special kind of sensitivity. But these qualities must be discoverable simply by examining the works themselves if they are discoverable at all. It is never even partly *in virtue* of the circumstances of a work's origin that it has a sense of mystery or is coherent or serene. Such circumstances sometimes provide hints concerning what to look for in a work, what we might reasonably expect to find by examining it. But these hints are always theoretically dispensable; a work's aesthetic properties must "in principle" be ascertainable without their help. Surely (it seems) a Rembrandt portrait does not have (or lack) a sense of mystery in virtue of the fact that Rembrandt intended it to have (or to lack) that quality, any more than a contractor's intention to make a roof leakproof makes it so; nor is the portrait mysterious in virtue of any other facts about what Rembrandt thought or how he went about painting the portrait or what his society happened to be like. Such circumstances are important to the result only insofar as they had an effect on the pattern of paint splotches that became attached to the canvas, and the canvas can be examined without in any way considering how the splotches got there. It would not matter in the least to the aesthetic properties of the portrait if the paint had been applied to the canvas not by Rembrandt at all, but by a chimpanzee or a cyclone in a paint shop.

The view sketched above can easily seem very persuasive. But the tendency of critics to discuss the histories of works of art in the course of justifying aesthetic judgments about them has been remarkably persistent. This is partly because hints derived from facts about a work's history, however dispensable they may be "in principle," are often crucially important in practice. (One might simply not think to listen for a recurring series of intervals in a piece of music, until he learns that the composer meant the work to be structured around it.) No doubt it is partly due also to genuine confusions on the part of critics. But I will argue that (some) facts about the origins of works of art have an *essential* role in criticism, that aesthetic judgments rest on them in an absolutely fundamental way. For this reason, and for another as well, the view that works of art should be judged simply by what can be perceived in them is seriously misleading, though there is something right in the idea that what matters aesthetically about a painting or a sonata is just how it looks or sounds.

II. STANDARD, VARIABLE, AND CONTRA-STANDARD PROPERTIES

I will continue to call tension, mystery, energy, coherence, balance, serenity, sentimentality, pallidness, disunity, grotesqueness, and so forth, as well as colors and shapes, pitches and timbres *properties* of works of art, though "property" is to be construed broadly enough not to beg any important questions. I will also, following Sibley, call properties of the former sort "aesthetic" properties, but purely for reasons of convenience I will include in this category "representational" and "resemblance" properties, which Sibley excludes—for example, the property of representing or being a picture of Napoleon, that of depicting an old man (as) stooping over a fire, that of resembling, or merely suggesting, a human face, claws (the petals of Van Gogh's sunflowers), or (in music) footsteps or conversation. It is not essential for my purposes to delimit with any exactness the class of aesthetic properties (if indeed any such delimitation is possible), for I am more interested in discussing particular examples of such properties than in making generalizations about the class as a whole. It will be obvious, however, that what I say about the examples I deal with is also applicable to a great many other properties we would want to call aesthetic.

Sibley points out that a work's aesthetic properties depend on its nonaesthetic properties; the former are "emergent" or "*Gestalt*" properties based on the latter.[8] I take this to be true of all the examples of aesthetic properties we will be dealing with, including representational and resemblance ones. It is because of the configuration of colors and shapes on a painting, perhaps in particular its dark colors and diagonal composition, that it has a sense of mystery and tension, if it does. The colors and shapes of a portrait are responsible for its resembling an old man and (perhaps with its title) its depicting an old man. The coherence or unity of a piece of music (for example, Beethoven's *Fifth Symphony*) may be largely due to the frequent recurrence of a rhythmic motive, and the regular meter of a song plus the absence of harmonic modulation and of large intervals in the voice part may make it serene or peaceful.

Moreover, a work *seems* or *appears* to us to have certain aesthetic properties because we observe in it, or it appears to us to have, certain nonaesthetic features (though it may not be necessary to notice consciously all the relevant nonaesthetic features). A painting depicting an old man may not look like an old man to someone who is color-blind, or when it is seen from an extreme angle or in bad lighting conditions so that its colors or shapes are distorted or obscured. Beethoven's *Fifth Symphony* performed in such a sloppy manner that many occurrences of the four-note rhythmic motive do not sound similar may seem incoherent or disunified.

I will argue, however, that a work's aesthetic properties depend not only on its non-aesthetic ones, but also on which of its nonaesthetic properties are "standard," which "variable," and which "contra-standard," in senses to be explained. I will approach this thesis by way of the psychological point that what aesthetic properties a work seems to us to have depends not only on what nonaesthetic features we perceive in it, but also on which of them are standard, which variable, and which contra-standard *for us* (in a sense also to be explained).

It is necessary to introduce first a distinction between standard, variable, and contra-standard properties relative to perceptually distinguishable categories of works of art. Such categories include media, genre, styles, forms, and so forth—for example, the categories of paintings, cubist paintings, Gothic architecture, classical sonatas, paintings in the style of Cézanne, and music in the style of late Beethoven—if they are interpreted in such a way that membership is determined solely by features that can be perceived in a work when it is experienced in the normal manner. Thus whether or not a piece of music was written in the eighteenth century is irrelevant to whether it belongs to the category of classical sonatas (interpreted in this way), and whether a work was produced by Cézanne or Beethoven has nothing essential to do with whether it is in the style of Cézanne or late Beethoven. The category of etchings as normally construed is not perceptually distinguishable in the requisite sense, for to be an etching is, I take it, simply to have been produced in a particular manner. But the category of *apparent* etchings, works which *look* like etchings from the quality of their lines, whether they are etchings or not, is perceptually distinguishable. A category will not count as "perceptually distinguishable" in my sense if in order to determine perceptually whether something belongs to it, it is necessary (in some or all cases) to determine which categories it is correctly perceived in partly or wholly on the basis of nonperceptual considerations. (See Section IV below.) This prevents, for example, the category of serene things from being perceptually distinguishable in this sense.

A feature of a work of art is *standard* with respect to a (perceptually distinguishable) category just in case it is among those in virtue of which works in that category belong to that category—that is, just in case the lack of that feature would disqualify, or tend to disqualify, a work from that category. A feature is *variable* with respect to a category just in case it has nothing to do with works' belonging to that category; the possession or lack of the feature is irrelevant to whether a work qualifies for the category. Finally, a *contra-standard* feature with respect to a category is the absence of a standard feature with respect to that category—that is, a feature whose presence tends to *disqualify* works as members of the category. Needless to say, it will not be clear in *all* cases whether a feature of a work is standard, variable, or contra-standard relative to a given category, since the criteria for classifying works of art are far from precise. But clear examples are abundant. The flatness of a painting and the motionlessness of its markings are standard, and its particular shapes and colors are variable, relative to the category of painting. A protruding three-dimensional object or an electrically driven twitching of the canvas would be contra-standard relative to this category. The straight lines in stick-figure drawings and squarish shapes in cubist paintings are standard with respect to those categories respectively, though they are variable with respect to the categories of drawing and painting. The exposition-development-recapitulation form of a classical sonata is standard, and its thematic material is variable, relative to the category of sonatas.

In order to explain what I mean by features being standard, variable, or contra-standard *for a person on a particular occasion*, I must introduce the notion of perceiving a work in, or as belonging to, a certain (perceptually distinguishable) category.[9] To perceive a work in a certain category is to perceive the "*Gestalt*" of that category in the work. This needs some explanation. People familiar with Brahmsian music—that is, music in the style of Brahms (notably, works of Johannes Brahms)—or impressionist paintings can frequently recognize members of these categories by recognizing the Brahmsian or impressionist *Gestalt* qualities. Such recognition is dependent on perception of particular features that are standard relative to these categories, but it is not a matter of *inferring* from the presence of such features that a work is Brahmsian or impressionist. One may not notice many of the relevant features, and he may be very vague about which ones are relevant. If I recognize a work as Brahmsian by first noting its lush textures, its basically traditional harmonic and formal structure, its superimposition and alternation of duple and triple meters, and so forth, and recalling that these characteristics are typical of Brahmsian works, I have not recognized it by hearing the Brahmsian *Gestalt*. To do that is simply to recognize it by its Brahmsian *sound*, without necessarily paying attention to the features ("cues") responsible for it. Similarly, recognizing an impressionist painting by its impressionist *Gestalt*, is recognizing the impressionist *look* about it, which we are familiar with from other impressionist paintings; not applying a rule we have learned for recognizing it from its features.

To *perceive* a *Gestalt* quality in a work—that is, to perceive it in a certain category—is not, or not merely, to *recognize* that *Gestalt* quality. Recognition is a momentary occurrence, whereas perceiving a quality is a continuous state which may last for a short or long time. (For the same reason, seeing the ambiguous duck-rabbit figure as a duck is not, or not merely, recognizing a property of it.) We perceive the Brahmsian or impressionist *Gestalt* in a work when, and as long as, it *sounds* (*looks*) Brahmsian or impressionist to us. This involves perceiving (not necessarily being aware of) features standard relative to that category. But it is not *just* this, nor this plus the intellectual realization that these features make the work Brahmsian, or impressionist. These features are perceived combined into a single *Gestalt* quality.

We can of course perceive a work in several or many different categories at once. A Brahms sonata might be heard simultaneously as a piece of music, a sonata, a romantic work, and a Brahmsian work. Some pairs of categories, however, seem to be such that one cannot perceive a work as belonging to both at once, much as one cannot see the duck-rabbit both as a duck and as a rabbit simultaneously. One cannot see a photographic image simultaneously as a still photograph and as (part of) a film, nor can one see something both in the category of paintings and at the same time in the category (to be explained shortly) of *guernicas*.

It will be useful to point out some of the *causes* of our perceiving works in certain categories. (*a*) In which categories we perceive a work depends in part, of course, on what other works we are familiar with. The more works of a certain sort we have experienced, the more likely it is that we will perceive a particular work in that category. (*b*) What we have heard critics and others say about works we have experienced, how they have categorized them, and what resemblances they have pointed out to us is also important. If no one has ever explained to me what is distinctive about Schubert's style (as opposed to the styles of, say, Schumann, Mendelssohn, Beethoven, Brahms, Hugo Wolf), or even pointed out that there is such a distinctive style, I may never have learned to hear the Schubertian *Gestalt* quality, even if I have heard many of Schubert's works, and so I may not hear his works as Schubertian. (*c*) How we are introduced to the particular work in question may be involved. If a Cézanne painting is exhibited in a collection of French Impressionist works, or if before seeing it we are told that it is French Impressionist, we are more likely to see it as French Impressionist than if it is exhibited in a random collection and we are not told anything about it beforehand.

I will say that a feature of a work is standard for a particular person on a particular occasion when, and only when, it is standard relative to some category in which he perceives it, and is not contra-standard relative to any category in which he perceives it. A feature is variable for a person on an occasion just when it is variable relative to *all* the categories in which he perceives it. And a feature is contra-standard for a person on an occasion just when it is contra-standard relative to *any* of the categories in which he perceives it.[10]

III. A POINT ABOUT PERCEPTION

I turn now to my psychological thesis that what aesthetic properties a work seems to have, what aesthetic effect it has on us, how it strikes us aesthetically often depends (in part) on which of its features are standard, which variable, and which contra-standard for us. I offer a series of examples in support of this thesis.

(*a*) Representational and resemblance properties provide perhaps the most obvious illustration of this thesis. Many works of art look like or resemble other objects—people, buildings, mountains, bowls of fruit, and so forth. Rembrandt's "Titus Reading" looks like a boy, and in particular like Rembrandt's son; Picasso's "Les Demoiselles d'Avignon" looks like five women, four standing and one sitting (though not *especially* like any particular women). A portrait may even be said to be a *perfect* likeness of the sitter, or to capture his image *exactly*.

An important consideration in determining whether a work *depicts* or *represents* a particular object, or an object of a certain sort (for example, Rembrandt's son, or simply *a* boy), in the sense of being a picture, sculpture, or whatever of it[11] is whether the work resembles that object, or objects of that kind. A significant degree of resemblance is, I suggest, a necessary condition in most contexts for such representation or depiction,[12] though the resemblance need not be obvious at first glance. If we are unable to see a similarity between a painting purportedly of a woman and women, I think we would have to suppose either that there is such a similarity which we have not yet discovered (as one might fail to see a face in a maze of lines), or that it simply is not a picture of a woman. Resemblance is of course not a *sufficient* condition for representation, since a portrait (containing only one figure) might resemble both the sitter and his twin brother equally but is not a portrait of both of them. (The title might determine which of them it depicts.)[13]

It takes only a touch of perversity, however, to find much of our talk about resemblances between works of art and other things preposterous. Paintings and people are *very* different sorts of things. Paintings are pieces of canvas supporting splotches of paint, while people are live, three-dimensional, flesh-and-blood animals. Moreover, except rarely and under special conditions of observation (probably including bad lighting) paintings and people *look* very different. Paintings look like pieces of canvas (or anyway flat surfaces) covered with paint and people look like flesh-and-blood animals. There is practically no danger of confusing them. How, then, can anyone seriously hold that a portrait resembles the sitter to any significant extent, let alone that it is a perfect likeness of him? Yet it remains true that many paintings strike us as resembling people, sometimes very much or even exactly—despite the fact that they look so very different!

To resolve this paradox we must recognize that the resemblances we perceive between, for example, portraits and people, those that are relevant in determining what works of art depict or represent, are resemblances of a somewhat special sort, tied up with the categories in which we perceive such works. The properties of a work which are standard for us are ordinarily irrelevant to what we take it to look like or resemble in the relevant sense, and hence to what we take it to depict or represent. The properties of a portrait which make it *so* different from, so easily distinguishable from, a person—such as its flatness and its *painted* look—are standard for us. Hence these properties just do not count with regard to what (or whom) it looks like. It is only the properties which are variable for us, the colors and shapes on the work's surface, that make it look to us like what it does. And these are the ones which are taken as relevant in determining what (if anything) the work represents.[14]

Other examples will reinforce this point. A marble bust of a Roman emperor seems to us to resemble a man with, say, an aquiline nose, a wrinkled brow, and an expression of grim determination, and we take it to represent a man with, or as having, those characteristics. But why don't we say that it resembles and represents a perpetually motionless man, of uniform (marble) color, who is severed at the chest? It is similar to such a man, it seems, and much more so than to a normally colored, mobile, and whole man. But we are not struck by the former similarity when we see the bust, obvious though it is on reflection. The bust's uniform color, motionlessness, and abrupt ending at the chest are standard properties relative to the category of busts, and since we see it as a bust they are standard for us. Similarly, black-and-white drawings do not look to us like colorless scenes and we do not take them to depict things as being colorless, nor do we regard stick-figure drawings as resembling and depicting only very thin people. A cubist work might look like a person with a cubical head to someone not familiar with the cubist style. But the standardness of such cubical shapes for people who see it as a cubist work prevents them from making that comparison.

The shapes of a painting or a still photograph of a high jumper in action are motionless, but these pictures do not look to us like a high jumper frozen in mid-air. Indeed, depending on features of the pictures which are variable for us (for example, the exact positions of the figures, swirling brush strokes in the painting, slight blurrings of the photographic image) the athlete may seem in a frenzy of activity; the pictures may convey a vivid sense of movement. But if static images exactly like those of the two pictures occur in a motion picture, and we see it as a motion picture, they probably would strike us as resembling a static athlete. This is because the immobility of the images is standard relative to the category of still pictures and variable relative to that of motion pictures. (Since we are so familiar with still pictures it might be difficult to see the static images as motion pictures for very long, rather than as [filmed] still pictures. But we could not help seeing them that way if we had no acquaintance at all with the medium of still pictures.) My point here is brought out by the tremendous aesthetic difference we are likely to experience between a film of a dancer moving *very* slowly and a still picture of him, even if "objectively" the two images are very nearly identical. We might well find the former studied, calm, deliberate, laborious, and the latter dynamic, energetic, flowing, or frenzied.

In general, then, what we regard a work as resembling, and as representing, depends on the properties of the work which are variable, and not on those which are standard for us.[15] The latter properties serve to determine what *kind* of a representation the work is, rather than what it represents or resembles. We take them for granted, as it were, in representations of that kind. This principle helps to explain also how clouds can look like elephants, how diatonic orchestral music can suggest a conversation or a person crying or laughing, and how a twelve-year-old boy can look like his middle-aged father.

We can now see how a portrait can be an *exact* likeness of the sitter, despite the huge differences between the two. The differences, insofar as they involve properties standard for us, simply do not count against likeness, and hence not against exact likeness. Similarly, a boy not only can resemble his father but can be his "spitting image," despite the boy's relative youthfulness. It is clear that the notions of resemblance and exact resemblance that we are concerned with are not even cousins of the notion of perceptual indistinguishability.

(*b*) The importance of the distinction between standard and variable properties is by no means limited to cases involving representation or resemblance. Imagine a society which does not have an established medium of painting, but does produce a kind of work of art called *guernicas*. *Guernicas* are like versions of Picasso's "Guernica" done in various bas-relief dimensions. All of them are surfaces with the colors and shapes of Picasso's "Guernica," but the surfaces are molded to protrude from the wall like relief maps of different kinds of terrain. Some *guernicas* have rolling surfaces, others are sharp and jagged, still others contain several relatively flat planes at various angles to each other, and so forth. Picasso's "Guernica" would be counted as a *guernica* in this society—a perfectly flat one—rather than as a painting. Its flatness is variable and the figures on its surface are standard relative to the category of *guernicas*. Thus the flatness, which is standard for us, would be variable for members of the other society (if they should come across "Guernica") and the figures on the surface, which are variable for us, would be standard for them. This would make for a profound difference between our aesthetic reaction to "Guernica" and theirs. It seems violent, dynamic, vital, disturbing to us. But I imagine it would strike them as cold, stark, lifeless, or serene and restful, or perhaps bland, dull, boring—but in any case *not* violent, dynamic, and vital. We do not pay attention to or take note of "Guernica"'s flatness; this is a feature we take for granted in paintings, as it were. But for the other society this is "Guernica"'s most striking and noteworthy characteristic—what is *expressive* about it. Conversely, "Guernica"'s color patches, which we find noteworthy and expressive, are insignificant to them.

It is important to notice that this difference in aesthetic response is not due *solely* to the fact that we are much more familiar with flat works of art than they are, and they are more familiar with "Guernica"'s colors and shapes. Someone equally familiar with paintings and *guernicas* might, I think, see Picasso's "Guernica" as a painting on some occasions, and as a *guernica* on others. On the former occasion it will probably look dynamic, violent, and so forth to him, and on the latter cold, serene, bland, or lifeless. Whether he sees the work in a museum of paintings or a museum of *guernicas*, or whether he has been told that it is a painting or a *guernica*, may influence how he sees it. But I think he might be able to shift at will from one way of seeing it to the other, somewhat as one shifts between seeing the duck-rabbit as a duck and seeing it as a rabbit.

This example and the previous ones might give the impression that in general only features of a work that are variable for us are aesthetically important—that these are the expressive, aesthetically active properties, as far as we are concerned, whereas features standard for us are aesthetically inert. But this notion is quite mistaken, as the following examples will demonstrate. Properties standard for us are not aesthetically lifeless, though the life that they have, the aesthetic effect they have on us, is typically very different from what it would be if they were variable for us.

(c) Because of the very fact that features standard for us do not seem striking or noteworthy, that they are somehow expected or taken for granted, they can contribute to a work a sense of order, inevitability, stability, correctness. This is perhaps most notably true of large-scale structural properties in the time arts. The exposition-development-recapitulation form (including the typical key and thematic relationships) of the first movements of classical sonatas, symphonies, and string quartets is standard with respect to the category of works in sonata-allegro form, and standard for listeners, including most of us, who hear them as belonging to that category. So proceeding along the lines of sonata-allegro form seems *right* to us; to our ears that is how sonatas are *supposed* to behave. We feel that we know where we are and where we are going throughout the work—more so, I suggest, than we would if we were not familiar with sonata-allegro form, if following the strictures of that form were variable rather than standard for us.[16] Properties standard for us do not always have this sort of unifying effect, however. The fact that a piano sonata contains only piano sounds, or uses the Western system of harmony throughout, does not make it seem unified to us. The reason, I think, is that these properties are *too* standard for us in a sense that needs explicating (see note 10). Nevertheless, sonata form is unifying partly because it is standard rather than variable for us.

(d) That a work (or part of it) has a certain determinate characteristic (for example, of size, speed, length, volume) is often variable relative to a particular category, when it is nevertheless standard for that category that the variable characteristic falls within a certain range. In such cases the aesthetic effect of the determinate variable property may be colored by the standard limits of the range. Hence these limits function as an aesthetic catalyst, even if not as an active ingredient.

Piano music is frequently marked *sostenuto*, *cantabile*, *legato*, or *lyrical*. But how can the pianist possibly carry out such instructions? Piano tones diminish in volume drastically immediately after the key is struck, becoming inaudible relatively promptly, and there is no way the player can prevent this. If a singer or violinist should produce sounds even approaching a piano's in suddenness of demise, they would be nerve-wrackingly sharp and percussive—anything but *cantabile* or lyrical! Yet piano music *can* be *cantabile*, *legato*, or lyrical nevertheless; sometimes it is extraordinarily so (for example, a good performance of the *Adagio Cantabile* movement of Beethoven's *Pathetique* sonata). What makes this possible is the very fact that the drastic diminution of piano tones cannot be prevented, and hence never is. It is a standard feature for piano music. A pianist can, however, by a variety of devices, control a tone's rate of diminution and length within the limits dictated by the nature of the instrument.[17] Piano tones may thus be *more or less* sustained within these limits, and *how* sustained they are, how quickly or slowly they diminish and how long they last, within the range of possibilities, is variable for piano music. A piano passage that sounds lyrical or *cantabile* to us is one in which the individual tones are *relatively* sustained, given the capabilities of the instrument. Such a passage sounds lyrical only because piano music is limited as it is, and we hear it as piano music; that is, the limitations are standard properties for us. The character of the passage is determined not merely by the "absolute" nature of the sounds, but by that in relation to the standard property of what piano tones can be like.[18]

This principle helps to explain the lack of energy and brilliance that we sometimes find even in very fast passages of electronic music. The energy and brilliance of a fast violin or piano passage derives not merely from the absolute speed of the music (together with accents, rhythmic characteristics, and so forth), but from the fact that it is fast *for that particular medium*. In electronic music different pitches can succeed one another at any frequency up to and including that at which they are no longer separately distinguishable. Because of this it is difficult to make electronic music *sound* fast (energetic, violent). For when we have heard enough electronic music to be aware of the possibilities we do not feel that the speed of a passage approaches a limit, no matter how fast it is.[19]

There are also visual correlates of these musical examples. A small elephant, one which is smaller than most elephants with which we are familiar, might impress us as charming, cute, delicate, or puny. This is not simply because of its (absolute) size, but because it is small *for an elephant*. To people who are familiar not with our elephants but with a race of mini-elephants, the same animal may look massive, strong, dominant, threatening, lumbering, if it is large for a mini-elephant. The size of elephants is variable relative to the class of elephants, but it varies only within a certain (not precisely specifiable) range. It is a standard property of elephants that they do fall within this range. How an elephant's size affects us aesthetically depends, since we see it as an elephant, on whether it falls in the upper, middle, or lower part of the range.

(e) Properties standard for a certain category which do not derive from physical limitations of the medium can be regarded as results of more or less conventional "rules" for producing works in the given category (for example, the "rules" of sixteenth-century counterpoint, or those for twelve-tone music). These rules may combine to create a dilemma for the artist which, if he is talented, he may resolve ingeniously and gracefully. The result may be a work with an aesthetic character very different from what it would have had if it had not been for those rules. Suppose that the first movement of a sonata in G major modulates to C-sharp major by the end of the development section. A rule of sonata form decrees that it must return to G for the recapitulation. But the keys of G and C-sharp are as unrelated as any two keys can be; it is difficult to modulate smoothly and quickly from one to the other. Suppose also that while the sonata is in C-sharp there are signs that, given other rules of sonata form, indicate that the recapitulation is imminent (for example, motivic hints of the return, an emotional climax, or a cadenza). Listeners who hear it as a work in sonata form are likely to have a distinct feeling of unease, tension, uncertainty, as the time for the recapitulation approaches. If the composer with a stroke of ingenuity accomplishes the necessary modulation quickly, efficiently, and naturally, this will give them a feeling of relief—one might say of deliverance. The movement to C-sharp (which may have seemed alien and brashly adventurous) will have proven to be quite appropriate, and the entire sequence will in retrospect have a sense of correctness and perfection about it. Our impression of it is likely, I think, to be very much like our impression of a "beautiful" or "elegant" proof in mathematics. (Indeed the composer's task in this example is not unlike that of producing such a proof.)

But suppose that the rule for sonatas were that the recapitulation must be *either* in the original key *or* in the key one half-step below it. Thus in the example above the recapitulation could have been in F-sharp major rather than G major. This possibility removes the sense of tension from the occurrence of C-sharp major in the development section, for a modulation from C-sharp to F-sharp is as easy as any modulation is (since C-sharp is the dominant of F-sharp). Of course, there would also be no special *release* of tension when the modulation to G is effected, there being no tension to be released. In fact, that modulation probably would be rather surprising, since the permissible modulation to F-sharp would be much more natural.

Thus the effect that the sonata has on us depends on which of its properties are dictated by "rules," which ones are standard relative to the category of sonatas and hence standard for us.

(*f*) I turn now to features which are contra-standard for us—that is, ones which have a tendency to disqualify a work from a category in which we nevertheless perceive it. We are likely to find such features shocking, or disconcerting, or startling, or upsetting, just because they are contra-standard for us. Their presence may be so obtrusive that they obscure the work's variable properties. Three-dimensional objects protruding from a canvas and movement in a sculpture are contra-standard relative to the categories of painting and (traditional) sculpture respectively. These features are contra-standard for us, and probably shocking, if despite them we perceive the works possessing them in the mentioned categories. The monochromatic paintings of Yves Klein are disturbing to us (at least at first) for this reason: we see them as paintings, though they contain the feature contra-standard for paintings of being one solid color. Notice that we find other similarly monochromatic surfaces—for example, walls of living rooms—not in the least disturbing, and indeed quite unnoteworthy.

If we are exposed frequently to works containing a certain kind of feature which is contra-standard for us, we ordinarily adjust our categories to accommodate it, making it contra-standard for us no longer. The first painting with a three-dimensional object glued to it was no doubt shocking. But now that the technique has become commonplace we are not shocked. This is because we no longer see these works as *paintings*, but rather as members of either (*a*) a new category—*collages*—in which case the offending feature has become standard rather than contra-standard for us, or (*b*) an expanded category which includes paintings both with and without attached objects, in which case that feature is variable for us.

But it is not just the rarity, unusualness, or unexpectedness of a feature that makes it shocking. If a work differs *too* significantly from the norms of a certain category we do not perceive it in that category and hence the difference is not contra-standard for us, even if we have not previously experienced works differing from that category in that way. A sculpture which is constantly and vigorously in motion would be so obviously and radically different from traditional sculptures that we probably would not perceive it as one even if it is the first moving sculpture we have come across. We would either perceive it as a *kinetic* sculpture, or simply remain confused. In contrast, a sculptured bust which is traditional in every respect except that one ear twitches slightly every thirty seconds would be perceived as an ordinary sculpture. So the twitching ear would be contra-standard for us and would be considerably more unsettling than the much greater movement of the other kinetic sculpture. Similarly, a very small colored area of an otherwise entirely black-and-white drawing would be very disconcerting. But if enough additional color is added to it we will see it as a colored rather than a black-and-white drawing, and the shock will vanish.

This point helps to explain a difference between the harmonic aberrations of Wagner's *Tristan and Isolde* on the one hand and on the other Debussy's *Pelleas et Melisande* and *Feux* and Schoenberg's *Pierrot Lunaire* as well as his later twelve-tone works. The latter are not merely *more* aberrant, *less* tonal, than *Tristan*. They differ from traditional tonal music in such respects and to such an extent that they are not heard as tonal at all. *Tristan*, however, retains enough of the apparatus of tonality, despite its deviations, to be heard as a tonal work. For this reason its lesser deviations are often the more shocking.[20] *Tristan* plays on harmonic traditions by selectively following and flaunting them, while *Pierrot Lunaire* and the others simply ignore them.

Shock then arises from features that are not just rare or unique, but ones that are contra-standard relative to categories in which objects possessing them are perceived. But it must be emphasized that to be contra-standard relative to a certain category is not merely to be rare or unique *among things of that category*. The melodic line of Schubert's song, "*Im Walde*," is probably unique; it probably does not occur in any other songs, or other works of any sort. But it is not contra-standard relative to the category of songs, because it does not tend to disqualify the work from that category. Nor is it contra-standard relative to any other category to which we hear the work as belonging. And clearly we do not find this melodic line at all upsetting. What is important is not the rarity of a feature, but its connection with the classification of the work. Features contra-standard for us are perceived as being misfits in a category which the work strikes us as belonging to, as doing *violence* to such a category, and being rare in a category is not the same thing as being a misfit in it.

It should be clear from the above examples that how a work affects us aesthetically—what aesthetic properties it seems to us to have and what ones we are inclined to attribute to it—depends in a variety of important ways on which of its features are standard, which variable, and which contra-standard for us. Moreover, this is obviously not an isolated or exceptional phenomenon, but a pervasive characteristic of aesthetic perception. I should emphasize that my purpose has not been to establish general principles about how each of the three sorts of properties affects us. How any particular feature affects us depends also on many variables I have not discussed. The important point is that in many cases whether a feature is standard, variable, or contra-standard for us has a great deal to do with what effect it has on us. We must now begin to assess the theoretical consequence of this.

IV. TRUTH AND FALSITY

The fact that what aesthetic properties a thing seems to have may depend on what categories it is perceived in raises a question about how to determine what aesthetic properties it really does have. If "Guernica" appears dynamic when seen as a painting, and not dynamic when seen as a *guernica*, is it dynamic or not? Can one way of seeing it be ruled correct, and the other incorrect? One way of approaching this problem is to deny that the apparently conflicting aesthetic judgments of people who perceive a work in different categories actually do conflict.[21]

Judgments that works of art have certain aesthetic properties, it might be suggested, implicitly involve reference to some particular set of categories. Thus our claim that "Guernica" is dynamic really amounts to the claim that it is (as we might say) dynamic *as a painting*, or for people who see it as a painting. The judgment that it is not dynamic made by people who see it as a *guernica* amounts simply to the judgment that it is not dynamic *as a guernica*. Interpreted in these days, the two judgments are of course quite compatible. Terms like "large" and "small" provide a convenient model for this interpretation. An elephant might be both small as an elephant and large as a mini-elephant, and hence it might be called truly either "large" or "small," depending on which category is implicitly referred to.

I think that aesthetic judgments are in *some* contexts amenable to such category-relative interpretations, especially aesthetic judgments about natural objects (clouds, mountains, sunsets) rather than works of art.

(It will be evident that the alternative account suggested below is not readily applicable to most judgments about natural objects.) But most of our aesthetic judgments can be forced into this mold only at the cost of distorting them beyond recognition.

My main objection is that category-relative interpretations do not allow aesthetic judgments to be mistaken often enough. It would certainly be natural to consider a person who calls "Guernica" stark, cold, or dull, because he sees it as a *guernica*, to be *mistaken*: he misunderstands the work because he is looking at it in the wrong way. Similarly, one who asserts that a good performance of the *Adagio Cantabile* of Beethoven's *Pathétique* is percussive, or that a Roman bust looks like a unicolored, immobile man severed at the chest and depicts him as such, is simply wrong, even if his judgment is a result of his perceiving the work in different categories from those in which we perceive it. Moreover, we do not accord a status any more privileged to our own aesthetic judgments. We are likely to regard, for example, cubist paintings, serial music, or Chinese music as formless, incoherent, or disturbing on our first contact with these forms largely because, I suggest, we would not be perceiving the works as cubist paintings, serial music, or Chinese music. But after becoming familiar with these kinds of art we would probably *retract* our previous judgments, admit that they were mistaken. It would be quite inappropriate to protest that what we meant previously was merely that the works were formless or disturbing for the categories in which we then perceived them, while admitting that they are not for the categories of cubist paintings, or serial, or Chinese music. The conflict between apparently incompatible aesthetic judgments made while perceiving a work in different categories does not simply evaporate when the difference of categories is pointed out, as does the conflict between the claims that an animal is large and that it is small, when it is made clear that the person making the first claim regarded it as a mini-elephant and the one making the second regarded it as an elephant. The latter judgments do not (necessarily) reflect a real disagreement about the size of the animal, but the former do reflect a real disagreement about the aesthetic nature of the work.

Thus it seems that, at least in some cases, it is *correct* to perceive a work in certain categories, and *incorrect* to perceive it in certain others; that is, our judgments of it when we perceive it in the former are likely to be true, and those we make when perceiving it in the latter, false. This provides us with absolute senses of "standard," "variable," and "contra-standard": features of a work are standard, variable, or contra-standard absolutely just in case they are standard, variable, or contra-standard (respectively) for people who perceive the work correctly. (Thus an absolutely standard feature is standard relative to some category in which the work is correctly perceived and contra-standard relative to none, an absolutely variable feature is variable relative to all such categories, and an absolutely contra-standard feature is contra-standard relative to at least one such category.)

How is it to be determined in which categories a work is correctly perceived? There is certainly no very precise or well-defined procedure to be followed. Different criteria are emphasized by different people and in different situations. But there are several fairly definite considerations which typically figure in critical discussions and fit our intuitions reasonably well. I suggest that the following circumstances count toward its being correct to perceive a work, W, in a given category, C:

(i) The presence in W of a relatively large number of features standard with respect to C. The correct way of perceiving a work is likely to be that in which it has a minimum of contra-standard features for us. I take the relevance of this consideration to be obvious. It cannot be correct to perceive Rembrandt's "Titus Reading" as a kinetic sculpture, if this is possible, just because that work has too few of the features which make kinetic sculptures kinetic sculptures. But of course this does not get us very far, for "Guernica," for example, qualifies equally well on this count for being perceived as a painting and as a *guernica*.

(ii) The fact, if it is one, that W is better, or more interesting or pleasing aesthetically, or more worth experiencing when perceived in C than it is when perceived in alternative ways. The correct way of perceiving a work is likely to be the way in which it comes off best.

(iii) The fact, if it is one, that the artist who produced W intended or expected it to be perceived in C, or thought of it as a C.

(iv) The fact, if it is one, that C is well established in and recognized by the society in which W was produced. A category is well established in and recognized by a society if the members of the society are familiar with works in that category, consider a work's membership in it a fact worth mentioning, exhibit works of that category together, and so forth—that is, roughly if that category figures importantly in their way of classifying works of art. The categories of impressionist painting and Brahmsian music are well established and recognized in our society; those of *guernicas*, paintings with diagonal composition containing green crosses, and pieces of music containing between four and eight F-sharps and at least seventeen quarter notes every eight bars are not. The categories in which a work is correctly perceived, according to this condition, are generally the ones in which the artist's contemporaries did perceive or would have perceived it.

In certain cases I think the mechanical process by which a work was produced, or (for example, in architecture) the non-perceptible physical characteristics or internal structure of a work, is relevant. A work is probably correctly perceived as an apparent etching[22] rather than, say, an apparent woodcut or line drawing, if it was produced by the etching process. The strength of materials in a building, or the presence of steel girders inside wooden or plaster columns counts toward (not necessarily conclusively) the correctness of perceiving it in the category of buildings with visual characteristics typical of buildings constructed in that manner. Because of their limited applicability I will not discuss these considerations further here.

What can be said in support of the relevance of conditions (ii), (iii), and (iv)? In the examples mentioned above, the categories in which we consider a work correctly perceived seem to meet (to the best of our knowledge) each of these three conditions. I would suppose that "Guernica" is better seen as a painting than it would be seen as a *guernica* (though this would be hard to prove). In any case, Picasso certainly intended it to be seen as a painting rather than a *guernica*, and the category of paintings is, and that of *guernicas* is not, well established in his (that is, our) society. But this of course does not show that (ii), (iii), and (iv) *each* is relevant. It tends to indicate only that one or other of them, or some combination, is relevant. The difficulty of assessing each of the three conditions individually is complicated by the fact that by and large they can be expected to coincide, to yield identical conclusions. Since an artist usually intends his works for his contemporaries he is likely to intend them to be perceived in categories established in and recognized by his society. Moreover, it is reasonable to expect works to come off better when perceived in the intended categories than when perceived in others. An artist tries to produce works which are well worth experiencing when perceived in the intended way and, unless we have reason to think he is totally incompetent, there is some presumption that he succeeded at least to some extent. But it is more or less a matter of chance whether the work comes off well when perceived in some unintended way. The convergence of the three conditions, however, at the same time diminishes the *practical* importance of justifying them individually, since in most cases we can decide how to judge particular works of art without doing so. But the theoretical question remains.

I will begin with (ii). If we are faced with a choice between two ways of perceiving a work, and the work is very much better perceived in one way than it is perceived in the other, I think that, at least in the absence of contrary considerations, we would be strongly inclined to settle on the former way of perceiving it as the *correct* way. The process of trying to determine what is in a work consists partly in casting around among otherwise plausible ways of perceiving it for one in which the work is good. We feel we are coming to a correct understanding of a work when we begin to like or enjoy it; we are finding what is really there when it seems to be worth experiencing.

But if (*ii*) is relevant, it is quite clearly not the *only* relevant consideration. Take any work of art we can agree is of fourth- or fifth- or tenth-rate quality. It is quite possible that if this work were perceived in some farfetched set of categories that someone might dream up, it would appear to be first-rate, a masterpiece. Finding such *ad hoc* categories obviously would require talent and ingenuity on the order of that necessary to produce a masterpiece in the first place. But we can sketch how one might begin searching for them. (*a*) If the mediocre work suffers from some disturbingly prominent feature that distracts from whatever merits the work has, this feature might be toned down by choosing categories with respect to which it is standard, rather than variable or contra-standard. When the work is perceived in the new way the offending feature may be no more distracting than the flatness of a painting is to us. (*b*) If the work suffers from an overabundance of clichés it might be livened up by choosing categories with respect to which the clichés are variable or contra-standard rather than standard. (*c*) If it needs ingenuity we might devise a set of rules in terms of which the work finds itself in a dilemma and then ingeniously escapes from it, and build these rules into a set of categories. Surely, however, if there are categories waiting to be discovered which would transform a mediocre work into a masterpiece, it does not follow that the work really is a hitherto unrecognized masterpiece. The fact that when perceived in such categories it would appear exciting, ingenious, and so forth, rather than grating, cliché-ridden, pedestrian, does not make it so. It *cannot* be correct, I suggest, to perceive a work in categories which are totally foreign to the artist and his society, even if it comes across as a masterpiece in them.[23]

This brings us to the historical conditions (*iii*) and (*iv*). I see no way of avoiding the conclusion that one or the other of them at least is relevant in determining in what categories a work is correctly perceived. I consider both relevant, but will not argue here for the independent relevance of (*iv*). (*iii*) merits special attention in light of the recent prevalence of disputes about the importance of artists' intentions. To test the relevance of (*iii*) we must consider a case in which (*iii*) and (*iv*) diverge. One such instance occurred during the early days of the twelve-tone movement in music. Schoenberg no doubt intended even his earliest twelve-tone works to be heard as such. But this category was certainly not then well established or recognized in his society; virtually none of his contemporaries (except close associates such as Berg and Webern), even musically sophisticated ones, would have (or could have) heard these works in that category. But it seems to me that even the very first twelve-tone compositions are correctly heard as such, that the judgments one who hears them otherwise would make of them (for example, that they are chaotic, formless) are mistaken. I think this would be so even if Schoenberg had been working entirely alone, if *none* of his contemporaries had any inkling of the twelve-tone system. No doubt the first twelve-tone compositions are much better when heard in the category of twelve-tone works than when they are heard in any other way people might be likely to hear them. But as we have seen this cannot *by itself* account for the correctness of hearing them in the former way. The only other feature of the situation which could be relevant, so far as I can see, is Schoenberg's intention.

The above example is unusual in that Schoenberg was extraordinarily self-conscious about what he was doing, having explicitly formulated rules—that is, specified standard properties—for twelve-tone composition. Artists are of course not often so self-conscious, even when producing revolutionary works of art. Their intentions as to which categories their works are to be perceived in are not nearly as clear as Schoenberg's were, and often they change their minds considerably during the process of creation. In such cases (as well as ones in which the artists' intentions are unknown) the question of what categories a work is correctly perceived in is, I think, left by default to condition (*iv*), together with (*i*) and (*ii*). But it seems to me that in almost all cases at least one of the historical conditions, (*iii*) and (*iv*), is of crucial importance.

My account of the rules governing decisions about what categories works are correctly perceived in leaves a lot undone. There are bound to be a large number of undecidable cases on my criteria. Artists' intentions are frequently unclear, variable, or undiscoverable. Many works belong to categories which are borderline cases of being well established in the artists' societies (perhaps, for example, the categories of rococo music—for instance, C. P. E. Bach—of music in the style of early Mozart, and of very thin metal sculptured figures of the kind that Giacometti made). Many works fall between well-established categories (for example, between impressionist and cubist paintings), possessing *some* of the standard features relative to each, and so neither clearly qualify nor clearly fail to qualify on the basis of condition (*i*) to be perceived in either. There is, in addition, the question of what relative weights to accord the various conditions when they conflict.

It would be a mistake, however, to try to tighten up much further the rules for deciding how works are correctly perceived. To do so would be simply to legislate gratuitously, since the intuitions and precedents we have to go on are highly variable and often confused. But it is important to notice just where these intuitions and precedents are inconclusive, for doing so will expose the sources of many critical disputes. One such dispute might well arise concerning Giacometti's thin metal sculptures. To a critic who sees them simply as sculptures, or sculptures of people, they look frail, emaciated, wispy, or wiry. But that is not how they would strike a critic who sees them in the category of thin metal sculptures of that sort (just as stick figures do not strike us as wispy or emaciated). He would be impressed not by the thinness of the sculptures, but by the expressive nature of the positions of their limbs, and so forth, and so no doubt would attribute very different aesthetic properties to them. Which of the two ways of seeing these works is correct is, I suspect, undecidable. It is not clear whether enough such works have been made and have been regarded sufficiently often as constituting a category for that category to be deemed well established in Giacometti's society. And I doubt whether any of the other conditions settle the issue conclusively. So perhaps the dispute between the two critics is essentially unresolvable. The most that we can do is to point out just what sort of a difference of perception underlies the dispute, and why it is unresolvable.

The occurrence of such impasses is by no means something to be regretted. Works may be fascinating precisely because of shifts between equally permissible ways of perceiving them. And the enormous richness of some works is due in part to the variety of permissible, and worthwhile, ways of perceiving them. But it should be emphasized that even when my criteria do not clearly specify a *single* set of categories in which a work is correctly perceived, there are bound to be possible ways of perceiving it (which we may or may not have thought of) that they definitely rule out.

The question posed at the outset of this section was how to determine what aesthetic properties a work has, given that which ones it seems to have depend on what categories it is perceived in, on which of its properties are standard, which variable, and which contra-standard for us. I have sketched in rough outline rules for deciding in what categories a work is *correctly* perceived (and hence which of its features are absolutely standard, variable, and contra-standard). The aesthetic properties it actually possesses are those that are to be found in it when it is perceived correctly.[24]

V. CONCLUSION

I return now to the issues raised in Section I. (I will adopt for the remainder of this paper the simplifying assumption that there is only one correct way of perceiving any work. Nothing important depends on this.) If a work's aesthetic properties are those that are to be found in it when it is perceived correctly, and the correct way to perceive it is determined partly by historical facts about the artist's intention and/or his society, no examination of the work itself, however thorough, will by itself reveal those properties.[25] If we are confronted by a work about whose origins we know absolutely nothing (for example, one lifted from the dust at an as yet unexcavated archaeological site on Mars), we would simply not be in a position to judge it aesthetically. We could not possibly tell by staring at it, no matter how intently and intelligently, whether it is coherent, or serene, or dynamic, for by staring we cannot tell whether it is to be seen as a sculpture, a *guernica*, or some other exotic or mundane kind of work of art. (We could attribute aesthetic properties to it in the way we do to natural objects, which of course does not involve consideration of historical facts about artists or their societies. [Cf. Section IV.] But to do this would not be to treat the object as a *work* of art.)

It should be emphasized that the relevant historical facts are not merely useful aids to aesthetic judgment; they do not simply provide hints concerning what might be found in the work. Rather they help to *determine* what aesthetic properties a work has; they, together with the work's nonaesthetic features, *make* it coherent, serene, or whatever. If the origin of a work which is coherent and serene had been different in crucial respects, the work would not have had these qualities; we would not merely have lacked a means for *discovering* them. And of two works which differ *only* in respect of their origins—that is, which are perceptually indistinguishable—one might be coherent or serene, and the other not. Thus, since artists' intentions are among the relevant historical considerations, the "intentional fallacy" is not a fallacy at all. I have of course made no claims about the relevance of artists' intentions as to the aesthetic properties that their works should have, and these intentions are among those most discussed in writings on aesthetics. I am willing to agree that whether an artist intended his work to be coherent or serene has nothing essential to do with whether it is coherent or serene. But this must not be allowed to seduce us into thinking that *no* intentions are relevant.

Aesthetic properties, then, are not to be found in works themselves in the straightforward way that colors and shapes or pitches and rhythms are. But I do not mean to deny that we perceive aesthetic properties in works of art. I see the serenity of a painting, and hear the coherence of a sonata, despite the fact that the presence of these qualities in the works depends partly on circumstances of their origin, which I cannot (now) perceive. Jones's marital status is part of what makes him a bachelor, if he is one, and we cannot tell his marital status just by looking at him, though we can thus ascertain his sex. Hence, I suppose, his bachelorhood is not a property we can be said to perceive in him. But the aesthetic properties of a work do not depend on historical facts about it in anything like the way Jones's bachelorhood depends on his marital status. The point is not that the historical facts (or in what categories the work is correctly perceived, or which of its properties are absolutely standard, variable, and contrastandard) function as *grounds* in any ordinary sense for aesthetic judgments. By themselves they do not, in general, count either for or against the presence of any particular aesthetic property. And they are not part of a larger body of information (also including data about the work derived from an examination of it) from which conclusions about the work's aesthetic properties are to be deduced or inferred. We must learn to *perceive* the work in the correct categories, as determined in part by the historical facts, and judge it by what we then perceive in it. The historical facts help to determine whether a painting is, for example, serene *only* (as far as my arguments go) by affecting what way of perceiving the painting must reveal this quality if it is truly attributable to the work.

We must not, however, expect to judge a work simply by setting ourselves to perceive it correctly, once it is determined what the correct way of perceiving it is. For one cannot, in general, perceive a work in a given set of categories simply by setting himself to do it. I could not possibly, merely by an act of will, see "Guernica" as a *guernica* rather than a painting, or hear a succession of street sounds in any arbitrary category one might dream up, even if the category has been explained to me in detail. (Nor can I imagine except in a rather vague way what it would be like, for example, to see "Guernica" as a *guernica*.) One cannot merely decide to respond appropriately to a work—to be shocked or unnerved or surprised by its (absolutely) contra-standard features, to find its standard features familiar or mundane, and to react to its variable features in other ways—once he knows the correct categories. Perceiving a work in a certain category or set of categories is a skill that must be acquired by training, and exposure to a great many other works of the category or categories in question is ordinarily, I believe, an essential part of this training. (But an effort of will may facilitate the training, and once the skill is acquired one may be able to decide at will whether or not to perceive it in that or those categories.) This has important consequences concerning how best to approach works of art of kinds that are new to us—contemporary works in new idioms, works from foreign cultures, or newly resurrected works from the ancient past. It is no use just immersing ourselves in a particular work, even with the knowledge of what categories it is correctly perceived in, for that alone will not enable us to perceive it in those categories. We must become familiar with a considerable variety of works of similar sorts.

When dealing with works of more familiar kinds it is not generally necessary to undertake deliberately the task of training ourselves to be able to perceive them in the correct categories (except perhaps when those categories include relatively subtle ones). But this is almost always, I think, only because we have been trained unwittingly. Even the ability to see paintings as paintings had to be acquired, it seems to me, by repeated exposure to a great many paintings. The critic must thus go beyond the work before him in order to judge it aesthetically, not only to discover what the correct categories are, but also to be able to perceive it in them. The latter does not require consideration of historical facts, or consideration of facts at all, but it requires directing one's attention nonetheless to things other than the work in question.

Probably no one would deny that *some* sort of perceptual training is necessary, in many if not all instances, for apprehending a work's serenity or coherence, or other aesthetic properties. And of course it is not only *aesthetic* properties whose apprehension by the senses requires training. But the kind of training required in the aesthetic cases (and perhaps some others as well) has not been properly appreciated. In order to learn how to recognize gulls of various kinds, or the sex of chicks, or a certain person's handwriting, one must usually have gulls of those kinds, or chicks of the two sexes, or examples of that person's handwriting pointed out to him, practice recognizing them himself, and be corrected when he makes mistakes. But the training important for discovering the serenity or coherence of a work of art that I have been discussing is not of this sort (though this sort of training might be important as well). Acquiring the ability to perceive a serene or coherent work in the correct categories is not a matter of having had serene or coherent things pointed out to one, or having practiced recognizing them. What is important is not (or not merely) experience with other serene and coherent things, but experience with other things of the appropriate categories.

Much of the argument in this paper has been directed against the seemingly common-sense notion that aesthetic judgments about works of art are to be based solely on what can be perceived in them, how they look or sound. That notion is seriously misleading, I claim, on two quite different counts. I do not deny that paintings and sonatas are to be judged solely on what can be seen or heard in them—when they are perceived correctly. But examining a work with the senses can by itself reveal neither how it is correct to perceive it, nor how to perceive it that way.

NOTES

1. Heinrich Wölfflin, *Principles of Art History*, trans. M. D. Hottinger (7th ed.; New York, 1929), p. 228.
2. ["W]e should all agree, I think, . . . that any quality that cannot even in principle be heard in it [a musical composition] does not belong to it as music." Monroe Beardsley, *Aesthetics: Problems in the Philosophy of Criticism* (New York, 1958), pp. 31–32.
3. Cf. Calvin Tompkins, *The Bride and the Bachelors* (New York, 1965), pp. 210–211.
4. Monroe Beardsley argues for a relatively strict separation (*op. cit.*, pp. 17–34). Some of the strongest recent attempts to enforce this separation are to be found in discussions of the so-called "intentional fallacy," beginning with William Wimsatt and Beardsley, "The Intentional Fallacy," *Sewanee Review*, vol. 54 (1946), which has been widely cited and reprinted. Despite the name of the "fallacy" these discussions are not limited to consideration of the relevance of artists' intentions.
5. The aesthetic properties of works of literature are not happily called "perceptual." For reasons connected with this it is sometimes awkward to treat literature together with the visual arts and music. (The notion of perceiving a work in a category, to be introduced shortly, is not straightforwardly applicable to literary works.) Hence in this paper I will concentrate on visual and musical works, though I believe that the central points I make concerning them hold, with suitable modifications, for novels, plays, and poems as well.
6. Frank Sibley distinguishes between "aesthetic" and "nonaesthetic" terms and concepts in "Aesthetic Concepts," *Philosophical Review*, vol. 68 (1959).
7. Cf. Paul Ziff, "Art and the 'Object of Art,'" in Ziff, *Philosophic Turnings* (Ithaca, N.Y., 1966), pp. 12–16 (originally published in *Mind*, n.s. vol. 60 [1951]).
8. "Aesthetic and Nonaesthetic," *Philosophical Review*, vol. 72 (1965).
9. This is a very difficult notion to make precise, and I do not claim to have succeeded entirely. But the following comments seem to me to go in the right direction, and, together with the examples in the next section, they should clarify it sufficiently for my present purposes.
10. In order to avoid excessive complexity and length, I am ignoring some considerations that might be important at a later stage of investigation. In particular, I think it would be important at some point to distinguish between different *degrees* or *levels* of standardness, variableness, and contrastandardness for a person; to speak, e.g., of features being *more* or *less* standard for him. At least two distinct sorts of grounds for such differences of degree should be recognized. (*a*) Distinctions between perceiving a work in a certain category to a greater and lesser extent should be allowed for, with corresponding differences of degree in the standardness for the perceiver of properties relative to that category. (*b*) A feature which is standard relative to more, and/or more specific, categories in which a person perceives the work should thereby count as more standard for him. Thus, if we see something as a painting and also as a French Impressionist painting, features standard relative to both categories are more standard for us than features standard relative only to the latter.
11. This excludes, e.g., the sense of "represent" in which a picture might represent justice or courage, and probably other senses as well.
12. This does not hold for the special case of photography. A photograph is a photograph of a woman no matter what it looks like, I take it, if a woman was in front of the lens when it was produced.

13. Nelson Goodman denies that resemblance is necessary for representation—and obviously not merely because of isolated or marginal examples of non-resembling representations (p. 5). I cannot treat his arguments here, but rather than reject *en masse* the common sense beliefs that pictures do resemble significantly what they depict and that they depict what they do partly because of such resemblances, if Goodman advocates rejecting them, I prefer to recognize a sense of "resemblance" in which these beliefs are true. My disagreement with him is perhaps less sharp than it appears since, as will be evident, I am quite willing to grant that the relevant resemblances are "conventional." Cf. Goodman, *Languages of Art* (Indianapolis, 1968), p. 39, n. 31.
14. The connection between features variable for us and what the work looks like is by no means a straightforward or simple one, however. It may involve "rules" which are more or less "conventional" (e.g., the "laws" of perspective). Cf. E. H. Gombrich, *Art and Illusion* (New York, 1960), and Nelson Goodman, *op. cit.*
15. There is at least one group of exceptions to this. Obviously features of a work which are standard for us because they are standard relative to some *representational* category which we see it in—e.g., the category of nudes, still lifes, or landscapes—do help determine what the work looks like to us and what we take it to depict.
16. The presence of clichés in a work sometimes allows it to contain drastically disorderly elements without becoming chaotic or incoherent. Cf. Anton Ehrenzweig, *The Hidden Order of Art* (London, 1967), pp. 114–116.
17. The timing of the release of the key affects the tone's length. Use of the sustaining pedal can lessen slightly a tone's diminuendo by reinforcing its overtones with sympathetic vibrations from other strings. The rate of diminuendo is affected somewhat more drastically by the force with which the key is struck. The more forcefully it is struck the greater is the tone's relative diminuendo. (Obviously the rate of diminuendo cannot be controlled in this way independently of the tone's initial volume.) The successive tones of a melody can be made to overlap so that each one's sharp attack is partially obscured by the lingering end of the preceding tone. A melodic tone may also be reinforced after it begins by sympathetic vibrations from harmonically related accompanying figures, contributed by the composer.
18. "[T]he musical media we know thus far derive their whole character and their usefulness as musical media precisely from their limitations." Roger Sessions, "Problems and Issues Facing the Composer Today," in Paul Henry Lang, *Problems of Modern Music* (New York, 1960), p. 31.
19. One way to make electronic music sound fast would be to make it sound like some traditional instrument, thereby trading on the limitations of that instrument.
20. Cf. William W. Austin, *Music in the 20th Century* (New York, 1966), pp. 205–206; and Eric Salzman, *Twentieth-Century Music: An Introduction* (Englewood Cliffs, N.J., 1967), pp. 5, 8, 19.
21. I am ruling out the view that the notions of truth and falsity are not applicable to aesthetic judgments, on the ground that it would force us to reject so much of our normal discourse and common-sense intuitions about art that theoretical aesthetics, conceived as attempting to understand the institution of art, would hardly have left a recognizable subject matter to investigate. (Cf. the quotation from Wölfflin, above.)
22. Cf. p. 284.
23. To say that it is incorrect (in my sense) to perceive a work in certain categories is not necessarily to claim that one *ought not* to perceive it that way. I heartily recommend perceiving mediocre works in categories that make perceiving them worthwhile whenever possible. The point is that one is not likely to *judge* the work correctly when he perceives it incorrectly.
24. This is a considerable oversimplification. If there are two equally correct ways of perceiving a work, and it appears to have a certain aesthetic property perceived in one but not the other of them, does it actually possess this property or not? There is no easy general answer. Probably in some such cases the question is undecidable. But I think we would sometimes be willing to say that a work is, e.g., touching or serene if it seems so when perceived in one correct way (or, more hesitantly, that there is "something very touching, or serene, about it"), while allowing that it does not seem so when perceived in another way which we do not want to rule incorrect. In some

cases works have aesthetic properties (e.g., intriguing, subtle, alive, interesting, deep) which are not apparent on perceiving it in any single acceptable way, but which depend on the multiplicity of acceptable ways of perceiving it and relations between them. None of these complications relieves the critic of the responsibility for determining in what way or ways it is correct to perceive a work.

25. But this, plus a general knowledge of what sorts of works were produced when and by whom, might.
[Ed.—Walton wishes to add the following note: "Since the original publication of this paper I have changed my views concerning resemblance in representational art. Cf. my 'Pictures and Make-Believe,' *Philosophical Review*, vol. 82 (1973)."]

Chaconne from *Partita No. 2 in D minor BWV 1004*. J. S. Bach (German). 1720.

What sort of thing is a musical work? Is it the written score, the autographed manuscript, the particular musical ideas of Bach, the musical sounds produced during the work's performance, or something else?

CHAPTER 6
What Sorts of Things Are Works of Art?

When thinking about the sort of thing which a work of art is, our intuitions are pulled in numerous directions at once. On the one hand, when we think of paintings and pieces of sculpture, we are apt to think of artworks as being a special sort of *physical* object—ones which can be created or destroyed, which are housed in various locations, which can be boxed up and shipped across the ocean, and so on. But when we are enthralled and awed by the emotive and other intentional properties which we perceive in artworks, or when we consider the ideas communicated in a great novel, or the reverberating metaphors offered in a fine poem, we tend to the opposite conclusion that works of art are mental entities, aesthetic objects which exist in one's head, as Collingwood said. When we think further and consider that the perception of these mental properties of artworks is not biologically innate but is culturally determined, we begin to think of artworks as culturally emergent entities, complex objects whose most valuable features cannot be reduced to (or understood at) any more elementary or naturalistic level. Finally, when we turn to artworks which are experienced only through multiple performances and copies, no one of which can be simply identical with *the* artwork in question (music and literature, for example), we may find ourselves toying with the conjecture that the artwork itself is some kind of Platonic Form, Idea, or universal.

These alternative considerations lead directly to the two main problems in attempting to determine the ontological status of various kinds of artworks.

First, in arts such as painting and sculpture, we seem to ascribe different and competing properties to these objects when we treat them *as* artworks than we do when we deal with them simply as physical objects among others. We touched on this point in Chapter 5. For example, as a painting, a certain canvas may be said to have great depth, but treated as a piece of canvas, it is a very thin object indeed. How can one and the same thing be both thin and of great depth?

Furthermore, there is a question of whether certain properties that we attribute to artworks can even be *sensibly* ascribed to "purely physical" objects such as canvases and marble blocks. For instance, one might argue that although a statue can be dignified, it is senseless to call the marble mass worked on by the sculptor dignified. The statue must, then, be something other than, something more than, the marble hulk, it might be concluded.

The second main ontological problem surrounding artworks arises in those arts wherein there is no single physical object that can be plausibly identified with the artwork. To read a novel, hear a concerto, see a play, or enjoy an opera, one must see, hear, and enjoy a certain *instance, performance,* or *copy* of that work. A musical work has its many performances, a literary work its many copies, a print its numerous impressions, and so on. What, then, is the relation between these numerous objects or events and the work of art itself? Solutions to this second problem frequently construe the artwork as some sort of abstract entity, a type, universal, or abstract particular of which performances, copies, and impressions are instantiations, examples, or approximations.

In the readings which follow, Wollheim addresses primarily (although the second problem is treated) the first main problem of art's ontology, while the other contributors debate proposed solutions to the second problem, with music figuring prominently as an example.

The fact that there *are* types of art in which no single, concrete object can naturally or plausibly be pointed to as *the* artwork is alone sufficient to undermine what Wollheim calls the "physical-object hypothesis" (and others have termed the "identity thesis") when this thesis is construed as the universal claim that every work of art, across the whole spectrum of art forms, is identical to some physical object. Trying to salvage the physical-object hypothesis by identifying the problem-causing sorts of art, such as music and literary works, with the *class* of correct performances or copies ultimately fails because we can meaningfully say things about the work which we cannot sensibly say about the class (for example, when it was begun and finished, who created it, and where it was composed).

But giving up the physical-object hypothesis as a completely general claim does not mean that it is necessarily wrong about *some* forms of art. Are there equally forceful reasons for denying that a painting just *is* the painted canvas, a sculpture just *is* a hunk of bronze or marble? Wollheim concentrates on evaluating a number of arguments that have been offered against this more restricted application of the physical-object hypothesis. His discussion opens many of the central questions of aesthetics, such as those concerning the expressiveness of art and the nature of aesthetic experience. Ultimately, Wollheim concludes that the arguments do not refute the idea that at least some works of art are identical with physical objects, but he nevertheless retains considerable doubt about endorsing the physical-object hypothesis, due to "the highly elusive notion of 'identity,' the analysis of which belongs to the more intricate part of general philosophy."

Margolis's work on the ontological status of the artwork is central to the history of analytic aesthetics. Focusing on the problem of the relation of the music to its performances and the literary works to their many copies, and relying on the type–token distinction, Margolis argues that the artwork is, ontologically speaking, a type whose tokens are the various performances, impressions, or copies of the work.

But what exactly is a type? Of course, we speak of types of coins, types of cars, types of flowers; the U.S. nickel is a type of coinage of which the two nickels in your pocket are tokens, but how should we classify types ontologically? According to Margolis, a type is "an abstract particular of a kind that can be instantiated." Artworks must be particulars rather than universals, if we are to be able to say, as we surely wish to, that they are created by artists. But creating a type, Margolis argues, requires that the artist create some token of that type, or at least provide an accepted notation for the creation of a correct token. That is to say, the type does not exist except as instantiated in its proper tokens.

In this way, Margolis rejects any "Platonic" construal of the existence of types and endorses a sort of Aristotelianism about such ontological matters. Beethoven did not instantiate a preexisting Platonic Essence when he wrote the *Fifth Symphony*; he created a work which had not existed before. And in the same way, musical works can be lost or destroyed (and also found again), no less than paintings or pieces of sculpture can.

The type–token distinction helps Margolis clarify the ontological status of those works with multiple instances, no one of which is identical to the work itself, but more generally, about all artwork. Margolis is prepared to deny their status as physical objects, being more convinced than Wollheim was by the arguments that art possesses properties that no mere physical objects can be said to have.

Unlike simple physical objects or, for that matter, natural types such as species, artworks are intentional, meaningful, and "culturally emergent" entities, Margolis asserts. As such, works of art cannot, strictly speaking, be identified with physical objects, but rather, should be conceived as "embodied" in those objects.

A particular impression of Dürer's *Melancholia I* is a token of *Melancholia I*, but the piece of paper with the ink on it is not a token of that type. Only objects having "intentional properties" (those, that is, which have meaning) can be tokens of a type. Again, this is "Aristotelian" in the sense that it insists that the embodied entity presupposes (but is nonidentical with) an embodying particular.

Margolis does not, however, make it persuasively clear why the possession of intentional and culturally freighted properties prohibits the identification of the artwork with a physical object or event. Consider some related cases. A tool, such as a tack hammer, is as much (if not as rich) a culturally emergent entity, replete with functional and intentional properties, as any artwork. Nevertheless, it seems correct to say that the hammer just is a physical object made of steel and wood. And, in spite of the old refrain that "it's not just a house, it's a home," the additional social features that make a house a home are true of that particular house, that particular wood and brick and plaster object.

There is, in general, much confusion surrounding the notion of a "purely physical object." If this is meant to refer exclusively to concrete objects possessing only the properties recognized by the primary physical sciences such as physics and chemistry, objects like boulders, rivers, or neutrinos, then surely no one would find it remotely plausible to identify any artwork with a physical object. But insofar as physical objects can come into complex relations with us, by being used in many and various ways, various types of more complicated properties, beyond the scope of the lower sciences, become true of them. Objects can come to represent other things for us, can be worked on to carry meaning and expressiveness for us, and can become symbolic and iconic, all without losing their ontological claim to physicality.

If a token print of Dürer's *Melancholia I* is not identical with a certain piece of printed paper, as Margolis is suggesting, then we are confronted with an embarrassment of entities in this case. Not only is there the abstract type, the artwork, *Melancholia I,* as well as its several token printings, but these particular tokens now must be distinguished from the actual pieces of inked paper in which they are "embodied," in Margolis's view.

It is certainly important to distinguish types from tokens regarding certain kinds of art, and it may be necessary to rely on some "embodiment" relation in other cases. But the results of combining these notions as Margolis does have struck some as too "ontologically rich" to swallow.

Wolterstorff sees clearly that all works of art do not have the same ontological status, that one account of the ontological status of artworks in general will not do. Instead he prefers to differentiate artworks into distinct types and to offer a separate account of the ontological status of each. Some works do not have a problematic ontological status—they are physical objects. Paintings, and sculpture, as well as the particular impressions of a print, or the particular prints of a photograph, are straightforwardly physical objects, in Wolterstorff's view. But he is more interested in those works which have multiple instances and in the differences among these works.

Wolterstorff begins by observing that there is a clear difference between the performance of an artwork and the artwork of which it is a performance, first because they have divergent properties and second because the same work can be performed many times. He calls a work of art which can be performed a "performance work," and performance works he says are "universals," at least in the sense that the same one can be performed many times. (Note how Wolterstorff takes the fact that a work can have multiple instances as sufficient for identifying it as a universal, while Margolis suggests that such works are abstract particulars, on the grounds that universals cannot, but artworks can, be created.)

A different distinction exists between the many printings of the same etching or different castings of the same bronze sculpture. This distinction is different from the performance/performance-work distinction in that each of the many instances of the "universal" in the case of the print or bronze casting is an "enduring physical object," while a musical performance is not an object at all but a physical event.

Wolterstorff proposes to call artworks whose instances are objects "object-works," and the particular impressions, copies, and so on the "objects" of object-works. Since literary works admit of copies as well as readings, both private and public, and films allow for numerous copies as well as numerous showings, these works are classified as both object-works and performance-works.

What is the basic ontological category to which object-works and performance-works belong, in Wolterstorff's view? His proposal is that they are *kinds* (types, sorts), in much the way that "The Grizzly" denotes a kind of bear, or "The Orchid" denotes a type of flower. Performance-works are, for Wolterstorff, a certain kind of performance, while an object-work is a certain kind of object. So, for example, the Bartok *Fifth String Quartet* is a kind of sound sequence whose instances are the correct performances of that work.

Kinds which admit of having correctly formed (as well as incorrectly formed) examples (i.e., which have some normative constraints as part of the concept of belonging to the kind) are termed "norm-kinds" by Wolterstorff. Performance-works and object-works are, from the ontological perspective, therefore, norm-kinds, if Wolterstorff is correct. A composer determines what will count as a correct performance of his or her work, usually through having written the score, which is a specification of the correctness conditions of performances.

What sort of thing is a musical work, asks Levinson? As we have already discussed, there is no concrete object one can point to as the work of art in cases such as music and literature. Levinson agrees with the consensus we already have noted (including Wollheim, Margolis, and Wolterstorff) that a musical work is some sort of abstract entity, specifically, "a structural type or kind." The question is, "precisely what sort of structural type?" One suggestion is that it is a sound structure—that is, a structure of certain sounds in certain relations to each other. Levinson finds this suggestion unacceptable and offers three objections to it.

First, if music is a pure sound structure, then, because sound structures are a sort of universal, they are something composers cannot compose, which is absurd. Like Margolis, Levinson rejects this Platonic idea as counterintuitive to our deeply held view that artworks are created by artists.

Second, a musical work is more than a sound structure. It also depends on "the total musico-historical context." The same sound structure composed at one time might be highly original, for example, but at a later time it would be unoriginal. Would we, for instance, value Haydn as highly as we do if he had been a composer of the 1980s (while Mozart was still to be found in the eighteenth century)? Conversely, the pieces composed by Haydn in the eighteenth century, which would be viewed as "old hat" if composed in the twentieth century, would be so advanced as to be unintelligible had they been composed in the thirteenth century.

Third, if musical works were simply sound structures, they would not involve specific means of performance, which they do. Scored musical works specify means of production, indicating that different instruments are to be played a certain way by musicians. So, Levinson argues, musical works cannot be divorced from either their musico-historical context or the instrumental means of production and therefore cannot be pure sound structures (which can be so divorced). Many properties that are true of works (e.g., their great virtuosity or their pushing of their medium to its extreme limits) may not have been true of those works if they involved performance means other than those specified by the composer.

What, then, are musical works? A musical work, Levinson says, is a type that is capable of being created, is individuated by context, and incorporates specific means of production. Consequently, Levinson concludes that a musical work is a "sound-performance means-structure," essentially indicated by a certain composer at a certain time.

Unlike pure sound structures, which exist eternally and are uncreated, "indicated structures" are what Levinson calls "initiated types," because they come into existence only through intentional action. It follows from Levinson's account that musical works must be created artifacts and, unlike Platonic Ideas, are objects which are designed primarily to be heard in or through their performances, and not merely grasped intellectually.

Bender's article acknowledges the advances in ontological clarity and precision made by Wolterstorff and Levinson, but argues that even greater clarity is possible if we distinguish types from patterns. To see the difference, consider that the design or pattern of the 1957 Ford Thunderbird is surely something different than the type of automobile: the 1957 Ford Thunderbird. Bender suggests that musical works are best conceived of as sound *patterns*, a kind of abstract particular which is *realized* in the works' various performances.

The work itself is not a type of performance, as Wolterstorff proposed, because the concept of a performance-kind or performance-type is simply the concept of all the work's performances, grouped together and considered as a unity. The concept of the musical work, however, is not this grouping notion, but rather the idea of an abstract sound pattern, describable in terms of indefinitely-referred-to musical notes and other values. The relation between a musical work and its performances is not the relation of type to token but is a relation of physical realization, Bender suggests.

This chapter, then, is another example of the nature of the dialogue in which analytic aestheticians are engaged and a good instance of that dialogue's potential for making philosophical progress on difficult issues surrounding the work of art.

From *Art and Its Objects: An Introduction to Aesthetics*

Richard Wollheim

1

Let us begin with the hypothesis that works of art are physical objects. I shall call this for the sake of brevity the "physical-object hypothesis." Such a hypothesis is a natural starting point: if only for the reason that it is plausible to assume that things are physical objects unless they very obviously aren't. Certain things very obviously aren't physical objects. Now though it may not be obvious that works of art are physical objects, they don't seem to belong among these other things. They don't, that is, immediately group themselves along with thoughts, or periods of history, or numbers, or mirages. Furthermore, and more substantively, this hypothesis accords with many traditional conceptions of Art and its objects and what they are.

2

Nevertheless the hypothesis that all works of art are physical objects can be challenged. For our purposes it will be useful, and instructive, to divide this challenge into two parts: the division conveniently corresponding to a division within the arts themselves. For in the case of certain arts the argument is that there is no physical object that can with any plausibility be identified as the work of art: there is no object existing in space and time (as physical objects must) that can be picked out and thought of as a piece of music or a novel. In the case of other arts—most notably painting and sculpture—the argument is that, though there are physical objects of a standard and acceptable kind that could be, indeed generally are, identified as works of art, such identifications are wrong.

The first part of this challenge is, as we shall see, by far the harder to meet. However it is, fortunately, not it, but the second part of the challenge, that potentially raises such difficulties for aesthetics.

3

That there is a physical object that can be identified as *Ulysses* or *Der Rosenkavalier* is not a view that can long survive the demand that we should pick out or point to that object. There is, of course, the copy of *Ulysses* that is on my table before me now, there is the performance of *Der Rosenkavalier* that I will go to tonight, and both these two things may (with some latitude, it is true, in the case of the performance) be regarded as physical objects. Furthermore, a common way of referring to these objects is by saying things like "*Ulysses* is on my table," "I shall see *Rosenkavalier* tonight": from which it would be tempting (but erroneous) to conclude that *Ulysses* just is my copy of it, *Rosenkavalier* just is tonight's performance.

From *Art and Its Objects* (New York: Harper and Row Publishers, 1968). Reprinted by permission of the publisher. Headings have been renumbered.

Tempting, but erroneous; and there are a number of very succinct ways of bringing out the error involved. For instance, it would follow that if I lost my copy of *Ulysses*, *Ulysses* would become a lost work. Again, it would follow that if the critics disliked tonight's performance of *Rosenkavalier*, then they dislike *Rosenkavalier*. Clearly neither of these inferences is acceptable.

We have here two locutions or ways of describing the facts: one in terms of works of art, the other in terms of copies, performances, etc. of works of art. Just because there are contexts in which these two locutions are interchangeable, this does not mean that there are no contexts, moreover no contexts of a substantive kind, in which they are not interchangeable. There very evidently are such contexts, and the physical-object hypothesis would seem to overlook them to its utter detriment.

4

But, it might now be maintained, of course it is absurd to identify *Ulysses* with my copy of it or *Der Rosenkavalier* with tonight's performance, but nothing follows from this of a general character about the wrongness of identifying works of art with physical objects. For what was wrong in these two cases was the actual physical object that was picked out and with which the identification was then made. The validity of the physical-object hypothesis, like that of any other hypothesis, is quite unaffected by the consequences of misapplying it.

For instance, it is obviously wrong to say that *Ulysses* is my copy of it. Nevertheless, there is a physical object, of precisely the same order of being as my copy, though significantly not called a "copy," with which such an identification would be quite correct. This object is the author's manuscript: that, in other words, which Joyce wrote when he wrote *Ulysses*.

On the intimate connection, which undoubtedly does exist, between a novel or a poem on the one hand and the author's manuscript on the other, I shall have something to add later. But the connection does not justify us in asserting that one just is the other. Indeed, to do so seems open to objections not all that dissimilar from those we have just been considering. The critic, for instance, who admires *Ulysses* does not necessarily admire the manuscript. Nor is the critic who has seen or handled the manuscript in a privileged position as such when it comes to judgment on the novel. And—here we have come to an objection directly parallel to that which seemed fatal to identifying *Ulysses* with my copy of it—it would be possible for the manuscript to be lost and *Ulysses* to survive. None of this can be admitted by the person who thinks that *Ulysses* and the manuscript are one and the same thing.

To this last objection someone might retort that there are cases (e.g., *Love's Labour Won*, Kleist's *Robert Guiscard*) where the manuscript is lost and the work is lost, and moreover the work is lost because the manuscript is lost. Of course there is no real argument here, since nothing more is claimed than that there are *some* cases like this. Nevertheless the retort is worth pursuing, for the significance of such cases is precisely the opposite of that intended. Instead of reinforcing, they actually diminish, the status of the manuscript. For if we now ask, When is the work lost when the manuscript is lost?, the answer is, When and only when the manuscript is unique: but then this would be true for any copy of the work were it unique.

Moreover, it is significant that in the case of *Rosenkavalier* it is not even possible to construct an argument corresponding to the one about *Ulysses*. To identify an opera or any other piece of music with the composer's holograph, which looks the corresponding thing to do, is implausible because (for instance), whereas an opera can be heard, a holograph cannot be. In consequence it is common at this stage of the argument, when music is considered, to introduce a new notion, that of the ideal performance, and then to identify the piece of music with this. There are many difficulties here: in the present context it is enough to point out that this step could not conceivably satisfy the purpose for which it was intended; that is, that of saving the physical-object hypothesis. For an ideal performance cannot be, even in the attenuated sense in which we have extended the term to ordinary performances, a physical object.

5

A final and desperate expedient to save the physical-object hypothesis is to suggest that all those works of art which cannot plausibly be identified with physical objects are identical with classes of such objects. A novel, of which there are copies, is not my or your copy but is the class of all its copies. An opera, of which there are performances, is not tonight's or last night's performance, nor even the ideal performance, but is the class of all its performances. (Of course, strictly speaking, this suggestion doesn't save the hypothesis at all: since a class of physical objects isn't necessarily, indeed is most unlikely to be, a physical object itself. But it saves something like the spirit of the hypothesis.)

However, it is not difficult to think of objections to this suggestion. Ordinarily we conceive of a novelist as writing a novel, or a composer as finishing an opera. But both these ideas imply some moment in time at which the work is complete. Now suppose (which is not unlikely) that the copies of a novel or the performances of an opera go on being produced for an indefinite period: then, on the present suggestion, there is no such moment, let alone one in their creator's lifetime. So we cannot say that *Ulysses* was written by Joyce, or that Strauss composed *Der Rosenkavalier*. Or, again, there is the problem of the unperformed symphony, or the poem of which there is not even a manuscript: in what sense can we now say that these things even *exist*?

But perhaps a more serious, certainly a more interesting, objection is that in this suggestion what is totally unexplained is why the various copies of *Ulysses* are all said to be copies of *Ulysses* and nothing else, why all the performances of *Der Rosenkavalier* are reckoned performances of that one opera. For the ordinary explanation of how we come to group copies or performances as being of this book or of that opera is by reference to something else, something other than themselves, to which they stand in some special relation. (Exactly what this other thing is, or what is the special relation in which they stand to it is, of course, something we are as yet totally unable to say.) But the effect, indeed precisely the point, of the present suggestion is to eliminate the possibility of any such reference: if a novel or opera just is its copies or its performances, then we cannot, for purposes of identification, refer from the latter to the former.

The possibility that remains is that the various particular objects, the copies or performances, are grouped as they are, not by reference to some other thing to which they are related, but in virtue of some relation that holds between them: more specifically, in virtue of resemblance.

But, in the first place, all copies of *Ulysses*, and certainly all performances of *Der Rosenkavalier*, are not perfect matches. And if it is now said that the differences do not matter, either because the various copies or performances resemble each other in all relevant respects, or because they resemble each other more than they resemble the copies or performances of any other novel or opera, neither answer is adequate. The first answer begs the issue, in that to talk of relevant respects presupposes that we know how, say, copies of *Ulysses* are grouped together: the second answer evades the issue, in that though it may tell us why we do not, say, reckon any of the performances of *Der Rosenkavalier* as performances of *Arabella*, it gives us no indication why we do not set some of them up separately, as performances of some third opera.

Secondly, it seems strange to refer to the resemblance between the copies of *Ulysses* or the performances of *Rosenkavalier* as though this were a brute fact: a fact, moreover, which could be used to explain why they were copies or performances of what they are. It would be more natural to think of this so-called "fact" as something that itself stood in need of explanation: and, moreover, as finding its explanation in just that which it is here invoked to explain. In other words, to say that certain copies or performances are of *Ulysses* or *Rosenkavalier* because they resemble one another seems precisely to reverse the natural order of thought: the resemblance, we would think, follows from, or is to be understood in terms of, the fact that they are of the same novel or opera.

6

However, those who are ready to concede that some kinds of work of art are not physical objects will yet insist that others are. *Ulysses* and *Der Rosenkavalier* may not be physical objects, but the *Donna Velata* and Donatello's *St. George* most certainly are.

I have already suggested (section 2) that the challenge to the physical-object hypothesis can be divided into two parts. It will be clear that I am now about to embark on the second part of the challenge: namely, that which allows that there are (some) physical objects that could conceivably be identified as works of art, but insists that it would be quite erroneous to make the identification.

(To some, such a course of action may seem superfluous. For enough has been said to disprove the physical-object hypothesis. That is true; but the argument that is to come has its intrinsic interest, and for that reason is worth developing. Those for whom the interest of all philosophical argument is essentially polemical, and who have been convinced by the preceding argument, may choose to think of that which is to follow as bearing upon a revised or weakened version of the physical-object hypothesis: namely, that some works of art are physical objects.)

7

In the Pitti there is a canvas (No. 245) 85 cm × 64 cm; in the Museo Nazionale, Florence, there is a piece of marble 209 cm high. It is with these physical objects that those who claim that the *Donna Velata* and the *St. George* are physical objects would naturally identify them.

This identification can be disputed in (roughly) one or other of two ways. It can be argued that the work of art has properties which are incompatible with certain properties that the physical object has, alternatively it can be argued that the work of art has properties which no physical object could have: in neither case could the work of art be the physical object.

An argument of the first kind would run: We say of the *St. George* that it moves with life (Vasari). Yet the block of marble is inanimate. Therefore the *St. George* cannot be that block of marble. An argument of the second kind would run: We say of the *Donna Velata* that it is exalted and dignified (Wölfflin). Yet a piece of canvas in the Pitti cannot conceivably have these qualities. Therefore the *Donna Velata* cannot be that piece of canvas.

These two arguments, I suggest, are not merely instances of these two ways of arguing, they are characteristic instances. For the argument that there is an incompatibility of property between works of art and physical objects characteristically concentrates on the representational properties of works of art. The argument that works of art have properties that physical objects could not have characteristically concentrates on the expressive properties of works of art. The terms "representational" and "expressive" are used here in a very wide fashion, which, it is hoped, will become clear as the discussion proceeds.

8

Let us begin with the argument about representational properties. An initial difficulty here is to see exactly how the argument is supposed to fit on to the facts. For, as we have seen from the *St. George* example, its tactic is to take some representational property that we ascribe to a work of art and then point out that there is some property that the relevant physical object possesses and that is incompatible with it, e.g. "being instinct with life" and "being inanimate." But if we consider how, in point of fact, we do talk or think of works of representational art, we see that by and large what we ascribe representational properties to are elements or bits of the picture: it is only peripherally that we make such an attribution to the work itself, to the work, that is, as a whole.

Let us take, for instance, the justly famous descriptions given by Wölfflin of Raphael's Stanze in *Classic Art*: in particular, that of the *Expulsion of Heliodorus*. Wölfflin is generally thought of as a formalist critic. But if he is, it is in a very restricted sense: since, even when he is most assiduous in using the vocabulary of geometry to describe compositional devices, it is significant how he identifies the shapes or forms whose arrangements he analyzes. He does so invariably by reference back to the characters or happenings that they depict. When, as in the Raphael descriptions, his aim is to bring out the dramatic content of a painting, he keeps extremely close to its representational aspect. What in such circumstances do we find him mentioning? The movement of the youths: the fallen Heliodorus, with vengeance breaking over him: the women and the children huddled together: the clambering pair of boys on the left who balance the prostrate Heliodorus on the right, and who lead the eyes backward to the centre where the High Priest is praying. Now all these particular elements, which seem the natural items of discourse in the description of a representational painting—or better, perhaps, of a painting in its representational function—provide no obvious point of application for the argument under consideration. For there would have to be, corresponding to each of these elements, a physical object such that we could then ask of it whether it possessed some property that is incompatible with the representational property we have ascribed to the element.

But, it will be objected, I have not given the situation in full. For even in the description of the *Expulsion of Heliodorus*, there are nonparticular or over-all representational attributions. Wölfflin, for instance, speaks of "a great void" in the middle of the composition.

This is true. But it looks as though the argument requires more than this. It requires not just that there should exist such attributions but that they should be central to the notion of representation: that, for instance, it should be through them that we learn what it is for something to be a representation of something else. I want to argue that, on the contrary, they are peripheral. First, in a weaker sense, in that they have no priority over the more particular or specific attributions. The very general attributions come out of a very large range of attributions, and it certainly does not look as though we could understand them without understanding the other judgments in the range. It is hard to see, for instance, how a man could "read" the void in the middle of Raphael's fresco if he was not at the same time able to make out the spatial relations that hold between Heliodorus and the youths who advance to scourge him, or between the Pope and the scene that he surveys in calm detachment. Secondly, a stronger argument could be mounted—though it would be too elaborate to do so here—to show that the representational attribution that we make in respect of the picture as a whole is dependent upon, or can be analysed in terms of, the specific attributions. The clearest way of exhibiting this would be to take simpler over-all attributions than Wölfflin's: for instance, that a picture has depth, or that it has great movement, or that it has a diagonal recession: and then show how these can be fully elucidated by reference to the spatial relations that hold between e.g., a tree in the foreground and the horizon, or the body of the saint and the crowd of angels through whom he ascends to heaven. A more dramatic way of exhibiting this would be to point out that we could not produce a sheet of blank paper and say that it was a representation of Empty Space. Though, of course, what we could do is to produce such a sheet and entitle it "Empty Space," and there could be a point to this title.

9

Reference was made in the last section to the wide range of representational attributions that we make, and it is important to appreciate quite how wide it is. It certainly extends well beyond the domain of purely figurative art, and takes in such things as geometrical drawings or certain forms of architectural ornament. And I now suggest that if we look at the opposite end of this range to that occupied by e.g. Raphael's Stanze, we may see our present problem in a fresh light.

It is said that Hans Hofmann, the doyen of New York painting, used to ask his pupils, on joining his studio, to put a black mark on a white canvas, and then observe how the black was on the white. It is clear that what Hofmann's pupils were asked to observe was not the fact that some black paint was physically on a white canvas. So I shall change the example somewhat to bring this out better, and assume that the young painters were asked to put a blue mark on a white canvas and then to observe how the blue was behind (as it was) the white. The sense in which "on" was used in the original example and "behind" in the revised example gives us in an elementary form the notion of what it is to see something as a representation, or for something to have representational properties. Accordingly, if we are going to accept the argument that works of art cannot be physical objects because they have representational properties, it looks as though we are committed to regarding the invitation to see the blue behind the white as something in the nature of an incitement to deny the physicality of the canvas. (This is imprecise: but the preceding section will have shown us how difficult it is to apply the argument we are considering with anything like precision.)

If it can be shown that it is quite wrong to treat the invitation in this way, that, on the contrary, there is no incompatibility between seeing one mark on the canvas as behind another and also insisting that both the marks and the canvas on which they lie are physical objects, then the present objection to the physical-object hypothesis fails. To establish this point would, however, require an elaborate argument. It might, though, be possible to avoid the need for such an argument by showing just how widespread or pervasive is the kind of seeing (let us call it "representational seeing"), to which Hofmann's pupils were invited. In fact, it would be little exaggeration to say that such seeing is coextensive with our seeing of any physical object whose surface exhibits any substantial degree of differentiation. Once we allow this fact, it then surely seems absurd to insist that representational seeing, and the judgments to which it characteristically gives rise, implicitly presuppose a denial of the physicality both of the representation itself and that on which it lies.

In a famous passage in the *Trattato* Leonardo advises the aspirant painter to "quicken the spirit of invention" by looking at walls stained with damp or at stones of uneven colour, and find in them divine landscapes and battle scenes and strange figures in violent action. This passage has many applications both for the psychology and for the philosophy of art. Here I quote it for the testimony it provides to the pervasiveness of representational seeing....

10

I have (it will be observed) presented the problem about representational properties and the prima facie difficulty they present for the physical-object hypothesis as though this was a problem that arose, at any rate in the first instance, only in connection with certain representational properties. There are, that is, cases where we attribute a representational property to a work of art and this clearly conflicts with some other property or properties that the corresponding physical object possesses. So, for instance, we say that a still-life has depth, but the canvas is flat; that a fresco has a void in the middle, but the wall on which it is painted is intact. And it is only where such a conflict occurs that, as I presented it, a problem occurs. It was for this reason that I amended the Hofmann case to that of a master who asked his students to put (blue) paint *on* the (white) canvas in such a way that they saw the blue (=colour of the paint) *behind* the white (=colour of the canvas). For though, of course, conflicts could arise if one pursued the original Hofmann case any distance (e.g. if someone asked, How far is the black in front of the white?), in the amended case the conflict arises immediately.

In presenting the problem thus, I coincided, I think, with the way it is generally conceived. In other words, representational properties are not regarded as being in general problematic. However, when we turn from the problem of representational properties to that of expressive properties and how they bear on the identification of works of art with physical objects, the situation somewhat changes. For the problem seems to be not, How can a work of art *qua* physical object of this or that kind express this or that emotion? but, How can a work of art *qua* physical object express emotion? . . .

If I am right in asserting the difference between the ways in which representational and expressive properties prove problematic—and I have no desire to be insistent here—the explanation may well lie in the fact that, though there is nothing other than a physical object that has representational properties, there is something other than a physical, or at any rate a purely physical, object that has expressive properties: namely, a human body and its parts, in particular the face and certain limbs. So now we wonder, How can anything other than this be expressive? More specifically, How can anything purely physical be expressive? . . .

11

Originally it was claimed that works of art were expressive of a certain state if and only if they had been produced in, and were capable of arousing to, that state. . . . So, for instance, the claim that certain music is sad because of what the composer felt is sometimes equated—by its proponents as well as by its critics—with the claim that at the time the composer was suffering from a bout of gloom. Or, again, to say that a certain statue is terrifying because of the emotions it arouses in the spectators is sometimes interpreted as meaning that someone who looks at it will take fight. In other words, to establish that the composer was not on the verge of tears or that the average spectator exhibits no desire to run away, is thought to be enough to refute this whole conception of expression. . . .

12

In the first place, and perhaps most primitively, we think of a work of art as expressive in the sense in which a gesture or a cry would be expressive: that is to say, we conceive of it as coming so directly and immediately out of some particular emotional or mental state that it bears unmistakable marks of that state upon it. In this sense the word remains very close to its etymology: *ex-primere*, to squeeze out or press out. An expression is a secretion of an inner state. I shall refer to this as "natural expression." Alongside this notion is another, which we apply when we think of an object as expressive of a certain condition because, when we are in that condition, it seems to us to match, or correspond with, what we experience inwardly; and perhaps when the condition passes, the object is also good for reminding us of it in some special poignant way, or for reviving it for us. For an object to be expressive in this sense, there is no requirement that it should originate in the condition that it expresses, nor indeed is there any stipulation about its genesis: for these purposes it is simply a piece of the environment which we appropriate on account of the way it seems to reiterate something in us. Expression in this sense I shall (following a famous nineteenth-century usage) call "correspondence." . . .

But though these two notions are logically distinct, in practice they are bound to interact: indeed, it is arguable that it goes beyond the limit of legitimate abstraction to imagine one without the other. We can see this by considering the notion of appropriateness, or fittingness, conceived as a relation holding between expression and expressed. . . .

When we endow a natural object or an artifact with expressive meaning, we tend to see it corporeally: that is, we tend to credit it with a particular look which bears a marked analogy to some look that the human body wears and that is constantly conjoined with an inner state.

13

To the question, Can a work of art be a physical object if it is also expressive?, it now looks as though we can, on the basis of the preceding account of expression, give an affirmative answer. For that account was elaborated with specifically in mind those arts where it is most plausible to think of a work of art as a physical object. But it may seem that with both the two notions of expression that I have tried to formulate, there remains an unexamined or problematic residue. And in the two cases the problem is much the same.

It may be stated like this: Granted that in each case the process I have described is perfectly comprehensible, how do we come at the end of it to attribute a human emotion to an object? In both cases the object has certain characteristics. In one case these characteristics mirror, in the other case they are caused by, certain inner states of ours. Why, on the basis of this, do the names of the inner states get transposed to the objects?

The difficulty with this objection might be put by saying that it treats a philosophical reconstruction of a part of our language as though it were a historical account. For it is not at all clear that, in the cases where we attribute emotions to objects in the ways that I have tried to describe, we have any other way of talking about the objects themselves. There is not necessarily a prior description in nonemotive terms, on which we superimpose the emotive description. Or, to put the same point in nonlinguistic terms, it is not always the case that things that we see as expressive, we can or could see in any other way. In such cases what we need is not a justification, but an explanation, of our language. That I hope to have given.

14

We have now completed our discussion of the physical-object hypothesis, and this would be a good moment at which to pause and review the situation.

The hypothesis, taken literally, has been clearly shown to be false: in that there are arts where it is impossible to find physical objects that are even candidates for being identified with works of art (sections 3–5). However, as far as those other arts are concerned where such physical objects can be found, the arguments against the identification—namely, those based on the fact that works of art have properties not predicable of physical objects—seemed less cogent (sections 6–13).

The general issue raised, whether works of art are physical objects, seems to compress two questions: the difference between which can be brought out by accenting first one, then the other, constituent word in the operative phrase. Are works of art *physical* objects? Are works of art physical *objects*? The first question would be a question about the stuff or constitution of works of art, what in the broadest sense they are made of: more specifically, Are they mental? or physical? are they constructs of the mind? The second question would be a question about the category to which works of art belong, about the criteria of identity and individuation applicable to them: more specifically, Are they universals, of which there are instances?, or classes, of which there are members?, are they particulars? Roughly speaking, the first question might be regarded as metaphysical, the second as logical. And, confusingly enough, both can be put in the form of a question about what kind of thing a work of art is.

Applying this distinction to the preceding discussion, we can now see that the method of falsifying the hypothesis that all works of art are physical objects has been to establish that there are some works of art that are not objects (or particulars) at all: whereas the further part of the case, which depends upon establishing that those works of art which are objects are nevertheless not physical, has not been made good. . . .

15

It needs, however, at this stage to be pointed out that the arguments in the [earlier] sections are less conclusive than perhaps they appeared to be. Certainly some conventional arguments to the effect that (certain) works are not (are not identical with) physical objects were disposed of. But it could be wrong to think that it follows from this that (certain) works of art are (are identical with) physical objects. The difficulty here lies in the highly elusive notion of "identity," the analysis of which belongs to the more intricate part of general philosophy.

The Ontological Peculiarity of Works of Art

Joseph Margolis

In the context of discussing the nature of artistic creativity, Jack Glickman offers the intriguing comment, "Particulars are made, types created."[1] The remark is a strategic one, but it is either false or misleading; and its recovery illuminates in a most economical way some of the complexities of the creative process and of the ontology of art. Glickman offers as an instance of the distinction he has in mind, the following: "If the chef created a new soup, he created a new kind of soup, a new recipe; he may not have made the soup [that is, some particular pot of soup]."[2] *If*, by 'kind,' Glickman means to signify a universal of some sort, then, since universals are not

created (or destroyed), it could not be the case that the chef "created" a new soup, a new kind of soup.[3] It must be the case that the chef, in making a particular (new) soup, created (to use Glickman's idiom) a kind of soup; otherwise, of course, that the chef created a new (kind of) soup may be evidenced by his having formulated a relevant recipe (which locution, in its own turn, shows the same ambiguity between type and token).

What is important, here, may not meet the eye at once. But if he can be said to create (to invent) a (new kind of) soup and if universals cannot be created or destroyed, then, in creating a kind of soup, a chef must be creating something other than a universal. The odd thing is that a kind of soup thus created is thought to be individuated among related creations; hence, it appears to be a particular of

---

From *The Journal of Aesthetics and Art Criticism*, 36 (1977). Reprinted with permission of the author and The American Society for Aesthetics.

some sort. But it also seems to be an abstract entity if it is a particular at all. Hence, although it may be possible to admit abstract particulars in principle,[4] it is difficult to concede that what the chef created is an abstract particular *if* one may be said to have *tasted* what the chef created. The analogy with art is plain. If Picasso created a new kind of painting, in painting *Les Demoiselles d'Avignon*, it would appear that he could not have done so *by using oils*.

There is only one solution *if* we mean to speak in this way. It must be possible to instantiate particulars (of a certain kind or of certain kinds) as well as to instantiate universals or properties. I suggest that the term 'type'—in all contexts in which the type/token ambiguity arises—signifies abstract particulars of a kind that can be instantiated. Let me offer a specimen instance. Printings properly pulled from Dürer's etching plate for *Melancholia I* are instances of *that* etching; but bona fide instances of *Melancholia I* need not have all their relevant properties in common, since later printings and printings that follow a touching up of the plate or printings that are themselves touched up may be genuine instances of *Melancholia I* and still differ markedly from one another—at least to the sensitive eye. Nothing, however, can instantiate a property without actually instantiating that property.[5] So to think of types as particulars (of a distinctive kind) accommodates the fact that we individuate works of art in unusual ways—performances of the same music, printings of the same etching, copies of the same novel—and that works of art may be created and destroyed. If, further, we grant that, in creating a new soup, a chef stirred the ingredients in his pot and that, in creating a new kind of painting, in painting *Les Demoiselles*, Picasso applied paint to canvas, we see that it is at least normally the case that one does not create a new kind of soup or a new kind of painting without (in Glickman's words) making a particular soup or a particular painting.

A great many questions intrude at this point. But we may bring this much at least to bear on an ingenious thesis of Glickman's. Glickman wishes to say that, though driftwood may be construed as a creation of "beach art," it remains true that driftwood was *made* by no one, is in fact a natural object, and hence that "the condition of artifactuality" so often claimed to be a necessary condition of being a work of art, is simply "superfluous."[6] "I see no conclusive conceptual block," says Glickman, "to allowing that the artwork [may] be a natural object."[7] Correspondingly, Duchamp's "ready-mades" are created out of artifacts, but the artist who created them did not actually make them. Glickman's thesis depends on the tenability of his distinction between making and creating; and as we have just seen, one does not, in the normal case at least, create a new kind of art (type) without making a particular work of that kind (that is, an instance of that particular, the type, not merely an instance of that kind, the universal). In other words, when an artist *creates* (allowing Glickman's terms) "beach art," a new kind of art, the artist *makes* a particular instance (or token) of a particular type—much as with wood sculpture, *this unique token of this driftwood composition.* He cannot create the universals that are newly instantiated since universals cannot be created. He can create a new type-particular, a particular of the kind "beach art" but he can do so only by making a token-particular of that type. What this shows is that we were unnecessarily tentative about the relation between types and tokens. We may credit an artist with having created a new type of art; but there are no types of art that are not instantiated by some token-instances or for which we lack a notation by reference to which (as in the performing arts) admissible token-instances of the particular type-work may be generated.

The reason for this strengthened conclusion has already been given. When an artist creates his work using the materials of his craft, the work he produces must have some perceptible physical properties at least; but it could not have such properties if the work were merely an abstract particular (or, of course, a universal). Hence, wherever an artist produces his work directly, even a new kind of work, he cannot be producing an abstract particular. Alternatively put, to credit an artist with having created a new *type* of art—a particular art-type—we must (normally) be thus crediting him in virtue of the particular (token) work he has made. In wood sculpture, the particular piece an artist makes is normally the unique instance of his work; in bronzes, it is more usually true that, as in Rodin's peculiarly industrious way, there are several or numerous tokens of the very same (type) sculpture. But though we may credit the artist with having created the type, the type does not exist except instantiated in its proper tokens. We may, by a kind of courtesy, say that an artist who has produced the cast for a set of bronzes has created an artwork-type; but the fact is: (i) he has *made* a particular cast, and (ii) the cast he's made is not the work *created*. Similar considerations apply to an artist's preparing a musical notation for the sonata he has created: (i) the artist makes a token instance of a type notation; and (ii) all admissible instances of his sonata are so identified by reference to the notations. The result is that, insofar as he creates a type, an artist must make a token. A chef's assistant may actually make the first pot of soup—of the soup the chef has created, but the actual soup exists only when the pot is made. Credit to the chef in virtue of his recipe is partly an assurance that his authorship is to be acknowledged in each and every pot of soup that is properly an instance of his creation, whether he makes it or not; and it is partly a device for individuating proper token instances of particular type objects. But only the token instances *of* a type actually exist and aesthetic interest in the type is given point only in virtue of one's aesthetic interest in actual or possible tokens—as in actual or contemplated performances of a particular sonata.

But if these distinctions be granted, then, normally, an artist makes a token of the type he has created. He could not create the type unless he made a proper token or, by the courtesy intended in notations and the like, he provided a schema *for* making proper tokens of a particular type. Hence, what is normally made, in the relevant sense, is a token of a type. It must be the case, then, that when Duchamp created his *Bottlerack*, although he did not make a bottlerack—that is, although he did not manufacture a bottlerack, although he did not first bring it about that an object instantiate being a bottlerack—nevertheless, *he did make a token of the Bottlerack*. Similarly, although driftwood is not a manufactured thing, when an artist creates (if an artist can create) a piece of "beach art," *he makes a token of that piece of "beach art."* He need not have made the driftwood. But that shows (i) that artifactuality is not superfluous, though it is indeed puzzling (when displaying otherwise untouched driftwood in accord with the developed sensibilities of a society can count as the creation of an artwork); and (ii) it is not the case (contrary to Glickman's claims) that a natural object can *be* a work of art or that a work can be created though *nothing* be made.

We may summarize the ontological peculiarities of the type/token distinction in the following way: (i) types and tokens are individuated as particulars; (ii) types and tokens are not separable and cannot exist separately from one another; (iii) types are instantiated by tokens and 'token' is an ellipsis for 'token-of-a-type'; (iv) types and tokens may be generated and destroyed in the sense that actual tokens of a novel type may be generated, the actual tokens of a given type may be destroyed, and whatever contingencies may be necessary to the generation of actual tokens may be destroyed or disabled; (v) types are actual abstract particulars in the sense only that a set of actual entities may be individuated as tokens of a particular type; (vi) it is incoherent to speak of comparing the properties of actual token- and type-particulars as opposed to comparing the properties of actual particular tokens of a type; (vii) reference to types as particulars serves exclusively to facilitate reference to actual and possible tokens-of-a-type. These distinctions are sufficient to mark the type/token concept as different from the kind/instance concept and the set/member concept.

Here, a second ontological oddity must be conceded. The driftwood that is made by no one is not the (unique) token that is made of the "beach art" creation; and the artifact, the bottlerack, that Duchamp did not make is not identical with the (probably but not necessarily unique) token that Duchamp did make of the creation called *Bottlerack*. What Duchamp made was a token of *Bottlerack*; and what the manufacturer of bottleracks made was a particular bottlerack that served as the material out of which Duchamp created *Bottlerack* by making a (probably unique) instance of *Bottlerack*. For, consider that Duchamp made something when he created *Bottlerack* but he did not make a bottlerack; also, that no one made the driftwood though someone (on the thesis) made a particular composition of art using the driftwood. If the bottlerack were said to be identical with Duchamp's *Bottlerack* (the token or the type), we should be contradicting ourselves; the same would be true of the driftwood case. Hence, in spite of appearances, there must be an ontological difference between tokens of artwork-types and such physical objects as bottleracks and driftwood that can serve as the materials out of which they are made.

My own suggestion is that (token) works of art are *embodied* in physical objects, not identical with them. I should argue, though this is not the place for it, that persons, similarly, are embodied in physical bodies but not identical with them.[8] The idea is that not only can one particular instantiate another particular in a certain way (tokens of types) but one particular can embody or be embodied in another particular with which it is (necessarily) not identical. The important point is that identity cannot work in the anomalous cases here considered (nor in the usual cases of art) and that what would otherwise be related by way of identity are, obviously, particulars. Furthermore, the embodiment relationship does not invite dualism though it does require a distinction among kinds of things and among the kinds of properties of things of such kinds. For example, a particular printing of Dürer's *Melancholia I* has the property of being a particular token of *Melancholia I* (the artwork type), but the physical paper and physical print do not, on any familiar view, have the property of being a token of a type. Only objects having such intentional properties as that of "being created" or, as with words, having meaning or the like can have the property of being a token of a type.[9]

What is meant in saying that one particular is embodied in another is: (i) that the two particulars are not identical; (ii) that the existence of the embodied particular presupposes the existence of the embodying particular; (iii) that the embodied particular possesses some of the properties of the embodying particular; (iv) that the embodied particular possesses properties that the embodying particular does not possess; (v) that the embodied particular possesses properties of a kind that the embodying particular cannot possess; (vi) that the individuation of the embodied particular presupposes the individuation of the embodying particular. The 'is' of embodiment, then, like the 'is' of identity and the 'is' of composition[10] is a logically distinctive use. On a theory, for instance a theory about the nature of a work of art, a particular physical object will be taken to embody a particular object of another kind in such a way that a certain systematic relationship will hold between them. Thus, for instance, a sculptor will be said to make a particular sculpture by cutting a block of marble: Michelangelo's *Pietà* will exhibit certain of the physical properties of the marble and certain representational and purposive properties as well; it will also have the property of being a unique token of the creation *Pietà*. The reason for theorizing thus is, quite simply, that works of art are the products of culturally informed labor and that physical objects are not. So seen, they must possess properties that physical objects, *qua* physical objects, do not and cannot possess. Hence, an identity thesis leads to palpable contradictions. Furthermore, the conception of embodiment promises to facilitate a nonreductive account of the relationship between physical nature and human culture, without dualistic assumptions. What this suggests is that the so-called mind/body problem is essentially a special form of a more general culture/nature problem. But that is another story.

A work of art, then, is a particular. It cannot be a universal because it is created and can be destroyed; also, because it possesses physical and perceptual properties. But it is a peculiar sort of particular, unlike physical bodies, because (i) it can instantiate another particular; and (ii) it can be embodied in another particular. The suggestion here is that all and only culturally emergent or culturally produced entities exhibit these traits. So the ontological characteristics assigned are no more than the most generic characteristics of art: its distinctive nature remains unanalyzed. Nevertheless, we can discern an important difference between these two properties, as far as art is concerned. For, the first property, that of being able to instantiate another particular, has only to do with individuating works of art and whatever may, contingently, depend upon that; while the second property has to do with the ontologically dependent nature of actual works of art. This is the reason we may speak of type artworks as particulars. They are heuristically introduced for purposes of individuation, though they cannot exist except in the sense in which particular tokens of particular type artworks exist. So we can never properly *compare* the properties of a token work and a type work.[11] What we may compare are alternative tokens of the same type—different printings of the same etching or different performances of the same sonata. In short, every work of art is a token-of-a-type; there are no tokens or types *tout court*. Again, this is not to say that there are no types or that an artist cannot create a new kind of painting. It is only to say that so speaking is an ellipsis for saying that a certain set of particulars are tokens of a type and that the artist is credited with so working with the properties of things, instantiated by the members of that set, that they are construed as tokens of a particular type.

So the dependencies of the two ontological traits mentioned are quite different. There are no types that are separable from tokens because there are no tokens except tokens-of-a-type. The very process for individuating tokens entails individuating types, that is, entails individuating different sets of particulars as the alternative tokens of this or that type. There is nothing left over to discuss. What may mislead is this: the concept of different tokens of the same type is intended, in the arts, to accommodate the fact that the aesthetically often decisive differences among tokens of the same type (alternative performances of a sonata, for instance) need not matter as far as the individuation of the (type) work is concerned.[12] But particular works of art cannot exist except as embodied in physical objects. This is simply another way of saying that works of art are culturally emergent entities; that is, that works of art exhibit properties that physical objects cannot exhibit, but do so in a way that does not depend on the presence of any substance other than what may be ascribed to purely physical objects. Broadly speaking, those properties are what may be characterized as functional or intentional properties and include design, expressiveness, symbolism, representation, meaning, style, and the like. Without prejudice to the nature of either art or persons, this way of viewing art suggests a very convenient linkup with the functional theory of mental traits.[13] Be that as it may, a reasonable theory of art could hold that when physical materials are worked in accord with a certain artistic craft then there emerges, culturally, an object embodied in the former that possesses a certain orderly array of functional properties of the kind just mentioned. Any object so produced may be treated as an artifact. Hence, works of art exist as fully as physical objects but the condition on which they do so depends on the independent existence of some physical object itself. Works of art, then, are culturally emergent entities, tokens-of-a-type that exist embodied in physical objects.

NOTES

1. Jack Glickman, "Creativity in the Arts," in Lars Aagaard-Mogensen, ed., *Culture and Art* (Nyborg and Atlantic Highlands, N.J.: F. Løkkes Forlag and Humanities Press, 1976), p. 140.
2. *Loc. cit.*
3. Difficulties of this sort undermine the recent thesis of Nicholas Wolterstorff's, namely, that

works of art are in fact kinds. Cf. Nicholas Wolterstorff, "Toward an Ontology of Art Works," *Nous* IX (1975), 115–142. Also, Joseph Margolis, *Art and Philosophy* (Atlantic Highlands, N.J.: Humanities Press, 1978), ch. 5.
4. Cf. Nelson Goodman, *The Structure of Appearance* (Indianapolis: Bobbs-Merrill, 2nd ed., 1966).
5. The subtleties of the type/token distinction are discussed at length in Margolis, *loc. cit.*
6. *Op. cit.*, p. 144.
7. *Ibid.*, p. 143.
8. A fuller account of the concept of embodiment with respect to art is given in *Art and Philosophy*, ch. 1. I have tried to apply the notion to all cultural entities—that is, persons, works of art, artifacts, words and sentences, machines, institutionalized actions, and the like—in *Persons and Minds* (Dordrecht: D. Reidel, 1977). Cf. also "On the Ontology of Persons," *New Scholasticism* X (1976), 73–84.
9. This is very close in spirit to Peirce's original distinction between types and tokens. Cf. *Collected Papers of Charles Sanders Peirce*, ed. Charles Hartshorne and Paul Weiss (Cambridge: Harvard University Press, 1939), vol. 4, par. 537.
10. Cf. David Wiggins, *Identity and Spatio-Temporal Continuity* (Oxford: Basil Blackwell, 1967).
11. This is one of the signal weaknesses of Wolterstorff's account, *loc. cit.*, as well as of Richard Wollheim's account: cf. *Art and Its Objects* (New York: Harper, 1968).
12. This counts against Nelson Goodman's strictures on the individuation of artworks. Cf. *Languages of Art* (Indianapolis: Bobbs-Merrill, 1968) and Joseph Margolis, "Numerical Identity and Reference in the Arts," *British Journal of Aesthetics* X (1970), 138–146.
13. Cf. for instance Hilary Putnam, "Minds and Machines," in Sidney Hook, ed., *Dimensions of Mind* (Englewood Cliffs, N.J.: Prentice-Hall, 1960), and Jerry Fodor, *Psychological Explanation* (New York: Random House, 1968).

Toward an Ontology of Art Works

Nicholas Wolterstorff

What sort of entity is a symphony? A drama? A dance? A graphic art print? A sculpture? A poem? A film? A painting?

Are works of art all fundamentally alike in their ontological status?

These are the questions to be discussed in this paper.

From *NOÛS*, 9 (1975). Reprinted with permission of the author and of the editor.

I. A PHENOMENOLOGY OF THE DISTINCTIONS AMONG WORKS OF ART

In several of the arts there is application for the distinction between a performance of something and that which is performed. In music, for example, one can distinguish between a performance of *Verklaerte Nacht* and that which is thereby performed, namely, Arnold Schoenberg's work *Verklaerte Nacht*. Similarly, in dance one can distinguish between a performance of *Swan Lake* and that which is thereby performed, namely, the ballet *Swan Lake*.

Some people will be skeptical as to whether, in the cases cited and others of the same sort, we really do have two distinct entities—a performance and that which is performed. But assuming it to be true that the concept of a performance of something and the concept of something performed both have application to the arts, there are two sorts of considerations which force one to the conclusion that that which is performed on a given occasion is distinct from the performance of it.

In the first place, a thing performed and a performance thereof will always diverge in certain of their properties. For example, *having been composed by Schoenberg* is a property of *Verklaerte Nacht* but not of any performance of *Verklaerte Nacht*. On the other hand, *taking place at a certain time and place* is a property of every performance of *Verklaerte Nacht* but not of *Verklaerte Nacht* itself. It is worth noting that a work performed may diverge from performances thereof not only in 'ontological' properties but also in 'aesthetic' properties. For example, it may be that *having the voice part begin on A natural* is not a property of any performance of Schoenberg's *Pierrot Lunaire*, though it is a property of the work itself, indeed, an *essential* one.

A second sort of consideration, one which is actually a specific application of the first, also leads to the conclusion that in certain of the arts one must distinguish between those entities which are performances and those entities which are works performed. This second sort of consideration hinges on applications of the concepts of identity and diversity. That which is performed on one occasion may be identical with that which is performed on another: George Szell, for example, may twice over have conducted a performance of *Verklaerte Nacht*. Thus, there may be two distinct performances of one single musical work. But two distinct things cannot each be identical with some one thing. Thus, the two distinct performances cannot both be identical with the work performed. But if one of them, call it A, was identified with the work performed, then the other, call it B, would, by virtue of being a performance of the work performed, be a performance of performance A. Not only that, but performance A would be capable of being performed on many other occasions as well. Both of these consequences, however, seem impossible.

Let us henceforth call a work of art which can be performed, a *performance-work*. Most if not all performance-works are universals, in that they can be multiply performed.

It would seem that performances in the arts are as correctly called "works of art" as are performance-works. The ontological status of performances is relatively clear, however, while that of performance-works is immensely perplexing. Performances are occurrences or events. They take place at a certain time and place, begin at a certain time and end at a certain time, last for a certain stretch of time, and have temporal parts in the sense that each performance is half over at a certain time, three-quarters over at a certain time, one-eighth over at a certain time, etc. But what sort of entity is a performance-work? That is something which we shall have to discuss in considerable detail. What should already be clear, though, is that performance-works are not occurrences (events). Thus, already we can answer one of our opening questions. Works of art are not all alike in their ontological status.

In certain of the nonperforming arts distinctions similar to the performance/performance-work distinction have application. Consider, for example, graphic-art prints. Here, a commonly applied distinction is that between a particular impression and the work of which it is an impression; between, for example, the tenth impression of *Obedient unto Death* and the print of which it is an impression, namely, George Rouault's *Obedient unto Death*. And consider those cases in which sculpture is produced from a mold. Here, a commonly applied distinction is that between a particular casting of, say, *The Thinker* and the sculptural work of which it is a casting, namely, Rodin's *The Thinker*.

And consider thirdly those cases in the field of architecture in which many different buildings are produced according to one set of specifications. Here, a commonly applied distinction is that between a given example of, say, the Tech-Bilt House No. 1 and that of which it is an example, namely, the Tech-Bilt House No. 1.

It may be noticed that an impression of a work of graphic art, a casting of a work of sculptural art, and an example of a work of architectural art are all enduring physical objects. This is why we have grouped these particular arts together. In order to have a convenient terminology, let us call the entities of which there can be impressions, castings, or examples, *object-works*. And let us say that impressions, castings, and examples are *objects of* object-works. Thus, as a counterpart to the performance/performance-work distinction, we have the distinction between impressions, castings, and examples on the one hand and object-works on the other.

The considerations which impel us to distinguish between an object-work and those entities which are objects thereof are parallel to those which impel us to distinguish between an entity which is a performance-work and those entities which are performances thereof. One consideration is again that of divergence in properties. For example, *having a thumbprint in the lower left corner* may be a property of a given impression of Rouault's print *Obedient unto Death*, or even of all impressions thereof, though it is not a property of the print *Obedient unto Death*. A second consideration is again to be derived from applications of the concepts of identity and diversity. For example, there can be two different castings of the same sculptural work; and neither both of these castings together nor either one singly can be identified with the work. In the case of object-works there is yet a third sort of consideration which may be adduced, one hinging on applications of the concepts of existence and nonexistence. Any one of the several objects of an object-work can be destroyed without the object-work thereby being destroyed. I could, for example, perform the horrifying operation of burning my impression of Rouault's *Obedient unto Death*, but I would not thereby put the print itself out of existence. Nor could I put the print out of existence by destroying any one of the other impressions, nor even by destroying the original etched plate.

It would seem that both object-works and the objects thereof are entitled to being called "works of art." Further, the ontological status of the latter is relatively unproblematic: They are physical objects. Of course, plenty of things about the nature of physical objects remain unclear. Yet we know what they are, and it is clear that impressions, castings, and examples are to be numbered among them. But what is an object-work? What is *its* ontological status? That is something which we shall have to discuss in detail.

There remain literary works, films, and paintings to consider. A literary work can be both written down and 'sounded out'. There can be both copies of it and utterances of it. Now, a copy is a physical object, whereas an uttering of something is a certain sort of event. Further, the *copy of* relation seems closely similar to the *example of, the impression of,* and the *casting of* relations. Accordingly, I shall say that a copy of a literary work is an object of it; and I shall add literary works to the group of entities to be called object-works. Furthermore, an utterance of a literary work is an event, very much like a performance. Accordingly, in the class of things to be called performance-works I shall include also literary works. Literary works, then, are both performance-works and object-works.

Saying this, however, makes one want to look back to see whether we do not have good ground for saying that works of music and drama are also both performance-works and object-works. In the case of dramatic works I think it is clear that we must say "No." A dramatic performance is a pattern of actions. The actions will in all but the most unusual cases include speech actions. But in all but the most unusual cases they will include other sorts of actions as well. More importantly, that pattern of actions which is a dramatic performance will always include actions of *role-playing*. For these reasons, a reading aloud or a recitation of the script of a drama is not yet a performance of the drama. A copy of the script for a drama is not a copy of the drama but instructions for proper performances thereof. The script may of course be a literary work in its own right. And that work can have both readings aloud and copies. But the drama is not the script. And a copy of the script is not a copy of the drama. The drama has no copies. All it has is performances. Dramas are only performance-works.

Music presents a somewhat less clear situation. The crucial question is this: Does a copy of the score stand to a work of music in a relationship similar enough to that in which a copy stands to a work of literature to justify us in calling the score-copy an object of the work? It seems to me not decisively clear one way or the other. What does seem clear is that a word can be both written down and uttered aloud, whereas a sound cannot be written down but only sounded out. The marks in a copy of a score are not instances of sounds but rather instructions for producing sounds. Of course, an instance of some sequence of words can also be treated as instructions for the utterance of that sequence; yet at the same time it is genuinely an instance of those words. Some words, especially those in primitive cultures, are never written down; some, especially those in technical languages, are never sounded out. Yet most words have a dual manifestation. The same is not true of sounds. But suppose someone suggests that music should be thought of as being composed of *notes* rather than sounds, and then goes on to argue that notes, like words, can be both sounded out and written down. Obviously, this is a suggestion worthy of further investigation. Whether it is true or false is not at once clear. But nothing that is said hereafter will depend essentially on whether or not it is true. So I shall continue to suppose that music consists of sounds.

The film seems to have a dual status similar to that of words. One and the same film may have many copies, a copy being a physical object; and it may also have many showings, a showing being an occurrence (event).

Thus, a film, like a literary work, has claim to being regarded as both an object-work and a performance-work. There is this difference worth noting, though: A showing of a film will always occur by way of the showing of a certain copy of the film, whereas the utterance of a literary work need not occur by way of the reading of some copy of the work. One can recite it from memory.

As for paintings, it seems that neither the object/object-work distinction nor the performance/performance-work distinction has application, nor does it seem that any close counterpart to these distinctions has application. There is, of course, the distinction between the work and reproductions of the work. But this is a quite different distinction, as can be seen from the fact that one can also have reproductions of each of the various impressions of a print. What is lacking in painting is any counterpart to the print/impression distinction. All one has is a counterpart to the impression/reproduction distinction. The point may be put by saying that all the impressions of a print are originals, none is a reproduction. The conclusion must be that a painting is a physical object. But more will be said on this matter later in our discussion.

To say this is not, of course, to deny that reproductions of paintings along with reproductions of sculpture are, in some cases at least, entitled to being called "works of art" in their own right. So too are films, though they are for the most part 'reproductive' of performances and of visible events and objects. And so too are recordings, though most recordings are 'reproductive' of sounds and of audible performances. It is interesting to note, however, that in the case of visual-art reproductions and sculpture reproductions one again often has application for the print/impression or the work/casting distinction, and that in the case of recordings (records) one can distinguish between the recording on the one hand and the various discs of the recording on the other and, in turn, between a given disc on the one hand and various playings of the disc on the other.

Though I have called what we have done

thus far *phenomenology*, what I have said is of course not free from ontological commitment. In saying that the distinction between performances and that which is performed can be applied to the arts, I said something which entails that there are performance-works. And I said that of most if not all of these it is true that they can be multiply performed. A thorough nominalist would deny that there are any multiply performable entities. Similarly, he would deny the existence of 'multiply-objectible' entities. I think it would be worthwhile to consider how the nominalist conviction that there are no such entities might most plausibly be developed; and I also think it would be worthwhile to consider whether any decisive arguments against such nominalism can be offered. But I shall not on this occasion attempt either of these. Rather, the question which I wish to discuss in detail is this: What is the ontological status of performance-works and object-works?

To simplify our terminology, I shall henceforth in this paper call only performance-works and object-works *art works*. And both performances of art works and objects of art works will be called examples of art works. I shall continue to use "work of art" to cover both art works and their examples, along with such things as paintings which are neither. Perhaps here is also a good place to remark that the fact that the performance/performance-work distinction or the object/object-work distinction applies to a certain art does not imply that it applies *throughout* that art. There may be works of that art which are neither. Those works of music, for example, which are *total* improvisations (as distinguished from those which are improvisations on a theme) are neither performances nor performance-works.[1]

II. THE SHARING OF PREDICATES AND PROPERTIES BETWEEN ART WORKS AND EXAMPLES

We cannot here discuss all competitors to the theory proposed in the following pages. But for an understanding of the theory, it will be useful briefly to consider and put behind us the view that performance-works and object-works are *sets* of their examples. The untenability of this suggestion can be seen by noticing that whatever members a set has it has necessarily, whereas a performance-work or object-work might always have had different and more or fewer performances or objects than it does have; and by noticing that if set α has no members and set β has no members, then α is identical with β, whereas it is not the case that if art work γ has no instances and art work δ has no instances, then γ is identical with δ.

That there is but one null set is clear enough. But that a set cannot have had a different membership from what it does have is a fact apt to be confused with related but different facts. The property, *having been a disciple of Saint Francis*, is a property shared in common by all and only the members of a certain set, that one, namely, whose members are all and only the disciples of Saint Francis. Let us for convenience name this set D. Now, whoever has the property of *having been a disciple of Saint Francis* has it only contingently. Accordingly, that set which is D might have been such that some of its members lacked this property; indeed, all might have lacked it. Alternatively, persons who are not members of D might have had this property. Thus, some other set than D might have been such that all and only its members have the property of *having been a disciple of Saint Francis*. But all these facts pertaining to what might have been in place of what is, are thoroughly compatible with the fact that D has its membership essentially.

To begin, consider some logical predicate which in normal usage can be predicated of two different things in such a way as to assert something true in both cases. Let us say that in such a case those two things *share that predicate*. One striking feature of the relationship between an art work and its examples is the pervasive sharing of predicates between the art work on the one hand and its examples on the other. "Is in the key of C minor" can be predicated truly of Beethoven's *Opus 111* and also of most if not all performances of Beethoven's *Opus 111*. "Has the figure slightly off-center to the right" can be predicated truly of Rouault's *Obedient unto Death* and likewise of most if not all impressions of *Obedient unto Death*. And so on, and on.

Of course, not every predicate which can be predicated truly of an art work or which can be predicated truly of examples of some art work, is shared by the work and its examples. "Is a performance" and "is an occurrence" are never shared, nor are "can be repeatedly performed" and "can repeatedly occur." Nor is "composed by Hindemith" ever shared. "Is thought about by me" is in some cases shared between a certain art work and all its examples, in other cases it is shared between a certain artwork and only some of its examples, while in yet other cases it is not shared between an art work and any of its examples. And "has 'no' as its third word" is unshared between the poem *Sailing to Byzantium* and my particular copy of it, whereas it is shared between the poem and *most* copies of it.

One naturally wonders, at this point, whether when a predicate is shared between an art work and some one or more of its examples, there is normally also a sharing of some property for which the predicate stands. If so, then the predicate is used *univocally*. On the other hand, if the predicate stands for two different properties but if there is some systematic relation between these, then the predicate is used *analogically*. If not even this is true, the predicate is used *equivocally*. Shortly, we shall discuss this issue pertaining to properties. Meanwhile, without yet committing ourselves on it, let us see whether we can find some pattern in this pervasive sharing of predicates. (See also Wolterstorff [9]: 250-254.)

From the start, one feels that there is some connection between a predicate's being true of the examples of an art work and its being true of the work. Can this feeling be substantiated? The example we have already used provides us with evidence for concluding that the following formula will not do: A predicate P is true of some art work W if P is true of every example of W. For "is a performance" is true of all the examples of performance-works but cannot be true, in its normal sense, of any of those art works themselves.

So suppose that from here on we discard from consideration those predicates which are true of one or more of the examples of some art work but which, in their normal meaning, *cannot* be true of the work itself. (When a predicate P used with normal meaning cannot be true of W, P will be said to be *excluded by* W. Likewise, when a property P cannot be possessed by W, P will be said to be *excluded by* W.) What then about the formula: For any predicate P which is not excluded by W, P is true of W if P is true of every example of W? One objection to this formula is that it is far more constricted in its application than what we were looking for. For we saw that "has a G sharp in its seventh measure" may be true of Bartok's *First Quartet* even though of many of its performances it is not true. Indeed, it may be true of none of the performances.

A clue to a better formula can be gotten by looking more closely at this example. Is it not the case that "has a G sharp in its seventh measure" is true of Bartok's *First Quartet* in case it is *impossible* that something should be a *correct* performance of Bartok's *First* and lack the property of having a G sharp in its seventh measure? Is it not the case that "has 'no' as its third word" is true of *Sailing to Byzantium* in case it is *impossible* that something should be a *correct* copy of *Sailing to Byzantium* and lack the property of having "no" as its third word?

These examples naturally suggest to us the following formula: For any predicate P which is not excluded by W, if there is some property *being* P which P expresses in normal usage and is such that it is impossible that something should be a correctly formed example of W and lack *being* P, then P is true of W.

But to this general formula as well, there are counterexamples. Consider for instance the predicate "is a performance or was highly thought of by Beethoven." There will be many works such that this predicate used in its normal sense will not be excluded by the work. Likewise, it is impossible that something should be a correctly formed example of some such work and lack the property of being either a performance or highly thought of by Beethoven; for it is impossible that that thing should lack the property of being a performance. Yet the predicate in question may very well not be true of the work. For the work cannot be a performance, and it may not have been highly thought of by Beethoven. And in general, take a predicate of the form "is either A or anti-W," where "is anti-W" represents a predicate such that (i) it is excluded by W and (ii) when predicated of examples of W it stands for a property such that necessarily if something is an example of W, then it has that property, and where "is A" represents any predicate whatsoever which is not excluded by W. Then the 'disjunctive predicate' represented by "is either A or anti-W" is itself not excluded by W and is itself such that when predicated of some example of W, it stands for a property such that it is impossible that something should be a correct example of W and lack it. Yet obviously the predicate may very well not be true of W.

The essence of the difficulty here would seem to be that some predicates stand for properties such that it is impossible that something should be an example of W at all, correct or incorrect, and lack the property. Such properties might be said to be *necessary to* examples of W. If we could eliminate from consideration predicates standing for such properties, then counterexamples of the sort suggested will be forestalled. So let us say that a predicate P is *acceptable with respect to* W if and only if P is neither excluded by W nor is such that any property for which it stands when truly predicated of examples of W is one which is necessary to examples of W. Then our proposed formula becomes this: For any predicate P which is acceptable with respect to W, if there is some property *being P* which P expresses in normal usage and is such that it is impossible that something should be a correctly formed example of W and lack *being P*, then P is true of W. (It should be noticed that the claim here is not *if and only if,* but just *if.*)

The core feature of this proposal is the suggestion that what is true of correctly formed examples of an art work plays a decisive role in determining what can be predicated truly of the work. Or, to put it yet more indefinitely, the core feature is the suggestion that the concept of an art work is intimately connected with the concept of a correctly formed example of the work.

Perhaps if we considered the matter in detail, we could find still more pattern to the sharing of predicates between artworks and examples than what we have thus far uncovered. But enough has been uncovered for our subsequent purposes. So let us now move from the level of language to the level of ontology and consider whether, when predicates are shared according to the general pattern uncovered, there is also a sharing of properties designated by those predicates.

One is naturally inclined to think that there is. Our dictionaries do not, after all, tell us that a certain word standardly means one thing when truly predicated of an art work and something else when truly predicated of an example of the work. Yet I think that we must in fact come to the conclusion that predicates shared between art works and their examples do not function univocally when the sharing follows the general pattern we have uncovered. For what one means, in truthfully predicating "has 'no' as its third word" of some copy of *Sailing to Byzantium* is that the third word-*occurrence* is "no." But when one truthfully predicates "has 'no' as its third word" of *Sailing to Byzantium* itself, one cannot mean this. For the poem does not consist of word-occurrences. Similarly, what one means in truthfully predicating "has a G sharp in its seventh measure" of some performance of Bartok's *Fifth* is that in its seventh measure there was an *occurrence* of the G-sharp pitch. But the *Quartet* itself does not consist of sound-occurrences. So I think it must be admitted that we have not discovered a systematic identity but only a systematic relation between the property designated by some predicate when it is truthfully predicated of some art examples and the property designated by that same predicate when truthfully predicated of the art work. Our conclusion must be that the sharing of predicates between art works and their examples pervasively exhibits *analogical* predication.

The situation is as follows. Suppose that P

is a predicate which can be shared between an art work W and its examples, and suppose further that a property for which P stands when truthfully predicated of examples of W is *being P*. Then for those cases in which the sharing of P fits the general pattern which we formulated, P when truthfully predicated of W stands for the property of *being such that something cannot be a correct example of it without having the property of being P*.

III. ART WORKS ARE KINDS

We have seen some of the fundamental relations which hold between an art work and its examples. But we have not yet gained much insight into the ontological status of art works. We are left so far without any satisfying answer to our question: What *is* an art work? We must take a next step.

The proposal I wish to make is that performance-works and object-works are *kinds (types, sorts)*—kinds whose examples are the performances or objects of those works. A performance-work is a certain kind of performance; an object-work is a certain kind of object.

A phenomenon which tends at once to confirm us in the suggestion that art works are kinds whose examples are the examples of those works is the fact that kinds which are not art works are like art works in just the ways that (as we saw earlier) sets of their examples are unlike art works. Just as an art work might have had different and more or fewer performances and objects than it does have, so too the kind Man, for example, might have had different and more or fewer examples than it does have. If Napoleon had not existed, it would not then have been the case that Man did not exist. Rather, Man would then have lacked one of the examples which in fact it had. And secondly, just as there may be two distinct unperformed symphonies, so too may there be two distinct unexampled kinds—e.g., the Unicorn and the Hippogriff.

Not only does it seem that art works are *kinds*. What is even more striking is their many close similarities to those special kinds of kinds familiarly known as *natural* kinds.

It has long been noticed by philosophers that in the case of natural kinds there is a pervasive sharing of predicates and/or properties between kinds and their examples. Let us look at the pattern of such sharing, beginning with a proposal made by Richard Wollheim. Having excluded from consideration those properties which cannot be shared between kinds, and examples, his suggestion is that the following is necessarily true: The K shares a certain property with all Ks if and only if it is impossible that something should be an example of the K and lack the property ([8]; 64–65).

What must be clearly perceived about this formula is that it speaks of *properties*, not of predicates. And in many if not most cases, a sharing of a predicate does not have, underlying it, a sharing of a property for which the predicate stands. That property which a grizzly possesses, of *being something that growls*, is not a property which the Grizzly could possess. Once one sees this, it becomes clear that the formula has an extremely limited application. Cases of shared predicates are common. Cases in which those predicates stand for properties which can be shared are relatively uncommon. Thus, the formula gives very little insight into the relation between kinds and their examples. Perhaps it's true that all grizzlies growl. And certainly it is true that the Grizzly growls (though at the same time it's true that something can be an example of the Grizzly while being mute). Yet this is not a counterexample to the formula; because what the Grizzly's growling consists of cannot be identical with what a grizzly's growling consists of. The tenability of the formula with respect to such cases is bought at the price of giving us no illumination with respect to them.

Even so, however, there are rather obvious counterexamples of other sorts to the formula. It could happen that a certain kind would share with all its examples the property of *having been referred to by someone or other*. Yet most kinds are such that something *could* be an example of them and still lack this property.

But now consider once again the sentence "The Grizzly growls." Is it not the case that "growls" is true of the Grizzly if it is impossible that something should be a *properly* formed grizzly and not growl? A grizzly muted is a malformed grizzly, and so also is grizzly born without a growl. What makes "growls" true of the Grizzly is that something cannot be a properly formed grizzly unless it growls. In botanical and zoological taxonomy books, one is not told about the features shared by all examples of a certain kind, nor about the essential features shared by all examples of a certain kind, but about the features which a thing cannot lack if it is to be a properly formed example of the kind. So already we have for natural kinds the same pattern which we earlier uncovered for art works: For any predicate P which is acceptable with respect to the K, if there is some property *being P* which P expresses in normal usage and which is such that it is impossible that something should be a properly formed example of the K and lack *being P*, then P is true of the K.

As in the case of art works, we must raise the question whether when we have a sharing of some predicate between a kind and its examples, we also have a sharing of some property for which that predicate stands. With respect to those cases which fit our general formula, I think the answer must be, "No, we do not." Predications in such cases are not univocal. But neither are they equivocal. They are analogical. When grizzlies growl, they emit from their throats certain characteristic sound-patterns which we English-speaking people call "growling." But the kind, Grizzly, does not do that. Its sound-emission cannot be caught on some record. Yet—the Grizzly growls. "Growls," when truly predicated of the Grizzly, would seem to stand for the property of *being such that something cannot be a properly formed example of it unless it growls.* Thus, there is a systematic non-univocality about "growls." The predicate "growls" stands naturally for two quite different properties, one holding of the Grizzly and one holding of at least every properly formed example thereof. In general, for those cases in which the sharing of predicates between a kind and its examples follows the general pattern which we have formulated, the predicates are used analogically in exactly the way in which they were seen to be used analogically in the corresponding cases for art works.

In concluding this section of our discussion, let us articulate an important assumption which we have been making throughout. Consider the kind: Red Thing. This does seem to be a genuine kind; it differs from the class of all red things in that it might have had different and more or fewer members than it does have. But now notice that there cannot be a distinction, among examples of this kind, between improperly formed examples and properly formed examples of the kind. For it is not possible that some of the examples of the Red Thing should be improperly formed examples of this kind (i.e., things improperly red), nor is it possible that some should be properly formed examples of the kind (i.e., things properly red). Or consider the two kinds: Properly Formed Orchid and Malformed Orchid. There seems no reason to doubt that there are such kinds as these. But neither of these can have properly formed examples, nor can either have improperly formed examples.

When a kind, the K, is such that it is possible that it should have properly formed examples and also possible that it should have improperly formed examples, let us say that the K is a *norm-kind*. We have assumed throughout our discussion that art works and natural kinds are both norm-kinds.

IV. WHAT KIND OF KINDS ARE ART WORKS?

Having suggested that art works are kinds, we must now take the next step of considering which kind a given art work is to be identified with. For the sake of convenience, I shall conduct the discussion by referring exclusively to music. But I shall have an eye throughout on the application to artworks generally.

In performing a musical work, one produces an occurrence of a certain sound-sequence, the sound-sequence itself being capable of multiple occurrences. Accordingly, that particular kind which is some musical work has as its examples various occurrences of sound-sequences. It is a kind whose examples are sound-sequences-occurrences.

But now more specifically, with which of those many kinds whose examples are sound-sequence-occurrences is a given musical work to be identified? An answer which comes immediately to mind is this:

(1) A musical work W is identical with that kind whose examples are occurrences of that sound-sequence which correct performances of W are occurrences of.[2]

About this it must be said, however, that for most if not all musical works there is no such sound-sequence. This is so, for one reason, because standards of correctness by no means wholly determine which sound-sequence must occur if W is to be performed correctly. Performances of a given work can all be correct in every detail—yet differ significantly. The musical works which come closest to permitting no divergence among their correct performances are those 'totally serialized' works of the last quarter century. Yet even these permit some divergence.

So (1) must be discarded. And the revised suggestion we should consider is this:

(2) A musical work W is identical with that kind whose examples are occurrences of members of that set of sound-sequences which correct performances of W are occurrences of.

But this suggestion, though it is better than (1), is also not satisfactory. On this view, an incorrect performance of some work W would not be an example thereof. Yet an incorrect performance of some work is, in spite of its incorrectness, a performance thereof. And is it not on that account an example of the work? Are not all performances of W to be counted among the examples of the kind with which W is identical?

So (2) must be revised by dropping the reference to *correct* performance, thus:

(3) A musical work W is identical with that kind whose examples are occurrences of members of that set of sound-sequences which performances of W are occurrences of.[3]

But now we must in turn raise a question concerning the satisfactoriness of (3), a question which plunges us into a whole nest of subtle matters. In performing a musical work one produces an occurrence of a certain sound-sequence. It is clear, however, that that very same sound-sequence can in principle occur in other ways than by way of someone performing that work—or indeed, *any* work. It can be made to occur, for example, by the blowing of the wind, or by someone's doodling on a piano, or by an electronic organ's going berserk. Performing is one way of producing occurrences of sound-sequences. But the very same sound-sequence which can be produced by the activity of performing can be produced in other ways as well. So a performance is not merely an occurrence of a certain sound-sequence. It is an occurrence produced by the activity of performing.

The question to consider now is whether a musical work is just a certain kind of sound-sequence-occurrence, no matter how produced, or whether a musical work is a certain kind of performance. Is (3) the formula we want, or the following:

(4) A musical work W is identical with that kind whose examples are performances of W (or, more simply stated, with the kind: Performance of W)?

To answer this question we shall have to look a bit into the nature of performing.

Performing is clearly an intentional act. But what is the nature of the intention involved? When someone performs Beethoven's *Opus 111*, what is it that he intends? Does he perhaps intend to follow the directions of the score in producing a sound-sequence-occurrence? Well, often he does indeed have this intent. But even success in this intent is seldom a sufficient condition for having performed the work. For though scores do, among their other functions, provide specifications for producing examples of the work, seldom are all the matters pertaining to correct performance specified in a score. Naturally, many are simply presupposed by the composer as part of the style and tradition in which he is working, and others are suggested without ever being specified. If the performer limits himself to following the specifications in the score, not even attempting in other respects to produce a correct example of the work, it is at the very least doubtful that he has performed the work.

An even more decisive objection is that one can perform some work without at all intending to follow the specifications of the score for the work. For there may be no score. If Beethoven had composed his *Opus 111* before scoring it, it would have been possible for him to perform the work without being guided by the score for that or any other work. That is, it would have been possible for him not merely to produce an occurrence of a sound-sequence which could also occur as a performance of *Opus 111*, but actually to perform the work. In fact, of course, there now is a score for *Opus 111*. But the vast bulk of indigenous folk music remains unscored. So in that case performers are never guided by the scores for the works. Yet those works can be performed.

It is true that specifications can be laid down to performers by means other than scores. The folk-music performer can be told verbally how some passage is to be performed. Or the rhythm can be stomped out for him by foot. But quite clearly it is no significant improvement over our first thought to say that the intention involved in performing a work is the intention to follow the specifications for producing examples of that work. For of most works it is true that even when we include *all* specifications, whether expressed in score notation or otherwise, these specifications are woefully insufficient for determining correct examples. Bartok, in his early career, set about scoring various Hungarian folk songs. His work did not consist of taking specifications which were expressed in something other than the Western scoring system and expressing them in score notation. On the contrary, his work consisted of providing those works, for the first time in their careers, with specifications for performance. And by and large our Western scores contain all the specifications we have for our musical works. But these are not enough. Correct performance requires knowledge of more matters than these.[4]

What emerges from all this is that to perform a work one must have knowledge of what is required for a correct example of the work; and one must then try to act on such knowledge in producing an occurrence of a sound-sequence. It is the producer's acting on his knowledge of the requirements that makes of some sound-sequence-occurrences a performance of the work, instead of merely an occurrence of a sound-sequence that *might also* have occurred in a performance of the work. Such knowledge may be gained in many ways—for example, from scores or other specifications. But seldom will it be gained wholly from specifications which have been expressed. And sometimes it may not be gained from these at all.

It is not necessary, though, if one is to perform a work, that one *succeed* in one's attempt to act on one's knowledge of what is required of a sound-sequence-occurrence if it is to be a correct example of the work. Even if one makes mistakes and so does not actually produce a correct example, still one may have performed the work. Of course there are limits, albeit rather indefinite ones, on how seriously one can fail and still have performed the work.

So my suggestion concerning the nature of performing is this: To perform a musical work W is to aim to produce a sound-sequence-occurrence in accord with one's knowledge of what is required of something if it is to be a correct example of W, and to succeed at least to the extent of producing an example of W.[5]

An implication of this understanding of the nature of performing is that when a performer deliberately departs from the requirements for a correct performance of some work W, he is then not performing W. Sometimes such departures are motivated by the performer's inability to negotiate some passage. In other cases they are motivated by the performer's belief that he can thereby produce an aesthetically better performance. But whatever the motive, if Anthony Newman, say, deliberately departs from what is necessary for a correct example of Bach's *Prelude and Fugue in D minor*, then (strictly speaking) he is not performing that work. He is probably instead performing Newman's variation on Bach's *Prelude and Fugue in D minor*.

We have been discussing at some length the concept of *performing*. It is time now to return to the question which led us into this discussion, namely, which is the correct view as to the nature of the musical work, (3) or (4)? Is a musical work just a certain kind of sound-sequence-occurrence, or is it a certain kind of performance?

What is worth noticing first is that on both (3) and (4), art works can be viewed as norm-kinds. That is evident on (4), but probably not so on (3). For on (3), W is just a kind whose examples are the occurrences of a certain set of sound-sequences. And sound-sequence-occurrences just are or are not occurrences of that sequence of which they are occurrences. It makes no sense to speak of some as correct occurrences thereof and some as incorrect occurrences. However, there seems to be nothing against thinking of certain of the 'member' sound-sequences as correct ones, and the rest as incorrect ones. Then correct examples of the work will be those which are occurrences of the former; incorrect examples will be those which are occurrences of the latter. Thus, the fact that art works are norm-kinds is as compatible with (3) as with (4).

What is also worth noting is that on both (3) and (4) those properties which a work has by virtue of what counts as correctness in examples belong to it essentially. A work which has a G natural in its seventh measure cannot fail to have had a G natural there, on pain of not being that work.

But in addition to the similarities, there are significant differences between the kinds which (3) proposes to identify with art works and those which (4) proposes to identify with them. So let us contrast some of the implications of each of these views. If (3) were true, then one would have to distinguish between examples and performances of works. As a matter of contingent fact, it might be that only performances of W were examples of W. But there would be no necessity in this. And as a corollary, on (3) one could hear Bartok's *Second Sonata* without anyone performing it. For, presumably, by hearing an example of the work one can hear the work; and on (3) a work can have nonperformance examples. Also, on (3) one could hear a work W without hearing a performance of W, by hearing a performance (correct or incorrect) of a distinct work W'. Further, one could hear several different musical works by listening to a performance of just one work. On (4), however, none of these results obtain.

Furthermore, if (3) were true, it would be possible for W to have among its examples sound-occurrences which are also examples of W'. For a sound-sequence which could occur as a correct (or indeed incorrect) performance of W might also occur as an incorrect performance of W'. One's first inclination is to say that on this point too, (3) and (4) differ. On (4), it would seem, distinct works cannot share any examples. But in fact this is false. On either view, musical works W and W' are identical if and only if whatever is necessary for something to be a correct example of W is also necessary for something to be a correct example of W', and vice versa. And on either view, something is a performance of a work W only if its production is guided by W's requirements for correct examples. But it seems clear that a given performance can be a performance of two distinct works; and so also it seems clear that the production of a given performance can be guided by the requirements for correct examples of two works at once. This can happen in two sorts of ways. If works W and W' are related in such a way that whatever W requires for correct performance W' also does, but not vice versa (there being matters which W settles in terms of correctness but which W' leaves optional), then, though W and W' are distinct works, whatever is a performance of W will also be one of W'. But even when works do not 'overlap' in this way, a group of performers, or even a single performer, can perform two works at once. This indeed is required by some of the works of Charles Ives. To perform them, hymns, folk songs, and patriotic songs must all be performed concurrently. Thus, on (4) as well as on (3), distinct works can share some, and even all, examples. However, on (4) the only cases of shared examples between two works W and W' will be those in which a performance is guided both by the criteria for correct examples of W and by those for correct examples of W'. And this limitation does not hold on (3).

But though there are a number of significant differences between the conception of a musical work offered us by (3) and that offered us by (4), none of the differences thus far pointed out seem to provide a solid reason for preferring either (3) or (4) to the other. On some issues, (3) may give us a more 'natural' understanding; on others, (4). But on none of these issues does either seem to give us a clearly mistaken understanding. And though the implications of the two views diverge on more issues than we have cited, I do not think that these other divergent implications yield any more decisive reason for preferring one view to the other. Though the kinds with which each view proposes to identify a given musical work both exist and are definitely distinct from each other, yet it is simply not clear which of these different kinds is identical with the work. The situation seems to be that when we refer to and speak of what we regard as art works, we, in all likelihood, do not with definiteness mean to pick out entities of either sort as opposed to those of the other. For on most matters entities of these two sorts do not differ. And the matters where they do differ are so far off on the edge of our normal concern in the arts that we have never had to make up our minds as to which of these sorts of entities we intend to be dealing with.

It is possible, of course, that future developments in the arts will force us to make up our minds. And perhaps those developments are already upon us. For example, John Cage's work 4' 33" requires no particular sorts of sounds, or sound-sequences whatsoever. There are requirements for a correct performance of the work; namely that the pianist keep his hands poised above a piano keyboard for 4 minutes and 33 seconds. And there are sounds to be listened to, namely, the sounds produced by the audience as they gradually realize what is being perpetrated. But the requirements include no specifications concerning sounds whatsoever. Thus, it is obvious that (3) simply lacks application to this case. (4), though, is still relevant. And if works such as this are eventually regarded as works of music, a decisive shift away from (3) toward (4) will have occurred.[6]

V. WHAT IS IT TO COMPOSE?

On either of the two views we have been considering, a composer of a musical work can be thought of as one who determines what constitutes correctness of performances of the work. And such determination of correctness has in turn two phases. The composer must think of, or consider, the correctness-conditions in question. And in addition, since in the course of composing a work he normally considers a great many more such than he actually settles on, he must certify these as those he wants. This much is essential to being a composer.

But normally a composer does more than determine what constitutes correctness of performance. Normally he also produces a score. Now, as we remarked earlier, a typical function of a score is to provide specifications for producing (correct) examples of the work associated with the score. Yet it does seem possible for a composer to determine a set of correctness-conditions which he knows to be impossible of being followed by any present performers on any extant or anticipated instruments. And it does seem possible for the composer to score such a work. Of course, he would not expect to hear it, and neither would he think of his score as providing specifications for performances. The score would just be the composer's *record* of his determination. It seems in fact that this is what every score is. Most scores function and are meant to function to guide performances. But what is true of every score is that it is a record of the artist's determination of correctness-conditions. If the record is in addition publicly legible, then it can also serve to communicate to others a knowledge of the conditions, and thus of the work. Musical aficionados can then become acquainted with the work by reading the score, and some may even thereby get some enjoyment from it.

Typically, then, there are at least these two activities involved in composing a work of music. The artist determines what constitutes correctness of performance, and he makes a record of his determination. Normally, of course, these two activities do not take place in neat separation. But sometimes they do. Mozart said that he imagined whole symphonies in his head. Housman said that he imagined poems while shaving. And concerning such cases, a question to consider is whether thereby an art work has been composed. Can one compose "in one's head"? Well, one can determine correctness-conditions in one's head, but one cannot in one's head *record* the determination. Thus, depending on whether one regards recording one's determination as necessary for composing a musical or literary work, different answers will be given.

A consequence of what we have been saying is that two people can compose the same work. For surely it is possible for two people to determine and record the same correctness-conditions. Thus, Beethoven's *Opus 111* is not necessarily just an opus of Beethoven. Indeed, it is not necessarily an opus of Beethoven at all. So also, the same musical work can in principle be known and performed in two different and independent cultures.

Does the artist, by composing his musical work, thereby also *create* it? That is, does he bring it into existence? If (4) is the correct theory as to the nature of the musical work, so that a musical work is a performance-kind, then it certainly seems plausible to hold that he does, at least if composing is understood as consisting just in the determination of correctness-conditions. For on (4) there can be no examples of a work which are not performances thereof. And to perform the work, one must know what is required of something if it is to be a correct example. But no one can know what these correctness-conditions are until they have been determined by someone or other. And for someone to determine the correctness-conditions is just to compose the work. On the other hand, composing the work would seem sufficient for bringing it into existence. Certainly it does not seem necessary that it also be performed. For there seems nothing contradictory in the notion of unperformed musical works.

But if (3) is the correct theory as to the nature of a musical work, it is not plausible to hold that in composing one creates. For on (3) a work may have examples which are not performances. And so there is nothing to prevent its having examples before performances have been made possible by the determination of correctness-conditions. But, surely, if there are examples of a work at a given time, then the work exists at that time. Thus, if (3) is correct, composing a work cannot in general be viewed as bringing it into existence.

But what, then, on (3), are the existence criteria for musical works? One possible view is that there exists such a work as W at time t if and only if W is being exemplified at t. But this view has the implausible consequence that musical works not only come into existence and go out, but that most of them exist intermittently. For on this view, the work exists when and only when it is being exemplified. And rare is the musical work which has no pair of exemplifications such that there is some time, between the occurrence of members of the pair, when the work is not being exemplified.

An alternative view would be that there exists such a work as W if and only if W is being exemplified or has been exemplified. But this view has the consequence that there cannot be a musical work which has not been exemplified. In fact, however, the contemporary literature concerning music is filled with the laments of composers whose works go unexemplified.

So perhaps the best view is that a musical work W exists just in case it is *possible* that there be an exemplification of W. For this view has none of the untoward consequences of the other views. On this view, it would not be possible for a work to be composed but not exist; on this view, a work would not cease to exist when all exemplifications ceased; and on this view, there could be unexemplified works.

It should be noticed, though, that on this view musical works exist everlastingly. For if it is ever possible that there be something which is an example of *Opus 111*, then it is always possible. Neither by composing nor by any other activity on his part does a composer bring his work into existence. Rather, if (3) is correct, the composer should be thought of as a selector rather than as a creator. To compose would be to select a certain kind of sound-occurrence. The only thing a composer would normally bring into existence would be a token (copy) of his score. Creation would be confined to token creation. Furthermore, since the selection of the work occurs in the process of determining its correctness-conditions, such determination would have to be viewed as consisting in *discovering* the conditions. By contrast, on the view that the artist brings his work into existence by composing it, determination of the conditions for correctness can best be thought of as consisting in *devising* the conditions.

It must be admitted that there is something odd in thinking of musical works as existing everlastingly, waiting to be selected and recorded. But perhaps the correct view is that though the entity which is a musical work *exists* everlastingly, it is not a *musical work* until some composer does something to it. If so, then in answer to the question. "What must be done to a kind in order to make it a musical work?" one can take one's stand at at least two different points. One can hold that it is not a musical work until someone has determined its correctness-conditions, or one can hold that it is not a musical work until its correctness-conditions have been recorded as well as determined.

VI. HOW TO TELL CORRECTNESS

Our discussion concerning the ontological status of art works has concentrated on music. The detailed application to the other arts of the points we have made can be left to the reader. But two final matters must be considered. One is this: Why can paintings and sculptures not be viewed as single-exampled kinds rather than as physical objects, thereby giving us a "unified theory" of art works? P. F. Strawson, after saying that "in a certain sense, paintings and works of sculpture" are types, adds this footnote:

The mention of paintings and works of sculpture may seem absurd. Are they not particulars? But this is a superficial point. The things the dealers buy and sell are particulars. But it is only because of the empirical deficiencies of reproductive techniques that we identify these with the works of art. Were it not for these deficiencies, the original of a painting would have only the interest which belongs to the original manuscript of a poem. Different people could look at exactly the same painting in different places at the same time, just as different people can listen to exactly the same quartet at different times in the same place ([6]:231.)

The situation is not quite as Strawson represents it, however. Of course there is nothing impossible in a certain object-work's having but one object. But object-works are norm-kinds, and being such they have associated with them certain requirements for something's being a correct example of the work. What is different in the case of paintings is that there are no such associated requirements. There simply are no requirements for something's being a correct example of some kind of which *The Odalesque* is the premier example. Of course, one can pick out things which to a certain close degree *resemble* this painting. There is a kind corresponding to them, and the painting is an example of it. But this is not a norm-kind, and none of our names of paintings are names of such entities.

Secondly, a question which has been pressing for a long time is this: How do we tell what constitutes a correct example of some art work? By now, however, the question has almost answered itself. In the case of works produced by some artist, the answer is that we try to discover the relevant features of that artifact which the artist produced (or which he arranged to have produced) as a record of his selection and as a guide or production-item for the making of examples. Of course, we will often discover that we cannot find out with any surety what the relevant features of that artifact were (are). We may no longer have the poet's original copy of the poem nor any very reliable evidence as to what it was like in crucial respects. Or we may have several copies from the poet's hand and not know which he authenticated. Or we may have an original authenticated copy but it may contain mistakes made by the poet, and we may find it impossible to determine which of various possibilities he had in mind. Or we may have an original, authenticated, and correct copy, but we may no longer know how to interpret all the symbols. In all such cases and many others we simply have to acknowledge that we are to some extent uncertain as to what constitutes a correct example. To that extent, we are also uncertain as to the character of the work. Yet it is clear what we must look for: the features of that original artifact.

In the case of those art works sustained in the memory of a culture and for which there is no artifact functioning as guide or production-item, we simply have to find out what the culture would regard as a correct and what it would regard as an incorrect example of the work—which is the same as finding out what the culture takes the art work to be like in those respects.[7]

NOTES

1. The general drift of the distinctions made above has been acquiring something of a consensus in recent years among those who have concerned themselves with the nature of works of art. See Harrison [2], MacDonald [3], Margolis [4], Stevenson [5], Wellek and Warren [7], and Wollheim [8].
2. The circular reference to W, in (1) and all that follows, is harmless. For we are not discussing how to identify (pick out) art works. Instead,

assuming that we are acquainted with art works and that we can identify them, we are discussing their ontological status. Also, this formula and the following ones are not meant to be restricted to works which *actually have* examples. Strictly, it should read "whose examples are or would be occurrences," and "are or would be occurrences of."

3. A question to consider is whether or not this kind is identical with the set of those sound-sequences. Of course the *kind* in question here, a kind whose examples are certain sound-sequence-occurrences, is not identical with the *set* of those same sound-sequence-occurrences—for reasons already rehearsed. But that is not what we are considering. Rather, the question is this: Might a certain set of sound-sequences be identical with the kind whose examples are the occurrences of the members of that set?

A view concerning the nature of a work of music which has a great deal of initial plausibility is that it is a certain sound-sequence. When one notices, however, that among correct performances there is often wide variation in the sound-sequences instantiated, then it is clear that this initial view must be modified. The least modification would seem to be that a work of music is a *set* of sound-sequences, namely, that set whose members can occur as a correct performance. Now this line of thought concerning the nature of the work of music is different from the line pursued in the paper. There, the line pursued is that a work of music is a certain *kind* of sound-sequence-occurrence, rather than a certain sound-sequence or set of sound-sequences. The question posed, however, is whether these two lines of thought are incompatible.

I see no reason for thinking that they are. So far as I can see, a set of sound-sequences is identical with the kind whose examples are occurrences of the members of the set. If this is correct, then the proposal made by (3) is identical with this:

W is identical with the set of those sound-sequences which performances of W are occurrences of.

4. Throughout, in speaking of specifications I have been thinking of specifications for *correct* performances. Possibly some of the specifications to be found in scores are not such but are instead specifications for *excellent* performances. This may be true, for example, for the registrations suggested in the scores for certain

organ works. I suspect that in the case of works of folk art for which no scores exist, it is often difficult or even impossible to distinguish between what is *correct* and what is *excellent*.
5. It should be remarked that what is required of something if it is to be a correct performance of some work of music is often not just that the performance *sound* a certain way. It may be required, for example, that the sounds be produced by certain specific instruments, whether or not other instruments could make the same sounds. Is this the case for electronic music? For a correct performance of some work for magnetic tape, must the sounds be produced by playing a tape (a tape, furthermore, which is either the original or genetically derived therefrom)?
6. More than just such a shift would be involved in such a change of concept. In addition, the claim that we made in beginning this discussion, 'In performing a musical work one produces an occurrence of a certain sound-sequence,' would then have become false.
7. In thinking through the issues discussed in this paper, I have received a great deal of assistance from my colleagues in the Philosophy Department at Calvin College. I have also received valuable advice from the editor of *Noûs*, from a reader for *Noûs*, and from Kendall Walton.

REFERENCES

[1] Collingwood, R. G., *The Principles of Art* (Oxford: Oxford University Press, 1938).
[2] Harrison, Andrew, "Works of Art and Other Cultural Objects," *Proceedings of the Aristotelian Society* XVIII (1967–1968), 105–128.
[3] MacDonald, Margaret, "Art and Imagination," *Proceedings of the Aristotelian Society* LIII (1952–1953), 205–226.
[4] Margolis, Joseph, *The Language of Art and Art Criticism* (Detroit: Wayne State University Press, 1965).
[5] Stevenson, C. L., "On 'What Is a Poem?'" *Philosophical Review* LXVI (1957): 329–362.
[6] Strawson, P. F., *Individuals* (London: Methuen, 1959).
[7] Wellek, R., and A. Warren, *Theory of Literature* (New York: Harcourt, Brace and World, 1956).
[8] Wollheim, Richard, *Art and Its Objects* (New York: Harper and Row, 1968).
[9] Wolterstorff, Nicholas, *On Universals* (Chicago: University of Chicago Press, 1970).

What a Musical Work Is

Jerrold Levinson

What *exactly* did Beethoven compose? That is the question I will begin with. Well, for one, Beethoven composed a quintet for piano and winds (flute, oboe, clarinet, horn) in E-flat, Opus 16, in 1797. But what sort of thing is it, this quintet which was the outcome of Beethoven's creative activity? What does it consist in or of? Shall we say that Beethoven composed actual *sounds*? No, for sounds die out, but the quintet has endured. Did Beethoven compose a *score*? No, since many are familiar with Beethoven's composition who have had no contact with its score.[1]

Philosophers have long been puzzled about the identity or nature of the art object in nonphysical arts, e.g., music and literature. In these arts—unlike painting and sculp-

---

From *The Journal of Philosophy*, 77 (1980). Reprinted by permission of the publisher and the author.

ture—there is no particular physical "thing" that one can plausibly take to be the artwork itself. This puzzlement has sometimes led philosophers (e.g., Croce) to maintain that musical and literary works are purely mental—that they are in fact private intuitive experiences in the minds of composers and poets. But this does not seem likely, since experiences can be neither played nor read nor heard. More generally, the Crocean view puts the objectivity of musical and literary works in dire peril—they become inaccessible and unsharable. Fortunately, however, there is a way of accepting the nonphysicality of such works without undermining their objectivity.

Those familiar with recent reflection on the ontological question for works of art will know of the widespread consensus that a musical work is in fact a variety of abstract object—to wit, a structural type or kind.[2] Instances of this type are to be found in the individual performances of the work. The type can be heard through its instances, and yet exists independently of its instances. I believe this to be basically correct. A piece of music is *some* sort of structural type, and as such is both nonphysical and publicly available. But *what* sort of type is it? I aim in this paper to say as precisely as I can what structural type it is that a musical work should be identified with.

The most natural and common proposal on this question is that a musical work is a *sound* structure—a structure, sequence, or pattern of sounds, pure and simple.[3] My first objective will be to show that this proposal is deeply unsatisfactory, that a musical work is more than just a sound structure *per se*. I will do this by developing three different objections to the sound-structure view. In the course of developing these objections, three requirements or desiderata for a more adequate view will emerge. The rightness—or at least plausibility—of those requirements will, I think, be apparent at that point. My second objective will then be to suggest a structural type that does satisfy the requirements, and thus can be identified with a musical work.[4]

At the outset, however, I should make clear that I am confining my inquiry to that paradigm of a musical work, the fully notated "classical" composition of Western culture, for example, Beethoven's Quintet for piano and winds in E-flat, Opus 16. So when I speak of a "musical work" in this paper it should be understood that I am speaking only of these paradigm musical works, and thus that all claims herein regarding musical works are to be construed with this implicit restriction.

I

The first objection to the view that musical works are sound structures is this. If musical works were sound structures, then musical works could not, properly speaking, be created by their composers. For sound structures are types of a pure sort which exist at all times. This is apparent from the fact that they—and the individual component sound types[5] that they comprise—can always have had instances.[6] A sound event conforming to the sound structure of Beethoven's Quintet, Opus 16 logically could have occurred in the Paleozoic era.[7] Less contentiously, perhaps, such an event surely could have taken place in 1760—ten years before Beethoven was born. But if that sound structure was capable of being *instantiated* then, it clearly must have *existed* at that time. Beethoven's compositional activity was not necessary in order for a certain sound-structure type to exist. It was not necessary to the possibility of certain sound events occurring which would be instances of that structure. Sound structures *per se* are not created by being scored—they exist before any compositional activity. Sound structures predate their first instantiation or conception because they are possible of exemplification *before* that point.[8] So, if composers truly create their works—i.e., bring them into existence—then musical works cannot be sound structures.

We can also defend the pre-existence of pure sound structures (i.e., existence prior to any instantiation or conception) in a somewhat different manner. We need only remind ourselves that purely sound structures are in effect mathematical objects—they are *sequences* of sets of sonic elements. (Sonic elements are such as pitches, timbres, durations, etc.). Now if the pre-existence of simple sonic element types be granted—and I think it must be—it follows automatically that all sets and all sequences of sets of these elements also pre-exist. Therefore pure sound structures are pre-existent. But if pure sound structures pre-exist, then it is not open for them to be objects of creational activity. So again, if composers are truly creators, their works cannot be pure sound structures.[9]

But why should we insist that composers truly create their compositions? Why is this a reasonable requirement? This question needs to be answered. A defense of the desideratum of true creation follows.

The main reason for holding to it is that it is one of the most firmly entrenched of our beliefs concerning art. There is probably no idea more central to thought about art than that it is an activity in which participants create things—these things being artworks. The whole tradition of art assumes art is creative in the strict sense, that it is a godlike activity in which the artist brings into being what did not exist beforehand—much as a demiurge forms a world out of inchoate matter. The notion that artists truly *add* to the world, in company with cake-bakers, house-builders, law-makers, and theory-constructors, is surely a deep-rooted idea that merits preservation if at all possible. The suggestion that some artists, composers in particular, instead merely *discover* or *select* for attention entities they have no hand in creating is so contrary to this basic intuition regarding artists and their works that we have a strong *prima facie* reason to reject it if we can. If it is possible to align musical works with indisputably creatable artworks such as paintings and sculptures, then it seems we should do so.

A second, closely related reason to preserve true creation *vis-à-vis* musical works is that some of the status, significance, and value we attach to musical composition derives from our belief in this. If we conceive of Beethoven's Fifth Symphony as existing sempiternally, before Beethoven's compositional act, a small part of the glory that surrounds Beethoven's composition of the piece seems to be removed. There is a special glow that envelops composers, as well as other artists, because we think of them as true creators. We marvel at a great piece of music *in part* because we marvel that, had its composer not engaged in a certain activity, the piece would (almost surely) not now exist; but it does exist, and we are grateful to the composer for precisely that. Ecclesiastes was wrong—there *are* ever some things new under the sun, musical compositions being among the most splendid of them—and splendid, at least in part, in virtue of this absolute newness.

Shall we then accept the creatability requirement as suggested? Before we do so a last qualm should be addressed. It is open for someone to admit the importance of musical composition being characterized by true creation and yet waive the creatability of works themselves. Such a person will point to entities associated with the compositional process which composers unequivocally bring into existence—e.g., thoughts, scores, performances—and claim that true creation need be extended no further. Now it is certainly true that these entities are strictly created, and we may also accord composers some recognition of their creativity in regard to these things. But the fact of the matter remains that *works* are the main items, the center and aim of the whole enterprise, and that since musical works are not identical with scores, performances, or thoughts,[10] if those are the only things actually created, then much is lost. "Composers are true creators" acquires a hollow ring. Creation in music shrinks to an outer veneer with no inner core.

I propose then that a most adequate account of the musical work should satisfy the following requirement, that of *creatability*[11]:

(Cre) Musical works must be such that they do *not* exist prior to the composer's compositional activity, but are *brought into* existence *by* that activity.

II

The second objection to the view that musical works are sound structures is this. (1) If musical works were just sound structures, then, if two distinct composers determine the same sound structure, they necessarily compose the same musical work. (2) But distinct composers determining the same sound structure in fact inevitably produce different musical works.[12] Therefore, musical works cannot be sound structures *simpliciter*. The rest of this section is devoted to supporting and elucidating the second premise of this argument.

Composers who produce identical scores in the same notational system with the same conventions of interpretation will determine the same sound structure. But the musical works they thereby compose will generally not be the same. The reason for this is that certain attributes of musical works are dependent on more than the sound structures contained. In particular, the aesthetic and artistic attributes of a piece of music are partly a function of, and must be gauged with reference to, the total musico-historical context in which the composer is situated while composing his piece. Since the musico-historical contexts of composing individuals are invariably different, then even if their works are identical in sound structure, they will differ widely in aesthetic and artistic attributes. But then, by Leibniz's law, the musical works themselves must be non-identical: if W_1 has any attribute that W_2 lacks, or *vice versa*, then $W_1 \neq W_2$.

I will not attempt to give a strict definition of musico-historical context, but will confine myself to pointing out a large part of what is involved in it. The total musico-historical context of a composer P at a time t can be said to include at least the following: (a) the whole of cultural, social, and political history prior to t,[13] (b) the whole of musical development up to t, (c) musical styles prevalent at t, (d) dominant musical influences at t, (e) musical activities of P's contemporaries at t, (f) P's apparent style at t, (g) P's musical repertoire[14] at t, (h) P's oeuvre at t, (i) musical influences operating on P at t. These factors contributing to the total musico-historical context might be conveniently divided into two groups, a–d and e–i. The former, which we could call the *general* musico-historical context, consists of factors relevant to anyone's composing at t; the latter, which we could call the *individual* musico-historical context, consists of factors relevant specifically to P's composing at t. In any event, all these factors operate to differentiate aesthetically or artistically musical works identical in sound structure, thus making it impossible to identify those works with their sound structures. I now provide several illustrations of this.[15]

(1) A work identical in sound structure with Schoenberg's *Pierrot Lunaire* (1912), but composed by Richard Strauss in 1897 would be aesthetically different from Schoenberg's work. Call it 'Pierrot Lunaire' As a Straussian work, *Pierrot Lunaire* would follow hard upon Brahm's *German Requiem*, would be contemporaneous with Debussy's *Nocturnes*, and would be taken as the next step in Strauss's development after *Also Sprach Zarathustra*. As such it would be more *bizarre*, more *upsetting*, more *anguished*, more *eerie* even than Schoenberg's work, since perceived against a musical tradition, a field of current styles, and an oeuvre with respect to which the musical characteristics of the sound structure involved in *Pierrot Lunaire* appear doubly extreme.[16]

(2) Mendelssohn's *Midsummer's Night Dream Overture* (1826) is admitted by all to be a highly *original* piece of music. Music of such elfin delicacy and feel for tone color had never before been written. But a score written in 1900 detailing the very same sound structure as is found in Mendelssohn's piece would clearly result in a work that was surpassingly *unoriginal*.

(3) Brahms's Piano Sonata Opus 2 (1852), an early work, is strongly *Liszt-influenced*, as any perceptive listener can discern. However, a work identical with it in sound structure, but written by Beethoven, could hardly have had the property of being Liszt-

influenced. And it would have had a visionary quality that Brahms's piece does not have.

(4) The symphonies of Johann Stamitz (1717–1757) are generally regarded as seminal works in the development of orchestral music. They employ many attention-getting devices novel for their time, one of which is known as the "Mannheim rocket"—essentially a loud ascending scale figure for unison strings. A symphony of Stamitz containing Mannheim rockets and the like is an *exciting* piece of music. But a piece written today which was identical in sound structure with one of Stamitz's symphonies, Mannheim rockets and all, would not be so much exciting as it would be exceedingly *funny*. Stamitz's symphony is to be heard in the context of Stamitz's earlier works, the persistence of late Baroque style, the contemporary activities of the young Mozart, and the Napoleonic wars. "Modern Stamitz"'s symphony would be heard in the context of "Modern Stamitz"'s earlier works (which are probably dodecaphonic), the existence of aleatory and electronic music, the musical enterprises both of Pierre Boulez and of Elton John, and the threat of nuclear annihilation.

(5) One of the passages in Bartok's *Concerto for Orchestra* (1943) satirizes Shostakovitch's *Seventh Symphony* ("Leningrad") of 1941, whose bombast was apparently not to Bartok's liking. A theme from that symphony is quoted and commented on musically in an unmistakable manner. But notice that if Bartok had written the very same score in 1939, the work he would then have composed could not have had the same property of satirizing Shostakovitch's *Seventh Symphony*. Nor would the work that would have resulted from *Shostakovitch's* penning that score in 1943.

These examples should serve to convince the reader that there is always some aesthetic or artistic difference between structurally identical compositions in the offing in virtue of differing musico-historical contexts. Even small differences in musico-historical context—e.g., an extra work in *P*'s oeuvre, a slight change in style dominant in *P*'s milieu, some musical influence deleted from *P*'s development as a composer—seem certain to induce some change in kind or degree in some aesthetic or artistic quality, however difficult it might be in such cases to pinpoint this change verbally.

For example, suppose there had been a composer (call him "Toenburg") in 1912 identical with Schoenberg in all musico-historical respects—e.g., birthdate, country, style, musical development, artistic intentions, etc., except that Toenburg had never written anything like *Verklarte Nacht* though he had in his oeuvre works structurally identical with everything else Schoenberg wrote before 1912. Now suppose simultaneously with Schoenberg he sketches the sound structure of *Pierrot Lunaire*. Toenburg has not produced the same musical work as Schoenberg, I maintain, if only because his work has a slightly different aesthetic/artistic content owing to the absence of a *Verklarte Nacht*-ish piece in Toenburg's oeuvre. Schoenberg's *Pierrot Lunaire* is properly heard with reference to Schoenberg's oeuvre in 1912, and Toenburg's *Pierrot Lunaire* with reference to Toenburg's oeuvre in 1912. One thus hears something in Schoenberg's piece by virtue of resonance with *Verklarte Nacht* that is not present in Toenburg's piece—perhaps a stronger reminiscence of Expressionist sighs?

Before formulating a second requirement of adequacy, as suggested by the fatal problem that contextual differentiation poses for the equation of musical works with pure sound structures, I must confront an objection that may be lurking in the wings. The objection in short is that the aesthetic and artistic differences I have been discussing are not really an obstacle to equating works and sound structures, because these supposed differences between *works* due to compositional context really just boil down to facts about their *composers*, and are not attributes of works at all. The objection is understandable, but I find it rather unconvincing for several reasons which I will briefly detail.

(1) Artistic and aesthetic attributions made of musical works are as direct and undisguised as attributions typically made of composers. It seems to be straightforwardly true that the *Eroica* symphony is noble, bold, original, revolutionary, influenced by Haydn, and reflective of Beethoven's thoughts about Napoleon, as it is that Beethoven had certain personal qualities, was a genius, changed the course of western music, studied with Haydn, and at one point idolized Napoleon. (2) Whereas we may admit some plausibility to reducing artistic attributions (e.g., 'original,' 'influenced by Haydn') to attributes of persons, there is no plausibility in so reducing aesthetic attributions; it is absurd to maintain that "W is scintillating," for example, is just a way of saying "W's composer is scintillating." (3) Finally, in the case of artistic attributions, not only do they appear as entrenched and legitimate as parallel attributions to composers, but, if anything, they often seem to be primary. Consider originality, for example, and imagine a composer and oeuvre that possess it. Surely the composer is original because *his works* are original; his works are not original because *he is*.

I thus propose a second requirement—that of *fine individuation*—to which any acceptable theory of the musical work should conform:

(Ind) Musical works must be such that composers composing in different musico-historical contexts[17] who determine identical sound structures invariably compose distinct musical works.

III

The third objection to the view that musical works are sound structures is this. If musical works were simply sound structures, then they would not essentially involve any particular means of performance. But the paradigm musical works that we are investigating in this paper, e.g., Beethoven's Quintet Opus 16, clearly *do* involve quite specific means of performance, i.e., particular instruments, in an essential way. The instrumentation of musical works is an integral part of those works. So musical works cannot be simply sound structures *per se*. Arguments in defense of the claim that performance means are an essential component of musical works now follow.

(1) Composers do not describe pure sound patterns in qualitative terms, leaving their means of production undiscussed. Rather, what they directly specify are means of production, through which a pure sound pattern is indirectly indicated. The score of Beethoven's Quintet, Opus 16, is not a recipe for providing an instance of a sound pattern *per se*, in whatever way you might like. Rather, it instructs one to produce an instance of a certain sound pattern through carrying out certain operations on certain instruments. When Beethoven writes a middle C for the oboe, he has done more than require an oboe-like sound at a certain pitch—he has called for such a sound as emanating from that quaint reed we call an "oboe." The idea that composers of the last 300 years were generally engaged in composing pure sound patterns, to which they were usually kind enough to append suggestions as to how they might be realized, is highly implausible. Composers are familiar with tone colors only insofar as they are familiar with instruments that possess them. We do not find composers creating pure combinations of tone color, and then later searching about for instruments that can realize or approximate these aural canvases; it would obviously be pointless or at least frustrating to do so. Composers often call for complex sounds that they have never heard before and can scarcely imagine—e.g., the sound of two trombones and three piccolos intoning middle C while four saxophones and five xylophones intone the C-sharp a half-step above; it is obvious here that what is primarily composed is not a pure untethered sound but an instrumental combination.[18]

(2) Scores are generally taken to be definitive of musical works, at least in conjunction with the conventions of notational interpreta-

tion assumed to be operative at the time of composition. It is hard to miss the fact that scores of musical works call for specific instruments in no uncertain terms. When we read in Beethoven's score the demand 'clarinet' (rather, 'Klarinett') we may wonder whether a clarinet of 1970 vintage and construction will do as well as one of 1800, but we have still been given a fairly definite idea of what sort of instrument is required. There is nothing in scores themselves that suggests that instrumental specifications are to be regarded as optional—any more than specifications of pitch, rhythm, or dynamics. Nor does the surrounding musical practice of the time encourage such a way of regarding them.[19] If we are not to abandon the principle that properly understood scores have a central role in determining the identity of musical works, then we must insist that the Quintet, Op. 16, without a clarinet is not the same piece—even if all sound-structural characteristics (including timbre) are preserved. To feel free to disregard as prominent an aspect of scores as performing means is to leave it open for someone to disregard any aspect of a score he does not wish to conform to—e.g., tempo, accidentals, accents, articulation, harmony—and claim that one nevertheless has the same work.[20] The only way it seems one could justify regarding performing-means specifications as just optional features of scores is to simply *assume* that musical works are nothing but sound structures *per se*.

Consider a sound event aurally indistinguishable from a typical performance of Beethoven's Quintet Opus 16, but issuing from a versatile synthesizer, or perhaps a piano plus a set of newly designed wind instruments, two hundred in number, each capable of just two or three notes. If performance means were not an integral aspect of a musical work, then there would be no question that this sound event constitutes a performance of Beethoven's Quintet Opus 16. But there is indeed such a question. It makes perfect sense to deny that it is such a performance on the grounds that the sounds heard did not derive from a piano and four standard woodwinds. We can count something as a performance of Beethoven's Quintet Opus 16 only if it involves the participation of the instruments for which the piece was written—or better—of the instruments that were written into the piece.

(3) To regard performing means as essential to musical works is to maintain that the sound structure of a work cannot be divorced from the instruments and voices through which that structure is fixed, and regarded as the work itself. The strongest reason why it cannot be so divorced is that the aesthetic content of a musical work is determined not only by its sound structure, and not only by its musico-historical context, but also in part by the actual means of production chosen for making that structure audible. The character of a musical composition, e.g., Beethoven's Quintet Opus 16 for piano and winds, is partly a function of how its sound structure relates to the potentialities of a certain instrument or set of instruments designated to produce that structure for audition. To assess that character correctly one must take cognizance not only of the qualitative nature of sounds heard but also of their source of origin. Musical compositions, by and large, have reasonably definite characters; that is to say, we can and do ascribe to them many fairly specific aesthetic qualities. But if prescribed performing forces were not intrinsic to musical compositions, then those compositions would not have the reasonably definite characters we clearly believe them to have. The determinateness of a work's aesthetic qualities is in peril if performing means are viewed as inessential so long as exact sound structure is preserved.

Consider a musical work W with specified performing means M which has some fairly specific aesthetic quality ϕ. The sound structure of W as produced by different performing means N, however, will invariably strike us either as not ϕ at all, or else as ϕ to a greater or lesser degree than before. Therefore, if means of sound production are not regarded as an integral part of musical works, then W cannot be said determinately to have the attribute ϕ. So if we wish to preserve a wide range of determinate aesthetic attributions, we must recognize performing means to be an essential component of musical works. I now provide two illustrations of this point.[21]

(a) Beethoven's Hammerklavier Sonata is a sublime, craggy, and heaven-storming piece of music. The closing passages (marked by ascending chordal trills) are surely among the most imposing and awesome in all music. However, if we understand the very sounds of the Hammerklavier Sonata to originate from a full-range synthesizer, as opposed to a mere 88-key piano of metal, wood, and felt, it no longer seems so sublime, so craggy, so awesome. The aesthetic qualities of the Hammerklavier Sonata depend in part on the strain that its sound structure imposes on the sonic capabilities of the piano; if we are not hearing its sound structure *as* produced by a piano then we are not sensing this strain, and thus our assessment of aesthetic content is altered. The closing passages of the Hammerklavier are awesome in part because we seem to hear the piano bursting at the seams and its keyboard on the verge of exhaustion. On a 10-octave electronic synthesizer those passages do not have quite that quality, and a hearing of them with knowledge of the source is an aesthetically different experience. The lesson here applies, I believe, to all musical works (of the paradigm sort). Their aesthetic attributes always depend, if not so dramatically, in part on the performing forces understood to belong to them.

(b) Consider a baroque concerto for two violins, such as Bach's Concerto in D minor, BWV1043. In such pieces one often finds a phrase (A) assigned to one violin, which is immediately followed by the *very same* phrase (B) assigned to the other violin. Now when one hears such passages *as* issuing from *two* violins (even if in a given performance there are no discernible differences between A and B in timbre or phrasing), a sense of question- and-answer, of relaxation and unhurriedness is communicated. But if one were to construe such passages as issuing from a *single* violin, that quality would be absent, and in its place the passages would assume a more emphatic, insistent, and repetitive cast.

(4) The dependence of aesthetic attributes on assumed or understood performing forces should now be apparent. The dependence of artistic attributes is even more plain. (a) Consider Paganini's Caprice Opus 1, No. 17. This piece surely deserves and receives the attribution 'virtuosic'. But if we did not conceive of the Caprice No. 17 as essentially for the violin, as inherently a *violin piece* (and not just a *violin-sounding piece*), then it would not merit that attribution. For, as executed by a computer or by some novel string instrument using nonviolinistic technique, its sound structure might not be particularly difficult to get through. (b) Imagine a piece written for violin to be played in such a way that certain passages sound more like a flute than they do like a violin. Such a piece would surely be accounted *unusual*, and to some degree, *original* as well. Understood as a piece for violin and occasional flute, however, it might have nothing unusual or original about it at all. Retaining the sound structure while setting actual performance means adrift completely dissolves part of the piece's artistic import. (c) According to one respected critic, Beethoven in the Quintet Opus 16 was interested in solving problems of balance between piano and winds—a nominally incompatible array of instruments —and succeeded in his own individual way.[22] It is not hard to agree with this assessment; thus, 'solves the problem of balance between piano and winds' is an attribution true of Beethoven's Quintet. It is difficult to see how this would be so if the Quintet is purely a sound structure, if piano and winds are not strictly part of the piece at all.[23]

I thus propose a third requirement for any account of the musical work: *inclusion of performance means*:

(Per) Musical works must be such that specific means of performance or sound production are integral to them.

IV

If musical works are not sound structures *simpliciter*, then what are they? The type that is a musical work must be capable of being created, must be individuated by context of composition, and must be inclusive of means of performance. The third desideratum is most easily met, and will be addressed first.

I propose that a musical work be taken to involve not only a pure sound structure, but also a structure of performing means. If the sound structure of a piece is basically a sequence of sounds qualitatively defined, then the performing-means structure is a parallel sequence of performing means specified for realizing the sounds at each point. Thus a musical work consists of at least two structures. It is a compound or conjunction of a sound structure and a performing-means structure. This compound is itself just a more complex structure; call it an "S/PM" structure, for short.[24] Beethoven's Opus 16 Quintet is at base an S/PM structure; the means of producing the sounds belonging to it are no more dispensable to its identity as a composition than the nature and order of those sounds themselves. This satisfies requirement (Per).

To satisfy the first and second requirements of adequacy we arrived at, it is necessary to realize that a musical work is not a structure of the *pure* sort at all, and thus not even a S/PM structure *simpliciter*. An S/PM structure is no more creatable or context-individuated than a sound structure is. I propose that we recognize a musical work to be a more complicated entity, namely this:

(MW) S/PM structure-as-indicated-by-X-at-t

where X is a particular person—the composer—and t is the time of composition. For the paradigmatic pieces we are concerned with, the composer typically indicates (fixes, determines, selects) an S/PM structure by creating a score. The *piece* he thereby composes is the S/PM structure-as-indicated by him on that occasion.

An S/PM structure-as-indicated-by-X-at-t, unlike an S/PM structure *simpliciter*, does not pre-exist the activity of composition and is thus capable of being created. When a composer θ composes a piece of music, he indicates an S/PM structure ψ, but he does not bring ψ into being. However, through the act of indicating ψ, he does bring into being something that did not previously exist—namely, ψ-as-indicated-by-θ-at-t_1. Before the compositional act at t_1, no relation obtains between θ and ψ. Composition establishes the relation of indication between θ and ψ. As a result of the compositional act, I suggest, the world contains a new entity, ψ-as-indicated-by-θ-at-t_1. Let me call such entities *indicated structures*. And let me represent indicated structures by expressions of form "S/PM*x*t." It is important to realize that indicated structures are entities distinct from the pure structures *per se* from which they are derived. Thus, in particular, $\psi^*\theta^*t_1$ is *not* just the structure ψ with the accidental property of having been indicated by θ at t_1—$\psi^*\theta^*t_1$ and ψ are strictly non-identical, though of course related. $\psi^*\theta^*t_1$, unlike ψ, can be and is created through θ's composing. Thus requirement (Cre) is satisfied.

Indicated structures also serve to satisfy our second requirement (Ind). If musical works are indicated structures of the sort we have suggested, then two such works, $\psi^*\theta^*t_1$ and $\alpha^*\phi^*t_2$ are identical if (i) $\psi = \alpha$, (ii) $\theta = \phi$, and (iii) $t_1 = t_2$. But if musical works are necessarily distinct if composed either by different people or at different times, then it certainly follows that works composed in different musico-historical contexts will be distinct, since any difference of musico-historical context from one work to another can be traced to a difference of composer or time or both. Put otherwise, musico-historical context (as explained in section II) is a function of time and person; given a time and person, musico-historical context is fixed. So requirement (Ind) is satisfied. That it is satisfied by our proposal with something to spare is a matter I will return to in section V. I now endeavor to increase the reader's grasp of what indicated structures are.

Indicated structures are a different class of type from pure structures. Types of the latter class we may call *implicit* types, and those of the former class *initiated* types. *Implicit* types include all purely abstract structures that are not inconsistent, e.g., geometrical figures, family relationships, strings of words, series of moves in chess, ways of placing five balls in three bins, etc. By calling them "implicit types" I mean to suggest that their existence is implicitly granted when a general framework of possibilities is given. For example, given that there is space, there are all the possible configurations in space; given there is the game of chess, there are all the possible combinations of allowed moves. Sound structures *simpliciter* are clearly implicit types. Given that there are sounds of various kinds, then all possible patterns and sequences of those sounds must be granted existence immediately as well. For a sound structure, in company with all pure structures, is always capable of instantiation before the point at which it is noticed, recognized, mentioned, or singled out. And thus its existence must predate that point. The same goes for a performance-means structure *simpliciter*. Given performing means (i.e., instruments) of various kinds, then all possible combinations and sequences of such means exist as well. The compound of these two, a sound/performance-means structure, thus, of course, also counts as an implicit type.

The other class of types, *initiated* types, are so called because they begin to exist only when they are initiated by an intentional human act of some kind. All those of interest can, I think, be construed as arising from an operation, like indication, performed upon a pure structure. Typically, this indication is effected by producing an exemplar of the structure involved, or a blueprint of it. In so indicating (or determining) the structure, the exemplar or blueprint inaugurates the type which is the *indicated* structure, the structure-as-indicated-by-*x*-at-*t*. All indicated structures are, perforce, initiated types.

Initiated types include such types as the Ford Thunderbird, the Lincoln penny, the hedgehog. The Ford Thunderbird is not simply a pure structure of metal, glass, and plastic. The pure structure that is embodied in the Thunderbird has existed *at least* since the invention of plastic (1870); there could certainly have been instances of it in 1900. But the Ford Thunderbird was created in 1957; so there could not have been instances of the Thunderbird in 1900. The Ford Thunderbird is an *initiated* type; it is a metal/glass/plastic structure-as-indicated (or determined) by the Ford Motor Company on such and such a date. It begins to exist as a result of an act of human indication or determination. The instances of this type are more than just instances of a pure structure—they are instances of an indicated structure. The Lincoln penny is similarly not a pure structure, an abstract pattern *tout court*, but a structure-as-indicated, a pattern-as-denominated-by-the-U.S. Government. Objects conforming to the pattern *tout court* but existing in 100 A.D. in Imperial Rome would not be instances of the Lincoln penny. Even the hedgehog is probably best understood, not as a pure biological structure, but rather as a biological structure-as-determined-or-fixed by natural terrestrial evolution at a particular point in history. The creatures we call "hedgehogs" possess a certain structure and stand in certain causal relations to some particular creatures which came into existence at a given past date. The biological structure of the hedgehog might have been instantiated in the Mesozoic era, or on Uranus, but nothing existing at that time, or at that place, could be an instance of the hedgehog as we understand it. Musical works, as I have suggested, are indicated structures too, and thus types that do not already exist but must instead be initiated. The same is true of poems, plays, and novels—each of these is an entity more individual and temporally bound than the pure verbal structure embodied in it.

The distinction between indicated structure and pure structure can perhaps be made clearer by analogy with the distinction between sentence and statement long enshrined in the philosophy of language.[25] These distinctions are motivated in similar ways. Statements were recognized partly in response to the need for entities individuated in some respects more finely than sentences, in order to provide bearers for the varying truth values that turned up in connection with a given sentence on different occasions.[26] Just so, indicated structures are recognized in response to the need for entities more finely individuated than pure structures, in order to provide bearers for various incompatible sets of aesthetic, artistic, cultural, semantic, and genetic properties. We allow that a given sentence can make different statements when uttered in different circumstances. Similarly, we realize that a given sound/performance-means structure yields different indicated structures, or musical works, when indicated in different musico-historical contexts.[27]

V

I have proposed that musical works be identified with rather specific indicated structures, in which a particular person and time figure ineliminably. The proposal MW was made, recall, in order to satisfy the creatability and individuation requirements. However, as I noted at that point, MW satisfies the individuation requirement with logical room to spare. Perhaps both requirements can be satisfied without invoking types that are quite so particularized? The obvious alternative is that a musical work is this sort of type:

(MW') S/PM structure-as-indicated-in-musico-historical context-C

Such types would be both creatable and sufficiently individuated. A type of this sort, like an MW type, comes into existence through some *actual* indication of an S/PM structure by a person at a time—a person who at that certain time is situated in a particular context. But the type's identity is not inherently tied to that of any individual as such. Thus, two composers composing simultaneously but independently in the same musico-historical context who determine the same S/PM structure create *distinct* MW types, but the *same* MW' type.

Given these two proposals, then, which satisfy all our desiderata, do we have reason to prefer one or the other? I will discuss one consideration in favor of MW', and three considerations in favor of MW.

(1) On the MW' proposal, it is at least logically possible for a musical work to have been composed by a person other than the person who actually composed it. If A is the actual composer of a musical work, ψ-as-indicated-in-C_1, then all we need imagine is that someone other than A was the person to first indicate the S/PM structure ψ in musico-historical context C_1. On the MW proposal, however, it becomes *logically impossible* for a work to have been composed by other than its actual composer. Could someone else have composed Beethoven's Quintet Opus 16, according to MW? For example, could Hummel have done so? No, because if ψ is the S/PM structure of the Quintet Opus 16, then all that Hummel might have composed is ψ-as-indicated-by-Hummel-in-1797, and not ψ-as-indicated-by-Beethoven-in-1797.[28] It must be admitted to be somewhat counterintuitive for a theory to make the composer of a work essential to that work.

(2) We can turn this consequence upside-down, however. One might cite as a virtue of the MW proposal that it gives a composer *logical insurance* that his works are his very own, that no one else has or ever could compose a work identical to any of his. If A's musical work is an MW type, then even a fellow composer situated in an identical musico-historical context determining the same S/PM structure composes a distinct musical work. It seems to me this is a desirable consequence, from the point of view of preserving the uniqueness of compositional activity. Why should a composer have to fear, how-

ever abstractly, that his work is not exclusively his, any more than a painter painting a painting or a sculptor sculpting a sculpture need be troubled about whether his work is at least numerically distinct from anyone else's? Why not adopt a construal of 'musical work' (and of 'poem', 'novel', 'dance', etc.) which, while maintaining musical works as abstract types, guarantees this individuation by artist for them as well? Considerations (1) and 2) thus appear to fairly well cancel each other out.

(3) A more decisive reason, however, for ensuring by proposal MW that composers A and B who determine the same S/PM structure in the same musico-historical context yet compose distinct works W_1 and W_2, is that, although W_1 and W_2 do not, it seems, differ structurally or aesthetically or artistically at the time of composition t, differences of an artistic sort are almost certain to develop after t. So, unless we wish to embrace the awkwardness of saying that two musical works can be identical when composed, but non-identical at some later point, we have a strong incentive to adopt MW. W_1 and W_2 will almost certainly diverge artistically because of the gross improbability that A and B will continue to be subject to the exact same influences to the same degree and that A's and B's oeuvres will continue to appear identical after the composition of W_1 and W_2. If A's and B's artistic careers do exhibit these differences after t, then W_1 and W_2 will acquire somewhat different artistic significance, since W_1 will eventually be seen properly against A's total development, and W_2 against B's total development. W_1 may turn out to be *a seminal work*, whereas W_2 turns out to be *a false start*. Or W_1 may turn out to be *much more influential* than W_2, owing to the fact that A comes to be much better known than B. In any case, there will be *some* divergence in artistic attributions, if not always so marked, unless A and B remain artistic duplicates of one another throughout their lives (and thereafter). Since circumstances subsequent to a work's composition are not comprised in musico-historical context of composition, proposal MW' leaves us open for the awkwardness mentioned above. MW forestalls this problem completely.[29]

(4) A last consideration inclining us to MW comprises certain intuitions concerning what would count as a performance of what. It seems that, in order for a performance to be a performance *of* W, not only must it fit and be intended to fit the S/PM structure of A's work W; there must also be some *connection*, more or less direct, between the sound event produced and A's creative activity. Whether this is primarily an intentional or causal connection is a difficult question,[30] but, unless it is present, I think we are loath to say that A's work has been performed. Consider two composers, Sterngrab and Grotesteen, who compose quartets with identical S/PM structures; suppose even that they share the same musico-historical context. Now imagine that the Aloysious Ensemble, who are great friends of Sterngrab, give the ill-attended première of Sterngrab's Quartet Opus 21. Clearly, the Aloysious have performed Sterngrab's Quartet Opus 21—but have they also performed Grotesteen's Quartet Opus 21? I think not. Why? For several reasons: they don't know Grotesteen; they weren't using Grotesteen's scores; they didn't believe themselves to be presenting Grotesteen's work—in short, there was no connection between their performance and Grotesteen the creator. Grotesteen's creating his Opus 21 Quartet had nothing whatever to do with the sound event produced by the Aloysious Ensemble on the afore-mentioned occasion. Now, if Sterngrab's Quartet has performances that Grotesteen's does not, and *vice versa*, then, again by Leibniz's law, Sterngrab's and Grotesteen's quartets cannot be identical. On proposal MW', Sterngrab and Grotesteen have composed the same musical work; on proposal MW, their works are distinct. That MW squares with this intuition regarding identification of performances is thus one more point in its favor.

I therefore rest with the account of musical works represented by MW. In the next section I offer some remarks on performances and transcriptions in light of this account.

VI

(1) On my view, the following must all be distinguished: (a) instances of W; (b) instances of the sound structure of W; (c) instances of the S/PM structure of W; (d) performances of W. An *instance* of a musical work W is a sound event which conforms *completely* to the sound/performance-means structure of W and which exhibits the required connection[31] to the indicative activity wherein W's composer A creates W. An instance of W is typically produced, either directly or indirectly, from a score that can be causally traced and is intentionally related by the performer, to the act of creation of W by A. Thus, all instances of W are instances of W's sound structure, and instances of W's S/PM structure—but the reverse is not the case.

Instances are a subclass of the set of performances of a work. A *performance* of a musical work W is a sound event which is *intended* to instantiate W—i.e., represents an attempt to exemplify W's S/PM structure in accordance with A's indication of it[32]—and which *succeeds to a reasonable degree*.[33] Since one cannot instantiate a musical work—an S/PM structure-as-indicated-by-X-at-t—without intending to, because instantiating *that* demands conscious guidance by instructions, memories, or the like which one regards as deriving from A's indicative act at t, it follows that the instances of W are all to be found among the performances of W. However, not all performances of W count as instances of W; many if not most attempts to exemplify S/PM structures fail by some margin. So these cannot count as instances of W, but they *are* performances—namely *incorrect* performances. (Of course, that they are strictly incorrect by no means entails that they are bad.) There are not, however, any incorrect *instances* of W; the *correct performances of* W are its instances, and no others.[34]

Finally, let me note that musical works as I understand them *can* be heard in or through their performances. One *hears* an S/PM structure-as-indicated-by-X-at-t whenever one hears an instance of that S/PM structure produced by performers who, roughly speaking, are guided by X's indication of the S/PM structure in question. And one *knows* precisely what musical work, i.e., structure-as-indicated, one is hearing if one knows what creative act is in effect the guiding source of the sound event being produced.

(2) On my view of what a musical work (of the paradigm sort) is, it follows immediately that a transcription of a musical work is a distinct musical work, whether it involves alteration of the sound structure (the normal case), or *even* of just the performance-means structure. It is a virtue of my view that it gives a clear answer to this question, which is often thought to be only arbitrarily decidable. If we want such pieces to have the definite aesthetic qualities we take them to have, instrumentation must be considered inseparable from them. Thus, we need not rely, in endorsing the distinctness position on transcriptions vis-à-vis original works, merely on the principle of fidelity to the composer's intended instrumentation. Rather we are also constrained by higher-order considerations of preserving the aesthetic integrity of such pieces.

In conclusion, let me stress some obvious consequences of accepting the theory of the musical work that I have proposed. First, composers would retain the status of creator in the strictest sense. Second, musical composition would be revealed as necessarily personalized. Third, musical composition could not fail to be seen as a historically rooted activity whose products must be understood with reference to their points of origin. Fourth, it would be recognized that the pure sound structure of a musical work, while graspable in isolation, does not exhaust the work structurally, and thus that the underlying means of performance must be taken into account as well if the work is to be corrrectly assessed.[35]

NOTES

I am indebted to several of my colleagues at the University of Maryland, both past and present, for helpful comments on earlier versions of this paper.

1. There are of course several other objections to these proposals, and to the Crocean proposal mentioned below. I do not mean to suggest that those I recall are clearly decisive by themselves.
2. See, for example, C. L. Stevenson, "On 'What Is a Poem?'," *Philosophical Review*, LXVI, 3 (July 1957): 329–362; J. Margolis, *The Language of Art and Art Criticism* (Detroit: Wayne State UP, 1965); R. Wollheim, *Art and Its Objects* (New York, Harper & Row, 1968).
3. It should be understood at the outset that sound structure includes not only pitches and rhythms, but also timbres, dynamics, accents—that is, all "purely aural" properties of sound.
4. The present paper owes a debt to two recent theories of the musical work: N. Wolterstorff, "Toward an Ontology of Artworks," *Noûs*, IX, 2 (May 1975): 115–142; and K. Walton, "The Presentation and Portrayal of Sound Patterns," *In Theory Only* (February 1977): 3–16. These writers are aware of some of the considerations that I adduce pointing to the complexity of a musical type. However, I believe they do not take them seriously enough, and thus are inclined to acquiesce in the view that musical works *are* or *may be* just sound structures. The present paper aims squarely to reject that view and to formulate one more adequate.
5. E.g., F# minor triad, three-note French-dotted rhythmic figure, middle C of bassoon timbre, etc.
6. This point is made by Wolterstorff, *op. cit.*, p. 138.
7. Though of course lack of suitable production facilities made this impossible in some nonlogical sense.
8. I am aware that someone might hold that in saying that a certain novel sound instance is possible at t, all we are committed to is that the sound structure of which it *would be* an instance might possibly *come into existence* at t, simultaneously with its first instance. But I do not think this is a plausible view; in saying that a certain sound event could occur at t we are saying something stronger than that the structure it would exemplify might come into existence—we are saying that that structure is right then available.
9. Some who yet resist the idea that pure sound structures pre-exist compositional activity are possibly failing to distinguish between *structure* and *construction*. It is true that constructions need to have been constructed in order to exist; it does not follow that structures need to have been constructed—i.e., actually put together from parts—in order to exist. The Brooklyn Bridge is a construction, and embodies a structure. The Brooklyn Bridge did not exist before its construction. But the geometrical structure it embodies, which required and received no construction, has always existed.

Given that there will still be some who are attracted to the view that pure sound structures are in some way created by composers, presumably through mental activity, and that these are their works, I will take this occasion to point out briefly two untoward consequences of such a view. The first is that instances of pure sound structures can always have been sounded accidentally before any composer thinks them into existence by directing his attention on the realm of sounds. In which case we would then be countenancing compositions that have instances before those compositions begin to exist. The second is that a person who conceives or sketches a sound structure new to him has no (logical) assurance that he has in fact composed *anything*. For if composing is bringing sound structures into existence, one may fail to do so in writing a score, provided someone else has conceived the same structure earlier. Notice that this is not a matter of the latecomer having composed the *same* work as his predecessor, but rather—what he and we would surely find incredible—a matter of his having composed *no* work at all.

10. Though composers compose their works *by* writing scores, having thoughts, or, less typically, producing performances.
11. It would be well to note here that, even if one rejects the requirement of creatability, abandonment of the sound-structure view in favor of something like the view I eventually propose will be demanded by the second and third requirements developed. And those requirements strike me as being nonnegotiable.
12. Notice that if we assume that composing musical works is strictly creating them, it follows immediately that two composers cannot compose the very same musical work (no matter what sound structures they determine) unless they are either composing jointly or composing independently but simultaneously. This is just a consequence of the fact that the same thing cannot be created both at t and at a later time t'. (The same goes for a single composer on temporally separate occasions; if composing is creating, a composer cannot compose the same work twice.) I will not, however, in

this section assume that composing is strict creation.
13. Cf. J. L. Borges, "Pierre Menard, Author of the Quixote" [in *Labyrinths* (New York: New Directions, 1962)] for a fictional demonstration of the dependence of artistic meaning on the historical context of creation.
14. Cf. Wollheim, *op. cit.*, pp. 48–54, for a discussion of the dependence of a work's expression on the artistic repertoire of the artist. The notion of "repertoire" is roughly that of a set of alternative decisions or choices within which an artist appears to be operating in creating his works. Wollheim extracts this idea from E. K. Gombrich's discussions of artistic expression in *Art and Illusion* and *Meditations on a Hobby-Horse*.
15. The convincingness of these examples depends crucially on accepting something like the following principle: "Works of art *truly have* those attributes which they *appear* to have when *correctly* perceived or regarded." I cannot provide a defense of this principle here, but it has been well argued for by C. Stevenson, "Interpretation and Evaluation in Aesthetics" [in W. E. Kennick, *Art and Philosophy* (New York: St. Martin's, 1964)], and Walton, "Categories of Art," *Philosophical Review*, LXVI, 3 (July 1970): 334–367, among others.
16. It is a mistake to regard this illustration as concerned with what *Pierrot Lunaire* would have been like if *it* had been composed by Strauss. (I am not even sure what *that* supposition amounts to.) The illustration rather concerns a possible musical work that possesses the same sound structure as *Pierrot Lunaire*, but is composed by Strauss in 1897. This work would be distinct from *Pierrot Lunaire*, because aesthetically divergent. But if musical works were identified with sound structures it could *not* be distinct.

Another way of casting the argument using this example would be as follows. Consider a possible world Q in which both Schoenberg's *Pierrot Lunaire* and Strauss's *Pierrot Lunaire* exist, and call the sound structure they have in common "K." In Q, the works diverge aesthetically and hence are non-identical. Clearly, the works cannot both be identified with their common sound structure, but to so identify only one of them would be perfectly arbitrary. So in Q, *Pierrot Lunaire* $\neq K$. But then in the actual world as well, *Pierrot Lunaire* $\neq K$. Why? Owing to the necessity that attaches to identity and difference. If two things are non-identical in any possible world, they are non-identical in every possible world in which they exist. Put otherwise, statements of identity and difference involving rigid designators are necessary. 'Pierrot Lunaire' and 'K' designate rigidly; they are proper names, not definite descriptions. Thus 'Pierrot Lunaire $\neq K$' is necessarily true, since true in Q. Therefore, in the actual world, *Pierrot Lunaire* $\neq K$. [The argument can be recast in this way, *mutatis mutandis*, for illustrations (2)–(5) as well.]
17. This includes a single composer on separate occasions.
18. It is inevitable that someone will object at this point that certain composers, in certain periods, did not compose with definite instruments in mind and did not make specific instrumentation integral to their works. This may be true to some extent. But two points must be noted. First, I have set out to define the nature of the *paradigmatic* musical composition in Western culture, of which Beethoven's Quintet, Opus 16 is an example. It is enough for my purpose that most "classical" compositions, and effectively all from 1750 to the present, integrally involve quite definite means of performance. Second, even in a case such as J. S. Bach, where controversy has long existed as to exactly what performing forces Bach intended, called for, or would have allowed in such compositions as *The Well-Tempered Clavier* or the Brandenburg Concerto No. 2, it is clear there are still more restrictions as to performing forces which must be considered part of those compositions. Thus, *The Well-Tempered Clavier* may not be a work belonging solely to the harpsichord (as opposed to the clavichord or fortepiano), but it is clearly a work for *keyboard*, and a performance of its sound structure on five violins would just for that reason not be a performance of *it*. And although the performance component of the Brandenburg Concerto No. 2 may be indeterminate between a trumpet and a natural horn in that prominent instrumental part, it certainly excludes the alto saxophone. Finally, a composition such as Bach's *Art of the Fugue*, for which perhaps no means of sound production are either prescribed or proscribed, is in this context merely the exception that proves the rule.
19. This should not be confounded with the fact that many composers were ready and willing

to adapt their works in response to exigencies—in short, to license transcriptions.
20. This is not to say that *everything* found in scores is constitutive of musical works. Some markings do not fix the identity of a work but are instead of the nature of advice, inspiration, helpful instruction, etc. However, the suggestion that instrumental specifications are of this sort is totally insupportable.
21. Cf. Walton, "Categories of Art," *op. cit.*, pp. 349/50, for related examples.
22. James Lyons, liner notes, phonograph record *Nonesuch* 71054.
23. The best one could say would be that the Quintet achieved a satisfactory blending of piano-ish sounds and woodwind-ish sounds.
24. One could alternatively speak of a single structure which, construed rightly, entails both the required sounds and the required means of sound production. This would be a structure of *performed sounds*, as opposed to "pure" sounds. For example, one such *performed sound* would correspond to the following specification: "Middle C of half-note duration played on oboe." Clearly this implies both a certain sound qualitatively defined and a means of producing it.

The main reason I favor the S/PM formulation is that it is more transparent. It preserves some continuity with the sound-structure view which it supersedes, and displays more clearly than the performed-sound formulation that, although a musical work is *more* than a sound structure, it most definitely *includes* a sound structure.
25. This analogy was brought to my attention by Warren Ingber.
26. See, for example, J. L. Austin's "Truth," *Proceedings of the Aristotelian Society*, supp. vol. XXIV (1950): 111–128.
27. The analogy might even be reversed, so as to illuminate the nature of statements. If musical works are structures-as-indicated . . . , then possibly statements just are: sentences-as-uttered . . .
28. I am assuming, of course, that Hummel could not possibly have *been* Beethoven. If he *could* have, then I suppose that, even on MW, Hummel might have composed Beethoven's Quintet.
29. I will take this opportunity to point out that although aesthetic and artistic attributes have played a large role in this paper, I have not insisted on them as *essential* to musical works, but only as relevant—in common with all other attributes—to *individuating* them. The argument has nowhere required as a premise that such attributes are essential attributes. It has assumed only that aesthetic/artistic attributes *truly belong* to works in a *reasonably determinate* fashion. As for what attributes *are* essential to musical works, given MW, it seems that certain structural and genetic attributes would have to be admitted: S/PM structure, composer, date of composition. But it is not obvious that aesthetic/artistic attributes will turn out to be essential, i.e., possessed by a work in all possible worlds it inhabits. Consider a possible world in which Schoenberg determines the S/PM structure of *Verklarte Nacht* during 1899 but in which Wagner had never existed. The resultant work might still be *Verklarte Nacht*, though some of its aesthetic/artistic attributes would be subtly different.
30. Quandaries arise when these considerations conflict, which I will not attempt to deal with here. For example, suppose the Aloysious Ensemble are actually reading copies of Grotesteen's score while believing themselves to be playing Sterngrab's score. Do they perform Sterngrab's Quartet, Grotesteen's Quartet, or both?
31. I will assume here that the required connection is primarily, if not wholly, intentional.
32. And thus an attempt to exemplify an S/PM-as-indicated-by-X-at-*t*.
33. What constitutes a "reasonable degree," and thus what differentiates poor or marginal performance from nonperformance, is for many compositions perhaps marked by the ability of an informed and sensitive listener to grasp, at least roughly, what S/PM structure is struggling to be presented. For example, even an especially informed and sensitive listener would grasp approximately nothing of the Hammerklavier Sonata from *my* attempt to present its structure, since my facility at the piano is next to nil—no performance (much less an instance) of the Hammerklavier Sonata can issue from me or my ilk.
34. Thus I am in opposition to Wolterstorff's suggestion, in "Toward an Ontology of Artworks," *op. cit.*, that musical works be construed as norm-kinds, i.e., as having correct and incorrect, or proper and improper, or standard and defective instances. What we say about musical works can, I think, be more perspicuously interpreted in terms of the distinction between instance and performance.

Further, construing instance as requiring full conformity to score (i.e., as an all-or-none proposition) has the virtue, as Nelson Goodman pointed out in *Languages of Art* (Indianapolis: Bobbs-Merrill, 1968), of assuring preservation of a work's identity from work to instance and from instance to work. But by also distinguishing between instance and performance (which Goodman does not do) one can sweeten the judgment, say, that Rubinstein's playing of the Chopin Ballade No. 3 with two mistakes is not an *instance* of the work, with the willing admission that it is surely a *performance* of it (and possibly a great one).

35. It is worth observing that, if the position developed in this paper is correct, it has interesting implications not only for the identity of other sorts of artwork (this I take to be obvious) but for the identity of abstract cultural objects of various sorts—e.g., scientific theories, speeches, laws, games. A physical theory, for example, can't be *simply* a set of sentences, propositions, or equations *if* it is in fact the possessor of properties such as brilliance, revolutionariness, derivativeness, immediate acceptance. For that very set of sentences, propositions, or equations might be found in another theory occurring fifty years earlier or later which lacked those properties.

Music and Metaphysics: Types and Patterns, Performances and Works

John W. Bender

Since the middle seventies, the thesis that musical works are, ontologically speaking, kinds or types has been widely received and persuasively argued. Although the details of their views differ, Margolis (1977), Wolterstorff (1970, 1975, 1980), and Levinson (1980, 1990) have each deftly defended this categorization. It is, however, time for a second look. Because Margolis' emphasis is less on the type/token relation between a musical work and its performances, and more on the different claim that artworks are "culturally emergent" entities which are "embodied" in physical objects, I will be focusing my attention on the other two writers.[1]

Although a musical work is, in my view, a created pattern of sound, I shall argue that Wolterstorff and Levinson are both incorrect in identifying the work with a kind or type whose examples or tokens are, or prominently include, the work's numerous performances.

It must be acknowledged at the outset that in dealing with ontological concepts such as universal, abstract particular, and kind, and with the broader framework in which they operate, we are entering a recognized philosophical danger zone, an area of enormous difficulty, disagreement and unclarity, where no one theory enjoys general acceptance and where it is notoriously hard to distinguish the superficial from the fundamental. It is well known that features of the language we employ do not reflect perfectly the structure of our ontological theory, but it certainly would be a virtue of such a theory that it handles systematically and makes consistent the things we say about various entities. We often

---

Reprinted from *Proceedings of the Ohio Philosophical Association*, April 1991, by permission of the author.

have little else to go on in clarifying our ontological claims and commitments.

The considerations and arguments I offer here are, then, driven by no special ontological agenda, but are guided simply by the goal of making consistent and sensible many of the things we commonly say about works of music. Conversely, to the extent that a proposed theory has odd-sounding or odd-seeming implications, suspicions, at least, are raised about its acceptability. Definitiveness, however, is as elusive in the metaphysics of music as it is in musical performances.

1. CONTRASTS BETWEEN WOLTERSTORFF'S AND LEVINSON'S VIEWS, AND WITH THE PRESENT VIEW

The detailed ontological positions of these two metaphysicians of music can each be expressed as a short sequence of principles.

Wolterstorff's Theory[2]

(Wa) Musical works are—like species, novels, words, states and actions—a certain sort of *universal* (a nonpredictable "substance universal").
(Wb) All universals are *kinds* (of one sort or another).
(Wc) Musical works are identical with (what I shall refer to here, for brevity's sake as) *Performance Kinds*, i.e. kinds whose examples are the works' individual performances (or "playings," as on a phonograph or player piano).

Since performances and playings are occurrences of sound-sequences, (Wc) is equivalent to:

(Wd) Musical work W is identical with the kind: Sound-Sequence-Occurrence Produced By Performing or Playing W.

So, rather as 'The Bengal Tiger' names a natural kind whose examples are particular tigers, 'Bartok's Fifth String Quartet' names the kind which I am calling a performance kind, viz., the kind: performance of Bartok's Fifth Quartet, and its examples prominently include the individual performances of the Fifth, each of which is an occurrence of a sound-sequence. Like a natural kind, a performance kind is what Wolterstorff calls a "norm-kind," i.e. a kind for which criteria can be specified for what is to count as a *correct* example. In writing the score or otherwise composing the work, musical composers lay down these correctness conditions by selecting sets of acoustical properties, as well as selecting certain methods of sound production, including instrumentation. In performing a work, one must, among other things, aim to satisfy the correctness conditions established by the composer's specifications (cf. 1980, 81).

Levinson's Theory[3]

(La) Musical works are *indicated performed-sound structures*.
(Lb) Such (PS) structures are *initiated types* (kinds, sorts) whose tokens are (at least some of) the works' performances and
(Lc) Initiated types are a sort of abstract particular, not a universal.

Unlike pure sound structures, which are non-creatable universals, and which Levinson would, I believe, categorize as *implicit* types or kinds, the performed-sound structures which are musical works are created or initiated by the acts of indication carried out by the composer. The intentional acts of indication are operations on pure sound structures by the individual composer and essentially "tether" that structure to the composer, a time, a musico-historical context, and a means of performance (1980, 21; 1990, 216). Something new is thus created: "Composers . . . don't create the sound (or other abstract) patterns involved in their activities, but they do nevertheless create the works —patterns-in-contexts—and so invest those works with meanings not possessed by the abstract patterns *tout court*" (1990, 218). Levinson now seems willing to think about this rather obscure "indication" relation along Wolterstorffean lines, as the specification of correctness conditions for a work's performances (1990, 260).

I can now say more specifically what I wish to accomplish in this paper. I shall argue that Levinson and Wolterstorff each have a bit of the truth, but also have their own, separate, problems. In addition, and central to the paper, I shall be arguing that they share the mistake of viewing a musical work as a kind/type whose examples/tokens include individual performances of the work. It is my contention that (Wa), (Wc), and (Wd) are false, while (Wb) may be correct (although I shall not argue for (Wb) here). Moreover, I find (Lb) unacceptable, and the truth or falsity of (Lc) not directly relevant to our issues. I do admit that there is *a sense* of the term, 'indicated performed-sound structure,' in which (La) can be maintained, but the sense is not quite Levinson's. I also will argue that a certain consequent of (La)-(Lc) is true, viz., that a musical work is an abstract particular. The positive position I shall be suggesting is this:

New Proposal

(Ba) A musical work is a sound-pattern, created by the composer.
(Bb) A sound pattern, in the sense intended here, is a series of sound-instances-in-relation, considered abstractly, i.e., no *particular* sound-instances are referred to in the creating of the pattern by the composer. (This will be explained below.)
(Bc) A musical work is an abstract particular, not a universal.
(Bd) A musical work is realized in/by its performances, but this realization relation is not identical to the relation of instantiating a universal or of tokening a type (exemplifying a kind).

2. PRIMA FACIE REASONS FOR DENYING THAT MUSICAL WORKS ARE KINDS OR TYPES

(a) Let's begin by assuming that the various performances of Bartok's String Quartet No. 5, Op. 102 are tokens of a type, or examples of a kind (I am using these concepts interchangeably here). The type they most obviously belong to is the type: Performance of the Bartok Fifth Quartet. When something is a token of a type, T, it is nearly always appropriate to say that the token is *a* T, and when a type has multiple tokens, to say that a certain token is *one T among others*, or that there are *numerous Ts*. For example, "This coin is an Indian Head U.S. nickel," and "Numerous Indian Head Nickels still exist, and this coin here is a very good example."

But last night's Chicago performance of the Bartok Fifth by the members of the Alban Berg String Quartet is not *a* Bartok Fifth, nor is it one among numerous Bartok Fifths, for there is only one musical work of that name. It is therefore problematic to identify the work with the type or kind: Performance of the Bartok Quartet No. 5.

(b) Musical performances are temporal events; they are the producing of specified sequences of sound in specified ways. Hence, performance-types to which the individual performances belong are event-types. But it is peculiar, I think, to call Beethoven's *Eroica* an event-type, in the way that the hurricane, for example, is an event-type. This is not to deny that the *Eroica* is an entity intimately related to its performance-type. This relational reading is certainly the transparent understanding of the construction we use to refer to individual performances as well as performance-types, viz., 'performance *of* M.' We use the name of one thing, the musical work, M, to insure definite reference to something else related to it, viz., the performances or performance-type. In this, we follow a widely used referential practice, one evident in referring expressions such as, 'eldest son of J. S. Bach,' where there is no question whether Carl Philip is identical to his father or to any *type* of relative.

(c) To further support the considerations in (b), it should be pointed out that there are certain properties true of musical works which are not truly, and perhaps not even sensibly, ascribed to performance-types. A work may have had its movements composed out-of-order, but a performance-type cannot be ascribed this feature. Indeed, performance-kinds or types do not have movements as their constituents at all; musical works are composed of notes and movements, but performance-kinds are "composed" of individual performances. Even a single performance can only be said to have *performed* movements as its parts, not *composed* movements.

(a)–(c) will gain additional forcefulness if a more theoretical underpinning can be provided for them. I turn now to a brief analysis of types in order to distinguish them from patterns.

3. TYPES AND PATTERNS

The types or kinds with which we are concerned have particulars as their tokens or examples. (Obviously not all types fit this description; for example, we can talk of a type of property such as "color properties," whose tokens are universals.) But having said what the types which interest us have as their tokens, we have said everything that is obvious about them; saying what the concept of the type itself amounts to is much more difficult. What are we to say, for instance, about the U.S. Indian Head Nickel?

The natural thing would be to say that the U.S. Indian Head Nickel is a type of U.S. currency, minted in Denver and San Francisco between 1913 and 1938, whose size, shape, weight and composition are _ _ _ _ _, and whose faces exhibit a certain engraving of the head of an native American on one side and a certain engraving of a buffalo on the other. Such a type, then, appears to be a *grouping* of particulars, in accordance with a specifiable set of satisfaction conditions, membership conditions which must be met by each token. And yet, if I were to amass every example of the Indian Head Nickel, being careful to weed out counterfeit, I would have literally grouped these coins in accordance with certain satisfaction conditions, but that pile of coins would not be the *type*.

Rather, the type seems to be a mental or conceptual grouping of certain particulars. The concept of a type is, as far as I can determine, the concept of "all particulars, x, that satisfy certain conditions, C, and considered as a unity."[4] If this is correct, we may say that a type is a mental grouping of entities (in our case, particulars) under certain satisfaction conditions. Perhaps this can be restated by saying that the types we are concerned with are "particulars-considered-collectively-as-a-unity-of-'all those x's satisfying conditions C'."

Performances that tolerably satisfy the conditions a composer lays down in specifying a work's structure are the particular events which we group together under the idea of a performance-kind. But we may now be able to see more clearly that, for the reasons cited above, the musical work itself is not a mental grouping of its performances. A performance is an intentional and tolerably successful attempt to realize the work in its entirety; a performance is not an attempt to realize a performance-kind in its entirety, or to realize a mental grouping of performances, whatever, if anything, that might mean.

It is not crucial to my argument that we determine the difficult issue whether a type or kind is a universal or a sort of abstract particular, but a few words on the problem are appropriate. That kinds or types are conceived as unities does not conclusively establish that they are a sort of particular, I think, since paradigm universals such as properties may also be conceived as unities. Kinds such as species or performance-kinds are, however, different from properties in being *nonpredicable*, at least if we follow Wolterstorff (and Aristotle) here (1970, 7, 221).

On the other hand, that they are repeatable in the sense of having tokens or examples does not conclusively establish that kinds are universals, for it is an open question whether the tokening or exemplification relation is the same relation as that connecting universals to their instances or cases.

Even the fact that works are *created* apparently does not deter Wolterstorff from the view that performance-types, like types and kinds generally, are universals. Composing a work is, for Wolterstorff, the selecting of a set of properties as criteria of correctness for the work's occurrences (1980, 62–64). How this amounts to creating the work, which is a kind, not a set of properties, is not made clear by Wolterstorff; perhaps he means for us to take our talk of *creating* the work less-than-literally.

In contrast, creatability is an important feature, in fact, a *sine qua non* of any acceptable theory of the musical work, according to Levinson (1980, 9). He certainly takes this condition seriously and literally, but instead of rejecting the idea that a created work is a type, Levinson distinguishes non-creatable (implicit) types, such as pure sound structures, from creatable (initiated) types, and then identifies musical works with the latter types, and spends no time fretting over the consequence that types thereby lose their univocal ontological status as universal or abstract particular (whichever it may be).

As I remarked, it is not crucial to my argument that we settle this matter of types' ontological status, because in spite of their disagreement over it, Wolterstorff and Levinson still agree that musical works are types or kinds with performances as their tokens or examples. What *is* crucial to my argument is that I now distinguish kinds/types from patterns, for it is my contention that musical works are created patterns of sound rather than performance-kinds.

A pattern is an arrangement of elements in certain relations to each other. Good examples would be the complex pattern of a beautiful Armenian rug, or the simpler patterns of geometrical shapes on Turkish ceramic tiles. These cases may place greater emphasis on repetition and economy of elements than we find in most musical works, but questions of complexity aside, they make a fundamental point that applies: a pattern is an arrangement of various elements situated in various relations to each other. The nature of the values and relations are, of course, different in the rung than they are in a musical work, the rug's pattern being composed of colored geometrical shapes in spatial relations, but the analogy is obvious: a musical work is (in part) a sequence of musical elements or values (values that can be specified along numerous dimensions, such as pitch, duration, intensity, timbre, instrumental source, etc.) in complex and precise temporal relations with each other.

There is much more to be said to clarify and augment this talk of musical patterns, and I will expand in the succeeding sections. But even in its present incomplete state, I think it is clear that sound-patterns are entities quite distinct from performance-kinds. Sound patterns are groupings of musical *elements*, not groupings of musical performances. Individual performances belong to a performance-kind; they do not "belong" to a sound pattern. The object of a musical performance is to *realize* a certain sound pattern; a performance is a performance *of* a certain sound pattern, it is not a performance *of* the performance-kind. ("Heifetz will now perform for us the performance-kind: Performance of the Mendelssohn E-flat Violin Concerto"!??) Realizing a specified sound pattern more-or-less exactly is a necessary physical condition if one's performance is to be an example of a certain kind; realizing the pattern, therefore, cannot be identical to instantiating a performance-kind.

Sound patterns, then, are not performance-types, and a work of music is a sort of sound pattern, not a kind of performance. But what sort of pattern exactly? The next three sections will try to answer this, and show how the concept of a pattern functions in the broader theory of a musical work as a created and performable entity.

4. INDICATED PATTERNS AND COMPOSING

Musical works are not pure sound structures according to Levinson, pure sound structures being, as they are, not creatable, and "akin to pure universals" (1990, 258). Musical works are indicated performed-sound structures, according to Levinson, and the compositional acts of indicating the musical structure and the performance means tie the work's identity inherently to its composer and to the musico-historical context of composition.

Am I suggesting that musical works *are* "pure" sound patterns? No. I mean 'sound pattern' in the sense in which it is natural to refer to such a pattern as a "specification" (i.e. the result of an act of specifying) and as something that is created by the composer; I do not mean it to refer to a "possible and implicit ordering of musical values, considered as universals." The pattern of the rug spoken of earlier was created by an anonymous 18th century Armenian, the design of the 1957 Ford Thunderbird was created by Ford's Dearborn design team in 1956, the design of the John Hancock Building in Boston was created by I.M. Pei and his architectural firm in the early 70's: it is a purely commonsense way of speaking to refer to patterns or designs as created by individuals at a certain time and in a specific relevant context. And it is one of Levinson's important contributions that he noticed the fact that unless we consider a musical work as an *indicated* or created structure, we cannot ascribe to it its full range of aesthetic properties (1980, 17–18; 1990, 241).

None of this, unfortunately, makes it very clear what an indicated structure is, ontologically speaking. And it is not very illuminating to speak, as Levinson does, of indication as an "operation . . . performed upon a pure structure" (1980, 21).[5] It is a puzzle why "indicating" a universal should be thought to bring into existence some non-universal abstract object. The property of weighing 175 pounds, as indicated by the doctor's scale, is nothing other than that property itself; the state of being dead as defined or indicated in Illinois law, is no less a state (a universal) for having been codified. In the following section, I will try to circumvent this problem by suggesting that creating a sound pattern does not have to be viewed in terms of an indication relation to a universal or "universal-like" object.

It is obvious that Levinson himself has not been entirely satisfied with his characterization of initiated types as "structures-as-indicated-by-x-at-t" (1990, 259–260), and hopes that the situation is improved by appropriation of Wolterstorff's idea that composing is the specifying of correctness conditions for properly formed performances or correct occurrences of the work, the selecting of certain properties and the rendering of them as normative (Wolterstorff 1980, 62). I have no doubt that when composing a work, the writer of music does specify conditions of correctness on performances of that work, but I am skeptical that these should be thought of as one and the same artistic act, to use Guy Sircello's phrase.[6]

A theory of artistic action would take us too far afield, but it is my contention that in the sense of 'basic' used in theory of action, composing a work is a more basic act than the specifying of conditions for correct performances of the work. Specification of correctness conditions is an act the artist does *through* performing the act of composition (as one specifies a rendezvous *through* passing a note that reads, "8:00 tonight".) I suggest that the (complex) act of composition be identified with the act of creating a musical pattern, and that this act is related to, but not identical with, the selection of performance criteria. Arguing for the identity or difference of intimately related actions is extremely difficult, so let me instead offer two examples, more to help fix intuitions than to establish my point conclusively.

When the President issues a communiqué, he is expressing his political ideas on some issue. In issuing his remarks he is also, presumably, specifying the conditions for accurate reporting, quotation or restatement of his position, but issuing the communiqué is not just the setting of these reporting standards. So too, a composer expresses his musical ideas when he composes a work, and also specifies performance standards, but the composing is not the setting of the standards.

Or again, a television art-instructor paints his landscape in certain ordered steps, and does so with the expectation that his viewers can follow and imitate his procedure. In painting his landscape, he also specifies what counts as correctly following his method, but this is not an act identical with his painting the landscape.

Creating a musical work is not, then, the specification of performance conditions, an act of indicating, performed on a pure sound structure, or the selecting of a set of properties. Composing a musical work is creating or specifying a musical pattern.

5. WHAT IS A MUSICAL SOUND PATTERN, AND WHAT ARE ITS COMPONENTS?

Frank Lloyd Wright designs the Robie House and in so doing creates an architectural artwork. Interestingly, part of the task of designing the house, beyond basic structure, floorplan, and detailing of rooms, is the specification of the construction materials. A grey cinder-block building in the shape of the Robie House would not be an adequate representation of Wright's work.

Music should be conceived in a similar fashion, and here I find myself in agreement with Levinson's rather purist position that performance means are an inherent element of the indicated structure which is the individual work. I see no reason to hesitate calling these specifications part of the created musical pattern, just as the specification of building materials is part of Wright's design, or the designation of the color of the various geometrical shapes is an element of the pattern of the Armenian rug.[7]

This broaches a more general question of the nature of the components involved in the sound patterns which are musical works. In writing his f minor Quintet the way he did, i.e., *for* piano and string quartet, Brahms was specifying that the performance forces are to be *a* piano and *a* string quartet. But may we not just as correctly say that the piece is for *the* piano and *the* string quartet, apparently relating the work to kinds (and groups) of instruments?

Imagine that the pattern of a Turkish ceramic tile is two circles above a triangle and square, with each pair flanked by vertical bars:

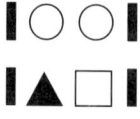

Can we just as easily describe the pattern in terms of The Circle, The Triangle, and The Square (i.e. in terms of types or perhaps universals, if we are Platonic in spirit)? The question I am asking is whether this created pattern should be conceived as types-and-properties-in-relation. Attempting to do so will, I think, run into trouble and oddity. Most generally, it is difficult to understand how types or properties as such can be thought to be in spatial relations to each other. And although it may be natural to describe the pattern as involving the Circle and the Triangle, is it as natural to say that the Vertical Line is a component? Moreover, if the circles are red, shall we say that The Red Circle, or stranger still, that Redness (and Circularity) is a component of the pattern? Specification of the relative sizes of the pattern's figures and the distances between them is certainly important, but problematic if we think of the pattern as types-in-relation. (The two-inch Red Circle one-half inch above The Blue Isosceles with two-inch Base, and . . . ??) Obviously, it is much easier and natural to describe the pattern as being composed of two 2-inch red circles one-half inch above a 2-inch blue isosceles and a white 2-inch square, with each pair bordered by single black vertical bars one-half inch thick and two inches long, etc. What I am suggesting is that in specifying a pattern, the creator refers indefinitely to tokens of certain types and to instances of properties and relations, rather than selecting or referring to universals of various sorts.

Even if types are not universals, I wish to suggest that in specifying the components of musical and other art works, the creative artist is not manipulating, ordering, sequencing, or relating *types*. Shakespeare begins *Twelfth Night* with the line, 'If music be the food of love, play on.' If this play is a pattern of English sentences or statements, shall we say that Shakespeare is specifying, selecting, or operating upon sentence-*types*, or is he arranging and thereby specifying sentence-tokens as he creates the pattern? What he writes, and what he sets down as correctness conditions for accurate copies of his play, are best conceived in terms of tokens, I claim.

By writing a token of this sentence at the start of his manuscript, Shakespeare implicitly specifies that any accurate copy of this play must begin with another token of this sentence, and any accurate performance of the play must begin with a token utterance of it. Specifying that a certain token must occur is not the same as referring to a sentence type in order to say something about *it*. When we say that *Twelfth Night* begins with the line, 'If music be . . . ,' we are not saying something about a sentence type, as we are when we say that the sentence, 'If music be the food of love, play on' contains nine words. The "line" which is part of the created pattern and to which we refer in talking about the play is not a sentence type.

Similarly, Beethoven's *Spring* Sonata for Violin and Piano begins with a half-note **a″** on the violin, and an eighth-note **a** and a whole-note **F** on the piano. This and the examples above can be systematically handled if we resist the temptation of thinking of musical pattern-building as the ordering of musical universals such as, "The note **A** two octaves above middle C," or "The piano chord, **a–F**." Much as Wright's design for the Kaufmann house calls for a rough-hewn sandstone floor in the living room, and two cantilevered terraces of specific proportions (not "The Rough-Sandstone Floor" and "The Cantilevered Terrace") Beethoven's sonata has an **a″** played ligato on the violin in its first bar.

Now, if musical patterns are not arrangements of types, it is clear that neither are they composed of the particular sound-tokens involved in any particular performance of the work. What exactly is the pattern, then? I suggest that we attempt to answer this by first thinking about the musical score, which codifies or notates the pattern.

A score is similar to an indefinite description. Consider the following indefinite description of a series of events: "A man is walking a black dog, when suddenly a squirrel appears in a tree ahead, and, seeing it, the dog growls." No particular man, dog, squirrel or tree is referred to here, nor is the description about Maleness or Treehood, or about species or kinds, such as *Canis Familiaris* or *The Grey Squirrel*. The description constructs a pattern of events but the pattern is *abstract* in the sense that particular men, animals, acts, and so forth, are not referred to. To *realize* this scene, however, certain conditions have now become necessary: some particular man must walk some black dog, for instance.[8]

Composing a musical work (something frequently done through writing a score) is making or specifying a musical pattern, I am arguing. The musical pattern is an abstract arrangement of specified-sound-instances-in-relation, i.e. it is a pattern of temporally related sound-instances as we conceive or describe them indefinitely. (Sound-instances so conceived I will call "abstracted sound-instances.") And just as an indefinite description of a man can specify many features without becoming a definite description, e.g., "A tall thin blonde man is walking a dog when . . . ," so too can a musical pattern fix features of the abstracted sound-instances composing it, and these may well include, as Levinson argues, their instrumental means of production.

In summary, then, a musical work is an abstract object, a sound pattern, created by an individual or individuals, and consisting of abstracted sound-instances-in-relation, with various properties of these sound-instances being open to the specification of the composer. It is also part of my proposal that the relation between the musical work or abstract pattern and its performances is a form of the realization relation, a relation that is different from the type-token relation. A performance of the work is the more-or-less correct realization of that sound pattern by performers intending to satisfy the composer's specifications of the pattern and its elements.

It is left to say something about the realization relation, in the hope of further distinguishing created abstracted sound patterns from performance-kinds.

6. PERFORMANCES REALIZE MUSICAL WORKS

Are there truly significant differences between the claim that a performance is an example or token of a musical work (conceived as a kind or type of performance) and the present thesis that a performance is a realization of a musical work, which is an abstract object, a pattern of a certain sort?

In order to slow any precipitate urge to reduce all one-many relations to the type-token relation, we should notice first that there are numerous such relations, and some are clearly not type-token in nature. Reference and designation relations are examples. The same entity can be referred to by numerous non-identical referring expressions while none of the expressions are tokens of that entity.

Furthermore, if one thinks of types as universals of some sort, and their tokens as instances of those universals, it should be pointed out that *particulars* can bear one-many relations to other particulars and on the assumption just made, therefore, these relations are not type-token relations. For example, many prints can be impressions of the same etched plate—as concrete a particular as one could hope for. Notice, further, that even if types are conceived as some sort of abstract particular, it would be mistaken to call the various impressions *tokens* of the *etched plate*. Consequently, the fact of the one-many relation between a musical work and its performances establishes neither that that relation is one of type-to-token, nor that the work, the sound-pattern as described above, is itself some sort of universal.

I have already suggested that musical works are particulars, on the grounds that, although each of many things can be green, and there can be numerous Bengal tigers, there cannot be more than one Beethoven *Eroica* Symphony, any more than there can be more than one George Bush, and nothing counts as *an Eroica* among many others.[9] Admittedly, this is not a conclusive argument, but the position it supports in regard to the unique identity of works of art is so intuitive that we should hold it, it seems to me, if we reasonably can.

I am proposing, then, that a musical work be conceived as an abstract particular, bearing a one-many relation other than the type-token relation to its performances.[10] A particular can bear a one-many relation to a group of objects even as those objects also stand as tokens of some type. Each coin in a certain run of U.S. nickels may be a striking from the same plate, as well as being tokens of the type: U.S. 5¢ piece, but clearly the type is not to be identified with that particular plate. I am claiming that an *abstract* particular can enter into an analogous situation: an indicated sound-pattern, musical work M, can be *realized* by various performances, even as those performances are also taken as tokens of the type: Performance of M. It does not follow that the sound pattern is identical to the performance-type, or that the performances are, precisely speaking, tokens or instances of M.

Realization of a musical sound pattern is a matter of "materializing" something that is abstractly specified; it is a matter of creating actual sound-instances-in-relation that possess the features and characteristics that are constituent of the pattern. Being a token of a type, in contrast, is a sort of membership or grouping relation. Tokens belong to their types or are said to be "in" the type. Realizations of patterns do not belong to, nor are they "in" the pattern. If anything, one says that the pattern is "in" the realizations. An animal can be *a* tiger, a sound event can be *a* performance of the Bartok Fifth Quartet by belonging to the right type, but no such event can be *a* Bartok Fifth, or "in" the Fifth because this musical work is a unique and abstract individual.

I cannot, at present, say much more about the realization relation, although more rather desperately needs to be said, if not for this paper, then for more general philosophical reasons. Versions of the realization relation play central roles in numerous philosophical theories in and beyond aesthetics. For example, computational states may be realized by electronic states in a computer, mental states may be realized by neurophysical states of the brain, cultural and aesthetic entities may be realized in certain physical objects, and so forth. But exactly how similar or different these specific relations are to that obtaining between musical works and their performances, I am not prepared to say at present. However, one point of apparent commonality in these cases is that the realization relation connects entities that are introduced at, and that occupy, different levels of theory or description, and perhaps also are entities whose ontological natures are significantly different. Realization acts as a theoretical bridge-relation and, as such, perhaps helps us to order our ontological commitments.

I believe, though, that enough has been said to make it apparent that the view presented here of musical works is different from both Wolterstorff's and Levinson's theories, although the differences are not quite the same in the two cases.

7. CONCLUSION

If my arguments, examples, and comparisons have been persuasive, we have seen that musical works are not performance-types or kinds, are not universals with many instances, but rather, are abstract particulars related to their performances (or other realizations).

Composing is not the selecting of certain properties, not the indication or manipulation of types or universals, but rather, is the specification of a musical pattern, whose elements are abstracted-sound-instances-in-relation—instances whose properties can be, to a greater or lesser extent, specified or determined by the composer. Since there is little ontological problem claiming that patterns are creatable things, we can continue to say, as common sense would have it, that musical works are created, not discovered, or merely "indicated." A robust notion of creation may well help to "tether" a given work to its composer and to certain relevant musicohistorical contexts, and I see no difficulty in this at all.

To perform a musical work is to realize intentionally the sound pattern and its specified features, in the manner indicated by the composer. For a performance to realize a musical work is not, ontologically speaking, the same thing as it is for the performance to belong to a certain performance-type.

The view that musical works are created sound-patterns, whose relation to their performances is not that of type-to-token, appears to satisfy our common sense modes of thought and discourse about music, while also being consistent and attractive at the level of closer ontological analysis. I suggest this view, then, not only for its intuitive appeal, but also as a philosophical improvement on the valuable and interesting work of Wolterstorff and Levinson.

NOTES

1. Another difference between Margolis, on one hand, and Wolterstorff and Levinson on the other, is that only Margolis distinguishes types from kinds. (In this paper, I side with Levinson and Wolterstorff and use these terms interchangeably.) Margolis' view, if I understand him, is that kinds are universals, are non-creatable, and exist even when unexemplified. Types are abstract particulars, existing only insofar as they are instantiated by their particular tokens, and are creatable (1977, 256). In addition, Margolis denies the status of physical object not only to the musical work but also to the particular performances of the work (cf. 257). Significant differences between Levinson and Wolterstorff will be noted in the text.
2. Although Wolterstorff (1975) makes most of these tenets clear, the full theory is in certain details more accessible from (1970), especially in its Introduction and Chapter 11. See pages 7, 252, 256–260. See also (1980) Part Two, especially 84–90. With (Wc), I have somewhat overstated Wolterstorff's position, or, more precisely, have reverted here to the 1970 statement of the position. Between that book and his later writings, Wolterstorff apparently came to see not only that some examples of a musical work are non-performance examples, but also that there is a difficult question whether to count as examples of a work occur-

rences of the proper sound sequence which are *neither* performances nor playings of the work. Wolterstorff's final position is that our references to works are likely to be indefinite as to whether they pick out the kinds indicated in (Wc) and (Wd) or the broader kind which allows as an example of a work any sound sequence that comes close enough to exemplifying the properties which define a correct performance of the work. Since the arguments of this paper apply to any kind which has performances among its instances, I will restrict myself to the simplified version of Wolterstorff's claims.

3. See Levinson (1980) and (1990, esp 216 and 216n). (La)'s reference to a "performed-sound structure" or (PSS) expresses Levinson's latest revision of his theory. In (1980) he referred instead to a combination of a sound structure and a performance-means structure, or "S/PM structure." The revision is meant to emphasize the unitary nature of the structure, relieving Levinson of the implication that works are combinations of two structures. The qualification noted in (Lb) captures Levinson's claim that some "performances" of a work are not instances of it; a performance of the Beethoven Op. 9 Trio on three tin whistles may be such a case (1990, 232, 236–237).

4. How is a type or kind different from a set, then, given that kinds or types do not satisfy the law of extensionality? We have to interpret the satisfaction conditions for a kind/type as supporting a certain subjunctive not supported by the membership conditions for a set. The kind K is the particulars—considered as a unity—that do satisfy C, and *would* be those particulars—considered as a unity—that *would* satisfy C, *were* the world different in certain respects (i.e., if K were to have had more or fewer examples).

5. On this point see Anderson (1985).

6. See Sircello (1972).

7. Doubtless, our intuitions regarding patterns may be overly influenced by the idea of a geometric pattern, whose components must be planar shapes, and therefore it may seem odd to call the specification of the color of those shapes "features" of a pattern. The fact is that some patterns or designs leave features such as color or means of implementation undesignated, while other patterns specify such features. Compare the pattern of the E-type Jaguar roadster to the pattern of the American flag. The "pattern theory" is therefore not inherently hostile to the idea that although timbre may be a specification of the pattern, the actual means of sound production are not essential to a work's identity. Although Levinson and I both are comfortable thinking of musical works as performance-specific, others disagree. For an argument against the inclusion of performance means as integral to the work, see Kivy (1988).

8. Thinking about either the score or the musical pattern as similar to an indefinite description is nicely compatible with my earlier point that the artistic acts of composing and specifying correctness conditions for performances are distinct but related acts. To continue with the example given of a man walking a dog, we distinguish the indefinite description of the scene or events from the imperative or command which might be given (say, by an instructor in Theater to his students) to perform or realize the scene. So too, there is a difference between the musical pattern itself and the implicit hypothetical imperative we may say the composer gives us: "If you wish to perform this work, *follow* the pattern."

9. Obviously, this claim does not deny that there can be both many performances of one work, as well as different versions of the same work, the latter point a complication I pass over here.

10. The abstractness of a particular does not stand in the way of its bearing a one-many relation to other particulars. Consider set membership. The set {1,2,3} embraces those three numbers as members, while none of them are tokens of the set. Another example: The Gettysburg Address is an abstract particular, in my view. It can be argued that it is necessarily related to both the following kind as well as the kind's examples: Kind: Screamed-out Rap renditions of the Gettysburg Address. There is, I take it, no desire to identify the Address with this kind.

REFERENCES

Anderson, James. "Musical Kinds," *British Journal of Aesthetics*, 25 (1985), 43–49.

Kivy, Peter. "Orchestrating Platonism," in T. Anderberg et al., eds., *Aesthetic Distinction*, Lund: Lund University Press, 1988, 42–55.

Levinson, Jerrold. "What a Musical Work Is," *The Journal of Philosophy*, LXXVII, No. 1 (1980), 5–28.

——. "What a Musical Work Is, Again," in Levinson's *Music, Art, and Metaphysics*, Ithaca: Cornell University Press, 1990.

Margolis, Joseph. "The Ontological Peculiarity of Works of Art," *The Journal of Aesthetics and Art Criticism*, XXXVI (1977), 45–50. Reprinted in Margolis' *Philosophy Looks at the Arts*, third edition, Philadelphia: Temple University Press, 1987. Page references are to this reprinting.

Sircello, Guy. "Expressive Properties of Art," in Sircello's *Mind and Art: An Essay on the Varieties of Expression*, Princeton: Princeton University Press, 1972, 16–46.

Wolterstorff, Nicholas. *On Universals*. Chicago: Chicago University Press, 1970.

——. "Toward an Ontology of Art Works," *Nous*, IX (1975), 115–142. Reprinted in Margolis (1987). Page references are to this reprinting.

——. *Works and Worlds of Art*. Oxford: The Clarendon Press, 1980.

Western Yoruba Gelede Mask (African). Early Twentieth Century. Gene Blocker Collection.

This mask was produced for religious ceremonial use. Before 1900, such artifacts were not valued as works of art and not appreciated aesthetically. How can such objects later be thought to possess such value?

CHAPTER 7
Aesthetic Experience and Art's Value

Roughly from the late eighteenth to the mid-twentieth century, aesthetics was approximately definable, more narrowly than it can be today, as the investigation of *aesthetic experience* and its phenomenological differences from other sorts of experience. And almost from the beginning, the outlines of the answer which would hold sway for some two hundred years were apparent. The three D's comprised the heart of this answer: disinterestedness, detachment, and distance.

Aesthetic experience was defined as the experience of objects that were to be appreciated, not because they fit in any way into our purposes or plans, and not because they fired up in us full-blooded emotional reactions in the way private events in our lives do. Aesthetic experience has a "coolness," a certain detachment. Think, for example, of the difference between appreciating someone's physical beauty and being infatuated with, or in love with, that person. Aesthetic appreciation of beauty need not bring with it the same "hot" emotions of love or infatuation. In fact, since personal feelings such as love can be very forgiving of the flaws of the loved one, one may think that a pure appreciation of beauty *requires* the kind of detachment or distance from the subject that a portraitist or photographer shows toward his or her subject.

Aesthetic experiences, however, are psychologically complex and seem to involve a broad range of human emotion, making the traditional answer seem superficial and not very clear. Consequently, it was an obvious target of analytic aesthetics' campaign against essentialism, psychologism, and conceptual confusion. The late 1950s and early 1960s saw various attempts (Vivas, Stolnitz, and Beardsley, among others) to give some clarity and precision to the conception of aesthetic experience.

Dickie sought a more radical solution in the mid-1960s. He rejected entirely the notion of a uniquely aesthetic experience as a useless and misleading "myth," the result of confused thinking and bad philosophical psychologizing. But the history of analytic aesthetics regarding aesthetic experience does not end here, for other analytic aestheticians, including Jerome Stolnitz and Beardsley, responded to Dickie by continuing to refine and remodel the concept in light of Dickie's criticisms.

Arthur Danto, as we shall see, reverses this trend, however, arguing that it is our belief that something is a work of art which determines what aesthetic properties are relevant and what the content of our aesthetic experiences will be. Danto suggests that any definition of art in terms of its capacity for producing aesthetic experience has things backwards, conceptually speaking.

In "The Myth of the Aesthetic Attitude," George Dickie asserts that it is not enough to clean up, logically speaking, the traditional notions of aesthetic experience, aesthetic attitude, and so on. All such notions are useless and misleading myths, in Dickie's view, which simply ought to be discarded, despite their impressive tradition in the history of aesthetic theory. Dickie concentrates especially on the distancing theory of Bullough (as defended by Sheila Dawson) and the theory of disinterestedness as interpreted by Stolnitz.

For Dickie it is not a question, as it was for Stolnitz, of how to describe aesthetic experience correctly, but of whether such an experience exists at all. "Are there actions denoted by 'to distance' or states of consciousness denoted by 'being distanced'?" Dickie himself can recall no such actions or experiences. The only truth in claims about distance, he says, are the obvious truisms that when we go to see a play we attend (or ought to attend) to the play and not to something else. But why introduce a confusing and misleading terminology of "distancing" and putting practical concerns "out of gear" when all you really want to say can be said much more simply and accurately in plain English?

According to Stolnitz's account of disinterestedness, we see an object with "no concern for any ulterior purpose." But what is the contrast, asks Dickie? What would it mean to listen to music interestedly? Of course, he points out, there are various reasons and motives we may have for listening to music (listening because it is a class assignment, or because one has season tickets or enjoys an occasional night out, and so on), but the *motive* or reason for listening is not a *kind* of listening. It is a separate issue which merely explains why one is listening.

Sometimes aesthetic-attitude theories are used to defend our excluding as aesthetically irrelevant certain distracting thoughts. But in that case, Dickie says, why not just say so; for if we are distracted by such thoughts, then we are no longer attending to the music or play. Concerning Bullough's famous example of the jealous husband unable to concentrate on *Othello* because of his suspicions about his wife, Dickie says the jealous husband is not attending to the play in some altered or new way, he simply is not attending to the play at all—he is thinking about his wife.

According to Dickie, it is psychologically senseless to say that the same object can be looked at in different ways or from different perspectives or points of view. In every case, Dickie argues, when we analyze such examples carefully we see that when the perspective shifts, so too does the object being attended to.

Dickie goes on to argue that by limiting aesthetically relevant attention to the perception of the object immediately in front of us, the myth of the aesthetic attitude has led us unduly to restrict what is relevant to our enjoyment of art, implying that we ought to be focused on the immediate object of perception and exclude any "distracting" contextual or background considerations, such as the moral dimension of the work. The only value the myth has had, according to Dickie, is its rhetorical role in reducing the prejudice many people had against abstract, nonobjective art, by focusing their attention on the formal and nonrepresentational aspects of such works.

Even if one finds forceful Dickie's argument that there is no particular attitude we assume when we approach art, we may not be persuaded that the concepts of aesthetic experience and uniquely aesthetic value should be jettisoned. No one has worked more persistently on such a theory than Monroe Beardsley. Beardsley suggests an interlocking set of definitions that relates the concepts of the aesthetic perspective, aesthetic value, and aesthetic experience or gratification to each other. It is an interesting example of a defense of embattled concepts through logical and definitional clarification.

Contrary to Dickie's suggestion, we often *do* apply more than one set of standards to the same object depending on our interests, needs, or desires, and our resulting judgments of the object may well vary, depending on the point of view we have adopted. A building, for example, may be well constructed but visually unattractive, good in the one sense, bad in the other. Or it may be perfect for warehousing goods, because of its size and layout, but mundane or even hideous from an architectural point of view.

In his first definition, Beardsley suggests that we understand the *aesthetic* point of view in terms of the kind of value or value-making features we are focusing on: "To adopt *an* aesthetic point of view with regard to X is to take an interest in whatever aesthetic value X may possess. . . . " This obviously moves us on to the conceptual question, "What is aesthetic value?," and Beardsley proposes a second definition: "The aesthetic value of an object is the value it possesses in virtue of its capacity to provide aesthetic gratification." As Beardsley says, he has deliberately switched from his earlier terminology of "aesthetic experience" to "aesthetic gratification" to avoid some of the difficulties raised by Dickie's critique.

While it is doubtful that anyone would object to the empirical fact that some people find certain works of art pleasing or gratifying, the central problem is to say what is meant by *aesthetic* gratification. Without this, the preceding definitions place their concepts in a logical order but give them very little substance.

And so, Beardsley proposes his final, most important definition: "Gratification is aesthetic when it is obtained primarily from attention to the formal unity and/or the regional qualities of a complex whole, and when its magnitude is a function of the degree of formal unity and/or the intensity of regional qualities."

Beardsley's clarification of aesthetic perception, aesthetic attitude, and so on, generally restricts the proper enjoyment of artworks to formal properties and excludes contextual properties, such as moral considerations.

Interestingly, Beardsley regards this feature of his theory as a plus, rather than a liability. He argues, in other words, that his account of aesthetic experience helps to clarify the idea of aesthetic relevance—strictly speaking, comments about an artwork are aesthetically relevant (as opposed to relevant from some other point of view, such as art historically, politically, culturally, biographically, etc.) only when they pertain to those features which affect aesthetic gratification—namely, the work's formal unity and regional qualities.

Goodman agrees with Beardsley that the value of art is to be found in the types of experiences it affords us, and therefore one may correctly call both of these writers "instrumentalists" regarding aesthetic value. But the sharing of this label is about all we find in common here, for Goodman holds a very different view of aesthetic experience. Generally speaking, Beardsley thinks of aesthetic experience as a private appreciation of a work's formal and regional qualities, as we have seen. Goodman, on the other hand, views aesthetic experience as a kind of cognitive decoding and understanding of the symbol that is the artwork. What we are trying to understand in aesthetic experience are the various referential functions of that symbol. The artwork, then, is not to be appreciated through any kind of mental detachment of it from everything else; on the contrary, we are trying to comprehend how it is related by its symbolic functions to other things.

Aesthetic experience is not emotional reaction, according to Goodman, and yet emotions are not irrelevant either. Rather, feeling functions *cognitively* within aesthetic experience (i.e., we identify, discriminate, and relate various emotions to grasp certain artworks and integrate them into the rest of our experience). We should not be misled, Goodman warns, by the old dichotomies of cognitive versus emotive or knowledge versus feeling. For all of its frequent emotional content, aesthetic experience is a form of cognitive inquiry and a potential source of knowledge.

But if this is so, what distinguishes the *aesthetic* experience from cognitive inquiries of a nonaesthetic nature? For Goodman, there is no special attitude or emotion which marks an experience as aesthetic. Aesthetic experience is not so much a distinctive cognitive mode as it is a cognitive activity focused on distinctive types of symbols. There are certain semantic and syntactic features of the symbol systems involved in the arts that can be treated as "symptoms" of the aesthetic. These include semantic and syntactic density, syntactic repleteness, exemplification, and multiple and complex reference. (For an explanation of these technical notions, see Dickie's second article in this chapter.) These symptoms are a far cry from any introspectible characteristics marking the reactions or thoughts we may have had in the presence of an artwork.

In "In Defense of Aesthetic Value," Beardsley again supports the instrumentalist or "functional" view, as he calls it in this later piece, attempting to bolster this position against the early counterarguments of Dickie and the competing picture of Goodman. This excerpt is valuable for its proposal (*contra* Goodman) of the phenomenological "symptoms" of an aesthetic experience, as well as for its general criticisms of Goodman's view that aesthetic value is not distinguishable from the *cognitive* value of an artwork.

As Dickie points out, Goodman's view of aesthetic *value* is a consequence of this picture of aesthetic experience. The value of art can be measured by its *cognitive efficacy*, according to Goodman, and efficacy has to do with how well the artwork participates in the making, manipulation, retention, and transformation of knowledge. Dickie takes exception to this view of aesthetic value and specifically tries to show that there must be other sources of value beyond that which accrues to the work of art as a result of the efficacy with which it exemplifies certain of its properties. Some degree of aesthetic value also derives from the fact that works often simply possess gorgeous features which are open to Beardslean appreciation, and sometimes the significance of what is represented in a work adds to its aesthetic value. Dickie claims (perhaps not wholly persuasively) that neither of these sources of value is captured by Goodman's position that aesthetic value is a matter of the work's cognitive efficacy. In "Instrumental Cognitivism," Dickie attempts a synthesis of Beardsley's and Goodman's views.

As we mentioned earlier, Danto believes that the logical "direction" of Beardsley's series of definitions is backwards. Art and the aesthetic point of view cannot be defined in terms of aesthetic experience or gratification, according to Danto, because the nature and quality of our aesthetic responses *presuppose* that we are viewing the objects of those responses as works of art.

Danto arrives at this conclusion as a consequence of his long-term interest in *perceptual indiscernibles*, that is, two objects that are perceptually identical, but only one of which is an artwork. If we respond to the two in aesthetically different ways, which Danto says we do, then aesthetic response cannot be a response to the objects' appearance alone since by hypothesis that is identical in two cases. Shouldn't our aesthetic responses to two objects be the same if the objects cannot be perceptually distinguished one from the other? Consider the famous case of Duchamp's urinal, *The Fountain*, which Duchamp exhibited as a work of art in 1917. As an artwork, *The Fountain*'s most important aesthetic properties are its wittiness, daring, impudence, and irreverence—hardly the features we would attribute to a visually identical urinal in its natural setting!

Danto's point is that these properties are revealed only if and when we first come to believe that this is an artwork. Before Duchamp, no amount of aesthetic perception or attention to a urinal from the aesthetic point of view would have revealed an impudent quality, though it might have caused us to notice its pleasing oval shape. Learning that *The Fountain* is a work of art does not simply shift our focus to properties which had previously been ignored in other urinals. Works of art, through their status as art, have qualities to attend to which their untransfigured counterparts simply lack, no matter how perceptually similar their surfaces may be. Artworks are, ontologically, a "different order of things" from their nonart counterparts, Danto claims.

It is debatable, however, whether either the ontological differences separating artworks from counterparts, or the psychological fact that we must first believe that an object *is* a work of art before being willing to ascribe certain aesthetic properties to it, establishes that Beardsley errs when he defines art ultimately in terms of aesthetic experience or gratification. Consider a different but related example. A specialized tool of some sort may be correctly defined *instrumentally* in terms of its intended function, even if it is true that we can recognize and respond to its particularly well-designed features or properties only after we identify it as the special tool it is.

The Myth of the Aesthetic Attitude

George Dickie

Some recent articles[1] have suggested the unsatisfactoriness of the notion of the aesthetic attitude and it is now time for a fresh look at that encrusted article of faith. This conception has been valuable to aesthetics and criticism in helping wean them from a sole concern with beauty and related notions.[2] However, I shall argue that the aesthetic attitude is a myth and while, as G. Ryle has said, "Myths often do a lot of theoretical good while they are still new,"[3] this particular one is no longer useful and in fact misleads aesthetic theory.

There is a range of theories which differ according to how strongly the aesthetic attitude is characterized. This variation is reflected in the language the theories employ. The strongest variety is Edward Bullough's theory of physical distance, recently defended by Sheila Dawson.[4] The central technical term of this theory is "distance" used as a verb to denote an action which either constitutes or is necessary for the aesthetic attitude. These theorists use such sentences as "He distanced (or failed to distance) the play." The second variety is widely held but has been defended most vigorously in recent years by Jerome Stolnitz and Eliseo Vivas. The *central* technical term of this variety is "disinterested"[5] used either as an adverb or as an adjective. This weaker theory speaks not of a special kind of action (distancing) but of an ordinary kind of action (attending) done in a certain way (disinterestedly). These first two versions are perhaps not as different as my classification suggests. However, the language of the two is different enough to justify separate discussions. My discussion of this second variety will for the most part make use of Jerome Stolnitz' book[6] which is a thorough, consistent, and large-scale version of the attitude theory. The weakest version of the attitude theory can be found in Vincent Tomas' statement "If looking at a picture and attending closely to how it looks is not really to be in the aesthetic attitude, then what on earth is?"[7] In the following I shall be concerned with the notion of *aesthetic* attitude and this notion may have little or no connection with the ordinary notion of an *attitude*.

I

Psychical distance, according to Bullough, is a psychological process by virtue of which a person *puts* some object (be it a painting, a play, or a dangerous fog at sea) "out of gear" with the practical interests of the self. Miss Dawson maintains that it is "the beauty of the phenomenon, which captures our attention, puts us out of gear with practical life, and forces us, if we are receptive, to view it on the level of aesthetic consciousness."[8]

Later she maintains that some persons (critics, actors, members of an orchestra, and the like) "distance deliberately."[9] Miss Dawson, following Bullough, discusses cases in which people are unable to bring off an act of distancing or are incapable of being induced into a state of being distanced. She uses Bullough's example of the jealous ("underdistanced") husband at a performance of

---

From *The American Philosophical Quarterly*, 1 (1964). Reprinted by permission of the publisher.

Othello who is unable to keep his attention on the play because he keeps thinking of his own wife's suspicious behavior. On the other hand, if "we are mainly concerned with the technical details of its [the play's] presentation, then we are said to be over-distanced."[10] There is, then, a species of action—distancing—which may be deliberately done and which initiates a state of consciousness—being distanced.

The question is: Are there actions denoted by "to distance" or states of consciousness denoted by "being distanced"? When the curtain goes up, when we walk up to a painting, or when we look at a sunset are we ever induced into a state of being distanced either by being struck by the beauty of the object or by pulling off an act of distancing? I do not recall committing any such special actions or of being induced into any special state, and I have no reason to suspect that I am atypical in this respect. The distance-theorist may perhaps ask, "But are you not usually oblivious to noises and sights other than those of the play or to the marks on the wall around the painting?" The answer is of course—"Yes." But if "to distance" and "being distanced" simply mean that one's attention is focused, what is the point of introducing new technical terms and speaking as if these terms refer to special kinds of acts and states of consciousness? The distance-theorist might argue further, "But surely you put the play (painting, sunset) 'out of gear' with your practical interests?" This question seems to me to be a very odd way of asking (by employing the technical metaphor "out of gear") if I attended to the play rather than thought about my wife or wondered how they managed to move the scenery about. Why not ask me straight out if I paid attention? Thus, when Miss Dawson says that the jealous husband underdistanced *Othello* and that the person with a consuming interest in techniques of stagecraft over-distanced the play, these are just technical and misleading ways of describing two different cases of inattention. In both cases something is being attended to, but in neither case is it the action of the play. To introduce the technical terms "distance," "under-distance," and "over-distance" does nothing but send us chasing after phantom acts and states of consciousness.

Miss Dawson's commitment to the theory of distance (as a kind of mental insulation material necessary for a work of art if it is to be enjoyed aesthetically) leads her to draw a conclusion so curious as to throw suspicion on the theory.

One remembers the horrible loss of distance in *Peter Pan*—the moment when Peter says "Do you believe in fairies? . . . If you believe, clap your hands!" the moment when most children would like to slink out of the theatre and not a few cry—not because Tinkerbell may die, but because the magic is gone. What, after all, should we feel like if Lear were to leave Cordelia, come to the front of the stage and say, "All the grown-ups who think that she loves me, shout 'Yes'."[11]

It is hard to believe that the responses of any children could be as theory-bound as those Miss Dawson describes. In fact, Peter Pan's request for applause is a dramatic high point to which children respond enthusiastically. The playwright gives the children a momentary chance to become actors in the play. The children do not at that moment lose or snap out of a state of being distanced because they never had or were in any such thing to begin with. The comparison of Peter Pan's appeal to the hypothetical one by Lear is pointless. *Peter Pan* is a magical play in which almost anything can happen, but *King Lear* is a play of a different kind. There are, by the way, many plays in which an actor directly addresses the audience (*Our Town, The Marriage Broker, A Taste of Honey*, for example) without causing the play to be less valuable. Such plays are unusual, but what is unusual is not necessarily bad; there is no point in trying to lay down rules to which every play must conform independently of the kind of play it is.

It is perhaps worth noting that Susanne Langer reports the reaction she had as a child to this scene in *Peter Pan*.[12] As she remembers it, Peter Pan's appeal shattered the illusion and caused her acute misery. However, she reports that all the other children clapped and laughed and enjoyed themselves.

II

The second way of conceiving of the aesthetic attitude—as the ordinary action of attending done in a certain way (disinterestedly)—is illustrated by the work of Jerome Stolnitz and Eliseo Vivas. Stolnitz defines "aesthetic attitude" as "disinterested and sympathetic attention to and contemplation of any object of awareness whatever, for its own sake alone."[13] Stolnitz defines the main terms of his definition: "disinterested" means "no concern for any ulterior purpose";[14] "sympathetic" means "accept the object on its own terms to appreciate it";[15] and "contemplation" means "perception directed toward the object in its own right and the spectator is not concerned to analyze it or ask questions about it."[16]

The notion of disinterestedness, which Stolnitz has elsewhere shown[17] to be seminal for modern aesthetic theory, is the key term here. Thus, it is necessary to be clear about the nature of disinterested attention to the various arts. It can make sense to speak, for example, of listening disinterestedly to music only if it makes sense to speak of listening interestedly to music. It would make no sense to speak of walking *fast* unless walking could be done *slowly*. Using Stolnitz' definition of "disinterestedness," the two situations would have to be described as "listening with no ulterior purpose" (disinterestedly) and "listening with an ulterior purpose" (interestedly). Note that what initially appears to be a perceptual distinction—listening in a certain way (interestedly or disinterestedly)—turns out to be a motivational or an intentional distinction—listening for or with a certain purpose. Suppose Jones listens to a piece of music for the purpose of being able to analyze and describe it on an examination the next day and Smith listens to the same music with no such ulterior purpose. There is certainly a difference between the motives and intentions of the two men: Jones has an ulterior purpose and Smith does not, but this does not mean Jones's *listening* differs from Smith's. It is possible that both men enjoy the music or that both be bored. The attention of either or both may flag and so on. It is important to note that a person's motive or intention is different from his action (Jones's listening to the music, for example). There is only one way to *listen* to (to attend to) music, although the listening may be more or less attentive and there may be a variety of motives, intentions, and reasons for doing so and a variety of ways of being distracted from the music.

In order to avoid a common mistake of aestheticians—drawing a conclusion about one kind of art and assuming it holds for all the arts—the question of disinterested attention must be considered for arts other than music. How would one look at a painting disinterestedly or interestedly? An example of alleged interested viewing might be the case in which a painting reminds Jones of his grandfather and Jones proceeds to muse about or to regale a companion with tales of his grandfather's pioneer exploits. Such incidents would be characterized by attitude-theorists as examples of using a work of art as a vehicle for associations and so on, i.e., cases of interested attention. But Jones is not looking at (attending to) the painting at all, although he may be facing it with his eyes open. Jones is now musing or attending to the story he is telling, although he had to look at the painting at first to notice that it resembled his grandfather. Jones is not now looking at the painting interestedly, since his is not now looking at (attending to) the painting. Jones's thinking or telling a story about his grandfather is no more a part of the painting than his speculating about the artist's intentions is and, hence, his musing, telling, speculating, and so on cannot properly be described as attending to the painting interestedly. What attitude-aestheticians are calling attention to is the occurrence of irrelevant associations which distract the viewer from the painting or whatever. But distraction is not a special kind of attention, it is a kind of inattention.

Consider now disinterestedness and plays.

I shall make use of some interesting examples offered by J. O. Urmson,[18] but I am not claiming that Urmson is an attitude-theorist. Urmson never speaks in his article of aesthetic attitude but rather of aesthetic satisfaction. In addition to aesthetic satisfaction, Urmson mentions economic, moral, personal, and intellectual satisfactions. I think the attitude-theorist would consider these last four kinds of satisfaction as "ulterior purposes" and, hence, cases of interested attention. Urmson considers the case of a man in the audience of a play who is delighted.[19] It is discovered that his delight is *solely* the result of the fact that there is a full house—the man is the impresario of the production. Urmson is right in calling *this* impresario's satisfaction economic rather than aesthetic, although there is a certain oddness about the example as it finds the impresario sitting *in the audience*. However, my concern is not with Urmson's examples as such but with the attitude theory. This impresario is certainly an interested party in the fullest sense of the word, but is his behavior an instance of interested attention as distinct from the supposed disinterested attention of the average citizen who sits beside him? In the situation as described by Urmson it would not make any sense to say that the impresario is attending to the play at all, since his *sole* concern at the moment is the till. If he can be said to be attending to anything (rather than just thinking about it) it is the size of the house. I do not mean to suggest that an impresario could not attend to his play if he found himself taking up a seat in a full house; I am challenging the sense of disinterested attention. As an example of personal satisfaction Urmson mentions the spectator whose daughter is in the play. Intellectual satisfaction involves the solution of technical problems of plays and moral satisfaction the consideration of the effects of the play on the viewer's conduct. All three of these candidates which the attitude-theorist would propose as cases of interested attention turn out to be just different ways of being distracted from the play and, hence, not cases of interested attention to the play. Of course, there is no reason to think that in any of these cases the distraction or inattention must be total, although it could be. In fact, such inattentions often occur but are so fleeting that nothing of the play, music, or whatever is missed or lost.

The example of a playwright watching a rehearsal or an out-of-town performance with a view to rewriting the script has been suggested to me as a case in which a spectator is certainly attending to the play (unlike our impresario) and attending in an interested manner. This case is unlike those just discussed but is similar to the earlier case of Jones (not Smith) listening to a particular piece of music. Our playwright—like Jones, who was to be examined on the music—has ulterior motives. Furthermore, the playwright, unlike an ordinary spectator, can change the script after the performance or during a rehearsal. But how is our playwright's *attention* (as distinguished from his motives and intentions) different from that of an ordinary viewer? The playwright might enjoy or be bored by the performance as any spectator might be. The playwright's attention might even flag. In short, the kinds of things which may happen to the playwright's attention are no different from those that may happen to an ordinary spectator, although the two may have quite different motives and intentions.

For the discussion of disinterested-interested reading of literature it is appropriate to turn to the arguments of Eliseo Vivas whose work is largely concerned with literature. Vivas remarks that "By approaching a poem in a nonaesthetic mode it may function as history, as social criticism, as diagnostic evidence of the author's neuroses, and in an indefinite number of other ways."[20] Vivas further notes that according to Plato "the Greeks used Homer as an authority on war and almost anything under the sun," and that a certain poem "can be read as erotic poetry or as an account of a mystical experience."[21] The difference between reading a poem *as* history or whatever (reading it nonaesthetically) and reading it aesthetically depends on how *we* approach or read it. A poem "does not come self-labelled,"[22] but presumably is a poem only when it is read in a certain way—when it is an object of aesthetic experience. For Vivas, being an aesthetic object means being the object of the aesthetic attitude. He defines the aesthetic experience as "an experience of rapt attention which involves the intransitive apprehension of an object's immanent meanings and values in their full presentational immediacy."[23] Vivas maintains that his definition "helps me understand better what I can and what I cannot do when I read *The Brothers [Karamazov]*" and his definition "forces us to acknowledge that *The Brothers Karamazov* can hardly be read as art. . . . "[24] This acknowledgment means that we probably cannot intransitively apprehend *The Brothers* because of its size and complexity.

"Intransitive" is the key term here and Vivas' meaning must be made clear. A number of passages reveal his meaning but perhaps the following is the best. "Having once seen a hockey game in slow motion, I am prepared to testify that it was an object of pure intransitive experience [attention]—for I was not *interested* in which team won the game and no external factors mingled with my interest in the beautiful rhythmic flow of the slow-moving men."[25] It appears that Vivas' "intrinsic attention" has the same meaning as Stolnitz' "disinterested attention," namely, "attending with no ulterior purpose."[26] Thus, the question to ask is "How does one attend to (read) a poem or any literary work transitively?" One can certainly attend to (read) a poem for a variety of different purposes and because of a variety of different reasons, but can one attend to a poem transitively? I do not think so, but let us consider the examples Vivas offers. He mentions "a type of reader" who uses a poem or parts of a poem as a spring-board for "loose, uncontrolled, relaxed day-dreaming, wool-gathering rambles, free from the contextual control" of the poem.[27] But surely it would be wrong to say such musing is a case of transitively attending to a poem, since it is clearly a case of not attending to a poem. Another supposed way of attending to a poem transitively is by approaching it "as diagnostic evidence of the author's neuroses." Vivas is right if he means that there is no critical point in doing this since it does not throw light on the poem. But this is a case of *using* information gleaned from a poem to make inferences about its author rather than attending to a poem. If anything can be said to be attended to here it is the author's neuroses (at least they are being thought about). This kind of case is perhaps best thought of as a rather special way of getting distracted from a poem. Of course, such "biographical" distractions might be insignificant and momentary enough so as scarcely to distract attention from the poem (a flash of insight or understanding about the poet). On the other hand, such distractions may turn into dissertations and whole careers. Such an interest may lead a reader to concentrate his attention (when he does read a poem) on certain "informational" aspects of a poem and to ignore the remaining aspects. As deplorable as such a sustained practice may be, it is at best a case of attending to certain features of a poem and ignoring others.

Another way that poetry may allegedly be read transitively is by reading it as history. This case is different from the two preceding ones since poetry often *contains* history (makes historical statements or at least references) but does not (usually) contain statements about the author's neuroses and so on nor does it contain statements about what a reader's free associations are about (otherwise we would not call them "*free* associations"). Reading a poem as history suggests that we are attending to (thinking about) historical events by way of attending to a poem—the poem is a time-telescope. Consider the following two sets of lines:

In fourteen hundred and ninety-two
  Columbus sailed the ocean blue.

Or like stout Cortez when with eagle eyes
  He star'd at the Pacific—and all his men
Look'd at each other with a wild surmise—
  Silent, upon a peak in Darien.

Someone might read both of these raptly and not know that they make historical references (inaccurately in one case)—might this be a case of intransitive attention? How would the above reading differ—so far as attention is concerned—from the case of a reader who recognized the historical content of the poetic lines? The two readings do not differ as far as attention is concerned. History is a part of these sets of poetic lines and the two readings differ in that the first fails to take account of an aspect of the poetic lines (its historical content) and the second does not fail to do so. Perhaps by "reading as history" Vivas means "reading *simply* as history." But even this meaning does not mark out a special kind of attention but rather means that only a single aspect of a poem is being noticed and that its rhyme, meter, and so on are ignored. Reading a poem as social criticism can be analyzed in a fashion similar to reading as history. Some poems simply are or contain social criticism, and a complete reading must not fail to notice this fact.

The above cases of alleged interested attending can be sorted out in the following way. Jones listening to the music and our playwright watching the rehearsal are both attending with ulterior motives to a work of art, but there is no reason to suppose that the attention of either is different in kind from that of an ordinary spectator. The reader who reads a poem as history is simply attending to an aspect of a poem. On the other hand, the remaining cases—Jones beside the painting telling of his grandfather, the gloating impresario, daydreaming while "reading" a poem, and so on—are simply cases of not attending to the work of art.

In general, I conclude that "disinterestedness" or "intransitiveness" cannot properly be used to refer to a special kind of attention. "Disinterestedness" is a term which is used to make clear that an action has certain kinds of motives. Hence, we speak of disinterested findings (of boards of inquiry), disinterested verdicts (of judges and juries), and so on. Attending to an object, of course, has its motives but the attending itself is not interested or disinterested according to whether its motives are of the kind which motivate interested or disinterested action (as findings and verdicts might), although the attending may be more or less close.

I have argued that the second way of conceiving the aesthetic attitude is also a myth, or at least that its main content—disinterested attention—is; but I must now try to establish that the view misleads aesthetic theory. I shall argue that the attitude-theorist is incorrect about (1) the way in which he wishes to set the limits of aesthetic relevance; (2) the relation of the critic to a work of art; and (3) the relation of morality to aesthetic value.

Since I shall make use of the treatment of aesthetic relevance in Jerome Stolnitz' book, let me make clear that I am not necessarily denying the relevance of the specific items he cites but disagreeing with his criterion of relevance. His criterion of relevance is derived from his definition of "aesthetic attitude" and is set forth at the very beginning of his book. This procedure leads Monroe Beardsley in his review of the book to remark that Stolnitz' discussion is premature.[28] Beardsley suggests "that relevance cannot be satisfactorily discussed until after a careful treatment of the several arts, their dimensions and capacities."[29]

First, what is meant by "aesthetic relevance?" Stolnitz defines the problem by asking the question: "Is it ever 'relevant' to the aesthetic experience to have thoughts or images or bits of knowledge which are not present within the object itself?"[30] Stolnitz begins by summarizing Bullough's experiment and discussion of single colors and associations.[31] Some associations absorb the spectator's attention and distract him from the color and some associations "fuse" with the color. Associations of the latter kind are aesthetic and the former are not. Stolnitz draws the following conclusion about associations:

If the aesthetic experience is as we have described it, then whether an association is aesthetic depends on whether it is compatible with the attitude of "disinterested attention." If the association reenforces the focusing of attention upon the object, by "fusing" with the object and thereby giving it added "life and significance," it is genuinely aesthetic. If, however, it arrogates attention to itself and away from the object, it undermines the aesthetic attitude.[32]

It is not clear how something could *fuse* with a single color, but "fusion" is one of those words in aesthetics which is rarely defined. Stolnitz then makes use of a more fruitful example, one from I. A. Richards' *Practical Criticism*.[33] He cites the responses of students to the poem which begins:

Between the erect and solemn trees
I will go down upon my knees;
I shall not find this day
So meet a place to pray.

The image of a rugby forward running arose in the mind of one student-reader on reading the third verse of this poem. A cathedral was suggested to a second reader of the poem. The cathedral image "is congruous with both the verbal meaning of the poem and the emotions and mood which it expresses. It does not divert attention away from the poem."[34] The rugby image is presumably incongruous and diverts attention from the poem.

It is a confusion to take compatibility with disinterested attention as a criterion of relevance. If, as I have tried to show, *disinterested attention* is a confused notion, then it will not do as a satisfactory criterion. Also, when Stolnitz comes to show why the cathedral image is, and the rugby image is not relevant, the criterion he actually uses is *congruousness with the meaning of the poem*, which is quite independent of the notion of disinterestedness. The problem is perhaps best described as the problem of relevance to a poem, or more generally, to a work of art, rather than aesthetic relevance.

A second way in which the attitude theory misleads aesthetics is its contention that a critic's relationship to a work of art is different in kind from the relationship of other persons to the work. H. S. Langfeld in an early statement of this view wrote that we may "slip from the attitude of aesthetic enjoyment to the attitude of the critic." He characterizes the critical attitude as "intellectually occupied in coldly estimating . . . merits" and the aesthetic attitude as responding "emotionally to" a work of art.[35] At the beginning of his book in the discussion of the aesthetic attitude, Stolnitz declares that if a percipient of a work of art "has the purpose of passing judgment upon it, his attitude is not aesthetic."[36] He develops this line at a later stage of his book, arguing that appreciation (perceiving with the aesthetic attitude) and criticism (seeking for reasons to support an evaluation of a work) are (1) distinct and (2) "psychologically opposed to each other."[37] The critical attitude is questioning, analytical, probing for strengths and weakness, and so on. The aesthetic attitude is just the opposite: "It commits our allegiance to the object freely and unquestioningly"; "the spectator 'surrenders' himself to the work of art."[38] "Just because the two attitudes are inimical, whenever criticism obtrudes, it reduces aesthetic interest."[39] Stolnitz does not, of course, argue that criticism is unimportant for appreciation. He maintains criticism plays an important and necessary role in preparing a person to appreciate the nuances, detail, form, and so on of works of art. We are quite right, he says, thus to read and listen perceptively and acutely, but he questions, "Does this mean that we must analyze, measure in terms of value-criteria, etc., *during* the supposedly aesthetic experience?"[40] His answer is "No" and he maintains that criticism must occur "*prior* to the aesthetic encounter,"[41] or it will interfere with appreciation.

How does Stolnitz know that criticism will always interfere with appreciation? His conclusion sounds like one based upon the observations of actual cases, but I do not think it is. I believe it is a logical consequence of his definition of aesthetic attitude in terms of disinterested attention (no ulterior purpose). According to his view, to appreciate an object aesthetically one has to perceive it with no ulterior purpose. But the critic has an ulterior purpose—to analyze and evaluate the object he perceives—hence, in so far as a person functions as a critic he cannot function as an appreciator. But here, as previously, Stolnitz confuses a perceptual distinction with a motivational one. If it were possible to *attend* disinterestedly or interestedly, then perhaps the critic (as percipient) would differ from other percipients. But if my earlier argument about attending is correct, the critic differs from other percipients only in his motives and intentions and not in the way in which he attends to a work of art.

Of course, it might just be a fact that the search for reasons is incompatible with the appreciation of art, but I do not think it is. Several years ago I participated in a series of panel discussions of films. During the showing of each film we were to discuss, I had to take note of various aspects of the film (actor's performance, dramatic development, organization of the screen-plane and screen-space at given moments, and so on) in order later to discuss the films. I believe that this practice not only helped educate me to appreciate subsequent films but that it enhanced the appreciation of the films I was analyzing. I noticed and was able to appreciate things about the films I was watching which ordinarily out of laziness I would not have noticed. I see no reason why the same should not be the case with the professional critic or any critical percipient. If many professional critics seem to appreciate so few works, it is not because they are critics, but perhaps because the percentage of good works of art is fairly small and they suffer from a kind of combat fatigue.

I am unable to see any significant difference between "perceptively and acutely" attending to a work of art (which Stolnitz holds enhances appreciation) and searching for reasons, so far as the experience of a work of art is concerned. If I attend perceptively and acutely, I will have certain standards and/or paradigms in mind (not necessarily consciously) and will be keenly aware of the elements and relations in the work and will evaluate them to some degree. Stolnitz writes as if criticism takes place and then is over and done with, but the search for and finding of reasons (noticing this fits in with that, and so on) is continuous in practiced appreciators. A practiced viewer does not even have to be looking for a reason, he may just notice a line or an area in a painting, for example, and the line or area becomes a reason why he thinks the painting better or worse. A person may be a critic (not necessarily a good one) without meaning to be or without even realizing it.

There is one final line worth pursuing. Stolnitz' remarks suggest that one reason he thinks criticism and appreciation incompatible is that they compete with one another for time (this would be especially bad in the cases of performed works). But seeking and finding reasons (criticism) does not compete for time with appreciation. First, to seek for a reason means to be ready and able to notice something and to be thus ready and able as one attends does not compete for time with the attending. In fact, I should suppose that seeking for reasons would tend to focus attention more securely on the work of art. Second, finding a reason is an achievement, like winning a race. (It takes time to run a race but not to win it.) Consider the finding of the following reasons. How much time does it take to "see" that a note is off key (or on key)? How long does it take to notice that an actor mispronounces a word (or does it right)? How much time does it take to realize that a character's action does not fit his already established personality? (One is struck by it.) How long does it take to apprehend that a happy ending is out of place? It does not take time to find any of these reasons or reasons in general. Finding a reason is like coming to understand—it is done in a flash. I do not mean to suggest that one cannot be mistaken in finding a reason. What may appear to be a fault or a merit (a found reason) in the middle of a performance (or during one look at a painting and so forth) may turn out to be just the opposite when seen from the perspective of the whole performance (or other looks at the painting).

A third way in which the attitude theory misleads aesthetic theory is its contention that aesthetic value is always independent of morality. This view is perhaps not peculiar to the attitude theory, but it is a logical consequence of the attitude approach. Two quotations from attitude-theorists will establish the drift of their view of morality and aesthetic value.

We are either concerned with the beauty of the object or with some other value of the same. Just as soon, for example, as ethical considerations occur to our mind, our attitude shifts.[42]

Any of us might reject a novel because it seems to conflict with our moral beliefs . . . When we do so . . . we have *not* read the book aesthetically, for we have interposed moral . . . responses of our own which are alien to it. This disrupts the aesthetic attitude. We cannot then say that the novel is *aesthetically* bad, for we have not permitted ourselves to consider it aesthetically. To maintain the aesthetic attitude, we must follow the lead of the object and respond in concert with it.[43]

This conception of the aesthetic attitude functions to hold the moral aspects and the *aesthetic* aspects of the work of art firmly apart. Presumably, although it is difficult to see one's way clearly here, the moral aspects of a work of art cannot be an object of aesthetic attention because aesthetic attention is by definition disinterested and the moral aspects are somehow practical (interested). I suspect that there are a number of confusions involved in the assumption of the incompatibility of aesthetic attention and the moral aspects of art, but I shall not attempt to make these clear, since the root of the assumption—disinterested attention—is a confused notion. Some way other than in terms of the aesthetic attitude, then, is needed to discuss the relation of morality and aesthetic value.

David Pole in a recent article[44] has argued that the moral vision which a work of art may embody is *aesthetically* significant. It should perhaps be remarked at this point that not all works of art embody a moral vision and perhaps some kinds of art (music, for example) cannot embody a moral vision, but certainly some novels, some poems, and some films and plays do. I assume it is unnecessary to show how novels and so on have this moral aspect. Pole notes the curious fact that while so many critics approach works of art in "overtly moralistic terms," it is a "philosophical commonplace . . . that the ethical and the aesthetic modes . . . form different categories."[45] I suspect that many philosophers would simply say that these critics are confused about their roles. But Pole assumes that philosophical theory "should take notice of practice"[46] and surely he is right. In agreeing with Pole's assumption I should like to reserve the right to argue in specific cases that a critic may be misguided. This right is especially necessary in a field such as aesthetics because the language and practice of critics is so often burdened with ancient theory. Perhaps *all* moralistic criticism is wrong but philosophers should not rule it out of order at the very beginning by use of a definition.

Pole thinks that the moral vision presented by a particular work of art will be either true or false (perhaps a mixture of true and false might occur). If a work has a false moral vision, then something "is lacking within the work itself. But to say that is to say that the [work] is internally incoherent; some particular aspect must jar with what—on the strength of the rest—we claim a right to demand. And here the moral fault that we have found will count as an aesthetic fault too."[47] Pole is trying to show that the assessment of the moral vision of a work of art is just a special case of coherence or incoherence, and since everyone would agree that coherence is an aesthetic category, the assessment of the moral vision is an aesthetic assessment.

I think Pole's conclusion is correct but take exception to some of his arguments. First, I am uncertain whether it is proper to speak of a moral vision being true or false, and would want to make a more modest claim—that a moral vision can be judged to be acceptable or unacceptable. (I am not claiming Pole is wrong and my claim is not inconsistent with his.) Second, I do not see that a false (or unacceptable) moral vision makes a work incoherent. I should suppose that to say a work is coherent or incoherent is to speak about how its parts fit together and this involves no reference to something outside the work as the work's truth or falsity does.

In any event, it seems to me that a faulty

moral vision can be shown to be an aesthetic fault independently of Pole's consideration of truth and coherence. As Pole's argument implies, a work's moral vision is a *part* of the work. Thus, any statement—descriptive or evaluative—about the work's moral vision is a statement about the *work*; and any statement about a *work* is a critical statement and, hence, falls within the aesthetic domain. To judge a moral vision to be morally unacceptable is to judge it defective and this amounts to saying that the work of art has a defective part. (Of course, a judgment of the acceptability of a moral vision may be wrong, as a judgment of an action sometimes is, but this fallibility does not make any difference.) Thus, a work's moral vision may be an aesthetic merit or defect just as a work's degree of unity is a merit or defect. But what justifies saying that a moral vision is a part of a work of art? Perhaps "part" is not quite the right word but it serves to make the point clear enough. A novel's moral vision is an essential part of the novel and if it were removed (I am not sure how such surgery could be carried out) the novel would be greatly changed. Anyway, a novel's moral vision is not like its covers or binding. However, someone might still argue that even though a work's moral vision is defective and the moral vision is part of the work, that this defect is not an *aesthetic* defect. How is "aesthetic" being used here? It is being used to segregate certain aspects or parts of works of art such as formal and stylistic aspects from such aspects as a work's moral vision. But it seems to me that the separation is only nominal. "Aesthetic" has been selected as a name for a certain sub-set of characteristics of works of art. I certainly cannot object to such a stipulation, since an underlying aim of this essay is to suggest the vacuousness of the term "aesthetic." My concern at this point is simply to insist that a work's moral vision is a part of the work and that, therefore, a critic can legitimately describe and evaluate it. I would *call* any defect or merit which a critic can legitimately point out an aesthetic defect or merit, but what we call it does not matter.

It would, of course, be a mistake to judge a work solely on the basis of its moral vision (it is only one part). The fact that some critics have judged works of art in this way is perhaps as much responsible as the theory of aesthetic attitude for the attempts to separate morality from the aesthetic. In fact, such criticism is no doubt at least partly responsible for the rise of the notion of the aesthetic attitude.

If the foregoing arguments are correct, the second way of conceiving the aesthetic attitude misleads aesthetic theory in at least three ways.

III

In answer to a hypothetical question about what is seen in viewing a portrait with the aesthetic attitude, Tomas in part responds "If looking at a picture and attending closely to how it looks is not really to be in the aesthetic attitude, then what on earth is?"[48] I shall take this sentence as formulating the weakest version of the aesthetic attitude. (I am ignoring Tomas' distinction between appearance and reality. See footnote 7. My remarks, thus, are not a critique of Tomas' argument; I am simply using one of his sentences.) First, this sentence speaks only of "looking at a picture," but "listening to a piece of music," "watching and listening to a play," and so on could be added easily enough. After thus expanding the sentence, it can be contracted into the general form: "Being in the aesthetic attitude is attending closely to a work of art (or a natural object)."

But the aesthetic attitude ("the hallmark of modern aesthetics") in this formulation is a great letdown—it no longer seems to say anything significant. Nevertheless, this does seem to be all that is left after the aesthetic attitude has been purged of *distancing* and *disinterestedness*. The only thing which prevents the aesthetic attitude from collapsing into simple attention is the qualification *closely*. One may, I suppose, attend to a work of art more or less closely, but this fact does not seem to signify anything very important. When "being in the aesthetic attitude" is equated with "attending (closely)," the equation neither involves any mythical element nor could it possibly mislead aesthetic theory. But if the definition has no vices, it seems to have no virtues either. When the aesthetic attitude finally turns out to be simply attending (closely), the final version should perhaps not be called "the weakest" but rather "the vacuous version" of the aesthetic attitude.

Stolnitz is no doubt historically correct that the notion of the aesthetic attitude has played an important role in the freeing of aesthetic theory from an overweening concern with beauty. It is easy to see how the slogan, "Anything can become an object of the aesthetic attitude," could help accomplish this liberation. It is worth noting, however, that the same goal could have been (and perhaps to some extent was) realized by simply noting that works of art are often ugly or contain ugliness, or have features which are difficult to include within beauty. No doubt, in more recent times people have been encouraged *to take an aesthetic attitude toward a painting* as a way of lowering their prejudices, say, against abstract and nonobjective art. So if the notion of aesthetic attitude has turned out to have no theoretical value for aesthetics, it has had practical value for the appreciation of art in a way similar to that of Clive Bell's suspect notion of significant form.

NOTES

1. See Marshall Cohen, "Appearance and the Aesthetic Attitude," *Journal of Philosophy*, vol. 56 (1959), p. 926; and Joseph Margolis, "Aesthetic Perception," *Journal of Aesthetics and Art Criticism*, vol. 19 (1960), p. 211. Margolis gives an argument, but it is so compact as to be at best only suggestive.
2. Jerome Stolnitz, "Some Questions Concerning Aesthetic Perception," *Philosophy and Phenomenological Research*, vol. 22 (1961), p. 69.
3. *The Concept of Mind* (London, 1949), p. 23.
4. " 'Distancing' as an Aesthetic Principle," *Australasian Journal of Philosophy*, vol. 39 (1961), pp. 155–74.
5. "Disinterested" is Stolnitz' term. Vivas uses "intransitive."
6. *Aesthetics and Philosophy of Art Criticism* (Boston, 1960), p. 510.
7. "Aesthetic Vision," *The Philosophical Review*, vol. 68 (1959), p. 63. I shall ignore Tomas' attempt to distinguish between appearance and reality since it seems to confuse rather than clarify aesthetic theory. See F. Sibley, "Aesthetics and the Looks of Things," *Journal of Philosophy*, vol. 56 (1959), pp. 905–15; M. Cohen, op. cit., pp. 915–26; and J. Stolnitz, "Some Questions Concerning Aesthetic Perception," op. cit., pp. 69–87. Tomas discusses only visual art and the aesthetic attitude, but his remarks could be generalized into a comprehensive theory.
8. Dawson, op. cit., p. 158.
9. Ibid., pp. 159–60.
10. Ibid, p. 159.
11. Ibid., p. 168.
12. *Feeling and Form* (New York, 1953), p. 318.
13. *Aesthetics and Philosophy of Art Criticism*, pp. 34–35.
14. Ibid., p. 35.
15. Ibid., p. 36.
16. Ibid., p. 38.
17. "On the Origins of 'Aesthetic Disinterestedness'," *The Journal of Aesthetics and Art Criticism*, vol. 20 (1961), pp. 131–143.
18. "What Makes a Situation Aesthetic?" in *Philosophy Looks at the Arts*, Joseph Margolis (ed.) (New York, 1962). Reprinted from *Proceedings of the Aristotelian Society*, Supplementary Volume 31 (1957), pp. 75–92.
19. Ibid., p. 15.
20. "Contextualism Reconsidered," *The Journal of Aesthetics and Art Criticism*, vol. 18 (1959), pp. 224–25.
21. Ibid., p. 225.
22. Loc. cit.
23. Ibid., p. 227.
24. Ibid., p. 237.
25. Ibid., p. 228. (Italics minc.)
26. Vivas' remark about the improbability of being able to read *The Brothers Karamazov* as art suggests that "intransitive attention" may sometimes mean for him "that which can be attended to at one time" or "that which can be held before the mind at one time." However, this second possible meaning is not one which is relevant here.
27. Vivas, op. cit., p. 231.
28. *The Journal of Philosophy*, vol. 57 (1960), p. 624.

29. Loc. cit.
30. Op. cit., p. 53.
31. Ibid., p. 54.
32. Ibid., pp. 54–55.
33. Ibid., pp. 55–56.
34. Ibid., p. 56.
35. *The Aesthetic Attitude* (New York, 1920), p. 79.
36. Op. cit., p. 35.
37. Ibid., p. 377.
38. Ibid., pp. 377–78.
39. Ibid., p. 379.
40. Ibid., p. 380.
41. Loc. cit.
42. H. S. Langfeld, op. cit., p. 73.
43. J. Stolnitz, op. cit., p. 36.
44. "Morality and the Assessment of Literature," *Philosophy*, vol. 37 (1962), pp. 193–207.
45. Ibid., p. 193.
46. Loc. cit.
47. Ibid., p. 206.
48. Tomas, op. cit., p. 63.

The Aesthetic Point of View

Monroe C. Beardsley

There has been a persistent effort to discover the uniquely aesthetic component, aspect, or ingredient in whatever is or is experienced. Unlike some other philosophical quarries, the object of this chase has not proved as elusive as the snark, the Holy Grail, or Judge Crater—the hunters have returned not empty-handed, but overburdened. For they have found a rich array of candidates for the basically and essentially aesthetic:

aesthetic experience   aesthetic objects
aesthetic value   aesthetic concepts
aesthetic enjoyment   aesthetic situations
aesthetic satisfaction

Confronted with such trophies, we cannot easily doubt that there *is* something peculiarly aesthetic to be found in our world or our experience; yet its exact location and its categorial status remain in question. This is my justification for conducting yet another raid on the ineffable, with the help of a different concept, one in the contemporary philosophical style.

I

When the conservationist and the attorney for Con Edison argue their conflicting cases before a state commission that is deciding whether a nuclear power plant shall be built beside the Hudson River, we can say they do not merely disagree; they regard that power plant from different points of view. When the head of the Histadrut Publishing House refused to publish the novel *Exodus* in Israel, he said: "If it is to be read as history, it is inaccurate. If it is to be read as literature, it is vulgar."[1] And Maxim Gorky reports a remark that Lenin once made to him:

'I know nothing that is greater than [Beethoven's] *Appassionata*. I would like to listen to it every day. A marvelous, superhuman music. I always say with pride—a naive pride perhaps: What miracles human beings can perform!' Then screwing his eyes [Lenin] added, smiling sadly, 'But I can't lis-

From *Contemporary Philosophic Thought*, 3 (1970). Reprinted by permission of the publisher.

ten to music too often; it affects your nerves. One wants to say stupid nice things and stroke on the head the people who can create such beauty while living in this vile hell. And now you must not stroke anyone on the head: you'll have your hands beaten off. You have to hit them on the head without mercy, though our ideal is not to use violence against anyone. Hmm, hmm,—an infernally cruel job we have.'[2]

In each of these examples, it seems plausible to say that one of the conflicting points of view is a peculiarly aesthetic one: that of the conservationist troubled by threats to the Hudson's scenic beauty; that of the publisher who refers to reading *Exodus* "as literature"; that of Lenin, who appears to hold that we ought to adopt the political (rather than the aesthetic) point of view toward Beethoven's sonata, because of the unfortunate political consequences of adopting the aesthetic point of view.

If the notion of the aesthetic point of view can be made clear, it should be useful from the philosophical point of view. The first philosophical use is in mediating certain kinds of dispute. To understand a particular point of view, we must envision its alternatives. Unless there can be more than one point of view toward something the concept breaks down. Consider, for example, the case of architecture. The classic criteria of Vitruvius were stated tersely by Sir Henry Wotton in these words: "Well-building hath three conditions: Commodity, Firmness, and Delight." Commodity is function: that it makes a good church or house or school. Firmness is construction: that the building holds itself up. Suppose we were comparing a number of buildings to see how well built they are, according to these "conditions." We would find some that are functionally effective, structurally sound, and visually attractive. We would find others—old wornout buildings or new suburban shacks—that are pretty poor in each of these departments. But also we would find that the characteristics vary independently over a wide range; that some extremely solid old bank buildings have Firmness (they are knocked down at great cost) without much Commodity or Delight, that some highly delightful buildings are functionally hopeless, that some convenient bridges collapse.

Now suppose we are faced with one of these mixed structures, and invited to say whether it is a good building, or how good it is. Someone might say the bank is very well built, because it is strong; another might reply that nevertheless its ugliness and inconvenience make it a very poor building. Someone might say that the bridge couldn't have been much good if it collapsed; but another might reply that it was a most excellent bridge, while it lasted—that encomium cannot be taken from it merely because it did not last long.

Such disputes may well make us wonder—as Geoffrey Scott wonders in his book on *The Architecture of Humanism*[3]—whether these "conditions" belong in the same discussion. Scott says that to lump them together is confusing: it is to "force on architecture an unreal unity of aim," since they are "incommensurable virtues." For clarity in architectural discussion, then, we might separate the three criteria, and say that they arise in connection with three different points of view—the practical, the engineering, and the aesthetic. In this way, the notion of a point of view is introduced to break up a dispute into segments that seem likely to be more manageable. Instead of asking one question—whether this is a good building—we divide it into three. Considering the building from the aesthetic point of view, we ask whether it is a good work of architecture; from the engineering point of view, whether it is a good structure; and from the practical point of view, whether it is a good machine for living.

Thus one way of clarifying the notion of a point of view would be in terms of the notion of being *good of a kind*.[4] We might say that to adopt the aesthetic point of view toward a building is to classify it as belonging to a species of aesthetic objects—namely, works of architecture—and then to take an interest in whether or not it is a *good* work of architecture. Of course, when an object belongs to one obvious and notable kind, and we judge it in relation to that kind, the "point of view" terminology is unnecessary. We wouldn't ordinarily speak of considering music from a musical point of view, because it wouldn't occur to us that someone might regard it from a political point of view. In the same way, it would be natural to speak of considering whiskey from a medical point of view but not of considering penicillin from a medical point of view. This shows that the "point of view" terminology is implicitly rejective: it is a device for setting aside considerations advanced by others (such as that the bridge will fall) in order to focus attention on the set of considerations that *we* wish to emphasize (such as that the sweep and soar of the bridge are a joy to behold).

The "point of view" terminology, however, is more elastic than the "good of its kind" terminology. To consider a bridge or music or sculpture as an aesthetic object is to consider it from the aesthetic point of view, but what about a mountain, a sea shell, or a tiger? These are neither musical compositions, paintings, poems nor sculptures. A sea shell cannot be *good* sculpture if it is not sculpture at all. But evidently we can adopt the aesthetic point of view toward these things. In fact, some aesthetic athletes (or athletic aesthetes) have claimed the ability to adopt the aesthetic point of view toward anything at all—toward *The Story of O* (this is what Elliot Fremont-Smith has called "beyond pornography"), toward a garbage dump, toward the murders of three civil-rights workers in Philadelphia, Mississippi. (This claim has been put to a severe test by some of our more far-out sculptors.) Perhaps even more remarkable is the feat recently performed by those who viewed the solemn installation of an "invisible sculpture" behind the Metropolitan Museum of Art. The installation consisted in digging a grave-size hole and filling it in again. "It is really an underground sculpture," said its conceiver, Claes Oldenburg. "I think of it as the dirt being loosened from the sides of a certain section of Central Park."[5] The city's architectural consultant, Sam Green, commented on the proceedings:

This is a conceptual work of art and is as much valid as something you can actually see. Everything is art if it is chosen by the artist to be art. You can say it is good art or bad art, but you can't say it isn't art. Just because you can't see a statue doesn't mean that it isn't there.

This, of course, is but one of countless examples of the current tendency to stretch the boundaries of the concept of "art."

The second philosophical use of the notion of the aesthetic point of view is to provide a broad concept of art that might be helpful for certain purposes. We might say:

A work of art (in the broad sense) is any perceptual or intentional object that is deliberately regarded from the aesthetic point of view.[6]

Here, "regarding" would have to include looking, listening, reading, and similar acts of attention, and also what I call "exhibiting"—picking up an object and placing it where it readily permits such attention, or presenting the object to persons acting as spectators.

II

What, then, is the aesthetic point of view? I propose the following:

To adopt the aesthetic point of view with regard to X is to take an interest in whatever aesthetic value X may possess.

I ask myself what I am doing in adopting a particular point of view, and acting toward an object in a way that is appropriate to that point of view; and, so far as I can see, it consists in searching out a corresponding value in the object, to discover whether any of it is present. Sometimes it is to go farther: to cash in on that value, to realize it, to avail myself of it. All this searching, seeking and, if possible, realizing, I subsume under the general phrase "taking an interest in." To listen to Beethoven's *Appassionata* with pleasure and a sense that it is "marvelous, superhuman music," is to seek—and find—aesthetic value in it. To read the novel *Exodus* "as literature," and be repelled because it is "vulgar," is (I take it) to seek aesthetic value in it, but not find very much of it. And when Geoffrey Scott makes his distinction between different ways of regarding a building, and between that "constructive integrity in fact" which belongs under Firmness, and that "constructive vividness in appearance" which is a source of architectural Delight, he adds that "their value in the building is of a wholly disparate kind"[7]; in short, the two points of view, the engineering and the aesthetic, involve two kinds of value.

This proposed definition of "aesthetic point of view" will not, as it stands, fit all of the ordinary uses of this phrase. There is a further complication. I am thinking of a remark by John Hightower, executive director of the New York State Council on the Arts, about the council's aim to "encourage some sort of aesthetic standards." He said, "There are lots of laws that unconsciously inhibit the arts. Architecture is the most dramatic example. Nobody has looked at the laws from an aesthetic point of view."[8] And I am thinking of a statement in the *Yale Alumni Magazine*[9] that the Yale City Planning Department was undertaking "a pioneering two-year research project to study highway environment from an aesthetic point of view." I suppose the attention in these cases was not on the supposed aesthetic value of the laws or of the present "highway environment," but rather in the aesthetic value that might be achieved by changes in these things. Perhaps that is why these examples speak of "*an* aesthetic point of view," rather than "*the* aesthetic point of view," And we could, if we wish, make use of this verbal distinction in our broadened definition:

To adopt *an* aesthetic point of view with regard to X is to take an interest in whatever aesthetic value that X may possess *or that is obtainable by means of X*.

I have allowed the phrase "adopting the aesthetic point of view" to cover a variety of activities. One of them is judging:

To judge X from the aesthetic point of view is to estimate the aesthetic value of X.

Those who are familiar with Paul Taylor's treatment of points of view in his book *Normative Discourse* will note how the order I find in these concepts differs from the one he finds. His account applies only to judging, which makes it too narrow to suit me. It also has, I think, another flaw. He holds that:

Taking a certain point of view is nothing but adopting certain canons of reasoning as the framework within which value judgments are to be justified; the canons of reasoning define the point of view. . . . We have already said that a value judgment is a moral judgment if it is made from the moral point of view.[10]

Thus we could ask of Taylor, What is an aesthetic value judgment? He would reply, It is one made from the aesthetic point of view. And which are those? They are the ones justified by appeal to certain "canons of reasoning," and more particularly the "rules of relevance." But which are the aesthetic rules of relevance? These are the rules "implicitly or explicitly followed by people" in using the aesthetic value-language—that is, in making judgments of aesthetic value. Perhaps I have misunderstood Taylor's line of thought here, but the path it seems to trace is circular. I hope to escape this trap by breaking into the chain at a different point.

I define "aesthetic point of view" in terms of "aesthetic value." And while I think this step is by no means a trivial one, it is not very enlightening unless it is accompanied by some account of aesthetic value. I don't propose to present a detailed theory on this occasion, but I shall extend my chain of definitions to a few more links, and provide some defense against suspected weaknesses. What, then, is aesthetic value?

The aesthetic value of an object is the value it possesses in virtue of its capacity to provide aesthetic gratification.

There are three points about this definition that require some attention.

First, it will be noted that this is not a definition of "value." It purports to distinguish *aesthetic* value from other kinds of value in terms of a particular capacity. It says that in judging the total value of an object we must include that part of its value which is due to its capacity to provide aesthetic gratification.

The second point concerns "aesthetic gratification." My earliest version of this capacity-definition of "aesthetic value" employed the concept of aesthetic experience.[11] I am still not persuaded that this concept must be abandoned as hopeless, but it needs further elaboration in the face of the criticism coming from George Dickie, whose relentless attack on unnecessarily multiplied entities in aesthetics has led him to skepticism about whether there is such a thing as aesthetic experience.[12] I have tried working with the concept of aesthetic enjoyment instead,[13] and that may be on the right track. For the present occasion, I have chosen a term that I think is somewhat broader in scope, and perhaps therefore slightly less misleading.

Again, however, the term "aesthetic gratification" is not self-explanatory. It seems clear that one kind of gratification can be distinguished from another only in terms of its intentional object: that is, of the properties that the pleasure is taken *in*, or the enjoyment is enjoyment *of*. To discriminate aesthetic gratification—and consequently aesthetic value and the aesthetic point of view—we must specify what it is obtained from. I offer the following:

Gratification is aesthetic when it is obtained primarily from attention to the formal unity and/or the regional qualities of a complex whole, and when its magnitude is a function of the degree of formal unity and/or the intensity of regional quality.

The defense of such a proposal would have to answer two questions. First, is there such a type of gratification? I think there is, and I think that it can be distinguished from other types of gratification, though it is often commingled with them. Second, what is the justification for calling this type of gratification "aesthetic"? The answer to this question would be more complicated. Essentially, I would argue that there are certain clear-cut exemplary cases of works of art—that is, poems, plays, musical compositions, etc.—that must be counted as works of art if anything is. There is a type of gratification characteristically and preeminently provided by such works, and this type of gratification is the type I have distinguished above. Finally, this type of gratification (once distinguished) has a paramount claim to be denominated "aesthetic"—even though there are many other things that works of art can do to you, such as inspire you, startle you, or give you a headache.

If this line of argument can be made convincing, we find ourselves with what might be called primary *marks* of the aesthetic: it is the presence in the object of some notable degree of unity and/or the presence of some notable intensity of regional quality that indicates that the enjoyments or satisfactions it affords are aesthetic—insofar as those enjoyments or satisfactions are afforded by these properties. I shall return to these marks a little later, and show the sort of use I think can be made of them.

III

But before we come to that, we must consider the third point about the capacity-definition of "aesthetic value"—and this is the most troublesome of them all.

The term "capacity" has been chosen with care. My view is that the aesthetic value of an object is not a function of the actual degree of gratification obtained from it. It is not an average, or the mean degree of gratification obtained from it by various perceivers. It is not a sum, or the total gratification obtained from it in the course of its existence. All these depend in part on external considerations, including the qualifications of those who happen to resort to libraries, museums, and concerts, and the circumstances of their visits. I am thinking in terms of particular exposures to the work—a particular experience of the music, of the poem, of the painting—and of the degree of aesthetic gratification obtained on each occasion. Aesthetic value depends on the highest degree obtainable under optimal circumstances. Thus my last definition should be supplemented by another one:

The amount of aesthetic value possessed by an object is a function of the degree of aesthetic gratification it is capable of providing in a particular experience of it.

My reason for holding this view is that I want to say that a critical evaluation is a judgment of aesthetic value, and it seems clear to me that estimating capacities is both the least and the most we can ask of the critical evaluator. I take it that when a literary critic, for example, judges the goodness of a poem (from the aesthetic point of view), and is prepared to back up his judgment with reasons, he must be saying something about the relationship of the poem to the experiences of actual or potential readers. The question is, What is this relationship? When a critic says that a poem is good, he is hardly ever in a position to predict the gratification that particular readers or groups of readers will receive from it. Moreover, he is usually not in a position to generalize about tendencies, to say, for instance, that readers of such-and-such propensities, preferences, or preparations will probably be delighted by the poem. If the critic has at his disposal the information required to support such statements, he is of course at liberty to say such things as: "This would have appealed to President Kennedy," or "This is an ideal Christmas gift for your friends who love mountain climbing." But when he simply says, "This is a good poem," we must interpret him as saying something weaker (though still significant) about the capacity of the work to provide a notable degree of aesthetic gratification. For *that* is a judgment he should be able to support, if he understands the poem.

The question, however, is whether the capacity-definition of "aesthetic value" is too weak, as a report of what actually happens in art criticism. I can think of three difficulties that have been or could be raised. They might be called (1) the unrecognized masterpiece problem, (2) the LSD problem, and (3) the Edgar Rice Burroughs problem. Or, to give them more abstract names, they are (1) the problem of falsification, (2) the problem of illusion, and (3) the problem of devaluation.

(1) Some people are troubled by one consequence of the capacity-definition—that objects can possess aesthetic value that never has been and never will be realized, such as the "gems of purest ray serene the dark unfathomed caves of ocean bear." This ought not to trouble us, I think. It is no real paradox that many objects worth looking at can never be looked at. But there is another kind of aesthetic inaccessibility in the highly complicated and obscure work that no critic can find substantial value in, though it may still be there. In Balzac's short story, "Le Chef-d'oeuvre inconnu," the master painter works in solitude for years, striving for the perfection of his greatest work; but in his dedication and delusion he overlays the canvas with so many brush strokes that the work is ruined. When his fellow artists finally see the painting, they are appalled by it. But how can they be sure that the painting doesn't have aesthetic value, merely because they have not found any? The capacity to provide aesthetic gratification of a high order may still be there, though they are not sharp or sensitive enough to take advantage of it.

If my proposed definition entailed that negative judgments of aesthetic value cannot even in principle be justified, then we would naturally mistrust it. But of course this consequence is not necessary. What does follow is that there is a certain asymmetry between negative and affirmative judgments, with respect to their degree of confirmation; but this is so between negative and affirmative existential statements in general. The experienced critic may have good reason in many cases not only for confessing that he finds little value in a painting, but for adding that very probably no one ever will find great value in it.

(2) If aesthetic value involves a capacity, then its presence can no doubt be sufficiently attested by a single realization. What a work *does* provide, it clearly *can* provide. And if my definition simply refers to the capacity, without qualification, then it makes no difference under what conditions that realization occurs. Now take any object you like, no matter how plain or ugly—say a heap of street sweepings awaiting the return of the street cleaner. Certainly we want to say that it is lacking in aesthetic value. But suppose someone whose consciousness is rapidly expanding under the influence of LSD or some other hallucinogenic drug happens to look at this heap and it gives him exquisite aesthetic gratification. Then it has the capacity to do so, and so it has high aesthetic value. But then perhaps every visual object has high aesthetic value, and all to about the same degree—if the reports may be trusted.

I cannot speak authoritatively of the LSD experience, but I gather that when a trip is successful, the object, however humble, may glow with unwonted intensity of color and its shapes assume an unexpected order and harmony. In short, the experience is illusory. This is certainly suggested by the most recent report I have run across.[14] Dr. Lloyd A. Grumbles, a Philadelphia psychiatrist,

said that while listening to Beethoven's *Eroica*, particularly the third movement, he felt simultaneously "insatiable longing and total gratification." . . . Dr. Grumbles said he also looked at prints of Picasso and Renoir paintings and realized, for the first time, "they were striving for the same goal."

Now you *know* he was under the influence of LSD.

This example suggests a modification of the definition given earlier:

The aesthetic value of X is the value that X possesses in virtue of its capacity to provide aesthetic gratification when *correctly experienced.*

(3) The problem of devaluation can perhaps be regarded as a generalization of the LSD problem.[15] When I was young I was for a time an avid reader of the Martian novels of Edgar Rice Burroughs. Recently when I bought the Dover paperback edition and looked at them again, I found that I could hardly read them. Their style alone is enough to repel you, if you really pay attention to it.

The problem is this: if on Monday I enjoy a novel very much, and thus know that it has the capacity to provide gratification, then how can I ever reverse the judgment and say the novel lacks that capacity? If the judgment that the novel is a good one is a capacity-judgment, it would seem that downward reevaluations (that is, devaluations) are always false—assuming that the original higher judgment was based on direct experience. There is no problem about upward reevaluations: when I say on Tuesday that the novel is better than I thought on Monday, this means that I have discovered the novel to have a greater capacity than I had realized. But how can we explain the lowering of an aesthetic evaluation and still maintain that these evaluations are capacity-judgments?

Some cases of devaluation can no doubt be taken care of without modifying the definition of "aesthetic value." The devaluation may be due to a shift in our value grades caused by enlargement of our range of experience. I might think that *Gone with the Wind* is a great novel, because it is the best I have read, but later I might take away that encomium and give it to *War and Peace*. Or the devaluation may be due to the belated recognition that my previous satisfaction in the work was a response to extra-aesthetic features. I now realize that my earlier enjoyment of detective stories was probably caused only in small part by their literary qualities, and was much more of a game-type pleasure.

But setting these cases aside, there remain cases where on perfectly sound and legitimate grounds I decide that the work, though it has provided a certain level of aesthetic gratification, is in fact not really that good. I have overestimated it. Evidently the definition of "aesthetic value" must be modified again. One thing we might do is insert a stipulation that the work be a reliable or dependable source of gratification: flukes don't count. We need not change the judgment into a straight tendency-statement. But we might insist that the enjoyment of the novel must at least be a repeatable experience. Something like this notion seems to underlie the frequent claim that our first reactions to a new work of art are not wholly to be trusted, that we should wait awhile and try it again; that we should see whether we can find at least one other person to corroborate our judgment; or that only posterity will be in a position to know whether the work is great.

I grant that all these precautions are helpful—indeed, they enable us to avoid the two sources of error mentioned a moment ago: having an inadequately formulated set of grading terms, and confusing aesthetic with nonaesthetic gratification. But I think it ought to be possible for a person, after a single experience of a work, to have excellent grounds for thinking it good and for commending it to others. And I think he would be justified in pointing out that he has found a potential source of aesthetic gratification that lies ready to be taken advantage of—even though he does not yet know how readily, how easily, how conveniently, or how frequently recourse may be had to it. Thus my escape from the difficulty is to revise the definition of "aesthetic value" again so as to stipulate that it is the value of the whole work that is in question:

The aesthetic value of X is the value that X possesses in virtue of its capacity to provide aesthetic gratification *when correctly and completely experienced.*

The youth who was carried away by the adventures of Thuvia and the green men of Mars and the other denizens of that strange planet may well have gotten greater aesthetic gratification than the elderly person who returned to them after so many years. For the youth was fairly oblivious to the faults of style, and he filled in the flat characterizations with his own imagination, giving himself up unself-consciously to the dramatic events and exotic scenery. But, though he was lucky in a way, his judgment of the *whole* work was not to be trusted.

IV

We saw earlier that the notion of a point of view plays a particular role in focusing or forwarding certain disputes by limiting the range of relevant considerations. We invoke the aesthetic point of view when we want to set aside certain considerations that others have advanced—as that a poem is pornographic, or that a painting is a forgery—or that (as Jacques Maritain remarks) "A splendid house without a door is not a good work of architecture."[16] But the person whose considerations are thus rejected may feel that the decision is arbitrary, and enter an appeal, in the hope that a higher philosophical tribunal will rule that the lower court erred in its exclusions. How do we know whether being pornographic, or being a forgery, or lacking a door, is irrelevant from the aesthetic point of view? I propose this answer:

A consideration about an object is relevant to the aesthetic point of view if and only if it is a fact about the object that affects the degree to which the marks of aesthetic gratification (formal unity and intensity of regional quality) are present in the object.

Thus: Is the fact that a painting is a forgery relevant to a judgment of it from the aesthetic point of view? No; because it has no bearing on its form or quality. Is the fact that a painting is a seascape relevant? Sometimes. It is when the subject contributes to, or detracts from, its degree of unity or its qualitative intensity. Is the biography of the composer relevant? According to a writer in *The Music Review*:

It is a well-known fact that knowledge of the circumstances surrounding the composition of a work enhances the audience's appreciation. . . .

It is because of this that programme notes, radio comments, and music appreciation courses are in such demand. To secure such knowledge is one of the important tasks of musical research.[17]

Now, I'm not sure that this "well-known fact" is really a fact, but let us assume that it is. Does it follow that information about the circumstances of composition is relevant to consideration of the work from an aesthetic point of view? We can imagine this sort of thing:

It was a cold rainy day in Vienna, and Schubert was down to his last crust of bread. As he looked about his dingy garret, listening to the rain that beat down, he reflected that he could not even afford to feed his mice. He recalled a sad poem by Goethe, and suddenly a melody sprang into his head. He seized an old piece of paper, and began to write feverishly. Thus was "Death and the Maiden" born.

Now even if everyone, or *nearly* everyone, who reads this program note finds that it increases his appreciation of the song, a condition of appreciation is not necessarily a condition of value. From this information—say, that it was raining—nothing can be inferred about the specifically aesthetic character of the song. (It is relevant, of course, that the words and music match each other in certain ways; however, we know that not by biographical investigation but by listening to the song itself.)

Here is one more example. In a very interesting article "On the Aesthetic Attitude in Romanesque Art," Meyer Schapiro has argued that:

Contrary to the general belief that in the Middle Ages the work of art was considered mainly as a vehicle of religious teaching or as a piece of craftsmanship serving a useful end, and that beauty of form and color was no object of contemplation in itself, these texts abound in aesthetic judgments and in statements about the qualities and structure of the work. They speak of the fascination of the image, its marvelous likeness to physical reality, and the artist's wonderful skill, often in complete abstraction from the content of the object of art.[18]

Schapiro is inquiring whether medieval people were capable of taking the aesthetic point of view in some independence of the religious and technological points of view. He studies various texts in which aesthetic objects are described and praised, to elicit the grounds on which this admiration is based, and to discover whether these grounds are relevant to the aesthetic point of view. Form and color, for example, are clearly relevant, and so to praise a work for its form or color is to adopt the aesthetic point of view. And I should think the same can be said for "the fascination of the image"—by which Schapiro refers to the extraordinary interest in the grotesque figures freely carved by the stonecutters in Romanesque buildings. These centaurs, chimeras, two-headed animals, creatures with feet and the tail of a serpent, etc., are the images deplored by Saint Bernard with an ambivalence like that in Lenin's remark about Beethoven:

In the cloister, under the eyes of the brethren who read there, what profit is there in those ridiculous monsters, in that marvelous and deformed beauty, in that beautiful deformity?[19]

But what of Schapiro's other points—the image's "marvelous likeness to physical reality, and the artist's wonderful skill"?

If a person admires skill in depiction, he is certainly not taking a religious point of view—but is he taking the aesthetic point of view? I should think not. No doubt when he notices the accuracy of depiction, reflects on the skill required to achieve it, and thus admires the artist, he may be placed in a more favorable psychological posture toward the work itself. But this contributes to the conditions of the experience; it does not enter into the experience directly, as does the perception of form and color, or the recognition of the represented objects as saints or serpents. So I would say that the fact that the medieval writer admired the skill in depiction is *not* evidence that he took the aesthetic point of view, though it is evidence that he took *an* aesthetic point of view, since skill was involved in the production of the work.

V

There is one final problem that may be worth raising and commenting upon briefly—although it is not at all clear to me how the problem should even be formulated. It concerns the justification of adopting the aesthetic point of view, and its potential conflicts with other points of view. On one hand, it is interesting to note that much effort has been spent (especially during recent decades) in getting people to adopt the aesthetic point of view much more firmly and continuously than has been common in our country. The conservationists are trying to arouse us to concern for the preservation of natural beauties, instead of automatically assuming that they have a lower priority than any other interest that happens to come up—such as installing power lines, or slaughtering deer, or advertising beer. And those who are concerned with "education of the eye," or "visual education," are always developing new methods of teaching the theory and practice of good design, the aim being to produce people who are aware of the growing hideousness of our cities and towns, and who are troubled enough to work for changes.

But the effort to broaden the adoption of the aesthetic point of view sometimes takes another form. According to its leading theoretician, the "Camp sensibility" is characterized by the great range of material to which it can respond: "Camp is the consistently aesthetic experience of the world," writes Susan Sontag. "It incarnates a victory of style over content, of aesthetics over morality, of irony over tragedy."[20]

Here is an extreme consequence of trying to increase the amount of aesthetic value of which we can take advantage. But it also gives rise to an interesting problem, which might be called "the dilemma of aesthetic education." The problem is pointed up by a cartoon I saw not long ago (by David Gerard), showing the proprietor of a junkyard named "Sam's Salvage" standing by a huge pile of junked cars, and saying to two other men: "Whattya mean it's an ugly eyesore? If I'd paid Picasso to pile it up, you'd call it a work of art."

The central task of aesthetic education, as traditionally conceived, is the improvement of taste, involving the development of two dispositions: (1) the capacity to obtain aesthetic gratification from increasingly subtle and complex aesthetic objects that are characterized by various forms of unity—in short, the response to beauty in one main sense; and (2) an increasing dependence on objects beautiful in this way (having harmony, order, balance, proportion) as sources of aesthetic satisfaction. It is this impulse that is behind the usual concept of "beautification"—shielding the highways from junkyards and billboards, and providing more trees and flowers and grass. As long as the individual's aesthetic development in this sense is accompanied by increasing access to beautiful sights and sounds, it is all to the good. His taste improves; his aesthetic pleasures are keener; and when he encounters unavoidable ugliness, he may be moved to eliminate it by labor or by law. On the other hand, suppose he finds that his environment grows uglier, as the economy progresses, and that the ugliness becomes harder to escape. Second, suppose he comes to enjoy another kind of aesthetic value, one that derives from intensity of regional quality more than formal fitness. And third, suppose he comes to realize that his aesthetic gratification is affected by the demands he makes upon an object—especially because the intensity of its regional qualities partly depends on its symbolic import. For example, the plain ordinary object may be seen as a kind of symbol, and become expressive (i.e., assume a noteworthy quality) if the individual attends to it in a way that invites these features to emerge. Suddenly, a whole new field of aesthetic gratification opens up. Trivial objects, the accidental, the neglected, the meretricious and vulgar, all take on new excitement. The automobile graveyard and the weed-filled garden are seen to have their own wild and grotesque expressiveness as well as symbolic import. The kewpie doll, the Christmas card, the Tiffany lampshade, can be enjoyed aesthetically, not for their beauty but for their bizarre qualities and their implicit reflection of social attitudes. This is a way of transfiguring reality, and though not everything can be transfigured, perhaps, it turns out that much can.

What I mean by the dilemma of aesthetic education is this: that we are torn between conflicting ways of redirecting taste. One is the way of love of beauty, which is limited in its range of enjoyment, but is reformist by implication, since it seeks a world that conforms to its ideal. The other is the way of aestheticizing everything—of taking the aesthetic point of view wherever possible—and this widens enjoyment, but is defeatist, since instead of eliminating the junkyard and the slum it tries to see them as expressive and symbolic. The conflict here is analogous to that between the social gospel and personal salvation in some of our churches—though no doubt its consequences are not equally momentous. I don't suppose this dilemma is ultimately unresolvable, though I cannot consider it further at the moment. I point it out as one of the implications of the tendency (which I have been briefly exploring) to extend the aesthetic point of view as widely as possible.

But there is another weighty tradition opposed to this expansion. Lenin and Saint Bernard stand witness to the possibility that there may be situations in which it is morally objectionable to adopt the aesthetic point of view. A man who had escaped from Auschwitz commented on Rolf Hochmuth's play: "*The Deputy* should not be considered as a historical work or even as a work of art, but as a moral lesson."[21] Perhaps he only meant that looking for historical truth or artistic merit in *The Deputy* is a waste of time. But he may also have meant that there is something blameworthy about anyone who is capable of contemplating those terrible events from a purely historical or purely aesthetic point of view.

Renata Adler, reporting in *The New Yorker*[22] on the New Politics Convention that took place in Chicago on Labor Day weekend, 1967, listed various types of self-styled "revolutionaries" who attended, including "the aesthetic-analogy revolutionaries, who discussed riots as though they were folk songs or pieces of local theatre, subject to appraisal in literary terms ('authentic,' 'beautiful')." That is carrying the aesthetic point of view pretty far.

This possibility has not gone unnoticed by imaginative writers—notably Henry James and Henrik Ibsen.[23] The tragedy of Mrs. Gereth, in *The Spoils of Poynton*, is that of a woman who could not escape the aesthetic point of view. She had a "passion for the exquisite" that made her prone "to be rendered unhappy by the presence of the dreadful [and] she was condemned to wince wherever she turned." In fact, the things that troubled her most—and she encountered them everywhere, but nowhere in more abundance than the country house known as Waterbath—were just the campy items featured by Miss Sontag: "trumpery ornament and scrapbook art, with strange excrescences and bunchy draperies, with gimcracks that might have been keepsakes for maid-servants [and even] a souvenir from some centennial or other Exhibition." The tragedy of the sculptor, Professor Rubek, in *When We Dead Awaken*, is that he so utterly aestheticized the woman who loved him and who was his model that she was not a person to him. As she says, "The work of art first—then the human being." It may even be—and I say this with the utmost hesitation, since I have no wish to sink in these muddy waters—that this is the theme of Antonioni's film, *Blow-Up*: the emptiness that comes from utter absorption in an aesthetic point of view of a photographer to whom every person and every event seems to represent only the possibility of a new photographic image. In that respect, Antonioni's photographer is certainly worse than Professor Rubek.

The mere confrontation of these two vague and general social philosophies of art will not, of course, take us very far in understanding the possibilities and the limitations of the aesthetic point of view. I leave matters unresolved, with questions hanging in the air. Whatever resolution we ultimately find, however, will surely incorporate two observations that may serve as a pair of conclusions.

First, there are occasions on which it would be wrong to adopt the aesthetic point of view, because there is a conflict of values and the values that are in peril are, in that particular case, clearly higher. Once in a while you see a striking photograph or film sequence in which someone is (for example) lying in the street after an accident, in need of immediate attention. And it is a shock to think suddenly that the photographer must have been on hand. I don't want to argue ethics of news photography, but if someone, out of the highest aesthetic motives, withheld first aid to a bleeding victim in order to record the scene, with careful attention to lighting and camera speed, then it is doubtful that that picture could be so splendid a work of art as to justify neglecting so stringent a moral obligation.

The second conclusion is that there is nothing—no object or event—that is *per se* wrong to consider from the aesthetic point of view. This, I think, is part of the truth in the art-for-art's-sake doctrine. To adopt the aesthetic point of view is simply to seek out a source of value. And it can never be a moral error to realize value—barring conflict with other values. Some people seem to fear that a serious and persistent aesthetic interest will become an enervating hyperaestheticism, a paralysis of will like that reported in advanced cases of psychedelic dependence. But the objects of aesthetic interest—such as harmonious design, good proportions, intense expressiveness—are not drugs, but part of the breath of life. Their cumulative effect is increased sensitization, fuller awareness, a closer touch with the environment and concern for what it is and might be. It seems to me very doubtful that we could have too much of these good things, or that they have inherent defects that prevent them from being an integral part of a good life.

NOTES

1. *New Republic* (Jan. 16, 1961), p. 23. Cf. Brendan Gill, in *The New Yorker* (March 5, 1966): "It is a lot easier to recommend attendance at 'The Gospel According to St. Matthew' as an act of penitential piety during the Lenten season than it is to praise the movie as a movie. Whether or not the life and death of Our Lord is the greatest story ever told, it is so far from being merely a story that we cannot deal with it in literary terms (if we could, I think we would have to begin by saying that in respect to construction and motivation it leaves much to be desired); our difficulty is enormously increased when we try to pass judgment on the story itself once it has been turned into a screenplay."
2. From Gorky's essay on Lenin, *Collected Works* XVII (Moscow, 1950), 39–40. My colleague Professor Olga Lang called my attention to this passage and translated it for me. Cf. *Days with Lenin* (New York: International Publishers, 1932), p. 52. *Time* (April 30, 1965, p. 50) reported that the Chinese Communists had forbidden the performance of Beethoven's works because they "paralyze one's revolutionary fighting will." A Chinese bacteriologist, in a letter to a Peking newspaper, wrote after listening to Beethoven, "I began to have strange illusions about a world filled with friendly love."
3. New York: Doubleday Anchor Books, 1954, p. 15, where he quotes Wotton.
4. In this discussion, I have been stimulated by an unpublished paper by J. O. Urmson on "Good of a Kind and Good from a Point of View," which I saw in manuscript in 1961. I should also like to thank him for comments on an earlier version of this paper. Cf. his note added to "What Makes a Situation Aesthetic?" in Joseph Margolis, ed., *Philosophy Looks at the Arts* [first edition] (New York: Charles Scribner's Sons, 1962), p. 26. I also note that John Hospers has some interesting remarks on the aesthetic point of view in "The Ideal Aesthetic Observer," *British Journal of Aesthetics* II (1962), 99–111.
5. *The New York Times*, Oct. 2, 1967, p. 55.

6. Cf. my "Comments" on Stanley Cavell's paper, in W. H. Capitan and D. D. Merrill, eds., *Art, Mind, and Religion* (Pittsburgh: University of Pittsburgh Press, 1967), esp. pp. 107–109.
7. *Op. cit.*, p. 89; cf. pp. 90–91, 95. In case it may be thought that architects who have the highest respect for their materials might repudiate my distinction, I quote Pier Luigi Nervi (in his Charles Eliot Norton lectures): "There does not exist, either in the past or in the present, a work of architecture which is accepted and recognized as excellent from the aesthetic point of view which is not also excellent from a technical point of view." From *Aesthetics and Technology in Building* (Cambridge: Harvard University Press, 1965), p. 2. Though arguing that one kind of value is a necessary (but not a sufficient) condition of the other, Nervi clearly assumes that there is a distinguishable aesthetic point of view.
8. *The New York Times*, April 2, 1967, p. 94.
9. Dec. 1966, p. 20.
10. Paul Taylor, *Normative Discourse* (Englewood Cliffs, N.J.: Prentice-Hall, Inc., 1961), p. 109.
11. See *Aesthetics: Problems in the Philosophy of Criticism* (New York: Harcourt, Brace & World, Inc., 1958), ch. 11.
12. See "Beardsley's Phantom Aesthetic Experience," *Journal of Philosophy* LXII (1965), 129–136, and my "Aesthetic Experience Regained," *Journal of Aesthetics and Art Criticism* XXVII (1969), 3–11.
13. "The Discrimination of Aesthetic Enjoyment," *British Journal of Aesthetics* III (1963), 291–300.
14. In the *Delaware County Daily Times* (Chester, Pa.), Feb. 10, 1967.
15. It was discussed briefly in my *Aesthetics* (New York: Harcourt, Brace, & World, 1958),pp. 534–535, but has since been called to my attention more sharply and forcefully by Professor Thomas Regan.
16. *L'Intuition Créatrice dans l'Art et dans la Poésie* (Paris: Desclée de Brouwer, 1966), p. 53.
17. Hans Tischler, "The Aesthetic Experience," *Music Review* XVII (1956), p. 200.
18. In K. Bharatha Iyer, ed., *Art and Thought* (London: Luzac, 1947), p. 138. I thank my colleague John Williams for calling my attention to this essay.
19. *Ibid.*, p. 133.
20. Susan Sontag, "Notes on Camp," *Partisan Review* XXXI (Fall 1964), p. 526.
21. *The New York Times*, May 4, 1966.
22. Sept. 23, 1967.
23. I set aside the somewhat indelicate verse by W. H. Auden called "The Aesthetic Point of View."

The Activity of Aesthetic Experience

Nelson Goodman

ACTION AND ATTITUDE

A persistent tradition pictures the aesthetic attitude as passive contemplation of the immediately given, direct apprehension of what is presented, uncontaminated by any conceptualization, isolated from all the echoes of the past and all the threats and promises of the future, exempt from all enterprise. By purification rites of disengagement and disinterpretation we are to seek a pristine, unsullied vision of the world. I need hardly recount the philosophic faults and aesthetic absurdities of such a view until someone seriously

From *Languages of Art* (Indianapolis: The Bobbs-Merrill Co., 1968). Reprinted by permission of Hackett Publishing Co. and the author.

goes so far as to maintain that the appropriate aesthetic attitude toward a poem amounts to gazing at the printed page without reading it.

I have held, on the contrary, that we have to read the painting as well as the poem, and that aesthetic experience is dynamic rather than static. It involves making delicate discriminations and discerning subtle relationships, identifying symbol systems and characters within these systems and what these characters denote and exemplify, interpreting works and reorganizing the world in terms of works and works in terms of the world. Much of our experience and many of our skills are brought to bear and may be transformed by the encounter. The aesthetic 'attitude' is restless, searching, testing—is less attitude than action: creation and re-creation.

What, though, distinguishes such aesthetic activity from other intelligent behavior such as perception, ordinary conduct, and scientific inquiry? One instant answer is that the aesthetic is directed to no practical end, is unconcerned with self-defense or conquest, with acquisition of necessities or luxuries, with prediction and control of nature. But if the aesthetic attitude disowns practical aims, still aimlessness is hardly enough. The aesthetic attitude is inquisitive as contrasted with the acquisitive and self-preservative, but not all nonpractical inquiry is aesthetic. To think of science as motivated ultimately by practical goals, as judged or justified by bridges and bombs and the control of nature, is to confuse science with technology. Science seeks knowledge without regard to practical consequences, and is concerned with prediction not as a guide for behavior but as a test of truth. Disinterested inquiry embraces both scientific and aesthetic experience.

Attempts are often made to distinguish the aesthetic in terms of immediate pleasure; but troubles arise and multiply here. Obviously, sheer quantity or intensity of pleasure cannot be the criterion. That a picture or poem provides more pleasure than does a proof is by no means clear; and some human activities unrelated to any of these provide enough more pleasure to render insignificant any differences in amount or degree among various types of inquiry. The claim that aesthetic pleasure is of a different and superior *quality* is by now too transparent a dodge to be taken seriously.

The inevitable next suggestion—that aesthetic experience is distinguished not by pleasure at all but by a special aesthetic emotion—can be dropped on the waste-pile of 'dormitive virtue' explanations.

This clears the way for the sophisticated theory that what counts is not pleasure yielded but pleasure 'objectified', pleasure read into the object as property thereof. Apart from images of some grotesque process of transfusion, what can this mean? To consider the pleasure as possessed rather than occasioned by the object—to say in effect that the object is pleased—may amount to saying that the object expresses the pleasure. But since some aesthetic objects are sad—express sadness rather than pleasure—this comes nowhere near distinguishing in general between aesthetic and nonaesthetic objects or experience.

Some of these difficulties are diminished and others obscured if we speak of satisfaction rather than pleasure. "Satisfaction" is colorless enough to pass in contexts where "pleasure" is ludicrous, hazy enough to blur counterinstances, and flexible enough to tolerate convenient vacillation in interpretation. Thus we may hope to lessen the temptation to conjure up a special quality or kind of feeling or to indulge in mumbo-jumbo about objectification. Nevertheless, satisfaction pretty plainly fails to distinguish aesthetic from nonaesthetic objects and experiences. Not only does some scientific inquiry yield much satisfaction, but some aesthetic objects and experiences yield none. Music and our listening, pictures and our looking, do not fluctuate between aesthetic and nonaesthetic as the playing or painting varies from exalted to excruciating. Being aesthetic does not exclude being unsatisfactory or being aesthetically bad.

The distinguishing feature, some say, is not satisfaction secured but satisfaction sought: in science, satisfaction is a mere by-product of inquiry; in art, inquiry is a mere means for obtaining satisfaction. The difference is held to be neither in process performed nor in satisfaction enjoyed but in attitude maintained. On this view the scientific *aim* is knowledge, the aesthetic *aim* satisfaction.

But how cleanly can these aims be separated? Does the scholar seek knowledge or the satisfaction of knowing? Obtaining knowledge and satisfying curiosity are so much the same that trying to do either without trying to do the other surely demands a precarious poise. And anyone who does manage to seek the satisfaction without seeking the knowledge will pretty surely get neither, while on the other hand abstention from all anticipation of satisfaction is unlikely to stimulate research. One may indeed be so absorbed in working on a problem as never to think of the satisfaction to be had from solving it; or one may dwell so fondly on the delights of finding a solution as to take no steps toward arriving at one. But if the latter attitude is aesthetic, aesthetic understanding of anything is foredoomed. And I cannot see that these tenuous, ephemeral, and idiosyncratic states of mind mark any significant difference between the aesthetic and the scientific.

THE FUNCTION OF FEELING

All these failures to arrive at an acceptable formulation in terms of pleasure or satisfaction, yielded or 'objectified' or anticipated, will hardly dislodge the conviction that the distinction between the scientific and the aesthetic is somehow rooted in the difference between knowing and feeling, between the cognitive and the emotive. This latter deeply entrenched dichotomy is in itself dubious on many grounds, and its application here becomes especially puzzling when aesthetic and scientific experience alike are seen to be fundamentally cognitive in character. But we do not easily part with the idea that art is in some way or other more emotive than is science.

The shift from pleasure or satisfaction to emotion-in-general softens some of the crudities of the hedonistic formulas but leaves us with trouble enough. Paintings and concerts, and the viewing and hearing of them, need not arouse emotion, any more than they need give satisfaction, to be aesthetic; and anticipated emotion is no better criterion than anticipated satisfaction. If the aesthetic is characteristically emotive in some way, we have yet to say in what way.

Any picture of aesthetic experience as a sort of emotional bath or orgy is plainly preposterous. The emotions involved tend to be muted and oblique as compared, for example, with the fear or sorrow or depression or exultation that arises from actual battle or bereavement or defeat or victory, and are not in general keener than the excitement or despair or elation that accompanies scientific exploration and discovery. What the inert spectator feels falls far short of what the characters portrayed on the stage feel, and even of what he himself would feel on witnessing real-life events. And if he leaps on the stage to participate, his response can no longer be called aesthetic. That art is concerned with simulated emotions suggests, as does the copy theory of representation, that art is a poor substitute for reality: that art is imitation, and aesthetic experience a pacifier that only partly compensates for lack of direct acquaintance and contact with the Real.

Often the emotions involved in aesthetic experience are not only somewhat tempered but also reversed in polarity. We welcome some works that arouse emotions we normally shun. Negative emotions of fear, hatred, disgust may become positive when occasioned by a play or painting. The problem of tragedy and the paradox of ugliness are made to order for ancient and modern Freudians, and the opportunity has not been neglected. Tragedy is said to have the effect of purging us of pent-up and hidden negative emotions, or of administering measured doses of the killed virus to prevent or mitigate the ravages of an actual attack. Art becomes not only palliative but therapeutic, providing both a substitute for good reality and a safeguard against bad reality. Theatres and museums function as adjuncts to Departments of Public Health.

Again, even among works of art and aesthetic experiences of evident excellence, the emotive component varies widely—from, say, a late Rembrandt to a late Mondrian, or from a Brahms to a Webern quartet. The Mondrian and the Webern are not obviously more emotive than Newton's or Einstein's laws; and a line between emotive and cognitive is less likely to mark off the aesthetic neatly from the scientific than to mark off some aesthetic objects and experiences from others.

All these troubles revive the temptation to posit a special aesthetic emotion or feeling or a special coloration of other emotions occurring in aesthetic experience. This special emotion or coloring may be intense when other emotions are feeble, may be positive when they are negative, and may occur in experience of the most intellectual art and yet be lacking in the most stirring scientific study. All difficulties are resolved—by begging the question. No doubt aesthetic emotions have the property that makes them aesthetic. No doubt things that burn are combustible. The theory of aesthetic phlogiston explains everything and nothing.

Thus two stubborn problems still confront us. First, despite our conviction that aesthetic experience is *some*how emotive rather than cognitive, the failure of formulae in terms of either yielded or anticipated emotions has left us with no way of saying *how*. Second, despite our recognition that emotion in aesthetic experience tends to be denatured and often even inverted, the obvious futility of explanations in terms of a special secretion of the aesthetic glands leaves us without any way of saying *why*. Perhaps the answer to the second question will be found in the answer to the first; perhaps emotion in aesthetic experience behaves as it does because of the role it plays.

Most of the troubles that have been plaguing us can, I have suggested, be blamed on the domineering dichotomy between the cognitive and the emotive. On the one side, we put sensation, perception, inference, conjecture, all nerveless inspection and investigation, fact, and truth; on the other, pleasure, pain, interest, satisfaction, disappointment, all brainless affective response, liking, and loathing. This pretty effectively keeps us from seeing that in aesthetic experience the *emotions function cognitively*. The work of art is apprehended through the feelings as well as through the senses. Emotional numbness disables here as definitely if not as completely as blindness or deafness. Nor are the feelings used exclusively for exploring the emotional content of a work. To some extent, we may feel how a painting looks as we may see how it feels. The actor or dancer—or the spectator—sometimes notes and remembers the feeling of a movement rather than its pattern, insofar as the two can be distinguished at all. Emotion in aesthetic experience is a means of discerning what properties a work has and expresses.

To say this is to invite hot denunciation for cold overintellectualization; but rather than aesthetic experience being here deprived of emotions, the understanding is being endowed with them. The fact that emotions participate in cognition no more implies that they are not felt than the fact that vision helps us discover properties of objects implies that color-sensations do not occur. Indeed, emotions must be felt—that is, must occur, as sensations must—if they are to be used cognitively. Cognitive use involves discriminating and relating them in order to gauge and grasp the work and integrate it with the rest of our experience and the world. If this is the opposite of passive absorption in sensations and emotions, it by no means amounts to canceling them. . . .

Although many puzzles are thus resolved and the role of emotion in aesthetic experience clarified, we are still left without a way of distinguishing aesthetic from all other experience. Cognitive employment of the emotions is neither present in every aesthetic nor absent from every nonaesthetic experience.

SYMPTOMS OF THE AESTHETIC

Repeated failure to find a neat formula for sorting experiences into aesthetic and nonaesthetic, in rough conformity with rough usage, suggests the need for a less simple-minded approach. Perhaps we should begin by examining the aesthetic relevance of the major characteristics of the several symbol processes involved in experience, and look for aspects or symptoms, rather than for a crisp criterion, of the aesthetic. A symptom is neither a necessary nor a sufficient condition for, but merely tends in conjunction with other such symptoms to be present in, aesthetic experience.

Three symptoms of the aesthetic may be syntactic density, semantic density, and syntactic repleteness. As we have seen, syntactic density is characteristic of nonlinguistic systems, and is one feature distinguishing sketches from scores and scripts; semantic density is characteristic of representation, description, and expression in the arts, and is one feature differentiating sketches and scripts from scores; and relative syntactic repleteness distinguishes the more representational among semantically dense systems from the more diagrammatic, the less from the more 'schematic'. All three features call for maximum sensitivity of discrimination. Syntactic and semantic density demand endless attention to determining character and referent, given any mark of the system; and relative syntactic repleteness in a syntactically dense system demands such effort at discrimination along, so to speak, more dimensions. Impossibility of finite determination may carry some suggestion of the ineffability so often claimed for, or charged against, the aesthetic. But density, far from being mysterious and vague, is explicitly defined; and it arises out of, and sustains, the unsatisfiable demand for absolute precision.

The fourth and final symptom of the aesthetic is the feature that distinguishes exemplificational from denotational systems and that combines with density to distinguish showing from saying. An experience is exemplificational insofar as concerned with properties exemplified or expressed—i.e., properties possessed and shown forth—by a symbol, not merely things the symbol denotes. Counting such exemplificationality as aesthetic may seem a concession to the tradition that associates the aesthetic with the immediate and nontransparent and so insists that the aesthetic object be taken for what it is in itself rather than as signifying anything else. But exemplification, like denotation, relates a symbol to a referent, and the distance from a symbol to what applies to or is exemplified by it is no less than the distance to what it applies to or denotes. As 'ineffability' upon analysis turns into density rather than mystery, 'immediacy' becomes a matter of exemplification rather than of intimacy—a function of direction rather than of distance. Nothing here implies that representation, in contrast with exemplification, is nonaesthetic. Exemplification contrasts with denotation rather than with representation. We saw that fictive representation and also representation-as are matters of exemplification; and representation in the arts is seldom explicitly factual and otherwise purely denotational. Moreover, an aesthetic experience need not exhibit all four symptoms.

The four symptoms probably tend to be present rather than absent, and to be prominent in aesthetic experience; but any of them may be absent from aesthetic or present in nonaesthetic experience. The symbolic vehicle of the literary arts, for example, is not syntactically dense, while the gauging of weights or temperatures may be dense both syntactically and semantically. Absence of some aesthetic or presence of some nonaesthetic symptom does not make for an aesthetically less pure totality, nor is an experience the more aesthetic the higher the concentration of aesthetic symptoms. Yet if the four symptoms listed are *severally* neither sufficient nor necessary for aesthetic experience, they may be *conjunctively* sufficient and *disjunctively* necessary; perhaps, that is, an experience is aesthetic if it has all these attributes and only if it has at least one of them.

I am not claiming that this proposal conforms faithfully to ordinary usage. Presystematic usage of "aesthetic" and "nonaesthetic" is even less clearly established by practice, and more seriously infected with inept theorizing, than in the case of most terms. I am rather suggesting that we have here an appropriate use for some badly abused terms. Density, repleteness, and exemplificationality, then, are earmarks of the aesthetic; articulateness, attenuation, and denotationality, earmarks of the nonaesthetic.

THE QUESTION OF MERIT

. . . Use of symbols beyond immediate need is for the sake of understanding, not practice; what compels is the urge to know, what delights is discovery, and communication is secondary to the apprehension and formulation of what is to be communicated. The primary purpose is cognition in and for itself; the practicality, pleasure, compulsion, and communicative utility all depend upon this.

Symbolization, then, is to be judged fundamentally by how well it serves the cognitive purpose; by the delicacy of its discriminations and the aptness of its allusions; by the way it works in grasping, exploring, and informing the world; by how it analyzes, sorts, orders, and organizes; by how it participates in the making, manipulation, retention, and transformation of knowledge. Considerations of simplicity and subtlety, power and precision, scope and selectivity, familiarity and freshness, are all relevant and often contend with one another; their weighting is relative to our interests, our information, and our inquiry.

So much for the cognitive efficacy of symbolization in general, but what of aesthetic excellence in particular? Distinguishing between the aesthetic and the meritorious cuts both ways. If excellence is not required of the aesthetic, neither is the excellence appropriate to aesthetic objects confined to them. Rather, the general excellence just sketched becomes aesthetic when exhibited by aesthetic objects; that is, aesthetic merit is such excellence in any symbolic functioning that, by its particular constellation of attributes, qualifies as aesthetic. This subsumption of aesthetic under cognitive excellence calls for one more reminder that the cognitive, while contrasted with both the practical and the passive, does not exclude the sensory or the emotive, that what we know through art is felt in our bones and nerves and muscles as well as grasped by our minds, that all the sensitivity and responsiveness of the organism participates in the invention and interpretation of symbols. . . .

Aesthetic merit, however, has by no means been my main concern in this book, and I am somewhat uncomfortable about having arrived at an incipient definition of what is often confusingly called 'beauty'. Excessive concentration on the question of excellence has been responsible, I think, for constriction and distortion of aesthetic inquiry.[1] To say that a work of art is good or even to say how good it is does not after all provide much information, does not tell us whether the work is evocative, robust, vibrant, or exquisitely designed, and still less what are its salient specific qualities of color, shape, or sound. Moreover, works of art are not racehorses, and picking a winner is not the primary goal. Rather than judgments of particular characteristics being mere means toward an ultimate appraisal, judgments of aesthetic value are often means toward discovering such characteristics. If a connoisseur tells me that one of two Cycladic idols that seem to me almost indistinguishable is much finer than the other, this inspires me to look for and may help me find the significant differences between the two. Estimates of excellence are among the minor aids to insight. Judging the excellence of works of art or the goodness of people is not the best way of understanding them. And a criterion of aesthetic merit is no more the major aim of aesthetics than a criterion of virtue is the major aim of psychology.

In short, conceiving of aesthetic experience as a form of understanding results both in resolving and in devaluing the question of aesthetic value.

NOTE

1. Cf. my "Merit as Means" in *Art and Philosophy*, ed. S. Hook (New York, New York University Press, 1966), pp. 56–57.

In Defense of Aesthetic Value

Monroe Beardsley

We come now to the most direct and serious attack on the functional account.[1] It has two parts:

(1) Talk of a *kind* of value, in a sense required by the functional account, is not intelligible.
(2) Even if there *are* kinds of value, there can be no such thing as aesthetic value, since we cannot isolate a special aesthetic character of experiences.

First as to the genus: how could things that have a value constitute a kind, within which we might mark out subordinate kinds? The most plausible answer can be summarized as follows: Toward anything whatever we may act in a variety of favoring ways, or adopt a variety of positive stances; helping to bring it into existence or to preserve and protect it, seeking it out, choosing or selecting it, making it more accessible to ourselves or others, borrowing or buying, taking advantage of its availability, etc. To act in any of these ways is to *elect* that thing, and anything that is or could be elected by someone is eligible. An act of electing something at some time may be one for which a justification can be given—i.e., there is an adequate reason for that act. Then we can say that the thing in question has *warranted eligibility*. A plausible view of value in general is that it is warranted eligibility. . . .

Thus we see how a value is a capacity (to contribute to the production of value), and how it is not circular to offer *this* as a definition, since "value" is not in turn defined by means of "a value."

I see no fatal flaw, then, in the conception of value-kinds. So our problem centers on the proposed species: whether one of these kinds can be aesthetic value. And this seems to depend on two things: identifying an aesthetic character in experience on which aesthetic value can be grounded, and showing that the possession of such a character is a valuable feature of such experiences. . . .

Those who have doubted or denied the existence of a special aesthetic character tend to rely on two negative arguments: first, that they have not succeeded in finding it, and second, that even its partisans cannot agree on what it is. To the first we may respond with commiseration, to the second with a legitimate excuse. It is fair to plead that to get at the aesthetic character is not necessarily a simple task. It may call for a good deal of subtle phenomenological inquiry, taking into account a wide range of experiences and carefully comparing our introspections with the reports of others. There is a serious problem of finding the right words to discriminate and articulate the noteworthy features of our interaction with outstanding artkind-instances. If there are continuing differences of opinion, or at least in emphasis, as for example about the precise nature of "disinterestedness" and its role in the experience of artworks, the fact is not surprising; and it neither belies the obvious truth that aestheticians have made progress in this direction nor mocks the persistent hope for further progress.

From *Proceedings and Addresses of the American Philosophical Association*, 52 (1979). Reprinted by permission of the publisher. Footnotes have been renumbered.

Although I am unready to relinquish more substantial claims concerning the analysis of aesthetic character, I am content here to advance a fairly modest one. Let us treat the aesthetic character as compound and disjunctive. It consists of five discernible features. Experience has an aesthetic character if it has at least four of these five features, including the first one.

1. A willingly accepted guidance over the succession of one's mental states by phenomenally objective properties (qualities and relations) of a perceptual or intentional field on which attention is fixed with a feeling that things are working or have worked themselves out fittingly. Since this awareness is directed *by*, as well as *to*, the object, we may call this feature, for short, *object-directedness*.
2. A sense of freedom, of release from the dominance of some antecedent concerns about past and future, a relaxation and sense of harmony with what is presented or semantically invoked by it or implicitly promised by it, so that what comes has the air of having been freely chosen. For short: *felt freedom*.
3. A sense that the objects of which interest is concentrated are set a little at a distance emotionally—a certain detachment of affect, so that even when we are confronted with dark and terrible things, and feel them sharply, they do not oppress but make us aware of our power to rise above them. For short: *detached affect*.
4. A sense of actively exercising constructive powers of the mind, of being challenged by a variety of potentially conflicting stimuli to try to make them cohere; a keyed-up state amounting to exhilaration in seeing connections between percepts and between meanings, a sense (which may be illusory) of achieved intelligibility. For short: *active discovery*.
5. A sense of integration as a person, of being restored to wholeness from distracting and disruptive impulses (but by inclusive synthesis as well as by exclusion), and a corresponding contentment, even through disturbing feelings, that involves self-acceptance and self-expansion. For short: *a sense of wholeness*.

If I may appropriate—or misappropriate—a colorful term introduced for a contrasting view (which I shall shortly acknowledge), I might call these five properties "symptoms" of the aesthetic in experience.

The limitations of these symptoms, as I have sketched them—object-directedness, felt freedom, detached affect, active discovery, and a sense of wholeness—are perhaps not so obscure that they need to be emphasized by me. (Others will cheerfully accept this labor.) Their vagueness is evident and essential. Yet I believe the descriptions apply to genuine realities, which we find in our experiences of many artworks, as well as other things. The symptoms are common (though not omnipresent) in experience; they are individually often present in play, sport, mathematics, and religion. These activities are sometimes accompanied by experiences with aesthetic character, though this is generally incidental to their central purpose. Here is one aspect of the aesthetic character that has made it difficult to manage—not that it is so rare, but that it turns up so widely, in mild or fleeting forms at least.

Despite their vagueness, these features allow for comparisons of degree among experiences with aesthetic character. The familiar dimensions apply here in usual ways: a feature may be more or less intense, sustained, pervasive, saturating, dominant over other aspects of the experience. More or fewer of the properties may be present, and they may cooperate more or less closely and powerfully. Not all comparisons of aesthetic value that might be attempted can be successful in this pluralistic scheme, so not all possible disputes about aesthetic value can be objectively resolved; but that was never promised. It seems to me, perhaps perversely, a merit of the proposal that it explains the considerable looseness and indeterminacy we actually encounter in the justification of art appraisals. Yet it remains true that the experience a well-qualified reader of poems obtains under favorable conditions, from reading Shakespeare's "Poor Soul! the center of my sinful earth" will have a decidedly more marked aesthetic character (considered all in all) than the experience that same reader, under similar conditions, will obtain from reading Michael Drayton's "To nothing fitter can I thee compare." That is evidence of greater aesthetic value.

One piece is still missing from the positive

case for aesthetic value. Although I have argued that objects possess this value in virtue of their capacity to impart marked aesthetic character to experience, I have so far merely assumed that experiences themselves possess value in virtue of having a capacity that is based on their aesthetic character. It may be evident that it is a good thing for an experience to have an aesthetic character—that this is *one* of the ways in which experiences can be worth having. But the question *why* this character confers value calls for a systematic answer—one that I am afraid is too long for this occasion. It calls for consideration of profoundly difficult questions about the nature of human goodness, what constitutes a good life, happiness, well-being and well-doing, and perhaps the meaning of life—though even if we differ in our answers to these questions, we may be able to agree that it is good for us to experience, at least occasionally, and to a degree seldom made possible except by artworks, the immediate sense (say) of inclusive self-integration and complex harmony with phenomenal objects. . . .

Having displayed, as I hope, some merits of the functional account of art appraisal, I would naturally like to make them stand out by contrasting this account with available alternatives. There is really only one serious alternative, I think: that put forward by Nelson Goodman. The present argument would be woefully incomplete without at least some attempt to meet his radical challenge.

Nelson Goodman's position rejects aesthetic value, as I have been analyzing and defending it, and proposes instead to base art appraisals on the cognitive value of artworks—their capacity to contribute to the "creation and comprehension of our worlds."[2] Artworks turn up in this account as characters, or classes of characters, in symbol systems, and like other symbols are to be judged primarily or centrally by their successful functioning as symbols, their "cognitive efficacy." In a memorable passage toward the end of *Languages of Art*, Goodman says that the use of symbols in making and meeting artworks "is for the sake of understanding. . . . What compels is the urge to know, what delights is discovery. . . . The primary purpose is cognition in and for itself."[3] And more recently, in *Ways of Worldmaking*, pursuing a related theme, he adds that "The arts must be taken no less seriously than the sciences as modes of discovery, creation, and enlargement of knowledge in the broad sense of advancement of the understanding."[4] Though, strictly speaking, truth is reserved for verbal claims, a broader category, "rightness of rendering," which involves both construing and constructing worlds, comprises the aims of both arts and sciences.

It is no small part of the debt we owe to *Languages of Art*—along with a few other books in recent decades—that we now recognize the extent to which the experience of artworks involves cognitive activities of many sorts—activities which do often in fact eventuate in knowledge and understanding. And much can be said for some arts as "modes of discovery." Yet when we bring together the results of many aesthetic inquiries, especially in our time, we cannot accede to these claims as stated. Instead of saying in general terms of artworks or artkind-instances that "the primary purpose is cognition in and for itself," we ought rather to say that the primary purpose is the aestheticizing of experience. In support of this rebuttal, I sketch three lines of argument.

First, it has not yet been shown, to my satisfaction, that instrumental musical works and nonrepresentational paintings are characters in symbol systems; it has not been adequately explained how they refer to anything. So I think their peculiar goodness has to be explained in some other way than by their successful symbol functioning in the service of cognition; what delights may be the discovery of the work itself, but not of other things via the work's reference. It would be temerarious to ascribe the artworks in general a primary purpose that cannot be fulfilled by such large and important subclasses of them.

Second, many natural objects, such as mountains and trees, are not characters in any symbol system, yet they seem to have a value that is closely akin to that of artworks.

This kinship can easily be explained in terms of aesthetic value, but hardly in terms of cognitive value.

Third, it is a commonplace (but I think well-placed here) that very widely in the arts, where cognitive concern is or could be present, we observe sacrifices in the cognitive dimension for the sake of other ends. Some aestheticians, of course, have tried to show that these apparent retreats are means to greater cognitive achievement (the novelist alters the newspaper facts that inspired his plot only in order to reveal deeper truths of human nature; and Poussin left the Biblical camels out of his famous painting of *Rebecca and Eleazer* the better to portray the essential human situation). This aiming at a "higher" truth certainly occurs in art, and is important; yet there is much that it will not explain (including the cases where the novelist changes the facts simply to make a better story—one that is more unified, or dramatic, or ironic, and thus more capable of fulfilling an aesthetic function; and perhaps Poussin found that he could make a better composition without the camels). The longer literature of this controversy supplies many such examples; they argue that cognition is not generally the overriding or dominant purpose of artworks.

And I will even go so far as to suggest—though with appropriate diffidence—that this point is tacitly conceded in Nelson Goodman's theory. It will be recalled that artworks, according to this theory, differ from other symbols basically in that they belong to symbol systems of a special sort, "aesthetic symbol systems." These systems possess one or more of those properties which he calls "symptoms of the aesthetic"—thus he is the victim of my terminological rip-off a little earlier. The symptoms are (1) syntactic and (2) semantic density, (3) a high degree of repleteness (in that more features of the symbol count), (4) exemplificationality (possession of predicates plus reference to them), and—as he has added in his most recent book—(5) "multiple and complex reference, where a symbol performs several integrated and interacting referential functions."[5] Now on the functional account it is understandable that artists creating artworks should often choose to make them symbols—that some types of symbol are very useful for the purpose of fashioning bearers of aesthetic value. And if we inquire what kinds of symbol lend themselves to this use, there is no better answer than Goodman's. But looking at the matter from within *his* system, it is fair to ask what justifies the selection and classification of these properties as "aesthetic."

To this question Goodman gives significant answers. The first three properties "call for maximum sensitivity of discrimination," since in a dense and replete symbol system minute differences between inscriptions make a difference in what symbols they are and in what they symbolize. Thus (I would suggest) the use of such symbols stimulates and exercises the cognitive faculties connected with perception to the highest degree and makes possible the construction of artworks of great subtlety and refinement, which are open to endless exploration. In an exemplificational symbol the properties referred to or expressed are "shown forth"—vividly presented for concentrated and prolonged affective apprehension.[6] Replete systems and multiple symbols carry complex meanings and compact them, giving an embracing unity to diverse elements of experience. As Goodman says in *Ways of Worldmaking*, "these [aesthetic] properties tend to focus attention on the symbol rather than, or at least along with, what it refers to"[7]—but to the extent that there is a tension here, it seems that our cognitive interests would tend to call for dominant attention to what is referred to, though our aesthetic interests might not. A symbol that attracts attention to itself, and rewards that attention, helps to detach our feelings from that to which it refers. "This emphasis upon the nontransparency of a work of art, upon the primacy of the work over what it refers to, far from involving denial or disregard of symbolic functions, derives from certain characteristics of a work as a symbol."[8] That's certainly true, and important. But also perfectly acceptable to anyone who maintains that the meanings and references in artworks are essential to their artistic nature. It is clearly consistent to emphasize the nontransparency of artworks while insisting on their symbolic character as well; but it is not so clearly consistent to emphasize the non-transparency of artworks and still insist that their cognitive symbolic function is their *primary* purpose.

It is, I think, some recommendation of aesthetic value (both of its reality and its importance) that the most powerful effort to dispense with it seems, in the end, to be driven back to reliance upon it. But I should not like to conclude with a mere dialectical flourish, even in this serious cause. It is rather the issue itself—underlying as it does so many current and promising controversies, yet, to my mind, still given too little serious discussion—that I wish to emphasize and stir into more active life.[9]

NOTES

1. By 'functional account,' Beardsley means to refer to his own position, as well as to any view which adheres to the following tenets: (a) in the case of at least some artworks, we can know that one is better than another; (b) in these cases there must be some way or manner in which the one work is better than the other; (c) there is something that can properly be called an artistic manner of goodness, that is, a kind of goodness typically associated with art; (d) the aesthetic character of certain experiences confers upon them aesthetic value; (e) such aesthetic value is a distinct kind of value; and (f) artworks are generally produced with the intention of providing conditions under which viewers of the art may have experiences with aesthetic value. [Eds.]
2. *Languages of Art*, Indianapolis: The Bobbs-Merrill Co., Inc., 1968, p. 265.
3. Ibid., p. 258.
4. *Ways of Worldmaking*, Indianapolis: Hackett, 1978, p. 102.
5. Ibid., p. 68.
6. *Languages of Art*, p. 253.
7. *Ways of Worldmaking*, p. 69.
8. Loc. cit.
9. I wish to acknowledge Elizabeth L. Beardsley's very helpful comments on this essay.

Instrumental Cognitivism

George Dickie

From *Evaluating Art* (Philadelphia: Temple University Press, 1988). Reprinted by permission of the publisher.

In 1968, at the very end of *Languages of Art*,[1] Goodman began sketching the broad outlines of an instrumentalist theory that like Beardsley's proposes to evaluate art on the basis of its ability to produce aesthetic experience. He continued sketching this theory in his 1978 article, "When Is Art?"[2] However, Goodman's conception of aesthetic experience is totally different from Beardsley's, and as a result of this difference, a dispute broke out between them.[3] This dispute is a clash between two very different conceptions of the nature of the proper experience of art. Beardsley's view, which is influenced by the Schopenhauerian tradition, conceives of the experience of art as detached and insulated from the rest of experience. Goodman's view, which revives a tradition antedating Schopenhauer, conceives of art as referring to the world and the experience of art as uninsulated from the rest of experience. Goodman's views, as sketchy and undeveloped as they are, are of the very greatest importance, because they challenge the conventional wisdom embodied in the theories of Beardsley and others that the experience of art ought to be detached and that cognitive features of art are not important in the evaluating of art.

The nub of the dispute is whether works of art, when properly experienced, are experienced as referring to things outside themselves. Because Beardsley maintains that aesthetic experience has a detached character, he claims that works of art are properly experienced as the center of a detached experience and that any reference a work of art makes to anything outside itself is nullified during the course of an aesthetic experience of the work. Since the references of works of art are nullified and cannot function in an aesthetic experience, works must be evaluated on the basis of their nonreferential aspects. Goodman, in contrast, maintains that works of art are symbols and, consequently, claims that works of art are essentially cognitive and are to be experienced as standing in cognitive relation to things outside of themselves. Thus, for Goodman, art is to be evaluated on the basis of its cognitive efficacy, that is, on the basis of how well it signifies what it signifies. Beardsley begins with a theory of aesthetic experience as detached and uses it to generate an account of the evaluation of art. Goodman, on the other hand, begins with a theory of art as symbol and uses it to generate an account of the evaluation of art.

Languages of Art's subtitle, *An Approach to a Theory of Symbols*, shows that Goodman sees the various arts as symbol systems. He wants to distinguish the art symbol systems from the nonart symbol systems, and he sees this as the problem of distinguishing the aesthetic from the nonaesthetic. Goodman rejects the traditional ways of making this distinction and makes the novel suggestion that the aesthetic/nonaesthetic distinction be made on the basis of the properties of symbol systems.

Goodman specifies five pairs of properties that symbol systems have. The first member of each of the pairs is an aesthetic symptom and the second is a nonaesthetic symptom. The first pair of symbol system properties is syntactic density and syntactic articulateness. A system is syntactically dense when it "provides for infinitely many characters so ordered that between each two there is a third."[4] Oil painting is a syntactically dense system because each painting is a character in a symbol system, and, for example, given two different paintings of Socrates, it is possible to paint a third that is different from each of the others and "falls between" them. A first painting might represent Socrates as having a large nose while a second might represent him as having a small nose. A third painting could be made representing Socrates as having a middle-sized nose. Between the middle-sized-nose painting and small-nose painting there could be a painting of Socrates with a nose neither middle-sized nor small but in between, and so on. Goodman cites an ungraduated mercury thermometer as an example of something that is syntactically dense and an electronic digital thermometer as an example of something that is syntactically articulate.[5]

The second pair of symbol system properties is semantic density and semantic articulateness. A system is semantically dense when "symbols are provided for things [referred to] distinguished by the finest differences in certain respects." English is cited as a semantically dense system, as presumably any natural language would be. Goodman also cites ungraduated mercury thermometers as semantically dense.[6]

The third pair of properties is syntactic repleteness and syntactic attenuation. A symbol system is replete when "comparatively many aspects of a symbol are significant."[7] An oil painting is replete because all of its features are important, and a chart of daily stock market averages is attenuated because only the height of the line above the baseline is important.

The fourth pair of properties is exemplification and denotation. Exemplification occurs when a symbol symbolizes by being a sample of a property it possesses—for example, a paint chip or a tailor's swatch. By "denotation" Goodman apparently means something like mere reference without any frills such as exemplification.

The final pair of symbol system properties is multiple and complex reference and its opposite. Multiple and complex reference occurs when "a symbol performs several integrated and interacting referential functions."[8]

Syntactic density, semantic density, syntactic repleteness, exemplification, and multiple and complex reference are the symptoms of the aesthetic. By the way, possession of these symptoms has nothing to do with the value of a work of art. In *Languages of Art*, Goodman asserts that the symptoms of the aesthetic "may be conjunctively sufficient and disjunctively necessary."[9] Ten years later in "When Is Art?" he is cagier about the matter, saying, "And for these five symptoms to come somewhere near being disjunctively necessary and conjunctively (as a syndrome) sufficient might well call for some redrawing of the vague and vagrant borderlines of the aesthetic."[10] In any event, all this suggests that if the symbols at the center of an experience have all five symptoms, then the experience is an aesthetic one, and in order for an experience to be an aesthetic experience, the symbol at its center must have at least one of the symptoms. Thus, any experience focused on symbols in English or even on an ungraduated thermometer may be an aesthetic experience, but, of course, it may not be.

Goodman is trying to work out some way of distinguishing those cognitive experiences that are aesthetic experiences from those that are not aesthetic experiences. What all this comes down to is that aesthetic experiences are those in which some attention is focused on the symbols as well as on that to which the symbols refer. How well this scheme works in sorting out cognitive experiences properly, while interesting, is not my primary concern. My main concern is with Goodman's claim that the value of art is to be measured by its cognitive efficacy.

The claims that make up Goodman's evaluational theory are as follows:

1. Every work of art is a symbol which symbolizes by means of either description, representation, expression, exemplification, or some combination of these four.
2. Symbols are for cognizing.
3. "The primary purpose [of art] is cognition in and for itself;. . . [art's] . . . practicality, pleasure, compulsion, and communicative utility all depend on this."
4. Art is to be evaluated by how well it serves its cognitive purpose.[11]

In number 3 above, Goodman's qualification "primary" in saying that the primary purpose of art is cognition and his mentioning of practicality, pleasure, compulsion, and communicative utility suggests that cognition is the primary criterion of art's value but that practicality, pleasure, compulsion, and communicative utility are secondary criteria of art's value. However, Goodman focuses entirely on cognitive efficacy in the remainder of his remarks in *Languages of Art* and in his later discussions of the evaluations of art.

Perhaps the first thing to note about Goodman's evaluational theory is that it contradicts Beardsley's theory at almost every point. For Goodman, the experience of art is cognitive and this means that it is not insulated or marked off sharply from the remainder of experience. A work of art refers unimpededly to things outside the immediate experience of the work, although this may be a somewhat misleading way of putting it since, for Goodman, the experience of art does not have an "edge" such that things can be inside or outside of it.

Assume for the moment that Goodman is right about art's always referring and being cognitive. How does the artistic value of works of art depend on their cognitive efficacy? One would expect from Goodman at this point a number of examples illustrating the cognitive efficacy of specific works of art. It would be particularly nice to have an example of a pair of works that illustrate how the cognitive efficacy of one is greater than the cognitive efficacy of the other—say, Cézanne's *The Sainte Victoire, Seen from the Quarry Called Bibemus* and Frith's *Paddington Station*. All that is given, however, is a general statement about cognitive efficacy:

Symbolization, then, is to be judged fundamentally by how well it serves the cognitive purpose: by the delicacy of its discriminations and the aptness of its allusions; by the way it works in grasping, exploring, and informing the world; by how it analyzes, sorts, orders, and organizes; by how it participates in the making, manipulation, retention, and transformation of knowledge. Considerations of simplicity and subtlety, power and precision, scope and selectivity, familiarity and freshness, are all relevant and often contend with one another; their weighting is relative to our interests, our information, and our inquiry.[12]

Lacking specific examples of the way in which the artistic value of art depends on cognitive efficacy, it is difficult to understand and, thus, to evaluate Goodman's theory. Nevertheless, there is a way to evaluate Goodman's claim about artistic value as cognitive efficacy. Underlying his claim about cognitive efficacy is the more basic claim that all art is referential: unless a work of art is referential in some way, the question of cognitive efficacy cannot arise for it. Thus, if there are nonreferential artworks, they cannot be evaluated according to Goodman's scheme. Goodman must show that there are no nonreferential works of art.

The most obvious candidates for nonreferential works of art are ones that come from the domains of nonobjective painting and instrumental music, works of art that are not usually referential in the obvious way that representative, descriptive, and even expressive works are. It is on such works that the controversy between Beardsley and Goodman regarding referentiality focuses. Thus, it is crucial for Goodman to show that nonobjective paintings that do not refer in any of the usual ways (representationally, for example) do in fact refer. Goodman seizes on the notion of exemplification.

Goodman maintains that a characteristic, such as the dominant color of a nonobjective painting, is referential because it exemplifies itself. His contention reveals the radical difference between his theory and Beardsley's: Beardsley maintains a work can have value by merely *possessing* a color that is, say, very intense, while Goodman maintains that, with respect to such a color, a work can have value only because the color it possesses refers by means of *exemplification*.

The issue, then, is whether the aesthetic value of works of art is always a function of the reference of their properties or whether in some cases their value may result from the simple possession of properties that do not refer. (Any value a work of art might have as a result of its expression is being ignored.)

Consider the following five Dantoesque objects: each is a flat rectangle two feet by four feet, each a gorgeous shade of blue, and all are visually indistinguishable from the distances at which they are seen. Three of the objects are paintings side by side on a wall. The fourth, on the floor below the paintings is a bundle of rug samples bound together and labeled "Rug Samples." The viewer sees only the topmost sample. The fifth object is a hole in the wall above the paintings into which an air conditioning duct is soon to be fitted, and through this hole the clear blue sky is seen.

The rug sample both possesses and exemplifies; that is, it both is a gorgeous blue and refers to, say, rug rolls of the same color. The well-established practice of choosing carpets based on such samples makes the reference possible. Beardsley and everyone else agrees with Goodman that exemplification occurs here. That is, everyone agrees that a rug sample is a sample. The painting on the left is titled *The Blue Sky*. This painting is representational and, hence, on Goodman's view symbolizes, that is, denotes. Let it be granted to Goodman that reference occurs here too.

The painting in the middle is titled *The Missing Shade of Blue*. This painting would presumably not be representational, but it does exemplify a shade of blue. The title provides a context analogous to that provided by the practice that surrounds rug selection. If the Humean title seems to complicate things too much, use the title *Cerulean Blue*, it will also supply a context sufficient for exemplification. Let it be granted to Goodman that reference occurs here too.

Move now to the hole in the wall above the paintings. The two by four foot rectangle of gorgeous blue is visually indistinguishable from the other four objects. However, this fifth object is neither a work of art nor a work of rug selection; it is just a section of sky. There can be no question that it merely possesses its color and does not exemplify its color and that it is gorgeous, that is, has aesthetic value. This is a clear case of the aesthetic experience of a bit of nature. Nothing needs to be granted Goodman in this case because no art is involved.

Move finally to the third painting, the one on the right. It is economically titled *#1*. Now, according to Goodman, (1) the blue of this painting exemplifies itself and (2) it is in virtue of this symbolizing that it has whatever aesthetic value it has. It is not clear to me that Goodman has yet presented any argument for the first claim that properties such as the blueness in this nonobjective painting exemplify. What he does do is to talk first about tailor's swatches, pointing out that they exemplify some of their properties (color, texture, pattern) but not other properties (shape, having pinked edges). He then moves on to, say, nonobjective paintings, pointing out that some of their properties are aesthetically important (color, pattern) and that some of their properties are not aesthetically important (being owned by Averell Harriman, being three hundred feet from Michigan Avenue). He notes that the aesthetically important properties of such paintings are shown forth, exhibited, and so forth. He then concludes that the important properties that are shown forth are exemplified and that the unimportant properties are not. Although this conclusion is consistent with what he has said, it does not follow from what he has said. What does follow is that there is something that distinguishes aesthetically important properties from aesthetically unimportant ones. More argument is required to show that that something is exemplification. Goodman needs to show that some kind of context (analogous to the practice surrounding rug samples) surrounds works of art and is specifically responsible for allowing exemplification. That this can be shown seems unlikely to me, especially in light of the fact that Goodman has made no move to do so. It will perhaps be instructive to see Goodman's own words on this point: "The properties that count in a purist [nonobjective] painting are those that the picture makes manifest, selects, focuses upon, exhibits, heightens in our consciousness—those that it shows forth—in short, those properties that it does not merely possess but *exemplifies*, stands as a sample of."[13] This is all by way of argument that Goodman gives. His remark, however, gives no more reason to say that the blue of *#1* exemplifies than to say that the blue seen through the hole in the wall exemplifies. So there is no reason to think that the aesthetic value *#1* has derives from exemplification or any other kind of reference. If *#1* has aesthetic value, it may well be because of the property of blueness it possesses. So, if *#1* has aesthetic value, Beardsley rather than Goodman seems to be right about why it has the value it has.

There is another argument distinct from the one just given that also shows that Goodman's view cannot have the generality that he claims for it. Suppose it is granted that *#1*, and every other nonobjective painting, exemplifies. Granted this claim, would Goodman's view that it is in virtue of exemplification that such paintings have whatever aesthetic value they have be acceptable? Suppose that *#1* is a gorgeous blue and exemplifies the gorgeous blue. Let it be granted for the moment that *#1* has aesthetic value because it exemplifies the gorgeous blue. *#1* must also have additional aesthetic value, because it is visually indistinguishable from the section of blue sky that has aesthetic value without exemplifying. Beardsley maintains that Goodman inadvertently concedes this point at the end of "When Is Art?" when he speaks of the five marks of the aesthetic.[14] Goodman writes:

Notice that these properties tend to focus attention on the symbol rather than, or at least along with, what it refers to. . . . This emphasis upon the nontransparency of a work of art, upon the primacy of the work over what it refers to, far from involving denial or disregard of symbolic functions, derives from certain characteristics of a work as a symbol.[15]

Goodman's remark about the nontransparency of a work of art and the primacy of the work over that to which it refers implies, according to Beardsley, that works of art have value independent of their references (even if they also have value because of their references). If, however, the mere possession of a property gets any aesthetic value points at all, then the generality of Goodman's theory of art evaluation is spoiled. I was at first convinced by Beardsley's argument, but I am not so sure now. Goodman might claim that the interest focused on the symbol (which is a work of art) is focused simply for the sake of accuracy of reference. But independently of whether Goodman concedes this point, #1 has additional aesthetic value that does not derive from exemplification.

There are two other related difficulties with Goodman's claim about cognitive efficiency as the criterion of artistic merit that are worth mentioning. The first is as follows. Assume that #1 has the value it has because its gorgeous blue exemplifies its color. Consider, however, a second nonobjective painting that like #1 is uniformly colored but is uniformly colored a dull, drab, muddy, brownish-grey. The second painting exemplifies its color just as well as the first painting does, because a painting is supposed to exemplify itself. There is, however, good reason to think that the first painting is superior. Thus, there has to be more to the evaluation of these two paintings than exemplification. Put in another way, according to Goodman's theory, every nonobjective, uniformly colored painting will have exactly the same value if the value of such paintings derives solely from exemplification, but surely all such paintings do not have the same value.

The other difficulty involves types of reference other than exemplification. If cognitive *efficacy* is the sole criterion of aesthetic merit, then the importance of what is signified can have no bearing on aesthetic merit. For example, any two equally efficacious representational paintings will have the same value, independently of what they represent. It is at least arguable that an important subject matter lends value to a work of art, although clearly it cannot be the whole story.

What is it then that makes art valuable? Beardsley and Goodman agree on one thing, namely, that art is valuable insofar as it can produce valuable experiences. That is, they agree that artistic value is instrumental value. I believe that they are right about the instrumental nature of artistic goodness.

Given that artistic value is instrumental value, what conclusions can be drawn about the evaluation of art on the basis of the analyses and criticisms of Beardsley's and Goodman's views that have been given so far?

First, Beardsley is right that some aspects of works of art are instrumentally valuable because they can produce valuable experiences without referring to anything outside the experience of the work of art. Examples of such aspects are the gorgeous blue of #1, the intense combinations of colors in many of Van Gogh's paintings, and the unity of form in a sonnet. Goodman is just wrong that an aspect of a work of art must refer in order to be valuable.

Goodman is right, however, that some aspects of works of art are instrumentally valuable because they can produce valuable experiences in which these aspects are experienced as standing in relation to things outside the immediate experience of the work. Examples of such aspects are the references in *The Adventures of Huckleberry Finn* to specific geographical locations and the depiction of the social and legal relations between slave and nonslave in the pre-Civil War United States. Beardsley is just wrong that an aspect of a work of art cannot be valuable to the experience of that work in virtue of its reference.

Both Beardsley and Goodman suffer from the philosopher's passion for theoretical neatness and simplicity. Each wants a theoretical explanation for the value of art that involves only one kind of feature: *possession* in Beardsley's case and *referentiality* in Goodman's case.

Beardsley's inability to recognize the value of reference derives from the view of aesthetic experience as the only proper product for the instrumentality of art, a view he inherited. The traditional picture of the aesthetic experience of a work of art goes like this: The work and the person or subject who is experiencing it are surrounded by an impenetrable, psychological wall "secreted" by the subject that experientially nullifies all relations that the work has to things outside the experience. Aspects of works of art may, and frequently do, refer, but a "proper" subject of aesthetic experience cannot take account of such references.

The roots of Goodman's inability to recognize the value of possessed properties are not so clear. His view that works of art are symbols, that is, have reference, has something to do with it. There is, however, nothing about being a symbol that prevents aspects of a symbol from having value independently of its symbol function, and Goodman may be admitting this when he speaks of the nontransparency of the symbols that are works of art. If so, he does not incorporate this admission into this theory. Perhaps Goodman has just not reflected sufficiently on the details of his own argument. There is a dialectical tendency that sometimes occurs when a philosopher opposes another view. The attacking philosopher will formulate his position as the exact opposite of the opposing view. Perhaps Goodman is caught up in this philosophical version of Newton's third law.

NOTES

1. Nelson Goodman, *Languages of Art: An Approach to a Theory of Symbols* (Indianapolis and New York: Bobbs-Merrill, 1968), pp. 255–265.
2. Nelson Goodman, "When Is Art?" in *Ways of Worldmaking* (Indianapolis and Cambridge: Hackett Publishing Co., 1978), pp. 57–70.
3. Monroe Beardsley, "Languages of Art and Art Criticism," *Erkenntnis* 12 (1978): 95–118; Nelson Goodman, "Reply to Beardsley," *Erkenntnis* 12 (1978): 169–173.
4. Goodman, *Languages of Art*, p. 136.
5. Goodman, *Ways of Worldmaking*, p. 68.
6. Ibid.
7. Ibid.
8. Ibid.
9. Goodman, *Languages of Art*, p. 254.
10. Goodman, *Ways of Worldmaking*, pp. 68–69.
11. Goodman, *Languages of Art*, pp. 255–265.
12. Ibid., p. 258.
13. Goodman, *Ways of Worldmaking*, p. 65.
14. Beardsley, "In Defense of Aesthetic Value," in *Proceedings and Addresses of the American Philosophical Association* (Newark, Del.: American Philosophical Association, 1979), p. 747.
15. Goodman, *Ways of Worldmaking*, p. 69.

Aesthetic Responses and Works of Art

Arthur Danto

It seems reasonable to suppose that if our aesthetic response to an object is a mere *Anschauung*, [perception] then if our *Anschauung* of an object x is A, our *Anschauung* of an object y should not especially differ when x and y are, in every outward particular, indiscernible: for the content of our perceptions should be much the same if whatever meets the senses is the same in the two instances. Since it is possible to imagine an artwork and a mere object to be similar in every observable respect, and if our aesthetic responses to the two differ when we know one of them to be an artwork, then it is reasonable to conclude

---

From *Philosophic Exchange*, Summer 1981. Reprinted by permission of the publisher.

that the difference in response must in part be a matter of that knowledge, and aesthetic response cannot accordingly always be a matter of mere *Anschauung*. Rather, aesthetic response will in part be a function of the concept(s) under which the object is perceived, and the beliefs appropriate to objects so conceived.

If this is true, there is a consequence of perhaps even greater moment to us. If knowledge that something is an artwork makes a difference in the mode of aesthetic response to an object—if there are differential aesthetic responses to indiscernible objects when one is an artwork and the other, say, a natural thing—then there would be a threat of circularity in any definition of art in which some reference to aesthetic response was intended to play a defining role. For it would not be just aesthetic response as such but a certain *kind* of aesthetic response which belonged to works of art in contrast with the kind which belongs to natural things, or to blasé artifacts like Brillo boxes (when not works of art)—and we should have to be able to distinguish works of art from natural things or mere artifacts in order to define the appropriate kind of response. Hence we could not *use that kind of response* to define the concept of the work of art.

Anyway, aesthetic considerations have always been viewed as having a natural place in discussions of art, and this is as good a place as any to come to terms with this easy association. The question is whether asthetic considerations belong to the definition of art. If they do not, then they simply will be among the things which go with the concept without pertaining to its logic, and not really more important, philosophically, than countless other things, like preciousness or collectability, which have also been felt part of the practice if not of the concept of art.

I

An aesthetic condition has been deemed necessary in the definition of art formulated by George Dickie in his influential discussion of the Institutional Theory of Art: a work of art is a "candidate for appreciation," a status conferred upon an artifact by what Dickie speaks of as "the art world"—an institutionally enfranchised group of persons who serve, so to speak, as trustees for the generalized *musee imaginaire*, the occupants of which are the artworks of the world. "If something cannot be appreciated," Dickie writes, "it cannot be a work of art." Dickie denies that he means specifically *aesthetic* appreciation, but he has been taken to mean just that by a prominent critic whose argument, if sound, has some meaning for us. It is that there are certain objects which *cannot* be appreciated, hence cannot be works of art by Dickie's own contrapositive formula. Hence the citizenry of the artworld is bounded by the constraints of appreciability and cannot by fiat declare just anything a work of art. . . .

There are two difficulties with this position as defended by Professor Ted Cohen. The first is this. Among the objects alleged immune to aesthetic appreciation, Cohen cites "ordinary thumbtacks, cheap white envelopes, the plastic forks given at some drive-in restaurants" and most particularly in view of the importance accorded one of them in the conceptual history of recent art, "urinals." Now I do not know whether the claim is that these cannot be appreciated, or simply cannot be appreciated favorably. Terms like "cheap," "ordinary," "plastic" are expressions of distaste, and it is not clear that even by Dickie's criterion, every object elevated to the stature of an artwork by the artworld must *ipso facto* be *favorably* appreciated. As a matter of textual fact, Dickie does say something like this: "I am saying that every work of art must have some minimal *potential* value or worthiness." But in fact aesthetic qualities compass, it seems to me, *negative* considerations: we are repelled, disgusted, even sickened by certain works of art. To restrict to the favorable cases the application of the epithet "work of art" would be parallel to regarding moral considerations as arising only with persons and actions which had some "minimal potential value or worthiness." And while there may indeed be good in everything, moral theory had better accommodate the swine, the wicked, the morally lazy, the bad, the evil, the revolting. So "appreciation," if aesthetic at least, can be negative, and the very use of the adjectives he does use tells us a lot about the way in which Professor Cohen appreciates throwaway forks, vulgar envelopes, and ordinary thumbtacks (in contrast with push-pins?). I should be astonished if negative aesthetic appreciation entailed that the objects which elicited it could not be works of art.

These questions can obviously not be settled without some discussion of aesthetic appreciation—or of appreciation *tout court*—but there is another and more damaging difficulty which would remain even if these questions were resolved in such a way as to leave Cohen's objection unshaken. Even were we to grant that an ordinary thumbtack could not be (aesthetically) appreciated (positively or negatively) it would not follow that a thumbtack—or an ordinary white envelope—or a plastic throwaway fork, could not be a work of art. Of course a thumbtack which *was* a work of art would have to differ in *some* way from a thumbtack otherwise like it in every external respect which was not a work of art. But in that case it is far from plain how things would stand with appreciation. Even granting the thumbtack itself was beneath appreciation, it would not follow that an artwork materially like a mere thumbtack could not be appreciated; and that to which we might respond appreciatively would be the properties of the artwork without necessarily being the properties of the thumbtack. To be sure the connection between the two may be very intricate to work out indeed—as intricate perhaps as the connection between a person and his body. We may see this somewhat more clearly perhaps by pondering the notorious example of Duchamp's *Fountain*, and Dickie's own analysis of it.

Dickie is adamant in insisting that there is no such thing as "a special kind of aesthetic consciousness, attention, or perception." And he goes on to say that "The only sense in which there is a difference between the appreciation of art and the appreciation of nonart is that the appreciations have different *objects*." Presumably he does not mean by "different objects" the difference between artworks and mere things, for then his definition would go circular: he would be defining appreciation of art in terms of its objects, whereas candidacy for appreciation was supposed to have gone into the explanation of why something is an artwork. So I gather he is trying to say that what we appreciate in artworks is just what we would appreciate in non-artworks, when in fact they happen materially to be the same, as *Fountain* is with countless many urinals distributed for the convenience of gentlemen wherever they congregate. "Why," Dickie says, "cannot the ordinary qualities of *Fountain*—its gleaming white surface, the depth revealed when it reflects images of surrounding objects, its pleasing oval shape—be appreciated? It has qualities similar to those of works by Brancusi and Moore which many do not balk at saying they appreciate." These *are* qualities of the urinal in question, as they are qualities of any urinal made of white porcelain, and which do resemble certain qualities of *Bird in Flight*. But the question is whether the artwork *Fountain* is indeed identical with that urinal, and hence whether those gleaming surfaces and deep reflections are indeed qualities of the artwork at all. Ted Cohen has supposed that Duchamp's work is not the urinal at all but the gesture of exhibiting it, and the gesture, if that indeed is the work, has no gleaming surfaces to speak of, and differs from what Moore and Brancusi did roughly as gestures differ from bits of brass and bronze. But the work, whatever it is, itself has properties that urinals themselves lack, it is daring, impudent, irreverent, witty, and clever and mere urinals are none of these. What would have provoked Duchamp to madness or murder, I should think, would be the sight of aesthetes mooning over the gleaming surfaces of the porcelain object he had manhandled into exhibition space: "How like Kilimanjaro! How like the white radiance of Eternity! How artistically sublime!" (Bitter laughter at the *Club des artistes*.) No: the properties of the object deposited in the artwork it shares with most items of industrial *porcelainerie*, while the properties *Fountain*, as an *artwork*, possesses, it shares with the Julian Tomb of Michaelangelo and the Great Perseus of Cellini. If what made *Fountain* an artwork were all and only the qualities it shared with urinals, the question would arise as to what makes it an artwork and not those. Is it just an oversight of the artworld? Should there be a mass transfiguration like a mass conversion to Buddhism of all the untouchables in Calcutta? I take the responsibility: herewith all the urinals in Greater New York along with those in Wichita *are artworks*! I shall get around to those in Baton Rouge and Oklahoma City when time permits. What Dickie has overlooked is an ambiguity in the term "makes" as it occurs in the question: What makes something a work of art? He has emphasized how something gets to be a work of art, which may be institutional, and neglected in favor of aesthetic considerations the question of what qualities constitute an artwork once something is one.

My own view is that a work of art has a great many qualities, indeed a great many qualities of a different sort altogether, than the qualities which belong to objects materially indiscernible from them but not themselves artworks. And some of these qualities may very well be aesthetic ones, or qualities one can experience aesthetically or find "worthy and valuable." But then in order to respond aesthetically to these one must first know the object is an artwork, and hence the distinction between what is art and what is not presumed available before the difference in response to that difference in identity is possible. Aristotle had an insight that the pleasure one derives from works of mimesis presupposes knowledge that they are imitations, for one will not derive that pleasure from the originals, however indiscernible originals and imitations may be. And Diderot has brilliantly argued that we may be moved to tears by representations of things which by themselves will move us not at all, or move us differently. We may cry at a representation of a mother's despair at the death of a child: but he would be hard-hearted who just wept at the correspondent reality: the thing is to *comfort and console*. What I shall proceed to argue, then, is that there are two orders of aesthetic response, depending upon whether the response is to an artwork or to a mere real thing which cannot be told apart from it. Hence we cannot appeal to aesthetic considerations in order to get our definition of art, inasmuch as we need the definition of art in order to identify the sorts of aesthetic responses appropriate to works of art in contrast with mere real things. True, something may not be a work of art without, as Dickie says, the minimal potential for aesthetic value: but I wonder if there is anything at all of which *that* is not true? He himself allows, against Cohen, that "thumbtacks, envelopes, and plastic forks have qualities that can be appreciated if one makes the effort to focus on them." So what cannot? Yet there is, I shall argue, a special aesthetics for works of art: indeed there is a special *language of artistic appreciation*; and inasmuch as both seem to be involved with the concept of art, it will not be amiss to address ourselves to some features of aesthetic and thence of artistic experience, even if it will not especially help us in finding the definition of art.

It will be an analytical convenience to begin by supposing, even if false, that there exists, just as a great many philosophers of merit have believed there to exist, an aesthetic sense, or a sense of beauty, or a faculty of taste; and that it is (or these are) as widely distributed among men as the so-called external senses, like sight and hearing, are. I should suppose them more widely distributed even than that, for there must be as much reason to suppose animals are driven by aesthetic preferences as that men are, and that if they are, there is evidence that we are dealing with something innate. I should on the other hand be astonished were someone to propose that there is an innate "sense of art." . . .

. . . [N]o knowledge of an object can make it look different, . . . an object retains its sensory qualities unchanged however it is classed and whatever it may be called. A rose is alleged to smell as sweet by whatever name it is called. To put it in a more contemporary idiom, one's sensory experiences would not be expected to undergo alteration with changes in the description of the object: that remains invariant under changes in description, as Santayana's useful if philosophically tendentious image of a 'mirroring intelligence' implies. If the aesthetic sense were like the other senses, the same, one would surmise, would be true of it, but in fact one's aesthetic responses are often a function of what one's beliefs about an object are, or the description under which the object is given. True, there may be cases where my sensory experience of an object may differ when the object is brought under a certain description, in the sense that knowing it to be of a certain kind, or knowing it to be described in that way, I may concentrate attention and pick up certain qualities I missed the first time around. Told that a certain wine has the taste of raspberries, I may learn to discriminate this taste which I did not discern when I first tasted it. Yet it was there to be tasted before as well as after it has been described that way: the object did not *acquire* these qualities by being described, nor did it change its status thereby. But the qualities an object has when an artwork are in fact so different from what an indiscernible counterpart has when a mere real thing that it is absurd to suppose I *missed* these qualities in the latter. They were not *there* to *be* missed. No sensory examination of an object will tell me that it is an artwork, since quality for quality it may be matched by an object which is not one, so far at least as the qualities to which the normal senses are responsive are concerned. If aesthetic response were constant as the difference between art and non-art, the same would be true of these. But in fact it is false. Our aesthetic responses will differ depending upon which it is because the qualities to which we respond are different.

I do not simply mean, even if it is incidentally true, that our *attitude* toward an object may alter when we discover it to have been an artwork. We may, upon learning that an artwork is before us, adopt an attitude of respect and awe. We may treat the object differently, as we may treat differently what we took to be an old derelict upon discovering him to be the pretender to the throne, or treat with respect a piece of wood described as from the true cross when we were about to use it for kindling. These changes indeed are "institutional" and social in character. Learning something to be an artwork, we may, just as Dickie says, attend to its gleaming surfaces or whatever. But if what we attend to could have been attended to before the transfiguration, the only change will have been adoption of an aesthetic stance, which we could in principle have struck before. It is a matter merely of attending to what was there to be perceived—like the taste of raspberries in the glass of Gigondas. No: learning it is a work of art means that it has qualities to attend to which its untransfigured counterparts just lacked; and that our aesthetic responses will be different. And this is not institutional, it is ontological. We are dealing with an altogether different *order* of things.

II

It is not difficult to construct examples in which this difference may be made plain, examples in which recognitionally indiscriminable objects prove to have very different qualities and indeed very different structures depending upon whether one of them is an artwork or not. Even if there is an innate aesthetic sense, the aesthetic response will differ, even in the same individual, depending upon how the indiscernible objects are classed. The differences are as deep as those between bodily movements and actions, between a person and a zombie, between a divinity and an idol.

Imagine six panels of ricepaper, used in the Japanese manner as a room divider, say in an apartment in Tokyo, a city whose air quality has degenerated alarmingly over recent years. Soot has been deposited on the roof which, one day, springs a leak in such a way that splotches and splashes and drips of soiled water get deposited in various irregular patterns while the apartment stands empty. The new tenant, an aesthete, suffers aesthetic recoil upon beholding the sordid sight: he demands removal and replacement with some nice clean panels, so the place "is fit to live in." Whereupon he is informed that a rare screen, six panels wide, by one of the great masters of the art, has come onto the market; that it would fit the space to perfection; that it is a once-in-a-lifetime opportunity. It is bought and installed and it is absolutely thrilling to look at it. To be sure, the same distribution of greys and blacks may be found as defaced its merely domestic predecessor, and for our purposes the panels in fact are exactly congruent. *These* blacks, however, are mountains, *those* grey smudges clouds. The fine splatterings in the panel to the extreme right compose a token representation of rain softening into mists. The irregular streak over here is a dragon ascending, at times indistinguishable from the mountains, at others from the clouds, making his mysterious way—W*ay*—through the boundless, softly articulated universe to whatever is its destiny and our own. It is a philosophical work, dense with depth and mystery and beauty: before it one is moved to the profoundest meditations: one is transfigured by its power—though its indistinguishable counterpart rightly provokes us only to revulsion and disgust. Our aesthete spends hour upon hour in contemplation of its bottomless wonder, now and again shuddering at the recollection of the desecration it replaced. Those dirty panels had no mystery and certainly no depth and absolutely no beauty. They were ugly beyond description.

It may be argued that the example is unfair. There may be a Japanese artist concerned with an oriental version of *l'art brut*. Flinging an epithet against the entire rotten preciosity of a decadent feudal tradition, he presents us with six panels of filthy rice paper, as offensive as bird-droppings on one of Guido's angel-struck maidens. It is nothing more than it pretends to be: so many stretches of soiled rice paper. Will it be beautiful, mysterious, cosmic, deep? I have no idea *what* aesthetic qualities it will have, for the object is insufficiently described and I cannot tell much from the small reproduction in *Art International*. I know that my responses to it will be different from those the great screen elicits. This work, I imagine will be described by connoisseurs as "sordid," without this being necessarily or at all an expression of disgust or even of aesthetic disprase. And I am certain that the logic of this expression's use will be different when applied as an artistic predicate, true of an artwork, than an aesthetic predicate true of a mere sordid thing. And it will go with quite different responses as well. I can do no more at this point in the present analysis than indicate that there is this difference, and to commit myself to work it out when I am in better position to map the semantics of the Language of Artistic Appreciation. But when I say that the object has been insufficiently described, I mean that a number of decisions must be made in identifying it as a work—decisions which do not come up at all in connection with its recognitionally congruent cousin, the long-since discarded set of soiled panels. Meanwhile how agreeable to have established that whatever the divisions between East and West, the identical philosophico-aesthetic questions can be raised for either tradition! . . .

Italian Comedians, **Antoine Watteau (French). Probably 1720. National Gallery of Art, Washington, D.C.**

Looking at this picture does not make us aware of certain facts that nonetheless may be relevant to interpreting it. Painted for his doctor and friend, this work represents a famous troupe who had been disbanded in 1697 but allowed to resume performance in 1716. Watteau, however, posed his acquaintances in the troupe's costumes. The center figure is thought to actually be Corneille van Cleve, Rector of the Royal Academy of Sculpture! How do we interpret this? Do you notice the subtle sadness that pervades this picture of gaiety? Watteau knew that he was dying at the time.

CHAPTER 8
Questions of Interpretation

As we suggested in the introduction to Chapter 2, analytic aesthetics has frequently been characterized as a second-order clarification of the concepts of art critics. Since the dominant art criticism during the period of early analytic aesthetics was New Criticism, aestheticians like Beardsley were concerned with clarifying, and to some extent justifying, the critical assumptions of that movement, including the assumption of the autonomy of the artwork and the rational objectivity of critical discourse. New Criticism assumed, in other words, that meaning is there in the poem, for example, objectively available to the sensitive reader.

On the other hand, from the "tradition of the aesthetic" (the eighteenth- and nineteenth-century account of aesthetic experience as fundamentally different from other types of experience in being more intuitive and perceptual rather than cognitive and intellectual) there came an insistence that the kind of objectivity of which the interpretation of art was capable was very different from that found elsewhere (in ethics, science, logic, or everyday "inductive" reasoning).

The problem for interpretation is primarily one of the role of reason-giving in art criticism. Is it, on the model of other sorts of reason-giving, providing necessary and sufficient conditions, one or the other but not both, or perhaps only defeasible conditions? Is it deductive or only inductive or neither? If neither, how can it be in some other sense (what other sense is there?) reasonable and objective? Is the central function of criticism perhaps only rhetorical, persuasive, or pragmatic, providing directions for perceiving, channeling canons of taste, getting one to look at things in certain ways, and the like?

Two of the most important early contributors and architects of this dialogue were Beardsley (who says, yes, interpretative criticism is basically a modified form of induction—objectively rational more or less in the same way as in ethics and everyday empirical reasoning) and Isenberg (who says, no, it is completely different and ultimately provides only rhetorical, persuasive, pragmatic directions for perceiving).

This debate turned mainly on the question of the role in art criticism of *general* critical reasons or criteria offered in interpretative arguments. One important consequence of this debate is the question of whether interpretations can be said to be true or false, correct or incorrect, or only reasonable, plausible, appropriate, or pragmatically useful.

Starting from an analytic analysis of the difference between descriptions and interpretations of works of art, Matthews argues forcefully that most interpretative assertions literally lack a truth value (i.e., they are neither true nor false, even though they can be construed as "plausible" or "implausible"). Unlike descriptions, critics' interpretations are made from an "epistemically weak" position (if you are interpreting something, then you are not in a position of categorical knowledge about that aspect of the thing), and this weakness derives from the fact that, in general, art critical interpretations are *radically underdetermined* by the interpreted work.

In some cases, this underdetermination may result from the vagueness of the interpretative statement, but in most cases it is because the work and its properties simply do not provide an evidential basis strong enough to support the categorical claim that the interpretative statement is true or false. Consider a novel, for example. Even clearcut interpretative claims suffering from little or no vagueness may nonetheless fail to be established by the novel since it may be neither asserted in the novel nor inferrable from or entailed by the fictional assertions of the novel. Just as in a conversation or interview, many things can be merely suggested, intimated, or alluded to.

As forceful as Matthews's arguments appear to be, there are two interesting questions that are left unresolved. First, since interpretations, in their best instances, outlast the initial critical acts of interpreting, does it really follow from the fact that the interpreting act goes on from an "epistemically weak" position that interpretations themselves generally lack truth value? Second, Matthews's claim about the underdetermination of interpretations is similar to a common thesis about the relation of scientific theories to their evidential or observational base. Nevertheless, many philosophers of science believe that theoretical statements can be either true or false. Why, then, can we not reason similarly about interpretative statements in art criticism? Is it a matter of *how* radically they are underdetermined by the artwork?

Whatever the outcome of the debate over whether interpretative criticism is basically like or unlike other sorts of rational arguments, which lead to conclusions that can be said to be straightforwardly true or false and that appeal to general reasons and are intellectually and abstractly understood, there is nonetheless general agreement at a very basic level within the analytic camp that art criticism is amenable to objective, rational standards.

There has, however, been an impact on this issue from Postmodernism. Although the longstanding more pragmatic side of analytic aesthetics should not be forgotten here, it is true that the Postmodern discussion has emphasized the claims that art criticism is unlike paradigm rational discourse in other areas and is not a truth-bearer. The main difference between analytic and Postmodern thinkers seems to lie in the degree of optimism or pessimism they exhibit toward the recovery of at least *some* form of rational objectivity in the discussion of art.

Moreover, there are some signs that under recent pressure of analytic scrutiny, Postmodernists may be backing off their more pessimistic and radical claims and settling into a more moderate position closer still to that of the analytic pragmatists. Van de Pitte's account of Gadamer's modified hermeneutical kind of objectivity in the reading included in this chapter is an example. Clearly, in the area of greatest exchange of ideas between analytic and Postmodern thinkers, namely, the theory of language (Searle and Derrida on Austin, comparisons between Wittgenstein and Heidegger), the more radical position of early Derrida that language is not connected referentially or epistemically to anything (the world, reality, etc.) is giving way to the more moderate position that there are at least conventional restraints on language, some of which may be at least indirectly constrained by reality. Yet a perceived crisis still exists.

Both Margolis and Van de Pitte seek to resolve the "crisis of modern critical practice," Van de Pitte through hermeneutics and Margolis by separating out the patently absurd interpretations of Postmodern theory from the more reasonable ground on which such theory rests.

Margolis offers us "three bits of advice." First, that it is impossible to separate a theory of interpretation from a theory of what that interpretation is *about*. Second, that there are two sorts of theories of interpretation—one which presupposes the existence of a relatively stable referent which interpretations are about, and a second which sees interpretation as creating what interpretations are about at the same time that they are creating the interpretations themselves. And third, that what we interpret in either of these two ways are cultural phenomena (what Margolis earlier referred to as "culturally emergent entities"). The first of the two sorts of interpretative enterprise is the more traditional and familiar one, while the second is the project of Postmodernism. While Margolis allows for both types of interpretation, he denies that the second can replace the first.

Margolis denies, in other words, that it is possible to say anything sensible without referring to an already existing object to which assertions have some epistemic ("adequational") obligation, and he denies that this elementary, but absolutely necessary, prerequisite of meaningful discourse privileges or biases any particular theory of the referent of interpretation.

Postmodern theories argue that traditional interpretations unconsciously assume many metaphysically, politically, and morally biased assumptions about art and literature which we must now become aware of and avoid assuming uncritically in the future. To avoid all such uncritical assumptions, we must even reject the most fundamental traditional assumption that interpretations describe (adequately or inadequately) some preexistent entity. We must become more sophisticated, it is claimed, and realize that the artwork only exists through historically biased interpretations (the second sort of theory above). Of course, many contemporary aestheticians, including Margolis, would acknowledge that in some sense or other artworks are culturally emergent entities, but this need not be interpreted to mean that nothing exists at all until someone begins to talk about it. It need only mean that what we think of as novels, poems, and plays exist in a complex contextual set of relationships involving, at least, some object, a human experiential capacity, and a set of social/cultural conventions. A poem will not be appreciated aesthetically as a poem by cows or Vulcans, and it will be understood differently by human beings enculturated in different societies, and it would mean something different within the same societies if the text itself were somehow altered. But that does not mean we are unable to identify the poem in question and criticize various interpretations of it.

Nonetheless, many Postmodernists interpret the culturally emergent nature of literary works to mean that critical language is cut off from any connection with an independent referent (the literary work) and that, as a result, the notion of an independently existing referent becomes vacuous—for all practical purposes, there is no literary work, only different interpretations, or "readings" (of *what*, it might be asked?).

In the midst of these confusing notions, Margolis makes what would otherwise be the rather innocuous claim that there simply cannot be any socially sustained, adjudicable discourse which in some sense does not enable "orderly reference and prediction." This minimal condition of interpretative discourse does not privilege any particular theory of the nature of the literary work. Of course, it is true that the interpretation of x at time t_1 may differ from the interpretation of x at time t_2. But that does not mean and cannot mean that x at time t_1 is not the same as x at time t_2. If they were completely different entities, the preceding story about the variability of interpretation could not be told. Saying that over time interpretations changed logically entails that the *same entity* was interpreted differently at different times. Suppose it turned out that the poem which was interpreted differently at different times was in fact two different poems. We would not in that case continue to talk about different interpretations. We can only speak of different interpretations of the same entity. Of course, it is also true that the words we use to describe that entity are not entirely theory-neutral. Even to call it a "poem" attributes some characteristics to the object. Nonetheless, Margolis argues, we have within our language well-established institutions for the use of proper nouns which allow us simply to refer to an object, which we can go on to describe or interpret.

Van de Pitte examines the "crisis of modern literature," which he identifies as the "failure of New Criticism," through hermeneutics. The problem is basically how to reconcile the "autonomy" of a literary work or artwork with some "objective" basis for resolving disputes over critical interpretations of it. To say that a work of art is autonomous seems to imply that it cannot be judged by anything "outside" that artwork. But this removes it from any basis on which to describe, interpret, or evaluate it. We would not be able to say it is about the First World War because that refers to something (the war) outside the poem. Nor could we say it expresses sorrow at the senseless loss of life in that war since that, too, refers to feelings existing outside the poem. According to Van de Pitte, any successful resolution to this problem must satisfy two necessary conditions, that literature be both autonomous and also objective. The "Old Criticism," he says, explained literature in terms of "outside" referents and so was objective but not autonomous, while New Criticism, by being autonomous, failed to be objective. Unfortunately, examined closely, Van de Pitte argues, hermeneutical theories fail to meet *either* condition (that is, providing neither autonomy *nor* objectivity).

Blocker's is another attempt to reconcile aesthetic autonomy with what Van de Pitte calls the "objective" reference to an outside world. Understood in a simplistic manner, both the New Critical claims of autonomy and the Postmodern rejection of autonomy in favor of maximal contextualization of the literary work are patently absurd, but when interpreted in a more sophisticated manner, which Blocker elaborates, both claims can be made plausible, *and* fully compatible, according to Blocker.

Critical Communication

Arnold Isenberg

That questions about meaning are provisionally separable, even if finally inseparable, from questions about validity and truth, is shown by the fact that meanings can be exchanged without the corresponding cognitive decisions. What is imparted by one person to another in an act of communication is (typically) a certain idea, thought, content, meaning, or claim—not a belief, expectation, surmise, or doubt; for the last are dependent on factors, such as the checking process, which go beyond the mere understanding of the message conveyed. And there is a host of questions which have to do with this message: its simplicity or complexity, its clarity or obscurity, its tense, its mood, its modality, and so on. Now, the theory of art criticism has, I think, been seriously hampered by a kind of headlong assault on the question of validity. We have many doctrines about the objectivity of a critical judgment but few concerning its import, or claim to objectivity, though the settlement of the first of these questions probably depends on the clarification of the second. The following remarks are for the most part restricted to meeting such questions as: What is the content of the critic's argument? What claim does he transmit to us? How does he expect us to deal with this claim?

A good point to start from is a theory of criticism, widely held in spite of its deficiencies, which divides the critical process into three parts. There is the value judgment or *verdict* (V): "This picture or poem is good—." There is a particular statement or *reason* (R): "—because it has such-and-such a quality—." And there is a general statement or *norm* (N): "—and any work which has that quality is *pro tanto* good."[1]

V has been construed, and will be construed here, as an expression of feeling—an utterance manifesting praise or blame. But among utterances of that class it is distinguished by being in some sense conditional upon R. This is only another phrasing of the commonly noted peculiarity of aesthetic feeling: that it is "embodied" in or "attached" to an aesthetic content.

R is a statement describing the content of an art work; but not every such descriptive statement will be a case of R. The proposition, "There are just twelve flowers in that picture" (and with it nine out of ten descriptions in Crowe and Cavalcaselle), is without critical relevance, that is, without any bearing upon V. The description of a work of art is seldom attempted for its own sake. It is controlled by some purpose, some interest; and there are many interests by which it might be controlled other than that of reaching or defending a critical judgment. The qualities which are significant in relation to one purpose—dating, attribution, archaeological reconstruction, clinical diagnosis, proving or illustrating some thesis in sociology—might be quite immaterial in relation to another. At the same time, we cannot be sure that there is any *kind* of statement about art, serving no matter what main interest, which cannot also act as R; or, in other words, that there is any *kind* of knowledge about art which cannot influence aesthetic appreciation.

From *Philosophical Review*, 58 (1949). Reprinted by permission of the publisher.

V and R, it should be said, are often combined in sentences which are at once normative and descriptive. If we have been told that the colors of a certain painting are garish, it would be astonishing to find that they were all very pale and unsaturated; and to this extent the critical comment conveys information. On the other hand, we might find the colors bright and intense, as expected, without being thereby forced to admit that they are garish; and this reveals the component of valuation (that is, distaste) in the critic's remark. This feature of critical usage has attracted much notice and some study; but we do not discuss it here at all. We shall be concerned solely with the descriptive function of R.

Now if we ask what makes a description critically useful and relevant, the first suggestion which occurs is that it is *supported by N*. N is based upon an inductive generalization which describes a relationship between some aesthetic quality and someone's or everyone's system of aesthetic response. Notice: I do not say that N *is* inductive generalization; for in critical evaluation N is being used not to predict or to explain anybody's reaction to a work of art but to vindicate that reaction, perhaps to someone who does not yet share it; and in this capacity N is a precept, a rule, a *generalized value statement*. But the *choice* of one norm, rather than another, when that choice is challenged, will usually be given some sort of inductive justification. We return to this question in a moment. I think we shall find that a careful analysis of N is unnecessary, because there are considerations which permit us to dismiss it altogether.

At this point it is well to remind ourselves that there is a difference between *explaining* and *justifying* a critical response. A psychologist who should be asked "why X likes the object y" would take X's enjoyment as a datum, a fact to be explained. And if he offers as explanation the presence in y of the quality Q, there is, explicit or latent in this causal argument, an appeal to some generalization which he has reason to think is true, such as "X likes any work which has that quality." But when we ask X as a critic "why he likes the object y," we want him to give us some reason to like it too and are not concerned with the causes of what we may so far regard as his bad taste. This distinction between genetic and normative inquiry, though it is familiar to all and acceptable to most of us, is commonly ignored in the practice of aesthetic speculation; and the chief reason for this—other than the ambiguity of the question "Why do you like this work?"—is the fact that some statements about the object will necessarily figure both in the explanation and in the critical defence of any reaction to it. Thus, if I tried to explain my feeling for the line

But musical as is Apollo's lute,

I should certainly mention "the pattern of *u*'s and *l*'s which reinforces the meaning with its own musical quality"; for this quality of my sensations is doubtless among the conditions of my feeling response. And the same point would be made in any effort to convince another person of the beauty of the line. The remark which gives a reason also, in this case, states a cause. But notice that, though as criticism this comment might be very effective, it is practically worthless as explanation; for we have no phonetic or psychological laws (nor any plausible "common-sense" generalizations) from which we might derive the prediction that such a pattern of *u*'s and *l*'s should be pleasing to me. In fact, the formulation ("pattern of *u*'s and *l*'s," etc.) is so vague that one could not tell just what general hypothesis it is that is being invoked or assumed; yet it is quite sharp enough for critical purposes. On the other hand, suppose that someone should fail to be "convinced" by my argument in favor of Milton's line. He might still readily admit that the quality of which I have spoken might have something to do with *my* pleasurable reaction, given my peculiar mentality. Thus the statement which is serving both to explain and to justify is not equally effective in the two capacities; and this brings out the difference between the two lines of argument. Coincident at the start, they diverge in the later stages. A *complete* explanation of any of my responses would have to include certain propositions about my nervous system, which would be irrelevant in any critical argument. And a critically relevant observation about some configuration in the art object might be useless for explaining a given experience, if only because the experience did not yet contain that configuration.[2]

Now it would not be strange if, among the dangers of ambiguity to which the description of art, like the rest of human speech, is exposed, there should be some which derive from the double purpose—critical and psychological—to which such description is often being put. And this is, as we shall see, the case.

The necessity for sound inductive generalizations in any attempt at aesthetic explanation is granted. We may now consider, very briefly, the parallel role in normative criticism which has been assigned to N. Let us limit our attention to those metacritical theories which *deny* a function in criticism to N. I divide these two kinds, those which attack existing standards and those which attack the very notion of a critical standard.

(1) It is said that we know of no law which governs human tastes and preferences, no quality shared by any two works of art that makes those works attractive or repellent. The point might be debated; but it is more important to notice what it assumes. It assumes that if N *were* based on a sound induction, it would be (together with R) a real ground for the acceptance of V. In other words, it would be reasonable to accept V on the strength of the quality Q if it could be shown that works which possess Q tend to be pleasing. It follows that criticism is being held back by the miserable state of aesthetic science. This raises an issue too large to be canvassed here. Most of us believe that the idea of progress applies to science, does not apply to art, applies, in some unusual and not very clear sense, to philosophy. What about criticism? Are there "discoveries" and "contributions" in this branch of thought? Is it reasonable to expect better evaluations of art after a thousand years of criticism than before?

The question is not a simple one: it admits of different answers on different interpretations. But I do think that some critical judgments have been and are every day being "proved" as well as in the nature of the case they ever can be proved. I think we have already numerous passages which are not to be corrected or improved upon. And if this opinion is right, then it could not be the case that the validation of critical judgments waits upon the discovery of aesthetic laws. Let us suppose even that we had some law which stated that a certain color combination, a certain melodic sequence, a certain type of dramatic hero has everywhere and always a positive emotional effect. To the extent to which this law holds, there is of course that much less disagreement in criticism; but there is no better method for resolving disagreement. We are not more fully convinced in our own judgment because we know its explanation; and we cannot hope to convince an imaginary opponent by appeal to this explanation, which by hypothesis does not hold for him.

(2) The more radical arguments against critical standards are spread out in the pages of Croce, Dewey, Richards, Prall, and the great romantic critics before them. They need not be repeated here. In one way or another they all attempt to expose the absurdity of presuming to judge a work of art, the very excuse for whose existence lies in its *difference* from everything that has gone before, by its degree of *resemblance* to something that has gone before; and on close inspection they create at least a very strong doubt as to whether a standard of success or failure in art is either necessary or possible. But it seems to me that they fail to provide a positive interpretation of criticism. Consider the following remarks by William James on the criticism of Herbert Spencer: "In all his dealings with the art products of mankind he manifests the same curious dryness and mechanical literality of judgment. . . . Turner's painting he finds untrue in that the earth-region is habitually as bright in tone as the air-region. Moreover, Turner scatters his detail too evenly. In Greek statues the hair is falsely treated. Renaissance painting

is spoiled by unreal illumination. Venetian Gothic sins by meaningless ornamentation." And so on. We should most of us agree with James that this is bad criticism. But *all* criticism is similar to this in that it cites, as reasons for praising or condemning a work, one or more of its qualities. If Spencer's reasons are descriptively true, how can we frame our objection to them except in some such terms as that "unreal illumination does not make a picture bad"; that is, by attacking his standards? What constitutes the relevance of a reason but its correlation with a norm? It is astonishing to notice how many writers, formally committed to an opposition to legal procedure in criticism, *seem* to relapse into a reliance upon standards whenever they give reasons for their critical judgments. The appearance is inevitable; for as long as we have no alternative interpretation of the import and function of R, we must assume *either* that R is perfectly arbitrary *or* that it presupposes and depends on some general claim.

With these preliminaries, we can examine a passage of criticism. This is Ludwig Goldscheider on *The Burial of Count Orgaz*:

Like the contour of a violently rising and falling wave is the outline of the four illuminated figures in the foreground: steeply upwards and downwards about the grey monk on the left, in mutually inclined curves about the yellow of the two saints, and again upwards and downwards about . . . the priest on the right. The depth of the wave indicates the optical centre; the double curve of the saints' yellow garments is carried by the greyish white of the shroud down still farther; in this lowest depth rests the bluish-grey armor of the knight.

This passage—which, we may suppose, was written to justify a favorable judgment on the painting—conveys to us the idea of a certain quality which, if we believe the critic, we should expect to find in a certain painting by El Greco. And we do find it: we can verify its presence by perception. In other words, there is a quality in the picture which agrees with the quality which we "have in mind"—which we have been led to think of by the critic's language. But the same quality ("a steeply rising and falling curve," etc.) would be found in any of a hundred lines one could draw on the board in three minutes. It could not be the critic's purpose to inform us of the presence of a quality as obvious as this. It seems reasonable to suppose that the critic is thinking of another quality, no idea of which is transmitted to us by his language, which he *sees* and which by his use of language he *gets us to see*. This quality is, of course, a wavelike contour; but it is not the quality designated by the *expression* "wavelike contour." Any object which has this quality will have a wavelike contour; but is not true that any object which has a wavelike contour will have this quality. At the same time, the expression "wavelike contour" *excludes* a great many things: if anything is a wavelike contour, it is not a color, it is not a mass, it is not a straight line. Now the critic, besides imparting to us the idea of a wavelike contour, gives us directions for perceiving, and does this *by means* of the idea he imparts to us, which narrows down the field of possible visual orientations and guides us in the discrimination of details, the organization of parts, the grouping of discrete objects into patterns. It is as if we found both an oyster and a pearl when we had been looking for a seashell because we had been told it was valuable. It *is* valuable, but not because it is a seashell.

I may be stretching usage by the senses I am about to assign to certain words, but it seems that the critic's *meaning* is "filled in," "rounded out," or "completed" by the act of perception, which is performed not to judge the truth of his description but in a certain sense to *understand* it. And if *communication* is a process by which a mental content is transmitted by symbols from one person to another, then we can say that it is a function of criticism to bring about communication at the level of the senses; that is, to induce a sameness of vision, of experienced content. If this is accomplished, it may or may not be followed by agreement, or what is called "communion"—a community of feeling which expresses itself in identical value judgments.

There is a contrast, therefore, between critical communication and what I may call normal or ordinary communication. In ordinary communication, symbols tend to acquire a footing relatively independent of sense-perception. It is, of course, doubtful whether the interpretation of symbols is at any time completely unaffected by the environmental context. But there is a difference of degree between, say, an exchange of glances which, though it means "Shall we go home?" at one time and place, would mean something very different at another—between this and formal science, whose vocabulary and syntax have relatively fixed connotations. With a passage of scientific prose before us, we may be dependent on experience for the definition of certain simple terms, as also for the confirmation of assertions; but we are not dependent on experience for the interpretation of compound expressions. If we are, this exposes semantical defects in the passage—obscurity, vagueness, ambiguity, or incompleteness. (Thus: "Paranoia is marked by a profound egocentricity and deep-seated feelings of insecurity"—the kind of remark which makes every student think he has the disease—is suitable for easy comparison of notes among clinicians, who know how to recognize the difference between paranoia and other conditions; but it does not explicitly set forth the criteria which they employ.) Statements about immediate experience, made in ordinary communication, are no exception. If a theory requires that a certain flame should be blue, then we have to report whether it is or is not blue—regardless of shades or variations which may be of enormous importance aesthetically. We are bound to the letters of our words. Compare with this something like the following:

"The expression on her face was delightful."
"What was delightful about it?"
"Didn't you see that smile?"

The speaker does not mean that there is something delightful about smiles as such; but he cannot be accused of not stating his meaning clearly, because the clarity of his language must be judged in relation to his purpose, which in this case is the *evaluation* of the immediate experience; and for that purpose the reference to the smile will be sufficient if it gets people to feel that they are "talking about the same thing." There is understanding and misunderstanding at this level; there are marks by which the existence of one or the other can be known; and there are means by which misunderstanding can be eliminated. But these phenomena are not identical with those that take the same names in the study of ordinary communication.

Reading criticism, otherwise than in the presence, or with direct recollection, of the objects discussed is a blank and senseless employment—a fact which is concealed from us by the cooperation, in our reading, of many non-critical purposes for which the information offered by the critic is material and useful. There is not in all the world's criticism a single purely descriptive statement concerning which one is prepared to say beforehand, "If it is true, I shall like that work so much the better"—and *this* fact is concealed by the play of memory, which gives the critic's language a quite different, more specific, meaning than it has as ordinary communication. The point is not at all similar to that made by writers who maintain that value judgments have no objective basis because the reasons given to support them are logically derivable from the value judgments themselves. I do not ask that R be related *logically* to V. In ethical argument you have someone say, "Yes, I would condemn that policy if it really did cause a wave of suicides, as you maintain." Suppose that the two clauses are here only psychologically related—still, this is what you never have in criticism. *The truth of R never adds the slightest weight to V*, because R does not designate any quality the perception of which might induce us to assent to V. But if it is not R, or what it designates that makes V acceptable, then R cannot possibly require the support of N. The critic is not committed to the general claim that the quality named Q is valuable because he never makes the particular claim that a work is good in virtue of the presence of Q.

But he, or his readers, can easily be misled into *thinking* that he has made such a claim. You have, perhaps, a conflict of opinion about the merits of a poem; and one writer defends his judgment by mentioning vowel sounds, metrical variations, consistent or inconsistent imagery. Another critic, taking this language at its face value in ordinary communication, points out that "by those standards" one would have to condemn famous passages in *Hamlet* or *Lear* and raise some admittedly bad poems to a high place. He may even attempt what he calls an "experiment" and, to show that his opponents' grounds are irrelevant, construct a travesty of the original poem in which its plot or its meter or its vowels and consonants, or whatever other qualities have been cited with approval, are held constant while the rest of the work is changed. This procedure, which takes up hundreds of the pages of our best modern critics, is a waste of time and space; for it is the critic abandoning his own function to pose as a scientist—to assume, in other words, that criticism explains experiences instead of clarifying and altering them. If he saw that the *meaning* of a word like "assonance"—the quality which it leads our perception to discriminate in one poem or another—is in critical usage never twice the same, he would see no point in "testing" any generalization about the relationship between assonance and poetic value.

Some of the foregoing remarks will have reminded you of certain doctrines with which they were not intended to agree. The fact that criticism does not actually designate the qualities to which it somehow directs our attention has been a ground of complaint by some writers, who tell us that our present critical vocabulary is woefully inadequate.[3] This proposition clearly looks to an eventual improvement in the language of criticism. The same point, in a stronger form and with a different moral, is familiar to readers of Bergson and Croce, who say that it is impossible by means of concepts to "grasp the essence" of the artistic fact; and this position has seemed to many people to display the ultimate futility of critical analysis. I think that by returning to the passage I quoted from Goldscheider about the painting by El Greco we can differentiate the present point of view from both of these. Imagine, then, that the painting should be projected on to a graph with intersecting co-ordinates. It would then be possible to write complicated mathematical expressions which would enable another person who knew the system to construct for himself as close an approximation to the exact outlines of the El Greco as we might desire. Would this be an advance towards precision in criticism? Could we say that we had devised a more specific terminology for drawing and painting? I think not, for the most refined concept remains a concept; there is no vanishing point at which it becomes a percept. It is the idea *of* a quality, it is not the quality itself. To render a critical verdict we should still have to perceive the quality; but Goldscheider's passage already shows it to us as clearly as language can. The idea of a new and better means of communication presupposes the absence of the sensory contents we are talking about; but criticism always assumes the presence of these contents to both parties; and it is upon this assumption that the vagueness or precision of a critical statement must be judged. Any further illustration of this point will have to be rough and hasty. For the last twenty or thirty years the "correct" thing to say about the metaphysical poets has been this: They think with their senses and feel with their brains. One hardly knows how to verify such a dictum: as a psychological observation it is exceedingly obscure. But it does not follow that it is not acute criticism; for it increases our awareness of the difference between Tennyson and Donne. Many words—like "subtlety," "variety," "complexity," "intensity"—which in ordinary communication are among the vaguest in the language have been used to convey sharp critical perceptions. And many expressions which have a clear independent meaning are vague and fuzzy when taken in relation to the content of a work of art. An examination of the ways in which the language of concepts mediates between perception and perception is clearly called for, though it is far too difficult to be attempted here.

We have also just seen reason to doubt that any aesthetic quality is ultimately ineffable. "What can be said" and "what cannot be said" are phrases which take their meaning from the purpose for which we are speaking. The aesthetics of obscurantism, in its insistence upon the incommunicability of the art object, has never made it clear what purpose or demand is to be served by communication. If we devised a system of concepts by which a work of art could be virtually reproduced at a distance by the use of language alone, what human intention would be furthered? We saw that *criticism* would not be improved: in the way in which criticism strives to "grasp" the work of art, we could grasp it no better then than now. The scientific *explanation* of aesthetic experiences would not be accomplished by a mere change of descriptive terminology. There remains only the *aesthetic* motive in talking about art. Now if we set it up as a condition of communicability that our language should *afford* the experience which it purports to describe, we shall of course reach the conclusion that art is incommunicable. But by that criterion all reality is unintelligible and ineffable, just as Bergson maintains. Such a demand upon thought and language is not only preposterous in that its fulfilment is logically impossible; it is also baneful, because it obscures the actual and very large influence of concepts upon the process of perception (by which, I must repeat, I mean something more than the ordinary *reference* of language to qualities of experience). Every part of the psychology of perception and attention provides us with examples of how unverbalized apperceptive reactions are engrained in the content and structure of the perceptual field. We can also learn from psychology how perception is affected by verbal cues and instructions. What remains unstudied is the play of critical comment in society at large; but we have, each of us in his own experience, instances of differential emphasis and selective grouping which have been brought about through the concepts imparted to us by the writings of critics.

I have perhaps overstressed the role of the critic as teacher, i.e., as one who affords *new* perceptions and with them new values. There is such a thing as discovering a community of perception and feeling which already exists; and this can be a very pleasant experience. But it often happens that there are qualities in a work of art which are, so to speak, neither perceived nor ignored but felt or endured in a manner of which Leibniz has given the classic description. Suppose it is only a feeling of monotony, a slight oppressiveness, which comes to us from the style of some writer. A critic then refers to his "piled-up clauses, endless sentences, repetitious diction." This remark shifts the focus of our attention and brings certain qualities which had been blurred and marginal into distinct consciousness. When, with a sense of illumination, we say "Yes, that's it exactly," we are really giving expression to the *change* which has taken place in our aesthetic apprehension. The post-critical experience is the true commentary on the pre-critical one. The same thing happens when, after listening to Debussy, we study the chords that can be formed on the basis of the whole-tone scale and then return to Debussy. New feelings are given which bear some resemblance to the old. There is no objection in these cases to our saying that we have been made to "understand" why we liked (or disliked) the work. But such understanding, which is the legitimate fruit of criticism, is nothing but a second moment of aesthetic experience, a retrial of experienced values. It should not be confused with the psychological study which seeks to know the causes of our feelings.

AUTHOR'S NOTE

In this article I have tried only to mark out the direction in which, as I believe, the exact nature of criticism should be sought. The task has been largely negative: it is necessary to correct preconceptions, obliterate false trials. There remain questions of two main kinds. Just to establish the adequacy of my analysis, there would have to be a detailed examination of critical phenomena, which present in the gross a fearful complexity. For example, I have paid almost no attention to large-scale or summary judgments—evaluations of artists, schools, or periods. One could quote brief statements about Shakespeare's qualities as a poet or Wagner's as a composer which seem to be full of insight; yet it would be hard to explain what these statements do to our "perception"—if that word can be used as a synonym for our appreciation of an artist's work as a whole.

But if the analysis is so far correct, it raises a hundred new questions. Two of these—rather, two sides of one large question—are especially important. What is the semantic relationship between the language of criticism and the qualities of the critic's or the reader's experience? I have argued that this relationship is not designation (though I do not deny that there *is* a relationship of designation between the critic's language and *some* qualities of a work of art). But neither is it denotation: the critic does not *point* to the qualities he has in mind. The ostensive function of language will explain the exhibition of *parts* or *details* of an art object but not the exhibition of abstract *qualities*; and it is the latter which is predominant in criticism. The only positive suggestion made in this paper can be restated as follows. To say that the critic "picks out" a quality in the work of art is to say that if there did exist a designation for that quality, then the designation which the critic employs would be what Morris calls an analytic implicate of that designation. (Thus, 'blue' is an analytic implicate of an expression '$H_3B_5S_2$' which designates a certain point on the colour solid.) This definition is clearly not sufficient to characterize the critic's method; but, more, the antecedent of the *definiens* is doubtful in meaning. A study of terms like "Rembrandt's chiaroscuro," "the blank verse of *The Tempest*," etc., etc., would probably result in the introduction of an idea analogous to that of the proper name (or of Russell's "definite description") but with this difference, that the entity uniquely named or labelled by this type of expression is not an object but a quality.

If we put the question on the psychological plane, it reads as follows: How is it that (*a*) we can "know what we like" in a work of art without (*b*) knowing what "causes" our enjoyment? I presume that criticism enlightens us as to (*a*) and that (*b*) would be provided by a psychological explanation; also that (*a*) is often true when (*b*) is not.

Contrary to Ducasse and some other writers I cannot see that the critic has any competence as a self-psychologist, a specialist in the explanation of his own responses. There is no other field in which we admit the existence of such scientific insight, unbridled by experimental controls and unsupported by valid general theory; and I do not think we can admit it here. (For that reason I held that critical insight, which does exist, cannot be identified with scientific understanding.) The truth is that, in the present stone age of aesthetic inquiry, we have not even the vaguest idea of the form that a "law of art appreciation" would take. Consider, "It is as a *colorist* that Titian excels"; interpret this as causal hypothesis—for example, "Titian colors give pleasure"; and overlook incidental difficulties, such as whether 'color' means tone or the hue (as opposed to the brightness and the saturation) of a tone. Superficially, this is similar to many low-grade hypotheses in psychology: "We owe the *color* of the object to the retinal rods and cones," "It is the *brightness* and not the color that infuriates a bull," "Highly *saturated* colors give pleasure to American schoolboys." But the difference is that we do not know what test conditions are marked out by our chosen proposition. Would it be relevant, as a test of its truth, to display the colors of a painting by Titian, in a series of small rectangular areas, to a group of subjects in the laboratory? I cannot believe this to be part of what is meant by a person who affirms this hypothesis. He is committed to no such test.

Anyone with a smattering of Gestalt psychology now interposes that the colors are, of course, pleasing *in* their context, not out of it. One has some trouble in understanding how in that case one could know that it is the *colors* that are pleasing. We may believe in studying the properties of wholes; but it is hard to see what scientific formulation can be given to the idea that a quality should have a certain function (that is, a causal relationship to the responses of an observer) in one and only one whole. Yet that appears to be the case with the color scheme in any painting by Titian.

We can be relieved of these difficulties simply by admitting our ignorance and confusion; but there is no such escape when we turn to criticism. For it *is* as a colorist that Titian excels—this is a fairly unanimous value judgment, and we should be able to analyze its meaning. (I should not, however, want the issue to turn on this particular example. Simpler and clearer judgments could be cited.) Now when our attention is called, by a critic, to a certain quality, we respond to that quality *in its context*. The context is never specified, as it would have to be in any scientific theory, but always assumed. Every descriptive statement affects our perception of—and our feeling for— the work as a whole. One might say, then, that we agree with the critic if and when he gets us to like the work about as well or as badly as he does. But this is clearly not enough. For he exerts his influence always through a specific discrimination. Art criticism is analytic, discriminating. It concerns itself less with over-all values than with merits and faults in specified respects. It is the quality and not the work that is good or bad; or, if you like, the work is good or bad "on account of its qualities." Thus, we may agree with his judgment but reject the critic's grounds (I have shown that the "grounds," to which he is really appealing are not the same as those which he explicitly states or designates); and when we do this, we are saying that the qualities which he admires are not those which we admire. But then we must know what we admire: we are somehow aware of the special attachment of our feelings to certain abstract qualities rather than to others. Without this, we could never reject a reason given for a value judgment with which we agree—we could never be dissatisfied with descriptive evaluation. There must therefore exist an analyzing, sifting, shredding process within perception which corresponds to the conceptual distinctness of our references to "strong form but weak color," "powerful images but slovenly meter," and so on.

This process is mysterious; but we can get useful hints from two quarters. Artists and art teachers are constantly "experimenting," in their own way. "Such a bright green at this point is jarring." "Shouldn't you add more detail to the large space on the right?" We can compare two wholes in a single respect and mark the difference in the registration upon our feelings. Implicit comparisons of this kind, with shifting tone of feeling, are what are involved in the isolation of qualities from the work, at least, in *some* critical judgments. I am afraid that as psychology, as an attempt to discover the causes of our feelings, this is primitive procedure; but as a mere analysis of what is meant by the praise and blame accorded to special qualities, it is not without value.

If, in the second place, we could discover what we mean by the difference between the "object" and the "cause" of an emotion, *outside* the field of aesthetics; if we could see both the distinction and the connection between two such judgments as "I hate his cheek" and "It is his cheek that inspires hatred in men"; if we knew what happens when a man says, "Now I know why I have always disliked him—it is his pretence of humility," there would be a valuable application to the analysis of critical judgments.

NOTES

1. Cf., for instance, C. J. Ducasse, *Art, the Critics, and You* [New York, 1944] (p. 116): "The statement that a given work possesses a certain objective characteristic expresses at the same time a judgment of value if the characteristic is one that the judging person approves or, as the case may be, disapproves; and is thus one that he regards as conferring, respectively, positive or negative value on any object of the given kind that happens to possess it." See, further, pp. 117–20.
2. I should like to add that when we speak of "justifying" or "giving reasons" for our critical judgments, we refer to something which patently does go on in the world and which is patently different from the causal explanation of tastes and preferences. We are not begging any question as to whether the critical judgment can "really" be justified; that is, established on an objective basis. Even if there were no truth or falsity in criticism, there would still be agreement and disagreement; and there would be argument which arises out of disagreement and attempts to resolve it. Hence, at the least there exists the purely "phenomenological" task of elucidating the import and intention of words like "insight," "acumen," "obtuseness," "bad taste," all of which have a real currency in criticism.
3. See D. W. Prall, *Aesthetic Analysis* [New York: Thomas Y. Crowell Co., 1929], p. 201.

The Testability of an Interpretation

Monroe C. Beardsley

Surely there are many literary works of which it can be said that they are understood better by some readers than by others. It is that fact that makes interpretation possible and (sometimes) desirable.

For if A understands *Sordello* better than B does, he may be able to help B understand what he understands but B does not. No doubt there are many ways in which A might do this. One is by reading the poem aloud in a manner that reflects his understanding of it. Another is by telling B what the work means; and any such statement, or set of statements, used to report discovered meaning in a literary text I shall call a "literary interpretation" or (for brevity in the present context) "interpretation."

Common usage among critics and literary theorists seems to sanction this broad definition of the term, and I resign myself to it here, though I hold out hope for distinguishing "interpretation" in a narrower sense from two other operations of literary exegesis.[1] I would prefer to reserve the term "interpretation" for exposing what I call the "themes" and "theses" of a literary work; the term "explication" for exposing the marginal or implicit meanings of words, phrases, and sentences (metaphors, for instance); and the term "elucidation" for exposing implied features of the world of the work (inferred motivations and character traits, for instance). On this occasion I shall conform to general practice by considering all three critical operations as acts of interpretation, and the sentences produced by these operations as interpretation-statements. Explication is evidently the most basic; since we can hardly be sure we know what is going on in a poem, much less what it symbolizes or says about the world, until we understand the interrelationships of meaning at the level of verbal texture.

1

One of the main and recurrent themes [here favored] might be called the vindication of critical rationality. Put less pretentiously, my thesis (or one of them) is that the processes of criticism, when they are performed well, have much reasonableness in them. The deliberations the critic goes through in his characteristic commerce with literary texts are rational deliberations, in important part; and the conclusions he reaches through them are (or can be) reasonable conclusions, in that reasons can be given to support their claims to truth.

Even if these generalizations have an appearance of acceptability when cast in abstract form, they may well become dubitable when applied to particular sorts of critical statement. That is what we have to find out. It must be acknowledged that the issues are complex and debatable.

For one thing, some critical theorists have recently emphasized the element of creativity in interpretation. By comparing literary interpretation with the performing artist's interpretation of score or script (which is a vital cooperation with the composer or dramatist in

From *The Possibility of Criticism* (Detroit: Wayne State University Press, 1970). Reprinted by permission of the publisher.

perfecting an actual aesthetic object), they have suggested that the literary interpreter, too, has a certain leeway, and does not merely "report" on "discovered meaning," as I said earlier, but puts something of his own into the work; so that different critics may produce different but equally legitimate interpretations, like two sopranos or two ingenues working from the same notations. I find myself rather severe with this line of thought. There is plenty of room for creativity in literary interpretation, if that means thinking of new ways of reading the work, if it means exercising sensitivity and imagination. But the moment the critic begins to use the work as an occasion for promoting his own ideas, he has abandoned the task of interpretation. Yet can we really draw a line here? That is the question.

The literary interpreter can be likened to practitioners of many other trades—not only to the singer and dancer but to the coal miner, the hunter, the pilgrim. . . . Each of these similitudes casts light on aspects of his work, but none is perfectly just. For his results, unlike theirs, issue in the form of statements. He claims to supply information we lack. And such a claim, when it could be challenged, calls for the support of reasons. The critic cannot avoid, in some way, *arguing*.[2]

Nevertheless, the view persists—and even grows—that there is something peculiar about interpretation-statements that gives them a distinct logical status and makes them undeserving of the adjectives that we apply to ordinary claims to provide information. Consider, for example, Stuart Hampshire's remark in a symposium on interpretation a few years ago:

If correctness is taken to imply finality, then I see no reason to accept this as the right epithet of praise for a critical interpretation. Some interpretations are impossible, absurd, unplausible, far-fetched, strained, inappropriate, and the object does not permit many of the interpretations that have been suggested. But the epithet of praise is more likely to be "illuminating," "plausible," even "original," also "interesting." "True interpretation" is an unusual form of words in the context of criticism. "Correct interpretation" does sometimes occur in these contexts; but it isn't standard and even less is it universal.[3]

That interpretations may be original and interesting, I would not wish to deny, though I would consider such praise faint enough to qualify as ironic condemnation. (If all you can say of my interpretation of a poem is that it is "interesting," I somehow do not feel I have convinced you.) It may be that we are not usually given to saying things like "Your interpretation is true," though "Your interpretation is false" strikes me as a little more familiar. Certainly interpretations are "right" or "wrong," and there are *mis*interpretations. Moreover, the statements that are given as interpretations ("This poem has such-and-such a meaning") can be called true or false without embarrassment at the idiom. Indeed, if they could not be true or false, I do not see how they could be illuminating or plausible. Hampshire objects to the phrase "correct interpretation" because it implies some rule of procedure to which the interpretative act conforms. I agree that the implication is there; I think it belongs there.

Hampshire's conditional at the beginning of the quotation "If correctness is taken to imply finality" brings out another reason why he thinks that interpretations are not true or false, strictly speaking: "it is typical of works of art that they should normally be susceptible of some interpretation and not susceptible of just one interpretation."[4] It is typical of the practice of criticism, especially in our own time (when the incentives to come up with novel interpretations, and the rewards of doing so, are great), that works of art are subjected to constant reinterpretation. But Hampshire's implication is that there can be no way of choosing among multiple interpretations, and no ground for regarding any particular one as most acceptable or exclusively acceptable. I do not agree. However, this question has been discussed more extensively by Joseph Margolis, to whose views I now turn.[5]

Margolis says that an interpretation can be "reasonable," but not "simply true or false."[6] I find this position puzzling. For I do not see how an interpretation could be reasonable unless reasons can be given to show its superiority to some alternatives; and I do not see how the reasons could count unless they are reasons for thinking it true. But Margolis's main thesis is that

> The philosophically most interesting feature of critical interpretation is its tolerance of alternative and seemingly contrary hypotheses. . . . Given the goal of interpretation, we do not understand that an admissible account necessarily precludes all others incompatible with it.[7]

Margolis points me out as one of those who has espoused the old-fashioned view that if two proposed interpretations of an aesthetic object are logically incompatible, then at least one of them must be rejected. It is, he says, a mistake to think that "there is some ideal object of criticism toward which all relevant experiences of a given work converge. . . . If we simply examine the practice of critics, I think we shall find no warrant at all for the claim."

My own examination of the practice of critics has led me to question this sweeping statement. I find the critic Samuel Hynes, for example, contrasting the opinions of Clark Emery and Hugh Kenner on the *Cantos* and adding: "Obviously they cannot both be right; if the passage describes an earthly paradise, then it cannot be a perversion of nature."[8] I find E. D. Hirsch remarking: "No doubt Coleridge understood *Hamlet* rather differently from Professor Kittredge. The fact is reflected in their disparate interpretations. . . . Both of them would have agreed that at least one of them must be wrong."[9] I find Frank Kermode commenting in a similar vein on the line between "liberty" and "license" in interpretation.[10]

We do not discover, according to Margolis's view, that interpretations are true or false, but only that they are "plausible"—and though two incompatible statements cannot both be true, they can both be plausible. But plausibility is at least an appearance of truth based upon some relevant evidence, and any statement that is plausible must be *in principle* capable of being shown to be true or false. Margolis does not deal with any of the sorts of real-life dispute over interpretation that exercise critics most—for example, Wordsworth's Lucy poem, discussed [earlier in Beardsley's text]. It seems that when he is talking about interpretations, he has in mind a Freudian or Marxist or Christian "interpretation." This is bringing to bear upon the work an "admissible myth,"[11] or looking at the work through the eyes of some such grand system. If that is the kind of thing that is in question, then I have no quarrel with his principle of tolerance. The story of "Jack and the Beanstalk," for example, can no doubt be taken as Freudian symbolism, as a Marxist fable, or as Christian allegory. I emphasize the phrase "can be taken as." It is true that "readings" such as these need not exclude each other. But the reason is surely that they do not bring out of the work something that lies momentarily hidden in it; they are rather ways of *using* the work to illustrate a preexistent system of thought. Though they are sometimes called "interpretations" (since this word is extremely obliging), they merit a distinct label, like *superimpositions*.

The issue between Margolis and myself, then, can be stated in this way: he holds that all interpretations have what he calls a "logical weakness," i.e., they tolerate each other even when they are incompatible. In contradiction to this view, I hold that there are a great many interpretations that obey what might be called the principle of "the Intolerability of Incompatibles," i.e., if two of them are logically incompatible, they cannot both be true. Indeed, I hold that *all* the literary interpretations that deserve the name obey this principle. But of course I do not wish to deny that there are cases of ambiguity where *no* interpretation can be established over its rivals; nor do I wish to deny that there are many cases where we cannot be sure that we have the correct interpretation.

2

Interpretations come in various sizes as well as shapes: some apply to individual words, phrases, or sentences, and thus concern what I call "local meanings" of the text; others purport to say what is meant by the work as a whole or some large part of it, and I shall call the meanings they claim to establish "regional meanings." The regional meanings (when they call for interpretation) evidently depend on the local ones. Consider once again the Lucy poem, and the question whether there is a hint of pantheism in its second stanza.

The poem is not explicitly pantheistic like, for example, the "Lines Composed a Few Miles above Tintern Abbey":

> And I have felt
> A presence that disturbs me with the joy
> Of elevated thoughts; a sense sublime
> Of something far more deeply interfused,
> Whose dwelling is the light of setting suns,
> And the round ocean and the living air,
> And the blue sky, and in the mind of man:
> A motion and a spirit, that impels
> All thinking things, all objects of all thought,
> And rolls through all things.

(It is interesting to note how "rolls" and "things" are used in this passage.) If there is pantheism in "A Slumber Did My Spirit Seal," [The relevant lines of Wordsworth's poem are: *No motion has she now, no force,/She neither hears nor sees;/Rolled round in earth's diurnal course,/With rocks, and stones, and trees.—Eds.*] it must be brought into the poem indirectly, either by the connotations of the words or by the suggestions (that is, the non-logical implications) of the syntax. Let us examine one problem of each type.

First, what I call *"suggestion."* The words "rocks" and "stones" and "trees" are placed in parallel syntactical situations, and this suggests, quite definitely, that the objects they denote are similar in some important respect. But a suggestion that two different things are similar can go in either direction, and we have to decide between them. Melvin Rader, in his recent book on Wordsworth's philosophy, says that Wordsworth (taking him as the speaker in this poem) "evidently felt that Lucy in her grave was wholly assimilated to inorganic things."[12] But is this evident? She is assimilated to rocks and stones and trees—but trees are certainly not inorganic things. Rader seems to take the parallelism as suggesting that the trees (and a fortiori the dead Lucy) are like rocks and stones, blind passive victims of external mechanical forces. But one could take the comparison the other way and come out with the opposite interpretation: by putting the word "trees" at the end, the speaker gives it emphasis; therefore, he is really suggesting that rocks and stones (and *a fortiori* the dead Lucy) are like trees in having an inner life of their own.

Thus we can bring the issue to a fairly sharp decision point. If the speaker is suggesting that Lucy and trees are like rocks and stones, we have a hint of mechanistic materialism. If he is suggesting that rocks and stones and Lucy are like trees, then we have a hint of pantheism (or at least animism).

Consider next a connotation problem. The speaker says that the dead Lucy has no force, no motion, and no sense-awareness—but then he says that she does have a motion, after all, since she lies near the surface of the earth and thus participates fully in its rotation. She is "rolled round in earth's diurnal course." The question is, How much can we legitimately find in the meaning of "rolled" here? Now the available repertoire of connotations for the word "rolled" is certainly quite rich. We can open up some of them by thinking of kinds of motion that we would strictly describe as "rolling"—that of the billiard ball, the snowball on the hill, the hoop propelled by a child. By exploring these familiar contexts for the term in its literal standard uses, we remind ourselves of the various forms of motion that can be classified as rolling. And by contrasting these forms of motion, we inventory the potential connotations of the term. There are steady boring motions, ungainly decelerating motions (the wagon rolling to a stop), scary accelerating motions (the car rolling downhill), etc. But what about the present context? Here what must strike us forcibly is the way the other words in this line qualify and specify the motion that Lucy has: it is a regular motion, with a constant rate; it is a comparatively slow and gentle motion, since one revolution takes twenty-four hours; it is an orderly motion, since it follows a simple circular path.

In none of these respects is it terrifying or demeaning; if anything, it is comforting and elevating. If we accept these connotations, the poem contains a hint of pantheism, or at least animism.

If these little exercises in close reading have a point, then, interpreting this poem is not a matter of willfully superimposing some precast intellectual scheme upon it. There really is something in the poem that we are trying to dig out, though it is elusive. And if we do come up with a decision, the interpretation-statement in which we express it will be subject to that fine principle of the Intolerability of Incompatibles. (If the poem is pantheistic, it is *not* non-pantheistic.)

In this discussion, I have strewn a number of ifs in my wake, and now is the time to convert them into categorical assertions. I have been giving a very simple model of a process of interpretation, showing how, if we can decide on the local meanings (connotations and suggestions), we can support the regional interpretations (such as that a poem is pantheistic). My defense of literary interpretation, then, has to go back to the basic premises and to the basic problem, which is the problem of meaning itself.

The issue we must now confront is precisely whether we ought to call these connotations and suggestions meanings at all—strictly speaking. It will no doubt be agreed that the word "rolled" does have a meaning, which the dictionary will supply: it applies to rotary motions of macroscopic objects, let us say, but not to other sorts of motion. To talk this way is indeed to talk about the meaning of a word, and such talk can be tested by empirical (that is, lexicographical) inquiry. But when it comes to the connotations of the word, are we on the same safe ground? When we say, for example, that the word can hint at a fearsome sort of motion or a gentle motion, at monotonous repetition or at steadiness and order—where do we get these ideas? The dictionary does not report them, and we are not obliged to take them into account when we ordinarily use the word in speaking of wheels, balls, hoops, etc.

Perhaps these connotations should not be considered part of meaning, strictly speaking, at all, but rather as psychological associations that individual readers may or may not be inclined to have when they read the word. In that case, no one could be told that he has to have these associations, or ought to have them, or that he has failed to understand the poem if he does not have them. The interpreter, according to that view, could only report his own associations, which might or might not chance to correspond with others'; and if another interpreter reported opposed associations, all we could ask is that he be equally sincere. Such reports would no longer be incompatible; nor would they give information about the meaning of the poem.

A consistent defender of this skeptical view of interpretation will no doubt extend his position to cover suggestions as well. Suppose one critic reports that Wordsworth's line about rocks and stones and trees suggests to him that the first two are as alive as the third, and another reports that it suggests to him that the third is as dead as the first two. Again both reports may be sincere, and therefore incorrigible, confessions of psychological response. But, according to the skeptic, the critics are not talking about anything that can be called the meaning of the poem; and so again their interpretations cannot be regarded as testable or as interpersonally valid.

If connotations and suggestions are not a part of meaning but something psychological and personal, then the alleged regional meanings that depend on them must be equally subjective and relative. It follows that the statement that Wordsworth's poem is pantheistic has the same status as the statements I have called "superimpositions." The interpreter is simply showing one way of taking the poem, and he cannot exclude others.

The question is, then, Are the connotations and the suggestions in poetry really part of the poem's meaning? To answer this question, we shall have to consider the nature of meaning.

3

I propose to bring to bear upon our present problem a most interesting and persuasive account of meaning that has been worked out by William Alston and the late J. L. Austin, following out Ludwig Wittgenstein's original insights into language.¹³ This account begins with the concept of a certain sort of verbal action, one that essentially requires the use of units of language, namely sentences or (in special cases) utterances that are understood to be substitutes for sentences. It has not so far been possible to give a satisfactory general characterization of these linguistic acts; the most helpful clue to recognizing them is that suggested by Austin. He distinguished between the acts that we perform *in* using sentences (these he called "illocutionary acts") and acts that we perform *by* using sentences (these he called "perlocutionary acts"). In using language, we may assert, argue, ask, order, promise, beg, appraise, implore, advise, consent, etc. *By means of* such acts, we may achieve certain effects upon other people: we may convince, inspire, enroll, please, enrage, inform, deceive, etc. In general, these results can also be obtained in other ways than by using language, but when they are obtained by means of language, then the language-user is performing a perlocutionary act. An illocutionary act may be intended to produce effects: for example, you argue to convince, you command to influence conduct. But whether or not you succeed in convincing, you have still argued, if you have used certain sentences in certain ways; and a command that is not obeyed is still a command.

The basic Wittgensteinian insight was that using language is a form of activity that is guided by rules—it was for this reason that he frequently used the analogy of playing games, and spoke of "language-games." Alston's proposal is that the difference between one type of illocutionary act and another is a matter of the rules that we tacitly submit ourselves to in choosing the appropriate form of expression. For example, suppose I want to tell someone to do something. I can say, "I command you to do it" or "I advise you to do it" (there are numerous alternatives, of course). The difference lies in what I implicitly "represent" to be the case in using these expressions.¹⁴ When I command I claim to be in a position of authority over the person I am speaking to; but I can advise without claiming authority.

Now I can, of course, command or advise without saying "I command" or "I advise." I may choose a form of words that, by some convention, represents the speaker as being, or as not being, in a position of authority—as certain forms of written discourse constitute military orders, or the prescription blank purports to be the issuance of a physician. If I simply say, "Send in your resignation," and this utterance by itself would be, under the circumstances, ambiguous, I can provide a context that makes it a command or a piece of advice. Suppose I say to someone, "Send in your resignation." He might ask whether I have any authority over him; and if I admit that I have none, then I am admitting that I was not commanding. Or, to put the matter another way, if I should say to him, "I know I have no authority over you, but I command you to send in your resignation," I would be talking a kind of nonsense.

By exploring the conditions that are represented as holding in performing a particular sort of illocutionary act, we can characterize each type of act and distinguish one type from another. Some of these sets of conditions are complicated and subtle, and require much careful analysis. For example, when I promise someone to do something, what are the represented conditions? Some of them can easily be stated:

In promising Y to do A, X represents

(1) that A is an action by X,
(2) that A is within X's power,
(3) that A is a future action,
(4) that Y wants X to do A,
(5) that X intends to do A.

There are others. Notice again that the act of promising does not depend on its results; even if X does not keep his word, he has still made the promise. But other elements of the illocutionary act are essential to its nature: X cannot promise (strictly speaking) that someone else will do something (he can promise that he will make the other person do it, though); X cannot promise today to do something yesterday. Such promises are void. It is true that in one sense X can promise to do something he knows he cannot do, or does not intend to do (then his promise is insincere), but to promise seriously is to make a commitment to sincerity.

We are to think of these conditions as so many rules that are tacitly recognized by the speech community in which these illocutionary acts are performed. When a sentence in a particular language can be used to perform a certain illocutionary act—when, that is, its use is understood as involving the speaker's representing certain conditions to hold—then it may be said to have a certain "illocutionary-act potential." This illocutionary-act potential of a sentence is what Alston identifies as its *meaning*. And further he proposes to say that when two sentences have the same illocutionary-act potential, then they have the same meaning.

It seems clear that we can speak of the meanings of sentences in this way, but ordinarily it is more common to speak of the meanings of words. Alston explains this notion ingeniously by pointing out that the words that appear in sentences make their distinctive contribution to the meanings of those sentences.

Thus it would seem plausible to think of two words as having the same meaning if and only if they make the same contribution to the illocutionary-act potentials of the sentences in which they occur; and whether or not they do can be tested by determining whether replacing one with the other would bring about any change in the illocutionary-act potentials of the sentences in which the replacements are carried out.[15]

Thus the meaning of a particular word or phrase is *its* (indirect) illocutionary-act potential. Not that a word or phrase can (normally) be used to perform an illocutionary act, but that it contributes in a distinctive way to the illocutionary-act potentials of sentences. The meaning of "milk" is its capacity to play a role in acts of describing milk, buying milk, explaining how to milk a cow, etc. And to say that a word has several meanings is to say that its total (indirect) illocutionary-act potential includes the capacity to make various distinct contributions to the illocutionary-act potentials of sentences in which it may occur.

All this is, of course, a mere sketch. Numerous complications are required for a fully developed theory of meaning. And there may be difficulties. But let us assume for the present that the theory is basically right—that when we are concerned with meaning, we are concerned with illocutionary-act potential. Then we must see whether this account offers help in resolving the issue stated earlier, whether the connotations of words and the suggestions of sentences are part of their meaning.

Consider suggestion first. Compare:

(1) He took the pill and became ill.
(2) He became ill and took the pill.

Now I hope it will be agreed that there is something that can be said by both these sentences; there is an illocutionary-act potential that they share. Moreover, each suggests something that the other does not: (1) suggests that the illness came after, and as a consequence of, the pill-taking; (2) suggests that the pill-taking came after, and as a remedy for, the illness. Is this difference in suggestion a difference in illocutionary-act potential—and therefore a difference in meaning? It seems to me that it is.

Now it is not clear just how illocutionary acts are to be divided and counted, or when we have one rather than two. But if we say that there is one illocutionary act performed in both (1) and (2), since in both cases the speaker represents that two actions were performed by a single person, then we must say that there is another illocutionary act performed in (1) and still another performed in (2)—for in (1) the speaker represents a certain temporal and causal order and in (2) its reverse. There is no doubt a further difference between what is stated and what is suggested by each sentence, but I think this is a difference in the force or intensity of the illocutionary act.

The notion that illocutionary acts can be performed with various degrees of force may be surprising, but it is not, I think, paradoxical. Take, for example, acts of engaging to do something. We can imagine a whole spectrum of these acts, ranging from the most solemn covenants, signed in blood, through promises and contracts, down to the most half-hearted, casual sort of commitment in which you can hardly be sure that a commitment has been made at all (as when someone says, in a tone carrying absolutely no conviction, that he reckons he will help you paint the house). Assertion can be made firmly and decidedly, or it can trail off into a mere insinuation or hesitant suggestion. Now when we have a sentence that is used to state one thing and to suggest another thing, there is a great difference in the force of the two simultaneous illocutionary acts. One is the primary illocutionary act; the other is secondary. This relationship is reversed in the case of irony, where the suggested ironic meaning is in fact put forth more intensely than the stated meaning. It might be said that the less intense the illocutionary act, the less responsibility the speaker assumes for its requisite conditions. But the main point I am concerned with here is that what is suggested by a sentence has a claim to be considered part of the illocutionary-act potential of the sentence.

Alston does not discuss suggestion, but he does discuss connotations (which he calls "associations"), and his conclusion is that they are not a part of meaning. He offers as his example some lines of Keats and a paraphrase of them:

Keats: "O, for a draught of vintage! that hath been Cooled a long age in the deep-delved earth!"

Alston: "O, for a drink of wine that has been reduced in temperature over a long period in ground with deep furrows in it."[16]

Alston concedes that the word "earth" has many special associations that are lacking in the word "ground," but he says,

I cannot see that in saying "It came from the earth" I am taking responsibility for any conditions over and above those for which I am taking responsibility in saying "It came out of the ground."[17]

And so, by his account of meaning, Alston concludes that the difference between "ground" and "earth" is not a difference of meaning.

Now there are two questions here that ought to be kept separate. First, do "earth" and "ground" differ in meaning? Second, do they have different meanings in this context?

As to the first question, if the meaning of each word is its total illocutionary-act potential, then there is no doubt that the words have different meanings. For there are many illocutionary acts performable with the help of one that will clearly fail if the other is substituted. I cannot conceive that Paul Tillich could have called his deity "the earth of being"; and we will not get the right picture if we substitute "earth" in the description of a house having a good deal of ground around it. On the other hand, "ground" will not do for "earth" in the phrase "earth-mother" (Alston's example) or in the phrase "salt of the earth."

The second question is whether earth and ground have different meanings, or only different associations, in the particular context of Alston's examples. Let us formulate part of the texts as imperatives:

(1) Bring me a draft of vintage that hath been cooled in the earth.
(2) Bring me a drink of wine that has been reduced in temperature in the ground.

I do not deny that both can be used to perform the same illocutionary act of ordering wine from the waiter. As far as that particular act is concerned, one will do as well as the other—provided the waiter is literate enough to understand all the words. If there is a difference of meaning embedded in the connotations of the different words, it will have to be because there is also a difference in *other* illocutionary acts simultaneously performed with these sentences.

To make clear the kind of difference I have in mind, I will introduce another example in which connotations are not involved. Compare:

(1) Bring me my slippers.
(2) Bring me my favorite slippers, which are such a comfort to me.

There is a particular illocutionary act which both of these sentences can be used to perform, under identical circumstances; and the nature of this act can be analyzed in terms of the represented conditions; for example, that there is one and only one pair of slippers singled out by the context; that the speaker does not already have them on; that the speaker wants them; that the hearer is in a position to bring them; etc. But obviously they do not have the same meaning, for the second one purveys information totally lacking from the first. A second illocutionary act is added in the second case: the act of praising the slippers on the ground that they comfort the speaker. The second case is a compound illocutionary act, though the syntax makes the ordering primary, the praising secondary.

This difference between the two slipper orders is like the difference between the two wine orders. I have to concede that the latter difference is somewhat more subtle. Keats's speaker does not use a set formula, like "Vintage is the most!" or "When you're out of vintage, you're out of wine." He relies on the connotations of "draft," "vintage," "cooled," and "earth." But he says something (though in a sense parenthetically) about the delicious flavor of the wine he wants, about the care required for its production, and about the satisfaction that drinking it is expected to give. He represents something to be the case. To ask for "vintage" is to ask for an old wine, but it is not to ask for any old wine. In short, the wine is praised in Keats's lines, but not in Alston's: a secondary illocutionary act is performed, as well as the primary one.[18]

4

The possibility of criticism depends not only on the existence of a text, an object susceptible of independent study, but also on the availability of a kind of method or principled procedure, by which proposed interpretations can be tested and can be shown to succeed or fail as attempts to make textual meanings explicit. I have not tried to set forth a whole interpretive procedure, and I have ignored many problems that must be tackled in working out and defending such a procedure. I have concentrated on one problem, which, though by no means the whole story, is (in my view) very basic: what sort of evidence can be appealed to in testing an interpretation? I have tried to answer this question, to show that public semantic facts, the connotations and suggestions in poems, are the stubborn data with which the interpreter must come to terms, even in his most elaborate, imaginative, and daring proposals.

Without such data to rely on, the interpretive process is in danger of degenerating into idle fancy or arbitrary invention. It is well known that when we come to a poem with an idea in mind of what it may be about to add up to, what we find in it will be much affected by our mental set. If we can pick and choose among the potential meanings of the work and arrange them to suit our mood, we can often spin out remarkable "readings." There is plenty of evidence to show what the ingenuity of critics can do when no semantic holds are barred. But I am arguing that there are some features of the poem's meaning that are antecedent to, and independent of, the entertaining of an interpretive hypothesis; and this makes it possible to check such hypotheses against reality, instead of letting them become self-confirming through circular reasoning.

If we make the distinction between regional interpretations of the work as a whole, or some large segment of it, and the more localized facts that support them, then we can formulate the interpretation problem as that of connecting macro-meanings with micro-meanings. In order to accept a proposed macro-meaning, we must be able to see it as emerging from the micro-meanings, as growing out of them and yet as making a whole that is more than the sum of the parts. Thus interpreting a poem is not like arranging a sack of children's blocks in a deliberately selected and imposed order. Nor is it like decoding a message bit by bit with the help of an appropriate code book. It is more like putting a jigsaw puzzle together, or tracing out contours on a badly stained old parchment map. But it can be done better or worse; and the results can be judged by reason.

In trying to resolve the problem I originally set for myself, I seem to have done something else. I have unexpectedly turned up a new answer to an old question. And though the answer may at first appear odd, it will, I think, prove more attractive on reflection. What is a poem? A poem is an imitation of a compound illocutionary act.

We have seen that even a single sentence may be used in performing two or more illocutionary acts, of rather different types, together. The speaker in a lyric poem may plead, threaten, cajole, deplore, reminisce, and pronounce a curse in sequence or almost simultaneously. Even in the Lucy poem, small as it is, the speaker compares two life-situations, praises Lucy, and expresses a mixture of resignation and regret. But the whole poem can be thought of as a single act, made up of several: the compound illocutionary act of its fictional speaker. Richard Wilbur has shown very clearly[19] how the shape of Robert Burns's poem "O My Luve's Like a Red, Red Rose" is defined by a series of illocutionary acts, such as praising, assuring, bidding farewell, promising, but with a rising curve of emotion in a single "thought or mood, which is developed to full intensity."[20]

It is surprising, and even unsettling, to find oneself reviving the term "imitation" after all its years of enforced retirement from most aesthetic circles. One of the problems in applying this concept to poems has been the difficulty of saying what it is that is imitated. The doctrine of illocutionary acts gives us a solution of this problem. The so-called "poetic use of language" is not a real use, but a make-believe use. A poem can, of course, be used in performing an illocutionary act—it may, for example, be enclosed in a box of candy or accompanied by a letter endorsing its sentiments. But the writing of a poem, as such, is not an illocutionary act; it is the creation of a fictional character performing a fictional illocutionary act.

But will this description really apply to all poems? The most serious counterexamples are didactic poems of various sorts—for example, *De rerum natura*.[21] Surely, it might be said, Lucretius in this poem is not merely imitating a series of illocutionary acts, but actually performing them, for he means to marshal actual facts and arguments, to preserve the memory of his master Epicurus, and to bring to mankind final liberation from the fear of death.

One way of meeting this objection would be to restrict the original generalization to lyric poems, setting aside the *Essay on Man*, *Paradise Lost*, and *English Bards and Scotch Reviewers*. I choose the bolder alternative of holding that even didactic poems are not to be taken as the verbal residues of real illocutionary acts. What makes them didactic is not, I think, that they are arguments rather than "expressions of emotion" (whatever that may be), but that they *imitate* arguments rather than pleadings, laments, or cries of joy.

Part of my reason for this view has been well stated by Paul Fussell, Jr.:

Meter, one of the primary correlatives of meaning in a poem, can "mean" in at least three ways. First, all meter, by distinguishing rhythmic from ordinary statement, objectifies that statement and impels it in the direction of a significant formality and even ritualism. The ritual "frame" in which meter encloses experience is like the artificial border of a painting: like a picture frame, meter reminds the apprehender unremittingly that he is not experiencing the real object of the "imitation" (in the Aristotelian sense) but is experiencing instead that object transmuted into symbolic form.[22]

It does not matter how sincerely the poet believes his doctrines, or how fondly he hopes to persuade others. If he goes about making speeches, writing letters, and distributing textbooks, then he is indeed arguing. But if he embodies his doctrines in a discourse that flaunts its poetic form (in sound and in meaning) and directs attention to itself as an object of rewarding scrutiny, then—so to speak—the illocutionary fuse is drawn. His utterance relinquishes its illocutionary force for aesthetic status, and takes on the character of being an appearance or a show of living language use. Of course, those of us who are interested in the history of philosophy can *read* Lucretius as a philosopher—can extract what he says about atoms and the void—and place these passages in other contexts where they can function as real arguments and can be judged as such. And because of this, there is perhaps no great harm in referring to these passages as arguments, even as they stand in *De rerum natura*—just as we speak of characters in a novel as disputing, even though we are aware that since the characters are nonexistent people, no real disputing is taking place.

To characterize poems in the way I have proposed is to give a genus, not the differentia. Not all imitations of illocutionary acts are poems: for example, to mimic what someone has said, to tell a joke, to say something for the purpose of testing a public address system. What makes a discourse a literary work (roughly speaking) is its exploitation to a high degree of the illocutionary-act potential of its verbal ingredients—or, in more usual terminology, its richness and complexity of meaning. And what makes a literary work a poem is the degree to which it condenses that complexity of meaning into compact, intense utterance.

It may seem that we have taken a very long way around to this final and familiar formula: that poems are distinguished by their complexity of meaning. But this commonplace ought to take on added significance from the route by which we reached it. For we see that the poem's complexity is not accidental or adventitious but a natural development of what it essentially is: the complex imitation of a compound illocutionary act.

NOTES

1. See my *Aesthetics*, pp. 129–130, 242–247, 401–403.
2. I say this notwithstanding the dogmatic denial of it by Frank Cioffi in "Intention and Interpretation in Criticism": "You don't show that a response to a work of literature is inadequate or inappropriate in the way that you show that the conclusion of an argument has been wrongly drawn." But it seems to me the literary interpreter is not concerned with the adequacy of our "response" to the work but only with the adequacy of our *understanding* of the work. It is true that a proposed interpretation often does not need to be argued, because we can see at once how it fits. But if we are hesitant about accepting it, we can always ask for a display of reasons—i.e., an argument.
3. Hampshire, in Sidney Hook, ed., *Art and Philosophy* (New York: New York University Press, 1966), p. 108.
4. Hampshire.
5. See Margolis, *The Language of Art and Art Criticism* (Wayne State University Press, 1965), part 3; and also his comments in Hook, ed., *Art and Philosophy*, pp. 265–268.
6. *Language of Art*, p. 76
7. *Ibid.*, pp. 91–92.
8. Hynes, "Whitman, Pound, and the Prose Tradition," in *The Presence of Walt Whitman*, English Institute Papers (Columbia University Press, 1962), pp. 129–130.
9. Hirsch, *Validity in Interpretation* (Yale University Press, 1967), p. 137.
10. *The New York Review of Books*, September 24, 1964, *apropos* of Jan Kott's *Shakespeare*.
11. Margolis, *Language of Art*, p. 93.
12. *Wordsworth: A Philosophical Approach* (Oxford: Clarendon Press, 1967), p. 172.
13. See William Alston, *Philosophy of Language* (Englewood Cliffs, N.J.: Prentice-Hall, 1964); J. L. Austin, *How to Do Things with Words* (Harvard University Press, 1962).
14. Alston speaks of "taking responsibility" for certain conditions in performing a particular illocutionary act; I prefer the term "represent," which has been suggested and used by Elizabeth Beardsley; see "A Plea for Deserts," *American Philosophical Quarterly* 6 (January 1969): 33–42.
15. Alston, p. 37.
16. *Ibid.*, p. 45.
17. *Ibid.*, p. 46.

18. Another way of analyzing the difference would perhaps be more congenial to Alston's view, though I think it would be oversimplified: we could say that in asking for "vintage . . . cooled in the earth" rather than "wine . . . reduced in temperature in the ground," he represents that what he desires is wine of high quality, and if this condition is taken to concern the attitude of the speaker, it would be assigned by Alston to the "emotive meaning" of the term (see Alston, pp. 47–48).
19. See "Explaining the Obvious," in "Speaking of Books" column of *The New York Times Book Review*, March 17, 1968.
20. One interesting use that can be made of this concept of a poem is to bring out the basic differences, sometimes called "rhetorical," between different kinds of poetry. English Augustan poetry, for example, gets its character largely from the preponderance of certain closely related kinds of pretended illocutionary acts: asserting, denying, judging, contrasting, arguing, etc.; see William K. Wimsatt, "The Augustan Mode in English Poetry," *ELH: A Journal of English Literary History* 20 (March 1953): 1–14.
21. I want to thank Joseph Margolis for bringing this counterexample and counterargument to my attention.
22. *Poetic Meter and Poetic Form* (New York: Random House, 1965), p. 14. A closely similar view has been well defended by Seymour Chatman: "Meter, then, is the sign of a certain kind of discourse. . . . It is one of the 'variety of well-understood conventions by which the fictional use of language is signalled'" (*A Theory of Meter* [The Hague: Mouton, 1965], p. 221).

Describing and Interpreting a Work of Art

Robert J. Matthews

Recent discussions of art criticism have repeatedly focused on the distinction between describing and interpreting. And clearly there is something to this distinction, for when someone requests a description of a work of art, he expects a response different from that appropriate to a request for an interpretation of that same work. It is, for example, one thing to ask for a description of Beckett's *Waiting for Godot*, but quite another to ask for an interpretation of it. But while most philosophers are agreed that there is a distinction to be made here, they remain unable to agree upon its nature.[1] Some have drawn the distinction in terms of content: whereas descriptions supposedly report on "non-meaning" properties of works of art, interpretations report on their meaning.[2] Others have emphasized the performative aspect of interpretation, as contrasted with the reportorial function of description.[3]

Though these philosophers are surely correct in much of what they say about descriptions and interpretations in art criticism, none seems to have succeeded in distinguishing them. The differentiae they propose fail. In the discussion that follows I present an alternative account of the distinction. I take as a point of departure the fact, apparently overlooked in earlier discussions, that descriptions and interpretations are products of the speech acts of describing and interpreting, respectively. Because descriptions and interpretations are individuated in terms of the

---

From *The Journal of Aesthetics and Art Criticism*, 36 (1977). Reprinted by permission of The American Society for Aesthetics.

speech acts that produce them, their distinction is to be found in a difference between these two types of speech act. This difference, I argue, is *epistemic* in nature: in order to be able to interpret an object (or event) the interpreter must be in a weaker epistemic position *vis-à-vis* the interpreted object (event) that is required if he is to be able to describe that same object (event). Having isolated this basic difference between the speech acts of describing and interpreting, I then proceed to characterize what I take to be its import within the domain of art criticism. In particular, I argue that a critic's interpretations, unlike his descriptions, are as a general rule epistemically weak in the way suggested because they are radically *underdetermined* by the interpreted work. The upshot of this underdetermination is that interpretive statements, and derivatively interpretations, in art criticism are typically neither true nor false. This fact explains the import of the distinction between description and interpretation in art criticism: the epistemic distinction between the products of two different speech acts typically marks an alethic distinction between statements that are either true or false and statements that are neither true nor false, i.e., a distinction between statements of putative fact about the work of art and statements that, in going beyond what is actually given, involve the added contribution of the critic. In my discussion I focus primarily on literary criticism; however, I assume that my remarks can easily be generalized to criticism of the other arts.

I

A brief exchange at the outset of a panel discussion of Henry James's *The Turn of the Screw* provides a suitable starting point, for it suggests the nature of the distinction that we wish to characterize. The exchange was initiated when Mark Van Doren offered a purported description of *The Turn of the Screw* as a "great and famous story [. . .] told by a governess, who lets us know how she saw two children under her charge, a little boy and a little girl, [. . .] corrupted by the ghosts of two evil servants."[4] The other two panelists, Allen Tate and Katherine Anne Porter, immediately took issue with Van Doren's characterization, implying that he had offered an interpretation of the story rather than a description of it. Such a criticism is not uncommon: we often have occasion to reject another's characterization of some situation or event as being only an interpretation. But what is it about interpretations that in some instances opens them to criticism? In what manner are they potentially deficient? If we consider those situations in which the disparaging "that's only an interpretation" is appropriate, the grounds for this criticism quickly become apparent. Of a piece with "that's mere speculation" or "that's an assumption on your part," this criticism is leveled against someone whose remarks go beyond the evidence at hand. Were I to offer a characterization of *The Turn of the Screw* similar to Van Doren's, a critic would certainly accept as descriptive the statement that the governess was charged with the care of two small children, Miles and Flora. Yet he might very well object to my considering as descriptive the statement that the children were corrupted by the ghosts of Miss Jessel and Peter Quint. After all, a continuing interpretive problem for James scholars has been that of explaining what precisely takes place in the story: Does the governess actually see the ghosts of Miss Jessel and Peter Quint, or are they, as Edmund Wilson suggests, "creatures of the governess's sex-starved imagination?" Yet in calling my second statement interpretive, this critic would not necessarily be expressing disapproval. Even if he supported my interpretation, he might nonetheless realize that textual evidence being what it is, this critical statement is interpretive and not descriptive. He might point out that it is not evident that it was ghosts, rather than the governess herself, who corrupted the children, citing those respected critics who have held just this view.

The point of the foregoing example, I take it, is that whether a critic succeeds in offering a description of *The Turn of the Screw* depends on the "epistemic basis" of his statements about the story. In order to offer a description, this critic must stand in the appropriate sort of epistemic relation to the object to which his statements refer. In particular, he must be in a position to know whether the statements constituting the description are true of James's story. Before attempting to defend this claim, let me explain what I mean by "being in a position to know." Suppose Nixon and Ford had a meeting shortly before Nixon's resignation at which Ford agreed to pardon Nixon in return for some specific favor. Unless you attended that meeting or learned from others, you will not know what favor Ford received from Nixon in return for the pardon. The problem is not simply that you do not know what happened at the meeting, but that you fail to satisfy a necessary condition for even being able to know: you fail to stand in the appropriate sort of epistemic relation to the happenings at the meeting. My point might be put more generally as follows: knowing that p is not simply a matter of thinking that p, where p is some true proposition; in order to know that p, one must think that p in virtue of standing in the appropriate sort of relation to the subject of p. In the imagined example, you fail to stand in that relation; hence, you could not *know*, for example, that Nixon promised Ford not to reveal an especially sensitive fact, even if you correctly thought this to be the case. You are simply not in a position to know this.[5]

Now, the conclusion I drew from the Van Doren example was that it is a necessary condition for A's being able to offer a description of x that A be in a position to know whether the statements constituting the description are true of x. I know of no conclusive argument for this claim, short of a full-blown theory of knowledge and of speech acts; however, the following considerations lend theoretical support to the inductive evidence provided by examples. Suppose someone hands you a package (in a plain, brown wrapper) and asks you to describe its contents. Unless you are in a position to know the contents, perhaps because you have looked inside, you will not be able to describe them. You will, of course, be able to offer a conjecture, and your conjecture may even prove correct; however, conjectures—even when correct—are not descriptions. Conjecturing is not describing. The difference lies in the fact that in order to describe an object the describer must stand in a special relation to that object. But what is the nature of that relation? Clearly, we do not want to characterize the relation either in terms of the truth of the statements constituting the putative description, nor in terms of the describer's beliefs regarding their truth. For the former consideration bears on the correctness of the description, while the latter bears on its sincerity; neither represents a necessary condition for something's being a description. The proper characterization of the relation between describer and object can, I think, be gleaned from the observation that in proffering a statement p as descriptive, a speaker conversationally implicates[6] that he knows that p. If I am right about the presence of such an implicature, then, by the analysis of knowing that p sketched above, this speaker implicates (1) that he thinks that p, (2) that p is true of the object described, and (3) that he stands in the appropriate sort of epistemic relation to that object. Now, the falsity of (1), (2), or (3) will defeat any claim that the speaker actually *knows* that p; however, only the falsity of (3) will defeat his claim to have offered a description. The falsity of (1) renders the description insincere, though no less a description, while the falsity of (2) renders it incorrect. Thus, while (1), (2), and (3) are all implicated by the speaker's characterization of p as descriptive, only (3) constitutes a necessary condition for p's being a description. But (3) requires that the speaker stand in precisely that epistemic relation that I earlier characterized as "being in a position to know." Hence, I find some support for my conclusion that it is a necessary condition for A's being able to offer a *description* of x that A be in a position to know whether the statements constituting the description are true of x.

We can gain some idea of what it is for a

critic to be in such a position vis-à-vis a literary work by considering once more the exchange between Van Doren and the other two panelists. The three panelists are agreed that on the basis of his reading of *The Turn of the Screw* Van Doren was able to describe certain aspects of the story; other aspects, however, he was not. Their debate centers on precisely which aspects he was (was not) able to describe. Tate and Porter accept as descriptive of James's story the statement that the governess was charged with the care of two small children, Miles and Flora; however, they do not accept as descriptive his statement that the governess saw two small children under her charge corrupted by the ghosts of two evil servants. Tate and Porter presumably base their rejection on the premise that no critic could possibly be in a position to know whether the statement in question was true, because there are no facts about James's story that would decide whether the children were corrupted by ghosts. Whatever the facts about James's story happen to be, they do not include either the children's being corrupted by ghosts or their not being corrupted by them. There is no fact of the matter here; hence, nothing that one could be in a position to know. Thus, given the aforementioned necessary condition for being able to offer a description, no critic—not even Van Doren—could possibly be *describing* James's story when he characterized it as one in which the children were corrupted by the ghosts of two evil servants.

Although Van Doren was unable to describe the children as having been corrupted by ghosts since he could not possibly have been in a position to know whether that was in fact the case, he was nevertheless able to offer an interpretation to that effect. For having read James's story he was in a position to know whether there were any grounds for thinking that the children were corrupted by ghosts. Indeed, he presumably knew that his statement was at least defensible, if not plausible, on evidence provided by the text. Here we begin to see what I am calling the "epistemic weakness" of interpretations relative to descriptions: we are sometimes in a position to interpret, when we are not in a position to describe. But interpretations are not for that reason to be assimilated to conjectures or guesses: their epistemic weakness is not total. In order to be able to offer an interpretation, the interpreter must stand in the proper epistemic relation to the interpretandum (the object of interpretation). In particular, he must know (and hence be in a position to know) that the statements constituting his interpretation are plausible, reasonable, or at least defensible on evidence provided by the interpretandum. This condition on interpreting legitimizes our expectation that the interpreter be able to justify his interpretation by appeal to the interpretandum. Demands that someone be able to justify conjectures or guesses enjoy no similar foundation.

The Van Doren example shows that in order to be able to interpret an object one need not be in as strong an epistemic position vis-à-vis that object as is required in order to be able to describe it. One need not be in a position to know whether the statements constituting the interpretation are true of the object. But this finding does not preclude the possibility that someone in a position to describe an object might not also be in a position to interpret that object in precisely the way that he describes it. The following sort of example rules out this possibility, thereby providing what I take to be the crucial differentia between describing and interpreting. Suppose that I am interested in Russell's views on the nature of facts, but am unaware of several letters in which Russell states explicitly (and sincerely) that when he wrote "On Propositions" he thought of facts as complexes of objects. I *interpret* the opening paragraphs of "On Propositions" as maintaining that facts are complexes of objects. (I am assuming that textual evidence is insufficient to permit me to describe the opening paragraphs in this way.) At the same time, another researcher discovers the imagined letters and subsequently *describes* the opening paragraphs of the essay in precisely the way that I have interpreted them. His description and my interpretation come to exactly the same statement, yet he has described the opening paragraphs of "On Propositions," whereas I have interpreted them. Clearly the difference does not lie in what is stated, for both of us have made the same statement. Rather it lies in the epistemic bases of our statements. In particular, the difference lies in our differing epistemic relation to evidence that would verify our statements. The other researcher is in a position to know whether the statement in question is true, whereas I am not. At best I am in a position to know that the statement is plausible. Because it is, I have argued, a necessary condition for A's being able to offer a description of x that A be in a position to know whether the statements constituting the description are true of x, I cannot be describing the opening paragraphs of Russell's essay when I make my statement. The other researcher can, because he is in a position to know whether his statement is true, since he has read the imagined letters.

But even though I am unable to describe these paragraphs as maintaining that facts are complexes of objects, I can interpret them in that way, which is something my colleague cannot do, presumably because he knows (and hence is in a position to know) whether his statement is true. In other words, it would seem to be a necessary condition for A's being able to interpret x (i.e., offer an interpretation of x) that A *not* be in a position to know whether the statements constituting the interpretation are true of x. Support for this condition on interpreting is found in our reluctance to characterize a statement as interpretive if we know that the person making the statement knew at the time that he made it, or at least was in a position to know then, whether it was true.[7] In the example at hand, we would accept the other researcher's statement as interpretive only if we had reason to believe that the information contained in the letters did not figure in the formulation of the interpretation, perhaps because he read them only after having completed his interpretation. Other examples point to the same conclusion. Suppose you interpret a friend's sudden coldness as a sign of irritation. Now suppose further that I happen to know that your friend's behavior is occasioned by worries about his family. In reporting this fact to you, do I provide yet a second interpretation? Surely not. Notice the oddity of my saying, "I would interpret his behavior differently, rather as a manifestation of his deep concern over his family," given that I know this to be the correct explanation of his behavior.

The two conditions on describing and interpreting formulated above do not specify a sufficient condition for something's being either a description or an interpretation; nevertheless, they do capture what seems to me to be the important distinction between describing and interpreting. Taken jointly these conditions require the non-identity of description and interpretation: if A is describing, then he is not interpreting, and vice-versa. (Of course, this leaves open the possibility that while A is not describing, he might not be interpreting either. Perhaps he is merely offering a conjecture or a guess.) Because descriptions and interpretations are individuated in terms of the speech acts that produce them, this distinction between the acts serves also to distinguish the act-products.

Thus far I have focused exclusively on the respective epistemic bases of describing and interpreting. This has been possible because there is no logically necessary distinction to be drawn between the propositional content of these two acts. An independent characterization of interpretation would certainly mention the fact that it is a necessary condition for something's being an interpretation that the statements constituting the interpretation make claims about the meaning, import, value, significance, etc. of the interpretandum; however, this characteristic of interpretations provides no basis for distinguishing description and interpretation. Descriptive claims about the meaning, import, significance, etc. of a descriptum are commonplace, as, for example, when we *describe* someone's behavior as goal-directed by saying, "Jones's behavior is goal-directed." Beardsley, it would seem, overlooks just this fact when he attempts to motivate the distinction between description and interpretation solely in terms of the propositional content of the statements constituting each. He takes a necessary condition for something's being an interpretation to be a sufficient condition for distinguishing, describing, and interpreting, which clearly it is not. Thus, he classes as interpretive the statement "the painting represents a Conestoga wagon," while he classes as descriptive the statement "the sculpture has a quality of barely contained frenzy."[8] Beardsley concedes that Charles Stevenson would regard the latter as interpretive rather than descriptive, while W. E. Kennick would regard the former as descriptive rather than interpretive. Perhaps they would. Nevertheless, one simply cannot decide whether a statement is descriptive or interpretive without information about the epistemic basis for the statement—any more than one can decide whether the statement "Jones is watching television" is descriptive or conjectural without knowing on what evidence the statement was based. The statement "the painting represents a Conestoga wagon" may or may not be interpretive: it depends on both the painting and the critic's epistemic relation to that painting. As a wild guess the statement would certainly be neither descriptive nor interpretive. But even if the critic were to study a painting closely, under ideal conditions of observation, etc., the nature of his statement would not thereby be decided. It would depend upon the painting itself: as a statement about a painting by Hurd, it would surely be descriptive; however, as a statement about an abstract painting, it might very well be interpretive.

The appeal of a content distinction derives from the fact that it does classify critics' statements in a manner that is roughly congruent with our usage of the terms "descriptive" and "interpretive." The statement "the painting includes a mauve elliptical area" is, as a matter of fact, typically descriptive, since critics are not given to conjecturing. (It cannot for logical reasons be interpretive.) A statement like "the object in the literary work symbolizes the separateness of human beings" is always (or at least almost always) interpretive. It is very easy to conclude from this that all statements about color are descriptive, all statements about symbolism interpretive, and so on. But such generalizations, even if correct, do not go to the heart of the matter. The crucial question of why *these* statements are interpretive (or generally so), but not those, remains unanswered. Also unaccounted for is the fact that the same sentence may be used descriptively in one context, but interpretively in another. The epistemic basis for a critic's statements has been overlooked.

Before turning to the question of the alethic distinction between description and interpretation in art criticism, let me emphasize that what I have said so far holds for all descriptions and interpretations, not just for those in art criticism.

II

In this section I shall defend the claim that interpretations, unlike descriptions, in art criticism are typically neither true nor false. Such an alethic distinction between descriptions and interpretations has been proposed by other philosophers; however, their defense of the distinction has been inadequate.[9] Lacking the epistemic distinction between describing and interpreting drawn in the preceding section, they have been unable to explain why descriptions should be either true or false, a consequence that we see to follow directly from the condition on describing. Nor have they been able to explain why interpretations should be neither true nor false. Indeed, the acknowledged fact that interpretations in art criticism can be plausible, reasonable, and the like, would seem to require that the statements constituting the interpretation be either true or false. Beardsley has raised just this objection to the claim that interpretations are neither true nor false, asserting that "any statement that is plausible must be *in principle* capable of being shown to be true or false."[10] Yet despite its initial plausibility, this objection is unsound; statements that are plausible are not necessarily either true or false. I shall demonstrate this fact before turning to the more difficult task of arguing that interpretations in art criticism are typically neither true nor false.

Imagine a context in which a speaker A states that p. A does not know that p is neither true nor false, because he is not in a position to know that fact. He does, however, know that p is plausible on the basis of other evidence. By hypothesis, then, p is a statement that is plausible yet neither true nor false; hence, we have a counterexample to the claim that statements that are plausible must be either true or false. Let me illustrate this argument-schema with an example. Jones is a middle-aged male, born to parents the male members of whose families all became bald at an early age. Knowing what we do of his parents' families (and of heredity), we can be reasonably confident that Jones himself is bald, even though we have no knowledge of this fact. That is, given what we know, it is plausible to suppose that Jones is bald. A statement to the effect that Jones is bald would itself be plausible. Now suppose that we meet Jones and find that though he is not bald, neither is he hirsute. In other words, it is not the case either that Jones is bald or that he is not bald (i.e., hirsute). He is, as we say, partly bald. Thus, we have an example of a plausible statement—*viz.*, "Jones is bald"—that turns out to be neither true nor false. Hence, statements that are plausible *can* be neither true nor false.

This brief demonstration underscores the independence of judgments of plausibility from judgments of truth: a statement that is plausible need not be true; nor must it be either true or false. Of course, interpretations would not be plausible, reasonable, admissible, and the like, if it were not that they often turn out to be factually correct or incorrect (i.e., either true or false) as well. But we cannot conclude from this that in order for a particular interpretation to be plausible, it must as well be either correct or incorrect; nor can we infer that a particular set of interpretations—namely, interpretations in art criticism—are necessarily either correct or incorrect.[11] If interpretive statements are necessarily either true or false, then they are so for reasons other than the fact that they are reasonable, plausible, or the like. Of course, I wish to argue that as a matter of contingent fact interpretive statements in art criticism are typically neither true nor false, so clearly I believe that such reasons cannot be forthcoming. But before setting out my argument for this conclusion, let me first sketch some general considerations about truth that will figure in the argument.

Both the claim that interpretive statements in art criticism are necessarily either true or false and the counterclaim that they are not are in the first instance claims about the applicability of the predicate "either true or false." Yet when the question of the applicability of this predicate is pressed, the issue fast becomes one of the applicability of the predicates "true" and "false." For the claim that an interpretive statement p is necessarily either true or false is logically equivalent to the claim that necessarily either p is true or p is false. But how are we to decide this question of the applicability of truth predicates to interpretive statements in art criticism? We cannot be guided here by the discourse of critics; for given its persuasive intent, these statements are typically, though perhaps not justifiably, advanced as verifiably true of the interpreted work. Rather we must look to the notion of truth itself, asking what classification of these statements would best preserve the point of truth ascriptions.[12] It is my contention that classifying interpretive statements in art criticism as "either true or false" typically fails to do just that. Statements are true (or false), when they are, in virtue of certain facts about the world, but "the facts" typically fail to decide the truth or falsity of interpretive statements in art criticism. To maintain that these statements are nonetheless "either true or false" is in effect to deny the special relation that true (and false) statements bear to the world. To accept these statements as "neither true nor false" is, on the other hand, to acknowledge them to bear a relation to the world that is strikingly different from that of statements that are either true or false. Let me try to support these claims, showing how they lead to the conclusion that interpretive statements in art criticism are as a general rule neither true nor false.

Most of us no longer accept a naive correspondence theory of truth, but we do retain a fundamentally *realist* conception of it; we believe that a statement is true (or false) only if there is something (else) in the world in virtue of which it is true (or false).[13] If one accepts this realist tenet, then it can easily be shown that the statement "*p* is either true or false" is true only if there is something in the world in virtue of which either *p* is true or *p* is false. (The argument uses a Tarskian premise to the effect that for any *k* where 'k' abbreviates the name of some statement *p*, *k* is true only if *p*.) But to say this is to say that "*p* is either true or false" is true only if relevant states of the world are (were, will be) such as to determine the truth or falsity of *p*. If we call statements whose truth or falsity is determined by relevant states of the world "determinate," then we can summarize the foregoing by saying that statements that are either true or false are determinate. This, of course, is not to say that the truth or falsity of such statements is known or even knowable; but if we did have knowledge of the relevant states, then clearly the truth or falsity of such statements would be decided one way or the other.

The virtue of the realist account of what it is for a statement to be either true or false is that it preserves the notion of truth ascriptions as classificatory of the way statements stand to the world. Statements that stand in a determinate, though perhaps as yet undetermined, relation to the world are clearly differentiated from those that do not. Moreover, they are differentiated in a way that captures the import of the ordinary-language ascriptions "either true or false" and "neither true nor false." The statement "seat A-13 was unoccupied during the last Met performance of *Elektra*," for example, can justifiably be neither asserted nor denied by those of us who have no knowledge of the relevant facts. Nevertheless, we could justifiably assert that this statement is either true or false, for presumably the statement is determinate. In other cases, however, the facts may fail to determine the truth or falsity of a statement for any of a number of different reasons: failure of reference or of presupposition, vagueness, etc. Philosophers who subscribe to a realist account of truth will find it very misleading, if not simply incorrect, to characterize such a statement as "either true or false," since that would imply its determinacy. Such a characterization would imply the existence of factual information, which, were it known, would decide the statement's truth or falsity. But clearly such information is non-existent. These, then, are cases in which as realists we should say that the statement is "neither true nor false." For since there is nothing in the world in virtue of which the statement is either true or false, if we are to hold to our realist tenet, we must conclude that the statement is *not* either true or false, i.e., that it is neither true nor false.

Interpretive statements in art criticism are as a general rule indeterminate, and hence neither true nor false. In some cases it is because these statements are vague, or even meaningless; however, in the majority of cases the critic's interpretive statements are not indeterminate for either of these reasons. There is, for example, nothing especially vague about the statement that the ghosts of Miss Jessel and Peter Quint corrupted Miles and Flora; nor is the statement meaningless. Rather these statements are indeterminate, and hence neither true nor false, because they are *radically underdetermined* by the interpreted work. By this I mean that interpretive statements in art criticism are underdetermined in precisely the way that theoretical statements in the empirical sciences have been alleged (falsely, I believe) to be underdetermined: relevant facts[14] fail to determine the truth or falsity of these statements, though they do provide them some measure of evidential support. The reason why interpretive statements in art criticism are (typically) underdetermined is quite simple: when a critic offers an interpretation of a work of art, he typically knows all relevant evidence bearing on his interpretation. Thus, if his statements are epistemically weak, which as interpretive statements they must be (cf. preceding section), then their weakness must lie in the evidential basis provided by the interpreted work, and not in the critic's knowledge of that basis. In other words, these statements are interpretive rather than descriptive, not because the critic happened not to be in a position to know whether the statements constituting his interpretation were true or false (perhaps because he read carelessly), but rather because given the relevant facts he could not possibly have been in such a position. There is simply no outstanding evidence, not known to the critic at the time of his interpretation, that would decide the truth or falsity of his statements.

Having full knowledge of the relevant evidence is not the momentous achievement that it first appears. Interpretations in art criticism are normally construed, and properly so given the purpose of art criticism, in such a way as to render "external evidence" (i.e., evidence not provided by the interpreted work) irrelevant. Thus, for example, there is no external evidence that would decide the truth or falsity of the statement that the governess saw, rather than imagined, the ghosts of Miss Jessel and Peter Quint—at least none that a critic would accept. Henry James's testimony, for example, would be of little help here. Critics never tire of reminding us (and themselves) that artists are notoriously bad interpreters of their own work. But the artist's failing is conceptual rather than empirical in nature.[15] The artist is not a privileged interpreter of his work, precisely because this would constitute an appeal to external evidence. He can say what he meant, but the work still means what it says. The art critical question is not, for example, whether James meant *The Turn of the Screw* to be read as a ghost story, but whether it can be read as one. The question of what James meant, or how he would have answered the art critical question, is left to the art historian or biographer.

Now, if art critical questions are properly construed in such a way as to render external evidence irrelevant, then a critic's interpretive statements must find their justification in internal evidence (i.e., in evidence provided by the interpreted work). Verification or falsification, when possible, will also rest only on internal evidence. There are only two possibilities: either this evidence will be sufficient to verify or falsify a critic's interpretive statements, or it will not. If it is not, then these statements are indeterminate, and hence neither true nor false. If it is sufficient, then this critic has made these statements without full knowledge of the relevant (internal) evidence bearing on them. For if he had been aware of this evidence at the time that he offered his interpretation, then he would not have been able to offer an interpretation, since he would have been in a position to know whether the statements constituting the interpretation were true. But critics typically *do* have full knowledge of the relevant (internal) evidence bearing on their interpretations. After all, given that it is *his* interpretation, a reasonably competent critic who reads carefully will almost certainly know what facts about the interpreted work bear on the interpretation. It is very unlikely that evidence sufficient to verify or falsify his interpretation would escape his notice. Hence, interpretations in art criticism will as a general rule be neither true nor false.

This does not preclude there being some interpretations that are simply right or wrong, correct or incorrect. But when a critic succeeds in providing a correct interpretation, his achievement is a minor one, made possible by his failure to apprise himself fully about the interpreted work.

The suggestion that art critical interpretations are as a general rule evidentially underdetermined, and hence neither true nor false, gives substance to the commonplace that interpretation involves "going beyond" what is actually given. The statements constituting these interpretations are interpretive rather than descriptive because they are not fully warranted by the interpreted work; relevant facts about the work fail to determine their truth or falsity. Clearly there is, as many have suggested, a similarity between the interpretations of the critic and those of the performing artist. But it is not one of virtuosity or artistry. (Would that it were!) Rather it is this: in both cases the interpretation is underdetermined by the interpretandum. In neither case does the interpretandum determine a unique interpretation; rather it constrains them only loosely. And precisely because interpretation does involve "going beyond" the given, interpretations require the added contribution of the interpreter.

NOTES

1. Richard Wollheim is notable in denying the distinction altogether; see his *Art and Its Objects* (New York, 1968), pp. 76–79.
2. Monroe Beardsley, "The Limits of Critical Interpretation," in S. Hook (ed.), *Art and Philosophy* (New York, 1966), p. 61.
3. Joseph Margolis, *The Language of Art and Art Criticism* (Detroit, 1965), p. 71. Stuart Hampshire advances a similar view in his "Types of Interpretation," in Hook (ed.), op. cit., pp. 101–108.
4. Gerald Willen (ed.), *A Casebook on Henry James's "The Turn of the Screw"* (New York, 1960), p. 160.
5. Being in a position to know whether p should not be confused with actually knowing whether p. The former is entailed by the latter, but not conversely. I may be in a position to know whether p, yet still not know whether p, if certain beliefs that I hold prevent me from thinking what is in fact the case (namely, that p or that not-p).
6. See H. P. Grice, "Logic and Conversation," in D. Davidson and G. Harman (eds.), *The Logic of Grammar* (Encino, Calif., 1975), pp. 64–75.
7. One person with whom I have discussed my proposed distinction between describing and interpreting has questioned my claim that interpretations are (necessarily) epistemically weak. He points out that we sometimes characterize as "interpretive" statements that we *know* to be true. His observation is correct, but it will not support the conclusion that my condition on interpreting is too strong. The observed use of "interpret" can be explained pragmatically in a way that actually lends support to my claim that interpretations are epistemically weak. The explanation is as follows: Characterizing a statement p as "descriptive" conversationally implicates that the person making the statement knows that p (cf. p. 446). Characterizing that same statement as "interpretive," on the other hand, generates the weaker implicature that the person has some grounds for thinking that p but that these grounds fall short of those necessary for knowing that p. Now, just as there are various politeness conventions that govern our discourse, so there are various *humility* conventions. In particular, there are conventions that require that we hedge first-person knowledge claims and implicatures, even when we are certain of their truth, *especially* when the claims or implicatures are likely to be controversial. It is precisely such a convention, I would argue, that leads speakers to use "interpret" when, according to my semantic analysis, epistemic considerations would dictate the use of "describe." Although final evaluation of this explanation must await further work in pragmatics, I find support for it in the fact that the use in question is typically first-person.

   There is a similar pragmatic phenomenon associated with certain uses of "describe." In polemical situations where claims are advanced with strong persuasive intent, speakers will often characterize as "descriptive" first-person statements that according to my analysis are interpretive. But, here too, there is a pragmatic explanation, though in this case it is one that appeals to certain rhetorical strategies.
8. "The Limits of Critical Interpretation," op. cit., pp. 61–62.
9. Cf., for example, Annette Barnes, "Half an Hour Before Breakfast," *Journal of Aesthetics and Art Criticism* XXXIV (Spring, 1976), 261–271.
10. *The Possibility of Criticism* (Detroit, 1970), p. 43.
11. What can be concluded is this: If interpretations in art criticism are neither true nor false, then our characterizations of those interpretations as "plausible," "reasonable," etc. derive their force from the practice of interpretation elsewhere in our lives, where interpretations are correct or incorrect, in addition to being reasonable, plausible, or the like. For without such cases there would be no reason to find a plausible interpretation in art criticism more compelling than one that is merely admissible. A plausible interpretation is more compelling, precisely because plausible interpretations elsewhere in our lives turn out to be correct more often than do those that are merely admissible. Interpretive practice in art criticism is, therefore, a derivative endeavor, dependent on other forms of interpretive practice.

12. Cf. Michael Dummett, "Truth," in George Pitcher (ed.), *Truth* (Englewood Cliffs, N.J., 1964), pp. 93–111.
13. Ibid., pp. 106–107.
14. The nature of facts about a work of art continues to be the focus of much controversy. I do not want to join that controversy here, except to suggest that statements of these facts are statements whose truth cannot *reasonably* be denied by anyone acquainted with the work these statements are about.
15. Cf. Wimsatt and Beardsley, "The Intentionalist Fallacy," reprinted in W. K. Wimsatt, Jr., *The Verbal Icon* (Lexington, Ky., 1967), p. 18.

I would like to thank Monroe Beardsley, Lars Hertzberg, and Joseph Margolis for their criticisms of an earlier draft of this paper.

Reinterpreting Interpretation

Joseph Margolis

Give or take a little in the way of precision, there are at least three bits of advice that ought not to be ignored in constructing a theory of interpretation of any size. First, it is impossible to disjoin the account of the nature or logic of interpretation from one's theory of the nature of what it is that may or must be submitted to interpretation. Second, there are only two sorts of pertinent theories of interpretation. One holds that interpretation is practiced *on* relatively stable, antecedently specifiable referents of some sort, and that the requisite account identifies the practice by which distributed claims about them are responsibly assigned truth-like values of some sort; the other holds that interpretation is a productive practice by which an entire "world" or what may be distributively referred to in that world is or are actually and aptly first constituted *for* certain sorts of further claim or use, possibly for interpretation in the first sense. These are not yet theories in their own right, but they are remarkably economi-

From *The Journal of Aesthetics and Art Criticism*, 47 (1989). Reprinted by permission of The American Society for Aesthetics.

cal directives about what to explore. The first sort of theory identifies the traditional genus of interpretation; the second is notably, even peculiarly, fashionable in our own time and is sometimes thought to disallow theories of the first sort. The latter move cannot possibly be right, for the simple reason that there is no socially sustained discourse that is not at least constative or enunciative in the sense of facilitating (in the sense of the French cognate verbs) orderly reference and predication. Since that is so, the familiar contemporary worry about statement, assertion, judgment, claim and the like on the grounds of the need to avoid any and all forms of cognitive privilege or transparency is a conceptually suicidal defense that misses the point of the ineliminability of the constative. One cannot do without reference, predication, description, interpretation, explanation, analysis, evaluation; although saying that disallows nothing in the way of arguable views about *what* may be described or interpreted or *how* description and interpretation actually proceed. The point would be entirely trivial except for the annoying fact that it is no longer unusual to hear it denied or implicitly rejected. In any case, the first sort of theory is the classical one. It admits the complexity of *what* we interpret, but it does not extend the notion of interpretation to include the very constitution of *that*. In contemporary theories, on the other hand, the cognitive intransparency of the world obliges us to make room for theories of the second sort. Characteristically, the work of such theories is thought to be inseparable from the work of theories of the first sort. You can appreciate, therefore, that the barest beginning of an account of interpretation plunges us at once into a conceptual swamp. For how can we interpret what has yet to be constituted and how can anything be constituted by way of interpretation? Still, there are no interesting theories of interpretation in our own time that do not—*or will not*—combine both senses of "interpret."

The third bit of advice reminds us that, whatever the slackness of linguistic usage, what are interpreted in either of the senses given are distinctly cultural phenomena or cultural entities of some sort, are interpretable in fact just in virtue of their having cultural features or because they are treated as having such features or because they have features sufficiently like cultural features to warrant being similarly treated.

These are all, of course, deliberately elusive but quite safe initial pronouncements that convey an air of imminent system and scope and a promise of detail that a streetwise audience is likely to be polite and patient enough about while awaiting full delivery from the vendor. Also, it is not likely to be ignored that, regarding all three bits of advice taken together, the first sort of theory of interpretation identifies referents conceptually apt in some antecedent sense *for* interpretation; whereas the second sort of theory treats interpretation as a process of actually constituting things *by* interpretation, by a constructive activity by which certain phenomena or entities are first and merely posited. This second usage enjoys a certain vogue as present, though, thus featured, it also has an odd ring. In any case, there is no incompatibility or equivalence between these two sorts of theory; also, it is worth considering that an adequate account of interpretation may need to incorporate elements of both sorts of theory. The kind of contribution the first might make can hardly be supposed to be entailed or precluded by the work of the second; and the point of the second would be entirely lost if it did not accommodate some generically constative discourse that could or actually would include interpretive discourse of the first sort.

Let us say that the first sort of theory is meant to be *adequational*, that is, to assign (for the purpose of interpretive constatation) a nature or features to the referents of our discourse such that *they* would be conceptually adequated to our making and supporting the kind of claim about them that we take interpretation to provide. Given the warning already collected, there is no reason to suppose that there is anything illicitly privileged in merely attempting to formulate an adequational theory. This is not to say that there is no metaphysical or epistemological bite to such a theory, only that it cannot reasonably be supposed that every metaphysics or epistemology necessarily violates the common injunction against privilege. Otherwise, since constative discourse cannot be avoided and since it cannot proceed without a stable practice of reference and predication, it appears that it could not fail to yield metaphysical and epistemological findings, privileged or not. Relativize such findings, however, to the mere saliencies or *Erscheinungen* of our shared world: one could then reject all the tricks of cognitive privilege without giving up the benefits of an adequational theory. The point is modest enough, though enormously potent. Indeed, it is almost universally ignored. What it signifies is that the admission of reference and predication is the logical or formal admission of a need *for* the processes of description and interpretation: it is the admission that a world apt for interpretation must be stable enough to support such processes. It is a complete *non sequitur*, therefore, to suppose that admitting that much is tantamount to admitting some further metaphysical or epistemological privilege. Correspondingly, we may characterize the second sort of theory as *constructive*, in the sense that we and the things of our cultural world may be taken to be constituted somehow, possibly serially reconstituted, as what they are, or thereby become, as a result of some initial interpretive act.

Interpretation in the adequational sense must be referentially reliable though it hardly requires, for that reason, that referents have fixed or unchanging natures; and interpretation in the second sense specifically admits an initial production or a constitutive change in the nature of certain things by virtue of some as yet unspecified activity. Clearly, there is no reason to suppose that there is a univocal sense of "interpret" that usefully serves both theories at once. But if a reasonable account of interpretation could be fashioned for both sorts of theory—which seems both promising and generous—then it would be a considerable convenience to be able to identify by the same term the referents addressed in the first sense of "interpret" and whatever may be constituted in the second sense. Call such referents *texts*. Recapitulating the above: texts and interpretation in the first sense must be adequated to one another; the ways in which texts are constituted yield referents apt for interpretation in the first sense; and texts are constituted as such by some suitable cultural activity, by interpretation in the second sense.

This is all very general but still noticeably tighter than our first intuitions. We may perhaps add one further preliminary distinction to save a little time later. The only other general constraints we should impose on what we mean to take texts to be—in order to accommodate interpretive discourse of a suitably comprehensive sort—are these: first, that texts must be taken to be sufficiently *unitary*, in a logical sense, that is, individuatable and reidentifiable numerically, though this hardly settles the question of *how unified* in a substantive way, how fixed or unchanging their internal natures must be; and second, that, however unified, variable, alterable, even enlarged or affected they may be or become as a result *of* interpretive activity, their nature must intrinsically include attributes of a suitably cultural sort that render them apt for interpretation in the first sense and that account for their peculiar alterability and openness in the second sense. They could not be unitary without *some* internal unity: so our warning about the distinction between a metaphysics and epistemology of privilege and a metaphysics and epistemology of salience is well taken. But equally, they could not be texts adequated for interpretation if they did not intrinsically possess linguistic, language-like, semiotic, symbolic, representational, expressive, rhetorical, intentional or similar properties: these are indeed just the sorts of property interpretive theories of the first sort and metaphysical theories of the second take for granted. Let us, for later convenience, say that texts intrinsically possess *Intentional* properties. A theory of interpretation is, then, a theory that: (i) accounts for originally constituting or reconstituting texts as such by constituting would-be referents possessing intrinsically Intentional natures; and (ii) accounts for the interpretation of such texts in virtue of which pertinent claims about them may be assigned truth-like values and may be duly supported in an evidentiary way. It is a matter of considerable importance that texts may, on an opposed theory, be said to be produced by some sort of socially pertinent labor (*poesis*) that is *not* originally interpretive itself—for instance, on the mimetic theory. In that case—classically, of course—only the adequational and constative notion of interpretation is needed. In our own time, because the world's transparency has been so radically denied, actually constituting *what* we can address by intelligent act or inquiry requires an original mixing of labor with the physical world or the repeated reclaiming of such a mixed world by further mixing of the same sort. In speaking of that process as interpretive, we anticipate (if only by way of a myth) the second, the constructive, sense of interpretation.

Once again, speaking in this way is no more than setting the stage for a suitable theory. Those already engaged in the advanced argument will find these first remarks little more than a postponement of the essential issue. Still, it cannot be denied that the point of managing things thus is to suggest very strongly than *any* alternative option is either defective, incomplete, inadequate, untenable, unresponsive, unconvincing, not pertinent—or worse. Much hangs on the presumption, of course, but we could never get started on an actual theory if we stopped here to examine with due care all the arguments that might lead us in other directions. There is a hubris in the undertaking. We may, therefore, anticipate an unavoidable barrage of puzzles that we may not actually address in selecting what is narrowly required for our topic.

I

So much for preliminaries. Now for a little scaffolding. Consider two very popular claims drawn from recent theoretically-minded views of texts (or, more narrowly, artworks). For one, Rosalind Krauss, pressing into service what (reflecting on the views of Roland Barthes and Jacques Derrida) she takes to be the postmodernist intention to "blur the distinction between literature and criticism," she speaks of "a kind of paraliterature," that is, a literature that is now neither criticism nor non-criticism but a sort of analogue of what criticism would have been for the modernist (preeminently, for Clement Greenberg) now that the distinction between artworks or texts and criticism has been blurred:

> The paraliterary space is the space of debate, quotation, partisanship, betrayal, reconciliation; but it is not the space of unity, coherence, or resolution that we think of as constituting the work of literature. For both Barthes and Derrida have a deep enmity toward that notion of the literary work. What is left is drama without the Play, voices without the Author, criticism without the Argument. It is no wonder that this country's critical establishment—outside the university, that is—remains unaffected by this work, simply cannot use it. Because the paraliterary cannot be a model for the systematic unpacking of the meanings of a work of art that criticism's task is thought to be . . . there is not *behind* the literal surface, a set of meanings to which [the paraliterary] points or models to which it refers, a set of originary terms onto which it opens and from which it derives its own authenticity.[1]

Clearly, in opposing the views of theorists like Greenberg, Krauss means to dismantle altogether (not merely to reverse) the high modernist thesis in all of its forms—for instance, as it appears in T.S. Eliot's famous remark, that a work of art "is autotelic" and that "criticism by definition is *about* something other than itself" (a notion Eliot considerably changed in due course)[2]; or to oppose what might be called the premodernist thesis of New Criticism—for instance, as it appears in Monroe Beardsley's so-called Principles of Independence and Autonomy: "that literary works exist as individuals and can be distinguished from other things" and "that literary works are self-sufficient entities whose properties are decisive in checking interpretations and judgments."[3] Krauss's thesis is at least a first specimen of what we have called the constructive or second sense of interpretation, although to admit that much is neither to support her particular thesis nor to suggest particular weaknesses in the second sort of theory as a result of weaknesses in her own version of that theory.

What is easy to miss, what Krauss misses, is that (a) the rejection of the fixed disjunction between criticism or interpretation and text or (b) the rejection of the fixed nature or fixedly bounded nature of texts independent of particular judgments or interpretation is not at all tantamount or equivalent to (c) the rejection of any functional (or logical) disjunction between criticism and texts. This may not be obvious. Roughly put: the paraliterary need not—indeed cannot logically—disallow, at any moment at which it is pertinently intruded, that last disjunction (c). The very nature of constative discourse forbids it. Krauss risks—the evidence of her extended discussions indicate that she more than risks, she actually loses—the point of the paraliterary insertion itself. When she says that what is "left" is "drama without the Play, voices without the Author, criticism without the Argument," we may understand that she thereby opposes the pertinence or adequacy of modernist (or premodernist) theories of the would-be referents of criticism—the object of distinctions (a) and (b); but in dismissing them, she *must* hold (so must we all) to some version of (c), the logical distinction of paraliterary comments (criticism or interpretation, if you like), *if*, as she obviously does, she means to speak (and does speak) of the work of Duchamp and Pollock and Stella and Serra and LeWitt and others. This is the reason, reviewing a variety of postmodernist work, she speaks of the "index," the "shifter," "traces, imprints, and clues" and similarly attenuated referential devices.[4] She shows by her discourse that she cannot—she is hardly disposed to—abandon the devices of reference (captions and titles included); but her dialectical maneuvers against modernists are intended to leave the impression (there is some reason to think she herself is convinced by the argument) that she *has* actually abandoned the logical referent we call "the play," in abandoning the high, complex, modernist entity "the Play"—as well as authors and criticism and the rest. Put as simply as we can: the logical distinction and pairing between interpretive discourse and interpreted referent is both entirely different in purpose from and perfectly compatible with the so-called postmodernist insistence on denying an unbridgeable disjunction between criticism and text or artwork.

What Krauss fails to notice (or to acknowledge) is that the constative constraints of discourse, whether paraliterary or highly critical, must retain an effective reference to what is sufficiently *unitary* (individuatable in a logical sense) to make such discourse pertinent; also, that it makes no difference at all what we suppose to be the internal *unity* or the order that remains when art departs from the high unity modernist or premodernist usage presumes, *so long as* our theory (and practice) permit reference and predication to continue to succeed. What postmodernists of Krauss's stripe merely confuse—which is not equivalent to an accusation against either Barthes or Derrida—is the difference between merely judging or interpreting artworks and trashing modernism, or the difference between formulating the difference between modernist and postmodernist art and judging or interpreting works of either sort, or even the difference between favoring or opposing, for cause, particular theories about art of either sort.

Fussy as it may appear, the quarrel being addressed is a more strategic one. Krauss's obvious intent—an objective she somewhat garbles in collecting Barthes's very interesting notion, which she means to apply in the visual artworld—is to reject the fixed demarcation between criticism or interpretation and text or artwork. The idea is that *what* in the paraliterary manner is said about a would-be artwork at time *t* may *need* to differ from *what* may be said about that "same" artwork at *t'* later than *t*, *as a result of already having defensibly interpreted (or commented on) the work at t.*

There are really two mistakes that Krauss commits here. First of all, she wrongly supposes, in rejecting what a critic offers in "a reading [of a particular painting] *by* proper names," that she is also somehow committed to rejecting the need *for* proper names or other referential devices in critically discussing that painting or its details. For example, she shows, regarding Picasso's *La Vie*, a 1904 Blue Period portrait of Picasso's friend Casagemas, which was modeled on an earlier self-portrait of Picasso himself, that a standard, somewhat psychoanalytic interpretation of the "meaning" of the work pretty well trades on what she herself wishes to avoid and rightly condemns as "the art history of the proper name." In context, she actually mentions and briefly discusses the principal philosophical theories of proper names and links them to what she terms disapprovingly "an aesthetics of extension."[5] But she thereby confuses the requirements of constatation with the presumptions of privilege; she slights the minima of unicity in her reasonable suspicions about modernist notions of unity. We *do not* settle the nature, essence, or boundaries of artworks merely by ensuring that we can identify and refer to them.

The truth is that the extensional function of proper names and referential devices may function within quite complex intentional contexts (for instance, as in the fragmenting of *Beaujolais* in a Juan Gris collage—which counts against modernist simplification); and where, as with titles or captions, it functions to individuate an artwork, we need not suppose that the very nature, structure, intentional detail or unity of the work is fixed or bounded by, or somehow determinately specified or specifiable in accord with, or unalterable with regard to, or unalterably linked to, that extensional function. The extensional function of proper names (naming *La Vie*, for instance) is not the same thing as the extension of what the name names (whatever we may suppose that to be, the "painting," say); and the extension of a name (whatever that is) is not the same thing as, and does not determine, the Intentional complexities of what the name names (for example, what one or many nonconverging interpretations of *La Vie* may reasonably impute, synchronically or diachronically, to *La Vie*).[6] This is precisely what is meant to be accommodated by distinguishing between the unicity and the unity of an artwork, where what "unity" designates may be contested, say, by modernist and postmodernist theorists of art, all the while *some* referential fixity regarding the bare logical "unicity" of a work enables that contest to be actually and first joined. It is entirely possible that the purely referential function be achieved by paying attention to reliable markings that are not even part, in any pertinent sense, of the painting in question. In a word, criticism and interpretation require referentially successful discourse; but providing for that says absolutely nothing about, and sets no significant constraints on (though it does require constraints on), the intrinsic nature of artworks and other cultural entities.

A theory of how to interpret the Picasso, eschewing a literal-minded "art history of the proper name" applied to the representational content of the painting, however, goes no distance at all toward demonstrating that the use of referential devices *for* fixing the painting's identity, or even for fixing certain of its details, commits us to the doctrine that paintings have or must have fixed natures. No, that is an utter *non sequitur* that draws us on to Krauss's second mistake, namely, her supposing that the play of paraliterary criticism in what she sketches as Barthes's spirit is, in its own turn, also incompatible with the mere referential fixity of the artwork itself. The truth is that many have been wrongly persuaded *that the extensional function of reference somehow fixes once and for all the substantive or Intentional complexities (the nature) of whatever are thus only logically individuated*—if, indeed, they actually are the sort of entity that possess such properties (as, of course, cultural phenomena all do).

The referential fixity of a text or artwork is a matter quite distinct from the substantive fixity of what may be referentially fixed. The two are doubtlessly closely linked, in the sense that nothing could be referentially fixed that did not exhibit a certain stability of nature; but how alterable (or by what means altered) the life of a person or the restored *Last Supper* or the oft interpreted *Hamlet* or the theoretically intriguing *Fountain* or the marvelously elastic *Sarrasine* may be is *not* a matter that can be decided, or that is actually determined merely, by fixing such texts or artworks *as* the reidentifiable referents they are. Modernism and premodernism do indeed appear to have been too naive or too conservative about the conceptual link between these two notions, and postmodernism may have liberated us in that respect; but, for its own part, postmodernism has failed (in Krauss at least) to acknowledge an *ontic* conservatism implied in referential success insofar as the possibility of such success affects the very nature of texts *apt for reference*—which of course (sadly perhaps) the modernists were never even tempted to disown. Unicity and unity are yoked concepts all right; but they need not, running in tandem, ever be taken for the same horse. By the same argument, to say that interpretation (in the sense of the first sort of theory we introduced) presupposes description is *not* to say that description must, to be valid or true, be timelessly fixed or unchangeable or designate the fixed or unchangeable properties of whatever we go on to interpret. That would depend on the particular *nature* of what we meant to describe or interpret—for whatever we describe or interpret must have a "nature" of some sort. Admitting description—or, better, describability—is, first, a purely logical concession to the minima of discourse; it is only secondarily, beyond that, disputatiously, a further—a hardly entailed—concession to modernism or to some other privileged metaphysics of art.[7] If so, then the requirement of the first sense of "interpret" the constative distinction, *cannot* be denied; and the modernist or premodernist thesis is at least not entailed by that concession. We may collect all this quite simply by acknowledging that the apparent formal fixities of discourse, the fixities of reference and predication, have nothing as such to do with deciding *what* the intrinsic nature of texts or particular texts may or must be—except for the fact (the hardly negligible fact) that whatever we say *is* the nature of a text must be compatible with so saying and with the interpretive discourse it is meant to support. Interpreted texts must have somewhat stable properties but they need not have altogether fixed natures. So we must go beyond Krauss.

II

Consider, now, a second claim, this time from Barthes's well-known essay, "From Work to Text," which is as close to a canonical formulation of what Krauss originally wished to borrow as one could possibly find:

In opposition to the notion of the *work* of art or literature there now arises a need for a new object, one obtained by the displacement or overturning of previous categories. This object is the Text. . . . The Text must not be thought of as a defined object. It would be useless to attempt a material separation of works and texts. . . . A very ancient work can contain "some text," while many products of contemporary literature are not texts at all. The difference is as follows: the work is concrete, occupying a portion of book-space (in a library, for example); the Text, on the other hand, is a methodological field.[8]

Two distinctions need to be made: first, there is no doubt that Barthes *never* means to abandon a constative reliance on referential facilities, all the while he clearly intends to subvert conventional views about reading a text (for instance, views somewhat like Beardsley's New Critical view of interpretive reading); second, there is no doubt that Barthes does mean *to constitute*, by a certain sort of reading and serial rereading, *that* "object" that thereby becomes (what he calls) the Text. The notion of the Text, for Barthes, therefore, is *not* the notion of an antecedent referent to which interpretation is directed but rather the notion of what is productively yielded by interpretatively addressing "something else" that, in the ongoing process of reading and rereading, *is* uniquely affected by that very process.

It is impossible to pursue the theme without citing Barthes's famous distinction between the readerly and the writerly (the *lisible* and *scriptible*) offered at the very opening of S/Z, which is close in spirit (and even language) to the paper just mentioned:

Why is the writerly our value? Because the goal of literary work (of literature as work) is to make the reader no longer a consumer, but a producer of the text. Our literature is characterized by the pitiless divorce which the literary institution maintains between the producer of the text and its user, between its owner and its customer, between its author and its reader. This reader is thereby plunged into a kind of idleness—he is intransitive; he is, in short, *serious*: instead of functioning himself, instead of gaining access to the magic of the signifier, to the pleasure of writing, he is left with no more than the poor freedom either to accept or reject the text: reading is nothing more than a *referendum*. Opposite the writerly text, then, is its countervalue, its negative, reactive value: what can be read, but not written: the *readerly*. We call any readerly text a classic text.[9]

Of course, Balzac's *Sarrasine* is the classic readerly text that Barthes marvelously shows us how to read as a writerly Text. In doing that, Barthes confirms: (i) that writerly reading does not eliminate readerly reading or its eligibility and contribution; (ii) that reading of either sort presupposes a referent—the point of mentioning the "signifier," necessary for both readerly and writerly reading; (iii) that the readerly text may have been, at some earlier time, a writerly Text in its own right but is now no longer such, is now a fixed or bounded text, the unity of which in the modernist or premodernist sense has become a function of its particular interpretive history; alternatively, its being reread now (as a readerly thing) commits us canonically to recovering what constitutes it as a properly fixed text; hence (iv) that even a readerly text is constituted (in our second sense) by interpreting something *else*—the "signifier," in Barthes's Saussurean usage; (v) that, for Barthes, the "Text," taken as the internal accusative of reading, is not an actual referent for further writerly reading (though the signifier is) but is collapsed into such a fixed referent only for readerly reading; and (vi) that reading in the writerly way is not in the least incompatible with admitting readerly texts; in fact, it may be practiced on such texts.

A great deal of nonsense has been spread abroad maligning Barthes's intelligence, when what is wanted is a careful understanding of the remarkable thesis Barthes has bequeathed us. As it happens, it affords the best clue we are likely to find regarding the second sort of theory of interpretation. In any case, in his terribly freewheeling way, Barthes shows us how to *entertain* the idea that a text (in our sense, not quite in his, though congruently enough with his own notion), need not be presumed to have a fixed nature throughout a responsible reading (that is, *in what we*—once again, not Barthes—are calling interpretation) in spite of the fact that, however that nature may change, it remains a changing or changeable nature *assignable to this* or *that text* (as *we* are prepared to say) or "signifier" (in Barthes's usage). What shall we make of that?

Barthes actually does speak of interpretation but only to dismiss it or to use the notion in what he calls "the Nietzschean sense of the word."[10] What he means is that ordinary interpretation (interpretation in our first sense) is addressed only to readerly texts, to texts construed as "products," referents with fixed natures; whereas writerly texts invite interpretation only in the "Nietzschean" sense (in something close to our second sense), in a sense applied to "production without product, structuration without structure":

> To interpret a text is not to give it a (more or less justified, more or less free) meaning, but on the contrary to appreciate what *plural* constitutes it. . . . This text is a galaxy of signifiers, not a structure of signifieds; it has no beginning; it is reversible; we gain access to it by several entrances, none of which can be authoritatively declared to be the main one; the codes it mobilizes extend as far as *the eye can reach*; they are interminable . . . their number is never closed, based as it is on the infinity of language.[11]

Barthes himself is most exact here: "as nothing exists outside the text [this remark follows Derrida's by about three years[12]], there is never a *whole* of the text [that is,] for the plural text, there cannot be a [fixed] narrative structure, a grammar, or a logic."[13] His meaning is plainly designed to preserve an adequacy of reference ("a galaxy of signifiers") but to disallow a complete fixity of predicable nature ("a structure of signifieds").

Interpretation in the "Nietzschean" sense subtends a responsive reading all right, but it is a reading that employs (as Barthes's own reading of S/Z shows) a *selection* from the codes of reading that obtain (somehow) in the life of our society—that do not and cannot lead to closure, to hierarchical preference, to correctness by way of reference to an antecedently closed textual nature. There is no longer an *explication de texte*: there is only a reading of the signifiers that thereby constitutes, reconstitutes, leaves infinitely or "plurally" open to endless further reconstitution, the signifiers that acquire *that very history*. This is the meaning of that otherwise impenetrable remark (playfully

Rousseauesque): "narrative is both merchandise and the relation of the contract of which it is the object."[14] So seen, *Sarrasine* is not a standard story or a two-part story that contains a story within a story inviting explanation: it *is* a story "of a contract of a force (the narrative) and the action of this force on the very contract controlling it": we are invited (in effect, *by* the writerly contract) to invent, by applying *to certain signifiers* the codes of reading *of our world*, whatever equivalences of structure may be imaginatively produced in an exchange of readings applied *to* the admitted structures of *Sarrasine* (the apparently "nested narratives").[15] It would be wrong, therefore, to deny that Barthes's sort of playful interpretation abandons reference *or* predication *or* a disciplined reading: it merely abandons *the full fixity of texts favored in readerly readings*, in standard modernist and premodernist accounts, and shifts reference from finished text to enabling signifier.

There are two pressure points in Barthes's theory of Texts pertinent to our second sense of interpretation. First, there *is* literally nothing that could be interpreted—*in the first sense* of "interpret"—until after the Text is "constituted" (Barthes's term) by work that is interpretive in the second sense; secondly, constituting a Text in that sense does not simply yield a "product," a specific fixed text in the ordinary sense, that could be further interpreted—in the first sense of "interpret." Remember—the point is regularly neglected by the would-be anarchists and irrationalists of interpretation—that Barthes never disallows the validity or disciplined option of readerly interpretation practiced on a textual product that is managed in accord with the first sense of "interpret." Barthes's thesis is only that the two sorts of reading arise together within the same societal practices and may even be regarded as sequentially ordered phases of reading (or interpretation) within the practice of an increasingly normalized use of particular texts (or "galaxies of signifiers"). Barthes's own emphasis is on the *jouissance* of preferring the writerly over the readerly, not the ineligibility of the latter.[16] Liberty with texts or signifiers does not escape the normal constraints of discourse—only the presumptions of *jejune* literary theory.

Consider the following observation (or, confession):

Reading a text cited by Stendhal (but not written by him) I find Proust in the minute detail. The Bishop of Lescars refers to the niece of his vicar-general in a series of affected apostrophes (*My little niece, my little friend, my lovely brunette, ah, delicious little morsel!*) which remind me of the way the two post girls at the Grand Hotel at Balbec, Marie Geneste and Celeste Albaret, address the narrator (*Oh, the little black-haired devil, oh, tricky little devil! Ah, youth! Ah, lovely skin!*) Elsewhere, but in the same way, in Flaubert, it is the blossoming apple trees of Normandy which I read *according to* Proust . . . this does not mean that I am in any way a Proust "specialist": Proust is what comes to me, not what I summon up; not an "authority," simply a *circular memory* [that is, a memory that "circles" or stalks a text]. Which is what the inter-text is: the impossibility of living outside the infinite text—whether this text be Proust or the daily newspaper or the television screen: the book creates the meaning, the meaning creates life.[17]

Reading in the writerly manner is a form of living, not a form of research; it involves know-how (*savoir-aller*, not *savoir*, at least not frontally). But it is disciplined, in at least the sense that it involves a form of play interesting to others (for instance, as in S/Z) only if the reader is really civilized and witty and inventive. We, then, can retrace the *play* of S/Z in order to become similarly motivated and (perhaps as) skillful. But reading in that way resists the "bifurcation" of the reader/read text—in order to allow that distinction to be made again in a freer way. There is no "explaining" that Text (Barthes's "Text") and there is no "knowledge" of the meaning of that Text: because, of course, there *is* (then) no definitive text and no one way of motivating readings "which would be definitive" of any meaning.[18] Nevertheless, there *are* "galaxies of signifiers," socially habituated practices, disciplined options of reading, and above all the customary meanings of sentences and sedimented readerly texts. One sees at once Krauss's mistake—as well as the mistake of such heavyhanded postmodernists as Jean-François Lyotard.[19] For, *savoir-faire* or *savoir-lire* presupposes *savoir*—at least distributively; similarly, writerly reading presupposes readerly reading—again at least distributively.

Barthes effectively acknowledges the point: it is the only possible condition on which a complete chaos of reading (or of cultural life in general) can be avoided. It is in part at least what Wittgenstein means by "forms of life," what Bourdieu means by *"habitus,"* what Marx means by *"praxis"* and "modes of production," what Hegel means by *"Sitten,"* what Gadamer means by *"wirkungsgeschichtliches Bewusstsein,"* what Husserl means by plural *"Lebensformen,"* what Foucault means by *"epistemes."* It is no more than the acknowledgement of the preformative historical practices by which culturally apt individuals first become apt. Their world is already culturally preformed *for them*; that is the reason they may be said to learn their native language and their native culture; that is the reason they can specify the "signifiers," the culturally (already) prepared materials, that, by interpreting (in the productive sense), they first constitute texts or artworks as such—what thereupon prove to be usable as referents apt for interpretation (in the adequational sense). Barthes's emphasis, of course, is on the initial process of doing just that. On the evidence (on his view), the process has been forgotten or ignored or misconstrued. Our own emphasis, for the moment at least, is focused rather on the option of continuing a critical discourse about whatever is thereby so constituted—without in the least reneging on Barthes's fine lesson. On the argument, we preserve both themes merely by distinguishing with care the logical requirements of unicity or individuation from the prejudice of certain substantive (premodernist or modernist) presumptions of unity or fixity of nature.

The constraints of reference and predication are not violated by Barthes, only displaced from produced texts to interpretable signifiers (in the second sense of "interpret").

Barthes himself does not tarry long enough to give us a theory of the social habituation of the practices of reading that support the distinctive discipline of readerly and writerly reading. He presupposes such a theory—or such theories—but he moves on only to offer examples of what he recommends. For our own part, we could easily pause to construct a theory of social practice—from Hegel or Marx, or Nietzsche or Foucault, or Weber or Lukács, or Husserl or Heidegger, or Adorno or Benjamin, or Lévi-Strauss or Althusser, or Wittgenstein or Bourdieu, or Gadamer or Kuhn.

The point remains quite constant, however; the waiving of texts in a sense suited to the first sort of interpretation does not eliminate constative discourse elsewhere (for readerly texts, say), does not preclude referential and predicative discipline within the *writerly* reading recommended (as in the identification of relevant signifiers, the identification of other readerly- and writerly-read texts, a certain civilized familiarity with the details of one's culture), and it does not even preclude a rapprochement between readerly and writerly reading *before and after* the play of a particularly agile exercise of the latter sort (the charm of S/Z, say). In short, Barthes's preference of the writerly is not even a denial of the ontology of texts—or, of the likely dawning of gradually normalized texts for which such an ontology could be retrospectively constructed (if we wished); *and* it does not itself supply an adequate analysis of what a signifier is, or a practice of reading, or even a human being capable of reading in either the readerly or writerly way. It is one thing to grasp the fresh discovery Barthes bequeaths us; it is quite another to make a shambles of every effort to understand interpretation. After all, the "bifurcation" of the signifier and the would-be reader remains, *after* the provisional "bifurcation" of the readerly text and the reader is first disallowed—and *then* (of course) civilly permitted to be recovered once again in Barthes's educated sense.

Barthes offers an instance (in S/Z)—after the fact of a readerly deposit of *Sarrasine* in the canon of conventional texts—*of* what it would be like *before* such a reading to read in the writerly way. The "galaxy of signifiers" itself lacks fixed meaning; but, as the competent readers we are, we do possess the know-how for grasping what may be taken to be their meaning. Barthes suppresses this hermeneutic or praxical or habituative dimension of reading—but it is surely there. The semantic and semiotic potentialities of signifiers are already built into the minima of any socialized habit of reading and using language. Nevertheless, Saussure, whom Barthes had taken his original departure from (but now supercedes), had never successfully explained the "original" relationship between writing and speech or writing and thought that he insisted on; and without that "originary" source—or the effective replacement for it more perspicuously advanced by Wittgenstein and Gadamer, say—there remains a critical lacuna in Barthes's own account. (Saussure's failing, of course, is just what Derrida had so mercilessly exposed in *Of Grammatology*.[20]) But the deeper theme, missing also in Derrida, is this: that the deconstructive or poststructuralist or antimodernist rejection of the bifurcation of reader and text itself entails a competent practice or activity *on the part of readers vis-à-vis something else* (signifiers, say) within a preformed or habituated cultural space in which (and by using the processes of which) what Barthes calls the "plural" or "infinite" Text *is first constituted*. In a sense, "the deconstruction of hermeneutics" is therefore reversed and aced by being shown to require and presuppose a "hermeneutics of deconstruction."[21] It is not, however, itself thereby disallowed or repudiated. What the argument shows is that the rejection of a cultural world bifurcated between inquiring subjects and subjects inquired into—or between such subjects and what they do or produce (texts, in the idiom we have adopted)—is itself the work of subjects active *in* such a bifurcated world. In short, *we* theorize in a critical moment about a preformative condition *we* cannot originally fathom (that Saussure thought he could fathom, that Husserl also thought he could fathom) within which the bifurcation of world and word (or text) and reader

first arises. Barthes's splendid game of writerly-readerly texts, therefore, serves a double purpose: for one thing, it affords a miniature exemplar of the impossibility of radically disjoining the double function of subjects as observer and observed (in much the same sense in which one cannot beat oneself at chess); and, for another, it subverts the fixities of privilege, of readerly reading, of the metaphysics of presence, of all the bugaboos of failing to remember *that* the steady structures of our now bifurcated world depend impenetrably on whatever *we* critically and mythically postulate as the preformed world within which our own salient world arises.

So seen, Barthes's invention is an attractive toy—no more than a toy, no more than a toy for Barthes himself: for we *could* easily (and would need to) interpose a conception of numbered, reidentifiable texts that could support interpretation in the first *and* second senses and that would, at the same time, subvert a metaphysics of privilege (the notion of fixed and bounded texts) just because—for reading purposes at least—texts do and must remain referentially accessible. Barthes's conceit of the infinite Text (that is not itself a referent) is, then, merely the deliberately posed extravagance of a disappearing limit *for* the more modestly interposed texts we are now recommending. Barthes nearly says as much:

The Text (if only because of its frequent "unreadability") decants the work from its consumption and gathers it up as play, task, production, and activity. This means that the Text requires an attempt to abolish (or at least to lessen) the distance between writing and reading, not by intensifying the reader's projection into the work, but by linking the two together in a single signifying process.[22]

The point is, a theory of texts adequate for interpretation at the present time must collect Barthes's double lesson—but must do so in an ampler and more systematic way than Barthes actually does. We must: (1) detach the full theory of the nature of texts (literary, visual, musical) from the mere constative constraints of discourse about them, so that all notions of fixity, essence, analogy with physical particulars are attenuated as far as possible or challenged as much as necessary; and (2) we must develop a positive theory of texts, of how texts (or culturally emergent phenomena and entities in general[23]) are actually constituted—first, from precultural physical materials and, second, from culturally prepared materials. (1) trades on the lesson drawn from Krauss and Barthes: that unity and unicity are distinct though not altogether separable notions; (2) requires an entirely fresh start and cannot fail to center on the peculiarities of Intentional properties and their incarnated relation to material properties.[24]

III

This has been a strenuous exercise. For one thing, it is always difficult to depend on the florid French. And for another, our thesis has its distinctly threatening side. But we may collect our findings now a little more lightly. An adequate theory of interpretation will seek to explain: (1) how it is that we can referentially fix, identify, or individuate artworks or texts for interpretation without at the same time insisting that their nature, their collected properties, their essential boundaries must also be supposed to be fixed, determined, changeless, or at least unaffected by merely interpreting them or commenting on them in the normal critical way; (2) how it is that artworks or texts are first constituted as such, so that they become the relatively stable referents of subsequent interpretive discourse; and (3) how it is that discursive interpretation *can* alter the natures of individuated texts and artworks and, in doing that, reconstitute their natures or properties without disorganizing their numerical identity and (of course) without inviting total chaos.

What we have at least shown is the sheer coherence of our intended answer to these questions: *the bare unicity of referents accommodates the absence of any fixed unity or fixed nature of the particulars thus identified.* In the biological world, for instance, we capture the limits of our tolerance for changing natures and fixed reference by adjusting our notions of natural kinds; spatio-temporal continuities, as Hume more or less admits, aid us in allowing fixity of identity to range over the shifting sequences of instantiated properties. In contemporary physics, among the quantum-mechanical puzzles of reconciling particle/wave anomalies, we exploit (with Heisenberg, for instance) punctual identification for the sake of descriptive control and then permit identification to become as story-relative as can be tolerated at a theoretical level at which such punctual identification would be altogether disallowed. In the cultural world, both with regard to persons and artworks, we borrow whatever similar conveniences we can; we maintain, for instance, wherever we may, "one person/one body," or "one sculpture/one block of marble," or "one poem/one inscription from a set of possible inscriptions." But texts and artworks do not form natural kinds and cannot be identified merely physically or as physical bodies. They differ essentially from natural objects in possessing Intentional properties. It is, in fact, just in virtue of that, paradigmatically, that texts *are subject to interpretation* in the two senses supplied *and* that those two senses are interrelated in the manner sketched.

Quite obviously, we have now come to the most strenuous part of the theory needed. Since we cannot possibly attempt here a full account of the ontology of artworks or cultural phenomena in general, we may as well be candid about the upshot of what such an account would yield.[25] It would make it possible to concede, *without endangering* the rigors of numerical identity *or* of the critical testing of particular claims *or* of coherent discourse in general, that texts may in principle be assigned infinitely many interpretations, that they may enter into infinitely many histories, and that interpretations and histories assigned them at t' later than t may well be affected by interpretations and histories assigned them at t. This *is* what accommodating Barthes's notion would require.

The fascinating thing is that it is entirely possible to make such a notion coherent, manageable, even quite plausible and disciplined. It would require quite a number of substantial concessions regarding the logic of general discourse that would not be narrowly occupied with the theory of art or interpretation. (These have elsewhere been shown to be entirely viable.) They could not fail to include at least: (i) abandoning as fixed principles the principles of excluded middle and *tertium non datur*; (ii) admitting the adequacy of, and the impossibility of exceeding the limitations of, story-relative reference; (iii) admitting the viability of relativistic truth-values and the compatibility of distributively employing such values together with the distributed use of bivalent or bipolar values where wanted; and (iv) challenging, if not repudiating, the adequacy of extensional canons for regimenting all languages descriptive of the real world. It would also require quite a number of substantial concessions of an ontological sort reconciled with the adjusted logic of discourse. For instance, it would require: (v) denying the adequacy of all physicalisms (as opposed to materialisms), whether reductive or not, in order to accommodate the reality of the artworld and the world of human culture in general; (vi) admitting cultural emergence, as distinct from physical emergence, as a process that yields indissolubly complex embodied or incarnated phenomena or properties; (vii) admitting that what distinguishes artworks, texts, and other cultural entities from natural entities depends essentially on the complex incarnation of Intentional properties; and (viii) admitting, in addition, that Intentional properties are such that they can be constituted, altered, affected, generated by the processes of critical discourse or interpretation applied to given texts or cultural referents, without adversely affecting the numerical fixity of such referents.

In a word, *if* physicalism and extensionalism are philosophically correct, or at least adequate (in real-time terms) for all discourse about the cultural world, then *everything* so far said is entirely pointless. That must be conceded straight off. But *if* they are neither correct nor demonstrated to be correct nor demonstrably correct nor even demonstrably adequate (in real-time terms), then we are left with a world for which theses (i)-(viii) are peculiarly apt, possibly even minimally required. It is certainly true that attacks on physicalism and extensionalism are widely and honorably resisted. But it is entirely fair to say that there is no known demonstration showing that opposition to those doctrines is as such incoherent, irresponsible, unfruitful, or calamitous. That is as honorable a stand as the other—probably a more resourceful one at least at the present time.[26] In any case, the admission of (i)-(viii) leads us directly to the startling finding that artworks or texts may be assigned infinitely many interpretations and may enter into infinitely many histories.[27] This is just what Barthes was getting at when, notoriously, he affirmed that "the Text . . . practices the infinite deferral of the signified."[28]

It is also, however, what a theorist like Gadamer means, speaking from the altogether different vantage of a hermeneutic ontology, when he declares that

to understand a text always means to apply it to ourselves and to know that, even if it must always be understood in different ways, it is still the same text presenting itself to us in these different ways. . . . The linguistic explicitness that the process of understanding gains through interpretation does not create a second sense apart from that which is understood and interpreted. The interpretative concepts are not, as such, thematic in understanding. Rather, it is their nature to disappear behind what they bring, in interpretation, into speech. Paradoxically, an interpretation is right when it is capable of disappearing in this way. The possibility of understanding is dependent on the possibility of this kind of mediating interpretation . . . interpretation is contained potentially in the understanding process. It simply makes the understanding explicit. Thus interpretation is not a means through which understanding is achieved, but it has passed into the content of what is understood.[29]

Notice that, unlike Barthes, Gadamer insists on the reidentification of one and the same text under plural, potentially infinite, interpretation and reinterpretation. The infinite openness of texts—in both an interpretive and historical sense (ultimately the same sense)—is ensured by the notion of reflexive application: the Intentional import *of* a text essentially incorporates into *its* developing, endlessly reconstituted meaning what its recovery for our own historical experience and prejudice can make it out to be. Its meaning is heuristically schematized in the intersection between *our* present power of reading and what, from that evolving perspective, we posit as *its* collected past. In this regard, our logical proposal about interpretable texts is closer to Gadamer's usage than to Barthes's. Quite unaccountably, however, Gadamer is, at every step, much more reluctant than he ought to be to accommodate a frank relativism—he is quite arbitrary about the point; and so, in this regard, our substantive proposal about interpretation is closer to Barthes's vision than to Gadamer's.

Still, it *is* Gadamer rather than Barthes who attempts to answer the third of the three questions we posed just a moment ago, namely, how it is that discursive interpretation can alter the nature of individuated texts without affecting their numerical identity and without producing conceptual chaos. Gadamer's answer depends, as is well known, on repudiating the Romantic recoverability of authorial intent, on reclaiming the historicity of human existence and cultural texts, on admitting the intransparency and preformative forces of the human world in which, in a Heideggerean sense, we are "thrown," and (most important) on featuring the natural or perspectival "prejudice" of all understanding and interpretation—in a word, on the function of "the fusion of horizons" (*Horizontverschmelzung*). Thus Gadamer maintains: "It is part of real understanding . . . that we regain the concepts of an historical past [understand or interpret a text] in such a way that they also include our own comprehension of them. [This is what is meant by] 'the fusion of horizons'."[30] The meaning *of* a text is the "fusion" of its perceived past and its perceived present application to ourselves; but it is *we* who monitor both elements of the effort.

The upshot is: (1) that it is in virtue of the Intentional nature of texts that they require interpretation in order to be understood; (2) that since interpretable texts and textual interpreters exist historically, preformatively, intransparently, there cannot be a uniquely correct or uniquely convergent reading or interpretation of a given text; and (3) that since interpretation and understanding require the historicized recovery of the Intentional import of a given text, it is quite impossible to fix that recovery except in terms of the salient or convincing fusion of—or what, from the perspective of present interpreters, is posited as the shared or continuous or intersecting—horizons of the past and the present. This resolution of our third question, rather along Gadamer's lines, reconciles the ontology of texts and the methodology of their interpretation.

Gadamer, however, without the least defense (as already remarked), affirms that there *is* a "universal" or "classical" tradition that can always be historically recovered—indeed, that must be recovered—for a successful resolution of the hermeneutic task.[31] Naturally, we reject his claim. But, more amiably for our present purpose, we may content ourselves with the knowledge that the conceptual strategy here adopted draws in its wake a large number of further questions we have not yet answered, having to do with claims of objectivity, supporting evidence, relativistic tolerance, the universality of cognitive claims, the specific ontology of art, the relationship of Intentional and physical attributes, and the like; and that strategy still accommodates in a dialectical way all the recent modernist/postmodernist quarrels, all the complexities of historicity and intransparency, Gadamer's own closet essentialism, and even such more daring conjectures as Michel Foucault for instance advances. For, puzzling over Velásquez's problem in representing pictorial representation within the Classical canon (in *Las Meninas*), Foucault remarks: "Before the end of the eighteenth century, *man* did not exist . . . He is a quite recent creature, which the demiurge of knowledge fabricated with its own hands less than two hundred years ago. [Before that time] there was no epistemological consciousness of man as such. The Classical *episteme* is articulated along lines that do not isolate, in any way, a specific domain proper to man."[32] The meaning of Foucault's remarkably apt perception (even if we should disagree with his interpretation of *Las Meninas*) is that the historical past, which is both real and *not* the same as the physical past in which it is incarnate, can be retroactively affected (without violating physical time or physical causality) by future sensibilities that could not have been recognized as potentiated in a particular past present. Merely to mention the complication is to appreciate the task of a seriously contemporary theory of interpretation.

Notions of historicity, therefore, as variable as Krauss's, Barthes's, Gadamer's, and Foucault's strongly favor the need for, and the plausibility of, a theory rather like the one here offered. The canonical view—what we have called interpretation restricted in the first sense—does not permit these subtle questions to be even honored or perceived; and interpretation in the sense here championed— that unites the first and second senses given—secures the stability of texts and interpretation by way of the salient habits of life of a society rather than by way of a privileged discovery of independently fixed entities. Without such a grounding, without the sheer conservative contingencies of life itself, human history would be an utter chaos; the disorder of critical interpretation would be instantly matched by the loss of science and rational prudence. That admission alone is much more than the recovery of a pragmatist aesthetics, but it is at least that.[33]

NOTES

1. Rosalind E. Krauss, "Postmodernism and the Paraliterary," in *The Originality of the Avant-Garde and Other Myths* (MIT Press, 1983), pp. 292–293.
2. T. S. Eliot, "The Function of Criticism," in *Selected Essays 1917–1932* (London: Faber and Faber, 1932), p. 19.
3. Monroe C. Beardsley, "The Authority of the Text," in *The Possibility of Criticism* (Wayne State University Press, 1970), p. 16.
4. See Krauss, "Notes on the Index: Part 1" and "Notes on the Index: Part 2," in *The Originality of the Avant-Garde*.
5. Krauss, "In the Name of Picasso," in *The Originality of the Avant-Garde*, pp. 28, 30, 32; italics added.
6. See Margolis, *Texts without Referents: Reconciling Science and Narrative* (Oxford: Blackwell, 1988), chs. 7, 8.
7. I confess that, in *The Language of Art and Art Criticism* (Wayne State University, 1965) and *Art and Philosophy* (Atlantic Highlands, N.J.: Humanities Press, 1980), I had not fully appreciated these complexities. I see that I was drawn, in effect, to allow more than I specifically wished to commit myself to. This essay is part of an attempt to make good my full escape—and, at the same time, to recover what is recoverable from those earlier accounts. I have, here, been very much influenced by the entire development of Continental European philosophy moving through Husserl and Heidegger and Gadamer and Derrida and Barthes and Foucault. But I am pleased to acknowledge the fairness of a criticism of the apparent force of my previously published position, in Richard Shusterman, "Interpretation, Intention, and Truth," in *Journal of Aesthetics and Art Criticism* 46 (1988): 399–411. I do believe that Shusterman himself fails to distinguish the logical and substantive issues, which gives a somewhat false impression of my earlier views. But that, doubtless, is due to my own former innocence; and, in any case, I should not protest too strenuously. See Joseph Margolis, *Texts without Referents*, part II.
8. Roland Barthes, "From Work to Text," in *Textual Strategies: Perspectives in Post-Structuralist Criticism*, trans. and ed. Josué V. Harari (Cornell University Press, 1979), p. 74.
9. Roland Barthes, S/Z, trans. Richard Miller (New York: Hill and Wang, 1974), p. 4. The closest English-language equivalent of Barthes's conception of "texts"—approached, however, from an entirely different point of view, one more disposed to the semantic than to the syntactic, though equally freewheeling in its attitude to codes or rules—is, of course, the one favored by Harold Bloom. The following brief passage from Harold Bloom, *A Map of Misreading* (Oxford University Press, 1975), "Introduction: A Meditation upon Misreading," makes this quite clear: "Reading . . . is a belated and all-but-impossible act, and if strong is always a misreading. Literary mean-

ing tends to become more underdetermined even as literary language becomes more overdetermined. . . . Influence, as I conceive it, means that there are *no* texts, but only relationships *between* texts. These relationships depend upon a critical act, a misreading or misprision, that one poet performs upon another, and that does not differ in kind from the necessary critical acts performed by every strong reader upon every text he encounters. The influence-relation governs reading as it governs writing, and reading is therefore a miswriting just as writing is a misreading. As literary history lengthens, all poetry necessarily becomes verse-criticism, just as all criticism becomes prose-poetry" (p. 3).
10. Barthes, S/Z, p. 5.
11. Ibid., pp. 5–6.
12. See Jacques Derrida, *Of Grammatology*, trans. Gayatri Chakravorty Spivak (Johns Hopkins Press, 1976), pp. 158, 161.
13. Barthes, *S/Z*, p. 6.
14. Ibid., p. 90.
15. Ibid.
16. See Roland Barthes, *The Pleasure of the Text*, trans. Richard Miller (New York: Hill and Wang, 1975).
17. Ibid., pp. 34–36.
18. Ibid., p. 34.
19. See Jean-François Lyotard, *The Postmodern Condition: A Report on Knowledge*, trans. Geoff Bennington and Brian Massumi (University of Minnesota Press, 1984), for instance, section 6.
20. Derrida, *Of Grammatology*, pt. I, ch. 2.
21. I am pleased to take this phrasing from John D. Caputo, *Radical Hermeneutics: Repetition, Deconstruction, and the Hermeneutic Project* (Indiana University Press, 1987), p. 187.
22. Barthes, "From Work to Text," p. 79.
23. This is, of course, a theme I have pursued in a great number of places. See Joseph Margolis, *Art and Philosophy*, Part One; *Culture and Cultural Entities* (Dordrecht: D. Reidel, 1984), ch. 1; *Texts without Referents*, ch. 6.
24. For a fuller account of intentionality, intensionality, Intentionality, see Joseph Margolis, *Science without Unity: Reconciling the Human and Natural Sciences* (Oxford: Blackwell, 1987), chs. 7, 9.
25. In *Texts without Referents*, chs. 6, 8, there appears the most compendious account of the matter I have been able to fashion to date.
26. Two specimen claims may be mentioned. In one, Daniel C. Dennett provocatively remarks: "Intentionality is not a mark that divides phenomena from phenomena, but sentences from sentences. . . . Intentional objects are not any kind of objects at all. [The tendency to treat them as distinct objects rests on] the dependence of Intentional objects on particular descriptions [that is, on the thesis that] to change the description is to change the object. What sort of thing is a different thing under different descriptions? Not any object. Can we not do without the objects altogether and talk most of descriptions? . . . Intentional sentences are *intensional* (nonextensional) sentences," Daniel C. Dennett, *Content and Consciousness* (London: Routledge and Kegan Paul, 1969), pp. 28–29. But this, though quite characteristic of a certain analytic stance, is remarkably weak. First of all, even with respect to ordinary descriptive contexts, it is not true that the intentionality thesis holds that things are altered by altering descriptions; it holds, rather, that, under differing descriptions, we cannot always tell *whether* we are dealing with the same thing or not. Secondly, in the context of *texts*, which Dennett nowhere considers, it may be claimed that, because texts possess Intentional properties inherently, they *are* interpretable and, *qua* interpretable, their properties may actually be changed or affected by *interpretation* but not in a way that would also change their merely physical features or change them for that reason alone. In a second claim, Donald Davidson, speaking of what he terms "radical interpretation"—effectively, understanding what another says, either intra-linguistically or inter-linguistically—flatly and without the least argument (here or anywhere) affirms that, since it is true enough that "interpretable speeches are nothing but (that is, identical with) actions performed with assorted nonlinguistic intentions (to warn, control, amuse, distract, insult), and these actions are in turn nothing but (identical with) intentional movements of the lips and larynx, . . . [these] nonlinguistic goings-on must supply the evidential base for interpretation" (regardless of the fact that saying so "provides no clue as to how the evidence is related to what it surely is evident for"), Donald Davidson, "Radical Interpretation," in *Inquiries into Truth and Interpretation* (Oxford University Press, 1984), pp. 126–127. But Davidson has never managed to show how to determine prior "non-linguistic"

intentions or how to distinguish them from linguistically expressed intentions or how to construe them in extensionally compliant physicalist terms or how to construe linguistically expressed intentions in extensionally compliant terms. Failure to achieve such results must effectively count as the failure of the doctrine actually advanced.
27. Theses (i)-(viii) are, in effect, defended in the trilogy that includes *Pragmatism without Foundations, Science without Unity, Texts without Referents*.
28. Barthes, "From Work to Text," p. 76.
29. Hans-Georg Gadamer, *Truth and Method*, 2d ed., trans. Garrett Barden and Robert Cumming (New York: Seabury Press, 1975), p. 359.
30. Ibid., p. 337. The entire argument is effectively collected in second part, part II, including Gadamer's resistance to relativism. It must be said as well, however, that, although Barthes clearly slights, and means to slight, the historical dimension of interpretation in his antimodernist (if not postmodernist) proposal, restoring that historical consideration—as with Gadamer—does *not* redeem the reliability of authorial intent *or* (against Gadamer) the reliability of a tradition's intent. The deeper puzzle involved here has somewhat eluded Alasdair MacIntyre's recent—and justified—critique of Barthes. So MacIntyre observes, against Barthes's "postmodernism" (Roland Barthes, *Critique et verité* [Paris: Seuil, 1966], particularly p. 56): "The understanding of the text is not controlled by authorial intention or by any relationship to an audience with specific shared beliefs, for it is outside context except the context of interpretation," Alasdair MacIntyre, *Whose Justice? Which Rationality?* (University of Notre Dame, 1988), p. 386. What MacIntyre fails to demonstrate—though his criticism of Barthes stands—is that the *recovery of tradition* itself entails, within any tradition, a historicized openendness of the sort Barthes explores, even if it is the case that Barthes himself, always suspicious of reliable histories, exaggerates the arbitrariness of writerly reading. It's reasonably clear that Barthes's own practice belies the rhetoric favored and that MacIntyre's corrective is committed to traditionalism.
31. Ibid., pp. 253–258, 316–325.
32. Michel Foucault, *The Order of Things: An Archaeology of the Human Sciences*, trans. (New York: Vintage Books, 1973), pp. 308–309.
33. Presidential Address, 46th Annual Meeting of the American Society of Aesthetics, October 28, 1988, Vancouver, British Columbia.

Hermeneutics and the 'Crisis' of Literature

M. M. Van de Pitte

I

The immediate cause of the much bruited crisis of literature is of course the evident failure of New Criticism.[1] The failure is sometimes attributed to the inappropriateness of New Critical practice in relation to theory,[2] but more often to the inadequacy of the theory itself. The majority view is likely the correct one. It is difficult to see how *any* specific critical practice is logically implied by a theory which centres on the notion of semantic autonomy. Poetics, to be worth having, should identify interpretative principles to regulate critical practice. But in a very fundamental sense, New Criticism cannot do this—certainly it cannot do so in a way consistent with the crucial tenet that the meaning of a text is irreducible to any particular person's understanding of it. Understanding a text is in that case unconditional—a simple seeing of 'what is there' behind and untouched by the critical process. However, objectivity of this sort has been forfeit since the publication of Kant's First Critique.

The purpose here is not to give yet another assessment of New Criticism though. Rather it is to explore a more fundamental issue that lurks in the background of such discussions. It is sufficiently important that if it is not settled, it is pointless to debate the merits of *any* specific critical theory, old or New. This prior issue is that of the viability, perhaps even of the intelligibility, of the notion of a discipline capable of developing methods adequate to literary analysis. The problem is this: to establish literature as a separate category, irreducible to the category of non-literary discourse, is usually to do so in terms of a notion—'metaphor,' 'symbol,' and 'irony' are among the common choices—which by definition cannot be cashed out in terms of ordinary, 'rationalistic' conceptual categories, that is, which cannot be cashed out without violating the 'irreducible to non-literary discourse' clause. Literature, even to the most sober-minded New Critic, is 'paradoxical,' 'magical,' 'miraculous'.[3] The fact (if it is one) that literary discourse is irreducible to non-literary discourse renders the critic's task seemingly hopeless, and so too the enterprise of formulating a coherent philosophy of criticism.

Fortunately the theoretical impossibility of propositionally extrapolating the meaning of literary works has never prevented theorists from trying to systematize the whole business, much less deterred critics from analysing the unsayable. But it seems that their efforts have been rewarded only if they have turned a blind eye to certain components which contribute to the paradox or dialectical tension or whatever it is which is the mark of literary meaning—or if, as is usually the case, they confine themselves to a negative characterization of their object, or to giving 'hints' which are as little susceptible of concise formulation as are the meanings hinted at.

The present situation in poetics is then not to be wondered at. And there is no reason to hope for improvement if it is the nature of

---

From *The British Journal of Aesthetics*, 24 (1984). Reprinted by permission of the publisher.

the case that anyone wishing to approach literature 'scientifically' is obliged to choose some elements while ignoring others, from among the sets of polarities which constitute the field of tension that is poetic meaning. Thus, as has long been recognized, distortion or falsification of the work is the necessary price for making its meaning discursive in accord with the canons of scientific discourse.

II

Is the situation for poetics quite as hopeless as this would indicate? Certainly there is no reason to anticipate the resuscitation of either of the critical perspectives dominant until now. The polarity around which they circled was that of immanent/transcendent meaning: 'Old' criticism had the text embodying or symbolizing a meaning exterior to it, while New Criticism affirmed the autonomously meaningful text. The reasons why neither position is satisfactory are well catalogued and need not concern us here. What must be noted is that neither position can satisfy both of what would seem to be necessary conditions for a science of literature. These conditions are that the discipline be both autonomous and objective. The transcendentalist cannot conform to the autonomy requirement, because he reduces literary meaning to non-literary (psychological, sociological, historical, philosophical . . .) meaning. Thus literary science is subsumed under one or more of the social scientific or humanistic disciplines. The immanentist, for his part, cannot establish objectivity. He can proclaim as much as he wants the meaningful *in se* text, but he can never demonstrate that meanings exist *in vacuo*, that they are predicates of physical things, of symbols or whatever, rather than being intentional objects. He cannot even afford to admit that they are both, without jeopardizing his theory. But to sever completely the connection between the text and people's intentions or uses precludes, rather than secures, the possibility of objective interpretation. There are then in principle as many viable interpretations as there are people who engage the text, simply because the theory cannot offer ground rules for confirmation or falsification of meaning hypotheses constructed in accord with it.

Of course the situation is much more complicated than this sketch would indicate. But it is at least clear that to return to the forms we have had is to circle endlessly around the form/content, subjective/objective dichotomies. We cannot, however, simply resign ourselves to the fact that the paradoxical, the essentially ambiguous, is not the stuff of which sciences are made. We must first examine the claim of some proponents of hermeneutical philosophy to have achieved an *Aufhebung* of the conflicting claims of old and New criticism.

Certainly if any position is likely to transcend the vitiating dichotomies at the heart of poetics it is that of the hermeneuticist. Hermeneutics directly addresses the crisis in literature particularly and in aesthetics generally. As one hermeneuticist puts it:

> Hermeneutical philosophy grows out of a dissatisfaction with the failure of aesthetics to transcend its perpetual dilemmas, its quarrels about whether to define art in terms of distinctions between sense and intellect, emotion and cognition, delight and deliberation, mediacy and immediacy, concreteness and abstraction, mimesis and expression, or truth and beauty.[4]

Indeed it represents the sole philosophical, meta-critical perspective with a direct bearing upon literature. Its ontological region of inquiry is the text and the text analogue, its basic epistemological category is interpretative understanding, its praxis is critical praxis. The hermeneuticist, rather than attempting to analyse literary interpretation on the model of scientific or common sense understanding, tries to make sense of these latter in terms of literary experience. It is thus both natural and necessary that the hermeneuticist should begin by laying out the fundamental concept of criticism—the concept of 'understanding a text'. He must do so not simply in order to provide the foundation for an aesthetics of literature and for literary criticism, but for the much more important work of grounding cognition generally. The hermeneuticist's work on this grander problem obliges him to analyse and criticize the conceptual framework in which the dichotomies that have plagued literary theory have their home. (Philosophers of science like Kuhn and Feyerabend call it the 'Cartesian' or 'foundationalist' framework, and mean it to comprehend, *inter alia*, metaphysical realism and correspondence truth theory.) Thus we have every reason to examine very carefully the hermeneuticist's claim to have resolved, or to be capable of resolving, the crisis of literature, before abandoning the problem.

It is important to note at the outset that the term 'hermeneutics' has been loosely applied to a spectrum of views. There are at least three different senses of it which crop up in writings on aesthetics. It is necessary to make our understanding of the term precise, at the same time that we ask whether it designates a viable *tertium quid* between old and New criticism. If we do not, we might well find that we have discredited the claim of one hermeneuticist to have put poetics on the right track, while leaving untouched the positions of other aestheticians who operate under the same rubric. We shall arbitrarily designate the three different species of hermeneutics as 'phenomenological', 'metaphysical', and 'transcendental', respectively (and admit at the outset that the neat distinctions between them are often confused in practice).

A. Phenomenological Hermeneutics

'Phenomenological hermeneutics' is here restricted to E. D. Hirsch's position, which is *sui generis* within hermeneutical aesthetics. Hirsch's position is in fact radically opposed to that of most aestheticians who likewise represent themselves as phenomenological hermeneuticists, but whom we shall call 'metaphysical' hermeneuticists. *Their* work has its provenance in *Sein und Zeit* and, despite superficial differences, is rooted squarely in Heideggerian ontology. Hirsch's work is not. Husserl is his intellectual ancestor, the Husserl who opposed himself to the 'subjectivism', 'psychologism', 'anthropologism', etc. of his renegade disciple, Heidegger. Hirsch's Husserl is not unlike Richard Rorty's, in that he champions a highly sophisticated version of the 'foundationalist' conceptual framework which modern hermeneutics is intent on surpassing.

However much his work differs from that of other hermeneutical aestheticians, Hirsch, in *Validity in Interpretation*, seeks to do for poetics what hermeneuticists since Dilthey have tried to do for the human sciences generally—that is, to determine 'the grounds by which their interpretations can be said to be valid and their insights true'.[5] As we know, Hirsch thinks he can do this by reintroducing the author's intention as the criterion for determining the meaning of a text.[6] But as is usually the case in aesthetics, his arguments against his opponents, the New Critics, are considerably more telling than his arguments for his own position. It is not difficult to show that, whatever the virtues of New Criticism, it clearly failed to produce canons of criticism which justify preferences among interpretations. The doctrine of semantic autonomy commits us, whether we will it or not, to a radically relativistic critical theory. Hirsch's alternative is to posit fixed meanings, meanings constituted historically by the authors of texts, but having the characteristics of Fregean or Husserlian ideas.[7] The word 'posit' is significant here—erhaps Hirsch is simply countering scepticism with dogmatism. Certainly his critics within and outside of hermeneutics have had little difficulty in exposing the inadequacies of his position.[8] If nothing else, he is plagued by the difficulty that has dogged hermeneutics since the time of Schleiermacher and which continues to dog those who, like Hirsch,[9] adhere to a rather simplistic version of the Dilthey/Weber model of interpretative understanding. This is the problem of justifying a claim to have understood an author's intention, supposing that is in fact what a text means. It would seem that if that problem is resolvable at all, it can only be so within the framework of a transcendental hermeneutics, a framework quite different from the one within which Hirsch operates.

Hirsch for his part cheerfully acknowledges this. He insists that 'rightly understanding what the author meant'[10] is the necessary normative principle underlying the ideal objective interpretation but grants that in fact no interpretation is certain—the ideal can never be demonstrated to have been satisfied.[11]

In fact, no matter which of the many weak points of Hirsch's interesting theory that his opponents parade forth—(many of them involve an instructive conflict between phenomenological (objectivist, idealist) and hermeneutical (subjectivist) principles)—we are likely to meet with a similar response from Hirsch. He knows the difficulties. He knows that his objectivist meta-critical stance is unverifiable and that particular interpretations executed from that perspective are unverifiable as well. He makes whatever case he can for objectivism not because he is convinced of the possibility of adequately grounding scientific (i.e., logically warranted) poetics, but because it is the only alternative available to the functional non-objectivism of New Criticism and the critical anarchy it promotes. And Hirsch is quite right in doing this.

In a sense then Hirsch's alternative to scepticism *is* dogmatism. But if we look under the theory presented in *Validity in Interpretation* the impression that it is entirely ungrounded (that objectivity is simply a matter of *fiat*) is somewhat dispelled. The theory can be weakly sanctioned in a way that the alternative cannot. The meta-theoretical foundations for the theory are frankly pragmatic and normative, with no pretence to being scientific. It is a matter of simple necessity that we must adopt an *als ob* objectivism if we want a distinctive literary science, an aesthetic of literature, at all. We must distinguish certain kinds of literary works—art works—from other kinds, and identify principles adequate to their analysis. 'But', Hirsch says, 'it is a philosophical mistake to argue that this procedure is sanctioned by a special ontological status for literature or that the methods of literary study are different in principle from other kinds of inquiry'.[12]

In the final analysis then, Hirsch's 'old' critical sort of poetics is rooted in orthodox post-positive or hermeneutical philosophy of science. Given that there is no semantically autonomous text to arbitrate among various understandings, given that interpreted meanings are ontologically equal (a function of the interpreter's purpose) then, in criticism—to borrow a phrase from Feyerabend—'anything goes'. In fact, according to Hirsch, 'hermeneutic theory has sanctioned just about every conceivable form of legitimacy in interpretation'. From this 'historical fact', he infers 'that interpretative norms are not really derived from theory, and that theory codifies *ex post facto* the interpretative norms we already prefer'.[13] This is Kuhn's *The Structure of Scientific Revolutions* fitted to poetics—the ultimate basis for the theories and methodological canons of poetics is the value preferences of the discipline's practitioners.

Hirsch's own value orientation is ethical in the narrow sense. He is deeply concerned with how poetics and criticism can contribute towards making individuals and societies better. What he has done in *Validity in Interpretation* is to formulate a concept of literature and of the study of literature appropriate to this. He has no illusions about its being the 'true' theory of criticism.

We might argue that there is no real inconsistency in adopting as Hirsch does a fundamentally relativist meta-critical position and a narrowly absolutist critical one. Hirsch has simply realized, as the author of *The Structure of Scientific Revolutions* has not, that a condition for the very possibility of any discipline is that one supposes it to have an object which can be genuinely known. Even if it requires a sort of methodological hypocrisy, one must affect ontological realism and correspondentist truth theory in order to get the job of any discipline done. It is a bonus for Hirsch that it happens to suit his moral and pedagogical interests to do so.

Hirsch's phenomenological hermeneutics

cannot 'solve' then the crisis of literature in the way demanded, that is, by establishing an autonomous and objective poetological science. His critics who regard the theory as a return to a soundly discredited 'old' criticism are disappointed because it failed to satisfy false expectations. They have missed the 'as if' character of Hirsch's position. In any case we shall have to look elsewhere for a logical grounding of poetics.

B. Metaphysical Hermeneutics

As already indicated, 'metaphysical' hermeneuticists are orthodox Heideggerians—for example, Emil Staiger and Beda Allemann. They differ from those other not-so-orthodox Heideggerians, whom we shall call 'transcendental' hermeneuticists, in that they are primarily concerned with understanding art in relation to ontology, rather than with addressing questions concerned with a (transcendental) logic of aesthetic interpretation.

Despite the popularity of this perspective, it only takes a moment's reflection to recognize it as *'der sich im Ansatz aufhebende Versuch, Wissenschaft mit einer Philosophie zu begründen, die selbst keinen Anspruch auf Wissenschaftlichkeit erhebt'*.[14] Heidegger's ontology is correlated with an epistemology that rejects scientific or logical reasoning as the standard of objectivity. Poetics and critical thinking in turn are tightly correlated with Heideggerian ontology and with the nonrational *Denken* appropriate to experiencing the 'Being' that is the core of that ontology.

For Heidegger, art, which is always in some sense poetry, is nothing but disclosure of this Being. And the truth of art, which is experienced in interpretation, is simply this 'being disclosed'. Criticism then is the *Auslegung of this truth*, of the ontological structure of the work.[15] It is always in a sense a resaying of the poem. Heidegger himself offers this account of critical explanation:

Whatever an explanation can or cannot do, this always applies: in order that what has been purely written of in the poem may stand forth a little clearer, the explanatory speech must break up each time both itself and what it has attempted. The final, but at the same time the most difficult step of every exposition consists in vanishing away altogether with its explanation in the fact of the pure existence of the poem.[16]

It goes without saying that the critic's task is then genuinely paradoxical. It is after all pointless if not impossible for him to resay the original in 'transcendental' speech (he could at best only produce a different poem), and in any case it is certainly impossible for him to resay it in terms of ordinary language. We are therefore obliged to conclude that, if critical discourse must have the same character as poetic discourse (which Monroe Beardsley aptly described as speech which simultaneously negates what it asserts), then we are in the awkward position of requiring another discipline in order to interpret criticism. Or—since we can no more have a 'scientific' discipline which transforms Heideggerian criticism into ordinary discourse without doing violence to its object than we can have 'scientific' criticism which transforms poetry into ordinary discourse—we do not need criticism at all.

In any case it is clear that Heidegger does not provide for either of two requirements for an aesthetic and critical theory: he does not offer criteria for identifying an autonomous class of literary art works, nor a basis for making meaningful, non-reductive claims about its members. The Heideggerian theory fails in the first regard not only because the poetry/criticism distinction is difficult or impossible to maintain, but more importantly because the poetry/philosophy distinction tends, despite Heidegger's efforts to maintain it, to disappear as well. Philosophy like poetry is the fruit of *Denken* rather than of rational thought. The philosopher too must reach beyond ordinary language for a language appropriate to *Denken*—a language free of the basic distinctions (subject/object, form/content, . . .) of the Cartesian or 'common sense' conceptual framework. (This is of course why Heidegger's own writing is so difficult.) The great poets (Hölderlin, Rilke, Trakl. . .) are philosophical; the great philosophers (the pre-Socratics, . . . ?) are poetical. It is only a matter of convention that we categorize Rilke's *Duineser Elegien* and Heraclitus' *Fragments* as we do.

It is this same relation, the relation between philosophy and poetry, which accounts for the failure of Heidegger's theory to satisfy the second requirement of a poetics—it does not provide a basis for meaningful non-reductive claims about literary works. In practice even more obviously than in theory, Heideggerian criticism like Heideggerian poetry is philosophy. Poetry is ontological speech. Criticism is speech about ontological speech. The Heideggerian critic calls to our attention the philosophical notions—temporality, historicity, finitude, death, . . .— embedded in the original. Surely since this is the case, poetics in practice if not in theory has lost its autonomy.

In the final analysis Heidegger, like Hirsch, has no illusions about what he is doing. It is ironic that his disciples advance his poetics as the solution to the crisis in literature.[17] For Heidegger himself, the task of poetics is simply to make manifest the essentially paradoxical character of literature.[18] As he puts it, the point is not to solve 'the riddle that is art itself. . . . The task is to see the riddle'.[19] And again like Hirsch, his ultimate interests (although he would object to our saying so) are moral and pedagogical. The poet, philosopher, and critic alike are priests, rather than scientists, of Being. Their function is to bring, with the incredibly limited linguistic means at their disposal, themselves or other potential 'preservers' into the house of Being.

Though it would seem that there is nothing here to follow New Criticism except a thorough-going scepticism about the possibility of a distinctive discipline to illuminate the nature of literature and of literary works, still metaphysical hermeneutics have not rejected the notion of a 'science' of literature. This, despite the fact that they have had enough experience of the limitations of a Heideggerian poetics—experience which has obliged them to continue their work of giving negative characterizations of the relevant concepts. These are concepts such as 'rhythm', 'irony' (Allemann) and 'time' (Staiger) which manifest the ambiguity, paradoxicality, dialecticity or whatever, that is the mark of the poetical. They have not abandoned poetics because they envision a simple resolution of their difficulties. They believe that although it is not presently possible to do so, it is in principle possible to ground poetics and to provide criteria for assessing critical claims. What is required for this is a language appropriate to *Denken*. It is merely contingently the case, owing to the limitations of present day Semiotics and Information Theory, that we do not have the language, free of the metaphysical prejudices of the Cartesian perspective, which is required for adequate hermeneutical science.[20] For anyone who questions the intelligibility of the notion of a non-rational science and correlative thought and language forms, this hope for a future hermeneutical poetics is difficult to understand.

C. Transcendental Hermeneutics

Although he transforms it almost beyond recognition, the transcendental hermeneuticist is less ready to abandon completely the traditional idea of science. He sees the force of Heidegger's critique of the conventional ideal of objectivity, but he sees also and attempts to avoid its radically sceptical and anti-scientific implications. He therefore endeavours to show that, while Heidegger *et al* are correct in holding that an individual's understanding of a poem is subjective, it is not viciously so. The poem itself sets limits to what can be understood of it.

We shall take as the paradigmatic transcendental hermeneuticist Hans-Georg Gadamer, whose work on hermeneutical aesthetics has given the focus to the debate among critical theorists about the possibility of truth within the hermeneutical framework. Is there anything in Gadamer's position to guarantee that the (what we at least take to be the) two elementary conditions for a genuine poetics—autonomy and objectivity—have been satisfied?

The answer to the question in regard to autonomy is 'no'. To establish autonomy requires a basis for distinguishing between non-literary and literary texts. But Gadamer and his followers agree with the other hermeneuticists discussed here that there is no real ground for this distinction. Influenced by Nietzsche and the post-positivists, they reject the classification of experience and texts into literary and non-literary, scientific and non-scientific. Again, it is merely a matter of convention, of custom or tradition, that certain texts are classified as art. It is (as Hirsch suggests) to *praxis*, the *praxis* of art and of art criticism, that theories of art, literature and criticism are made *ex post facto* to conform. (None the less they do affirm a *naively* discernible difference between art and non-art which is not less genuine for being unsanctioned in the manner required for a scientific poetics.)

The answer to the question concerning objectivity is also 'no'. To adequately justify that answer would require a careful analysis of the argument in Gadamer's *Truth and Method*, but the basic reason for the negative answer can be quickly indicated—ermeneuticists reject the foundationalist ideal of objectivity, instead insisting on the perspectival (Nietzsche), historical (Dilthey), value-orientated (Weber), and essentially circular (Heidegger) nature of understanding. Still they are credited with having provided a new basis for grounding science,[21] a basis to supplant the discredited positivist one. But Gadamer for his part sees each attempt within and without hermeneutics at salvaging a tag-end of objectivity as employing a *deus ex machina* which serves to mask, rather than to eliminate, the essential and hence irreducible situatedness and individuality of understanding. He has in mind solutions to the difficulty of endemic scientific relativism which invoke a Kantian-Husserlian transcendental ego, or the *consensus omnium*, or the ideal of the last historian or the last scientist, or a cybernetic 'black box' model, or the empirically identifiable community of the practitioners of a specific discipline. And he is likely correct in thinking that objectivity won by such means is always abstract, perhaps theoretically impossible, and hence merely putative.

But what does Gadamer offer in place of this spurious objectivity? What *can* he offer, compatible with his insistence that one must keep clearly in the centre of focus when fashioning a theory of interpretation the quintessential hermeneutical insight—interpretation is determined by the particularity of the interpreter's situation? This insistence constrains him to make what would appear to be hopelessly relativistic claims—that, for example, there can be indefinitely many different understandings of a text without any one of them (certainly not the author's) being 'better' than another. Or that the meaning of a text varies with the 'belief horizon' of an interpreter, with his time, place, language, culture, socio-economic status, etc. Or that it varies with the way in which previous interpreters, previous times, have understood the text. Or that it varies with the interests or purposes of its readers, . . . and so on. He does not hesitate to acknowledge that interpretation is always inadequate, that it is never strictly speaking 'true' of the work, and even that it is always viciously circular when viewed from an ordinary logical standpoint.

The most important and certainly the most surprising of the several notions which Gadamer introduces to ameliorate this relativism of his position is a variant of the notion of semantic autonomy. Texts have an 'immanence' of their own when observed in the context of the reading situation. That situation can be perceived as a sort of dialogue between the reader and the text which presents itself to him as autonomous, with belief horizons of its own.

There are obvious difficulties with this anthropomorphic model of the text. The 'rapport' in our 'dialogue' with a text is a felt rapport and is, needless to say, onesided. The ideal of objectivity would seem to require that this feeling of understanding be warranted on the basis of an insight into what the text 'really' means, an insight which can be made discursive. But Gadamer, despite his talk of the immanence of the text, holds that it is in principle impossible to effect this. We cannot somehow step outside of our interpretation into the presence of the noumenal, the inherently meaningful text. That is precisely the sort of dogmatism which the hermeneuticist strives to discredit once and for all. Thus he seems on the surface of things to be naïvely inconsistent. As the only available expedient which will save his position from a vitiating subjectivism he seems constrained to affirm, in violation of the central dictum of hermeneutics, the dogma of the inherently meaningful text.

But Gadamer is not the sort to naïvely contradict himself. His postulation of objectivity, of the immanently meaningful text, must be the product of pragmatic rather than of logical considerations. His American apologist, D. C. Hoy, reads him thus. Hoy is doubtless correct in regarding Gadamer's subjectivism as genuine and his objectivism as 'als ob'. He says:

Because of the insistence on the essential interconnections between the concepts of linguisticality and historicity, hermeneutic theory can reconcile the apparent conflict . . . between the immanence of the poetic text and the historicity of interpretation. There is no contradiction in asserting both that some texts need to be treated *as if* they were completely immanent and that those texts can appear to us only in the partial perspective of inadequate interpretations.[22]

This seems a lame defence of Gadamer against the charge of subjectivism levelled against him by hermeneuticist and non-hermeneuticist alike. That the subjectivism remains intact is apparent even from Hoy's concluding remarks to his defence of Gadamer's concept of immanence. He offers this desperately paradoxical description of hermeneuticist immanence:

Thus, immanence of the poetic text turns out to be another name for the historicity of interpretation. That a poetic text *appears* to transcend particular interpretive understandings leads us to call it immanent.[23]

Can we find in Gadamer a better basis for objectivity than the same sort of 'as if' objectivity we found in Hirsch? Perhaps it lies in the concept of 'facts' (*Sache*) which he invokes in defence of his new objectivism. In general the 'facts' are just what one would suppose them to be—the objects, events, states of affairs which one purports to understand and describe. In the case of literature, however, the facts have to do with the subject-matter, with what is meant in the poetic text, rather than with the meanings themselves. The 'facts' correlated with the immanent meaning of the text are, like immanent meaning itself, postulatory only. They are postulated, perforce, as a principle of integration for the various perspectives represented in the history of the understanding of the work.

But this is merely a variant reading of the postulatory dogmatism associated with the notion of the immanently meaningful text. Dogmatic realism saves meta-critics of literature from ending in the nihilism which is the corollary of their radical perspectivism. But it does not warrant the truth of interpretations or ground the hope that criteria for validating interpretations might one day be specified. By introducing the notions of 'immanent meaning' and 'facts' to which the meanings correlate, Gadamer has appropriated two essential elements of the correspondence truth theory which he so decisively rejects. It is not surprising then that the notions remain inoperative—the immanent meaning cannot be known 'in itself' and hence neither can the fact it points to. Perhaps he has invoked the two concepts because he recognizes that belief (however groundless) in certain features of the foundationalist position is a necessary condition if there is to be understanding at all, and is certainly necessary for the prosecution of any discipline.

Gadamer employs two additional, closely related, notions in his attempt to limit the scope of his subjectivism. These are 'tradition' and 'linguisticality' (*Sprachlichkeit*). Interpretation is a linguistic phenomenon and specific interpretations emerge out of a tradition, a history of the interpretation of the text. These truisms are meant to guarantee a measure of universality to the hermeneutical position. Whether a concept like 'history' or 'tradition' or 'linguisticality' can be established as a root concept of hermeneutics, conditioning its other notions and meliorating the relativism of the position is presently a matter of considerable debate among hermeneuticists. Some, notably Habermas, believe that some such concept (he opts for a theory of universal history) must be taken as foundational. But the argument against this is persuasive. Although this may indeed be the only way to confine the apparently vicious subjectivism of hermeneutics, the cost would be too high. To successfully break the hermeneutic circle is to destroy hermeneutics. Notions like 'tradition' and 'linguisticality' will not rescue the theory because consciousness cannot escape the circle, it cannot reflect objectively, outside of its history and situation, specific language, etc., on the nature of tradition, history, linguisticality. . . . Whether we like it or not, 'the interpreting word is the word of the interpreter; it is not the language and the dictionaries [Lexikon] of the interpreted text'.[24]

There is nothing here upon which to ground a scientific poetics but then, as in the case of Heidegger, it is unreasonable to expect that there should be. Transcendental hermeneuticists such as Gadamer deny that they can provide what those looking to hermeneutics for a grounded poetics are seeking. Their real interests—certainly Gadamer's interests—are more properly described as meta-hermeneutical rather than as hermeneutical. They are not concerned with generating canons of interpretation for literary critics, historians, etc. Rather they are concerned with the prior business of identifying the conditions for thinking about thinking. Hence the concern with the role of the interpreter in conditioning the data, with the historicity of interpreters and texts, with the contribution of tradition to the constitution of meaning, and with the endemic circularity of understanding. This self-imposed restriction of the scope of hermeneutics is a disappointment to those with false expectations. Hoy remarks only too truly that '[s]ome philosophers will find this transcendental, meta-hermeneutical claim rather empty, but they will also run into difficulties in attempting to specify more concrete and normative appropriateness conditions [for understanding a text]'.[25] The failure of all attempts to specify concrete, logically warranted and hence adequate conditions for literary understanding and criticism suggests that we must after all make do with whatever it is that the transcendental philosopher can provide. If he has in fact successfully identified the components of human understanding generally, then surely he has said something very important about literary understanding as well. What we learn from hermeneutics directly is how inappropriate and misguided is the standard concept of science *tout court*, and how especially inappropriate it is to a science of literature. What we glean from it indirectly is how impossible it is to function, or in any case to talk, without presupposing at least some of the elements of the 'discredited' Cartesian framework—without, that is, thinking that there are aesthetic objects and experiences which are specifically different from other sorts of objects and experiences, and that we can go some way towards saying what they are 'really' like. Beyond that, the critic can learn from hermeneutics that one can only approximate that unattainable ideal—an understanding of the immanent meaning of the work—by a systematic refinement of self-awareness. This means, by identifying in so far as possible and as accurately as possible the subjective and intersubjective contribution to the constituted *cum* pre-constituted (already meaningful) work.

Hermeneutics is first and foremost critical philosophy, in a narrow and obvious sense. And any methodology that might issue from it is also perforce critical—taking us crabwise towards genuine understanding of the work by means of the identification of the inessential, the idiosyncratic and provincial elements of that understanding. In that respect, it is much more Socratic than 'scientific'.

To sum up, the 'crisis' of literature can be attributed to the failure of either of the seemingly exhaustive approaches (by way of transcendent or immanent meaning) to literature to satisfy *both* of what would seem to be the minimal requirements for a genuine science of poetics. 'Old' criticism could account for objectivity but not for autonomy. New Criticism provides autonomy but not objectivity. Hermeneutics fails on both counts. To urge this view is hardly to suggest that we ignore or reject the hermeneutic approach to problems in aesthetics. It is, however, to suggest that those who look to hermeneutics for a solution to the 'crisis' of literature would be well advised to look elsewhere.

NOTES

1. The issue of the proximate and more profound causes of the crisis of literature is extremely interesting but is ignored here. See Michael Murray, *Modern Critical Theory: A Phenomenological Introduction* (The Hague, 1975), 7, who attributes it to the failure of art, Erwin Leibfried, *Kritische Wissenschaft vom Text* (Stuttgart, 1970), 4, who attributes it to the failure of science, and Beda Allemann, *Hölderlin und Heidegger* (Zurich, 1956), 188f., who attributes it to the failure of man.
2. See Murray Krieger, 'Meditation, Language and Vision in the Reading of Literature,' in *Interpretation: Theory and Practise* (Baltimore, 1969), 211–42, 213.
3. Ibid., 238–9.
4. D. C. Hoy, *The Critical Circle: Literature, History, and Philosophical Hermeneutics* (Berkeley, 1978), 74.
5. E. D. Hirsch, *Validity in Interpretation* (New Haven, 1967), 4.
6. See the important qualification of the notion of the author's intention in Appendix I of *Validity in Interpretation*, 244.
7. Ibid., 214.
8. E.g., Chapter 1 of Hoy's *The Critical Circle* traces some of the circles in Hirsch's reasoning.
9. And Peter Winch in the social sciences, for that matter.
10. *Validity in Interpretation*, 26.
11. Ibid., 173.
12. E. D. Hirsch, 'Some Aims of Criticism,' *The Aims of Interpretation* (Chicago, 1976), 124–45, 137.
13. 'Three Dimensions of Hermeneutics', *Aims of Interpretation*, 74–92, 76.
14. Erwin Leibfried, op. cit., 48. (Staiger and Allemann are, appropriately enough, the targets of this remark.)
15. See e.g. M. Heidegger, 'The Origin of the Work of Art,' In *Philosophies of Art and Beauty*, ed. A. Hofstadter and R. Kuhns (New York: 1964), 649–701.
16. M. Heidegger, 'Remembrance of the Poet,' *Existence and Being*, ed. W. Brock (Chicago: 1967), 233–69, 234–5.
17. See e.g. Michael Murray, op. cit.
18. What he says of Trakl's poetry is true of all poetry: 'The poetic work speaks out of an ambiguous ambiguousness. Yet the multiple ambiguousness of the poetic saying does not scatter in vague equivocations. The ambiguous tone of Trakl's poetry arises out of a gathering, that is, out of a unison which, meant for itself alone, always remains unsayable. [It] is not lax imprecision, but rather the rigor of him who leaves what is as it is, who has entered into the "righteous vision" and now submits to it' (M. Heidegger, *On The Way to Language* (New York: 1971), 92). The critic/reader can recapture the vision, but he cannot make it sayable.
19. M. Heidegger, 'Epilogue' to 'The Origin of the Work of Art,' 699.
20. See e.g. Beda Allemann, 'Ironie als literarisches Prinzip,' *Ironie und Dichtung* (Pfullingen, 1956), 22.
21. Specifically the social sciences and humanities are meant, but the claim is also made (by Mary Hesse, Gerard Radnitzky, *et al*) that hermeneutics can provide the elements of an adequate meta-theoretical account of the natural sciences as well.
22. D. C. Hoy, op. cit., 99 (my emphasis).
23. Ibid., 100 (my emphasis).
24. H-G. Gadamer, *Truth and Method* (London: 1975), 430.
25. D. C. Hoy, op. cit., 122.

Interpreting Art

H. Gene Blocker

One of the most perennially troubling questions of recent aesthetics concerns the possibility of adequate interpretations of art. Specifically, do works of art *have* meaning? Can we *know* what they mean? And, can we *say* what they mean?

Representational art works appear to operate on two distinct levels—on the more immediate level, particular, concrete objects of sight and sound (a horse, a violet, a bird) are presented and described, but these objects are generally understood to mean something of a quite different nature which is not directly mentioned or described in the art work. On the first level, *The Old Man and the Sea* is a story of an old Cuban fisherman who finally lands the big one he has dreamed about only to have the huge fish eaten by sharks; but on another level the story is understood more universally to signify or symbolize the struggle between Man and Nature, and between Man and himself. On one level *Dover Beach* describes the action of the surf at night steadily wearing away the cliffs of Dover, but this is understood to refer to the loss of Christian faith in the modern age. Stephen Spender describes this relationship using an early draft of one of his own poems.

From *The Journal of Aesthetic Education*, 24 (1990). Reprinted by permission of the publisher. Parts of this paper have previously appeared in "The Meaning of a Poem," *The British Journal of Aesthetics*, 10 (1970), *Philosophy of Art* (New York: Scribners, 1979), and "The Medium of Poetry," *Philosophy and Literature*, Bolling, ed. (New York: Haven, 1987).

There are some days when the sea lies like a harp
Stretched flat beneath the cliffs. The waves,
Like wires burn with the sun's copper glow
Between whose spaces every image
Of sky and hedge and field and boat
Dwells like the huge face of the afternoon.
When the heat grows tired, the afternoon
Out of the land may breathe a sigh
Which moves across the wires like a soft hand
Between whose spaces the vibration holds
Every bird-cry, dog's bark, man-shout
And creak of rollock from the land and sky
With all the music of the afternoon.

The idea of this poem is a vision of the sea. The faith of the poet is that if this vision is clearly stated it will be significant. The vision is of the sea stretched under a cliff. On top of the cliff there are fields, hedges, houses. Horses draw carts along lanes, dogs bark far inland, bells ring in the distance. The shore seems laden with hedges, roses, horses and men, all high above the sea, on a very fine summer day when the ocean seems to reflect and absorb the shore. Then the small strung-out glittering waves of the sea lying under the shore are like the strings of a harp which catch the sunlight. Between these strings lies the reflection of the shore. Butterflies are wafted out over the waves, which they mistake for the fields of the chalky landscape, searching them for flowers. On a day such as this, the land, reflected in the sea, appears to enter into the sea, as though it lies under it, like Atlantis. The wires of the harp are like a seen music fusing seascape and landscape.

Looking at this vision in another way, it obviously has symbolic value. The sea represents death and eternity, the land represents the brief life of the summer and of the one human generation which passes into the sea of eternity. But let me here say at once that although the poet may be conscious of this aspect of his vision, it is exactly what he wants to avoid stating, or even being too concerned with. His job is to recreate his vision, and let it speak its moral for itself. The poet must distinguish clearly in his own mind between that which most definitely must be said and that which must not be said. The unsaid inner meaning is revealed in the music and the tonality of the poem, and the poet is conscious of it in his knowledge that a certain tone of voice, a certain rhythm, are necessary.[1]

On the one hand, then, there is a strong tendency on the part of people who read and enjoy poetry to ascribe meaning either to the parts or to the whole of the poem. In Wordsworth's poem, "She dwelt among the untrodden ways" the "violet by a mossy stone" signifies or symbolizes Lucy's shy and retiring nature despite her quiet but distinctive charm. Frost's poem "Stopping by Woods on a Snowy Evening," we feel inclined to say, is a reflection on death.

Whose woods these are I think I know.
His house is in the village though;
He will not see me stopping here
To watch his woods fill up with snow.

My little horse must think it queer
To stop without a farmhouse near
Between the woods and frozen lake
The darkest evening of the year.

He gives his harness bells a shake
To ask if there is some mistake.
The only other sound's the sweep
Of easy wind and downy flake.

The woods are lovely, dark and deep,
But I have promises to keep,
And miles to go before I sleep,
And miles to go before I sleep.

We suspect that the last part of Dylan Thomas' "A Winter's Tale" has something to do with resurrection, an idea also reflected in the lines of Yeats' poem, "Death," "Many times he died, Many times rose again."

Nor dread nor hope attend
A dying animal;
A man awaits his end
Dreading and hoping all;
Many times he died,
Many times he rose again.

A great man in his pride
Confronting murderous men
Casts derision upon
Supersession of breath;
He knows death to the bone—
Man has created death.

On the other hand, there is an equally strong reaction on the part of certain critics against any such suggestion, and a very skeptical attitude on the part of the poets themselves. It was customary to ask Robert Frost on his lecture tours whether the last lines of "Stopping by Woods on a Snowy Evening" were a reflection on death. Did he mean, in other words, that the desirability of death was offset by the more onerous duties in the here and now? To which Frost always replied "No." The lines, he said, described a man stopping his carriage to view a field newly filled with snow before going on into town. Picasso is similarly reported to have denied that his painting of a red bull's head depicted the dangerous emergence of Fascism. What the painting showed, he maintained, was the head of a red bull. Faulkner, who was always suspicious of academics, is said to have replied to the suggestion that the spotted horse in *As I Lay Dying* referred to the morally blemished nature of man: "Well, I wouldn't know, I never had much education."

Certainly few critics then or now would fault such a response, which seems a straightforward, if naive, support of the critics' own defense of the essential unity of poetic form and content. As the formalists and imaginationists have been saying for years, what a poem means or is about cannot be isolated from the particular way it has actually been said in that particular poem. Hence, as T. S. Eliot saw, a poem is untranslatable. To offer a translation of a poem is to propose two different expressions identical in meaning—that is, two forms of speech having the same content or meaning. In the case of poetry, the contention is, this simply cannot be done. The meaning of a poem is unique and internal to it and cannot lie in anything outside the poem, such as Christian imagery, sexuality, death or responsibility. As A. C. Bradley put it, a poem

should express perfectly the writer's perception, feeling, image or thought; so that, as we read a descriptive phrase of Keats's, we exclaim, "That is the thing itself"; so that, to quote Arnold, the words are "symbols equivalent with the thing symbolized," or, in our technical language, a form identical with its content. Hence in true poetry it is, in strictness, impossible to express the meaning in any but its own words, or to change the words without changing the meaning. A translation of such poetry is not really the old meaning in a fresh dress; it is a new product.[2]

And this is something we must all applaud. How awful for the ghost of Tolstoy for someone to put aside *War and Peace* with the remark: "Right, war is bad; now what else has he got to say?" Or to abandon Picasso's painting with a brusque: "Oh yes, the Fascists. Terrible time that was." Or worse, in the case of Frost and Yeats: "How true, how true." If it seems difficult to see how meaning can be unique to a particular utterance, how it can be internal to a particular form of words, then some critics are prepared to go the whole hog and declare with Archibald MacLeish that, in that case, poems don't mean anything, or with Susan Sontag that what is important in contemporary art is not meaning but effect. Obviously, the problems surrounding artistic meaning are enormous—first, the meaning is never stated directly in the art work. How then do we know a proposed interpretation is the real meaning? Might it not simply be a figment of the critic's imagination? Even if we agree there is some deeper meaning beneath the surface, the relation of the "manifest" to the "latent" content is far from clear. Finally, doesn't this idea of a latent, hidden meaning contradict the internal principle of poetic autonomy? Wouldn't such a latent content lie outside the poem? For this reason contemporary critics and poets are inclined to say, "back to the art work," "a poem means nothing but itself." As Bradley says,

Pure poetry is not the decoration of a preconceived and clearly defined matter: it springs from the creative impulse of a vague imaginative mass pressing for development and definition. If the poet already knew exactly what he meant to say, why should he write the poem? The poem would in fact already be written. . . . The growing of this body into its full stature and perfect shape was the same thing as the gradual self-definition of the meaning. . . . This is . . . the reason why, if we insist on asking for the meaning of such a poem, we can only be answered, "It means itself."[3]

But it is one thing to applaud a slogan and quite another to defend its truth as a sober proposition. "A poem should not mean but be." Good for MacLeish; but is this strictly true? "Form is inseparable from content." "A poem means itself." "The medium is the message." Again, while we agree entirely with the spirit of these slogans, we may question whether aesthetic values are strictly "unique" and "internal." What exactly do we mean when we say this? We must clarify these claims and make whatever qualifications are necessary.

With what, for example, is the internal-uniqueness criterion of poetry meant to be contrasted? With prose statements, presumably. But surely what is said linguistically always depends on the way it is said. If I change "slammed the door" to "shut the door" the meaning is different. Similarly, there are important shades of difference in the meaning of expressions like: "come if you possibly can," "come if you can," "come if you like," "come if you want," "come if you really want," "come if you must," and so on. So if the meaning of poetry is internal and inseparable from its form, then the same seems to be true more or less outside of poetry.

Conversely, we can turn the argument round and ask if the meaning of *poetic* language ever is or can be strictly "internal." Bell says we must bring nothing of our own experience of the world to the poem. But the poet's comparison of old men to spaniels who mumble the game,

So well-bred spaniels civilly delight
In mumbling of the game they dare not bite,

will mean little to one who doesn't already know, outside the poem, that spaniels are game dogs noted for the care they take in retrieving birds without mangling the flesh. Similarly, assuming the lines "Many times he died,/Many times rose again," have some implied reference to the crucifixion and resurrection of Christ, this will mean little to the ordinary Burmese Buddhist. And one totally unfamiliar with snow or English violets will scarcely understand much of the poems of Frost or Wordsworth mentioned above. Nor are these examples exceptional. The poet, like any writer, must rely on a wealth of common experience and understanding that are completely general and external to the poem.

Indeed, the point is so obvious it would scarcely need mentioning were it not for the tendency to embrace extreme slogans when their time is ripe. In reaction to a generation of critics probing beneath the surface of the poem for its hidden "inner" reality of psychoanalytic, religious or Marxist meanings, we are only too happy to rally round the banner: "back to the work of art." But in the first excited blush of enthusiasm there is a tendency to make assertions which are plain nonsense in the sober light of day. Consider again Fry's remark, "Now I venture to say that no one who has a real understanding of the art of painting attaches any importance to what we call the subject of a picture—what is represented." Right in spirit; wrong in fact. Once again, today, we are hearing the strident pleas of the opposite sort of extremists, this time urging us to discount any intrinsic quality of the work of art in favor of its contextual meaning in its entire socio-political-economic setting. Between this extreme of broad social context and the opposite extreme of the art work itself works of art exist in every possible intermediary context—within the context of the other work of that artist, of other work of that genre, in that art historical period, and so on. It is pointless to try to determine which of these contexts is *in general* most appropriate; each can and is appropriate in a defined area of interest. The fact that paintings or film can shed light on prevailing social and economic conditions of the time does not preclude the possibility of critically analyzing the structure of the art work or discussing its relation to other work by the same artist or its relation to other work in the same genre, or geographical-temporal type. Part of the task of the philosophy of art is to separate out the obvious falseness of such extreme positions from the sound basis on which they rest and to reformulate the latter in a clear and unambiguous way.

So, in this case, while we must accept in principle the idea that the meaning of a poem cannot be given entirely in some other, say, prose statement, we must reject the suggestion supposedly implied by this, that it is always wrong to discuss the meaning of a poem, or that poems don't mean anything. Rejecting in a strict or literal sense the distinction between meaning which is "internal" and unique to a work of art and that which is external and generalizable outside that work of art, we might begin by trying to define and defend this distinction in a looser and relative sense.

Let us say that if understanding a line of poetry or the poem as a whole requires no more common experience or understanding outside the poem than what we could reasonably expect any educated adult of that society to possess (the boundaries of which are admittedly much open to question), and if the meaning of these lines is not exhausted by the "external" meaning presupposed for any qualified reader, then we will say that the meaning is "internal" and "unique." If understanding a line of Pound's "Cantos" depends on an extensive knowledge of ancient Indian or Chinese philosophic thought, then I think we can safely assume that this meaning lies "outside" the poem. And if there is no more, or little more, to be got from a poem than some commonplace moral or religious sentiment with which we are all too familiar outside the poem, then we are surely justified in withholding our approval on the grounds that this meaning is extraneous to the poem. But if the common meaning already understood "outside" the poem is only presupposed, is only necessary but not sufficient to an understanding of the poem—if the poem's meaning is "filled in', 'rounded out' . . . by the act of perception,"[4] then we can say that the meaning is "internal" and "unique" to the poem in our new, more cautiously defined sense.

This is one example of the general problem of reconciling aesthetic autonomy and heteronomy. We start from a common basis of understood meanings, meanings which ordinary objects have in daily life independently of art and aesthetic experience. There is an enormous range of meanings which ordinary objects suggest or connote in everyday life. Take an ordinary styrofoam cup, for instance. What kind of cup is it? What does it suggest about the quality or style of life of which it is a part? It is cheap, disposable, polluting, anonymous, belonging to no one in particular. The cup says a lot about the society in which it has a natural place, a society of fast-food chains, environmental pollution, frozen dinners, interchangeability, alienation, lack of identity, and so on. But is this what the cup means? Do physical objects have meaning?

In ordinary English "means" signifies a variety of different things besides the more familiar meaning of words and sentences. Sometimes meaning signifies purpose and intention, as in "I mean to help him if I can," "What is the meaning of this?" or "It was meant to be a footstool." Sometimes "meaning" refers to the interrelationships between things, as "Passage of this bill will mean the end of second-class citizenship," "Dark clouds mean rain," "Buzzing means bees and bees mean honey," or "Little things mean a lot." In addition to these kinds of meaning, every object in our environment has a recognizable identity, a class or category to which it properly belongs (a cup, a table, a tree, etc.). In addition to linguistic meaning, then, there are at least three other kinds of meaning—purposive, contextual, and identity meaning. There is nothing strange in a cup having meaning in the sense of its purpose or function, its recognizable identity as a cup, or, most important, its place in our ordinary world. In its contextual sense a single ordinary object can call to mind the entire world or environment to which it belongs. In this sense there is no familiar object which is without meaning.

This rich source of ordinary meaning becomes a potential pool of material to be incorporated in an art work. As we have seen, the ordinary object is transformed by its new context within the work of art, although this new context is in part the product of what each particular object contributes to the work from its ordinary context. In fact, the rich associative meaning of objects is enhanced, as Schopenhauer first discovered, by its dislocation from its ordinary utilitarian role.

The cup, for example, taken out of its ordinary context and placed, say, in a piece of sculpture, retains an aura of its ordinary contextual meaning. But now this meaning can be strengthened and reinforced through its combination with other everyday objects. So, for example, an empty TV dinner container or a paper milk carton can reinforce the sense of the artificiality, interchangeability, and cheapness, not just of these particular objects, but of modern life in general. Indeed this sense or meaning becomes much more pronounced in art than it is in everyday life, because of the disinterestedness of aesthetic perception which invites reflection on the general significance, or essence of things. When this is combined with its contextual reinforcement within the art object, its sharp clarity can produce a striking, dramatic effect.

Thus, the ordinary purposive, identity, and contextual meaning of objects is external and heteronomous, while the meaning created by the new context of the art work is autonomous, internal, and unique to that art work.

The conception of meaning underlying this view of poetry is obviously not the ordinary sort of conceptual or classificatory meaning. Somehow, the meaning we find in poetry works in just the opposite way from our usual conceptual, classificatory understanding of things. Ordinarily we start with the general concept or category and then see if the particular item in question falls within that category. As I stand on the corner I know precisely what I am waiting for—namely, a bus. The general nature of the bus is clear in my mind; my only concern is to correctly sort the particular items I find into the right category—bus or nonbus. As Kant pointed out long ago, in his distinction of determinate and reflective judgments, the process appears to operate in just the opposite way in the case of poetry. Here I begin with what I am presented—a concrete particular, a line, a color, a violet, a bus, a clock, and work my way as best I can toward the general, but in an indeterminate manner. The poem presents me with an image of snow—a particular, not a universal; and the image of snow does connote (quite independently of this poem) an indefinite range of general ideas—death, quiet, softness, purity, and on and on. As Kant put it, the imagination here stimulates the understanding to reflect on an indefinite string of associated notions but which can nonetheless never be completed and so determined by the understanding. An important function of the poetic conventions governing the medium is to release this deeper level of meaning and to lead it in a certain direction.

Consider as an example the special sense of resurrection internal to the last stanza of Dylan Thomas' poem "A Winter's Tale."

For the bird lay bedded
In a choir of beings, as though she slept or died,
And the wings glided wide and he was hymned and wedded,
And through the thighs of the engulfing bride,
The woman breasted and the heaven headed
Bird, he was brought low,
Burning in the bride bed of love, in the whirl-
Pool at the wonting centre, in the folds
Of paradise, in the spun bud of the world.
And she rose with him flowering in her melting snow.

The particular, unique meaning of this work is strictly dependent on every part of the poem and the particular way in which these parts hang together. And aside from the background of common experience presupposed for understanding the general meaning of the objects referred to, this meaning does not depend on anything else. The meaning is determined solely by the impact of each part on every other. In fact the precise meaning of practically every word and phrase is determined by its relation to every other word and phrase in the poem, and it's not until we imaginatively reconstruct the totality of these relationships that we get the particular sense of the poem.

Just to indicate a few of these relationships, the "bird" of the first line is a bird in the ordinary sense, but in conjunction with the "choir of beings" in the second and the notion of "hymned" in the third, the bird also takes on the meaning of the heavenly angels and the Holy Spirit as represented in the Christian symbolism of the dove. This amplified meaning is reinforced and further modified by the expressions "bedded," "slept," "thighs," "bride," "breasted," "bride bed of love," and others that, in their obvious suggestions of love, sex, and marriage, connote further the quasi-sexual relation of the dove of the Holy Spirit and Mary, the mother of Jesus. The meaning of this bird is amplified further by the expressions "burning" and "melting snow" which suggest the image of the phoenix bird arising from its own ashes. This forms the transition to another set of relationships. The notion of "bud" and "flowering," taken in conjunction with the phoenix image and the expression "rose" in the last line, suggests the idea of resurrection, though a very special sense of resurrection which we have never encountered before. The unique meaning internal to the poem is determined contextually by the organic form of the work.

This is true even of individual words in the poem. What does "rose," for example, mean? First that she got up from this sexual union with the bird (which may also suggest the myth of Leda raped by the swan), second the resurrection, and finally a flower, now conveying all the overtones of the bud-flowering image, and especially of a particular kind of flower, one intimately related to the passion of romantic love, a "red, red rose." The poem, we may surely say, has something to do with resurrection, but a kind of all-encompassing, life-renewing resurrection which we can only learn from the poem, and to which the word "resurrection" does scant justice—though it is probably as good as any other. Thomas has managed to integrate in a tightly knit poem normally disparate images of spring, sex and religion into a total imaginative vision, comparable in its richness perhaps only to mythology.

In many ways this type of meaning resembles what we call "symbolic" meaning, at least in some of the standard uses of that word. But there are also enormous differences between the way we understand symbols in poetry and outside of poetry which should make us cautious in characterizing poetic meaning as symbolic. Because of the conventional nature of symbolic meaning, as it is ordinarily understood, the symbol itself is transparent. If I am reading a book, I do not notice the letters themselves; they are a mere vehicle for me to the underlying meaning of the passage. I seem to see through the symbols, as it were, focusing, not on the marks on the page, but on their meaning. The poem, by contrast, is not like this at all. Here our attention is riveted on the icon itself. Our focus is on the image, on the concrete presentation of objects for our imagination. In Roger Fry's language, we don't just *see* the concrete image before us, we *look* at it.

Secondly, poetic images are unlike other types of symbols in that while the latter can be very definite and precise in their reference and meaning, the former are not. In Van Eyck's painting we know that the bleeding lamb refers to Christ. But in Frost's poem, there is no definite sense of what the poem is about; there is no direct, obvious, well-known, conventional connection between snow and death. It is indeed debatable whether the poem is about death at all. Frost denied that it was. The poem evokes a feeling of many things, including death, but also of stillness, quietness, peace, tranquility, and so on. And our understanding of what the poem is about is therefore much more closely tied to that particular poem and the way it constructs those particular images. We say in the tradition of the "aesthetic" that the transformation of the image as given is a product of imagination, but this is primarily a way of contrasting the poetic construction of meaning with the ordinary. Despite its indefinite range and nonconceptual nature, we are not individually free to imagine whatever we like in reading this or any other poem. It is only the *range* of associations which cannot be pinned down, or restricted in advance, not the question of which images belong and which do not. The meaning is closely controlled, though in a special, poetic way, by the ordinary, though normally suppressed secondary, associational meanings of words, and by the conventions governing poetic manipulations of the medium.

Another major difference between poetic meaning and "symbolic" meaning is that symbols, in some senses at least, are, within a given community, consistently bearers of fixed meaning, whereas the secondary meanings of the images we utilize in poetry only come into prominence by being placed in a poetic context. Whereas symbols of the first sort are understood because of long-established conventions, the only conventions which appear to operate in the poetic context are that the object will be treated symbolically when it appears in the context of a poem, along with the additional and very general convention that we interpret the generalized significance of objects in a poem in terms of the overall harmony or context of the poem. If I write home to my mother that I stopped to look at some newly fallen snow, the secondary meanings associated with snow (quietness, purity, death) remain submerged, suppressed, overwhelmed by the more ordinary matter-of-fact meaning of cold weather in this part of the country recently, and this is primarily because mine is a letter and not a poem. As soon as we know it is a poem, then, through the conventions of modern poetry, the whole range of secondary meanings associated with snow begin to predominate. This broad range of associations is controlled and focused by the contextual considerations within the poem itself. It is because of the context Frost establishes with "deep" and "sleep" that the quietness of the snow allies itself with the notion of death, virtually removing at the same time the association of snow with purity, which is given no chance within the contextual arrangement of words within the poem.

Sometimes poems, plays and stories are based on actual events, and the differences between the context of the poem, play or story, on the one hand, and the context of a letter, or newspaper report can be easily and starkly observed. *The Old Man and the Sea*, for example, is based on an actual event reported in a Havana newspaper, just as Peter Shaffer's *Equus* was based on an actual event reported in Great Britain. But when these events appear in a newspaper, they are not "symbols," that is, they are not bearers of generalized meaning of profound significance. When we read in a British newspaper that a young teenager blinded some horses in a stable where he worked, we are merely intrigued, titillated by this bizarre behavior. But merely by appearing in a play, this same event suddenly takes on profound significance. Of course, Shaffer does not merely take the newspaper report and place it in a play; he transforms the reality within the confines of his media, and here the structuring of events in the play certainly does much to reinforce the almost Romantic meaning Shaffer wishes to attach to this unusual event. We see clearly from the construction of the play the contrast between the doctor and the boy, for example, the doctor interested in primitive magic power, but from an intellectual, adult perspective, while the boy is immersed in the prerational, mythical vision and cannot stand back from it to gain a philosophical insight into its general cultural meaning. Nonetheless, the mere placement of an ordinary mundane event in an art context by itself is sufficient to transform that object from a mundane particular into an aesthetic image or symbol of vast significance, as has been amply shown in the work of certain minimalists, Dadaists, and Concept artists.

An interesting experiment would be to take the same newspaper story and reproduce it, *as is*, as a short story, in a documentary style. Or a piece of news film, say from a war zone, as an art film, or an ordinary snapshot as an art photo. The results would be somewhat limited due to the lack of media manipulation by the artist; but the object would nonetheless be transfigured, to use Danto's phrase, from an ordinary event to an aesthetic image, a transformation which necessarily involves a shift from a particular, classificatory meaning to an image of broad and quite profound meaning.

There is often confusion in the literature as to whether the poetic meaning is particular or general. As contrasted with conceptual, classificatory meaning, the image presents itself as a unique individual; but in the range of associational meanings conjured up by the image, many of which are allowed to operate contextually within the poem, the image has very generalized meaning. As Schopenhauer said, when the ordinary classificatory, conceptual meaning is blocked in aesthetic perception, we see the individual before us, both as a unique particular and as Idea.

Here again, this ability of the poetic context to release and to control the range of secondary meanings associated with the image is a major difference between poetic meaning and what is often understood by "symbolic" meaning. What gives a symbol meaning is a conventional rule adopted by members of a community agreeing to let that symbol stand for that categorical meaning. What gives an image universal meaning in a poem is a much more general rule which has nothing to do with that particular image but which tells us in a very general way to treat concrete objects and events in poetry in generalized terms, that is, to release the string of secondary associations as controlled by poetic conventions.

Granted that works of art may be said to *have* meaning, how do we *know* what that meaning is? That is, how objective and intersubjective is our understanding of the meaning of a poem, for example, and how subjective and idiosyncratic? If the theory I have sketched above is correct, we can see that interpretations of art works may be objective first in the sense that the associative meanings of individual elements borrowed from the world external to the art work are reasonably fixed, at least among members of a particular social community, and second in the conventions which dictate how those meanings are to be combined, again, at least relative to a particular social group familiar with the conventions peculiar to a specific art genre. Interpretations are therefore subjective only in the individual freedom to range within these fluid boundaries. Within these boundaries we may reasonably argue whether the last lines of Frost's poem are about death, quietude or nihilism, but we can be reasonably certain that these lines are *not* about political assassination.

But granting that one can make out the distinction between "inner" and "outer" meaning along these lines, can one *say* what the internal meaning of a poem is? As we have seen before, if the internal meaning of the poem is unique, while words for saying what it means are general, how can we say what it means? As Collingwood puts it,

The reason why description, so far from helping expression, actually damages it, is that description generalizes. To describe a thing is to call it a thing of such and such a kind: to bring it under a conception, to classify it. Expression, on the contrary, individualizes. (Expressed) anger . . . is no doubt an instance of anger, and in describing it as anger one is telling truth about it; but it is much more than mere anger: it is a peculiar anger, not quite like any anger that I ever felt before, and probably not quite like any anger I shall ever feel again . . . The poet, therefore, in proportion as he understands his business, gets as far away as possible from merely labelling his emotions as instances of this or that general kind, and takes enormous pains to individualize them by expressing them in terms which reveal their difference from any other emotion of the same sort.[5]

And if we can't say what it means, does it make any sense to speak of the meaning of a poem? "If the poem has a meaning that is unique to it, then tell us what the meaning is!" This seems a reasonable demand. Either we can't say what it means and thereby demonstrate our acceptance of an apparently vacuous philosophical position, or else we say what the meaning is and tacitly contradict our previous assertion that the meaning is truly internal and unique.

How to get around the dilemma? Can we say what a poem means? It all depends on what we mean by "saying" what something means. If saying means providing an alternative form of words identical in meaning, then we cannot say what a poem means. But neither can we "say" what anything means in this sense. But if by "saying" we mean something like suggesting, indicating or illuminating, then we surely can say what a poem means. We can at least place the meaning within certain limits on which most of us can agree. Frost's poem has to do with death, nihilism, quietude, or something of the sort. "Resurrection" brings out the meaning of the last stanza of "A Winter's Tale" in a way "assassination" does not. Opinions will vary as to the precise meaning of Yeats' poem, but most of us can agree that its meaning falls within a closely knit group of related attitudes toward death. While we may disagree among ourselves as to which of the possible interpretations within this limit is best, we can agree more or less on what the range of meanings should be. The poem has something to do with a sardonic, or realistic attitude toward death. This expresses fairly well the range of more or less adequate interpretations. For example, the poem can be seen to describe an attitude typical of Hemingway's heroes, of a person who lives in such constant danger, where fear and anxiety have so thoroughly pervaded everything he does and thinks, that he has learned to live with and in a sense to overcome the ordinary man's fear of death. Or it could be read to fit the sort of hero in Camus' *The Myth of Sisyphus*, seeing there is no final hope and coming to terms with this. Either interpretation could be useful in pointing to the unique meaning internal to the poem, but of course neither "just is" that meaning.

The theme of *Howard's End* is the synthesis of the opposites represented in the Wilcox and Schlegel families. But what are these opposites, and can we say what they are? We can suggest what they are by means of a series of related contrasts: materialism and spiritualism, practical and romantic, realistic and idealistic, scientific and artistic, imperialism and socialism, and so on. Each of these points in the right direction, though none pinpoints that sense of opposition precisely. More important, the items in the list are complementary rather than competitive. Together they form a coherent group focusing, from different standpoints, on different aspects of that single and unique vision of social opposition Forster achieves in *Howard's End*. From a historical point of view we see the relationship as one of imperialism versus socialism, but this does not rule out the contrast of scientific versus artistic way of life, nor the philosophical opposition of realism and idealism. These represent parallel expressions on compatible levels of meaning. Most of us, for example, if given the first three pairs, could go on to name the others, and this is because materialism, for example, is associated in our minds with a scientific and realistic temperament, while the spiritualist will tend to be lumped with romantic and idealistic attitudes. Just as an actual society is an intricate web of social, political, historical, temperamental, philosophical, and religious strands, so the fictional re-creation of that society can be analyzed on similarly complementary planes.

In this sense, then, there seems no reason to deny that one can say what a poem means. The anxiety of the poet and the hostility of the critic stem from the other sense of "saying," i.e., providing a complete and exact translation identical in meaning. But can one ever say what anything means in that sense? After a generation of "language philosophers" we are inclined to say no. We are accustomed now to disparage the view that language, even ideally, just "states facts" or "mirrors the world." Meanings, we are now prepared to say, are ways of understanding things, words being the tools we use to illuminate, suggest, point out aspects of things which interest us in one way or another—and this is no more true of poetry and criticism than of science and everyday speech.

Wittgenstein claimed in the *Tractatus* a clear distinction between what could be "said" in language and what could only be "shown." What could be said simply reported or pictured the facts and was strictly true or false; what could only be shown or suggested was strictly nonsense, being neither literally true nor false. But in the attempt to refine and clarify this distinction it became increasingly clear that one couldn't just "say" what one meant, as opposed to "sketching" or "showing" it. And this collapsed the distinction, undermining the implied view of language, no longer considered, even ideally, as naming or registering facts, reading off the world's labels; but rather as a tool we use for our own ends, on the descriptive side, to display, point, elucidate, or indicate.

So the fact that works of art have no meaning in one sense does not imply that they have no meaning in some other sense, just as the fact that a poem is untranslatable in one sense does not mean that we cannot say what it means in some other sense. In the same vein, we can put into words, roughly and with a clear sense of inadequacy, thoughts which are in another sense inexpressible. Those who complain that their thoughts are inexpressible usually go on at great length to put those very thoughts into words. "Language is incapable of expressing the union of man and nature." But language has already been used to express this idea. "Union" is already used to suggest a kind of relation; there is already the suggestion of things being joined together in a certain way. To say that X is inexpressible, then, is not to be understood as disallowing any talk about X, but as a warning about the sort of meaning which "cannot" be given. It serves to mark a recognized inadequacy of language and to caution against confusing what we can and cannot do with words.

Similarly, the assertion that a poem is untranslatable should not be understood to mean either the impossibility of translating a poem into a prose statement or the inadvisability of such. The assertion that a poem is untranslatable should be taken as a warning not to mistake a suggestion of the meaning of a poem, which we can give, for an exact equivalent of its meaning, which we cannot. What, for example, do writers like Sontag mean when they say that in contemporary art it is the "effect" rather than the meaning which is important? If they mean that the interpretation of a poem is never an adequate substitute for the poem, that one can never say exactly what a poem means, that the meaning of a work of art is internal to it, or that the meaning of art is inseparable from the organic structure of that particular work of art, then, of course, they are right, though all of this has been said before. But if they mean that works of art, even the most contemporary, have no meaning at all, then they have been misled by an oversimplified view of meaning. Just as Robbe-Grillet's "no-comment" is itself a comment, so an artist may be concerned to strip away "heavy" or "deep" layers of social or romantic meanings to get down to some more fundamental level. But this in itself constitutes a meaning, signifying the artist's concern for what is "basic" and what is "real"—some of the more powerful meanings in the New Realist vocabulary. The worry over saying what a poem means, then, is an implied rejection of a naive view of language as applied to criticism. It is primarily a statement of the limitations of critical discourse, an attempt to define the boundaries between what critical discourse can and cannot do. Once we acknowledge these limitations and the dangers involved in ignoring them, then we are free to go on using language in this admittedly limited and potentially dangerous way, though now aware of its dangers and limitations.

NOTES

1. Stephen Spender, "The Making of a Poem," *Partisan Review* 13 (1946), pp. 297–98, reprinted in *Creativity in the Arts*, Vincent Thomas, ed. (Englewood Cliffs, N.J.: Prentice-Hall, 1964), pp. 38–39.
2. A. C. Bradley, "Poetry for Poetry's Sake," from *Oxford Lectures on Poetry* (London: Macmillan & Co., 1909).
3. *Ibid.*
4. Arnold Isenberg, "Critical Communication," *The Philosophical Review* 58 (1949).
5. R. G. Collingwood, *The Principles of Art* (New York: Oxford University Press, 1958).

Boy on the Rocks, Henri Rousseau (French). 1895/97. National Gallery of Art, Washington, D.C.

Is this poorly painted by traditional European standards? It seems primitive or naive in its style. If this effect was intentional, should that fact alter our evaluation of the painting?

CHAPTER 9
Evaluating Art and the Relativism Controversy

The traditional problem of aesthetic evaluation has, at least since the eighteenth century, been perceived as the question of whether such evaluation could ever be anything more than expressions of personal, subjective preference, and, if so, then how precisely and in what sense *can* aesthetic evaluations be said to be universally valid and objective. As Hume noted in "On the Standard of Taste," the problem is that, on the one hand, much of our ordinary talk about the value of artworks seems to presuppose some universal, objective basis of assessment, and yet, on the other hand, we cannot find sufficiently widespread areas of agreement among critics to support such an assumption. The pretension of objectivity may never be justified in actual critical practice. Kant reformulated Hume's problem as the logical expectation that, unlike expressions of personal preference, value judgments about an object ought to be universally accepted. There is no contradiction in the assertion that you like something which I do not like. These are just two different facts about two different people. But if I say an object is good and you say the same object is not good, we seem to be contradicting one another, asserting contradictory properties of the same object. Our views seem to be in conflict with one another; we therefore assume that something has gone wrong either in the assessment or communication process, and we naturally look for ways for resolving this clash (for example, through art critical debate).

More recently, this problem has presented itself as the widespread challenge of subjective and cultural relativism. Because relativism is a popular view of such importance, including as it does skepticism regarding ethical and political knowledge, and appearing, moreover, to challenge the very possibility of rational aesthetic assessment presupposed in any art critical debate, it has been a prominent topic of discussion among analytic aestheticians. In many ways relativism is a paradigm of the kind of problem analytic philosophy is best equipped to solve. To many philosophers, relativism is a complex tangle of confused issues naively thrown together in a jumble of vagueness; if analytic philosophy has any useful role to play it ought to be able to sort out conceptual muddles like this. Unfortunately, untangling the mess requires uncompromising logical rigor and conceptual finesse. The result therefore makes for some rather difficult philosophical reading.

Beardsley's careful but difficult argument against aesthetic relativism admits the obvious facts on which relativists base their case but reformulates them in a way which denies the relativists' thesis. An aesthetic relativist would say that the same object could be good in one society and not good in another society. Of course, it is not enough for the relativist to say merely that the same object could be enjoyed in one society and fail to be enjoyed in another society. This is obviously true, simply as a matter of fact. What the relativist claims is something far more interesting and controversial, which Beardsley claims is false, namely that the same object can be good in some societies and not good in others; that is, its goodness is "relative" to the society in which the judgment is made.

Beardsley's well-known analysis of aesthetic value (see Chapter 5) asserts that an object has aesthetic value if it has "the capacity to provide an experience with marked aesthetic character," and an object is a "good aesthetic object" if it "has the capacity to provide an aesthetic experience better than average." Beardsley argues that the relativist must specify not only the respect in which two contradictory claims (the artwork is good and the artwork is not good) can both be true, but must also explain how such a relativizing condition could result in such apparently contradictory judgments. The relativist cannot therefore simply say, "This artwork is good and not good." He or she must go on to say "good and not good relative to what?"

Suppose the relativist says the same artwork is good relative to one society or culture and not good relative to some other society or culture. Beardsley insists that the burden of proof is now on the relativist to tell us why it is reasonable to think that a difference in the cultural bases of different societies could result in contradictory judgments of the worth of the artwork. In this case it is not difficult to see how the relativist would likely try to proceed—cultural conditions influence how a person perceives, understands, and appreciates things. Even if human beings were very much alike, across different cultures, they would not look at the same objects in the same way because they have been differently acculturated. But this obvious truism is inadequate to establish relativism, even though it is often confused with it. The fact that people of different cultures *react* differently to a work of art is a different matter than the relativistic claim that the work is good in one culture but not good in another. Does it follow from the fact that I cannot understand or appreciate Chinese opera that this particular Chinese opera is not good? If aesthetic appreciation depends on cultural conditioning, we must ask how I would respond to the Chinese opera if I knew more about Chinese opera, had grown up watching and listening to them, knew the stories on which they were based, and in short understood and appreciated the conventions governing this type of art. In that case, there is little reason to think that my opinion of this particular opera would differ from the majority of Chinese experts.

This argument is even more compelling when we remember Beardsley's definition of "aesthetically good" in terms of a "capacity" to produce an enriching aesthetic experience. The question of whether this object is aesthetically good therefore becomes the question of whether this object has the capacity to produce a kind of aesthetic experience. The fact that a limited art education has inhibited my actualizing aesthetic experiences in the presence of certain artworks does not show that these objects lack the capacity to provide such experiences. The proof of the existence of such a capacity would be to see how it would be actualized in *similar* cases—that is, by human beings *similarly educated*.

As Beardsley notes, properly understood (analyzed), the facts on which relativism invalidly argues amount to a "relationalism" rather than a "relativism." It has been known at least since the thirteenth century that certain properties exist only in a complex relationship with other properties. This does not mean (as relativists, for example, suppose) that such properties are subjective or relative, but that they have a universal objectivity within a complex of relationships. Does the word *halt* mean stop? It does not, if taken out of the wider context of its relationships with a particular language and its socially accepted conventions of linguistic usage. But given the rules of English language at a particular point in time in a particular society, then it is "universally," "objectively" true that *halt* does indeed mean stop.

It is interesting to note that Beardsley, as an "analytic philosopher," does not *deny* contextuality but rather *analyzes* and tries to *explain* it. Since Beardsley is known for his defense of the "autonomy" of art, it may come as a surprise that he defends art's autonomy in a sophisticated way consistent with its contextuality. As he says, "relativising relativism," that is, embracing its full contextuality, removes its epistemic sting. Relativism, properly understood, would have damaging consequences for art criticism only if aesthetic properties were thought to be "one-place" predicates which existed in objects unrelated to human psychology or social enculturation. Once the "relationality" or "contextuality" of aesthetic properties is acknowledged, relativism is simply a confused way of stating some very obvious facts about our experience of aesthetic value.

For Margolis, arguments like Beardsley's, which refute relativism by demonstrating its eventual collapse into logical contradiction are "impeccable but indecisive" in that they consider only the truth values of aesthetic judgments, when in fact aesthetic judgments take "values of other sorts or [take] 'truth-values' other than true and false." Looking at these other values, Margolis attempts to formulate a "robust relativism" which can withstand the aforementioned arguments of Beardsley and others—"robust" in the sense that it will successfully reject any notion of "cognitivism" in art criticism, the view that judgments of artworks can give us knowledge, that we could in principle know whether such judgments are true or false, that it is conceivable, however difficult in practice, to determine which are true and which are false.

Margolis claims that Sibley's account of aesthetic terms which are not in any way condition-governed, such as "graceful" and "moving," are robustly relativistic. (See Chapter 5 for Sibley's view.) When a critic says the work is "graceful," he or she need not intend to make a cognitive assertion which we are to judge as either true or false (it may be intended to get us to see the work in a certain light, to suggest an aesthetic path to the work, to privilege one kind of art over others, etc.). And even if the critic *is* attempting to make a truthful claim, there is no way we can ever determine whether the statement is true or false, no way we can ever show that those who dispute the claim are mistaken.

Margolis argues, against Beardsley, for greater latitude and creativity in interpretation. For any given artwork there will be many different interpretations, all of which, or at least many of which, could be said to be "good" in some sense other than their being "true"—for example, an interpretation might be said to be good in the sense that it helps us to see an older artwork in terms of contemporary concerns. Margolis rejects Beardsley's insistence that the meaning is somehow there in the poem, however elusive. As Beardsley himself admits, the meaning of crucial words of the poem can shift over time with the gradual evolution of the language generally. Margolis argues that this shows the possibility of incompatible and "nonconverging . . . literary interpretations."

Of course, Beardsley could respond in terms of his account, just discussed, of contextual relationality. At one time x means Y; at a different time x means Z—once we specify the date, the meaning is objectively fixed. And there is no reason for Beardsley or others who argue against relativism to deny that of a dozen interpretations of a given poem, there are three or four reasonably good ones. This could be maintained without embracing relativism by saying, for example, that these interpretations represent different ways of saying essentially the same thing, or that each represents an important partial truth, or "aspect," of the total meaning which none of the interpretations completely captures. If we can demonstrate that any of this is the case, we have escaped relativism in favor of an admittedly difficult cognitivism.

Margolis also argues that relativism must be accepted to account for the fact that art is a "culturally emergent entity." But, we might imagine Beardsley suggesting a "relational" construal of the concept of the work of art similar to the view he propounds of aesthetic value. "Being a work of art" is not a one-place but a many-place predicate, it might be suggested, involving at least a physical object, human psychology, and social conventions and cultural conditions. If there were no human beings and no artistic conventions there could be no works of art, but relativism hardly follows. Given the art object, what we know of human psychology, and the conventions of a particular society at a given time, it is objectively determinable that such and such is a work of art and, more or less, that it has a certain meaning. Of course, it is true that we live in a society which is undergoing unusually rapid changes, so that at any given moment there is doubt and confusion as to what exactly *are* the operative conventions. But this just complicates the situation, making it more difficult to determine what is going on; it does not, however, prove or make plausible what is required for the robust relativist's claim that there is no way in principle to decide such things.

This is precisely Novitz's argument. Against Margolis's robust relativism,

Novitz defends a "realist account" of the interpretation of fictional literature. The most controversial, but also interesting, kind of literary interpretation, Novitz argues, is the attempt to solve what individual readers find puzzling about the text. Here the reader/critic offers imaginative hypotheses, or conjectures, provisionally projected onto the text and then "tested" by the interpretation's conformity to the text and either "falsified" or "verified." Verification of such "tests," Novitz argues, results in cognitive knowledge of the text. Interpretations of this sort are verified against objective constraints in the text itself—well-established fictional conventions, the meanings of words, commonplace empirical and historical knowledge referred to in the work, widely believed psychological generalizations, and so on. As Novitz admits, there will be individual variability as to what constitutes a puzzle in a given text, and this depends partly on variability among readers as to what is objectively known in a given society concerning the textual constraints just mentioned.

Thus, *contra* Margolis, Novitz believes that a distinction can be drawn between description and interpretation. Whatever is relatively puzzling for a given reader will give rise to the need for "interpretations" as hypotheses for solving that puzzle, and reports of whatever is relatively obvious and clear for that same reader will be for that reader "descriptions." Insofar as there is a large measure of shared common cultural conventions by members of the same society, there will be a large measure of agreement within that society as to what is a description and what is an interpretation. (Matthew's article in the previous chapter is also relevant to this distinction.)

Robust relativism means that there is no way in principle to resolve disputes over the truth and falsity of varying interpretations. In Novitz's account, on the other hand, "verification" of different interpretations does ultimately turn on answerable questions of truth and falsity. Debates of this sort over the relativity or objectivity of aesthetic interpretations are clearly important to the related issues surrounding our evaluations of art, since those evaluations are often, perhaps always, based on our interpretation.

Meager raises the question, not of how we evaluate a particular art work, but of how we evaluate art in general. Since art is not instrumentally valued, like craft, it is difficult to pin down its value. Following Wittgenstein's discussion of "forms of life," Meager suggests that to appreciate the value of art we need to see its role in the entire context of our culture, and perhaps in the still larger context of human life as a whole. This leads either to a "relativized concept of a culturally sophisticated form of art as a medium of communication within a [culture]," the idea that art is the primary means by which a society comes to understand itself (Meager calls this conception, "Level A") or to a view of art as a form of *human* life, that is, more broadly, "as relating to a near-universal human responsive framework within which we can understand the intelligibility of a non-utilitarian kind, of art as a distinct human activity" (Level B).

On the level A interpretation, art speaks a "language" shared and understood by members of a particular society and therefore, within that society, enjoys a measure of objective communicability. But, Meager argues, in the modern period, having achieved autonomy from utilitarian pursuits, the contemporary artist's pursuit of originality has often broken these bonds of social communication and is thereby driving contemporary art "to suicide."

But this death of *art* (on Level A) may instill new interest in, and give new life to, *beauty* (on Level B); that is, as art ceases to speak for a particular society, defining its aspirations and sense of self, art may come to be seen as a way of understanding what it is to be human.

If there are such "Level B" universal concerns treatable by art, relativism would lose much of its threat, and the objectivity of aesthetic evaluations would find a firm basis. Needless to say, not all thinkers will agree that such a transcendent "Level B" exists.

Another major problem affecting the rationality of art criticism is the question of the generality of reasons offered in criticism. Generally speaking, if a reason is offered for why something is good or bad, that reason ought to apply to anything else with similar properties. If a knife is good because it is sharp, then any other sharp knife ought also to be judged good, at least in this one respect. But such generality is hard to come by in aesthetic reasoning. What is said to make one work of art good may not contribute to the value of a second work of art and may even detract from the goodness of a third artwork. But if there are no generalizable reasons in art criticism, then many aestheticians are prepared to deny art criticism any rational basis. In that case, say these philosophers of art, critics may offer what appear to be reasons in support of his or her judgment, not to prove its truth but to get us to see the work in the proper light, to endorse the kind of art represented by that work, and so on.

The great defender of the generality of reasons in art criticism in the twentieth century has been Monroe Beardsley. Beardsley argued consistently over many years that if art criticism is to be rationally, objectively based it must be based on reasons which apply generally. That means that a reason which a critic offers in support of one work must always count toward the goodness of another work and never detract from its goodness. On that ground, Beardsley distinguished two types of critical reasons—one, which he called primary, which always contributed to the work's goodness, and another sort of reason, which he called secondary, which could count for or against the goodness of the work, depending on how it interacted with other good-making features. The main difference between primary and secondary, therefore, is that primary features operate independently of other features, whereas secondary features can only operate in conjunction with other features. Unity, complexity, and intensity of regional quality, Beardsley thought, were the only primary properties, while a much larger group of secondary properties, like delicacy and comic hilarity, would count toward the value of the work unless they clashed with and disrupted some other secondary features, such as energetic robustness or tragic sadness.

Sibley, who supports Beardsley's general position that art critical reasons have generality, thinks Beardsley has gone too far in a "heroic" attempt to identify primary features which always count toward and never count against a work's goodness. In effect, Sibley argues against Beardsley's distinction of primary and secondary features, believing that all features function as "secondary"; that is, they are generally good-making features, but not when they clash with other features which are dominant in the work. Beardsley's "heroic" defense of primary features, Sibley argues, is both unnecessary and also inadequate. Insistence on these primary features also tends to reduce aesthetic experience to watery-thin abstractions—as though the main enjoyment of music, for example, is simply to perceive its unity, complexity, and intensity of regional qualities. More specific features, such as romping gaiety, inventiveness, and humor, Beardsley must exclude as being secondary—that is, running the "risk" of sometimes counting for and sometimes counting against a work's goodness. But, Sibley wonders, how can we consider a work's unity except as a unity of secondary features? It is better, Sibley thinks, to drop the distinction of primary and secondary features and to consider them all together as enjoying a richer though more limited sort of generality.

Dickie suggests that Beardsley could avoid Sibley's criticism by saying that good-making primary features always count toward the goodness of the work if considered "in isolation from other properties." This would treat the notion of a primary feature as similar to Ross's notion of a "*prima facie*" moral duty. For example, considered in isolation from other prima facie duties, promise keeping is indeed a duty, but when considered along with other, possibly conflicting, prima facie duties (for example, aiding someone in danger), it may not be the duty we are "strictly" obliged to carry out on a particular occasion.

But, of course, by this qualification nothing remains of the distinction of primary and secondary features. As Dickie points out, part of Beardsley's concern for primary features is to provide the correlates in the artwork of the features Beardsley believes characterize our aesthetic experiences. But since Dickie does not believe there is such a thing as an aesthetic experience, he is rather indifferent to this consequence for Beardsley's overall aesthetic theory.

The Refutation of Relativism

Monroe C. Beardsley

I

One way of looking at relativism is this. If Smith holds that a certain predicate, P, is an *n*-place predicate, and Jones holds that P is an (*n* + 1)-place predicate, then Jones is a P-relativist, relative to Smith. This relativizes the concept of relativism in two ways, one more familiar than the other, I think. First, as most would agree, one is a relativist with respect to a particular predicate, or type of predicate, and hence to a certain class of sentences: attributions of moral wrongness, or historical importance, or aesthetic qualities, or whatever. Second, one is a relativist with respect to a certain alternative theory about the degree of polyadicity of the predicate, that is, a theory which considers the predicate to be one degree (or perhaps we should say, at least one degree) lower.

Since no applicable predicate has zero places, it cannot be relativism to claim that a particular predicate is monadic. And, in general, if everyone agrees that a particular predicate has *n* places ("It takes two to tango"), one who asserts this is a relativist relative to no one, and hence no relativist at all.

There is a characteristic form of argument, well known to all of us, which is used to settle disputes about the correct degree of a predicate. Indeed, it would not be unreasonable to stipulate that one is a relativist only if

---

From *The Journal of Aesthetics and Art Criticism*, 41 (1983). Reprinted by permission of The American Society for Aesthetics.

he supports his conclusion by an argument of this form. The principle presupposed is that the predicate P must be construed to have at least that degree of polyadicity which is necessary to conserve the same truth-value for all occurrences of any sentence in which it is combined with the same referring terms. Consider a simple example, the predicate "is hungry." We can say,

(1) Henry is hungry.
(2) Henry is not hungry.

And it may turn out that both of these sentences are true, though they are verbally contradictory. To evade the contradiction (or, which is the same thing, to insure that the truth of sentence (1) remains constant), we introduce another variable, ranging over times, and re-exhibit the original one-place predicate as a two-place predicate "x is hungry at time t." Now we can say,

(3) Henry is hungry at 11:00 A.M.
(4) Henry is not hungry at 1:00 P.M.

—giving Henry plenty of time for lunch.

Thus the argument for concluding that the predicate "is hungry" is really a two-place predicate "is hungry at time t" is that this interpretation of the predicate is required for truth-constancy, and hence for logical consistency. But then three lessons are clearly suggested. First, if Jones wants to prove that P is an (*n* + 1)-place predicate, he can do so (perhaps can *only* do so) by showing that as an n-place predicate, it would not be truth-constant. He must cite at least one example, such as the case of Henry. Second, since by the Occam principle the simplest interpretation that does the job is to be preferred, the burden of proof is borne by Jones, rather than by Smith, who has the simpler interpretation of P. Third, Jones cannot merely argue, in general terms, that P is an $(n + 1)$-place predicate; he must make a proposal about the kind of entity over which the $(n + 1)$th variable is to range, and he must show exactly how the addition of this variable to a certain kind of sentence renders constant a truth-value that would otherwise vary. Thus in the hunger case, we resolved the issue by selecting a pair of sentences, which, though verbally contradictory, could both be true, and then proposing a variable ranging over times (rather than, say, geographical locations).

To narrow the concept of relativism to issues that have been of greatest moment to aestheticians, let us at this point introduce a further stipulation. In this narrower sense, the relativist is one who insists that the $(n + 1)$th variable range over individual human beings or groups of human beings. This claim is the focus of the most continuing and intense dispute. We could give it a special name, such as "human relativism," but in this context we may as well call it plain "relativism" for short, so long as the stipulation is kept in mind.

I believe there is also a fourth lesson to be learned—one more cloudy in outline but potentially more worth learning. In the hunger case, Jones (if we let him represent the defender of the thesis that "is hungry" is a two-place predicate) is propounding a *general* thesis about the predicate, but he supports it with a *single* example—Henry's change of state. The example illustrates the way in which his proposal is supposed to solve the problem of keeping truth-values constant. But he must convince us that the same proposal will have the same result in *all* sentential contexts containing the same predicate—or, to be more flexible, in some large and identifiable class of such contexts. This he can only do, as far as I can see, by appealing to an empirical generalization of a particular sort: that is, one that explains, in a causal way, why hunger may be expected to vary from time to time, so that it will be true of Henry at some times that he is hungry but false of him at other times. (Whereas, by contrast, we do not expect his hunger to depend on whether he is in Philadelphia or Camden.) Jones will, of course, invoke our general knowledge about how hunger tends to vary in relation to the interval of time since one has most recently eaten (among other things, to be sure)—because the mechanism that gives rise to hunger is triggered by certain physiological conditions. Thus the required generalization is that length of time elapsed since previous meal affects intensity of hunger state at any given time.

II

It may be tedious to dwell on this rather remote example, but I believe the lessons it teaches are well worth our attention. Though I have chosen for illustration an example that involves variation in time, the same conclusion might have been reached by considering an example of variability in space—or, indeed, from culture to culture. I do not deal here with ethical relativism (because, despite having the best teacher, Elizabeth Beardsley, I still don't know what makes an action right or wrong), but I think I know what gives an object aesthetic value (which is the capacity to provide an experience with marked aesthetic character), and I think I know what makes an object a good aesthetic one (which is the capacity to provide an aesthetic experience better than average, or a very good aesthetic experience—it being assumed here that aesthetic experiences are well worth having).

It follows from my definition of "relativism" that an object can have aesthetic value in, or for, one society, but not in, or for, another; and, indeed, this is sometimes taken as the definition of "relativism." But my argument, which is simple, is that this consequence is false. But I concede that to establish this, I must rely on what I said above about the burden of proof, and come down rather heavily on the "capacity"—element of my definition. A great deal, as will be seen, depends on the latter. The inclusion of the term "capacity" makes the definition *relational*, but not *relativistic*.

This may be the best point at which to pause for a brief discussion of the concept of capacity, which I take to be a dispositional term, in both its application to objects and persons—for it is applied to both. There is the capacity of the object to afford some special sort of satisfaction—"id quod visum placet," in the familiar Thomistic definition of "Beauty"—and there is the capacity of the person to realize in experience what the object has to offer—which requires a complex of abilities and sensibilities and training and previous experience. But capacities differ from other dispositional properties in requiring an act of voluntary attention, I suppose—that of using the tool or attending the play, or that of initially listening to the music, even though one may be carried away by it helplessly. The only exceptions I can think of are the flower which one runs across inadvertently, and the snatch of music heard without preparation—but perhaps even these may be said to presuppose some effort, at least to get to the appropriate location.

I'll take "is artistically good" as the value predicate to conjure with—and we see at once an advantage of relativizing relativism, since it enables us to evade the problem of deciding the absolute degree of polyadicity of this predicate. Thus let Smith be cast in his usual role of (comparative) nonrelativist. It doesn't matter whether he holds that "is artistically good" is a simple monadic predicate or holds that this is a shorthand expression for "is a good y," where this variable ranges over species (types or genres) or works of art. In either case, Jones is, as usual, one variable ahead of him, insisting that for the expression

(5) x is a good y

to be complete, still one more variable must be supplied, even if it gives us a triadic predicate:

(6) x is a good y with respect to z

—where, as I said earlier, z ranges over individual people or groups of people.

But now it is time to apply the lessons that we learned earlier in discussing hunger. For Jones the relativist cannot stop at this point, after making a bare claim. He must answer a few questions for us.

First, then, why cannot we be content to leave (5) as it is, and regard it as perfectly complete without further reconstruction or remodelling? The relativist must begin by giving us the name of an artwork which can be substituted for x in (5), so that (5) turns out to be both true and false. He might, for example, propose:

(7) Jackson Pollock's *Autumn Rhythm* is artistically good (or, a good painting).
(8) Jackson Pollock's *Autumn Rhythm* is not artistically good (or, a good painting).

Now, the relativist has to show us how both (7) and (8) can be true, though contradictory. This is tantamount to deciding what kind of relativist he wants to be—that is, what is the range of the variable he proposes to introduce as another place in the predicate. Does he claim, for example, that *Autumn Rhythm* was not artistically good when it was first painted in the 1950s, but after 1960 it was artistically good? Or that it is good in the United States but not, say, in Soviet Russia, where nonrepresentational art is officially (and no doubt popularly) condemned? Or that it is good in the West, but not in a very different cultural setting—say, Saudi Arabia, or Thailand, or among the Bantu? Or that it is good in relation to one art critic but not in relation to another?

To decide upon an answer to this question is, as I say, to adopt one or another form of relativism. Whence the hydraheaded character of relativism and the Herculean task of refuting it. But perhaps in discussing briefly just one form of relativism, we can uncover difficulties of sufficient generality to cast doubt on all forms. Suppose, then, that Jones elects to insert a societal variable; what he claims is that the same work of art may be artistically good in one society (or to people insofar as they are members of that society) but not in another. The complete predicate, spelled out, then will be

x is artistically good in society z.

But, as we saw earlier, the relativist must discharge one more duty to finish his task: he must explain why he chooses this range for the new variable; he must justify his choice. Now it has been well established, but still it is sometimes forgotten, that this cannot be done by side-stepping into another question. It won't do to say, for example, that what people like in the way of paintings is partly determined by their cultural milieu and upbringing, so that liking may be expected to vary from society to society. We did not ask how *likeability* is correlated with difference of society, for we already know that

is liked by

is a 2-place (or $2 + n$)-place predicate. We want to know what in a society affects artistic goodness (not likeability)— how variations in artistic goodness can be caused (at least in part) by moving the painting from society to society. This is the proper challenge to the relativist, and as you can see it is no easy challenge to meet. We can understand, to give a contrastive example, how the artistic goodness of a painting might be affected by "restoring" it or by leaving it out in the rain; but how is artistic goodness affected by giving the painting different societal settings?

The most plausible sort of reply on behalf of the relativist, I think, is that artistic goodness is partly a function of the receiver's capacity to understand and enjoy. Isn't that obviously true of technological objects—if we allow them as suggestive analogues? Transfer the tractor to mid-Manhattan, the army tank to the Hopi reservation, the atomic power plant to Mozambique—don't they lose their worth by that transferral? If they cannot be used by the members of the new society, how can they retain their goodness? And if *Autumn Rhythm* cannot be understood and used aesthetically (so to speak) by members of a given society, then (it may be argued) it simply lacks artistic goodness in that society. That is why, to be complete and truth-constant, the predicate "is artistically good" requires the extra place marked by the variable z.

We must concede, of course, that societies condition their members in such a way that they are unable to understand and enjoy artworks of various kinds. No doubt you would be doing a friend no favor if you sent him a set of the Yale Shakespeare, knowing that he reads only Hindi. He couldn't use it. Are we then to say that Shakespeare's plays, when placed in his library, are not in that location good plays? Or should we not say that he is simply in no position to appreciate them? He is not even in a position to form an opinion of their artistic worth. But then we have a kind of paradox. For the very circumstance (namely, his linguistic limitation) that would, on the relativist's argument, qualify the Hindi-reader to report that Shakespeare's plays have no artistic goodness in his group will at the same time disqualify him from making a judgment of their artistic goodness.

Artistic goodness is a form of *eligibility*: it is what is worth taking advantage of, choosing, appropriating. But it seems that the relativist is in danger of confusing eligibility with *availability*—a rather different thing. To say that an artwork is available to society z is to say that members of society z are capable of understanding and enjoying it—or, if you like, appreciating it. *Hamlet* is not available to a society whose members read only Hindi or to a society with no concept of drama or fiction; and it is at least partly unavailable to a society whose members utterly fail so see what was wrong with Claudius's marrying his brother's widow or why anyone could possibly want revenge.[1]

But my accusation of confusion may be unfair. For the relativist may reply that he is perfectly aware of the distinction; but he holds that availability is a necessary condition of artistic goodness—an artwork can be artistically good only in a context (societal or personal) in which it is available. What good is it if no one can take advantage of it? The truth is, it seems to me, that its goodness remains the same, whether or not advantage can be taken. Poetry is not argument, but it may testify as expert witness on meanings and differences of meaning. You recall Thomas Gray's examples of another sort of unavailability:

Full many a gem of purest ray serene,
The dark unfathomed caves of ocean bear:
Full many a flower is born to blush unseen
And waste its sweetness on the desert air.

The speaker evidently does not doubt that the unseen and unseeable gem possesses those aesthetic qualities that ground its aesthetic value. And unless the unsmelt desert flowers' sweetness also retains its value, in what sense is that sweetness wasted?

A refrigerator may be taken to a place where there is no electricity. It is there quite useless. But if it was a good refrigerator to start with, it does not become a less good refrigerator (a poor one, or a bad one) by being removed to that debilitating context. If two Jackson Pollock paintings are equally good, we cannot make one less good by transporting it to a society whose members are blind to its merits or incapable of reacting to it sympathetically. I do not know what else is required to show that eligibility does not entail availability, and that, therefore, the relativity of the latter does not entail the relativity of the former.

Thus I deny that the two contradictory sentences about *Autumn Rhythm*—(7) and (8) above—are both true; and I deny that relativists have succeeded in proving (as it is their burden to do) that any such pair of sentences is true—much less in explaining causally how they could both be true. And I think the same line of argument will undermine all other attempts to supply a rationale for introducing an extra z-variable in the predicate "is artistically good"—whether z be allowed to range over epochs, cultures, subcultures, social classes, or individuals. As I have said, it is demonstrable (but beside the point) that such things as liking, enjoying, appreciating, admiring, taking pleasure in, deriving satisfaction from, are variable. It does not follow that artistic goodness is also variable. Until the relativist can prove that, he has not established relativism. And because of the asymmetry in the burden of proof, this failure of proof leaves nonrelativism victorious.

III

I can't forbear adding a reminder of one more error that we have often been warned against but that still looms up from time to time to add a specious plausibility to the relativistic account of judgments of artistic goodness. The moral of the story—to get that on the record first—is that you can't plausibly be too many kinds of relativist at once. Although I thought of my example independently, I have since encountered an interesting character in Kurt Vonnegut, Jr.'s *Breakfast of Champions*—the minimal painter Rabo Karabekian, who was paid fifty-thousand dollars "for sticking a piece of yellow tape to a green piece of canvas," apparently in a vertical position, if I understand his rhapsodic speech.[2] I suspect that the work of the fictional Karabekian was a far cry from that of the real Barnett Newman, who has produced many canvases, sometimes called "field paintings," with narrow vertical bands. But I beg leave to introduce a couple of fictional painters of my own.

Imagine a painting by a New York follower of Barnett Newman: a broad white expanse some ten by fifteen feet, with a single vertical band of red. It is called *Definition*. It expresses openness, your avant-garde critic will assure you, adding that this painter represents the self as a vertical line, which stands alone, while the field reaches out hopelessly for communication with other distant selves. Now suppose an Eskimo in the far North chances upon a large canvas and some paint. He has always admired a bright red utility pole set up long ago by visiting Westerners for some mysterious purpose. He sets out to paint a picture of it, standing amid the snow—thus unintentionally producing an exact duplicate of the painting in Manhattan. It is called *Pole in Snow*. The two paintings are of the same kind, in a strict sense; you can't tell them apart. Yet what a world of difference! The Eskimo, never having experienced the existential angst peculiar to a faltering Western civilization, could not express the feelings of the lonely crowd and the modern communication-gap. His painting lacks this deep meaning, and thus is merely a representation of a red pole in snow. It is not a particularly good painting. But *Definition* is a fine painting, rich in suggested meaning.

This is rather fanciful, but not merely so; some contemporary aestheticians have made a good deal of this sort of transformation—notably Arthur Danto.[3] I have doubts about it myself, but I don't want to argue that issue now. A dilemma will suffice. If we refuse to include "artistic acts." as Guy Sircello has called them,[4] in the work itself, and stick to what we can actually discern in it, then the Eskimo's work becomes just as good as the New Yorker's, for they have the same visual properties and hence the capacity to provide the same aesthetic satisfaction to anyone equipped to appreciate them. However, if we say they have radically different meanings, because of their different cultural contexts, then they are no longer paintings of the same kind, so it is not surprising that one is a better painting than the other.

Here is an important kind of possible relativism, though not a relativism of value-judging, such as we have been concerned with. The simpler examples involve aesthetic qualities. Take openness, for example. To us, living in our crowded urban culture, the canvases of Barnett Newman may appear very open and empty—even terrifyingly so—and the force of that single vertical line becomes enormously intensified. To the Eskimo, on the other hand, familiar with vast expanses of snow, the painting may not look especially open or empty at all. Then we would be saying that the perception of aesthetic qualities varies from society to society; and we become relativists if we go on to say that the *existence* of such qualities also varies—that the very same painting (or visual design) *is* open in one culture, but not open (or not so open) in another. Such a view might be called "aesthetic quality relativism," to distinguish it from artistic goodness relativism.

The issue over aesthetic-quality relativism is an important one. In case my example strikes you as too artificial, I'll cite an actual one: Bernini's famous sculpture of St. Teresa (c. 1647) in Rome. Bernard Heyl has compared the comments of six art historians, all writing during the nineteen-fifties.[5] One describes the work as cold, arid, and unpoetical; another, as suffused with worldly passion rather than mystic fervor; another, as merely pretty and sentimental; another, as expressing ardent mysticism, true piety, and divine joy. Evidently these writers have seen very different qualities in the same physical object. And, of course, we could conclude that some of them must be mistaken—or we could adopt a relativistic view of their divergence.

Now suppose we were to grant, for the sake of argument, that aesthetic quality relativism is true. Then we have in effect distinct *St. Teresa*s, with quite different qualities; and because of this difference, some may be aesthetically better than others. But to say this is not to adopt artistic goodness relativism; for there is nothing relativistic in conceding that objects of very different kinds can also differ in artistic goodness. So with the two indistinguishable paintings we imagined a moment ago: if we accept aesthetic quality relativism, they are no longer of the same kind, in important respects. For the one in Manhattan is expansive, open, empty: the one in Alaska is not. It is not the same work that is being judged differently by the two societies.

One can be a relativist about both aesthetic qualities and artistic goodness, but it seems that if one is both sorts of relativist with respect to the same artwork and the same range of variables, there is a danger of some logical embarrassment.

NOTES

1. See Laura Bohannon, "Shakespeare in the Bush," in *Theme and Form*, ed. M. C. Beardsley, R. W. Daniel, and G. Leggett (Englewood Cliffs, 1975): reprinted from *Conformity and Conflict: Readings in Cultural Anthropology*, ed. J. P. Spradley and D. W. McCurdy (Boston, 1971).
2. Kurt Vonnegut, Jr., *Breakfast of Champions* (New York, 1975), pp. 214,221.
3. See his essay, "The Transfiguration of the Commonplace," *Journal of Aesthetics and Art Criticism*, 33, no. 1 (1974), 139–48.
4. See Guy Sircello, *Mind and Art* (Princeton University Press, 1972), ch. 1.
5. "'Relativism' and 'Objectivity' in Stephen C. Pepper's Theory of Criticism," *Journal of Aesthetics and Art Criticism*, 18, no. 4 (1960), 387–88.

Robust Relativism

Joseph Margolis

There seems to be a simple way to refute relativism. Construe it as a conservative thesis: that, for some set of judgments, it is not the case that no judgments can in principle be valid (skepticism) or that judgments can be validly defended on one principle only (what Richard Henson has recently termed "universalism").[1] Assign truth-values, then, to judgments on relativistic grounds and assume that, in relevantly significant disputes, the correct assignment of incompatible truth-values depends on the use of competing (relativistic) "principles." There is no need to attempt to individuate such principles. The point of the exercise is that, on the hypothesis, relativism leads to contradiction, since judgments would then be able to be validly shown to be both true and false.

The argument is impeccable but indecisive—for an elementary reason. Grant only that a putatively relativistic set of judgments lacks truth-values (true and false) but takes values of other sorts or takes "truth-values" other than true and false. For example, if judgments are said to be probable (on the evidence) rather than true, then it is quite possible that judgments otherwise incompatible—as true or false—are equiprobable (on the evidence).[2] This is not to say that considerations of probability entail relativism; but it is also not to deny that they could be construed relativistically. In any case, the refutation of relativism fails so far forth if there is a set of judgments that relativism claims for its own, to which not truth and falsity but values that, interpreted on the model of truth-assignments, would lead to contradiction do not therefore thus do so. It is of course also possible to hold that judgments are relativized in the sense that every validating "principle" is said to subtend its own sector of judgments and that no two principles have intersecting sectors.[3] But, although this is a possible strategy, it is quite uninteresting,

From *The Journal of Aesthetics and Art Criticism*, 35 (1976). Reprinted by permission of The American Society for Aesthetics.

since what we want to consider are the prospects of a *robust* relativism, that is, a relativism that admits some range of *competing* claims, claims for which there are at least minimal grounds justifying the joint application of competing principles—hence, that admits not only incompatible judgments relative to any particular principle but also what may be called "incongruent" judgments, judgments that construed in terms of truth and falsity would be incompatible *and* that involve the use of predicates jointly accessible to competing principles. The weaker form of relativism is uninteresting whether truth itself is thought to be relativized to a particular language[4] or whether a restricted range of judgments is thought to be defensible only in terms of some particular convention of "implicit agreement."[5]

Still, the distinction between the two sorts of relativism suggests some necessary constraints that a viable and robust relativism would entail: (1) the rejection of skepticism and universalism for a given set of judgments; (2) the provision that such a set of judgments takes values other than truth and falsity and includes incongruent judgments; (3) the rejection of cognitivism (entailed by [(2)], in any case—that is, the rejection of the view that, for the properties ascribed in the judgments in question, we possess a matching cognitive faculty [perception, for instance] the normal exercise of which enables us to make veridical discriminations of their presence or absence)[6]; (4) the admission of the joint relevance of competing principles in validating the ascriptions or appraisals in question (entailed by [(2)], in any case—that is, the admission of some theory explaining such tolerance).[7] On reflection, these four conditions appear to be sufficient as well as necessary for the provision of a robust relativism. They are, in any case, jointly compatible and, together, they undercut what may fairly be taken to be the least specialized attack on relativism that could be mounted. I shall take a theory to be relativistic, therefore, if it meets our four conditions—which, on the analysis sketched, is equivalent to the first two. It is important and useful to note that no constraints at all are placed on the kinds of judgment that may be construed relativistically, for instance, as between judgments that are and are not value judgments.

Having said this much, let me proceed, first, polemically, to provide grounds for thinking that, in the context of aesthetics or of the aesthetic appreciation of the arts, there are at least three distinct ranges of judgment that may be strongly defended as tolerating or even requiring a relativistic construction; and secondly, more affirmatively but very briefly, to sketch a theory in virtue of which those findings may be sustained. In the first portion of the argument, then, I shall try to show that, for each of the three domains to be marked out, well-known arguments (at least implicitly) opposed to a relativistic construction are inherently indecisive. In the second portion of the argument, then, I shall try to say what it is about the nature of art and judgment that sustains a relativistic thesis. It should be said at once, however, that it is no part of my thesis that *all* judgments (taken collectively) may be defensibly construed as behaving relativistically—which of course would involve construing truth relativistically. That would be tantamount to retreating to a radical version of the weaker sense of relativism; and, in any case, I am persuaded that such a view is incoherent. So it may be insisted that a further condition (5) should be appended, namely, that relativistic sets of judgments presuppose some range of non-relativistic judgments, or that relativistic judgments are dependent on there being some viable range of non-relativistic judgments. But I take (5) to be entailed by (1). In any case, the provision precludes the possible embarrassment of conceding that we may wish to hold it *true* that relativistic judgments ("incongruent" in the sense supplied) do have the values (other than true and false) that they are said to have. It may also be claimed that genuinely relativistic theories should be distinguished sharply from theories that merely admit that the validity of any range of judgments is relative to the supporting evidence or supporting considerations on which that is said to depend. So a further condition

(6) may be required, namely, that a set of judgments is relativistic if their validation is determined by considerations bearing on the individual sensibilities of anyone who relevantly judges. (This may in fact be the fair sense of the relativistic interpretation of Protagoras' dictum.) But, the thesis to which (6) is contrasted is itself tautological; and, also, (6) appears to be entailed by (2). Still, (6) is essential, since it is surely with regard to varying personal sensibilities that we anticipate the relevant specimens to arise; and (6) precludes mere expressions of differing preference, since the expression of a preference is not as such a judgment.

Turn, now, to our specimens.

Frank Sibley, in a well-known series of papers, has argued that a particularly important set of aesthetic properties are not in any positive way "condition-governed" and that their discrimination requires the exercise of taste or perceptiveness. As he puts it,

We say that a novel has a great number of characters and deals with life in a manufacturing town; that a painting uses pale colors, predominantly blues and greens, and has kneeling figures in the foreground; that the theme in a fugue is inverted at such a point and that there is a stretto in the close; that the action of a play takes place in the span of one day and that there is a reconciliation scene in the fifth act. Such remarks may be made by, and such features pointed out to, anyone with normal eyes, ears, and intelligence. On the other hand, we also say that a poem is tightly-knit or deeply moving; that a picture lacks balance, or has a certain serenity and repose, or that the grouping of the figures sets up an exciting tension; or that the characters in a novel never really come to life, or that a certain episode strikes a false note. It would be neutral enough to say that the making of such judgments as these requires the exercise of taste, perceptiveness, or sensitivity, of aesthetic discrimination or appreciation; one would *not* say this of my first group. Accordingly, when a work or expression is such that taste or perceptiveness is required in order to apply it, I shall call it an *aesthetic* term or expression, and I shall, correspondingly, speak of *aesthetic* concepts or *taste* concepts.[8]

About these, Sibley claims, "there are no non-aesthetic features which serve in *any* circumstances as logically *sufficient* conditions for applying aesthetic terms. Aesthetic or taste concepts are not in *this* respect condition-governed at all."[9] Of course, Sibley clearly means to hold that the discrimination involved is, in some sense, perceptual or perception-like—informed by taste or perceptiveness—*and* that the capacity in question is not to be understood in terms of any form of intuitionism.[10]

It is, admittedly, not clear whether Sibley can escape intuitionism; and it is entirely reasonable to claim that *some* of the concepts that Sibley regards as aesthetic *are* condition-governed and that some that he regards as nonaesthetic (and that are also condition-governed) *are*, on a perfectly reasonable usage, actually aesthetic or aesthetically important—for instance, the discrimination of the fugal form and its complications and the discrimination of musical unity.[11] The central question remains, what of those uses of aesthetic terms that are not condition-governed, in Sibley's sense? Can these be reasonably construed as objectively discerned *in* the work in question? Here, Sibley himself concedes the possibility that ascriptions of the sort he has in mind ("graceful," "dainty," "moving," "plaintive," "balanced," "lacking in unity," and the like—what he sometimes calls "tertiary or *Gestalt* properties, among others") may merely be *"apt* rather than *true."*[12] Sibley himself opts for the objectivity of such qualities on the basis of considerations that quite clearly fail to exclude a decisive alternative. He notices that simple qualities like color admit of "ultimate proof" (that is, proof that they are present) only in the way in which that proof is "tied to an overlap of agreement in sorting, distinguishing and much else which links people present and past; . . . where different sets of people agree amongst themselves thus (e.g., groups of similarly color-blind people), it is reference to the set with the most detailed discrimination that we treat as conclusive."[13]

His argument continues in the following way:

When I say the only ultimate test or proof, I mean that, since colors are simple properties in the sense that no other visible feature makes something the color it is, one cannot appeal to other features of an object in virtue of possessing which, by some rule of meaning, it can be said to be red or blue, as one can with such properties as triangular, etc. With colors there is no such intermediate appeal; only directly an appeal to agreement. But *if* there are aesthetic properties—the supposition under investigation—they will, despite dissimilarities, be like colors in this respect. For though, unlike colors, they will be dependent on other properties of things, they cannot, since they are not entailed by the properties responsible for them, be ascribed by virtue of the presence of other properties and some rule of meaning. Hence a proof will again make no intermediate appeal to other properties of the thing, but directly to agreement.[14]

Sibley adds that "this agreement is not easy to describe. Not *any* agreement will do; the fact that some of us, here and now, make identical discriminations need not settle the color of things."[15] This shows reasonably clearly that Sibley thinks that the "perception" of aesthetic or tertiary qualities is not dissimilar in an essential regard from the perception of colors: the agreement involved is an agreement about perceived (though dependent) qualities. And so, in effect, Sibley subscribes to some form of cognitivism (if not intuitionism); he must reject our condition (3)—hence, relativism. But that's just it. What Sibley needs is a *theory* of perception and perceptual qualities that would justify construing the qualities in question as perceptual qualities and not merely as qualities such that, in a sense that conforms to the enormous variability of such judgments, it would be *apt* but not *true* to say that this poem or sculpture "has" it. In an earlier paper, Sibley says quite explicitly that "aesthetics deals with a kind of perception," and appeals to the case of the color-blind man to clarify the nature of defective aesthetic perception.[16] On the other hand, in spite of his insistence that "some aesthetic judgments may be characterized as right, wrong, true, false, undeniable," he actually favors the alternative theory at times, conceding that, even for his own cases, "for some range of judgments we prefer terms like 'reasonable,' 'admissible,' 'understandable' or 'eccentric' to 'right' and 'wrong.'"[17]

Sibley also has considerable difficulty in explaining how to select the aesthetic "elite" whose discrimination is relatively reliable simply because he fails to supply a theory of the requisite perception in terms of which to account for and to correct the discrimination of any would-be aesthetic percipient. But the absence of such a theory places his advocacy of cognitivism in doubt, since, for *any* claim that putatively relies on the exercise of a cognitive faculty (perceptual, for instance), a theoretical basis must be provided for distinguishing between what actually *is* the case and what only *seems* to be so.[18] This condition must be satisfied whether the properties in question are said to be simple or complex. Sibley's admission, however, of what it may be *apt* but not true to say is incompatible with his particular claims of aesthetic objectivity, since judgments of what may be apt but not true to say cannot preclude incongruence (in the sense supplied). His concession, in short, precludes the application of the requisite "is"/"seems" contrast, where the concession has force; and where he would deny its force, he lacks the requisite theory. Hence, Sibley's position is subject to a complex dilemma: either (a) his aesthetic concepts are condition-governed (since dependent) and thus enter inferentially into judgments that are straightforwardly true or false; or else (b) they are not condition-governed (though dependent) and, since they enter into judgments that are straightforwardly true or false, Sibley is committed to some sort of intuitionism; or else (c) they are not condition-governed (though dependent) and enter into judgments that can be apt or inapt or the like but not true or false.

It is, I think, fair to say that the concepts Sibley is chiefly concerned with ("graceful," "moving," "balanced," "unified," and the like) have a definite use in judgments that depend on the individual sensibilities of different persons. He himself concedes the point, which is tantamount to conceding a relativistic thesis. Some of his opponents (Peter Kivy, for instance)[19] wish to show that these concepts are used in an ordinary condition-governed way, but they have not shown (and it is difficult to imagine how they could possibly show) that such concepts are never, or are not even characteristically, used in a way that is either not condition-governed (in Sibley's sense) or if condition-governed not governed in such a way as to lead to judgments that are straightforwardly true or false. Let it suffice, then, that judgments that Sibley says involve taste or perceptiveness or sensibility—ranging over much of what is typically noted in appreciative discourse, without directly involving (but not necessarily excluding) evaluative distinctions[20]—may be construed, and may even need to be construed, relativistically.

The other two quarrels I wish to pick are drawn from Monroe Beardsley's relatively recent book, *The Possibility of Criticism*.[21] Again, I mean to argue in each case primarily on the basis of internal evidence.

In speaking about a critic's judgments (he confines himself here to judgments of literature), Beardsley has the following straightforward view to present:

What is the point of making a literary judgment and arguing for it? My answer to this question—which I shall defend here—is simple and old-fashioned. It is to inform someone how good a literary work is. But philosophers are rightly suspicious of this so-called "informing," if it merely evokes verbal agreement but brings no further satisfaction to the hearer. . . . [Still] there is a proximate end in judging—namely, to provide information about value.[22]

Judgments of course call for supporting reasons. Beardsley claims that the reasons a critic supplies in order to justify his judgment conform to the "'ordinary' sense" of reasons; that is, they "have a bearing on the *truth* of the judgments." He adds that "the relevance of such reasons presupposes that the judgments can be true or false"; but he concedes in the very same context, noting that this runs contrary to his own view about criticism, that "there might be reasons for making a certain judgment that are not reasons for saying it is true, if it should be the case that judgments cannot be true or false."[23] So Beardsley in effect concedes our condition (2) or at least an essential part of it. He even concludes as a result: "So our first question is whether in fact critical judgments have a truth-value—i.e., are either true or false"[24]—which, under the circumstances, we must understand to mean, whether all relevant judgments are true or false.

But he never does show that they are. He does mention P. H. Nowell-Smith's account purporting to show that even so-called verdictives (in J. L. Austin's sense), estimates, for instance, though not usually said to be true or false, nevertheless "surely involve a claim to truth, which may be allowed or disallowed."[25] But he considers no other possibilities. His principal effort is actually directed against an argument of Michael Scriven's, which purports to show that critical reasoning is impossible, in the sense that justifying or explaining reasons is impossible to supply in the way required to support ascriptions of truth.[26] Scriven's argument, as Beardsley summarizes it, holds that "it must be possible for us to know that the reason is true, and also to know that it *is* a reason for the conclusion, *before* knowing that the conclusion is true" (the so-called "independence requirement").[27] Beardsley seems to take it that the refutation of Scriven's thesis entails his own favored view—that critical judgments (in particular, estimates, as he puts it, of "the greatest amount of artistic goodness that [e.g.,] the poem allows of actualizing in any one encounter with it") have truth-value. "This," he says, "I am convinced, is what the critic estimates."[28] Again, his argument against Scriven runs as follows:

But *if*, as I claim, these judgments are estimates, then some reasons *must* be used by the critics in arriving at them, and *therefore* there must be some basic features of literary works that are always merits or defects.[29]

But this begs the question with which Beardsley originally began. For, *if* justification or explanatory reasons may be provided for utterances (judgments) that lack truth-value, then it cannot be shown that if judgments include estimates and if estimates call for supporting reasons, then all judgments have truth-value. Some estimates may and some may not, in the sense given; and some critical judgments may not behave in the way Beardsley claims estimates do. Also, it is difficult to see how, unless by some sort of cognitivism or the weaker version of relativism, judgments of the kind mentioned above ("concerning the greatest amount of artistic goodness," etc.) could possibly be said to be straightforwardly true or false. In fact, what Scriven's argument tends to show, as a by-benefit, is that a significant range of critical value judgments, though they call for supporting reasons, rests on considerations that actually preclude the ascription of the value *true*; for, as Scriven says, agreement about how some valuational condition must be satisfied often (Scriven apparently thinks, always) "does not exceed the degree of our initial agreement about the merit of the work of art."[30] I take this to accord with what I have elsewhere termed "appreciative judgments," that is, judgments that call for pertinent justifying or explanatory reasons but that, depending as they do on personal taste, cannot be binding on another, cannot be simply true, cannot be said to support the relevant distinction between a work's actually having the value in question or only appearing to.[31] With respect to such judgments, I claim, we may say only that it is reasonable, extreme, eccentric, etc., *to say* that a work has this or that degree of merit rather than that it demonstrably *has* it. Hence, even such judgments conform to whatever semantic constraints obtain on the use of the predicates in question. There are, therefore, judgments (including some that Beardsley himself considers) that would support the relativistic view, and that might even require it—the view, that is, that justifying reasons may be admitted where particular judgments cannot take the value "true" (and do not, in Nowell-Smith's sense, involve a claim to truth).

The third quarrel concerns the nature of the interpretation, as opposed to the description, of a work of art; and here, I am simply responding to Beardsley's criticism of my own earlier statements on the matter.[32] The issue directly concerns what may be definitely found *in* a work and what lies *outside* it. Beardsley opposes what I and others emphasize as "the element of creativity in interpretation." He says, "I find myself rather severe with this line of thought," that is, the suggestion "that the literary interpreter, too [like the performing artist] has a certain leeway, and does not merely 'report' on 'discovered meaning,' . . . but puts something of his own into the work; so that different critics may produce different but equally legitimate interpretations, like two sopranos or two ingenues working from the same notations."[33]

But there are difficulties in his account. For one thing, though he subscribes to what he terms "the Principle of Independence" (that is, "that literary works exist as individuals and can be distinguished from other things"), he claims that what he terms "the Principle of Autonomy" is a postulate "that is logically complementary to the first" (that is, that literary works are self-sufficient entities, whose properties are decisive in checking interpretations and judgments.[34]) But I would maintain—and have tried to demonstrate elsewhere[35]—that problems about the numerical identity of a work of art can be managed without any commitment respecting the demarcation between description and interpretation, the demarcation between what is in a work and what is not. Only if one held, in addition to a theory about individuating works of art, a compelling theory about the nature and properties of works of art, could one hope to sustain the so-called Principle of Autonomy—by actually providing criteria for determining putatively internal properties to be or actually not to be internal. Beardsley offers no such theory, as far as I know. But then, it follows, as a second consideration, that he may well have misdescribed the "latitudinarian" view of interpretation; interpretations (in the sense he rejects) may not be simple "superimpositions," as he says, that is, "interpretations" that are merely "ways of *using* the work to illustrate a pre-existent system of thought [say, in taking the story of 'Jack and the Beanstalk' as Freudian symbolism or as a Marxist fable]"[36]; they may actually be needed precisely because there is no sharp demarcation line between what is internal and what is external to a work of art *and because what is uncertain in this respect may be important in terms of aesthetic appreciation*. Thirdly, the admission of so-called superimpositions would itself be a telling concession if (as is in fact the case) Beardsley has not yet provided the requisite theory in virtue of which superimpositions and "genuine" interpretations can be logically demarcated. Fourthly, the implied admission that there *is* a certain latitude that holds in music and the other performing arts raises (unresolved) questions both about whether there is a clear sense, for all the arts, of the tenability of the Principles of Independence and Autonomy and about what may be the formulable (and relevant) differences between literature and the performing arts. Fifthly, Beardsley himself concedes, in a context in which he opposes an extreme view ingeniously supported by Frank Cioffi,[37] that

Some things are definitely said in the poem and cannot be overlooked; others are suggested, as we find on careful reading; others are gently hinted, and whatever methods of literary interpretation we use, we can never establish them decisively as "in" or "out." Therefore whatever comes from without, but yet can be taken as an interesting extension of what is surely in, may be admissible. It merely makes a larger whole. But this concession will not justify extensive borrowings from biography.[38]

I cannot see how this concession, generously advanced though it may be, can fail to undermine Beardsley's Principle of Autonomy. Even the question of biographical reference and of intentional interpretation surely becomes moot—which is not to say of course that critical interpretation lacks rigor altogether.

A sixth consideration concerns the nature of language itself, since Beardsley here restricts himself to literary interpretation. First of all, he rests his case on the strength of the thesis that the interpretation of "textual meaning" (as opposed to "authorial meaning"—in the sense proposed by E. D. Hirsch)[39] is "the proper task of the literary interpreter" and that such meaning "lies momentarily hidden" in, say, some poem, "really is something in the poem that we are trying to dig out, though it is elusive."[40] But even apart from his confidence about determining textual meaning, Beardsley seems entirely prepared to concede that meanings may accrue to a literary text because of the historical conditions under which a living language is used. In his effort to contrast textual and authorial meaning, for instance, he says that "the meaning of a text can change after its author has died. . . . The *OED* furnishes abundant evidence that individual words and idioms acquire new meanings and lose old meanings as time passes; these changes can in turn produce changes of meaning in sentences in which the words appear." He offers a curious instance from the work of Mark Akenside, acknowledges that a certain eighteenth-century phrase "has . . . acquired a new meaning," and even speaks of "today's textual meaning of the line" (in question).[41]

But *if* he allows changing textual meanings, he *cannot* preclude the possibility of incompatible and non-converging literary interpretations in rendering a coherent account, unless he also maintains that there is an executive rule (unformulated) for determining which textual meaning (changing through diachronic changes in language itself) to prefer; after all, large portions of an entire text may be subject to similar changes and may therefore support plural interpretations. But secondly, in this regard, the very theory of linguistic meaning to which he subscribes—William Alston's theory of "illocutionary act potentials" (regardless of its own defensibility)[42]—depends precisely on speakers' intentions; consequently, once again, Beardsley cannot, on his own principles, preclude the prospect of defending non-converging ("creative") literary interpretations. Finally, with regard to literature (*and* certainly with regard to the other arts), the critic's interpretation is *not* restricted, as Beardsley claims, merely to ferreting out textual meanings; it is often concerned (as even the admission of diachronic changes in meaning confirm) with plausible ways in which what may be called the artistic design (the internal coherent order of work) may be construed.[43] In fact, the case that Beardsley puts before us (introduced by Hirsch) of Cleanth Brooks's and F. W. Bateson's incompatible interpretations of Wordsworth's *A Slumber Did My Spirit Seal* bears this point out convincingly.[44] Unfortunately, neither interpretation, however plausible, is entirely unproblematic. Bateson's pantheistic interpretation cannot be supported on the basis solely of the so-called textual meaning of the lines *No motion has she now, no force,/She neither hears nor sees;/Rolled round in earth's diurnal course,/With rocks, and stones, and trees*. And Brooks's interpretation (which, rightly understood, emphasizes the lover's shock—almost in a clinical sense—reacting to Lucy's death and consequent inertness) is somewhat careless about textual meanings but not in a way that vitiates his interpretation. The upshot is that Wordsworth's Lucy poem, contrary to Beardsley's claim, does appear to support two different interpretations of the poem's larger meaning or design (that is, roughly the picture of the imaginative world disclosed in the poem), *without even entailing different interpretations of the poem's textual meaning.* There seems to be no way to preclude the possibility.

There is then no reason to deny that interpretation sometimes serves to convey a sense of virtuosity in fathoming what is hidden (but describable) in a work of art. But there is no reason to insist that interpretation functions only thus. Beardsley discounts incompatible interpretations in accord with what he calls "the principle of 'the Intolerability of Incompatibles,' i.e., if two [interpretations] are logically incompatible, they cannot both be true [and they implicitly claim to be true]." "Indeed," Beardsley says, "I hold that *all* of the literary interpretations that deserve the name obey the principle."[45] He does not deny that there are "interpretations" that could not be jointly true and yet may be said to be plausible; but these are not true interpretations, are merely what he calls "superimpositions." And he fails to notice that falsity may be opposed to both truth and plausibility.[46] Also, he has not provided either an explicit theory of the nature of a work of art or the requisite criteria for determining what is internal and what external to the work of art itself; consequently, he cannot in principle preclude plural and incompatible interpretations of a literary work just as he cannot in principle distinguish between superimpositions and interpretations that specify what is "momentarily hidden" in a piece of literature. Hence, he cannot preclude a relativistic conception of interpretation—which may well be not merely tolerated but required.

I have now, I hope, shown (polemically) that a relativistic conception of aesthetic appreciation, of critical judgments (of value), and of literary interpretations is viable, not unreasonable, and possibly even required by the ways in which we attend to works of art. I shall have to be extremely brief about my reasons for thinking that a relativistic account is actually required for these and related distinctions. The argument centers on two considerations. First of all, works of art are what I should call culturally emergent entities.[47] I wish to avoid here theorizing in too detailed a way about the nature of art, since our issue does not require it and since controversial details may easily deflect us from our purpose. But the most familiar properties of art, its artifactuality, its internal purposiveness, its being assignable meanings (in various senses), forms, designs, styles, symbolic and representational functions, and the like all call for a sensitivity to cultural distinctions that cannot in any obvious way be directly accessible (unless by postulating some *ad hoc* intuitionism) to any cognitive faculty resembling sensory perception. But culturally freighted phenomena are notoriously open to intensional quarrels, that is, to identification under alternative descriptions; and there is no obvious way in which to show that plural, non-converging, and otherwise incompatible characterizations of cultural items can be sorted as correct or incorrect in such a way that a relativistic account would be precluded. The proliferation of intensional divergences is as close to the heart of the cultural as anything we might otherwise suggest. One has only to think of ideologies, ideals, schools of thought, traditions as well as the deep informality of the so-called rules of language and of artistic creation. This suggests why it is that the appreciation, the interpretation, and the evaluation of art should behave in accord with relativistic expectations. In particular, the relativistic theory of interpretation is sometimes resisted because one wishes to avoid the somewhat unfortunate habit of speaking of art's being inherently incomplete or defective and awaiting the interpretive critic's contribution in order actually to *finish* the work. What is initially defective or incomplete, of course, is our understanding, not the work; but the nature of the defect is such that, for conceptual reasons, we cannot be certain that what is supplied by way of interpretation is really in principle descriptively available in the work itself—on the basis of any familiar perceptual or perception-like model, which after all offers us the best prospect of the requisite control. One can expect, therefore, a certain conceptual congruence between the theory of art and the latitude tolerated in the practice of critical interpretation.

The second consideration concerns the nature of values themselves. I should hold (controversially, I admit) that persons like works of art are culturally emergent entities—not natural creatures like the members of *Homo sapiens*: chiefly, because the mastery of language is essential to being a person.[48] If this were granted, then the possibility of defending *any* form of cognitivism (moral, aesthetic, or any other) with respect to the values appropriate to persons or to their characteristic work is radically undermined. Consequently, the prospects of avoiding a relativistic account of values (and of value judgments), even were it possible to avoid such an account of the presumably descriptive and interpretive levels of our appreciative concern with art, is nearly nil. But noticeably with respect to values, if cognitivism is defeated,[49] then we can either retreat to the robust or weaker form of relativism or else, even further but with inevitable dissatisfaction, to a skepticism about values.

There appear to be no other promising strategies.[50]

NOTES

1. In an untitled and as yet unpublished book on ethical relativism.
2. Cf. C. G. Hempel, "Inductive Inconsistencies," in *Aspects of Scientific Explanation* (New York, 1965). Cf. also G. H. von Wright, "Remarks on the Epistemology of Subjective Probability," in Ernest Nagel *et al.*, eds., *Logic, Methodology and Philosophy of Science* (Stanford University Press, 1962).
3. This is, roughly, the theme of conventionalism in values.
4. Cf. Alfred Tarski, "The Semantic Conception of Truth," *Philosophy and Phenomenological Research* IV (1944), 341–376; cf. also W. V. Quine, *Word and Object* (Cambridge, 1960), pp. 23–24; and Donald Davidson, "Truth and Meaning," *Synthese* III (1967), 304–322. The requirements of the coherence of interlinguistic communication entail the inadequacy of such a conception: even if ascriptions of "truth" are relativized, we require a conception of truth that is not language-relative even if what is true can only be formulated in a way that is subject to the local features of particular languages.
5. The thesis has been defended most recently by Gilbert Harman, "Moral Relativism Defended," *Philosophical Review* LXXXIV (1975), 3–22. Harman's thesis is relativistic not merely in the trivial sense that supporting reasons are relative to considerations of some sort but because "the source of the reasons" (for doing something—Harman's concern here is with moral relativism) is one's "sincere intention to observe a certain agreement," ibid., 10.
6. The argument is indifferent to the kind of property considered, though moral properties have traditionally been the principal object of concern. Cf. Joseph Margolis, "Moral Cognitivism," *Ethics* LXXXV (1975), 136–141.
7. It is possible that one might argue that (2) signifies only that, were the relevant judgments interpreted so as to take truth and falsity as truth-values, we should be committed to a single arena of dispute; that the admission of other values does not entail the relevance of competing validating principles. But the intention here is to formulate constraints for the

robust, not the weaker, version of relativism. Hence, provision must be made—even if separately, via (4)—for the joint relevance of competing principles.
8. Frank Sibley, "Aesthetic Concepts," *Philosophical Review* LXVIII (1959), 421–450; reprinted (with extensive minor revisions) in Joseph Margolis, *Philosophy Looks at the Arts* (New York, 1962).
9. *Loc. cit.*
10. Cf. Frank Sibley, "Objectivity and Aesthetics," *Proceedings of the Aristotelian Society*, Supplementary XLII (1968), 31–54.
11. Cf. Peter Kivy, *Speaking of Art* (The Hague, 1973), chs. 1–3; also Joseph Margolis, *The Language of Art and Art Criticism* (Detroit, 1965), ch. 8.
12. "Objectivity and Aesthetics."
13. *Loc. cit.*
14. *Loc. cit.*
15. *Loc. cit.*
16. Cf. Frank Sibley, "Critical Judgments of Aesthetic Value," *Philosophical Review* LXXIV (1965), 135–159.
17. "Objectivity and Aesthetics."
18. Cf. Isabel Hungerland, "The Logic of Aesthetic Concepts" (Presidential Address of the Pacific Division of the American Philosophical Association, 1962), *Proceedings and Addresses of the American Philosophical Association* XXXVI, 43–66. Hungerland's statement is, however, too extreme in that it fails to provide for condition-governed concepts.
19. *Loc. cit.*
20. Cf. Kivy, *op. cit.*, p. 17.
21. Detroit, 1970.
22. *Ibid.*, pp. 63–64.
23. *Ibid.*, p. 71.
24. *Ibid.*
25. *Ibid.*
26. Cf. Michael Scriven, "The Objectivity of Aesthetic Evaluation," *The Monist* L (1969), 159–187.
27. Beardsley, *op. cit.*, pp. 77f.
28. *Ibid.*, p. 75.
29. *Ibid.*, p. 82.
30. Scriven, *op. cit.*, p. 179.
31. Cf. Joseph Margolis, *The Language of Art and Art Criticism* (Detroit, 1965), ch. 10; and *Values and Conduct* (Oxford, 1971), ch. 1.
32. *The Language of Art and Art Criticism*, chs. 5–6.
33. Beardsley, *op. cit.*, pp. 39–40.
34. *Ibid.*, p. 16.
35. *The Language of Art and Art Criticism*, ch. 4.
36. Beardsley, *op. cit.*, pp. 43–44.
37. Cf. Frank Cioffi, "Intention and Interpretation in Criticism," *Proceedings of the Aristotelian Society* LXIV (1963–1964), 85–103. Cf. also, Stuart Hampshire, "Types of Interpretation," in Sidney Hook, ed., *Art and Philosophy*.
38. Beardsley, *op. cit.*, p. 36.
39. Cf. E. D. Hirsch, *Validity in Interpretation* (New Haven, 1967); also Joseph Margolis, review of above, in *Shakespeare Studies* II (1970), 407–414.
40. Beardsley, *op. cit.*, pp. 32, 44, 47.
41. *Ibid.*, pp. 19–20.
42. Cf. William Alston, *Philosophy of Language* (Englewood Cliffs, 1964); and Joseph Margolis, "Meaning, Speakers' Intentions, and Speech Acts," *Review of Metaphysics* XIX (1973), 1007–1022.
43. Cf. *The Language of Art and Art Criticism*, ch. 3.
44. Cf. Cleanth Brooks, "Irony as a Principle of Structure," in M. D. Zabel, ed., *Literary Opinion in America* (New York, 1951); and F. W. Bateson, *English Poetry: A Critical Introduction* (London, 1950).
45. Beardsley, *op. cit.*, p. 44.
46. *Ibid.*, pp. 42–44.
47. Cf. Joseph Margolis, "Works of Art as Physically Embodied and Culturally Emergent Entities," *British Journal of Aesthetics* XIV (1974), 187–196.
48. Cf. "Works of Art as Physically Embodied and Culturally Emergent Entities"; also Joseph Margolis, "Mastering a Natural Language: Rationalists vs. Empiricists," *Diogenes* no. 84 (1973), pp. 41–57.
49. Cf. "Moral Cognitivism"; also *Values and Conduct*.
50. I had seen, in manuscript, Professor Annette Barnes's paper, "Half an Hour Before Breakfast," criticizing my theory of the logic of interpretive judgments (Journal of Aesthetics and Art Criticism, Spring, 1976). I have taken no account of her charges here, both because the paper had not been published at the time this essay was completed (it was in fact completed before I saw her paper) and because I had attempted to answer her in detail, by letter. Suffice it to say that her charges go wrong in a number of ways: (i) I do not maintain that contradictory accounts of anything can be defended as true, either separately or jointly; only that what would, on a model of truth and falsity, be contradictory, may be jointly defended as plausible or reasonable or the like;

(ii) Barnes offers a set of alternative versions of a tolerance principle for admitting diverging interpretations, that she wrongly takes to be exhaustive and therefore, to capture my own view in a multiple dilemma; not exhaustive both because several of her alternatives involve self-contradictory features (which I explicitly avoid) and because no provision is made for truth-values other than "true" and "false"; (iii) Barnes makes no provision for what I term the asymmetry of truth and falsity: that, for instance, the "false" is opposed both to the "true" and the "plausible" and the considerations of plausibility do not entail the relevance of considerations of truth; (iv) my argument regarding the logic of interpretation is only applied to those entities that we call works of art; it does not presuppose any theory of the nature of a work of art, though it is compatible with an independent theory that I also support; (v) on my view, it *follows* that, *if* interpretation behaves as I claim it does, the properties ascribed to a work of art by way of interpretive criticism cannot be said to be *in* the work in the sense in which description would require; some of the paradoxes that Barnes attributes to my position simply fail to take account of this important point.

Towards a Robust Realism

David Novitz

Some relativists argue that there can be no way of deciding between competing literary interpretations: no way, that is, of deciding which (if any) is true and which false. Although this doctrine takes a variety of forms, it usually draws strength from the claim that since the beliefs and concepts central to an interpretation are either wholly or largely determined by the situation of the critic, there can be no neutral way of verifying competing interpretations.[1]

Needless to say, this view has been widely discussed and seriously challenged.[2] Of late, however, a new, supposedly more robust, relativism has emerged which claims not only to avoid these challenges, but to vindicate a kind of scepticism about interpretation.[3] My aim in this paper is to defend a realist account of the interpretation of fictional literature against the claims of the so-called "robust" relativist. In order to do this I shall try to show that the arguments adduced in support of "robust" relativism altogether misconstrue the epistemic structure of interpretation. I shall begin, therefore, with an explanation of this structure: an explanation which effectively undermines all varieties of relativism about interpretation.

1. INTERPRETATION, IMAGINATION, AND DESCRIPTION

Readers of fiction are often required to solve certain puzzles, to dispel confusions or eliminate doubts about the meanings of individual words, phrases, or sentences in a text, about

From *The Journal of Aesthetics and Art Criticism*, 41 (1982). Reprinted by permission of The American Society for Aesthetics.

the theme of a work or its plot, about the actions, motives and machinations of fictional characters, or about the political or religious significance of the work to a certain group of people. Attempts to dispel such puzzles are commonly regarded by critics and readers alike as interpretations, and it is my claim that the creative, originative, or fanciful imagination plays a crucial role in the interpretation of fictional literature.

On my view, whenever existing knowledge and belief fail to bridge the gap between ignorance and insight, we are forced, if we are curious enough, to conjecture, fantasize, or hypothesize as to the solution of our puzzle.[4] One might, for instance, be puzzled by aspects of certain fictional works, and so might suppose or imagine, say, that Willoughby intends to seduce Marianne Dashwood, or that the word "apeneck" conveys Sweeney's bestiality. Yet again, one might imagine that *The Turn of the Screw* is a story of sexual repression, or that Falstaff hopes, through his antics, to rise to prominence in Hal's entourage. These are all guesses: imaginative construals designed to solve certain problems. Each is tentatively projected on to the work, and to the extent that it removes our confusion or eases our bewilderment, it is adopted as a provisional solution to our puzzle. We gradually come to rely on it, to believe it, and if it enables us to negotiate the work the better—that is, to understand other sequences within it, or to have appropriate expectations about future events in the narrative—we will eventually treat it as knowledge.

Of course, such solutions are not derived, either deductively or inductively, from our existing knowledge or beliefs, for *ex hypothesi* we do not have sufficient knowledge or the requisite beliefs to solve these problems.[5] Rather, the solutions are the product of our creative or fanciful imaginings.[6] Having said this, though, we must take care not to confuse these imaginings with those which merely elaborate and develop the fictional world sketched by an author. A reader may quite gratuitously imagine that Anna Karenina has pearly teeth, jet-black hair, and a very straight nose—even though Tolstoy does not describe her in this way, and even though no puzzle is solved by imagining her in this way. Here the reader contributes to the fiction by fantasizing within the "limits" set by Tolstoy's descriptions. Should the reader transgress these "limits" by imagining Karenina to be (or to do) other than Tolstoy's descriptions allow, we will maintain that the reader does not properly understand the novel. Nonetheless, these imaginings are not designed to explain the work. They are interpretations in a very different sense of this word.

Indeed, it would seem that we often operate with two quite different senses of "interpretation": one in which interpretations involve fanciful conjectures intended to solve certain puzzles; and another in which interpretations involve the fanciful, largely subjective and entirely gratuitous elaboration of the work. The trouble is that in speaking of interpretation we often confuse these two senses. The performances of concert pianists, for instance, are frequently regarded as interpretations—where this may mean two quite different things. In some cases pianists perform, and so interpret, certain works without experiencing any puzzlement at all. Theirs is an elaborative contribution to the work: they merely weave their fanciful variations within the "limits" of the score, and so come to perform the work in ways which they regard as straightforward and uncontrived. There are, however, situations in which pianists may quite properly be puzzled about how best to play a piece, and in these cases their performances (interpretations) involve problem solving of one sort or another. Confusion between these two kinds of interpretation is encouraged by the fact that they often (contingently) affect each other. Interpretative problem solving may be strongly influenced by one's (interpretative) elaboration of a work; while one's elaborations, in their turn, may be influenced by one's solutions to earlier puzzles that one may have had about the piece. But all of this, quite clearly, is a reason for emphasizing, not blurring, the distinction between these two types of interpretation.

My interest, of course, is with interpretations which attempt to solve certain puzzles about a work; for it is only in these cases—where elucidations and explanations are offered—that questions about empirical adequacy, plausibility, truth, and falsity properly arise. A reader's subjective elaborations of *Anna Karenina* are not candidates for empirical appraisal, for they plainly are not offered as substantive claims about the work but are the private fantasies of one reader. The moment, however, that they influence an explanation of the work, or are challenged by someone else's explanation, they may themselves be treated as attempts to explain, and will be subjected to assessment of one sort or another.

Interpretation in this sense always involves the fanciful formulation of conjectures or hypotheses which are designed to solve certain puzzles. If an initial conjecture fails to remove our bewilderment, is wild and wide of the mark, we are forced to think again, to imagine anew—but on this occasion our imagining will be directed or controlled by our knowledge of at least one failure. It is therefore true that wild and uninhibited leaps of fancy, far from promoting an adequate understanding of the fiction, will in all likelihood mislead us as to its import and content. Nonetheless, as we have just seen, the fanciful imagination may be progressively constrained and directed by knowledge and beliefs bred of past experience, and as a result may eventually afford new insights and understanding.[7]

There are, needless to say, many different experiences which may serve to constrain a reader's fanciful response to fiction. Perhaps the most trivial of these constraints is the perceived word on the printed page which when taken together with our knowledge of the English language, inevitably limits the scope of the reader's imaginings. Thus, for instance, the rules of reading English require that on perceiving the letters "d," "o," and "g" clustered together, one should read "dog," and that one should normally understand this word in terms of its standard or dictionary sense. Still more, anyone who is acquainted with the genre of the novel knows that one should respond to the novel in virtue of the words and sentences of which it is composed. And such knowledge inevitably directs and constrains the reader's fanciful imaginings so that not any imaginative response to the work will be an appropriate or useful response.

Not only does such knowledge inhibit our flights of fancy, but, more important for my purposes, it also helps determine what we find puzzling in a fictional work. A person who knows the meaning of the sentence "The dog is barking" will be less puzzled by a work containing this sentence than a person who is ignorant of this fundamental. Indeed, the reader in the know may be said to understand the meaning of the sentence without in any sense having to decode, decipher, or interpret it. In the sense of "interpretation" with which I am concerned, it is simply inappropriate to speak of readers interpreting the meaning of a sentence if its meaning is already known to them. The need for interpretation only arises when one does not, or is unable to, understand . . . although the quest for understanding, I hasten to add, is not always linked to a quest for meaning.[8]

There is, of course, a vast body of belief which pertains to fictional literature. Some of these beliefs are widely regarded as true and often pass as knowledge. They may include beliefs about, or knowledge of, the function of a comma, a paragraph, or a chapter; about the dictionary meaning of certain words, of the letters of the alphabet, or of certain aspects of the genre that we call the novel. When once in possession of such beliefs, certain features of the fictional work no longer stand in need of explanation: they are features which we regard as "given" in the work, and which are "transparent" in the sense that they can be understood without recourse to interpretation.

Clearly, though, not everyone is in possession of the same beliefs or items of knowledge. Consequently, what puzzles one person about a work may be obvious to another. Thus, for instance, if you know that Willoughby is deceiving Marianne (in *Sense and Sensibility*) you will regard this as a "transparent" feature of the work; and your statement "Willoughby is deceiving Marianne" will count as a description of one aspect of this work. But if what you know is unknown to me, I may very well be mystified by Willoughby's behavior. As a result I merely conjecture or fantasize when I utter the words "Willoughby is deceiving Marianne." Even though we both utter the same words, it is plain, I think, that we perform different speech acts: you *describe* and I *interpret* an aspect of the work. The difference between these two acts is not merely, as Robert J. Matthews has cogently argued, that interpretation is "epistemically weaker" than description.[9] It is also that interpretation involves fanciful imaginings of one sort or another which are designed to take us beyond what we already know or believe. Descriptions, on the other hand, merely involve the linguistic application of our recalled knowledge or beliefs.

By arguing in this way, I am able, I think, to avoid many of the problems which often beset the search for a distinction between interpretation and description. If, as Monroe Beardsley suggests, the distinction is to be based on the content of an utterance, we are left with the difficulty not just of determining which contents are descriptive, which interpretative, but also of explaining why one and the same sentence can be used both to describe and to interpret.[10]

Nor will it do to distinguish description from interpretation on the basis of the relative stability of their respective objects. According to Joseph Margolis stable objects are *described*; unstable ones "whose properties pose something of a puzzle" are *interpreted*.[11] But the trouble with this, of course, is that our perception of stabilities is itself unstable. How we see the world depends importantly on the beliefs that we bring to perception: so much so that objects are only taken to have certain properties for as long as our beliefs (and theories) about them endure. Since these are variable there can be no way of knowing which properties of any object are stable, which unstable. Unless "stability" (and hence "description") is to be explained in terms of enduring beliefs and knowledge, Margolis runs the risk of reducing all empirical descriptions to interpretations. Indeed, C. L. Stevenson seems to take Margolis's position to its logical conclusion, and despairs of ever distinguishing description from interpretation. Description, he argues, is always selective, and always involves construing certain marks or shapes in certain ways; and this, he maintains, amounts to a low-level interpretation of the work.[12]

It is plain, however, that describing cannot be reduced to interpreting. The epistemic structure of the one is manifestly different from that of the other. Interpretation, we have seen, involves the controlled exercise of what I have called the creative or fanciful imagination in an attempt to dispel confusion and bewilderment bred of ignorance. It involves flights of fancy which are mediated and constrained by our past or present experience. Description, on the other hand, does not require the exercise of the fanciful imagination. It is not intended to solve one's puzzles or banish one's confusions. On the contrary, a serious or sincere description presupposes the absence of bewilderment, puzzlement, or confusion, and hence neither involves the formation nor the refinement of hypotheses.[13] Rather, as we have seen, it involves the linguistic application of our recalled knowledge and beliefs.

One might be tempted to contest this way of drawing the distinction either on the grounds that we can interpret without in any sense being puzzled or curious; or on the grounds that we can sincerely describe an entity even when we do not know what it is that we are describing. But this onslaught soon flounders. In the latter case—the case of describing—it is plain that when we sincerely describe an entity without knowing anything about it, it is merely that we wrongly take ourselves to know something about the object, and so misdescribe it. Sincere descriptions can, of course, be incorrect, but even when we describe incorrectly we must, as I have stressed, *believe* that we are acquainted with, or know certain things about, the object of the description. If we are aware that we do not know anything about it, then we cannot seriously attempt to describe it. We may tentatively construe it in one way or another, but this, I have been at pains to show, is quite different from describing.

The claim that we can interpret a work without being puzzled or curious about it, is similarly misplaced. Sometimes the confusion resides in a failure to distinguish elaborative interpretations from those which attempt to elucidate and explain. Since my concern, in this paper, is to know whether interpretations can bear a truth-value, and since this question gains currency only when asked of elucidatory interpretations, my claim pertains only to elucidatory, not elaborative, interpretations. And it is plain that an interpretation which seeks to explain, can only do so if the interpreter is puzzled, bewildered or curious about the object of interpretation. After all, why should one seek to explain or elucidate if one already knows, or believes that one knows, the answer to one's puzzle?

Despite the triteness of this observation, it is sometimes suggested that we do read, understand, and therefore interpret novels in the elucidatory sense without being the least bit puzzled by their contents. But this is misleading. Of course one can read and understand a linguistic construction without being puzzled by it. Nothing that I have said is intended to deny this and I have already affirmed the possibility. My point, though, is that in any such case we do not come to understand the construction by interpreting it. Rather, one understands it in virtue of what one already knows or believes. The mere fact, therefore, that I have understood (or misunderstood) does not entail that I have interpreted. We only suppose that it does because when one's grasp of a work is challenged, one often defends it by using locutions like "On my reading . . ." or "On this interpretation . . ." where this suggests that in reading the work I must have interpreted it. But such an inference is unwarranted. My understanding may simply be the product of what I already know or believe; although now that it (and hence some of my beliefs) are being called into question, I will no doubt be inclined to regard it more tentatively, and may in the end be forced to offer my reading as an elucidatory interpretation of the work.

I have now come some of the way towards providing what is hopefully an adequate account of the epistemic structure of interpretation. There is, of course, much more that can be said. Nonetheless, my claim is that when once minimally acquainted with this structure, we have at our disposal an instrument with which to demolish relativistic arguments against interpretation.

2. A ROBUST RELATIVISM?

On my view a coherent relativism can only ever entail that critics who subscribe to different systems of belief and value will frequently offer different interpretations of the same work. This is as obvious as it is true, and for a philosopher it is both uninteresting and unproblematic. The interesting claim is that there can be no way of resolving these differences, of discovering that one interpretation is correct, and another false. However, it has been widely argued that on close inspection this claim turns out to be radically incoherent.[14]

Joseph Margolis disagrees.[15] True enough, he insists that a robust relativism must allow disputing critics access to a common conceptual scheme. And he stresses as well that it is no part of his thesis to maintain that all judgments should be construed relativistically, for this, he correctly observes, would have the embarrassing reflexive consequence of relativizing truth (p. 38). In this way Margolis avoids the incoherence of a radical relativism.

Nonetheless, he is adamant that it is inappropriate to describe interpretations as true or false (p. 44). Rather, they should be understood as taking values like probable, improbable, or equiprobable (p. 37). The reason for this is that since fictional works are "culturally freighted phenomena" (p. 44), a number of "competing principles" may be jointly relevant to the validation of any interpretation of such a work (p. 38). The "competing principles" which Margolis has in mind are presumably derived from those culturally determined "myths" . . . from Freudianism to Catholicism and Zen Buddhism . . . which, he has argued elsewhere, color our perception not only of sizeable portions of reality, but of works of literature as well.[16] Interpretation, on this view, involves the imaginative application of such principles: an imaginative exercise which is sometimes thought of as being akin to that of the practicing artist since it is supposed to add to, or even complete, the work.[17] Thus Margolis tells us that "interpreting" suggests "a touch of virtuosity, an element of performance."[18] Moreover, since in assessing interpretations "we are more interested in certain powers of imagination, the logical rigor associated with truth and falsity simply does not apply."[19]

These observations together constitute the cornerstone of Margolis's relativism. But it is not an entirely secure cornerstone. Part of the trouble is that from the very outset Margolis tends to confuse elaborative with elucidatory interpretations. While it is true that cultural considerations may color both our elaborations and elucidations of a fictional work, it is only in the former case that interpreting suggests "a touch of virtuosity" to which truth and falsity do not properly apply. In the latter case—where interpretations are intended to explain—questions of truth and falsity are still very much alive. It is, of course, true that cultural backgrounds influence both the contents and goals of interpretation, but this has no bearing on whether or not an individual interpretation with a specific explanatory goal can be true or false. Even within one and the same culture interpretations can have an indefinitely large number of aims: as many aims, in fact, as there are possible puzzles about a work. And it is obvious, I think, that discussions about the adequacy of any elucidatory interpretation must be informed by a knowledge of the puzzle which the interpretation seeks to solve. I shall argue that once given this knowledge, there is no reason why one cannot assess the truth or falsity of the interpretation.

If one's aim is to know the meaning or theme of a work, then a given interpretation either will or will not afford knowledge of this. It is Margolis's reluctance to acknowledge this fact which has made his remarks the target of sustained criticism. According to Monroe Beardsley, while "the story of 'Jack and the Beanstalk' . . . can no doubt be taken as Freudian symbolism, as a Marxist fable, or as Christian allegory," this is far from being a genuine interpretation of the work, and is no more than a "superimposition" on it.[20] Or, as E. D. Hirsch tells us, it involves determining the "significance" of the work, its relevance, that is, to our current concerns and favored theories, but it does not give us the meaning of the work.[21] The point, presumably, of Hirsch's remark is that since one can only determine the relevance of a literary work to a particular concern (i.e., its "significance") if one has already grasped its meaning, interpretation can never be a matter of discerning the relevance of a work to a particular historical or cultural concern.

But these criticisms, while they do not altogether miss their mark, fail to observe a number of crucial distinctions. We should notice, for a start, that readers are frequently puzzled by the relevance of a work, say, to their religious beliefs, or, perhaps, to a particular event; and they may seek to dispel this puzzle imaginatively—that is, through interpretation. Thus, for example, one may feel that *Macbeth* ought to be able to 'say something' about the assassination of Anwar Sadat, but one may be puzzled as to what exactly it does say about this event. As a result, and contrary to Hirsch's claim, one may attempt, interpretatively, to determine the relevance of the play to this event. Despite Beardsley's suggestion, this clearly is not a "superimposition" on the work. It is a genuine (elucidatory) interpretation of an aspect of the work; although it is not, of course, an interpretation of the meaning concealed within the work.

Second, we should notice that there will be occasions when one is not at all puzzled by the relevance of a work to a particular theory or religion, but where one chooses nonetheless to elaborate the work in terms of that theory or religion. Thus, for instance, one may think of Emma Woodhouse and her relationship to her father and Mr. Knightley entirely in terms of Freudian theory. And this, of course, is an instance of elaborative, not elucidatory, interpretation. While it may perhaps constitute what Beardsley calls a superimposition, it is not of itself an attempt to explain the meaning of the work, and does not therefore distort the meaning which "lies hidden" within it.

Such distortions only occur when one's goal in interpretation is to explain the meaning of a work or its parts. According to Beardsley, it is when this goal is subverted by the "myths" which mediate the interpretation, that we have a "superimposition" which distorts the true meaning of the work. Suppose, for example, that a critic wishes to grasp the meaning of *Hamlet*, where this is construed (according to established critical practice) as the meaning which Shakespeare and his contemporaries would have attached to the play. Beardsley's contention is that any attempt to achieve this goal in terms, say, of Marxian economic theory, must constitute a distortion of the meaning—a "superimposition" on the meaning—which "lies hidden in the work." It must do so because Marxian theory, not being of the appropriate time and place, cannot reveal anything about the Elizabethan understanding of *Hamlet*. At best it imposes an anachronistic conception on the meaning which is properly a part of the work.

Margolis, however, will have none of this. On his view, anyone who claims that a critical tract does not give the meaning of a work, but is merely a superimposition on it, must be able to tell where the meaning of a work ends and where superimpositions begin. But to do this, he informs us, requires a comprehensive theory of the identity and individuation of literary works and their properties. The trouble, according to Margolis, is that it is difficult to come by such a theory. Literary works of art, he tells us, enjoy a cultural existence. They are "culturally emergent entities," and since "culturally freighted phenomena are notoriously open to intentional quarrels, that is to identification under alternative descriptions" (p. 44), there can be "no sharp demarcation line between what is internal and what is external" to them (p. 42). Consequently, Margolis would have it that there is no obvious way of telling which meanings lie concealed within, and which are external to, a literary work. On his view, therefore, until we have a "theory in terms of which superimpositions and 'genuine' interpretations can be demarcated," interpretations in terms of cultural "myths" (that is, so-called superimpositions) may well enable us to attribute a perfectly plausible meaning to a literary work (p. 42).

As a result, since it is always possible for different critics to use equally plausible and yet competing principles (or cultural "myths") when interpreting a fictional work, Margolis believes that it must also be possible for them to arrive at equiprobable and yet incompatible interpretations of the meaning of a work. Given the cultural dimension of a literary work, and given, as a consequence, the fact that different critics individuate works and distinguish their properties differently, Margolis maintains that there can be no question of deciding which, if any, of these interpretations is true. It is this claim which lies at the heart of his "robust" relativism.

The case for a "robust" relativism, therefore, depends crucially on the assumption that since literary works enjoy a cultural habitat, they cannot be neatly individuated. For when once we are able to individuate a work, we will also be able to discern what is internal to it, and will, as a result, be able to speak, and speak properly, of meanings concealed within it, and meanings superimposed upon it.

But is it true that we cannot furnish an adequate theory in terms of which to identify and individuate literary works? I think not. Strange though it may seem, Margolis has himself furnished us with an excellent theory which, when taken together with some of my remarks about the epistemic structure of interpretation, is adequate to the task. Literary works of art, he argues, are physically embodied and culturally emergent entities.[22] "A work of art," he tells us, "can be identified as such only relative to a favorable culture with respect to the traditions of which it actually exists" (p. 193). And earlier he tells us that "the recognition that a given work of art actually exists *and has the properties it has* depends on the cultural traditions in terms of which a particular physical object may justifiably be said to embody a particular work of art . . ." (p. 191, my emphasis).

If Margolis is to be believed, therefore, it ought to be possible to individuate a literary work, and so determine its properties, provided always that one knows which cultural traditions are operative at a given time. On his view, such knowledge, inasmuch as it gives us access to the (culturally emergent) properties of a literary work, must also allow us to decide which properties are internal and which are external to it. And this, in its turn, will allow us to determine the meaning of a work or its parts, and to distinguish it from meanings which, in Beardsley's words, are merely superimposed on the work.

But Margolis denies that his observations can be applied in any straightforward way to literary works of art. He does not, of course, deny that one can have the relevant cultural knowledge in terms of which to identify a work and its properties, for to deny this, he fears, is to embrace a radical and incoherent relativism. Nor is his denial founded on the fact that it is difficult to acquire the pertinent knowledge. Such difficulties are undeniable, but they are also undeniably contingent; and the contingent difficulties involved in coming to acquire the relevant cultural knowledge cannot establish a relativism. Rather, his is a conceptual objection: one founded on what he takes to be the "logic" of interpretation. Literary works of art, he says, "often cannot themselves be ascribed a coherent design . . . without imputing by interpretation properties that yield a plausible" account of the work as a whole (p. 193). In other words, the ascription of certain kinds of properties to a literary work depends "on the identification of the work *under a certain description* (or interpretation)" (pp. 193–94). It follows from this that we cannot claim to know, independently of a specific interpretation, that properties of a certain sort (culturally significant properties) inhere in the work. "The nature of the work," Margolis tells us, "is not first fixed and then interpreted." Rather, the work is "identified *for* relevant description and appraisal *when* 'it' is interpreted" (p. 194). It is this above all which makes it impossible for us to verify an interpretation by appealing to the properties of a literary work.

So while Margolis believes himself to have offered a theory of the identity of literary works and their properties, he plainly does not believe that his theory in any way supports the view that it is possible to determine the truth of a literary interpretation. It is time, now, to show that Margolis is wrong.

The claim is that because the ascription of some properties to a literary work of art depends on the identification of that work under a certain description or interpretation, one can only have interpretative access to these properties. The reason for this, you will remember, is that works of art are "culturally freighted phenomena" and do not enjoy a stable set of properties. The properties that they are taken to have will always depend on the culturally determined values, beliefs and theories—and hence interpretations and descriptions—that we bring to the work. And since all of these may vary, the properties of the work must also be taken to vary.

But this conclusion is patently misleading. The plain fact of the matter is that there *are* cultural stabilities: enduring beliefs, theories, values in terms of which we perceive all manner of objects—whether they be ashtrays, sea shells or works of art. Against the background of these stabilities natural objects are seen to have, and cultural artifacts do have, a stable range of properties.

It would seem, then, that in order to perceive the properties of an artwork, one needs to acquaint oneself with the relevant cultural stabilities. And one can do so in a variety of ways: by consulting dictionaries, encyclopaedias, history books, anthropological investigations, sociological studies, and so on. Of course, not every critic will have easy or immediate access to such sources, and may, as a result, be puzzled by certain aspects of the work. It is in such situations, I have argued, that (elucidatory) interpretations are called for: interpretations which may subsequently be verified by acquainting oneself with the cultural background against which the work and its properties emerge.

So it simply is not true that the process of discerning and describing the properties of a literary work of art amounts merely to interpreting the work. In my view, Margolis is much too impressed by the fact that culturally based theories and beliefs mediate our descriptions and interpretations of works of art. It is this, I suspect, which leads him to overlook certain important distinctions between describing and interpreting, and to speak, at times, as if the two are the same. What he fails to appreciate is that cultural "myths" do not only enter into our descriptions of artworks, but thoroughly mediate our descriptions of all artifacts and natural objects—so that whether Margolis knows it or not, he is, in the end, committed to treating all descriptions as covert interpretations.

It follows, therefore, that unless the distinction between describing and interpreting is to collapse altogether, Margolis must concede its application to literary works of art. And, as we have seen, there are good reasons for doing so. Elucidatory interpretations of a literary work, I argued at the outset of this paper, are only ever called for when our available knowledge and beliefs are unable to banish whatever puzzles or confusions we have regarding the work. In such cases we are required to engage in imaginative or fanciful speculation in order to alleviate our curiosity and cure our ignorance. Descriptions of a literary work, by contrast, never involve speculation, but merely involve the verbal application of what we already take ourselves to know. Acknowledged ignorance, in other words, while a condition of (elucidatory) interpretation, precludes description. Consequently, while it is true that interpretations imaginatively impute certain properties to works, descriptions never do. They merely mention the properties which we recognize in the light of what we already know or believe.

Contrary to Margolis's suggestion, therefore, the fact that we identify a literary work under a certain description does not entail that we thereby interpret the work and so merely "impute" properties to it. If it is true, to use Margolis's example, that Stanislavsky was *describing* Chekov's plays when he identified them as tragedies, then Chekov's famous rejoinder can only amount to the claim that Stanislavsky had misdescribed his plays.[23] Identifying descriptions can, of course, be false or misleading, but this is not to say that they are interpretations. Conversely, to interpret a work is never thereby to identify it under, or by means of, a certain *description*. It is true, of course, that if an interpretation is to be comprehensible, the interpreter must identify whatever is being, or is to be, interpreted. This is frequently done with the help of noncontroversial descriptive phrases like "The object on the wall . . ." or "The novel you are reading . . . ," where what follows is a set of interpretative statements. To say this, of course, is not to say that descriptions are interpretative; still less that a work is "identified for relevant description . . . when 'it' is interpreted" (p. 194). It is only to concede what must already be obvious, namely that descriptive and interpretative phrases can inhabit the same critical tract.

There is, then, no reason at all to suppose that the identification of a work under a certain description ever involves the interpretative imputation of properties to it. Nor, of course, is there reason to think, as Margolis undoubtedly does, that critical interpretations somehow complete the literary work, and so create certain of its properties. Indeed, if Margolis's theory of the individuation and identity of works of art has any virtue at all, it is the virtue of explaining how we can discern the properties of a fictional work independently of interpretation. On his view, such properties are jointly a function of the physical object in which the work is embodied (the printed pages), and of the culture in which the work emerges. If this is correct, and I think that it is, knowledge of the physical object and its cultural setting will allow us to discern, to know, and hence to describe, the properties of the work. And this is important, for it furnishes us with an independent means of verifying any given interpretation: it provides us with a way of coming to know whether interpretatively imputed properties actually inhere in a particular work. It is, of course, true that the ability to discern these properties on any given occasion may itself be the result of prior interpretative acts which have produced knowledge of (or established beliefs about) the work and its properties. However, I argued earlier that the act of applying such knowledge or beliefs is never itself interpretative. To claim that it is, is merely to confuse description with interpretation, and is to misconstrue the epistemic structure of both.

If I am right, the case for a robust relativism fails. Since we can know the properties of a work independently of any specific attempt to interpret it, we have at our disposal a means of verifying different interpretations of the work. Not only can interpretations be true or false, but they can be known to be true or false.[24] Needless to say, there will be cases in which we are undecided as to the truth or falsity of an interpretation, but such uncertainties will always be the result of a contingent, and usually remediable, lack of knowledge. As such they neither entail a radical nor a robust relativism.

3. VERIFICATION

It is one thing to interpret a work, but altogether another to verify it. In my view, Margolis's theory of literary works as physically embodied and culturally emergent entities comes a long way towards explaining the process of verification. And I have already shown, if only in skeletal form, how this is possible. It is time now to fill in some of the detail, and to explain more fully one of the major preoccupations of literary criticism.

Literary works of art are physically embodied. In most cases they inhabit white pages suitably inscribed with black ink. When once given the appropriate linguistic and literary conventions, these pages may properly be regarded as a sequence of words—that is, what we standardly call a text. Normally we assume that the text furnishes us with a good deal of evidence necessary for discerning the theme of a work and the meaning of its parts. This is why we begin the task of coming to understand a novel by attending in the first instance to its vocabulary and syntactical constructions. It should come as no surprise, then, to find that we frequently begin the task of verifying an interpretation by attending to sentences on the printed page. In my view it is always necessary to appeal to the text of a work, and to use it as an arbiter of correctness, when attempting to verify an interpretation of the theme of a work or the meaning of its parts.

This, of course, is not to deny that a literary text standardly conveys whatever its author intends it to convey. If H. P. Grice is to be believed, success in linguistic communication involves the hearer's or reader's recognition of whatever the speaker or author intended to convey by using a particular linguistic device.[25] However, it needs to be stressed that recognition of the author's very complex intention is facilitated by the development of linguistic conventions which are used by an author in the (not infallible) belief that they will convey to a reader whatever the author intends or means to convey. Reciprocally, the reader will suppose (again not infallibly) that the use of specific conventional devices on a particular occasion conveys whatever the author intended to convey.

There is, then, much to commend the view that linguistic meaning is an affair of human consciousness.[26] However, it is a vastly different matter to suppose, as E. D. Hirsch unquestionably does, that the interpretation of literature, inasmuch as it involves a search for "determinate meaning," is always, in the last resort, a matter of uncovering authorial intention.[27] The trouble with such a view, as Monroe Beardsley has pointed out, is that authors, like speakers, make mistakes.[28] Occasionally authors will invoke the wrong convention. They may be guilty of malaprops or of unintentionally ambiguous constructions, and as a result they may fail to say what they mean. In such cases the resultant passages have a meaning which is different from the authors' meaning; and any appeal to authorial intention, while it may tell us what an author meant to convey, will tell us very little, if anything, about the meaning of the passage in question.

Even though Hirsch correctly emphasizes an important genetic relation between linguistic meaning and human mental states, his scepticism about the text as a source of meaning and as a criterion for verifying interpretations is largely misplaced. Hirsch simply overlooks the well known fact that in any natural language there are many established devices which are used in a range of standardized ways in order to convey authorial intention. Such devices enjoy what H. P. Grice calls a "timeless," as opposed to an "utterer's occasion," meaning: and they are used by an author precisely because he believes that they will serve to convey whatever it is that he means or intends.[29] Certainly the origin of these devices must be explained in terms of human intention, but they have long since escaped the complete influence of the individuals who use them. They have acquired an independence which allows them to be the bearers of meanings which may be left entirely untouched by the particular intentions of an author on a specific occasion.[30] It is no longer the intention which gives the device meaning: rather, it is frequently the standard meaning of the device which allows us to attribute a particular intention to the author.

If I am right, any text which is written in a natural language must contain a vast number of conventional linguistic devices. Consequently, acquaintance with the relevant linguistic conventions (which are themselves partly definitive of a culture) will enable us to discern the meaning of some of the words, phrases and sentences used in the text. Meaning, quite clearly, is itself a culturally emergent property. So too, of course, are the theme and plot of the work, as well as its ambiguities and vaguenesses. Having said this, though, it is tempting, but totally mistaken, to conclude that any interpretation of a literary work which its text is "able to bear"—that is, which reflects the conventional meanings of its various words and phrases—is to that extent true or correct. The trouble with this is that a word can only bear its standard meaning if it is used in accordance with established usage.[31] Since it need not always be obvious from the text alone whether or not a given word is being used conventionally, we may not be able to tell whether the word bears its standard meaning on this occasion. And if we cannot tell from the text alone, it would seem that the text cannot be regarded as a touchstone for correctness in interpretations.

Despite this, it would be unnecessarily precipitate to dismiss the text as a source of meaning or as a ground for asserting the validity of an interpretation. While it is true that a consideration of the text alone is never sufficient for ascertaining the theme of a work or the adequacy of its interpretations, we have already seen that a consideration of the text plays a necessary part in this process. However, since it only plays *a part*, something else must be required if we are ever to know that an interpretation is true or false.

Well, what is it that is required? In a recent article Jack Meiland tells us that we must consider the text in "relation to impersonal (social) linguistic conventions."[32] A similar view is held by Svante Nordin who maintains that texts must be considered in their social context. Nordin is of the opinion that interpretations can be known to be true if we attend both to the text and to the linguistic conventions of the community in which the texts occurs.[33] Both views seem to me to be basically sound, but neither is developed in sufficient detail. The main problem is that there is no explanation of how social and linguistic conventions help determine whether a given interpretation 'fits' the text. Nor is there any clear account of the nature of these conventions. Clearly, not any conventions will do, but little has been done to delineate the requisite conventions.

A moment's reflection, however, will suffice to show that when once we know that a work is a tragedy and not a parody, an allegory and not a comedy, we are immediately able to tell how certain of its words and sentences are being used: literally or figuratively, metaphorically, ironically and so on. Moreover, just as the utterance "You are about to die" has one meaning when we take it as having the illocutionary force of a threat, and another when we take it as a prediction, so *Goldilocks* has one theme or meaning when we take it as a child's adventure story, and another when we take it as a psychological or political statement. And, of course, if we know to which genre, category or class the story belongs, then we can appeal to this knowledge, as well as to our knowledge of the conventional devices used in the text, in order to validate certain interpretations of the tale and eliminate others.

But how, you will ask, are we to tell to which genre, or set of genres, a work belongs? Is this not itself the object of interpretation? The short answer is that it may, but need not, be. Not all art lovers come to a work swaddled in ignorance. The trained observer is usually acquainted with many genres and, of course, with the tell-tale signs of genre membership. Not only can audiences tell a painting from a novel, but they can usually distinguish kinds of paintings and kinds of novels. This (cultural) knowledge, Kendall Walton argues, often mediates our perception of the work: we see it as belonging to, or as being in, a particular category, and this both affects what we look for in the work and, most importantly, what we see in it.[34] So while it certainly is true, as Margolis has argued, that "no distinction of genres, periods, art forms, styles and the like can be supposed to be discovered *simpliciter*"—that is without the benefit of some knowledge of the relevant culture; it need not follow from this that "some suitably selected alternative system of categories" can always displace the genre to which the work is seen to belong.[35] By Margolis's own admission, a rational critic's knowledge of the culture in which the work appears must prevent the arbitrary displacement of our critical categories.[36]

Needless to say there will be occasions when we cannot readily classify a work: occasions when we are puzzled about the appropriateness of confining the work to one genre rather than another. Any resolution of this puzzle invariably requires close attention to a range of conventional clues which (when taken together with some knowledge of the appropriate period of a culture) will enable us to tell to what genre or set of genres, if any, the work belongs. A critic may consider the title of a work, the manner in which a story is told, its written style and formal composition. He may consider its choice of vocabulary, date of publication, and even its length. Anyone conversant with literary art forms will invariably look to certain of these (and other) conventional clues when attempting to determine genre membership. Of course, not everyone knows that these are salient features of literary genres. Nonetheless, this is something that can be learned, and provided that we have acquired the requisite knowledge, there is no reason why we cannot come to know to which category of art, if any, a work belongs.

Context, of course, need not be explicated solely in terms of genres, art forms, styles and their conventional signs. Should we wish to verify the interpretation of a work which does not obviously belong to any established genre or style, we would almost certainly turn our attention from generic to genetic considerations. In such a case we try to discern the various properties of the work by attending perhaps to the biography or autobiography jottings of an author, or, possibly, to the linguistic conventions governing the period in which he or she wrote. We may attend, too, to the history of the period, to other of its literary products, or to the works of writers known to have influenced our author. And it is clear from this that attempts to verify an interpretation may become increasingly esoteric. A critical dispute which starts with apparently innocuous questions about the proper way of reading a contemporary work—whether to stress it in this way rather than that—may quickly lead to a specialized enquiry into the proper way of reading hexameter verse in the fourth century. It would seem, then, that our attempts to verify interpretations may acquire the form of a social or historical enquiry, and provided that we allow that social and historical knowledge are possible, it must also be possible to furnish grounds which help establish that a given interpretation of a literary work is true.

4. CONCLUSION

Any elucidatory interpretation of a literary work may be said to be true if the properties which it imputes to the work can be independently discovered within it. The process of discovery, we have now seen, depends crucially on the acquisition of the relevant cultural knowledge: knowledge of conventions, practices and traditions of one sort or another. It is only in the light of such knowledge that it is possible to discover and observe those features of the work which help determine its character and identity, and which furnish a touchstone for correctness in interpretation.

If this is correct, Margolis's relativism fails. It is a relativism, we have seen, which depends crucially on the belief that works of art are "culturally freighted" objects, the properties of which are not always "well-defined" or available for inspection. Indeed, if Margolis is to be believed, these properties only emerge in contexts where culturally based beliefs and theories (so-called "myths") are interpretatively applied to the works. On Margolis's view, therefore, works of art are incomplete, and the task of completing them falls to those who attend to, and wish to understand, the works. The resultant interpretations, we have been told, involve a "touch of virtuosity, an element of performance," for in interpreting a literary work of art the reader is required to imagine properties which can plausibly be imputed to the work, and which, in being imputed, actually become a part of it.[37] However, as we have seen, Margolis is of the opinion that these interpretations are importantly, indeed vitally, influenced by the cultural baggage that each individual brings to the work, and since not everyone carries the same baggage, the view is that at least some of the properties of an artwork are inherently unstable.

It is, I am convinced, the spectre of instability which brings Margolis to the view that interpretations can never properly be said to be true. What is more, since the "myths" involved in interpretation are thought to determine the nature of some of the properties of an artwork, Margolis has argued that no description of the properties of an artwork can ever serve to validate an interpretation of it since it can never be interpretatively neutral. Indeed, we have seen that in the final analysis Margolis cannot countenance any clear distinction between describing and interpreting the culturally significant properties of a literary work of art.

My aim, of course, has been to show that Margolis is mistaken. His relativism, I have argued, fails not only to distinguish elaborative from elucidatory interpretation, but fails as well to draw appropriate epistemic distinctions between description and interpretation. It is no doubt true that culturally determined "myths" may influence the way in which we interpret artworks. What Margolis overlooks, though, is the fact that to interpret a work may *either* be to elaborate *or* to elucidate it; and that in the latter case questions of truth or adequacy *do* properly arise. If the aim of an interpretation is to elucidate, to solve a problem or a puzzle, then it is in principle possible, I have argued, to verify the interpretation—even where this is an interpretation of the culturally significant properties of the work.

On my view all objects, and not just "culturally freighted" ones, are perceived in terms of cultural "myths" of one sort or another. Margolis's mistake, I have argued, is to suppose that these are chronically unstable, for they plainly are not. They are often enduring and form part of those stabilities which help characterize a society and its culture. It is our knowledge of these stabilities which allows us to discern and describe the properties of the (natural and cultural) objects which surround us.

By adopting Margolis's theory of works of art as physically embodied and culturally emergent entities, therefore, I have, I think, shown that an elucidatory interpretation of a work of art may be verified simply by acquiring the appropriate knowledge of the cultural traditions against which the work and its properties emerge. To know, or to be acquainted with, the appropriate aspects of a culture is to be in a position to describe the properties of the work: and these descriptions will, of course, serve to verify an elucidatory interpretation of it.

Of course, what we look for when verifying an interpretation will very largely be determined by the interpretation itself, but this does not entail that what we find is wholly determined by the interpretation. It is a commonplace of everyday experience that we do not always find what we look for, or look for what we find. The properties of a literary work are no exception, and, we have seen, can be known independently of any given interpretation.

If I am acquainted with the meanings of certain words and the rules of accepted behavior in eighteenth-century England, I will know, on reading *Sense and Sensibility*, that the Dashwood family had lived in Sussex for many years, that Mrs. Dashwood has recently been widowed, that Elinor is older than Marianne, and that Willoughby treats Marianne shabbily. Like so many other readers who are acquainted with the relevant cultural knowledge, I do not hesitate to assent to these propositions and to assert their truth. They describe what, for me, are "given" or "transparent" features of the work: features which will serve as a touchstone for the correctness of any interpretation offered by a person who is puzzled by the work or by certain of its parts. Any interpretation of *Sense and Sensibility*, therefore, which accurately reflects any one of these features, is to that extent true: this despite the fact that it need not be an exhaustive interpretation of the work.

It is simply false, then, that there is "no clear-cut agreement about what is in . . . " a literary work of art.[38] Certainly critics may disagree about this, just as they may disagree about what period of a culture is appropriate to the work. But there is no reason why such disputes cannot be resolved. We can and often do discover that particular beliefs and ideas are inappropriate to the interpretation of a particular play. The critic who maintains that Lear is properly thought of as the victim of his own illiberal and non-democratic form of government, can easily be shown by appeal to historical evidence that he is interpreting the play in terms of concepts which are wholly foreign to the Elizabethan conception of a sound political order. There are historical facts, often reliably recorded, to which critics can and do appeal in order to resolve critical disputes. Nor is it simply that the critic calls these facts "into play *if he wishes.*"[39] Rational disputation is essential to critical elucidation, and it is this that forces the critic to consider the available facts and to bow to the weight of evidence.

I do not, of course, wish to suggest that every interpretative disagreement will, in time, be happily resolved . . . although I have argued that those which resist rational resolution do so for purely contingent reasons. Nor do I wish to suggest that literary works are never highly complex, vague or ambiguous, or that a true interpretation can never find them so. Of course literary works and their parts can bear many (more or less determinate) meanings. To acknowledge this is to acknowledge their interest and their charm, but is not to accept either a radical or a 'robust' relativism.

NOTES

1. See, for example, T. S. Eliot, "Tradition and the Individual Talent" (1919), in *Selected Essays*, London, 1950; Lionel Trilling, "The Sense of the Past," in *The Liberal Imagination* (New York, 1940); Joseph Margolis, "Describing and Interpreting Works of Art," in *Contemporary Studies in Aesthetics*, ed. F. J. Coleman (New York, 1968).
2. Among the more prominent opponents of interpretative relativism are Monroe C. Beardsley, *The Possibility of Criticism* (Wayne State University Press, 1970); E. D. Hirsch, Jr., *Validity in Interpretation* (Yale University Press, 1967), and *The Aims of Interpretation* (University of Chicago Press, 1976); Anthony Savile, "Tradition and Interpretation," *The Journal of Aesthetics and Art Criticism*, XXXVI (1978), 303–16; P. D. Juhl, *Interpretation: An Essay*

in the Philosophy of Literary Criticism (Princeton University Press, 1980).
3. Joseph Margolis, "Robust Relativism," *The Journal of Aesthetics and Art Criticism*, XXXV (1976), 37–46.
4. For a detailed account of the fanciful or creative imagination, and its role in the acquisition and growth of empirical knowledge, see my "Of Fact and Fancy," *American Philosophical Quarterly*, 17 (1980), 143–49.
5. Cf. C. L. Stevenson, "On the Reasons Which Can Be Given for the Interpretation of a Poem," in *Philosophy Looks at the Arts*, First Edition, edited by Joseph Margolis (New York, 1962), where Stevenson defends the view that interpretation proceeds inductively.
6. See my "Of Fact and Fancy," op. cit., pp. 145–47. It should be stressed that in speaking of the fanciful or creative imagination, I am speaking of a mental ability or capacity, but not of an ontic entity or faculty.
7. Ibid., pp. 147–48.
8. Attempts to understand the theme of a work or the motives of a fictional character cannot plausibly be construed as a search for (linguistic) meaning. This point is very clearly made by Stuart Hampshire, "Types of Interpretation," in *Art and Philosophy*, ed. Sidney Hook (New York, 1966). Despite this we do often speak of attempts to grasp the theme of a work as attempts to understand *the meaning* of the work. I shall adopt this convention in the present paper.
9. Robert J. Matthews, "Describing and Interpreting a Work of Art," *The Journal of Aesthetics and Art Criticism*, XXXVI (1977), 5–14.
10. Monroe C. Beardsley, "The Limits of Critical Interpretation," in *Art and Philosophy*, ed. Sidney Hook, pp. 61–62. The point is taken up by Robert J. Matthews, op. cit.
11. Joseph Margolis, *Art and Philosophy* (Atlantic Highlands, 1980), p. 111.
12. C. L. Stevenson, "Interpretation and Evaluation in Aesthetics," *Philosophical Analysis*, ed. Max Black (Englewood Cliffs, 1950).
13. An insincere description will contain the very strong suggestion or "conversational implicature" that the speaker knows or believes whatever is conveyed by the description. See H. P. Grice, "Logic and Conversation" in *The Logic of Grammar*, ed. by D. Davidson and G. Harman (Encino, California, 1975), pp. 64–75. I am indebted to Robert J. Matthews, op. cit., for drawing my attention to this point.
14. See, for example, Roger Trigg, *Reason and Commitment* (Cambridge University Press, 1973); as well as Anthony Savile, op. cit.
15. Joseph Margolis, "Robust Relativism," op. cit. Page references to this article will be given in the text.
16. Joseph Margolis, *The Language of Art and Art Criticism*, p. 88. The same view is advanced in his more recent *Art and Philosophy*, pp. 148–49.
17. This view is shared by M. MacDonald, "Some Distinctive Features of Arguments Used in Criticism of the Arts" in *Aesthetics and Language*, ed. W. Elton (London, 1954); and Richard Wollheim, *Art and Its Objects* (Harmondsworth, 1970), p. 103.
18. Joseph Margolis, *The Language of Art and Art Criticism*, p. 71; *Art and Philosophy*, p. 111.
19. Joseph Margolis, *The Language of Art and Art Criticism*, p. 88. See his *Art and Philosophy*, pp. 120–21.
20. M. C. Beardsley, op. cit., pp. 43–44.
21. E. D. Hirsch, Jr., *Validity in Interpretation*, pp. 140 ff., and *The Aims of Interpretation*, pp. 1–13.
22. Joseph Margolis, "Works of Art as Physically Embodied and Culturally Emergent Entities," *The British Journal of Aesthetics*, 14 (1974), 187–96. Page references to this article will be given in the text.
23. Joseph Margolis, *Art and Philosophy*, p. 167.
24. In this respect I differ not only from relativists, but from less sceptical theorists such as E. D. Hirsch, Jr., *Validity in Interpretation*, p. 173, where he writes: "Correctness is precisely the goal of interpretation and may in fact be achieved, even though it can never be known to be achieved."
25. H. P. Grice, "Meaning," *The Philosophical Review*, 66 (1957), 377–88; and "Utterer's Meaning and Intentions," *The Philosophical Review*, 78 (1969), 147–77.
26. E. D. Hirsch, Jr., *Validity in Interpretation*, p. 23.
27. Ibid., Chapter 1.
28. M. C. Beardsley, op. cit., pp. 18–19. See as well, Laurent Stern, "On Interpreting," *The Journal of Aesthetics and Art Criticism*, XXXIX (1980), 119–29, esp. p. 123, where he offers two interesting arguments designed to undermine Hirsch's view.
29. See H. P. Grice, "Utterer's Meaning and Intentions," op. cit., pp. 147–48.
30. It is true, of course, that the context in which such a device is used may reveal a tension between its standard meaning and the au-

thorial intention made apparent in the rest of the text. However, this is always contingent on the structure of the text, and it remains possible that such a tension may be undetectable.
31. Cf. Anthony Savile, "The Place of Intention in the Concept of Art," in *Aesthetics*, ed. H. Osborne (Oxford University Press, 1972).
32. Jack W. Meiland, "Interpretation as a Cognitive Discipline," *Philosophy and Literature*, 2 (1978), 22–45, esp. p. 38.
33. Svante Nordin, *Interpretation and Method: Studies in the Explication of Literature* (Lund, 1978).
34. Kendall Walton, "Categories of Art," *The Philosophical Review*, LXXXIX (1970), esp. 340–41.
35. Joseph Margolis, "Critics and Literature," *The British Journal of Aesthetics*, 11 (1971), 369–84, esp. p. 378.
36. Joseph Margolis, "Works of Art as Physically Embodied and Culturally Emergent Entities," op. cit.
37. Joseph Margolis, *Art and Philosophy*, p. 111.
38. Joseph Margolis, "Describing and Interpreting Works of Art," op. cit., p. 186.
39. Joseph Margolis, "Critics and Literature," op. cit., p. 381.

I am grateful to Don Callen for his comments on an earlier draft of this paper.

Art and Beauty

Ruby Meager

The pursuit of the fine arts, as productive activities distinct from vocational engagement in techniques and crafts of various kinds, is a rather local phenomenon in human history. Moreover from classical times it has been recognized that to the extent that such very fine art separates itself off from the various crafts it involves, and distinguishes itself as answerable to no clear demand for specifiable end products or for accuracy to specification in those end products which it allows patrons to specify for it, it is an activity for which no adequate principles of production can be drawn up, learned and taught. Consequently its intelligibility as a human activity is threatened, even if the threat is thought of under the ambivalent form of Plato's 'divine madness'. Crafts, after all, have the clearest possible title to intelligibility for our telcologically functioning minds. Human activity itself is essentially goal-directed and a craft precisely is a goal-directed activity *intelligently* ordered and carried out with regard to materials, means and ends. And while it was possible to regard artists as supercraftsmen, carrying out perhaps very difficult orders for the most exalted patrons with practised and attested if not supreme skill, no question could arise as to what it was they were about, what their efforts were directed at, what constituted success or failure, glory or defect, at least in an obvious because utilitarian sense. No doubt such artists also worked with greater or less individual felicity in the exercise of their particular craft, earning themselves greater or less renown for the

From *The British Journal of Aesthetics*, 14 (1974). Reprinted by permission of Oxford University Press.
This paper was first read at the Seventh International Congress of Aesthetics, Bucharest, and to The British Society of Aesthetics in November 1973.

beauty or perfection of their work; but this gilt upon their gingerbread could be comfortably accommodated as an added perfection only to be expected in works dedicated to the service of such exalted causes or persons. But since artists have liberated themselves from subservience to craftsmanlike tasks and ends, however exalted, and have raised the banner of the autonomy of art, this obvious utilitarian-type intelligibility is lost to them and no replacement presents itself clearly as inherent in the nature of art itself. The '*ratio*' of 'Art' as an independently valuable activity seems obstinately to resist analysis. The proclaimed autonomy of art has accordingly ushered in a reign of conceptual anarchy. Attempts to find a unifying end for art itself in such previously means-like tasks as representation or expression prove restrictive or vacuous and recently, in the empiricist camp at least, defeat has actually been welcomed, with characteristic philosophical masochism, in the adoption of Wittgenstein's 'family resemblance' model for a concept, with its explicit instruction *not* to look for any one unifying principle relating every instance to every other instance of the concept over its whole range, as just the thing for the concept of art.

However, the merely negative force of this proposal from Wittgenstein has been supplemented by the more positive claim from his followers that we should view art as what Wittgenstein called a 'form of life.' I suspect at least a two-level admonition here, corresponding to at least two of the levels at which Wittgenstein speaks of 'forms of life'. (A) The more obvious reference is that to be found in his treatment, in *Lectures and Conversations on Aesthetics*, of an artistic culture (such as could be elitist or popular, decadent or healthy) as a 'form of life.' So we find him reported as maintaining that 'what belongs to a language-game belongs to a whole culture', and that to say what 'appreciation' consists in we would need to know the whole social complex of activities and attentions within which such 'appreciation' emerges: 'whether children give concerts, whether women do or only men do, etc.' as the lecture-notes illustrate. We could add: whether and how children are formally and informally introduced to the arts generally; whether one dresses for the opera; whether churches, priests, liturgical procedures are elaborately adorned; whether there are national galleries for the exhibition of paintings, and if so whether they contain paintings by contemporary artists; whether, and if so relatively how much, one has to pay for entry to them (the Tories have much to answer for!), etc. The theory is that only a grasp of the whole social complex of activities concerned in the production, display, performance, discussion, defence of, attacks on, material support for, collection or storage of, what people in some roughly homogeneous social group treat as art—and not merely a grasp such that one could *describe* these but a grasp such that one can feel oneself drawn into participating in them, engaging in them from the heart as a form of one's own life: only on the basis of such a grasp does the conception of 'art' related to such a socially based 'appreciation' acquire intelligibility and the title of 'work of art' a definite sense in which it operates not merely as a description applied with certain truth-conditions but also as a regulative idea in the thought of artists and public alike.

In this account of the role of art in our lives—parallel for example, to the account which people have found in Wittgenstein of religious belief as an expression of a whole 'form of life' rather than a claim to dogmatic truth—we have a prescription for a relativized concept of a culturally sophisticated form of art as a medium of communication within a culturally prepared group. Such a concept accommodates very easily the autonomy claimed for art, or rather for the artist, in post-Renaissance western European culture, providing him with just the social basis for intelligible work which he otherwise would lack. This is made clear in, for example, the penetrating study *Art and Its Objects* by Richard Wollheim, in which he celebrates this concept of art and the artist. A crude summary of the derived account of the art of painting, adapted from a radio talk by Professor Wollheim, may help to show how this concept of art works out in practice.

Painting, we may say, is necessarily at least the making of marks on a plane surface. This, simply as a voluntary activity, is (or can be) fun for the painter, and would have a point just as such. But painting is this *plus* the leaving of a trace which can be seen. So the painter can *deepen* his fun by so directing his activity as to leave a trace which he *intends to be seen*, and in which spectators (himself included) may *recognize his intentions* in leaving such a trace to be seen, so that the painter's deeper fun in intention-realization in a trace will be matched by the spectators' deeper fun in intention-recognition in the trace. Such an exchange of intentions realized and recognized in a trace constitutes *sense* of a sort in the trace. But presupposed to the possibility of such an exchange of understood intentions in a trace is the existence of, and on the part of both painter and spectator the internalized understanding of, ranges of already available forms for traces to take: available media, available techniques, available ways of forming images or patterning compositions, ways of alluding to aspects of natural or social life, to history, to geography, etc., etc. That is, presupposed to the deeper potentialities of intention-realization and intention-recognition conferring sense of this sort on paintings is a hierarchy of what Wollheim calls 'stringencies' accepted and used by the painter, each constituting at once a limiting and a signifying factor to be taken into account in determining where and how his marks shall fall; each representing a range of alternatives among which the marks he actually makes represent significantly expressive *choices*. The painter *must* use such recognized media, techniques, images, etc., to make his individual point in his individual mark; the spectator *must* understand the trace as representing *this* choice among well understood alternatives if he is to recognize the individual point the painter is making in this choice. But both use and understanding must be (or must at least give the effect of) an exercise of an *internalized spontaneous* judgement in the making of, and in the interpretation of, marks; must represent an expression of a (highly sophisticated, no doubt) form of life. Otherwise the traces will be inscribed, and 'read off', in ways appropriate rather to the characters in a written document than to the directly experienced forms of a work of art.

Now it is indeed possible to use Wittgenstein's 'form of life' recipe at this sophisticated level in giving an account of the intelligibility of certain forms (typically elitist, of course) of art; but there is also the less obvious, and more interesting, deeper level of reference to 'forms of life' (B) in Wittgenstein's writings which he equates, for example, with that 'agreement in judgments' (*Philosophical Investigations*, Part I, 241–2) on which the possibility of agreed *or* disputed opinions in any area of communication of experience depends. Thus 'agreement in judgments' in spontaneous colour-discrimination is necessarily presupposed to the possibility of the determinable disputes we have in opinions as to the colour of particular coloured objects, and of the truth-condition governed colour-concepts which make such determinable disputes possible. The theory that art operates also, and perhaps primarily, as a 'form of life' at this basic level, a form of life shared almost universally, mediating and making intelligible the communication of experiences of all kinds—perceptions, sentiments, exaltations and disgusts—from the simplest to the most complex, would provide an explanation at least of the temptation to think of art as a universal language. It resembles, no doubt, Kant's conception of the 'universal voice' making intelligible the judgment of *beauty*. Now the Wittgenstein followers' emphasis is on *art* as communication in a more sophisticated framework and at a more local, culturally relativized level of response, and is seemingly far from Kant's concern with the communicability of the sense of beauty, whether in nature or in art. But if we could draw together the traditional twin concerns of art and beauty, it might be because we could treat art also as a form of human life (B), as relating to a near-universal human responsive framework within which we can understand the intelligibility, of a non-utilitarian kind, of art as a distinct human activity.

Now if we take the level (A) claim that art should be seen as articulating a whole particular culture, this in itself unexceptionable plea for all-round and deep understanding of the whole range of the actual social phenomena articulated by our particular concern with art effectively underwrites the currently accepted selective principles and limitations on that range; and if, like Wollheim, we derive our concept of art from reflection on an art-scene in which art is taken as essentially autonomous, I suggest that at least two factors supervene which tend to drive art, so conceived, to suicide.

First, having thrown off in the name of the autonomy of art such external goals as producing beauty in the service of God or of Mammon, artists have necessarily themselves assumed responsibility for self-directed spontaneous concerns, whether in wrestling with the angel of their art or more generally in wrestling with life-exploration through their art. But this has placed an awful onus of spontaneity and originality on the individual artist. Certainly he can use the ordered systems of expression afforded him by his art, his time, his society; but it is his own thing he is expected to do with these trappings. He must become an Adrian Leverkühn or a Tonio Kröger, dedicating his life to self-directed artistic innovation, or self- or life-exploration. But in the former case there is a limit of tolerance in both artist and public for the interest to be found in the in-group excitements of paint-surface swearing at paint-surface, paint-edge cutting paint-edge; in the regress of films about films, plays about plays, novels about novels and so on through the permutations; and in the latter case artistic order comes to be seen as inhibiting genuine exploration and expression: the gap between art and life demands to be closed, and we are presented with exhibitions in which it is *logically* impossible to distinguish the exhibits from the gallery furnishings or accidental detritus without recourse to the catalogue and with concerts at which it is logically impossible to distinguish the new work from the surrounding silences except by John Cage's say-so. But it seems fair to call this situation a kind of death of art.

Secondly, taking to heart the thought that art can only be understood in the light of the whole social form of life which it articulates, let us consider the relationship between such autonomous artists, so necessarily original, and their critics and the public; for now the public must all perforce like sheep look up and wait for pre-feeding by responsive and articulate professional critics, who alone have the time and training necessary to feel their way into the ever newer art forms, before they can have any hope of appreciating what the artist is up to. To survive at all, therefore, our original artist must attract to himself critics who will take the trouble so to immerse themselves in his work that like sensitive midwives they can deliver this strange offspring in its new form whole and clear to the patient public, who may be as well disposed, as open and receptive as you please (though many, alas, are not) but will inevitably need guidance to adjust their ears and expectations to, say, the new 12-tone structures placed before them. Now such critics develop a vested interest in those artists whose minds they come to understand; and behind them lie dealers or media men with vested interests in regular producers of works which can be rendered distinctively recognizable, even to a certain extent predictably describable, and so treated as a roughly predictable marketable product. Thus as the erstwhile external support of the artist by church or public dignitary for works of glorification is replaced by supposedly internal support for the sake of his art alone, there is a built-in temptation to both critics and dealers or promoters to attend to and value art works primarily according to *whose* works they are, reinforcing the orthodoxy anyway of the primacy of the artist as originator. This apotheosis of the artist once recognized as a great name is complete, of course, only in the international auction rooms and only in regard to Old Masters safely dead. But with autonomous art the same tendency operates all the way down the scale, putting some severe strain on the spontaneity and originality of New Masters, still but half way through their contract with their dealer-investor. Under such strain it is understandable that we find the narcissistic regressions of art upon art, and of art devoted to The Artist's Problem, already adverted to; and also, of course, the various repudiations of these in the anti-art gestures in which Duchamp's ready-mades join silent music, auto-destructive mechanical absurdities meet vasty 'earth-art' projects, and at the farthest remove from medium-delight the marvellous conceptual art arises in typescript upon labels.

It is indeed tempting to regard such phenomena as marking that death of art so ambivalently decreed by Plato, so cheerfully announced by Hegel, its heir-presumptive. But they might rather be a signal to make us reconsider our concept of art; to put in question at least *this* autonomous, auto-publicizing conception of the artist fostered in the associated conception of art as a necessarily sophisticated, culturally circumscribed, individual-to-individual form of communication of experience. Rather than throw ourselves to the anti-art wolves, we might at least recall the possibility that art may also operate as a form of life at the (B) level, in a sense in which it would have intelligibility born not merely of a local fashionable culture-phase but of a universal mode of communication relating to some universally shared human sensitivity—say, even, to beauty. True, the concept of beauty is itself still obscure to us; the power and the *modus operandi* of the beautiful is as mysterious, if not as terrible, to us as to Plato (unless indeed one allows Kant some credit here). But does it not have more to do with what we have chosen and valued as art through the ages of human production than individual sophistication, autonomy, originality, spontaneity, etc., in the artist? It is not, after all, because Shakespeare is superior in these, or in political or practical wisdom, or in self-awareness, or in many-layered ambiguity, to, say, Dr. Johnson, that Shakespeare's poetry is memorable and the articulate and learned Doctor's is forgettable.

General Criteria and Reasons in Aesthetics

Frank Sibley

It is a somewhat daunting task to attempt to discuss the work of Monroe Beardsley, especially his work on aesthetics. Over a long period he has been more than prolific; he has pursued many issues with a wholly admirable pertinacity, developing and modifying his views bit by bit and in detail, with great good sense and sensitivity, not only as he has come to think his own positions need amending, but also in the light of criticism directed at him by others. There is a vast amount of his work with which I agree, and I doubt that I can say much that he has not already himself thought of, even if he may have rejected it as unsatisfactory. Given the bulk, subtlety, and complexity of his writings, it is almost inevitable that at some point I shall misrepresent him or do him an injustice. It is likely that I

From *Essays on Aesthetics*, John Fisher, ed. (Philadelphia: Temple University Press, 1983).

may simply have overlooked or forgotten some important points he has made. I shall have to risk this and rely on his customary appreciation of those who tend to support views similar to his own from their own particular standpoint as well as his constant interest in and generosity toward those who either misunderstand him or attempt to oppose his views.

Throughout his writings Beardsley has steadily sought to uphold the view that in criticism there are and can be general reasons for aesthetic judgments. On this point I stand and have always stood on the same side as he does. Thus, basically, we face together those many writers over several decades—I dub them "particularists"—who have argued that in criticism there are no such general reasons. The dispute arises because both we and those we oppose agree that reasons, to be reasons, must have a consistency about them; but our opponents allege that any "reason" offered to support the judgment that one work has aesthetic merit may be offered to support the judgment that another work has an aesthetic defect. To debate this issue adequately would require several complex chapters; so in the space available I can indicate my defense of the "generalist" position only in the sketchiest way and with the simplest of examples. I shall argue that through not making certain distinctions adequately, Beardsley adopts an extreme and heroic position that is unnecessary even to dispose of the most serious of the denials of consistency just mentioned. Later I shall argue that the particular kind of heroic attempt he makes is inadequate to establish a deeper claim; that by means of it he can isolate ultimate criteria of aesthetic merit from ultimately negative aesthetic criteria. On the first question he attempts more than is necessary to defeat our common adversaries; and for the second question, the line of defense he adopts through the bulk of his work is unsatisfactory.

The line of defense that he employs for both questions consists in claiming that there are three primary or basic positive criteria—unity, complexity, and intensity of regional quality—that can never in any circumstances count otherwise than in a positive

direction. These criteria he regards as ultimately "safe"; all other (secondary) criteria are "risky."[1] To make any of the latter safe in a given case, they must be linked to one or more of the primary criteria. I shall argue that a sharp distinction is essential within the criteria that Beardsley allows to be risky, a distinction he at times hovers on the brink of making. To take some of his examples, the presence of puns (or four-letter words) in a work may be either a merit or a defect; equally, he allows, may the presence of dramatic intensity (or a touch of humor).[2] Each is a secondary criterion. To show that either is, in a particular work, a merit, he maintains, ultimately requires a linkage to the primary criteria. But this, I claim, overlooks a vital difference. "X contains many puns" (I use x throughout to mean an artwork, not any specific kind of work like a tragedy, a pastoral poem, a sonnet, a statue, or a fugue) attributes to x a property or feature that is in itself entirely *neutral*. To claim that the puns are a merit in x, I agree, demands a linking explanation—they are striking, vivid, evocative, and so on. To claim that they are a defect also demands some such explanation—they are distracting, insipid, etc. So "X contains many puns (metaphors, etc.)," *tout court*, carries no implication of aesthetic merit or defect. But this is not so, I maintain, with "X has dramatic intensity." The attribution to an artwork of dramatic intensity, *tout court*, like the attribution of grace or elegance, is the attribution to it of a property that inherently possesses aesthetic merit. I would say that there are a whole host of properties that inherently possess a positive aesthetic polarity when applied to works of art, not just those I have mentioned, which seem to me aesthetic *par excellence*, but many, like witty, balanced, and joyous, that have applications of another kind entirely outside the arts. Similarly there are a host of inherently negative properties, like garish, sentimental, bombastic, and ugly. If these properties are not themselves grounds of aesthetic value (positive or negative respectively) in the realm of the arts, I cannot conceivably see what could be.[3] They are like "honest," "conscientious," "considerate," in the realm of ethics. Whereas the neutral properties that can be offered in reasons for merit or demerit possess, without linking explanation, no inherent polarity whatever, these do inherently possess an aesthetic evaluative polarity. One cannot intelligibly say *tout court*, and with this Beardsley certainly agrees, "This work is bad because it is graceful," or "This work is good because it is garish." I would want to say that all these, not Beardsley's three, are basic or primary aesthetic criteria, some of merit, some of demerit.

But now the question arises why Beardsley should suppose them inadequate as basic or primary general aesthetic criteria and why he should regard them as "risky." The reason is clear. He is only too aware, as are the particularists, that grace or elegance or dramatic intensity need not necessarily be a merit, may even be a defect, in a particular work. And for this too, most certainly, an explanation is needed in each particular case. But this time it is not an explanation of why an inherently neutral feature (the presence of puns or metaphors) is a reason for merit in a work; it is an entirely different kind of explanation: why a feature, inherently a merit when taken *tout court*, is, in the context of a particular work, a defect. Beardsley, I think, never adequately distinguishes the two cases. He regularly lumps them together. He therefore tries the same sort of explanation with the second group, linking them again to his one-way criteria. But though an explanation is needed, it does not have to be of this sort. Indeed, it is here that the second crucial distinction not explicitly emphasized by Beardsley must be made. To save what I have called general evaluative criteria from the attack of the particularists, Beardsley supposes it necessary to perform what I called the heroic task of finding certain criteria to fall back on: not merely ones that, applied to a work *tout court*, inherently count one way, but ones that always, in every work, can count only one way.

It is clear that, and why, Beardsley makes this move. If there are genuine reasons, there must be generality; if generality, consistency; and if consistency, the reasons given must always count one way only. As he says about butchers' knives, "if a certain degree of sharpness is a merit . . . then to say that a knife has that degree of sharpness must *always* be a reason to support the conclusion that it is good, and it will apply to *all* knives of the relevant sort. . . . *It will, at least, never be a fault in a knife*" (my italics).[4] And so what I called his heroic task is to find primary positive criteria that are such that "the addition of any one of them or an increase in it, without a decrease in any of the others, will always make the work a better one."[5] But the distinction that must be made clearly here is that between overall judgments of things, like butchers' knives, where the relevant criteria are *independent* of each other, and overall judgments of those many things, including artworks, where the relevant criteria are *interacting*.[6] In the former, once the thing is discovered to have certain merit-qualities and if it possesses enough, the judgment that the thing is good is merely summative; the inherent merit-qualities do not interact. If the blade is sharp, the knife well balanced, the handle convenient to hold, and so on, then in the absence of overriding or defeating negative qualities (for example, that it breaks after one day's use), it is a good one. But with very many things, though we can set out criteria of merit, these are not independent; they can interact within the whole in various ways. What are merit-features *tout court* or *in vacuo* for that *sort* of thing may not work satisfactorily together with other such *tout court* merit-features in a *particular* thing of that sort. It is the sort of object sometimes spoken of as an "organic whole." This is not a case of defeasibility, inherent positive features being overridden or defeated by inherent negative features. With defeasibility, inherently positive features never become negative in a particular instance: duress may defeat a contract, but offer and acceptance never count against a contract. But where there is possible interaction in a complex whole, as in artworks, what *in vacuo* is inherently an aesthetic merit may *itself*, in conjunction with other inherently positive features in that complex, become a *defect*.

For this an explanation will be necessary, but it can be a perfectly intelligible, though special, sort of explanation. It will be a *reversing* explanation, not the sort that showed why the occurrence of puns or metaphors (neutral in themselves) gave merit to a work. And such reversing explanations are common. Indeed, the sorts of cases needing detailed discussion are legion. Here I can take only one of the simplest, suggested by one of Beardsley's examples. When someone has decided that certain parts of a work are highly comic and other parts intensely tragic—both *tout court*, or inherent, or, in my usage, primary criteria of merit—he has to judge for himself whether the comic episodes detract from or enhance the tragic character, or vice versa. If he decides that the comic elements do detract from and dilute the tragic intensity, *and* that the tragic element is predominant, the comic elements, though of aesthetic worth in themselves, will be defects in that work precisely because they dilute the predominant tragic intensity.

I have argued elsewhere that there are no sure-fire rules by which, referring to the neutral and nonaesthetic qualities of things, one can infer that something is balanced, tragic, comic, joyous, and so on. One has to look and see. Here, equally, at a different level, I am saying that there are no sure-fire mechanical rules or procedures for deciding which qualities are actual defects in the work; one has to judge for oneself. But if the critic does decide that the comic elements are defects in this work, a perfectly general reason can be given. A work that might otherwise have excelled by its tragic intensity is marred by certain (inherently valuable) comic elements that dilute and weaken that (inherently valuable) tragic intensity; or vice versa. It is a matter for deciding, judging, that one dilutes, rather than contributes to, the other, for deciding which of the elements is on balance predominant, and hence deciding that a feature, in itself valuable, is the detracting feature, or defect, in the context of that work. This is a built-in and unavoidable phenomenon, not only in artworks, but wherever inherent merit-qualities may interact, and not one we need or should regret.

Beardsley comes closest to this position perhaps in his article "On the Generality of Critical Reasons." There he adequately refutes several of the more simple-minded arguments of the particularists. But I think it is clear that by ultimately striving for what I called the heroic solution, he falls back on his three primary criteria, and in doing so fails to convince where conviction is possible. It is precisely in dealing with the most crucial case, where an inherent merit-quality constitutes a defect in a particular work, that he hovers on the brink of the right answer. He claims that "the General Criterion Theory [by "general" he means criteria that *always* count only one way] can easily take account of such variations."[7] Rightly he says, just as I do, that a general criterion theory "does not mean that this desirable feature can be *combined* with all other desirable features," or that "all plays that lack a high degree of [dramatic intensity] would necessarily become better by increasing it, for some plays might thereby lose some other quality that *especially* adorns them" (my italics).[8] But here his argument falters. In his Shakespeare examples (*Hamlet* and *Macbeth*), having agreed that humor is a merit in one context but a defect in another, he, in my view, wrongly concedes that a "touch of humor is not a *general* merit" (my italics), because something else, namely, high dramatic tension, is.[9] But he should not have given way thus on the generality of the merit of humor, especially as in the next sentence he in effect concedes equally that high dramatic tension is not a general aesthetic merit either; for some plays that lack it would, if it were increased, "thereby lose some other quality that especially adorns them." So by parity of reasoning dramatic intensity is not a general criterion either.

My claim is that humor and dramatic intensity are *both* inherently general aesthetic merits, though either may be a defect, given an appropriate explanation, in the context of a given work. Instead, Beardsley falls back onto his three "always positive" primary criteria, a position that I am arguing is unnecessary. (It is true that Beardsley then says that even secondary criteria are general "in an important sense," which may seem to coincide with the view I am espousing.) But his secondary criteria, though general, are "subordinate and conditional." "X is a *secondary (positive) criterion* . . . if there is a certain set of other properties such that, whenever they are present . . . the addition of X . . . will always produce an increase in one or more of the primary criteria."[10] I would deny that any such "set of other properties" can ever be specified.

Incidentally, if the particularist's fear is that the admission of general criteria of the sort I admit—grace, elegance, humor, subtle characterization, dramatic intensity, which I have called basic aesthetic criteria—would make evaluative judgments a mere matter of mechanically testing a work against rules, or that it would preclude the possibility of these inherently valuable aesthetic qualities being defects in a particular work, my answer to him has already been given. In fact, my answer amounts to a direct denial of the claim of one particularist, Mary Mothersill, who says that "there is no analogue in criticism to what in moral philosophy have been called '*prima facie* duties'"—or, we might add, virtues.[11] The general qualities that, when mentioned *tout court* or *in vacuo*, I have called inherent merit-qualities are, in the context of a particular work, *prima facie* merits, but not necessarily *actual* merits.

The situation is analogous—I stress analogous, not identical—to that in ethics (and many other areas where criteria interact). If one accepts that promise keeping, truth telling, honesty, and so on are inherently moral virtues, it may nevertheless be necessary, even right in certain circumstances, *either* to lie or to break a promise.[12] Unless one accepts some fixed hierarchy of virtues or some plausible overriding principle like Utilitarianism, one is left to a non-rule-governed decision, weighing, for example, the seriousness or relative unimportance of the lie against that of the promise breaking, rather as one has to decide, in a hypothetical play containing both comic and tragic episodes, which are the defects and which therefore ought to have been expunged. (The disanalogy with ethics is that telling the truth may exclude keeping the promise, whereas the comic and tragic episodes are not mutually exclusive.) So I would call primary or basic those sorts of inherent aesthetic merit-qualities I have indicated, just as I would call the cited moral virtues or general duties primary or basic. And this is to use "primary" and "basic" in a way quite different from Beardsley's, for in the context of a particular work these qualities will be only *prima facie* merits, not necessarily actual merits of that work—though they will be actual merits too if no appropriate reversing explanation is available.

I have said that Beardsley's heroic attempt to find (three) always-one-way basic criteria is not necessary to refute the particularist who raises the reversibility phenomenon. I can now say why. I take three different kinds of examples. If we can say that x is hilariously comic *tout court* (being made so by the puns, etc., in it), if we can say that x is exceedingly graceful *tout court*, or if we can say that x has a tragic intensity (enhanced by its comic episodes) *tout court*, we have thereby given fully adequate and sufficient reasons for attributing aesthetic merit to x. Yet all of these fully adequate reasons—being hilariously comic, being exceedingly graceful, and having tragic intensity—cite Beardsley's "secondary" criteria, which could, in certain circumstances, count negatively. But not here. There is no necessity, when these reasons are given, to secure them yet further by linking them to permanently one-way positive criteria.

I turn now to my second claim: that Beardsley's appeal to his three basic criteria is inadequate for isolating ultimate criteria of aesthetic merit from ultimately negative aesthetic criteria. Again, to justify this claim fully would need lengthy argument. I can attempt only the briefest sketch. I shall have to concentrate on unity and intensity of regional quality, saying little about complexity. It is only fair to point out that Beardsley has always admitted the possibility that his three canons might not be adequate, and he has frequently attempted to rebut possible criticisms. He admits that it might be argued that "some [human regional] qualities are cited as grounds for dispraise"; he regards the question whether "*all* Objective Reasons can be subsumed under these three Canons" as "a very bold question"; but he is prepared "even to go as far as to say" that they can, adding, "This may be too sweeping a claim," but "at any rate, it is stated explicitly enough so that it can be attacked or defended."[13] It is certainly the case that through most of his work he has adhered to the claim and has not conceded any insuperable objections.

I shall consider unity first. Unity must be unity *of* something[14] and for some *purpose* or of some *kind*. Unity in itself is an empty concept. For, first, we cannot employ the criterion of unity except in a second-order way. We cannot just look for unity. If we have before us a simple poem exhibiting—to use one of Beardsley's examples—"heroic strength," we find this latter quality exhibited in the work either intensely or confusedly. If the former, we can conclude that the basic elements (words, rhythms, etc.) possessed unity; if the latter, they did not. If we are considering the play containing both tragic and comic episodes, we decide whether the episodes enhance or dilute each other. If the former, the work is unified; if the latter, it is not. So the judgment that the work has one or more of the qualities that I have called inherently aesthetic qualities is logically prior to the judgment of unity. Second, unity, unlike grace or elegance, is not a criterion that is inherently aesthetic at all. Almost anything may exhibit unity (organization, completeness, etc.): for example, a political rally. But even if we seek unity in what is in fact a work of art, that work may still exhibit a unity that is not an aesthetic or artistic unity. A very bad novel, its episodes thrown together haphazardly, could be unified in the sense that it preaches a single, coherent political doctrine throughout. It may have a unity, coherence, even a developing complexity of political viewpoint, but no artistic worth. But if we have to qualify unity by saying *artistic* or *aesthetic* unity, unity itself can hardly be an aesthetic criterion, and, *a fortiori*, it cannot be a primary aesthetic criterion. So as a basic one-way aesthetic criterion, unity cannot fill the bill. Somewhat similar comments can be made about complexity. We cannot necessarily decide independently that a work is complex or varied; this may also be second-order in the way unity is. And for complexity to be an *aesthetic* merit, the work must have a (reasonably unified) complexity that yields inherently valuable *aesthetic* properties. Like unity, complexity or variety can characterize political rallies and political points of view within an atrocious novel, as well as technical manuals, sporting activities, and so on.

If we now try to give appropriate content to unity, interpreting it, say, as unity of an intense regional quality or unity of a variety of such qualities, we come to difficulties over both intensity and regional qualities. "Intense" is ambiguous. The most common understanding of this term would be "extreme." A work may have an intensity of sadness, calm, tragedy, gaiety ("intensely graceful" and "intensely elegant" sound somewhat odd). But Beardsley cannot mean that regional qualities are, *ceteris paribus*, aesthetically better for always being intense in this sense. Some fine works are not intense in this way; they have a gentle humor, a hint of wistfulness, a faint suggestion of melancholy underlying a peaceful calm or quiet serenity. We value these regional qualities too and would not be without them. In the sense in which "intense" means "extreme," intensity is not necessarily what we seek in qualities of aesthetic value. So perhaps we must sometimes take "intense" to mean something like "pure," "quintessential," "epitomized," a clear expression of some regional quality. Intensity may mean simply that some regional quality has been securely grasped; characterlessness, insipidity, unclarity, and confusion have been avoided.[15] I shall say no more about this, but use "intensity" hereafter allowing it to take whichever sense is appropriate.

The far more serious question concerns regional qualities. Do we transform unity and complexity into clearly *aesthetic* qualities (and hence perhaps aesthetic merits) if we simply say unity (and complexity) of an intense regional quality? This question goes deeper than the one I began with, whether the "reversibility" of criteria emphasized by the particularists must always be met by a linkage to one or more of the three always-one-way primary positive criteria, of which intensity of regional quality is one. It calls in question the very claim that intensity of regional quality *is* a primary or always-one-way criterion of aesthetic value. And the reason it does this is that only some (intensive) regional qualities would seem to be aesthetic in character at all, and of those that are, only some are inherently positive, while others are inherently negative. In his various accounts and lists of regional qualities, Beardsley has given examples as different as triangularity, squareness, lyric grace, heroic strength, and dramatic intensity, as well as the qualities pompous, precious, subtle, garish; and I suppose we could add a few thousand more: mottled, pin-striped, leering, face-like, politically biased, ugly, sentimental, boring, and irritating (though I believe Beardsley would exclude the last three as "affective," not "objective"). All these, I think, could be (unlike perhaps insipid and characterless) more or less intense in one or another of the senses of "intense" indicated. But I would suppose that triangular, mottled, pin-striped, face-like, and politically biased are aesthetically neutral; and that while some of the intensive regional qualities listed above are aesthetically positive, others, like ugly, garish and sentimental are aesthetically negative. (Beardsley has been aware of these problems from the start;[16] at times he restricts positive regional qualities to "human" regional qualities, but he admits even then problems that I touch on below.) It would seem clear therefore that intensity of regional quality is far from being a primary positive criterion; only those regional qualities that are not aesthetically neutral and not aesthetically negative are positive. But, put thus, this is vacuous, and we seem forced to limit ourselves to some selected list containing only the sort of examples I gave earlier as primary positive criteria in my sense.

If the position I have presented so sketchily is correct, *some* (even "human") regional qualities possessing unity, complexity, and intensity are negative, capable of being "independently cited as a ground" of *negative* evaluations. Unless Beardsley can meet these objections, he fails to reduce the "very large variety" of positive reasons to his three primary criteria, a move that he regards as important—though I do not—to support a generalist position that in a broad way we equally accept. I believe that this kind of underpinning is not only inadequate but unnecessary. It is interesting to see how, characteristically, Beardsley has turned on several occasions in his more recent writings to these problems, which he recognized, as I have said, as early as the publication of *Aesthetics* in 1958. In all his relevant articles up till 1968, with one exception, he adheres regularly to the view that there are "exactly three basic criteria" that always count positively, never negatively. But in the 1966 article[17] the difficulty reappears, at least for the reader, though Beardsley does not tackle it: properties (like unity and intensity) are "instrumental"; they have the capacity to provide aesthetic enjoyment. But, the reader is forced to ask himself, "What if some instances of unity and intensity have the capacity to provide aesthetic revulsion?" In 1968 he returns again to face directly the question "Why are some aesthetic qualities artistically objectionable?"[18] He himself speaks of, and so admits, "defects due to negative regional qualities." He still tries to cope with them by reference to his three criteria, but with some lack of confidence ("Some of the other negative qualities are difficult to accommodate to this scheme. . . . But I hope that even those can be dealt with by dint of more sensitive and precise analysis").

I believe his attempt fails, as it did earlier. If intensity of some regional quality is to be a merit, then certainly, as he says, it is easy to see why *privative* qualities (e.g., insipidity, which entails lack of intensity) would be defects. Perhaps we can also admit that the qualities he calls *disruptive* (e.g., franticness) are destructive of unity (and hence of a pervasive intensity of desirable regional quality). But those he calls *reductive*, that is, lacking in complexity (crudeness, pomposity), along with others he finds hard to accommodate (grossness, preciousness), to which I would add bombast, garishness, sentimentality, and ugliness, seem to me capable of intensity (i.e., not privative), and not necessarily disruptive of unity or for that matter exclusive of complexity (i.e., reductive). A novel might contain a complex variety of kinds of sentimentality, not internally discordant but uniting, and so "enhancing" each other, to yield an overall and intense sentimentality. A vase might have a variety of ugly features—shape, decoration, color combinations—a uniting or mutually reinforcing complex of ugly elements adding up to an intensity of ugliness. Such works, it seems to me, would have unity, complexity, and a resulting intense regional quality—but a wholly negative one. If Beardsley cannot evade such cases, his position becomes similar to mine: some intense unified and complex regional qualities are defects, basic and primary defects. In what seems to me a tell-tale remark, he seems almost to concede this: for he speaks of a good poem as one that "generates a regional quality of aesthetic *interest*"[19] (my italics), where "interest" strongly suggests "value." But within a few lines he is resorting again to his three basic criteria: "the critic . . . must have the taste to tell how unified and complex a pattern is, how intensely it glows with regional qualities"—unless the word "glows" surreptitiously gives the game away.

The last relevant paper I know of fairly and squarely faces the difficulty.[20] He admits with his usual candor that he is left with a large problem, "how to explain why certain qualities, but not others, *can* be cited in reasons supporting judgments of aesthetic value." He refers us back to his previous attempt (just discussed) "to come to grips with this problem," but admits characteristically that "it is far from being solved." I feel this to be an admission that appeal to his three canons never solves (I should say, cannot solve) this problem. The "hint of a solution" he then offers is that certain value-grounding qualities, in particular "human qualities" (he concedes a possible difficulty about some others), are properties "naturally *interesting* to us . . . we can work up feelings about them. They touch us where we live." These are, of course, the ones that are positive, but I find this no more than a hint; and here, so far as I know, the discussion of this particular problem ends to date. One might hope that Beardsley had at last abandoned as unnecessary and inadequate the Three Canons view; but as we shall see in a moment, they reappear in another context even more recently.

Perhaps, with his customary persistence and ingenuity, Beardsley will yet offer an acceptable account of why some aesthetic criteria are inherently positive and others negative. This, as he has always recognized, is an additional and difficult task. It is just as necessary for him to show *why* his basic criteria (which, I have argued, fail to do the trick of collecting all positive criteria under three heads) are aesthetically positive as it is for me to show why my suggested host of inherent merit and demerit qualities are respectively positive and negative aesthetically. No doubt he would regard it as an added difficulty for the position I have outlined "that there seems no way of demonstrating that any particular list of qualities is an exhaustive inventory of those that are aesthetically valuable."[21] I cannot attempt to offer any suggestion here. Nor is it my present task to discuss the persistent endeavors he has made to deal with this problem, starting in chapter 11 of *Aesthetics* and continuing through many more recent papers. Consistently he has adhered to the view that positive aesthetic qualities are instrumental capacities that provide, in certain conditions, a certain state of mind, for which he has used, variously, the terms "aesthetic experience," "aesthetic enjoyment," "aesthetic interest," "aesthetic gratification," and so on. This state of mind he has in turn tried at various times to isolate and define by reference to *its* unity, completeness, complexity, intensity, and pleasure. To me it seems that these attempts result in difficulties, parallel to those I have discussed, breaking out again at a new level. Nevertheless, it strikes me as right that of the two available kinds of moves, he should at least attempt this one. The alternative, which Beardsley has several times rejected,[22] is to discriminate the state of mind—aesthetic enjoyment, or satisfaction—by reference to the set of aesthetic criteria we employ and the kind of properties we take aesthetic satisfaction in; instead, he wants to distinguish an aesthetic experience "in terms of its own internal properties," not by reference to the properties of the object that are instrumental in giving rise to aesthetic experience. For the latter course would be analogous to a moral philosopher's accepting as not further explainable that honesty and considerateness are virtues and cruelty a vice without, as a philosopher should, continuing to seek an explanatory principle. To do otherwise is to do what Gilbert Ryle once said about "family resemblance," to accept a position that should be adopted only as a last resort. It is odd therefore to find, though I must be misunderstanding him, that in one of his later papers he looks as if he is reversing his position and reviving his primary criteria: "Gratification is aesthetic when it is obtained primarily from attention to the formal unity and/or regional qualities of a complex whole."[23]

I fear that in the foregoing my admiration for Beardsley's work may have been obscured by the fact that I have been critical, not of his staunchly maintained position that there are general aesthetic criteria, for I share this view and regard myself as an ally, but of the detail by which he supports the position. I can only say that this is because I regard his work as so important that it merits careful critical scrutiny. My regret is that I must inevitably have done him far less than justice in so brief a paper.

I shall end with the more congenial task of trying to strengthen Beardsley's defense against a criticism that would, were it sound, endanger any general criterion theory, whether his or mine. Again my account must be schematic in the extreme. The objection is that made by Michael Scriven: that in aesthetic evaluation the independence requirement is "difficult" to meet. This requirement "demands that we be able to know the reason or reasons for a conclusion without first having to know the conclusion; otherwise we can never use the reasons as a means of getting to the conclusion."[24] I shall ignore the word "difficult" and the temporal suggestion of "first." The only claim of genuine interest would be the logical claim that in aesthetics we cannot meet the independence requirement since we cannot know the reason for an evaluative conclusion unless we already know this conclusion. I shall assume Scriven to be making this stronger claim because he also says that reasons must be "such that we *can* know them without knowing the conclusion." I think Beardsley also understands Scriven's claim in this strong sense, since he says that if Scriven were right, "it would follow that critics *cannot* use reasons to arrive at their judgment."[25] Beardsley's reply to Scriven is somewhat complex, and I find it hard to assess it; but at one point (p. 83) it takes the form of reiterating his own view that "some reasons *must* be used by critics in arriving at" their judgments (which does not refute but simply denies Scriven's claim about aesthetic reasons) and that "therefore there must be some basic features . . . that are always merits or defects"—unity and intensity of regional quality again. I do not see this as an adequate reply to Scriven, not do I see that Beardsley's appeal to his three basic criteria, already criticized, either helps or is needed, as he seems to suppose.

But I do think that Scriven's claim about aesthetic reasons is false, that nothing he says establishes it, and that it can indeed be refuted. We must, however, distinguish and set aside certain questions, important to discuss in their own right, but irrelevant to the central issue. We are not concerned, for instance, (1) with the ways in which, by various means, we can enable someone else to see for himself that a work is good; or (2) with the giving to someone of reasons that, if he accepts our statements as true, would require him to admit that a work must be good, though he cannot see that it is for himself; or (3) with the person who finds a work good and later looks for the reasons why it is, in order to justify his initial judgment. Our concern is with the critic who attends to the work for himself and in doing so finds in it qualities that serve as reasons for deciding or "concluding" that it is good (or poor, flawed, indifferent, etc.).

I shall concede Scriven's claim at its strongest: that a reason must be logically prior to a conclusion. I shall argue that, even so, Scriven's skepticism about aesthetic reasons fails at least in some cases, and possibly in all, and fails because of an easily committed confusion. The possible cases to consider for a full refutation are legion. I can here consider only one sort of case, though I think the general principle could be invoked differently in other examples. The case I discuss is in one respect an extremely simple one, but in another respect one of the most troubling, since it is a case where a *prima facie* merit is judged on actual defect. Scriven, I believe, is involved in an ambiguity involving two sorts of conclusions. For him, rightly, the ultimate conclusion is an evaluation that the work is good, perfect, flawed, and so on; that is, it is an overall judgment of *value*. But it is essential to distinguish this from an overall judgment of the *character* or *characteristics* of the work. (I deliberately use these terms rather than Beardsley's "quality" to avoid any possible suggestion of evaluation.)

The crucial kind of case to consider (though there are many others of interest) is that of the critic who approaches an artwork looking for the character or characteristics it has (elegance, grace, garishness, etc.) but who also actively accepts for himself (not merely on someone else's word) that some of these characteristics are *prima facie* aesthetic merits, others *prima facie* aesthetic defects. In the work he approaches (call it x), he finds predominantly a build-up of characteristic P (say, tragic intensity); he also finds in it episodes with characteristic Q (hilarious comedy). In the case under consideration, he decides that these latter do not heighten, but dilute (render less intense), the predominant character P. He therefore judges these to be defects. Note, however, that he did not simply judge the episodes with characteristic Q to be detractions from the *value* of the work. This *in vacuo* would be impossible; there must be some reason why he judges them defects. What he judges is that they dilute or weaken the predominant (tragic) character P, a judgment of the *character* of the work. But he also himself accepts, *ex hypothesi* in our simplified case, that P is a characteristic of inherent aesthetic value. So his overall judgment of the value of x—that x is not perfect, but flawed—follows from his judgment that the predominant character P is weakened (in Beardsley's terminology, made less intense) by the presence in x of episodes with the character Q. But this latter was a judgment about the overall *character* of the work. It is from *this* that it follows that, since he regards P as a characteristic of aesthetic value, x is less valuable than it would have been without Q and that Q is therefore a defect in the work. But he could not have decided that Q was a defect in its overall value, and that x was flawed, *without* having decided that characteristic Q in this case weakened the predominant characteristic P. The overall judgment of (somewhat defective) value rested on his judgment that characteristic P was weakened by Q. This, together with his accepted premise that P is a characteristic of aesthetic merit, yields the value conclusion that x is of less aesthetic value than it would have been without Q. Schematically, then, his overall judgment of value—that x was flawed, and that Q was its defect—rested on his judgments (1) that P is the predominant characteristic of x; (2) that P is weakened, not intensified, by the presence of characteristic Q; (3) that P is inherently a *prima facie* aesthetic merit; and (4) that though Q is also a *prima facie* aesthetic merit, its presence dilutes the intensity of P. In short, an overall judgment of character is distinguishable from an overall judgment of value and logically precedes it.

Beardsley in fact put the position exactly enough, without the trimmings, when he said, "A reason is some *descriptive* or interpretative proposition about the work. . . . Thus a reason always cites some *property* of the work, and we may say that this property is then employed as a *criterion of value* by the critic who presents that reason" (my italics).[26] This form of argument is in no way controverted by the fact that a person might, in temporal order, feel sure at the outset that x is flawed, without yet being able to say why. For when he does come to see why he initially thought it *flawed*, it will be because, in our simplified case, he realizes that P, the predominant characteristic, and one he accepts as aesthetically valuable, was rendered less intense by Q. Thus, though I have proved it for only certain sorts of cases, implicit or explicit acceptance of certain characteristics as being of aesthetic merit, and implicit or explicit recognition that x either intensely has, or in a diluted way has, some such predominant characteristic, function as the reason for, and have logical priority over, the overall conclusion as to the value of x. (This of course is only the simplest of cases; it has also to be distinguished from the sort of case already mentioned where hints of melancholy interposed within the gaiety, as in a Mozart movement, do not diminish or weaken the predominant gaiety, but unite to give the work a different and in itself valuable character, for example, the quintessence of a gaiety tinged with an underlying melancholy.)

One further point about Scriven's remarks. There is often a kind of absurdity involved in speaking, as he does, of reasons for a "conclusion." Ordinarily there need be no movement of inference to conclusion from reasons or premises. The critic does not normally say to himself, "X has strong and undiluted tragic intensity (or whatever); I regard this as aesthetic merit; so I must conclude that the work is good." When you already accept that the characteristic P is one with inherent aesthetic merit, in seeing or deciding that x has P you are *ipso facto* seeing or deciding that x has some merit, just as the butcher, finding his knife sharp, has, in doing so, found it, at least in that respect, good. He does not argue by a process of inference from premise to conclusion, "It is sharp; I accept sharpness as a merit; so I must admit that to that extent it is a good knife," even though an argument with premises and conclusion could always be constructed in this form. I cannot here deal with the many different and often highly complex examples that one can think of, but I am confident that an analogous answer can be made in most, if not all, cases to rebut Scriven's claim against the independence of reasons and evaluative "conclusions" in aesthetics. Thus, I think Scriven's charge is the result of inadequate analysis, a failure to distinguish overall character from overall value. I hope therefore to have at least sketched a strategy that any upholder of general criteria, Beardsley included, can successfully develop against one objection that, if true, would be serious for us all.

In this short paper I have tried to outline, and defend against certain criticisms, a General Criterion theory, a kind of theory to which both Beardsley and I are adherents. Though this has involved considerable criticism of the substructure of Beardsley's views, I cannot end without emphasizing again my high admiration for his range, variety, ingenuity, fertility, and persistence in pursuing, with subtlety and determination, what seem to me the central questions of aesthetics. The corpus of his work, which I hope will be added to for a long while to come, will inevitably remain a storehouse of important ideas and arguments for anyone seriously interested in the subject.

NOTES

1. Monroe C. Beardsley, "The Discrimination of Aesthetic Enjoyment," *British Journal of Aesthetics* 2 (1963): 297.

2. Monroe C. Beardsley, "On the Generality of Critical Reasons," *Journal of Philosophy* LIX (1962): 484–85.
3. Beardsley, of course, constantly admits that there is a very large variety of reasons (see, e.g., *Aesthetics: Problems in the Philosophy of Criticism* [New York, 1958], p. 462, and elsewhere), but he thinks we can find room for them in his three main groups. He would probably reject my line of argument here as "a simple appeal to paradigm cases" ("On the Generality of Critical Reasons," p. 478).
4. "On the Generality of Critical Reasons," p. 479.
5. Ibid., p. 485.
6. Beardsley hints at this, but little more, in *Aesthetics*, p. 465, where he says, "It does not seem that the contribution of each feature of an aesthetic object can be considered in an atomistic fashion," and in several other places, including his remarks about secondary criteria in "On the Generality of Critical Reasons," p. 485.
7. "On the Generality of Critical Reasons," p. 485.
8. Ibid.
9. Ibid.
10. Ibid.
11. Mary Mothersill, "Critical Reasons," *Philosophical Quarterly* 11 (1961): 77.
12. Again Beardsley comes very close to this position in what he says about ethics in "On the Generality of Critical Reasons," p. 481.
13. *Aesthetics*, pp. 464–70.
14. This is implicit in various things Beardsley says, e.g., in *Aesthetics*, pp. 198–200.
15. Beardsley seems to note this point briefly, e.g., in *Aesthetics*, where he says, "The essential thing is that the work have some quality that stands out, instead of being vapid, characterless" (p. 298), and speaks of both "higher intensity and greater purity" (p. 382).
16. *Aesthetics*, pp. 463–64.
17. "The Aesthetic Problem of Justification," *Journal of Aesthetic Education* 1 (1966): 32, 39.
18. "Bad Poetry," published in *The Possibility of Criticism* (Detroit, 1970), pp. 98–100.
19. Ibid., p. 110.
20. "What Is an Aesthetic Quality?" *Theoria* 39 (1973): 65, 69.
21. *Aesthetics*, p. 509.
22. "The Discrimination of Aesthetic Enjoyment," p. 296, and "Aesthetic Experience Regained," *Journal of Aesthetics and Art Criticism* 28 (1969–70): 5.
23. "The Aesthetic Point of View" (1970), reprinted in *Philosophy Looks at the Arts*, ed. Joseph Margolis, rev. ed. (Philadelphia, 1978), p. 12.
24. Michael Scriven, *Primary Philosophy* (New York, 1966), pp. 57–59.
25. *The Possibility of Criticism*, pp. 77–85.
26. "On the Generality of Critical Reasons," p. 479.

Beardsley, Sibley, and Critical Principles

George Dickie

There is a long-standing controversy in aesthetics as to whether the evaluation of art requires general principles. Monroe Beardsley has played a prominent role in this debate.

From *The Journal of Aesthetics and Art Criticism*, 41 (1987). Reprinted by permission of The American Society for Aesthetics.

Beardsley's account of critical reasoning involves a commitment to critical principles, that is, to general criteria, and he devoted considerable time and energy to combating those who deny that such generality is involved in evaluative criticism. In this paper, although I shall not challenge the importance of critical principles, I shall call into question the particular view that Beardsley has worked out. In part, I shall rely on an argument recently published by Frank Sibley, but I shall also examine and criticize some aspects of the view that Sibley offers as an alternative to Beardsley's theory.

I shall begin by outlining Beardsley's arguments and conclusions concerning generality. There is a certain amount of discussion of the justification of the generality involved in critical reasons in Beardsley's book, *Aesthetics: Problems in the Philosophy of Criticism*.[1] However, his fullest treatment of the topic occurs in his later article, "On the Generality of Critical Reasons,"[2] where he states and responds to a series of arguments that the opponents of generality have raised against the use of principles in art criticism.

The first argument of his opponents that Beardsley responds to is the claim that there are no single features of works of art "that are either necessary or sufficient conditions of goodness."[3] The word "goodness" in this kind of context can mean either "has value" or "is good," but in connection with this first argument Beardsley and his opponents intend "is good." The distinction here is between the nonspecific predicate "has value," which if predicated of a work of art indicates only that it has some degree of value which may range from very low to very high, and the specific predicate "is good," which if predicated of a work of art indicates that it has a specific relatively high degree of value. The predicate "has value" simply indicates that a work has some unspecified position on the value scale, while the predicate "is good" indicates that a work has a specific position at a relatively high point on the value scale. So the question is, "Are there any features which are necessary or sufficient for a work of art's being good?" Beardsley notes that unity is a necessary condition of having artistic value because unity is a necessary condition of being a work of art (as it is of being an individuated thing), but he agrees that there is no single condition which is necessary for being artistically good. He also agrees that there is no single feature which is sufficient for being artistically good. Beardsley's response to this first objection against principles is, then, to agree that no single feature is either necessary or sufficient for a work of art's being good, but to maintain that nevertheless it is possible that there are single features which always contribute to the value of a work of art. Later in his article he calls such features "primary (positive) criteria," characterizing them as features that "always contribute positively to the value of a work, in so far as they are present."[4] Of course, at the beginning of his article, he is only asserting the possibility of primary (positive) criteria; later in his article he goes further.

This first argument of the opponents of principles concerns the conditions of being good and denies the possibility of principles, i.e., principles that involve single features of works of art which are necessary or sufficient for their being good. Beardsley responds by agreeing that there are no necessary or sufficient conditions of a work of art's being good. He goes on, however, to maintain that there may be sufficient conditions of value, i.e., features which always contribute positively to the value of works of art. Thus, he maintains the possibility of sufficiency principles such as "a unified work of art always has some value."

The second argument of his opponents maintains that the same particular feature may be a merit in one artwork and a defect or even neutral in another.[5] From these alleged facts they argue that such features must lack the generality which is required for them to be incorporated into principles. Beardsley's answer is to accept his opponents' contention that a particular feature may be a merit in one artwork and a defect or neutral in another, but he goes on to argue that a feature may be a merit in one work of art because of the way it interacts with other features of the work and be a defect or neutral in another work of art because of the way it interacts with the different features of the second work. According to Beardsley, then, a feature may be a merit in one work of art because it contributes to a higher order value but a defect or neutral in another work because it does not contribute to a higher order value. If a feature does contribute to a higher order value and the higher order value is always a merit, then the feature in question has what I will call dependent generality. (Using this terminology, a higher order value which is always a merit has independent generality.)

The third argument of the opponents of principles is that one feature may be a merit in one work and a different feature may be a merit in another work.[6] The Beardsleyan answer to this claim is that such merits may have dependent generality through their interactions with other features which produce higher order value (as in the case of the second argument), or the two features may both be different higher order values which are always merits. This last possibility requires that there is more than one higher order independent value.

Up to this point in "On the Generality of Critical Reasons," Beardsley's answers to the opponents of generality are entirely conditional. To the first objection, he answers that while there are no necessary or sufficient conditions for being a good work of art, it is possible that some feature or features may always contribute to the value of a work of art. This answer argues for the possibility of independent generality. His answer to the second objection, that the same feature may be a merit, a defect, or neutral in different contexts, argues for the possibility of dependent generality, if there is independent generality. His answer to the third objection, that two different features may be merits in two different works, argues that there is dependent generality (if there is independent generality) or that there is independent generality if there are two features which are independently general. To complete his argument Beardsley needs to show 1) that there are at least two independently general merits and 2) that all dependent merits are merits because they interact with other features of works of art to produce one of the two or more independent merits.

Beardsley formulates his definitions of independent generality (his term is "primary criteria") and dependent generality (his term is "secondary criteria") as follows.

Let us say that the properties A, B, C are the primary (positive) criteria of aesthetic value if the addition of any one of them or an increase in it, without a decrease in any of the others, will always make the work a better one.

And let us say that a given property X is a secondary (positive) criterion of aesthetic value if there is a certain set of other properties such that, whenever they are present, the addition of X or an increase in it will always produce an increase in one or more of the primary criteria.[7]

Two things can be noted about these definitions: 1) they are both concerned only with sufficiency for aesthetic value, and 2) the criteria speak only of having value.

At the very end of "On the Generality of Critical Reasons," Beardsley goes a little way toward removing the conditionality of his arguments. He quotes Paul Ziff's remark:

Some good paintings are somewhat disorganized: they are good in spite of the fact that they are somewhat disorganized. But no painting is good because it is disorganized and many are bad primarily because they are disorganized.[8]

Beardsley says of this remark, "Ziff is precisely correct. . . . Disorganization, by this exact description, is a primary (negative) critical criterion."[9] By implication, Beardsley is claiming that being organized (unified) is a primary (positive) critical criterion. If these remarks suffice, they establish that there is one primary (positive) critical criterion (unity). However, to complete his argument, as noted earlier, Beardsley needs to establish that there are at least two primary positive criteria.

As is well known, Beardsley in fact maintains that there are exactly three primary criteria: unity, intensity, and complexity. Beardsley never proves that his trinitarian view is the case, but if it is true, it removes the conditionality of his argument in "On the Generality of Critical Reasons." There is, of course, no logical connection between his definition of "primary (positive) critieria" and his view that there are three and only three primary criteria; it is possible, given the definition, that there is only one primary (positive) criterion or that there are two, three, four, or even more such criteria.

There is, however, a problem with Beardsley's definition of "primary criteria." It is a defining characteristic of secondary criteria that they must interact with other features of the work so as to contribute to a higher order value, which is itself either a primary criterion or ultimately leads to a primary criterion. Because interaction is necessary for secondary criteria, their generality is conditional or dependent. In contrast, a primary criterion in Beardsley's view must have the independent generality which is required if there are to be principles at all. As noted earlier, Beardsley characterizes such generality as follows: "The primary criteria . . . always contribute positively to the value of a work, in so far as they are present."[10] Beardsley's definition of "primary criteria," however, does not guarantee independent generality as he conceives of it. Recall his definition.

Let us say that the properties A, B, C are the primary (positive) criteria of aesthetic value if the addition of any one of them or an increase in it, without a decrease in any of the others, will always make the work a better one.

Notice that the definition contains the qualification "without a decrease in any of the others." The word "others" here must refer to "the other primary (positive) criteria," and this raises a question of whether one can use the definition as a test of whether a given feature is a primary positive criterion. That is, if one uses the definition to see if a given property, say unity, is a primary positive criterion, one must already know what the other primary positive criteria are. But perhaps this problem can be avoided by applying the definition to a set of properties all at once, say unity, intensity, and complexity. So back to the qualification itself and the problem of whether Beardsley's definition of "primary criteria" guarantees independent generality as he conceives of it.

Unity, intensity, and complexity seem to fit the description well enough. The addition or increase of any of them would, no doubt, make a work better, if it does not decrease any other primary positive criterion. But because the definition allows for interaction among the primary positive criteria, there could be cases of works of art in which the addition or increase of one of the primary positive criterion, say unity, could cause a sufficient decrease of another, say complexity, so that a work does not become better. Beardsley has asserted that primary criteria "always contribute positively to the value of a work, in so far as they are present . . . ," but his definition of "primary (positive) criteria" allows for interaction so that something can satisfy the definition without contributing positively to the value of a work. Thus, Beardsley's definition of "primary (positive) criteria" does not really accomplish what he wants it to do: it does not really define independent generality as he actually conceives of it.

Frank Sibley opens his recent article, "General Criteria and Reasons in Aesthetics,"[11] by acknowledging his agreement with Beardsley about the necessity of generality (i.e., principles) for evaluative criticism, but he argues that Beardsley tries to do more than is actually required. Sibley claims that Beardsley mistakenly supposes it necessary to find criteria that, when present in a work of art, always count only in a positive way, the so-called primary positive criteria. Sibley is right that Beardsley desires such criteria, and I believe that Beardsley thinks his definition of "primary positive criteria" realizes his desired goal for he explicitly says, "The primary criteria . . . always contribute positively to the value of a work, in so far as they are present." I have shown, however, that the definition of "primary positive criteria" that Beardsley formulates does not accommodate his desire. Without his realizing it, Beardsley's definition fails to satisfy his goal because it allows for the interaction of his primary criteria and the consequent possibility of the diminution of the value of a work by the addition or increase of a property which fits the definition of "primary positive criterion."

Beardsley is led to the desire for ultimate criteria that always, in every work, count only in one way, because, according to Sibley, he fails to make an important distinction. Beardsley, Sibley notes, treats two very different features of works of art as secondary criteria. Beardsley treats such features as "containing many puns," "having a touch of humor," and "having dramatic intensity" as secondary criteria because each may be a merit in one work of art and a defect in another work. Such features, according to Beardsley, are merits or defects because of the way they interact with other aspects of the works. Sibley agrees that a feature such as "containing many puns" requires interaction with other properties to be either a merit or a defect, because "having many puns" is entirely neutral and "carries no implication of aesthetic merit or defect."[12] On the other hand, he maintains that such properties as "having a touch of humor" and "having dramatic intensity" "inherently possess . . . aesthetic merit."[13] Beardsley fails to notice, according to Sibley, that he has collected radically different kinds of features under the same heading. Of course, features with inherent aesthetic merit can interact with one another (and presumably with neutral features) to produce greater or lesser value, but they are not in themselves neutral. There are, Sibley asserts, an indefinitely large number of inherently positive aesthetic merits (elegance, grace, wittiness, balance) and an indefinitely large number of inherently negative aesthetic defects (garishness, sentimentality, bombast, ugliness), and he asserts that "all these . . . are basic or primary aesthetic criteria, some of merit, some of demerit."[14] Thus, the real distinction to be drawn here is the distinction between inherently neutral features which may in given cases interact with other properties to produce value or disvalue in art, and inherently charged (aesthetic) features, which may also in given cases interact with other properties to produce value or disvalue.

Why does Beardsley refuse to accept such properties as a touch of humor, dramatic intensity, elegance, and garishness as primary criteria? Sibley maintains it is because 1) Beardsley realizes that such features can be a merit in one work of art and a defect in another work, and 2) Beardsley supposes that he must find features that in every work always count only one way, if they are to be primary criteria. Sibley maintains that Beardsley's supposition is unnecessary. Elegance, garishness, and the like always have aesthetic polarity, i.e., are aesthetically charged positively or negatively, although because of their interactions with other properties they can be either merits or defects in actual works of art. It is just unnecessary, Sibley claims, to find features which in every work always count only one way. Also, it is apparently impossible to find the sort of thing Beardsley wants. As noted earlier, Beardsley's definition of "primary (positive) criteria" fails to achieve the goal he was aiming at. (Sibley does not notice that the definition fails because it allows for interaction of primary criteria—just the thing that he wants.)

There is a way to reformulate the definition of "primary positive criterion" which avoids the criticism made above. The trick is to leave out all reference to interaction within a work of art. The definition then goes as follows:

A property is a primary positive criterion of aesthetic value if it is a property of a work of art and if in isolation from other properties it is valuable.

The isolation qualification is to be understood in the following way: the property being considered is to be considered as if it were the property of a work of art which has only one value property. Please note that the isolation clause in the definition does not imply that the value properties of works of art are experienced independently of one another. Given this new definition of "primary positive criterion," generality is preserved even though a primary positive criterion property can interact in a given case not to increase or even to lower the overall value of a work of art in which it occurs.

If unity in itself is valuable, then it is a primary positive criterion. So are intensity and complexity, if they are valuable. Of course, it remains an open question whether these three will turn out to be valuable. And, if these three are valuable, there is the further question of whether they are the only primary positive criteria.

Given the new definition of "primary positive criterion," however, there is as much reason to think that the property "touch of humor" satisfies the definition as there is to think that unity, intensity, and complexity do. Once the isolation clause is inserted into the definition, there are, in fact, any number of properties which fit it and, of course, an equally large number that would satisfy a parallel definition of "primary negative criterion."

Once the definition of "primary positive criterion" is altered so that it will include many of the properties Beardsley wanted to designate "secondary [positive] criteria," the distinction between primary and secondary criteria of aesthetic value, as Beardsley has made it, evaporates; the new definition preserves independent generality (the goal of the definition of "primary [positive] criteria") as well as allows for interaction among properties in works of art (the goal of the definition of "secondary positive criterion").

As noted earlier, there is no logical connection between Beardsley's definition of primary positive criteria and his trinitarian view that there are exactly three such criteria, so that the reformulation of the definition of "primary positive criteria" does not have any effect on the trinitarian view. So, even if Beardsley's distinction between primary and secondary criteria must be abandoned, it is possible that he can still hold to his trinitarian view that every merit is an instance of unity, intensity, or complexity (either explicitly or disguisedly) or an element which links up with other elements to produce unity, intensity, or complexity. Nevertheless, it does seem to be a fact that there are a large number of properties which satisfy the newly formulated definition of "primary positive criterion."

With the new definition of "primary positive criterion," there remain two questions unresolved between Beardsley and Sibley. The first question is, "Are all properties that satisfy the new definition of 'primary positive criterion' either explicitly or disguisedly instances of either unity, intensity, or complexity?" The second question is "Are there primary negative criteria which are not merely low degrees of primary positive criteria?" As noted just above, Beardsley answers the first question in the affirmative, and will want to argue in something like the following way: elegance is just a kind of, say, intensity; balance is just a kind of, say, unity; and so on. Sibley can agree that in many cases of a value property, for example, balance will turn out to be an instance of one of Beardsley's big three, say, unity. Sibley, however, is skeptical that all positive value properties will so neatly sort out in Beardsley's trinitarian way. Moreover, Sibley argues that unity, intensity, and complexity are not "inherently aesthetic at all," but I shall not discuss his contention and arguments at this point. How important is it that there are exactly three primary positive criteria and that they are unity, intensity, and complexity, as opposed to there being a large number of primary positive criteria? If the trinitarian view is true, it would be interesting to know that it is true, but it would be a long, tedious, perhaps impossible task to show that it is true. One would have to show that each of a long list of value properties (elegance, balance, and so on) is an instance of one of the trinity. Beardsley himself never makes a serious attempt to to this. But even if the trinitarian view is true, what does it add to the reason-statement "that painting has value because it is balanced" to say "and balance is a kind of unity"? As a principle for use in critical reasoning, "balance in a work of art (in isolation from other properties) always has some value" is just as good as "unity in a work of art (in isolation from other properties) always has some value."

Of course, Beardsley has a deep, underlying reason for desiring the truth of his trinitarian thesis: in his evaluational theory, the perceptible objective features of unity, intensity, and complexity are supposed to cause the subjective phenomenal features of aesthetic experience, namely, subjective phenomenal unity, intensity, and complexity. The unity, intensity, and complexity of works of art exhibit a symmetry with the unity, intensity, and complexity they are alleged to cause within aesthetic experience. And, presumably his view (never discussed) is that the value features in the subject must mirror their causes in the object in order to be caused by them. It is not self-evident to me that even if the subjective features of aesthetic experience are as Beardsley maintains, it is necessary that they be mirror images of their objective causes. In any event, this deep reason cannot function as an argument for the trinitarian view unless it is worked out in some detail.

In addition to the dispute over the trinitarian thesis and related to it, there is the second question at issue between Beardsley and Sibley: "Are there primary negative criteria which are not merely low degrees of primary positive criteria?" Beardsley, because of his conception of aesthetic experience and his trinitarian view, must answer in the negative. He must argue that each negative property, such as garishness, bombast, and the like, is a low degree of unity, intensity, or complexity. Sibley can agree that in many cases a value property, such as insipidness, will turn out to be an instance of a low degree of one of Beardsley's big three, say, intensity, but Sibley is skeptical that all negative value properties can be shown to be low degrees of the positive value properties of unity, intensity, or complexity. In fact, Sibley argues that there are wholly negative value complexes which are not just low degrees of unity, intensity, or complexity, or any other positive value property, but I shall not discuss his contention and arguments at this point. Again, how important is it that there are exactly three primary positive criteria and that they are unity, intensity, and complexity, as opposed to there being some primary criteria which are totally negative and not just low degrees of unity, intensity, or complexity? Even if the trinitarian view is true, what does it add to the reason-statement "that painting is defective because it is insipid" to say "and insipidness is a way of lacking intensity." As a principle of critical reasoning, "insipidness in a work (in isolation from other properties) is always a defect" is just as good as "the lack of intensity in a work (in isolation from other properties) is always a defect."

While I am not persuaded by all of Sibley's arguments, I am inclined toward his view that there are a large number of positive and negative criteria. I do not think that Beardsley's view has been definitely refuted, but its neatness and its lack of support lead me to suspect the view. Furthermore, I am very suspicious of Beardsley's notion of aesthetic experience, and, therefore, I do not find his deep reason involving the symmetry of the three objective and three subjective features within aesthetic experience at all persuasive. My "solution" to the debate between Beardsley and Sibley about the number of primary criteria is to bypass it, arguing that it is most plausible to follow Sibley's lead. If in the long run it turns out that Beardsley's view is right, it is a simple logical matter to reduce critical arguments worked out in Sibley's terminology to the neater terminology of Beardsley.

A basic question remains unresolved at the end of Sibley's article: In what way is it justified to claim that a long list of positive and negative primary criteria do, to use his terminology, inherently possess positive and negative polarity? Beardsley, as Sibley notes, has tried to justify his trinity by contending that they are instrumentally valuable in producing a certain kind of valuable experience—aesthetic experience as he conceives of it. Sibley indicates that he thinks the instrumentalist route Beardsley chooses is the right kind of approach, but he believes that the particulars of Beardsley's account are inaccurate. Sibley, however, does not give any detailed criticism of Beardsley's account of aesthetic experience nor does he attempt to work out an instrumentalist account of his own.

Sibley does, however, suggest something which comes close to being for him a test of inherent aesthetic polarity when he asserts, "One cannot intelligibly say *tout court* . . . 'This work is bad because it is graceful,' or 'This work is good because it is garish.'"[15] Assuming, as Sibley must be doing, that such properties are not neutral, the test shows that gracefulness has positive inherent aesthetic polarity and that garishness has negative inherent aesthetic polarity. (The test assumes that the property being tested is being considered independently of its relations to other properties of the work.)

What I shall call "the Sibley test for aesthetic polarity" is very similar to the "test" embedded in the passage which Beardsley quotes from Paul Ziff's "Reasons in Art Criticism." The passage, quoted earlier, reads as follows:

Some good paintings are somewhat disorganized: they are good in spite of the fact that they are somewhat disorganized. But no painting is good because it is disorganized, and many are bad primarily because they are disorganized.

Ziff is saying (I weaken the value predicates), that one must say,

1. No work will have value because it is disorganized.
2. Any work will lack value because it is disorganized.

And I think Ziff implies that

3. Any work will have value because it is organized.

Ziff and Beardsley are clearly talking about the same sort of thing when Ziff speaks of paintings being organized and disorganized and Beardsley speaks of works of art being unified, but they conceive of these value aspects in different ways. Ziff seems to think that only relatively high degrees of unity or organization have positive value, and he seems to think that low degrees of unity have negative value. In "On the Generality of Critical Reasons" Beardsley appears to endorse Ziff's view. He says, "Disorganization, by this exact description [Ziff's], is a primary (negative) critical criterion."[16] But this apparently wholehearted endorsement cannot be Beardsley's considered view, for he thinks every degree of unity no matter how low is positively valuable. Beardsley's conception is to be preferred, because Ziff's view faces the problem of how the same thing (unity) can be positively valuable in one degree and negatively valuable in another. What could be called the "Ziff-Beardsley test of the aesthetic polarity of unity" can be formulated as follows:

One must say (insofar as being organized is considered in isolation from other properties of the work),

1. No work can increase its value by becoming less organized.
2. Any work will decrease its value by becoming less organized.
3. Any work will increase its value by becoming more organized.

Both the Ziff-Beardsley test and the Sibley test are tests for positive and negative aesthetic polarity. However, the types of properties considered by the three philosophers differ in kind. Sibley discusses gracefulness, garishness, elegance, and the like; Ziff and Beardsley discuss unity or organization. Unity or organization is a property that every work of art will have in some degree or other, whereas garishness and the other properties Sibley is concerned with may not be exemplified at all in a given work of art. Unity is a standard feature of works of art (and of any other individuated thing), whereas garishness and the other properties Sibley is concerned with are only occasional features of works of art (and other things).

Complexity, another of the Beardsleyan trinity, is also a standard feature; it is a property that every work of art will have in some degree. Although it is not so straightforward and easy to see whether this is so, the third member of the trinity—intensity—may also be a standard feature of works of art. If unity, complexity, and the Sibley properties have aesthetic polarity, then there are two different kinds of properties with aesthetic polarity—standard and occasional. Sibley has an argument with two aspects to the effect that unity and complexity are not positive aesthetic polarities. He writes concerning unity, that

unity, unlike grace or elegance, is not a criterion that is inherently aesthetic at all. Almost anything may exhibit unity (organization, completeness, etc.): for example, a political rally. But even if we seek unity in what is in fact a work of art, that work may still exhibit a unity that is not an aesthetic or artistic unity. A very bad novel, its episodes thrown together haphazardly, could be unified in the sense that it preaches a single, coherent political doctrine throughout. It may have a unity, coherence, even a developing complexity of political viewpoint, but no artistic worth. But if we have to qualify unity by saying *artistic* or *aesthetic* unity,

unity itself can hardly be an aesthetic criterion, and, *a fortiori*, it cannot be a primary aesthetic criterion.[17]

There is an aspect of unity (and complexity) which must be mentioned again at this point. Unity is a property that every individuated thing possesses; it is what I have just called a standard feature. For Beardsley, any degree of unity, however low, is still a positive value. Hence, a very bad work of art with a very low degree of unity (very disorganized) will still have some positive value derived from what little unity it possesses.

Consider the first aspect of Sibley's argument. It is true that any individuated thing exhibits unity, including a political rally, but this does not show that unity is not inherently aesthetic. Things other than works of art—animal movements, sunsets, and even political rallies—can exhibit aesthetic properties, such as gracefulness, colorfulness, and comicness, for example. For Sibley's argument to work he would have to show that a political rally cannot have aesthetic properties, but a political rally can have the property of being tense, comic, dramatic, or any other of a large number of aesthetic properties. Even if unity is not an inherently aesthetic property, it might be a positive artistic value because it is a positive value whenever it occurs in a work of art. Thus, a unity that occurs in art will be a value in art, i.e., an artistic value. Further, Sibley seems to be assuming that the only value that a work of art can have is an aesthetic value, but this conclusion requires an additional argument. In fact, I want to deny that the aesthetic properties of the kind Sibley and Beardsley talk about are the only artistic values, although I shall not pursue this point in this paper.

The second aspect of Sibley's argument, involving the example of the very bad political novel, draws too strong a conclusion: such a work would probably not have "no artistic worth," but rather a low artistic worth. I suspect that Sibley is here thinking in terms of strong evaluational predicates, and he moves from the undoubtedly correct conclusion that such a novel would not be a good work to the unwarranted conclusion that such a novel would not have any worth.

Sibley uses the same argument against complexity with, I think, the same result. In fact, it seems to me that both unity and complexity pass the positive part of what I shall now call "the Ziff-Sibley test of aesthetic and/or artistic polarity."

Sibley has a final argument against unity and complexity as positive aesthetic criteria. He gives the following example as a counterexample:

A vase might have a variety of ugly features—shape, decoration, color combinations—a uniting and mutually reinforcing complex of ugly elements adding up to an intensity of ugliness. Such works, it seems to me, would have unity, complexity, and a resulting intense regional quality—but a wholly negative one.[18]

I grant that the intense regional quality of the vase Sibley is envisaging would be extremely low in aesthetic value. Consider, however, a second vase which has a similar variety of ugly features (shape, decoration, color combination) but in which these various elements are incoherent. Such a vase would have even less value than the one Sibley conceives of. These two cases show that the unity of the vase conceived of by Sibley must have a positive value despite the vase's overall badness.

It is not clear to me whether an argument of the kind I have just given can salvage complexity as a primary positive artistic criterion, but perhaps it could. Intensity, however, is another matter. The vase case that Sibley envisages shows that the intense regional quality of the vase would be "a wholly negative one." (It does not, however, show that the unity which underlies the regional quality is itself negative.) As Sibley notes, Beardsley himself has shown great uneasiness about the possibilities of intensities of regional quality that are negative.

How do things now stand? Beardsley's definitions of "primary positive criteria" and "secondary positive criteria" must be abandoned, but I have formulated a new definition of "primary positive criterion" which preserves the generality he desired for both primary and secondary criteria and allows for the interaction he desired for secondary criteria. It seems that a large number of properties satisfy the new definition of primary positive criterion of aesthetic value and that a large number of properties satisfy the definition of primary negative criterion of aesthetic value. Further, unity is both a primary positive artistic criterion and a standard feature of works of art, and perhaps complexity which is clearly a standard feature of works of art is also a primary positive artistic criterion. We have, then, a kind of compromise between the views of Beardsley and Sibley.

On Beardsley's view, there are three positive sufficiency principles.

1. Unity in a work of art is always valuable;
2. Complexity in a work of art is always valuable; and
3. Intensity in a work of art is always valuable.

On Sibley's view, many positive and negative sufficiency principles derive from his test of aesthetic polarity. For example,

1. Elegance in a work of art (in isolation from other properties) is always valuable;
2. Garishness in a work of art (in isolation from other properties) is always disvaluable.

On the compromise view, there are many positive and negative sufficiency principles of the kind entailed by Sibley's view. However, among the positive sufficiency principles of the compromise view, there will also be unity and complexity principles.

1. Unity in a work of art (in isolation from other properties) is always valuable;
2. Complexity in a work of art (in isolation from other properties) is always valuable.

Furthermore, since unity and complexity are standard features of a work of art, there will be at least two necessity principles.

1. A valuable work of art is always unified; and
2. A valuable work of art is always complex.

I conclude this paper by noting an interesting historical parallel. In the eighteenth century, Frances Hutcheson and David Hume, although working in the same tradition, provided a striking contrast. Hutcheson presented a tidy theory in which uniformity in variety is the only property which triggers the sense of beauty, and this single but complex property is wholly positive. Hume, in addressing the same question, gave a long, clearly incomplete list of positive and negative properties which trigger the faculty of taste. Beardsley's and Sibley's theories provide a present-day parallel to the eighteenth-century phenomenon. Beardsley divides Hutcheson's uniformity in variety into its two component parts, adds intensity, and arrives at the tidy view that there are just three primary positive aesthetic criteria and no negative ones. In contrast, Sibley (like Hume) claims that there are many positive and negative aesthetic criteria. An important difference between Hume and Sibley is that Hume includes many different instances of unity and complexity on his list of properties that trigger the faculty of taste.

NOTES

1. Monroe Beardsley, *Aesthetics: Problems in the Philosophy of Criticism* (New York, 1958).
2. Monroe Beardsley, "On the Generality of Critical Reasons," *The Journal of Philosophy* 59 (1962): 477–86.
3. Ibid., 483.
4. Ibid., 485.
5. Ibid., 484.
6. Ibid., 483–84.
7. Ibid., 485.
8. Ibid., 486.
9. Ibid., 485.
10. Ibid., 485.
11. Frank Sibley, in *Essays on Aesthetics*, ed. John Fisher (Temple University Press, 1983), pp. 3 20.
12. Ibid., p. 4.
13. Ibid., p. 5.
14. Ibid., p. 5.
15. Ibid., p. 16.
16. Beardsley, p. 486.
17. Sibley, p. 10.
18. Ibid., p. 13.

This paper was presented as the annual Monroe Beardsley Memorial Lecture on April 24, 1987 at Temple University and as a version of a chapter of a manuscript on the theory of art evaluation.

Stations of the Cross (1–6), Barnett Newman (American). 1960. National Gallery of Art, Washington, D.C.

Can we come to know anything about spirituality from what Newman offers us here? Can art, generally speaking, be a source of important knowledge?

CHAPTER 10
Art, Science, and Knowledge: Knowing the World through Art

We value art for a broad variety of reasons. It yields rich pleasure, exercises our perceptual and imaginative faculties, expands our emotional and affective capacities, is the bearer and sometimes the breaker of traditions, and reflects individuals' and cultures' images of themselves. Is it also correct to claim that art is or can be a source of *knowledge* about the world, about reality, about ourselves? Our answer to this question is central not only to our view of art, but also to the way we conceive of its relation to science. Science certainly yields knowledge—empirical knowledge of the way things are, the actual structure and order of things. If nothing similar can be claimed for the arts, then an essentially dichotomous view must be taken of the arts and sciences, and this, of course, is a well-known position: Science deals with knowledge, art with emotions; science concerns truths, art concerns values; science establishes facts, art suggests perspectives.

Some thinkers find this attitude quite natural; others naturally find it quite mistaken. Still others claim that any simple comparison or contrast of art and science will be too simple, since both are highly diverse and complex intellectual enterprises.

The articles in this chapter contain a wide and interesting range of views on the relation between science and the arts, as well as on whether art can correctly be called a source of knowledge. The follow-up question of what *kind* of knowledge might result from our understanding and appreciation of the arts is also given careful attention.

Louis Arnaud Reid warns us that knowledge of facts or true propositions—so-called discursive or *propositional knowledge*—is not the only form of knowledge we need to acknowledge, even if it is the paradigm for the sciences. There are forms of direct knowledge or knowledge by acquaintance which are not reducible or translatable into propositional knowledge, and these nonpropositional forms are of particular importance when discussing our knowledge of values, morals, other persons, and aesthetic objects, according to Reid. Knowing many things about a person or many facts about an artwork is simply not equivalent to knowing that person or work.

Contrary to the traditional analyses of knowledge, Reid believes that holding or being able to state true propositions is not a condition which gets to the heart of the nature of knowledge. Knowledge, Reid says, is a kind of cognitive grasping, a "getting into" an object's nature, and such grasping is not always expressible in words. Part of the reason for this is that our cognitive "grasp" of objects often involves our feelings or affective awareness, which are nonpropositional.

One might object, "But to *know* something, mustn't what we are grasping be *true*, and isn't it excessive to think that when we grasp art, we grasp truth?" Reid attempts to circumvent this criticism (in our view unsuccessfully) by proposing that truth is not a measure of reality or independent fact, as it is construed in the sciences, but is actually a measure of the efficiency or efficacy of our acts of cognitive grasping. Since aesthetic understanding is susceptible to standards of efficacy, it can be thought of as true and as possibly affording us knowledge. Aesthetic interpretations can also be viewed as *objective* because they must answer to similar standards, and yet, unlike scientific propositions, which are tested against independent facts, interpretations are and must be *personal* because they can only be made on the basis of the interpreter's acquaintance with the work and related to his or her individual experiences. (Compare Kant's claim that aesthetic judgments are universal but subjective.)

Although Reid's conclusions are, we believe, based on an implausible conception of truth, and his views of knowledge are left impressionistic and imprecise, saying little or nothing of the kinds of (nonpropositional?) things we can supposedly come to know when we grasp artworks, we nevertheless find in this essay (1) a defense of art as a knowledge-giving source; (2) the proposal that this knowledge is different in significant ways from scientific, factual, or empirical knowledge; (3) the claim that the cognitive grasping of art is not contradicted by, but indeed requires, the engagement of feeling or affect (and in this seems distinct from science); and (4) that the usual propositional conception of truth must be expanded or altered when it is applied to the arts, and this, in part, constitutes a difference between scientific knowledge and knowledge delivered by the arts. These claims resonate in most of the succeeding articles and, perhaps most interestingly, find very direct, if somewhat clearer, analogues in the views of Goodman, a philosopher of very different stripe from Reid.

Scientific theories can, naturally enough, be called interpretations of the world or reality, and artworks and artists are often described as interpreting nature and providing us with a view of the world and ourselves. Osborne asks how far the similarity extends and notes six points of comparison, some indicating an abstract similarity but others amounting to important differences between science and the arts. This list could easily and instructively be expanded, but the points Osborne selects are unquestionably worthy of discussion, and any effort toward refining them will quickly indicate how elusive clarity can be in these matters.

1. Science and art both bring new order into the world for us. It is Osborne's view that art brings *perceptual* order, and science brings *intellectual* order. Art's aim is to exercise and expand our powers of percipience; science's goal is understanding the world. Many aestheticians may take exception to Osborne's characterizations here. Although most kinds of art obviously do emphasize perceptual properties and abilities, this is not universally true, and as we already have seen in Chapter 5, a work's aesthetic properties are often not simple surface or perceptual properties at all. Neither is it clear that there is any serious categorical distinction between a perceptual and an intellectual ordering; aren't perceptual structures or orderings a *type* of intellectual ordering? Furthermore, it could be observed that art and science "bring order" in very different senses of *bring*. It is typical (though hardly uncontested) to claim that science *discovers* the underlying, preexisting order in nature, while an artist *creates* or suggests something new and original, ordering things in unpredictable and novel ways. It is debatable, then, whether either the similarity or the difference Osborne cites in this first point are precisely as he describes them.

2. Scientific theories, once established, are *intersubjective* or shared— they are common intellectual properties employed and worked on by many. Artists' interpretations of the world, in contrast, are expressions of individuality and may have little claim on intersubjective validity and do not await general adoption or elaboration by others in the same way that scientific theories do. Osborne is surely onto one sense in which science is objective while art is subjective. The conflicts or contradictions among artists' various "interpretations" of the world do not demand, nor can they often find, resolution in the way that competing scientific theories do. The tribunal of fact or experimental confirmation cannot conclusively establish one artistic or humanistic perspective over another, primarily because these alternative views of our world and ourselves embody and express value judgments and normative attitudes that facts alone cannot conclusively adjudicate. Even if science is "value-laden" in the many ways which recent philosophers of science have propounded, especially regarding methodology and protocol, its theories are not, or should not be, laden with the private attitudes or values of the scientists regarding the object of their investigation.

3. Artworks and scientific theorizing are both the result of creative, imaginative thinking of a sort that cannot be reduced to rules or procedures. This is not to say that each practice is not crucially served by numerous rule-governed or tradition-governed procedures, but the successful end products of scientific and artistic activity embody original, creative, synthetic, and nondeductive reasoning which resists codification in terms of rule following.

4. As important as imagination is in the production of both science and art, science is ultimately not about imagined or possible worlds, but about the real, actual one in all its rich contingency. Art, in contrast, Osborne points out, is free to invent the fictional and concern itself with the possible and the ideal. The legitimate "reach" of the imagination is longer in the arts than in science. In the sciences, imagination remains in the service of the empirical facts—how things *are*; in the arts, the imagination can be employed

to show us how things *should* be, *could* be, or *might* have been. Interpretation of *existing* reality need not be the focus of art, though it often is; science has a stronger bond to the facts. This should not be understood as suggesting that science is bound to the *status quo*, since future physical possibilities often are the focus of its attention. Rather the point is that science explicates the general, lawful nature of the empirical world, rather than moral ideals, social, cultural aspirations, or private human hopes and fears, as art often does.

5. Osborne intimates that science is accessible to anyone who can comprehend its formal languages and techniques. Art, however, requires more than a kind of cognitive competence—it requires the exercise of sensitivity and special perceptual abilities different from those demanded by the sciences. This appears to be Osborne's way of suggesting that some notion of *taste* operates in aesthetic appreciation that is not required by scientific comprehension.

6. The representations of science are fundamentally quantitative, general, and abstract (i.e., they focus on things, states, and properties that are quantifiable and phenomena that are repeatable and lawful). The interpretations of the artist, on the other hand, are generally qualitative, not quantitative, and are unique and concrete, Osborne suggests.

No doubt, artistic renderings are usually not quantifiable in any clear way, and they are frequently *about* nonquantifiable situations, experiences, and emotions. They also are unique individual objects, though whether they are, in every case, *concrete* is a matter we have examined in Chapter 6. And artworks do not have generality in the sense that one *subsumes* particular phenomena under them, as we do in the case of scientific theory. However, at least some artworks propound or express general themes or theses which can be thought to apply to later experiences, even if this application is in no way lawlike or universal.

Because they are related to the aforementioned points, let us add two more that are equally worth considering.

7. Scientific interpretations and theories frequently (though not always) function *predictively*. Their predictive power is a consequence of their generality. Artworks, considered as interpretations of reality, are rarely predictive in nature, and it is unclear that they could, in any sense, be ascribed predictive *power*, since they cannot easily be said to have logical consequences.

8. An artwork itself cannot be claimed to be *confirmed* or *disconfirmed* by experience or observation in the way that theories are subjected to confirmation. Sometimes, however, works of art state, express, or suggest themes that may well be confirmed or disconfirmed, to some degree and in a less rigorous sense, by life experience, it seems. It should be remembered, however, that art is not always in the business of making claims or propounding theses or morals, so nothing is offered in such cases that *could* be confirmed or disconfirmed.

Without denying these specific differences, Goodman (whose views we introduced in Chapters 3 and 7) emphasizes the similarities, and believes that there is no deep schism between art and science. Both are or involve symbol systems for "creation and comprehension of our worlds," and what differences there are, according to Goodman, come down to rather specific differences in the characteristics of the symbols employed.

Claimed distinctions, for example, that science's goal is truth, while art is never tested against the truth, or that science accumulates knowledge, while art is for pleasure or for emotional release, fail upon examination, Goodman argues. Although we admittedly tend to restrict the notion of truth to symbol systems that are sentential, Goodman suggests that a broader notion of "aptness of fit"—"aptness in conforming to and reforming our knowledge and our world"—is equally applicable to aesthetic and scientific symbol systems. (Recall Reid's roughly similar idea mentioned above.) We also see here that Goodman has no fear of thinking of art in *epistemic* terms; in fact, the cognitive efficacy of aesthetic symbols is a source of knowledge in Goodman's view, much as we saw in Reid's case.

In the brief yet multi-theme excerpt of Putnam's, a number of interesting claims are made, if not elaborated upon and integrated. It will not do, Putnam remarks, simply to say that novels do or do not give knowledge (especially moral or psychological knowledge). No matter how profound, a novelist's insight is not *knowledge* if it is not *tested*. You cannot know what it was like to be a communist in the 1940s by reading Doris Lessing's *The Golden Notebook*, no matter how convincing and plausible you find that novel, unless you have some independent way of checking that account's truth. Hence, it is incorrect to say that *in reading* a novel, one *acquires* knowledge. At least one does not, through reading the novel, acquire a confirmed, tested claim or hypothesis.

We can, however, acquire the hypothesis, as it were. We have been presented with a certain *possibility* by the novel; it has shown us how things *would be* or *may be* if the "hypothesis" *were* true. Putnam is willing to consider a discovery of a kind of knowledge, though it is not knowledge of fact but only of possibility. He calls this *conceptual* knowledge. Novels are often highly valuable in giving us conceptual knowledge of difficult moral situations or complexities, and this kind of knowledge can be important in our practical reasoning, our reasoning about how to live.

Admittedly, this is "nonscientific" knowledge, but this is not any shortcoming blameable on literature—in fact, Putnam accuses the social sciences themselves of the shortcoming. In their desire to remain value free, their reluctance to take up questions of how we might possibly live rather than how we in fact live, the sciences have cut themselves off from our moral and practical reasoning. Putnam seems to be suggesting at the end of this piece that practical knowledge and theoretical knowledge should interpenetrate more. Such thinking may provide the means of "testing" that could convert the contributions of literature into empirical knowledge.

In "Fiction and the Growth of Knowledge," Novitz systematically describes the various things we may be said to *learn* from reading fiction, and it is, as he says, "a veritable medley" of attitudes, skills, values, and beliefs. We learn conceptual, cognitive, and imaginative skills, we absorb attitudes and values from seeing them embodied and elaborated on in fiction, we learn of different world views, and so on.

However, it is Novitz's view that the forming of factual beliefs and the acquisition of *propositional knowledge,* though they are a component, do not constitute a major component of what we learn from fiction. Novitz rather emphasizes practical knowledge and what he calls *empathic* knowledge.

Empathic knowledge is knowledge of *what it is like* to be in certain situations, or have certain experiences, what it *feels* like to be caught in the anguish of a moral dilemma or the treachery of deceit, for example. The power of fiction lies in its ability to create "worlds" or situations and give us a sense of what it is like to inhabit them. Empathic knowledge, then, appears to be a notion quite similar to Putnam's conceptual knowledge, although somewhat greater emphasis is placed on feeling here than with Putnam. There is nothing, for example, which prevents us from thinking of conceptual knowledge as propositional in nature, while Novitz clearly distinguishes empathic from propositional knowledge.

Bender is interested in further elaborating on the possibility that the arts can, among their many ways of functioning, act as sources of propositional knowledge. He tries to show that the usual analytic conceptions of knowledge, truth, and justification are compatible with the contention that we can come to know valuable truths of many different sorts through aesthetic appreciation of artworks.

In arguing for this claim, it is important to see the work of art, not as an isolated messenger or deliverer of the facts but as an object suspended in a complex epistemic web of beliefs and inferences of various sorts.

Perception, description, interpretation, and evaluation of art are all inferential procedures, without which there can be no understanding *of* art, nor any understanding *through* it. But once inferences of various degrees and to various kinds of conclusions are operating, it becomes an intelligible question whether one may warrantedly draw inferences from what is presented in an artwork, and from the way it is presented, to general propositions whose truth can be tested or confirmed by judging their coherence with other parts of one's background system of warranted beliefs. Bender suggests that at least in some cases the upshot of this procedure can make a legitimate claim to the term "knowledge."

Art and Knowledge

Louis Arnaud Reid

A philosophically familiar account of 'knowledge' is that if one believes a proposition and the proposition is true, and one is justified in believing it true, then one has knowledge. The 'justification' condition poses a difficulty (also familiar, and ancient). How does one 'know' that the justification justifies? By further justification? And the justification of that? There is a regress, *unless* one postulates that at some point one directly and intuitively 'sees' that the justification is a sufficient justification. This direct intuitive 'seeing' seems to be 'knowledge' in another sense.

If this is valid, it is important, because it shows that the opening statement above is describing not 'knowledge' in the most general sense, but one *kind* of knowledge, the discursively propositional kind, with its own presuppositions about truth. The major importance of this kind of knowing and knowledge no one in his senses would dispute; still, it is but one kind. And it is a kind that makes special, and limited, demands upon the personal mind. All knowing is a function of personal minds, and all knowledge, on one side of it, is, at some stage of coming to know and knowing, a personal experience, though once acquired, it becomes dispositional. The kind of knowledge which is expressed in propositional statements about matters of fact is of a kind, naturally, which focuses upon matters of fact, upon 'what is the case'. The focus is upon a certain kind of objectivity.

Because, as I have just said, all cognizing, all knowing, is a function of personal minds,

---

From *The British Journal of Aesthetics*, 25 (1985). Reprinted by permission of Oxford University Press.

so of course is discursive and propositional knowing. But since the purpose of it is objective and impersonal truth, 'public' truth which can be understood and shared (at least potentially) with other minds, one has to be on one's guard against subjective factors which might bias, obscure, or in any way conflict with what T. H. Huxley called the 'cold clear logic of the mind', or subjective misapprehensions of what may really be the facts. Such subjective factors as feelings, emotions, desires may have to be suppressed if they are in danger of distorting the apprehension of facts. This does not imply, of course, that feelings and emotions are necessarily absent from clear thinking about facts. The passionate excitements of great scientific discoveries are familiar enough. There can be 'aesthetic' delight in a 'beautiful' hypothesis. But for science itself it is the *intellectually* apprehended validity of objective impersonal truth which counts, and its contribution to the building up of systematic impersonal knowledge.

The domination of this account of knowledge, not just as one, crucially important, *kind* of knowledge, but as the paradigm of anything that has the right to call itself 'knowledge' in any serious sense, is overwhelming. It is an inheritance of our culture and is endemic in our culture and our ideas of education. If 'knowledge', or 'cognition,' or the 'cognitive' is mentioned, this image of it almost automatically springs to mind. There are, of course, claims to other kinds of knowing and knowledge—of values, moral or aesthetic, of other persons. We do say, with serious intent, 'He has deep moral insight', 'He understands his friend', 'His knowledge and understanding of music is masterly.' But all these claims, to the academic epistemologist whose model of knowledge is of the propositional-truth kind, are suspect. Scepticism is rife, and not merely about whether such claims are true or false, but whether 'true' and 'false' are relevant to the claims, whether 'knowledge' is the right word. Values are certainly linked in various ways to matters of fact; but values as such are not mere matters of fact. If so the propositional truth-criterion, that it 'states the facts' cannot be applicable.

Unless we are prepared to swallow, line, hook and sinker, the propositional-truth model as a paradigm for all 'knowledge,' the dismissal of these other claims to be knowledge seems dogmatic, sweeping, and far too simple. But further than that, I think it can be shown that the account of knowledge and truth *intrinsic* to the propositional view is in itself invalid, and that its invalidity is at the root of a false denial of truth-claims and knowledge-claims of other kinds of knowledge and knowing.

On the propositional view, truth is thought to *be* a relationship between statement and fact, and if there is to be knowledge a true statement must be made. Knowledge, on this view, is made dependent on the (supposedly) independent truth of propositional statements.

I think this is a mistake, even on the assumptions of the propositional theory of knowledge. Moreover, if we cling to this mistake, it seems perfectly clear that the way is closed to even a *prima facie* consideration of there being 'true' or 'valid' knowledge of art, or even degrees of it.

In elucidation of what I think is the 'mistake' of the propositional account of knowledge and truth, I return here to a book I wrote a long time ago—*Knowledge and Truth*, published by Macmillan in 1923. Reviewing critically a number of views then current (Coherence, American *New Realism*, S. Alexander's theory of truth and error, Russell's earlier and later theories, and 'Critical Realism'), I sketched a positive account of truth and knowledge which opened the way to recognizing what was called in the last chapter 'Non-propositional Truth,' referring specially to the arts. (I think now that some of my remarks about the arts there were crude. But I still hold that the substance of my theory of knowledge and truth is valid.)

Two main factors were criticized. One was general, that knowledge is *defined* in terms of propositional statements. The other was particular, that knowledge was defined in terms of the justifiable *truth* of propositional statements. Knowledge was being made dependent (almost a depend*ant*!) on the making of true statements. This, I thought, was putting the cart before the horse. The verbal—or other symbolic—statements of propositions are but the expression of something more basic, more fundamental, namely the mind's self-transcending power of being aware of a world which is not itself. It was not of course denied then (nor has it been denied now in this paper) that for a great deal of knowledge it is of the utmost importance that it should be expressed explicitly in verbal statements, and that this kind of knowledge could not be clearly grasped without it. But the mind's transcendent power, the everyday mystery, of being able to cognize, to *know*, is basic and central. It was this *living* fact, of which statements are one kind of necessary articulation, deposited publicly, as it were, in an already shared public language, that was central.

So that instead of making knowledge—even this kind of propositional knowledge—a function of the truth of propositional statements, I reversed it and said that truth is a function, or attribute, or quality, of the personal mind's living cognitive apprehension of the 'world' independent of mind. I used the metaphor of 'prehension' or cognitive grasping. Physically, when we stretch out to grasp something, we may get a firm hold of it, or we may fumble and slip. The metaphor of cognitive prehension was meant to suggest that when it was working efficiently, the character of the cognitive prehension was, in some degree at any rate, 'true,' and when working inefficiently, in various degrees false. Truth and falsity were, I suggested, finally characters of the living self-transcending cognitive activity of mind apprehending its object. The truth of propositions was dependent on and in part (though in part only) derivative from that. Truth was, therefore, ultimately adverbial rather than adjectival, the character of a successful self-transcending cognitive mental activity, rather than of a statement—however important in the realm of propositional knowledge statements may be.

The advantage of this view is that it opens up the way to understanding the knowledge-claims of different kinds of knowing and knowledge. The claim of the propositional form to be the paradigm of knowledge generally cuts us off from this. Knowledge of other persons, of moral values, of art cannot be reduced to impersonal statements 'that something is the case'. All knowledge, if I am right in what has so far been said, is, on one side of it, the possession of a person: 'truth' and 'knowledge' have no meaning apart from knowing human persons. Sometimes, in coming to know, there is the experience of coming to know; this becomes assimilated into dispositional knowing—present when we are asleep. In either case knowledge is the possession of a person.

This applies to propositional knowledge as well as to other kinds of knowing. But, as was suggested at the beginning, in propositional knowledge of what is the case, and in discursive knowledge generally, the feelings of the knower, though feeling of some sort is probably always present, are not directly relevant to the knowing of impersonal objective fact. But in other kinds of knowledge, they are not only relevant; they can be crucial. One cannot know, in any full sense, a friend, moral good or evil, works of art, without sensitive feeling. One may of course know many things *about* persons, moral values, works of art. And we may, and do, talk about all these things. But without a basis of direct experiential knowledge, in which the whole person (including the feeling person) is involved, sometimes very deeply involved, in the cognitive apprehension, we cannot even begin to know what we are talking about. In a good deal of propositional thinking we divide ourselves in two, the thinking part of 'mind,' analysing, detachedly surveying, with feelings and emotions largely quiescent. Other kinds of knowing—for example the knowing of art, are *holistic*, as cool discursive thinking in conceptual abstractions is not.

This difference is, incidentally, of great cultural and educational importance. If the detachment from feeling which is so necessary a part of discursive thinking is too exclusively pursued, becomes too obsessive, it can damage personal life irreparably. Darwin, speaking in grief of the atrophy of a part of his brain which to him seemed 'to have become a kind of machine for grinding general laws out of large collections of facts' complained that 'for many years I cannot endure to read a line of poetry.' J. S. Mill, reared from early childhood in habits of analysis, laments that his education acted like a worm both at the root of the passions and of the virtues, had undermined all desires and all pleasures, and had failed to create these feelings in sufficient strength to resist the dissolving influence of analysis. (There is an urgent message here for contemporary education!)

In the experience-knowledge of works of art, feeling and knowing are inseparable. To make this clearer, and because 'feeling' is a word very loosely used, and there is little agreement about use, I must say what I mean by feeling.

Psychologists earlier in the century—Ward and Stout, for example—defined feeling as hedonic tone positive or negative, pleasure or unpleasure. But though feeling may have hedonic tone, the identification of feeling with hedonic tone is far too limited and thin: it does no justice to the part which feeling plays throughout the whole of conscious life. To say for example that the purpose of art is to give 'pleasure' may contain some important truth. In itself it tells us nothing about art; and a hedonistic theory of art can lead us in exactly the wrong direction. We have to think again about feeling.

My own general theme is that feeling is an inseparable part of everything that happens in the conscious life of the psychophysical organism. A most important aspect of this is the relation of feeling to cognition.

Feeling, on one side of it, is the most immediate, the most private, the most intimate thing we know. 'I feel'; I feel, alone; alone, I feel. No one else can know my 'I feel.' And if I feel, I feel *something*. The something I feel is the process of human life becoming aware of itself, or as aware of itself. As I wrote in a paper[1] some years ago: 'Feeling is the immediate awareness of, potentially, the whole content of human experience as it is lived by a particular human being. Feeling is the immediate awareness, from the "inside," of conscious human experience in the widest and most usually accepted sense of that term, conscious experience which includes bodily sensations, actions of various kinds, thinking, imagining, willing, having moral and aesthetic experiences, perhaps religious ones, loving, hating, coming to know and coming to terms with the external world, ourselves and other people . . . Feeling is the immediate awareness of indwelling in that conscious life in its most inclusive sense. To symbolise the conceptual distinction between feel*ing*, the participle, be*ing* immediately aware, and its *content*, it is sometimes useful to use the symbols "IA" for the participles denoting the process or event of feeling or immediate awareness, and "C" to stand for the content of feeling. Feeling as it actually occurs is always IA(C).'

What I am saying here, that feeling's immediate awareness is 'cognitive,' is in contradiction to the current propositional view that we cannot be said to *know* anything unless we can state it under a named category or concept. I am merely implying, once again, that this is a too limited view of knowing and knowledge. The content of what we are immediately aware is unlimited, whilst the range of our categorial language is extremely limited. A few of the contents of our feelings can be named but only in a general way. Many are not, and some cannot be. The content of our cognitive feeling for art, for instance, can never be translated adequately into words or symbols other than those of the art itself.

Feeling is present throughout conscious life. But caution is needed here. This does not mean that we are focally conscious of it all the time. Usually we are not. Sometimes it is marginal, and sometimes it *seems* to be absent altogether—lacing one's shoes for example. Again, though we *can* be aware of feeling ourselves inhabiting our bodies, for the most part there is no such conscious awareness.

I am, then, *not* saying that we always feel ourselves feeling, are immediately aware of ourselves as immediately aware, or feel *that* we are feeling or being immediately aware. Sometimes we can be: and *afterwards* in retrospection we may be able to discern the presence of the factor of feeling of which we were perhaps not at all conscious at the time.

In the normal situation attention is not turned inwards but outwards. If, for instance, we are engaged in or attending to an interesting argument, or listening to a piece of fine music, our attention is completely absorbed in what is being attended to, the argument, or the music. The object of attention completely fills up the field. But though this is certainly true, and very important, retrospection, which we can carry out as self-conscious human beings, does not bear out any impression that there was no feeling present at the time. There was cognitive feeling, the 'feeling through' of the argument, the feeling through of the structured music. And there was affect. The argument was perhaps exciting, and we enjoyed it. In the objective, holistic absorption in the music, there was enjoyment, perhaps enraptured enjoyment.

It will be noticed that I am distinguishing feeling (I.A.) from *affect*. This is important, for in common psychological parlance 'feeling' and 'affect' are used indiscriminately as meaning the same thing. And because, as we have seen, the word 'affect' is used commonly to denote hedonic tone positive or negative, the identification of feeling simply with affect would take us back to the view I have rejected, that feeling just *is* pleasure-unpleasure. But feeling is not to be identified with affect, though it can *have* affect. And I am repeating that if so, the affect which feeling may have is not adequately described as hedonic tone, pleasure-pain—though the terms 'pleasure' and 'pain' do have some use as rough indicators. We all recognize what they mean. But they are far too general to give any idea of the unlimited range of the *concrete* qualities of affect. We have to remember that feeling (I.A.) is cognitive. If, as I have suggested, feeling is the immediate awareness 'from the inside' of all that goes on in conscious human experience, then the affect of feeling, inseparable from it, is as wide in concrete content as the range of human experience itself. To repeat, feeling is not, *qua* immediate awareness, identical with affect. Feeling is immediate awareness of human experience from the inside, and as such cognitive. As this, it *has* affect, sometimes. So, generalizing, feeling has (at least) two distinguishable aspects, the cognitive and the affective. If, sometimes, I speak of 'affective feeling' and 'cognitive feeling', this has to be understood as shorthand for feeling in its affective, or in its cognitive, aspect.

I have, so far, merely mentioned the *conative* side of mind—its interest, activity of striving, etc. But of course, since mind works as a unity, it is involved all the time, in all cognitive awareness whether of fact or value. Feeling, as I have suggested, plays a particularly important part at some stages in the knowing of values, both as affective and cognitive. In intellectual or matter-of-fact thinking affective feeling tends to be incidental, though in such activities we may often be said to be (cognitively) 'feeling our way,' positive hedonic tone encouraging us to proceed in the same direction, negative tone, perhaps, to pause and take stock. But in all this, though it is sometimes convenient to speak of cognitive feeling or perhaps of conative thinking, these are only shorthand expressions of an emphasis. It is not 'cognition' that knows. It is the whole person, the human psychophysical organism who apprehends through these modes of itself.

Though it is quite true to say that in every kind of knowing and knowledge it is the 'person' who experiences and possesses the knowledge, it may sometimes sound a little pompous, even sentimental, to insist on the word being used when the knowledge is of some simple or commonplace truth. If one does apply the word 'person' in speaking (correctly) of the possession of some obvious piece of propositional knowledge, it is only as a counter to the much too exclusive stress on the seemingly total neutral impersonality of propositional truth. But when we think of the knowing and knowledge of works of *art*, it becomes vital to stress the potential totality of the involvement of the person, and the direct intuition of the work in its complex wholeness.

The creation, and the discriminating understanding of given works of art, draws upon knowledge of many kinds, but all of them are conditions of, or subservient to knowing, knowledge, understanding of a kind which is unique, *sui generis*. The different kinds of knowledge and equipment are familiar to all experienced artists and critics, and can only be mentioned here and without elaboration, for they are highly complex and interrelated in ways far too subtle to be adequately described, even at length. And of course they vary as between the different arts. I have such things in mind as acute sense perception, intimate knowledge of, and (for the artist) ability to use materials and ability to use techniques of different kinds. Knowledge of art history, conceptual thinking, familiarity with the use of conceptual language in critical discussion, empathy, imagination . . . But none of them, or all put together, are sufficient. In the making of art and in the appreciation of given art, we address the work as a particular, not in the sense of its being merely a particular instance of a class (though it can, in conceptual language, also be an instance, say, of Post-impressionism), but as *this individual*.

At this stage, a new and unique kind of knowing and knowledge emerges, conditioned by what went before, but never sufficiently so conditioned. If we consider the process of artistic construction, we find that the conventional distinction between *knowing* and *making* breaks down, or is transformed in existential unity. It is true too that in discursive thinking (say in science) knowledge is achieved through constructive activity. Here also there is a 'knowing' through 'making.' In our attempts better to know the facts of the world we 'make' hypotheses, and our making is a necessary way of developing our knowledge and understanding of the world. But the difference between the union of knowing and making in (say) scientific knowing and in artistic knowing is that in science, making is in aid of getting a better (constructed) perspective of a world which independently *is*. The 'world' we seek to know better transcends the constructed instruments of understanding, whereas the created constructions of art are attended to aesthetically 'for their own sake,' for their (relatively speaking) 'opaque' intrinsic quality. Scientifically created constructions are instrumental as artistically created constructions are not. Making and knowing (and the made and the known) are for art, as I suggested, in existential unity.

One may emphasize another aspect of the same thing. The constructions of art are discoveries, but, paradoxically, they are discoveries of what was not, in any sense at all, 'there' before the process of creation began. In one sense or aspect, the creative activity of art 'makes' its reality—as scientifically creative activity does not make the independent reality of the world—and in the making 'discovers' the new thing made. The new thing made is, on one side of it physical (a picture, a piece of sounding music, dance . . . and of course there are the 'scores' for music, literature, drama, dance). The perceived physical is an essential factor in all the arts as traditionally understood: and *qua* physical it is matter of fact. But the *raison d'être* of art is of course not merely physical or factual, but imaginative rendering of *value*, the world of man and nature seen, felt, imagined, judged, by fully living persons. Art is imaginative symbolic embodiment in perceptual phenomena, in physical forms-as-perceived, of unlimited ranges of meaning (of different kinds and ranges in the different arts) as apprehended by the sensitive and imaginative minds of artists, and offered to us if we will (and can) espouse it. In its meaning-embodied, the riches of the physical and the spiritual are gathered in, transmuted, transsubstantiated, metamorphosed, so that the division between physical and spiritual is dissolved. Meanings are drawn in, transformed in aesthetic embodiment, and, as *embodied*, become *localized* in perceived space and time. Shakespeare, as usual, has said it:

The poet's eye, in a fine frenzy rolling,
Doth glance from heaven to earth, from earth to heaven;
And, as imagination bodies forth
The forms of things unknown, the poet's pen
Turns them to shapes, and gives to airy nothing
A local habitation and a name.
(Note the 'local'!)

What the artist discovers through making is not properly known till the making has been completed. Of course he often (not always) has ideas or some tentative general plan. But the concrete final form of his work is not known, and cannot be known, beforehand. There is not even a simple *telos* to guide him, as a craftsman may have a pattern to work to or a house builder a plan. If we are talking of creation—and in spite of the commonly cheap use of this word everywhere, art making *is* truly creative—we have to realize that the *telos* is changing all the time whilst the artist is working in dialogue with his medium. There is evolution whilst he works; and it is not simply the unfolding of a plan, but *creative* evolution. There is a parallel process, though not exactly so, in the experience of the *spectator* of given art. In the experiencing of a piece of music new to us, for example, we cannot, musically, come to know and understand it till we have heard it all to its conclusion, and in fact not until we have heard it a number of times and studied it—and even then only in a high degree if we are sufficiently musical. In musical understanding 'the end is in the beginning' and throughout every flowing part. It is an aesthetic organism in which every part is internally related to every other part and to the whole. The same kind of thing, *mutatis mutandis*, applies to other (so-called) non-temporal arts. It is equally true of pictures and sculptures—though this is often not recognized in practice as in a gallery we pass rapidly from one work to the next.

In considering the appreciation of art (as well as, in another form, its creation) there is, of course, the problem of *interpretation*. A presented structure engages the full attention and study of a person, in which his senses, imagination, thought, feeling cognitive and affective, perhaps emotion are involved with one another in this complex attention of the person to what is given. As personal it is and must be a private experiencing of the given object, but as directed to the object is self-transcending. The focus of attention is upon the work. But as the work is a complex phenomenon-as-apprehended-by-the-spectator, the 'interpretation' is *his* interpretation. A musical score, a complex presentation with many aspects, can be 'seen' to have different and musically viable interpretations by different masters. They are different because, since the musical composition is complex and *has* many aspects, this musician is bringing out certain aspects of the music, and that musician others. And, if we speak of an interpretation as being 'musically viable' (or artistically satisfying) we mean that the performer has created (he is the creator-after-the-Creator) an artistically organic unity based on his study of the composer's given score. This is not saying that the rendering is a good one because it corresponds exactly to the original composer's interpretation of his own music. That we do not know, unless indeed it happens that the composer is alive and is interpreting his own score. But even then—as composers have often admitted—another musician may bring out aspects of his music which he, the composer, had not fully realized. What counts, it would seem, is that the performing musician must study assiduously the composer's works (and not only the particular work he is to play), gather the composer's musical intentions as far as he can from the written score, and then perform it in terms of his (necessarily) personal understanding. The question then of its musical 'viability' may be put in the form: 'Does the interpretative playing of this particular piece of music artistically "come off?"' The answer must come in the first place from the artistic judgement of each competently sensitive musical listener. But such judgement must be put alongside other competent musical judgements. Though there will always be healthy disagreements, the consensus of competent critical judgements builds up through time a critical canon, a stabilizing, but never a final authority.[2]

The adequacy of artistic understanding is perhaps easier to judge in the case of a performative art like music, where performance is itself an art, or in the sensitive reading aloud of poetry, likewise an interpretative art, than it is in nonperformative arts. When looking at pictures or sculptures, or watching dance, we have to judge indirectly the adequacy of others' artistic understanding through their use of words, metaphors, perhaps by their gestures or the manner of speaking or other expressive bodily dispositions.

But it is clear that the 'objectivity' of the knowledge and understanding of art has to be *personally* judged. In this it can be contrasted, once again, with the objectivity of scientific knowledge and understanding. Here too there is personal judgement, particularly shown in the assessment of new theories. But validity and truth in science are in the end controlled by impersonal matter of fact, logical and empirical. In spite of the tentativeness (stressed by Popper and others) of scientific judgements, it is the factual foundation of scientific and other propositional statements of fact (and the extraordinary success of technology as applied science) which gives to propositional knowledge and truth its deserved prestige, and which also produces the mistaken *idée fixe* that this is the only respectably valid and true 'knowledge.' Judgements of value—including judgements of art—are suspect as knowledge because human values, whatever their (metaphysically speculative) status *qua* their *ratio essendi*, have their *ratio cognoscendi* not simply in logical reason or empirical matter of fact, but require, at least at some stages of their apprehension, a personally human feeling for them. One may accept, on authority, *that* to be compassionate is commonly reckoned a virtue, or *that* a Rembrandt self-portrait is said to be a great painting. But if one has never *felt* the goodness of compassion or the quality of Rembrandt's painting, one cannot know their intrinsic or inherent value. If one has not, cognitively and affectively, *felt*, in playing it or listening to it, the tremendously dramatic working up, from a simple and almost naïve beginning, the three-part fugue in Beethoven, Op. 110, one cannot have fully *known* it. It is not, as I mentioned at the beginning, speaking of science, that there is an intellectual apprehension *and*, perhaps, an emotion about it. The cognitive-affective feeling is intrinsic to the knowing and understanding. Knowing about pure matters of fact, as we have been saying, involves, relatively speaking, only a part of one's self. Knowing of value, and here particularly the knowing of art, which calls on all the resources of the psychophysical person, is essentially holistic. It is knowledge, but far more than knowledge; it is one of the supreme forms of life.

NOTES

1. 'Feeling, Thinking, Knowing,' *Aristotelian Society Proceedings* (1976–7), pp. 165–84. In this quotation I have slightly modified the original.
2. A remark of Aaron Copland is apposite here. Commenting on how performances of his work may vary, he says: 'But each different reading must in itself be convincing, musically and psychologically—it must be within the limits of one of the possible ways of interpreting the works.' Aaron Copland, *Music and Imagination* (New York: Mentor Books, 1952). The quotation is taken from the typescript of a paper by Carl Hausman, 'Insight in the Arts.'

Interpretation in Science and in Art

Harold Osborne

I

I have always been a bit sceptical about the value that is ascribed to the amateur analyses of linguistic usage with which it has become customary to preface philosophical discourse. Everyday language is not a model of consistency and philosophers are not always experts in linguistic matters. Nor is it always the case that a distinct concept lurks tantalizingly concealed beneath the general acceptation of a word; there is more often than not a range of indeterminacy, a penumbra of uncertainty. Nevertheless, or perhaps for this very reason, it will be helpful as a guide to what I mean to discuss in this paper if I first eliminate some of the main uses of the word 'interpret' with which I shall *not* be centrally concerned. In doing this I shall take note of points made in papers read at the symposium of the New York University Institute of Philosophy on Art and Philosophy in 1964.[1]

The basic meaning of 'interpret' is, then, to elucidate or, in the words of Monroe C. Beardsley in his opening paper on 'The Limits of Critical Interpretation,' 'verbally to unfold or disclose' the information encoded in any

From *The British Journal of Aesthetics*, 23 (1983). Reprinted by permission of Oxford University Press.

communication be it in written or spoken words, gestures, smoke signals or pulses of light from a laser beam. In this paper Beardsley laid down the two principles that interpretation is essentially connected with meaning and that a person who offers an interpretation of anything tacitly claims correctness for it. Both these principles no doubt apply pretty generally in ordinary life although, as will be seen, considerable modification is necessary in connection with the fine arts. Interpretations of works of art are valued, not so much for correctness, as for their validity and perspicacity.

The translation of a message from one language into another is a special case of this basic usage and although we no longer employ the verb in this sense, we still speak of a person who translates the spoken word as an 'interpreter.' In the fine arts translation in a rather wider sense is a matter of far-ranging importance, for a considerable part of criticism is concerned precisely with the attempt to convey the message or meaning of a work of art in prose language. And, although this is not part of my present purpose, it is interesting to investigate the somewhat similar constraints which apply when attempts are made to reproduce the 'spirit' of a work of art in a different sensory medium as, for instance, colour-music or dance interpretations of music or drama.

It should be noted that implicit in this basic usage is an assumption that a communication of which an interpretation is offered does have a meaning and that the interpretation is correct or incorrect in relation to that meaning. The meaning is determined by the common conventions operative in that mode of signalling, for example the rules of a language. It need not be identical with the meaning intended by the signaller for the signaller may have made mistakes in encoding the meaning he intended to convey or he may have been imperfectly versed in the mode of signalling used. In this context—again in contrast with the fine arts—it is regarded as a defect, the defect of ambiguity, if a communication allows of a multiplicity of meanings. But explicitness must not be confused with superficiality or ease of apprehension. Meaning may be profound or difficult of access without being ambiguous. Kant was often both obscure and profound. Spinoza's writing was perspicuous though his meaning was often profound. These principles and assumptions may be admirably illustrated from the medieval Christian heresies, which usually purported to be correct interpretations of passages in the Bible but were condemned by others, who believed that the interpretations were false. Both parties shared the assumptions that the Bible is not ambiguous and that it has a true meaning although that meaning is often difficult to come by.

The word carries a still more extended meaning when historians and newsmen are said to interpret events by putting them into a wider context, indicating what they signify or portend or explaining their occurrence by pointing to what Stuart Hampshire called 'weak causal dependencies' among them. Similarly a man's behaviour or mental state may be interpreted by attributing hidden motives or finding hidden causes. As an example of this usage, in his review of Dr Phyllis Greenacre's Freud Anniversary Lecture 'The Quest for the Father' (1963) Peter Medawar contrasted the psychogenic and psychoanalytical 'interpretations' of Darwin's illness proposed by Sir Arthur Keith, Dr Edward Kempf and others with the 'interpretation' of Professor Saul Adler, who attributed it to the little known Chagas disease.[2] In his paper 'Types of Interpretation,' Stuart Hampshire also mentions this kind of interpretation, saying: 'A psychoanalyst is par excellence an interpreter.' Reverberations of this extended usage are also to be found in the literature of the arts, as when an artist's biography or beliefs are adduced for the supposed elucidation of his works.

In the main, however, when we come to the interpretation of works of art we enter a very different mental landscape. We are accustomed to speak of interpretations by critics and also in the performing arts a performer is said to 'interpret' or 'give an interpretation of' a composition by his rendering of a musical or choreographic score or a part in a drama. The assumption that the object to be interpreted has or should have a single meaning in relation to which the interpretation is correct or incorrect no longer holds good in these contexts. When the notion of meaning is recognized at all in connection with the fine arts it is pretty generally believed nowadays that works of art, including poems and literary art in general, contain a multiplicity of valid but not always completely compatible meanings which become apparent only in the course of time and not all of which were consciously known to the artist or intended by him. Among others Roman Ingarden made a point of this in his doctrine of concretization. Some suggested meanings will be dismissed as false on the ground that they involve misapprehensions of the 'spirit' of the work or misreadings of the text. Many others may be accepted as plausible and some as illuminating. We assess this kind of interpretation for its insight and interest rather than for correctness. It is not assumed that there is one only 'true' interpretation and it is regarded as a merit not a defect in a work of art if it is replete with an abundance of meanings which are thus gradually disclosed. This, for example, is the major difference between poetry and prose, between writing which appeals to the attention as art and writing which does not.

The function of interpretation in art criticism depends on the view that is taken of art itself. Beardsley distinguished two extremes, which he called the Significance Theory and the Immanence Theory respectively and between which most other theories lie. According to the Immanence Theory works of art are to be attended to for their intrinsic qualities alone, including of course their expressive qualities, and any attention to external reference disturbs the aesthetic attitude which is proper to their appreciation. Lacking external reference they also lack meaning or significance, and since interpretation is linked to the elucidation of meaning the interpretation of works of art is, according to this theory, either impossible or improper. The theory is rarely maintained in its most rigorous form, although it is widely believed that artistic meaning can at best be approximated but cannot be precisely formulated in prose discourse. The Significance Theory allows of interpretation but imposes the necessity to distinguish interpretation from description. The distinction is a fine one and aestheticians who have applied themselves to the matter are far from agreed exactly where the line of demarcation should be drawn.[3] The arguments advanced to show on the one hand that all works of art, however abstract, do have external reference and on the other hand that no works of art, even literary works, have external reference *qua* art are fascinating in their ingenuity if something less than convincing. But I want to suggest that their interest is quite esoteric, a private corner in the philosophers' playground. Not even the most sensitive critic, let alone his readers, cares a rap whether his remarks are more properly called descriptions or interpretations. What matters is whether they are enlightening and whether they further appreciation of the art work.

A distinction is sometimes drawn between interpretation of a score or text and interpretation of the work, whether by the critic or by a performer. But since the text or score is usually our only clue to the meaning of the work, such a distinction is without practical import. There can be no interpretation of a score which is not an interpretation of the work except for purely technical explications of the conventions of coding used—which may, of course, have their own importance.[4] The work itself is represented by a perduring text or score consisting of encoded instructions for performance and has no independent existence apart from the series of performances arising from these instructions. To express this philosophers say that individual performances are tokens of a type, but this formula does not enlarge our understanding of the importance of imprecision in allowing latitude to talented performers for bringing to light new meanings and shades of meaning in scores which others have interpreted differently. Except in the case of such electronic music as is recorded once for all instead of being scored, musical scores are imperfectly specific. Even when a metronome reading is given, variations in tempo are only vaguely indicated by such terms as 'accelerando' and retardando, variations in loudness by 'crescendo,' 'diminuendo,' etc., and timbre merely by the mention of the instrument to be used. Indications of phrasing are loose and everywhere scope for interpretation is open for the performer. Choreographic and dramatic scores are still less specific. Only with film drama is a single synthetic performance recorded and perpetuated as 'the' work. Thus interpretation enters into the very being of most works in the performing arts.

In this area the renderings of different performers bear an obvious analogy to the 'readings' of a poem. But it is an analogy with a difference. In contrast to the imprecision of musical and choreographic scores it is assumed that the meaning or meanings of a poem are inseparable from the actual words of which it consists together with their immediate and more distant associations, their subtle implications, their sonorous rhythms, etc. All this is regarded as germane to its meaning, which is intrinsic to the words in the way that the meaning of a non-iconic work of abstract visual art is intrinsic to its actual forms. Therefore, it is held, a poem cannot be successfully paraphrased or translated into another language.

Having thus rapidly run over these various common uses of 'interpret' I now come to two equally familiar senses of the word which it will be the main purpose of this paper to discuss and compare.

(i) A representational artist—which, of course, includes all literary artists—is said to 'interpret' nature or human nature by the manner in which he presents that segment of experienced or imagined actuality which forms the subject of his work. Henri Matisse, for example, once said that 'even when an artist consciously departs from nature he must do it with the conviction that it is only the better to interpret her.' And he added: 'Underneath the succession of moments which constitutes the superficial existence of things animate and inanimate and which is continually obscuring and transforming them, it is still possible to search for a truer, more essential character which the artist will seize so that he may give to reality a more lasting interpretation.' In this usage of the word the work of art becomes the interpretation instead of being the subject of interpretation. It is with the way in which the work interprets its subject that I shall henceforward be concerned.

(ii) In a similar if even more extended sense scientific theories are referred to as interpretations of actuality. To quote one example of this, the astrophysicist David Layzer wrote: 'If we regard the Cosmological Principle as an approximate description of that part of the universe we have so far been able to observe, what shall we say about the universe as a whole? To refuse to make any assumption at all is to abandon any attempt to interpret cosmological observations or to understand the connection between locally unaccelerated frames of reference and distant matter.'[5]

In the former of these usages artists are said to 'interpret' when they impose a coherent *perceptual* order upon a segment of perceived or imagined actuality or when they bring such a segment within a *perceptually* ordered structure. In the latter scientists are said to 'interpret' when they bring a section of experienced facts or observations within the ambit of a coherent *intellectual* structure, usually mathematically expressed, with still wider implications. It is the object of this paper to probe this analogy further in the hope of discovering whether it can lead to a deeper understanding of either or both of these activities.

II

The theoretical sciences interpret the world by bringing order and regularity into the kaleidoscopic variety of experience, subduing its vagaries in the interest of understanding. A scientific theory is an intellectual construct consisting of a few basic concepts united by fundamental principles which are assumed to have general validity. From these axioms are deduced theorems which are then tested against a new range of experience to which they point. Experienced fact and observation are the ultimate criterion of all theory. Therefore, as Karl Popper liked to emphasize, to be useful, indeed to be properly called scientific at all, a theory must be falsifiable by fact. No theory can be definitively proved empirically for there may always arise new facts by which it is controverted. But unless it is in principle falsifiable, it cannot be validated by conformity with known experience.

Then besides the fact that it is not falsified by known experience, the acceptability of a scientific theory is measured by its lucidity for the understanding, its comprehensiveness or scope and its predictive power or fertility in leading to new avenues of knowledge. The ultimate aim is to unite all knowable facts within one all-embracing theoretical system which displays the maximum simplicity and elegance. As Einstein once said: 'It is the grand object of all theory to make these irreducible elements (i.e. the fundamental axioms and postulates) as simple and as few in number as possible, without having to renounce the adequate representation of any empirical content whatever.'[6]

The basic principles and the concepts with which contemporary science works are not deduced from experience or reasoned out by logical rule but are mental creations reached intuitively against a background of highly specialized experience. As Einstein again said: 'There is no logical path to these laws: only intuition, resting on sympathetic understanding of experience, can reach them.' And further: 'Experience may suggest the appropriate mathematical concepts, but they most certainly cannot be deduced from it.' Max Planck's quantum hypothesis, which he himself called 'an act of sheer desperation' arising from his work on black-body radiation, was described by H. R. Pagels in his book *The Cosmic Code* (1982) as 'an incredible leap of intuition . . . one of the great leaps of rational intuition.' On more than one occasion intuitive insights have led to predictions which were afterwards verified by observation. The most famous case was Einstein's own attribution of the deflection of light in the neighbourhood of a massive body to the curvature of space. Other examples are de Broglie's suggestion of the wavelike behaviour of elementary particles, Pauli's exclusion principle and Yukawa's prediction in 1935 of the pion, which was first discovered in 1947.

Of course the work of creative imagination was not foreign to traditional science. There is, for example, no such thing in experience as a dimensionless point, a line without breadth or a plane without thickness. But we do have visual experience of an end, an edge, a surface and three-dimensional solidity, and by abstraction and extrapolation from these we can picture the basic concepts of Euclidean geometry. With rather more difficulty we can visualize the elements of Lobachevskii's geometry of the surface of a sphere. But it is otherwise with the mathematical concepts of modern physics. We can come to terms intellectually with the idea of a three-dimensional universe which is both finite and unbounded; but we can form no visual analogue of Einstein's hypersphere, while the idea of an infinite dimensional vector space is completely opaque to concrete imagination. We know curvature in space but curvature *of* space lies beyond the powers of human imagination. The apparent paradoxicality of an elementary constituent of matter which behaves both as a discrete particle and as a wave is not mitigated by any possibility of calling up a concrete perceptible analogue, the more so when we hear that the wave is not a wave in any substance but, as Max Born first suggested, a wave of probability. In fact it seems likely that we can conceive probability itself only negatively as the absence of detailed knowledge. The metaphors of modern science (waves, particles, fields, forces, etc.) are generally taken from the field of perception but they are metaphors which defy perceptible application in their scientific functions.

Scientists are not unaware of these things, but they are concerned with the understanding and are overwhelmed by the novelty of discovery. In his book *Other Worlds*,[7] Paul Davies said: 'There is no everyday counterpart of a "wave-particle", so the microworld is not merely a Lilliputian version of the macroworld, it is something qualitatively different—almost paradoxically so. In this strange world of the quantum, intuition deserts us, and seemingly absurd or miraculous events can occur.' It has become common form to speak of the 'schizophrenic behaviour' of elementary particles and J. E. Dodd warns of the 'constant challenge to shrug off our everyday imaginings in the microworld and learn to think in terms of these unfamiliar ideas.'[8] Even an innovator of the stature of J. A. Wheeler applied to contemporary physics what Gertrude Stein once said of modern art: 'It looks strange and it looks strange and it looks very strange; and then suddenly it doesn't look strange at all and you can't understand what made it look strange in the first place.'[9] One can indeed habituate oneself to new conceptions, train oneself to manipulate strange ideas by the equally strange laws of logic implicit in them, but only at the expense of creating a world of thought isolated from the common world of experience. By confining attention to verification within the esoteric experience of the laboratory and the observatory one may constrain oneself to feel at home with strange and novel concepts, but to do so helps in no way to bridge the gulf between this new world of physical science and the world of common life and percipience. The prevailing indifference of scientists to perceptibility in the choice of their metaphors—for example the use of colours and tastes for the classification of imperceptible quarks—emphasizes this divorce between the two worlds. And this divorce is certainly a major reason why what is the most important revolution that has ever taken place in man's understanding of the world in which we live has made so little impact on the general and artistic imagination of our time. In no previous age has scientific belief played so small a part in fashioning contemporary outlook or the direction of poetic imagination. Even the minor genre of science fiction wallows in the shallows of projective technology. The advances in certain areas of science have brought about a schizophrenic outlook, the beginnings of a mental sickness that bids well to spread more widely. And if the comparison which I am attempting to institute between the two modes of interpretation serves to highlight this dangerous gulf, its main purpose will be served.

III

As the scientist creates ordered conceptual systems, working for the extension of understanding and incidentally for the greater powers of control over the environment which understanding can bestow, the artist creates perceptible[10] constructs each with its own perceptible beauty, working for the enhancement of percipience, the enrichment of perceptual experience, and adding to the cultural heritage of mankind. The representational artist makes a recognizable depiction or description of a segment of the phenomenal world, real or imagined. This is what is meant by calling his work representational. He also brings into being a perceptible construct which claims appreciation as an aesthetic object in its own right. This is what is meant by calling it a work of art. The conditions for success are that it shall have sufficient individuality to stand apart as something unique in its kind, sufficient complexity to sustain attention at a high level of voltage and sufficient perceptual unity to be contemplated as a single presentation.

Perceptual unity is an elusive notion which can be little more than adumbrated here. It must not be confused with simplicity or with coherence for analytical understanding. Compare a landscape from classical antiquity with one by Poussin or Constable. The former displays, typically, a collection of natural objects without visual cohesion. A river-god may stand for a river, a mermaid tower over a trireme, and so on. Naïve art and the art of children often exhibits a similar incoherence. What we dignify with the title of landscape art, however, not only depicts an assemblage of natural objects but presents a visually coherent structure of colours, shapes, directional lines, etc., with emergent properties which dominate and give character to the whole. Provided the latter is achieved, a measure of incoherence in the represented material is permitted. Similarly, to be accepted as a work of art, a still life must be more than a haphazard collection of edibles set before edacious Dutch eyes. It is a coherent composition made distinctive by the sort of emergent properties which give character also to non-iconic abstract art. A portrait is more than an accurately depicted assembly of individual features; by its own emergent properties it helps to interpret character and personality. Often indeed we apprehend perceptual unity by becoming aware of the emergent properties of the greater whole. For just as a simple melody may have qualities of liveliness, tenderness or melancholy which do not belong to the individual intervals of which the melody is composed but lend unity and character to the whole melody, so a more complex work, if it is to be successful as a work of art, must be unified by characterizing emergent qualities, giving distinctive individuality to the whole thing. It is this possibility of being perceived not merely as a collection of items, whether representational or not, but as a coalescing and coherently compact whole that enables it to expand vision and extend our perceptual powers. Otherwise, as in life generally, we perceive isolated 'bits,' relating them together theoretically instead of perceptually, and percipience remains meagre and desolate.

Within the constraints imposed by this general requirement for perceptual unity there is unlimited scope for variety of interpretation. Although in the past the depiction of reality has been the predominant motive of those who have made and those who have commissioned works of art, the modern outlook of course no longer regards representation as a necessary condition at all except in the case of literary and dramatic art, where it is a built-in feature. And when works of art *are* representational, exactness, verisimilitude and completeness of detail are no longer considered an artistic merit, while originality and insight are prized more highly. Despite the partial perpetuation of national styles and other representational conventions most—perhaps all—works of acknowledged artistic excellence display some distinctiveness and originality in their ways of looking at what they represent. Some artists and schools (Caravaggio, Spanish *tenebrismo*, Velazquez, Manet) emphasized the light/dark dimension of colour while others (Seurat, Signac, Pissarro) made this dimension recessive and gave prominence to structures of unmodified hue. One could enumerate such conventions of representation endlessly and within them all artists of distinction have had their personal ways of interpreting that which they depicted. There seems to be no logical necessity why this must have been so. Much Chinese art theory valued originality less highly than adherence to the practices of the past and medieval European theory set most store by the emulation of antiquity. But so it has been in more recent Western judgement and here is to be found the element of truth in the common affirmation of representational artists that their work is a form of self-expression.

One of the more powerful if less obvious instruments of interpretation in the hands of the artist is to endow his works with aesthetic or emotional qualities which are then, if the works are representational, reflected upon the subject of representation. Thus a forest pool might be depicted as peaceful and calm or as sinister and strangely threatening. In this way representation itself becomes interpretation. Inherent characteristics of ordinary things may be brought to prominence—as was done by the Kitchen Sink school and by some Pop art—and people may thus be induced to notice and *see* what they had hitherto taken blindly for granted. Alternatively scenes and objects may be presented with qualities of aesthetic beauty (or ugliness) which they are not usually seen to possess or with an emotional aura that grips the observer's attention as strange and unexpected. Language is meagre of words with which to express and discriminate finer shades of aesthetic flavour or emotional complexion. These qualities of things can be brought to attention only through art and by art alone can people be helped to richer and more sensitive experience of their world. By the powers of interpretation open to the arts aspects of the world can be communicated which could not otherwise be described and by their powers of interpretation the fine arts widen and enrich men's perceptual experience of their world.

Human beings are not yet completely stereotyped. Individuality persists and is reflected in our attitudes to our fellowmen and our common world. So long as these are not regimented to a stereotyped uniformity, individual sensibility will continue to achieve its culminating expression in the arts of representation. Science by contrast eliminates from its purview whatever cannot be reduced to rule.

IV

Having given some account of the ways in which science and art go about interpreting their material, I will now in this final section attempt to highlight the more important comparisons and contrasts between them.

(i) Both the artist and the scientist bring new order into the world, responding to a basic human compulsion.

The aim and the justification of the fine arts reside in their capacity to exercise and extend the powers of percipience. In the disciplines of pure mathematics, logic and metaphysics the claims of the intellect are paramount. In the theoretical sciences the goal is understanding for the satisfaction of our intellectual curiosity about the universe in which we live. A scientific theory is a mental product which may have its own beauty of coherence, lucidity, elegance and scope. Scientists have often shown themselves to be highly sensitive to intellectual beauty in their theories.[11] But, as has been shown, this value is secondary to that of relevance and all scientists are aware that the dividing line between a scientific theory and a non-scientific speculation is that between a theory which is testable against the actuality of experience and that which is not. This is inherent in our conception of what science is. And those theories which do not pass the test are abandoned, however beautiful they may be. Lamarck's theory of evolution was described by Schrödinger as 'beautiful, elating, encouraging and invigorating,' but untenable because it wrongly assumes that acquired characteristics are physically inheritable.[12] Dennis Sciama said of Hoyle's 'steady state' theory of the universe that 'it is very beautiful but it is now in serious conflict with observation.' Unlike the pure mathematicians, no scientist is interested in producing theories of however great beauty which will turn out to be not in keeping with the facts of observation or barren of further discovery.

By contrast the artist, with the help of craftsmanship, brings new things into being, adding to the contents of the perceptible world. Unlike those of the scientist, his products are subject to no criterion of relevance. Although they may carry many and important extra-aesthetic values, as art they are assessed solely by their own perceptible beauty, that is by their qualities of unity, coherence and complexity, which are the measure of their power to extend and enlarge percipience. If the work is representational, the artist's creations will inevitably interpret that section of the world, real or imaginary, which they represent. But this is not essential to their being as art and when works of art *are* representational neither exactness nor completeness of correspondence are criteria of their excellence. Nevertheless vigour and delicacy of interpretation are one of the more important extra-aesthetic values which works of art may possess. As science can alert and nourish men's intellectual curiosity, art can by this means induce them to cultivate a more sensitive and satisfying experience of their world.

(ii) Arising from the above is the fact that a scientific theory once formulated and accepted is in principle common property, not varying from man to man; but in the arts interpretation is always subjective, carrying the stamp of the artist's personality. It is an expression of his individuality, for others to acclaim or deplore. This is why works of art do not become obsolete when new ones are created as do scientific theories.

(iii) While much routine work is involved in working out the implications of scientific theories and then testing them, and much craftsmanship goes into the production of works of art, both originate in an act of creative insight which cannot be reduced to rule.

Despite the canons of beauty which have existed from the time of the ancient Greeks and theories of symmetry based on the Golden Section which have been propounded since the Renaissance,[13] the principles of order which underlie perceptual beauty cannot be brought within the purview of theoretical understanding. There are no theoretical, no mathematically expressible rules for the creation of works of art and it is not possible to analyse with scientific rigour in what their beauty consists. Every work of art is the result of a separate creative act, however much calculation may have followed or preceded that act, just as the fundamental concepts of a scientific theory are reached by an act of creative intuition. This holds good whether the work involves highly personal or mainly traditional modes of interpretation.

If the principles of perceptual order cannot be rationalized, neither do the concepts of the contemporary physical science lend themselves to perceptual imagination. The mathematical ideas of particle physics cannot be concretely imaged and the metaphorical language in use leads to paradox or contradiction if removed from its mathematical and experimental background. Even the magnitudes in which science now deals evade imaginative grasp. We can understand, but there are few if any people who can realize concretely, the difference between five million and three billion years ago on earth. The difference between a distance of a hundred million light years and twenty billion light years away from earth can be understood theoretically but cannot be apprehended concretely. A popular exposition of particle physics contains the statement that 'in familiar units, a typical nuclear diameter might be, say, 0.000000000000006 meter . . .' and that the time it would take for light to cross a typical nucleus is '$2.0 * 10^{-23}$ sec.' If a few '0's' were added or removed, it would make no difference to imaginative apprehension, although these things are not opaque to a trained understanding.

This chasm between the two modes of apprehension, perceptual cognition and analytical understanding, has increased out of all measure in the present century and is a major reason why the unprecedented advances in knowledge that modern science has so rapidly achieved have made little if any impact on the popular or artistic imagination of the age. Artistic imagination remains impoverished and deprived, no longer able to give concrete expression to what is most typical of our time, though scientists are not similarly impeded from contact with what art has to offer.

(iv) Although imagination of its own kind plays an indispensable role in the origination and elaboration of scientific theories, science has no place for the imaginary in the sense of what might be but is not. In the interpretations offered by the arts, however, this makes a major contribution. By inventing fictional, even impossible, situations the arts widen men's experience, engendering new and more sensitive attitudes with which to face the realities. They create possibilities of emotional and perceptual experience which life does not otherwise afford except to the very few. And in its own way this too amounts to interpretation. Through its enrichment of personality aesthetic experience is no longer divorced from life.

(v) As has been said, science *is* interpretation, and scientific interpretation is open and invariant for every man who has learned to comprehend the formal language in which it is expressed. If such men are now few, this does not invalidate the principle. Art on the other hand has a twofold function. Its primary purpose is to create new objects for the exercise of aesthetic awareness. The interpretation of existing reality is secondary and not essential—though some artists, such as Malevich, Gabo, Kandinsky and Mondrian, have thought that their non-iconic abstract works were interpretations of fundamental, non-perceptible features of cosmic reality. The ability to appreciate the products of the arts is not common to all men even in principle. It is a perceptual *skill* which arises from a special ability often restricted in its ambit and always needing to be cultivated and trained. Without the cultivation of the appropriate skill the kinds of interpretation embodied in the fine arts remain a closed book.

(vi) The most radical difference between the kind of interpretation provided by the sciences and that with which the fine arts are concerned depends upon the nature of their respective subject-matter and is at once so obvious and so far-reaching that it often escapes specific mention. It is the outcome of what historians of thought describe as a movement from quality to quantity. From its origins with Galileo and Newton modern science pursues its aims by dealing with abstractions. It limits itself to those aspects of things which can be quantified, banishing all else beyond its orbit. The theories and the formulae apply, but apply only to those aspects of experience which can be reduced to number. In his address to the Physical Society of Berlin on the occasion of Max Planck's sixtieth birthday Einstein said: 'As regards his subject-matter, on the other hand, the physicist has to limit himself very severely; he must content himself with describing the most simple events which can be brought within the domain of our experience; all events of a more complex order are beyond the power of the human intellect to reconstruct with the subtle accuracy and logical perfection which the theoretical physicist demands. Supreme purity, clarity and certainty are attained only by the sacrifice of completeness . . . .' This aspect of scientific method is familiar also to those who are interested in the new technologies of microelectronics. In his book *The Silicon Idol* (1984), for example, Michael Shallis quotes René Guénon: 'The chief characteristic of the [scientific] point of view is that it seeks to bring everything down to quantity, anything that cannot be so treated is not taken into account and is regarded as more or less non-existent.' It is this which explains the dominant position given to statistics from quantum physics to molecular biology, to psychology, to economics and the sociological sciences. It is important indeed to bear in mind that the profound insights and the surprisingly deep understanding achieved by science are restricted in their scope to those aspects of things which can be quantified, that is, to those features which are common to a multiplicity of individuals, and that in the human and sociological sciences the results mimic a pseudo-precision only by the suppression of the individual and immediate. For what can be quantified is that only which is common to individuals in the mass while concrete individuality is reduced to a cipher.

Contrary to this, interpretation in the arts is supremely individual and concrete. Not only is every work of art the outcome of an original creative event, although works of art are sharable objects, every act of appreciation is private and personal. It cannot be communicated in ordinary language. This is why books on art history are so dull. Works of art cannot be described and the interpretations of the world which they carry are too concrete to be put into words, for language is the conceptualization of experience. Yet the arts bring back into life the richness and variety which scientific understanding has abstracted from the world. Their interpretations are less useful for the practical manipulation of the environment but they are more immediate, more precise, more concrete, like the contacts of persons with persons.

NOTES

1. See Sidney Hook (ed.), *Art and Philosophy*, Columbia University Press (1966).
2. The review is reprinted in Peter Medawar, *Plato's Republic* (1982) with the title 'Darwin's illness.'
3. See, for example, Charles Stevenson, 'Interpretation and Evaluation in Aesthetics,' in Max Black (ed.), *Philosophical Analysis* (1950) and W. E. Kennick, *Art and Philosophy* (1964), p. 498.
4. I have in mind such works as Stanley Boorman (ed.), *Studies in the Performance of Late Medieval Music* (1964).
5. David Layzer, *Constructing the Universe* (1984), p. 255.

6. This and the following quotations from Einstein are from the essays and addresses incorporated in A. Einstein, *The World as I See It* (Eng. Trans., 1935).
7. Paul Davies, *Other Worlds* (1980), p. 75.
8. J. E. Dodd, *The Ideas of Particle Physics* (1984), p. 23.
9. John Archibald Wheeler and Wojciech Hubert Zurek (eds.), *Quantum Theory and Measurement* (1983), p. 185.
10. Here and elsewhere in this paper I use the word 'perception' and its cognates to cover all forms of direct apprehension, including apprehension of the intellectual beauty of scientific or philosophical theories as opposed to theoretical 'knowledge about.'
11. See H. Osborne, 'Mathematical Beauty and Physical Science,' *The British Journal of Aesthetics*, Vol. 24, No. 4 (1984).
12. Erwin Schrödinger, *Mind and Matter* (1958).
13. See H. Osborne, 'Symmetry as an Aesthetic Factor,' *Computers and Mathematics with Applications* (1985, The University of Connecticut).

Art and the Understanding

Nelson Goodman

In saying that aesthetic experience is cognitive experience distinguished by the dominance of certain symbolic characteristics and judged by standards of cognitive efficacy, have I overlooked the sharpest contrast: that in science, unlike art, the ultimate test is truth? Do not the two domains differ most drastically in that truth means all for the one, nothing for the other?

Despite rife doctrine, truth by itself matters very little in science. We can generate volumes of dependable truths at will so long as we are unconcerned with their importance; the multiplication tables are inexhaustible, and empirical truths abound. Scientific hypotheses, however true, are worthless unless they meet minimal demands of scope or specificity imposed by our inquiry, unless they effect some telling analysis or synthesis, unless they raise or answer significant questions. Truth is not enough; it is at most a necessary condition. But even this concedes too much; the noblest scientific laws are seldom quite true. Minor discrepancies are overridden in the interest of breadth or power or simplicity.[1] Science denies its data as the statesman denies his constituents—within the limits of prudence.

Yet neither is truth one among competing criteria involved in the rating of scientific hypotheses. Given any assemblage of evidence, countless alternative hypotheses conform to it. We cannot choose among them on grounds of truth; for we have no direct access to their truth. Rather, we judge them by such features as their simplicity and strength. These criteria are not supplemental to truth but applied hopefully as a means for arriving at the nearest approximation to truth that is compatible with our other interests.

Does this leave us with the cardinal residual difference that truth—though not enough, not necessary, and not a touchstone for choosing among hypotheses—is neverthe-

From *Languages of Art* (Indianapolis: The Bobbs-Merrill Co., 1968). Reprinted by permission of the publisher.

less a consideration relevant in science but not in art? Even so meek a formulation suggests too strong a contrast. Truth of a hypothesis after all is a matter of fit—fit with a body of theory, and fit of hypothesis and theory to the data at hand and the facts to be encountered. And as Philipp Frank liked to remind us, goodness of fit takes a two-way adjustment—of theory to facts and of facts to theory—with the double aim of comfort and a new look. But such fitness, such aptness in conforming to and reforming our knowledge and our world, is equally relevant for the aesthetic symbol. Truth and its aesthetic counterpart amount to appropriateness under different names. If we speak of hypotheses but not of works of art as true, that is because we reserve the terms "true" and "false" for symbols in sentential form. I do not say this difference is negligible, but it is specific rather than generic, a difference in field of application rather than in formula, and marks no schism between the scientific and the aesthetic.

None of this is directed toward obliterating the distinction between art and science. Declarations of indissoluble unity—whether of the sciences, the arts, the arts and sciences together, or of mankind—tend anyway to focus attention upon the differences. What I am stressing is that the affinities here are deeper, and the significant differentia other, than is often supposed. The difference between art and science is not that between feeling and fact, intuition and inference, delight and deliberation, synthesis and analysis, sensation and cerebration, concreteness and abstraction, passion and action, mediacy and immediacy, or truth and beauty, but rather a difference in domination of certain specific characteristics of symbols.

The implications of this reconception may go beyond philosophy. We hear a good deal about how the aptitudes and training needed for the arts and for the sciences contrast or even conflict with one another. Earnest and elaborate efforts to devise and test means of finding and fostering aesthetic abilities are always being initiated. But none of this talk or these trials can come to much without an adequate conceptual framework for designing crucial experiments and interpreting their results. Once the arts and sciences are seen to involve working with—inventing, applying, reading, transforming, manipulating—symbol systems that agree and differ in certain specific ways, we can perhaps undertake pointed psychological investigation of how the pertinent skills inhibit or enhance one another; and the outcome might well call for changes in educational technology. Our preliminary study suggests, for example, that some processes requisite for a science are less akin to each other than to some requisite for an art. But let us forego foregone conclusions. Firm and usable results are as far off as badly needed; and the time has come in this field for the false truism and the plangent platitude to give way to the elementary experiment and the hesitant hypothesis.

Whatever consequences might eventually be forthcoming for psychology or education would in any case count as by-products of the theoretical inquiry begun here. My aim has been to take some steps toward a systematic study of symbols and symbol systems and the ways they function in our perceptions and actions and arts and sciences, and thus in the creation and comprehension of our worlds.

[The symbolic characteristics symptomatic of aesthetic systems that Goodman refers to here are discussed more extensively by him in the selection reprinted in Chapter 7 above.—Eds.]

NOTE

1. See my "Science and Simplicity" in *Philosophy of Science Today*, ed. S. Morgenbesser (New York, Basic Books, Inc., 1967), pp. 68–78.

Literature, Science, and Reflection

Hilary Putnam

In a world in which revealed books no longer command general acceptance, very few people would deny that scientific knowledge must play some role in the resolution of moral problems on both a social and an individual level. But it is easy to be puzzled about what role literature can and should play. At the same time, the social and psychological sciences tend to disappoint us. Thus we tend to be at once disillusioned with science and unclear as to the bearing of literature. I suggest that until we arrive at a better view of moral reasoning than we have recently been fed, we will not be able to arrive at any kind of reasoned consensus as to what either literature or the sciences can contribute to our deepest concerns. . . .

It seems to me wrong either to say that novels give knowledge of man or to say categorically that they do not. The situation is more complicated than a single simple affirmation on either side can suggest. No matter how profound the psychological insights of a novelist may seem to be, they cannot be called *knowledge* if they have not been tested. To say that the perceptive reader can just *see* that the psychological insights of a novelist are not just plausible, but that they have some kind of universal truth, is to return to the idea of knowledge by intuition about matters of empirical fact, to The Method of What is Agreeable to Reason. To take some examples of novels less difficult than Dostoevsky's: if I read Celine's *Journey to the End of the Night* I do not *learn* that love does not exist, that all human beings are hateful and hating (even if—and I am sure this is not the case—those propositions should be true). What I learn is to see the world as it looks to someone who is sure that hypothesis is correct. I see what plausibility that hypothesis has; what it would be like if it *were* true; how someone could possibly think that it *is* true. But all this is still not empirical knowledge. Yet it is not correct to say that it is not knowledge at all; for being aware of a new interpretation of the facts, however repellent, of a construction that can—I now see—be put upon the facts, however perversely—is a kind of knowledge. It is knowledge of a possibility. It is *conceptual* knowledge.

It may seem strange to describe something as real and 'empirical' as a vision of how humans behave and of what 'makes them tick' as *conceptual* knowledge; but that is all it is unless it is tested, if not scientifically, at least tested in the actual experience of intelligent and sensitive men and women. Thinking of a hypothesis that one had not considered before is *conceptual* discovery; it is not empirical discovery, although it may result in empirical discovery if the hypothesis turns out to be correct. Yet the 'knowledge of a possibility' that literature gives us should not be knowledge of a *mere* possibility. That the possibility Celine holds before us *is* a 'mere' possibility is, after all, one of the reasons we do not rate Celine higher than we do as a novelist. So again the situation is complicated, there are both empirical and conceptual elements in the knowledge we gain from literature.

From *Meaning and the Moral Sciences* (Boston: Routledge and Kegan Paul, 1978). Reprinted by permission of the publisher.

But, it may be objected, the novelist's 'hypothesis' is not subject to scientific testing. It is not that *sort* of hypothesis. This is often, but not always, true. If Celine were right—if all apparent instances of love were really disguised self-interest of the most selfish kind—I have little doubt that one could find empirical evidence for this of many kinds. Perhaps the difficulty here is that operationists have convinced too many people that all scientific hypotheses bear their testability on their face, and hence that any statement that it is not obvious how to test cannot be in the sphere of science at all. But this is a gross caricature of science, even if it is one that many scientists have been taught to believe. Very often the genius of a scientist lies precisely in thinking of a way of testing a statement that did not seem testable at all.

To take a different, and more plausible, example than Celine: it is one of the virtues of *The Golden Notebook* that it presents an extremely plausible account of how it felt to be a communist in the 1940s. Yet it cannot be said that after reading it one has acquired *knowledge* of what it was like to be a communist in the 1940s, unless one has some independent source of knowledge that Doris Lessing's account is factually true. You may feel convinced upon reading *The Golden Notebook*; you may say to yourself *this is what it must have been like*; but unless you want to substitute subjective plausibility and conformity with What is Agreeable to Reason for answering to the objective facts and being shown by adequate evidence to so answer as the criteria for 'knowledge,' you have no right to say 'I *know* that this is what it was like.' You do not *know*; and the very next week you may be convinced by an equally plausible novel that it must have all been entirely different from Doris Lessing's description.

There is, however, something Doris Lessing does in *The Golden Notebook* which is very important and whose value does not depend on the correctness or incorrectness of her description of the British Communist Party (although it does depend on the correctness of her description of how that Party was perceived, and on the correctness of part of her criticism of the communists—that they were totalitarian and manipulative, for example). She represents to us a certain moral perplexity, a problem or a group of moral problems, some of them connected with being a woman in the present century, some of them connected with being a person with a social conscience in the present century, as that moral perplexity might have been felt by one perfectly possible person in a perfectly definite period. What I am suggesting is that if we want to reason rationally about feminism, communism, liberalism, or just about life in the twentieth century, then what Doris Lessing does for our sensibility is enormously important.

To think of the novel itself as presenting us with some kind of nonscientific knowledge of man is making it all somehow too much like *propositions*. I said at the outset that there is a sense in which there is such a thing as 'nonscientific knowledge of man'; moral knowledge, if not 'nonscientific knowledge of man' in the sense of the people just alluded to, is practical knowledge of how to live; and practical knowledge is not 'scientific' in the sense of being theoretical knowledge. Moreover, practical knowledge . . . involves our full capacities of feeling and imagination. . . .

Literature somehow ties up with a kind of knowledge which is close to the centre of moral concern and which is not 'scientific knowledge' in any reasonably standard sense. But saying that literature 'gives' nonscientific knowledge of man makes the matter too simple.

Just as some thinkers tend to view literature as knowledge, so today other thinkers tend to view science as a philosophy. The tendency to view science as a philosophy is an understandable one. Many traditional philosophical questions—for example, the infinity of space and time, and the nature of space, time, and matter—have been abandoned to physics, by most realistically minded philosophers. At most, the professional philosopher hopes to be able to clarify the results the physicist obtains. The social sciences are, for many reasons, in a less impressive state than the physical sciences; but here there is already the hope if not the achievement—the hope that social and psychological science may one day shed some real light on the nature of society and man. Certainly few philosophers from any perspective would today write about justice without considering the bearing of economic theory, or about the parts of the psyche without considering psychological theory. But if science is a philosophy, it suffers from being all metaphysics and no ethics; and metaphysics without ethics is blind. Social science often seems sterile precisely because it is interested in the mere description of what we have in the way of society now, and not in the possibility of a society which is at once feasible and just; and psychological science rarely discusses man in society, or the possibility, in *any* society, of ways of life which are at once moral, feasible, and rewarding.

I am not urging that science should be pursued only for practical ends or only for moral enlightenment. Of course, knowledge for its own sake is and should be a 'terminal value' for educated men and women. But I contend that even the *philosophical* significance of science, let alone the practical significance, becomes hard to see without distortion when science and moral reflection are as sharply separated as they have become in our culture.

Relativity theory bears on the nature of matter, space, and time, to be sure; but it also bears on the whole nature and possibility of human certainty, for example. The overthrow of Euclidean geometry was not *just* the overthrow of a theory of space. Euclidean geometry was the paradigm of certainty attained through *a priori* reasoning, and, more than that, the paradigm held up to the moral philosopher by Plato as well as by Spinoza. Understanding the role played by the ideal of certainty in our intellectual and moral life for over two thousand years and considering carefully the implications of its demise for moral (and social and religious) argument as well as for pure science is not incompatible with appreciating Relativity 'for its own sake'—in fact it is inseparable from doing this properly. And much of the emptiness of current social science arises from the attempt to study social and psychological questions with an entirely false ideal of 'objectivity' which misses even the connections of the social sciences with each other, in addition to missing the questions of the greatest importance to moral reflection.

One caution is in order, however. Dropping false ideals of 'objectivity' does not mean viewing all social science from the standpoint of getting the world out of the mess it is in during, say, the next hundred years. Important as that is, it still falls far short of the ultimate question, which is not how to make individual reforms—even reforms as big as 'socialism'—but *where* do we want to go?

Let me try to summarize these somewhat ranging reflections. I have not tried to demonstrate in this paper that emotive theories of ethical discourse are wrong or that ethical relativism is wrong. That is a subject for technical philosophical papers. I have indicated that, in my opinion, these fashionable and by now widely disseminated philosophical views are wrong, and that some ethical principles at least are likely to have a large measure of objectivity. I have suggested, following the lead of Judy Baker and Paul Grice, that the 'objectivity' of ethical principles, or, more broadly, of 'moralities,' is connected with such things as width of appeal, ability to withstand certain kinds of rational criticism (which I have not tried to spell out), feasibility, ideality, and, of course, with how it actually *feels* to live by them or attempt to live by them. I have also pointed out that moral knowledge is what philosophers call 'practical knowledge' as opposed to theoretical knowledge, and that imagination and sensibility are essential *instruments* of practical reasoning. My purpose has not been to defend these views here, but to see what difference these views make, if they are right, not for philosophy but for literature and science.

I have contended that the idea that morality is just 'subjective' and the corollary idea that moral reasoning is either just instrumental (concerned with the selection of means to *arbitrarily* selected ends) or else a contradiction in terms, is terribly destructive not just for morality itself but for all of culture. We can only understand the way in which the literary imagination does really help us to understand ourselves and life, on the one hand, and the way in which science does really bear on metaphysical problems on the other, if we have an adequate view of moral reasoning, where, by moral reasoning, I mean not just reasoning about duty or virtue, but moral reasoning in the widest sense—reasoning about how to live.

Fiction and the Growth of Knowledge

David Novitz

Perhaps the most obvious legacy of the Enlightenment is the widely held belief that empirical science alone can furnish us with useful knowledge about the world. Any claim to knowledge which is not based on, or amenable to, scientific enquiry is generally regarded as bogus, as a kind of quackery to be shunned by all who are not simple-minded or superstitious. David Hume, as a figure of the Enlightenment, persuaded his heirs that the deductive arguments of traditional metaphysics, while perhaps logically certain, were empirically vacuous. On his view, if our claims about the world were to be properly founded and justifiable, they would have to be derived not from deductive system-building, but from sense experience. On this view . . . the fanciful imagination turns out to be no more than a source of error which, if relied on, will lead to the total destruction of human nature.

We are already acquainted with the romantic reason to all of this, and we have seen how easily it tumbles into an untenable idealism. Perhaps because they are reassured by the failure of romantic metaphysics,

Anglo–American philosophers of this century continue, for the most part, to speak of the growth of knowledge only in the context of scientific enquiry. As a result, those working in the wake of Popper and W. V. Quine have tended to concentrate on the growth of propositional (or sentential) knowledge, as if to suggest that it is the only knowledge that matters, or, still worse, that it is the only knowledge that grows.[1] This tendency has not only hampered the epistemological enterprise, but has encouraged many to ignore the products of the fanciful imagination, and especially works of art, as a potential source of knowledge. As I have already intimated, my aim . . . is to reverse the trend, and I shall do so [here] by attending to one art form in particular, namely, fictional literature.

LEARNING FROM FICTION

Novels are typically regarded as works of fiction, but it is well known that not all statements in a novel need be fictional. Some may be assertions about the actual world—assertions that, if true, afford knowledge of that world. Others, however, express the author's creative or fanciful imaginings. They express fabrications, inventions, fantasies, and are

---

From *Knowledge, Fiction and Imagination* (Philadelphia: Temple University Press, 1987). Reprinted by permission of the publisher. Footnotes have been renumbered.

properly regarded as fictional statements. If they cohere, they will describe and delineate what I shall call a "world" of the author's imagining—a fictional or an imaginary world.[2] Attentive readers who understand the text of a fictional work will derivatively imagine this world, and may very well be moved by what they imagine.

It is of considerable interest that readers who respond to fiction in this way frequently claim to have learned something from the fiction. The claim is not merely that they have acquired knowledge about the fictional work and its imaginary world, but that they have learned something about the actual world in which we live. Not only does fiction impart knowledge of the real world, we are told, but it helps us to understand and to come to terms with what would otherwise be baffling. It imparts insights, skills, and values of one sort or another, and in so doing helps us to see the world differently.

That we learn about our world from fiction seems clear enough. The problem is to know how this is possible, for if fictional statements are not true of the world we inhabit, it is difficult to understand how we can learn about the world from such statements. And while there have been many attempts to answer this question, even a cursory glance at the literature reveals a tendency for explanation to cease at the very point at which one might have expected it to begin.[3] Although I cannot examine this literature here, it would seem that one reason for this failure is that many theorists uncritically suppose that there can be only one way in which we learn from fiction. This assumption compels them to explain a range of diverse phenomena by appeal to a single principle, and what better way of doing so than with the help of unexplained metaphors and obscure expressions?

It goes without saying, though, that there are many different things that one can learn, and that they are not all learned in the same way. One does not learn tennis in the way that one learns history; nor does one learn science in the way that one learns to be moral. Similarly, since there is a number of different sorts of things that one may learn about the world from fiction, it seems unreasonable to suppose that they must all be learned in a single way.

What is it that we learn from fiction? First, I think it plain enough that people sometimes acquire propositional beliefs about their world from the novels and stories that they encounter. Such beliefs—propositional beliefs about the furniture of the world and what has happened in it—I shall call factual beliefs, and it is clear that some of these beliefs may be true and others false. Hence we may say that in learning from fiction we sometimes acquire true or false factual beliefs. Of course, the mere acquisition of a true factual belief does not amount to the acquisition of propositional knowledge. It is only when we are justified in believing that p that we can appropriately be said to know that p. And although I shall have more to say about the process of justification later on, it is my claim that in learning from fiction we can acquire propositional knowledge about our world.

Of course, as I have already hinted, factual beliefs and propositional knowledge are by no means the major component of what we learn from fiction. As we know from the many censorship boards all over the world, it is possible to acquire certain values or attitudes from fictional works. These may, of course, affect and be affected by one's beliefs, and will at times be integrally related to them.

In addition, it should be stressed that a good deal of what we learn from fiction is practical rather than propositional or attitudinal. We often acquire not just factual beliefs and values, but also a range of skills from the novels that we read. These skills fall into at least two classes. First, there are skills of strategy. A favorite hero may furnish us with purely practical strategies for handling a tricky situation: strategies which we may adopt when we find ourselves in a similar situation. Alternatively, a fictional work may impart intellectual strategies by enabling us to take more aspects of a problem into account, and in this way to think more comprehensively and efficiently about it. In the latter case fiction extends our thinking by drawing to our attention previously unconsidered aspects of a problem.

The second class of skills, however, does not merely extend our thinking, but radically alters it. Fiction may impart what, for want of a better term, I shall call conceptual or cognitive skills: skills which offer radically new ways of thinking about or perceiving aspects of our environment. Novels and plays, we shall see, may enable us to place new and helpful constructions on an otherwise baffling array of events. They enable us to see old and familiar objects in a radically different light. In this way, fiction may help us to notice qualities of, or relations between, objects, persons, and events where these were previously unnoticed.

Finally, fiction often enables its readers to acquire beliefs about, indeed knowledge of, what it feels like to be in certain complex and demanding situations. Empathic beliefs and knowledge of this sort are derived from, and have to be explained in terms of, our awareness or experience of what is sometimes termed a direct object. A feature of such awareness is that it is irreducibly nonpropositional, in the sense that it cannot be captured or adequately conveyed in linguistic descriptions. For instance, no matter how precise and vivid my descriptions are, they will never acquaint you with my feelings as an orphan, or with the strains of Mozart's *Te Deum*, K. 141, or with the anguish of a moral dilemma. In these cases we often say that one can come to know Mozart's music only by listening to it, or that one does not know what it feels like to be bereaved until one has, in one way or another, experienced bereavement.

I have already explained how our imaginative involvement in fiction allows us to respond emotionally or feelingly to the tribulations and triumphs of creatures of fiction. It is as a result of these experiences, I can now add, that we often come to hold certain beliefs about what it must feel like to occupy situations akin to those of our favorite heroes and heroines. Such beliefs are invariably nonpropositional. They are derived from felt experience and are about the felt nature of the experiences which we can expect to have in certain other situations. Consequently, if I am right, they cannot adequately be conveyed by description. This is not to say that such experiences are never brought under concepts. It is only to say that the expression of such concepts in language will not serve to convey beliefs about what it actually feels like to have these experiences. It is such beliefs that I have dubbed empathic, and if they turn out to have some basis in, or to cohere with, our future or past experiences, they will pass as empathic knowledge.[4]

It would seem, then, that we learn many different things from fiction. We acquire factual beliefs, propositional knowledge, values, attitudes, and skills of one sort or another, as well as empathic beliefs and knowledge. . . .

SKILLS FROM FICTION

It would seem, then, that readers acquire factual beliefs and propositional knowledge from fiction in much the way that scientists gather knowledge about the fabric of the universe. Both rely extensively on hypotheses and their corroboration. The only difference is that scientists can and do invent their own hypotheses, whereas readers of fiction are very much less inventive. They merely borrow the fabrications of authors, and their sole contribution is to conjecture or hypothesize that these fabrications apply to the actual world. This difference aside, though, it would seem that I have reduced the epistemology of fiction to that of science, and that I therefore regard the acquisition of factual beliefs and propositional knowledge in each case as fundamentally similar.

To some this must appear implausible. We learn from fiction, we are told, in a way which is much richer than the mere dispassionate formulation and testing of hypotheses.[5] We become involved in the fiction, "caught up in" it, we "lose ourselves" in the lives and situations of its creatures. We "identify" with them, share their hopes, fears, and joys. This, we are told, contributes to and enhances the learning experience. Since I have so far ignored this dimension, the view is taken that my account of learning from fiction must be inadequate.

Although there is considerable substance to this objection, I want to insist that my account so far is incomplete rather than seriously defective. Until now I have attempted only to explain the acquisition of factual beliefs and propositional knowledge from fiction. These, I have argued, are not acquired analogically or inductively, but are the products of certain speculations induced by the fiction. Now, if one believes, as I do, that a speculative, conjectural, or fanciful element is essential to the growth of our body of empirical knowledge and beliefs, then, in this fundamental respect at least, the acquisition of factual beliefs from fiction will resemble their acquisition in science. If this is what is meant by the claim that I have "reduced the epistemology of fiction to that of science," then I must remain entirely unrepentant.

Nonetheless—and here the objection hints at something important—factual beliefs form only a minor and relatively insignificant component of what we learn from fiction. Fiction is not, for the most part, a source of propositional beliefs and knowledge about the world. We consult encyclopaedias and chemistry, geography, and history books, not novels and plays, when we require such information. Certainly fiction is often lauded as a source of insight and knowledge, but a closer look reveals that it is praised for the practical and empathic knowledge that it affords and seldom, if ever, for propositional knowledge. From fiction, I have said, we may acquire certain strategic and conceptual skills (practical knowledge); and we may learn what it feels like to be caught up in certain situations (empathic beliefs and knowledge). It is when we ask how all of this is possible that we are forced to tell a story which is very different from the one told in the case of factual beliefs and propositional knowledge: a story, moreover, which emphasizes our imaginative and emotional involvement in the fiction.

There can be little doubt that readers often respond to fiction by imagining the various events and situations described by an author. Tolstoy's words, one might say, become the occasion of a reader's imaginative entry into the world of his fictional creatures; one derivatively imagines the world of Anna Karenina by considering Tolstoy's descriptions without a mind to their truth-value. In other words, one considers what it is like to be caught up in Anna's situation, one considers her quandaries, her perplexities and moral dilemmas, and arguably as a result, one is able to experience the dread and hopelessness of her situation. Such a reader may very well acquire certain empathic beliefs about what it is like to be in this or a similar situation. It is partly as a result of these beliefs, I now wish to argue, that the reader is able to acquire certain skills from the work.

How is this possible? Well, consider the following example.[6] Suppose that I want to retrieve a ball which has lodged itself in the upper branches of a walnut tree. I gaze upward trying to fathom which branches will best provide a foothold and which a secure grip. Clearly, if I can imaginatively re-create the situation—that is, if I can "see" myself in my mind's eye moving from this branch to that, holding here and stepping there, and if I can imagine what it feels like to stand on a high, swaying branch while reaching for a ball, I will not only have some idea of, but will have developed what is in effect a complex hypothesis about, what it is like to be in such a situation. To the extent that I assent to this hypothesis, I may be said to have acquired certain empathic beliefs about what it is like to retrieve a ball from the upmost branches of a tree. Not only do these beliefs allow me to construe my predicament in a certain way, but they also allow me to develop plans of action appropriate to it. I will now attend to what I believe are the likely difficulties in the situation, the possible risks, and I will try to conceive of ways of avoiding them.

Of course, the best-laid plans can and do go awry, and in this case I could break my neck simply because my imaginings, and the empathic beliefs derived from them, are wayward and inaccurate. As a result I acquire a range of inappropriate expectations about my task, and this, of course, is the key to failure. Usually, though, our imaginings are guided and constrained by what we already know, and if the resultant empathic beliefs cohere with present or past experiences, we will be tempted to rely on them. They will be used as a foundation on which to base our understanding of, and our actions in, the situation. Those of us, therefore, who have climbed the masts of sailing ships, or have clung to a rope off the Caroline Face of Mount Cook, are better placed to gauge the accuracy of beliefs about what it is like to retrieve a ball from the upmost branches of a tree. Such persons can claim a certain insight into the situation—an understanding bred both of their imaginative involvement in it, and of their past experience.

My claim, of course, is that much the same thing happens when we respond imaginatively to fiction. Readers of *Anna Karenina* do not only imagine or re-create the heroine's quandaries, but given sufficient interest, they actually ponder and explore them. They imagine what it is like to be assailed by such problems, they feel the fright and despair that accompany them, and, arguably as a result, they are able to discern their overwhelming complexity.

Clearly, then, those readers who are curious enough will have at hand a set of hypotheses about what it is like to be ensnared in a situation akin to Anna Karenina's. Like all hypotheses, these may tentatively be projected onto the world, and if they enable us to make sense of specific events and situations, they will most likely be adopted or believed. Empathic beliefs of this sort will no doubt be assessed in terms of the extent to which they cohere with our past and future experiences. If they do cohere with our past experience, with what we already know or believe of people in similar nonimaginary situations, we will not only regard the action of the novel as plausible, but we might even claim to know what it would be like to be in a situation such as Anna's. Still more, empathic beliefs of this sort will mediate a reader's assessment of the risks involved in the heroine's various responses to her predicament, and from time to time such readers will no doubt offer solutions of their own, which are then tentatively imposed on the fictional situation in order to assess their adequacy. As we saw in the case of our vagrant ball, readers who engage in this imaginative activity acquire what might be termed a set of practical hypotheses: that is to say, they have at their disposal a range of possible ways of responding to, or negotiating, a certain sort of problem.

Needless to say, though, not all of these envisaged responses will be adequate to the problem. Indeed, some may be rejected without ever being tried in practice, rather in the way that, after further consideration, one rejects potential moves in a game of chess. Others, however, will be put to the test. If found wanting, they will simply be abandoned, but if they are helpful they will be tried on successive occasions, will eventually come to be relied upon, and will be adopted as proven strategies.

Clearly, then, if the problems which confront fictional characters are seen to arise in the actual world, any reader who has acquired empathic beliefs pertinent to such problems may well be more aware of, and hence more sensitive to, the difficulties involved in solving them. If this turns out to be the case, we are justified in saying that the fiction has imparted empathic *knowledge* of the situation, that it has given readers a "pretty good idea of," or enabled them to know something about, what it feels like to be ensnared in such a situation. . . .

My argument has been that it is our imaginative participation in the fiction which furnishes us with empathic beliefs, and, partly as a result, with a set of practical hypotheses for tackling similar quandaries in the actual world. Such hypotheses may amount either to possible ways of *considering* such problems, or they may amount to possible ways of *tackling* them. Either way, they help furnish practical rather than purely propositional knowledge and belief. . . .

THE EXPLORATION OF VALUES

And what of values? At least part of the charm and fascination of fictional literature resides in the fact that it forces us to look anew at, and to reconsider, certain of our attitudes and values. All sorts of values are up for scrutiny—economic, ecological, intellectual, architectural, religious, and moral values are only some that become candidates for exploration and reassessment. Nonetheless, moral values enjoy a certain primacy, and it is these that I am concerned with at present.

Fiction, I think it true to say, often explores, teases, and tests our moral standards and attitudes. Occasionally a work will undermine attitudes, confound our moral beliefs, and instill new or different moral values. And in such situations a reader can properly be said to have learned something from the fiction. No doubt there will be those who think that the acquisition of values never amounts to the acquisition of knowledge, and that such learning can therefore have little to do with the topic of . . . fiction and the growth of knowledge. But such an objection is premature. Even though I cannot argue the case here, it seems that we can know that certain actions are right or wrong. Certainly we often claim to know this, just as we often claim to know how we ought to behave. Equally important for my argument is the fact that we can and do come to know that to make a moral decision in a certain situation is often complicated and difficult. We can come to know, too, that we are no longer as certain as we once were about our moral attitudes; and, of course, we can come to know that we have revised these attitudes. Such knowledge, I now want to argue, is often acquired from fiction, and is acquired in a number of different ways.

First of all, we know that factual beliefs are often integrally related to values, so that to acquire a factual belief from fiction is, on occasions, to acquire a value of one sort or another. If, as a result of seeing Athol Fugard's *Marigolds in August*, I come to believe that the South African political system dehumanizes black people, I thereby acquire a certain moral attitude toward that system. I think of it as wrong, iniquitous, or unjust. As a result I now know that I have a particular, perhaps a revised, moral attitude toward the South African political system.

There is, though, an altogether different way of acquiring values from fiction. Suppose, for instance, that in the light of Defoe's *Robinson Crusoe*, I come to think of isolation no longer as unproductive and arduous, but as a spur to human resourcefulness. Now, if I set great store by the latter, if I value it highly, I am very likely to place a similar value on isolation, which I now see as promoting human resourcefulness. Of course, such a transfer of values need not always be something of which I am aware. I might simply discover that my attitude toward isolation has changed, and, on reflection, I might locate *Robinson Crusoe* as the source of that change. It should be stressed, too, that I need not transfer my values in this way at all, and that whether I do will depend on what I happen to know or believe. Thus, for instance, if I believe that isolation is responsible for much human suffering, or that it is inconducive to good mental health, I am hardly likely to value it very highly, no matter how highly I regard human resourcefulness.

There clearly is a sense, then, in which *Robinson Crusoe*, rather than pontificating on the virtues and ills of human loneliness, invites us to reconsider, explore, and test our current attitudes to isolation. The best fiction, or at least the fiction which earns the most praise, seldom pronounces decisively on moral issues. It does not offer dogmatic or authoritative solutions to problems of value. Rather, as we shall see, fiction is often at its most exciting, and instructs us most adequately in matters of value, when it explores moral problems and brings its readers to see them in their fullness and complexity. And this brings us to a third—perhaps the most important—way of acquiring values from fiction.

The comprehending reader, I suggested earlier, imaginatively re-creates the fictional world delineated by an author, and in so doing "enters into" the life of that world. We consider what it is like to be faced with the problems which confront the hero, the villain, the school master and his mistress. We share their fears, elation, and sadness, and the tears that we shed are bred of a close and intimate understanding of their situation. Step by step we explore their quandaries, their dilemmas, the consequences of their untoward actions, and, as we saw earlier, the resultant empathic beliefs and knowledge enable us to develop strategies for negotiating similar situations in the actual world. Not only this, for readers are also in a position to grasp the extent and force of the moral problems that assail fictional characters ensnared in such situations. They are able, for instance, to appreciate the extent to which Raskolnikov becomes a victim of circumstance, and they are made acutely aware of Anna Karenina's anguish in having to choose between alternative courses of action.

It is plain, I think, that when once we involve ourselves imaginatively in Anna Karenina's world, we become acquainted not only with the complexities, but also with the exigencies, of her situation. As a result we are brought to consider the extent of her duties and obligations, and in so doing we invariably ponder the moral question, "How ought she to behave?" It is in attempting to answer this question that our own values are held up for scrutiny and reassessment, and it goes without saying that our answer to the question will determine whether we retain these values.

Clearly, then, whatever the values extracted from the fiction, it is not as if Tolstoy instructs us in morality or imposes his own moral values on us. Rather, he brings us to reconsider our existing values and attitudes by tempting us to apply these to a complex and very lifelike situation, which he has sketched in abundant detail and with consummate skill. If a reader believes that his or her values are adequate to the fictional situation, they will merely have been reinforced by the novel and will remain unaltered. At times, though, one may come to believe, indeed know, that one's attitudes are unsatisfactory: that they do not do justice to the complexity of the situation. As a result there is a shift or alteration of values. One might acquire new, very specific, moral principles, or, rather more likely, one may modify existing principles or their application in the light of the fiction. Thus, for instance, one may now believe, even know, that adultery is not always as wrong as one had previously supposed; or one may believe that one ought always to acquaint oneself with the facts of an adulterous situation before venturing to judge it.

Of course, fiction is not the only source of new or altered values. Actual experience of the real world can have a similar effect, for when one is ensnared in a morally complex and demanding situation, one's attitudes and values are invariably called into question. The difference is that fiction allows us to do so with minimal cost to ourselves and others. Our vicarious concern for a favorite heroine, the moral judgments we make about her and the moral decisions we take on her behalf, the scorn and derision, the praise and blame that we heap upon her, can all occur without the anguish and painful consequences that are often attendant in the actual world. We acquire moral insights without having to live in the situations which occasion them. What is more, they are insights which are often more easily acquired from fiction than from their actual counterparts. A narrative sequence can be so designed as to give us much more knowledge about a complex fictional situation than we could reasonably hope to attain if ensnared in its nonfictional equivalent. Thus, for instance, when reading *Crime and Punishment* we do not only see matters from Raskolnikov's point of view, but from that of Sasha and Razumikhin as well. It would, of course, be very difficult for a man guilty of a crime such as Raskolnikov's in the actual world to adopt so broad a perspective.

There clearly are a number of different ways in which we acquire values from fiction. In my view, it is when readers become imaginatively "caught up in" the fiction that it best allows them to explore and reassess their values. And this, it seems, is an important aspect of fiction, for in fostering reasoning of this sort, fiction helps sharpen our sensitivity to moral issues and increases our awareness of the sorts of quandaries and difficulties encountered by people who would otherwise be the victims of ill-considered judgments. Good fiction, it is sometimes said, explores the human condition, but this, Hilary Putnam correctly contends, is just another, somewhat more pretentious, way of saying that it explores the moral problems and dilemmas which many of us experience in our actual lives.[7] Its worth here is to be found not just in imparting values, but in getting its readers to grasp the difficulties involved in adequately judging certain human situations.

CONCLUSION

In all, there is no one way in which we learn from literary works of art. There is, rather, a *pot-pourri* of ways, a veritable medley of methods, for acquiring beliefs, knowledge, skills, and values of one sort or another. Each of these methods needs careful scrutiny, and while I take myself to have pointed to some of their salient features, much work remains to be done.

One thing that must now be apparent is that propositional beliefs and knowledge form only a fragment of what is learned from fiction. Still more, they are by no means the most useful aspect of what is learned. The practical knowledge acquired from a fictional work, as well as one's empathic knowledge or beliefs about the situations akin to those in which fictional creatures find themselves, is, we have seen, profoundly useful. And yet, such knowledge is not scientific.

This is important, for as I said at the outset . . . philosophers have tended in the wake of the Enlightenment to the view that because propositional knowledge and belief are the stuff of science, they alone constitute the province of epistemology. Much of this chapter may be seen as antidote to that view, one which is bred of my attempt to resuscitate a romantic epistemology.

NOTES

1. See, for example, W. V. Quine, "Epistemology Naturalized," in *Ontological Relativity and Other Essays* (Columbia University Press, New York, 1969), pp. 69–90; Karl Popper, "Epistemology Without a Knowing Subject," in *Objective Knowledge: An Evolutionary Approach* (Oxford University Press, Oxford, 1972), pp. 106–52. See, as well, Ian Hacking, *Why Does Language Matter to Philosophy?* (Cambridge University Press, Cambridge, 1975), pp. 160ff.
2. The coherence in question need not be logical, for it is well known that not all fictional worlds are logically possible. The world of Dr. Who, for instance, is clearly not a logically coherent world since it involves time travel and so breaches the law of contradiction. In such a case, the requirement of coherence amounts to no more than that the sentences of the fiction should "hang together" in a way which presents a unified narrative. There is, of course, a good deal more to be said about fictional worlds, but I shall not address this topic here.
3. See, for example, John Hospers, "Implied Truths in Literature," in Francis J. Coleman, ed., *Contemporary Studies in Aesthetics* (McGraw-Hill, New York, 1968), pp. 233–46; John Hospers, *Meaning and Truth in the Arts* (University of North Carolina Press, Chapel Hill, 1946), p. 206; Dorothy Walsh, "The Cognitive Content of Art," in Coleman, ed., *Contemporary Studies in Aesthetics*, pp. 285, 296–97; Dorothy Walsh, *Literature and Knowledge* (Wesleyan University Press, Middletown, Conn., 1969), chs. 6–8; Jacob Bronowski, *The Visionary Eye* (MIT Press, Cambridge, 1978), pp. 117–20; Julian Mitchell, "Truth and Fiction," in *Philosophy and the Arts*, Royal Institute of Philosophy Lectures, vol. 6, 1971–72 (Macmillan, London, 1973), pp. 1–22.
4. There is a sense in which such beliefs are self-fulfilling, for they can condition our emotional responses to future situations. For this reason it is arguable, although I will not argue

the case here, that in some instances first-person empathic beliefs constitute empathic knowledge.
5. See, for example, Walsh, "The Cognitive Content of Art," p. 287.
6. This is an adaptation of an example employed by Hilary Putnam, "Literature, Science and Reflection," in *Meaning and the Moral Sciences* (Routledge & Kegan Paul, London, 1978), pp. 83–94.
7. Putnam, "Literature, Science and Reflection," p. 87.

Art as a Source of Knowledge: Linking Analytic Aesthetics and Epistemology

John W. Bender

> *Art fixes a kind of knowledge of which science has no understanding, and which gentlemen too confined within the scientific habit cannot approach intelligently.*
> J. C. Ransom, *The Kenyon Review*, Spring 1939

> [T]*here is no persuasive reason for supposing that music cannot be sung and loved directly, without pretending that we must scratch up some queer kind of knowledge and truth in music in order to justify our love. . . . The fine arts are adventures that deserve to be taken seriously. To subordinate them to the sciences, by reducing each work of art to the status of a truth-vehicle, is to take each art less than seriously.*
> Douglas N. Morgan, *Journal of Aesthetics and Art Criticism*, Fall 1967

> *It seems wrong to me either to say that novels give knowledge of man or to say categorically that they do not.*
> Hilary Putnam, *Meaning and the Moral Sciences*, 1978

I. ART, KNOWLEDGE, AND PHILOSOPHERS

It is in no way remarkable that, as an epistemologist and aesthetician, I happen to think that not enough has been done by philosophers to relate aesthetic experience and aesthetic appreciation to epistemic states such as knowledge and justified belief. It is of more interest, perhaps, that as an epistemologist and aesthetician, I am puzzled and dissatisfied by our tradition's handling of the question, "Does art give us knowledge?" Although traditions are never univocal on big questions, in this instance there is a disturbingly deep current of denial of art's epistemic efficacy, to which we have adapted, perhaps because that current has been for the most part also warm and gentle, attributing other valuable functions to the arts and only rarely turning cold and turbulent, as in Plato's case. In addition to this denial, there is an unusual amount of polite philosophical skirting and sidestepping of the issue to be found here. It is ironic that philosophers, so often liable to charges of overintellectualizing an issue, have for so long been reluctant to validate their enjoyment and valuing of art, even partially, in terms of the knowledge it can impart.

I do not think the explanation for this is that philosophers, being experts on the nature of knowledge, have seen more clearly and quickly than others, that art is simply not cut out to transmit knowledge, even though some have claimed as much. Rather, I suggest that much of the dismissing of art as an epistemic vehicle arises from two common philosophical dispositions: our ability to say (and penchant for saying) what art is *not*, and a persistent essentialist hope that whatever it *is*, its nature is singular and definable. These work together in the following familiar ways. "Art is *not* philosophy (which is the contemplative search for knowledge); all art is imitation of reality, and a mere imitation cannot bring real knowledge." "Art is *not* science (which is the paradigm of knowledge); all art is expressive, and nothing devoid of factual content can transmit knowledge." "Art is *not* objective; all art is subjective, impressionistic, intuitive. We can adopt an attitude toward it, but cannot come to know things through it." "Art is *not* a language; all art is iconic or presentational or metaphoric in its use of symbols, not discursive or literal. Art is not propositional enough to communicate knowledge." And so on.

One can see these dispositions at work in the opening quote from Douglas Morgan and feel their influence even on those few defenders of art's epistemic powers, such as J. C. Ransom, for whom art does yield knowledge (but, of course, of a qualified, "special" sort). For Dorothy Walsh, it is knowledge of possibilities only; for L. A. Reid, it is an "experience knowledge" that is nonpropositional in character; for David Novitz, it is "empathic knowledge," while Hilary Putnam will admit only that fiction may yield "conceptual knowledge" but not knowledge of empirical fact (Walsh, *Literature and Knowledge*, Ch. 10, and "Cognitive Content," 610; Reid, 118; Novitz, Ch. 1; Putnam, 90).

For the most part, ours is an intellectual history of distinguishing art from some paradigm of knowledge and then salving the split by redirecting attention to some nonepistemic function plausibly attributable to art. We seem to all but ignore the danger of implicitly committing two fallacies here: dissimilarity to some favored field of knowledge does not establish that art is not epistemic; moreover, attributing other functions or values to art different from the communication of knowledge does not exclude the possibility of the latter.

The claim I wish to defend is not novel but does run against the current, seeks to avoid the fallacies mentioned, and, to mix metaphors, does take something of an intellectual high road regarding aesthetic appreciation and experience. It is the claim that art, in general, functions in a multiplicity of cognitive, perceptual, and expressive ways, and frequently, though certainly not always, this includes, or should include, the conveyance of propositional knowledge, when those appreciating the works are sufficiently thoughtful. I wish to suggest that viewing art as a source of knowledge (whether it is unique knowledge available only through art, as Martha Nussbaum seems to suggest, I doubt but leave aside) is a natural supposition if we see artworks as intentional objects and symbols which ground various inferences and from which we draw (many more) inferences. The picture I propose we paint of art is one of a complex intentional object suspended in an even more complex inferential web, some strands of which lead to knowledge.

The knowledge which art can give us is sometimes empirical and about the world; it can be general or specific in scope, abstract or concrete in its content. It is sometimes psychological or social and about ourselves; often it is of a normative, value-oriented nature or, in some other way, is a version of what I will call "modal" knowledge, knowledge that something is necessary, lawful, probable, possible, or impossible. Modal knowledge tells us about how things could or would or should be, under certain conditions or in a certain context, and often concerns tendencies, potentialities, and generalities.

I will defend these suggestions by responding to a trio of complex objections that can be made to the idea that art conveys knowledge, and in the course of doing this I hope to provide a variety of examples of what we come to know through different artworks and to elaborate on the thesis that artworks are symbols suspended in an inference net.

II. THE HERITAGE OF DENIAL

I should first comment on the current I am resisting. This is a very incomplete sampling (since a full treatment would require rolling out much of the history of aesthetics), but it will suffice to give us a sense of direction.

1. Plato is a philosopher beguiled, fearful, and denying of art, dazzled by its power but suspicious of its place in the ideal scheme of things, including the pursuit of knowledge. Artworks, being only imitations and illusions of real things, house no knowledge because knowledge is a relation we strive to obtain to Reality. As Plato jealously but dismissively describes them, artists are magnetic madmen who are directly acted on by the Muses but who do not know what they are doing. Perhaps the ultimate explanation for this characterization is that artists propose no strategy, no Socratic methodology which others can follow in their rational and systematic pursuit of knowledge. Art, in short, is not philosophy for Plato, but is mere imitation. (See *Republic* 598d–599a; *Ion* 533–535, 540a–542b.)

2. Like Plato, Aristotle views the arts as skills of making (*poiesis*)—the making of imitations and representations, in particular—and distinguishes them at least as categorically as Plato from knowing (*theoria*). Knowledge answers *why* questions, while excellence in art answers *how* questions. To call an artist "wise" is to say only that he is excellent in his art; it is not to attribute to him knowledge of first principles or their consequences. Scientific knowledge is the capacity to demonstrate, and its object is necessity; art is the capacity to make and is concerned not with necessity but with coming into being. The artist, in this scheme, appears to be in the wrong category of activity to discover and convey much in the way of knowledge. And what about the artwork itself—does it not transmit knowledge as one of its benefits? The function of a good tragedy, Aristotle tells us, is the production of a certain kind of proper *pleasure* that comes from our feeling pity and fear when the tragedy's plot and the behavior of its characters are rendered plausibly and comply with psychological law. (See *Metaphysics* 1.1; *Nichomachean Ethics* 1139b, 1141a; *Poetics*, esp. Chps. 13–15.)

Pleasure, whether proper or not, is surely a nonepistemic consequence of the artist's excellence or know-how. Perhaps I am not doing justice here to the cognitive and didactic functions of tragedy, which are not lost on Aristotle. It may well be true that he distinguishes theoretical knowledge from art because of his theory of practical reasoning (a theory which emphasizes our experiences of and emotional reactions to concrete and particular situations rather than our theoretical understanding of things general and universal) and because it is Aristotle's view that what we can learn through tragedy is *knowledge how* we ought to act in certain concrete situations, *how* to live a good life, *how* to be and behave excellently. It may well be, as Martha Nussbaum has argued ("Discernment," 79–84; "Form," 36–42) that Aristotle's primary point is that practical knowledge of what to do cannot be arrived at by use of theoretical reasoning alone, that emotional responsiveness to particular circumstances is necessary. Nonetheless, it seems plausible to characterize Aristotle's position here as being focused on art as a learning source regarding virtuous or excellent action rather than as a source of propositional knowledge.

3. For Kant, there is one clear sense in which there is no aesthetic knowledge at all. In the realm of the aesthetic, our cognitive machinery is not properly engaged to make epistemic judgments. Treating an object aesthetically does not involve our capacity for subsuming sensory manifolds under determinate concepts, a prerequisite for empirical knowledge. Aesthetic judgments are judgments of the beautiful, judgments which we make when we find ourselves moved to aesthetic satisfaction by a work's purposiveness of form in the absence of any real purpose. These are judgments which express a certain pleasure one experiences when perceiving art.

All this may be well and good as a logic of judgments of the beautiful, and Kant is rightly famous for so brilliantly arguing that the beauty of a work is not deducible from its cognizable properties. But the issue of whether we can get knowledge from art seems to have gotten lost somewhere between the *Critique of Pure Reason* and the *Critique of Judgment*. Nevertheless, Kant seems compelled to say that if we *do* come to know, it is only through treating the artwork as an object of the understanding and not as a subject of aesthetic judgment. What Kant would not and cannot claim is that we can come to important knowledge *through* our aesthetic perception and appreciation of an artwork, or that our aesthetic sensitivities may be prerequisites to the discovery of this knowledge. (See *Critique of Judgment*, Introduction, §10, §65; also Meerbote for the convoluted relationships between Kant's aesthetics and epistemology.)

4. The influential Romantic interests in myth and symbolism, on the one hand, and in art as the expression of the artist's emotions, on the other, richly fed positivist aesthetics during philosophy's so-called linguistic turn and beyond. After Ogden and Richards carefully delineated the different functions of language and warned not to confuse its symbolic with its emotive use, aestheticians developed numerous theories which may have heeded the warning but certainly did not hesitate in revolving around the themes of expression, symbol, and language. Two examples will show the anti-epistemic consequences for art.

The simplest position, one arguably held by I. A. Richards, Rudolph Carnap, and (regarding some of the arts) A. J. Ayer, is the theory that art is always a purely emotive use of language or symbols. In this view, art should, as Richards suggested, abandon as confused and unreachable its quest for knowledge and truth. And even though Ayer admits that literature and poetry have cognitive as well as emotive content, the prospects for knowledge still seem poor and distant, since these art forms are, for Ayer, bodies of sentences which are *false*.

The second and much more sophisticated view is that of Susanne Langer. Reacting against both the German-Romantic conceit that music is a true *language* of emotions in which composers could write (some claimed quite specific) expositions of feelings, and against the idea that music is a form of self-expression, Langer suggests that music is a *presentational symbol* which does not *refer* to human emotions but which logically and morphologically resembles emotions and other dynamic patterns of human experience. (A presentational symbol is a nondiscursive symbol that is not analyzable into basic, discrete, independently meaningful units but is nevertheless meaningful by presenting its constituents in structural relations that bear some similarity to that which is represented.) Music can articulate forms which language cannot set forth and can therefore reveal the nature of feelings in a way language cannot approach, Langer claims. But this relevation, it seems, must be one of acquaintance rather than being in any way propositional, for music is a nondiscursive, nonreferential, and "unconsummated" symbol, its meaning remaining unfixed and its significance implicit.

The question to ask, though, is whether certain propositional knowledge (perhaps knowledge about human emotions) can come to us through presentational symbols like music. Can the properties presented and exemplified by the artwork, along with contextual facts that surround and frame it, ground inferences about the work's meaning and significance which may in some cases constitute knowledge? Can we project "analytical hypotheses" about artworks in a way similar to what Quine suggests we must do about others' sentences in order to cope with their referential indeterminancy? (See Ayer, 44–45, 113–14; Langer, Chps. 3 and 8; Ogden and Richards, Ch. VII; and Weitz.)

5. Recently, in the book *Contingency, Irony, and Solidarity*, Richard Rorty put forward a postmodern "ironist" view of philosophical problems which is pragmatist, pluralist, and relativist about language, truth, knowledge, and most other matters, and which holds that philosophy, as well as liberal society more generally, has much to learn from certain types of literature and literary criticism. The ironist is one who has come to grips with the utter contingency of our conceptual schemes, language, and indeed, life, and has broken away from the metaphysician's desire for discovering fundamental realities or truth, replacing this with a personal search for autonomy through a process of "redescription" of significant matters into one's own "final vocabulary." (A paradigm of such redescription, to which Rorty often returns, is to be found in Proust's *Remembrance of Things Past*.) These alternative descriptions and redescriptions are, of course, incommensurable, and no independent criteria of adequacy or truth can be used to adjudicate among them. The following passages provide a sketch:

Metaphysicians think that human beings by nature desire to know. They think this because the vocabulary they have inherited, their commonsense, provides them with a picture of knowledge as a relation between human beings and "reality." . . . It also tells us that "reality," if properly asked, will help us determine what our final vocabulary should be. . . . By contrast, ironists do not see the search for a final vocabulary as (even in part) a way of getting something distinct from this vocabulary right. They do not take the point of discursive thought to be *knowing*, in any sense that can be explicated by notions like "reality," "real essence," "objective point of view," and "the correspondence of language to reality." (75)

[Ironists are] never quite able to take themselves seriously because [they are] always aware that the terms in which they describe themselves are subject to change, always aware of the contingency and fragility of their final vocabularies. (73f)

. . . although the thoroughgoing ironist can use the notion of a "better description," he has no criterion for the application of this term and so cannot use the notion of "the right description." (99)

Rorty's full view not only gives special place to literature (e.g., literature is far more effective in arguing for a liberal, caring society than is any social philosophy) but also appears to have anti-epistemic consequences for aesthetics. In this relativist scheme, it would seem that the function of art could hardly be anything other than a Proustian redescription of one aspect or another of the world, of one form of life or another, perhaps with the goal of personal autonomy. "Proust's job was done," Rorty says, "when he put the events of his own life in his own order, made a pattern out of all the little things" (105). The impression is strong that art conveys no knowledge because there is no knowledge to convey—only redescription. On this point, Rorty stands as representative for numerous postmodernist writers. The current, it seems, is still strong.

III. NOTWITHSTANDING OBJECTIONS, ART CAN YIELD KNOWLEDGE

In the remainder of this paper, I will elaborate on my positive view that art can be the source of important and valuable propositional knowledge, but I will do so from the defensive posture of answering three complex and interrelated objections. Certain elements in these objections, it should be clear, are associated with the sample theories of the previous section, some are characteristic of other well-known positions, and others are simply commonsensical but important nonetheless.

1. *Art, surely, provides us with valuable and pleasurable experiences of rather vast variety, but not knowledge per se, except in trivial or secondary ways. In this, our experience of art is similar to other types of aesthetic or enjoyable experiences. When one drives a fast car fast, or attends a tennis match, for example, one may be after the exciting experience but is not, except in peculiar circumstances, after knowledge; even Saturday's "thoughtful" hike in a subalpine meadow is not a botanical hunt for knowledge. Likewise, the gaining of knowledge is not the point or heart of aesthetic experience. Let's not overintellectualize art or view it too didactically.*

The complete answer to this objection will require the whole of this paper. But we can begin with a few of its points. Construed as a statement of the naive idea that art is a source of pleasure and little more, this is not a serious objection and, at any rate, has already been thoroughly trounced by many writers. (See Nelson Goodman's *Languages of Art*, VI, 4, for a sample.) Art is far too cognitive and serious an intellectual pursuit to be treated as a simple stimulus for pleasure. It is true that some warm themselves with music as well as with a fire in the den, or relax with a novel, but it is also true that this is a simple-minded use of art.

It is much more interesting to view this first objection in a different way, perhaps as a restatement of Douglas Morgan's point with which I began, namely, that art should not be subordinated to science and treated like a mere "truth vehicle." This is, of course, correct, but it is not my intention to scientize art or to claim that knowledge is art's sole goal or that its function is always didactic; rather it is to take art seriously and on its own terms (as Morgan wishes)—terms, however, that sometimes include truth and knowledge, I argue. This is strikingly different from viewing art as a neutral conduit or messenger of cold facts, itself to be "factored out" once the information is received. That would be absurd, and if Morgan alludes to this with his term, *truth vehicle*, he is alluding to a straw man. Significant knowledge comes to us through art *only* when we pay the greatest attention to the work itself. Unlike science, where it is possible (if unadvisable) to learn the conclusions of experiments and ignore their design, with art there is no way to ignore the aesthetics and absorb the knowledge. *Having* the experience is, indeed, crucial. But this in no way negates the fact that, as in science, the knowledge to be found in art comes to us through the process of inference. It is time for an example.

There is such a powerful reflectiveness, a meta-cognitive and meta-emotional quality to certain movements of Beethoven's late string quartets, that it would be perverse, I think, to deny that there is a strong communicative intent behind them. Specifically, the opening fugue of the *Quartet in C-sharp minor, Op. 131*, can teach one this: that the deepest, most concentrated, profound, and personal thoughtfulness does not destroy or preclude light, engaged, "public" joy, and that, in discovering such unities of oppositions, one can find a kind of calm in the face of life's fatefulness.

This is a very complex lesson, to be sure, but that is part of the work's greatness and value as well as why the lesson can plausibly be said to be *learned* from the work. But how do we learn it, and is it right to call it knowledge?

To learn anything from the work, indeed, to be in the position to learn, requires that we engage in *interpreting* the work. We first must hear the music as exemplifying the relevant properties such as profundity and depth, lightness and innocent joyfulness, and hear (or cognize) these various elements as being related to each other in specific ways. For example, we must interpret the profound and light passages as contrasting but not in opposition, and we must judge that the piece exhibits a convincing and natural way of moving from one to the other, if we are going to claim that ultimately we have learned something.

Our judgment of the cogency of these relations among affects—perhaps what some mean when they say the music "speaks the truth"—surely derives at least in part from, and may presuppose, our comprehension of the work's *musical* cogency. In fact, the relevant mental processes of identification, comprehension, interpretation, and so forth, though often immediate-seeming and perhaps subconscious to a degree, can be construed logically as various forms of inference from the more basic sensory information the artwork presents. Hearing the music as profound requires a projection of the musical content onto a terrain or map of psychological possibilities, not unlike our ability to recognize (hypothesize about) a person's current emotional state from his or her facial gestures. Conclusions or interpretations of this sort clearly rely on an antecedent knowledge of, or a scheme for, possible emotive states and hence can be thought of as inferences.

Can we speak of such interpretative inferences being justified or unjustified? I believe so, although it must be admitted that there is no accepted psychological model of the structure of such complex, sensory-cognitive inferences; nor is there any generally accepted epistemic theory of inferential justification. All that I wish to suggest, to return to the example, is that it is sensible to ask for a defense of our inference that the Beethoven quartet is profound (and not, say, morose), and sometimes, I think, we can give an answer that justifies our claim. If musically adept, we may justify ourselves at the piano by pointing out that the passage goes like *this* and does *not* go like *that*, playing a revised version which is indeed morose. Or, we may point out that the surrounding musical context of the passage is less "consistent" with the morose hypothesis in the sense that acceptance of that interpretation reduces the degree of unity that can be claimed for the movement as a whole. There are numerous strategies.

It is an accepted fact of art criticism that such inferences and interpretations are *underdetermined* by the basic sensory data of an artwork (see Matthews). This means that our inferences are in for competition and that justification is not a deductive matter, but epistemologists know these lessons well from other knowledge areas and yet do not conclude (at least *some* do not conclude) that standards of justification are hopeless. The underdetermination thesis also, I think, argues in favor of the relevance of certain kinds of background, contextual, historical, and biographical information to the justifiability of our inferences. Any strong claim of the "autonomy of art" is untenable, in my view, because it denies obvious facts such as that we often make valuable inferences from art to artist and from artist to art, and that what an artist intends to do or not to do, as well as the contexts in which he or she is working, affect what the artist in fact accomplishes. It is only when we take seriously the picture of the work of art as a presentational symbol (a symbol exhibiting some of the properties it refers to) centered in a complex inferential web that we come to accept the demand for inferential justification as itself legitimate, and the possibility that knowledge is communicated as real.

Our discussion thus far has only suggested that, in regard to art and aesthetic experience, we can appropriately talk of inferences and justification without fear of necessarily neutering, overscientizing, or overintellectualizing the experience. We can rejoin the argument now by taking up another objection, closely related to the first.

2. *The cognitive nature of art's functions can be granted, certainly. There have been, after all, numerous theories emphasizing this: Langer, as already noted, conceived of artworks as presentational symbols that articulate the human emotional landscape, and Charles Morris before her saw art as iconic signs that signify certain properties by exhib-*

iting them. Nelson Goodman, the leading current cognitivist, takes art to literally and metaphorically exemplify many properties, some formal, some emotional, and claims that art's value is a matter of its cognitive, symbolic efficacy. But when we experience these functions of art, we can feel or understand what they express without formulating some lesson, some truth, something propositional. You may be right that in experiencing art we are involved in cognitive inferences about it, and that our claims about this content are open to and in need of justification in some sense of that term. But what we "know" through art we "know" in experiencing it; it is knowledge by acquaintance, as it were; it is more like knowing how the Eiffel Tower looks at night than it is like knowing that the Eiffel Tower is a symbol of modernity or that it is riveted together. The upshot of the processes of aesthetic appreciation and interpretation is an enriched experience, not a propositional conclusion.

There is some truth to this objection, but also much romance. Artworks *are* experienced and can be entered into, lived, even "inhabited," as Steven Smith has suggested (Smith, 95). Art can "create worlds," as Goodman would say, or at least create parts or aspects of worlds, in which we can immerse ourselves. One does indeed *sense* the overwhelming depth of the *Cavatina* from Beethoven's B-flat quartet, Op. 130, and *feel* its reflective peace. And, I would admit that, in many cases, one's work is done when the formal and expressive features and relationships of a piece of art have been noticed and experienced. But sometimes, it seems to me, there is more to do, more to be had. There is a difference between being transported into Beethoven's world and knowing where you are, or, perhaps more accurately, there are varying degrees of understanding of that world. It is possible to *feel* Beethoven's music intelligently, to inhabit *The World According to Garp* with familiarity, but not know what to make of it. Learning more and more what to make of it is a process which, at least in part, involves making intricate and unobvious inferences to propositional conclusions, some of which, to my mind, constitute knowledge. It is no threat to this knowledge that the artworks which can yield it are often themselves not composed of propositions. Vast reaches of our propositional knowledge are grounded in the nonpropositional, and the most natural of signs (e.g., the ubiquitous bear's footprint), can give us propositional knowledge.

When we understand the symbolic intent of an image, the metaphorical force of a poetic line, the thematic content of a literary work, the "depth meaning" of a passage (to use DeWitt Parker's concept; Parker, 32), we are inferring content.

Sometimes we stop at the point of understanding that the piece contains a visual or verbal metaphor for death or pleasure, a damning representation of a person, an ambiguous depiction of two lovers, and so on, but often we are motivated to ask *why* these features are present and feel justified in drawing some conclusions, hazarding a guess about a unifying theme or about the work's significance or "meaning." It has been common (prior to recent postmodern denials to the contrary) to agree to this thesis in regard to the literary and theatrical arts, but its force is more general, applying, I believe, to every art form, although not to every artwork. Superb as pure abstractionist art can be, for example, I admit that the "knowledge" we derive from a certain example may be nothing more than an acquaintance with *this* particular way of achieving balance or intensity, *this* way of exemplifying energy, tension, or void.

But even here, we must be careful not to be too "minimalist" about knowledge. Maybe there is nothing more to do in front of a Morris Louis painting than to absorb its cool sensuality, or, while viewing the Rothko triptych, to feel "metaphysical" or contemplative. But would it be wrong to say that through Mondrian's compositions in his reduced style of the 1920s and 1930s we can come to know that our sense of physical structure and unity is as much *created* by color as it is filled in by it? "But the unifying principles internal to a Mondrian do not apply generally to objects," one may object. A quick, justificatory reply may be, "Have you noticed how many everyday objects and structures can be seen as one sees a Mondrian?" Again, one can hardly fail to sense and marvel at the exquisite balance of a Mozart middle symphony, such as *Symphony #25 in G minor, K. 183*—it is the property most clearly and resoundingly exemplified by this work. But one can go beyond simply feeling this symmetry and discover through repeated attention that this feature is not adequately explained in the usual terms of the Classical symmetry of the composition's melodic lines, but also and more strikingly is due to the shapes, lengths, and orchestral "weights" of the four movements and the relations among these abstract values. That is to say, one can learn something *architectural* from Mozart: that the perceived weight, shape, and length of component and noncontiguous elements of a whole can contribute to a subtle sense of balance.

Consequently, it is not at all clear to me that aesthetic apprehension and appreciation *is* more like knowing what the Eiffel Tower looks like than it is like knowing that it is a symbol of modernity. The situation may better be described by saying that aesthetic experiences with significant epistemic content are like recognizing that the Eiffel Tower is a symbol of modernity *through* knowing, among other things, how it looks.

3. *But, surely, there remain two very large obstacles in the way of your thesis, not surprisingly, one having to do with truth and the other with justification. If we put aside certain analytic niceties, we can think of knowledge as justified true belief. The problem over truth is this: What art expresses, presents, communicates to us, implies, insinuates, or "argues for" must be construed as one point of view, one perspective, one "way the world is," and, in some cases, perhaps, as a statement of the artist's beliefs, attitudes, outlook, fears, and aspirations. But all this belongs to the Platonic realm of "opinion," as it were, not to the realm of truth. The second problem, about justification, is related to the truth problem: Even if we grant that analyses and interpretations of an artwork's content can be justified, that only provides us with grounds for conclusions of the form, "The painting expresses the importance and centrality of x," "The novel's most important claim is p," "The symphony seems to be the composer's most concise statement of the fear that q and of his confidence that r." Having justification for conclusions such as these is a wholly different matter from being justified in believing that x is important, or that p, q, or r are true. But these latter beliefs are what are necessary if art gives us knowledge.*

In her excellent, insightful, and now slightly greying article, "The Cognitive Content of Art," Dorothy Walsh makes an observation which seems to give weight to what I am calling the "truth problem." Even though artists and artworks put forward radically different and, according to Walsh, incompatible, views and visions, we do not treat them as competing truth claims, as we do when we encounter theoretical incompatibilities in science or philosophy:

The plain fact is that works of art are never competitive in the sense in which scientific hypotheses and philosophical theories may be. . . . [C]ontradiction in philosophical doctrine does indeed necessitate choice, whereas radical diversity, amounting to incompatibility, in the content of two different works of art does not necessitate rejection of either. . . . It is, of course, not only poets who say incompatible things without mutual contradiction. Cézanne's vision of three-dimensional space and of the objects in that space is radically incompatible with the vision of Turner. In passing from the music of Bach to the music of Debussy we realize that we have made a transition from one world into another. . . . In the visual world of Cézanne's creation the graceful vistas of Watteau's landscapes are not merely absent or neglected; they are specifically rejected. (Walsh, 608–10)

Walsh resists the proposal that would resolve the apparent incompatibility among artworks' cognitive content by claiming that each work is only a *partial* articulation of the world and human experience, and hence may each be true. She concludes, instead, that the solution lies in conceiving of art not as a *truth* vehicle but as a vehicle of *possibility*. Art's cognitive role, in this view, is to present us with certain diverse possibilities. This idea is also to be found in (but does not exhaust) the more recent views of Novitz, Nussbaum, and Putnam. (See Novitz; Putnam; and Nussbaum, "Finely Aware.")

Given my earlier reference to art's conveyance of "modal" knowledge, one might expect that I must concur with Walsh on this point, but my agreement with her is limited. First, although a statement of possibility may be some artworks' sole intent, art frequently is at least an attempt at conveying more than mere possibility. Concerns with how the actual world may be, would be, should be, under certain conditions, are not the same as elaborations of how a possible world is. Many artists are thinking about actual tendencies, probabilities, generalities, and potentials. These are not the same as mere possibilities and can be empirically true or false. Cézanne was not painting a possible world that looked like his canvases; he was painting the actual world. And he was (we must be realistic) focusing only on some aspects of the visual world. It is, therefore, not obvious to me that there is the radical incompatibility Walsh describes between Cézanne's world and Turner's or Watteau's. What Cézanne specifically rejects, it seems to me, is Watteau's painting *style* rather than anything Watteau may be "saying" with his art.

Indeed, as soon as we resist the evaporation of art's cognitive content into the realm of mere possibility, it also becomes wise to resist describing every difference as radical incompatibility. If we do not, it becomes difficult to explain, short of postulating a kind of aesthetic schizophrenia, the ease with which we embrace both Bach and Debussy, Shostokovich and Schubert. It is better, when we can do it, to say things like this: "Following Bach, Mozart, and Beethoven, as Brahms did, his emphases are as different and new as they are natural, and those earlier voices had their various influences on his focus and concern."

This means that we may want to be more precise in our phrasing of the knowledge we believe we derive from certain artworks, and not claim, for example, that work X teaches us that the world is total misery and darkness and that Y helps us discover that the world is continual joy and pure light.

None of this is meant to deny, however, that different works can and perhaps frequently do bring forward contradictory or conflicting "claims." Earlier, I suggested that Beethoven's Op. 131 allows us the knowledge that a resolving unity is achievable between one's most personal and profound efforts and feelings and an engaged, even affable, sense of humanity. Something approaching the contradiction of this claim can be found in Vladimir Nabokov's *Pale Fire*. There is, in that novel, an irresolvable antithesis between the artist's personal search for fulfillment and profoundity and the development of any sense of humanity and kindness. Now, who is to say whether the truth lies with Beethoven or Nabokov? Isn't it better that we acknowledge these conflicting points of view and leave the matter of truth aside?

Only, it seems to me, if we are prepared to believe that there is no important difference between what a valuable but false point of view has to offer, and what a truth has to offer us—only, that is, if we are prepared to be epistemological subjectivists and ironists, for which there are only descriptions and redescriptions, as Richard Rorty would say.

The problems of truth and justification as I have described them, and as they exist more generally in epistemology, are the source of Rorty's position and are paraphrased in his objections to metaphysical urges, which, by the way, would certainly be his "redescription" of the motivations behind this paper.

Rorty is bound to chide, "You have simply not taken to heart postmodernism in philosophy, or, for that matter, in art and literary criticism either. The hunt for knowledge in art is the metaphysician's urge for general ideas and final vocabularies." Art, or at least good art, or at least good *Proustian* art, is not involved in this search. "Proust . . . was a perspectivalist who did not have to worry about whether perspectivalism was a true theory" (Rorty, 107). The position which Rorty seems to be endorsing here and throughout his book is that art has done a better job than philosophy of freeing itself from metaphysical urges, and philosophy should either follow this lead, or at the very least stop imposing those urges on art.

I cannot at this point embark on a wholesale debate of relativism and ironism, but I think what I am defending here is at least somewhat more mundane than what Rorty's metaphysician craves. I already have suggested that the knowledge we derive from art is diverse in its nature and its logic; it is not all knowledge of "real essences" or necessities, nor is it directly intuitable from the work or deducible as a certainty from it; it is *inferred* and *revisable*, as most of our knowledge claims are. And nothing that I am suggesting commits us to the idea that every issue which may engage an artist has a single answer or is monological in its nature, and that the artist's work either "gets" the answer or not. To think of art as a source of knowledge, and epistemology as relevant to aesthetics, it is not necessary, as far as I can see, to be a Platonist about knowledge and the knowable world, but Rorty intimates as much.

I wish to say only what Rorty in other places seems to acknowledge (although I am unsure how he can, given his views of truth and descriptions). In fact, my earlier comments on Nabokov's work intentionally followed Rorty's own on this author, to highlight my present point. Rorty says,

. . . Nabokov knew quite well that ecstasy and tenderness not only are separable but tend to preclude each other—that most nonobsessed poets are, like Shade, second rate. This is the "moral" knowledge that his novels help us acquire . . . (159). [Nabokov] creates characters who are both ecstatic and cruel, noticing and heartless. . . . This particular sort of genius-monster—the monster of incuriosity—is Nabokov's contribution to our knowledge of human possibilities. (160–61)

If we can come to this kind of knowledge through our understanding of art, in Rorty's view, then there may be less separating us than seems to separate the ironist and metaphysician in Rorty's own characterization of these positions. It is interesting to note in passing that Nabokov himself said of *Lolita* something quite in opposition to the preceding passage:

I am neither a reader nor a writer of didactic fiction, and . . . *Lolita* has no moral in tow. For me a work of fiction exists only insofar as it affords me what I shall bluntly call aesthetic bliss, that is a sense of being somehow, somewhere, connected with other states of being where art (curiosity, tenderness, kindness, ecstasy) is the norm. ("On a Book Entitled *Lolita*," 314–15)

One may think that Nabokov's view better fits Rorty's *theory* than Rorty's does. (I also hope that, by now, you share with me the belief that art goes beyond "aesthetic bliss.")

But, back now to the truth problem. How *are* we to handle conflicting or contradictory cognitive content within artworks? Rather like we handle and evaluate the conflicting mass of individual opinions and attitudes confronting us everywhere, I would say. We critically examine the grounds on which they are held, and more broadly estimate their likelihood of truth, by calling on our own relevant knowledge and experience and checking for coherence and other epistemic virtues. The process is fallabilistic, to be sure, and it is often wise to plead indecision regarding the truth of conflicting claims.

Moreover, it should not be forgotten that, for the inferences which we make on the basis of our experience of an artwork, there are numerous stopping points, some being more local, some more global. We first infer from a work's basic content what properties, relationships, and emotions are being exemplified and then try to piece together some unifying interpretation which makes it intelligible why those things occur as they do, are organized and related as they are. In some instances, we find reason for inferring that the artwork is proposing, asserting, implying certain ideas or conclusions. In addition, there may be grounds, either internal to the work or external but part of the work's aesthetic-historical context or the biography of the artist, which justify an inference to the *artist's* beliefs, convictions, hopes, attitudes, etc., although such inferences can easily turn fallacious. (But some cases, this sort of ancillary knowledge about the artist can help to clarify the content of the work and add justification to the interpretations we project.)

We may, however, disagree with the artwork's vision, find it unconvincing, or simply be confused by it. In some cases, we stop at conclusions such as, "Arnulf Rainer's photoseries 'Body Language' construes art as a form of self-mutilation, but this I reject." In intermediate instances, we may engage in a kind of conceptual dialogue with a work and decide that we *have* learned from it, but learned less than what was proffered. We may infer, for example, that in *Pale Fire* Nabokov views artists as necessarily inattentive and cruel persons but we may be willing to take away, as something of value, not the belief that artists *are* cruel, but a more circumscribed lesson with which we can agree—namely, that intense, obsessive, personal projects, even among the most intelligent, bring with them the significant threat of inattention and cruelty to others. We turn what may have been presented as a categorical or universal truth into a claim of tendency or probability, whose truth we find more likely.

In other cases a work may present, in the most aesthetically beautiful manner, a moving vision or scheme of things, which we can appreciate and savor but which we ultimately find too naive or mystical, passé or prescientific. In one of the supreme works of music, the *Sonata #2 in A minor for Unaccompanied Violin*, BWV 1003, J. S. Bach presents a sparkling but unscientific and religious vision of humanity's place in the world (and manages to create this wonder with a single violin playing Baroque dance movements). Bach unites the feeling of human contingency to a divine and eternal pattern: within the architecture of divinely created nature, a very large place is reserved for human activity and sentiment, but one never forgets that, as deep and poignantly beautiful as Bach's "humanity" is, ours is a contingent and subservient place in God's world. If we can no longer accept the truth of this vision, we stop our inferences after we have drawn our conclusion about what Bach *thought* he knew and wished to convey about the structure of the world. We may, of course, try to place a more abstract and secular interpretation on the music in order to attribute more "truth" to the great Bach, and this may or may not work.

Sometimes, though, we can wholly accept a work on its own terms and infer from it, undiluted, an important, and maybe revelatory, truth. Perhaps what I have claimed about Beethoven's late quartet is a case; perhaps Irving's *The World According to Garp*, to select an example with particular relevance to the issues in this paper, allows us to see that art can assist us in dealing with the chaos of experience, because art *is* an effort to structure, order, and find meaning. (See Harter and Thompson, 88–97.) (Perhaps *Garp* also teaches us that this effort is doomed, but I think my sentiment about this should be obvious.)

What we are prepared to call or identify as the knowledge inherent in art clarifies itself only as we think critically about the work—not only trying to make sense of *it*, but also trying to place it, or what it seems to be teaching us, within the rest of our epistemic field. This is the process by which we can become *justified* in believing something that has been put forward to us in the context and form of art. Knowledge is not the same as the receipt of information, as Keith Lehrer and many other epistemologists are fond of pointing out, and, at least concerning the type of knowledge we are discussing here, it is safe to say that to have it, there must be some critical and conscious thought about, some epistemic evaluation of, the inferences we make in coming to grips with an artwork.

The problem of justification, as I stated earlier, is the correct observation that having a justified interpretation of what a work is "up to" is not the same thing as having reasons or justification for believing that what it "says" is true. But once we admit this, I think we can see how it is possible to be justified in accepting what the work offers. What is noteworthy here is that reaching a justified *interpretation of the work is a necessary part, and the uniquely aesthetic part of the process.* (This explains why art and literary criticism, which deal with the canons of interpretation, can correctly be said to add to the knowledge we derive from the arts.) We must notice the work's subtle features, weigh and evaluate different hypotheses about their interconnections, argue about their meanings, and engage in numerous other cognitive labors in casting a justifiable interpretation. *Evaluation* of the work's artistic prowess and merit is also relevant to the ultimate question of knowledge and justification. How convincingly a theme is handled in the work, and how natural and coherent the work's progress is toward its conclusions, can affect the warrant we have for our knowledge claims, though a detailed articulation of this procedure would be difficult at present. But surely, the breathtaking clarity and seamless unity with which a great artwork can sometimes explore new horizons, new claims about the human condition, rightfully weighs in the positive toward our acceptance of its lessons.

Finally, though, there are the "external" checks which we must go through if we are not to be indoctrinated by a work's forcefulness or infatuated with its charm or cachet. The rest of what we know or take ourselves to know can act as epistemic "defeating conditions" on the interpreted claims of art and bring further confirmation to them or provide a fuller and systematic context in which the themes and hypotheses of the artwork gain plausibility. (On defeasibility theories of knowledge, see Lehrer, and Pollock, Chps. 2, 5, 7, and Appendix.) It is this broader epistemic network or background which is in operation when a work "rings true" to us.

In a sense then, knowledge that has an artistic source is not "in" the work in some isolated or atomistic fashion, not only because we must *infer* it from the work's more basic features, but also because as Quine and others have argued, few if any propositions constitute knowledge in isolation; the status of knowledge is a relational status, linking propositions holistically to the rest of our network or web of belief. Knowledge through art is no different, better, or worse in this respect.

IV. CONCLUSION: THE FUNCTIONS OF ART

Here is a partial list of the possible functions of art, none of which I would deny. Art

Gives us unique perceptual and cognitive experiences;
Offers new ways of perceiving and conceiving things;
Exhibits, expresses, and evokes emotions in us;
Gives us pleasure—sensory, sensual, and intellectual in kind;
Represents things;
Communicates intentional states and attitudes of the artist;
Exemplifies properties and relations of very abstract sorts;
Functions as a presentational sign;
Creates "worlds" and points of view;
Is an exercise of and exercises the imagination;
Utilizes verbal, visual, auditory, and kinesthetic metaphors;
Matures and deepens our aesthetic sensibilities;
Is a "working out" of some problem or concern of the artist;

Portrays and manifests values, hopes, aspirations, ideals;

Gives us knowledge of the world, sometimes factual, sometimes normative, and sometimes "modal."

Any theory of art which denies these functions is bound to fail, simply because, like life (which cannot be encompassed by one science), art is too varied and complex to be exhausted by a simple and singular view of its rewards and lessons. Art is perhaps more profitably viewed as more similar in its complexity to philosophy than to science, if only because it is a common mistake to assign science a singular function: the pursuit of, and accumulation of, truth or knowledge. It seems to many that more divergent things (sometimes embarrassingly divergent) go on in philosophy: seeing issues from different perspectives, meeting argument with counterargument, developing conceptual and analytical abilities, striving to understand a multiplicity of views, manipulating and relating concepts and abstractions. But philosophy's range of activities and functions has not caused us (not all of us, at least) to dismiss the idea that there is philosophical knowledge, and a similar conclusion is warranted, I believe, in the case of art. Among its many other values, art brings us knowledge—or so I have tried to argue.

REFERENCES

Aristotle. *Metaphysics. Nichomachean Ethics. Poetics.* In Richard McKeon, ed., *The Basic Works of Aristotle.* Cambridge: Oxford University Press, 1941.

Ayer, Alfred J. *Language, Truth, and Logic.* New York: Dover Publications, 1952.

Goodman, Nelson. *Languages of Art.* Indianapolis: Bobbs-Merrill Company, 1968.

———. *Ways of Worldmaking.* Indianapolis: Hackett Publishing Company, 1978.

Harter, Carol C., and Thompson, James R. *John Irving.* Boston: Twayne Publishers, 1986.

Kant, Immanuel. *The Critique of Judgment.* Translated by James C. Meredith. Oxford: Oxford University Press, 1952.

Langer, Susanne. *Philosophy in a New Key.* Cambridge, Mass.: Harvard University Press, 1942.

Lehrer, Keith. "Meta-Knowledge: Undefeated Justification," *Synthese*, 74 (1988), 329–47.

Matthews, Robert J. "Describing and Interpreting a Work of Art," *Journal of Aesthetics and Art Criticism*, 36 (1977), 5–14.

Meerbote, Ralf. "Reflection in Beauty." In Ted Cohen and Paul Guyer, eds., *Essays in Kant's Aesthetics.* Chicago: Chicago University Press, 1982, 55–86.

Morgan, Douglas. "Must Art Tell the Truth?," *Journal of Aesthetics and Art Criticism*, XXVI, No. 1 (Fall 1967), 17–27.

Morris, Charles W. *Foundations of the Theory of Signs.* Chicago: University of Chicago Press, 1938.

Nabokov, Vladimir. *Lolita.* New York: Vintage International, 1989.

Novitz, David. *Knowledge, Fiction and Imagination.* Philadelphia: Temple University Press, 1987.

Nussbaum, Martha. "The Discernment of Perception: An Aristotelian Conception of Private and Public Rationality." In M. Nussbaum, *Love's Knowledge: Essays on Philosophy and Literature.* New York: Oxford University Press, 1990.

———. "Form and Content: Philosophy and Literature." In *Love's Knowledge*.

———. "'Finely Aware and Richly Responsible': Literature and the Moral Imagination." In *Love's Knowledge*.

Ogden, C. K., and Richards, I. A. *The Meaning of Meaning*, 8th ed. New York: Harcourt, Brace and Co., 1956.

Parker, DeWitt. *The Principles of Aesthetics*, 2nd ed. New York: F. S. Crofts and Co., 1946.

Plato. *The Republic. The Sophist. Ion.* In Edith Hamilton and Huntington Cairns, eds., *The Collected Dialogues of Plato.* Princeton: Princeton University Press, 1961.

Pollock, John L. *Contemporary Theories of Knowledge.* Totowa, N.J.: Rowman and Littlefield, 1986.

Quine, W. V. "Two Dogmas of Empiricism." In W. V. Quine, *From a Logical Point of View.* New York: Harper and Row, 1953, 20–46.

———, and Ullian, Joseph. *The Web of Belief*, 2nd ed. New York: Random House, 1978.

Ransom, J. C. "The Arts and the Philosophers," *The Kenyon Review*, Spring 1939, 194–99.

Reid, Louis A. "Art and Knowledge," *British Journal of Aesthetics*, 25 (1985), 115–24.

Rorty, Richard. *Contingency, Irony, and Solidarity*. Cambridge: Cambridge University Press, 1989.

Smith, Steven. "The Quality of Aesthetic Convention." In Michael Mitias, ed., *Aesthetic Quality and Aesthetic Convention*. Amsterdam: Rudolphi Publishers, 1988, 91–104.

Walsh, Dorothy. "The Cognitive Content of Art," *Philosophical Review*, LII (1943), 433–51. Reprinted in Eliseo Vivas and Murray Krieger, eds., *The Problems of Aesthetics*. New York: Holt, Rinehart, and Winston, 1953.

——. *Literature and Knowledge*. Middletown, Conn.: Wesleyan University Press, 1969.

Weitz, Morris. "Art, Language, and Truth." In Morris Weitz, *Philosophy of the Arts*. Cambridge, Mass.: Harvard University Press, 1950, 134–152.

BH 39 .C666 1993

Contemporary philosophy of art